The
B&B Guide
2010

AA Lifestyle Guides

40th edition

© AA Media Limited 2009.
AA Media Limited retains the copyright in the current edition
© 2009 and in all subsequent editions, reprints and amendments to editions.
The information contained in this directory is sourced from the AA's establishment database.
All rights reserved. No part of this publication may be reproduced, stored in a retrieval system, or transmitted in any form or by any means - electronic, photocopying, recording, or otherwise - unless the written permission of the publishers has been given beforehand. This book may not be sold, resold, hired out or otherwise disposed of by way of trade in any form of binding or cover other than that in which it is published, without the prior written consent of all relevant Publishers. The contents of this publication are believed correct at the time of printing. Nevertheless the Publisher cannot be held responsible for any errors or omissions or for changes in the details given in this guide or for the consequences of any reliance on the information provided in the same. This does not affect your statutory rights. Assessments of AA inspected establishments are based on the experience(s) of the hotel and restaurant inspectors on the occasion(s) of their visit(s), therefore the descriptions in this guide represent an element of subjective opinion that may not reflect a reader's own opinion on another occasion.

Please use one of the Readers' Report Forms at the end of the guide or contact:
The Editor, AA B&B Guide, Fanum House, Floor13, Basing View, Basingstoke, Hampshire RG21 4EA
lifestyleguides@theAA.com

Advertisement Sales: advertisingsales@theAA.com

The Automobile Association would like to thank the following photographers and companies for their assistance in the preparation of this book.
Abbreviations for the picture credits are as follows: (t) top; (b) bottom; (l) left; (r) right; (c) centre
(AA) AA World Travel Library.
Front cover: (t) Sea View Villa, Lynmouth; (bl) The Gallery, London SW7; (br) Fauhope House, Melrose.
Back cover: (l) Butler House, Kilkenny; (c) Photolibrary Group; (r) Chestnut House, Bath.
Every effort has been made to trace the copyright holders, and we apologise in advance for any accidental errors. We would be happy to apply the corrections in the following edition of this publication.

Typeset by Servis Filmsetting Ltd, Stockport, Greater Manchester
Printed by Printer Industria Grafica S.A., Barcelona
This directory is compiled by AA Lifestyle Guides, managed in the Librios Information Management System and generated by the AA establishment database system.

Published by AA Publishing, which is a trading name of AA Media Limited
whose registered office is:
Fanum House, Basing View, Basingstoke, Hampshire RG21 4EA
Registered number 06112600

A CIP catalogue record for this book is available from the British Library.
ISBN: 978-0-7495-6280-9
A03990

Maps prepared by the
Mapping Services Department of
AA Publishing.

Maps © AA Media Limited 2009.

This product includes mapping data licensed from Ordnance Survey® with the permission of the Controller of Her Majesty's Stationery Office.
© Crown copyright 2009.
All rights reserved.
Licence number 100021153.

Land & Property Services.
This is based upon Crown Copyright and is reproduced with the permission of Land & Property Services under delegated authority from the Controller of Her Majesty's Stationery Office.
© Crown copyright and database rights 2009
Licence number 100,363.
Permit number 90031

Republic of Ireland mapping based on
© Ordnance Survey Ireland/Government of Ireland
Copyright Permit number MP000109

Information on National Parks in England provided by the Countryside Agency (Natural England). Information on National Parks in Scotland provided by Scottish Natural Heritage. Information on National Parks in Wales provided by The Countryside Council for Wales.

Contents

How to Use the Guide

1 LOCATION, MAP REFERENCE & NAME

Each country is listed in alphabetical order by county then town/village. The Channel Islands and Isle of Man follow the England section and the Scottish islands follow the rest of Scotland. Establishments are listed alphabetically in descending order of Stars with any Yellow Stars first in each rating.

The map page number refers to the atlas at the back of the guide and is followed by the National Grid Reference. To find the town/village, read the first figure across and the second figure vertically within the lettered square. You can find routes at theAA.com or AAbookings.ie. Farmhouse entries also have a six-figure National Grid Reference, which can be used with Ordnance Survey maps or **www.ordnancesurvey.co.uk**.

We also show the name of the proprietors, as often farms are known locally by their name.

2 CLASSIFICATION & DESIGNATOR

See pages 6 and 7.

Five Star establishments are highlighted as Premier Collection, and they are listed on page 24.

If the establishment's name is shown in *italics*, then details have not been confirmed by the proprietor for this edition.

⊛ **Rosettes** The AA's food award, see page 11.

🍶 **Egg cups and 🥧 pies** These symbols indicate that, in the experience of the inspector, either breakfast or dinner are really special, and have an emphasis on freshly prepared local ingredients.

3 E-MAIL ADDRESS & WEBSITE

E-mail and website addresses are included where they have been specified by the establishment. Such websites are not under the control of AA Media Limited, who cannot accept any responsibility or liability in respect of any and all matters whatsoever relating to such websites.

BERKSHIRE

1 | HUNGERFORD | Map 5 SU36 | **1**

The Swan Inn

2 ★★★★ 🍶 🥧 INN

5

Craven Rd, Inkpen RG17 9DX
☎ 01488 668326 📠 01488 668306
3 e-mail: enquiries@theswaninn-organics.co.uk
web: www.theswaninn-organics.co.uk
4 dir: *3.5m SE of Hungerford. S on Hungerford High St past rail bridge, left to Hungerford Common, right signed Inkpen*

6 This delightful village inn dates back to the 17th century has open fires and beams in the bar, and the bonus of a smart restaurant. Bedrooms are generally spacious and well equipped. Organic produce is available from the on-site farm shop, so the bar, restaurant and breakfast menus all feature local organic produce too.

7 **Rooms** 10 en suite (2 fmly) S £60-£70; D £80-£95*
8 **Facilities** tea/coffee Dinner available Direct Dial Cen ht Wi-fi **Conf** Max 40 Thtr 40 Class 40 Board 12 **Parking** 50 | **9**
Notes ⊗ Closed 25-26 Dec

10

---

4 DIRECTIONS & DISTANCES

Distances in **directions** are given in miles (m) and yards (yds), or kilometres (km) and metres (mtrs) in the Republic of Ireland.

5 PHOTOGRAPHS

Establishments may choose to include a photograph

6 DESCRIPTION

Written by the inspector at the time of his or her visit.

---

7 ROOMS

The number of letting bedrooms (rms), or rooms with a bath or shower en suite are shown. Bedrooms that have a private bathroom (pri facs) adjacent are indicated.

The number of bedrooms in an annexe of equivalent standard are also shown. Facilities may not be the same as in the main building.

Charges are per night:
S bed and breakfast per person
D bed and breakfast for two people sharing a room. If an asterisk (✳) follows the prices this indicates 2009 prices.

The euro is the currency of the Republic of Ireland.

Prices are indications only, so check before booking. Some places may offer free accommodation to children provided they share their parents' room.

8 FACILITIES

Most bedrooms will have TV. If this is important to you, please check when booking. If **TV4B** appears, this means that there are TVs in four bedrooms.

If **Dinner** is shown, you may have to order in advance. Please check when booking. For other abbreviations and symbols, see the table on the right.

9 PARKING

Parking is usually followed by the number of spaces. Motorists should be aware that some establishments may charge for parking. Please check when booking.

10 NOTES

Although many hotels allow dogs, they may be excluded from some areas of the hotel and some breeds, particularly those requiring an exceptional license, may not be acceptable at all. Under the Disability Discrimination Act 1995 access should be allowed to guide dogs and assistance dogs. Please check the hotel's policy when making your booking.

No children - children cannot be accommodated, or a minimum age may be specified, e.g. No children 4yrs means no children under four years old.

Establishments with special facilities for children (**ch fac**) may include a babysitting service or baby-intercom system, playroom or playground, laundry facilities, drying and ironing facilities, cots, high chairs and special meals. If you have very young children, check before booking.

No coaches is published in good faith from details supplied by the establishment. Inns have well-defined legal obligations towards travellers; in the event of a query the customer should contact the proprietor or local licensing authority.

Additional facilities such as lifts or any leisure activities available are also listed. **LB** indicates that Short or Leisure Breaks are available. Contact the establishment for details.

Establishments are open all year unless **Closed** days/dates/months are shown. Some places are open all year but offer a restricted

service (**RS**) in low season. If the text does not say what the restricted services are you should check before booking.

Civ Wed 50 The establishment is licensed for civil weddings and can accommodate 50 guests for the ceremony.

⊛ shows that **credit/debit cards are not accepted**, but check when booking. Where credit cards are accepted there may be an extra charge.

Smoking Since July 1st 2007 smoking is banned in all public places in the United Kingdom and Ireland. The proprietor can designate one or more bedrooms with ventilation systems where the occupants can smoke, but communal areas must be smoke-free. Communal areas include the interior bars and restaurants in pubs and inns. We indicate number of smoking rooms (if any).

Conference facilities Conf indicates that facilities are available. Total number of delegates that can be accommodated is shown, plus maximum numbers in various settings.

Key to Symbols and abbreviations

★ ✦	Classification (see page 6)
⊛	AA Rosette award (see page 11)
A	Associate entry (see page 7)
U	Unclassified rating (see page 7)
☎	Phone number
📄	Fax number
🍴	A very special breakfast, with an emphasis on freshly prepared local ingredients
🍽	A very special dinner, with an emphasis on freshly prepared local ingredients
S	Single room
D	Double room (2 people sharing)
pri fac	Private facilities
fmly	Family bedroom
GF	Ground floor bedroom
LB	Short/Leisure breaks
✱	2009 prices
Cen ht	Full central heating
ch fac	Special facilities for children
TVL	Lounge with television
TV4B	Television in four bedrooms
STV	Satellite television
FTV	Freeview television
Wi-fi	Wireless internet
⊛	Credit cards not accepted
tea/coffee	Tea and coffee facilities
Conf	Conference facilities
rms	Bedrooms in main building
Etr	Easter
fr	From
RS	Restricted service
⊗	No dogs
〰	Indoor swimming pool
〰	Heated indoor swimming pool
⤳	Outdoor swimming pool
⤳	Heated outdoor swimming pool
✋	Croquet lawn
⚘	Tennis court
⚑	Putting green

AA Inspected Guest Accommodation

The AA inspects and classifies more than 3,000 guest houses, farmhouses and inns for its Guest Accommodation Scheme, under common quality standards agreed between the AA, VisitBritain, VisitScotland and VisitWales.
AA recognised establishments pay an annual fee according to the classification and the number of bedrooms. The classification is not transferable if an establishment changes hands.

The AA presents several awards within the Guest Accommodation scheme, including the **AA Friendliest Landlady of the Year**, which showcases the very finest hospitality in the country, **Guest Accommodation of the Year Awards**, presented to establishments in Scotland, Ireland, Wales and England, **AA London B&B of the Year**, and **AA Funkiest B&B of the Year**. See pages 12 and 14 for this year's winners.

Stars

AA Stars classify guest accommodation at five levels of quality, from one at the simplest, to five offering the highest quality. In order to achieve a one Star rating an establishment must meet certain minimum entry requirements, including:

• A cooked breakfast, or substantial continental option is provided.
• The proprietor and/or staff are available for your arrival, departure and at all meal times.
• Once registered, you have access to the establishment at all times unless previously notified.
• All areas of operation meet minimum quality requirements for cleanliness, maintenance and hospitality as well as facilities and the delivery of services.
• A dining room or similar eating area is available unless meals are only served in bedrooms.

Our research shows that quality is very important to visitors. To obtain a higher Star rating, an establishment must provide increased quality standards across all areas, with particular emphasis in four key areas:
• Cleanliness and housekeeping
• Hospitality and service
• Quality and condition of bedrooms, bathrooms and public rooms
• Food quality

There are also particular requirements in order for an establishment to achieve three, four or five Stars, for example:

Three Stars and above
• access to both sides of all beds for double occupancy
• bathrooms/shower rooms cannot be used by the proprietor
• there is a washbasin in every guest bedroom (either in the bedrooms or the en suite/private facility)

Four Stars
• half of bedrooms must be en suite or have private facilities

Five Stars
• all bedrooms must be en suite or have private facilities

Establishments applying for AA recognition are visited by one of the AA's qualified accommodation inspectors as a mystery guest. Inspectors stay overnight to make a thorough test of the accommodation, food, and hospitality. After paying the bill the following morning they identify themselves and ask to be shown round the premises. The inspector completes a full report, resulting in a recommendation for the appropriate Star rating. After this first visit, the establishment will receive an annual visit to check that standards are maintained. If it changes hands, the new owners must re-apply for classification, as standards can change.

Guests can expect to find the following minimum standards at all levels:

- Pleasant and helpful welcome and service, and sound standards of housekeeping and maintenance
- Comfortable accommodation equipped to modern standards
- Bedding and towels changed for each new guest, and at least weekly if the room is taken for a long stay
- Adequate storage, heating, lighting and comfortable seating
- A sufficient hot water supply at reasonable times
- A full cooked breakfast. (If this is not provided, the fact must be advertised and a substantial continental breakfast must be offered)

When an AA inspector has visited a property, and evaluated all the aspects of the accommodation for comfort, facilities, attention to detail and presentation, you can be confident the Star rating will allow you to make the right choice for an enjoyable stay.

★ Highly Commended

Yellow Stars indicate that an accommodation is in the top ten percent of its Star rating. Yellow Stars only apply to 3, 4 or 5 Star establishments.

Accommodation Designators

Along with the Star ratings, six designators have been introduced. The proprietors, in discussion with our inspectors, choose which designator best describes their establishment:

B&B

A private house run by the owner with accommodation for no more than six paying guests.

GUEST HOUSE

Run on a more commercial basis than a B&B, the accommodation provides for more than six paying guests and there are usually more services; for example staff as well as the owner may provide dinner.

FARMHOUSE

The B&B or guest house accommodation is part of a working farm or smallholding.

INN

The accommodation is provided in a fully licensed establishment. The bar will be open to non-residents and can provide food in the evenings.

RESTAURANT WITH ROOMS

This is a destination restaurant offering overnight accommodation, with dining being the main business and open to non-residents. The restaurant should offer a high standard of food and restaurant service at least five nights a week. A liquor licence is necessary and there is a maximum of 12 bedrooms.

GUEST ACCOMMODATION

Any establishment that meets the minimum entry requirements is eligible for this general category.

U Unclassified entries

A small number of establishments in this guide have this symbol because their Star classification was not confirmed at the time of going to press. This may be due to a change of ownership or because the establishment has only recently joined the AA rating scheme. For up-to-date information on these and other new establishments check **theAA.com**.

A Associate entries

These establishments have been inspected and rated by VisitBritain, VisitScotland or VisitWales, and have joined the AA scheme on a marketing-only basis. A limited entry for these places appears in the guide, while descriptions for these establishments appear on **theAA.com**.

Book into AA rated hotels from the comfort of your home. How very accommodating

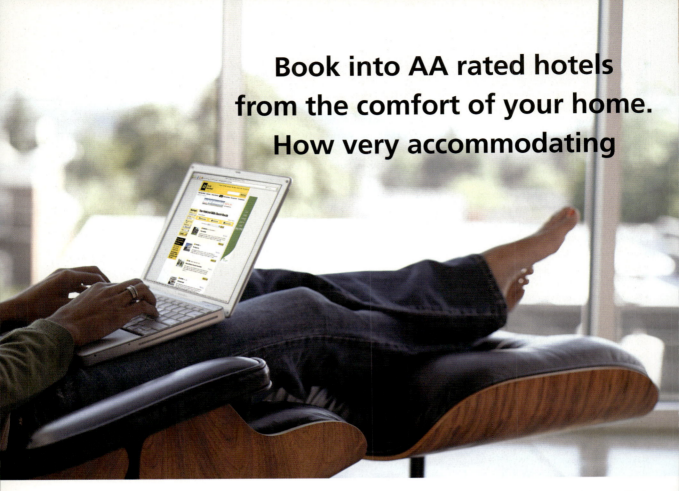

If you're looking for a hotel or B&B visit theAA.com/travel first. You can book hundreds of AA rated establishments there and then

- All accommodation is rated from one to five stars with detailed listings
- 5% discount available for AA Members at many hotels – look for the Members' 5% off – book it buttons
- Fantastic offers also available on the hotel and B&B homepage

AA Route Planner – guides you through every step of your journey

If you're planning on going on a long journey and need to find a stop over or two on the way, simply go to the AA's new and improved Route Planner. With its new mapping powered by Google™, you just scroll over your route to find available hotels at every step of your journey.

Visit **theAA.com/travel**

For the road ahead

Useful Information

There may be restricted access to some establishments, particularly in the late morning and the afternoon, so do check when booking.

London prices tend to be higher than outside the capital, and normally only bed and breakfast is provided, although some establishments do provide a full meal service.

Farmhouses: Sometimes the land has been sold and only the house remains, but many are working farms and some farmers are happy to allow visitors to look around, or even to help feed the animals. However, you should always exercise care and never leave children unsupervised. Although the directory entry states the acreage and the type of farming, do check when booking to make sure that it matches your expectations. The farmhouses are listed under towns or villages, but do ask for directions when booking.

Inns: Traditional inns often have a cosy bar, convivial atmosphere, and good beer and pub food. Those listed in the guide will provide breakfast in a suitable room, and should also serve light meals during licensing hours. The character of the properties vary according to whether they are country inns or town establishments. Check before you book, including arrival times as these may be restricted to opening hours.

Booking

Book as early as possible, particularly for the peak holiday period (early June to the end of September) and for Easter and other public holidays. In some parts of Scotland the skiing season is also a peak holiday period. Some establishments only accept weekly bookings from Saturday, and some require a deposit on booking.

Prices

Minimum and maximum prices are shown for one (S) and two people (D) per night and include a full breakfast. If dinner is also included this is indicated in brackets (incl dinner). Where prices are for the room only, this is indicated.

Useful Information *continued*

Prices in the guide include VAT (and service where applicable), except the Channel Islands where VAT does not apply.

Where proprietors have been unable to provide us with their 2010 charges we publish the 2009 price as a rough guide (shown by an asterisk ✳). Where no prices are given, please make enquiries direct.

Cancellation

If you have to cancel a booking, let the proprietor know at once. If the room cannot be re-let you may be held legally responsible for partial payment; you could lose your deposit or be liable for compensation, so consider taking out cancellation insurance.

Food and drink

Some guest accommodation provides evening meals, ranging from a set meal to a full menu. Some even have their own restaurant. You may have to arrange dinner in advance, at breakfast, or on the previous day, so do ask when booking.

If you book on bed, breakfast and evening meal terms, you may find that the tariff includes only the set menu. If there is a carte you may be able to order from this and pay a supplement.

On Sundays, many establishments serve the main meal at midday, and provide only a cold supper in the evening. In some parts of Britain, particularly in Scotland, high tea (i.e. a savoury dish followed by bread and butter, scones and cakes) is sometimes served instead of, or as an alternative to, dinner.

Facilities for Disabled Guests

The Disability Discrimination Act (access to Goods and Services) means that service providers may have to consider making adjustments to their premises. For further information see www.direct.gov.uk/en/ DisabledPeople/RightsAndObligations/ DisabilityRights/DG_4001068.

Ground-floor rooms are noted under Facilities. The establishments in this guide should all be aware of their responsibilities under the Act. Always phone in advance to ensure that the establishment you have chosen has appropriate facilities. See also www.tourismforall.org.uk.

AA Rosette Awards

The AA awards Rosettes to some 2,000 restaurants as the best in the UK.

Excellent local restaurants serving food prepared with care, understanding and skill, using good quality ingredients.

The best local restaurants, which aim for and achieve higher standards and better consistency, and where a greater precision is apparent in the cooking. There will be obvious attention to the selection of quality ingredients.

Outstanding restaurants that demand recognition well beyond their local area.

Among the very best restaurants in the British Isles, where the cooking demands national recognition.

The finest restaurants in the British Isles, where the cooking compares with the best in the world.

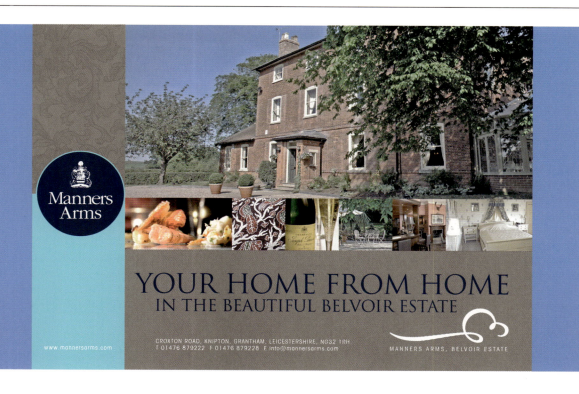

Manners Arms

YOUR HOME FROM HOME
IN THE BEAUTIFUL BELVOIR ESTATE

www.mannersarms.com

CROXTON ROAD, KNIPTON, GRANTHAM, LEICESTERSHIRE, NG32 1RH
T 01476 879222 F 01476 879228 E info@mannersarms.com

MANNERS ARMS, BELVOIR ESTATE

AA B&B Awards

Each year the AA likes to celebrate the cream of the Guest Accommodation scheme crop. Held at **The Langham,** *London, the event recognised and rewarded 27 very deserving finalists for demonstrating all-round excellence and unfailing standards, and for providing outstanding service to their guests. All finalists were treated to a champagne reception followed by a formal four course celebratory luncheon, and received a personalised certificate and an engraved Villeroy & Boch decanter as well as a goody bag to take home with them.*

Above: Giovanna Grossi, AA Hotel Services, Group Area Manager presenting Carole with her award, accompanied by Nigel David, CEO of eviivo, sponsors of the AA Friendliest Landlady of the Year Award.

FRIENDLIEST LANDLADY OF THE YEAR

Sponsored by **eviivo**

Carole Edney,
WEST MARDEN FARMHOUSE ★★★★
West Marden, West Sussex PAGE 355

Carole Edney and her husband Martin have been welcoming guests to their 16th-century farmhouse, nestled in a small village in the South Downs, since 1995. Set in an Area of Outstanding Natural Beauty, the spacious property is on a working arable farm which has been in the Edney family for several generations. Carole goes to great lengths to ensure that she sources the very best of everything, from the finest toiletries and Egyptian cotton bedlinen, to meat from the most reputable local producers, to make sure that her guests feel as relaxed and 're-charged' as possible; and is always happy to offer guests advice on the local area and to recommend the best pubs and restaurants to visit.

FUNKIEST B&B OF THE YEAR

WINDERMERE SUITES ★★★★★

PAGE 103

Windermere Suites is a unique B&B in the Lake District that also acts as a designer showcase of the very best cutting edge furniture, furnishings and accessories. Run by husband and wife team Colin and Victoria Monk, who both have a background in design, Windermere Suites certainly differs from the average B&B, with guests offered the opportunity to order everything within the suites, from a Kartel Phillippe Starck Ghost Chair to Villeroy & Boch crockery. Each of the eight suites has its own lounge and dining area, where guests can take breakfast, as well as large walk-in wardrobes and stunning bathrooms combining oversized air baths with flat-screen TVs, mood lighting and under-floor heating.

LONDON B&B OF THE YEAR

THE SUMNER ★★★★

PAGE 242

Established in 2006, The Sumner is a townhouse in the heart of London, just minutes from Oxford Street, the bright lights of the West End, and the green expanse of Hyde Park. Part of a Georgian terrace dating from the 1820s, The Sumner has been fitted to the highest standards whilst also preserving many of the building's historical characteristics. This independent establishment combines tradition with modern comfort, and all 20 rooms are designer-decorated and luxuriously appointed. The Sumner's centrepiece is an intimate and elegant sitting room with an original fireplace and timber flooring, ideal for enjoying a drink before or after any excursion into central London.

AA Guest Accommodation of the Year

Every year we ask our inspectors to nominate those establishments they feel come closest to the ideal of what a B&B should be. They consider location, food standards and quality of furniture and fittings, as well as charm and hospitality. From a shortlist of around 20, one is selected from each country in the guide.

ENGLAND

CHATTON PARK HOUSE ★★★★★
PAGE 265

Once home to the Duke of Northumberland, Chatton Park House is a beautiful Georgian property, converted to a Bed & Breakfast in 2007. Run by husband and wife team Paul and Michelle Mattinson, the house offers luxurious accommodation with uninterrupted views over the Northumberland countryside to the Cheviot Hills. The perfect base for rest, peace and tranquillity, situated in close proximity to stunning white sand beaches, historic castles, idyllic walks and cosy village pubs.

SCOTLAND

LOCH NESS LODGE ★★★★★
PAGE 433

Loch Ness Lodge is an elegant and intimate exclusive-use retreat in the heart of the Scottish Highlands overlooking the mysterious and beautiful Loch Ness. A small family-run business, Loch Ness Lodge brings together the very best of traditional Scottish architecture and contemporary design, boasting elegant reception rooms, a spa and therapy area, and fine dining in its two Rosette-awarded restaurant. The lodge's seven bedrooms have been individually styled and are inspired by the natural beauty of the surrounding Highlands, each named after a well-loved Highland loch or glen.

WALES

TAN-YR-ONNEN ★★★★★
PAGE 467

IRELAND

ROSQUIL HOUSE, KILKENNY ★★★★
PAGE 509

Husband and wife team Patrick and Sara Murphy have been welcoming guests to their guest house since 2006. Set in the heart of North Wales in the Vale of Clywd, this welcoming establishment is within easy reach of the local attractions. Sara and Patrick go to every effort to make sure that their guests enjoy their stay, ensuring that food is sourced locally where they can, and offering customers everything they might require, from providing a lift to a good pub or spending five minutes chatting over a cup of tea.

A purpose-built house within walking distance of the city centre, Rosquil House is contemporary and stylish, with an airy vaulted breakfast room and carefully decorated, spacious bedrooms. Owners Rhoda and Phil Nolan are passionate about their business, genuinely warm, welcoming and very helpful. Rhoda bakes breads and scones each morning while Phil is responsible for the delightful breakfast which is a real treat; an excellent choice available on the cold buffet, stewed and fresh fruits, yoghurts, homemade muesli, and the range of hot dishes changes weekly.

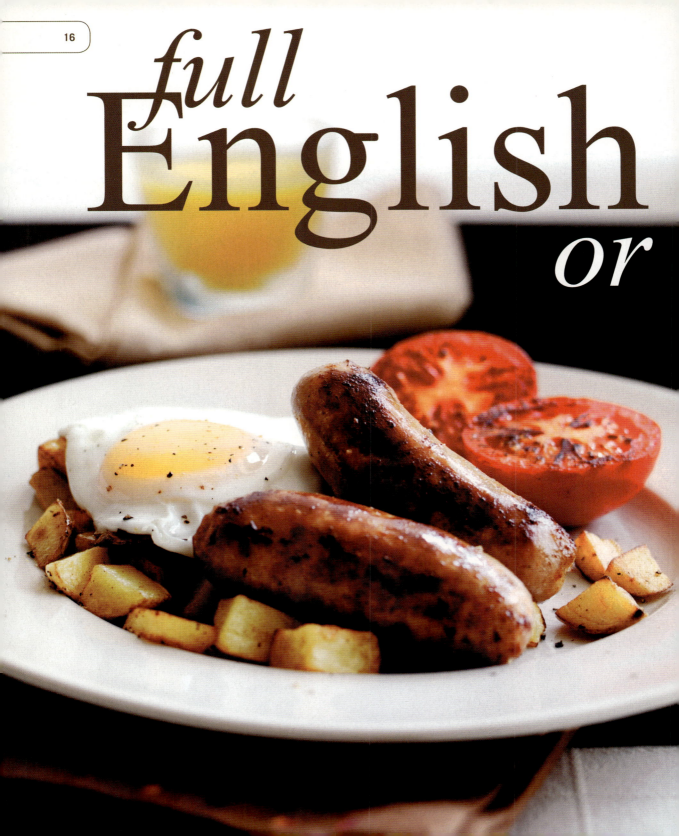

full English *or*

> ❛ *The only way to eat well in England is to have breakfast three times a day* ❜
>
> *Somerset Maugham*

goat omelette?

by **Phil Bryant**

What's for breakfast? How about mashed boiled plantains? No? Goat omelette, maybe? OK, not that either. Slow-cooked fava beans, then?

To British tastes, greeting the new day with such delights may seem a bit strange, but not to the people of, respectively, the Dominican Republic, Ghana and Egypt. For them a bowl of cornflakes and milk, or a boiled egg with soldiers, would seem equally alien.

Wherever in the world we are, breakfast – a word first recorded in 1463 – is an essential part of the day. As a word its origin is simple enough - we can't eat while we are asleep, so we fast, albeit involuntarily, until we break it with the day's first meal. If only all etymology was so simple.

Our great affection for a good old traditional fry-up, known colloquially throughout the land (well, almost) as a Full English, often transcends our knowledge that far healthier options are available. This is why we may ration ourselves to one at weekends, or to when we stay in a hotel or B&B (an abbreviation that means only one thing in Britain, unless you were a Beavis & Butthead fan!).

Breakfast has inspired some memorable quotes. That grand old man of letters, Somerset Maugham, had the meal taped when he said: "The only way to eat well in England is to have breakfast three times a day." Then there was novelist C S Lewis who rather biblically observed: "He that but looketh on a plate of ham and eggs to lust after it hath already committed breakfast with it in his heart." And it was an old German proverb that advised: "Eat breakfast like a king, lunch like a prince, and dine like a pauper."

Of course, it's not just kings who can eat regally. Some years ago, when Her Majesty The Queen started wearing glasses, to illustrate her new look, one of the tabloids published a photo of her with them on. The caption read: "The Queen, seen here at breakfast". Nothing wrong with that, you might think, except that she was also wearing her crown. It must have been quite a breakfast to warrant getting out the ceremonial headgear!

The Full English

Most commercial establishments, whether swanky hotel, modest B&B or ▷

Left: The ultimate full English?

'greasy spoon' café, are likely to offer a Full English, typically of eggs, bacon, sausages, tomatoes, mushrooms and fried bread. Thankfully, there is no British Standard, thus permitting the addition or subtraction of any item, depending on the establishment you're eating in, where in Britain you are, and what you actually like.

This freedom from official standardisation can cause controversy, however, with some insisting that a Full English isn't complete without, say, baked beans, while others would protest at the absence of fried potatoes. It would be interesting to know how many different combinations are offered by the 3100 establishments in this guide.

AA Egg Cup-holder Jennifer Coombes runs Hollow Tree Farm near Wells in Somerset. Her breakfast, which "absolutely delighted" an AA inspector, consists of a choice of 14 cereals, fruit juices, fresh fruit, eggs any style with three rashers of bacon, sausages, vine tomatoes and mushrooms, and "old-fashioned" bread, or croissants. "I charge far too little, but it's a great way to start the day," she says.

Cross-border breakfast

Regional differences soon become apparent to anyone who travels around the country. Black pudding, for example, although associated more with the north of England, could quite easily appear on your plate in Truro, Chelmsford or even Llandudno in North Wales, where the Welshness of Christina Ward's cooked breakfasts at Glenavon Guest House is impeccable. Her black pudding, however, is Scottish!

Traditionally, Welsh breakfasts include laverbread, a seaweed purée mixed with oatmeal, formed into patties and fried in bacon fat, but it can be hard to find on B&B menus, even in the south of the country where it comes from.

North of the Border, your Full English (perish the thought that it should be called that!) might include a lorne slice, which is a kind of flat sausage, Ayrshire (sweet-cured) bacon, or even haggis. The "Highland breakfast" offered by Margaret Capsomidis, an AA Friendliest Landlady finalist in 2008, includes locally grown raspberries (available virtually all year round), and a fry-up with black pudding made by her Aviemore butcher to a recipe passed on by her neighbour, a former Scottish black pudding champion. Anyone who asks for baked beans, though, will "ruin their breakfast", she says.

Porridge, of course, is inextricably associated with Scotland, although it is popular throughout Britain, especially in winter. Your Caledonian hosts may well give it a lift with whisky (putting paid to all that nonsense about the sun and yardarms).

In his book *Great Railway Journeys*, actor, comedian and writer Michael Palin travels along what has been called the Cholesterol Coast of Northern Ireland. This rather unfair soubriquet was coined in recognition of the Ulster Fry, the marvellous cooked breakfasts served in the seaside hotels and B&Bs of Antrim and Down. But think of it as just another Full English, with perhaps the addition of farls, little potato scones cooked on a hot plate.

The Poor Relation?

Health considerations apart, our breakfasts more than stand their ground against the Continental breakfast, an often-lacklustre croissant or brioche, accompanied by a pat of butter, a mini-pot of jam and a cup of coffee. Depending on your location, you may also find salami or ham, slices of soap-like cheese, a bit of fruit, or occasionally a hard-boiled egg. Frankly, though, Continental breakfasts don't cut the mustard in the same way as ours at least, when served in Britain.

Which brings us neatly to condiments and sauces. In addition to salt or pepper to taste, no Full English is truly complete without a splodge of tomato ketchup, a dollop of brown sauce, or a smear of English mustard. There are also those who will absolutely insist on drizzling everything with Worcestershire sauce, although the bottle may have to be painstakingly unearthed from the back of the sideboard.

Of course, none of us would have to worry about where the Worcestershire is hiding if we didn't eat a cooked breakfast, but let's face it, boiled plantains simply aren't in the same league. □

This freedom from official standardisation can cause controversy

With more than 230 farmhouse B&Bs in this edition and many of them set on working farms, we asked several farmers why they opened their gates to paying guests and which were the hardest work – the animals or the people?

It's an early start for Heather Hughes at Cwmanog Isaf Farm in Betws-y-Coed, north Wales. "We're up before 6am and first of all we feed the sheep and cattle and check they're OK," she says. "Then we start on the breakfasts for up to half a dozen guests." Cwmanog Isaf Farm is one of a growing number of working farms welcoming guests for bed and breakfast and, despite the hard work looking after both humans and animals, it seems that everyone enjoys the arrangement.

The Hughes family bought their farmland, which includes the enchanting Fairy Glen gorge on the River Conwy, in 1994 with the intention of opening a B&B. "If you're farming people, unless you have a huge farm the only way to keep your way of life is to diversify," says Heather. "We've only got 30 acres but people do book us because we're a real working farm. Our sheep are very tame and guests go out to talk to them and feed them biscuits. But they also come here because it's peaceful: they don't

Worki

hear traffic and there are no streetlights so it is dark. They hear owls at night and birdsong in the morning. Or they can just go down to the river and listen to that."

Rural multi-tasking

Most small to medium-sized farms will have considered some form of diversification, such as running a B&B or farm shop. Foot and mouth disease, unpredictable market prices and international exchange rates are all

out of the control of farmers and have conspired to make it harder to earn a living from the land. In the decade from 1993 100,000 farmers and farm workers left farming and, according to Defra, by 2006 at least 50 percent of Britain's farmers had diversified. Among these farmers, on average, their diversified income is greater than the income from solely farming.

For many small farms, offering bed and breakfast to countryside-loving guests is the only way to survive. An important side effect is that the countryside itself benefits: small farms are more diverse and sustainable. Rare breed livestock is nurtured on small farms, which are also more supportive ▷

ng Farms
By Robin Barton

of wildlife and local communities than industrial-scale farms.

Dianne Bickle of Crowtrees Farm near Stoke-on-Trent in Staffordshire agrees: "Without the B&B we wouldn't be farming. It's lucky that we love doing the B&B – as you get older you're not as physically able to run after cattle. Bed and breakfast has been a good option and we love meeting new people."

Alton Towers is just 10 minutes away by car. "We opened the summer that the Nemesis ride was opened, which was unplanned on our part," says Dianne. They've grown the B&B from two rooms to seven, converting a barn into four more rooms in 2003 with the help of a Rural Enterprise Grant.

The season at Crowtrees Farm, from March to October, follows that of Alton

"We've always had good experiences with guests and many come back year after year and have become friends. You can feel a bit isolated on a farm otherwise."

It's a feeling shared by many of the B&B-owning farms we spoke to, including Lilwen McAllister at Erw-Lon near Fishguard, Pembrokeshire, famous for her warm welcome.

Lilwen has been running her B&B for 34 years and is proof that diversification is not a new idea: "We started it for myself and for the extra income. Fortunately we live in such a wonderful area with castles, walking, St David's cathedral and dolphin watching that we've always been hugely popular."

Erw-Lon, with beautiful views of the Preseli Hills, is set in the Pembrokeshire Coast National Park. Cattle are raised on the farm's 128 acres and when families stay, Lilwen's husband takes children for rides on the tractor. "Sometimes they might see a cow calving and their eyes open wide and they ask all sorts of questions," she laughs.

In 34 years of business Lilwen has worked out what people are looking for in

> ❝If you're farming people, unless you have a huge farm the only way to keep your way of life is to diversify❞

Crowtrees Farm opened its B&B in 1993 but the Bickles had been farming their 70 acres since 1969. "We farmed dairy cows for 25 years then went into beef, then sheep, but we both had to work full time to make ends meet." But the Bickles had an ace up their sleeve:

Towers; lambing comes during a quiet period for the B&B and the animals are in the fields over the summer. Families come to enjoy the open space and the rollercoasters of the theme park nearby.

For Dianne, meeting people is part of the appeal of running a farmhouse B&B.

a B&B: "Hospitality. That's what it comes down to." Lilwen's hospitality begins in the kitchen. "We try to serve good, wholesome food we've grown ourselves and I try to buy local produce where I can. I serve our own beef at the dinner table. All the meat is traceable and guests ask about that now. Several years ago it was all about cordon bleu cooking but tastes have gone right back to simple, traditional food – people appreciate the true taste of meat and the true taste of vegetables."

It's a win-win

Everyone it seems is a winner: guests can experience a working farm in action, the farmers get some much-needed income and some company, wildlife thrives without the intensive practices of larger farms and money is ploughed back into the local community. What about the animals? Well, they're still the priority. "Last thing at night we check the animals again," says Heather Hughes, "but we leave our guests in peace." □

★★★★★ Premier Collection

ENGLAND

BUCKINGHAMSHIRE
BEACONSFIELD
Crazy Bear Beaconsfield

CAMBRIDGESHIRE
ELTON
The Crown Inn

CHESHIRE
CHESTER
Oddfellows
MALPAS
Tilston Lodge

CORNWALL & ISLES OF SCILLY
BOSCASTLE
Trerosewill Farm
DRYM
Drym Farm
FALMOUTH
Dolvean House
LAUNCESTON
Primrose Cottage
LOOE
The Beach House
PADSTOW
The Seafood Restaurant
PENZANCE
Camilla House
Ennys
The Summer House
PERRANUTHNOE
Ednovean Farm
POLPERRO
Trenderway Farm
ST AUSTELL
Anchorage House
Highland Court Lodge
Lower Barn
ST BLAZEY
Nanscawen Manor House
Penarwyn House
ST IVES
Beachcroft
Jamies
Primrose Valley

CUMBRIA
AMBLESIDE
Drunken Duck
ARNSIDE
Number 43
BORROWDALE
Hazel Bank Country House
BOWNESS-ON-WINDERMERE
Oakbank House
BRAMPTON
The Hill On The Wall
CARTMEL
L'enclume
CONISTON
Coniston Lodge
Wheelgate Country Guest House
CROSTHWAITE
The Punchbowl Inn at Crosthwaite
GRASMERE
Moss Grove Organic
KESWICK
The Grange Country Guest House
KIRKBY LONSDALE
Hipping Hall
The Sun Inn
LORTON
New House Farm
Winder Hall Country House
NEAR SAWREY
Ees Wyke Country House
NEWBY BRIDGE
The Knoll Country House
PENRITH
Brooklands Guest House
TROUTBECK
Broadoaks Country House
WINDERMERE
Beaumont House
The Cranleigh
The Howbeck
Low House
Newstead
Windermere Suites
The Woodlands

DERBYSHIRE
ASHBOURNE
Turlow Bank
BELPER
Dannah Farm Country House
BRADWELL
The Samuel Fox Country Inn
BUXTON
Grendon Guest House
HOPE
Underleigh House
MATLOCK
Holmefield
NEWHAVEN
The Smithy
WESTON UNDERWOOD
Park View Farm
WIRKSWORTH
The Old Manor House

DEVON
AXMINSTER
Kerrington House
BUDLEIGH SALTERTON
Heath Close
CHAGFORD
Parford Well
CHILLATON
Tor Cottage
DARTMOUTH
Nonsuch House
Strete Barton House
HONITON
West Colwell Farm
HORNS CROSS
The Round House
LUSTLEIGH
Eastwrey Barton
Woodley House
LYDFORD
Moor View House
LYNMOUTH
Bonnicott House
The Heatherville
Sea View Villa
LYNTON
Highcliffe House
Victoria Lodge

SIDMOUTH
The Salty Monk
SOUTH MOLTON
Kerscott Farm
TEIGNMOUTH
Thomas Luny House
TORQUAY
Linden House
The Marstan

DORSET

BLANDFORD FORUM
Portman Lodge
BRIDPORT
The Roundham House
The Shave Cross Inn
CHRISTCHURCH
Druid House
The Lord Bute & Restaurant
Seawards
DORCHESTER
Little Court
FARNHAM
Farnham Farm House
FRAMPTON
Frampton House
POOLE
Luminiere Boutique Bed & Breakfast
STURMINSTER NEWTON
The Crown Inn
WAREHAM
Kemps Country House
WIMBORNE MINSTER
Les Bouviers Restaurant with Rooms

CO DURHAM

BARNARD CASTLE
Greta House
Number 34

ESSEX

CHIPPING ONGAR
Diggins Farm
WIX
Dairy House

GLOUCESTERSHIRE

BLOCKLEY
Lower Brook House

CHELTENHAM
Beaumont House
Cleeve Hill House
Georgian House
Lypiatt House
CHIPPING CAMPDEN
The Malt House
Staddlestones
ST BRIAVELS
Prospect Cottage
TETBURY
Beaufort House

HAMPSHIRE

BENTLEY
Bentley Green Farm
BROCKENHURST
The Cottage Lodge
LYMINGTON
The Olde Barn
MILFORD ON SEA
Ha'penny House
SOUTHAMPTON
Riverside Bed & Breakfast
WINCHESTER
Giffard House
Orchard House

HEREFORDSHIRE

HEREFORD
Somerville House
LEOMINSTER
Hills Farm
MOCCAS
Moccas Court

HERTFORDSHIRE

DATCHWORTH
Farmhouse B&B
HERTFORD HEATH
Brides Farm
Rushen

KENT

CANTERBURY
Magnolia House
Yorke Lodge
DEAL
Sutherland House

DODDINGTON
The Old Vicarage
DOVER
The Marquis at Alkham
FARNINGHAM
Beesfield Farm
FOLKESTONE
The Relish
HAWKHURST
Southgate-Little Fowlers
IVYCHURCH
Olde Moat House
MARDEN
Merzie Meadows
ROYAL TUNBRIDGE WELLS
Danehurst House

LANCASHIRE

PRESTON
Whitestake Farm
WHITEWELL
The Inn at Whitewell

LEICESTERSHIRE

KEGWORTH
Kegworth House
SHEPSHED
The Grange Courtyard

LINCOLNSHIRE

HEMSWELL
Hemswell Court
HOUGH-ON-THE-HILL
The Brownlow Arms
LINCOLN
Bailhouse & Mews
Charlotte House
Minster Lodge
MARKET RASEN
Blaven
NORMANTON
La Casita
STAMFORD
Rock Lodge
WINTERINGHAM
Winteringham Fields

★★★★★ Premier Collection *continued*

LONDON POSTAL DISTRICTS
SW3
San Domenico House

NORFOLK
ALDBOROUGH
Aldborough Hall
BLAKENEY
Blakeney House
CLEY NEXT THE SEA
Old Town Hall House
CROMER
Incleborough House
GREAT YARMOUTH
Andover House
HINDRINGHAM
Field House
HOLT
Plantation House
NORTH WALSHAM
White House Farm
SHERINGHAM
Ashbourne House
The Eiders Bed & Breakfast
The Eight Acres
Fairlawns
THURSFORD
Holly Lodge

NORTHAMPTONSHIRE
STANWICK
The Courtyard Luxury Lodge

NORTHUMBERLAND
BELFORD
Market Cross
BERWICK-UPON-TWEED
West Coates
CHATTON
Chatton Park House
CORNHILL-ON-TWEED
Ivy Cottage
ROTHBURY
The Orchard House
WOOLER
The Old Manse

NOTTINGHAMSHIRE
ELTON
The Grange
HOLBECK
Browns
NOTTINGHAM
Greenwood Lodge City Guest House
Restaurant Sat Bains with Rooms

OXFORDSHIRE
ABINGDON
B&B Rafters
BURFORD
Burford House
GORING
The Miller of Mansfield
HENLEY-ON-THAMES
Crowsley House
OXFORD
Burlington House
STADHAMPTON
The Crazy Bear
WANTAGE
Brook Barn

SHROPSHIRE
BRIDGNORTH
The Albynes
CHURCH STRETTON
Field House
The Orchards
Rectory Farm
Willowfield Guest House
CLUN
Birches Mill
IRONBRIDGE
The Library House
LLANFAIR WATERDINE
The Waterdine
LUDLOW
The Clive Bar & Restaurant with Rooms
De Greys of Ludlow
Line Farm
MARKET DRAYTON
Ternhill Farm House &
The Cottage Restaurant
OSWESTRY
Greystones

SOMERSET
BATH
Apsley House
Athole House
Ayrlington
Cheriton House
Chestnuts House
Dorian House
Meadowland
One Three Nine
Paradise House
The Villa Magdala
CHARD
Bellplot House
CHEDDAR
Batts Farm
DULVERTON
Tarr Farm Inn
FROME
Lullington House
The Place To Stay
TAUNTON
Elm Villa
WELLS
Beaconsfield Farm
WESTON-SUPER-MARE
Church House
WITHYPOOL
Kings Farm
YEOVIL
Little Barwick House

STAFFORDSHIRE
CHEDDLETON
Choir Cottage and Choir House
RUGELEY
Colton House
TAMWORTH
Oak Tree Farm

SUFFOLK
BURY ST EDMUNDS
Clarice House
HADLEIGH
Edge Hall
HOLTON
Valley Farm
LAVENHAM

Lavenham Great House 'Restaurant With Rooms'
Lavenham Old Rectory
Lavenham Priory
SOUTHWOLD
Sutherland House
STOWMARKET
Bays Farm
YAXLEY
The Auberge

SURREY
CAMBERLEY
Maywood House
CHIDDINGFOLD
The Crown Inn
FARNHAM
Bentley Mill

EAST SUSSEX
DITCHLING
Tovey Lodge
EASTBOURNE
The Berkeley
The Gables
The Manse B & B
Ocklynge Manor
HALLAND
Tamberry Hall
HASTINGS & ST LEONARDS
The Laindons
Stream House
HERSTMONCEUX
Wartling Place
RYE
Jeake's House
Manor Farm Oast
White Vine House

WEST SUSSEX
ARUNDEL
Brooklands Country Guest House
CHICHESTER
Rooks Hill
The Royal Oak
West Stoke House
CHILGROVE
The Fish House
LINDFIELD

The Pilstyes
MIDHURST
Park House
Rivermead House
ROGATE
Mizzards
SIDLESHAM
The Crab & Lobster
Landseer House
WEST MARDEN
West Marden Farmhouse

TYNE & WEAR
GATESHEAD
The Stables Lodge
SUNNISIDE
Hedley Hall Country House

WARWICKSHIRE
ATHERSTONE
Chapel House Restaurant With Rooms
ETTINGTON
Fulready Manor
GREAT WOLFORD
The Old Coach House
STRATFORD-UPON-AVON
Cherry Trees

WEST MIDLANDS
BIRMINGHAM
Westbourne Lodge

ISLE OF WIGHT
BONCHURCH
Winterbourne Country House
GODSHILL
Godshill Park Farm House
Koala Cottage
NITON
Enchanted Manor
VENTNOR
The Hambrough
Horseshoe Bay House
The Leconfield

WILTSHIRE
BOX
Foggam Barn Bed and Breakfast
Spinney Cross

BRADFORD-ON-AVON
Bradford Old Windmill
DEVIZES
Blounts Court Farm
HIGHWORTH
Jesmonds of Highworth
WHITLEY
The Pear Tree Inn

WORCESTERSHIRE
BEWDLEY
Number Thirty
BROADWAY
Mill Hay House
Russell's

EAST RIDING OF YORKSHIRE
BEVERLEY
Burton Mount Country House
BRIDLINGTON
Marton Grange

NORTH YORKSHIRE
AMPLEFORTH
Shallowdale House
APPLETREEWICK
Knowles Lodge
BEDALE
Mill Close Farm
BYLAND ABBEY
The Abbey Inn
GOLDSBOROUGH
Goldsborough Hall
GRASSINGTON
Ashfield House
KNARESBOROUGH
General Tarleton Inn
LEYBURN
Thorney Hall
Capple Bank Farm
PICKERING
17 Burgate
RIPON
Mallard Grange
SCARBOROUGH
Holly Croft

★★★★★ Premier Collection *continued*

THIRSK
Spital Hill
THORNTON WATLASS
Thornton Watlass Hall

CHANNEL ISLANDS

JERSEY
ST AUBIN
The Panorama

ISLE OF MAN
PORT ST MARY
Aaron House

SCOTLAND

ARGYLL & BUTE
BOWMORE
The Harbour Inn and Restaurant
CARDROSS
Kirkton House
CONNEL
Ards House
HELENSBURGH
Lethamhill
OBAN
Blarcreen House

DUMFRIES & GALLOWAY
MOFFAT
Well View
THORNHILL
Gillbank House

CITY OF EDINBURGH
EDINBURGH
Elmview
Kew House
The Witchery by the Castle

FIFE
PEAT INN
The Peat Inn
ST ANDREWS
The Paddock

HIGHLAND
ABRIACHAN
Loch Ness Lodge
AVIEMORE
The Old Minister's House
BRORA
Glenaveron
DAVIOT
Daviot Lodge
DORNOCH
2 Quail Restaurant and Rooms
FORT WILLIAM
The Grange
GRANTOWN-ON-SPEY
An Cala
INVERNESS
Trafford Bank
KINGUSSIE
The Cross at Kingussie
NEWTONMORE
Ard-Na-Coille
POOLEWE
Pool House
STRUAN
Ullinish Country Lodge

PERTH & KINROSS
ALYTH
Tigh Na Leigh Guesthouse
PITLOCHRY
Easter Dunfallandy House

SCOTTISH BORDERS
MELROSE
Fauhope House

SOUTH AYRSHIRE
AYR
The Crescent
MAYBOLE
Ladyburn

STIRLING
STRATHYRE
Creagan House

WEST LOTHIAN
EAST CALDER
Ashcroft Farmhouse
LINLITHGOW
Arden Country House

WALES

CARMARTHENSHIRE
ST CLEARS
Coedllys Country House

CEREDIGION
ABERAERON
The Harbourmaster
Ty Mawr Mansion
ABERYSTWYTH
Awel-Deg

CONWY
ABERGELE
The Kinmel Arms
BETWS-Y-COED
Penmachno Hall
Tan-y-Foel Country House
BYLCHAU
Hafod Elwy Hall
CONWY
The Groes Inn
The Old Rectory Country House
Sychnant Pass Country House
RHOS-ON-SEA
Plas Rhos

DENBIGHSHIRE
LLANDYRNOG
Pentre Mawr Country House
RUTHIN
Firgrove Country House B&B
ST ASAPH
Tan-Yr-Onnen Guest House

GWYNEDD
DOLGELLAU
Tyddynmawr Farmhouse

ISLE OF ANGLESEY
BEAUMARIS
Ye Olde Bulls Head Inn

MONMOUTHSHIRE
SKENFRITH
The Bell at Skenfrith
WHITEBROOK
The Crown at Whitebrook

NEWPORT
CAERLEON
Radford House

PEMBROKESHIRE
SOLVA
Crug-Glas Country House
Lochmeyler Farm Guest House
ST DAVID'S
Ramsey House

POWYS
BRECON
Canal Bank
The Coach House
Peterstone Court
CAERSWS
The Talkhouse
CRICKHOWELL
Glangrwyney Court
LLANDRINDOD WELLS
Guidfa House
WELSHPOOL
Moors Farm B&B

SWANSEA
MUMBLES
Little Langland
PARKMILL
Maes-Yr-Haf Restaurant with Rooms
REYNOLDSTON
Fairyhill

NORTHERN IRELAND

ANTRIM
BUSHMILLS
Whitepark House

DOWN
BANGOR
Hebron House

HOLYWOOD
Rayanne House

LONDONDERRY
COLERAINE
Greenhill House

TYRONE
DUNGANNON
Grange Lodge

REPUBLIC OF IRELAND

CLARE
DOOLIN
Ballyvara House
LAHINCH
Moy House

CORK
BLARNEY
Ashlee Lodge
CLONAKILTY
An Garran Coir
KINSALE
Friar's Lodge
Old Bank House
Perryville House
SHANAGARRY
Ballymaloe House
YOUGHAL
Ahernes

DUBLIN
DUBLIN
Aberdeen Lodge
Blakes Townhouse
Butlers Town House
Glenogra
Harrington Hall
Merrion Hall
Pembroke Townhouse

KERRY
BALLYBUNION
Cashen Course House
CASTLEGREGORY
Shores Country House

DINGLE
Castlewood House
Emlagh House
Gormans Clifftop House & Restaurant
Milltown House
KILLARNEY
Foleys Town House
Fairview
Old Weir Lodge
KILLORGLIN
Carrig House Country House & Restaurant

KILDARE
ATHY
Coursetown Country House

LIMERICK
KILMALLOCK
Flemingstown House

SLIGO
ENNISCRONE
Seasons Lodge

TIPPERARY
THURLES
The Castle
Inch House Country House & Restaurant

WATERFORD
BALLYMACARBRY
Glasha Farmhouse
Hanoras Cottage
DUNGARVAN
Castle Country House
Sliabh gCua Farmhouse
WATERFORD
Sion Hill House & Gardens

WEXFORD
CAMPILE
Kilmokea Country Manor & Gardens
GOREY
Woodlands Country House
ROSSLARE HARBOUR
Churchtown House

WICKLOW
DUNLAVIN
Rathsallagh House

England

Cliff Ridge above Great Ayton, North York Moors National Park

BEDFORDSHIRE

DUNSTABLE
Map 11 TL02

The Highwayman

★★ Ⓐ INN

London Rd LU6 3DX
☎ 01582 601122 📠 01582 603812
e-mail: 6466@greeneking.co.uk
web: www.oldenglish.co.uk
dir: N'bound: M1 junct 9, A5, 6m on right. S'bound: M1 junct 11, A505, left on A5 towards London. Property on left.

Rooms 52 en suite (3 fmly) (24 GF) S £45–£49; D £50–£65 **Facilities** tea/coffee Direct Dial **Parking** 76

MARSTON MORETAINE
Map 11 SP94

Twin Lodge

★★★★ Ⓐ BED AND BREAKFAST

Lower Shelton Rd, Lower Shelton MK43 0LP
☎ 01234 767597
e-mail: pwillsmore@waitrose.com
dir: Off A421 into Lower Shelton

Rooms 4 en suite S £35–£40; D £60–£70* **Facilities** FTV TVL tea/coffee Cen ht **Parking** 5 **Notes** ⊗ ⊜

SANDY
Map 12 TL14

Highfield Farm (TL166515)

★★★★★ Ⓐ FARMHOUSE

Tempsford Rd SG19 2AQ
☎ 01767 682332 **Mrs M Codd**
e-mail: margaret@highfield-farm.co.uk
web: www.highfield-farm.co.uk
dir: 1.5m N of Sandy, driveway off E side of A1

Rooms 3 en suite 3 annexe rms 2 annexe en suite (1 pri facs) (2 fmly) (3 GF) S £51.75–£65; D £75–£90* **Facilities** FTV TVL tea/coffee Cen ht Wi-fi **Parking** 7 **Notes** ⊗ 300 acres arable

BERKSHIRE

BEENHAM
Map 5 SU56

The Six Bells

★★★★ INN

The Green RG7 5NX
☎ 0118 971 3368
e-mail: info@thesixbells.net
web: www.thesixbells.net
dir: Off A4 between Reading/Newbury, follow signs for Beenham Village

Traditional village pub with a restaurant and bedrooms. Good access to Thatcham and Newbury, good atmosphere, friendly service and comfortable, well appointed accommodation.

Rooms 4 en suite **Facilities** FTV tea/coffee Dinner available Cen ht **Conf** Max 40 Thtr 40 Class 40 Board 25 **Parking** 20 **Notes** ⊗ No coaches

BOXFORD
Map 5 SU47

High Street Farm Barn (SU424714)

★★★★ FARMHOUSE

RG20 8DD
☎ 01488 608783 & 07768 324707 **Mr & Mrs Boden**
e-mail: nboden@uk2.net
dir: 0.5m W of village centre. Off B4000 to Boxford, farm 1st on left opposite pub

A converted barn situated on a small holding in the Berkshire village of Boxford. Bedrooms are smartly furnished and a comfortable lounge is available for guests use. Breakfast, which is served at one table, includes free-range eggs from the farm and home-made breads and marmalades.

Rooms 2 en suite (2 GF) S £50; D £65* **Facilities** tea/coffee Cen ht **Parking** **Notes** ⊗ ⊜ 15 acres sheep

White Hart Cottage

★★★ BED AND BREAKFAST

Westbrook RG20 8DN
☎ 01488 608410
e-mail: gillian@jones-parry.orangehome.co.uk
dir: 0.3m NW of Boxford. Off B4000 to Boxford, left for Westbrook, premises on right

Guests are ensured of a friendly welcome at this pretty cottage, peacefully located in the delightful village of Boxford. Newbury and the M4 are both just a short drive away. Bedrooms are attractively appointed and guests have access to a small TV lounge. A hearty breakfast is served at the large kitchen table.

Rooms 3 rms (1 en suite) (2 pri facs) S £30–£35; D £60–£65* **Facilities** TV2B TVL tea/coffee Cen ht **Parking** 6 **Notes** ⊗ No Children Closed 12 Dec–12 Jan ⊜

Bell @ Boxford

★★★ Ⓐ INN

Lambourn Rd RG20 8DD
☎ 01488 608721
e-mail: paul@bellatboxford.com
dir: M4 junct 14 onto A338 towards Wantage. Turn right onto B4000 to x-rds, signed Boxford

Rooms 11 en suite (4 GF) S £50–£75; D £65–£85 **Facilities** FTV tea/coffee Dinner available Direct Dial Cen ht Wi-fi Pool Table **Conf** Max 12 Board 12 **Parking** 35

BRACKNELL
Map 5 SU86

Angel Farm

★★★★ BED AND BREAKFAST

Monks Alley RG42 5PA
☎ 01344 455539 📠 01344 484629
e-mail: sj@angelfarm.co.uk
dir: In centre of Binfield, at rdbt turn onto Forest Rd signed Hurst. Right at 1st rdbt onto Wicks Green. Left onto Monks Alley, 3rd house on right

This alluringly named farmhouse is the home of delightful Mrs Muir and her equally welcoming canine friends. The accommodation has been stylishly and thoughtfully converted. Breakfast is taken around a large imposing dining table and includes home-produced free-range eggs. Although close to the motorway network, the farm enjoys a tranquil country setting.

Rooms 2 rms (2 pri facs) (2 GF) **Facilities** tea/coffee Cen ht Wi-fi ➴ **Parking** 2 **Notes** ⊗ No Children 10yrs RS Sat & Sun No accommodation available ⊜

CHIEVELEY
Map 5 SU47

The Crab at Chieveley

★★★★ ⊛⊛ GUEST ACCOMMODATION

Wantage Rd RG20 8UE
☎ 01635 247550 📠 01635 247440
e-mail: info@crabatchieveley.com
dir: 1.5m W of Chieveley on B4494

The individually themed bedrooms at this former pub have been appointed to a very high standard and include a full range of modern amenities. Ground-floor rooms have a small private patio area complete with a hot tub. The warm and cosy restaurant offers an extensive and award-winning range of fish and seafood dishes.

Rooms 9 en suite 5 annexe en suite (8 GF) **Facilities** FTV tea/coffee Dinner available Direct Dial Cen ht Licensed Wi-fi Hot Tub, Japanese spa suite **Conf** Max 14 Thtr 14 Class 14 Board 14 **Parking** 60 **Notes** LB

COOKHAM DEAN
Map 5 SU88

The Inn on the Green

★★★★ ⊛⊛ RESTAURANT WITH ROOMS

The Old Cricket Common SL6 9NZ
☎ 01628 482638 📠 01628 487474
e-mail: reception@theinnonthegreen.com
dir: In village centre

A traditional English country inn set in rural Berkshire. Bedrooms are spacious and comfortable, with antique furnishings adding to the character. The building retains many traditional features including a wood panelled dining room and Old English bar with log fire. Food is imaginative and noteworthy and can be enjoyed outside in the garden or terrace in warmer months.

Rooms 9 en suite (4 GF) **Facilities** STV FTV tea/coffee Dinner available Direct Dial Cen ht Wi-fi Hot tub, Outdoor games **Conf** Max 70 Thtr 70 Class 30 Board 20 **Parking** 50 **Notes** ⊗ RS Sun & Mon Close at 5pm Sun, Restaurant closed Mon Civ Wed 100

HUNGERFORD Map 5 SU36

Crown & Garter

★★★★ 🍴 INN

Great Common, Inkpen RG17 9QR
☎ 01488 668325
e-mail: gill.hern@btopenworld.com
web: www.crownandgarter.com
dir: 4m SE of Hungerford. Off A4 into Kintbury, opp corner stores onto Inkpen Rd, straight for 2m

Peacefully located in the attractive village of Inkpen, this charming 17th-century inn has a bar with large inglenook log fire where interesting well-prepared dishes are offered. The bedrooms surround a pretty garden, and are comprehensively equipped and attractively decorated in a country cottage style.

Rooms 8 annexe en suite (8 GF) S £69.50; D £99* **Facilities** FTV tea/coffee Dinner available Cen ht Wi-fi **Parking** 40 **Notes** LB ⊗ No Children 7yrs RS No lunch Mon/Tue or evening meal Sun No coaches

The Swan Inn

★★★★ 🛏🍴 INN

Craven Rd, Inkpen RG17 9DX
☎ 01488 668326 📠 01488 668306
e-mail: enquiries@theswaninn-organics.co.uk
web: www.theswaninn-organics.co.uk
dir: 3.5m SE of Hungerford. S on Hungerford High St past rail bridge, left to Hungerford Common, right signed Inkpen

This delightful village inn dates back to the 17th century has open fires and beams in the bar, and the bonus of a smart restaurant. Bedrooms are generally spacious and well equipped. Organic produce is available from the on-site farm shop, so the bar, restaurant and breakfast menus all feature local organic produce too.

The Swan Inn

Rooms 10 en suite (2 fmly) S £60-£70; D £80-£95* **Facilities** tea/coffee Dinner available Direct Dial Cen ht Wi-fi **Conf** Max 40 Thtr 40 Class 40 Board 12 **Parking** 50 **Notes** ⊗ Closed 25-26 Dec

Beacon House

★★★ BED AND BREAKFAST

Bell Ln, Upper Green, Inkpen RG17 9QJ
☎ 01488 668640 📠 01488 668640
e-mail: l.g.cave@classicfm.net
web: www.beaconhouseinkpen.com
dir: 4m SE of Hungerford. Off A4 S into Kintbury, left onto Inkpen Rd, 1m over x-rds, right to common, 3rd left after Crown & Garter pub

This large house is set in peaceful countryside. Bedrooms are comfortably furnished and overlook fields. As well as the lounge, there is usually an art exhibition and sale featuring watercolours, textiles, printmaking and pottery in the adjoining Gallery. Guests are always invited to view.

Rooms 3 rms S fr £34; D fr £68* **Facilities** TVL Cen ht Art studio & gallery **Parking** 6 **Notes** LB ⊗

HURLEY Map 5 SU88

Black Boys Inn

★★★★ 🌻🌻 RESTAURANT WITH ROOMS

Henley Rd SL6 5NQ
☎ 01628 824212
e-mail: info@blackboysinn.co.uk
web: www.blackboysinn.co.uk
dir: 1m W of Hurley on A4130

Just a short drive from Henley, the traditional exterior of this friendly establishment is a contrast to the smart modernity within. Popular with locals, the restaurant is the stage for Simon Bonwick's imaginative cuisine, and offers a buzzing atmosphere. The well-appointed bedrooms are situated in converted barns close by.

Rooms 8 annexe en suite (5 GF); D £87.50-£140* **Facilities** FTV tea/coffee Dinner available Cen ht Wi-fi **Conf** Max 8 Board 8 **Parking** 40 **Notes** ⊗ No Children 12yrs No coaches

NEWBURY Map 5 SU46

Pilgrims Guest House

★★★★ GUEST ACCOMMODATION

Oxford Rd RG14 1XB
☎ 01635 40694 📠 01635 44873
e-mail: office@pilgrimsgh.co.uk
web: www.pilgrimsnewbury.co.uk
dir: Off Waitrose A4 rdbt onto B4494 towards Wantage, 0.5m on left

Located close to the town centre, this smartly presented house has stylish bedrooms with modern bathrooms, and some rooms are in a new annexe. Hearty breakfasts are served in the bright dining room. Large car park.

Rooms 13 rms (9 en suite) 4 annexe en suite (1 fmly) (3 GF) S £42-£55; D £55-£65* **Facilities** tea/coffee Cen ht Wi-fi **Parking** 17 **Notes** ⊗ Closed 24 Dec-2 Jan

Rookwood Farm House

★★★★ GUEST ACCOMMODATION

Stockcross RG20 8JX
☎ 01488 608676 📠 01488 657961
e-mail: charlotte@rookwoodfarmhouse.co.uk
dir: 2m W of Newbury, at junct A4 & A34 onto B4000, 0.75m to Stockcross, 1st right signed Woodspeen, bear left, 1st on right

This farmhouse enjoys wonderful views and is very much a family home. Bedrooms are attractively presented and feature fine pieces of furniture. Breakfast is served on one large table in the kitchen. The coach house has a kitchen and sitting room, and during the summer visitors can enjoy the beautiful gardens and outdoor pool.

Rooms 1 en suite 2 annexe en suite (1 fmly) **Facilities** TVL tea/coffee Cen ht 🏇 ⛵ **Conf** Max 12 Board 12 **Parking** 3 **Notes** ⊗

NEWBURY *continued*

Dolphin Inn

★★★ GUEST ACCOMMODATION

113 Bartholomew St RG14 5DT
☎ **01635 232425** 🖶 **01635 230356**
e-mail: room@dolphin-inns.com
dir: *In town centre. Off A339 Sainsbury's rdbt into town centre, signs for council offices, inn opposite*

A warm welcome and attentive service are assured at this renovated 17th-century coaching inn, located within easy walking distance of the historic centre. Thoughtfully furnished bedrooms feature smart modern bathrooms, and spacious public areas include an attractive conservatory restaurant.

Rooms 4 en suite **Facilities** STV FTV tea/coffee Dinner available Direct Dial Cen ht Licensed **Conf** Max 50 Thtr 50 Class 50 Board 40 **Parking** 20 **Notes** ⊗ No Children 16yrs

The Limes Guest House

★★★ GUEST HOUSE

368 London Rd RG14 2QH
☎ **01635 33082** 🖶 **01635 580023**
e-mail: s.j.sweeney@btinternet.com
web: www.limesguesthouse.co.uk
dir: *M4 junct 13, 3m S towards Newbury. Take A4 to towards Thatcham/Reading, 400yds past Newbury Business Park on left*

Built in 1910, the Edwardian house is convenient for Newbury and Thatcham, and Newbury Racecourse is only a mile away. The en suite bedrooms are individually decorated. Wi-fi internet access and ample parking are available. Dinner and breakfast are served in the light dining room overlooking the spacious gardens.

Rooms 17 en suite (2 fmly) (9 GF) **Facilities** FTV TVL tea/coffee Dinner available Direct Dial Cen ht Wi-fi **Parking** 20 **Notes** ⊗

Weir View House

★★★★ GUEST ACCOMMODATION

9 Shooters Hill RG8 7DZ
☎ **0118 984 2120** 🖶 **0118 984 3777**
e-mail: info@weirview.co.uk
web: www.weirview.co.uk
dir: *A329 N from Pangbourne, after mini rdbt under rail bridge, opp Swan pub*

A warm welcome is guaranteed at this delightful house, situated in the village of Pangbourne overlooking the River Thames. The spacious modern bedrooms have been finished to a very high standard and the thoughtful extras include a well-stocked minibar. A continental breakfast is served in the bright and airy dining room, and freshly cooked meals can be delivered to your room from the pub across the road.

Rooms 9 en suite (6 fmly) (3 GF); D £80-£95*
Facilities FTV TVL tea/coffee Direct Dial Cen ht Wi-fi
Parking 10 **Notes** ⊗ Closed 23 Dec-1 Jan

The New Inn

★★★★ 🏠🍽 INN

Chalkhouse Green Rd, Kidmore End RG4 9AU
☎ **0118 972 3115** 🖶 **0118 972 4733**
e-mail: thenewinn@live.co.uk
web: www.thenewinnrestaurant.co.uk
dir: *Near Reading Golf Club*

This delightful village inn successfully combines traditional charm with stylish sophistication. The popular bar offers real ales and a selection of snacks, while more formal meals are available in the restaurant. Bedrooms

---

are modern and peaceful and some have their own patios and balconies.

Rooms 6 en suite (3 GF); D £75-£95* **Facilities** FTV tea/coffee Dinner available Direct Dial Cen ht Wi-fi **Parking** 60 **Notes** LB

Chestnuts Bed & Breakfast

★★★ BED AND BREAKFAST

Basingstoke Rd, Spencers Wood RG7 1AA
☎ **0118 988 6171** & **07903 956397**
e-mail: chestnuts4bb@hotmail.com
dir: *M4 junct 11, A33 for Basingstoke, next rdbt onto B3349 Three Mile Cross, over white-spot rdbt, Chestnuts 1m on left between chemist & bakery*

This detached Georgian house is convenient for the business parks of Reading, just 1.5 miles from the M4 and with easy access to the M3. The non-smoking house provides spacious bedrooms, warm hospitality, a good breakfast, and off-road parking.

Rooms 2 rms 2 annexe en suite S £35-£45; D £50-£60 **Facilities** FTV tea/coffee Cen ht Wi-fi **Parking** 4 **Notes** ⊗ No Children 16yrs 🖶

La Baguette Reading

★★ GUEST HOUSE

7 Blagrave St RG1 1PJ
☎ **0118 956 0882** 🖶 **0118 951 1447**
e-mail: sales@ccare.co.uk

Located a moments walk from Reading town centre, close to the main train station. Bedrooms vary in size and provide comfortable accommodation for the traveller. A varied choice of breakfast is served in the popular 'La Baguette' sandwich shop below.

Rooms 6 rms (6 pri facs) **Facilities** tea/coffee Cen ht Wi-fi **Notes** LB

Furnival Lodge

★★★★ 🅰 GUEST HOUSE

53-55 Furnival Av SL2 1DH
☎ **01753 570333** 🖶 **01753 670038**
e-mail: info@furnival-lodge.co.uk
web: www.furnival-lodge.co.uk
dir: *Just off A355 (Farnham Rd) adjacent to BP garage*

Rooms 10 en suite (1 fmly) (3 GF) **Facilities** TVL Cen ht Wi-fi **Parking** 7 **Notes** ⊗

WINDSOR
Map 6 SU97

Park Farm
★★★★ GUEST ACCOMMODATION

St Leonards Rd SL4 3EA
☎ 01753 866823
e-mail: stay@parkfarm.com
dir: *M4 junct 6, at end of dual-carriageway take 3rd exit. At junct, turn right, Park Farm on left*

Ideally situated between Windsor and Legoland, Park Farm offers a warm welcome and traditionally styled accommodation. Each bedroom has a lot of useful facilities. Some rooms also have romantic wrought-iron beds. The owners aim to offer guests a friendly and personal service including advice and information on where to eat or what to do in the area. Bunkbeds can be added for children.

Rooms 4 rms (3 en suite) (1 pri facs) (2 fmly) (2 GF) **Facilities** FTV tea/coffee Cen ht Wi-fi **Parking** 8 **Notes** ⊗ ⊜

Clarence Guest House
★★★ GUEST HOUSE

9 Clarence Rd SL4 5AE
☎ 01753 864436 🖷 01753 857060
e-mail: clarence.hotel@btconnect.com
web: www.clarence-hotel.co.uk
dir: *M4 junct 6, dual-carriageway to Windsor, left at 1st rdbt onto Clarence Rd*

This Grade II listed Victorian house is in the heart of Windsor. Space in some rooms is limited, but all are well maintained and offer excellent value for money. Facilities include a lounge with a well-stocked bar, and a steam room. Breakfast is served in the dining room overlooking attractive gardens.

Rooms 20 en suite (6 fmly) (2 GF) (18 smoking) S £40-£72; D £45-£82* **Facilities** FTV TVL tea/coffee Cen ht Licensed Wi-fi Sauna Steam room **Parking** 4

WOKINGHAM
Map 5 SU86

Quarters
★★★★ GUEST ACCOMMODATION

14 Milton Rd RG40 1DB
☎ 0118 979 7071 🖷 0118 977 0057
e-mail: elaineizod@hotmail.com
dir: *From town centre on A321 towards Henley/Twyford. Left at 1st mini-rdbt onto Milton Rd*

Located just a short walk from the town centre, a guaranteed warm welcome is assured here. Stylishly decorated bedrooms are well equipped and spacious. A hearty breakfast is served around the communal dining table.

Rooms 3 en suite **Facilities** FTV tea/coffee Cen ht Wi-fi **Notes** ⊗ ⊜

BRISTOL

BRISTOL
Map 4 ST57

Westfield House
★★★★ ⊜ BED AND BREAKFAST

37 Stoke Hill, Stoke Bishop BS9 1LQ
☎ 0117 962 6119 🖷 0117 962 6119
e-mail: admin@westfieldhouse.net
web: www.westfieldhouse.net
dir: *1.8m NW of city centre in Stoke Bishop*

A genuine welcome is assured at this friendly, family-run guest house in a quiet location on the edge of Durdham Downs. The very well-equipped bedrooms offer high levels of quality and comfort. Home-cooked dinners are available by arrangement, and in summer these can be enjoyed on the patio overlooking the large rear garden.

Rooms 3 en suite S £69-£79; D £79-£108 **Facilities** FTV TVL tea/coffee Dinner available Direct Dial Cen ht Wi-fi ⤵ **Conf** Max 10 Board 10 **Parking** 5 **Notes** LB ⊗ No Children 11yrs

Downlands House
★★★★ GUEST ACCOMMODATION

33 Henleaze Gardens, Henleaze BS9 4HH
☎ 0117 962 1639
e-mail: info@downlandshouse.co.uk
web: www.downlandshouse.com
dir: *2m NW of city centre off A4018. M5 junct 17, follow Westbury-on-Trym/City Centre signs, pass Badminton private girls' school. Henleaze Gdns on left*

This elegant Victorian property is convenient for Durdham Downs, Clifton village and Bristol Zoo. The attractive bedrooms have lots of extra touches, there is a smart lounge, and breakfast is served in either the conservatory or the stylish dining room.

Rooms 10 rms (7 en suite) (3 pri facs) (1 fmly) (1 GF) S £40-£55; D £70-£75* **Facilities** FTV TVL tea/coffee Cen ht Wi-fi

Downs Edge
★★★★ GUEST HOUSE

Saville Rd, Stoke Bishop BS9 1JA
☎ 0117 968 3264 & 07885 866463 🖷 0117 968 7063
e-mail: welcome@downsedge.com
dir: *M5 junct 17, A4018, 4th rdbt right onto B4054 Parrys Ln, 1st left onto Saville Rd, 3rd right onto Hollybush Ln, left after 2nd speed ramp into Downs Edge Drive*

This fetching country house has a quiet countryside setting in the heart of the city, on the edge of Durdham Downs. It stands in glorious gardens and is furnished with period pieces and paintings. The pleasant, well-equipped bedrooms have en suite facilities and the added bonus of sweeping views across the Downs - a nice finishing touch to each room is a basket full with life's little necessities. Breakfast is an impressive variety of hot and cold dishes. There is a drawing room with an

continued

BRISTOL *continued*

open fire, and a library containing many books about Bristol.

Rooms 4 en suite 3 annexe en suite **Facilities** tea/coffee Cen ht Wi-fi **Conf** Board 12 **Parking** 8 **Notes** ⊗ No Children 6yrs Closed Xmas & New Year

Greenlands *(ST597636)*

★★★★ FARMHOUSE

BS39 4ES
☎ 01275 333487 ▤ 01275 331211 Mrs J Cleverley

(For full entry see Stanton Drew (Somerset))

Valley Farm

★★★★ BED AND BREAKFAST

Sandy Ln BS39 4EL
☎ 01275 332723 & 07799 768161 ▤ 01275 332723
e-mail: valleyfarm2000@tiscali.co.uk

(For full entry see Stanton Drew (Somerset))

Westbury Park Guest House

★★★★ GUEST HOUSE

37 Westbury Rd, Westbury-on-Trym BS9 3AU
☎ 0117 962 0465 ▤ 0117 962 8607
e-mail: westburypark@btconnect.com
dir: *M5 junct 17, A4018, 3.5m opp gates of Badminton School*

On the edge of Durdham Downs, this detached guest house is ideally located for many of Bristol's attractions. Breakfast is served in the spacious dining room overlooking the front garden. Bedrooms and bathrooms come in a range of shapes and sizes, including one room on the ground floor.

Rooms 8 en suite (3 fmly) (1 GF) **Facilities** tea/coffee Cen ht Licensed **Parking** 4

Mayfair Lodge

★★★ GUEST HOUSE

5 Henleaze Rd, Westbury-on-Trym BS9 4EX
☎ 0117 962 2008 ▤ 0117 962 2008
e-mail: mayfairlodge@blueyonder.co.uk
dir: *M5 junct 17, A4018, after 3rd rdbt onto Henleaze Rd, Lodge 50yds on left*

This charming Victorian house is in a residential area close to Durdham Downs and Bristol Zoo. Mayfair Lodge has well-equipped bedrooms of varying sizes and a relaxed, friendly atmosphere. Breakfast is served at separate tables in the bright dining room. Off-road parking is available behind the property.

Rooms 9 rms (6 en suite) S £36-£55; D £68-£70* **Facilities** tea/coffee Cen ht Wi-fi **Parking** 6 **Notes** ⊗ No Children 10yrs Closed Xmas & New Year

Washington

★★★ GUEST HOUSE

11-15 St Pauls Rd, Clifton BS8 1LX
☎ 0117 973 3980 ▤ 0117 973 4740
e-mail: washington@cliftonhotels.com
dir: *A4018 into city, right at lights opp BBC, house 200yds on left*

This large terrace house is within walking distance of the city centre and Clifton village. The bedrooms, many recently refurbished, are well equipped for business guests. Public areas include a modern reception lounge and a bright basement breakfast room. The property has secure parking and a rear patio garden.

Rooms 46 rms (40 en suite) (4 fmly) (10 GF) (7 smoking) S £39-£69; D £48-£87* **Facilities** STV tea/coffee Direct Dial Cen ht Licensed Wi-fi Reduced rate pass for local health club **Parking** 16 **Notes** Closed 23 Dec-3 Jan

Downs View

★★★ ◭ GUEST HOUSE

38 Upper Belgrave Rd, Clifton BS8 2XN
☎ 0117 973 7046 ▤ 0117 973 8169
e-mail: bookings@downsviewguesthouse.co.uk
dir: *1m NW of city centre. A4018 onto A4176, just before zoo*

Rooms 16 rms (9 en suite) (1 fmly) (2 GF) S £45-£60; D £60-£75* **Facilities** FTV tea/coffee Cen ht Wi-fi **Notes** ⊗ Closed Xmas & New Year

Shirehampton Lodge

★★ GUEST HOUSE

62-64 High St, Shirehampton BS11 0DJ
☎ 0117 907 3480 ▤ 0117 907 3481
dir: *M5 junct 18, B4054 to Shirehampton for 1m, premises on left opp Texaco garage, entrance up ramp*

Situated above shops, this imaginatively converted warehouse offers easy access to the motorway and the city centre. The modern bedrooms are thoughtfully equipped for business and leisure, and there is a well-furnished lounge/dining room.

Rooms 11 en suite (3 fmly) **Facilities** STV tea/coffee Cen ht **Parking** 10 **Notes** No Children

EASTON-IN-GORDANO   Map 4 ST57

The Tynings B & B

★★★ BED AND BREAKFAST

Martcombe Rd BS20 0QE
☎ 01275 372608
e-mail: elizabeth.bleaken@virgin.net
dir: *M5 junct 19, A369 towards Bristol (signed Clifton), 0.5m on right opp Rudgleigh Inn*

The Tynings is just ten minutes drive away from central Bristol. Bedrooms and bathrooms here offer a range of sizes and all are well decorated and comfortably furnished. Off-street car parking is available and guests may wish to opt for dinner in the pub just across the road. Breakfast is served in the small but comfortable dining room.

Rooms 6 rms (3 en suite) (3 pri facs) (4 fmly) (1 GF) S £40-£45; D £50-£55* **Facilities** TVL tea/coffee Cen ht Wi-fi **Parking** 8 **Notes** ⊗ Closed 25 & 26 Dec ▣

BUCKINGHAMSHIRE

AMERSHAM   Map 6 SU99

Wildhatch

★★★★ BED AND BREAKFAST

Coles Hill Ln, Winchmore Hill HP7 0NT
☎ 01494 722611 ▤ 01494 722611
e-mail: ci.john.wildhatch@btinternet.com
dir: *M40 junct 2 N on A355, after 1.5m left at Magpies public house. Fork left at Coleshill & continue to Winchmore Hill, house 2nd on left after 30mph sign*

This beautifully presented modern house offers well-equipped bedrooms and comfortable public rooms, hospitality is a major strength. Delicious, freshly cooked breakfasts are served in the dining room overlooking the gardens and surrounding countryside. Weather permitting breakfast may be taken on the terrace. Close to major motorway links.

Rooms 2 en suite (1 fmly) S £45-£50; D £60-£65 **Facilities** TVL tea/coffee Dinner available Cen ht Wi-fi **Parking** 4 **Notes** Closed 23 Dec-17 Jan ▣

BEACONSFIELD   Map 6 SU99

PREMIER COLLECTION

Crazy Bear Beaconsfield
★★★★★ GUEST ACCOMMODATION

75 Wycombe End, Old Town HP9 1LX
☎ 01494 673086 📠 01494 730183
e-mail: enquiries@crazybear-beaconsfield.co.uk
dir: M40 junct 2, 3rd exit from rdbt, next rdbt 1st exit.
Over 2 mini-rdbts, on right

Located in the heart of the old town, this former inn
dating from Tudor times has been completely restored
to create an exciting and vibrant environment. Good
food in both the Thai and the English Restaurants,
classic cocktails and an extensive wine list can be
enjoyed. The rooms are individually appointed with
unusual fabrics and dazzling colours.

Rooms 6 en suite 4 annexe en suite (2 GF) S £170;
D £215-£380 **Facilities** STV Dinner available Direct
Dial Cen ht Licensed Wi-fi ⚡ Jacuzzi **Conf** Max 40
Board 22 **Parking** 12 **Notes** ⊗

BRILL   Map 11 SP61

Poletrees Farm *(SP660160)*
★★★★ FARMHOUSE

Ludgershall Rd HP18 9TZ
☎ 01844 238276 📠 01844 238276   Mrs A Cooper
e-mail: poletrees.farm@virgin.net
dir: S off A41 signed Ludgershall/Brill, after railway
bridge 0.5m on left

Located between the villages of Ludgershall and Brill,
this 16th-century farmhouse retains many original
features including a wealth of exposed beams. The
bedrooms are in converted outbuildings. Breakfast is
served in the cosy dining room, the setting for a
wholesome breakfast.

Rooms 4 annexe en suite (4 GF); D £70-£80*
Facilities FTV TVL tea/coffee Cen ht **Parking** 6 **Notes** LB
⊗ No Children 10yrs 110 acres beef/sheep

DENHAM   Map 6 TQ08

The Falcon Inn
★★★★ 🍺 INN

Village Rd UB9 5BE
☎ 01895 832125
e-mail: mail@falcondenham.com
web: www.falcondenham.com
dir: M40 junct 1 signed A40 Gerrards Cross. After approx
200yds, turn right into Old Mill Rd, follow road, pub opp
village green

The 18th-century inn stands in the heart of the
picturesque village, opposite the green. The bedrooms,
with smart shower rooms en suite, are well equipped and
display original features. Carefully prepared dishes and a
good selection of wines are available for lunch and dinner
in the cosy restaurant.

Rooms 4 en suite **Facilities** tea/coffee Dinner available
Cen ht Wi-fi **Notes** LB ⊗ No Children 10yrs

London Road, Great Missenden, Bucks HP16 0DG
Tel/Fax: 01494 862200   Fax: 01494 862685
Email: goodfood@nagsheadbucks.com
Website: www.nagsheadbucks.com

AA
★★★★

The 4 star, Nags Head Inn has tastefully been
refurbished to a high standard retaining its original
15th century country inn features including low
oak beams and a large inglenook fireplace.

It's now an award-winning Rosette gastro pub
and restaurant with beautifully furnished double and twin
bedrooms all with private ensuite facilities.

Situated in the valley of the River Misbourne within the
glorious Chilterns, it's ideally located within walking
distance of the picturesque village of Great Missenden,
Buckinghamshire near all major road and rail routes.

Highly regarded for their English and French fusion dishes,
the menu is extensive with starters, salads, main dishes,
desserts and daily specials, as well as a pub menu. Enjoy!

FORD
Map 5 SP71

Dinton Hermit
★★★ INN

Water Ln HP17 8XH
☎ **01296 747473** ▤ **01296 748819**
e-mail: mary@passionpubs.co.uk
dir: 2m from A418

A restored 400-year-old, Grade II listed property that now provides a smart restaurant and atmospheric bedrooms in both the old inn and in the 200-year-old barn conversion. Bedrooms are well equipped and comfortable, and the restaurant is popular with locals and guests alike.

Rooms 7 en suite 6 annexe en suite (8 GF) S £90–£130; D £90–£130* **Facilities** FTV tea/coffee Dinner available Direct Dial Cen ht Wi-fi **Parking** 40 **Notes** LB

GAYHURST
Map 11 SP84

Mill Farm (SP852454)
★★★ FARMHOUSE

MK16 8LT
☎ **01908 611489** & **07714 719640**
▤ 01908 611489 **Mrs K Adams**
e-mail: adamsmillfarm@aol.com
web: www.millfarmgayhurst.co.uk
dir: B526 from Newport Pagnell, 2.5m left onto Haversham Rd, Mill Farm 1st on left

Within easy reach of Newport Pagnell and the M1, this historic farmhouse has a peaceful setting with wonderful views over farmland. Bedrooms are decorated in a homely style and have a host of thoughtful extras. The sumptuous lounge-dining room is enhanced with fine antiques, and the extensive grounds include a tennis court.

Rooms 3 rms (2 en suite) 1 annexe en suite (1 fmly) (1 GF) S £25–£35; D £50–£60* **Facilities** TVL tea/coffee Cen ht 🎣 🚤 Fishing **Parking** 13 **Notes** 🚭 550 acres mixed

GREAT MISSENDEN
Map 6 SP80

Nags Head Inn & Restaurant
★★★★ 🏵 INN

London Rd HP16 0DG
☎ **01494 862200** ▤ **01494 862685**
e-mail: goodfood@nagsheadbucks.com
web: www.nagsheadbucks.com
dir: N of Amersham on A413, turn left at Chiltern hospital onto London Rd signed Great Missenden

A delightful 15th-century inn located in the picturesque Chiltern Hills, has a popular reputation locally thanks to its extensive menu with local produce and carefully prepared dishes plus the wine list. Individually designed bedrooms are comfortable with a modern twist ensuring a home-from-home feel. Ample parking is available.

Rooms 5 en suite (1 fmly) S £90–£120; D £90–£120 **Facilities** FTV tea/coffee Dinner available Cen ht Wi-fi **Conf** Max 50 **Parking** 40

See advert on page 37

HIGH WYCOMBE
Map 5 SU89

The Tree at Cadmore
★★★★ INN

Marlow Rd HP14 3PF
☎ **01494 881183** & **882269** ▤ **01494 882269**
e-mail: cadmore@treehotel.co.uk

Newly refurbished to meet the expectations of modern guests, the bedrooms are spacious and well equipped. The stylish pub retains a real traditional, country atmosphere and offers a well-balanced menu together with a fine range of wines, beers and spirits. Guests can also relax on the patio area in warmer weather.

Rooms 16 en suite S £45–£75; D £50–£95* **Facilities** Dinner available Direct Dial Wi-fi **Parking**

Clifton Lodge
★★★ GUEST HOUSE

210 West Wycombe Rd HP12 3AR
☎ **01494 440095** & **529062** ▤ **01494 536322**
e-mail: sales@cliftonlodgehotel.com
web: www.cliftonlodgehotel.com
dir: A40 from town centre towards Aylesbury, on right after BP station & opp phone box

Located west of the town centre, this long-established, owner-managed establishment provides a range of bedrooms, popular with a regular commercial clientele. Public areas include an attractive conservatory-dining room and a cosy lounge. Ample parking behind the property.

Rooms 32 rms (20 en suite) (1 fmly) (7 GF) **Facilities** TVL tea/coffee Dinner available Direct Dial Cen ht Licensed **Conf** Max 30 Thtr 30 Class 20 Board 15 **Parking** 28 **Notes** 🚭

IVINGHOE
Map 11 SP91

The Brownlow B&B
★★★★ GUEST ACCOMMODATION

LU7 9DY
☎ **01296 668787**
e-mail: info@thebrownlow.com
dir: A41 to Tring onto B488 to Ivinghoe/Dunstable. Follow Leighton Buzzard sign on B488

The Brownlow at Ivinghoe was built in the early 1800s to serve the newly finished Grand Union Canal, it has remained in the same family ever since. The old stables have now been converted into well-appointed bedrooms, which offer plenty of modern amenities. Breakfast is served at the communal table overlooking the canal.

Rooms 5 en suite (5 GF) S £45–£55; D £75–£85* **Facilities** FTV TVL tea/coffee Cen ht Wi-fi **Parking** 6 **Notes** 🚭 No Children 6yrs

CAMBRIDGESHIRE

BOXWORTH
Map 12 TL36

The Golden Ball Inn
★★★★ INN

High St CB23 8LY
☎ **01954 267397** ▤ **01954 267497**
e-mail: info@goldenballhotel.co.uk
dir: In village centre

The Golden Ball is a delightful 17th-century thatched inn with modern accommodation. The bedrooms are well appointed and each bathroom has a bath and power shower. The inn is very popular for its restaurant, pub meals and real ales, and service is helpful and friendly.

Rooms 11 en suite (1 fmly) (9 GF) S £79–£79; D £89–£89 **Facilities** tea/coffee Dinner available Direct Dial Cen ht **Conf** Max 20 **Parking** 75 **Notes** 🚭

CAMBRIDGE
Map 12 TL45

The Gate Lodge
★★★★ BED AND BREAKFAST

2 Hinton Rd, Fulbourn CB1 5DZ
☎ 01223 881951 📠 01223 881952
e-mail: bandb@thegatelodge.co.uk
dir: *5m E of Cambridge. W side of Fulbourn village opp corner to Bakers Arms pub.*

This restful, lovingly restored house is in a sleepy village not far from Cambridge and the M11. The spacious bedrooms are well appointed with useful extras including internet connections, flat screen TV with Freeview and DVD facilities in all rooms. Breakfast is a feature, served round a large oak table in the attractive dining room.

Rooms 3 rms (1 en suite) (2 pri facs) (2 fmly) S £60-£80; D £80-£85* **Facilities** FTV tea/coffee Cen ht 🛟 **Parking** 5 **Notes** ⊗ No Children 5yrs

Lynwood House
★★★★ 🏠 GUEST HOUSE

217 Chesterton Rd CB4 1AN
☎ 01223 500776
e-mail: info@lynwood-house.co.uk
web: www.lynwood-house.co.uk
dir: *M11 N junct 13, A1303 towards city centre, left at mini-rdbt, house 1m on left*

Located close to the river and central attractions, this constantly improving guest house provides a range of thoughtfully equipped bedrooms, most of which have the benefit of modern en suite shower rooms. Organically sourced produce is a feature of the wholesome breakfasts which are taken in a stylish dining room. A warm welcome is assured.

Rooms 7 rms (5 en suite) (1 fmly) (2 GF) S £35-£75; D £75-£105* **Facilities** FTV tea/coffee Cen ht Wi-fi **Parking** 3 **Notes** ⊗ No Children 12yrs

Rose Corner
★★★★ BED AND BREAKFAST

42 Woodcock Close, Impington CB24 9LD
☎ 01223 563136 📠 01223 233886
e-mail: wsalmon.rosecorner@virgin.net
web: www.rose-corner.co.uk
dir: *4m N of Cambridge. A14 junct 32, B1049 N into Impington, off Milton Rd*

The detached property is in a quiet cul-de-sac in the popular village of Impington, north of the city. Its spacious bedrooms are carefully furnished and thoughtfully equipped, and breakfast is served in the comfortable lounge/dining room overlooking the rear gardens.

Rooms 5 rms (3 en suite) S £30; D £60-£65* **Facilities** FTV TVL tea/coffee Cen ht Wi-fi **Parking** 5 **Notes** ⊗ No Children 11yrs

Angela's B & B
★★★ BED AND BREAKFAST

40 Leys Av CB4 2AW
☎ 01223 709695 & 691088 📠 01223 363297
e-mail: prague2@live.co.uk
dir: *From A14 onto A1309 (Milton Rd). 1.5m right onto Hurst Park Av*

A friendly, family-run bed and breakfast situated in a quiet street close to the heart of the city centre. The dining room overlooks the garden and guests have the use of a cosy lounge; breakfast is served on the terrace in the summer months. The smartly appointed bedrooms have co-ordinated soft furnishings and a good range of useful extras.

Rooms 2 rms (1 en suite) (1 pri facs) S £45-£60; D £60-£80* **Facilities** TVL Cen ht Wi-fi Sauna Jacuzzi **Parking** 2 **Notes** ⊗

Alpha Milton
★★★ GUEST HOUSE

61-63 Milton Rd CB4 1XA
☎ 01223 311625 📠 01223 565100
e-mail: info@alphamilton.com
dir: *0.5m NE of city centre*

The Alpha Milton is in a residential area just a short walk from the city centre. The attractive lounge-dining room overlooks the rear garden, and the pleasant bedrooms have a good range of facilities.

Rooms 8 rms (6 en suite) (1 pri facs) (2 fmly) (2 GF) S £40-£70; D £60-£90* **Facilities** TVL tea/coffee Cen ht Wi-fi **Parking** 8 **Notes** LB ⊗

Benson House
★★★ GUEST HOUSE

24 Huntingdon Rd CB3 0HH
☎ 01223 311594 📠 01223 311594
e-mail: bensonhouse@btconnect.com
dir: *0.5m NW of city centre on A604*

The popular guest house is well placed for the city centre and New Hall and Fitzwilliam colleges. Its pleasant bedrooms vary in size and style and are well equipped. Limited private parking behind the property.

Rooms 7 rms (6 en suite) (1 pri facs) (1 GF) S £65-£75; D £70-£95 **Facilities** FTV tea/coffee Cen ht Wi-fi **Parking** 5 **Notes** ⊗ No Children 12yrs

Fairways
★★★ GUEST HOUSE

143 Cherry Hinton Rd CB1 7BX
☎ 01223 246063 📠 01223 248306
e-mail: michaelslatter@btconnect.com
web: www.fairwaysguesthouse.com
dir: *M11 junct 11 onto A1309 to A1134. Left onto A1307, right onto Cherry Hinton Rd*

The large Victorian house provides well-equipped bedrooms convenient for the city centre and the ring road. Many of the rooms have attractive, handcrafted pine furniture, and the en suite rooms have modern showers. Breakfast is served in an attractive ground-floor dining room and ample car parking is available to the rear of property.

Rooms 16 rms (9 en suite) (3 fmly) (4 GF) S £34-£42; D £56-£70 **Facilities** tea/coffee Cen ht Wi-fi **Parking** 20 **Notes** ⊗ Closed 22 Dec-2 Jan

CAMBRIDGE *continued*

Hamden
★★★ GUEST HOUSE

89 High St, Cherry Hinton CB1 9LU
☎ 01223 413263 📠 01223 245960
e-mail: info@hamdenguesthouse.co.uk
web: www.hamdenguesthouse.co.uk
dir: *3m SE of city centre. Off A1134 to Cherry Hinton*

Expect a warm welcome at this small, family-run guest house, which is just a short drive from the city centre. The pleasant bedrooms are generally quite spacious and equipped with many thoughtful extras. Public rooms include a large kitchen-dining room where breakfast is served at individual tables.

Rooms 3 en suite (2 fmly) (1 GF) S £40-£45; D £60-£70*
Facilities FTV tea/coffee Direct Dial Cen ht **Parking** 6
Notes LB ⊗ No Children 5yrs

See advert on opposite page

Hamilton Lodge
★★★ GUEST HOUSE

156 Chesterton Rd CB4 1DA
☎ 01223 365664 📠 01223 314866
e-mail: hamiltonhotel@talk21.com
dir: *1m NE of city centre, off A1134 ring road*

Smartly maintained property situated just a short walk from the city centre. The pleasantly appointed bedrooms have co-ordinated fabrics and a good range of facilities to enhance guest comfort. The relaxing public areas include a large open-plan restaurant/bar, where breakfast, evening meals and a range of snacks are available.

Rooms 25 rms (19 en suite) (4 fmly) (8 GF) S £32-£60; D £60-£85* **Facilities** tea/coffee Dinner available Direct Dial Cen ht Licensed Wi-fi **Parking** 20 **Notes** ⊗ Closed 25 & 26 Dec

Southampton Guest House
★★★ GUEST HOUSE

7 Elizabeth Way CB4 1DE
☎ 01223 357780 📠 01223 314297
e-mail: southamptonhouse@btinternet.com
web: www.southamptonguesthouse.com
dir: *0.5m E of city centre*

The proprietors provide a friendly service at their terrace guest house, which is on the inner ring road, just a short walk from the Grafton Centre. The property has well-equipped bedrooms, and a comprehensive English breakfast is served.

Rooms 5 en suite (3 fmly) (1 GF) S £35-£45; D £48-£58*
Facilities tea/coffee Direct Dial Cen ht Wi-fi **Parking** 8
Notes ⊗ 🚭

Ashtrees Guest House
★★ GUEST HOUSE

128 Perne Rd CB1 3RR
☎ 01223 411233 📠 01223 411233
e-mail: ashtrees@cscuk.net
web: www.ashtreesguesthouse.co.uk
dir: *1.5m SE of city centre on A1134*

Service is informal, cheerful and helpful at Ashtrees, and the en suite bedrooms come in a variety of styles and sizes. A continental or full cooked breakfast is served at individual tables in the pleasant breakfast room. Some private parking is available to the rear of the property.

Rooms 5 en suite (1 fmly) (2 GF) **Facilities** tea/coffee Cen ht **Parking** 5

ELTON Map 12 TL09

PREMIER COLLECTION

The Crown Inn
★★★★★ 🍴 INN

8 Duck St PE8 6RQ
☎ 01832 280232
e-mail: inncrown@googlemail.com
web: www.thecrowninn.org
dir: *A1 junct 17 onto A605 W. In 3.5m right signed Elton, 0.9m left signed Nassington. On village green*

Expect a warm welcome at this delightful village pub which is situated opposite the village green. The property dates back to the 16th century, and has recently undergone major refurbishment yet retains many of its original features, such as a large inglenook fireplace and oak-beamed ceilings. The smartly decorated bedrooms are tastefully appointed and thoughtfully equipped. Public rooms include a large open-plan lounge bar, a small relaxed dining area to the front, and a tastefully appointed circular restaurant.

Rooms 3 en suite 2 annexe en suite (2 fmly) (2 GF) S £60-£80; D £80-£120* **Facilities** tea/coffee Dinner available Cen ht Wi-fi **Conf** Max 40 Thtr 25 Class 40 Board 25 **Parking** 15 **Notes** LB RS Sun eve & Mon (ex BH) Restaurant only closed No coaches

---

ELY Map 12 TL58

The Anchor Inn
★★★★ 🌑 RESTAURANT WITH ROOMS

Sutton Gault CB6 2BD
☎ 01353 778537 📠 01353 776180
e-mail: anchorinn@popmail.bta.com
dir: *6m W of Ely. Sutton Gault signed off B1381 at S end of Sutton*

Located beside the New Bedford River with stunning country views, this 17th-century inn has a wealth of original features enhanced by period furniture. The spacious bedrooms are tastefully appointed and equipped with many thoughtful touches. The friendly team of staff offer helpful and attentive service.

Rooms 4 en suite (2 fmly) **Facilities** FTV tea/coffee Dinner available Direct Dial Cen ht Wi-fi **Parking** 16 **Notes** ⊗ No coaches

The Nyton

★★★★ 😐 GUEST ACCOMMODATION

7 Barton Rd CB7 4HZ
☎ 01353 662459 📄 01353 666217
e-mail: nytonhotel@yahoo.co.uk
dir: *From S, A10 into Ely on Cambridge Rd, pass golf course, 1st right*

Set in two acres of mature gardens, this family-run establishment offers comfortable bedrooms in a range of sizes and styles. The pleasant public rooms include a wood-panelled restaurant, a smart bar, and a conservatory-lounge overlooking the gardens. Meals are available in the dining room and informal light meals are served in the lounge bar.

Rooms 9 en suite (3 fmly) (2 GF) S £45-£60; D £70-£90*
Facilities FTV TVL tea/coffee Dinner available Direct Dial Cen ht Licensed Wi-fi Golf 18 **Conf** Max 40 Thtr 40 Class 20 Board 40 **Parking** 25 **Notes** LB ⊗ Civ Wed 100

The Three Pickerels

★★★★ INN

19 Bridge Rd, Mepal CB6 2AR
☎ 01353 777777 📄 01353 777891
e-mail: info@thethreepickerels.co.uk
web: www.thethreepickerels.co.uk

Situated in the tranquil village of Mepal on the outskirts of Ely, this property sits on the banks of the New Bedford River and has views of the surrounding grassland. Public rooms include a smart bar, a dining room and a lovely lounge overlooking the river. The smartly appointed bedrooms are comfortable and well equipped.

Rooms 4 en suite (3 fmly) S fr £40; D fr £75
Facilities FTV TVL tea/coffee Dinner available Cen ht Fishing Pool Table **Notes** ⊗

Castle Lodge

★★★ GUEST HOUSE

50 New Barns Rd CB7 4PW
☎ 01353 662276 📄 01353 666606
e-mail: castlelodgehotel@supanet.com
dir: *Off B1382 Prickwillow Rd, NE from town centre*

Located within easy walking distance of the cathedral, this extended Victorian house offers well-equipped bedrooms in a variety of sizes. Public areas include a traditionally furnished dining room and a comfortable air-conditioned bar lounge. Service is friendly and helpful.

Rooms 11 rms (6 en suite) (3 fmly) S £32.50-£55; D £75*
Facilities TVL tea/coffee Dinner available Direct Dial Cen ht Licensed Wi-fi **Conf** Max 40 Board 40 **Parking** 6

HILTON   Map 12 TL26

Prince of Wales

★★★ INN

Potton Rd PE28 9NG
☎ 01480 830257 📄 01480 830257
dir: *A14 onto B1040 towards Biggleswade, 2m into village, Prince of Wales on left*

This popular village inn offers a choice of cosy traditional bars serving good food and real ales. The pleasantly decorated bedrooms are equipped with modern facilities.

A hearty breakfast is served in the dining room at individual tables.

Rooms 4 en suite **Facilities** tea/coffee Dinner available Direct Dial Cen ht Pool Table **Parking** 12 **Notes** No Children 5yrs

HINXTON   Map 12 TL44

The Red Lion Inn

★★★★ 😐 INN

32 High St CB10 1QY
☎ 01799 530601 📄 01799 531201
e-mail: info@redlionhinxton.co.uk

The Red Lion Inn is a 16th-century privately-owned free house pub-restaurant, with high quality purpose-built accommodation, set in the pretty conservation village of Hinxton. In the winter guests can relax by the well-stoked fire, while in summer there is an attractive walled garden, overlooked by a dovecote and the village church.

Rooms 8 annexe en suite (2 fmly) (8 GF) S £75-£95; D £95-£125* **Facilities** FTV tea/coffee Dinner available Direct Dial Cen ht Wi-fi **Parking** 43 **Notes** LB

HUNTINGDON   Map 12 TL27

Cheriton House

★★★★★ 🅰 GUEST ACCOMMODATION

Mill St, Houghton PE28 2AZ
☎ 01480 464004 📄 01480 496960
e-mail: sales@cheritonhousecambs.co.uk
dir: *In village of Houghton, through village square, signed to river & mill*

Rooms 2 en suite 3 annexe en suite (3 GF) **Facilities** tea/coffee Cen ht Wi-fi ⚓ **Conf** Max 15 Thtr 15 Class 6 Board 8 **Parking** 7 **Notes** ⊗ No Children 14yrs

AA ★★★
Guest House

HAMDEN
GUEST HOUSE

Comfortable en-suite bedrooms 2½ miles from Cambridge City Centre. Frequent bus service. Car park. Local shops. Pubs and restaurants within walking distance.

89 High Street, Cherry Hinton, Cambridge CB1 9LU

Tel: (01223) 413263

e-mail: info@hamdenguesthouse.co.uk
web: www.hamdenguesthouse.co.uk

HUNTINGDON continued

The Three Horseshoes

★★★★ INN

Moat Ln, Abbots Ripton PE28 2PD
☎ 01487 773440 📄 01487 773440
e-mail: thethreehorseshoes.com@btconnect.com
web: www.thethreehorseshoes.com
dir: 3m N of Huntingdon. Off B1090 in Abbots Ripton

Delightful 17th-century, Grade II-listed inn situated in the heart of the attractive village of Abbots Ripton on the outskirts of Huntingdon. The spacious public rooms include a lounge bar, two smaller lounges with plush sofas, a bright dining room and a further small bar area to the front. The individually decorated bedrooms are comfortably appointed and well equipped.

Rooms 5 en suite S £65-£75; D £90-£120* Facilities FTV tea/coffee Dinner available Cen ht Wi-fi Conf Max 60 Parking 100 Notes LB

See advert on this page

KIRTLING   Map 12 TL65

Hill Farm Guest House

★★★ BED AND BREAKFAST

CB8 9HQ
☎ 01638 730253 📄 01638 731957
dir: 0.5m NW of Kirtling

Located on arable land south of Newmarket, in the heart of horse-breeding country, this 400-year-old property retains many original features. Public areas are furnished in keeping with the building's character, and hearty breakfasts are served at a family table in the elegant dining room.

Hill Farm Guest House

Rooms 3 en suite Facilities TVL tea/coffee Direct Dial Cen ht Wi-fi 🐾 Parking 15 Notes 🐕

PETERBOROUGH   Map 12 TL19

Aaron Park

★★★ GUEST ACCOMMODATION

109 Park Rd PE1 2TR
☎ 01733 564849 📄 01733 564855
e-mail: aaronparkhotel@yahoo.co.uk
dir: A1 onto A1139 to junct 5, to city centre on Boongate, over rdbt onto Crawthorne Rd, over lights, next left

Family service is both friendly and helpful at this Victorian house, which is situated in a tree-lined avenue just a short walk from the city centre and cathedral. Bedrooms come in a variety of styles and sizes; each room is nicely presented and has a good range of modern facilities. Freshly cooked breakfasts are carefully presented and provide a good start to the day.

Rooms 10 en suite (3 fmly) (2 GF) Facilities FTV tea/coffee Cen ht Licensed Parking 8 Notes ⊗ Closed Xmas

STETCHWORTH   Map 12 TL65

The Old Mill

★★★★ BED AND BREAKFAST

Mill Ln CB8 9TR
☎ 01638 507839 & 07831 179948
e-mail: gbell839@aol.com
dir: In village centre off Tea Kettle Ln

Situated in a delightful village, the accommodation comprises a thoughtfully equipped self-contained flat sleeping four, with a small kitchen, quality pine furniture and a DVD player. Access is via a private staircase leading to a sun terrace overlooking mature gardens. Breakfast is served at a large communal table in the main house.

Rooms 1 annexe en suite Facilities FTV TVL tea/coffee Cen ht Wi-fi 🐾 Parking 2 Notes LB 🐕

UFFORD   Map 12 TF00

The White Hart

Ⓤ

Main St PE9 3BH
☎ 01780 740250 📄 01780 740927
e-mail: info@whitehartufford.co.uk

Currently the rating for this establishment is not confirmed. This may be due to a change of ownership or because it has only recently joined the AA rating scheme.

Rooms 6 en suite S £55-£80; D £65-£90* Notes Closed 24-26 Dec

---

The Three Horseshoes

Village pub with fine dining restaurant and 5 quality ensuite rooms.

The Three Horseshoes is located in the heart of the attractive village of Abbots Ripton, Huntingdon, Cambridgeshire and has recently been sympathetically refurbished and extended.

With origins dating back from the 17th Century, The Three Horseshoes is a grade II listed building including two detached letting accommodation buildings to the side of the main building.

Abbots Ripton, Moat Lane, Huntingdon PE28 2PA
Tel: 01487 773440
Email: thethreehorseshoes.com@btconnect.com
Website: www.thethreehorseshoes.com

WILLINGHAM
Map 12 TL47

Willingham House

★★★★ 😋 GUEST ACCOMMODATION

50 Church St CB4 5HT
☎ 01954 260606 📠 01954 260603
e-mail: info@cimcol.com
web: www.cimcol.com
dir: A14 junct 29 onto B1050 to Willingham

A former rectory, this elegant Victorian house has been sympathetically renovated and extended to provide high standards of comfort and facilities. Bedrooms are thoughtfully furnished and imaginative dinners are served in an attractive dining room. Extensive conference facilities and pretty mature grounds are additional features.

Rooms 16 en suite 6 annexe en suite (7 GF) **Facilities** TVL tea/coffee Dinner available Cen ht Licensed Wi-fi Pool Table **Conf** Max 40 Thtr 40 Class 23 Board 24 **Parking** 25 **Notes** ⊗

CHESHIRE

AUDLEM
Map 15 SJ64

Little Heath Farm (SJ663455)

★★★★ FARMHOUSE

CW3 0HE
☎ 01270 811324   Mrs H M Bennion
e-mail: hilaryandbob@ukonline.co.uk
dir: Off A525 in village onto A529 towards Nantwich for 0.3m. Farm opposite village green

The 200-year-old brick farmhouse retains much original character, including low beamed ceilings. The traditionally furnished public areas include a cosy sitting room and a dining room where you dine family style. The refurbished bedrooms are stylish, and the friendly proprietors create a relaxing atmosphere.

Rooms 3 en suite (1 fmly) S £25-£40; D £50-£60*
Facilities TVL tea/coffee Cen ht **Conf** Max 10 Board 10 **Parking** 6 **Notes** LB ⊗ 50 acres mixed

BOLLINGTON
Map 16 SJ97

The Church House Inn

★★★ 😋 INN

Church St SK10 5PY
☎ 01625 574014 📠 01625 562026
e-mail: info@thechurchhouseinn-bollington.co.uk

A traditional village inn with beams and log fires and lots of character and local history, The Church House Inn has comfortable, well equipped accommodation. An extensive range of imaginative and popular dishes are served in

the bar or dining room, which also offers a fine choice of real ales and wines.

Rooms 5 en suite (1 fmly) S £45; D £55* **Facilities** FTV tea/coffee Dinner available Cen ht Wi-fi **Parking** 4 **Notes** ⊗

BURWARDSLEY
Map 15 SJ55

Cheshire Cheese Cottage

★★★★ BED AND BREAKFAST

Burwardsley Rd CH3 9NS
☎ 01829 770887 📠 01829 770887
e-mail: r.rosney@yahoo.co.uk

A very warm welcome awaits at this delightful little cottage, which is set in its own extensive grounds and colourful gardens on the outskirts of the village. The accommodation consists of two modern bedrooms on ground floor level. There is also a conservatory which doubles as both lounge and breakfast room. Breakfasts are freshly cooked and hearty. Owner Rose Rosney is a qualified masseur and guests can book treatments if they wish.

Rooms 2 en suite (2 GF) **Facilities** FTV TVL tea/coffee Direct Dial Cen ht Wi-fi Golf 18 Riding **Parking** 4 **Notes** ⊗ No Children 🐾

Sandhollow Farm B&B

★★★★ BED AND BREAKFAST

Harthill Rd CH3 9NU
☎ 01829 770894
e-mail: paul.kickdrum@tiscali.co.uk
dir: From A41, turn off to Tattenhall, follow signs to Burwardsley. Continue past post office, 0.25m on right

Sandhollow Farm is an award-winning, recently converted farmhouse commanding spectacular views of the Cheshire Plain and Welsh hills. Bedrooms have been carefully renovated and there is a comfortable lounge with a log fire. Substantial breakfasts using organic, homemade and local produce are served in the adjoining dining room with views across the garden and surrounding countryside.

Rooms 3 en suite (1 GF) S £55-£60; D £76-£90*
Facilities tea/coffee Cen ht Wi-fi **Parking** 4 **Notes** LB ⊗ No Children 12yrs Closed annual holiday

The Pheasant Inn

★★★★ INN

Higher Burwardsley CH3 9PF
☎ 01829 770434 📠 01829 771097
e-mail: info@thepheasantinn.co.uk
dir: From A41, left to Tattenhall, right at 1st junct & left at 2nd Higher Burwardsley. At post office left, signed

This delightful 300-year-old inn sits high on the Peckforton Hills and enjoys spectacular views over the Cheshire Plain. Well-equipped, comfortable bedrooms are housed in an adjacent converted barn. Creative dishes are served either in the stylish restaurant or in the traditional, beamed bar. Real fires are lit in the winter months.

Rooms 2 en suite 10 annexe en suite (2 fmly) (5 GF)
Facilities tea/coffee Dinner available Cen ht Wi-fi Fishing **Parking** 80

CHESTER
Map 15 SJ46

See also Malpas

PREMIER COLLECTION

Oddfellows

★★★★★ 😋 🍴 RESTAURANT WITH ROOMS

20 Lower Bridge St CH1 1RS
☎ 01244 400001
e-mail: reception@oddfellows.biz

Surrounded by designer shops and only a few minutes' walk from the Chester Rows, old meets new at this stylish Georgian mansion. The upper ground floor comprises a walled garden with ornamental moat, Arabic tents, a roofed patio, a cocktail bar with an excellent wine selection, a bustling brasserie and an Alice in Wonderland tea room. Fine dining, featuring local produce, is skilfully prepared in a second-floor formal restaurant and a sumptuous 'members' lounge is also available to diners and resident guests. Bedrooms have the wow factor with super beds and every conceivable extra to enhance the guest experience. Oddfellows was a Runner-up in the AA Funkiest B&B of the Year 2009-2010 Award.

Rooms 4 en suite **Facilities** FTV tea/coffee Dinner available Direct Dial Cen ht Wi-fi **Conf** Max 40 Thtr 40 **Parking** 4 **Notes** LB ⊗ No coaches Civ Wed 60

CHESTER *continued*

Mitchell's of Chester

★★★★★ Ⓐ GUEST HOUSE

28 Hough Green CH4 8JQ
☎ 01244 679004   📄 01244 659567
e-mail: mitoches@dialstart.net
web: www.mitchellsofchester.com
dir: *1m SW of city centre. A483 onto A5104, 300yds on right in Hough Green*

Rooms 7 en suite (1 fmly) (1 GF) S £40-£45; D £69-£85
Facilities FTV TVL tea/coffee Cen ht Wi-fi **Parking** 5
Notes LB ⊗ No Children 8yrs Closed 21-29 Dec

Cheltenham Lodge

★★★★ GUEST ACCOMMODATION

58 Hoole Rd, Hoole CH2 3NL
☎ 01244 346767
e-mail: cheltenhamlodge@btinternet.com
web: www.cheltenhamlodge.co.uk
dir: *1m NE of city centre on A56*

A small, personally-run guest house lmidway between the city centre and M53, Cheltenham Lodge offers attractive modern bedrooms, which include some on the ground floor, and a family room. All are well equipped, and a substantial breakfast is served in the smart dining room.

Rooms 5 en suite (2 fmly) (2 GF) S £30-£65; D £65-£85*
Facilities FTV tea/coffee Cen ht **Parking** 5 **Notes** LB ⊗
Closed 23 Dec-7 Jan 🅴

Chester Brooklands

★★★★ GUEST ACCOMMODATION

8 Newton Ln CH2 3RB
☎ 01244 348856   📄 01244 348856
e-mail: enquiries@chester-bandb.co.uk
dir: *M53 junct 12, A56 towards city, 1m right onto Newton Ln, on right*

Located in a mainly residential area close to Hoole village centre, this well-presented house has been carefully renovated to provide a range of thoughtfully furnished bedrooms with modern shower rooms en suite. Breakfast is served in the attractive dining room and a warm welcome is assured.

Rooms 5 en suite (1 fmly) **Facilities** FTV TVL tea/coffee Cen ht Wi-fi **Parking** 5 **Notes** LB ⊗ RS 2-3 wks in the year

Golborne Manor

★★★★ BED AND BREAKFAST

Platts Ln, Hatton Heath CH3 9AN
☎ 01829 770310 & 07774 695268   📄 01829 770370
e-mail: info@golbornemanor.co.uk
dir: *5m S off A14 (Whitchurch road). Right onto Platts Ln, 400yds on left*

The elegant Edwardian house stands in beautiful gardens with spectacular views across open countryside. Accommodation is in spacious bedrooms with either brass bedsteads or a richly carved antique Arabian bed. Breakfast is served around a large table in the dining room, and there is also a comfortable lounge.

Rooms 2 en suite (1 fmly); D £60-£80 **Facilities** FTV tea/coffee Cen ht 🍴 table tennis **Conf** Max 10 **Parking** 6
Notes LB ⊗ RS wknds 🅴

Green Gables

★★★★ GUEST HOUSE

11 Eversley Park CH2 2AJ
☎ 01244 372243   📄 01244 376352
e-mail: perruzza_d@hotmail.com
web: www.greengableschester.co.uk
dir: *Off A5116 Liverpool Rd signed Countess of Chester Hospital, right at 3rd pedestrian lights to Eversley Park*

The attractive Victorian house, set in pretty gardens, is in a quiet residential area close to the city centre. The well-equipped bedrooms include a family room, and there is a choice of sitting rooms. The bright breakfast room is strikingly decorated.

Rooms 2 en suite (1 fmly) S £42-£59; D £59*
Facilities FTV TVL tea/coffee Cen ht Wi-fi **Parking** 8
Notes ⊗ 🅴

Hamilton Court

★★★★ GUEST ACCOMMODATION

5-7 Hamilton St CH2 3JG
☎ 01244 345387   📄 01244 317404
e-mail: hamiltoncourth@aol.com
dir: *From town centre, All Saints church on left, 2nd turning on left*

Hamilton Court is a family-run establishment, only ten minutes walk from the city centre. All bedrooms are en suite and have useful facilities. Children are welcome and pets can be accommodated by arrangement.

Rooms 11 en suite (4 fmly) (1 GF) **Facilities** FTV tea/coffee Cen ht Licensed Wi-fi **Parking** 4 **Notes** Closed 24 Dec-3 Jan

Lavender Lodge

★★★★ GUEST ACCOMMODATION

46 Hoole Rd CH2 3NL
☎ 01244 323204   📄 01244 329821
e-mail: bookings@lavenderlodgechester.co.uk
web: www.lavenderlodgechester.co.uk
dir: *1m NE of city centre on A56, opp All Saints church*

A warm welcome is assured at this smart late Victorian house located within easy walking distance of central attractions. The bedrooms are equipped with thoughtful extras and have modern bathrooms. Quality breakfasts are served in the attractive dining room.

Rooms 5 en suite (2 fmly) **Facilities** FTV tea/coffee Cen ht Wi-fi **Parking** 7 **Notes** Closed 24 Dec-2 Jan

The Old Farmhouse B&B

★★★★ BED AND BREAKFAST

9 Eggbridge Ln, Waverton CH3 7PE
☎ 01244 332124
e-mail: jmitchellgreenwalls@hotmail.com
web: www.chestereggbridgefarm.co.uk
dir: *From A41 at Waverton turn left at Moor Ln, left onto Eggbridge Ln and over Canal Bridge, on the right*

A warm welcome is assured at this 18th-century former farmhouse, located in a village community three miles south of the city centre. Cosy bedrooms are equipped with a wealth of thoughtful extras and hearty breakfasts feature local or home-made produce.

Rooms 2 rms (1 en suite) (1 pri facs) S £45; D fr £65*
Facilities FTV TVL tea/coffee Cen ht Wi-fi **Parking** 5
Notes LB ⊗ No Children 10yrs Closed 15 Feb-1 Mar RS 24-26 Dec continental bkfst only

Summerhill Guest House

★★★ GUEST HOUSE

4 Greenfield Ln, Hoole Village CH2 2PA
☎ 01244 400020 & 400334
e-mail: capricorn@taurusuk.net
dir: 1.5m NE of city centre. A56 onto A41, 1st right

Summerhill is a converted Edwardian house with comfortable, well-equipped accommodation. The helpful owners provide a friendly atmosphere and hearty breakfasts in the attractive dining room.

Rooms 4 en suite (1 fmly) S £30-£45; D £60-£80* Facilities FTV TVL tea/coffee Cen ht Parking 4 Notes LB ⊗ No Children 8yrs

Glen Garth

★★★ GUEST ACCOMMODATION

59 Hoole Rd CH2 3NJ
☎ 01244 310260 📄 01244 310260
e-mail: glengarth@chester63.fsnet.co.uk
dir: Exit M53 onto A56, 0.5m E of city

Situated within easy walking distance of the city, family-run Glen Garth provides well-equipped bedrooms and hearty breakfasts served in the pleasant rear dining room. Friendly, attentive service is a strength here.

Rooms 5 rms (3 en suite) (2 pri facs) (3 fmly) S £30-£35; D £50-£70* Facilities FTV tea/coffee Cen ht Parking 5 Notes LB ⊗ ⊜

Dragonfly

Ⓤ

94 Watergate St CH1 2LF
☎ 01244 346740 📄 01244 346740
e-mail: sleep@hoteldragonfly.com
dir: M53 junct 12 follow A56 signed Chester. Take 2nd exit from rdbt - St Oswalds Way, next rdbt take 1st onto St Martin's

Currently the rating for this establishment is not confirmed. This may be due to a change of ownership or because it has only recently joined the AA rating scheme.

Rooms 4 en suite S £50-£70; D £80-£105* Facilities FTV tea/coffee Cen ht Wi-fi Parking 2 Notes ⊗

The Plough At Eaton

★★★★ ⊜ INN

Macclesfield Rd, Eaton CW12 2NH
☎ 01260 280207 📄 01260 298458
e-mail: theploughinn@hotmail.co.uk
dir: On A536 (Congleton to Macclesfield road), 1.5m from Congleton town centre

A renovated traditional inn offering high quality meals and high class bedrooms in an adjacent building. Bedrooms and bathrooms are very new and offer modern facilities, while the gardens include discreet sitting areas. The restaurant is housed in a restored barn to the rear of the inn.

Rooms 17 annexe en suite (2 fmly) (8 GF) S £60-£65; D £75-£85 Facilities tea/coffee Dinner available Direct Dial Cen ht Wi-fi Parking 78 Notes LB RS 25-26 Dec & 1 Jan Close at 6pm Civ Wed 60

Egerton Arms Country Inn

★★★★ INN

Astbury Village CW12 4RQ
☎ 01260 273946 📄 01260 277273
e-mail: egertonastbury@totalise.co.uk
dir: 1.5m SW of Congleton off A34, by St Mary's Church

This traditional country inn stands opposite the church in the pretty village of Astbury. The creative, good-value menus in the bars and restaurant attract a strong local following, and the bedrooms have been refurbished to provide high standards of comfort and facilities.

Rooms 6 en suite (1 fmly) S £50-£55; D £70-£80* Facilities tea/coffee Dinner available Cen ht Wi-fi Conf Max 40 Thtr 40 Class 30 Board 20 Parking 100 Notes LB ⊗ No coaches

---

Sandhole Farm

★★★★ Ⓐ GUEST ACCOMMODATION

Hulme Walfield CW12 2JH
☎ 01260 224419 📄 01260 224766
e-mail: veronica@sandholefarm.co.uk
dir: 2m N of Congleton. Off A34 down driveway

Rooms 16 annexe en suite (3 fmly) (7 GF) S £60-£70; D £80* Facilities TVL tea/coffee Direct Dial Cen ht Wi-fi Conf Thtr 80 Class 80 Board 50 Parking 50 Notes RS Xmas wk Self-catering only Civ Wed 150

Valleybrook Guest House

★★★★ BED AND BREAKFAST

29 Nevis Dr, Woolstanwood CW2 8UH
☎ 01270 588977
e-mail: mail@valleybrookguesthouse.co.uk
web: www.valleybrookguesthouse.co.uk
dir: A530 onto A532 towards Crewe, 1st right, then 1st left, then 2nd right, 50yds on left

Located between Crewe and Nantwich, Valleybrook offers comfortable well equipped accommodation and a friendly welcome. Breakfast, using home-made and local produce, is served in the attractive dining room overlooking the garden.

Rooms 2 rms (1 en suite) (1 pri facs) S £35-£40; D £45-£50* Facilities FTV tea/coffee Cen ht Wi-fi Parking 2 Notes ⊗

The Farndon

★★★★ INN

High St CH3 6PU
☎ 01829 270570 📄 01829 272060
e-mail: enquiries@thefarndon.co.uk
web: www.thefarndon.co.uk
dir: Just off A534

Located close to Chester and the North Wales coast, The Farndon is a family-run 16th-century coaching inn which has been tastefully renovated to create a traditional inn with a modern twist. The modern, attractive bedrooms are well equipped and downstairs the bar still offers open log fires and a selection of real ales and fine wines, together with a wide range of attractive imaginative dishes.

Rooms 5 rms (4 en suite) (1 pri facs) (2 fmly) S £55-£70; D £60-£95 (room only)* Facilities FTV TVL tea/coffee Dinner available Direct Dial Cen ht Wi-fi spa treatments Conf Max 50 Thtr 50 Class 40 Board 30 Parking 25 Notes LB

The Hinton

★★★★ GUEST HOUSE

Town Ln, Mobberley WA16 7HH
☎ 01565 873484
e-mail: the.hinton@virgin.net
dir: 1m NE on B5085 in Mobberley

This well-proportioned house offers a range of comfortable bedrooms with thoughtful extras. Comprehensive breakfasts, and dinners by arrangement, are served in the attractive dining room and a lounge is available.

Rooms 6 en suite (1 fmly) S £48; D £62* **Facilities** FTV tea/coffee Dinner available Cen ht Licensed Wi-fi **Parking** 8 **Notes** ⊗

The Cottage Restaurant & Lodge

★★★★ GUEST ACCOMMODATION

London Rd, Allostock WA16 9LU
☎ 01565 722470 📄 01565 722749
e-mail: reception@thecottageknutsford.co.uk
dir: M6 junct 18/19 onto A50, between Holmes Chapel & Knutsford

This well presented family-run establishment enjoys a peaceful location on the A50 between Knutsford and Holmes Chapel. Smart, spacious lodge-style bedrooms complement an attractive open-plan restaurant and bar lounge. Bedrooms are thoughtfully equipped and offer good levels of comfort. Conference and meeting facilities, as well as ample parking, are available.

Rooms 12 annexe en suite (4 fmly) (6 GF) S £55-£79; D £60-£95* **Facilities** FTV tea/coffee Dinner available Direct Dial Cen ht Licensed Wi-fi **Conf** Max 50 Thtr 50 Class 25 Board 25 **Parking** 40 **Notes** LB ⊗

The Dog Inn

★★★★ INN

Well Bank Ln, Over Peover WA16 8UP
☎ 01625 861421 📄 01625 864800
e-mail: thedog-inn@paddockinnsfsnet.co.uk
web: www.doginn-overpeover.co.uk
dir: 4m SE of Knutsford. Off A50 at Whipping Stocks 2m to Peover Heath

Set in delightful Cheshire countryside, the front of this popular 18th-century inn is adorned with hanging baskets and tubs. The attractive bedrooms have many extras, while the lounge bar and restaurant offer a wide selection of ales and an extensive all-day menu using local produce.

Rooms 6 en suite S £50-£60; D £60-£80* **Facilities** FTV tea/coffee Dinner available Direct Dial Cen ht Wi-fi Pool Table **Parking** 80

Laburnum Cottage

★★★★ GUEST HOUSE

Knutsford Rd, Mobberley WA16 7PU
☎ 01565 872464
e-mail: laburnum.cottage@hotmail.co.uk
dir: 1m NE of Knutsford on B5085 towards Mobberley

Set in attractive gardens, this cottage-style property is within easy reach of the M6, M56 and Manchester Airport. The attractive bedrooms are thoughtfully equipped, and imaginative and carefully prepared evening meals are available by arrangement. There is also a comfortable lounge.

Rooms 5 en suite S £46; D £64* **Facilities** FTV TVL tea/coffee Dinner available Cen ht Wi-fi **Parking** 6 **Notes** ⊗

Rose Cottage Guest House

★★★★ BED AND BREAKFAST

Newton Hall Ln, Mobberley WA16 7LL
☎ 01565 872430
e-mail: davies.rosecottage@yahoo.co.uk
web: www.rose-cottage-guesthouse.com
dir: 3m NE of Knutsford. B5085 E through Mobberley, before Bird in Hand pub left onto Newton Hall Ln, 0.5m on right

Standing in extensive mature gardens on the outskirts of Mobberley, this Victorian house has an extension which offers bedrooms with thoughtful extras. Comprehensive breakfasts are served in the attractive lounge-dining room, overlooking a wildlife pond.

Rooms 3 en suite (2 GF) S £49; D £59* **Facilities** FTV tea/coffee Cen ht Wi-fi **Parking** 10 **Notes** LB ⊗ No Children 12yrs Closed 24 Dec-1 Jan

Rostherne Country House

★★★★ GUEST ACCOMMODATION

Rostherne Ln, Rostherne WA16 6RY
☎ 01565 832628
e-mail: info@rosthernehouse.co.uk

Set in its own spacious gardens in the village of Rostherne, this elegant Victorian house retains much original charm with spacious, well-equipped bedrooms and character lounges with open fires. It is a wonderful relaxing base for exploring the delights of Cheshire and dinner is available by arrangement. Other facilities include an honesty bar and a paddock for guests' horses. Courses in various subjects are also available.

Rooms 4 rms (3 en suite) (1 pri facs) (1 fmly) S fr £49.50; D £75-£95* **Facilities** FTV TVL tea/coffee Dinner available Cen ht Wi-fi Guest arrangement for indoor swimming pool & spa **Conf** Max 20 Thtr 20 **Parking** 12

See advert on opposite page

Holly Tree Farm *(SJ802709)*

★★★★ FARMHOUSE

Holmes Chapel Rd SK11 9DT
☎ 01477 571257 📄 01477 571257 Mrs Venables
web: www.hollytreefarm.org
dir: On A535 Holmes Chapel Rd in front of Jodrell Bank

Located close to Jodrell Bank, Holly Tree Farm offers a good base for the business person or for touring the local attractions. Rooms are located in the house adjacent to the farm and are attractive and well equipped. Hearty breakfasts are taken in the farmhouse, and the emphasis is on local produce from the farm's own shop.

Rooms 4 en suite (1 fmly) (1 GF) S £30-£35; D £60-£65* **Facilities** TVL tea/coffee Cen ht Wi-fi **Parking** 3 **Notes** LB ⊗ 🐾 100 acres beef/sheep/poultry

---

MACCLESFIELD   Map 16 SJ97

See also Rainow

Penrose Guest House

★★ GUEST HOUSE

56 Birtles Rd, Whirley SK10 3JQ
☎ 01625 615323 📄 01625 432284
e-mail: info@penroseguesthouse.co.uk
web: www.penroseguesthouse.co.uk
dir: A537 to rdbt and follow signs leisure centre, left at mini rdbt. 1st left into Birtles Rd

Peacefully located in the suburb of Whirley, yet convenient for the hospital and the centre of town, this delightful home offers spacious comfortable bedrooms. Healthy breakfast is taken at one table looking over the lawned gardens, which are popular with an array of wild birds.

Rooms 3 rms S fr £25; D fr £50 (room only) **Facilities** FTV tea/coffee Cen ht Wi-fi **Parking** 5 **Notes** LB ⊗ No Children 7yrs

---

MALPAS   Map 15 SJ44

PREMIER COLLECTION

Tilston Lodge

★★★★★ 🏛 GUEST ACCOMMODATION

Tilston SY14 7DR
☎ 01829 250223 📄 01829 250223
dir: A41 S from Chester for 10m, turn right for Tilston. Left at T-junct. Lodge 200yds on right

A former hunting lodge, this impressive Victorian house stands in 16 acres of rolling orchards and pasture, which are home to rare breeds of sheep and poultry. The spacious bedrooms are furnished with fine period pieces and a wealth of thoughtful extras. Ground-floor areas overlook immaculate gardens and a choice of lounges is available in addition to the elegant dining room, the setting for memorable breakfasts.

Rooms 3 en suite (1 fmly) S £46-£52; D £76-£84 **Facilities** FTV TVL tea/coffee Cen ht 🛁 Hot tub **Parking** 8 **Notes** LB ⊗ 🚭

Hampton House (SJ505496)

★★★★ FARMHOUSE

Stevensons Ln, Hampton SY14 8JS
☎ 01948 820588 📄 01948 820588 Mrs E H Sarginson
e-mail: enquiries@hamptonhousefarm.co.uk
dir: 2m NE of Malpas. Off A41 onto Cholmondeley Rd, next left

Parts of this house are reputed to date from 1600 and quality furnishing styles highlight the many retained period features including a wealth of exposed beams. It is located on a quiet dairy farm and offers thoughtfully appointed accommodation and a warm welcome.

Rooms 3 rms (2 en suite) (1 pri facs) S £30-£35; D £55-£60* **Facilities** TVL tea/coffee Cen ht Wi-fi **Parking** 10 **Notes** ⊗ No Children 12yrs 🚜 180 acres mixed

---

Rostherne Country House

Rostherne Lane, Rostherne, nr Knutsford WA16 6RY

Rostherne, a beautiful grade 2 listed, country residence situated in its own grounds, offers overnight stay accommodation in beautiful, en-suite rooms in the heart of Cheshire.

A unique retreat for visitors or corporate clients, it is close to Hale, Bowden, Knutsford and Altrincham whilst also being only 25 minutes drive-time from Chester and central Manchester.

Convenient for Manchester airport, and offering car-parking facilities and transfers by arrangement, it is also an ideal touring base. Guest passes are available for the local spa, beauty salon and pool.

Fishing, riding, falconry, cycling, polo, golf, cricket, croquet, tennis, BBQ by arrangement.

Breakfasts and evening Meals are made from locally sourced produce (we are able to suit any specific dietary needs).

Various courses are also held at Rosthern House including cookery, well-being, holistic beauty, gardening and art. The House is also available for private weekend parties, with, or without staff. Ideal venue for reunions, corporate away days etc.

Telephone: 01565 832628
Email: info@rosthernehouse.co.uk
Web: www.rosthernehouse.co.uk

MALPAS *continued*

Mill House & Granary

★★★ ⬛ GUEST HOUSE

Mill House, Higher Wych SY14 7JR
☎ 01948 780362 📠 01948 780566
e-mail: angela@videoactive.co.uk
web: www.millhouseandgranary.co.uk
dir: *3m S of Malpas. A41 onto B5395, next left by bus shelter, Mill House 1m on left*

Rooms 3 rms (2 en suite) (1 pri facs) S £25-£30;
D £50-£60* **Facilities** TVL tea/coffee Dinner available Cen ht **Parking** 6 **Notes** ✿ Closed Dec 🐾

MIDDLEWICH — Map 15 SJ76

The Boars Head

★★★ INN

Kinderton St CW10 0JE
☎ 01606 833191 📄 01606 833198
e-mail: boarshead hotel@hotmail.com
dir: *On A54 in town centre, E of bridge*

Set close to the centre of Middlewich, the Boars Head offers well-appointed accommodation and is popular with canal boat visitors. A good selection of real ales and meals is available in the attractive bar.

Rooms 8 en suite (3 fmly) (1 GF) (1 smoking) S £40;
D £50* **Facilities** FTV tea/coffee Dinner available Cen ht Pool Table **Conf** Max 50 Thtr 50 Class 40 Board 40
Parking 15

NANTWICH — Map 15 SJ65

See also Wybunbury

Henhull Hall *(SJ641536)*

★★★★ FARMHOUSE

Welshmans Ln CW5 6AD
☎ 01270 624158 📄 01270 624158 Mr & Mrs Percival
e-mail: philippercival@hotmail.com
dir: *M6 junct 16 onto A500 towards Nantwich, then A51 past Rease Heath, turn left onto Welshmans Ln, 0.25m on left*

Expect a warm welcome at Henhull Hall, which has been in the Percival family since 1924. The Hall stands on the site of the Battle of Nantwich fought in 1644. The farmhouse is amidst 250 acres of farmland with beautiful grounds and gardens surrounding the house. Bedrooms are spacious and individually decorated; breakfast is served in the attractive dining room and features fresh farm produce.

Rooms 2 rms (1 en suite) (1 pri facs) (1 fmly) S £35-£40;
D £70-£80 **Facilities** TV1B TVL tea/coffee Cen ht 🐾
Conf Max 10 Thtr 10 Class 10 Board 10 **Parking** 4
Notes ✿ 345 acres dairy/arable

Oakland House

★★★★ GUEST ACCOMMODATION

252 Newcastle Rd, Blakelow, Shavington CW5 7ET
☎ 01270 567134
e-mail: enquiries@oaklandhouseonline.co.uk
dir: *2m E of Nantwich. Off A500 into Shavington, house 0.5m W of village*

Oakland House offers a friendly and relaxed atmosphere. Bedrooms, some of which are in a separate chalet, are attractively furnished and well equipped. There is a spacious sitting room, and a modern conservatory overlooks the pretty garden and the Cheshire countryside beyond. Substantial breakfasts are served either around one large table or at separate tables.

Rooms 3 en suite 6 annexe en suite (1 fmly) (6 GF)
S £34-£40; D £50-£56 **Facilities** TVL tea/coffee Cen ht
Wi-fi **Parking** 13 **Notes** LB Closed 31 Dec

NORTHWICH — Map 15 SJ67

The Red Lion

★★★ INN

277 Chester Rd, Hartford CW8 1QL
☎ 01606 74597
e-mail: cathy.iglesias@tesco.net
web: www.redlionhartford.com
dir: *From A556 take Hartford exit. Red Lion at 1st junct on left next to church*

Located in the community of Hartford opposite the parish church, this popular inn provides a range of real ales and traditional pub food in the cosy public areas and neat beer garden during the warmer months. Smart new bedrooms feature many thoughtful extras in addition to efficient en suite shower rooms.

Rooms 3 en suite (1 fmly) S £44.95; D £60*
Facilities tea/coffee Dinner available Cen ht Wi-fi Pool Table **Parking** 6 **Notes** ✿ No coaches

---

RAINOW — Map 16 SJ97

Common Barn Farm B&B *(SJ965764)*

★★★★ FARMHOUSE

Smith Ln SK10 5XJ
☎ 01625 574878 & 07779 816098 Mrs R Cooper
e-mail: g_greengrass@hotmail.com
web: www.cottages-with-a-view.co.uk
dir: *B5470 through Rainow towards Whaley Bridge, right onto Smith Ln, 0.5m on right down drive*

Located high in the Pennines and straddling the border of Cheshire and the Peak District, this new barn conversion provides a popular destination for walkers. Bedrooms are spacious and stylish and all bathrooms offer modern power showers. A conservatory lounge is ideal for relaxation while enjoying stunning views. Hearty breakfasts are as memorable as the warmth of welcome.

A coffee shop during the day provides light snacks and home-baked fayre.

Rooms 5 annexe en suite (1 fmly) (3 GF) **Facilities** TVL tea/coffee Cen ht Wi-fi Fishing **Conf** Max 25 **Parking** 40
Notes LB ✿ 250 acres sheep

TARPORLEY — Map 15 SJ56

Alvanley Arms Inn

★★★★ 🍴 INN

Forest Rd, Cotebrook CW6 9DS
☎ 01829 760200
web: www.alvanleyarms.co.uk
dir: *2m NE of Tarporley on A49 in Cotebrook*

Records show that there has been a pub on this site since the 16th century, and renovations have uncovered original beams in some of the stylish, well-equipped bedrooms. Wide-ranging menus are available in the cosy bars, and the adjoining Shire Horse Centre and Countryside Park is popular with families. Delamere Forest Park and Oulton Park race circuit are nearby.

Rooms 7 en suite **Facilities** tea/coffee Dinner available Cen ht Wi-fi free entry for residents to Shire Horse Centre
Parking 70 **Notes** No coaches

Hill House Farm *(SJ583626)*

★★★★ FARMHOUSE

Rushton CW6 9AU
☎ 01829 732238 📄 01829 733929 Mrs C Rayner
e-mail: aa@hillhousefarm-cheshire.co.uk
web: www.hillhousefarm-cheshire.co.uk
dir: *1.5m E of Tarporley. Off A51/A49 to Eaton, take Lower Ln, continue E for Rushton, right onto The Hall Ln, farm 0.5m*

This impressive brick farmhouse stands in very attractive gardens within 14 acres of rolling pastureland. The stylish bedrooms have en suite facilities, and there is a spacious lounge and a traditionally furnished breakfast room.

Rooms 3 en suite 1 annexe en suite (1 fmly) S £50-£60;
D £80-£100* **Facilities** TVL tea/coffee Cen ht Wi-fi
Parking 6 **Notes** LB Closed Xmas & New Year 14 acres non-working

The Tollemache Arms

★★★★ INN

Nantwich Rd, Alpraham CW6 9JE
☎ 01829 261716
e-mail: enquiries@tollemachearms.co.uk
web: www.tollemachearms.co.uk
dir: *On A51 Chester to Crewe road, 2.5m from Tarporley*

Located on the main road between Crewe and Chester (city centre 10 miles) the Tollemache Arms is a convenient base for business or for exploring local attractions such as Oulton Park or Tatton Gardens, and the accommodation is attractive and well equipped. The 18th-century inn has recently been refurbished to a high standard with log fires, oak beams and many interesting features, and offers a large selection of interesting meals using local produce, fine wines and real ales.

Rooms 4 en suite S £50-£60; D £55-£60* Facilities TVL tea/coffee Dinner available Cen ht Wi-fi Conf Max 15 Board 15 Parking 38 Notes LB

WARRINGTON   Map 15 SJ68

Rams Head Inn

★★★ INN

Church Ln, Grappen Hall WA4 3EP
☎ 01925 262814   ▤ 01925 860876
e-mail: mail@ramshead-inn.co.uk
dir: *A50 Warrington 1.5m, 1st left onto Bell House Ln 0.5m, Inn on left*

Located close to the church in this historic village close to Warrington, the Rams Head Inn offers comfortable accommodation in a friendly atmosphere. Breakfast and a wide choice of meals are served in the character lounges and small functions are catered for.

Rooms 4 en suite (1 fmly) Facilities FTV tea/coffee Dinner available Direct Dial Cen ht Wi-fi Conf Max 25 Thtr 25 Class 25 Board 25 Parking 80 Notes ⊗

WILMSLOW

See Manchester Airport (Greater Manchester)

WYBUNBURY   Map 15 SJ64

Lea Farm *(SJ717489)*

★★★ FARMHOUSE

Wrinehill Rd CW5 7NS
☎ 01270 841429   Mrs J E Callwood
e-mail: leafarm@hotmail.co.uk
dir: *1m E of Wybunbury village church on unclassified road*

This working dairy farm is surrounded by delightful gardens and beautiful Cheshire countryside. The spacious bedrooms have modern facilities and there is a cosy lounge. Hearty breakfasts are served in the attractive dining room, which looks out over the garden, with its resident peacocks.

Rooms 3 rms (2 en suite) (1 fmly) S £28-£35; D £48-£58* Facilities TVL tea/coffee Cen ht Fishing Pool Table Parking 24 Notes ⊛ 150 acres dairy/beef

CORNWALL & ISLES OF SCILLY

BODMIN   Map 2 SX06

Talamayne

★★★★ ☒ BED AND BREAKFAST

Helland PL30 4PX
☎ 01208 264519   ▤ 01208 264519
e-mail: martyn@talamayne.co.uk
dir: *From A30 follow signs for Helland, 2nd house on right on entering the village*

A professionally run B&B with an emphasis on high quality, comfortable accommodation in a home-from-home environment. Located within easy reach of many of the West Country's attractions to the north and south coasts. On arrival guests are greeted with a warm welcome and freshly prepared Cornish cream tea. Award-winning breakfasts are Aga-cooked and feature local free-range eggs and produce.

Rooms 3 rms (2 en suite) (1 pri facs) (1 GF) S £40-£65; D £60-£75 Facilities FTV TVL tea/coffee Cen ht Parking 7 Notes ⊗ No Children ⊛

Castle Canyke Farm

★★★★ BED AND BREAKFAST

Priors Barn Rd PL31 1HG
☎ 01208 79109
e-mail: bookings@castlecanykefarm.co.uk
web: www.castlecanykefarm.co.uk
dir: *On A389/A38 Priory Rd between church & Carminow Cross rdbt*

A traditional bed and breakfast operation with very friendly hosts offering comfortable, well appointed rooms in a very handy location, with off-street parking. Hearty breakfasts are served in the conservatory, guests have their own lounge and are also welcome to use the pretty garden to the rear.

Rooms 3 en suite (1 fmly) S £40-£45; D £60-£65* Facilities FTV TVL tea/coffee Cen ht Wi-fi Parking 3 Notes ⊗ No Children 5yrs ⊛

Roscrea

★★★★ ☒ BED AND BREAKFAST

18 Saint Nicholas' St PL31 1AD
☎ 01208 74400   ▤ 01208 72361
e-mail: roscrea@btconnect.com
dir: *From Bodmin take B3268 to Lostwithiel. Roscrea 0.25m on left*

Dating back to 1805, this fascinating house was once the home of a celebrated local schoolmaster. Now sympathetically restored to its former glory, this is an excellent location for anyone wishing to explore all that Cornwall has to offer. Comfort and quality are evident throughout all areas, matched by the warmth of the welcome. Breakfast is a treat here, featuring local produce and eggs from the resident hens. Dinner is also available by prior arrangement.

Rooms 3 rms (2 en suite) (1 pri facs) S £38-£43; D £66-£76* Facilities FTV TVL tea/coffee Dinner available Cen ht Wi-fi Parking 2 Notes LB ⊗ ⊛

The Stables at Welltown

★★★★ ☒ BED AND BREAKFAST

Cardinham PL30 4EG
☎ 01208 821316   ▤ 01208 821673
e-mail: thestables@welltown.orangehome.co.uk

Enjoying a peaceful location away from hustle and bustle, this is a wonderful place to relax and enjoy the unspoilt delights of this rugged area. Guests are assured of a rewarding and pleasurable stay. Converted from stables, there is character and comfort in equal measure with an uncluttered contemporary feel. Breakfast from the Aga is a real treat with local produce in abundance. Additional facilities include a snug lounge and attractive garden.

Rooms 2 en suite S £30-£35; D £50-£55* Facilities FTV TVL tea/coffee Dinner available Cen ht Parking 2 Notes No Children 12yrs ⊛

BODMIN *continued*

Tranack

★★★ GUEST ACCOMMODATION

26 Castle St PL31 2DU
☎ 01208 269095
e-mail: sandrambutler@onetel.com
dir: *A30 to St Petroc church, 2nd exit at mini rdbt, 1st right, 1st left, 150yds on left*

Situated in a quiet location within walking distance of the centre of town, this friendly and welcoming establishment combines comfort and character. Bedrooms are attractively furnished and equipped with useful extras. Breakfast is a real treat, served around the dining room table and featuring local produce and eggs fresh from the resident hens.

Rooms 2 en suite (2 fmly) S £40; D £60* **Facilities** tea/coffee Cen ht **Parking** 1 **Notes** ⊗ Closed 23-27 Dec 🖼

Mount Pleasant Farm

★★★ GUEST ACCOMMODATION

Mount PL30 4EX
☎ 01208 821342
e-mail: info@mountpleasantcottages.co.uk
dir: *A30 from Bodmin towards Launceston for 4m, right signed Millpool, continue 3m*

Set in ten acres, this is a wonderfully peaceful base from which to explore the delights of Cornwall. Originally a farmhouse dating back to the 17th-century, there is something here for all the family with extensive facilities including a games barn and heated swimming pool. Cosy bedrooms are well furnished, while public areas include a spacious sun lounge and extensive gardens. Breakfast, served in the well-appointed dining room, features local produce and is a highlight of any stay; home-cooked evening meals are available by prior arrangement.

Rooms 6 en suite (3 fmly) S £32-£42; D £54-£74* **Facilities** FTV TVL tea/coffee Dinner available Cen ht 🖼 Pool Table Games barn **Parking** 8 **Notes** LB 🖼

BOSCASTLE Map 2 SX09

PREMIER COLLECTION

Trerosewill Farm *(SX095905)*
★★★★★ 🏠 FARMHOUSE

Paradise PL35 0DL
☎ 01840 250545 📄 01840 250727
Mr & Mrs Nicholls
e-mail: enquiries@trerosewill.co.uk
web: www.trerosewill.co.uk
dir: *Take B3266 at junct with B3263, towards Tintagel. After 0.2m, turn left by brown sign, 100yds along lane*

A genuine Cornish welcome, complete with tea and cake, is assured at the home of the Nicholls family. From this elevated position, the views over the village below to the sea beyond are truly spectacular. Bedrooms offer a host of thoughtful and generous extras from bath robes to Wi-fi access. Breakfast is a showcase of locally sourced and home-made produce including eggs, sausages, breads and jams. Additional facilities include a hot tub.

Rooms 6 en suite 2 annexe en suite (2 fmly) (2 GF); D £68-£99* **Facilities** TVL tea/coffee Direct Dial Cen ht Licensed Wi-fi Hot tub **Parking** 10 **Notes** LB ⊗ No Children 7yrs Closed mid Dec-mid Jan 50 acres beef/lamb

Boscastle House

★★★★★ 🅰 GUEST ACCOMMODATION

Tintagel Rd PL35 0AS
☎ 01840 250654 📄 01840 250654
e-mail: relax@boscastlehouse.com
dir: *In village, junct B3266 & B3263*

Rooms 6 en suite S £36-£59; D £54-£98*

Old Coach House

★★★★ GUEST ACCOMMODATION

Tintagel Rd PL35 0AS
☎ 01840 250398 📄 01840 250346
e-mail: stay@old-coach.co.uk
web: www.old-coach.co.uk
dir: *In village at junct B3266 & B3263. 150yds from petrol station towards Tintagel*

Over 300 years old, the Old Coach House has lovely views over the village and the rolling countryside. The comfortable bedrooms are well equipped and include two rooms on the ground floor. A hearty breakfast is served in the conservatory, which overlooks the well-kept garden.

Rooms 8 en suite (3 fmly) (2 GF) S £35-£45; D £60-£70* **Facilities** FTV TVL tea/coffee Cen ht Wi-fi **Parking** 9 **Notes** LB Closed Xmas

---

Pencarmol

★★★ BED AND BREAKFAST

5 Penally Ter, The Harbour PL35 0HA
☎ 01840 250435
e-mail: info@pencarmol.co.uk
dir: *Off B3263 to Boscastle harbour*

This lovely cottage has super views of the harbour and dramatic cliffs. The friendly proprietors are most welcoming and attentive hosts. There is a lovely garden and car parking is available. Bedrooms are compact and provide a good range of facilities. Breakfast features fresh mackerel, if any have been caught.

Rooms 3 en suite (1 fmly) **Facilities** TVL tea/coffee Cen ht **Parking** 3 **Notes** Closed 25 Dec-2 Jan 🖼

BUDE Map 2 SS20

Bangors Organic

★★★★ GUEST HOUSE

Poundstock EX23 0DP
☎ 01288 361297
e-mail: info@bangorsorganic.co.uk
dir: *4m S of Bude. On A39 in Poundstock*

Located a few miles south of Bude, this renovated Victorian establishment offers elegant accommodation with a good level of comfort. Bedrooms are furnished to a high standard and are located both in the main house and in an adjacent coach house, the latter being more contemporary in style. Bathrooms are a particular feature here, offering impressive levels of space and luxury. Breakfast and dinner, featuring organic, local and home-made produce, are served in the pleasant dining room. The establishment is Certified Organic by the Soil Association.

Rooms 2 en suite 2 annexe en suite (1 GF) D £120-£170 **Facilities** FTV TVL tea/coffee Dinner available Cen ht Licensed Wi-fi Badminton **Parking** 10 **Notes** ⊗ No Children 12yrs

Dylan's Guest House

★★★★ GUEST HOUSE

12 Downs View EX23 8RF
☎ 01288 354705
e-mail: dylansbude@tiscali.co.uk
dir: *From A39 onto A3073 at Stratton, at 2nd rdbt turn right to town centre, through town centre, signed to Downs View*

Recently refurbished to a high standard, this late Victorian house overlooks the golf course and is just a five minute walk from the beach. There is a refreshing and appealing style here, derived from a combination of original features and a crisp, contemporary décor. The well equipped bedrooms are light and airy with impressive levels of comfort. Plenty of choice is offered at breakfast, which is carefully prepared from quality produce and served in the attractive dining room.

Rooms 4 rms (2 en suite) (2 pri facs) (2 fmly)
Facilities FTV TVL tea/coffee Cen ht **Parking** 2 **Notes** LB ⊗ ⊠

Fairway House

★★★★ GUEST HOUSE

8 Downs View EX23 8RF
☎ 01288 355059

e-mail: enquiries@fairwayguesthouse.co.uk
dir: N through town to Flexbury, follow brown tourist signs to Downs View from golf course

Genuine hospitality and attentive service await you at this delightful Victorian terrace property, which overlooks the golf course and is close to the beach and town centre. The comfortable bedrooms are of a high standard and have many thoughtful extra facilities. A hearty breakfast, using local produce, is served at separate tables.

Rooms 7 rms (5 en suite) (1 fmly) S £26-£40; D £50-£63* **Facilities** FTV tea/coffee Cen ht **Notes** LB ⊗ Closed Dec-Jan ⊠

Oak Lodge B&B

★★★★ BED AND BREAKFAST

Oak Lodge, Stratton EX23 9AT
☎ 01288 354144

e-mail: julie@oaklodgebude.com
web: www.oaklodgebude.com
dir: At junct of A3072 & A39, at Stratton turn right, 100yds on right

This stylish, contemporary home has a wonderfully light and airy feel throughout. Impressive architecture, combined with a warm and genuine welcome, ensures a rewarding and relaxing stay. Bedrooms offer bags of comfort, allied with superb bathrooms of high quality. A guest lounge is also provided with lovely views across the village and rolling fields beyond. Weather permitting, breakfast can be enjoyed on the deck, with eggs provided by the resident hens.

Rooms 3 rms (2 en suite) (1 pri facs) S £25-£45; D £50-£70* **Facilities** FTV TVL tea/coffee Cen ht Wi-fi **Parking** 3 **Notes** LB ⊗ No Children ⊠

Bude Haven

★★★★ GUEST ACCOMMODATION

Flexbury Av EX23 8NS
☎ 01288 352305   📄 01288 352662

e-mail: enquiries@budehavenhotel.com
web: www.budehavenhotel.com
dir: 0.5m N of Bude in Flexbury centre

This charming, refurbished Edwardian property is in a quiet area within easy walking distance of Bude centre and Crooklets Beach. Bedrooms are bright and airy, and the restaurant offers an interesting menu at dinnertime. You can also relax in the lounge or the bar.

Rooms 10 en suite (1 fmly) S £32.50-£45; D £65-£90*
Facilities FTV TVL tea/coffee Dinner available Cen ht Licensed Wi-fi Hot tub **Parking** 4 **Notes** LB ⊗

The Cliff at Bude

★★★★ GUEST HOUSE

Maer Down, Crooklets Beach EX23 8NG
☎ 01288 353110   & 356833   📄 01288 353110

e-mail: cliff-hotel@btconnect.com
web: www.cliffhotel.co.uk
dir: A39 through Bude, left at top of High St, pass Somerfields, 1st right between golf course, over x-rds, premises at end on left

Overlooking the sea from a clifftop location, this friendly and efficient establishment provides spacious, well-equipped bedrooms. The various public areas include a bar and lounge and an impressive range of leisure facilities. Delicious dinners and tasty breakfasts are available in the attractive dining room.

Rooms 15 en suite (15 fmly) (8 GF) S £45.54; D £75.90*
Facilities FTV TVL tea/coffee Dinner available Direct Dial Cen ht Licensed ⊠ 🏊 ♨ Gymnasium Pool Table **Parking** 18 **Notes** LB Closed Nov-Mar

Pencarrol

★★★★ GUEST HOUSE

21 Downs View EX23 8RF
☎ 01288 352478

e-mail: pencarrolbude@aol.com
dir: 0.5m N of Bude. N from Bude into Flexbury village

This cosy guest house is only a short walk from Bude centre and Crooklets Beach, and has glorious views over the golf course. Bedrooms are attractively furnished and there is a first-floor lounge. Breakfast is served at separate tables in the dining room.

Rooms 7 rms (3 en suite) (2 pri facs) (2 fmly) (2 GF) S £28.50-£33.50; D £66-£73 **Facilities** FTV TVL tea/coffee Cen ht **Notes** LB ⊗ Closed Nov-Jan ⊠

Stratton Gardens House

★★★★ GUEST ACCOMMODATION

Cot Hill, Stratton EX23 9DN
☎ 01288 352500

e-mail: moira@stratton-gardens.co.uk
web: www.stratton-gardens.co.uk
dir: From Holsworthy take A3072 to Stratton. Up hill far side of Kings Arms. Take 3rd right

Tucked away in a quiet corner of this small town of Stratton, a mile from Bude, Stratton Gardens is a 16th-century house which was formerly owned by the church. Each of the bedrooms is distinctively furnished, and very comfortable. In the candlelit restaurant a varied menu is provided, offering innovative fare using the best of local produce. Specific diets can be catered for. Ample on-site parking is an added bonus.

Rooms 7 rms (6 en suite) (2 fmly) S £29-£36; D £62-£76* **Facilities** TVL tea/coffee Dinner available Cen ht Licensed **Parking** 14 **Notes** ⊗

Surf Haven Guest House

★★★★ 🅐 GUEST HOUSE

31 Downs View EX23 8RG
☎ 01288 353923

e-mail: info@surfhaven.co.uk
web: www.surfhaven.co.uk
dir: From A3072 follow signs to Bude town centre then follow sign for Crooklets Beach

Rooms 8 rms (7 en suite) (1 pri facs) (4 fmly) (1 GF)
Facilities TVL tea/coffee Dinner available Cen ht Wi-fi **Parking** 8 **Notes** LB

Sea Jade Guest House

★★★ GUEST ACCOMMODATION

15 Burn View EX23 8BZ
☎ 01288 353404

e-mail: seajadeguesthouse@yahoo.co.uk
dir: A39 turn right follow signs for Bude & golf course

A very well located guesthouse within a few minutes walk of both town and beaches. Very friendly hosts, comfortable bedrooms and hearty breakfast make this a very popular venue.

Rooms 8 rms (7 en suite) (1 pri facs) (4 fmly) (2 GF) S £28-£35; D £56-£62* **Facilities** FTV TVL tea/coffee Cen ht **Notes** LB ⊗ ⊠

CALLINGTON — Map 3 SX36

Woodpeckers
★★★★ GUEST HOUSE

Rilla Mill PL17 7NT
☎ 01579 363717
e-mail: alisonmerchant@virgin.net
dir: 5m NW of Callington. Off B3254 at Upton Cross x-rds for Rilla Mill

Set in a conservation village, in a wooded valley, by a tumbling stream, this modern, detached house offers cosy, well equipped bedrooms with numerous thoughtful extras. Home-cooked dinners, using the best of local ingredients, are available by arrangement. The hot tub in the garden is a welcome feature.

Rooms 3 en suite **Facilities** STV FTV tea/coffee Dinner available Cen ht Gymnasium Spa/Hot Tub **Parking** 7 **Notes** LB ⊗ ⊜

Green Pastures Bed & Breakfast
★★★ BED AND BREAKFAST

Longhill PL17 8AU
☎ 01579 382566
e-mail: greenpast@aol.com
dir: 0.5m E of Callington on A390 to Tavistock

Located on the southern side of Kit Hill, this friendly, homely establishment has panoramic views across the Tamar Valley and distant views of Dartmoor. The modern bungalow stands in five acres of land, where Shetland ponies contentedly graze. Bedrooms are comfortably furnished and there is a large lounge.

Rooms 3 rms (2 en suite) (1 pri facs) (3 GF) **Facilities** tea/coffee Cen ht **Parking** 8 **Notes** ⊗ No Children 18yrs ⊜

The Olive Tree Bed & Breakfast
★★★ BED AND BREAKFAST

Maders PL17 7LL
☎ 01579 384392   ▤ 01579 384392
e-mail: kindredspirits@blueyonder.co.uk
dir: From M5 junct 31 A38 Plymouth A388 Callington through town up hill on left

A warm welcome is assured at this single storey property, a mile north of Callington. The attractive accommodation is spacious, and well equipped with numerous extras. At breakfast an interesting choice is offered, featuring home-produced eggs from the hens in the garden.

Rooms 3 rms (2 en suite) (1 pri facs) (3 GF) **Facilities** tea/coffee Dinner available Cen ht Wi-fi Massage & reflexology available on site **Parking** 10 **Notes** ⊜

CAMELFORD — Map 2 SX18

Sea View Farm
★★★ BED AND BREAKFAST

Otterham Station PL32 9SW
☎ 01840 261433
e-mail: dawnandcarl@rock.com
dir: From A30 take A395 at Hallworthy, then B3262 at A39 turn right, 1st on left

A former farmhouse on the edge of the main A39 with easy access to Bude, Camelford and Launceston. Comfortable bedroom, friendly hosts and a hearty breakfast, using home-produced eggs. Guests have the use of private lounge, and Reiki treatments are also available.

Rooms 1 rms (1 pri facs) S £35; D £60* **Facilities** FTV TVL tea/coffee Cen ht Riding **Parking** 8 **Notes** LB ⊗ ⊜

CAWSAND — Map 3 SX45

Wringford Down
★★★ GUEST ACCOMMODATION

Hat Ln PL10 1LE
☎ 01752 822287
e-mail: a.molloy@virgin.net
dir: A374 onto B3247, pass Millbrook, right towards Cawsand & sharp right, 0.5m on right

This family-run establishment has a peaceful location near Rame Head and the South West Coast Path, and is particularly welcoming to families. There is a nursery, swimming pool, games room, and gardens with play areas. A range of rooms, and some suites and self-catering units are available. Breakfast and dinner are served in the dining room.

Rooms 7 en suite 4 annexe en suite (8 fmly) (4 GF) S £46-£56; D £72-£92* **Facilities** FTV TVL tea/coffee Dinner available Cen ht Licensed Wi-fi ⊗ ⊰ Pool Table Table tennis **Parking** 20 **Notes** LB Civ Wed 100

CONGDON'S SHOP — Map 2 SX27

Trevadlock Farm (SX262793)
★★★★ FARMHOUSE

PL15 7PW
☎ 01566 782239   Mrs Sleep
e-mail: trevadlock@farming.co.uk
dir: W of Launceston exit A30 onto B325 towards Callington. After garage on right take 3rd right. Pass old chapel and sign for Trevadlock, 0.5m, farm down hill on right

A working dairy farm near to Launceston and Callington just off the A30. Rooms are well appointed and comfortable and guests are made to feel very welcome with tea and scones on arrival. Breakfast is served in the dining room and features lots of local produce.

Rooms 2 en suite; D £60-£75 **Facilities** FTV TVL tea/coffee Cen ht Wi-fi **Parking** 2 **Notes** LB ⊗ No Children Closed Xmas & New Year 150 acres mixed/sheep/dairy

CONSTANTINE — Map 2 SW72

Trengilly Wartha Inn
★★★ ⊛ INN

Nancenoy TR11 5RP
☎ 01326 340332   ▤ 01326 340332
e-mail: reception@trengilly.co.uk
web: www.trengilly.co.uk
dir: Follow signs to Nancenoy, left towards Gweek until 1st sign for inn, left & left again at next sign, continue to inn

Located in a very peaceful wooded valley, just one and a half miles from the village of Constantine, this inn offers cosy, comfortable accommodation with nicely appointed and well equipped bedrooms. An interesting menu is offered in the restaurant together with a well balanced wine list; there is also a wide selection of bar meals available at lunch and dinner.

Rooms 6 en suite 2 annexe en suite (2 fmly) (2 GF) S £50-£65; D £80-£96* **Facilities** tea/coffee Dinner available Direct Dial Cen ht Wi-fi Boules **Conf** Max 30 Class 30 Board 30 **Parking** 60 **Notes** LB RS 25 Dec No food

CRACKINGTON HAVEN · Map 2 SX19

Lower Tresmorn Farm *(SX164975)*

★★★★ FARMHOUSE

EX23 0NU
☎ 01840 230667 📄 01840 230667 Rachel Crocker
e-mail: rachel.crocker@talk21.com
web: www.lowertresmorn.co.uk
dir: *Take Tresmorn turn off coast road 2m N of Crackington Haven*

Set in the North Cornwall Heritage Coast area, parts of this charming farmhouse date back to medieval times. The welcome is warm and genuine with a reviving cup of tea and piece of cake always on offer. Bedrooms are located in the main house and an adjacent converted barn, and all provide plenty of comfort. Breakfast and dinner (by prior arrangement) use local or farm produce.

Rooms 3 rms (2 en suite) 3 annexe en suite (2 fmly) (2 GF) S £36-£60; D £60-£76* **Facilities** FTV TV4B TVL tea/coffee Dinner available **Parking** 6 **Notes** ⊗ No Children 8yrs RS 20 Dec-5 Jan B&B only 432 acres beef/sheep

Bears & Boxes Country Guest House

★★★★ GUEST HOUSE

Penrose, Dizzard EX23 0NX
☎ 01840 230318
e-mail: rwfrh@btinternet.com
web: www.bearsandboxes.com
dir: *1.5m NE of St Gennys in Dizzard*

Dating in part from the mid 17th century, Bears & Boxes is a small, family-run guest house situated 500yds from the coastal path. You are welcomed with a tray of tea and home-made cake, and the caring owners are always around to help and advise about the locality. The cosy bedrooms have numerous thoughtful extras, and evening meals, using the very best of local ingredients and cooked with flair, are served by arrangement.

Rooms 3 en suite 1 annexe rms (1 pri facs) (1 fmly) (1 GF) S £28.80-£32; D £57.60-£64* **Facilities** FTV TVL tea/coffee Dinner available Cen ht Wi-fi **Parking** 6

CRAFTHOLE · Map 3 SX35

The Liscawn

★★★★ GUEST ACCOMMODATION

PL11 3BD
☎ 01503 230863
e-mail: enquiries@liscawn.co.uk
web: www.liscawn.co.uk
dir: *A374 onto B3247 to Crafthole, through village, left at rdbt, 0.3m on left*

A well established, friendly, family-run establishment with comfortable rooms. Serving food every night of the week, The Liscawn sits in mature grounds and is a few minutes from the Coastal Path and Whitsand Bay.

Rooms 8 en suite 5 annexe en suite (3 fmly) (2 GF) S £50-£55; D £60-£90* **Facilities** FTV tea/coffee Dinner available Cen ht Licensed Children's play area **Conf** Max 60 Thtr 60 Class 40 Board 35 **Parking** 50 **Notes** Civ Wed 70

CRANTOCK · Map 2 SW76

Carrek Woth

★★★ GUEST ACCOMMODATION

West Pentire Rd TR8 5SA
☎ 01637 830530
web: www.carrekwoth.co.uk
dir: *W from Crantock towards West Pentire*

Many guests return to this friendly, family-run house where hospitality and service are keynotes. Carrek Woth takes its name from the Cornish for Goose Rock, which can be seen in Crantock Bay. All the rooms are on the ground floor and the bedrooms are neatly furnished and some have good views. The lounge looks toward Newquay and the sea. Breakfast is served in the attractive dining room, where Sunday lunch is also available.

Rooms 6 en suite (1 fmly) (6 GF) S fr £44; D fr £66* **Facilities** FTV TVL tea/coffee Cen ht **Parking** 6 **Notes** LB ⊗

DEVORAN · Map 2 SW73

Pentrig

★★★ BED AND BREAKFAST

Greenbank Rd TR3 6PQ
☎ 01872 863597
dir: *A39 (Truro to Falmouth), dual carriageway down hill to rdbt. Take exit signed Devoran*

Guests are assured of a warm welcome at this dormer bungalow, family home. Conveniently situated mid-way between Truro and Falmouth, Pentrig is an ideal centre from which to explore numerous attractions. A hearty breakfast is served, using free range eggs and local produce wherever possible, at a communal table overlooking the well tended gardens. The comfortable bedrooms are well equipped.

Rooms 2 rms; D £50-£60* **Facilities** FTV TVL tea/coffee Cen ht **Parking** 10 **Notes** ⊗ No Children 12yrs Closed 21 Dec-1 Jan ⊗

DRYM · Map 2 SW63

PREMIER COLLECTION

Drym Farm

★★★★★ BED AND BREAKFAST

Drym, Praze, Camborne TR14 0NU
☎ 01209 831039
e-mail: drymfarm@hotmail.co.uk
web: www.drymfarm.co.uk
dir: *Off B3302 at Leedstown to Drym. Follow until right turn to Drym. Farm drive on right after Drym House*

This delightful granite house stands in mature grounds and gardens in a lush, secluded valley. Guests are assured of a warm, friendly welcome. Bedrooms are stylishly simple and carefully furnished, with an emphasis on good linen and comfort. The comfortable lounge has a relaxing atmosphere; and breakfasts use local and organic produce.

Rooms 2 rms (2 pri facs) S £50-£70; D £75-£90* **Facilities** FTV tea/coffee Cen ht Wi-fi **Parking** 6 **Notes** LB ⊗ ⊗

FALMOUTH
Map 2 SW83

PREMIER COLLECTION

Dolvean House
★★★★★ GUEST ACCOMMODATION

50 Melvill Rd TR11 4DQ
☎ 01326 313658 📠 01326 313995
e-mail: reservations@dolvean.co.uk
web: www.dolvean.co.uk
dir: *On A39 near town centre & Maritime Museum*

A Victorian house with high standards throughout. Rooms are comfortable and well equipped and there is a guest lounge. Well located for the beach and town alike with ample off-street parking.

Rooms 10 en suite (2 GF) S £36-£42; D £72-£94 **Facilities** FTV TVL tea/coffee Cen ht Licensed Wi-fi **Parking** 11 **Notes** LB Closed Xmas

Prospect House
★★★★ GUEST ACCOMMODATION

1 Church Rd, Penryn TR10 8DA
☎ 01326 373198 📠 01326 373198
e-mail: stay@prospecthouse.co.uk
web: www.prospecthouse.co.uk
dir: *Off A39 at Treluswell rdbt onto B3292, turn right at Penryn town centre sign. Left at junct to town hall, left onto Saint Gluivas St, at bottom on left*

Situated close to the waterside, Prospect House is an attractive building, built for a ship's captain around 1820. The original charm of the house has been carefully maintained, and the attractive bedrooms are well equipped. A comfortable lounge is available, and freshly cooked breakfasts are served in the elegant dining room. Small friendly dogs only accepted.

Rooms 3 en suite; D £65-£70* **Facilities** FTV TVL tea/coffee Dinner available Cen ht Wi-fi **Conf** Max 6 **Parking** 4

The Rosemary
★★★★ GUEST ACCOMMODATION

22 Gyllyngvase Ter TR11 4DL
☎ 01326 314669
e-mail: therosemary@tiscali.co.uk
web: www.therosemary.co.uk
dir: *A39 Melvill Rd signed to beaches & seafront, right onto Gyllyngvase Rd, 1st left*

Centrally located with splendid views over Falmouth Bay, this friendly establishment provides comfortable accommodation. The attractive bedrooms are thoughtfully equipped and some enjoy the benefit of the views. Guests can relax in the lounge with a drink from the well stocked bar. Also available is a sunny decking area at the rear in the pretty garden, facing the sea.

Rooms 10 en suite (4 fmly) S £39-£45; D £68-£80* **Facilities** FTV tea/coffee Cen ht Licensed Wi-fi **Parking** 3 **Notes** Closed Nov-Jan

See advert on opposite page

Bosanneth Guest House
★★★★ GUEST HOUSE

Gyllyngvase Hill TR11 4DW
☎ 01326 314649 📠 01326 314649
e-mail: stay@bosanneth.co.uk
dir: *From Truro on A39 follow signs for beaches/docks, 3rd right mini-rdbt Melvil Rd, 3rd right onto Gyllyngvase Hill*

Well situated Edwardian property with stylish, comfortable rooms and very friendly hosts. Most rooms, including the lounge and dining room, have beautiful sea views and dinner is served nightly. A full Cornish breakfast is served in the dining room.

Rooms 8 en suite S £35-£45; D £75-£90* **Facilities** FTV tea/coffee Dinner available Cen ht Licensed Wi-fi **Parking** 7 **Notes** LB ⊗ No Children 15yrs

Cotswold House
★★★★ GUEST HOUSE

49 Melvill Rd TR11 4DF
☎ 01326 312077
e-mail: info@cotswoldhousehotel.com
dir: *On A39 near town centre & docks*

This smart Victorian house has splendid sea views, and is just a short walk from the town. The atmosphere is relaxed, the bar is popular, and the lounge provides a good level of comfort. A hearty breakfast is served in the dining room and dinner, featuring home-cooked dishes, is available by prior arrangement.

Rooms 10 en suite (1 fmly) (1 GF) **Facilities** FTV TVL tea/coffee Dinner available Cen ht Licensed **Parking** 10 **Notes** ⊗ Closed Xmas

Esmond House

★★★★ GUEST HOUSE

5 Emslie Rd TR11 4BG
☎ 01326 313214
e-mail: esmondhouse@btopenworld.com
web: www.esmondhouse.com
dir: *Off A39 Melvill Rd left onto Emslie Rd*

The friendly and comfortable Edwardian house is just a short easy walk from the beach. Bedrooms vary in size and some have sea views; the rooms are on the first and second floors. A hearty, freshly cooked breakfast is served in the spacious, traditionally furnished front room, whose large bay windows create a light and airy environment.

Rooms 4 en suite S £30-£35; D £60-£65 **Facilities** FTV tea/coffee Cen ht **Notes** LB ⊗ No Children 3yrs Closed Nov-Jan

Gayhurst

★★★★ GUEST ACCOMMODATION

10 Pennance Rd TR11 4EA
☎ 01326 315161
e-mail: jfjgriffin@yahoo.co.uk
web: www.falmouth-gayhurst.co.uk
dir: *A39 towards town centre, at end of Western Ter right at mini-rdbt onto Pennance Rd*

Many guests return to this friendly home, located in a quiet residential area close to the beaches. The spacious bedrooms are comfortably appointed, and some have sea views. Freshly cooked breakfasts are served in the bright dining room, which overlooks the attractive garden.

Rooms 5 en suite; D £60-£70* **Facilities** FTV tea/coffee **Parking** 5 **Notes** ⊗ No Children 10yrs Closed Nov-Etr

Hawthorne Dene Guest House

★★★★ GUEST HOUSE

12 Pennance Rd TR11 4EA
☎ 01326 311427   🖷 01326 311994
e-mail: enquiries@hawthornedenehotel.co.uk
web: www.hawthornedenehotel.com
dir: *A39 towards town centre, at end of Western Ter right at mini-rdbt onto Pennance Rd*

Picture windows in the lounge, dining room and many of the bedrooms of this late Victorian house look out over the sea. Cuisine is a feature, and dishes focus on the best of local and organic produce. A log fire burns in winter in the comfortable lounge. Sign language is understood.

Rooms 10 en suite (1 fmly) (1 GF) S £40; D £80-£95 **Facilities** FTV tea/coffee Dinner available Cen ht Licensed Wi-fi **Parking** 7 **Notes** LB ⊗

Lugo Rock

★★★★ GUEST ACCOMMODATION

59 Melvill Rd TR11 4DF
☎ 01326 311344   🖷 01326 311567
e-mail: info@lugorockhotel.co.uk
dir: *On A39 near town centre & docks*

The proprietor of this pleasant house provides comfortable and spacious accommodation and a friendly atmosphere. Bedrooms are attractively decorated and well equipped. There is a smart lounge and terrace overlooking the well-tended garden and ample car parking space is provided, there is also a small bar. Breakfast is served in the stylish dining room.

Rooms 12 en suite (3 fmly) (2 GF) S £35-£50; D £50-£79* **Facilities** FTV TVL tea/coffee Cen ht Licensed Wi-fi **Parking** 12 **Notes** No Children 12yrs

Melvill House

★★★★ GUEST ACCOMMODATION

52 Melvill Rd TR11 4DQ
☎ 01326 316645   🖷 01326 211608
e-mail: melvillhouse@btconnect.com
dir: *On A39 near town centre & docks*

Well situated for the beach, the town centre and the National Maritime Museum on the harbour, Melvill House is a family-run establishment with a relaxed atmosphere. Some bedrooms have four-poster beds, and breakfast is served in the smart dining room. Ample parking.

Rooms 7 en suite (2 fmly) (1 GF) S £28-£35; D £56-£65 **Facilities** TVL tea/coffee Cen ht Wi-fi **Parking** 8 **Notes** LB ⊗

The Rathgowry

★★★★ GUEST ACCOMMODATION

Gyllyngvase Hill TR11 4DN
☎ 01326 313482
e-mail: enquiries@rathgowry.co.uk
dir: *A39 from Truro bypass Penryn follow signs for docks & beaches (avoid town centre). A39 into Dracaena Ave, Melvill Rd & right into Gyllyngvase Hill*

A spacious Edwardian house, situated within easy walking distance of the town centre and beach. Bedrooms are bright, well maintained and comfortable, and four have sea views. A spacious lounge is available, and in the attractive dining room, evening meals are served by prior arrangement. The resident proprietors offer helpful and friendly service, and forecourt parking is provided.

Rooms 10 rms (8 en suite) (2 pri facs) (2 fmly) (1 GF) **Facilities** FTV tea/coffee Dinner available Cen ht **Parking** 10 **Notes** LB ⊗ Closed Oct-Apr ⊗

The ROSEMARY

Gyllyngvase Terrace, Falmouth, Cornwall TR11 4DL

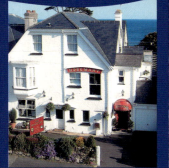

RUN by a Cornish family, the Rosemary is a charming Victorian house with a big welcome. Situated on one of the quietest roads in Falmouth, yet central, its garden is a haven of tranquillity and the views will bring you back time and again. All the bedrooms are light and airy, ensuite, and attractively decorated. Just a gentle stroll from the beach, harbour and town centre. Non-smoking throughout.

Tel: 01326 314669   email: therosemary@tiscali.co.uk
Website: www.therosemary.co.uk

FALMOUTH *continued*

Rosemullion

★★★★ GUEST ACCOMMODATION

Gyllyngvase Hill TR11 4DF
☎ 01326 314690 🖷 01326 210098
e-mail: gail@rosemullionhotel.demon.co.uk

Recognisable by its mock-Tudor exterior, this friendly establishment is well situated for both the town centre and the beach. Some of the comfortable bedrooms are on the ground floor, while a few rooms on the top floor have views to Falmouth Bay. Hospitality and service are strengths. Breakfast, served in the panelled dining room, is freshly cooked and there is a well appointed lounge.

Rooms 13 rms (11 en suite) (2 pri facs) (3 GF)
Facilities FTV tea/coffee Cen ht Wi-fi **Parking** 18
Notes ⊗ No Children Closed 23-29 Dec 🖼

The Westcott

★★★★ 🅰 GUEST ACCOMMODATION

Gyllyngvase Hill TR11 4DN
☎ 01326 311309 🖷 01326 330222
e-mail: westcotthotel@btinternet.com
web: www.westcotthotelfalmouth.co.uk
dir: *A39 from Truro to Falmouth. Gyllyngvase Hill on right 600yds before Princess Pavillion*

Rooms 10 en suite S £35-£40; D £60-£70* **Facilities** FTV TVL tea/coffee Cen ht Wi-fi **Parking** 7 **Notes** LB ⊗ No Children 5yrs

Boswyn

★★★ BED AND BREAKFAST

1 Western Ter TR11 4QN
☎ 01326 314667
e-mail: eric.jermyn@sky.com

A traditional bed and breakfast with genuine hospitality and friendly service. Rooms are well equipped and furnished, a guest lounge is available, and a separate dining room is the venue for breakfast. Conveniently located just a few minutes walk from the sea front with on-street parking nearby.

Rooms 4 en suite (2 fmly) S £25-£30; D £50-£55*
Facilities FTV TVL tea/coffee Cen ht Wi-fi **Notes** LB ⊗ 🖼

The Oasis Guest House

★★★ GUEST HOUSE

15 Dracaena Av TR11 2EG
☎ 01326 311457
web: www.theoasisguesthouse.com
dir: *From A30 take A390 through Truro into Falmouth, through lights, at Esso garage. House 200yds on left*

Guests are assured of a warm friendly welcome at this comfortable establishment. Conveniently situated for the town centre, the beaches and the numerous local attractions, the Oasis is an ideal location for both business and leisure guests. Some ground floor bedrooms are available, and a freshly cooked breakfast is served in the cosy dining room.

Rooms 7 rms (6 en suite) (1 pri facs) (2 fmly) (3 GF) S £30-£35; D £50-£55* **Facilities** FTV TVL tea/coffee Cen ht Wi-fi **Parking** 6 **Notes** LB ⊗

The Observatory

★★★ GUEST HOUSE

27 Western Ter TR11 4QL
☎ 01326 314509
web: www.theobservatoryguesthouse.co.uk
dir: *On A39, Dracaena Av onto Western Ter*

This interesting house is in a pleasant location, close to the town and harbour. The proprietors are very friendly hosts. Bedrooms come in a range of sizes, and freshly cooked breakfasts, with vegetarian options, are served in the dining room. On-site parking is an added bonus.

Rooms 6 en suite (2 fmly) (3 GF) S £35-£40; D £55*
Facilities FTV tea/coffee Cen ht **Parking** 6 **Notes** LB ⊗ 🖼

Penwarren

★★★ GUEST HOUSE

3 Avenue Rd TR11 4AZ
☎ 01326 314216
e-mail: penwarren@btconnect.com

Penwarren is in the heart of Falmouth, not far from Gyllyngvase beach. This friendly establishment is a winner of a Green Award for environmental awareness. Service is attentive and thoughtful and the fresh accommodation comes with considerate extras. A varied choice is offered at breakfast; a cosy lounge is also available.

Rooms 7 rms (6 en suite) (1 pri facs) (1 fmly)
Facilities TVL tea/coffee Cen ht **Parking** 7 **Notes** ⊗
Closed 20 Dec-6 Jan

Trevoil Guest House

★★★ GUEST HOUSE

25 Avenue Rd TR11 4AY
☎ 01326 314145 & 07966 409782 🖷 01326 314145
e-mail: alan.jewel@btconnect.com
dir: *Off A39 Melvill Rd left onto Avenue Rd, 150yds from Maritime Museum*

Located within walking distance of the town centre, the friendly Trevoil is a comfortable and relaxed environment. Breakfast is enjoyed in the light, pleasant dining room.

Rooms 8 rms (4 en suite) (3 fmly) (1 GF) S £23-£25; D £46-£50* **Facilities** tea/coffee Cen ht Wi-fi **Parking** 6 **Notes** LB

The Tudor Court

★★★ GUEST HOUSE

55 Melvill Rd TR11 4DF
☎ 01326 312807
e-mail: enquiries@tudorcourthotel.com
dir: *A39 to Falmouth straight through Dracaena Ave, onto Melvill Road. Tudor Court 300yds on right*

This mock-Tudor establishment offers bright, well-equipped bedrooms, some having the benefit of distant sea views. A comfortable bar/lounge is available for guests and in the dining room, which overlooks the attractive garden, a freshly cooked, full English breakfast is served.

Rooms 10 rms (9 en suite) (1 pri facs) (1 fmly)
Facilities TVL tea/coffee Cen ht **Parking** 10 **Notes** ⊗

Eden Lodge

★★ GUEST HOUSE

54 Melvill Rd TR11 4DQ
☎ 01326 212989 & 07715 696218
e-mail: edenlodge@hotmail.co.uk
dir: *On A39, on left 200yds past Fox Rosehill Gardens*

Very well located on Melvill Road with off-road parking, Eden Lodge boasts comfortable rooms and a swimming pool. The friendly hosts serve dinner by arrangement and do all they can to ensure a comfortable stay. Rooms are well equipped and offer very good value-for-money.

Rooms 5 rms (4 en suite) (2 fmly) (1 GF) S £25-£35; D £50-£70* **Facilities** FTV TVL tea/coffee Dinner available Cen ht Licensed Wi-fi 🔲 Gymnasium Massage & aromatherapy by appointment **Parking** 9 **Notes** LB 🖼

FLUSHING · Map 2 SW83

Trefusis Barton Farmhouse B&B (SW815341)

★★★ FARMHOUSE

TR11 5TD
☎ 01326 374257 & 07866 045646
🖨 01326 374257 Mrs J Laity
e-mail: trefusisbarton@aol.com
dir: Off A39 towards Carclew, follow signs to Mylor Bridge, left at mini-rdbt, after 0.5m straight across at x-rds

This working farm is easily reached high above the village of Flushing. The friendly home is convenient for a relaxing break or for touring, and the comfortable bedrooms have many thoughtful extras. Breakfast is served at the farmhouse kitchen table, fresh from the Aga.

Rooms 3 en suite (1 GF) S fr £40; D fr £65* Facilities FTV tea/coffee Cen ht Parking 6 Notes ⊗ ⊛ 400 acres dairy/arable

FOWEY · Map 2 SX15

Trevanion

★★★★ GUEST ACCOMMODATION

70 Lostwithiel St PL23 1BQ
☎ 01726 832602
e-mail: alisteve@trevanionguesthouse.co.uk
web: www.trevanionguesthouse.co.uk
dir: A3082 into Fowey, down hill, left onto Lostwithiel St, Trevanion on left

This 16th-century merchant's house provides friendly, comfortable accommodation within easy walking distance of the historic town of Fowey and is convenient for visiting the Eden Project. A hearty farmhouse-style cooked breakfast, using local produce, is served in the attractive dining room and other menu options are available.

Rooms 5 rms (4 en suite) (1 pri facs) (2 fmly) (1 GF) S £35-£40; D £50-£70* Facilities FTV tea/coffee Cen ht Wi-fi Parking 5 Notes LB ⊛

GOLDSITHNEY · Map 2 SW53

Penleen

★★★ GUEST ACCOMMODATION

South Rd TR20 9LF
☎ 01736 710633
e-mail: jimblain@penleen.com
web: www.penleen.com
dir: A30 towards Penzance, left onto A394 at rdbt. Left into Goldsithney, 1st right onto South Rd

Penleen is a quiet home close to Penzance and Mount's Bay. The friendly proprietors ensure you have a comfortable stay. The lounge overlooks an attractive garden and freshly cooked breakfasts are served in the

dining room. Bedrooms come with a good range of facilities.

Rooms 2 rms (1 en suite) (1 pri facs) S £35-£40; D £57-£60* Facilities FTV tea/coffee Cen ht Parking 2 Notes ⊗ No Children 8yrs Closed 19 Dec-5 Jan ⊛

GORRAN · Map 2 SW94

Tregerrick Farm B&B (SW992436)

★★★★ FARMHOUSE

PL26 6NF
☎ 01726 843418 🖨 01726 843418 Mrs C Thomas
e-mail: fandc.thomas@btconnect.com
web: www.tregerrickfarm.co.uk
dir: 1m NW of Gorran. B3273 S from St Austell, right after Pentewan Sands campsite to The Lost Gardens of Heligan, continue 3m, farm on left

Near many attractions, the family-run Victorian farmhouse offers a high standard of accommodation in peaceful countryside. Two of the attractive bedrooms are in the main house, the other is in a self-contained, two-bedroom suite. Delicious breakfasts, featuring home-made breads and preserves, are served around the large dining table.

Rooms 2 en suite 2 annexe rms (2 pri facs) (1 fmly) (2 GF) S £45; D £68-£75 Facilities FTV TVL tea/coffee Cen ht Wi-fi Parking 4 Notes LB ⊗ No Children 4yrs Closed Nov-Jan ⊛ 280 acres arable/beef

GORRAN HAVEN · Map 2 SX04

The Mead

★★★★ BED AND BREAKFAST

PL26 6HU
☎ 01726 842981
e-mail: maureengoff@tiscali.co.uk
dir: A30 signed to St Austell continue towards Mevagissey. Signed for Gorran Haven, 1st right Wansford Meadows

Guests are welcomed at this new, comfortable home, with a complimentary cream tea. Peacefully situated in Gorran Haven, within a ten-minute walk of the sandy beach, Heligan and the Eden Project are a short drive away. The bedrooms feature larger than average beds and numerous extra facilities. Hearty breakfasts are served in the ground floor dining room, with free-range eggs from the owner's hens in the garden, when possible.

Rooms 2 en suite S £40; D £60 Facilities FTV tea/coffee Cen ht Wi-fi Parking 2 Notes ⊗ No Children Closed Xmas ⊛

GRAMPOUND · Map 2 SW94

Perran House

★★★ GUEST ACCOMMODATION

Fore St TR2 4RS
☎ 01726 882066 🖨 01726 882936
dir: On A390 in village centre

Convenient for Truro or St Austell, Perran House dates from the 17th century and offers brightly decorated and co-ordinated bedrooms equipped with modern facilities. Breakfast is served in the airy dining room and there is ample off-road parking.

Rooms 5 rms (3 en suite) S fr £22; D fr £48* Facilities FTV tea/coffee Cen ht Parking 8 Notes ⊗ No Children 7yrs

GWEEK · Map 2 SW72

Barton Farm (SW692279)

★★★ FARMHOUSE

TR13 0QH
☎ 01326 572557 & 07814 942471 Mrs P Jenkin
e-mail: bartonfarm@talk21.com
dir: 1m NW of Gweek. Off A394 at Manhay x-rds towards Gweek, 1m left at T-junct, farm 150yds on left

This dairy farm in a peaceful location near Gweek has been in the same family for four generations. The proprietors' warm hospitality brings guests back year after year. Scrumptious breakfasts are served in the traditionally furnished dining room.

Rooms 3 rms (1 pri facs) Facilities TVL tea/coffee Parking 5 Notes ⊗ Closed Nov-Feb ⊛ 178 acres beef/dairy

HAYLE · Map 2 SW53

Calize Country House

★★★★ GUEST ACCOMMODATION

Prosper Hill, Gwithian TR27 5BW
☎ 01736 753268 🖨 01736 753268
e-mail: jilly@calize.co.uk
dir: 2m NE of Hayle. B3301 in Gwithian at Red River Inn, house 350yds up hill on left

The refurbished establishment has superb views of the sea and countryside, and is well located for the beaches and coves of West Penwith, walking, birdwatching, and the many gardens in the area. The attentive proprietors provide a most welcoming environment and invite you to share their comfortable lounge, which has a log-burning fire during colder months. Enjoyable breakfasts featuring delicious home-made fare are served around a communal table with sea views.

Rooms 4 en suite S £50-£60; D £80-£90 Facilities FTV TVL tea/coffee Cen ht Wi-fi Parking 6 Notes ⊗ No Children 12yrs ⊛

HAYLE *continued*

Treglisson Guest House

★★★★ GUEST HOUSE

Wheal Alfred Rd TR27 5JT
☎ 01736 753141
e-mail: steve@treglisson.co.uk
dir: *A30 Hayle rdbt, 4th exit, 1st left at mini rdbt, guest house 1m on left*

This fine period house sits in the middle of some 130 acres of working arable farmland. The house has recently been sympathetically restored and the charming bedrooms are each individually furnished. Guests can relax and enjoy the warmth of the log-burning stove during the colder months or make use of the swimming pool in the summer.

Rooms 4 en suite (2 fmly) S £40; D £55-£75*
Facilities FTV tea/coffee Cen ht Wi-fi🐾 Children's play area **Parking** 6 **Notes** ⊗ Closed 23 Dec-2 Jan RS Nov-Feb Phone for availability

---

HELSTON   Map 2 SW62

See also St Keverne

PREMIER COLLECTION

Drym Farm
★★★★★ BED AND BREAKFAST

Drym, Praze, Camborne TR14 0NU
☎ 01209 831039
e-mail: drymfarm@hotmail.co.uk
web: www.drymfarm.co.uk

(For full entry see Drym)

LANLIVERY   Map 2 SX05

The Crown Inn

★★★ INN

PL30 5BT
☎ 01208 872707   🖷 01208 871208
e-mail: thecrown@wagtailinns.com
web: www.wagtailinns.com
dir: *Signed off A390, 2m W of Lostwithiel. Inn 0.5m down lane into village, opp church*

This characterful inn has a long history, reflected in its worn flagstone floors, aged beams, ancient well and open fireplaces. Dating in part from the 12th century, the Crown has recently undergone faithful restoration. Dining is a feature and menus offer a wide choice of fresh fish, local produce and interesting dishes. The bedrooms are more contemporary and are attractively and impressively appointed. The garden is a delight.

Rooms 2 en suite 7 annexe en suite (7 GF) S £49.95-£79.95; D £49.95-£79.95* **Facilities** FTV tea/ coffee Dinner available Cen ht Wi-fi **Parking** 50

LAUNCESTON   Map 3 SX38

See also Congdon's Shop

PREMIER COLLECTION

Primrose Cottage
★★★★★ 🛏 BED AND BREAKFAST

Lawhitton PL15 9PE
☎ 01566 773645
e-mail: enquiry@primrosecottagesuites.co.uk
web: www.primrosecottagesuites.co.uk
dir: *Exit A30 Tavistock, follow A388 through Launceston for Plymouth then B3362, Tavistock 2.5m*

Originally a cottage, this impressive property has been imaginatively developed to provide stylish accommodation. From its elevated position, views across the lush countryside are wonderful. Two of the spacious suites have external entrances, while the third is in the main house. All provide high levels of comfort with separate seating areas. Breakfast makes use of excellent local produce and a guest lounge is also available. Outside, guests can enjoy the garden, or perhaps take a stroll down to the River Tamar for a spot of fishing.

Rooms 2 en suite 1 annexe en suite (1 GF) S £70-£90; D £80-£130 **Facilities** FTV tea/coffee Dinner available Cen ht Fishing **Parking** 5 **Notes** ⊗ No Children 12yrs

Hurdon *(SX333828)*

★★★★ 🍴 FARMHOUSE

PL15 9LS
☎ 01566 772955   Mrs M Smith
dir: *A30 onto A388 to Launceston, at rdbt exit for hospital, 2nd right signed Trebullett, premises 1st on right*

Genuine hospitality is assured at this delightful 18th-century granite farmhouse. The bedrooms are individually furnished and decorated, and equipped with numerous extras. The delicious dinners, by arrangement, use only the best local produce, and include home-made puddings and the farm's own clotted cream.

Rooms 6 en suite (1 fmly) (1 GF) S £32-£36; D £54-£64 **Facilities** FTV TVL tea/coffee Dinner available Cen ht **Parking** 10 **Notes** ⊗ Closed Nov-Apr 🐾 400 acres mixed

Bradridge Farm *(SX328938)*

★★★★ FARMHOUSE

PL15 9RL
☎ 01409 271264   Mrs A Strout
e-mail: angela@bradridgefarm.co.uk
dir: *5.5m N of Launceston. Off B3254 at Ladycross sign for Boyton, Bradridge 2nd farm on right after Boyton school*

The late Victorian farmhouse stands in glorious countryside on the border of Devon and Cornwall. The well-presented bedrooms have numerous thoughtful extras, and the Aga-cooked breakfasts feature farm-fresh eggs.

Rooms 4 rms (3 en suite) (1 fmly) S £28-£30; D £56-£60* **Facilities** FTV TVL tea/coffee Cen ht Fishing **Parking** 6 **Notes** LB Closed Nov-Feb 🐾 250 acres arable/ beef/sheep/hens

Tyne Wells House

★★★★ BED AND BREAKFAST

Pennygillam PL15 7EE
☎ 01566 775810
e-mail: btucker@talktalk.net
web: www.tynewells.co.uk
dir: *0.6m SW of town centre. Off A30 onto Pennygillam rdbt, house off rdbt*

Situated on the outskirts of the town, Tyne Wells House has panoramic views over the countryside. A relaxed and friendly atmosphere prevails and the bedrooms are neatly furnished. A hearty breakfast is served in the dining room, which overlooks the garden. Evening meals are available by arrangement.

Rooms 3 rms (2 en suite) (1 pri facs) (1 fmly) S £30-£40; D £48-£60* **Facilities** tea/coffee Cen ht Wi-fi **Parking** 4 **Notes** LB ⊗ 🐾

Oakside Farm Bungalow

★★★★ Ⓐ BED AND BREAKFAST

Oakside, South Petherwin PL15 7JL
☎ **01566 86733**
e-mail: janetcrossman415@btinternet.com
dir: *3m SW of Launceston. A30 W, 1st left after passing under Kennards House (A395) flyover*

Rooms 3 rms (2 en suite) (1 pri facs) (3 GF)
S £27.50-£30; D £55-£60* **Facilities** FTV TVL tea/coffee
Cen ht Wi-fi **Parking** 6 **Notes** ⊗ ☺

B&B@ Rose Cottage

★★★ BED AND BREAKFAST

Rose Cottage, 5 Lower Cleaverfield PL15 8ED
☎ **01566 779292**
e-mail: info@rosecottagecornwall.co.uk
dir: *Exit A30 at Launceston onto A388. Lower Cleaverfield 200yds on left after 2nd mini rdbt*

A warm and genuine welcome is extended to all guests at this charming cottage, parts of which date back several hundred years. A homely atmosphere ensures a relaxing and enjoyable stay with every effort made to help with any local information required. Bedrooms are very comfortable and breakfast is served in the attractive dining room with lovely views across the valley. Wi-fi access is also available.

Rooms 3 rms (2 en suite) (1 pri facs) S £29-£37;
D £58-£74 **Facilities** FTV TVL tea/coffee Cen ht Wi-fi
Parking 4 **Notes** LB ⊗ No Children 9yrs

LISKEARD Map 2 SX26

See also Callington

Pencubitt Country House

★★★★ GUEST HOUSE

Lamellion Cross PL14 4EB
☎ **01579 342694**
e-mail: hotel@pencubitt.com
dir: *From A38 head towards Liskeard and follow signs to railway station, signed on the right*

Located on the southern edge of the town, this well appointed property is peacefully set in two and a half acres of gardens; overlooking the rolling countryside of Looe Valley. The comfortable bedrooms feature numerous extra facilities. A spacious lounge and separate bar area are delightful areas for guests to relax in after a day exploring the many attractions in the area.

Rooms 8 en suite S £55-£65; D £95-£120* **Facilities** FTV
tea/coffee Direct Dial Cen ht Licensed Wi-fi 🏊
Parking 15 **Notes** LB ⊗ No Children 12yrs

Redgate Smithy

★★★★ 🛏 BED AND BREAKFAST

Redgate, St Cleer PL14 6RU
☎ **01579 321578**
e-mail: enquiries@redgatesmithy.co.uk
web: www.redgatesmithy.co.uk
dir: *3m NW of Liskeard. Off A30 at Bolventor/Jamaica Inn onto St Cleer Rd for 7m, B&B just past x-rds*

This 200-year-old converted smithy is on the southern fringe of Bodmin Moor near Golitha Falls. The friendly accommodation offers smartly furnished, cottage style bedrooms with many extra facilities. There are several dining options nearby, and a wide choice of freshly cooked breakfasts are served in the conservatory.

Rooms 3 rms (2 en suite) (1 pri facs) S £45; D £70*
Facilities FTV tea/coffee Cen ht **Parking** 3 **Notes** LB No
Children 12yrs Closed Xmas & New Year ☺

Trecarne House

★★★★ GUEST ACCOMMODATION

Penhale Grange, St Cleer PL14 5EB
☎ **01579 343543** 🖷 **01579 343543**
e-mail: trish@trecarnehouse.co.uk
dir: *B3254 N from Liskeard to St Cleer. Right at Post Office, 3rd left after church, 2nd right, house on right*

A warm welcome awaits you at this large family home, peacefully located on the edge of the village. The stylish and spacious bedrooms, which have magnificent country views, feature pine floors and have many thoughtful extras. The buffet-style breakfast offers a wide choice, which can be enjoyed in the dining room and sun-filled conservatory overlooking rolling countryside.

Rooms 3 en suite (2 fmly) **Facilities** TVL tea/coffee Cen ht
Table tennis Trampoline **Conf** Max 12 **Parking** 6 **Notes** ⊗

Elnor

★★★ GUEST HOUSE

1 Russell St PL14 4BP
☎ **01579 342472** 🖷 **01579 345673**
e-mail: infoelnorguesthouse@talktalk.net
dir: *Off A38 from Plymouth into town centre, house on right opp florist on road to railway station*

This well-established, friendly guest house is close to the town centre and railway station, and is just a short drive from Bodmin Moor and other places of interest. Bedrooms are neatly presented and well equipped, and some are on the ground floor. A cosy lounge and a small bar are available.

Rooms 6 rms (4 en suite) 3 annexe en suite (3 fmly) (4
GF) S £27-£32; D £58* **Facilities** FTV TVL tea/coffee
Direct Dial Cen ht Licensed **Parking** 7 **Notes** ⊗ ☺

Moor Gate

★★★ BED AND BREAKFAST

Higher Rd, Pensilva PL14 5NJ
☎ **01579 362386**
e-mail: sylviadoney@hotmail.co.uk
dir: *B3254 N from Liskeard for 4m, right to Pensilva, Moor Gate on right*

Enjoying excellent country views, this friendly house stands in attractive grounds on the edge of the pleasant village of Pensilva, and the recently designated World Heritage Site of Caradon Hill. The two attractive bedrooms are well equipped, and freshly cooked breakfasts are served in the lounge overlooking the garden.

Rooms 2 rms (1 en suite) (1 pri facs) **Facilities** tea/
coffee Cen ht **Parking** 4 **Notes** ⊗ ☺

LIZARD Map 2 SW71

Penmenner House

★★★ GUEST ACCOMMODATION

Penmenner Rd TR12 7NR
☎ **01326 290370**
dir: *A3083 into Lizard, right at green to sea, last house on right*

Interesting tales abound at this Victorian house, which has a splendid coastal setting. A friendly welcome is assured and the comfortable bedrooms, some having sea views, are equipped with modern facilities. Breakfast is a treat with local produce used whenever possible, thus ensuring a tasty and satisfying start to the day.

Rooms 6 rms (5 en suite) **Facilities** tea/coffee Dinner
available Cen ht Licensed **Parking** 10 **Notes** ⊗

BARCLAY HOUSE
ROOMS   RESTAURANT   COTTAGES

"Food for which any metropolitan restaurant would expect a Michelin star"
– Richard Madeley and Judy Finnigan, Daily Express, 2007

High on the hill above the East Looe River stands Barclay House – just minutes from the Historic Fishing port of Looe. Choose between smart, contemporary rooms or luxurious cottages – all enjoying spectacular views. Set in 6 acres of peaceful gardens with heated outdoor pool, gymnasium and sauna, this is a really special place to stay. Award Winning restaurant – superb atmosphere – freshest "day boat" fish – we have it all!

***

St Martin's Road, East Looe, PL13 1 LP
Tel: 01503 262929
Website: www.barclayhouse.co.uk
Email: info@barclayhouse.co.uk

LOOE
Map 2 SX25

PREMIER COLLECTION

The Beach House
★★★★★ 🏠 GUEST ACCOMMODATION

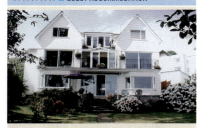

Marine Dr, Hannafore PL13 2DH
☎ 01503 262598 📠 01503 262298
e-mail: enquiries@thebeachhouselooe.co.uk
web: www.thebeachhouselooe.co.uk
dir: From Looe W over bridge, left to Hannafore &
Marine Dr, on right after Tom Sawyer Tavern

This peaceful property has panoramic sea views and is
just a short walk from the harbour, restaurants and
town. Some rooms have been refurbished with stylish
hand-made furniture, and the bedrooms are well
equipped and have many extras. Hearty breakfasts are
served in the first-floor dining room, a good start for
the South West Coast Path that goes right by the
house.

Rooms 5 en suite (4 GF) S £75-£120; D £100-£130*
Facilities FTV tea/coffee Cen ht Wi-fi Beauty treatment
room Parking 6 Notes LB ⊗ No Children 16yrs

Barclay House
★★★★ ⊛ GUEST ACCOMMODATION

St Martin's Rd PL13 1LP
☎ 01503 262929 📠 01503 262632
e-mail: reception@barclayhouse.co.uk
web: www.barclayhouse.co.uk
dir: 1st house on left on entering Looe from A38

This establishment stands in six acres of grounds
overlooking Looe Harbour, and is within walking distance

of the town. The thoughtfully furnished bedrooms have
modern facilities, and there is a sitting room, a spacious
bar, and a terrace where guests can enjoy an aperitif in
the summer months. Enjoyable freshly prepared dinners
are served in the light and airy restaurant that proves
popular with locals and tourists alike. A heated
swimming pool is also available.

Rooms 10 en suite 1 annexe en suite (1 fmly) (1 GF)
S £75-£120; D £89-£160* Facilities STV tea/coffee
Dinner available Direct Dial Cen ht Licensed Wi-fi 🏌
Sauna Gymnasium Conf Max 40 Thtr 20 Class 10 Board
18 Parking 25 Notes LB ⊗

See advert on opposite page

Bay View Farm (SX282548)
★★★★ 🍽 FARMHOUSE

St Martins PL13 1NZ
☎ 01503 265922 📠 01503 265922 Mrs E Elford
e-mail: mike@looebaycaravans.co.uk
web: www.looedirectory.co.uk/bay-view-farm.htm
dir: 2m NE of Looe. Off B3253 for Monkey Sanctuary,
farm signed

The renovated and extended bungalow has a truly
spectacular location with ever-changing views across
Looe Bay. The spacious bedrooms have many thoughtful
extras. Add a genuine Cornish welcome, tranquillity and
great food, and it's easy to see why guests are drawn
back to this special place.

Rooms 3 en suite (3 GF) S £35-£40; D £60-£65*
Facilities TVL tea/coffee Dinner available Cen ht
Parking 3 Notes LB ⊗ No Children 5yrs 🐴 56 acres
mixed/shire horses

Bucklawren Farm (SX278540)
★★★★ FARMHOUSE

St Martin-by-Looe PL13 1NZ
☎ 01503 240738 📠 01503 240481 Mrs J Henly
e-mail: bucklawren@btopenworld.com
web: www.bucklawren.co.uk
dir: 2m NE of Looe. Off B3253 to Monkey Sanctuary, 0.5m
right to Bucklawren, farmhouse 0.5m on left

The spacious 19th-century farmhouse stands in 400
acres of farmland just a mile from the beach. The
attractive bedrooms, including one on the ground floor,
are well equipped, and the front-facing rooms have
spectacular views across fields to the sea. Breakfast is
served in the dining room, and tempting home-cooked
evening meals are available at the nearby Granary
Restaurant.

Rooms 7 rms (6 en suite) (1 pri facs) (3 fmly) (1 GF)
S £37.50-£50; D £60-£75 Facilities TVL tea/coffee Cen ht
🐴 Parking 6 Notes LB ⊗ No Children 5yrs Closed Nov-
Feb 400 acres arable/beef

Polgover Farm (SX277586)
★★★★ FARMHOUSE

Widegates PL13 1PY
☎ 01503 240248 Mrs L Wills
e-mail: enquiries@polgoverfarm.co.uk
dir: 4m NE of Looe. A38 S onto B3251 & B3252, B&B
0.5m on right

This attractive house stands in peaceful farmland with
fine views. The welcoming proprietors ensure guests feel
at home. Comfortable bedrooms are tastefully decorated
with numerous thoughtful extras, and hearty breakfasts
are served in the very pleasant lounge.

Rooms 3 rms (2 en suite) (1 pri facs); D £60-£76*
Facilities FTV TVL tea/coffee Cen ht Parking 9 Notes LB
⊗ No Children 12yrs Closed Nov-Feb 🐴 93 acres arable/
sheep

LOOE *continued*

South Trelowia Barns

★★★★ GUEST HOUSE

Widegates PL13 1QL
☎ 01503 240709
e-mail: relax@southtrelowiabarns.co.uk
dir: *A387 W from Hessenford, 1m left signed Trelowia, 0.75m down lane on right*

Set in a very peaceful rural location, this home offers a relaxing environment and is full of character. The proprietors provide a warm welcome and guests are made to feel at home. The comfortable bedrooms have lots of extra facilities. Cooking is accomplished and features home-grown and local produce.

Rooms 1 en suite 1 annexe en suite (2 fmly) S £30-£40; D £50-£54 **Facilities** FTV TV1B TVL tea/coffee Dinner available Cen ht **Parking** 6 **Notes** LB 🐾

Trehaven Manor

★★★★ 🏠 🍽 GUEST ACCOMMODATION

Station Rd PL13 1HN
☎ 01503 262028 ☎ 01503 265613
e-mail: enquiries@trehavenhotel.co.uk
web: www.trehavenhotel.co.uk
dir: *In East Looe between railway station & bridge. Trehaven's drive adjacent to The Globe PH*

Run by a charming family, the former rectory has a stunning location with magnificent views of the estuary. Many of the attractive bedrooms have views, and all are particularly well equipped. There is also a cosy lounge bar. Dinner, by arrangement, specialises in Oriental cuisine, and breakfast features traditional fare; both meals are memorable.

Rooms 7 en suite (1 fmly) (1 GF) **Facilities** TVL tea/coffee Dinner available Cen ht Licensed **Parking** 8 **Notes** 🐾

Anchor Lights Bed & Breakfast

★★★★ GUEST ACCOMMODATION

The Quay, West looe PL13 2BU
☎ 01503 262334
e-mail: info@anchorlights.co.uk
web: www.anchorlights.co.uk
dir: *A38 signed Liskeard then B3253 signed Looe, situated on The Quay*

A recently renovated Edwardian house with great views across the estuary in an elevated position. Comfortable bedrooms and bathrooms and a light, airy breakfast room. Breakfast offers quality local produce including local kippers when available.

Rooms 4 rms (2 en suite) (2 pri facs) S £55-£65; D £60-£95* **Facilities** FTV tea/coffee Cen ht Wi-fi **Notes** LB 🐾 No Children 12yrs 🐾

Coombe Farm

★★★★ GUEST ACCOMMODATION

Widegates PL13 1QN
☎ 01503 240223
e-mail: coombe_farm@hotmail.com
web: www.coombefarmhotel.co.uk
dir: *3.5m E of Looe on B3253 just S of Widegates*

Set in ten acres of grounds and gardens, Coombe Farm has a friendly atmosphere. The bedrooms are in a converted stone barn, and are comfortable and spacious. Each has a dining area, with breakfast delivered to your room.

Rooms 3 annexe en suite (1 fmly) (3 GF) S £50-£60; D £70-£84* **Facilities** STV FTV tea/coffee Direct Dial ☎ **Parking** 20 **Notes** Closed 15 Dec-5 Jan

Down Ende Country House

★★★★ GUEST ACCOMMODATION

Widegates PL13 1QN
☎ 01503 240213 📠 01503 240213
e-mail: teresa@downende.com
web: www.downende.com
dir: *A374 towards Looe, right A387 road becomes B3253 on left after Coombe Farm*

Set in its own grounds, guests are assured of a warm welcome here, at this young family's home. Bedrooms are comfortable and well equipped, the majority overlooking the gardens, to the front of the property. Home-cooked evening meals are a highlight and use the best of local produce, prepared with care and skill.

Rooms 7 en suite 1 annexe en suite (1 fmly) (2 GF) S £40-£55; D £70-£80* **Facilities** tea/coffee Dinner available Cen ht Licensed Wi-fi **Conf** Max 20 **Parking** 9 **Notes** LB 🐾 RS 21-28 Dec

Polraen Country House

★★★★ 🏠 🍽 GUEST ACCOMMODATION

Sandplace PL13 1PJ
☎ 01503 263956
e-mail: enquiries@polraen.co.uk
web: www.polraen.co.uk
dir: *2m N of Looe at junct A387 & B3254*

This 18th-century stone house, formerly a coaching inn, nestles in the peaceful Looe Valley. The charming hosts provide friendly service in a relaxed atmosphere, and bedrooms and public areas are stylishly co-ordinated and

well equipped. The licensed bar, lounge and dining room overlook the garden, and there are facilities for children. Excellent evening meals feature local produce.

Rooms 5 en suite (2 fmly) D £64-£99* **Facilities** STV FTV TVL tea/coffee Dinner available Cen ht Licensed Wi-fi **Conf** Max 20 Thtr 16 Class 16 Board 16 **Parking** 20 **Notes** LB 🐾 Closed 25-27 Dec RS Nov-Feb (dinner by prior arrangement)

Shutta House

★★★★ GUEST ACCOMMODATION

Shutta PL13 1LS
☎ 01503 264233
e-mail: enquiries@shuttahouse.co.uk
web: www.shuttahouse.co.uk
dir: *From A58 Liskeard, follow A387 to Looe, opposite railway station*

This fine Victorian house was once the vicarage and has been sympathetically refurbished by the owners to create appealing and contemporary accommodation. Bedrooms all offer high standards of comfort with elegant styling and original character. Breakfast utilises locally sourced produce where possible, and is served in the light and airy dining room. Guests are also welcome to use the garden which overlooks the East Looe River.

Rooms 3 en suite S £38-£50; D £60-£80* **Facilities** tea/coffee Cen ht Wi-fi **Conf** Class 6 Board 6 **Parking** 1 **Notes** 🐾 No Children 11yrs

Southdown

★★★★ BED AND BREAKFAST

Meadway PL13 1JT
☎ 01503 262222
e-mail: gjkmason@tiscali.co.uk
web: www.looebandb.com
dir: *A387 onto B3252, left onto Barbican Rd, left onto Hay Ln and right onto Meadway*

With spectacular views over the bay, Southdown is quietly situated on the East Cliff Downs, and is a ten minute walk along the coastal path from Looe beach and the town. The accommodation is ideally suited for a family or couple, with two bedrooms, one enjoying the superb view, the other overlooking the attractive rear garden. Guests are assured of a warm welcome and a hearty breakfast.

Rooms 2 en suite (1 fmly) D £56-£60* **Facilities** FTV TVL tea/coffee Cen ht Wi-fi **Notes** LB 🐾 🐾

Tremaine Farm (SX194558)

★★★★ FARMHOUSE

Pelynt PL13 2LT
☎ 01503 220417 📠 01503 220417 Mrs R Philp
e-mail: tremainefarm@tiscali.co.uk
web: www.tremainefarm.co.uk
dir: 5m NW of Looe. B3359 N from Pelynt, left at x-rds

Convenient for Fowey, Looe and Polperro, this pleasant
working farm offers a comfortable stay. The proprietors
provide friendly hospitality and attentive service, and the
spacious bedrooms are well equipped. A hearty breakfast
is served in the dining room and there is a particularly
pleasant lounge. This is a non-smoking house.

Rooms 2 rms (1 en suite) (1 pri facs) (1 fmly);
D £64-£68* Facilities TVL tea/coffee Cen ht Wi-fi
Parking 6 Notes LB ⊗ ⊗ 300 acres arable/sheep/
potatoes

Woodlands

★★★★ GUEST HOUSE

St Martins Rd PL13 1LP
☎ 01503 264405
e-mail: rlundy@btinternet.com
web: www.looedirectory.co.uk/woodlands.htm
dir: On B3253, after Looe sign, St Martin's church on
right. 1m further on left

The charming Victorian country house looks over
woodland and the Looe estuary, and is within walking
distance of the harbour and beaches. The cosy bedrooms
are well equipped, and public rooms include a lounge and

the elegant dining room where dinner is served by
arrangement.

Woodlands

Rooms 4 en suite (2 fmly); D £60-£80 Facilities FTV tea/
coffee Dinner available Cen ht Licensed Parking 6
Notes LB ⊗ No Children 7yrs Closed Dec-Jan

Little Harbour

★★★ GUEST HOUSE

Church St PL13 2EX
☎ 01503 262474
e-mail: littleharbour@btinternet.com
web: www.looedirectory.co.uk
dir: From harbour West Looe, right into Princess Sq, guest
house on left

Little Harbour is situated almost on Looe's harbourside in
the historic old town; it has a pleasant and convenient
location and parking is available. The proprietors are
friendly and attentive, and the bedrooms are well
appointed and attractively decorated. Breakfast is served
freshly cooked in the dining room.

Rooms 5 en suite (1 fmly) S £20-£45; D £40-£60
Facilities STV FTV tea/coffee Cen ht Parking 3 Notes LB
No Children 12yrs

The Old Chapel

★★★ BED AND BREAKFAST

4 Summer Ln PL13 2LP
☎ 01503 220500
e-mail: mail@the-old-chapel.co.uk
web: www.the-old-chapel.co.uk
dir: A390 onto B3359 7m. Reach Pelynt and Old Chapel,
on right down hill

Closed as a chapel since 1935, this attractive building
was then used as a school canteen for the County
Council. Sympathetically converted to a village house, the
friendly owners welcome guests to their home. Bedrooms
are comfortable, making best use of the available space.
A hearty breakfast is served at a communal table in the

dining room. This is an ideal base for exploring the
numerous attractions the area has to offer.

Rooms 2 rms (1 en suite) (1 pri facs) S £40; D £60
Facilities FTV tea/coffee Cen ht Wi-fi Parking 4 Notes ⊗
No Children ⊗

The Old Malt House

★★★ BED AND BREAKFAST

West Looe Hill PL13 2HE
☎ 01503 264976
e-mail: oldmalt@tiscali.co.uk
web: www.oldmalthouselooe.co.uk
dir: A387 to Looe, 1st left after bridge, right behind fire
station, 100yds on left

A short, level stroll from the harbour front, the Old Malt
House dates back to 1650 and is very conveniently
situated for all of Looe's amenities. The cosy bedrooms
are well equipped and are approached via an external
stone staircase, while a hearty breakfast using local
produce is served in the ground floor dining room.

Rooms 3 en suite (3 fmly) S £30-£50; D fr £50*
Facilities FTV tea/coffee Cen ht Wi-fi Parking 3 Notes LB
⊗ No Children

The Ship Inn

★★★ INN

Fore St PL13 1AD
☎ 01503 263124 📠 01503 263624
e-mail: reservations@smallandfriendly.co.uk
web: www.smallandfriendly.co.uk

This lively, family pub is located in the very heart of
bustling East Looe and has a local following. The
bedrooms are comfortable and equipped with all the
expected facilities. A wide range of popular dishes is
served at lunch times and during the evenings, with light
refreshments available throughout the day.

Rooms 8 en suite (1 fmly) Facilities tea/coffee Dinner
available Cen ht Pool Table Notes LB ⊗

LOOE *continued*

St Johns Court

Ⓤ

East Cliff PL13 1DE
☎ 01503 265811
e-mail: b&b@stjohnscourtlooe.co.uk
dir: *300yds S of Looe bridge. Through Fore St, left at Ship Inn, 200yds on left*

Currently the rating for this establishment is not confirmed. This may be due to a change of ownership or because it has only recently joined the AA rating scheme.

Rooms 3 en suite; D £56–£70* **Facilities** TVL tea/coffee Cen ht **Parking** 2 **Notes** LB

LOSTWITHIEL Map 2 SX15

Penrose B&B

★★★★ GUEST ACCOMMODATION

1 The Terrrace PL22 0DT
☎ 01208 871417 🖷 01208 871101
e-mail: enquiries@penrosebb.co.uk
web: www.penrosebb.co.uk
dir: *A390 Edgecombe Rd, Lostwithiel onto Scrations Ln, 1st right for parking*

Just a short walk from the town centre, this grand Victorian house offers comfortable accommodation and a genuine homely atmosphere. Many of the bedrooms have the original fireplaces and all are equipped with thoughtful extras. Breakfast is a generous offering and is served in the elegant dining room, with views over the garden. Wi-fi access is also available.

Rooms 7 rms (6 en suite) (1 pri facs) (3 fmly) (2 GF); D £40–£80 **Facilities** FTV tea/coffee Cen ht Wi-fi **Parking** 8 **Notes** LB

Hartswell Farm *(SX119597)*

★★★ FARMHOUSE

St Winnow PL22 0RB
☎ 01208 873419 🖷 01208 873419 **Mrs W Jordan**
e-mail: hartswell@connexions.co.uk
web: www.connexions.co.uk/hartswell
dir: *1m E of Lostwithiel. S off A390 at Downend Garage, farm 0.25m up hill on left*

This 17th-century farmhouse has a wonderfully peaceful setting, and offers generous hospitality and a homely atmosphere. The cosy bedrooms look across rolling countryside, and breakfast includes tasty eggs fresh from the farm. A self-catering barn conversion is available, one with the Access Exceptional award. Hartswell Farm boasts a small herd of Red Poll cows and calves.

Rooms 3 rms (2 en suite) (1 pri facs) (1 fmly) S £32–£44; D £56–£70 **Facilities** STV TV1B TVL tea/coffee Cen ht Wi-fi Sailing days for 5 night stays **Parking** 3 **Notes** LB ⊗ No Children 6yrs 🌐 52 acres rare breed cattle

MANACCAN Map 2 SW72

The Hen House

★★★★ BED AND BREAKFAST

Tregarne TR12 6EW
☎ 01326 280236
e-mail: henhouseuk@aol.com
web: www.thehenhouse-cornwall.co.uk
dir: *A3083 onto B3293 left into Newtown, right at T-junct. After 2.3m, take left fork, then 1st right, last house*

Cleverly converted from former farm buildings, this delightful little bed and breakfast is a haven of peace and tranquillity. The spacious and thoughtfully equipped modern bedrooms are both on ground floor level. However, by far the greatest strength here is the warm and friendly hospitality. Self-catering accommodation is also available.

Rooms 1 en suite 1 annexe en suite (2 GF) S £60–£70; D £70–£85 **Facilities** FTV tea/coffee Cen ht Wi-fi Tai-Chi workshops, Reflexology & Reiki therapies **Parking** 5 **Notes** LB No Children 12yrs

MARAZION Map 2 SW53

Glenleigh

★★★★ GUEST HOUSE

Higher Fore St TR17 0BQ
☎ 01736 710308
e-mail: info@marazionhotels.com
dir: *Off A394 to Penzance, opp Fire Engine Inn*

This proud granite house has an elevated position with wonderful views towards St Michael's Mount. The welcoming proprietors have owned this house for more than 30 years and many guests return. Dinners, by arrangement, are served in the comfortable dining room and feature fresh local produce where possible.

Rooms 9 en suite (1 fmly) (1 GF) **Facilities** FTV TVL tea/coffee Dinner available Cen ht Licensed **Parking** 9 **Notes** LB ⊗ No Children 3yrs Closed Nov–Mar 🌐

Godolphin Arms

★★★★ INN

TR17 0EN
☎ 01736 710202 🖷 01736 710171
e-mail: enquiries@godolpharms.co.uk
dir: *From A30 follow Marazion signs for 1m to B&B. At end of causeway to St Michael's Mount*

A traditional inn overlooking St Michael's Mount and beyond, The Godolphin is the heart of the community and caters for all ages. Bedrooms have recently been refurbished, staff are friendly staff and there's good reserved parking for guests. Food served is served daily, and there are often special themed evenings.

Rooms 10 en suite (2 fmly) (2 GF) S £65–£110; D £85–£145* **Facilities** STV tea/coffee Dinner available Direct Dial Cen ht Wi-fi Direct access to beach **Parking** 10 **Notes** LB No coaches Civ Wed 75

Blue Horizon

★★★ GUEST ACCOMMODATION

Fore St TR17 0AW
☎ 01736 711199
e-mail: holidaybreaksmarazion@freeola.com
web: www.holidaybreaksmarazion.co.uk
dir: *E end of village centre*

Located in the heart of this market town, the rear of this establishment is almost at the water's edge and offers superb views of the sea from its garden, some of the bedrooms and the breakfast room. The atmosphere is laid back and relaxed. There are a number of additional facilities (charged), including a laundry room, sauna cabin and barbecue facilities. Ample parking is also available.

Rooms 6 rms (5 en suite) (1 pri facs) (2 GF) S £34; D £58–£68* **Facilities** FTV TVL tea/coffee Wi-fi Sauna Hot tub, bike hire **Parking** 7 **Notes** LB ⊗ Closed Nov–mid Feb

St Michaels Bed and Breakfast

★★★ GUEST ACCOMMODATION

The Corner House, Fore St TR17 0AD
☎ 01736 711348
e-mail: jhopkins005@aol.com

Very well located on Fore Street with off-street parking and some rooms with sea views, this family-run accommodation offers bright well-equipped bedrooms and quality breakfasts. The owners are very friendly and helpful, and the beds extremely comfortable.

Rooms 6 en suite (1 fmly) S £65–£75; D £70–£80* **Facilities** FTV tea/coffee Cen ht Wi-fi **Parking** 6 **Notes** ⊗ No Children 12yrs 🌐

MEVAGISSEY
Map 2 SX04

Kerryanna Country House
★★★★ BED AND BREAKFAST

Treleaven Farm, Valley Rd PL26 6SA
☎ 01726 843558 ▤ 01726 843558
e-mail: enquiries@kerryanna.co.uk
dir: *B3273 St Austell to Mevagissey road, right at bottom of hill, next to playground*

Located on the peaceful outskirts of this fishing village, Kerryanna stands in two acres of gardens and looks across the countryside to the sea. The attractive bedrooms are comfortably furnished, with one room on the ground floor. There are three cosy lounges, a swimming pool and a putting green.

Rooms 3 en suite; D £70-£74* **Facilities** FTV tea/coffee Cen ht ❧ **Parking** 6 **Notes** LB ⊗ No Children 15yrs Closed Oct-Apr ☺

Headlands
★★★ GUEST ACCOMMODATION

Polkirt Hill PL26 6UX
☎ 01726 843453
e-mail: headlandshotel@talk21.com
dir: *One-way through village & ascend towards Port Mellon, Headlands on right*

Set on an elevated position with spectacular views over the bay, this family-run establishment offers friendly service and comfortable accommodation. The colourful bedrooms are well equipped, with many having sea views. Public rooms include a stylish lounge bar and dining room.

Rooms 14 rms (12 en suite) (1 fmly) (4 GF) S £40-£50; D £80-£90* **Facilities** FTV tea/coffee Cen ht Licensed **Parking** 10 **Notes** LB ⊗ Closed Dec-Jan

The Ship
★★★ INN

Fore St PL26 6UQ
☎ 01726 843324 ▤ 01726 844368
e-mail: reservations@smallandfriendly.co.uk
dir: *B3273 S from St Austell to Mevagissey, in central square*

The 400-year-old Ship Inn stands in the centre of this delightful fishing village. The popular bar, with low-beamed ceilings, flagstone floors and a strong nautical feel, offers a choice of menu or blackboard specials. The pine-furnished bedrooms are attractively decorated. Car park nearby.

Rooms 5 en suite (2 fmly) **Facilities** tea/coffee Dinner available Cen ht

MITCHELL
Map 2 SW85

The Plume of Feathers
★★★★ INN

TR8 5AX
☎ 01872 510387 & 511122 ▤ 01872 511124
e-mail: enquiries@theplume.info
dir: *Just off A30 & A3076, follow signs*

A very popular inn with origins dating back to 16th century, situated close to Newquay and the beaches. The restaurant offers a varied menu which relies heavily on local produce. The stylish bedrooms are decorated in neutral colours and have wrought-iron beds with quality linens. The garden makes an ideal place to enjoy a meal or a Cornish tea. The staff are very friendly.

Rooms 7 annexe en suite (1 fmly) (5 GF) S £53.75-£83.75; D £75-£115* **Facilities** FTV tea/coffee Dinner available Cen ht Wi-fi **Parking** 40 **Notes** LB No coaches

MORWENSTOW
Map 2 SS21

West Point B&B
★★★★ BED AND BREAKFAST

West Point, Crimp EX23 9PB
☎ 01288 331594
e-mail: bramhill@supanet.com
dir: *Take A361 to Barnstaple onto A39 towards Bude. 7m past Clovelly rdbt on right*

Ideally placed for exploring the beautiful countryside and coasts of north Cornwall and north Devon, this smartly appointed establishment is surrounded by colourful gardens with far reaching views to the rear. Guests are assured of a genuine welcome plus the freedom of all-day access. Both bedrooms are comfortable, light and airy, with one having a four-poster bed and patio doors leading to the garden. Additional facilities include a guest lounge and dining room where local farm produce is utilised whenever possible.

Rooms 2 en suite (1 fmly) (2 GF) S £35; D £60 **Facilities** FTV TVL tea/coffee Cen ht **Parking** 4 **Notes** LB ⊗ Closed 22 Dec-2 Jan ☺

MOUSEHOLE
Map 2 SW42

The Cornish Range Restaurant with Rooms
★★★★ ◉◉ RESTAURANT WITH ROOMS

6 Chapel St TR19 6BD
☎ 01736 731488
e-mail: info@cornishrange.co.uk
dir: *Coast road through Newlyn into Mousehole, along harbour past Ship Inn, sharp right, then left, establishment on right*

This is a memorable place to eat and stay. Stylish rooms, with delightful Cornish home-made furnishings, and attentive, friendly service create a relaxing environment. Interesting and accurate cuisine relies heavily on freshly-landed, local fish and shellfish, as well as local meat and poultry, and the freshest fruit and vegetables.

Rooms 3 en suite; D £80-£110* **Facilities** FTV tea/coffee Dinner available Cen ht Wi-fi **Notes** ⊗ No coaches

MULLION
Map 2 SW61

Colvennor Farmhouse
★★★★ BED AND BREAKFAST

Cury TR12 7BJ
☎ 01326 241208
e-mail: colvennor@aol.com
web: www.colvennorfarmhouse.com
dir: *A3083 (Helston-Lizard), over rdbt at end of airfield, next right to Cury/Poldhu Cove, farm 1.4m on right at top of hill*

The friendly proprietors ensure guests have a comfortable stay at this Grade II listed building, which dates from the 17th century. Set in an acre of attractive and tranquil grounds, the house is a good base for touring the Lizard peninsula. Freshly cooked breakfasts are served in the dining room.

Rooms 3 en suite (1 GF) S £38-£40; D £58-£66* **Facilities** FTV tea/coffee Cen ht Wi-fi **Parking** 4 **Notes** LB ⊗ No Children 10yrs Closed Dec & Jan

NEWQUAY
Map 2 SW86

Degembris Farmhouse (SW852568)

★★★★ FARMHOUSE

St Newlyn East TR8 5HY
☎ **01872 510555** **Mrs H Elford**
e-mail: thefarmhouse@degembris.co.uk
dir: *3m SE of Newquay. A30 onto A3058 towards Newquay, 3rd left to St Newlyn East & 2nd left*

This Grade II listed, 16th-century farmhouse is convenient for both the Eden Project and Newquay. Well located, with ample off-road parking, it offers a friendly atmosphere. The comfortable, well-appointed bedrooms have lovely country views, and there is a guest sitting room.

Rooms 5 rms (3 en suite) (1 fmly) **Facilities** FTV TVL tea/coffee Cen ht Wi-fi **Conf** Max 12 **Parking** 8 **Notes** LB ⊗ Closed Xmas 30 acres non-working

Dewolf Guest House

★★★★ GUEST HOUSE

100 Henver Rd TR7 3BL
☎ **01637 874746**
e-mail: holidays@dewolfguesthouse.com
dir: *A392 onto A3058 at Quintrell Downs rdbt, guest house on left just past mini-rdbts*

Making you feel welcome and at home is the priority here. The bedrooms in the main house are bright and well equipped, and there are two more in a separate single storey building at the rear. One bedroom has a private enclosed area and a small fridge The cosy lounge has pictures and items that reflect the host's interest in wildlife. The guesthouse is just a short walk from Porth Beach.

Rooms 4 en suite 2 annexe en suite (2 fmly) (3 GF) S £30-£45; D £60-£90 **Facilities** FTV tea/coffee Cen ht Licensed **Parking** 6 **Notes** LB

Fairview House

★★★★ GUEST HOUSE

2 Fairview Ter TR7 1RJ
☎ **01637 871179** **&** **07968 680957**
e-mail: lindasheppsh@aol.com
web: www.fairviewhouse.org.uk
dir: *From A30 exit at Newquay onto A392. Right onto Trevemper Rd. At rdbt turn left. At top of hill right at lights, left onto Fairview Terrace. Continue to bottom. House on left*

This very friendly guesthouse is conveniently located for access to the town centre, beaches and other amenities. It provides soundly maintained modern bedrooms and facilities include a lounge and bar.

Rooms 5 rms (3 en suite) (2 fmly) (1 GF) **Facilities** FTV tea/coffee Cen ht Licensed **Notes** LB ⊗ ⊗

Kallacliff

★★★★ GUEST ACCOMMODATION

12 Lusty Glaze Rd TR7 3AD
☎ **01637 871704**
e-mail: kallacliffhotel@btconnect.com
dir: *0.5m NE of town centre. A3058 to Newquay, right off Henver Rd onto Lusty Glaze Rd, 350yds on right*

This popular establishment is in a peaceful area close to the South West Coast Path. There are stunning views of the Atlantic from the bar and the breakfast dining room, and some of the attractive bedrooms also have sea views. Beaches and eateries are just a stroll away.

Rooms 8 en suite (3 fmly) (2 GF); D £72-£92 **Facilities** TVL tea/coffee Cen ht Licensed **Parking** 10 **Notes** LB ⊗

Windward

★★★★ GUEST ACCOMMODATION

Alexandra Rd, Porth Bay TR7 3NB
☎ **01637 873185** **▤** **01637 851400**
e-mail: enquiries@windwardhotel.co.uk
dir: *1.5m NE of town centre. A3058 towards Newquay, right onto B3276 Padstow road, 1m on right*

Windward is pleasantly located almost on Porth Beach and is convenient for the airport. It offers spectacular views, friendly hospitality, and a pleasant bar and terrace for relaxing. The spacious bedrooms, some with balcony, and many with sea views, are well equipped, and breakfast is served in the restaurant overlooking the beach.

Rooms 13 en suite (1 fmly) (3 GF) S £66-£76; D £86-£120* **Facilities** FTV TVL tea/coffee Dinner available Cen ht Licensed Wi-fi **Conf** Max 30 Thtr 30 Class 30 Board 30 **Parking** 15 **Notes** LB ⊗

The Three Tees

★★★ GUEST ACCOMMODATION

21 Carminow Way TR7 3AY
☎ **01637 872055** **▤** **01637 872665**
e-mail: greg@3tees.co.uk
web: www.3tees.co.uk
dir: *A30 onto A392 Newquay. Right at Quintrell Downs rdbt signed Porth, over x-rds & 3rd right*

Located in a quiet residential area just a short walk from the town and beach, this friendly family-run accommodation is comfortable and well equipped. There is a lounge, bar and a sun lounge for the use of guests. Breakfast is served in the dining room, where snacks are available throughout the day. Light snacks are available in the bar during the evenings.

Rooms 8 rms (7 en suite) (1 pri facs) 1 annexe en suite (4 fmly) (2 GF); D £60-£70* **Facilities** FTV TVL tea/coffee Cen ht Licensed Wi-fi **Parking** 11 **Notes** LB Closed Nov-Feb

Tregarthen Guest House

★★★ GUEST ACCOMMODATION

1 Arundel Way TR7 3BB
☎ **01637 873554**
e-mail: info@tregarthen.co.uk
web: www.tregarthen.co.uk
dir: *From A30 onto A392, at Quintrell onto A3058 Henver Rd, Arundel Way 4th right*

Located in a quiet residential area just a short walk from the beaches and town centre of Newquay. The owners of this delightful detached property provide warm hospitality along with comfortable accommodation which is smartly furnished and well-equipped. Evening meals can be provided by arrangement, and the hearty breakfast is served at individual tables in the spacious ground floor dining room. There is also a cosy lounge facility where guests can sit and relax. Parking is ample to the front of the property.

Rooms 5 en suite 2 annexe en suite (2 fmly) (6 GF) S £30-£50; D £40-£70* **Facilities** FTV tea/coffee Dinner available Cen ht Wi-fi **Parking** 7 **Notes** LB ⊗ Closed Xmas RS Oct-Jun No evening meal

Wenden

★ ★ ★ GUEST HOUSE

11 Berry Rd TR7 1AU
☎ 01637 872604 📠 01637 872604
e-mail: wenden@newquay-holidays.co.uk
web: www.newquay-holidays.co.uk
dir: *In town centre off seafront Cliff Rd, near station*

The family-run guest house offers bright, modern accommodation near the beach and the town centre. Bedrooms have been carefully designed to make best use of space, and each is individually styled. Breakfast, served in the stylish dining room, is a filling start to the day.

Rooms 7 en suite; D £45-£65 **Facilities** FTV tea/coffee Cen ht Wi-fi **Parking** 7 **Notes** LB ⊗ No Children 16yrs Closed 1wk Xmas

Avalon

★ ★ ★ GUEST ACCOMMODATION

4 Edgcumbe Gardens TR7 2QD
☎ 01637 877522
e-mail: enquiries@avalonnewquay.co.uk

Conveniently situated within walking distance of the town centre and the beaches, Avalon provides comfortable accommodation. Located in a quiet, residential area, with the benefit of on-site parking, guests enjoy the front-facing sun terrace during the summer months. Golfing holiday offers are available.

Rooms 6 rms (5 en suite) (1 pri facs) (1 fmly) S £20-£30; D £50-£60 **Facilities** tea/coffee **Parking** 6 **Notes** LB ⊜

Copper Beech

★ ★ ★ GUEST HOUSE

70 Edgcumbe Av TR7 2NN
☎ 01637 873376
e-mail: info@copperbeechnewquay.co.uk
web: www.copperbeechnewquay.co.uk
dir: *Exit A30 signed RAF St Mawgan, at rdbt take A3059 exit 6m. Right at T-junct, left at 1st mini-rdbt, straight over 2nd. 3rd on right opp tennis courts*

Set amidst pleasant gardens, Copper Beech is located in a peaceful area of the town opposite Trenance Gardens. Bedrooms are light and airy, with ground floor rooms available. Comprehensive breakfasts are served in an attractive dining room and a warm welcome is assured.

Rooms 13 en suite (2 fmly) (3 GF) **Facilities** TVL tea/coffee Dinner available Cen ht Licensed **Parking** 13 **Notes** ⊗

The Croft

★ ★ ★ GUEST ACCOMMODATION

37 Mount Wise TR7 2BL
☎ 01637 871520 📠 01637 871520
e-mail: info@the-crofthotel.co.uk
web: www.the-crofthotel.co.uk
dir: *In town centre nr Towan Beach, junct Mount Wise & Mayfield Rd*

Located just minutes away from the town centre and beach, this accommodation is comfortable and the friendly host creates a homely atmosphere. A full English breakfast is served in the informal bar-dining room.

Rooms 8 rms (6 en suite) (2 pri facs) (4 fmly); D £50-£70* **Facilities** tea/coffee Dinner available Cen ht Licensed Wi-fi **Parking** 7 **Notes** LB ⊗

Lazy Days Guest House

★ ★ ★ GUEST HOUSE

36 St Annes Rd TR7 2SA
☎ 01637 876074 📠 01637 876074
e-mail: susan.baker07@btinternet.com
dir: *A30 onto A392 towards Quintrell Downs. A3088 towards Newquay, Henver Rd 3rd left, 1st right*

Within walking distance of the town centre, this quietly situated, single storey property has recently been extended and extensively refurbished. In the stylishly decorated bedrooms, the best possible use has been made of the available space. Guests are assured a relaxed and friendly welcome, hearty breakfasts being served in the rear conservatory.

Rooms 4 en suite (3 GF) S £25-£35; D £50-£70 **Facilities** FTV TVL tea/coffee Cen ht **Parking** 5 **Notes** LB ⊗ No Children 18yrs Closed 21-29 Dec

Meadow View

★ ★ ★ GUEST ACCOMMODATION

135 Mount Wise TR7 1QR
☎ 01637 873132
e-mail: meadowview135@hotmail.com
web: www.meadowviewguesthouse.co.uk
dir: *A392 into Newquay to Mountwise, Meadow View on left before rdbt to Pentire*

Expect a warm welcome at this detached property which is ideally located just a short walk from the town of Newquay and the famous Fistral Beach, renowned for its surfing. A short drive away are Waterworld, the Eden Project, and the Pentire Peninsular with its rolling green coastline. Accommodation is comfortable with some rooms having a countryside view. A hearty breakfast is served in the pleasant dining room and there is a cosy sun lounge to relax in.

Rooms 7 en suite (2 fmly); D £54-£64* **Facilities** tea/coffee Cen ht **Parking** 7 **Notes** LB ⊗ No Children 5yrs Closed 7 Nov-mid Feb ⊜

Milber Guest House

★ ★ ★ GUEST HOUSE

11 Michell Av TR7 1BN
☎ 01637 872825
e-mail: suemilber@aol.com
dir: *A392 Newquay straight ahead at Quintrell rdbt to Henver Rd/Berry Rd. Turn right onto Mount Wise, 2nd right to Michell Av*

This small and friendly guest house is situated in the centre of Newquay. Bedrooms are comfortable and offer lots of useful facilities. The bar is open most reasonable times, and guests get their own keys so they can come and go as they please.

Rooms 6 rms (4 en suite) (6 fmly) (1 GF) S £20-£35; D £40-£70* **Facilities** FTV tea/coffee Cen ht Licensed **Notes** LB ⊗ ⊜

Pencrebar

★ ★ ★ GUEST ACCOMMODATION

4 Berry Rd TR7 1AT
☎ 01637 872037
e-mail: enquiries@pencrebar.com
web: www.pencrebar.com
dir: *A30 onto A392, then right at boating lake on entering Newquay*

This friendly family-run house is a short walk from Newquay's popular beaches and the town centre. Bedrooms are all spacious and well planned. Delicious breakfasts are served in the attractive dining room. Secure car parking is available for guests.

Rooms 7 en suite (2 fmly) S £27-£33; D £44-£56 **Facilities** FTV tea/coffee Cen ht Parking charged all year **Parking** 5 **Notes** LB ⊗

The Pippin

★ ★ ★ GUEST ACCOMMODATION

2 Godolphin Way TR7 3BU
☎ 01637 873979
e-mail: thepippins@btinternet.com
dir: *A3058 to Newquay (Henver Rd), 1st right after double rdbt*

Well located establishment just a short walk from Newquay's north beaches. Staff are very friendly and bedrooms are very comfortable. Freshly cooked breakfasts are served in the light and airy dining room which overlooks the well tended garden. Good off-road parking is a bonus.

Rooms 6 rms (3 en suite) (3 pri facs) (3 GF) **Facilities** tea/coffee Cen ht **Parking** 6 **Notes** ⊗ No Children 2yrs Closed Nov-Apr ⊜

NEWQUAY *continued*

Porth Lodge

★★★ GUEST ACCOMMODATION

Porth Bean Rd TR7 3LT
☎ **01637 874483**
e-mail: info@porthlodgehotel.co.uk

A popular venue with its own bowling alley. The property has recently been totally refurbished to provide bedrooms that are even more comfortable and well equipped. Food is served daily and the team are friendly and helpful.

Rooms 16 en suite S £30-£40; D £60-£80* **Facilities** FTV tea/coffee Dinner available Cen ht Licensed Wi-fi Pool Table Ten pin bowling alley **Conf** Thtr 40 Class 30 Board 20 **Parking** 20 **Notes** LB

Rolling Waves

★★★ GUEST HOUSE

Alexandra Rd, Porth TR7 3NB
☎ **01637 873236** ▯ **01637 873236**
e-mail: enquiries@rollingwaves.co.uk
dir: *A30 onto A392, A3058 towards Newquay, then B3276 to Porth, pass Mermaid public house*

A family owned and run guest house with great views across the bay. Rooms are comfortable, the hosts friendly and welcoming, and dinner is available on request.

Rooms 7 rms (6 en suite) (1 pri facs) (1 fmly) (3 GF); D £56-£72* **Facilities** FTV TVL tea/coffee Dinner available Cen ht Licensed **Parking** 7 **Notes** ⊗

St Breca

★★★ GUEST HOUSE

22 Mount Wise TR7 2BG
☎ **01637 872745**
e-mail: enquiries@stbreca.co.uk
dir: *A30 onto A392. Follow signs to Newquay, then to Mount Wise*

This friendly guesthouse is conveniently located a few minutes walk from the town centre, beaches and other amenities. It provides soundly maintained, modern bedrooms and separate tables are provided in the attractive breakfast room.

Rooms 10 rms (8 en suite) (2 pri facs) (3 fmly) (2 GF) S £20-£35; D £40-£70* **Facilities** tea/coffee Cen ht **Parking** 8 **Notes** LB ⊗

The Silver Jubilee

★★★ GUEST HOUSE

13 Berry Rd TR7 1AU
☎ **01637 874544**
e-mail: andrew.hatton@tiscali.co.uk
dir: *Follow A3058 into Newquay. After railway station, left at lights, 3rd house on left*

Silver Jubilee is a small establishment situated on the level in the heart of Newquay. All amenities including shopping centre and beaches are about three minutes walk away. Breakfast and dinner (Easter to September) are served in the dining room. There is also a bar/lounge for a pre-dinner drink or post-meal relaxation.

Rooms 7 en suite (3 fmly) S £34-£50; D £48-£80* **Facilities** tea/coffee Dinner available Cen ht Licensed Wi-fi **Parking** 3 **Notes** LB ⊗

Summer Breeze

★★★ GUEST HOUSE

20 Mount Wise TR7 2BG
☎ **01637 871518**
e-mail: summer-breeze@sky.com
web: www.summer-breeze.info
dir: *A30 onto A392 signed to Newquay, turn right at Pentire rdbt, 0.5m on left*

Guests are assured of a warm welcome at this centrally located guest house; just a couple of minutes from the town centre and not much further from the beaches. Bedrooms are neatly furnished and decorated, all equipped with modern facilities. Freshly cooked, hearty breakfasts are served each morning in the sunny breakfast room; prior notice is appreciated for the vegetarian option.

Rooms 6 en suite (3 fmly) (1 GF); D £50-£80* **Facilities** tea/coffee Cen ht **Parking** 4 **Notes** LB ⊗

Tir Chonaill

★★★ GUEST ACCOMMODATION

106 Mount Wise TR7 1QP
☎ **01637 876492**
e-mail: tirchonailhotel@talk21.com
web: www.tirchonaill.co.uk
dir: *A392 into Newquay, last rdbt right onto Mount Wise*

Expect a warm welcome at the long-established and family-owned Tir Chonaill, situated close to the beaches and the town centre. Some of the neat bedrooms have wonderful views across town to the sea, and the hearty breakfasts are sure to satisfy.

Rooms 9 en suite (9 fmly) (1 GF) S £35-£50; D £60-£90* **Facilities** TVL tea/coffee Cen ht Licensed **Parking** 10 **Notes** LB

PADSTOW   Map 2 SW97

PREMIER COLLECTION

The Seafood Restaurant

★★★★★ ◉◉◉ RESTAURANT WITH ROOMS

Riverside PL28 8BY
☎ **01841 532700** ▯ **01841 532942**
e-mail: reservations@rickstein.com
dir: *Padstow town centre down hill, follow road round sharp bend, on left*

Food lovers continue to beat a well-trodden path to this legendary establishment that has benefited from considerable recent investment. Situated on the edge of the harbour, just a stone's throw from the shops, the Seafood Restaurant offers stylish and comfortable bedrooms that boast numerous thoughtful extras; some have views of the estuary and a couple have stunning private balconies. Service is relaxed and friendly, perfect for that break by the sea; booking is essential for both accommodation and a table in the restaurant.

Rooms 14 en suite 6 annexe en suite (6 fmly) (3 GF); D £132.18-£264.26* **Facilities** STV tea/coffee Dinner available Direct Dial Cen ht Lift Cookery School **Parking** 12 **Notes** LB Closed 24-26 Dec RS 1 May restaurant closed No coaches

The Old Mill House

★★★★ GUEST HOUSE

PL27 7QT
☎ 01841 540388 📄 01841 540406
e-mail: enquiries@theoldmillhouse.com
web: www.theoldmillhouse.com
dir: 2m S of Padstow. In centre of Little Petherick on A389

Situated in an Area of Outstanding Natural Beauty, the Old Mill House is a 16th-century corn mill with attractive secluded gardens beside a gentle stream. Guests enjoy an English breakfast in the mill room where the mill wheel still turns.

Rooms 7 en suite S £80-£120; D £80-£120 Facilities TVL tea/coffee Cen ht Licensed Parking 20 Notes ⊗ No Children 14yrs Closed Dec-Feb

Penjoly Guest House

★★★★ 🏠 GUEST HOUSE

Padstow Rd PL28 8LB
☎ 01841 533535 📄 01841 532313
e-mail: penjoly.padstow@btopenworld.com
dir: 1m S of Padstow. Off A389 near Padstow Holiday Park

A professionally run establishment, where attention to detail and quality are trademarks throughout. Bedrooms are carefully decorated and complemented by a impressive range of extras. Guests have the convenience of off-road parking. Breakfast is served in the attractive breakfast room or the conservatory, and a guest lounge is also available. This is a perfect base for exploring the West Country's delights, and for seeking out the gastronomic attractions of Cornwall.

Rooms 3 en suite (3 GF); D £77-£90* Facilities STV FTV TVL tea/coffee Cen ht Wi-fi Parking 10 Notes ⊗ No Children 16yrs 🚭

Rick Stein's Café

★★★★ BED AND BREAKFAST

10 Middle St PL28 8AP
☎ 01841 532700 📄 01841 532942
e-mail: reservations@rickstein.com
dir: A389 into town, one way past church, 3rd right

Another Rick Stein success story, this lively café by day, restaurant by night, offers good food, quality accommodation, and is just a short walk from the harbour. Three rooms are available, all quite different but sharing high standards of cosseting comfort. Friendly and personable staff complete the picture.

Rooms 3 en suite (1 fmly) Facilities tea/coffee Dinner available Cen ht Licensed Notes LB Closed 1 May BH RS 24-26 Dec

Roselyn

★★★★ BED AND BREAKFAST

20 Grenville Rd PL28 8EX
☎ 01841 532756
e-mail: padstowbbroselyn@bushinternet.com
web: www.padstowbbroselyn.co.uk
dir: After blue 'Welcome to Padstow' sign, Grenville Rd 1st left

This charming small guest house is in a quiet residential area just a 10-minute walk from the centre of the delightful fishing port. Guests are assured of warm hospitality, and smartly furnished, well-equipped bedrooms. A good choice of breakfast options is available.

Rooms 3 en suite S £40-£45; D £65-£70* Facilities FTV tea/coffee Cen ht Wi-fi Parking 4 Notes LB ⊗ RS Xmas

Treravel House

★★★★ BED AND BREAKFAST

PL28 8LB
☎ 01841 532931
e-mail: mandytreravel@tiscali.co.uk

Located just a few minutes outside Padstow, Treravel House provides rooms that are light and well furnished. Breakfast uses the house's own free-range eggs and is served in the bright breakfast room. Mandy Eddy provides a very warm welcome to all her guests and a pleasant stay is assured.

Rooms 3 en suite S £40; D £60-£75* Facilities FTV tea/coffee Cen ht Wi-fi Parking 6 Notes LB ⊗ 🚭

Little Pentyre

★★ BED AND BREAKFAST

6 Moyle Rd PL28 8DG
☎ 01841 532246
e-mail: JujuLloyd@aol.com
dir: From A389, right onto Dennis Rd, bear right onto Moyle Rd

Within easy, level walking distance of the town centre, Little Pentyre is situated in a quiet residential area, adjacent to the Camel Estuary and Trail. The comfortable bedrooms are well equipped and guests enjoy a freshly cooked breakfast, featuring eggs from the hens in the rear garden.

Rooms 2 en suite (2 GF) S £30; D £55* Facilities FTV tea/coffee Cen ht Parking 2 Notes No Children 10yrs 🚭

PAR   Map 2 SX05

Elmswood House

★★★★ GUEST ACCOMMODATION

73 Tehidy Rd, Tywardreath PL24 2QD
☎ 01726 814221 📄 01726 814399
e-mail: enquiries@elmswoodhousehotel.co.uk
web: www.elmswoodhousehotel.co.uk
dir: Right from Par station, then 1st left to top of hill, opp village church

Elmswood is a fine Victorian house set in the middle of the village opposite the church, where many guests return for the warm welcome. Bedrooms have quality furnishings and many extra facilities, and the attractive dining room, lounge and bar overlook a beautiful garden.

Rooms 7 rms (6 en suite) (1 pri facs) (1 fmly) (1 GF) S £35-£42; D £64-£74* Facilities FTV TVL tea/coffee Cen ht Licensed Wi-fi Parking 7 Notes ⊗ No Children 10yrs Closed Jan

The Royal Inn

★★★★ INN

66 Eastcliffe Rd, Tywardreath PL24 2AJ
☎ 01726 815601 📄 01726 816415
e-mail: info@royal-inn.co.uk
dir: Adjacent to Par railway station

Set opposite the local rail station, on the edge of the village of Tywardreath, this fully refurbished freehouse provides high standards of comfort and quality. Only 5 minutes from Par Sands and 4 miles from the Eden Project, this is an ideal base for exploring Cornwall. The open-plan bar area has slate floors and a large open fire. The atmosphere is relaxed and diners can choose from the bar menu or more formal dining in the restaurant or conservatory. All rooms have en suite facilities, along with tv, clock radio, direct dial telephone, hairdryer and refreshment tray. All twin rooms have sofa beds (suitable for children under 14), and the family suite is suitable for families of 4 or 5.

Rooms 15 en suite (8 fmly) (4 GF) S £45-£68; D £65-£90* Facilities tea/coffee Dinner available Direct Dial Cen ht Wi-fi Pool Table Parking 17 Notes LB Closed 23-26 Dec & 30 Dec-1 Jan

PREMIER COLLECTION

Camilla House
★★★★★ 🏠 GUEST HOUSE

12 Regent Ter TR18 4DW
☎ 01736 363771 📠 01736 363771
e-mail: enquiries@camillahouse.co.uk
web: www.camillahouse.co.uk
dir: A30 to Penzance, at rail station follow road along harbour front onto Promenade Rd. Opp Jubilee Bathing Pool, Regent Ter 2nd right

The friendly proprietors at this attractive Grade II listed terrace house do their utmost to ensure a comfortable stay. Wi-fi access is available throughout the house, and there is also access to computers in the lounge. Bedrooms and bathrooms are attractive, providing many added extras. Some bedrooms and the dining room provide delightful sea views.

Rooms 8 rms (7 en suite) (1 pri facs) (1 GF)
S £35-£37.50; D £75-£85* Facilities FTV TVL tea/coffee Dinner available Cen ht Licensed Wi-fi Parking 6 Notes LB ⊗

PREMIER COLLECTION

Ennys
★★★★★ 🏠 GUEST ACCOMMODATION

Trewhella Ln TR20 9BZ
☎ 01736 740262 📠 01736 740055
e-mail: ennys@ennys.co.uk
web: www.ennys.co.uk

(For full entry see St Hilary)

PREMIER COLLECTION

The Summer House
★★★★★ ◉◉ GUEST ACCOMMODATION

Cornwall Ter TR18 4HL
☎ 01736 363744 📠 01736 360959
e-mail: reception@summerhouse-cornwall.com
web: www.summerhouse-cornwall.com
dir: A30 to Penzance, at rail station follow along harbour onto Promenade Rd, pass Jubilee Pool, right after Queens Hotel. Summer House 30yds on left

This house, in a delightful residential location close to the seafront and harbour, is decorated in a Mediterranean style. The walled garden also reflects the theme, with sub-tropical plantings and attractive blue tables and chairs; dinner and drinks are served here on summer evenings. Expect warm hospitality and attentive service. Fresh local produce is simply prepared to provide memorable dishes on the daily changing menu.

Rooms 5 en suite Facilities FTV TVL tea/coffee Dinner available Cen ht Licensed Wi-fi Parking 6 Notes ⊗ No Children 13yrs Closed Nov-Feb

Blue Seas
★★★★ 🏠 GUEST ACCOMMODATION

13 Regent Ter TR18 4DW
☎ 01736 364744
e-mail: blueseas@ukonline.co.uk
dir: A30 to Penzance, at rail station along harbour front onto Promenade Rd, opp Jubilee Bathing Pool, Regent Ter 2nd right

Located on an elegant Regency terrace with stunning views across Mounts Bay, this is an ideal location for exploring the local area. There is an appealing contemporary style throughout with bedrooms providing a combination of comfort and quality, most with wonderful sea views. A guest lounge is also available, where you'll find lots of useful local information, books and magazines to peruse. Breakfast is a real treat here, featuring excellent local produce and a range of options from the generous continental buffet, vegetarian, fish options or the full English.

Rooms 8 en suite (2 fmly) (2 GF) S £38-£45; D £76-£90
Facilities FTV tea/coffee Cen ht Wi-fi Parking 9 Notes LB ⊗ Closed 15 Dec-Jan

Chy-an-Mor
★★★★ GUEST ACCOMMODATION

15 Regent Ter TR18 4DW
☎ 01736 363441
e-mail: reception@chyanmor.co.uk
dir: From railway station, take left lane to promenade, 1st right in front of Stanley House

This elegant Grade II listed Georgian house has been refurbished to provide high standards throughout. Bedrooms are individually designed and equipped with thoughtful extras, and many have spectacular views over Mounts Bay. The spacious lounge has similar views and tasty and satisfying breakfasts are served in the dining room. Ample off-street parking is available.

Rooms 9 en suite S £37-£40; D £70-£85* Facilities FTV tea/coffee Cen ht Wi-fi Parking 15 Notes ⊗ No Children

The Dunedin
★★★★ GUEST ACCOMMODATION

Alexandra Rd TR18 4LZ
☎ 01736 362652 📠 01736 360497
e-mail: info@dunedinhotel.co.uk
web: www.dunedinhotel.co.uk
dir: A30 to Penzance, at rail station along harbour front onto Promenade Rd, right onto Alexandra Rd, Dunedin on right

The house is in a tree-lined avenue just a stroll from the promenade and town centre. The friendly proprietors provide a relaxed atmosphere. Bedrooms are well equipped and smartly decorated to a high standard. There is a cosy lounge and hearty breakfasts are served in the dining room.

Rooms 8 rms (8 pri facs) (2 fmly) (2 GF) S £30-£37.50; D £55-£70* Facilities FTV TVL tea/coffee Cen ht Wi-fi Notes LB ⊗ Closed 15 Dec-2 Jan 🏧

The Old Vicarage
★★★★ BED AND BREAKFAST

Churchtown, St Hilary TR20 9DQ
☎ 01736 711508 & 07736 101230 📠 01736 711508
e-mail: johnbd524@aol.com
dir: 5m E of Penzance. Off B3280 in St Hilary

Feel at home with a friendly welcome at this home. The spacious bedrooms are thoughtfully equipped, and there is a snooker room, a comfortable lounge and extensive gardens. Also available to guests, a trekking and riding school, run by the proprietors, who run a small stud farm as well.

Rooms 3 en suite (1 fmly); D £55-£70* **Facilities** FTV TVL tea/coffee Cen ht Riding Snooker **Parking** 8 **Notes** LB

Rose Farm *(SW446290)*

★★★★ FARMHOUSE

Chyanhal, Buryas Bridge TR19 6AN
☎ 01736 731808 🖃 01736 731808 Mrs P Lally
e-mail: penny@rosefarmcornwall.co.uk
web: www.rosefarmcornwall.co.uk
dir: *1.5m S of Penzance. Off A30 at Drift (behind phone box), 0.75m on left*

Situated in peaceful countryside near Penzance, this working farm provides cosy accommodation with a genuine welcome and relaxed atmosphere. Bedrooms are attractively designed and well equipped, and some rooms have a private entrance. A hearty breakfast is served in the lounge-dining room at a refectory table.

Rooms 2 en suite 1 annexe en suite (1 fmly) (1 GF) **Facilities** FTV tea/coffee Cen ht **Parking** 8 **Notes** ⊗ Closed 24-27 Dec 23 acres beef/sheep

The Carlton

★★★ GUEST HOUSE

Promenade TR18 4NW
☎ 01736 362081 🖃 01736 362081
e-mail: carltonhotelpenzance@talk21.com
dir: *From A30 signs for harbour & Newlyn, on right after rdbt*

Situated on the pleasant promenade and having sea views from some of its rooms, The Carlton is an easy stroll from the town centre and amenities. Bedrooms are traditionally styled. There is a guest lounge and spacious dining room, both sea facing.

Rooms 12 rms (9 en suite) (3 smoking) S £25-£30; D £30-£60 **Facilities** FTV TVL tea/coffee **Notes** ⊗

Mount Royal

★★★ GUEST ACCOMMODATION

Chyandour Cliff TR18 3LQ
☎ 01736 362233 🖃 01736 362233
e-mail: mountroyal@btconnect.com
dir: *Off A30 onto coast road into town*

Part Georgian and part Victorian, the spacious Mount Royal has splendid views over Mount's Bay and is convenient for the town's attractions. The elegant dining room retains its original fireplace and ornate sideboard. Parking available to the rear of the property.

Rooms 7 en suite (3 fmly) (1 GF) S £60; D £70-£80* **Facilities** FTV tea/coffee Cen ht **Parking** 10 **Notes** LB ⊗ Closed Nov-Mar 📧

Mount View

★★★ INN

Longrock TR20 8JJ
☎ 01736 710416 🖃 01736 710416
dir: *Off A30 at Marazion/Penzance rdbt, 3rd exit signed Longrock. On right after pelican crossing*

This Victorian inn, just a short walk from the beach and half a mile from the Isles of Scilly heliport, is a good base for exploring West Cornwall. Bedrooms are well equipped, including a hospitality tray, and the bar is a popular with locals. Breakfast is served in the dining room and a dinner menu is available.

Rooms 5 rms (3 en suite) (2 fmly) (2 smoking) **Facilities** tea/coffee Dinner available Pool Table **Conf** Max 20 **Parking** 8 **Notes** RS Sun Closed 4.30-7pm

Penmorvah

★★★ GUEST ACCOMMODATION

61 Alexandra Rd TR18 4LZ
☎ 01736 363711
dir: *A30 to Penzance, at railway station follow road along harbour front pass Jubilee pool. At mini-rdbt, right onto Alexandra Rd*

A well situated bed and breakfast offering comfortable rooms, all of which are en suite. Penmorvah is just a few minutes walk from the seafront with convenient on-street parking nearby.

Rooms 10 en suite (2 fmly) (3 GF) **Facilities** FTV TVL tea/coffee Cen ht **Notes** 📧

Southern Comfort

★★★ GUEST HOUSE

Seafront, 8 Alexandra Ter TR18 4NX
☎ 01736 366333
dir: *0.5m SW of town centre. Follow seafront road, right after Lidl store, establishment signed*

This grand Victorian house is in a quiet location overlooking the bay and St Michael's Mount. A pleasant welcome awaits all guests, both tourist and business. Breakfast is served in the lower-ground dining room, and guests can enjoy a drink either outside in summer or in the bar or lounge.

Rooms 12 en suite (2 fmly) **Facilities** STV FTV TVL tea/coffee Dinner available Cen ht Licensed **Parking** 6 **Notes** 📧

The Stanley

★★★ GUEST ACCOMMODATION

23 Regents Ter TR18 4DW
☎ 01736 362146
e-mail: info@thestanleypenzance.co.uk

A well established property on the seafront with off-road parking available. Very handy for the Scillonian ferry and close to town. Rooms are comfortable, the hosts are friendly and cooked breakfasts are served in the dining room overlooking the seafront.

Rooms 10 en suite S £28-£35; D £56-£70* **Facilities** FTV

The Swordfish Inn

★★★ INN

The Strand, Newlyn TR18 5HN
☎ 01736 362830
e-mail: info@swordfishinn.co.uk
dir: *1m SW of Penzance*

Situated in the very heart of the fishing village of Newlyn, The Swordfish was totally renovated a couple of years ago. The spacious, comfortable bedrooms are well appointed, as are the en suite shower rooms. This establishment is a popular venue for locals and tourists alike.

Rooms 4 en suite (1 smoking) **Facilities** FTV tea/coffee Cen ht Wi-fi **Notes** ⊗ No coaches

PERRANARWORTHAL — Map 2 SW73

Blankednick Farm

★★★★ BED AND BREAKFAST

Ponsanooth TR3 7JN
☎ 01872 863784
dir: *A39 Truro to Falmouth road, at Perranarworthal, 2nd right turn after Norway Inn. B&B signed*

A traditional bed and breakfast of very high standards throughout plus a very warm welcome from experienced hosts, Blankednick Farm is in a quiet yet accessible location and sits in 16 acres of grounds and gardens. The bedrooms are very well appointed, and hearty Aga-cooked breakfasts are served at a large table in the dining room.

Rooms 2 en suite S £60; D £75* **Facilities** FTV tea/coffee Cen ht **Parking Notes** ⊗ 🐾

PERRANPORTH — Map 2 SW75

St Georges Country House

★★★★ GUEST ACCOMMODATION

St Georges Hill TR6 0ED
☎ 01872 572184
e-mail: info@stgeorgescountryhouse.co.uk

Situated in an elevated position above Perranporth, St Georges is a very friendly and comfortable establishment. The owners and staff are attentive, and very welcoming. Food is served most evenings and there is also a bar and large sitting room with comfy sofas and lots of books.

Rooms 7 en suite (2 fmly) **Facilities** FTV TVL tea/coffee Dinner available Cen ht Licensed Wi-fi **Conf** Max 20 Board 20 fred **Notes** LB Closed 1wk fr 23 Dec

PERRANUTHNOE — Map 2 SW52

PREMIER COLLECTION

Ednovean Farm *(SW538295)*

★★★★★ 🏡 FARMHOUSE

TR20 9LZ
☎ 01736 711883   Mr & Mrs C Taylor
e-mail: info@ednoveanfarm.co.uk
web: www.ednoveanfarm.co.uk
dir: *Off A394 towards Perranuthnoe at Dynasty Restaurant, farm drive on left on bend by post box*

Tranquillity is guaranteed at this 17th-century farmhouse, which looks across the countryside towards Mount's Bay. The bedrooms are individually styled and are most comfortable. The impressive Mediterranean style gardens are ideal to relax in. In addition to the sitting room, there is also a garden room and several patios. Breakfast is served at a magnificent oak table.

Rooms 3 en suite (3 GF) S £90-£105; D £90-£105* **Facilities** FTV tea/coffee Cen ht Wi-fi **Parking** 4 **Notes** LB ⊗ No Children 16yrs Closed 24-28 Dec & New Year 22 acres grassland/horticultural

Ednovean House

★★★★ GUEST ACCOMMODATION

TR20 9LZ
☎ 01736 711071
e-mail: clive@ednoveanhouse.co.uk
dir: *Off A394 at Perran x-rds between Penzance and Helston, 1st lane left, continue to end past farm*

Ednovean House is in a tranquil location with spectacular views of Mount's Bay and St Michael's Mount. It is ideal for a relaxing break or for touring the area. This establishment offers comfortable lounges and well-tended gardens and terraces. Bedrooms are comfortable and attractively decorated; ask for a room with a view.

Rooms 7 en suite S £33-£35; D £56-£90* **Facilities** TVL TV1B tea/coffee Cen ht **Parking** 12 **Notes** No Children 7yrs Closed Xmas & New Year

The Victoria Inn

★★★ 🍽 INN

TR20 9NP
☎ 01736 710309
e-mail: enquiries@victoriainn-penzance.co.uk
dir: *Off A394 into village*

The attractive and friendly inn, popular with locals and visitors alike, reputedly originates from the Middle Ages. Daily specials in the cosy bar or the dining room include local fish, while the bedrooms are small but well equipped.

Rooms 2 en suite S £45-£65; D £65* **Facilities** tea/coffee Dinner available **Parking** 10 **Notes** No Children 18yrs Closed 1wk Jan

POLPERRO — Map 2 SX25

PREMIER COLLECTION

Trenderway Farm *(SX214533)*

★★★★★ FARMHOUSE

Pelynt PL13 2LY
☎ 01503 272214   📠 0870 705 9998 Mr Yaron Peled & Jacq Harris
e-mail: stay@trenderwayfarm.com
web: www.trenderwayfarm.co.uk
dir: *Take A387 from Looe to Polperro, pass petrol station on left, right at farm sign & follow road across ford*

Set in 300 acres on a working farm, warm hospitality is offered in this delightful 16th-century farmhouse. Stylish bedrooms, both in the farmhouse and in the adjacent barns, offer high levels of comfort and include Wi-fi access. Hearty breakfasts are served in the conservatory overlooking the lake, and free-range eggs from the farm, as well as high quality local produce, are served.

Rooms 2 en suite 4 annexe en suite (1 GF); D £95-£155* **Facilities** FTV tea/coffee Cen ht Wi-fi Lakes **Conf** Max 15 Thtr 12 Class 12 Board 15 **Parking** 6 **Notes** LB ⊗ No Children 200 acres beef/sheep/orchards

Trenake Manor Farm *(SX190555)*

★★★★ FARMHOUSE

Pelynt PL13 2LT
☎ 01503 220835 🖹 01503 220835 **Mrs L Philp**
e-mail: lorraine@cornishfarmhouse.co.uk
dir: 3.5m N of Polperro. A390 onto B3359 for Looe, 5m left at small x-rds

The welcoming 15th-century farmhouse is surrounded by countryside and is a good base for touring Cornwall. Bedrooms have considerate finishing touches and there is a comfortable lounge. Breakfast, using local produce, is enjoyed in the cosy dining room (you may just spot the milking cows quietly passing the end of the garden).

Rooms 3 en suite (1 fmly) **Facilities** TVL tea/coffee Cen ht Wi-fi **Parking** 10 **Notes** LB ⊗ 400 acres dairy/beef/arable

Penryn House

★★★ GUEST ACCOMMODATION

The Coombes PL13 2RQ
☎ 01503 272157 🖹 01503 273055
e-mail: chrispidcock@aol.com
web: www.penrynhouse.co.uk
dir: A387 to Polperro, at mini-rdbt left down hill into village (ignore restricted access). 200yds on left

Penryn House has a relaxed atmosphere and offers a warm welcome. Every effort is made to ensure a memorable stay. Bedrooms are neatly presented and reflect the character of the building. After a day exploring, enjoy a drink at the bar and relax in the comfortable lounge.

Rooms 12 rms (11 en suite) (1 pri facs) (3 fmly) S £35-£40; D £70-£100* **Facilities** FTV tea/coffee Licensed Wi-fi **Parking** 13 **Notes** LB

PORTHLEVEN   Map 2 SW62

Kota Restaurant with Rooms

★★★ ◉ RESTAURANT WITH ROOMS

Harbour Head TR13 9JA
☎ 01326 562407 🖹 01326 562407
e-mail: kota@btconnect.com
dir: B3304 from Helston into Porthleven, Kota on harbour head opposite slipway

Overlooking the Harbour Head, this 300-year-old building is the home of Kota Restaurant (Kota being Maori for

shellfish). The bedrooms are approached from a granite stairway to the side of the building. The family room is spacious and has the benefit of harbour views, while the smaller, double room is at the rear of the property. The enthusiastic, young owners ensure guests enjoy their stay here and a meal in the restaurant is not to be missed. Breakfast features the best of local produce.

Rooms 2 annexe en suite (1 fmly) S £50-£70; D £50-£90* **Facilities** tea/coffee Dinner available Wi-fi **Parking** 1 **Notes** ⊗ Closed Jan RS Nov-Mar Closed for lunch Mon-Thu & all day Sun No coaches

PORT ISAAC   Map 2 SW98

The Corn Mill

★★★★ BED AND BREAKFAST

Port Isaac Rd, Trelill PL30 3HZ
☎ 01208 851079
dir: Off B3314, between Pendoggett & Trelill

Dating from the 18th century, this mill has been lovingly restored to provide a home packed full of character. The bedrooms are individually styled and personal touches create a wonderfully relaxed and homely atmosphere. The farmhouse kitchen is the venue for a delicious breakfast.

Rooms 2 en suite (1 fmly); D £75 **Facilities** tea/coffee Cen ht TV1B **Parking** 3 **Notes** Closed 24 Dec-5 Jan ⊜

PORTLOE   Map 2 SW93

Carradale

★★★★ BED AND BREAKFAST

TR2 5RB
☎ 01872 501508
e-mail: barbara495@btinternet.com
dir: Off A3078 into Portloe, B&B 200yds from Ship Inn

Carradale lies on the outskirts of this picturesque fishing village, a short walk from the South West Coast Path. It provides warm hospitality, a good level of comfort and well equipped bedrooms. There is an upper-floor lounge with a television. Breakfast is served around a communal table in the pleasant dining room.

Rooms 2 en suite (1 fmly) (1 GF) S £40; D £65* **Facilities** TVL TV1B tea/coffee Cen ht **Parking** 5 **Notes** ⊗ ⊜

REDRUTH   Map 2 SW64

Old Railway Yard

★★★★ BED AND BREAKFAST

Lanner Hill TR16 5SZ
☎ 01209 314514
e-mail: graham@s-collier.freeserve.co.uk
dir: A393 Redruth/Falmouth road, at brow of hill before Lanner village, turn right, 125mtrs

A traditional bed and breakfast off Lanner Hill with easy access to the main A30. The hosts are friendly and attentive and make their guests really feel at home. Rooms are very well appointed, and there is a small guest lounge and a conservatory as well as the garden for guests to enjoy.

Rooms 4 rms (2 en suite) (2 pri facs); D £50-£65* **Facilities** FTV TVL tea/coffee Dinner available Cen ht **Parking** 8 **Notes** ⊗ No Children 6yrs ⊜

Lanner Inn

★★ INN

The Square, Lanner TR16 6EH
☎ 01209 215611 🖹 01209 214065
e-mail: info@lannerinn.co.uk
web: www.lannerinn.co.uk
dir: 2m SE of Redruth. In Lanner on A393

Conveniently situated for Redruth and the A30 this traditional inn is about to undergo refurbishment and is now under new ownership. Bedrooms are comfortable and staff very friendly.

Rooms 5 en suite 1 annexe en suite (2 fmly) (1 GF) S £40; D £70* **Facilities** FTV tea/coffee Cen ht Pool Table **Parking** 16

ROCHE   Map 2 SW96

Saffron Park

★★★ BED AND BREAKFAST

Belowda PL26 8NL
☎ 01726 890105 & 07930 572536
e-mail: saffron.park@btinternet.com
dir: *Exit new A30 at Victoria junct, after rdbt continue
W along former A30. Pass Victoria Inn & Lodge 0.75m,
right into narrow lane before Roche Cross junct, on left
within 200yds*

Saffron Park is midway between the north and south
coasts and very convenient for the Eden Project. Friendly
hospitality and attentive service are provided, and there
is a comfortable lounge and pleasant bedrooms. A hearty
breakfast is served in the dining room.

Rooms 2 en suite (1 fmly) S £30; D £60* Facilities TVL
tea/coffee Cen ht Wi-fi Sauna Spa bath Parking 5
Notes Closed 22 Dec-2 Jan

RUAN MINOR   Map 2 SW71

The Coach House

★★★★ GUEST ACCOMMODATION

Kuggar TR12 7LY
☎ 01326 291044
e-mail: mjanmakin@aol.com
dir: *1m N of Ruan Minor in Kuggar*

This 17th-century house is close to Kennack Sands and
Goonhilly Downs nature reserve. The friendly proprietors
provide a warm welcome for their guests, who can relax
in the spacious lounge-dining room where a fire burns in
colder months. Bedrooms, two of which are in a converted
stable block, are attractively decorated.

Rooms 3 en suite 2 annexe en suite (2 GF); D £70*
Facilities STV TVL tea/coffee Cen ht Wi-fi Parking 10
Notes LB ⊗ Closed Xmas ⊜

ST AGNES   Map 2 SW75

The Aramay

★★★★ GUEST ACCOMMODATION

Armay House, Quay Rd TR5 0RP
☎ 01872 553546
e-mail: amie@thearamay.com

Newly refurbished to very high standards The Aramay
offers stylish, contemporary surroundings with an
intimate feel. Service is relaxed and informal, and an
award-winning breakfast is served till late. Very well
located with off-road parking.

Rooms 5 en suite (1 GF) S £90-£105; D £90-£105*
Facilities STV TVL tea/coffee Cen ht Licensed Wi-fi
Parking 5 Notes ⊗ No Children 16yrs

Driftwood Spars

★★★★ ⊜ GUEST ACCOMMODATION

Trevaunance Cove TR5 0RT
☎ 01872 552428   📠 01872 553701
e-mail: driftwoodspars@hotmail.com
dir: *A30 to Chiverton rdbt, right onto B3277, through
village. Driftwood Spars 200yds before beach*

Partly built from ship-wreck timbers, this 18th-century
inn attracts locals and visitors alike. The attractive
bedrooms, some in an annexe, are decorated in bright,
sea-side style and have many interesting features. Local
produce served in the informal pub dining room or in the
restaurant, ranges from hand-pulled beers to delicious,
locally landed seafood.

Rooms 9 en suite 6 annexe en suite (4 fmly) (5 GF)
S £45-£66; D £86-£102* Facilities tea/coffee Dinner
available Direct Dial Cen ht Licensed Wi-fi Pool Table
Conf Max 50 Thtr 50 Class 25 Board 20 Parking 40
Notes LB RS 25 Dec no lunch/dinner, no bar in evening

Penkerris

★★ GUEST HOUSE

Penwinnick Rd TR5 0PA
☎ 01872 552262   📠 01872 552262
e-mail: info@penkerris.co.uk
web: www.penkerris.co.uk
dir: *A30 onto B3277 to village, 1st house on right after
village sign*

Set in gardens on the edge of the village, Penkerris is an
Edwardian house with a relaxed atmosphere. The best
possible use is made of space in the bedrooms, and
home-cooked evening meals using local produce are
served by arrangement. Ample parking available.

Rooms 6 rms (4 en suite) (3 fmly) S fr £22.50;
D £45-£65* Facilities TVL tea/coffee Dinner available
Licensed Parking 9 Notes LB

ST AUSTELL   Map 2 SX05

See also Gorran Haven, Roche & St Blazey

PREMIER COLLECTION

Anchorage House

★★★★★ 🏠 ⊜ GUEST ACCOMMODATION

Nettles Corner, Tregrehan Mills PL25 3RH
☎ 01726 814071   📠 01726 813462
e-mail: info@anchoragehouse.co.uk
web: www.anchoragehouse.co.uk
dir: *2 m E of town centre off A390, opposite St Austell
Garden Centre*

This Georgian style house is set in an acre of carefully
landscaped gardens at the end of a private lane.
Guests are met upon arrival with afternoon tea, often
served on the patio, and dinner is served in the evening
by arrangement. The luxurious bedrooms are equipped
to the highest standard and thoughtful extras include
satellite television, fresh fruit, magazines, bottled
water and chocolates. Guests also have use of the pool,
hot tub, gym and sauna. The house is a short distance
from the Eden Project, the Lost Gardens of Heligan,
Carolyn Bay and Charlestown Harbour.

Rooms 4 en suite 1 annexe en suite (1 GF) S £85-£135;
D £115-£160 Facilities STV FTV tea/coffee Dinner
available Cen ht Wi-fi 🏊 Sauna Gymnasium Spa
treatments, Hot tub Parking 6 Notes ⊗ No Children
16yrs Closed Dec-Feb

PREMIER COLLECTION

Penarwyn House

★★★★★ 🏠 GUEST ACCOMMODATION

PL24 2DS
☎ 01726 814224   📠 01726 814224
e-mail: stay@penarwyn.co.uk
web: www.penarwyn.co.uk

(For full entry see St Blazey)

PREMIER COLLECTION

Highland Court Lodge
★★★★★ GUEST ACCOMMODATION

Biscovey Rd, Biscovey, Par PL24 2HW
☎ 01726 813320 📄 01726 813320
e-mail: enquiries@highlandcourt.co.uk
web: www.highlandcourt.co.uk
dir: *2m E of St Austell. A390 E to St Blazey Gate, right onto Biscovey Rd, 300yds on right*

Highland Court Lodge is an extremely well presented and maintained contemporary building with stunning views over St Austell Bay, and is just over one mile from the Eden Project. Its impressive en suite bedrooms have luxurious fabrics and each room opens onto a private patio. There is a lounge with deep sofas, and the terrace shares the fine views. The local Cornish catch features strongly in the freshly prepared dinners, which, like breakfast are not to be missed.

Rooms 5 en suite (2 fmly) (5 GF) S £75-£115; D £90-£190 **Facilities** FTV tea/coffee Dinner available Cen ht Licensed Wi-fi **Conf** Max 12 Class 12 Board 12 **Parking** 10 **Notes** LB ⊗

PREMIER COLLECTION

Lower Barn
★★★★★ GUEST ACCOMMODATION

Bosue, St Ewe PL26 6ET
☎ 01726 844881
e-mail: janie@bosue.co.uk
web: www.bosue.co.uk
dir: *3.5m SW of St Austell. Off B3273 at x-rds signed Lost Gardens of Heligan, Lower Barn signed 1m on right*

This converted barn, tucked away in countryside with easy access to local attractions, has huge appeal. Warm colours create a Mediterranean feel, complemented by informal and genuine hospitality. Bedrooms have a host of extras. Breakfast is served around a large table or on the patio deck overlooking the garden, which also has a hot tub.

Rooms 3 en suite (1 fmly) (1 GF) **Facilities** tea/coffee Dinner available Cen ht Sauna Gymnasium Hot tub Spa treatments **Parking** 7 **Notes** LB ⊗ Closed Jan

PREMIER COLLECTION

Nanscawen Manor House
★★★★★ GUEST ACCOMMODATION

Prideaux Rd, Luxulyan Valley PL24 2SR
☎ 01726 814488
e-mail: keith@nanscawen.com
web: www.nanscawen.com

(For full entry see St Blazey)

Hunter's Moon
★★★★ GUEST HOUSE

Chapel Hill, Polgooth PL26 7BU
☎ 01726 66445 📄 01726 66445
e-mail: enquiries@huntersmooncornwall.co.uk
dir: *1.5m SW of town centre. Off B3273 into Polgooth, pass village shop on left, 1st right*

Hunter's Moon lies in a quiet village just a few miles from Heligan and within easy reach of the Eden Project. Service is friendly and attentive and the bedrooms are well equipped for business or leisure. There is a conservatory-lounge and a pretty garden to enjoy during warmer

weather. Breakfast is served in the cosy dining room and the nearby village inn serves freshly prepared meals.

Rooms 4 en suite (2 fmly) S £48-£50; D £66-£70* **Facilities** FTV tea/coffee Cen ht **Parking** 5 **Notes** ⊗ No Children 14yrs ⊗

Sunnyvale Bed & Breakfast
★★★★ BED AND BREAKFAST

Hewas Water PL26 7JF
☎ 01726 882572
e-mail: jm.uden@hotmail.com
dir: *4m SW of St Austell. Off A390 in Hewas Water*

This house has pleasant gardens in a peaceful location, and the very friendly proprietor makes you feel most welcome. The bedrooms are both ground floor, one specifically designed for the disabled, and have an extensive range of facilities. Breakfast is either taken in the main house at separate tables, or for the less able in the bedroom, by prior arrangement.

Rooms 2 annexe en suite (2 GF) S £40-£45; D £60-£65 **Facilities** FTV tea/coffee Cen ht **Parking** 4 **Notes** ⊗ No Children 16yrs ⊗

Cooperage
★★★★ BED AND BREAKFAST

37 Cooperage Rd, Trewoon PL25 5SJ
☎ 01726 70497 & 07854 960385
e-mail: lcooperage@tiscali.co.uk
web: www.cooperagebb.co.uk
dir: *1m W of St Austell. On A3058 in Trewoon*

Situated on the edge of the town, this late Victorian, semi-detached granite house has been renovated in a contemporary style. The comfortable bedrooms are well equipped and feature beautifully tiled en suites. Guests are assured of a friendly and relaxed welcome here and the property is conveniently positioned for the numerous amenities and attractions locally. Cooperage is suitable for both business and leisure guests. Pets welcome by arrangement.

Rooms 4 rms (3 en suite) (1 pri facs) S £35-£40; D £55-£60 **Facilities** FTV tea/coffee Cen ht Wi-fi **Parking** 6 **Notes** LB

ST AUSTELL *continued*

The Elms

★★★★ BED AND BREAKFAST

14 Penwinnick Rd PL25 5DW
☎ 01726 74981 📄 01726 74981
e-mail: pete@edenbb.co.uk
web: www.edenbb.co.uk
dir: *0.5m SW of town centre. On A390 junct Pondhu Rd*

Well located for the Eden Project or for touring Cornwall, this accommodation offers a relaxed and friendly environment for leisure and business guests. Bedrooms, one with a four-poster bed, are well equipped and there is an inviting lounge. Breakfast is served in the conservatory dining room.

Rooms 3 annexe en suite (1 GF) S £30–£35; D £60–£70*
Facilities FTV TVL tea/coffee Cen ht Wi-fi Golf 18
Parking 3 **Notes** LB ⊗

Elmswood House

★★★★ GUEST ACCOMMODATION

73 Tehidy Rd, Tywardreath PL24 2QD
☎ 01726 814221 📄 01726 814399
e-mail: enquiries@elmswoodhousehotel.co.uk
web: www.elmswoodhousehotel.co.uk

(For full entry see Par)

Polgreen

★★★★ BED AND BREAKFAST

Trelowth PL26 7DZ
☎ 01726 64546
e-mail: office@polgreenguesthouse.co.uk
dir: *Off A390 to Truro, signed Trelowth, 1st left to Polgooth, entrance 200yds on right*

Located just outside St Austell with easy access to the town, beaches and the Eden Project, Polgreen offers high quality rooms and friendly, attentive service. Off-road parking, established gardens, and hearty breakfasts make this an ideal base for touring Cornwall.

Rooms 3 en suite S £60–£80; D £70–£80 **Facilities** FTV tea/coffee Cen ht Summerhouse available for guests use **Parking** 3 **Notes** ⊗ No Children 12yrs Closed Xmas

Polgreen Farm

★★★★ GUEST ACCOMMODATION

London Apprentice PL26 7AP
☎ 01726 75151
e-mail: polgreen.farm@btinternet.com
web: www.polgreenfarm.co.uk
dir: *1.5m S of St Austell. Off B3273, turn left entering London Apprentice & signed*

Guests return regularly for the friendly welcome at this peaceful accommodation located just south of St Austell. The spacious and well-equipped bedrooms are divided between the main house and an adjoining property, and each building has a comfortable lounge. Breakfast is served in a pleasant conservatory overlooking the garden.

Rooms 3 rms (2 en suite) (1 pri facs) 4 annexe en suite (1 fmly) (1 GF) S £30–£40; D £56–£64 **Facilities** FTV TVL tea/coffee Cen ht **Parking** 8 **Notes** LB ⊗ ⊕

Poltarrow (SW998518)

★★★★ FARMHOUSE

St Mewan PL26 7DR
☎ 01726 67111 📄 01726 67111 Mrs J Nancarrow
e-mail: enquire@poltarrow.co.uk
dir: *1.5m W of town centre. Off A390 to St Mewan, pass school, 2nd farm on left after 0.5m*

Set in 45 acres of gardens and pasture, this delightful traditional farmhouse retains many of original features, including open fires. The attractive bedrooms are comfortably furnished and decorated with style. Breakfast, cooked in the Aga, is served in the conservatory overlooking the gardens. An impressive indoor pool is available, together with a sports hall for badminton, bowls and short tennis.

Rooms 3 en suite 2 annexe en suite (1 fmly) S £45–£50; D £75* **Facilities** FTV TVL tea/coffee Cen ht Wi-fi ⊗ Fishing Pool Table Indoor short tennis, badminton, bowls **Parking** 10 **Notes** LB ⊗ No Children 5yrs Closed 16 Dec-5 Jan 45 acres mixed

T'Gallants

★★★ GUEST HOUSE

6 Charlestown Rd, Charlestown PL25 3NJ
☎ 01726 70203 📄 01726 70203
e-mail: enquiries@tgallants.co.uk
dir: *0.5m SE of town off A390 rdbt signed Charlestown*

The fine Georgian house partly dates from 1630. It overlooks the historic port of Charlestown, with its fleet of square-rigged sailing ships. Bedrooms are well presented and spacious, and one has a four-poster bed and views of the port. Breakfast is served in the attractive dining room with a choice of traditional or continental offered. A guest lounge is also available.

Rooms 7 en suite **Facilities** FTV TVL tea/coffee Cen ht Wi-fi **Notes** ⊗

ST BLAZEY	Map 2 SX05

PREMIER COLLECTION

Penarwyn House

★★★★★ GUEST ACCOMMODATION

PL24 2DS
☎ 01726 814224 📄 01726 814224
e-mail: stay@penarwyn.co.uk
web: www.penarwyn.co.uk
dir: *A390 W through St Blazey, left before 2nd speed camera into Doubletrees School, Penarwyn straight ahead*

This impressive house stands in tranquil surroundings close to main routes, the Eden Project and many attractions. Painstakingly restored, the spacious house offers a host of facilities, and the bedrooms are particularly comfortable and delightfully appointed. Breakfast is another highlight here, and along with the proprietor's most welcoming hospitality, Penarwyn provides a memorable stay.

Rooms 4 en suite (1 fmly) S £55–£75; D £110–£150* **Facilities** FTV tea/coffee Cen ht Wi-fi 3/4 size snooker table **Parking** 6 **Notes** LB ⊗ No Children 10yrs

PREMIER COLLECTION

Nanscawen Manor House
★★★★★ GUEST ACCOMMODATION

Prideaux Rd, Luxulyan Valley PL24 2SR
☎ 01726 814488
e-mail: keith@nanscawen.com
web: www.nanscawen.com
dir: A390 W to St Blazey, right after railway,
Nanscawen 0.75m on right

This renovated manor house originates from the 14th century and provides a high standard of accommodation, with elegant bedrooms and bathrooms with spa baths. There are extra touches throughout to pamper you, a spacious lounge with a well-stocked honesty bar, and five acres of pleasant gardens with splendid woodland views. Breakfast, served in the conservatory, features fresh local produce.

Rooms 3 en suite S £45–£110; D £79–£122*
Facilities STV tea/coffee Direct Dial Cen ht Wi-fi ⏁
Parking 8 Notes ⊗ No Children 12yrs

ST GENNYS   Map 2 SX19

Rosecare Villa Farm
★★★★ GUEST ACCOMMODATION

EX23 0BG
☎ 01840 230474
e-mail: info@northcornwallholidays.com
dir: 9m S of Bude on A39, S of Wainhouse Corner

This family-run establishment is close to the spectacular North Cornish coast, an area with a host of activities on offer. Dating back several hundred years, the house was once a slate captain's house and is now a smallholding complete with a small menagerie. Woodland walks are also available. Bedrooms are situated in the original stone barns surrounding the courtyard, and each has its own separate entrance. Breakfast features locally sourced produce with eggs from the resident hens. Dinner is also available by prior arrangement.

Rooms 5 annexe en suite (5 GF) S £33; D £66*
Facilities FTV tea/coffee Dinner available Cen ht
Parking 8 Notes LB Closed 22–28 Dec

ST HILARY   Map 2 SW53

PREMIER COLLECTION

Ennys
★★★★★ ⬛ GUEST ACCOMMODATION

Trewhella Ln TR20 9BZ
☎ 01736 740262   📠 01736 740055
e-mail: ennys@ennys.co.uk
web: www.ennys.co.uk
dir: 1m N of B3280 Leedstown-Goldsithney road at end of Trewhella Ln

Set off the beaten track, this 17th-century manor house is a perfect place to unwind. A friendly welcome awaits you, and a complimentary afternoon tea is laid out in the kitchen. Ennys retains much original character and the rooms are impressively furnished. A delightful Cornish breakfast is served in the dining room, using a wealth of fresh local ingredients and home-produced fresh eggs. Three self-catering cottages available.

Rooms 3 en suite 2 annexe en suite (2 fmly) (1 GF)
S £70–£115; D £90–£135 Facilities FTV tea/coffee
Cen ht Wi-fi ⏁ 🏊 Parking 8 Notes ⊗ No Children 5yrs Closed Nov–28 Mar

ST IVES   Map 2 SW54

PREMIER COLLECTION

Beachcroft
★★★★★ GUEST ACCOMMODATION

Valley Rd, Carbis Bay TR26 2QS
☎ 01736 794442
e-mail: info@beachcroftstives.co.uk
web: www.beachcroftstives.co.uk
dir: From A30/A3074 rdbt, follow signs to St Ives, through Carbis Bay, turn right onto Valley Rd

After a total refurbishment and transformation Beachcroft now offers a tranquil haven of peace and calm in truly top class surroundings. The hosts offer genuine warmth and hospitality and their focus is guest relaxation and enjoyment. Egyptian cotton, flat screen televisions, Villeroy Boch bathrooms and Molton Brown toiletries are only a few examples of the quality to be expected here.

Rooms 5 en suite; D £140–£170* Facilities FTV TVL tea/coffee Cen ht Licensed Wi-fi Parking 5 Notes ⊗ No Children 12yrs

PREMIER COLLECTION

Jamies
★★★★★ GUEST ACCOMMODATION

Wheal Whidden, Carbis Bay TR26 2QX
☎ 01736 794718
e-mail: info@jamiesstives.co.uk
web: www.jamiesstives.co.uk
dir: A3074 to Carbis Bay, onto Pannier Ln, 2nd left

Accomplished hosts, Felicity and Jamie, provide a most pleasant home for their guests at this attractive Cornish Villa, which has been thoughtfully renovated and stylishly appointed. Bedrooms are spacious and comfortable, all have sea views, and lots of thoughtful extras have been provided. Breakfast is a feature here and is taken in the elegant dining room at a large round table providing a memorable aspect to a stay at Jamies.

Rooms 3 en suite (1 GF) S £75–£95; D £110*
Facilities FTV tea/coffee Cen ht Parking 4 Notes ⊗ No Children 12yrs RS Dec–Feb optional opening ☺

PREMIER COLLECTION

Primrose Valley
★★★★★ ⬛ GUEST ACCOMMODATION

Porthminster Beach TR26 2ED
☎ 01736 794939   📠 01736 794939
e-mail: info@primroseonline.co.uk
web: www.primroseonline.co.uk
dir: A3074 to St Ives, 25yds after town sign right onto Primrose Valley, left under bridge, along beach front, turn left back under bridge, property on left

St Ives is just a short walk from this friendly, family-run establishment close to Porthminster Beach. The atmosphere is light and airy and modernisation provides a good level of comfort. Some bedrooms have balconies with stunning views. There is a lounge and bar area, and dinner is available. Breakfast features local produce and home-made items.

Rooms 9 en suite (1 fmly); D £100–£165*
Facilities tea/coffee Dinner available Cen ht Licensed Wi-fi REN treatment & therapy room Parking 13 Notes LB ⊗ No Children 8yrs Closed 23–27 Dec RS 2–29 Jan

ST IVES *continued*

Glanmor

★★★★ GUEST ACCOMMODATION

The Belyars TR26 2BX
☎ 01736 795613
e-mail: margaret@glanmor.net
dir: A3074 to St Ives, left at Porthminster Hotel & up Talland Rd

The relaxed and friendly atmosphere at the Glanmor draws guests back time after time. It is just a short walk from the town centre and beaches, and offers attractive, well equipped bedrooms. There is a comfortable lounge and conservatory, and the pretty landscaped gardens have seating on warm sunny days. Carefully prepared breakfasts are served in the light and airy dining room.

Rooms 6 en suite (3 fmly) (2 GF) S £35; D £60-£76*
Facilities TVL tea/coffee Cen ht Wi-fi **Parking** 6 **Notes** ✖ No Children 3yrs 🐾

Lamorna Lodge

★★★★ GUEST ACCOMMODATION

Boskerris Rd, Carbis Bay TR26 2NG
☎ 01736 795967
e-mail: lamorna@tr26.wanadoo.co.uk
dir: A30 onto A3074, right after playground in Carbis Bay, establishment 200yds on right

A truly genuine welcome is assured at this quietly situated establishment which is just a short walk from Carbis Bay beach. Wonderful views over St Ives Bay to Godrevy Lighthouse can be enjoyed from the spacious lounge, a view also shared by some of the stylish bedrooms. Breakfast and dinner are served in the elegant surroundings of the dining room where home-cooked food is prepared from local produce.

Rooms 9 en suite (4 fmly) (2 GF) S £48-£52; D £76-£96*
Facilities FTV tea/coffee Dinner available Cen ht
Conf Max 18 Thtr 18 Class 18 Board 18 **Parking** 9
Notes LB ✖ Closed 5 Nov-10 Mar

The Nook

★★★★ GUEST ACCOMMODATION

Ayr TR26 1EQ
☎ 01736 795913
e-mail: info@nookstives.co.uk
web: www.nookstives.co.uk
dir: A30 to St Ives left at Natwest, right at rdbt & left at top of hill

Recently the subject of extensive refurbishment, the Nook is an ideal base for exploring Cornwall's spectacular coastline, gardens and countryside. The comfortable bedrooms are furnished in a modern, contemporary style and are equipped with numerous facilities. Guests enjoy a wide variety on offer at breakfast, from full English or continental, to scrambled eggs with smoked salmon.

Rooms 11 en suite (1 fmly) (1 GF) S £38-£46;
D £72-£98* **Facilities** FTV TVL tea/coffee Cen ht Wi-fi
Parking 10 **Notes** LB ✖

Treliska

★★★★ 🏠 GUEST ACCOMMODATION

3 Bedford Rd TR26 1SP
☎ 01736 797678 📠 01736 797678
e-mail: info@treliska.com
web: www.treliska.com
dir: A3074 to St Ives, fork at Porthminster Hotel into town, at T-junct facing Barclays Bank left onto Bedford Rd, house on right

This stylish, friendly and relaxed home is close to the seafront, restaurants and galleries. There is a refreshing approach here with a contemporary feel throughout. Impressive bathrooms have invigorating showers, while the attractive bedrooms are configured to maximise comfort. Enjoyable, freshly cooked Cornish breakfasts are served in the lounge-dining room with a choice of coffee available at all times to guests. Additional facilities include internet and Wi-fi connections.

Rooms 5 en suite **Facilities** FTV tea/coffee Cen ht Wi-fi
Notes ✖ No Children 10yrs 🐾

Bay View Guest House

★★★★ GUEST ACCOMMODATION

5 Pednolver Ter TR26 2EL
☎ 01736 796765
e-mail: jamesvictorsimmons@hotmail.com
dir: A30/A3704 to St Ives, follow signs for leisure centre, Pednolver Ter off Albert Rd

Situated within 250 yards of Porthminster Beach, this small, friendly guesthouse provides comfortable accommodation and a warm welcome. Rear on-site car parking is a bonus.

Rooms 5 rms (3 en suite) (2 pri facs) (1 fmly) S £33-£35;
D £66-£70* **Facilities** TVL tea/coffee Wi-fi **Parking** 5
Notes ✖ No Children 5yrs Closed Oct-Etr 🐾

Borthalan

★★★★ GUEST ACCOMMODATION

Off Boskerris Rd, Carbis Bay TR26 2NQ
☎ 01736 795946 📠 01736 795946
e-mail: borthalanhotel@btconnect.com
dir: A3074 into Carbis Bay, right onto Boskerris Rd, 1st left onto cul-de-sac

Quietly situated, this welcoming establishment is just a short walk from Carbis Bay station, from where you can take the 3-minute journey to St Ives without the hassle of car parking. The friendly proprietors provide a relaxing environment, with every effort made to ensure an enjoyable stay. Bedrooms are all well equipped and smartly presented, some with lovely sea views. There is a cosy lounge and an attractive garden, and breakfast is served in the bright dining room.

Rooms 7 en suite **Facilities** TVL tea/coffee Cen ht
Licensed **Parking** 7 **Notes** ✖ No Children 12yrs Closed
Xmas

Coombe Farmhouse

★★★★ BED AND BREAKFAST

TR27 6NW
☎ 01736 740843
e-mail: coombefarmhouse@aol.com
web: www.coombefarmhouse.com
dir: 1.5m W of Lelant. Off A3074 to Lelant Downs

Built of sturdy granite, this early 19th-century farmhouse is in a delightful location tucked away at the southern foot of Trencrom Hill, yet convenient for St Ives. The comfortable bedrooms are attractively decorated. There is a cosy lounge, and substantial breakfasts, featuring farm-fresh eggs, are served in the dining room overlooking the garden.

Rooms 3 rms (2 en suite) (1 pri facs) S £40; D £72-£80
Facilities TVL tea/coffee Cen ht **Parking** 3 **Notes** ✖ No
Children 12yrs Closed Dec 🐾

Edgar's

★★★★ GUEST ACCOMMODATION

Chy-an-Creet, Higher Stennack TR26 2HA
☎ 01736 796559 📄 01736 796559
e-mail: stay@edgarshotel.co.uk
web: www.edgarshotel.co.uk
dir: *0.5m W of town centre on B3306, opp Leach Pottery*

High standards of comfort are provided at this friendly, family-run property. Public areas are spacious and include two comfortable guest lounges, and bedrooms, some on the ground floor, are well equipped. Breakfast, served in the dining room, includes home-made preserves and makes good use of local produce. Good off-road parking available.

Rooms 8 en suite (2 fmly) (4 GF) S £39-£75; D £59-£120* **Facilities** FTV TVL tea/coffee Cen ht Wi-fi **Parking** 8 **Notes** LB ⊗ Closed Nov-Feb

Headland House

★★★★ GUEST ACCOMMODATION

Headland Rd, Carbis Bay TR26 2NS
☎ 01736 796647 📄 01736 796647
e-mail: headland.house@btconnect.com
dir: *A30 onto A3074 towards St Ives, at Carbis Bay right to Porthepta Rd & 3rd on right*

Newly renovated and furnished house with great views over Carbis Bay from many rooms. Headland House is a stylish and comfortable operation with very friendly hosts. Breakfast can be taken in the conservatory, and it benefits from off-road parking.

Rooms 6 en suite 1 annexe en suite (1 fmly) **Facilities** FTV TVL tea/coffee Cen ht Licensed Wi-fi **Parking** 7 **Notes** LB ⊗ No Children 14yrs 📧

The Mustard Tree

★★★★ GUEST HOUSE

Sea View Meadows, St Ives Rd, Carbis Bay TR26 2JX
☎ 01736 795677
e-mail: enquiries@mustard-tree.co.uk
dir: *A3074 to Carbis Bay, The Mustard Tree on right opp Methodist church*

Set in delightful gardens and having sea views, this attractive house is just a short drive from the centre of St Ives. Alternatively, the coastal path leads from Carbis Bay to St Ives. The pleasant bedrooms are very comfortable and have many extra facilities. A splendid choice is offered at breakfast, with vegetarian or continental options; a range of 'lite bites' are available in the early evening.

Rooms 7 rms (6 en suite) (1 pri facs) (2 fmly) (4 GF) S £32-£40; D £64-£85* **Facilities** FTV TVL tea/coffee Dinner available Cen ht Wi-fi **Conf** Max 16 **Parking** 7 **Notes** ⊗

Nancherrow Cottage

★★★★ BED AND BREAKFAST

7 Fish St TR26 1LT
☎ 01736 798496
e-mail: peterjean@nancherrowcottage.fsnet.co.uk
dir: *A30 onto A3074, through Lelant to St Ives, along Harbour to Sloop Inn. Turn left onto Fish St*

Situated a stone's throw from the harbour, in the centre of the town, Nancherrow Cottage is an attractive period property, with friendly, enthusiastic owners. The comfortable bedrooms are well equipped and boast numerous, thoughtful extras. Breakfast is served around a communal table, an interesting and varied choice is offered, including a full English cooked breakfast, scrambled eggs and smoked salmon on toasted muffin, and lots more.

Rooms 3 en suite S £50-£65; D £75-£90* **Facilities** tea/coffee Cen ht **Notes** LB ⊗ No Children 12yrs Closed mid Nov-mid Feb 📧

The Old Count House

★★★★ GUEST HOUSE

1 Trenwith Square TR26 1DQ
☎ 01736 795369 📄 01736 799109
e-mail: counthouse@btconnect.com
web: www.theoldcounthouse-stives.co.uk
dir: *Follow signs to St Ives, house between leisure centre & school*

Situated in a quiet residential area with on-site parking, the Old Count House is a granite stone house, where mine workers collected their wages in Victorian times. Guests are assured of a warm welcome and an extensive choice at breakfast. Bedrooms vary in size, with all rooms being

well equipped. The town centre and all its restaurants is only a five minute walk away.

The Old Count House

Rooms 10 en suite (2 GF) S £38-£42; D £72-£88* **Facilities** TVL tea/coffee Cen ht Sauna **Parking** 9 **Notes** ⊗ No Children Closed 20-29 Dec

Old Vicarage

★★★★ GUEST HOUSE

Parc-an-Creet TR26 2ES
☎ 01736 796124
e-mail: stay@oldvicarage.com
web: www.oldvicarage.com
dir: *Off A3074 in town centre onto B3306, 0.5m right into Parc-an-Creet*

This former Victorian rectory stands in secluded gardens in a quiet part of St Ives and is convenient for the seaside, town and the Tate. The bedrooms are enhanced by modern facilities. A good choice of local produce is offered at breakfast, plus home-made yoghurt and preserves.

Rooms 5 en suite (4 fmly) S £60-£65; D £80-£90* **Facilities** TVL tea/coffee Cen ht Licensed ♿ **Parking** 12 **Notes** Closed Dec-Jan Civ Wed 40

The Regent

★★★★ GUEST ACCOMMODATION

Fernlea Ter TR26 2BH
☎ 01736 796195 📄 01736 794641
e-mail: keith@regenthotel.com
web: www.regenthotel.com
dir: *In town centre, near bus & railway station*

This popular and attractive property stands on an elevated position convenient for the town centre and seafront. The Regent has well-equipped bedrooms, some with spectacular sea vistas, and the comfortable lounge also has great views. The breakfast choices, including vegetarian, are excellent.

Rooms 10 rms (8 en suite) (1 fmly) S £35-£48; D £73-£98* **Facilities** TVL tea/coffee Cen ht Wi-fi **Parking** 12 **Notes** LB ⊗ No Children 16yrs

ST IVES *continued*

Rivendell Guest House

★★★ GUEST HOUSE

7 Porthminster Ter TR26 2DQ
☎ 01736 794923 📄 01736 794923
e-mail: rivendellstives@aol.com
web: www.rivendell-stives.co.uk
dir: *A3074 to St Ives, left at junct, left again & up hill,
over road, 50yds on right*

Just a short walk from the town centre and harbour, this
friendly and welcoming establishment has much to offer
those visiting this lovely area. Bedrooms are all well
appointed with contemporary comforts; some also have
the benefit of sea views. Breakfast and dinner (by prior
arrangement) are served in the attractive dining room
which leads through to the guest lounge.

Rooms 7 rms (6 en suite) (1 pri facs) S £28-£34;
D £60-£80* **Facilities** FTV TVL tea/coffee Dinner available
Cen ht Wi-fi **Parking** 5 **Notes** LB ⊗ Closed 23-26 Dec

The Rookery

★★★★ GUEST ACCOMMODATION

8 The Terrrace TR26 2BL
☎ 01736 799401
e-mail: therookerystives@hotmail.com
dir: *A3074 through Carbis Bay, right fork at Porthminster
Hotel, The Rookery 500yds on left*

This friendly establishment stands on an elevated
position overlooking the town and sandy beach. The
attractive bedrooms include one on the ground floor and a
luxurious suite, all of which are well equipped and offer a
good level of comfort. Breakfast is served in the first-floor
dining room at separate tables.

Rooms 7 en suite (1 GF) S £35-£45; D £60-£90*
Facilities FTV tea/coffee Cen ht Wi-fi **Parking** 7 **Notes** ⊗
No Children 7yrs

St Dennis

★★★★ 🏠 BED AND BREAKFAST

6 Albany Ter TR26 2BS
☎ 01736 795027
e-mail: stdennis007@btopenworld.com
dir: *A3074 to St Ives, pass St Ives Motor Co on right,
continue down hill, Albany Ter 1st left, signed Edward
Hain Hospital*

St Dennis is a friendly and comfortable place to stay
within walking distance of the town and beaches.
Breakfast is a real treat with an emphasis upon excellent
local organic produce. The comprehensive menu includes
plenty of variety for both meat eaters and vegetarians
with lighter, healthier options also offered. Bedrooms are
attractively decorated and have many thoughtful touches.
Ample parking is available.

Rooms 3 en suite; D £66-£88 **Facilities** FTV tea/coffee
Cen ht **Parking** 5 **Notes** ⊗ No Children 12yrs Closed Nov-
Feb

Thurlestone Guest House

★★★★ GUEST ACCOMMODATION

St Ives Rd, Carbis Bay TR26 2RT
☎ 01736 796369
e-mail: mandycartwright@btopenworld.com
dir: *A3074 to Carbis Bay, pass convenience store on left,
0.25m on left next to newsagent*

The granite chapel built in 1843 now offers stylish,
comfortable accommodation. The welcoming proprietors
provide a relaxed environment, and many guests return
regularly. Recently totally upgraded, there is a cosy
lounge bar, and some of the well-equipped bedrooms
have sea views.

Rooms 7 en suite (1 fmly) (1 GF) **Facilities** TVL tea/coffee
Cen ht Licensed **Parking** 5 **Notes** ⊗

The Tregorran

★★★★ GUEST ACCOMMODATION

Headland Rd, Carbis Bay TR26 2NU
☎ 01736 795889
e-mail: book@carbisbay.com
web: www.carbisbay.com
dir: *Right at Carbis Bay to beach, along Porthrepta Rd,
last right onto Headland Rd, Tregorran halfway along*

There are wonderful views of Carbis Bay and St Ives from
the friendly, family-run Tregorran. Relax by the pool, in
the garden or in the pleasant bar, and there is also a
comfortable lounge, and a games room and a gym.
Breakfast is served in an airy dining room, which has
superb views.

Rooms 18 en suite (5 fmly) (4 GF) S £36-£50;
D £74-£100 **Facilities** FTV TVL tea/coffee Cen ht Licensed
🏋 Gymnasium Pool Table **Parking** 20 **Notes** LB Closed
Nov-Etr

Wheal-e-Mine Bed & Breakfast

★★★★ BED AND BREAKFAST

9 Belmont Ter TR26 1DZ
☎ 01736 795051 📄 01736 795051
e-mail: whealemine@btinternet.com
web: www.whealemine.co.uk
dir: *A3074 into town, left at x-rds onto B3306, right at
rdbt, left at top of hill*

Guests are assured of a warm, friendly welcome at this
Victorian, terraced property, which over the last few years
has been fully upgraded with style and flair. Bedrooms
are well appointed and each boasts distant sea views. A
hearty breakfast is served each morning in the attractive
dining room. On-site parking at the rear of the property is
an added bonus.

Rooms 3 rms (2 en suite) (1 pri facs) D £60-£76*
Facilities FTV tea/coffee Cen ht **Parking** 3 **Notes** LB ⊗
No Children 18yrs Closed Nov-Mar ✉

The Woodside

★★★★ GUEST ACCOMMODATION

The Belyars TR26 2DA
☎ 01736 795681
e-mail: woodsidehotel@btconnect.com
dir: *A3074 to St Ives, left at Porthminster Hotel onto
Talland Rd, 1st left onto Belyars Ln, Woodside 4th on
right*

This attractive house is in a peaceful location overlooking
St Ives Bay. The friendly proprietors provide a welcoming
and relaxing environment, and the bedrooms, some with
sea views, come in a range of sizes. Hearty breakfasts are
served in the dining room, and there is a comfortable
lounge and a well-stocked bar.

Rooms 10 en suite (3 fmly) S £40-£55; D £80-£120*
Facilities FTV TVL tea/coffee Cen ht Licensed 🏋 Pool
Table **Parking** 12 **Notes** LB ⊗ No Children 5yrs

Atlantic

★★★ GUEST ACCOMMODATION

8 Atlantic Ter TR26 1JQ
☎ 01736 793957
e-mail: mail@atlantichouse.org.uk
dir: *In town centre via A3306 Fore St*

Situated on the hill above Tate St Ives, the Atlantic has
sea views from all rooms. The property is beside a car
park and within walking distance of the town's beaches.
Bedrooms are well equipped, and a hearty breakfast
featuring home-made bread is served in the pleasant
front dining room around two large tables.

Rooms 3 en suite **Facilities** tea/coffee Cen ht **Notes** ⊗
✉

The Hollies

★★★ GUEST ACCOMMODATION

4 Talland Rd TR26 2DF
☎ 01736 796605 & 793495
e-mail: theholliesstives@aol.com
dir: *A3074 to St Ives, left at Porthminster Hotel, 500yds bear left, bear left again, 3rd property on right*

The Hollies has an elevated position with fine views, and is within easy walking distance of the town and harbour. Some of the homely bedrooms have sea views, and families are particularly welcome. A hearty breakfast is served in the pleasant dining room.

Rooms 10 en suite (4 fmly) S £40-£76; D £60-£90*
Facilities FTV TVL tea/coffee Cen ht **Parking** 10 **Notes** LB
⊗ No Children 3yrs Closed Xmas

Horizon

★★★ GUEST ACCOMMODATION

5 Carthew Ter TR26 1EB
☎ 01736 798069

With an elevated position, this family home affords pleasant sea views and is within walking distance of the town centre and beaches. The host welcomes guests as friends and creates a most homely atmosphere. Some of the attractive bedrooms have wonderful views, and there is a comfortable lounge. A traditional English cooked breakfast is served around a communal table. Dinner is available by prior arrangement and is house-party style.

Rooms 3 en suite **Facilities** TVL Dinner available Cen ht
Parking 2 **Notes** ⊗ No Children Closed Nov-Apr ⊜

Penlee International Guest House

★★★ GUEST ACCOMMODATION

St Ives Rd, Carbis Bay TR26 2SX
☎ 01736 795497
e-mail: enquiries@penleeinternational.co.uk
dir: *A30 onto A3074, 75yds after Carbis Bay sign left onto Polmennor Dr, 1st left into car park*

Situated in Carbis Bay, with distant coastal views, Penlee International is a small friendly establishment. In the comfortable bedrooms, the best possible use has been made of the available space. Guests can relax and spend enjoyable evenings in the cosy bar, with its pool table and 42 inch widescreen TV.

Rooms 8 en suite (3 fmly) **Facilities** FTV TVL tea/coffee
Cen ht Licensed **Parking** 6 **Notes** LB ⊗

Portarlington

★★★ GUEST ACCOMMODATION

11 Parc Bean TR26 1EA
☎ 01736 797278 📠 01736 797278
e-mail: info@portarlington.co.uk
web: www.portarlington.co.uk

This pleasant home is convenient for the town, beaches and Tate St Ives. The friendly proprietors have long welcomed guests to their home and many return regularly. Bedrooms are well furnished and some have sea views. There is a comfortable lounge, and enjoyable breakfasts are served in the attractive dining room.

Rooms 4 en suite (3 fmly); D £60-£64* **Facilities** FTV TVL
tea/coffee Cen ht **Parking** 4 **Notes** LB ⊗ No Children 3yrs
Closed Nov-Jan ⊜

Porthminster View

★★★ GUEST ACCOMMODATION

13 Draycott Ter TR26 2EF
☎ 01736 795850 📠 01736 796811
e-mail: enquiry@porthminster.com
web: www.porthminster.com
dir: *A3074 entering town, 300yds past Ford station right onto Draycott Ter*

Built around 1896, this relaxed, family-friendly establishment was formerly home to the local stationmaster. It stands high above Porthminster Beach and has spectacular views. The bedrooms are thoughtfully equipped. Guests can use a well-appointed lounge, which has many books and videos. The portions at breakfast are generous.

Rooms 6 en suite (1 fmly) **Facilities** TVL tea/coffee Cen ht
Parking 1 **Notes** ⊗ No Children 11yrs

St Margaret's Guest House

★★★ GUEST HOUSE

3 Parc Av TR26 2DN
☎ 01736 795785
e-mail: btrevena@aol.com
web: www.stmargaretsguesthouse.co.uk
dir: *A3074 to town centre, left onto Gabriel St & The Stennack, left onto Parc Av*

Guests feel comfortable at St Margaret's, with its panoramic views of the town and bay, and just a short walk from the sandy beaches. Breakfast is served in a pleasant dining room and dinner is available by arrangement.

Rooms 4 en suite (1 fmly) **Facilities** tea/coffee Dinner
available **Parking** 3

Skidden House

★★★ GUEST ACCOMMODATION

Skidden Hill TR26 2DU
☎ 01736 796899
e-mail: skiddenhouse@tiscali.co.uk
web: www.skiddenhouse.co.uk
dir: *A3074 to St Ives, 1st right after bus/railway station*

Skidden House is in the heart of town and is reputed to have formerly been a jail, brothel and a pub, as well as St Ives' oldest hotel. The accommodation is now much more comfortable and welcoming, with pleasant, well-equipped rooms. Some parking is available.

Rooms 7 en suite (3 fmly) (2 GF) S £35-£42; D £70-£84*
Facilities TVL tea/coffee Direct Dial Cen ht Licensed
Parking 4 **Notes** LB ⊗

Sloop

★★★ INN

The Wharf TR26 1LP
☎ 01736 796584 📠 01736 793322
e-mail: sloopinn@btinternet.com
web: www.sloop-inn.co.uk
dir: *On St Ives harbour by middle slipway*

This attractive, historic inn has an imposing position on the harbour. Each of the guest rooms has a nautical name, many with pleasant views, and all have impressive modern facilities. A good choice of dishes is offered at lunch and dinner in the atmospheric restaurant-bar.

Rooms 18 rms (15 en suite) (6 fmly) (2 GF) (5 smoking)
Facilities FTV tea/coffee Dinner available Cen ht Wi-fi
Parking 6 **Notes** No coaches

ST JUST (NEAR LAND'S END)   Map 2 SW33

The Wellington

★★ INN

Market Square TR19 7HD
☎ 01736 787319 ▤ 01736 787906
e-mail: wellingtonhotel@msn.com
dir: 6m W of Penzance

This friendly inn, situated in busy Market Square, offers comfortable accommodation and is popular with locals and visitors alike. Bedrooms are spacious and well equipped. Home-cooked food and local ales from the well-stocked bar make for a pleasant stay.

Rooms 5 en suite 6 annexe en suite (4 fmly) (3 GF) S £40; D £60–£75* **Facilities** tea/coffee Dinner available Direct Dial Cen ht Pool Table **Conf** Max 20fred **Notes** LB

ST KEVERNE   Map 2 SW72

Gallen-Treath Guest House

★★★ GUEST HOUSE

Porthallow TR12 6PL
☎ 01326 280400 ▤ 01326 280400
e-mail: gallentreath@btclick.com
dir: 1.5m S of St Keverne in Porthallow

Gallen-Treath has super views over the countryside and sea from its elevated position above Porthallow. Bedrooms are individually decorated and feature many personal touches. Guests can relax in the large, comfortable lounge complete with balcony. Hearty breakfasts and dinners (by arrangement) are served in the bright dining room.

Rooms 5 rms (4 en suite) (1 pri facs) (1 fmly) (1 GF) S £25–£32; D £50–£64* **Facilities** FTV TVL tea/coffee Dinner available Cen ht Licensed **Parking** 6

ST MAWGAN   Map 2 SW86

The Falcon Inn

★★★★ INN

TR8 4EP
☎ 01637 860225 ▤ 01637 860884
e-mail: info@thefalconinn-stmawgan.co.uk
dir: A30 towards Newquay airport, follow signs for St Mawgan

Traditional village pub serving good food and drink along with two well presented and comfortable en suite bedrooms. Pleasant atmosphere, friendly owners and staff and a quiet location with plenty of off-street parking make this a popular venue. The pub is closed between 3-6pm, access for accommodation can be arranged outside of these times.

Rooms 2 en suite **Facilities** STV FTV tea/coffee Dinner available Direct Dial Cen ht Wi-fi Pool Table **Parking** 20 **Notes** Closed 25 Dec RS 24 Dec No B&B available No coaches

SALTASH   Map 3 SX45

Smeaton Farm *(SX387634)*

★★★★ 🏠 🍴 FARMHOUSE

PL12 6RZ
☎ 01579 351833 ▤ 01579 351833   Mr & Mrs Jones
e-mail: info@smeatonfarm.co.uk
web: www.smeatonfarm.co.uk
dir: 1m N of Hatt & 1m S of St Mellion just off A388

This elegant Georgian farmhouse is surrounded by 450 acres of rolling Cornish farmland, providing a wonderfully peaceful place to stay. Home to the Jones family, the atmosphere is relaxed and hospitable, with every effort made to ensure a comfortable and rewarding break. Bedrooms are spacious, light and airy. Enjoyable dinners often feature home-reared meats and the sausages at breakfast come highly recommended.

Rooms 3 en suite (1 fmly) S £45–£50; D £60–£80* **Facilities** FTV TVL tea/coffee Dinner available Cen ht Licensed Wi-fi Riding Cornish maze, guided farm tours **Parking** 8 **Notes** LB ⊗ 450 acres arable/beef/sheep/organic

Crooked Inn

★★★ GUEST ACCOMMODATION

Stoketon Cross, Trematon PL12 4RZ
☎ 01752 848177 ▤ 01752 843203
e-mail: info@crooked-inn.co.uk
dir: 1.5m NW of Saltash. A38 W from Saltash, 2nd left to Trematon, sharp right

The friendly animals that freely roam the courtyard add to the relaxed country style of this delightful inn. The spacious bedrooms are well equipped, and freshly cooked dinners are available in the bar and conservatory. Breakfast is served in the cottage-style dining room.

Rooms 18 annexe rms 15 annexe en suite (5 fmly) (7 GF) **Facilities** tea/coffee Dinner available Cen ht Licensed 🎣 Please telephone for details **Conf** Max 60 **Parking** 45 **Notes** Closed 25 Dec

See advert on opposite page

The Holland Inn

★★★ INN

Callington Rd, Hatt PL12 6PJ
☎ 01752 844044 ▤ 01752 849701
e-mail: hollandinn@myopal.net
web: www.hollandinn.co.uk
dir: 2m NW of Saltash on A388

This popular country inn provides spacious and comfortable accommodation in countryside near the A38. The attractive bedrooms are in an annexe. The wide choice for lunch and dinner includes a carvery, and a good selection of ales and wines is available at the bar.

Rooms 30 en suite (5 fmly) (30 GF) (11 smoking) S £52.50–£57.50; D £60–£65* **Facilities** FTV tea/coffee Dinner available Direct Dial Cen ht Wi-fi Pool Table 9 hole crazy golf **Conf** Max 50 Thtr 50 Class 50 **Parking** 30 **Notes** LB ⊗ Civ Wed 50

SCILLY, ISLES OF

ST MARY'S   Map 2 SV91

Crebinick House

★★★★ GUEST HOUSE

Church St TR21 0JT
☎ 01720 422968
e-mail: aa@crebinick.co.uk
web: www.crebinick.co.uk
dir: House 500yds from quay through Hugh Town; (airport bus to house)

Many guests return time and again to this friendly, family-run house close to the town centre and the seafront. The granite-built property dates from 1760 and has smart, well equipped bedrooms; two are on the ground floor. There is a quiet lounge for relaxing.

Rooms 6 en suite (2 GF); D £74–£90* **Facilities** FTV TVL tea/coffee Cen ht **Notes** ⊗ No Children 10yrs Closed Nov-Mar ▨

TRESCO   Map 2 SV81

New Inn

★★★★ 🏮 INN

TR24 0QQ
☎ 01720 422844 & 423006 ▤ 01720 423200
e-mail: newinn@tresco.co.uk
web: www.tresco.co.uk
dir: By New Grimsby Quay

This friendly, popular inn is located at the island's centre point and offers bright, attractive and well-equipped bedrooms, many with splendid sea views. Guests have an extensive choice from the menu at both lunch and dinner and can also choose where they take their meals - either in the airy bistro-style Pavilion, the popular bar which serves real ales, or the elegant restaurant. A heated outdoor pool is also available.

Rooms 16 rms (15 en suite) (2 GF) S £70-£172; D £140-£230* **Facilities** Dinner available Wi-fi 🛁 **Notes** ⊗

SENNEN
Map 2 SW32

Mayon Farmhouse

★★★★ BED AND BREAKFAST

TR19 7AD
☎ 01736 871757
e-mail: mayonfarmhouse@hotmail.co.uk
web: www.mayonfarmhouse.co.uk
dir: A30 into Sennen, driveway opp Post Office

Guests receive a genuine welcome and a cream tea at this 19th-century, granite former farmhouse. About one mile from Land's End, and conveniently situated for visiting the Minack Theatre, it has country and distant coastal views. The attractive bedrooms are comfortable and well equipped, and an imaginative choice is offered at breakfast.

Rooms 4 rms (3 en suite) (1 pri facs) (1 fmly) S £50; D £80-£90 **Facilities** FTV TVL tea/coffee Cen ht Wi-fi **Parking** 30 **Notes** LB ⊗ No Children 8yrs

TINTAGEL
Map 2 SX08

Pendrin House

★★★★ GUEST HOUSE

Atlantic Rd PL34 0DE
☎ 01840 770560
e-mail: info@pendrintintagel.co.uk
dir: Through village, pass entrance to Tintagel Castle, last house on right before Headlands Caravan Park

Located close to coastal walks, castle and the town centre, this Victorian house provides comfortable accommodation with most rooms having sea or country views. Delicious evening meals, using quality fresh ingredients, are available by arrangement. There is a cosy lounge.

Rooms 9 rms (5 en suite) (4 pri facs) (1 fmly) S £28-£32; D £55-£65* **Facilities** FTV TVL tea/coffee Cen ht **Parking** 6 **Notes** ⊗ No Children 12yrs

The Bluff Centre

★★★★ 🅰 GUEST HOUSE

Treknow PL34 0EP
☎ 01840 770033 & 770920 📠 01840 770033
e-mail: book@bluffcentre.co.uk
web: www.bluffcentre.co.uk
dir: A39 take B3314 over x-rds, right onto B3263 to Tintagel, left into Treknow

Rooms 8 rms (5 pri facs) (1 fmly) (5 GF) S £33; D £66* **Facilities** FTV TVL tea/coffee Dinner available Cen ht Licensed Wi-fi Games room & library **Conf** Max 20 **Parking** 6 **Notes** LB ⊗ Closed 22 Dec-3 Jan

The Cottage Teashop

★★★★ 🅰 BED AND BREAKFAST

Bossiney Rd PL34 0AH
☎ 01840 770639
dir: Off A30, 2m past Launceston junct onto A395. Follow signs to Camelford then Tintagel

Rooms 3 en suite 1 annexe en suite (1 GF) D £50-£60* **Facilities** FTV tea/coffee Cen ht **Parking** 4 **Notes** LB No Children 12yrs Closed 24-26 Dec

Tregosse House

★★★ BED AND BREAKFAST

Treknow PL34 0EP
☎ 01840 779230
e-mail: enquiries@tregossehouse.co.uk
web: www.tregossehouse.co.uk
dir: A30 onto A395 to Tintagel, signed Treknow. At Atlantic View Hotel bear right, 0.5m on right

Surrounded by open farmland, Tregosse House boasts probably one of the best views of the sea in North Cornwall. This family home, which has undergone extensive upgrading over the last few years, welcomes guests throughout the year, and offers a hearty, freshly cooked breakfast served at separate tables.

Rooms 3 en suite S £40-£45; D £60-£64* **Facilities** FTV tea/coffee Cen ht **Parking** 1 **Notes** LB ⊗ No Children 14yrs

CROOKED INN

Pets & Children Welcome

TREMATON SALTASH CORNWALL

TEL: 01752 848177 and ask for Tony or Sandra or FAX: 01752 843203

Swimming Pool available for Guests

AA
★★★

Our luxury en-suite accommodation is available all seasons. Extensive menu of home cooked food: many traditional ales. Set in 10 acres of lawns and woodland overlooking the beautiful Lyner Valley, yet only 15 minutes from Plymouth City centre. We have vast play areas for children and many unusual family pets.

Bulland House B&B

★★★★ BED AND BREAKFAST

Nr Antony PL11 2PE
☎ 01752 813823
e-mail: info@averywarmwelcome.co.uk
dir: 2.3m from Torpoint ferry heading E on A364; from W, 1m from Antony on A364

Well situated for Tor Point and National Trust's Antony House and within easy reach of Plymouth, this establishment offers comfortable rooms, friendly hospitality and a peaceful location. The freshly cooked breakfast includes a range of organic produce and is served at a large table in the breakfast room.

Rooms 2 rms (1 en suite) (1 pri facs) S fr £45; D fr £70*
Facilities TVL tea/coffee Cen ht Wi-fi **Parking** 6 **Notes** ⊗ ⊛

Bissick Old Mill

★★★★ GUEST HOUSE

Ladock TR2 4PG
☎ 01726 882557
e-mail: enquiries@bissickoldmill.plus.com
dir: 6m NE of Truro. Off B3275 in Ladock village centre by Falmouth Arms pub

This charming, family-run mill dates back some 300 years. Low ceilings, beams, stone walls and an impressive fireplace all contribute to its character. Equally inviting is the hospitality extended to guests, who are instantly made welcome. The breakfast menu offers a range of hot dishes, is freshly prepared and is a memorable aspect of any stay.

Rooms 3 en suite 1 annexe en suite (1 fmly) (1 GF) S £52-£60; D £70-£90 **Facilities** FTV TVL tea/coffee Direct Dial Cen ht Wi-fi **Parking** 6 **Notes** LB ⊗

The Haven

★★★★ BED AND BREAKFAST

Truro Vean Ter TR1 1HA
☎ 01872 264197
e-mail: thehaven7@btinternet.com
dir: Entering Truro from A39 or A390, right at 1st rdbt, through 2 sets of lights, next right then immediately left. On left (no through road)

A recently refurbished and extended property within a few minutes walk of the city centre with off-street parking and views of the cathedral. The owners are very friendly, rooms are bright and well furnished, beds are very comfortable and bathrooms very well equipped. Freshly cooked hearty breakfasts are served at a large table in the separate breakfast room.

Rooms 3 rms (2 en suite) (1 pri facs) (3 GF) D £62-£68*
Facilities FTV tea/coffee Cen ht Wi-fi **Parking** 3 **Notes** ⊗ No Children 7yrs Closed 20 Dec-4 Jan ⊛

Manor Cottage

★★★★ GUEST ACCOMMODATION

Tresillian TR2 4BN
☎ 01872 520212
e-mail: manorcottage@live.co.uk
dir: 3m E of Truro on A390, on left opp river

Located just a few minutes drive from Truro this well-run establishment is friendly and comfortable. Breakfast is served in the conservatory and dinner is available with prior notice.

Rooms 5 rms (2 en suite) (1 pri facs) (1 fmly) S £32-£39; D £58-£74* **Facilities** tea/coffee Dinner available Licensed Wi-fi **Parking** 8 **Notes** LB ⊗

Oxturn House

★★★★ BED AND BREAKFAST

Ladock TR2 4NQ
☎ 01726 884348
e-mail: oxturnhouse@hotmail.com
web: www.oxturnhouse.co.uk
dir: 6m NE of Truro. B3275 into Ladock, onto lane opp Falmouth Arms, up hill 200yds, 1st right after end 30mph sign, Oxturn on right

A friendly welcome is assured at this large family house, set slightly above the village and close to a pub and several dining venues. Bedrooms are spacious and a pleasant lounge is available. In summer you can enjoy the country views from the patio. Hearty breakfasts are served in the dining room.

Rooms 2 rms (1 en suite) (1 pri facs); D £58-£70*
Facilities TVL tea/coffee Cen ht Wi-fi **Parking** 4 **Notes** ⊗ No Children 12yrs Closed Dec-Jan ⊛

The Whitehouse Inn & Luxury Lodge

★★★★ INN

Penhallow TR4 9LQ
☎ 01872 573306 📠 01872 572062
e-mail: whitehouseinn@btconnect.com
web: www.whitehousecornwall.co.uk
dir: A3075 between Newquay & Redruth

This popular inn now offers recently constructed, very well appointed bedrooms. Conveniently located mid-way between Truro and Newquay, the Whitehouse Inn has a busy bar and restaurant, appealing to all palates and pockets. In addition to the local and international artists performing at weekends, widescreen TVs, pool tables and both indoor and outdoor children's play areas are provided. A wide range of meals is available, including the carvery which offers great value for money.

Rooms 12 en suite (3 fmly) (6 GF) S £48-£55; D £65-£75* **Facilities** FTV tea/coffee Dinner available Direct Dial Cen ht Lift Wi-fi Golf 9 Pool Table Go-Karts Crazy golf **Parking** 200 **Notes** ⊗

Spires

★★★ BED AND BREAKFAST

45 Treyew Rd TR1 2BY
☎ 01872 277621
dir: 0.5m W of town centre on A39, opp Truro City Football Club

This comfortable establishment enjoys a homely atmosphere and friendly host. The city centre is just a short drive away, or a walk for the more energetic (downhill there, uphill back). Bedrooms are light and airy; one room is spacious and has a splendid view of the city and cathedral. Breakfast is served in the cosy dining room. The nearby pub-restaurant offers an extensive choice of meals.

Rooms 2 rms (1 en suite) (1 pri facs) (1 fmly) S £35-£40; D £58-£60* **Facilities** FTV tea/coffee Cen ht Wi-fi **Parking** 2 **Notes** ⊗ ⊛

Cliftons

★★★ GUEST ACCOMMODATION

46 Tregolls Rd TR1 1LA
☎ 01872 274116 📠 01872 274116
e-mail: cliftonsbandb@hotmail.com
dir: 0.5m NE of city centre on A390

This lovely Victorian property has character, provides a relaxed atmosphere and is within walking distance of the city centre. Bedrooms, including one on the ground floor, have considerate extras. There is a lounge for guests, with a large tropical fish tank. The breakfast menu offers a good choice of dishes in the bright dining room.

Rooms 6 en suite (1 fmly) (1 GF) S £40-£43; D £60-£63* **Facilities** TVL tea/coffee Cen ht **Parking** 6 **Notes** ⊗

Coronation Guest House

★★★ BED AND BREAKFAST

2 Coronation Ter TR1 3HJ
☎ 01872 274514
e-mail: theterracecornwall@hotmail.co.uk
dir: Opp railway station

Located just a short distance from the city centre and close to the railway station, this Victorian accommodation is attentively cared for. Bedrooms, although not spacious, are clean and bright. A freshly prepared traditional English breakfast is taken in the pleasant dining room at the rear of the house.

Rooms 3 rms S fr £30; D fr £60* **Facilities** FTV tea/coffee Cen ht **Notes** ⊗ No Children 8yrs ⊛

Donnington Guest House

★★★ GUEST ACCOMMODATION

43 Treyew Rd TR1 2BY
☎ 01872 222552
e-mail: info@donnington-guesthouse.co.uk

A well located property within 12 minutes walk of the city centre. It is actually two houses operating as one, with breakfast being taken in the breakfast room of one of them. Well-appointed rooms, a friendly host and good off-road parking make this a very popular venue.

Rooms 14 rms (12 en suite) (2 pri facs) (5 fmly) (3 GF) S £30-£35; D £60-£65* **Facilities** FTV tea/coffee Cen ht Lift Wi-fi **Parking** 11

Polsue Manor Farm (SW858462)

★★★ FARMHOUSE

Tresillian TR2 4BP
☎ 01872 520234 📠 01872 520616 Mrs G Holliday
e-mail: geraldineholliday@hotmail.com
dir: 2m NE of Truro. Farm entrance on A390 at S end of Tresillian

The 190-acre sheep farm is in peaceful countryside a short drive from Truro. The farmhouse provides a relaxing break from the city, with hearty breakfasts and warm hospitality. The spacious dining room has pleasant views and three large communal tables. Bedrooms do not offer televisions but there is a homely lounge equipped with a television and video recorder with a selection of videos for viewing.

Rooms 5 rms (2 en suite) (3 fmly) (1 GF) S £30-£35; D £54-£58* **Facilities** TVL tea/coffee **Parking** 5 **Notes** LB Closed 21 Dec-2 Jan 190 acres mixed/sheep/horses/working

Resparveth Farm (SW914499)

★★★ FARMHOUSE

Grampound Rd TR2 4EF
☎ 01726 882382 📠 01726 882382 Ms Lisa Willey
e-mail: lisawilley83@hotmail.com

New, young owners of this traditional farmhouse bed and breakfast do all they can to make your stay as comfortable as possible. Handy location for St Austell, the Eden Project and Truro, offering comfortable rooms and freshly cooked breakfasts at one large table in the breakfast room featuring an original Cornish Range.

Rooms 3 en suite S £42; D £56* **Facilities** TVL tea/coffee Cen ht **Parking** 4 **Notes** 65 acres

The Bay Tree

★★ GUEST ACCOMMODATION

28 Ferris Town TR1 3JH
☎ 01872 240274

A well established friendly property within a few minutes walk of the railway station and the city centre. Rooms are comfortable and have shared facilities, and breakfast is served at large tables in the dining room.

Rooms 4 rms (1 fmly) S £35; D £55* **Facilities** STV FTV tea/coffee Direct Dial Cen ht Wi-fi **Notes** ⊛

VERYAN   Map 2 SW93

Elerkey Guest House

★★★★ GUEST HOUSE

Elerkey House TR2 5QA
☎ 01872 501261 & 501160 📠 01872 501354
e-mail: enquiries@elerkey.co.uk
web: www.elerkey.co.uk
dir: In village, 1st left after church & water gardens

This peaceful home is surrounded by attractive gardens in a tranquil village. The proprietors and their family provide exemplary hospitality and many guests return time and again. The pleasantly appointed bedrooms have many considerate extras.

Rooms 4 en suite (1 fmly) S £45-£70; D £60-£70* **Facilities** tea/coffee Direct Dial Cen ht Art gallery & gift shop **Parking** 4 **Notes** LB ⊗ Closed Dec-Feb

---

ZENNOR   Map 2 SW43

The Gurnard's Head

★★★ ◎◎ INN

Treen TR26 3DE
☎ 01736 796928
e-mail: enquiries@gurnardshead.co.uk
dir: 5m from St Ives on B3306, 4.5m from Penzance via New Mill

Ideally located for enjoying the beautiful coastline, this inn offers atmospheric public areas. The style is relaxed and very popular with walkers, keen to rest their weary legs. A log fire in the bar provides a warm welcome on colder days and on warmer days, outside seating is available. Lunch and dinner, featuring local home-cooked food, is available either in the bar or the adjoining restaurant area. The dinner menu is not extensive but there are interesting choices and everything is home-made, including the bread. Breakfast is served around a grand farmhouse table.

Rooms 7 en suite S £65-£75; D £85-£150* **Facilities** tea/coffee Dinner available Wi-fi **Parking** 40 **Notes** Closed 25 Dec & 4 days mid Jan No coaches

---

CUMBRIA

ALSTON   Map 18 NY74

See also Cowshill (Co Durham)

Lowbyer Manor Country House

★★★★ GUEST HOUSE

Hexham Rd CA9 3JX
☎ 01434 381230 📠 01434 381425
e-mail: stay@lowbyer.com
web: www.lowbyer.com
dir: 250yds N of village centre on A686. Pass South Tynedale Railway on left, turn right

Located on the edge of the village, this Grade II listed Georgian building retains many original features, which are highlighted by the furnishings and decor. Cosy bedrooms are filled with a wealth of thoughtful extras and day rooms include an elegant dining room, a comfortable lounge and bar equipped with lots of historical artefacts.

Rooms 9 en suite (1 fmly) S £33-£55; D £66-£80 **Facilities** tea/coffee Cen ht Licensed **Parking** 9 **Notes** LB

ALSTON *continued*

Nent Hall Country House

★★★ GUEST ACCOMMODATION

CA9 3LQ
☎ 01434 381584 📠 01434 382668
e-mail: info@nenthall.com
web: www.nenthall.com
dir: *From A1 junct 58 onto A68, then A689. Nent Hall 2m beyond Nenthead*

Enthusiastic new owners have considerably upgraded this delightful old house that stands in well-kept gardens. Warm and friendly hospitality is provided, with well-appointed and comfortable accommodation, some rooms being on the ground floor and others being suitable for families. There are two comfortable lounges and a pleasant bar serving meals and light snacks as well as a more formal dining room.

Rooms 18 en suite (2 fmly) (9 GF); D £69-£159*
Facilities TVL tea/coffee Dinner available Direct Dial Cen ht Licensed Wi-fi DVD library Conf Max 200
Parking 100 Notes ⊗ Civ Wed 200

AMBLESIDE — Map 18 NY30

PREMIER COLLECTION

Drunken Duck
★★★★★ ◉◉ INN

Barngates LA22 0NG
☎ 015394 36347 📠 015394 36781
e-mail: info@drunkenduckinn.co.uk
web: www.drunkenduckinn.co.uk
dir: *B5285, S from Ambleside towards Hawkshead, 2.5m signed right, 0.5m up hill*

This 400-year-old, traditional coaching inn has been stylishly modernised to offer a high standard of accommodation. Superior rooms are in a courtyard house looking out over private gardens and a tarn. The bar retains its original character and is the hub of the inn. Fresh, local produce features on the imaginative menus served there and in the cosy restaurant. The on-site brewery ensures a fine selection of award-winning ales.

Rooms 8 en suite 9 annexe en suite (5 GF) S £90-£275; D £90-£275* Facilities FTV Dinner available Direct Dial Cen ht Wi-fi Fishing Parking 40 Notes ⊗ Closed 25 Dec No coaches

The Fisherbeck

★★★★ 🏠 GUEST ACCOMMODATION

Lake Rd LA22 0DH
☎ 015394 33215 📠 015394 33600
e-mail: email@fisherbeckhotel.co.uk
web: www.fisherbeckhotel.co.uk

Set on the southern approach to the town, this well-presented and friendly establishment offers a high standard of accommodation. Many of the spacious, modern bedrooms have fine views. There is a choice of lounges, where refreshments are served, and the split-level breakfast room provides many interesting dishes.

Rooms 18 en suite (2 fmly) (4 GF) S £41-£49; D £72-£130* Facilities TVL tea/coffee Direct Dial Cen ht Licensed Wi-fi Use of nearby leisure club, free fishing available Conf Max 20 Class 20 Board 20 Parking 20 Notes LB ⊗ Closed 24 Dec-24 Jan

Riverside

★★★★ GUEST HOUSE

Under Loughrigg LA22 9LJ
☎ 015394 32395 📠 015394 32440
e-mail: info@riverside-at-ambleside.co.uk
web: www.riverside-at-ambleside.co.uk
dir: *A593 from Ambleside to Coniston, over stone bridge, right onto Under Loughrigg Ln, Riverside 150yds left*

A friendly atmosphere prevails at this refurbished Victorian house, situated on a quiet lane by the River Rothay, below Loughrigg Fell. Bedrooms, all with lovely views, are very comfortable, stylishly furnished and feature homely extras; some have spa baths. A log-burning stove warms the lounge in winter. Guests can use the garden, which has seating for morning and evening sun.

Rooms 6 en suite (1 fmly) Facilities TVL tea/coffee Cen ht Licensed Fishing Jacuzzi Parking 15 Notes ⊗ No Children 5yrs Closed Xmas & New Year

Wateredge Inn

★★★★ INN

Waterhead Bay LA22 0EP
☎ 015394 32332 📠 015394 31878
e-mail: rec@wateredgeinn.co.uk
web: www.wateredgeinn.co.uk
dir: *On A59, at Waterhead, 1m S of Ambleside. Inn at end of promenade by lake*

This modern inn has an idyllic location on the shore of Windermere at Waterhead Bay. The pretty bedrooms are particularly smart and generally spacious, and all offer a high standard of quality and comfort. The airy bar-restaurant opens onto attractive gardens, which have magnificent lake views. There is also a comfortable lounge, bar and dining area.

Rooms 15 en suite 7 annexe en suite (4 fmly) (3 GF)
Facilities tea/coffee Dinner available Cen ht Wi-fi Complimentary membership of nearby leisure club
Parking 40 Notes Closed 25-26 Dec

Ambleside Lodge

★★★★ GUEST HOUSE

Rothay Rd LA22 0EJ
☎ 015394 31681 📠 015394 34547
e-mail: enquiries@ambleside-lodge.com
web: www.ambleside-lodge.com

Located close to the centre of this historic market town, this Grade II listed 18th-century residence has a peaceful atmosphere. The stylishly decorated, elegant accommodation includes attractive bedrooms with antique and contemporary pieces, including four-poster beds. Attentive, personal service is provided.

Rooms 18 en suite (8 GF) S £40; D £70-£75*
Facilities FTV tea/coffee Cen ht Wi-fi Parking 20
Notes LB

Brathay Lodge

★★★★ GUEST ACCOMMODATION

Rothay Rd LA22 0EE
☎ 015394 32000
e-mail: info@brathay-lodge.co.uk
dir: *One-way system in town centre. Lodge on right opp tennis courts*

This traditional property has been refurbished in a bright contemporary style. The pine-furnished bedrooms are mainly very spacious; some share a communal balcony and some of the ground-floor rooms have their own entrance. All rooms have spa baths. Breakfast is continental, self-service in the lounge or can be taken to your bedroom.

Rooms 12 en suite 7 annexe en suite (5 fmly) (6 GF); D £55–£139* **Facilities** FTV tea/coffee Cen ht Wi-fi Use of Langdale Country Club **Parking** 24 **Notes** LB

Broadview Guest House

★★★★ 🏠 GUEST HOUSE

Lake Rd LA22 0DN
☎ 015394 32431
e-mail: enquiries@broadviewguesthouse.co.uk
web: www.broadviewguesthouse.co.uk
dir: On A591 S side of Ambleside, on Lake Rd opposite Garden Centre

Just a short walk from the centre of Ambleside a warm welcome is assured at this popular guest house, where regular improvements enhance the guest experience. Bedrooms are thoughtfully furnished and comprehensive breakfasts provide an excellent start to the day.

Rooms 6 rms (3 en suite) (1 pri facs) S £30–£100; D £50–£100* **Facilities** tea/coffee Cen ht Wi-fi Access to nearby leisure club **Notes** LB ⊗

Cherry Garth

★★★★ GUEST HOUSE

Old Lake Rd LA22 0DH
☎ 015394 33128 📠 015394 33885
e-mail: reception@cherrygarth.com
dir: A591 N into Ambleside, over lights, B&B 800yds on right

Set on the southern approach to the town, this detached house sits in well-landscaped gardens giving views of Loughrigg Fell and Wetherlam. Bedrooms offer a range of styles, are spacious and have modern fittings with all of the expected facilities. Traditional Lakeland breakfasts are served in the lounge-breakfast room overlooking the front garden.

Rooms 11 en suite (2 fmly) (3 GF) S £40–£65; D £75–£120 **Facilities** tea/coffee Cen ht Licensed **Parking** 14 **Notes** LB

Elterwater Park

★★★★ GUEST HOUSE

Skelwith Bridge LA22 9NP
☎ 015394 32227
e-mail: enquiries@elterwater.com
dir: A593 from Ambleside to Coniston, 1m past Skelwith Bridge Hotel, layby on right fronts estate road to Elterwater Park, signed at gate

This 18th-century Lakeland house is set in 119 acres of parkland, and offers a unique setting and stunning views. The friendly proprietors are dedicated to becoming carbon neutral so the house has geothermal heating and its own water supply. Attractive, comfortable bedrooms include a ground floor annexe room. Evening meals are available by arrangement and there is a useful drying room too.

Rooms 4 en suite 5 annexe en suite (5 GF) S £42–£52; D £64–£84 **Facilities** STV tea/coffee Dinner available Cen ht Licensed Wi-fi **Parking** 10 **Notes** ⊗ No Children 10yrs

Kent House

★★★★ GUEST HOUSE

Lake Rd LA22 0AD
☎ 015394 33279
e-mail: mail@kent-house.com
web: www.kent-house.com
dir: From town centre, by Post Office on one-way system 300yds on left on terrace above main road

From an elevated location overlooking the town, this traditional Lakeland house offers comfortable, well-equipped accommodation with attractive bedrooms. Traditional breakfasts featuring the best of local produce are served at individual tables in the elegant dining room.

Rooms 5 rms (4 en suite) (1 pri facs) (2 fmly) **Facilities** tea/coffee Cen ht **Parking** 2

Lake House

★★★★ GUEST ACCOMMODATION

Waterhead Bay LA22 0HD
☎ 015394 32360 📠 015394 31474
e-mail: info@lakehousehotel.co.uk
dir: From S: M6 junct 36, A590, then A591 towards Kendal & Windermere. House 3m N of Windermere. From N: M6 junct 40, A66 to Keswick, then A591 to Ambleside. House just S of town

Set on a hillside with lake views, this delightful house has very stylish accommodation and a homely atmosphere. The bedrooms are all individual in style and include many homely extras. Dinner is available at the nearby sister property with complimentary transport, and leisure facilities are available there too. Breakfast is an interesting and substantial cold buffet.

Rooms 12 en suite (3 fmly) (2 GF) S £75–£95; D £99–£160* **Facilities** TVL tea/coffee Cen ht Licensed Wi-fi Use of pool at Regent Hotel **Parking** 12 **Notes** LB ⊗

Lakes Lodge

★★★★ GUEST ACCOMMODATION

Lake Rd LA22 0DB
☎ 015394 33240 📠 015394 31474
e-mail: info@lakeslodge.co.uk
dir: Enter Ambleside on A59, right around one-way system, on exiting town turn right onto Lake Rd

Located in the centre of Ambleside, friendly service and simply furnished, contemporary bedrooms, in a range of sizes are offered. Wine, beer and champagne can be served to bedrooms during the day and evening, until 9pm. A continental breakfast buffet is served in the café-style breakfast room. Guests can arrange use of an indoor pool at a nearby hotel.

Rooms 12 en suite (4 fmly) (2 GF) **Facilities** tea/coffee Cen ht Licensed Wi-fi **Parking** 12 **Notes** LB ⊗

The Log House

★★★★ ⚜ 🏠 RESTAURANT WITH ROOMS

Lake Rd LA22 0DN
☎ 015394 31077
e-mail: nicola@loghouse.co.uk
web: www.loghouse.co.uk
dir: On left after Hayes Garden Centre on A591 (Lake Rd)

This charming and historic Norwegian building is located midway between the town centre and the shore of Lake Windermere, just five minutes' walk to each. Guests can enjoy delicious meals in the attractive restaurant, which also has a bar area. There are three comfortable bedrooms, each equipped with thoughtful accessories such as DVD/VCR players, Wi-fi and hairdryers.

Rooms 3 en suite S £60–£90; D £60–£90* **Facilities** FTV tea/coffee Dinner available Cen ht Wi-fi **Parking** 3 **Notes** LB ⊗ Closed 7 Jan-7 Feb No coaches

AMBLESIDE *continued*

Rysdale Guesthouse

★★★★ GUEST ACCOMMODATION

Rothay Rd LA22 0EE
☎ 015394 32140 📠 015394 33999
e-mail: info@rysdalehotel.co.uk
dir: *A591 into Ambleside, one-way system to A593, Rysdale on right facing church*

The comfortable Edwardian house is only a stroll from the village centre and overlooks the church and the park. The friendly proprietors offer attractive, well-equipped bedrooms, most of which enjoy superb mountain views, as does the smart dining room. There is also a cosy lounge with an inglenook fireplace.

Rooms 9 rms (7 en suite) (2 pri facs) (1 fmly) S £33-£45; D £66-£96* **Facilities** tea/coffee Cen ht **Parking** 1 **Notes** ⊗ No Children 4yrs Closed 23-27 Dec RS Jan 📷

Wanslea Guest House

★★★★ GUEST HOUSE

Low Fold, Lake Rd LA22 0DN
☎ 015394 33884 📠 015394 33884
e-mail: information@wanslea.co.uk
dir: *On S side of town, opp garden centre*

Located between town centre and lakeside pier, this Victorian house provides a range of thoughtfully furnished bedrooms, some of which are individually themed and equipped with spa baths. Comprehensive breakfasts are served in the spacious dining room and a cosy lounge is available.

Rooms 8 en suite (2 fmly) S £35-£50; D £50-£90 **Facilities** FTV TVL tea/coffee Cen ht Wi-fi **Notes** LB ⊗ No Children 6yrs Closed 23-26 Dec

The Old Vicarage

★★★★ ⚑ GUEST ACCOMMODATION

Vicarage Rd LA22 9DH
☎ 015394 33364 📠 015394 34734
e-mail: info@oldvicarageambleside.co.uk
web: www.oldvicarageambleside.co.uk
dir: *In town centre. Off Compston Rd onto Vicarage Rd*

Rooms 15 en suite (4 fmly) (2 GF) S fr £55; D fr £90* **Facilities** STV tea/coffee Cen ht Wi-fi 🐾 ♨ Riding Sauna Pool Table Hot tub **Parking** 17 **Notes** LB Closed 23-28 Dec

The Rothay Garth

★★★★ ⚑ GUEST ACCOMMODATION

Rothay Rd LA22 0EE
☎ 015394 32217 📠 015394 34400
e-mail: book@rothay-garth.co.uk
dir: *M6 junct 36, A591 to Ambleside. 1st lights straight over, then left onto Wansfell Rd. At T-junct turn right, located on right*

Rooms 14 en suite 1 annexe en suite (3 fmly) (4 GF); D £74-£112* **Facilities** FTV TVL tea/coffee Direct Dial Cen ht Licensed **Parking** 18 **Notes** LB

Fell View

★★★ BED AND BREAKFAST

Church St LA22 0BT
☎ 01539 431343
e-mail: fellview@sky.com

Located in the centre of Ambleside this cosy and well maintained house offers two well furnished en suite bedrooms with thoughtful accessories provided. Tasty breakfasts are served in the charming dining room at individual tables. The proprietors are friendly and welcoming.

Rooms 2 en suite **Facilities** tea/coffee Cen ht **Parking** 2 **Notes** ⊗ No Children Closed 24-29 Dec

Haven Cottage Guest House

★★★ GUEST HOUSE

Rydal Rd LA22 9AY
☎ 015394 33270
e-mail: enquiries@amblesidehavencottage.co.uk
web: www.amblesidehavencottage.co.uk
dir: *250yds N of town centre on A591*

A warm welcome awaits along with home baking and refreshments served on arrival. Claire and Tim create a definite home-away-from-home, making their guests feel very welcome, with plenty of extras provided. Haven Cottage is located on the edge of Ambleside and benefits

from off-road parking. Very good breakfast; see how many puzzles you can work out!

Haven Cottage Guest House

Rooms 7 rms (5 en suite) (2 fmly) S £30-£37; D £60-£80 **Facilities** tea/coffee Cen ht Wi-fi **Parking** 6 **Notes** LB ⊗ No Children 8yrs

---

APPLEBY-IN-WESTMORLAND   Map 18 NY62

Hall Croft

★★★★ ⬛ BED AND BREAKFAST

Dufton CA16 6DB
☎ 017683 52902
e-mail: r.walker@leaseholdpartnerships.co.uk
dir: *3m N of Appleby. In Dufton by village green*

Standing at the end of a lime-tree avenue, Hall Croft, built in 1882, has been restored to its original glory. Bedrooms are comfortably proportioned, traditionally furnished and well equipped. Breakfasts, served in the lounge-dining room, are substantial and include a range of home-made produce. Guests can enjoy the lovely garden, which has views of the Pennines.

Rooms 3 rms (2 en suite) (1 pri facs) S fr £33; D fr £56* **Facilities** FTV tea/coffee Cen ht **Parking** 3 **Notes** Closed 24-26 Dec 📷

North End Farmhouse

★★★★ GUEST HOUSE

Bolton CA16 6AX
☎ 017683 61959 📠 017683 619598
e-mail: mary@northendfarmhouse.co.uk
web: www.northendfarmhouse.co.uk
dir: *Off A66 into Bolton midway between Kirkby Thore & Appleby. At x-rds in Bolton turn right into North End*

A warm welcome awaits at this traditional and thoughtfully extended Westmorland style farmhouse set in a small country village. Bedrooms are spacious and well equipped; there is a cosy lounge with a log-burning stove. Breakfast offers traditional home-cooked fare served in the conservatory room overlooking the Pennines. Dinner is available by arrangement.

Rooms 2 en suite S £29-£35; D £58-£70* **Facilities** FTV TVL tea/coffee Dinner available Cen ht Golf 18 Fishing Riding **Parking** 6 **Notes** LB ⊗ No Children 11yrs

ARMATHWAITE Map 18 NY54

The Dukes Head Inn

★★★ INN

Front St CA4 9PB
☎ 016974 72226
e-mail: info@dukeshead-hotel.co.uk
web: www.dukeshead-hotel.co.uk
dir: *In village centre opp post office*

Located in the peaceful village of Armathwaite close to the River Eden, the Dukes Head offers comfortable accommodation in a warm friendly atmosphere. There is a relaxing lounge bar with open fires and a wide choice of meals are available either here or in the restaurant.

Rooms 5 rms (3 en suite) (2 pri facs) S fr £42.50; D fr £62.50* **Facilities** FTV TV4B tea/coffee Dinner available Cen ht Wi-fi **Parking** 20 **Notes** LB Closed 25 Dec

ARNSIDE Map 18 SD47

PREMIER COLLECTION

Number 43

★★★★★ GUEST ACCOMMODATION

The Promenade LA5 0AA
☎ 01524 762761 ▤ 01524 761455
e-mail: lesley@no43.org.uk
web: www.no43.org.uk

Number 43 is a contemporary townhouse located on the promenade. Recently renovated to please the most discerning of guests, this is a retreat that has sheer elegance and comfort in a contemporary and exciting way, luxurious surroundings and excellent guest care from Lesley and her team. The two suites come with coastal views from the bed and one from the bath

Rooms 6 en suite; D £110-£180 **Facilities** TVL Dinner available Cen ht Licensed **Notes** ⊗

BARROW-IN-FURNESS Map 18 SD26

Ambrose

★★★ INN

Duke St LA14 1XT
☎ 01229 830990 ▤ 01229 830991
e-mail: info@ambrosehotel.co.uk
dir: *On A590, pass Asda, take 1st left onto Duke St. 200yds on right*

Situated on the fringe of the Lake District and only a short walk from the town centre, Ambrose offers comfortable, well equipped accommodation in a relaxed environment. The popular bar has a changing selection of cask beers and there is a games room. Freshly cooked

breakfasts and evening meals are served in the bar or elevated dining area.

Rooms 12 en suite (3 fmly) S £50-£60; D £55-£65 (room only) **Facilities** STV tea/coffee Dinner available Direct Dial Cen ht Wi-fi Pool Table **Notes** LB

BOOT Map 18 NY10

Brook House Inn

★★★★ INN

CA19 1TG
☎ 01946 723288 ▤ 01946 723160
e-mail: stay@brookhouseinn.co.uk
web: www.brookhouseinn.co.uk
dir: *In village centre. 0.5m NE of Dalegarth station*

Located in the heart of Eskdale, this impressive inn dates from the early 18th century and has been renovated to offer comfortable accommodation with smart, modern bathrooms for weary walkers and travellers. Wholesome meals using local produce are served in the traditionally furnished dining room or attractive bar, the latter featuring real ales and country memorabilia.

Rooms 7 en suite (2 fmly) S £52.50-£60; D £72-£90* **Facilities** FTV tea/coffee Dinner available Cen ht **Conf** Max 35 **Parking** 24 **Notes** LB Closed 25 Dec

The Woolpack Inn

★★★ INN

CA19 1TH
☎ 019467 23230
e-mail: enquiries@woolpack.co.uk
dir: *From Eskdale Green follow single track road towards Hardknott, 1m on left*

A traditional Lake District inn, at the head of Eskdale which dates back to the 16th century. A friendly welcome is guaranteed along with true peace, relaxation and tastefully modernised bedrooms. Enjoy the residents or walkers bar with beer from the Woolpack's own micro-brewery. Restaurant offers imaginative home-made produce.

Rooms 8 rms (6 en suite) (2 fmly) **Facilities** STV tea/coffee Dinner available Cen ht Wi-fi **Parking** 40 **Notes** No coaches

BORROWDALE Map 18 NY21

PREMIER COLLECTION

Hazel Bank Country House

★★★★★ ◉ ☕ GUEST HOUSE

Rosthwaite CA12 5XB
☎ 017687 77248
e-mail: info@hazelbankhotel.co.uk
dir: *From Keswick, follow B5289 towards Borrowdale, turn left after sign for Rosthwaite*

Arrival at this grand Victorian house is impressive, reached via a picturesque hump back bridge and winding drive. Set on an elevated position surrounded by four acres of gardens and woodland, Hazel Bank enjoys magnificent views of Borrowdale. Carefully cooked dishes are served in the elegant dining room; the daily-changing, four-course dinner menu featuring fresh, local ingredients. There is a friendly atmosphere here and the proprietors are very welcoming.

Rooms 8 en suite (2 GF) S £65-£79.50; D £130-£159* (incl.dinner) **Facilities** tea/coffee Dinner available Cen ht Licensed ⤵ **Parking** 12 **Notes** ⊗ No Children 12yrs Closed 30 Nov-23 Dec

BOWNESS-ON-WINDERMERE

See Windermere

BRAITHWAITE   Map 18 NY22

The Cottage in the Wood
★★★★ ◉◉ 🍴 RESTAURANT WITH ROOMS

Whinlatter Pass CA12 5TW
☎ 017687 78409
e-mail: relax@thecottageinthewood.co.uk
dir: M6 junct 40 onto A66 W. After Keswick turn off for
Braithwaite via Whinlatter Pass (B5292), located at top
of pass

This charming property sits amid wooded hills with
striking views of Skiddaw, and is in a convenient location
for Keswick. The professional owners provide excellent
hospitality in a relaxed manner and offer a freshly
prepared dinner from a set menu that includes a
vegetarian choice. There is a cosy lounge and a small
bar. The bedrooms are individually decorated, and the
superior rooms include many useful extras.

Rooms 9 en suite (1 fmly) (1 GF) S £75-£90;
D £90-£140* Facilities FTV tea/coffee Dinner available
Cen ht Wi-fi Parking 15 Notes LB ⊗ No Children 10yrs
Closed Jan No coaches

The Royal Oak
★★★★ INN

CA12 5SY
☎ 017687 78533 📠 017687 78533
e-mail: info@royaloak-braithwaite.co.uk
web: www.royaloak-braithwaite.co.uk
dir: In village centre

The Royal Oak, in the pretty village of Braithwaite, has
delightful views of Skiddaw and Barrow, and is a good
base for tourists and walkers. Some of the well-equipped
bedrooms are furnished with four-poster beds. Hearty
meals and traditional Cumbrian breakfasts are served in
the restaurant, and there is an atmospheric, well-stocked
bar.

Rooms 10 en suite (1 fmly) S £40-£45; D £70-£76*
Facilities STV tea/coffee Dinner available Cen ht Wi-fi 🏊
Parking 20 Notes LB

BRAMPTON   Map 21 NY56

See also Castle Carrock & Gilsland (Northumberland)

PREMIER COLLECTION

The Hill On The Wall
★★★★★ GUEST ACCOMMODATION

Gilsland CA8 7DA
☎ 016977 47214 📠 016977 47214
e-mail: info@hadrians-wallbedandbreakfast.com
web: http://hadrians-wallbedandbreakfast.com
dir: A69 into Gilsland & follow brown tourist signs for
Birdoswald, The Hill on the Wall 0.5m on right

Overlooking Hadrian's Wall, this elegant house was
originally built in the 16th century as a fortified
farmhouse. The spacious, attractive bedrooms are well
equipped. The lounge is comfortably furnished and
stocked with books and games. Breakfast, using good
local produce, is served in the smart dining room.

Rooms 3 rms (2 en suite) (1 pri facs) (1 GF);
D £80-£90 Facilities FTV TVL tea/coffee Cen ht Wi-fi
Golf 18 Parking 8 Notes LB ⊗ No Children 10yrs
Closed Dec & Jan ◉

The Blacksmiths Arms
★★★★ INN

Talkin Village CA8 1LE
☎ 016977 3452 & 42111 📠 016977 3396
e-mail: blacksmithsarmstalkin@yahoo.co.uk
web: www.blacksmithstalkin.co.uk
dir: B6413 from Brampton to Castle Carrock, after level
crossing 2nd left signed Talkin

Dating from the early 19th century and used as a smithy
until the 1950s, this friendly village inn offers good
home-cooked fare and real ales, with two Cumbrian cask
beers always available. Bedrooms are well equipped, and
three are particularly smart. An extensive menu and daily

specials are offered in the cosy bar lounges or the smart,
panelled Old Forge Restaurant.

Rooms 5 en suite 3 annexe en suite (2 fmly) (3 GF)
S £45-£55; D £60-£75 Facilities FTV tea/coffee Dinner
available Direct Dial Cen ht Wi-fi Parking 20 Notes ⊗ No
coaches

Hullerbank
★★★★ GUEST ACCOMMODATION

Talkin CA8 1LB
☎ 016977 46668 📠 016977 46668
e-mail: info@hullerbank.co.uk
web: www.hullerbank.co.uk
dir: B6413 from Brampton for 2m, over railway & after
golf club left to Talkin, onto Hallbankgate Rd & signs to
Hullerbank

Dating from 1635, Hullerbank is a delightful farmhouse
set in well-tended gardens, convenient for Hadrian's
Wall, the Lake District and the Borders. Bedrooms are
comfortably proportioned, attractively decorated and well
equipped. There is a cosy ground-floor lounge with an
inglenook fireplace, and traditional hearty breakfasts are
served in the dining room.

Rooms 3 rms (2 en suite) (1 pri facs); D £66-£68*
Facilities TVL tea/coffee Cen ht Parking 6 Notes ⊗ No
Children 12yrs Closed Dec-Mar

BRIGSTEER   Map 18 SD48

The Wheatsheaf
★★★★ ◉ INN

LA8 8AN
☎ 015395 68254
e-mail: wheatsheaf@brigsteer.gb.com
web: www.brigsteer.gb.com
dir: Off A591 signed Brigsteer, Wheatsheaf at bottom
of hill

Lying in the peaceful little hamlet of Brigsteer to the west
of Kendal, just off the A591, the Wheatsheaf offers
attractive, well-equipped en suite bedrooms, all of which
have been refurbished to offer modern comforts. There is
a cosy, well-stocked bar, and a spacious, charming
dining room where delicious home-cooked fare is served
at individual tables.

Rooms 3 en suite Facilities tea/coffee Dinner available
Cen ht Parking 25 Notes ⊗ No coaches

BROUGHTON-IN-FURNESS Map 18 SD28

The Old Kings Head

★★★★ 🍴 INN

Church St LA20 6HJ
☎ 01229 716293 📠 01229 715165
e-mail: russelleclar7jw@wanadoo.co.uk
dir: M6 junct 36, onto A591. After 2m onto A5900 signed
Barrow, turn right at Greenodd (A5092) to Broughton

This traditional family-run country inn offers a warm
welcome, charming public areas and real ales. A wide
choice of freshly cooked meals are served in the bar,
restaurant or, during warmer months, the attractive beer
garden. Bedrooms are varied in size but all are
comfortable and tastefully presented.

Rooms 6 rms (5 en suite) (1 fmly) Facilities tea/coffee
Dinner available Cen ht Parking 6 Notes LB ⊗

CALDBECK Map 18 NY34

Swaledale Watch Farm

★★★★ GUEST ACCOMMODATION

Whelpo CA7 8HQ
☎ 016974 78409 📠 016974 78409
e-mail: nan.savage@talk21.com
web: www.swaledale-watch.co.uk
dir: 1m SW of Caldbeck on B5299

This attractive farmhouse, set in its own nature reserve,
is in a peaceful location with a backdrop of picturesque
fells. The en suite bedrooms are spacious and well
equipped. Two rooms are in an adjacent converted farm
building and share a comfortable sitting room.
Traditional hearty breakfasts are served in the attractive
dining room overlooking the garden, with views of the
fells.

Rooms 2 en suite 2 annexe en suite (2 fmly) (4 GF)
S £28-£33; D £56-£60* Facilities TVL tea/coffee Cen ht
100 acre Nature Reserve, badger watching evenings
Parking 8 Notes Closed 24-26 Dec

CARLISLE Map 18 NY35

See also Brampton & Castle Carrock

Cambro House

★★★★ GUEST ACCOMMODATION

173 Warwick Rd CA1 1LP
☎ 01228 543094
e-mail: davidcambro@aol.com
dir: M6 junct 43, onto Warwick Rd, 1m on right before St
Aidan's Church

This smart Victorian house is close to the town centre and
motorway. The beautifully refurbished and spacious
bedrooms are brightly decorated, smartly appointed and
thoughtfully equipped. A hearty Cumbrian breakfast is
served in the cosy morning room.

Rooms 3 en suite (1 GF) S £30-£35; D £50-£60
Facilities FTV tea/coffee Cen ht Wi-fi Parking 2 Notes LB
⊗ No Children 5yrs

No1 Guest House

★★★★ BED AND BREAKFAST

1 Etterby St CA3 9JB
☎ 01228 547285 & 07899 948711
e-mail: sheila@carlislebandb.co.uk
dir: M6 junct 44 onto A7, right at 7th lights onto Etterby
St, house 1st on left

This small friendly house is on the north side of the city
within walking distance of the centre. The attractive,
well-equipped en suite bedrooms consist of a double, a
twin-bed and a single room. Hearty traditional breakfasts
featuring the best of local produce are served in the
ground-floor dining room.

Rooms 3 en suite S £30-£35; D £60-£70* Facilities FTV
tea/coffee Dinner available Cen ht Wi-fi Parking 1
Notes LB ⊗

Angus House & Almonds Restaurant

★★★ 🍴 GUEST ACCOMMODATION

14-16 Scotland Rd CA3 9DG
☎ 01228 523546 📠 01228 531895
e-mail: hotel@angus-hotel.co.uk
web: www.angus-hotel.co.uk
dir: 0.5m N of city centre on A7

Situated just north of the city, this family-run
establishment is ideal for business and leisure. A warm
welcome is assured and the accommodation is well
equipped. Almonds Restaurant provides enjoyable food
and home baking, and there is also a lounge and a large
meeting room.

Rooms 10 en suite (2 fmly) S £52; D £74* Facilities FTV
tea/coffee Dinner available Direct Dial Cen ht Licensed
Wi-fi Conf Max 25 Thtr 25 Class 16 Board 16fred
Notes LB

Marlborough House

★★★ GUEST ACCOMMODATION

2 Marlbourgh Gardens, Stanwix CA3 9NW
☎ 01228 512174
e-mail: ian_mc_brown@hotmail.com
dir: M6 junct 44, 2m to Carlisle, left at Crown Inn

A warm welcome awaits you at Marlborough House
situated within easy walking distance of the city centre.
This friendly guest house offers individually decorated,
pleasantly furnished, and thoughtfully equipped
bedrooms. There is a comfortable conservatory breakfast
room where hearty breakfasts are served at individual
tables. Parking is available.

Rooms 4 en suite (1 fmly) (1 GF) Facilities TVL tea/coffee
Dinner available Cen ht Wi-fi Golf 18 Parking 8 Notes LB
⊗

CARTMEL — Map 18 SD37

PREMIER COLLECTION

L'enclume
★★★★★ ⚜⚜⚜⚜ RESTAURANT WITH ROOMS

Cavendish St LA11 6PZ
☎ 015395 36362
e-mail: info@lenclume.co.uk
dir: From A590 turn for Cartmel before Newby Bridge

A delightful 13th-century property in the heart of this delightful village offering 21st-century cooking that is worth travelling for. Simon Rogan cooks imaginative, adventurous food in this stylish restaurant. Individually designed, modern, en suite rooms vary in size and style, and are either in the main property or dotted about the village only a few seconds' walk from the restaurant.

Rooms 7 en suite 5 annexe en suite (3 fmly) (3 GF) S £68-£169; D £98-£199 (room only)* **Facilities** STV tea/coffee Dinner available Direct Dial Cen ht **Parking** 11 **Notes** No coaches

CASTLE CARROCK — Map 18 NY55

Gelt Hall Farm *(NY542554)*

★★ FARMHOUSE

CA8 9LT
☎ 01228 670260 📠 01228 670260 **Mrs Annie Robinson**
e-mail: robinson@gelthall.fsnet.co.uk
dir: B6413 to Castle Carrock, farm in village centre

This working farmhouse retains much of its original 17th-century character. The cheerful bedrooms are traditionally furnished and overlook the farmyard. Breakfast is served at a communal table in the cosy lounge, and warm hospitality is a particular feature.

Rooms 3 rms (1 en suite) (1 fmly) **Facilities** TV2B TVL tea/coffee **Parking** 7 **Notes** ⊛ 400 acres beef/dairy/sheep/mixed

COCKERMOUTH — Map 18 NY13

Highside Farmhouse
★★★★ BED AND BREAKFAST

Embleton CA13 9TN
☎ 01768 776893
e-mail: enquiries@highsidefarmhouse.co.uk
web: www.highsidefarmhouse.co.uk
dir: A66 (Keswick to Cockermouth), left at sign Lorton/Buttermere, left at T-junct. 300yds turn right opp church, farm at top of hill

True to its name, this 17th-century farmhouse stands over 600 feet up Ling Fell with breathtaking views across to the Solway Firth and Scotland. Add warm hospitality, great breakfasts, an inviting lounge-dining room with open fire in winter, and pine-furnished bedrooms, and the trip up the narrow winding road is well worth it.

Rooms 2 en suite S £42-£46; D £62-£66* **Facilities** FTV tea/coffee Cen ht **Parking** 2 **Notes** No Children 10yrs ⊛

Rose Cottage
★★★★ GUEST HOUSE

Lorton Rd CA13 9DX
☎ 01900 822189 📠 01900 822189
e-mail: bookings@rosecottageguest.co.uk
dir: A5292 from Cockermouth to Lorton/Buttermere, Rose Cottage on right

This former inn is on the edge of town and has been refurbished to provide attractive, modern accommodation. The smart, well-equipped en suite bedrooms include a self-contained studio room with external access. There is a cosy lounge, and a smart dining room where delicious home-cooked dinners are a highlight.

Rooms 6 en suite 1 annexe en suite (2 fmly) (3 GF) S £45-£65; D £65-£90 **Facilities** FTV tea/coffee Dinner available Cen ht Licensed Wi-fi **Parking** 12 **Notes** LB Closed 13-20 Feb RS 24-27 Dec

CONISTON — Map 18 SD39

PREMIER COLLECTION

Coniston Lodge
★★★★★ 🚆 🍵 GUEST HOUSE

Station Rd LA21 8HH
☎ 015394 41201 📠 015394 41201
e-mail: info@coniston-lodge.com
web: www.coniston-lodge.com
dir: Off A593 x-rds near fuel station up hill onto Station Rd

Coniston Lodge stands in mature gardens and is adorned with artistic touches, collectables and beautiful fresh and dried flower arrangements. An open staircase leads to the lounge (with a balcony overlooking the gardens) and the dining room. The well-proportioned bedrooms are in an extension on columns above the car park. Breakfasts are memorable, as are dinners (by arrangement).

Rooms 6 en suite **Facilities** tea/coffee Dinner available Direct Dial Cen ht Licensed **Parking** 9 **Notes** ⊛ No Children 10yrs RS Sun-Tue dinner not served

PREMIER COLLECTION

Wheelgate Country Guest House
★★★★★ 🚆 GUEST HOUSE

Little Arrow LA21 8AU
☎ 015394 41418 📠 015394 41114
e-mail: enquiry@wheelgate.co.uk
dir: 1.5m S of Coniston, on W side of road

Dating from the 17th century, this charming farmhouse has original oak beams, panelling and low ceilings. An intimate bar, laundry facilities and a comfortable lounge with open fire are provided. There are impressive views over the well-tended gardens and the beautiful Lakeland countryside. A warm welcome can be expected.

Rooms 4 en suite 1 annexe en suite (1 GF) S £40-£45; D £70-£90* **Facilities** tea/coffee Cen ht Licensed **Parking** 5 **Notes** LB ⊛ No Children 8yrs Closed Nov-Apr

CROSTHWAITE — Map 18 SD49

PREMIER COLLECTION

The Punchbowl Inn at Crosthwaite
★★★★★ @ INN

Lyth Valley LA8 8HR
☎ 015395 68237 📄 015397 68875
e-mail: info@the-punchbowl.co.uk
dir: *M6 junct 36 signed Barrow, on A5074 towards Windermere, turn right for Crosthwaite. At E end of village beside church*

Located in the stunning Lyth Valley alongside the village church, this historic inn has been renovated to provide excellent standards of comfort and facilities. Its sumptuous bedrooms have a wealth of thoughtful extras, and imaginative food is available in the elegant restaurant or in the rustic-style bar with open fires. A warm welcome and professional service is assured.

Rooms 9 en suite S £93.75-£183.75; D £125-£310*
Facilities Dinner available Direct Dial Cen ht Wi-fi
Parking 25 **Notes** No coaches Civ Wed 50

Crosthwaite House
★★★★ GUEST HOUSE

LA8 8BP
☎ 015395 68264 📄 015395 68264
e-mail: bookings@crosthwaitehouse.co.uk
web: www.crosthwaitehouse.co.uk
dir: *A590 onto A5074, 4m right to Crosthwaite, 0.5m turn left*

Enjoying stunning views across the Lyth Valley, this friendly Georgian house is a haven of tranquillity. Bedrooms are spacious and offer a host of thoughtful extras. The reception rooms include a comfortable lounge and a pleasant dining room with polished floorboards and individual tables.

Rooms 6 en suite S £27.50-£32; D £55-£64*
Facilities FTV TVL tea/coffee Cen ht **Parking** 10
Notes Closed mid Nov-Jan RS early Nov & Feb-Mar

CULGAITH — Map 18 NY62

Laurel House
★★★★ 🅰 BED AND BREAKFAST

CA10 1QL
☎ 01768 88638
e-mail: laurelhouse@fsmail.net
dir: *A66 onto B6412, following Culgaith, 1st right past 30mph signs, 50yds on left*

Rooms 3 en suite S £45-£50; D £70-£75* **Facilities** FTV tea/coffee Dinner available Cen ht **Parking** 3 **Notes** ⊗ No Children 16yrs

FAUGH — Map 18 NY55

The String of Horses Inn
★★★ 🅰 INN

CA8 9EG
☎ 01228 670297
e-mail: info@stringofhorses.com
web: www.stringofhorses.com
dir: *A69 turn towards Heads Nook at Corby Hill lights. 1m through Heads Nook, turn left*

Rooms 11 en suite (1 fmly) S £40-£55; D £60-£70*
Facilities FTV TVL tea/coffee Dinner available Direct Dial Cen ht Wi-fi **Conf** Max 60 Thtr 60 Class 30 Board 30 **Parking** 30 **Notes** LB ⊗

GRANGE-OVER-SANDS — Map 18 SD47

Corner Beech House
★★★★ 🏠 GUEST ACCOMMODATION

Methven Ter, Kents Bank Rd LA11 7DP
☎ 015395 33088
e-mail: info@cornerbeech.co.uk
web: www.cornerbeech.co.uk
dir: *M6 junct 36 onto A590, then off B5277, Kents Bank Rd*

Overlooking Morecambe Bay this Edwardian house is well maintained and offers a friendly atmosphere. Hearty breakfasts featuring home-made and local produce are served in the attractive dining room. All bedrooms are en suite and well equipped with sitting area, widescreen digital televisions and DVD players.

Rooms 3 en suite S £49; D £74* **Facilities** FTV tea/coffee Cen ht **Parking** 5 **Notes** ⊗ No Children 14yrs

GRASMERE — Map 18 NY30

PREMIER COLLECTION

Moss Grove Organic
★★★★★ 🏠 GUEST ACCOMMODATION

LA22 9SW
☎ 015394 35251 📄 015394 35306
e-mail: enquiries@mossgrove.com
web: www.mossgrove.com
dir: *From S, M6 junct 36 onto A591 signed Keswick, from N M6 junct 40 onto A591 signed Windermere*

Located in the centre of Grasmere, this impressive Victorian house has been refurbished using as many natural products as possible with ongoing dedication to causing minimal environmental impact. The stylish bedrooms are decorated with beautiful wallpaper and natural clay paints, featuring handmade beds and furnishings. Bose home entertainment systems, flat screen TVs and luxury bathrooms add further comfort. Extensive continental breakfasts are served in the spacious kitchen, where guests can help themselves and dine at the large wooden dining table in the guest lounge.

Rooms 11 en suite (2 GF) S £125-£250; D £125-£250*
Facilities STV tea/coffee Cen ht Licensed Wi-fi
Parking 11 **Notes** LB No Children 14yrs Closed 24-25 Dec

Silver Lea Guest House
★★★★ GUEST HOUSE

Easedale Rd LA22 9QE
☎ 015394 35657 📄 015394 35657
e-mail: info@silverlea.com
dir: *Easedale Rd opp village green, Silverlea 300yds on right*

A friendly welcome is assured at this ivy-clad Lakeland-stone house, just a short walk from the village. Delicious, freshly cooked breakfasts are served in the cosy cottage dining room. Bedrooms, some having their own sitting area, are fresh in appearance and very comfortable. Silverlea is an ideal base for walking and exploring the Lake District.

Rooms 4 en suite S £60-£96; D £80-£96* **Facilities** FTV tea/coffee Cen ht Wi-fi **Parking** 4 **Notes** LB ⊗ No Children 11yrs

GRASMERE *continued*

White Moss House

★★★ 🏠 ⬛ GUEST HOUSE

Rydal Water LA22 9SE
☎ 015394 35295 📄 015394 35516
e-mail: sue@whitemoss.com
web: www.whitemoss.com
dir: *On A591 1m S of Grasmere, 2m N of Ambleside*

This traditional Lakeland house was once bought by Wordsworth for his son. It benefits from a central location and has a loyal following. The individually styled bedrooms are comfortable and thoughtfully equipped. There is also a two-room suite in a cottage on the hillside above the house. Afternoon tea is served in the inviting lounge. It is possible to book all five rooms for a private 'house party', dinner is then available by arrangement.

Rooms 5 en suite S £62-£84; D £84-£108* **Facilities** FTV tea/coffee Direct Dial Cen ht Licensed Wi-fi Fishing Free use of local leisure club & fishing permits **Parking** 10 **Notes** LB ⊗ Closed Dec-Jan

GRIZEDALE   Map 18 SD39

Grizedale Lodge

★★★★ GUEST ACCOMMODATION

LA22 0QL
☎ 015394 36532 📄 015394 36572
e-mail: enquiries@grizedale-lodge.com
web: www.grizedale-lodge.com
dir: *From Hawkshead follow signs S to Grizedale. Lodge 2m on right*

Set in the heart of the tranquil Grizedale Forest Park, this charming establishment provides particularly comfortable bedrooms, some with four-poster beds and splendid views. Hearty breakfasts are served in the attractive dining room, which leads to a balcony for relaxing on in summer.

Rooms 8 en suite (1 fmly) (2 GF) S £55-£75; D £95-£110* **Facilities** STV TVL tea/coffee Dinner available Cen ht Licensed Wi-fi **Conf** Max 10 **Parking** 20 **Notes** LB

HAWKSHEAD   Map 18 SD39

See also Near Sawrey

PREMIER COLLECTION

Ees Wyke Country House

★★★★★ ◉ ⬛ GUEST HOUSE

LA22 0JZ
☎ 015394 36393
e-mail: mail@eeswyke.co.uk
web: www.eeswyke.co.uk

(For full entry see Near Sawrey)

Sawrey Ground

★★★★ 🏠 GUEST ACCOMMODATION

Hawkshead Hill LA22 0PP
☎ 015394 36683
e-mail: mail@sawreyground.com
dir: *B5285 from Hawkshead, 1m to Hawkshead Hill, sharp right after Baptist chapel, signs to Tarn Hows for 0.25m. Sawrey Ground on right*

Set in the heart of the Lake District, this charming 17th-century farmhouse has a superb setting on the doorstep of Tarn Hows. The flagstone entrance hall leads to a sitting room with a beamed ceiling, where an open fire burns on winter nights. Hearty breakfasts featuring fresh fruit and home-baked bread are served in the dining room. The traditional bedrooms are furnished in pine and oak.

Rooms 3 en suite; D £74-£86* **Facilities** FTV tea/coffee Cen ht Wi-fi **Parking** 6 **Notes** ⊗ No Children 8yrs ⊜

The Sun Inn

★★★★ INN

Main St LA22 0NT
☎ 015394 36236 📄 015394 36747
e-mail: rooms@suninn.co.uk
web: www.suninn.co.uk

This 16th-century inn features a wood-panelled bar with low, oak-beamed ceilings and an open log fire. Substantial, carefully prepared meals are served in the bar and dining room. The bedrooms, three of which are in an adjacent cottage, are attractively furnished and include some four-poster rooms.

Rooms 8 en suite (1 fmly) **Facilities** tea/coffee Dinner available Cen ht Wi-fi Fishing Pool Table **Conf** Max 20 Thtr 20 Class 20 Board 12fred **Notes** LB

Kings Arms

★★★ INN

LA22 0NZ
☎ 015394 36372 📄 015394 36006
e-mail: info@kingsarmshawkshead.co.uk
web: www.kingsarmshawkshead.co.uk
dir: *In main square*

A traditional Lakeland inn in the heart of a conservation area. The cosy, thoughtfully equipped bedrooms retain much character and are traditionally furnished. A good choice of freshly prepared food is available in the lounge bar and the neatly presented dining room.

Rooms 8 en suite (3 fmly) S £41-£49; D £72-£88* **Facilities** tea/coffee Dinner available Direct Dial Cen ht Fishing **Parking** **Notes** LB Closed 25 Dec

HELTON   Map 18 NY52

Beckfoot Country House

★★★★ GUEST ACCOMMODATION

CA10 2QB
☎ 01931 713241 📄 01931 713391
e-mail: info@beckfoot.co.uk
dir: *M6 junct 39, A6 through Shap & left to Bampton. Through Bampton Grange & Bampton, house 2m on left*

This delightful Victorian country house stands in well-tended gardens surrounded by beautiful open countryside, and is only a short drive from Penrith. Bedrooms are spacious and very well equipped. The four-poster room is particularly impressive. Public areas include an elegant drawing room, where guitar workshops are occasionally held, an oak-panelled dining room and a television lounge.

Rooms 7 en suite 1 annexe en suite (1 fmly) (1 GF) **Facilities** STV TVL tea/coffee Cen ht Licensed Wi-fi Childrens play area **Conf** Max 20 **Parking** 12 **Notes** LB Closed Dec-Feb

HOLMROOK   Map 18 SD09

The Lutwidge Arms

★★★ INN

CA19 1UH
☎ 019467 24230 📄 019467 24100
e-mail: mail@lutwidgearms.co.uk
dir: *M6 junct 36 onto A590 towards Barrow. Follow A595 towards Whitehaven/Workington, in centre of Holmrook*

This Victorian roadside inn is family run and offers a welcoming atmosphere. The name comes from the Lutwidge family of Holmrook Hall, who included Charles Lutwidge Dodgson, better known as Lewis Caroll. The bar and restaurant offer a wide range of meals during the evening. Bedrooms are comfortably equipped.

Rooms 11 en suite 5 annexe en suite (5 fmly) (5 GF) **Facilities** FTV TVL tea/coffee Dinner available Direct Dial Cen ht Wi-fi Pool Table **Parking** 30 **Notes** LB ⊗

See also Brigsteer

Burrow Hall Country Guest House

★★★★ BED AND BREAKFAST

Plantation Bridge LA8 9JR
☎ 01539 821711 📠 01539 821711
e-mail: burrow.hall@virgin.net
web: www.burrowhall.co.uk
dir: *3m NW of Kendal on A591*

Dating from 1648, this charming country house has been restored to provide comfortable, modern accommodation. Some of the en suite bedrooms have lovely views of the fells, and all are neatly furnished and well equipped. Guests have a separate entrance to a comfortable lounge and the breakfast room.

Rooms 4 en suite **Facilities** TVL tea/coffee Cen ht **Parking** 8 **Notes** ⊗ No Children 12yrs Closed 23-26 Dec

The Glen

★★★★ 🅰 GUEST ACCOMMODATION

Oxenholme LA9 7RF
☎ 01539 726386 📠 01539 724434
e-mail: greeninthe glen@btinternet.com
web: www.glen-kendal.co.uk
dir: *2m S of Kendal. B6254 to Oxenholme, past railway station, driveway on right up hill*

Rooms 6 en suite (2 fmly) (1 GF) **Facilities** STV tea/coffee Cen ht Wi-fi Hot tub **Parking** 10

Gilpin Bridge

★★★ INN

Bridge End, Levens LA8 8EP
☎ 015395 52206 📠 015395 52444
e-mail: info@gilpinbridgeinn.co.uk
dir: *M6 junct 36, 7m on A5074, 100yds from A590*

Situated just outside Levens, this modern Tudor-style inn offers a creative and appealing bar and restaurant menu. The bedrooms offer comfortable accommodation, and

there is a games room, a function suite, and an outside playground for children.

Gilpin Bridge

Rooms 9 en suite (1 fmly) **Facilities** FTV tea/coffee Dinner available Cen ht Pool Table **Conf** Max 80 Thtr 80 Class 60 Board 40 **Parking** 50

See also Lorton

PREMIER COLLECTION

The Grange Country Guest House

★★★★★ GUEST HOUSE

Manor Brow, Ambleside Rd CA12 4BA
☎ 017687 72500 📠 0707 500 4885
e-mail: info@grangekeswick.com
web: www.grangekeswick.com
dir: *M6 junct 40, A66 15m. A591 for 1m, turn right onto Manor Brow*

This stylish Victorian residence stands in beautiful gardens just a stroll from the town centre and offers a relaxed atmosphere and professional service. The spacious bedrooms are well equipped and some have beams and mountain views. Spacious lounges and ample parking are available. The proprietors are keen to give advice on walks and local activities.

Rooms 10 en suite (1 GF) S £72-£85; D £90-£108 **Facilities** FTV tea/coffee Direct Dial Cen ht Licensed Wi-fi **Parking** 10 **Notes** LB ⊗ No Children 10yrs Closed Jan

Dalegarth House

★★★★ 🍽 GUEST ACCOMMODATION

Portinscale CA12 5RQ
☎ 017687 72817
e-mail: allerdalechef@aol.com
dir: *Off A66 to Portinscale, pass Farmers Arms, 100yds on left*

The friendly family-run establishment stands on an elevated position in the village of Portinscale, and has fine views from the well-tended garden. The attractive bedrooms are well equipped, and there is a peaceful lounge, a well-stocked bar, and a spacious dining room

where the resident owner-chef produces hearty breakfasts and delicious evening meals.

Dalegarth House

Rooms 8 en suite 2 annexe en suite (2 GF) S £40-£45; D £80-£90* **Facilities** FTV tea/coffee Dinner available Cen ht Licensed Wi-fi **Parking** 14 **Notes** LB ⊗ No Children 12yrs Closed Dec-1 Mar

Howe Keld

★★★★ 🏡 GUEST ACCOMMODATION

5/7 The Heads CA12 5ES
☎ 017687 72417 & 0800 783 0212 📠 017687 80378
e-mail: david@howekeld.co.uk
web: www.howekeld.co.uk
dir: *From town centre towards Borrowdale, right opp main car park, 1st on left*

Howe Keld has been completely refurbished to create spacious, contemporary accommodation. Many rooms have solid wood floors and bespoke furniture made by local furniture maker Danny Frost along with local Herdwick carpets. On the ground floor there is a bright new spacious dining room and lounge area where guests can relax. Breakfast is another highlight, with local and home-made produce a feature.

Rooms 15 en suite (3 fmly) (2 GF) S £45-£75; D £70-£120* **Facilities** FTV tea/coffee Cen ht Licensed Wi-fi **Parking** 7 **Notes** LB Closed Xmas & Jan

Amble House

★★★★ GUEST HOUSE

23 Eskin St CA12 4DQ
☎ 017687 73288
e-mail: info@amblehouse.co.uk
web: www.amblehouse.co.uk
dir: *400yds SE of town centre. Off A5271 Penrith Rd onto Greta St & Eskin St*

An enthusiastic welcome awaits you at this Victorian mid-terrace house, close to the town centre. The thoughtfully equipped bedrooms have co-ordinated decor and are furnished in pine. Healthy breakfasts are served in the attractive dining room.

Rooms 5 en suite; D £60-£64* **Facilities** tea/coffee Cen ht **Notes** LB ⊗ No Children 16yrs Closed 24-26 Dec

KESWICK *continued*

Avondale

★★★★ GUEST ACCOMMODATION

20 Southey St CA12 4EF
☎ 017687 72735
e-mail: enquiries@avondaleguesthouse.com
web: www.avondaleguesthouse.com
dir: *A591 towards town centre, left at war memorial onto Station St, sharp left onto Southey St, Avondale 100yds on right*

Expect efficient and friendly service at this pristine terrace house just a short walk from the town centre. Bright, modern, well-equipped bedrooms come in a variety of sizes. The cosy lounge has a collection of books and there is an airy dining room.

Rooms 6 en suite S £34-£38; D £68-£76 **Facilities** tea/coffee Cen ht **Notes** ⊗ No Children 12yrs

Badgers Wood

★★★★ GUEST HOUSE

30 Stanger St CA12 5JU
☎ 017687 72621 ☎ 017687 72621
e-mail: enquiries@badgers-wood.co.uk
web: www.badgers-wood.co.uk
dir: *In town centre off A5271 (main street)*

A warm welcome awaits you at this delightful Victorian terrace house, located in a quiet area close to the town centre. The smart bedrooms are nicely furnished and well equipped, and the attractive breakfast room at the front of the house overlooks the fells.

Rooms 6 en suite **Facilities** tea/coffee Cen ht **Parking** 2 **Notes** ⊗ No Children 12yrs Closed 3-31 Jan 🚲

Claremont House

★★★★ GUEST ACCOMMODATION

Chestnut Hill CA12 4LT
☎ 017687 72089
e-mail: claremonthouse@btinternet.com
web: www.claremonthousekeswick.co.uk
dir: *A591 N onto Chestnut Hill, Keswick. Pass Manor Brow on left, Claremont House 100yds on right*

This attractive and well-maintained family home stands in mature grounds overlooking the town. Bedrooms are pine furnished and thoughtfully equipped, while the welcoming dining room has good views towards the fells.

Rooms 6 en suite S £40-£75; D £60-£75* **Facilities** tea/coffee Cen ht **Parking** 6 **Notes** LB ⊗ No Children 12yrs Closed 23-26 Dec 🚲

Craglands Guest House

★★★★ GUEST ACCOMMODATION

Penrith Rd CA12 4LJ
☎ 017687 74406
e-mail: craglands@msn.com
dir: *0.5m E of Keswick centre on A5271 (Penrith Rd) at junct A591*

This Victorian house occupies an elevated position within walking distance of the town centre. The good value accommodation provides attractive, well equipped bedrooms. Pauline and Mark offer a warm welcome and serve delicious breakfasts with local produce and homemade breads.

Rooms 7 rms (5 en suite) **Facilities** tea/coffee Dinner available Cen ht Wi-fi **Parking** 6 **Notes** LB ⊗ No Children 8yrs

Cragside

★★★★ GUEST ACCOMMODATION

39 Blencathra St CA12 4HX
☎ 017687 73344 ☎ 017687 73344
e-mail: wayne-alison@cragside39blencathra.fsnet.co.uk
dir: *A591 Penrith Rd into Keswick, under rail bridge, 2nd left*

Expect warm hospitality at this guest house, located within easy walking distance of the town centre. The attractive bedrooms are well equipped, and many have fine views of the fells. Hearty Cumbrian breakfasts are served in the breakfast room, which overlooks the small front garden. Visually or hearing impaired guests are catered for, with Braille information, televisions with teletext, and a loop system installed in the dining room.

Rooms 4 en suite (1 fmly) S £35-£40; D £50-£60* **Facilities** FTV tea/coffee Cen ht Wi-fi **Notes** No Children 4yrs

Dorchester House

★★★★ GUEST ACCOMMODATION

17 Southey St CA12 4EG
☎ 017687 73256
e-mail: dennis@dorchesterhouse.co.uk
dir: *200yds E of town centre. Off A5271 Penrith Rd onto Southey St, 150yds on left*

A warm welcome awaits you at this guest house, just a stroll from the town centre and its amenities. The comfortably proportioned, well-maintained bedrooms offer pleasing co-ordinated decor. Hearty breakfasts are served in the attractive ground-floor dining room. This is a non-smoking establishment.

Rooms 8 rms (7 en suite) (2 fmly) S £28-£37; D £62-£68* **Facilities** tea/coffee Cen ht **Notes** LB ⊗

Eden Green

★★★★ GUEST HOUSE

20 Blencathra St CA12 4HP
☎ 017687 72077 ☎ 017687 80870
e-mail: enquiries@edengreenguesthouse.com
web: www.edengreenguesthouse.com
dir: *A591 Penrith Rd into Keswick, under railway bridge, 2nd left, house 500yds on left*

This mid-terrace house, faced with local stone, offers well-decorated and furnished bedrooms, some suitable for families and some with fine views of Skiddaw. Traditional English and vegetarian breakfasts are served in the neat breakfast room, and packed lunches can be provided on request.

Rooms 5 en suite (1 fmly) (1 GF) S £30-£35; D £56-£70* **Facilities** tea/coffee Cen ht Wi-fi **Notes** LB ⊗ No Children 8yrs

Hazelmere

★★★★ GUEST ACCOMMODATION

Crosthwaite Rd CA12 5PG
☎ 017687 72445 ☎ 017687 74075
e-mail: info@hazelmerekeswick.co.uk
web: www.hazelmerekeswick.co.uk
dir: *Off A66 at Crosthwaite rdbt (A591 junct) for Keswick, Hazelmere 400yds on right*

This large Victorian house is only a short walk from Market Square and within walking distance of Derwentwater and the local fells. The attractive bedrooms are comfortably furnished and well equipped. Hearty Cumbrian breakfasts are served at individual tables in the ground-floor dining room, which has delightful views.

Rooms 6 en suite (1 fmly) S £32-£37; D £64-£74* **Facilities** FTV tea/coffee Cen ht Wi-fi **Parking** 7 **Notes** No Children 8yrs

Hedgehog Hill Guest House

★★★★ GUEST HOUSE

18 Blencathra St CA12 4HP
☎ 017687 80654
e-mail: keith@hedgehoghill.co.uk
dir: *M6 junct 40, take A66 to Keswick. Left onto Blencathra St*

Expect warm hospitality at this Victorian terrace house. Hedgehog Hill is convenient for the town centre, the many walks and local attractions. Bedrooms are comfortably equipped and offer thoughtful extras. Hearty breakfasts are served in the light and airy dining room with vegetarians well catered for.

Rooms 6 rms (4 en suite) S £26-£28; D £56-£64* **Facilities** tea/coffee Cen ht **Notes** ⊗ No Children 12yrs

The Hollies

★★★★ GUEST ACCOMMODATION

Threlkeld CA12 4RX
☎ 017687 79216 📠 017687 79216
e-mail: info@theholliesinlakeland.co.uk
web: www.theholliesinlakeland.co.uk
dir: 3m E of Keswick. Off A66 into Threlkeld, The Hollies opp village hall

Built in 1900 using local stone, The Hollies is an impressive detached property in the heart of Threlkeld. Lying at the foot of Blencathra, it is on the coast-to-coast walk, and the sea-to-sea cycle route. The attractive bedrooms are well equipped, and hearty breakfasts served in the dining room feature the best of local produce and home-made bread.

Rooms 4 en suite Facilities STV tea/coffee Cen ht Parking 6 Notes ⊗

Honister House

★★★★ 🏠 BED AND BREAKFAST

1 Borrowdale Rd CA12 5DD
☎ 017687 73181
e-mail: honisterhouse@btconnect.com
web: www.honisterhouse.co.uk
dir: 100yds S of town centre, off Market Sq onto Borrowdale Rd

This charming family home is one of the oldest properties in Keswick, dating from the 18th century, and has attractive and well-equipped bedrooms. John and Susie Stakes are the friendly proprietors, who offer a warm welcome and serve hearty breakfasts utilising high quality local, organic and Fair Trade produce wherever possible.

Rooms 3 en suite; D £70-£75* Facilities FTV tea/coffee Cen ht Wi-fi Notes LB ⊗

Keswick Lodge

★★★★ INN

Main St CA12 5HZ
☎ 017687 74584
e-mail: info@keswicklodge.co.uk

Located on the corner of the vibrant market square this large, friendly 18th-century coaching inn offers a wide range of meals throughout the day and evening, fully stocked bar and cask ales. Bedrooms vary in size but all are contemporary, smartly presented and feature quality accessories such as LCD TVs. There is also a drying room.

Rooms 18 en suite (1 fmly) S £90; D £90* Facilities FTV tea/coffee Dinner available Cen ht Wi-fi Notes LB ⊗

Keswick Park

★★★★ GUEST ACCOMMODATION

33 Station Rd CA12 4NA
☎ 017687 72072 📠 017687 74816
e-mail: reservations@keswickparkhotel.com
web: www.keswickparkhotel.com
dir: 200yds NE of town centre. Off A5271 Penrith Rd onto Station Rd

A friendly welcome awaits you at this comfortable Victorian house, situated within a short walking distance of the town centre. Bedrooms are mostly of a good size, and have homely extras. The breakfast room is in two sections, one with a good outlook, and there also is a cosy bar. Fine days can be enjoyed sitting on the front garden patio with a refreshment.

Rooms 16 en suite (2 fmly) Facilities TVL tea/coffee Direct Dial Cen ht Licensed Wi-fi Parking 8 Notes ⊗

Sunnyside Guest House

★★★★ GUEST HOUSE

25 Southey St CA12 4EF
☎ 017687 72446
e-mail: enquiries@sunnysideguesthouse.com
web: www.sunnysideguesthouse.com
dir: 200yds E of town centre. Off A5271 Penrith Rd onto Southey St, Sunnyside on left

This stylish guest house is in a quiet area close to the town centre. Bedrooms, which have been refurbished to a high standard, include a family room, and are comfortably furnished and well equipped. There is a spacious and comfortable lounge with plenty of books and magazines. Breakfast is served at individual tables in the airy and attractive dining room, and private parking is available.

Rooms 7 en suite (1 fmly); D £60-£74* Facilities FTV tea/coffee Cen ht Parking 8 Notes LB ⊗ No Children 12yrs

West View Guest House

★★★★ GUEST HOUSE

The Heads CA12 5ES
☎ 017687 73638
e-mail: info@westviewkeswick.co.uk
web: www.westviewkeswick.co.uk
dir: From Penrith on A66, 2nd exit for Keswick at rdbt. Follow signs for Borrowdale

Close to Derwentwater and the centre of Keswick this Victorian house benefits from stunning views, particularly from the spacious guest lounge. Bedrooms vary in size with some more compact than others but all are suitably equipped and comfortable. The friendly proprietors also offer drying facilities and secure storage for bikes.

Rooms 8 en suite (1 GF) S £50; D £70* Facilities FTV TVL tea/coffee Cen ht Wi-fi Notes ⊗ No Children 12yrs

The Edwardene

★★★★ 🅰 GUEST ACCOMMODATION

26 Southey St CA12 4EF
☎ 017687 73586 📠 017687 73824
e-mail: info@edwardenehotel.com
dir: A591 towards Keswick town centre. Left at lights into Southey St

Rooms 11 en suite (1 fmly) S £40-£46; D £78-£90* Facilities TVL tea/coffee Direct Dial Cen ht Licensed Wi-fi Parking 2 Notes LB ⊗

Sandon Guesthouse

★★★★ 🅰 GUEST HOUSE

13 Southey St CA12 4EG
☎ 017687 73648
e-mail: enquiries@sandonguesthouse.com
dir: 200yds E of town centre. Off A5271 Penrith Rd onto Southey St

Rooms 6 rms (5 en suite) (1 pri facs) S £30-£36; D £60-£72 Facilities tea/coffee Cen ht Notes ⊗ No Children 4yrs Closed 24 Dec (day), 25-26 Dec

Watendlath

★★★★ 🅰 GUEST HOUSE

15 Acorn St CA12 4EA
☎ 017687 74165 📠 017687 74165
e-mail: info@watendlathguesthouse.co.uk
dir: 350yds SE of town centre. Off A5271 Penrith Rd onto Southey St, left onto Acorn St

Rooms 4 en suite (2 fmly); D £56-£70* Facilities tea/coffee Cen ht Notes ⊗ Closed Xmas ⊗

Brierholme

★★★ GUEST ACCOMMODATION

21 Bank St CA12 5JZ
☎ 017687 72938
e-mail: enquiries@brierholme.co.uk
web: www.brierholme.co.uk
dir: On A591, 100yds from Post Office

This lovely Victorian house is only a minute's walk from the town centre, and the friendly owners have extensive knowledge of the local area. Bedrooms are neatly presented, well equipped and all have lovely views of the surrounding fells. Guests also have the added benefit of private parking, and a lock-up garage for bikes or motorcycles is also available.

Rooms 6 en suite (2 fmly) Facilities tea/coffee Cen ht Parking 6 Notes LB No Children 5yrs

KESWICK *continued*

Low Nest Farm B&B *(NY282224)*

★★★ FARMHOUSE

Castlerigg CA12 4TF
☎ 017687 72378 **Mrs A True**
e-mail: info@lownestfarm.co.uk
dir: *2m S of Keswick, off A591 (Windermere road)*

Low Nest Farm is a small, family-run farm set in some typically breath-taking Cumbrian scenery. Bedrooms are comfortable, en suite and benefit from views of the aforementioned landscape. There are of course, any number of walks available in the area, and Keswick is just two miles away.

Rooms 8 en suite (4 GF) S £33-£45; D £50-£90*
Facilities FTV TV6B TVL tea/coffee Cen ht Wi-fi
Parking 10 **Notes** No Children 16yrs RS Nov-Mar Renovations taking place ⊛ 120 acres mixed

---

PREMIER COLLECTION

Hipping Hall

★★★★★ ⊛⊛ 🏠 RESTAURANT WITH ROOMS

Cowan Bridge LA6 2JJ
☎ 015242 71187 📄 015242 72452
e-mail: info@hippinghall.com
dir: *M6 junct 36 take A65 through Kirkby Lonsdale towards Skipton. On right after Cowan Bridge*

Close to the market town of Kirkby Lonsdale, Hipping Hall offers spacious feature bedrooms, designed in tranquil colours with sumptuous textures and fabrics. Bathrooms use natural stone, slate and limestone and are the perfect place to relax. The sitting room, with large, comfortable sofas, paintings and patterned wallpaper, has a traditional feel. The restaurant is a 15th-century hall with tapestries and a minstrels' gallery that is as impressive as it is intimate.

Rooms 6 en suite 3 annexe en suite (1 GF);
D £215-£335* (incl.dinner) **Facilities** Dinner available Direct Dial Cen ht ⬇ **Parking** 30 **Notes** No Children 12yrs Closed 3-8 Jan No coaches Civ Wed 42

PREMIER COLLECTION

The Sun Inn

★★★★★ ⊛ INN

6 Market St LA6 2AU
☎ 015242 71965 📄 015242 72485
e-mail: email@sun-inn.info
web: www.sun-inn.info
dir: *From A65 follow signs to town centre. Inn on main street*

A 17th-century inn situated in a historic market town, overlooking St Mary's Church. The atmospheric bar features stone walls, wooden beams and log fires with real ales available. Delicious meals are served in the bar and more formal, modern restaurant. Traditional and modern styles are blended together in the beautifully appointed rooms with excellent en suites.

Rooms 11 en suite (2 fmly) S £65-£130; D £90-£150*
Facilities tea/coffee Dinner available Cen ht Wi-fi
Notes No coaches

The Snooty Fox Inn

★★★★ 🍽 INN

33 Main St LA6 2AH
☎ 01524 271308 📄 01524 272642
e-mail: snootyfoxhotel@talktalk.net
dir: *M6 junct 36, A65 towards Skipton for 5.5m. At Kirkby Lonsdale follow signs for town centre, next to Market Sq*

Located on the Main Street, this charming Jacobean inn offers traditional yet fully equipped bedrooms. Public areas include a well furnished bar and restaurant, with log fires lit in the colder months. A variety of dishes are served utilising fresh local produce.

Rooms 9 en suite **Facilities** tea/coffee Dinner available Cen ht Wi-fi **Parking** 5 **Notes** No coaches

---

The Copper Kettle

★★★ 🅰 GUEST ACCOMMODATION

3-5 Market St LA6 2AU
☎ 015242 71714 📄 015242 71714
e-mail: gamble_p@btconnect.com
dir: *In town centre, down lane by Post Office*

Rooms 5 en suite (2 fmly) S £29; D £42-£49*
Facilities tea/coffee Dinner available Licensed **Parking** 3 **Notes** LB

Brownber Hall Country House

★★★★ GUEST HOUSE

Newbiggin-on-Lune CA17 4NX
☎ 01539 623208
e-mail: enquiries@brownberhall.co.uk
web: www.brownberhall.co.uk
dir: *6m SW of Kirkby Stephen. Off A685 signed Great Asby, 60yds right through gatehouse, 0.25m sharp left onto driveway*

Having an elevated position with superb views of the surrounding countryside, Brownber Hall, built in 1860, has been restored to its original glory. The en suite bedrooms are comfortably proportioned, attractively decorated and well equipped. The ground floor has two lovely reception rooms, which retain many original features, and a charming dining room where traditional breakfasts, and by arrangement delicious dinners, are served.

Rooms 6 en suite (1 GF) **Facilities** tea/coffee Dinner available Cen ht Lift **Conf** Max 20 Board 20 **Parking** 12

Three Shires Inn

★★★★ INN

LA22 9NZ
☎ 015394 37215 📄 015394 37127
e-mail: enquiry@threeshiresinn.co.uk
web: www.threeshiresinn.co.uk
dir: *Turn off A593, 3m from Ambleside at 2nd junct signed for Langdales. 1st left after 0.5m, 1m along lane*

Enjoying an outstanding rural location, this family-run inn was built in 1872. The brightly decorated bedrooms are individual in style and many offer panoramic views. The attractive lounge features a roaring fire in the cooler months and there is a traditional style bar with a great selection of local ales. Meals can be taken in either the bar or cosy restaurant.

Rooms 10 en suite (1 fmly) S £50-£100; D £78-£106*
Facilities TVL tea/coffee Dinner available Cen ht Wi-fi Use of local country club **Parking** 15 **Notes** LB Closed 25 Dec RS Dec & Jan wknds & New Year only No coaches

---

Home from Home

★★★★ GUEST HOUSE

6 English St CA6 5SD
☎ 01228 792474
e-mail: joy762bnb@yahoo.co.uk
dir: *M6 junct 44, follow signs for A7 Longtown. House on main road next to chip shop*

A property that really lives up to its name, a warm and genuine welcome on arrival is assured and throughout your stay. Bedrooms are comfortable and well presented with good attention to detail. A hearty breakfast with ingredients locally sourced offers a great start to the day.

Rooms 5 en suite (2 fmly) (1 GF) S fr £30; D £56*
Facilities tea/coffee Cen ht **Parking** 5 **Notes** ⊗ No Children 4yrs 🅿

LORTON Map 18 NY12

PREMIER COLLECTION

New House Farm *(NY159227)*
★★★★★ FARMHOUSE

CA13 9UU
☎ 01900 85404 📠 01900 85478 Ms H Thompson
e-mail: hazel@newhouse-farm.co.uk
web: www.newhouse-farm.com
dir: *6m S of Cockermouth on B5289 between Lorton & Loweswater*

A warm welcome awaits you at this restored Grade II listed, 17th-century farmhouse, situated in Lorton Vale. The inviting public areas and bedrooms have been stylishly decorated to complement the original features. Bedrooms are spacious and have thoughtful extras including home-baked biscuits, and many have period-style beds and romantic bathrooms. The daily changing, delicious five-course dinner menu and hearty breakfasts are highlights.

Rooms 3 en suite 2 annexe en suite (2 GF) S £70–£120; D £140–£170 **Facilities** tea/coffee Dinner available Cen ht Licensed Wi-fi Hot spa in the garden **Conf** Max 12 **Parking** 30 **Notes** LB No Children 6yrs 15 acres non-working

PREMIER COLLECTION

Winder Hall Country House
★★★★★ 🏠 🍽 GUEST ACCOMMODATION

CA13 9UP
☎ 01900 85107 📠 01900 85479
e-mail: stay@winderhall.co.uk
web: www.winderhall.co.uk
dir: *A66 W from Keswick, at Braithwaite onto B5292 to Lorton, left at T-junct signed Buttermere, Winder Hall 0.5m on right*

Impressive Winder Hall dates from the 14th century. The lounge is luxuriously furnished and the elegant, spacious dining room is the venue for skilfully prepared meals using local produce. The smart, individually styled bedrooms are thoughtfully equipped, and all are furnished with fine antiques or pine. Two rooms have beautiful four-poster beds.

Rooms 7 en suite 3 annexe rms (3 pri facs) (4 fmly) S £65–£165; D £105–£185* **Facilities** FTV TV7B tea/coffee Dinner available Direct Dial Cen ht Licensed Wi-fi Fishing Sauna Hot tub **Conf** Max 25 Class 25 Board 25 **Parking** 10 **Notes** LB ⊗ Closed 2-31 Jan Civ Wed 65

The Old Vicarage
★★★★ 🏠 🍽 GUEST HOUSE

Church Ln CA13 9UN
☎ 01900 85656
e-mail: enquiries@oldvicarage.co.uk
web: www.oldvicarage.co.uk
dir: *B5292 onto B5289 N of Lorton. 1st left signed Church, house 1st on right*

This delightful Victorian house offers spacious accommodation in the peaceful Lorton Vale, at the heart of the Lake District National Park. A converted coach-house offers two rooms with exposed stone walls, and is ideal for families with older children. Bedrooms in the main house are well equipped and have excellent views of the distant mountains. Delicious home cooking is served in the bright dining room.

Rooms 5 en suite 2 annexe en suite (1 GF) S £75–£80; D £110–£120* **Facilities** tea/coffee Dinner available Cen ht Licensed Wi-fi **Parking** 10 **Notes** ⊗ No Children 8yrs

LOWESWATER Map 18 NY12

Kirkstile Inn
★★★★ INN

CA13 0RU
☎ 01900 85219 📠 01900 85239
e-mail: info@kirkstile.com
web: www.kirkstile.com
dir: *A66 onto B5292 into Lorton, left signed Buttermere. Signs to Loweswater, left signed Kirkstile Inn*

This historic 16th-century inn lies in a valley surrounded by mountains. Serving great food and ale, its rustic bar and adjoining rooms are a mecca for walkers. There is also a cosy restaurant offering a quieter ambiance. Bedrooms retain their original character. A spacious family suite in an annexe, with two bedrooms, a lounge and a bathroom.

Rooms 7 en suite 1 annexe en suite (1 fmly) S £59.50-£89; D £89-£99* **Facilities** TV2B TVL tea/coffee Dinner available Cen ht **Parking** 30 **Notes** LB Closed 25 Dec No coaches

MUNGRISDALE Map 18 NY33

The Mill Inn
★★★ 🍽 INN

CA11 0XR
☎ 01768 79632 📠 017687 79981
e-mail: info@the-millinn.co.uk
dir: *A66, 1m from main road*

This popular 16th-century inn stands beside a tranquil stream with a woodland backdrop. The modern bedrooms provide good levels of comfort and facilities. A wide selection of home-cooked dishes are served in the restaurant and lounge bar areas.

Rooms 6 rms (5 en suite) (1 pri facs) (1 fmly) S £35-£47.50; D £70-£75 **Facilities** tea/coffee Dinner available Cen ht Pool table (winter only) **Conf** Max 20 **Parking** 20 **Notes** LB Closed 25-26 Dec

NEAR SAWREY Map 18 SD39

PREMIER COLLECTION

Ees Wyke Country House
★★★★★ 🏅 🏠 GUEST HOUSE

LA22 0JZ
☎ 015394 36393
e-mail: mail@eeswyke.co.uk
web: www.eeswyke.co.uk
dir: *On B5285 on W side of village*

A warm welcome awaits you at this elegant Georgian country house with views over Esthwaite Water and the surrounding countryside. The thoughtfully equipped bedrooms have been decorated and furnished with care. There is a charming lounge with an open fire, and a splendid dining room where a carefully prepared five-course dinner is served. Breakfasts have a fine reputation due to the skilful use of local produce.

Rooms 8 en suite (1 GF) S £50-£82; D £100-£132* **Facilities** tea/coffee Dinner available Cen ht Licensed **Parking** 12 **Notes** LB ⊗ No Children 12yrs

NEAR SAWREY *continued*

Buckle Yeat

★★★ GUEST HOUSE

LA22 0LF
☎ 015394 36446 & 36538
e-mail: info@buckle-yeat.co.uk
web: www.buckle-yeat.co.uk
dir: *In village centre*

Close to Beatrix Potter's former home, Buckle Yeat is mentioned in some of the author's well-known tales. This charming 200-year-old cottage retains many original features, including a beamed dining room where freshly cooked breakfasts and cream teas are served. Bedrooms are pretty and there is an elegant lounge.

Rooms 7 rms (6 en suite) (1 pri facs) (1 fmly) (1 GF)
S £38-£40; D £76-£80* **Facilities** TVL tea/coffee Cen ht
Wi-fi **Parking** 9 **Notes** Closed Jan RS Nov-Dec wknds only

NEWBY BRIDGE — Map 18 SD38

PREMIER COLLECTION

The Knoll Country House

★★★★★ 🏠 🍽 GUEST ACCOMMODATION

Lakeside LA12 8AU
☎ 015395 31347 📠 015395 30850
e-mail: info@theknoll-lakeside.co.uk
dir: *A590 W to Newby Bridge, over rdbt, signed right for Lake Steamers, house 0.5m on left*

This delightful Edwardian villa stands in a leafy dell on the western side of Windermere. Public areas have many original features, including an open fire in the cosy lounge and dining room. The attractive bedrooms vary in style and outlook, all are very stylish. The welcome, from Jenny and her enthusiastic team, is caring and natural and Jenny also prepares a good range of excellent dishes at breakfast and dinner.

Rooms 8 en suite **Facilities** TVL tea/coffee Dinner available Direct Dial Cen ht Licensed Wi-fi Use of nearby hotel leisure spa **Parking** 8 **Notes** ⊗ No Children 16yrs Closed 24-26 Dec

Hill Crest

★★★★ 🛏 BED AND BREAKFAST

Brow Edge LA12 8QP
☎ 015395 31766 📠 015395 31986
e-mail: enquiries@hillcrest.gbr.cc
dir: *1m SW of Newby Bridge. Off A590 onto Brow Edge Rd, house 0.75m on right*

Set in picturesque surroundings with stunning views offering a high standard of en suite accommodation at this well kept Lakeland home. All rooms are individual and well maintained. The lounge doubles as a breakfast room and opens out on to a large patio to the rear. The breakfast menu makes good use of fresh local produce. Warm and genuine hospitality is guaranteed.

Rooms 3 en suite (2 fmly) (1 GF) S £45-£60; D £60-£90 **Facilities** TVL tea/coffee Cen ht Free use of local leisure club if staying 5 nights **Parking** 4 **Notes** LB ⊗ Closed 22-26 Dec

Lyndhurst Country House

★★★★ 🛏 GUEST HOUSE

LA12 8ND
☎ 015395 31245
e-mail: chris@lyndhurstcountryhouse.co.uk
dir: *On junct of A590 & A592 at Newby Bridge rdbt*

This 1920s house is situated close to the southern tip of Lake Windermere. Accommodation consists of three comfortable, tastefully decorated bedrooms, each with en suite shower room. Hearty breakfasts feature local produce and are served in the pleasant dining room, which also has a lounge area opening onto the garden.

Rooms 3 en suite; D £65-£75 **Facilities** tea/coffee Cen ht **Parking** 3 **Notes** ⊗ No Children 8yrs Closed 23-28 Dec

The Coach House

★★★★ BED AND BREAKFAST

Hollow Oak LA12 8AD
☎ 015395 31622
e-mail: coachho@talk21.com
web: www.coachho.com
dir: *2.5m SW of Newby Bridge. Off A590 onto B5278 signed Cark & 1st left into rear of white house*

This converted coach house stands in delightful gardens south of Lake Windermere. The hosts offer a warm welcome and are a good source of local knowledge. The modern bedrooms are light and airy, and there is a cosy lounge. Breakfast is served in a converted stable.

Rooms 3 rms (2 en suite) (1 pri facs) S £35; D £55 **Facilities** TVL tea/coffee Cen ht **Parking** 3 **Notes** LB ⊗ No Children 10yrs 🐾

Lakes End

★★★ GUEST HOUSE

LA12 8ND
☎ 015395 31260 📠 015395 31260
e-mail: info@lakes-end.co.uk
web: www.lakes-end.co.uk
dir: *On A590 in Newby Bridge, 100yds from rdbt*

In a sheltered, wooded setting away from the road, Lakes End is convenient for the coast and the lakes. The bedrooms have been thoughtfully furnished and equipped. Traditional English breakfasts are served, and delicious home-cooked evening meals can be provided by arrangement.

Rooms 4 en suite (1 fmly) (1 GF) S £35-£45; D £60-£75* **Facilities** STV FTV tea/coffee Dinner available Cen ht Licensed **Parking** 6 **Notes** LB ⊗

PENRITH — Map 18 NY53

See also Culgaith

PREMIER COLLECTION

Brooklands Guest House

★★★★★ 🏠 GUEST HOUSE

2 Portland Place CA11 7QN
☎ 01768 863395 📠 01768 863395
e-mail: enquiries@brooklandsguesthouse.com
web: www.brooklandsguesthouse.com
dir: *From town hall onto Portland Place, 50yds on left*

In the bustling market town of Penrith this beautifully refurbished house offers individually furnished bedrooms with high quality accessories and some luxury touches. Nothing seems to be too much trouble for the friendly owners, and from romantic breaks to excellent storage for cyclists, all guests are very well looked after. Delicious breakfasts featuring Cumbrian produce are served in the attractive dining room.

Rooms 6 en suite (1 fmly) S £35; D £70-£80 **Facilities** FTV tea/coffee Cen ht Wi-fi **Parking** 2 **Notes** LB ⊗ Closed 24 Dec-4 Jan

Roundthorn Country House

★★★★★ 🅰 GUEST ACCOMMODATION

Beacon Edge CA11 8SJ
☎ 01768 863952 📠 01768 864100
e-mail: enquiries@roundthorn.co.uk
dir: *1.2m NE of town centre. Off A686 signed Roundthorn*

Rooms 10 en suite (3 fmly) S £72.50-£91; D £103.50-£115* **Facilities** tea/coffee Dinner available Direct Dial Cen ht Licensed Wi-fi **Conf** Max 200 Thtr 200 Class 200 Board 50 **Parking** 60 **Notes** LB ⊗ Civ Wed 100

Brandelhow

★★★★ GUEST HOUSE

1 Portland Place CA11 7QN
☎ 01768 864470
e-mail: enquiries@brandelhowguesthouse.co.uk
web: www.brandelhowguesthouse.co.uk
dir: *In town centre on one-way system, left at town hall*

Situated within easy walking distance of central amenities, this friendly guest house is also convenient for the Lakes and M6. The bedrooms are thoughtfully furnished and some are suitable for families. Breakfasts, utilising quality local produce, are served in a Cumbria-themed dining room overlooking the pretty courtyard garden. Afternoon and High teas are available by arrangement.

Rooms 5 rms (4 en suite) (1 pri facs) (2 fmly) S £35; D £70-£80* **Facilities** FTV tea/coffee Cen ht Wi-fi **Notes** ⊗ Closed 31 Dec & 1 Jan

Acorn Guest House

★★★★ GUEST HOUSE

Scotland Rd CA11 9HL
☎ 01768 868696
e-mail: acornguesthouse@fsmail.net
web: www.acorn-guesthouse.co.uk

This house, newly refurbished, is on the edge of the town and is popular with walkers and cyclists. Bedrooms are generally spacious and a substantial, freshly cooked breakfast is offered. Drying facilities are available.

Rooms 8 en suite (2 fmly) **Facilities** FTV tea/coffee Cen ht Licensed **Parking** 8 **Notes** ⊗

Beckfoot Country House

★★★★ GUEST ACCOMMODATION

CA10 2QB
☎ 01931 713241 🖷 01931 713391
e-mail: info@beckfoot.co.uk

(For full entry see Helton)

Glendale

★★★★ GUEST HOUSE

4 Portland Place CA11 7QN
☎ 01768 210061
e-mail: glendaleguesthouse@yahoo.co.uk
web: www.glendaleguesthouse.com
dir: *M6 junct 40, follow town centre signs. Pass castle, turn left before town hall*

This friendly family-run guest house is part of a Victorian terrace only a stroll from the town centre and convenient for the lakes and Eden Valley. Drying facilities are available. Bedrooms vary in size, but all are attractive, and well equipped and presented. Hearty breakfasts are served at individual tables in the charming ground-floor dining room.

Rooms 7 rms (6 en suite) (1 pri facs) (3 fmly) **Facilities** FTV tea/coffee Cen ht Wi-fi

Tymparon Hall

★★★★ 🅰 GUEST ACCOMMODATION

Newbiggin, Stainton CA11 0HS
☎ 017684 83236
e-mail: margaret@tymparon.freeserve.co.uk
web: www.tymparon.freeserve.co.uk
dir: *M6 junct 40, A66 towards Keswick for 1.75m, right turn for Newbiggin, Tymparon Hall on right*

Rooms 3 rms (2 en suite) (1 pri facs) (2 fmly) S £40-£50; D £70-£80* **Facilities** TVL tea/coffee Cen ht **Parking** **Notes** LB ⊗ No Children 3yrs 🐾

Albany House

★★★ GUEST HOUSE

5 Portland Place CA11 7QN
☎ 01768 863072
e-mail: info@albany-house.org.uk
dir: *Left at town hall onto Portland Place. 30yds on left*

A well maintained Victorian house located close to Penrith town centre. Bedrooms are spacious, comfortable and thoughtfully equipped. Wholesome breakfasts utilising local ingredients are served in the attractive breakfast room.

Rooms 5 rms (2 en suite) (3 fmly); D £50-£70 **Facilities** FTV tea/coffee Cen ht Wi-fi **Notes** ⊗

Abbey House

★★★ GUEST HOUSE

7 Victoria Rd CA11 8HR
☎ 01768 863414 & 07949 771548 🖷 01768 863414
e-mail: anneabbeyhouse@aol.com
web: www.abbeyhousebandb.co.uk
dir: *500yds SE of town centre on A6 Victoria Rd*

Located close to the centre of town, Abbey House offers a warm atmosphere and comfortable accommodation. Breakfast is served in the attractive downstairs dining room.

Rooms 4 en suite (1 fmly) (1 GF) **Facilities** FTV tea/coffee Cen ht **Parking** 4 **Notes** LB ⊗

POOLEY BRIDGE — Map 18 NY42

Elm House

★★★★ GUEST HOUSE

High St CA10 2NH
☎ 017684 86334
e-mail: enquiries@stayullswater.co.uk
web: www.stayullswater.co.uk
dir: *B5320 into village, next to church*

Mark and Anne offer a friendly welcome at this delightful stone built house at the edge of the village. The attractive bedrooms are thoughtfully equipped with ground floor and family room available. A good range is offered at breakfast in the conservatory style dining room looking over unspoilt gardens.

Rooms 8 rms (7 en suite) (1 pri facs) (1 fmly) (3 GF) S £45-£70; D £64-£100* **Facilities** FTV tea/coffee Cen ht Wi-fi **Parking** 9 **Notes** ⊗

RAVENSTONEDALE — Map 18 NY70

The Black Swan

★★★★ ≜ ⊜ INN

CA17 4NG
☎ 015396 23204 🖷 015396 23204
e-mail: enquiries@blackswanhotel.com
dir: *M6 junct 38. Black Swan on A685, W of Kirkby Stephen*

Set in the heart of this quiet village, the inn is popular with visitors and locals and offers a very friendly welcome. Bedrooms are individually styled and comfortably equipped. There is an informal atmosphere in the bar areas and home-made meals can be taken in the bar or the stylish dining room. Relax by the fire in the cooler months and enjoy the riverside garden in the summer.

Rooms 7 rms (6 en suite) (1 pri facs) 3 annexe en suite (3 fmly) (3 GF) **Facilities** tea/coffee Dinner available Cen ht Wi-fi ⚲ Golf 9 Fishing Snooker **Conf** Max 14 Thtr 14 Class 14 Board 14 **Parking** 20

RYDAL

See Ambleside

Cumbrian Lodge

★★★★ ⬤ RESTAURANT WITH ROOMS

Gosforth Rd CA20 1JG
☎ 019467 27309 🖩 019467 27158
e-mail: cumbrianlodge@btconnect.com
web: www.cumbrianlodge.com
dir: Off A595 at Gosforth onto B5344 signed Seascale, 2m on left

A relaxed and friendly atmosphere prevails at this well-run restaurant with rooms, where tasty, well-prepared dinners prove popular locally. The decor and fixtures are modern throughout, and the bedrooms are well-equipped for both business and leisure guests. The thatched garden buildings provide a delightful opportunity for dining alfresco under canvas panels, for up to 12 diners.

Rooms 6 en suite (1 fmly) S £78.50; D £90*
Facilities STV tea/coffee Dinner available Direct Dial Cen ht Wi-fi 🛏 **Parking** 15 **Notes** ⊗

Cross Keys Temperance Inn

★★★ GUEST ACCOMMODATION

Cautley LA10 5NE
☎ 015396 20284 🖩 015396 21966
e-mail: clowes@freeuk.com
dir: 4m NE of Sedbergh on A683

Built in the 1732, this charming inn retains many original features. No alcohol is sold at this temperance inn, though you can bring your own to go with the ambitious home-cooked dishes. Bedrooms are traditionally presented and thoughtfully equipped, and the conservatory has delightful views of the Dales.

Rooms 2 en suite (1 fmly) S £37.50-£42.50; D £75
Facilities tea/coffee Dinner available Direct Dial Cen ht Riding **Parking** 9 **Notes** LB ⊗

Brookfield

★★★★ GUEST HOUSE

CA10 3PZ
☎ 01931 716397 🖩 01931 716397
e-mail: info@brookfieldshap.co.uk
dir: M6 junct 39, A6 towards Shap. 1st accommodation off motorway, on right

Having a quiet rural location within easy reach of the M6, this inviting house stands in well-tended gardens. Bedrooms are thoughtfully appointed and well maintained. There is a comfortable lounge, and a small bar area next to the traditional dining room where substantial, home-cooked breakfasts are served at individual tables.

Rooms 4 rms (3 en suite) S £35-£45; D £70 **Facilities** FTV TVL tea/coffee Cen ht Licensed Wi-fi **Conf** Max 20 **Parking** 20 **Notes** ⊗ No Children 12yrs Closed Jan 🖾

Fell House Guest House & Mango Restaurant

★★ GUEST HOUSE

Shap Main St CA10 3NY
☎ 01931 716343 🖩 01931 716343
e-mail: louis_mushandu@talk21.com

Conveniently located for Coast to Coast walkers or exploring the Lake District, this friendly house dates back to 1900. Bedrooms are practically furnished and guests also have use of a lounge. The cosy, brightly decorated restaurant features a varied choice of cuisines. The house is also a popular venue for live music.

Rooms 5 rms (2 en suite) (3 pri facs) (3 fmly) (1 GF) S £30-£45; D £50-£70 **Facilities** tea/coffee Dinner available Cen ht Licensed **Conf** Max 20 Class 20 **Parking** 5 **Notes** LB ⊗

Skygarth Farm (NY612261)

★★★ FARMHOUSE

CA10 1SS
☎ 01768 361300 🖩 01768 361300 Mrs Robinson
e-mail: enquire@skygarth.co.uk
dir: Off A66 at Temple Sowerby for Morland, Skygarth 500yds on right, follow signs

Skygarth is just south of the village, half a mile from the busy main road. The house stands in a cobbled courtyard surrounded by cowsheds and with gardens to the rear, where red squirrels feed. There are two well-proportioned bedrooms and an attractive lounge where tasty breakfasts are served.

Rooms 2 rms (2 fmly) S £25-£30; D £46-£56*
Facilities FTV TVL tea/coffee Cen ht **Parking** 4 **Notes** ⊗ Closed Dec-Jan 🖾 200 acres mixed

---

Lane Head Farm

★★★★ GUEST HOUSE

CA11 0SY
☎ 017687 79220
e-mail: info@laneheadfarm.co.uk
web: www.laneheadfarm.co.uk
dir: On A66 between Penrith & Keswick

This delightful converted farmhouse dates from the 18th century and enjoys a peaceful location with magnificent views. Bedrooms are comfortable and well equipped, and two are furnished with four-poster beds. One bedroom is on the ground floor. Public areas are well presented and include a comfortable lounge and spacious dining room with an open log fire. Meals are freshly prepared using local ingredients, and hosts Josette and Mark offer a warm welcome to all.

Rooms 7 en suite (1 GF) S £45-£90; D £70-£90
Facilities FTV tea/coffee Dinner available Cen ht Licensed **Parking** 9 **Notes** LB ⊗ No Children 12yrs

---

PREMIER COLLECTION

Broadoaks Country House

★★★★★ ⬤ GUEST ACCOMMODATION

Bridge Ln LA23 1LA
☎ 015394 45566 🖩 015394 88766
e-mail: enquiries@broadoakscountryhouse.co.uk
web: www.broadoakscountryhouse.co.uk
dir: Exit A591 junct 36 pass Windermere. Filing station on left, 1st right 0.5m

This impressive Lakeland stone house has been restored to its original Victorian grandeur and is set in seven acres of landscaped grounds with stunning views of the Troutbeck Valley. Individually furnished bedrooms are well appointed and en suite bathrooms feature either whirlpool or Victorian roll top baths. Spacious day rooms include the music room, featuring a Bechstein piano. Meals are served by friendly and attentive staff in the elegant dining room.

Rooms 11 en suite 3 annexe en suite (5 fmly) (4 GF)
Facilities FTV tea/coffee Dinner available Direct Dial Cen ht Licensed Wi-fi 🛏 ⚓ Fishing Snooker Arrangement with local leisure facility **Conf** Max 62 Thtr 40 Class 45 Board 45 **Parking** 40 **Notes** Civ Wed 62

Queens Head

★★★★ ⊜ INN

Town Head LA23 1PW
☎ 015394 32174 📠 015394 31938
e-mail: feast@queensheadhotel.com
web: www.queensheadhotel.com
dir: *M6 junct 36 onto A591, past Windermere towards Ambleside. At mini-rdbt, right onto A592 for Ullswater*

This 17th-century coaching inn has stunning views of the Troutbeck valley. The delightful bedrooms, several with four-poster beds, are traditionally furnished and equipped with modern facilities. Beams, flagstone floors, and a bar that was once an Elizabethan four-poster, provide a wonderful setting in which to enjoy imaginative food, real ales and fine wines.

Rooms 10 en suite 5 annexe en suite (1 fmly) (2 GF)
S £70-£80; D £110-£130* **Facilities** tea/coffee Dinner available Cen ht Wi-fi **Parking** 100 **Notes** LB No coaches

ULVERSTON   Map 18 SD27

Church Walk House

★★★★ BED AND BREAKFAST

Church Walk LA12 7EW
☎ 01229 582211
e-mail: martinchadd@btinternet.com
dir: *In town centre opp Stables furniture shop on corner of Fountain St and Church Walk*

This Grade II listed 18th-century residence stands in the heart of the historic market town. Stylishly decorated, the accommodation includes attractive bedrooms with a mix of antiques and contemporary pieces. Service is attentive, and there is a small herbal garden and patio.

Rooms 3 rms (2 en suite) S £30-£45; D £60-£75
Facilities TVL tea/coffee Cen ht **Notes** LB ⊛

WATERMILLOCK   Map 18 NY42

Brackenrigg

★★★ INN

CA11 0LP
☎ 017684 86206 📠 017684 86945
e-mail: enquiries@brackenrigginn.co.uk
web: www.brackenrigginn.co.uk
dir: *6m from M6 onto A66 towards Keswick & A592 to Ullswater, right at lake & continue 2m*

An 18th-century coaching inn with superb views of Ullswater and the surrounding countryside. Freshly prepared dishes and daily specials are served by friendly staff in the traditional bar and restaurant. The bedrooms include six attractive rooms in the stable cottages.

Rooms 11 en suite 6 annexe en suite (8 fmly) (3 GF)
Facilities tea/coffee Dinner available Cen ht Wi-fi
Conf Max 48 Thtr 36 Class 12 Board 16 **Parking** 40

WHITEHAVEN   Map 18 NX91

Glenfield Guest House

★★★★ GUEST HOUSE

Back Corkickle CA28 7TS
☎ 01946 691911 & 07810 632890 📠 01946 694060
e-mail: glenfieldgh@aol.com
web: www.glenfield-whitehaven.co.uk
dir: *0.5m SE of town centre on A5094*

The imposing, family-run Victorian house is in a conservation area close to the historic town centre and harbour. Margaret and Andrew provide a relaxed environment with friendly but unobtrusive service, and this is a good start point for the Sea to Sea (C2C) cycle ride.

Rooms 6 en suite (2 fmly) S £35; D £60-£75*
Facilities FTV TVL tea/coffee Dinner available Cen ht Licensed Wi-fi

WINDERMERE   Map 18 SD49

PREMIER COLLECTION

The Cranleigh

★★★★★ GUEST HOUSE

Kendal Rd, Bowness LA23 3EW
☎ 015394 43293 & 44245 📠 015394 47283
e-mail: enquiries@thecranleigh.com
web: www.thecranleigh.com
dir: *Lake Rd onto Kendal Rd, 150yds on right*

Just a short walk from Lake Windermere this smartly appointed period property is being transformed to provide stylish accommodation. Bedrooms are divided between the main house and adjacent building. Luxury and superior rooms are impressive, featuring spa baths, illuminated showers and an excellent range of accessories. Guests have complimentary use of leisure facilities at a nearby hotel.

Rooms 11 en suite 6 annexe en suite (3 GF)
S £75-£170; D £82-£220* **Facilities** FTV tea/coffee Direct Dial Cen ht Licensed Wi-fi ⊛ Squash Snooker Sauna Solarium Gymnasium **Parking** 13 **Notes** LB ⊛ No Children 15yrs

AA Funkiest B&B of the Year

PREMIER COLLECTION

Windermere Suites

★★★★★ BED AND BREAKFAST

New Rd LA23 2LA
☎ 015394 44739
e-mail: pureluxury@windermeresuites.co.uk
dir: *Through village on one-way system towards Bowness-on-Windermere. 0.25m on left after The Howbeck*

Close to Windermere and Bowness, Windermere Suites is a very special boutique town house which offers eight individual suites, all combining contemporary designer furniture with cutting edge entertainment technology and sheer elegance. Each suite has its own lounge area, and the bathrooms have large spa baths complete with TV, mood lighting and power showers. Rooms also have mini-bars and room service up to 10 at night. An unusual feature is the 'living showroom' element, if you like an item of furniture or decoration you can order it at a discount.

Rooms 8 en suite (3 GF); D £170-£260* **Facilities** STV FTV TV3B TVL tea/coffee Dinner available Cen ht Licensed Wi-fi **Parking** 9 **Notes** LB ⊛

PREMIER COLLECTION

Beaumont House

★★★★★ GUEST HOUSE

Holly Rd LA23 2AF
☎ 015394 47075 📠 015394 88311
e-mail: enquiries@lakesbeaumont.co.uk
web: www.lakesbeaumont.co.uk
dir: *After one-way system left onto Ellerthwaite Rd & 1st left*

A warm welcome awaits you at this smart, traditional house, in a peaceful location just a stroll from the town centre. Bedrooms, some with four-poster beds, are individually furnished to a high standard, as are the modern bathrooms. The spacious lounge has an honesty bar, and hearty breakfasts are served in the smartly appointed dining room.

Rooms 10 en suite (4 GF) S £60-£80; D £80-£150
Facilities TVL tea/coffee Cen ht Licensed Wi-fi
Parking 10 **Notes** LB ⊛ No Children 12yrs

WINDERMERE *continued*

PREMIER COLLECTION

The Howbeck
★★★★★ GUEST HOUSE

New Rd LA23 2LA
☎ 015394 44739
e-mail: relax@howbeck.co.uk
dir: *A591 through Windermere town centre, left towards Bowness*

Howbeck is a delightful Victorian villa, convenient for the village and the lake. Bedrooms are well appointed and feature lovely soft furnishings, along with new luxurious spa baths in some cases. There is a bright lounge with internet access and an attractive dining room where home-prepared dinners and hearty Cumbrian breakfasts are served at individual tables. This house is non-smoking.

Rooms 10 en suite 1 annexe en suite (3 GF) S £57.50-£149; D £85-£209 **Facilities** STV TVL tea/coffee Dinner available Cen ht Licensed Wi-fi **Parking** 12 **Notes** LB ⊗ No Children 12yrs Closed 24-25 Dec

PREMIER COLLECTION

Low House
★★★★★ BED AND BREAKFAST

Cleabarrow LA23 3NA
☎ 015394 43156
e-mail: info@lowhouse.co.uk
web: www.lowhouse.co.uk
dir: *A591 N past Kendal, 1st left B5284 signed Crook. After 5m, past Windermere Golf Club, 1st right signed Heathwaite, Low House on right*

This delightful 17th-century house is in a quiet location just off the road that passes the golf club and a 25-minute country walk from Bowness. Restored to create a homely atmosphere, the bedrooms are well equipped and there are two lounges in addition to the breakfast room. An optional extra is the hire of the family's 1965 Bentley to visit local restaurants and attractions.

Rooms 3 rms (2 en suite) (1 pri facs); D £80-£130* **Facilities** tea/coffee Dinner available Cen ht Wi-fi 🕊 **Parking** 5 **Notes** LB ⊗ No Children 12yrs Closed 23-27 Dec

PREMIER COLLECTION

Newstead
★★★★★ GUEST HOUSE

New Rd LA23 2EE
☎ 015394 44485 📄 015394 88904
e-mail: info@newstead-guesthouse.co.uk
dir: *0.5m from A591 between Windermere & Bowness*

A family home set in landscaped gardens, this spacious Victorian house offers very comfortable well-equipped accommodation. The attractive bedrooms are very individual and retain original features such as fireplaces and include many thoughtful extra touches. There is an elegant lounge and a smart dining room where freshly cooked breakfasts are served at individual tables.

Rooms 9 en suite (1 fmly) S £40-£70; D £50-£125* **Facilities** FTV TV7B tea/coffee Cen ht Wi-fi Free use of Parklands Leisure Club **Parking** 10 **Notes** LB ⊗ No Children 7yrs ✉

PREMIER COLLECTION

Oakbank House
★★★★ 🏠 GUEST HOUSE

Helm Rd LA23 3BU
☎ 015394 43386 📄 015394 47965
e-mail: enquiries@oakbankhousehotel.co.uk
web: www.oakbankhousehotel.co.uk
dir: *Off A591 through town centre into Bowness, Helm Rd 100yds on left after cinema*

Oakbank House is just off the main street in Bowness village, overlooking Windermere and the fells beyond. Bedrooms are individually styled, attractive and very well equipped; most have stunning lake views. There is an elegant lounge with a perpetual coffee pot, and delicious breakfasts are served at individual tables in the dining room.

Rooms 12 en suite (3 GF) S £50-£100; D £50-£110* **Facilities** tea/coffee Cen ht Licensed Wi-fi Free membership of local country club **Parking** 14 **Notes** LB ⊗ RS 20-26 Dec

PREMIER COLLECTION

The Woodlands
★★★★★ GUEST HOUSE

New Rd LA23 2EE
☎ 015394 43915 📄 015394 43915
e-mail: enquiries@woodlands-windermere.co.uk
web: www.woodlands-windermere.co.uk
dir: *One-way system through town down New Rd towards lake, premises by war memorial clock*

Just a short walk from Lake Windermere, guests can expect stylish accommodation and friendly, attentive service. Bedrooms (including two contemporary 4-poster rooms) have been individually decorated and feature quality furnishings and accessories, such as flat screen televisions. Guests are welcome to relax in the comfortable lounge where there is also a well stocked bar offering beers, wine, champagnes and rich Italian coffees. A wide choice is offered at breakfast which is served in the spacious dining room.

Rooms 14 en suite (2 fmly) (3 GF) **Facilities** tea/coffee Dinner available Cen ht Licensed Free facilities at local leisure/sports club **Parking** 17

Storrs Gate House

★★★★★ 🅰 GUEST HOUSE

Longtail Hill LA23 3JD
☎ 015394 43272
e-mail: enquiries@storrsgatehouse.co.uk
web: www.storrsgatehouse.co.uk
dir: *At junct A592 & B5284, opposite Windermere Marina*

Rooms 7 en suite (2 GF); D £80-£120* **Facilities** STV tea/coffee Cen ht Licensed Wi-fi **Parking** 7 **Notes** LB ⊗ No Children 10yrs Closed Xmas & New Year

See advert on opposite page

Dene House

★★★★ GUEST ACCOMMODATION

Kendal Rd LA23 3EW
☎ 015394 48236 📄 015394 48236
e-mail: denehouse@ignetics.co.uk
dir: 0.5m S of Bowness centre on A5074, next to Burnside Hotel

A friendly welcome awaits you at this smart Victorian house, in a peaceful location just a short walk from the centre of Bowness. The elegant bedrooms are generally spacious, individually decorated and are particularly well equipped. Afternoon tea is served on the patio, which overlooks a well-tended garden. A car park is available.

Rooms 7 rms (5 en suite) (2 pri facs) (1 fmly) (1 GF) S £36-£42; D £75-£85* **Facilities** FTV TVL tea/coffee Cen ht Wi-fi Free use of adjacent leisure centre **Parking** 7 **Notes** LB ⊗ No Children 12yrs

Fairfield House and Gardens

★★★★ 🏛 GUEST HOUSE

Brantfell Rd, Bowness-on-Windermere LA23 3AE
☎ 015394 46565 📄 015394 46564
e-mail: tonyandliz@the-fairfield.co.uk
web: www.the-fairfield.co.uk
dir: Into Bowness town centre, turn opp St Martin's Church & sharp left by Spinnery restaurant, house 200yds on right

Situated just above Bowness and Lake Windermere this Lakeland country house is tucked away in a half acre of secluded, peaceful gardens. The house has been beautifully refurbished to combine Georgian and Victorian features with stylish, contemporary design. Guests are shown warm hospitality and can relax in the delightful lounge. Bedrooms are well furnished, varying in size and style with some featuring luxurious bathrooms. Delicious breakfasts are served in the attractive dining room or on the terrace in warmer weather.

Rooms 10 en suite (2 fmly) (3 GF) **Facilities** TVL tea/coffee Dinner available Cen ht Licensed ⚓ **Conf** Max 20 Thtr 20 Class 10 Board 12 **Parking** 10 **Notes** No Children 10yrs

See advert on this page

Storrs Gate House

Winner of Bed and Breakfast of the Year in the Cumbria Tourism Awards 2009 • Five Stars with a Silver Award
• Delightful, detached 19C luxury guesthouse, opposite Lake Windermere. • Family run, with a friendly atmosphere and personal service.
• Beautiful king-size four poster suites and stunning power showers. • Scrumptious breakfasts using local and home-made produce.
• Ample parking. • Romantic gardens. • Wheelchair accessible ground floor accommodation.
• Voted in the top 5 B&B's in the UK by Period Living Magazine Awards. • Recommended by *Which? Good B&B Guide.*

Longtail Hill, Bowness-on-Windermere, Cumbria LA23 3JD   Tel: 015394 43272   Website: www.storrsgatehouse.co.uk   Email: enquiries@storrsgatehouse.co.uk

---

Fairfield House and Gardens

The Fairfield is a charming Georgian house set in quiet secluded grounds with its own car park. Located in a quiet cul-de-sac, yet just a few steps from the waterfront, shops, pubs, clubs and restaurants of Bowness.

A spacious terrace and a large lounge, where we are licensed for alcohol, and free Internet access and Wi-fi are available. We have four-poster rooms, deluxe rooms with spa bath's and a roofspace penthouse.

Brantfell Road, Bowness Bay, Windermere, Cumbria LA23 3AE
Tel: 015394 46565   Fax: 015394 46564
Website: www.the-fairfield.co.uk

WINDERMERE *continued*

The Hideaway at Windermere

★★★★ ● RESTAURANT WITH ROOMS

Phoenix Way LA23 1DB
☎ 015394 43070
e-mail: eatandstay@thehideawayatwindermere.co.uk
web: www.thehideawayatwindermere.co.uk
dir: *Exit A591 at Ravensworth B&B, onto Phoenix Way, The Hideaway 100mtrs on right*

Tucked away quietly this beautiful Victorian Lakeland house is personally run by owners Richard and Lisa. Delicious food, individually designed bedrooms and warm hospitality ensure an enjoyable stay. There is a beautifully appointed lounge looking out to the garden and the restaurant is split between two light and airy rooms; here guests will find the emphasis is on fresh, local ingredients and attentive, yet friendly service. Bedrooms vary in size and style, with the largest featuring luxury bathrooms.

Rooms 10 en suite 1 annexe en suite S £67-£150; D £90-£190 **Facilities** tea/coffee Dinner available Direct Dial Cen ht **Parking** 15 **Notes** LB ⊗ No Children 12yrs Closed Jan-mid Feb RS Mon & Tue Restaurant closed for dinner ex New Year No coaches

Blenheim Lodge

★★★★ GUEST ACCOMMODATION

Brantfell Rd, Bowness-on-Windermere LA23 3AE
☎ 015394 43440
e-mail: enquiries@blenheim-lodge.com
dir: *From Windermere to Bowness village, left at mini rdbt, 1st left & left again, house at top*

From a peaceful position above the town of Bowness, Blenheim Lodge has some stunning panoramic views of Lake Windermere. Bedrooms are well equipped featuring antique furnishings and pocket-sprung mattresses. Most beds are antiques themselves and include two William IV four-posters and three Louis XV beds. There is a comfortable lounge and a beautifully decorated dining room.

Rooms 11 rms (10 en suite) (1 pri facs) (2 fmly) (2 GF) S £50-£59; D £79-£138* **Facilities** TVL tea/coffee Licensed Two free fishing permits **Parking** 11 **Notes** LB ⊗ Closed 25 Dec RS 20-27 Dec may open - phone for details

The Coach House

★★★★ GUEST ACCOMMODATION

Lake Rd LA23 2EQ
☎ 015394 44494
e-mail: enquiries@lakedistrictbandb.com
web: www.lakedistrictbandb.com
dir: *A591 to Windermere house 0.5m on right opp St Herbert's Church*

Expect a relaxed and welcoming atmosphere at this stylish house, which has a minimalist interior with bright decor and cosmopolitan furnishings. The attractive bedrooms are well equipped. There is a reception lounge, and a breakfast room where freshly prepared breakfasts feature the best of local produce.

Rooms 5 en suite (1 fmly) S £45-£70; D £60-£80 **Facilities** FTV tea/coffee Cen ht Wi-fi Use of local health & leisure club **Parking** 5 **Notes** LB ⊗ No Children 5yrs Closed 24-26 Dec

The Coppice

★★★★ 🔒 🍴 GUEST HOUSE

Brook Rd LA23 2ED
☎ 015394 88501 📄 015394 42148
e-mail: chris@thecoppice.co.uk
web: www.thecoppice.co.uk
dir: *0.25m S of village centre on A5074*

This attractive detached house lies between Windermere and Bowness. There are colourful public rooms and bedrooms, and a restaurant serving freshly prepared local produce. The bedrooms vary in size and style and have good facilities.

Rooms 9 en suite (2 fmly) (1 GF) S £40-£65; D £68-£120* **Facilities** tea/coffee Dinner available Cen ht Licensed Wi-fi Private leisure club membership **Parking** 10 **Notes** LB

The Cottage

★★★★ 🔒 GUEST ACCOMMODATION

Elleray Rd LA23 1AG
☎ 015394 44796
e-mail: enquiries@thecottageguesthouse.com
dir: *A591, past Windermere Hotel, in 150yds turn left onto Elleray Rd. The Cottage 150yds on left*

Built in 1847, this attractive house has been extensively refurbished to offer a blend of modern and traditional styles. The tastefully furnished bedrooms are well equipped and comfortable. A wide choice of freshly cooked breakfasts are served in the spacious dining room at individual tables.

Rooms 8 en suite (2 GF); D £58-£98* **Facilities** FTV tea/coffee Cen ht **Parking** 8 **Notes** ⊗ No Children 11yrs Closed Nov-Jan

Fair Rigg

★★★★ GUEST ACCOMMODATION

Ferry View LA23 3JB
☎ 015394 43941
e-mail: stay@fairrigg.co.uk
web: www.fairrigg.co.uk
dir: 0.5m S of village centre at junct A5074 & B5284

This late Victorian house has been refurbished to provide spacious accommodation, while retaining many original features. The elegant dining room and many of the bedrooms have delightful views of the lake and to the mountains. Bedrooms are attractively decorated and well equipped.

Rooms 6 en suite (1 GF) S £35-£55; D £62-£88*
Facilities tea/coffee Cen ht Wi-fi **Parking** 6 **Notes** LB ⊗
No Children 14yrs Closed 22-27 Dec

Fir Trees

★★★★ GUEST HOUSE

Lake Rd LA23 2EQ
☎ 015394 42272 📠 015394 42512
e-mail: enquiries@fir-trees.com
web: www.fir-trees.co.uk
dir: Off A591 through town, Lake Rd in 0.5m, Fir Trees on left after clock tower

Located halfway between Windermere town and the lake, this spacious Victorian house offers attractive and well equipped accommodation. Bedrooms are generously proportioned and have many thoughtful extra touches. Breakfasts, featuring the best of local produce, are served at individual tables in the smart dining room.

Rooms 9 en suite (2 fmly) (3 GF) S £45-£55; D £64-£72*
Facilities tea/coffee Dinner available Cen ht Wi-fi Free use of local country club (2 nights stay) **Parking** 9
Notes LB ⊗

Glencree

★★★★ GUEST HOUSE

Lake Rd LA23 2EQ
☎ 015394 45822
e-mail: h.butterworth@btinternet.com
web: www.glencreelakes.co.uk
dir: From town centre signs for Bowness & The Lake, Glencree on right after large wooded area on right

Colourful hanging baskets and floral displays adorn the car park and entrance to Glencree, which lies between

Windermere and Bowness. Bedrooms are brightly decorated and individually furnished. The attractive lounge, with an honesty bar, is next to the dining room, where breakfasts are served at individual tables.

Rooms 6 en suite (1 fmly) (1 GF) S £45-£65; D £60-£90*
Facilities TVL tea/coffee Dinner available Cen ht Licensed Wi-fi **Parking** 6 **Notes** LB ⊗

Glenville House

★★★★ GUEST HOUSE

Lake Rd LA23 2EQ
☎ 015394 43371 📠 015394 48457
e-mail: mail@glenvillehouse.co.uk
dir: Off A591 into Windermere, B5074 to Bowness, Glenville 0.5m on right next to St John's Church

This traditional Lakeland stone house has a relaxing and friendly atmosphere, and is just a short walk from the town centre and Lake Windermere. Breakfast, including a wide choice of cooked dishes, is served in the pleasant dining room. Bedrooms are attractively decorated and furnished with good quality en suite bathrooms.

Rooms 7 en suite (1 GF) S £65-£99; D £60-£125
Facilities tea/coffee Cen ht Wi-fi **Parking** 7 **Notes** LB ⊗
No Children Closed Xmas

The Haven

★★★★ BED AND BREAKFAST

10 Birch St LA23 1EG
☎ 015394 44017
e-mail: thehaven.windermere@btopenworld.com
dir: On A5074 enter one-way system, 3rd left onto Birch St

Built from Lakeland slate and stone, this Victorian house is just a stroll from the town centre and shops. The bright, spacious bedrooms offer en suite or private facilities, and one has a Victorian brass bed. A hearty Cumbrian breakfast is served in the well-appointed dining room that doubles as a lounge.

Rooms 3 en suite (1 fmly); D £44-£84 **Facilities** tea/coffee Cen ht Wi-fi **Parking** 3 **Notes** LB ⊗ No Children 7yrs

Holly-Wood Guest House

★★★★ GUEST HOUSE

Holly Rd LA23 2AF
☎ 015394 42219
e-mail: info@hollywoodguesthouse.co.uk
web: www.hollywoodguesthouse.co.uk
dir: A591 towards Windermere, left into town, left again onto Ellerthwaite Rd, next left into Holly Rd

This attractive Victorian end terrace is located in a quiet residential area just a few minutes walk from the town centre. Guests are offered a friendly welcome, comfortable, well equipped bedrooms and a freshly prepared breakfast. Limited off street parking is also available.

Rooms 6 en suite (1 fmly) S £35-£45; D £70-£80
Facilities tea/coffee Cen ht **Parking** 3 **Notes** ⊗ No Children 10yrs Closed 22-28 Dec

Invergarry Guest House

★★★★ GUEST HOUSE

3 Thornbarrow Rd LA23 2EW
☎ 015394 44561 📠 015394 43960
e-mail: invergarryguesthouse@btinternet.com
web: www.invergarrywindermere.com
dir: Towards Bowness, turn left onto Thornbarrow Road

Just 10 minutes' walk from the villages of Windermere and Bowness-on-Windermere, this 19th-century traditional Lakeland house offers a warm welcome to all guests. Bedrooms and bathrooms are comfortable, well equipped and include a chalet room in the courtyard garden. Guests also have use of a cosy lounge. A wide choice is offered at breakfast.

Rooms 4 en suite 1 annexe en suite (1 GF) S £45; D £60-£90 **Facilities** tea/coffee Cen ht **Parking** 2
Notes LB ⊗ No Children 16yrs

WINDERMERE *continued*

Jerichos at The Waverley

★★★★ ◉◉ ✿ RESTAURANT WITH ROOMS

College Rd LA23 1BX
☎ 015394 42522 📠 015394 88899
e-mail: info@jerichos.co.uk
dir: *A591 to Windermere, 2nd left onto Elleray Rd then 1st right onto College Rd*

Dating back to around 1870, this centrally located property has been lovingly restored by its current owners over the last twelve years. All the elegantly furnished bedrooms are en suite and the top floor rooms have views of the fells. Breakfast is served in the Restaurant Room, and the comfortable lounge has a real fire to relax by on chillier days. The chef/proprietor has established a strong reputation for his creative menus that use the best local and seasonal produce. The restaurant is always busy so booking is essential. Wi-fi is available.

Rooms 10 en suite (1 fmly) S £35-£45; D £68-£100*
Facilities tea/coffee Dinner available Cen ht Wi-fi
Parking 12 **Notes** LB ⊗ No Children 4yrs Closed 1-14 Nov & 3wks from 10 Jan No coaches

The Old Court House

★★★★ GUEST HOUSE

Lake Rd LA23 3AP
☎ 015394 45096
e-mail: alison@theoch.co.uk
dir: *On Windermere-Bowness road at junct Longlands Rd*

Guests are given a warm welcome at this attractive former Victorian police station and courthouse, located in the centre of Bowness. Comfortable, pine-furnished bedrooms offer a good range of extra facilities. Freshly prepared breakfasts are served in the bright ground-floor dining room.

Rooms 6 en suite (2 GF) S £40-£60; D £60-£80*
Facilities tea/coffee Cen ht Wi-fi **Parking** 6 **Notes** LB ⊗ No Children 10yrs

The Willowsmere

★★★★ ✿ GUEST HOUSE

Ambleside Rd LA23 1ES
☎ 015394 43575 📠 015394 44962
e-mail: info@thewillowsmere.com
web: www.thewillowsmere.com
dir: *On A591, 500yds on left after Windermere station, towards Ambleside*

Willowsmere is a friendly, family-run establishment within easy walking distance of the town centre. It stands in a colourful, well-tended garden, with a patio and water feature to the rear. The attractive bedrooms are spacious, and there is a choice of inviting lounges and a well-stocked bar. Delicious breakfasts are served at individual tables in the stylish dining room.

Rooms 12 en suite (1 GF) S £38-£66; D £64-£132*
Facilities TVL tea/coffee Cen ht Licensed Wi-fi Free use of pool, sauna and gym at local hotel **Parking** 15 **Notes** LB ⊗ No Children 12yrs

St Johns Lodge

★★★ ✿ GUEST ACCOMMODATION

Lake Rd LA23 2EQ
☎ 015394 43078 📠 015394 88054
e-mail: mail@st-johns-lodge.co.uk
web: www.st-johns-lodge.co.uk
dir: *On A5074 between Windermere & lake*

Located between Windermere and Bowness, this large guest house offers a refreshingly friendly welcome. Bedrooms vary in size and style but all are neatly furnished and decorated. Freshly prepared traditional breakfasts, including vegetarian, vegan, gluten and dairy free options, are served in the well-appointed basement dining room. Facilities include free internet access.

Rooms 12 en suite (1 fmly) **Facilities** tea/coffee Cen ht Wi-fi Free access to local leisure club **Parking** 3 **Notes** ⊗ No Children 12yrs Closed Xmas

Adam Place Guest House

★★★ GUEST HOUSE

1 Park Av LA23 2AR
☎ 015394 44600 📠 015394 44600
e-mail: adamplacewindermere@yahoo.co.uk
web: www.adam-place.co.uk
dir: *Off A591 into Windermere, through town centre, left onto Ellerthwaite Rd & Park Av*

Located in a mainly residential area within easy walking distance of lake and town centre, this stone Victorian house has been renovated to provide comfortable and homely bedrooms. Comprehensive breakfasts are served in the cosy dining room and there is a pretty patio garden.

Rooms 5 en suite (2 fmly) S £30-£40; D £50-£70
Facilities tea/coffee Cen ht **Notes** ⊗ No Children 6yrs

Broadlands

★★★ GUEST HOUSE

19 Broad St LA23 2AB
☎ 015394 46532
e-mail: enquiries@broadlandsbandb.co.uk
dir: *From A591 follow one-way system, left onto Broad St after pedestrian crossing*

A friendly welcome is offered at this attractive house opposite the park and library and convenient for central amenities. Bedrooms are pleasantly co-ordinated and comfortably furnished, and freshly prepared breakfasts are served in the ground-floor dining room.

Rooms 5 en suite (2 fmly) S £27-£32; D £54-£65*
Facilities FTV tea/coffee Cen ht Wi-fi **Notes** LB ⊗ No Children 12yrs Closed Jan & Feb

Eagle & Child Inn

★★★ INN

Kendal Rd, Staveley LA8 9LP
☎ 01539 821320
e-mail: info@eaglechildinn.co.uk
web: www.eaglechildinn.co.uk
dir: *A591 from Kendal towards Windermere, sign for Staveley, pub 500yds on left*

Close to the beautiful Kentmere valley, this delightful village pub offers comfortable accommodation and good food. A choice of local cask ales can be enjoyed in either the tranquil riverside garden or the spacious bar. Breakfast is served in the Redmond Suite, which is available for functions.

Rooms 5 en suite (1 fmly) **Facilities** tea/coffee Dinner available Cen ht Local Leisure Club facilities can be arranged **Conf** Max 60 Board 40 **Parking** 16 **Notes** ⊗

Elim House

★★★ GUEST ACCOMMODATION

Biskey Howe Rd LA23 2JP
☎ 015394 42021 📠 015394 42021
e-mail: elimhouse@btopenworld.com
web: www.elimhouse.co.uk
dir: *Left off A5074, 150yds past police station, turn left onto Biskey Howe Rd, 1st house on left*

A short walk from the bustling village of Bowness and the lake, this attractive house has a colourful, well-kept garden. Bedrooms, some in an annexe, vary in size and style, but all offer sound levels of comfort. A hearty Cumbrian breakfast is served in the cheerful breakfast room.

Rooms 6 en suite 3 annexe en suite; D £60-£100
Facilities FTV tea/coffee Wi-fi **Parking** 7 **Notes** LB ⊗ No Children Closed 1-26 Dec RS Jan-Mar wknds only ex 14 Feb

Green Gables Guest House

★★★ GUEST HOUSE

37 Broad St LA23 2AB
☎ 015394 43886
e-mail: info@greengablesguesthouse.co.uk
dir: Off A591 into Windermere, 1st left after pelican crossing, opp car park

Aptly named, Green Gables is a friendly guest house looking onto Elleray Gardens. Just a short walk from the centre, the house is attractively furnished and offers bright, fresh and well appointed bedrooms. There is a comfortable bar-lounge, and substantial breakfasts are served in the spacious dining room.

Rooms 7 rms (4 en suite) (3 pri facs) (3 fmly) (1 GF) **Facilities** TVL tea/coffee Cen ht Licensed **Notes** ⊗ Closed 23-27 Dec

DERBYSHIRE

ALFRETON Map 16 SK45

Oaktree Farm

★★★ BED AND BREAKFAST

Matlock Rd, Oakerthorpe, Wessington DE55 7NA
☎ 01773 832957 & 07999 876969
e-mail: katherine770@btinternet.com
dir: 2m W of Alfreton. A615 W under railway bridge & past cottages, farmhouse on left

Set in 22 acres, including a fishing lake, chicken run and kitchen garden, this mellow-stone house provides thoughtfully equipped bedrooms complemented by modern bathrooms. Breakfasts using the freshest ingredients are served in an attractive cottage-style dining room. The pretty floral patio is a bonus in summer.

Rooms 3 en suite S £30-£32; D £50-£52* **Facilities** STV TVL tea/coffee Cen ht Fishing **Parking** 10 **Notes** ⊗ Closed 24-26 Dec ✉

ASHBOURNE Map 10 SK14

PREMIER COLLECTION

Turlow Bank

★★★★★ ■ BED AND BREAKFAST

Hognaston DE6 1PW
☎ 01335 370299 ▤ 01335 370299
e-mail: turlowbank@w3z.co.uk
web: www.turlowbank.co.uk
dir: Off B5035 to Hognaston (signed Hognaston only), through village towards Hulland Ward, Turlow Bank 0.5m, look for clock tower

Set in delightful gardens on a superb elevated position close to Carsington Water, this extended 19th-century farmhouse provides high levels of comfort with excellent facilities. Bedrooms are equipped with many thoughtful extras and feature quality modern bathrooms. Comprehensive breakfasts, which include free-range chicken or duck eggs, are served at a family table in the cosy dining room. A spacious lounge is available. Hospitality is memorable.

Rooms 2 en suite S £45-£55; D £70-£90 **Facilities** TVL tea/coffee Cen ht Wi-fi ⌣ **Parking** 6 **Notes** ⊗ No Children 12yrs Closed 25-27 Dec ✉

Bramhall's of Ashbourne

★★★★ GUEST ACCOMMODATION

6 Buxton Rd DE6 1EX
☎ 01335 346158 ▤ 01335 347453
e-mail: info@bramhalls.co.uk
dir: From market square N onto Buxton Rd up hill, on left

Located in the heart of this historic market town, Bramhall's occupies a conversion of two cottages and an Edwardian house. It is increasingly popular for its imaginative food and excellent value for money.

Bedrooms are filled with thoughtful extras and there is a pleasant courtyard garden at the rear.

Rooms 10 rms (8 en suite) (2 pri facs) (2 fmly) (1 GF) **Facilities** FTV tea/coffee Dinner available Cen ht Licensed Wi-fi **Conf** Max 25 **Parking** 5 **Notes** LB ⊗

Compton House

★★★★ GUEST ACCOMMODATION

27-31 Compton DE6 1BX
☎ 01335 343100
e-mail: jane@comptonhouse.co.uk
web: www.comptonhouse.co.uk
dir: A52 from Derby into Ashbourne, over lights at bottom of hill, house 100yds on left opp garage

Within easy walking distance of the central attractions, this conversion of three cottages has resulted in a house with good standards of comfort and facilities. Bedrooms are filled with homely extras and comprehensive breakfasts are served in the cottage-style dining room.

Rooms 5 en suite (2 fmly) (1 GF) S £35-£40; D £60-£70 **Facilities** TVL tea/coffee Cen ht Wi-fi **Parking** 6 **Notes** LB

Mercaston Hall (SK279419)

★★★★ FARMHOUSE

Mercaston DE6 3BL
☎ 01335 360263   Mr & Mrs A Haddon
e-mail: mercastonhall@btinternet.com
dir: Off A52 in Brailsford onto Luke Ln, 1m turn right at 1st x-rds, house 1m on right

Located in a pretty hamlet, this medieval building retains many original features. Bedrooms are homely, and additional facilities include an all-weather tennis court and a livery service. This is a good base for visiting local stately homes, the Derwent Valley mills and Dovedale.

Rooms 3 en suite S fr £50; D fr £70 **Facilities** FTV tea/coffee Cen ht ⌣ **Parking** **Notes** No Children 8yrs Closed Xmas ✉ 60 acres mixed

Mona Villas Bed & Breakfast

★★★★ BED AND BREAKFAST

1 Mona Villas, Church Ln, Middle Mayfield DE6 2JS
☎ 01335 343773 ▤ 01335 343773
e-mail: info@mona-villas.fsnet.co.uk
web: www.mona-villas.fsnet.co.uk
dir: 2.5m SW of Ashbourne. B5032 to Middle Mayfield, onto Church Ln, 400yds on right

This well-furnished house overlooks open fields close to the village. The bedrooms are very well equipped and have good facilities. Substantial breakfasts are served in the bright dining room and hospitality is a major strength.

Rooms 3 en suite (1 GF) S £30-£35; D £48-£56* **Facilities** FTV tea/coffee Cen ht **Parking** 6 **Notes** LB ⊗ ✉

ASHBOURNE *continued*

The Wheel House

★★★★ 🏠 BED AND BREAKFAST

Belper Rd, Hulland Ward DE6 3EE
☎ 01335 372837   📠 01335 372837
e-mail: thewheelhouse@btinternet.com
dir: *Between Ashbourne & Belper on A517*

This comfortably furnished house is set in open countryside on the main road between Ashbourne and Belper. The bedrooms are well furnished and a cosy lounge is also available. Breakfasts are hearty, and guests can expect friendly and attentive service.

Rooms 3 en suite (1 fmly) S £45-£55; D £60-£70*
Facilities TVL tea/coffee Cen ht Wi-fi **Parking** 5 **Notes** LB ⊗

Homesclose House

★★★ BED AND BREAKFAST

DE6 2DA
☎ 01335 324475
e-mail: gilltomlinson@tiscali.co.uk
dir: *Off A52 into village centre*

Stunning views of the surrounding countryside and manicured gardens are a feature of this beautifully maintained dormer bungalow. Bedrooms are filled with homely extras, and an attractive dining room with one family table is the setting for breakfast.

Rooms 3 rms (2 en suite) (1 fmly) (1 GF) **Facilities** TVL tea/coffee Cen ht **Parking** 4 **Notes** LB Closed Dec-Jan ⊗

Thistle Bank Guest House

★★★ GUEST ACCOMMODATION

24A Derby Rd DE6 1BE
☎ 01335 300451
e-mail: cindy.swann@hotmail.co.uk
dir: *M1 junct 25, A52 to Derby, A52 to Ashbourne, located at bottom of hill on right*

Set on the outskirts of Ashbourne, Thistle Bank offers four spacious, well equipped, modern en suite bedrooms. Breakfasts are hearty, and guests can expect friendly and attentive service. An ideal location to explore the Peak District National Park.

Rooms 4 en suite (3 fmly) S £30-£35; D £60-£65*
Facilities TVL Cen ht Wi-fi **Parking** 5 **Notes** ⊗

The Old Barn at Common End Farm

★★★ GUEST ACCOMMODATION

Common End Farm, Swinscoe DE6 2BW
☎ 01335 342342
e-mail: commonendbarn@hotmail.co.uk
web: www.commonendbarn.co.uk
dir: *4m W of Ashbourne. Off A52 at Swinscoe*

This converted barn provides a range of pine-furnished bedrooms with modern shower rooms en suite. Breakfast is served in the cosy dining room and a lounge is available.

Rooms 6 en suite (2 fmly) (4 GF) S £40-£42.50; D £60-£65 **Facilities** TVL tea/coffee Cen ht **Parking** 10 **Notes** LB ⊗

Stone Cottage

★★★ BED AND BREAKFAST

Green Ln, Clifton DE6 2BL
☎ 01335 343377
e-mail: info@stone-cottage.fsnet.co.uk
web: www.stone-cottage.fsnet.co.uk
dir: *1m from Ashbourne on A52 (Leek-Uttoxeter). Left at sign for Clifton, 2nd house on right*

A good base for touring and only a short drive from the town centre, this well-maintained stone house stands in pretty gardens and provides homely bedrooms. Freshly cooked breakfasts are served in an attractive conservatory, and tourist information is available.

Rooms 3 en suite (1 fmly) S £28-£45; D £50-£64*
Facilities STV TVL tea/coffee Cen ht **Parking** 4 **Notes** ⊗

Air Cottage Farm *(SK142523)*

★★ FARMHOUSE

Ilam DE6 2BD
☎ 01335 350475   Mrs J Wain
dir: *A515 from Ashbourne, left signed Thorpe/Dovedale/ Ilam, in Ilam right at memorial stone to Alstonfield, right at 1st cattle grid gate on right leaving village, 2nd farm on drive*

This 18th-century farmhouse has a magnificent elevated position with stunning views over the countryside and Dovedale. It provides traditional standards of accommodation and is very popular with serious walkers, climbers and artists visiting this beautiful part of the Peak District.

Rooms 3 rms (3 GF) S £26-£29; D £52-£58 **Facilities** TVL tea/coffee Cen ht **Parking** 4 **Notes** ⊗ Closed Dec-Feb ⊗ 320 acres cattle/sheep

---

BAKEWELL   Map 16 SK26

Avenue House

★★★★ GUEST ACCOMMODATION

The Avenue DE45 1EQ
☎ 01629 812467
dir: *Off A6 onto The Avenue, 1st house on right*

Located a short walk from the town centre, this impressive Victorian house has original features complemented by the décor and furnishings. Bedrooms have many thoughtful extras and the modern bathrooms contain power showers. Hearty English breakfasts are served in the traditionally furnished dining room.

Rooms 3 en suite S £38-£45; D £55-£65 **Facilities** STV tea/coffee Cen ht **Parking** 3 **Notes** ⊗ ⊛

Bourne House

★★★★ GUEST HOUSE

The Park, Haddon Rd DE45 1ET
☎ 01629 813274
dir: *300yds S of town centre on A6, on left before park*

This impressive former manse stands in mature gardens and is located overlooking the park a few minutes' walk from the town centre. Bedrooms are spacious and lots of thoughtful extras enhance guest comfort. Breakfast is taken in an attractive period-furnished dining room and a warm welcome is assured.

Rooms 3 en suite; D fr £56 **Facilities** tea/coffee Cen ht **Parking** 5 **Notes** ⊗ No Children 7yrs Closed Dec-Feb ⊛

Croft Cottages

★★★★ GUEST ACCOMMODATION

Coombs Rd DE45 1AQ
☎ 01629 814101
e-mail: croftco@btinternet.com
dir: *A619 E from town centre over bridge, right onto Station Rd & Coombs Rd*

A warm welcome is assured at this Grade II listed stone building close to the River Wye and town centre. Thoughtfully equipped bedrooms are available in the main house or in an adjoining converted barn suite. Breakfast is served in a spacious lounge dining room.

Rooms 3 rms (2 en suite) (1 pri facs) 1 annexe en suite (1 fmly); D £60-£78 **Facilities** tea/coffee Cen ht **Parking** 2 **Notes** ⊛

Holly Cottage

★★★★ BED AND BREAKFAST

Pilsley DE45 1UH
☎ **01246 582245** 📠 **01246 583177**
e-mail: hollycottagebandb@btinternet.com
dir: *Follow brown tourist signs for Chatsworth & Pilsley. Holly Cottage next to post office*

A warm welcome is assured at this mellow stone cottage, part of a combined Post Office and shop in the conservation area of Pilsley, which is owned by the adjacent Chatsworth Estate. The cosy bedrooms feature a wealth of thoughtful extras, and comprehensive breakfasts, utilising quality local produce, are taken in an attractive pine-furnished dining room.

Rooms 3 en suite S £60-£70; D £65-£75* **Facilities** tea/coffee Cen ht Wi-fi **Notes** LB ⊗ No Children 10yrs

Wyedale

★★★★ BED AND BREAKFAST

Wyedale House, 25 Holywell DE45 1BA
☎ **01629 812845**
dir: *500yds SE of town centre, off A6 (Haddon Rd)*

Wyedale is close to the town centre and is ideal for relaxing or touring. Bedrooms, one of which is on the ground floor, are spacious and freshly decorated. Breakfast is served in the attractive dining room, which overlooks the rear patio.

Rooms 4 en suite (1 fmly) (1 GF); D £50-£60* **Facilities** tea/coffee Cen ht **Parking** 5 **Notes** ⊗ Closed 31 Dec RS 24 Dec

Everton

★★★ GUEST HOUSE

Haddon Rd DE45 1AW
☎ **01629 815028**
e-mail: trish@evertonbandb.co.uk
dir: *S of Bakewell on A6*

Ideally located opposite a public park and a few minutes walk from central attractions, this large semi-detached house provides comfortable homely bedrooms and an attractive pine-furnished dining room, the setting for comprehensive breakfasts.

Rooms 3 rms (2 en suite) (1 pri facs) (1 fmly) S £30-£45; D £50-£65* **Facilities** tea/coffee Cen ht **Parking** 6 **Notes** LB Closed 24-26 Dec RS 30-31 Dec 🐾

The George

★★★ INN

Church St, Youlgreave DE45 1UW
☎ **01629 636292** 📠 **01632 636292**
dir: *3m S of Bakewell in Youlgreave, opp church*

The public bars of the 17th-century George are popular with locals and tourists. Bedroom styles vary, and all have shower rooms en suite. Breakfast is served in the lounge bar, and a range of bar meals and snacks is available.

Rooms 3 en suite (1 fmly) **Facilities** tea/coffee Dinner available Cen ht Fishing **Parking** 12 **Notes** 🐾

Wyeclose

★★★ BED AND BREAKFAST

5 Granby Croft DE45 1ET
☎ **01629 813702** 📠 **01629 813702**
e-mail: h.wilson@talk21.com
dir: *Off A6 Matlock St onto Granby Rd & Granby Croft*

Located in a quiet cul-de-sac in the town centre, this Edwardian house provides thoughtfully furnished bedroom accommodation with smart modern bathrooms and an attractive dining room, the setting for comprehensive breakfasts. Original family art is a feature in the ground-floor areas.

Rooms 2 rms (1 en suite) (1 pri facs); D £56* **Facilities** STV FTV tea/coffee Cen ht **Parking** 3 **Notes** ⊗ No Children 8yrs Closed Xmas & New Year 🐾

Yorkshire Bridge Inn

★★★★ INN

Ashopton Rd S33 0AZ
☎ **01433 651361** 📠 **01433 651361**
e-mail: info@yorkshire-bridge.co.uk
web: www.yorkshire-bridge.co.uk

A well-established country inn, ideally located beside Ladybower Dam and within reach of the Peak District's many beauty spots, the Yorkshire Bridge Inn offers a wide range of excellent dishes in both the bar and dining area, along with a good selection of real ales. Bedrooms are attractively furnished, comfortable and well-equipped.

Rooms 14 en suite (3 fmly) (4 GF) **Facilities** STV tea/coffee Dinner available Direct Dial Cen ht **Conf** Max 20 **Parking** 50

See advert on this page

• Glorious Peak District location
• Fantastic real ales
• Fine food prepared to order
• Fresh local produce
• 14 comfortable bedrooms
• Friendly atmosphere for all

Freehouse of the year
finalist 2000, 2001 & 2004

Call 01433 651361 for a brochure
web: www.yorkshire-bridge.co.uk

AA ★★★★ INN

BAMFORD *continued*

Thornhill View

★★★ GUEST ACCOMMODATION

Hope Rd, Bamford, Hope Valley S33 0AL
☎ 01433 651823
e-mail: thornhill4bb@aol.com
dir: 0.5m SW of Bamford. On A6187 at Thornhill Ln junct

Comfortable accommodation in a secluded location, set back from the main road running through the Hope Valley nearby to the Rising Sun Inn. Compact bedrooms are well equipped, and Jo Fairbairn is a caring hostess.

Rooms 3 rms (2 en suite) (1 pri facs) (2 GF) D £55–£60 **Facilities** tea/coffee Cen ht **Parking** 3 **Notes** LB ⊗

The White House

★★★ BED AND BREAKFAST

Shatton Ln S33 0BG
☎ 01433 651487 📠 01433 651487
dir: A6187 (Hathersage to Hope), left opp High Peak Garden Centre into Shatton. White House 250yds on left

Set in a secluded lane among attractive gardens, this large detached family home offers spacious, nicely laid out bedrooms. Breakfast is served around a large communal table in the neat dining room, which overlooks the garden. The comfortable lounge has a television.

Rooms 5 rms S fr £30; D fr £50* **Facilities** TVL tea/coffee Cen ht **Parking** 4 **Notes** ⊗

BEELEY
Map 16 SK26

Devonshire Arms-Beeley

★★★★ ⚙️⚙️ INN

Devonshire Square DE4 2NR
☎ 01629 733259 📠 01629 734542
e-mail: enquiries@devonshirebeeley.co.uk
web: www.devonshirebeeley.co.uk
dir: B6012 towards Matlock, pass Chatsworth House. After 1.5m turn left, 2nd entrance to Beeley village

The Devonshire Arms is a picturesque country inn at the heart of village life. It offers all the charm and character of an historic inn with a warm and comfortable interior full of oak beams and stone crannies, but venture inside a little further and you will find the startlingly different décor of the brasserie with its contemporary bar, glass fronted wine store and colourful furnishings. For the ultimate escape, there are four stylish cottage bedrooms.

Rooms 4 en suite 4 annexe en suite (1 fmly) (2 GF) **Facilities** STV tea/coffee Dinner available Direct Dial Cen ht Wi-fi **Parking** 40 **Notes** No coaches

BELPER
Map 11 SK34

PREMIER COLLECTION

Dannah Farm Country House

★★★★★ 🍴 GUEST ACCOMMODATION

Bowmans Ln, Shottle DE56 2DR
☎ 01773 550273 & 550630 📠 01773 550590
e-mail: reservations@dannah.co.uk
web: www.dannah.co.uk
dir: A517 from Belper towards Ashbourne, 1.5m right into Shottle after Hanging Gate pub on right, over x-rds & right

Part of the Chatsworth Estates at Shottle, on an elevated position with stunning views, this impressive Georgian house and outbuildings have been renovated to provide high standards of comfort and facilities. Many original features have been retained, and are enhanced by quality decor and furnishings. The bedrooms are filled with a wealth of thoughtful extras. One room has an outdoor hot tub. The Mixing Place restaurant is the setting for imaginative dinners and memorable breakfasts, which make use of the finest local produce.

Rooms 8 en suite (1 fmly) (2 GF) S £75–£95; D £150–£200* **Facilities** FTV tea/coffee Dinner available Direct Dial Cen ht Licensed Wi-fi Sauna Leisure cabin, hot tub **Conf** Max 10 Thtr 10 Class 10 Board 10 **Parking** 20 **Notes** LB ⊗ Closed 24–26 Dec

See advert on opposite page

Chevin Green Farm *(SK339471)*

★★★★ FARMHOUSE

Chevin Rd DE56 2UN
☎ 01773 822328 📠 01773 822328 Mr & Mrs Postles
e-mail: davidrmarley@btinternet.com
web: www.chevingreenfarm.org.uk
dir: Off A6 opp Strutt Arms at Milford onto Chevin Rd, 1.5m on left

You can be sure of a warm welcome at this 300-year-old farm overlooking the Derwent valley. Bedrooms are furnished with thoughtful extras and smart modern bathrooms. There is a comfortable lounge, and breakfast is served at separate tables in the cosy dining room. Self-catering units are also available.

Rooms 5 en suite (1 fmly) (1 GF) **Facilities** TVL tea/coffee Cen ht **Parking** 5 **Notes** ⊗ Closed Xmas & New Year 38 acres non-working

The Hollins

★★★★ BED AND BREAKFAST

45 Belper Ln DE56 2UQ
☎ 01773 823955
e-mail: emery.christine@googlemail.com
dir: A6 onto A517 W, over bridge, right onto Belper Ln, 300yds up hill

This immaculately maintained house is a 10-minute walk from the town centre. The bedroom is comfortable and equipped with many extras, and the dining room can be used for evening work or take-away food. The full English breakfast is a highlight.

Rooms 1 en suite (1 fmly) S £30–£35; D £55–£60* **Facilities** tea/coffee Cen ht **Parking** 1 **Notes** ⊗ No Children 4yrs ⊗

BIRCH VALE
Map 16 SK08

The Waltzing Weasel Inn

★★★ INN

8 New Mills Rd SK22 1BT
☎ 01663 743402 📠 01663 744397
e-mail: w-weasel@zen.co.uk
web: www.w-weasel.co.uk

Located between Glossop and Chapel-en-le-Frith in the High Peak District, this mellow stone inn enjoys a good local reputation for its range of real ales and imaginative food. Some of the spacious bedrooms offer fine rural views and a warm welcome is assured.

Rooms 8 en suite (1 fmly) (2 GF) **Facilities** tea/coffee Dinner available Cen ht **Conf** Thtr 15 Class 12 Board 10 **Parking** 42

BONSALL
Map 16 SK25

Pig of Lead

★★★★ GUEST ACCOMMODATION

Via Gellia Rd DE4 2AJ
☎ 01629 820040 📠 01629 820040
e-mail: pigoflead@aol.com
dir: 0.5m SE of Bonsall on A5012

This delightful property dating back over two hundred years was once an inn named after a measurement of lead, which used to be mined locally. Only five minutes from Matlock Bath, this is a good base for exploring the area. Individually styled bedrooms are comfortable and well appointed. A warm welcome and hearty breakfasts featuring local produce can be assured here.

Rooms 3 en suite **Facilities** tea/coffee Cen ht Wi-fi **Parking** 3 **Notes** No Children 14yrs ⊗

BRADWELL
Map 16 SK18

PREMIER COLLECTION

The Samuel Fox Country Inn
★★★★★ ◉ INN

Stretfield Rd S33 9JT
☎ 01433 621562 ▤ 01433 623770
e-mail: thesamuelfox@hotmail.co.uk
dir: M1 junct 29, A617 towards Chesterfield, A619
signed Baslow & Buxton, 2nd rdbt A623 for 7m, take
B6049 to Bradwell, through village on left

Recently renamed after Bradwell's most famous son,
industrial magnate Samuel Fox, who built the
steelworks at Stocksbridge. The Samuel Fox has
undergone a full refurbishment and is modern and
stylish while retaining its rustic charm. Bedrooms are
immaculately presented and extensively equipped.
Service is highly attentive. Modern British cuisine is
served in the restaurant with breathtaking views over
Bradwell.

Rooms 4 en suite S £75; D £115* Facilities tea/coffee
Dinner available Direct Dial Cen ht Parking 15
Notes LB ⊗ No coaches

BUXTON
Map 16 SK07

PREMIER COLLECTION

Grendon Guest House
★★★★★ 🍽 GUEST HOUSE

Bishops Ln SK17 6UN
☎ 01298 78831
e-mail: grendonguesthouse@hotmail.co.uk
web: www.grendonguesthouse.co.uk
dir: 0.75m from Buxton centre. Turn right off A53 (St
Johns Rd), just past Otter Hole development

A warm welcome is assured at this non-smoking
Edwardian house, set in immaculate grounds just a
short walk from the town centre. The spacious,
carefully furnished bedrooms are filled with thoughtful
extras and lots of local information. Stunning country
views can be enjoyed from the elegant lounge-dining
room, where imaginative dinners are served. The
attractive breakfast room is the setting for
comprehensive breakfasts using local produce.

Rooms 5 en suite; D £65-£90* Facilities FTV TVL tea/
coffee Dinner available Cen ht Wi-fi Parking 8
Notes LB No Children 10yrs

The Grosvenor House
★★★★ 🏠 GUEST HOUSE

1 Broad Walk SK17 6JE
☎ 01298 72439
e-mail: grosvenor.buxton@btopenworld.com
dir: In town centre

This Victorian house is centrally located overlooking the
Pavilion Gardens and Opera House. Bedrooms are
carefully furnished and have many thoughtful extras.
There is a comfortable period-style sitting room, and
freshly prepared imaginative breakfasts are served in the
cosy dining room.

Rooms 8 en suite (1 fmly) S £45-£50; D £65-£80*
Facilities tea/coffee Cen ht Wi-fi Conf Max 8 Parking 2
Notes ⊗ Closed Xmas

Dannah Farm
C O U N T R Y   H O U S E

*Superb award-winning accommodation, set amidst the
beautiful Derbyshire countryside on the Chatsworth
Estates at Shottle. Nestling just below Alport Heights
with its panoramic views over the surrounding six
counties, the discerning guest will find something a
little out of the ordinary at DannahFarm. From our
luxurious Spa Cabin to rooms oozing with the WOW
factor - unique detail waits around every corner. Sample
"The Studio Hideaway" with fantastic Canadian Spa
outdoor hot tub set on a private terrace, "The
Ecclesbourne" with wet room, double spa bath,
and private sauna, or even the stunning Red Room!*

AA
Highly Commended
★★★★★
Guest Accommodation
2009 - 2010

east midlands tourism
SILVER enjoy england
excellence
awards 2008

*Take a peek at our
website and discover
sheer unadulterated
luxury in The
Derbyshire Dales.*

**Dannah Farm, Bowmans Lane, Shottle, Nr Belper,
Derbyshire DE56 2DR. Tel: 01773 550 273.
slack@dannah.co.uk   www.dannah.co.uk**

BUXTON *continued*

Oldfield

★★★★ GUEST HOUSE

8 Macclesfield Rd SK17 9AH
☎ 01298 78264
e-mail: avril@oldfieldhousebuxton.co.uk
web: www.oldfieldhousebuxton.co.uk
dir: *On B5059 0.5m SW of town centre*

Located within easy walking distance of the centre, this impressive Victorian house provides spacious bedrooms with modern en suites. Comprehensive breakfasts are served in the bright dining room, and a cosy lounge is available.

Rooms 5 rms (3 en suite) (2 pri facs) (1 GF) D £75*
Facilities FTV TVL tea/coffee Cen ht **Parking** 7 **Notes** LB ⊗ Closed Xmas

Roseleigh

★★★★ GUEST HOUSE

19 Broad Walk SK17 6JR
☎ 01298 24904 🖷 01298 24904
e-mail: enquiries@roseleighhotel.co.uk
web: www.roseleighhotel.co.uk
dir: *A6 to Safeway rdbt, onto Dale Rd, right at lights, 100yds left by Swan pub, down hill & right onto Hartington Rd*

This elegant property has a prime location overlooking Pavilion Gardens, and quality furnishings and décor highlight the many original features. Thoughtfully furnished bedrooms have smart modern shower rooms and a comfortable lounge is also available.

Rooms 14 rms (12 en suite) (2 pri facs) (1 GF) S £35-£88; D £74-£88 **Facilities** tea/coffee Cen ht Wi-fi **Parking** 9 **Notes** ⊗ No Children 6yrs Closed 16 Dec-16 Jan

The Old Manse Guesthouse

★★★★ Ⓐ GUEST HOUSE

6 Clifton Rd, Silverlands SK17 6QL
☎ 01298 25638
e-mail: info@oldmanse.co.uk
web: www.oldmanse.co.uk
dir: *From A6 approach Buxton via Morrisons rdbt onto B5059 Dale Rd, 200yds before bridge right onto Peveril Rd & Clifton Rd*

Rooms 7 rms (6 en suite) (1 pri facs) (2 fmly) S £30-£32; D £60-£70* **Facilities** FTV TVL tea/coffee Cen ht Wi-fi **Conf** Max 20 Thtr 20 Class 15 Board 14 **Parking** 4 **Notes** LB ⊗

Wellhead Farm

★★★ GUEST ACCOMMODATION

Wormhill SK17 8SL
☎ 01298 871023 🖷 0871 236 0267
e-mail: wellhead4bunkntrough@cbits.net
dir: *Between Bakewell & Buxton. Off A6 onto B6049 signed Millers Dale/Tideswell & left to Wormhill. From A623 Chesterfield then left in Peak Forest, left to Wormhill*

This 16th-century farmhouse is in a peaceful location, and has low beams and two comfortable lounges. The bedrooms, some with four-poster beds, come with radios, beverage trays and many thoughtful extras. The proprietors provide friendly and attentive hospitality in their delightful home.

Rooms 4 en suite (1 fmly) S £45-£49; D £68-£70 **Facilities** TVL tea/coffee Dinner available Cen ht **Parking** 4 **Notes** LB 🕭

CALVER	Map 16 SK27

Valley View

★★★★ GUEST HOUSE

Smithy Knoll Rd S32 3XW
☎ 01433 631407
e-mail: sue@a-place-2-stay.co.uk
web: www.a-place-2-stay.co.uk
dir: *A623 from Baslow into Calver, 3rd left onto Donkey Ln*

This detached stone house is in the heart of the village. It is very well-furnished throughout and delightfully friendly service is provided. A hearty breakfast is served in the cosy dining room, which is well-stocked with local guide books.

Rooms 3 en suite 1 annexe en suite (1 GF); D £50-£80 **Facilities** tea/coffee Cen ht Wi-fi **Parking** 6 **Notes** LB No Children 5yrs

CARSINGTON	Map 16 SK25

Henmore Grange

★★★★ BED AND BREAKFAST

Hopton DE4 4DF
☎ 01629 540420 🖷 01629 540420
e-mail: henmoregrange@hotmail.com
dir: *B5035 into Hopton, Henmore Grange 2nd house on left*

Ideally located very close to Carsington Water, this stone built farmhouse has been tastefully restored and retains many original features. Bedrooms are comfortable and well appointed and a freshly cooked breakfast is served in the farmhouse style dining room. An ideal touring centre, offering secure cycle storage and ample parking.

Rooms 3 en suite (1 fmly) S £40-£50; D £70* **Facilities** tea/coffee Cen ht **Parking** 10 **Notes** LB ⊗ 🕭

CASTLETON	Map 16 SK18

See also Hope

The Rising Sun

★★★★ INN

Hope Rd S33 0AL
☎ 01433 651323 🖷 01433 651601
e-mail: info@the-rising-sun.org
dir: *On A625 from Sheffield to Castleton*

Located at Thornhill Moor in the Hope Valley, this 18th-century inn has been renovated to provide high standards of comfort and facilities. Spacious luxury bedrooms offer quality furnishings and efficient modern bathrooms, and some have stunning views of the surrounding countryside. The staff are friendly and capable, and imaginative food is offered in the comfortable public areas.

Rooms 12 en suite (2 fmly) S £55.50-£69.50; D £70-£140* **Facilities** STV tea/coffee Dinner available Cen ht Wi-fi **Conf** Max 200 Thtr 200 Class 200 Board 24 **Parking** 120 **Notes** LB Civ Wed 220

See advert on opposite page

CHESTERFIELD — Map 16 SK37

Batemans Mill

★★★★ Ⓐ INN

Mill Ln, Old Tupton S42 6AE
☎ 01246 862296 📠 01246 865672
e-mail: info@batemansmill.co.uk
dir: *6.5m S of Chesterfield. Off A61 at Clay Cross onto Holmgate Rd to Valley Rd & Mill Ln*

Rooms 8 en suite (1 fmly) (4 GF) **Facilities** FTV tea/coffee Dinner available Direct Dial Cen ht Wi-fi **Conf** Max 50 Thtr 50 Class 30 Board 30 **Parking** 50 **Notes** Closed 1st wk Jan

CROMFORD — Map 16 SK25

Alison House

★★★★ GUEST ACCOMMODATION

Intake Ln DE4 3RH
☎ 01629 822211 📠 01629 822316
e-mail: info@alison-house-hotel.co.uk

This very well furnished and spacious 18th-century house stands in seven acres of grounds just a short walk from

the village. Public rooms are comfortable and bedrooms are mostly very spacious.

Rooms 16 en suite (1 fmly) (4 GF) S £49; D £79-£99* **Facilities** tea/coffee Dinner available Direct Dial Cen ht Licensed Wi-fi 🌊 **Conf** Max 40 Thtr 40 Class 40 Board 40 **Parking** 30 **Notes** LB Civ Wed 50

DARLEY DALE — Map 16 SK26

Meadow House

★★★★ BED AND BREAKFAST

Dale Road North DE4 2HX
☎ 01629 734324
dir: *0.5m N of village centre on A6*

Located within a short distance of Matlock, this friendly, non-smoking house stands in grounds and is well furnished throughout. Guests can enjoy substantial tasty breakfasts in the cosy lounge-dining room.

Rooms 3 rms (2 en suite) (1 pri facs) (1 fmly) S £30-£35; D £50-£58* **Facilities** tea/coffee Cen ht **Parking** 6 **Notes** ⊗ No Children 8yrs 🚭

DERBY — Map 11 SK33

See also Belper & Melbourne

Chambers House

★★★ GUEST ACCOMMODATION

110 Green Ln DE1 1RY
☎ 01332 746412
web: www.chambershouse.co.uk
dir: *In city centre on Green Lane. Approach car park via Abbey St & Wilson St*

Located a short walk from the centre, this impressive double-fronted Victorian house retains many original features. The attractive bedrooms are generally spacious, some are en suite while others have shared facilities. A car park is available.

Rooms 12 rms (4 en suite) (2 fmly) (2 GF) **Facilities** TVL tea/coffee **Parking** 6 **Notes** ⊗ 🚭

The Derby Conference Centre

★★★ GUEST ACCOMMODATION

London Rd DE24 8UX
☎ 01332 861852 📠 01322 264410
e-mail: reservations@thederbyconferencecentre.com
web: www.thederbyconferencecentre.com
dir: *A50/A52 onto A6, located at rdbt with Pride Park*

Formerly a railway training centre, this Grade II-listed art deco building has undergone a major refurbishment to modernise the public areas, meeting rooms and accommodation, yet it still retains original features such as the wall paintings by Norman Wilkinson. Day rooms offer good flexibility and comforts, while updated conference facilities can cater for small to very large gatherings. The studio bedroom accommodation is soundly appointed and equipped.

Rooms 50 en suite (10 GF) S £45; D £55 **Facilities** FTV TVL tea/coffee Dinner available Cen ht Licensed Wi-fi Pool Table **Conf** Max 1000 Thtr 400 Class 80 Board 50 **Parking** 200 **Notes** ⊗ Closed 24 Dec-4 Jan Civ Wed 400

AA ★★★★

The Rising Sun

Silver ETC

'Winner of the East Midlands Small Hotel of Excellence Award 2005'

The Rising Sun, Thornhill Moor, Hope Road, Nr. Bamford, Hope Valley, Derbyshire S33 0AL
Telephone: 01433 651323 • Fax: 01433 651601
E-Mail: info@the-rising.sun.org • www.the-rising-sun.org

THIS IS NOT JUST ANOTHER INN THIS IS AN EXPERIENCE!

The Rising Sun, an 18th Century Inn situated in the heart of the Peak District National Park, is privately owned and family run. The inn has been sympathetically restored with 12 individually designed deluxe bedrooms yet maintains its authentic country atmosphere. Fresh flowers in abundance and antiques together with friendly and efficient staff make this the place to stay. Quality fresh food, real ales and fine wines served daily in a relaxed and comfortable bar. Civil ceremonies & wedding receptions a speciality.

FENNY BENTLEY — Map 16 SK14

Bentley Brook Inn

★★★ INN

DE6 1LF
☎ 01335 350278 📠 01335 350422
e-mail: all@bentleybrookinn.co.uk
dir: 2m N of Ashbourne at junct of A515 & B5056

This popular inn is located in the Peak District National Park, just north of Ashbourne. It is a charming building with an attractive terrace, sweeping lawns, and nursery gardens. A well-appointed family restaurant dominates the ground floor, where a wide range of dishes is available all day. The character bar serves beer from its own micro-brewery. Bedrooms are well appointed and thoughtfully equipped.

Rooms 11 en suite (1 fmly) (2 GF) **Facilities** TVL tea/coffee Dinner available Direct Dial Cen ht Wi-fi **Conf** Max 11 Thtr 11 Class 11 Board 11 **Parking** 60 **Notes** LB Civ Wed 40

FOOLOW — Map 16 SK17

The Bulls Head Inn

★★★★ INN

S32 5QR
☎ 01433 630873 📠 01433 631738
e-mail: wilbnd@aol.com
dir: Off A623 into Foolow

Located in the village centre, this popular inn retains many original features and offers comfortable, well-equipped bedrooms. Extensive and imaginative bar meals are served in the traditionally furnished dining room or in the cosy bar areas. The inn welcomes well-behaved dogs in the bar (and even muddy boots on the flagstone areas).

Rooms 3 en suite (1 fmly) **Facilities** tea/coffee Dinner available Cen ht **Parking** 20

FROGGATT — Map 16 SK27

The Chequers Inn

★★★★ ⊛ INN

S32 3ZJ
☎ 01433 630231 📠 01433 631072
e-mail: info@chequers-froggatt.com
dir: On A625 between Sheffield & Bakewell, 0.75m from Calver

A very popular 16th-century inn offering an extensive range of well-cooked food. The bedrooms are comprehensively equipped with all modern comforts and the hospitality is professional and sincere. A good location for touring Derbyshire, the Peak Park, and visiting Chatsworth.

Rooms 5 en suite S £70-£100; D £70-£100*
Facilities tea/coffee Dinner available Direct Dial Cen ht **Parking** 45 **Notes** LB ⊗ Closed 25 Dec No coaches

GLOSSOP — Map 16 SK09

Allmans Heath Cottage Bed & Breakfast

★★★★ 🏠 BED AND BREAKFAST

Woodhead Rd SK13 7QE
☎ 01457 857867
e-mail: julie@allmansheathcottage.co.uk
dir: From Glossop town centre lights, proceed up Nolfolk St towards Woodhead for 1m. Continue through tunnel of trees, on left turning in at farm gate

Just one mile from Glossop, this converted farm cottage has beamed ceilings, open fires and many original features. All the rooms command spectacular views over open countryside, and hospitality is warm and friendly. Julie Naylor was a finalist for the AA Friendliest Landlady of the Year 2009-2010 Award.

Rooms 2 rms (1 en suite) (1 pri facs); D £60*
Facilities TVL tea/coffee Cen ht Wi-fi **Parking** 6 **Notes** ⊗ ⊛

Woodlands

★★★★ BED AND BREAKFAST

Woodseats Ln, Charlesworth SK13 5DP
☎ 01457 866568
e-mail: brian.mairs@sky.com
web: www.woodlandshighpeak.co.uk
dir: 3m SW of Glossop. Off A626, 0.5m from Charlesworth towards Marple

This delightful Victorian house stands in well-tended grounds and offers very well-equipped and delightfully furnished bedrooms. There is a comfy lounge and a conservatory serving very good breakfasts, lunches and cream teas.

Rooms 3 rms (2 en suite) (1 pri facs) S £40-£45; D £60-£70* **Facilities** FTV TVL tea/coffee Cen ht Licensed **Parking** 5 **Notes** ⊗ No Children 12yrs ⊛

Rock Farm (SK027907)

★★★★ FARMHOUSE

Monks Rd SK13 6JZ
☎ 01457 861086 & 07780 670568
📠 01457 861086 Mrs Dennett
e-mail: rockfarmbandb@btinternet.com
dir: Off A624 onto Monks Rd, signed Charlesworth. After 1m, Rock Farm on left, follow farm track past Higher Plainsteads Farm

Located down a winding track, with spectacular views over Kinder Scout and the surrounding hills from all rooms, Rock Farm is a restored family home. Walkers, horses, and riders, as well as young families, are offered a particularly warm welcome. Fresh eggs are used at breakfast.

Rooms 2 rms S £40; D £60* **Facilities** TVL tea/coffee Dinner available Cen ht Stabling & grazing available for guests horses **Parking** 4 **Notes** ⊗ ⊛ 6 acres non-working

The Old House

★★★ BED AND BREAKFAST

Woodhead Rd, Torside SK13 1HU
☎ 01457 857527
e-mail: oldhouse@torside.co.uk
dir: 2m N of Glossop. On B6105 between sailing club & hairpin bend

Set on the northwest-facing slopes above a reservoir, this smallholding commands superb views and offers all mod cons, including a drying room for people who are walking the nearby Pennine Way. Oak beams and rough plastered walls date from the 17th century, and hospitality is warm.

Rooms 3 en suite (1 fmly) (1 GF) S £25-£35; D £50-£60*
Facilities TVL tea/coffee Dinner available Cen ht **Parking** 5 **Notes** LB ⊛

White House Farm *(SK031963)*

★★★ FARMHOUSE

Padfield SK13 1ET
☎ 01457 854695 📄 01457 854695 Mrs S Wynne
dir: *A628 from Sheffield to Tintwistle, signed to Padfield*

A 200-year-old farmhouse standing on the edge of Padfield village with fine views across the Longdendale Valley. The bedrooms are pleasantly furnished and comfortable. Breakfast is served around a large table in the dining room. There is a lounge and ample parking.

Rooms 1 rms 2 annexe rms (1 GF) **Facilities** FTV TVL tea/coffee Cen ht **Parking** 10 **Notes** 🐾 40 acres mixed

---

GREAT HUCKLOW   Map 16 SK17

The Queen Anne

★★★ INN

SK17 8RF
☎ 01298 871246 📄 01298 873504
e-mail: angelaryan100@aol.com
web: www.queenanneinn.co.uk
dir: *Off A623 onto B6049 to Great Hucklow*

Set in the heart of this pretty village, the Queen Anne has been a licensed inn for over 300 years and the public areas retain many original features. The bedrooms are in a separate building with direct access, and have modern shower rooms en suite.

Rooms 2 annexe en suite (2 GF) S £40-£50; D £60-£65* **Facilities** TVL tea/coffee Dinner available Cen ht **Parking** 20 **Notes** LB 🐾 No Children 10yrs Closed Xmas & New Year

---

HARTINGTON   Map 16 SK16

Bank House

★★★★ GUEST ACCOMMODATION

Market Place SK17 0AL
☎ 01298 84465
dir: *B5054 into village centre*

Bank House is a very well-maintained Grade II listed Georgian building that stands in the main square of this delightful village. Bedrooms are neat and fresh in appearance, and there is a comfortable television lounge. A hearty breakfast is served in the ground-floor cottage-style dining room.

Rooms 5 rms (3 en suite) (3 fmly) S £27-£34; D £50-£56* **Facilities** TVL tea/coffee Dinner available Cen ht **Parking** 2 **Notes** LB 🐾 Closed Xmas RS 22-28 Dec 🐾

HARTSHORNE   Map 10 SK32

The Mill Wheel

★★★★ 🍽 INN

Ticknall Rd DE11 7AS
☎ 01283 550335 📄 01283 552833
e-mail: info@themillwheel.co.uk
web: www.themillwheel.co.uk
dir: *M42 junct 2 follow signs for A511 to Woodville, left onto A514 towards Derby to Hartshorne*

This popular inn and restaurant provides a wide range of well-prepared food and has a large mill wheel in the bar. Bedrooms are modern and well-equipped while friendly and attentive service is provided.

Rooms 4 en suite (2 GF) D fr £58.95* **Facilities** FTV tea/coffee Dinner available Cen ht Wi-fi **Parking** 55 **Notes** 🐾

HATHERSAGE   Map 16 SK28

Cannon Croft

★★★★ 🛏 BED AND BREAKFAST

Cannonfields S32 1AG
☎ 01433 650005
e-mail: soates@cannoncroft.fsbusiness.co.uk
dir: *From George Hotel in village centre, 150yds W right onto single-track lane before bridge, Cannon Croft 130yds*

Set on the edge of the village with superb views of the surrounding countryside, this non-smoking home offers well-furnished and comprehensively equipped en suite bedrooms. An extensive choice of carefully prepared breakfasts is served in the conservatory-lounge. The enthusiastic hosts always offer a warm welcome.

Rooms 3 en suite (1 fmly) (3 GF) D £64-£68* **Facilities** tea/coffee Cen ht **Parking** 5 **Notes** LB 🐾 No Children 12yrs 🐾

Hillfoot Farm

★★★★ GUEST ACCOMMODATION

Castleton Rd S32 1EG
☎ 01433 651673
e-mail: hillfootfarm@hotmail.com
web: www.hillfootfarm.com
dir: *On A625 0.5m W from Hathersage on right*

This 16th-century former inn and tollhouse is at the end of an old packhorse route, and you can expect a welcome from the friendly dog. The house has been extended to offer spacious, comfortable bedrooms and there is also a cosy lounge. Breakfast is served in the adjacent beamed dining room. This is a non-smoking establishment.

Rooms 4 en suite (1 fmly) (2 GF) D £50-£60 **Facilities** tea/coffee Cen ht **Parking** 12 **Notes** LB 🐾 No Children 12yrs 🐾

Millstone

★★★★ INN

Sheffield Rd S32 1DA
☎ 01433 650258 📄 01433 651664
e-mail: jerry@millstoneinn.co.uk
web: www.millstoneinn.co.uk
dir: *0.5m SE of village on A6187*

This timber and stone inn stands on an elevated position overlooking the Hope Valley. It offers modern, well-equipped bedrooms, and real ales and exciting food are served in the friendly bar. The smart Terrace fish restaurant offers fine dining with great views over the valley. Wi-fi and free use of the local gym are benefits.

Rooms 8 en suite (3 fmly) **Facilities** tea/coffee Dinner available Direct Dial Cen ht Wi-fi Gym membership free to guests **Conf** Max 40 Thtr 40 Class 40 Board 40 **Parking** 80

Plough

★★★★ 🍴 INN

Leadmill Bridge S32 1BA
☎ 01433 650319 📄 01433 651049
e-mail: sales@theploughinn-hathersage.co.uk
web: www.theploughinn-hathersage.co.uk
dir: *1m SE of Hathersage on B6001. Over bridge, 150yds beyond at Leadmill*

This delightful 16th-century inn with beer garden has an idyllic location by the River Derwent. A selection of real ales and imaginative food is served in the spacious public areas, and original open fires and exposed beams have been preserved. The thoughtfully equipped, well-appointed bedrooms include two impressive suites.

Rooms 3 en suite 2 annexe en suite (1 GF) **Facilities** tea/coffee Dinner available Direct Dial Cen ht **Parking** 50 **Notes** LB 🐾 Closed 25 Dec No coaches

HATHERSAGE *continued*

The Scotsman's Pack Inn

★★★★ INN

School Ln S32 1BZ

☎ 01433 650253 ⓘ 01433 650712

e-mail: scotsmans.pack@btinternet.com

dir: *A625 into Hathersage, turn right onto School Ln towards the church, Scotsman's Pack 100yds on right*

This comfortable inn on the edge of the village provides a wide range of well-prepared food. The bedrooms are compact, well-furnished and thoughtfully equipped, while the bar, which contains Little John's chair, is a great place to meet the locals. Hearty breakfasts are served in the separate dining room, and the staff are very friendly.

Rooms 5 en suite **Facilities** tea/coffee Dinner available Cen ht **Conf** Max 20 **Parking** 17 **Notes** LB ⊗ RS 25 Dec eve no food served

---

HAYFIELD Map 16 SK08

Spinney Cottage B&B

★★★★ BED AND BREAKFAST

Spinnerbottom SK22 1BL

☎ 01663 743230

dir: *A6 onto A6015 towards Hayfield, 2m turn left, 400yds on right*

Spinney Cottage lies a short distance from the picturesque village of Hayfield and is a good base for touring the area. Hospitality is warm, the attractive bedrooms are well equipped, and hearty breakfasts are served in the cottage-style dining room.

Rooms 3 rms (2 en suite) (1 pri facs) (1 fmly) S £27; D £54 **Facilities** TVL tea/coffee Cen ht **Notes** ⊗ Closed Xmas & New Year ✾

HOPE Map 16 SK18

PREMIER COLLECTION

Underleigh House

★★★★★ GUEST ACCOMMODATION

Off Edale Rd S33 6RF

☎ 01433 621372 ⓘ 01433 621324

e-mail: info@underleighhouse.co.uk

web: www.underleighhouse.co.uk

dir: *From village church on A6187 onto Edale Rd, 1m left onto lane*

Situated at the end of a private lane, surrounded by glorious scenery, Underleigh House was converted from a barn and cottage that dates from 1873, and now offers carefully furnished and attractively decorated bedrooms with modern facilities. One room has a private lounge and others have access to the gardens. There is a very spacious lounge with comfortable chairs and a welcoming log fire. Memorable breakfasts are served at one large table in the dining room. Vivienne and Philip Taylor were finalists in the AA Friendliest Landlady of the Year 2009-2010 Award

Rooms 5 en suite (2 GF) S £60-£80; D £80-£100* **Facilities** TVL tea/coffee Direct Dial Cen ht Licensed Wi-fi **Parking** 6 **Notes** LB No Children 12yrs Closed Xmas, New Year & 4 Jan-4 Feb

---

Stoney Ridge

★★★★ GUEST ACCOMMODATION

Granby Rd, Bradwell S33 9HU

☎ 01433 620538

e-mail: toneyridge@aol.com

web: www.stoneyridge.org.uk

dir: *From N end of Bradwell, Gore Ln uphill past Bowling Green Inn, turn left onto Granby Rd*

This large, split-level bungalow stands in attractive mature gardens at the highest part of the village and has extensive views. Hens roam freely in the landscaped garden, and their fresh eggs add to the hearty breakfasts. Bedrooms are attractively furnished and thoughtfully equipped, and there is a spacious comfortable lounge and a superb indoor swimming pool.

Rooms 4 rms (3 en suite) (1 pri facs) S £45-£55; D £54-£70* **Facilities** TVL tea/coffee Cen ht Wi-fi ⟨⟩ **Parking** 3 **Notes** LB No Children 10yrs RS Winter Pool may be closed for maintenance

---

Poachers Arms

★★★★ Ⓐ INN

95 Castleton Rd S33 6SB

☎ 01433 620380

e-mail: btissington95@aol.com

web: www.poachersarms.co.uk

dir: *On A625/A6187 between Hope & Castleton*

Rooms 4 en suite S £50-£80; D £50-£80 **Facilities** tea/coffee Dinner available Cen ht Wi-fi **Parking** 30 **Notes** LB ⊗ No coaches

---

Round Meadow Barn

★★★ BED AND BREAKFAST

Parsons Ln S33 6RB

☎ 01433 621347 & 07836 689422 ⓘ 01433 621347

e-mail: rmbarn@bigfoot.com

dir: *Off A625 Hope Rd N onto Parsons Ln, over railway bridge, 200yds right into Hay barnyard, through gates, across 3 fields, house on left*

This converted barn, with original stone walls and exposed timbers, stands in open fields in the picturesque Hope Valley. The bedrooms are large enough for families and there are two modern bathrooms. Breakfast is served at one large table adjoining the family kitchen.

Rooms 4 rms (1 en suite) (1 fmly) S £30-£40; D £60-£70* **Facilities** tea/coffee Cen ht Golf 18 Riding **Parking** 8 **Notes** LB ✾

LONGFORD Map 10 SK23

Russets

★★★★ BED AND BREAKFAST

Off Main St DE6 3DR

☎ 01335 330874 ⓘ 01335 330874

e-mail: geoffreynolan@btinternet.com

web: www.russets.com

dir: *A516 in Hatton onto Sutton Ln, at T-junct right onto Long Ln. next right into Longford & right before phone box on Main St*

An indoor swimming pool is available at this beautifully maintained bungalow, which is in a peaceful location near Alton Towers. Bedrooms are well-equipped and have smart modern bathrooms. Comprehensive breakfasts are served at a family table in a homely dining room, and a comfortable lounge is available.

Rooms 2 en suite (1 fmly) (2 GF) S £40-£63; D £60-£63 **Facilities** STV TVL tea/coffee Cen ht Wi-fi ⟨⟩ Gymnasium **Parking** 4 **Notes** Closed 3rd wk Dec-1st wk Jan ✾

MATLOCK   Map 16 SK35

PREMIER COLLECTION

Holmefield
★★★★★ 🍴 GUEST HOUSE

Dale Road North, Darley Dale DE4 2HY
☎ 01629 735347
e-mail: holmefieldguesthouse@btinternet.com
web: www.holmefieldguesthouse.co.uk
dir: *Between Bakewell & Matlock on A6. 1m from Rowsley & Chatsworth Estate, 0.5m from Peak Rail*

Standing on mature grounds between Matlock and Bakewell, this elegant Victorian house has been furnished with flair to offer good levels of comfort and facilities. Imaginative dinners feature seasonal local produce, some from The Chatsworth Estate, and warm hospitality and attentive service are assured.

Rooms 4 en suite (2 fmly) **Facilities** tea/coffee Dinner available Cen ht Pool Table badminton, table tennis **Parking** 4 **Notes** ⊗ Closed 23 Dec-2 Jan

Yew Tree Cottage
★★★★ 🏠 BED AND BREAKFAST

The Knoll, Tansley DE4 5FP
☎ 01629 583862 & 07799 541903
e-mail: enquiries@yewtreecottagebb.co.uk
dir: *1.2m E of Matlock. Off A615 into Tansley centre*

This 18th-century cottage has been renovated to provide high standards of comfort while retaining original character. Memorable breakfasts are served in the elegant dining room and a cosy lounge is available. A warm welcome and attentive service are assured.

Rooms 3 en suite S £65; D £75-£95 **Facilities** TVL tea/coffee Cen ht Wi-fi Sauna **Parking** 3 **Notes** LB ⊗ No Children 12yrs

Glendon
★★★★ GUEST HOUSE

Knowleston Place DE4 3BU
☎ 01629 584732
e-mail: sylvia.elliott@tesco.net
dir: *250yds SE of town centre. Off A615, car park before Glendon sign*

Glendon is set beside a park just a short walk from the town centre. The spacious bedrooms are pleasantly decorated and well equipped, and one is suitable for families. The comfortable third-floor lounge has lovely views over Bentley Brook and the local church.

Rooms 4 rms (2 en suite) (1 fmly) S £35-£40; D £59-£63 **Facilities** TVL tea/coffee Cen ht **Parking** 4 **Notes** ⊗ No Children 3yrs Closed Dec 🐾

Hearthstone Farm *(SK308583)*
★★★★ FARMHOUSE

Hearthstone Ln, Riber DE4 5JW
☎ 01629 534304   📄 01629 534372   Mrs Gilman
e-mail: enquiries@hearthstonefarm.co.uk
web: www.hearthstonefarm.co.uk
dir: *A615 at Tansley 2m E of Matlock, turn opp Royal Oak towards Riber, at gates to Riber Hall left onto Riber Rd and 1st left onto Hearthstone Ln, farmhouse on left*

Situated on a stunning elevated location, this traditional stone farmhouse retains many original features and is stylishly decorated throughout. Bedrooms are equipped with a wealth of homely extras and comprehensive breakfasts feature the farm's organic produce. There is a very comfortable lounge, and the farm animals in the grounds are an attraction.

Rooms 3 en suite S £45-£50; D £65-£70* **Facilities** FTV TVL tea/coffee Cen ht Wi-fi **Parking** 6 **Notes** LB Closed Xmas & New Year 🐾 150 acres organic beef/lamb/pigs

Mount Tabor House
★★★★ BED AND BREAKFAST

Bowns Hill, Crich DE4 5DG
☎ 01773 857008   & 07813 007478   📄 01773 857008
e-mail: mountabor@msn.com
dir: *6m SE of Matlock. On B5035 in centre of Crich*

This former Victorian Methodist chapel has fine surroundings. The first floor is a spacious living-dining area, where dinner and breakfast are served at one table - leaded Gothic windows and a superb wrought-iron balcony look across the Amber Valley. Interesting meals are created from quality local and organic produce, with dietary needs willingly catered for. The two bedrooms have a useful range of facilities, and the larger room has a king-size antique pine bed.

Rooms 2 en suite (2 fmly) (1 GF) S £60; D £75-£80 **Facilities** FTV tea/coffee Dinner available Cen ht Wi-fi jacuzzi **Parking** 3 **Notes** ⊗ No Children

Old Sunday School
★★★★ BED AND BREAKFAST

New St DE4 3FH
☎ 01629 583347   📄 01629 583347
e-mail: davhpatrick@hotmail.com
dir: *In town centre. Off A6 rdbt to Crown Sq, turn right onto Bank Rd, New St 4th on right*

A warm welcome is assured at this converted Victorian chapel, built of mellow sandstone and just a short walk from central attractions. The homely bedroom is complemented by a modern shower room, and the spacious living area includes a period dining table, the setting for comprehensive breakfasts and (by arrangement) imaginative dinners.

Rooms 1 en suite (1 fmly) S £30; D £55* **Facilities** TVL tea/coffee Dinner available Cen ht Wi-fi **Notes** LB ⊗ 🐾

The Red Lion
★★★★ INN

Matlock Green DE4 3BT
☎ 01629 584888
dir: *500yds SE of town centre on A632*

This comfortable inn is a good base for exploring Matlock and the surrounding Derbyshire countryside. Each bedroom is comfortable and furnished in quality pine. Public areas include a character bar with open fire and a restaurant where a wide selection of meals is on offer.

Rooms 6 en suite S £40; D £65-£70* **Facilities** tea/coffee Dinner available Cen ht Pool Table **Parking** 20 **Notes** ⊗

MATLOCK *continued*

Sunnybank Guest House

★★★★ GUEST ACCOMMODATION

37 Clifton Rd, Matlock Bath DE4 3PW
☎ 01629 584621
e-mail: mark@sunnybank.mail1.co.uk
dir: *Take A6 Matlock towards Cromford, on right between Temple and Newbath Hotels*

A warm and friendly welcome awaits you in this attractive Victorian residence. Sunnybank is characterful, comfortable and charming. Situated in a quiet cul-de-sac amidst mature woodland surroundings. It has stunning views of the Derwent Valley and Wildcat Craggs, and is central to numerous walks, waterways and attractions.

Rooms 5 rms (4 en suite) (1 pri facs) (1 fmly) (1 GF) S £40-£45; D £60-£74* **Facilities** tea/coffee Cen ht **Notes** LB ⊗ No Children 12yrs

Woodside

★★★★ BED AND BREAKFAST

Stanton Lees DE4 2LQ
☎ 01629 734320 ▤ 01629 734320
e-mail: kathpotter8378@woodsidestantonlees.co.uk
web: www.woodsidestantonlees.co.uk
dir: *4m NW of Matlock. A6 onto B5057 into Darley Bridge, opp pub right to Stanton Lees & right fork*

Located on an elevated position with stunning views of the surrounding countryside, this mellow-stone house has been renovated to provide high standards of comfort and facilities. Carefully decorated bedrooms come with a wealth of thoughtful extras, and ground-floor areas include a comfortable lounge and conservatory overlooking the garden, which is home to a variety of wild birds.

Rooms 3 en suite S £36-£40; D £56-£62* **Facilities** FTV TVL tea/coffee Cen ht **Parking** 3 **Notes** ⊗ No Children 3yrs 🕮

Bradford Villa

★★★ BED AND BREAKFAST

26 Chesterfield Rd DE4 3DQ
☎ 01629 57147
dir: *500yds NE of town centre on A632, opp Lilybank hamlet*

This non-smoking, semi-detached Victorian house is situated on an elevated position in neat gardens on the north edge of the town. Bedrooms are comfortably furnished and suitable for families. Small car park at rear.

Rooms 2 rms (1 en suite) (1 pri facs) (2 fmly); D £56-£60* **Facilities** tea/coffee Cen ht **Parking** 4 **Notes** ⊗ Closed 22 Dec-3 Jan 🕮

Farley *(SK294622)*

★★★ FARMHOUSE

Farley DE4 5LR
☎ 01629 582533 & 07801 756409
▤ 01629 584856 Mrs Brailsford
e-mail: eric.brailsford@btconnect.com
dir: *1m N of Matlock. From A6 rdbt towards Bakewell, 1st right, right at top of hill, left up Farley Hill, 2nd farm on left*

You can expect a warm welcome at this traditional stone farmhouse. In addition to farming, the proprietors also breed dogs and horses. The bedrooms are pleasantly decorated and equipped with many useful extras. Breakfast is served round one large table, and dinner is available by arrangement.

Rooms 2 en suite (3 fmly) S £35-£55; D fr £55* **Facilities** TVL tea/coffee Dinner available Cen ht Riding **Parking** 8 **Notes** LB 🕮 165 acres arable/beef/dairy

Red House Carriage Museum

★★★ GUEST ACCOMMODATION

Old Rd, Darley Dale DE4 2ER
☎ 01629 733583 ▤ 01629 733583
e-mail: redhousestables@hotmail.co.uk
dir: *2m N of Matlock, left off A6, 200yds on left*

Located in a famous working carriage-driving school and museum, this detached house provides homely and thoughtfully equipped bedrooms, one on the ground floor and one in a former stable. Comprehensive breakfasts are served at a family table in an attractive dining room, and the comfortable lounge area overlooks the spacious gardens.

Rooms 2 rms (1 en suite) 2 annexe en suite (1 fmly) (1 GF) S £40; D £70-£75* **Facilities** tea/coffee Cen ht Horse & carriage trips **Parking** 5 **Notes** ⊗ 🕮

The Coach House

★★★★ GUEST HOUSE

69 Derby Rd DE73 1FE
☎ 01332 862338 ▤ 01332 695281
e-mail: enquiries@coachhouse-hotel.co.uk
web: www.coachhouse-hotel.co.uk
dir: *Off B587 in village centre*

Located in the heart of a conservation area and close to Donington Park and East Midlands Airport, this traditional cottage has been restored to provide good standards of comfort and facilities. Bedrooms are thoughtfully furnished, and two are in converted stables. A lounge and secure parking are available.

Rooms 6 en suite (1 fmly) (3 GF) S £35-£40; D £50-£64* **Facilities** TVL tea/coffee Cen ht Wi-fi **Parking** 6 **Notes** LB ⊗

The Melbourne Arms

★★★ INN

92 Ashby Rd DE73 8ES
☎ 01332 864949 ▤ 01332 865525
e-mail: info@melbournearms.co.uk
web: www.melbournearms.co.uk
dir: *3m from East Midlands Airport*

Well located for the airport and Donington Park, this Grade II listed inn provides modern, thoughtfully equipped bedrooms, one of which is in a converted outbuilding. Ground-floor areas include two bars, a coffee shop and an elegant Indian restaurant.

Rooms 7 en suite (1 fmly) S £40-£50; D £60-£70* **Facilities** TVL tea/coffee Dinner available Cen ht Wi-fi Bouncy Castle for children (weather permitting) **Conf** Max 25 Thtr 15 Class 15 Board 15 **Parking** 52 **Notes** ⊗

See advert on opposite page

NEWHAVEN Map 16 SK16

PREMIER COLLECTION

The Smithy
★★★★★ GUEST ACCOMMODATION

SK17 0DT
☎ 01298 84548 📄 01298 84548
e-mail: lynnandgary@thesmithybedandbreakfast.co.uk
web: www.thesmithybedandbreakfast.co.uk
dir: 0.5m S of Newhaven on A515. Next to Biggin Ln, private driveway opp Ivy House

Set in a peaceful location close to the Tissington and High Peak trails, the 17th-century drovers' inn and blacksmith's workshop have been carefully renovated. Bedrooms, which are in a former barn, are well equipped. Enjoyable breakfasts, which include free-range eggs and home-made preserves, are served in the forge, which features the original bellows on the vast open hearth.

Rooms 4 en suite (2 GF); D £74-£90* **Facilities** TVL tea/coffee Cen ht **Conf** Max 20 Thtr 15 Board 10 **Parking** 8 **Notes** LB ⊗ ⛔

NEW MILLS Map 16 SK08

Pack Horse Inn
★★★★ 🅰 INN

Mellor Rd SK22 4QQ
☎ 01663 742365 📄 01663 741674
e-mail: info@packhorseinn.co.uk
dir: A6 onto A6015, left at lights. Right at rdbt, after 0.5m left, onto Mellor Rd

Rooms 7 en suite 5 annexe en suite (1 fmly) (2 GF) **Facilities** tea/coffee Dinner available Cen ht Wi-fi **Parking** 50 **Notes** ⊗ No coaches

RISLEY Map 11 SK43

Braeside Guest House
★★★★ GUEST HOUSE

113 Derby Rd DE72 3SS
☎ 0115 939 5885
e-mail: bookings@braesideguesthouse.co.uk
web: www.braesideguesthouse.co.uk
dir: W end of village on B5010

Located on a leafy avenue, a few minutes' drive from junction 25 of the M1, this elegant detached house provides a range of thoughtfully furnished bedrooms, located in sympathetically renovated former outbuildings. Breakfast is served in an attractive conservatory dining room overlooking immaculately maintained mature gardens, and a warm welcome is assured.

Rooms 6 annexe en suite (6 GF) **Facilities** tea/coffee Cen ht **Parking** 10 **Notes** ⊗ Closed 25-26 Dec

ROWSLEY Map 16 SK26

The Grouse and Claret
★★★★ INN

Station Rd DE4 2EB
☎ 01629 733233 📄 01629 735194
e-mail: grouseandclaret.matlock@marstons.co.uk
dir: M1 junct 28, A6 5m from Matlock, 3m from Bakewell

A busy inn with a wide range of dishes available in the spacious bars. Bedrooms are pleasantly furnished and staff are friendly and attentive.

Rooms 8 en suite (2 fmly) **Facilities** STV FTV tea/coffee Dinner available Cen ht Wi-fi **Parking** 78 **Notes** ⊗ No coaches

SWADLINCOTE Map 10 SK21

Overseale House
★★★ BED AND BREAKFAST

Acresford Rd, Overseal DE12 6HX
☎ 01283 763741 📄 01283 760015
e-mail: oversealehouse@hotmail.com
web: www.oversealehouse.co.uk
dir: On A444 between Burton upon Trent & M42 junct 11

Located in the village, this well-proportioned Georgian mansion, built for a renowned industrialist, retains many original features including a magnificent dining room decorated with ornate mouldings. The period-furnished ground-floor areas include a cosy sitting room, and bedrooms contain many thoughtful extras.

Rooms 4 en suite 1 annexe en suite (3 fmly) (2 GF) S £30-£35; D £60-£70* **Facilities** tea/coffee Cen ht **Conf** Max 14 Board 14 **Parking** 6 **Notes** ⛔

THE MELBOURNE ARMS
CUISINE INDIA

INDIAN, CONTINENTAL FOODS / BAR SNACKS

01332 - 864949 & 863990

AA
★★★
INN

92 Ashby Road, Melbourne, Derbyshire.
DE73 8ES. Fax : 01332 - 865525
Email us :- info@melbournearms.com
Find us :- www.melbournearms.com

Offers the Best Standard Accommodation.

Nine individually designed En-suite bedrooms.

Room with disabled facilities on ground floor for easy access.

The Best Indian & Continental Cuisines.

Free WI-FI zone, access on request.

Fully air Conditioned restaurant with two well-stocked Bars, CCTV covers the whole car park up to 60 cars.

Easy access to East Midlands Airport, Pride park Donington Park race track, Calke Abbey, A42, M42, M1, A50, A453, Peak District.

TIDESWELL — Map 16 SK17

Poppies
★★★ GUEST ACCOMMODATION

Bank Square SK17 8LA
☎ 01298 871083
e-mail: poptidza@dialstart.net
dir: On B6049 in village centre opp NatWest bank

A friendly welcome is assured at this non-smoking house, located in the heart of a former lead-mining and textile community, a short walk from the 14th-century parish church. Bedrooms are homely and practical.

Rooms 3 rms (1 en suite) (1 fmly) S £23-£27.50; D £46-£55* **Facilities** tea/coffee Cen ht **Notes** ✉

WESTON UNDERWOOD — Map 10 SK24

PREMIER COLLECTION

Park View Farm (SK293425)
★★★★★ FARMHOUSE

DE6 4PA
☎ 01335 360352 & 07771 573057
🖷 01335 360352 **Mrs Adams**
e-mail: enquiries@parkviewfarm.co.uk
web: www.parkviewfarm.co.uk
dir: From A52/A38 rdbt W of Derby, take A38 N, 1st left to Kedleston Hall. Continue for 1.5m past x-rds

An impressive Victorian farmhouse surrounded by beautiful gardens and 370 acres of arable land. Each bedroom has an antique four-poster bed, attractive decor, period furniture and a wealth of homely extras. Quality ornaments and art enhance the many original features and ground-floor rooms include a spacious comfortable lounge and an elegant dining room.

Rooms 3 en suite S £55-£60; D £80-£85* **Facilities** TVL tea/coffee Cen ht Wi-fi **Parking** 10 **Notes** LB ⊗ No Children 5yrs Closed Xmas ✉ 370 acres Organic arable/sheep

WINSTER — Map 16 SK26

Brae Cottage
★★★★ 🅰 GUEST ACCOMMODATION

East Bank DE4 2DT
☎ 01629 650375
dir: A6 onto B5057, driveway on right past pub

Rooms 2 annexe en suite (1 fmly) (2 GF) S £40-£50; D £50-£60* **Facilities** tea/coffee Cen ht **Parking** 2 **Notes** ⊗ No Children 11yrs ✉

WIRKSWORTH — Map 16 SK25

PREMIER COLLECTION

The Old Manor House
★★★★★ BED AND BREAKFAST

Coldwell St DE4 4FB
☎ 01629 822502
e-mail: ivan@spurrier-smith.fsnet.co.uk
dir: On B5035 Coldwell St off village centre

Located on the village edge, this impressive period house has been lovingly renovated to provide high standards of comfort and facilities. Quality furnishing and décor highlight the many original features and the spacious bedroom has a wealth of thoughtful extras. Comprehensive breakfasts are served in the elegant dining room and a spacious drawing room is available.

Rooms 1 rms (1 pri facs) S £50-£60; D £80-£85* **Facilities** tea/coffee Cen ht 🍴 Pool Table **Parking** 1 **Notes** ⊗ No Children 12yrs Closed Xmas & New Year ✉

YOULGREAVE — Map 16 SK26

The Old Bakery
★★★ BED AND BREAKFAST

Church St DE45 1UR
☎ 01629 636887
e-mail: corcot@tiscali.co.uk
dir: Off A515/A6, in village centre

Located in the heart of this unspoiled village, the former bakery has been renovated to provide a range of thoughtfully furnished bedrooms, one of which is in a converted barn. Breakfast is served in the original baker's shop and furnishings enhance the retained features.

Rooms 2 rms 1 annexe en suite S £32-£60; D £50-£70 **Facilities** TV2B TVL Cen ht **Parking** 2 **Notes** Closed Xmas ✉

DEVON

ASHBURTON — Map 3 SX77

Greencott
★★★★ GUEST HOUSE

Landscove TQ13 7LZ
☎ 01803 762649
dir: 3m SE of Ashburton. Off A38 at Peartree junct, Landscove signed on slip road, village green 2m on right, opp village hall

Greencott has a peaceful village location and superb country views. Your hosts extend a very warm welcome and there is a relaxed home-from-home atmosphere. Service is attentive and caring and many guests return time and again. Bedrooms are attractive, comfortable and very well equipped. Delicious country cooking is served around an oak dining table.

Rooms 2 en suite **Facilities** TVL tea/coffee Dinner available Cen ht **Parking** 3 **Notes** LB ⊗ Closed 25-26 Dec ✉

Gages Mill Country Guest House
★★★★ GUEST ACCOMMODATION

Buckfastleigh Rd TQ13 7JW
☎ 01364 652391 🖷 01364 652641
e-mail: richards@gagesmill.co.uk
dir: Off A38 at Peartree junct, turn right then left at fuel station, Gages Mill 500yds on left

Set in delightful grounds and well-tended gardens, Gages Mill lies on the edge of Dartmoor National Park and is an attractive former wool mill dating back to the 14th century. This family-run house offers a warm welcome and a home-from-home atmosphere. Breakfast is served in the dining room at individual tables, and there is a lounge where you can play games or watch television.

Rooms 7 en suite (1 fmly) (1 GF) S £45-£55; D £62-£70* **Facilities** TVL tea/coffee Cen ht Licensed Wi-fi **Parking** 7 **Notes** ⊗ No Children 8yrs Closed 23 Oct-1 Mar ✉

The Rising Sun
★★★★ 🍽 INN

Woodland TQ13 7JT
☎ 01364 652544
e-mail: admin@therisingsunwoodland.co.uk
dir: A38, exit signed Woodland/Denbury, continue straight on for 1.5m Rising Sun on left

Peacefully situated in scenic south Devon countryside, this inn is just a short drive from the A38. A friendly welcome is extended to all guests; business, leisure and families alike. Bedrooms are comfortable and well equipped. Dinner and breakfast feature much local and organic produce. A good selection of homemade puddings, West Country cheeses, local wines and quality real ales are available.

Rooms 5 en suite (2 fmly) (2 GF) **Facilities** FTV tea/coffee Dinner available Cen ht **Parking** 30 **Notes** No coaches

Turtley Corn Mill has had a varied history, originally built as a mill, then converted into a famous chicken hatchery, finally becoming a pub in the 1970's.

Turtley was completely renovated in 2005. The interiors are light and fresh, with a noticeable absence of music, fruit machines or pool tables, all thoughtfully replaced with newspapers to read, books to browse, good food to eat, great local beers and interesting wines.

The setting of the Mill is idyllic; located in the beautiful and varied area of Avonwick, South Hams the original Mill is set in six acres of grounds bordered by the River Glazebrook, we even have our own small lake complete with an island, perfect for sunny days and idle wandering!

The menu changes daily and features a wealth of local produce, served from 12:00noon until 9:30pm (9:00pm on Sundays) although on busy nights, chef's ability to take orders may end a little earlier.

In 2008 Turtley added four double en-suite bedrooms, one with a bath, all are designed and fitted out to a standard now expected by those who travel regularly. Each room comes complete with king-size bed, duck feather and down duvets, Egyptian cotton linen, Sky free view, flat screen TV's, free internet connection, powerful, spacious showers and other thoughtful additions carefully chosen for your comfort and relaxation.

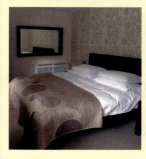

The Turtley Corn Mill, Avonwick, Devon, TQ10 9ES
Tel: 01364 646100
Email: mill@avonwick.net
Website: www.avonwick.net

Room rates; £89.00 to £110.00 B&B per room

ASHBURTON *continued*

Sladesdown Farm *(SX765684)*

★★★★ FARMHOUSE

Landscove TQ13 7ND
☎ 01364 653973 ▤ 01364 653973 Mr & Mrs Mason
e-mail: sue@sladesdown.co.uk
dir: *2m S of Ashburton. Off A38 at Peartree junct, Landscove signed on slip road, left at 2nd x-rds, farm 100yds right*

Set in 50 acres of tranquil pasture and well-tended gardens, and convenient for the A38, this modern farmhouse offers very spacious, attractive accommodation. There's a friendly atmosphere, with relaxation assured either in the lounge or on the terrace in finer weather. Guests are welcome to wander across the land where a series of ponds have been created attracting abundant wildlife. A hearty breakfast featuring delicious local and home-made produce is the perfect start to the day.

Rooms 4 rms (2 en suite) (2 pri facs) (1 fmly)
Facilities tea/coffee Cen ht **Parking Notes** ⊗ ⊜ 14 acres beef/turkeys/chickens

---

West Down *(SS582228)*

★★★★ ⊜ FARMHOUSE

Little Eastacombe EX37 9HP
☎ 01769 560551 ▤ 01769 560551 Mr & Mrs Savery
e-mail: info@westdown.co.uk
web: www.westdown.co.uk
dir: *0.5m from Atherington on B3227 to Torrington, turn right, 100yds on left*

Set in 25 acres of lush Devon countryside, this establishment makes a good base for exploring the area. Peace and caring hospitality are assured. Bedrooms are equipped with a host of thoughtful extras, and every effort is made to ensure an enjoyable stay. A choice of homely lounges is available, and breakfast and scrumptious dinners are served in the sun lounge.

Rooms 2 en suite 2 annexe en suite (2 GF) S £32-£36; D £64-£72* **Facilities** TVL tea/coffee Dinner available Cen ht Wi-fi **Parking** 8 **Notes** LB ⊗ ⊜ 25 acres sheep/chickens

---

Turtley Corn Mill

★★★★ ⊜ INN

TQ10 9ES
☎ 01364 646100 ▤ 01364 646101
e-mail: mill@avonwick.net
web: www.avonwick.net
dir: *From A38, S towards Avonwick, 0.5m on left*

Located just off the A38 in a beautiful area, this fine mill is set within six acres of grounds bordered by the River Glazebrook, complete with a small lake and its own

---

island. The four, en suite bedrooms are modern contemporary design with king-size beds. There are some thoughtful extras provided, including flat-screen TVs. The food offered is high quality, served all day in a variety of relaxed dining areas or outside if preferred, by friendly, efficient staff. Breakfast provides a hearty start to the day.

Rooms 4 en suite (1 fmly) S £89-£110; D £89-£110
Facilities STV FTV tea/coffee Dinner available Cen ht Wi-fi **Parking** 90 **Notes** ⊗ Closed 25 Dec No coaches

See advert on page 123

PREMIER COLLECTION

Kerrington House

★★★★★ ▤ ⊜ GUEST ACCOMMODATION

Musbury Rd EX13 5JR
☎ 01297 35333 ▤ 01297 35345
e-mail: jareaney@talktalkbusiness.net
web: www.kerringtonhouse.com
dir: *0.5m from Axminster on A358 towards Seaton, house on left*

Set in landscaped gardens, this delightful house has been lovingly restored. The carefully decorated bedrooms are equipped with many thoughtful touches, and personal treasures adorn the light and airy drawing room. Breakfast offers a good selection of dishes prepared with flair and imagination. The house is available with exclusive use for small house parties.

Rooms 5 en suite **Facilities** tea/coffee Dinner available Direct Dial Cen ht Licensed **Conf** Max 12 Board 12 **Parking** 6 **Notes** ⊗

The Bark House

★★★★ ⊜ GUEST ACCOMMODATION

Oakfordbridge EX16 9HZ
☎ 01398 351236
web: www.thebarkhouse.co.uk
dir: *A361 to rdbt at Tiverton onto A396 for Dulverton, then onto Oakfordbridge. House on right*

Located in the stunning Exe Valley, this is a perfect place to relax and unwind, surrounded by wonderful unspoilt countryside. Hospitality is a hallmark here and a cup of tea by the fireside is always on offer. Both breakfast and

---

dinner make use of the excellent local produce, and are served in the attractive dining room, overlooking fields and the river. Bedrooms all have a homely, cottage-style feel with comfy beds to ensure a peaceful night's sleep.

Rooms 6 rms (5 en suite) (1 pri facs) S £52-£68; D £84-£130* **Facilities** tea/coffee Dinner available Cen ht Licensed **Parking** 6 **Notes** LB

Newhouse Farm *(SS892228)*

★★★★ ⊜ FARMHOUSE

EX16 9JE
☎ 01398 351347 Mrs A Boldry
e-mail: anne.boldry@btconnect.com
web: www.newhouse-farm-holidays.co.uk
dir: *5m W of Bampton on B3227*

Set in 42 acres of rolling farmland, this delightful farmhouse provides a friendly and informal atmosphere. The smart, rustic-style bedrooms are well equipped with modern facilities, and imaginative and delicious home-cooked dinners, using the best local produce, are available by arrangement. Home-made bread and preserves feature at breakfast which can be enjoyed outside on the patio in the summer months.

Rooms 3 en suite (1 GF) S £35; D £60-£70 **Facilities** FTV tea/coffee Dinner available Cen ht Fishing **Parking** 3 **Notes** LB ⊗ No Children 10yrs Closed Xmas & New Year 42 acres beef/sheep

---

Cresta Guest House

★★★ GUEST HOUSE

26 Sticklepath Hill EX31 2BU
☎ 01271 374022
e-mail: peter.davis170@virgin.net
dir: *On A3215, 0.6m W of town centre, top of hill on right*

A warm welcome is assured at this family-run establishment, situated on the western outskirts of Barnstaple. The well-equipped, individually styled bedrooms are comfortably appointed and include ground-floor rooms. A hearty breakfast is served in the modern and comfortable dining room.

Rooms 6 rms (4 en suite) (2 pri facs) 2 annexe en suite (2 fmly) (2 GF) S £25; D £49* **Facilities** FTV tea/coffee Cen ht Wi-fi **Parking** 6 **Notes** ⊗ Closed 2wks Xmas

Rowden Barton *(SS538306)*

★★★ FARMHOUSE

Roundswell EX31 3NP
☎ 01271 344365 Mrs VJ Dallyn
dir: *2m SW of Barnstaple on B3232*

Rowden Barton offers a friendly and homely environment where guests can feel they are part of the family. The two comfortable bedrooms share an adjoining bathroom, and both rooms have views of the surrounding countryside. Delicious breakfasts, featuring home-made bread and preserves, provide a fine start to the day. Vivienne Dallyn was a finalist for the AA Friendliest Landlady of the Year 2009-2010 Award.

Rooms 2 rms S £25-£28; D £45-£50* **Facilities** TVL Cen ht **Parking** 4 **Notes** ⊗ No Children 12yrs 🐾 90 acres beef/sheep

---

BEER Map 4 SY28

Anchor Inn

Ⓤ

Fore St EX12 3ET
☎ 01297 20386 🖹 01297 24474
e-mail: 6403@greeneking.co.uk

Currently the rating for this establishment is not confirmed. This may be due to a change of ownership or because it has only recently joined the AA rating scheme.

Rooms 8 rms (5 en suite)

BEESANDS Map 3 SX84

The Cricket Inn

★★★★ ⚙ INN

TQ7 2EN
☎ 01548 580215
e-mail: enquiries@thecricketinn.com
dir: *From Kingsbridge follow A379 towards Dartmouth, at Stokenham mini-rdbt turn right for Beesands*

Dating back to 1867 this charming seaside inn is situated almost on the beach at Start Bay. The well appointed bedrooms have fantastic views, comfortable beds and flatscreen TVs. A daily changing fish menu offers with locally caught crabs, lobster and perhaps hand-dived scallops.

Rooms 4 en suite (1 fmly) S £40-£55; D £60-£90* **Facilities** tea/coffee Dinner available Cen ht Wi-fi **Notes** No coaches

---

BERRYNARBOR Map 3 SS54

Berry Mill House

★★★★ GUEST ACCOMMODATION

Mill Ln EX34 9SH
☎ 01271 882990
e-mail: enquiries@berrymillhouse.co.uk
web: www.berrymillhouse.co.uk
dir: *500yds NW of village centre. A399 W through Combe Martin, 2nd left at bottom of the hill, house on left*

In a wooded valley on the edge of the village, this former grain mill is a 5-minute walk on the coastal path. Guests are assured of a warm reception from the owners, who enjoy welcoming guests to their home. The freshly-cooked breakfast provides a substantial start to the day while home-cooked evening meals are available by arrangement.

Rooms 3 en suite; D £65-£70* **Facilities** TVL tea/coffee Dinner available Cen ht Licensed 🍷 **Parking** 6 **Notes** LB ⊗ No Children 12yrs Closed Nov & Xmas 🐾

BIDEFORD Map 3 SS42

See also Westward Ho!

The Mount

★★★★ GUEST HOUSE

Northdown Rd EX39 3LP
☎ 01237 473748 🖹 01271 373813
e-mail: andrew@themountbideford.co.uk
web: www.themountbideford.co.uk
dir: *Bideford turning off A39, right after Rydon garage, premises on right after 600yds at mini-rdbt*

A genuine warm welcome is assured at this delightful, centrally located Georgian property. Bedrooms are comfortably furnished and well equipped, and a ground-floor room is available for easier access. A hearty breakfast is served in the elegant dining room and there is a cosy sitting room.

Rooms 8 en suite (3 fmly) (1 GF) S £32-£38; D £65-£76* **Facilities** FTV tea/coffee Cen ht Licensed Wi-fi **Parking** 5 **Notes** LB ⊗ Closed Xmas

---

Pines at Eastleigh

★★★★ 🏠 GUEST ACCOMMODATION

The Pines, Eastleigh EX39 4PA
☎ 01271 860561 🖹 01271 861689
e-mail: pirrie@thepinesateastleigh.co.uk
dir: *A39 onto A386 signed East-the-Water. 1st left signed Eastleigh, 500yds next left, 1.5m to village, house on right*

Friendly hospitality is assured at this Georgian farmhouse, set in seven acres of gardens. Two of the comfortable bedrooms are located in the main house, the remainder in converted barns around a charming courtyard, with a pretty pond and well. A delicious breakfast featuring local and home-made produce is served in the dining room, and a lounge and honesty bar are also available.

Rooms 6 en suite (1 fmly) (4 GF) S £39-£45; D £75-£90 **Facilities** tea/coffee Direct Dial Cen ht Licensed Wi-fi 🍷 Table Tennis, Archery, Table Football **Conf** Max 25 Thtr 20 Board 20 **Parking** 20 **Notes** LB No Children 9yrs

---

BOVEY TRACEY Map 3 SX87

The Cromwell Arms

★★★ INN

Fore St TQ13 9AE
☎ 01626 833473 🖹 01626 836873
e-mail: enquiries@thecromwell.co.uk
dir: *In town centre*

A traditional country inn situated in the heart of Bovey Tracey, on the southern edge of Dartmoor and approximately 3 miles from Newton Abbot. The Cromwell dates back to the 1600s, is full of original charm and has been enhanced with facilities brought up to 21st century standards. This is an atmospheric, friendly pub with lots of character, suitable for all ages and open all day every day.

Rooms 12 en suite (2 fmly) S £52.50-£60; D £65-£70 **Facilities** FTV tea/coffee Dinner available Direct Dial Cen ht **Conf** Max 40 Thtr 40 Class 25 Board 25 **Parking** 25

BRAUNTON Map 3 SS43

Denham House

★★★★ 🄰 BED AND BREAKFAST

North Buckland EX33 1HY
☎ 01271 890297 🖹 01271 890106
e-mail: info@denhamhouse.co.uk
web: www.denhamhouse.co.uk
dir: *From Barnstaple A361, 2nd left after Knowle, follow lane into North Buckland, house on right*

Rooms 6 en suite (2 fmly) S £35-£40; D £60-£70 **Facilities** FTV TVL tea/coffee Cen ht Licensed Snooker Pool Table Table tennis Skittle Alley **Parking** 7 **Notes** LB ⊗

BRIXHAM
Map 3 SX95

Anchorage Guest House
★★★★ GUEST HOUSE

170 New Rd TQ5 8DA
☎ 01803 852960
e-mail: enquiries@brixham-anchorage.co.uk
dir: A3022, enter Brixham, left at lights, 1st on right

This smartly appointed establishment is conveniently located within walking distance of the town centre and harbour. The Anchorage stands in its own grounds and guests have use of the garden; there is also ample safe parking. The dining room and bedrooms all have a light, bright contemporary style with many extra facilities provided to ensure a comfortable stay.

Rooms 7 rms (6 en suite) (1 pri facs) (1 fmly) (4 GF) S £23-£34; D £52-£68* Facilities TVL Cen ht Wi-fi Parking 7 Notes LB ⊗

Harbour View Brixham
★★★ GUEST ACCOMMODATION

65 King St TQ5 9TH
☎ 01803 853052 🖳 01803 853052
dir: A3022 to town centre/harbour, left at lights, right at T-junct, premises on right of inner harbour

This comfortable house looks across the harbour towards Torbay. The friendly proprietors provide attractive, well-equipped accommodation, and there is a pleasant lounge area in the dining room. Breakfasts are traditional, well-cooked and appetising.

Rooms 8 rms (7 en suite) (1 pri facs) (1 fmly) S £31-£45; D £50-£66* Facilities FTV tea/coffee Cen ht Parking 7 Notes LB ⊗

BUCKFAST
Map 3 SX76

Furzeleigh Mill
★★★ GUEST ACCOMMODATION

Old Ashburton Rd TQ11 0JP
☎ 01364 643476
e-mail: enquiries@furzeleigh.co.uk
web: www.furzeleigh.co.uk
dir: Off A38 at Dartbridge junct, right at end slip road, right opp Little Chef signed Ashburton/Prince Town (do not cross River Dart bridge), 200yds right

This Grade II listed 16th-century converted corn mill stands in its own grounds and is a good base for touring Dartmoor. Spacious family rooms are available as well as a lounge and a bar. All meals are served in the dining room and use local produce.

Rooms 14 en suite (2 fmly) S £42-£47.50; D £68-£80* Facilities FTV TVL tea/coffee Dinner available Cen ht Licensed Wi-fi Conf Max 20 Thtr 20 Parking 32 Notes LB No Children 8yrs Closed 23 Dec-2 Jan

BUCKFASTLEIGH
Map 3 SX76

Kilbury Manor
★★★★ 🏠 GUEST ACCOMMODATION

Colston Rd TQ11 0LN
☎ 01364 644079
e-mail: visit@kilburymanor.co.uk
web: www.kilburymanor.co.uk
dir: Off A38 onto B3380 to Buckfastleigh, left onto Old Totnes Rd, at bottom turn right, Kilbury Manor on left

Dating back to the 17th century, this charming Devon longhouse is situated in the tranquil surroundings of the Dart Valley with access to the river across the meadow. Bedrooms have lots of character and are located in the main house or in adjacent converted barns, all of which provide high levels of comfort with period furnishings. Breakfast is served in the elegant dining room with local produce very much in evidence.

Rooms 4 rms (3 en suite) (1 pri facs) (1 fmly) (1 GF) S £45-£65; D £65-£85 Facilities FTV tea/coffee Cen ht Wi-fi Parking 5 Notes ⊗ No Children 8yrs ⌨

Kings Arms
★★★ INN

15 Fore St TQ11 0BT
☎ 01364 642341
dir: In town centre opp tourist office & The Valiant Soldier

This long-established, friendly and popular inn provides a well-appointed base from which to explore this picturesque area. Bedrooms are comfortably furnished, while public areas include a choice of bars, dining area and an attractive patio and garden.

Rooms 4 rms (1 en suite) S £35-£45; D £55-£75* Facilities tea/coffee Dinner available Conf Max 20 Thtr 20 Class 14 Board 14 Parking 1 Notes No coaches

Dartbridge Inn
★★★ 🅰 INN

Totnes Rd TQ11 0JR
☎ 01364 642214 🖳 01364 643839
e-mail: dartbridgeinn@oldenglishinns.co.uk
web: www.oldenglishinns.co.uk
dir: 0.5m NE of town centre. A38 onto A384, 250yds on left

Rooms 10 en suite (1 fmly) Facilities tea/coffee Direct Dial Conf Max 150 Thtr 150 Class 75 Board 40 Parking 100

BUDLEIGH SALTERTON
Map 3 SY08

PREMIER COLLECTION

Heath Close
★★★★★ BED AND BREAKFAST

Lansdowne Rd EX9 6AH
☎ 01395 444337
e-mail: info@heathclose.com
web: www.heathclose.com

On the outskirts of picturesque Budleigh Salterton and just a short walk from the South West Coastal Path, this delightful house offers high quality accommodation and a generous welcome. Bedrooms are located both in the main house and an adjacent self-contained cottage; all providing an engaging blend of style, comfort and luxury. A light and airy lounge opens onto the garden, and breakfast can be served either in the attractive dining room or on the terrace in summer months.

Rooms 4 en suite (1 fmly) (2 GF) S £79-£89; D £89-£95 Facilities FTV TVL tea/coffee Cen ht Wi-fi Parking 12 Notes LB ⊗ No Children 16yrs

Hansard House
★★★★ GUEST ACCOMMODATION

3 Northview Rd EX9 6BY
☎ 01395 442773 🖳 01395 442475
e-mail: enquiries@hansardhotel.co.uk
web: www.hansardhouseinns.co.uk
dir: 500yds W of town centre

Hansard House is quietly situated a short walk from the town centre. Many of the well-presented bedrooms have commanding views across the town to the countryside and estuary beyond. Several are located on the ground floor and have easier access. Guests enjoy a varied selection at breakfast including a range of healthy options. The dining room and lounge are both comfortably furnished, and dinners are sometimes available with prior notification.

Rooms 12 en suite (1 fmly) (3 GF) S £39-£49; D £84-£91* **Facilities** STV TVL tea/coffee Direct Dial Cen ht Lift Licensed Wi-fi **Parking** 11 **Notes** LB

CHAGFORD Map 3 SX78

PREMIER COLLECTION

Parford Well
★★★★★ BED AND BREAKFAST

Sandy Park TQ13 8JW
☎ 01647 433353
e-mail: tim@parfordwell.co.uk
web: www.parfordwell.co.uk
dir: A30 onto A382, after 3m left at Sandy Park towards Drewsteignton, house 50yds on left

Set in delightful grounds on the edge of Dartmoor, this attractive house is a restful and friendly home. Quality and style are combined in the comfortable bedrooms, the lounge overlooks the well-tended gardens, and breakfast is served at tables dressed with silverware and crisp linen in one of two dining rooms. Carefully cooked, top local ingredients are hallmarks of a breakfast that's a perfect start to a day exploring the moors.

Rooms 3 rms (2 en suite) (1 pri facs) S £45-£90; D £75-£90 **Facilities** TVL Cen ht Wi-fi **Parking** 4 **Notes** ⊗ No Children 8yrs 🐾

Easton Court
★★★★ GUEST ACCOMMODATION

Easton Cross TQ13 8JL
☎ 01647 433469
e-mail: stay@easton.co.uk
web: www.easton.co.uk
dir: 1m NE of Chagford at junct A382 & B3206

Set in Dartmoor National Park, the age of this picturesque house is evident in the oak beams and thick granite walls. Guests can come and go via a separate entrance. Relaxation is obligatory, either in the lovely garden or in the snug surroundings of the lounge. The delightful bedrooms all have country views.

Rooms 5 en suite (2 GF) S £50-£65; D £65-£80* **Facilities** FTV tea/coffee Cen ht Wi-fi **Parking** 5 **Notes** No Children 10yrs

---

CHERITON FITZPAINE Map 3 SS80

Lower Burrow Coombe Farm *(SS883054)*
★★★ FARMHOUSE

EX17 4JS
☎ 01363 866220 Mrs Kekwick
dir: M5 junct 27 to Tiverton, follow signs to Exeter. At Bickleigh take A3072 towards Crediton, 3m on right, sign for farm

Situated in one of Devon's most beautiful valleys, this is an unspoilt smallholding, conveniently located midway between Exmoor and Dartmoor. Guests receive a warm and friendly welcome here and will enjoy the tranquillity of this home. While two of the bedrooms are in the original Elizabethan part of the property, the other room benefits from its own private sitting room.

Rooms 3 rms (1 pri facs) (1 fmly) S £25-£40; D £50-£75* **Facilities** FTV TVL tea/coffee Cen ht **Parking** **Notes** ⊗ Closed Oct-Mar 🐾 48 acres sheep/poultry

---

CHILLATON Map 3 SX48

PREMIER COLLECTION

Tor Cottage
★★★★★ GUEST ACCOMMODATION

PL16 0JE
☎ 01822 860248 📠 01822 860126
e-mail: info@torcottage.co.uk
web: www.torcottage.co.uk
dir: A30 Lewdown exit through Chillaton towards Tavistock, 300yds after Post Office right signed 'Bridlepath No Public Vehicular Access' to end

Tor Cottage, located in its own valley with 18 acres of grounds, is a welcome antidote to the fast pace of everyday life. Rooms are spacious and elegant; the cottage-wing bedroom has a separate sitting room, and the garden rooms have their own wood burners. The gardens are delightful, with a stream and heated outdoor pool. An exceptional range of dishes is offered at breakfast, which can be enjoyed either in the conservatory dining room or on the terrace.

Rooms 1 en suite 3 annexe en suite (3 GF) S £98; D £140-£150 **Facilities** FTV TVL tea/coffee Dinner available Cen ht Wi-fi 🎣 **Parking** 8 **Notes** LB ⊗ No Children 14yrs Closed 17 Dec-7 Jan

---

CHULMLEIGH Map 3 SS61

Old Bakehouse
★★★★ 🍴 GUEST HOUSE

South Molton St EX18 7BW
☎ 01769 580074 & 580137 📠 01769 580074
e-mail: oldbakehouse@colinandholly.co.uk
web: www.colinandholly.co.uk
dir: A377 onto B3096 into village, left into South Molton St, 100yds on left

This 16th-century thatched house is situated in the centre of the medieval town. The cosy licensed restaurant offers fixed-price menus which feature local produce; dishes are imaginative and made with care. Some of the charming bedrooms are located across a courtyard in the former village bakery.

Rooms 3 en suite (1 GF) S £50; D £70 **Facilities** FTV tea/coffee Dinner available Cen ht Licensed **Notes** LB ⊗ No Children 11yrs

---

CLOVELLY Map 3 SS32

East Dyke Farmhouse (SS312235)
★★★★ 🏠 FARMHOUSE

East Dyke Farm, Higher Clovelly EX39 5RU
☎ 01237 431216 Mrs H Goaman
e-mail: steve.goaman@virgin.net
web: www.bedbreakfastclovelly.co.uk
dir: A39 onto B3237 at Clovelly Cross rdbt, farm 500yds on left

Adjoining Clovelly's Iron Age hill fort, the working farm has glorious views across Bideford Bay in the distance. The farmhouse has a friendly atmosphere and offers attractively co-ordinated bedrooms. A major attraction is the breakfast, where local produce and delicious home-made preserves are served around one large table.

Rooms 3 rms (2 en suite) (1 pri facs) (1 fmly) **Facilities** FTV TVL tea/coffee Cen ht Wi-fi **Parking** 6 **Notes** ⊗ Closed 24-26 Dec 🐾 350 acres beef/arable

COLEFORD Map 3 SS70

The New Inn

★★★★ INN

EX17 5BZ

☎ 01363 84242 📠 01363 85044

e-mail: enquiries@thenewinncoleford.co.uk

dir: Off A377 into Coleford, inn after 1.5m

Originally dating back to the 13th century, this charming thatched village inn has much to offer, and provides a relaxing base from which to explore this beautiful corner of Devon. Bedrooms are spacious, comfortable and well appointed with lovely snugly beds and lots of period features retained. Roaring fires, flagged floors and 'Captain', the resident parrot, all combine to engaging effect. A choice of carefully prepared dishes is on offer in the bar and lounges, with local produce strongly featured.

Rooms 6 en suite (1 fmly) (1 GF) S £60-£65; D £80-£85* **Facilities** tea/coffee Dinner available Direct Dial Cen ht **Parking** 50 **Notes** LB Closed 25-26 Dec

COLYFORD Map 4 SY29

Lower Orchard

★★★★ BED AND BREAKFAST

Swan Hill Rd EX24 6QQ

☎ 01297 553615

e-mail: booking@lowerorchard.com

web: www.lowerorchard.com

dir: On A3052 in Colyford, between Lyme Regis & Sidmouth

This modern ranch-style family home looks over the Axe Valley. The spacious ground-floor bedrooms are very well equipped. Breakfast is served in the lounge-dining room with patio doors leading to a private sun terrace, well-tended gardens and splash pool. The owners have also

created a motoring memories museum and a classic car showroom nearby.

Rooms 2 rms (1 en suite) (1 pri facs) (2 GF) S £45-£55; D £55-£65 **Facilities** TVL tea/coffee Cen ht ⚗ **Parking** 3 **Notes** ⊛

CROYDE Map 3 SS43

The Whiteleaf

★★★★ 🛏 🍽 GUEST HOUSE

Croyde Rd EX33 1PN

☎ 01271 890266

dir: On B3231 entering Croyde, on left at 'Road Narrows' sign

A warm, family welcome awaits guests at this attractive house within easy walking distance of the pretty village and the sandy beach. Each of the well-equipped bedrooms has its own charm, and three rooms have decked balconies. Ambitious and imaginative dinners, using fresh seasonal produce, are served every evening in the restaurant.

Rooms 5 en suite (2 fmly) S £56-£60; D £74-£86* **Facilities** tea/coffee Dinner available Direct Dial Cen ht Licensed **Parking** 10 **Notes** LB ⊛ Closed 24-26 Dec

CULLOMPTON Map 3 ST00

Weir Mill Farm (ST040108)

★★★★ FARMHOUSE

Jaycroft, Willand EX15 2RE

☎ 01884 820803 Mrs R Parish

e-mail: rita@weirmill-devon.co.uk

web: www.weirmill-devon.co.uk

dir: 2m N of Cullompton. M5 junct 27, B3181 to Willand, left at rdbt onto B3340 signed Uffculme, 50yds right onto Willand Moor Rd, after Lupin Way left onto lane

Set in extensive farmland, this charming 19th-century farmhouse offers comfortable accommodation with a relaxed and homely atmosphere. The spacious bedrooms are attractively decorated and equipped with an impressive range of thoughtful extras. A good choice is offered at breakfast in the well-appointed dining room. The farmhouse is non-smoking.

Rooms 3 en suite (1 fmly) S £35; D £55 **Facilities** TVL tea/coffee Cen ht **Parking** 5 **Notes** ⊛ 100 acres arable/beef

Wishay Farm (SS994056)

★★★ FARMHOUSE

Trinity EX15 1PE

☎ 01884 33223 📠 01884 33223 Mrs Baker

e-mail: wishayfarm@btopenworld.com

web: www.wishayfarm-bandb-devon.co.uk

dir: 2m SW of Cullompton. From town centre onto Colbrock Ln, 1.5m to junct, continue over, farm 200yds on left

This is a 280-acre, working arable and beef farm with a modernised Grade II listed farmhouse. The house has a peaceful location with pleasant, country views. The two bedrooms are spacious and comfortably furnished. A traditional farmhouse breakfast is served in the dining room, and a separate guest lounge is also available.

Rooms 2 rms (1 en suite) (1 pri facs) (2 fmly) S £32; D £48-£52* **Facilities** TVL tea/coffee Cen ht Wi-fi **Parking** 3 **Notes** LB ⊛ 280 acres arable/beef

DARTMEET Map 3 SX67

Hunter's Lodge B & B

★★★★ 🛏 🍽 GUEST ACCOMMODATION

PL20 6SG

☎ 01364 631173 & 07840 905624

e-mail: huntlodge@pobox.com

dir: A38 at Ashburton onto B3357 to Dartmeet, Hunter's Lodge 1st right after 3rd bridge over Dart River

Situated between the East and West Dart rivers, Hunter's Lodge is at the very heart of Dartmoor. The house offers splendid views, and the bedrooms are attractively and comfortably presented. Dinner, available by arrangement, features a wide range of fresh foods and local farm produce. German, French and Spanish are spoken here.

Rooms 3 rms (2 en suite) 1 annexe en suite (1 fmly) S £35-£45; D £50-£80* **Facilities** FTV TV1B tea/coffee Dinner available Cen ht Spa bath **Parking** 6 **Notes** LB Closed 24-26 Dec RS Mon & Tue closed in low season

Brimpts Farm

★★★ GUEST ACCOMMODATION

PL20 6SG
☎ 01364 631450 📠 01364 631179
e-mail: info@brimptsfarm.co.uk
web: www.brimptsfarm.co.uk
dir: *Dartmeet at E end of B3357, establishment signed on right at top of hill*

A popular venue for walkers and lovers of the great outdoors, Brimpts is peacefully situated in the heart of Dartmoor and has been a Duchy of Cornwall farm since 1307. Bedrooms are simply furnished and many have wonderful views across Dartmoor. Dinner is served by arrangement. Additional facilities include a children's play area and sauna and spa. Brimpts is also home to the Dartmoor Pony Heritage Trust.

Rooms 10 en suite (2 fmly) (7 GF) S £32.50; D £55 **Facilities** TV1B TVL tea/coffee Dinner available Cen ht Licensed Wi-fi Sauna Pool Table Farm walks & trails, Hot tub **Conf** Max 60 Thtr 60 Class 40 Board 25 **Parking** 50 **Notes** LB

DARTMOUTH   Map 3 SX85

PREMIER COLLECTION

Nonsuch House

★★★★★ ⬛⬛ GUEST ACCOMMODATION

Church Hill, Kingswear TQ6 0BX
☎ 01803 752829 📠 01803 752357
e-mail: enquiries@nonsuch-house.co.uk
web: www.nonsuch-house.co.uk
dir: *A3022 onto A379 2m before Brixham. Fork left onto B3205. Left up Higher Contour Rd, down Ridley Hill, house on bend on left at top of Church Hill*

This delightful Edwardian property has fabulous views across the Dart estuary. The marvellous hosts combine friendliness with unobtrusive service. Bedrooms are spacious and superbly appointed, each with a spectacular panorama of the harbour. Fresh, local ingredients are served at dinner, including top-quality meat and fish, along with farmhouse cheeses. Breakfast, on the patio in good weather, features freshly squeezed juice, local sausages and home-baked bread.

Rooms 4 en suite (2 GF) S £80-£110; D £105-£135* **Facilities** FTV tea/coffee Dinner available Cen ht Wi-fi **Parking** 4 **Notes** LB ⊗ No Children 10yrs RS Sat & Tue-Wed no dinner available

PREMIER COLLECTION

Strete Barton House

★★★★★ GUEST HOUSE

Totnes Rd TQ6 0RU
☎ 01803 770364 📠 01803 771182
e-mail: info@stretebarton.co.uk
web: www.stretebarton.co.uk

(For full entry see Strete)

The New Angel Rooms

★★★★ RESTAURANT WITH ROOMS

51 Victoria Rd TQ6 9RT
☎ 01803 839425 📠 01803 839505
e-mail: info@thenewangel.co.uk
dir: *In Dartmouth take one-way system, 1st left at NatWest Bank*

Just a level stroll from the acclaimed New Angel restaurant, this terrace property offers very comfortable, contemporary accommodation, equipped with numerous extra facilities including a complimentary half bottle of Champagne. Breakfast is a feature, with freshly squeezed orange juice: specials such as eggs Benedict and scrambled eggs with smoked salmon should not be missed.

Rooms 6 en suite (2 fmly); D £85-£125* **Facilities** FTV TVL tea/coffee Dinner available Cen ht **Notes** ⊗ Closed Jan No coaches

Woodside Cottage

★★★★ ⬛ BED AND BREAKFAST

TQ9 7BL
☎ 01803 898164
e-mail: theaa@woodsidedartmouth.co.uk
web: www.woodsidedartmouth.co.uk
dir: *Off A3122 to Dartmouth. After golf club brown sign right to house, sharp right, 0.5m on right*

This delightful and comfortable house lies in a scenic valley within easy reach of Dartmouth, and is ideal for walkers and for touring. The charming proprietors are very welcoming, and the bedrooms are attractive. Local and organic produce, cooked on an Aga, and home-made marmalade and fresh eggs feature at breakfast.

Rooms 3 en suite; D £80-£90 **Facilities** FTV tea/coffee Cen ht Wi-fi Concessions at Dartmouth Golf Club **Parking** 4 **Notes** ⊗ No Children 18yrs Closed 25-26 Dec

---

Strete Barton House - South Hams Luxury Coastal Guest House

16th Century Manor House set in the picturesque village of Strete, near Dartmouth. Panoramic sea views. Only one mile from award winning beaches of Blackpool Sands and Slapton Sands. The South West Coast Path a mere 50 metres away. Contemporary interior; Egyptian cotton sheets; fluffy white towels; feather-down pillows; luxury toiletries; beverage tray; flat screen TV and DVD/CD player.

T: 01803 770364 **F:** 01803 771182 **E:** info@stretebarton.co.uk **W:** www.stretebarton.co.uk

AA ★★★★★ Guest House

DARTMOUTH *continued*

Captain's House

★★★★ GUEST ACCOMMODATION

18 Clarence St TQ6 9NW
☎ **01803 832133**
e-mail: thecaptainshouse@aol.com
web: www.captainshouse.co.uk
dir: *B3122 into Dartmouth, Clarence St parallel with river*

Dating from 1730, this charming house retains many original features and is only a short walk from the quayside and town centre. The attractive bedrooms are comfortable and well-equipped. Enjoyable breakfasts are served in the dining room and include local produce and a large selection of quality preserves.

Rooms 5 en suite **Facilities** tea/coffee Cen ht **Notes** ⊗ No Children 5yrs

Cherub's Nest

★★★★ GUEST ACCOMMODATION

15 Higher St TQ6 9RB
☎ **01803 832482**
e-mail: cherubsnest4bb@aol.com
web: www.cherubsnest.co.uk
dir: *From Lower Dartmouth ferry along Lower St, left onto Smith St, left onto Higher St, Cherub's Nest 50yds on left*

Dating from 1710, this former merchant's house, bedecked with flowers during the summer, is located in the very heart of historic Dartmouth. Full of character, the individually decorated bedrooms vary in size, but all are attractive and well equipped. A choice of breakfasts is served in the cosy dining room.

Rooms 3 en suite **Facilities** tea/coffee Cen ht Wi-fi **Notes** ⊗ No Children 10yrs

Triatic

★★★★ BED AND BREAKFAST

13a Ridge Hill TQ6 9PE
☎ **01803 833954**
web: www.triatic.co.uk
dir: *From Riverside via A3122/A379, 1st right then 2nd left onto Ridge Hill*

Just a five minute walk from the historic town centre of Dartmouth, Triatic enjoys a prominent position overlooking the town and the harbour. Accommodation is of a high standard and the guest bedroom is equipped with a host of thoughtful extras. A warm welcome is assured from the conscientious owners of this lovely house.

Rooms 1 en suite S £50-£55; D £60-£75 **Facilities** FTV tea/coffee Cen ht **Parking** 1 **Notes** LB ⊗ No Children Closed 2 Jan-mid Mar ⊗

DAWLISH — Map 3 SX97

Old Dawlish Brewery

★★★ GUEST ACCOMMODATION

45 High St EX7 9HF
☎ **01626 889611** 📄 **01626 867263**
e-mail: enquiries@dawlishbrewery.com
web: www.dawlishbrewery.com
dir: *From A379 (Exeter road) entering town, bear right onto High St*

As the name implies this was once a brewery, and indeed the tradition continues with a beer on offer that is unique to this establishment. The atmosphere is relaxed and welcoming with both the bar and restaurant having a rustic charm. Much of the food is locally sourced including excellent pork products from the proprietor's nearby farm. Bedrooms are located in a separate building directly opposite, and include an impressive and stylish suite.

Rooms 2 annexe rms 1 annexe en suite (1 pri facs) (2 GF); D £70-£125* **Facilities** STV tea/coffee Dinner available Cen ht Licensed Wi-fi **Parking** 1 **Notes** LB ⊗

DODDISCOMBSLEIGH — Map 3 SX88

The Nobody Inn

★★★★ INN

EX6 7PS
☎ **01647 252394** 📄 **01647 252978**
e-mail: info@nobodyinn.co.uk
web: www.nobodyinn.co.uk
dir: *From A38 turn off at top of Haldon Hill, follow signs to Doddiscombsleigh*

Dating back to the 16th century, this fascinating inn is something of a mecca for lovers of wine, whisky and local ale - the choices are extensive. Of course, that's not forgetting the impressive food of which much is locally sourced including an extensive selection of cheese. Bedrooms and bathrooms have now been totally refurbished to provide high levels of quality, comfort and individuality. Reassuringly, the bars and lounges remain unchanged with charmingly mis-matched furniture, age-darkened beams and inglenook fireplace, all adding up to an engaging place to visit.

Rooms 5 rms (4 en suite) (1 pri facs) S £45-£70; D £60-£95* **Facilities** tea/coffee Dinner available Direct Dial Wi-fi **Parking** 50 **Notes** No Children 5yrs Closed 25-26 Dec & 31 Dec pm No coaches

---

EXETER — Map 3 SX99

See also Rockbeare

Chi Restaurant & Bar with Accommodation

★★★★ 🍴 RESTAURANT WITH ROOMS

Fore St, Kenton EX6 8LD
☎ **01626 890213** 📄 **01626 891678**
e-mail: enquiries@chi-restaurant.co.uk
web: www.chi-restaurant.co.uk
dir: *5m S of Exeter. M5 junct 30, A379 towards Dawlish, in Kenton centre*

This former pub has been spectacularly transformed into a chic and contemporary bar, allied with a stylish Chinese restaurant. Dishes are beautifully presented with an emphasis on quality produce and authenticity, resulting in a memorable dining experience. Bedrooms are well equipped and all provide good levels of space and comfort, along with modern bathrooms.

Rooms 5 en suite (2 fmly) S £33.30-£37; D £53.10-£59 (room only)* **Facilities** FTV TVL tea/coffee Dinner available Direct Dial Cen ht Wi-fi **Parking** 26 **Notes** ⊗ No coaches

Holbrook Farm

★★★★ GUEST ACCOMMODATION

Clyst Honiton EX5 2HR
☎ **01392 367000** 📄 **01392 367000**
e-mail: heatherglanvill@holbrookfarm.co.uk
web: www.holbrookfarm.co.uk
dir: *M5, A3052 for Sidmouth, pass Westpoint (county showground) & Cat and Fiddle pub, 500yds left at Hill Pond caravans, signed for 1m*

This friendly, modern farmhouse stands in lush rolling countryside and has spectacular views. All bedrooms are located on the ground floor, have their own entrance and offer bright, attractive and spacious accommodation. Breakfast features the best fresh local produce. Holbrook Farm is convenient for Exeter, the coast and moor, and there are several popular inns and restaurants nearby.

Rooms 3 en suite (1 fmly) (3 GF) S £30-£50; D £55-£60* **Facilities** tea/coffee Cen ht Wi-fi **Parking** 4 **Notes** LB ⊗

Mill Farm (SX959839)

★★★★ FARMHOUSE

Kenton EX6 8JR
☎ 01392 832471 **Mrs D Lambert**
e-mail: info@millfarmstay.co.uk
dir: *A379 from Exeter towards Dawlish, over mini-rdbt by Swans Nest, farm 1.75m on right*

Located just a short drive from the Powderham Estate, this imposing working farmhouse is surrounded by pastureland. Each of the spacious bedrooms (single, twin, double and family) is stylishly and comfortably furnished and has co-ordinated decor; all rooms have views across the countryside. Breakfast (including vegetarian options) is served in the sunny dining room and a lounge is also provided. A packed breakfast can be prepared if a very early start is required.

Rooms 5 en suite (3 fmly) S £40-£50; D £65
Facilities tea/coffee Cen ht Wi-fi **Parking** 12 **Notes** LB ⊗
No Children 6yrs Closed Xmas 30 acres horses

Rydon (SX999871)

★★★★ FARMHOUSE

Woodbury EX5 1LB
☎ 01395 232341 📠 01395 232341 **Mrs S Glanvill**
e-mail: sallyglanvill@aol.com
web: www.rydonfarmwoodbury.co.uk
dir: *A376 & B3179 from Exeter into Woodbury, right before 30mph sign*

Dating from the 16th century, this Devon longhouse has been run by the same family for eight generations. A stay here is an opportunity to experience a farming lifestyle complete with patient cows steadfastly waiting to be milked. The spacious bedrooms are equipped with many useful extra facilities and one has a four-poster bed. There is a television lounge and a delightful garden in which to relax. Breakfast is a treat, served in front of an inglenook fireplace.

Rooms 3 en suite (1 fmly) S £52-£55; D £74-£80*
Facilities FTV TVL tea/coffee Cen ht **Parking** 3 **Notes** LB
450 acres dairy

Raffles

★★★★ 🅰 GUEST HOUSE

11 Blackall Rd EX4 4HD
☎ 01392 270200 📠 01392 270200
e-mail: raffleshtl@btinternet.com
dir: *M5, exit at Exeter services, follow signs for Middlemore & City Centre*

Rooms 6 en suite (2 fmly) S £42-£45; D £72-£75
Facilities STV FTV TVL tea/coffee Cen ht Licensed Wi-fi
Parking 6 **Notes** LB

Chimneys

★★★ GUEST HOUSE

The Strand, Starcross EX6 8PA
☎ 01626 890813
e-mail: tuckmrgrt@aol.com
web: www.chimneys-bandb.co.uk
dir: *M5 junct 30, follow signs for A379 (Dawlish). On entering Starcross, 3rd house on right*

This grand house dates back to the 1880s and looks out across the Exe Estuary. All bedrooms offer good levels of comfort, and some also have the bonus of lovely views across the river. Elegant public rooms have plenty of character with a very welcoming and homely feel. Breakfast provides a satisfying start to the day, and dinner is also available by prior arrangement.

Rooms 5 en suite (2 fmly) S £35-£45; D £55-£70*
Facilities FTV tea/coffee Dinner available Cen ht Licensed Wi-fi **Parking** 5 **Notes** LB ⊗ Closed Dec-Feb

Culm Vale Country House

★★★ BED AND BREAKFAST

Culm Vale, Stoke Canon EX5 4EG
☎ 01392 841515 📠 01392 841615
e-mail: culmvale@hotmail.com
web: www.culmvaleaccommodation.co.uk
dir: *A396 from Exeter towards Tiverton, after Stoke Canon sign, Culm Vale 5th property on right*

A warm welcome is extended at this impressive house situated on the edge of pretty Stoke Canon. Family-run, the Culm Vale is full of character and offers very spacious, comfortable accommodation. Breakfast, featuring eggs laid by the family's own hens, can be enjoyed in the grand dining room.

Rooms 4 rms (1 en suite) S £30-£35; D £40-£45*
Facilities FTV tea/coffee Cen ht Wi-fi ⟋ **Parking** 4
Notes ⊗

Dunmore Guest House

★★★ GUEST HOUSE

22 Blackall Rd EX4 4HE
☎ 01392 431643 📠 01392 431643
e-mail: dunmorehtl@aol.com
web: www.dunmorehotel.co.uk
dir: *M5 junct 29, through city centre, right at mini-rdbt, house on left*

Convenient for the city centre, Exeter College and the railway station, this guest house provides comfortable accommodation. The bedrooms are attractive and well presented, and many have been redecorated to provide very good standards. Traditional English breakfasts are served in the dining room.

Rooms 9 rms (6 en suite) (3 fmly) (1 GF) S £40; D £52-£60*
Facilities FTV tea/coffee Cen ht Wi-fi **Notes** LB ⊗

The Sunnymede Guest House

★★★ GUEST HOUSE

24 New North Rd EX4 4HF
☎ 01392 273844 📠 01392 273844
e-mail: seldonsnnymds@aol.com
dir: *600yds N of cathedral. On one-way system pass Central Station in Queen St, at clocktower rdbt turn right, Sunnymede on left*

The Sunnymede has a central location in this historic city and is convenient for the college, shopping centre and attractions. A compact guest house, it offers well-presented, comfortable bedrooms, ideal for business or leisure guests. A good choice is available at breakfast.

Rooms 7 rms (4 en suite) (1 fmly) S £30-£35;
D £52-£60* **Facilities** FTV TVL tea/coffee Cen ht **Notes** ⊗
Closed 20 Dec-15 Jan

EXMOUTH Map 3 SY08

Barn

★★★★ 🏠 GUEST ACCOMMODATION

Foxholes Hill, Marine Dr EX8 2DF
☎ 01395 224411 📠 01395 225445
e-mail: exmouthbarn@googlemail.com
web: www.barnhotel.co.uk
dir: *From M5 junct 30 take A376 to Exmouth, then follow signs to seafront. At rdbt last exit into Foxholes Hill. Located on right*

This Grade II-listed establishment has a prime location, close to miles of sandy beaches. Equally pleasant is the immaculate rear garden, which is sea-facing and features a terrace and swimming pool for use during the summer. Service is attentive and friendly, and spectacular sea views are enjoyed from most of the well-equipped bedrooms and public rooms. Breakfast, featuring freshly squeezed juices and local produce, is served in the pleasant dining room.

Rooms 11 en suite (4 fmly) **Facilities** FTV tea/coffee Direct Dial Cen ht Licensed Wi-fi ⟋ **Parking** 30 **Notes** LB Closed 23 Dec-10 Jan

DARTMOUTH *continued*

The Devoncourt

★★★★ GUEST ACCOMMODATION

16 Douglas Av EX8 2EX
☎ 01395 272277 📄 01395 269315
e-mail: enquiries@devoncourt.com
web: www.devoncourthotel.com
dir: M5/A376 to Exmouth, follow seafront to Maer Rd, right at T-junct

The Devoncourt stands in four acres of mature, subtropical gardens, sloping gently towards the sea and overlooking two miles of sandy beaches. It offers extensive leisure facilities, and the smartly furnished bedrooms are exceptionally well equipped. Public areas are spacious and shared with timeshare owners. For meals you can choose between the informal bar and the restaurant.

Rooms 10 en suite (1 fmly) **Facilities** FTV TVL tea/coffee Dinner available Direct Dial Cen ht Lift Licensed Wi-fi 🔄 🏌 🎱 🏊 🎿 Snooker Sauna Solarium Gymnasium Sun shower, Jacuzzi **Parking** 50 **Notes** ⊗ Civ Wed

---

HARTLAND Map 2 SS22

Fosfelle

★★★ GUEST HOUSE

EX39 6EF
☎ 01237 441273 📄 01237 441273
dir: 500yds SE of village on B3248

Dating from the 17th century, this delightful manor house offers comfortable accommodation close to the village of Hartland. It is set in six acres of gardens that has two fishing lakes. Guests can enjoy pool or darts in the welcoming bar, and the restaurant offers a range of freshly prepared dishes.

Rooms 7 rms (4 en suite) (2 fmly) S £35-£42; D £65-£70 **Facilities** TV6B TVL tea/coffee Dinner available Cen ht Licensed Fishing Pool Table **Parking** 20 **Notes** LB

HOLSWORTHY Map 3 SS30

Leworthy Farm House

★★★★ GUEST ACCOMMODATION

Lower Leworthy, Nr Pyworthy EX22 6SJ
☎ 01409 259469 📄 01409 259469
e-mail: leworthyfarmhouse@yahoo.co.uk
web: www.leworthyfarmhouse.co.uk
dir: From Holsworthy onto Bodmin St towards North Tamerton, 4th left signed Leworthy/Southdown

Located in an unspoiled area of north Devon with three acres of gardens, meadows, a copse and a fishing lake, this delightful farmhouse provides bright, comfortable accommodation with numerous extra facilities. Breakfast is served in the large lounge-dining room.

Rooms 7 en suite (1 fmly) S £45-£65; D £65* **Facilities** FTV TVL tea/coffee Wi-fi Fishing **Parking** 8 **Notes** LB ⊗ 🍽

Bickford Arms

★★★★ 🍴 INN

Brandis Corner EX22 7XY
☎ 01409 221318 📄 01409 220085
e-mail: info@bickfordarms.com
dir: 4m E of Holsworthy on A3072

This roadside inn has been providing rest and sustenance for weary travellers for many years, and the tradition continues today with a genuine welcome and relaxed atmosphere. The spacious bar is warmed by a crackling fire in cooler months and guests can choose to eat either here or in the restaurant, with a choice of bar menu and specials board. The attractive bedrooms provide high levels of comfort, likewise the impressive and well-appointed bathrooms.

Rooms 5 en suite (1 fmly) S £50-£90; D £70-£100* **Facilities** tea/coffee Dinner available Cen ht Wi-fi **Conf** Max 40 Thtr 40 Board 20 **Parking** 50 **Notes** ⊗ RS Mon-Wed (Jan & Feb) closed 3-5.30pm No coaches

---

Clawford Vineyard

★★★★ GUEST HOUSE

Clawton EX22 6PN
☎ 01409 254177 📄 01409 254177
e-mail: john.ray@clawford.co.uk
dir: A388 (Holsworth to Launceston road), left at Clawton x-rds, 1.5m to T-junct, left, 0.5m left again

Situated in the peaceful Claw Valley and with splendid views over fishing lakes and woods, this working cider orchard and vineyard offers spacious and comfortable bedrooms. There is a large lounge, a well-stocked bar, a conservatory and a restaurant. Freshly cooked dishes are well prepared and attractively presented at dinner and breakfast. Self-catering apartments, overlooking the lakes, are also available.

Rooms 11 en suite (7 fmly) **Facilities** TVL tea/coffee Dinner available Cen ht Licensed Fishing Pool Table Coarse & game fishing **Parking** 60 **Notes** ⊗ No Children 6yrs

---

The Hollies Farm Guest House (SS371001)

★★★ FARMHOUSE

Clawton EX22 6PN
☎ 01409 253770 & 07929 318033 Mr & Mrs G Colwill
e-mail: theholliesfarm@hotmail.com
web: www.theholliesfarm.co.uk
dir: Off A388 at Clawton village signed vineyard, after 2m Hollies in lane on left after T-junct, signed

This sheep and beef farm offers comfortable, modern accommodation in a family atmosphere. There are pleasant views across the countryside from most bedrooms; all are well appointed. Breakfast is served in the conservatory, and dinner is available by arrangement. There is also a barbecue area with a gazebo.

Rooms 3 en suite (3 fmly) S £26-£30; D £46-£54* **Facilities** TVL tea/coffee Dinner available Cen ht Hot tub **Parking** 6 **Notes** LB ⊗ Closed 24-25 Dec 🍽 25 acres beef/sheep

PREMIER COLLECTION

West Colwell Farm
★★★★ 🏠 BED AND BREAKFAST

Offwell EX14 9SL
☎ 01404 831130 📠 01404 831769
e-mail: stay@westcolwell.co.uk
dir: *Off A35 to village, at church downhill, farm 0.5m on right*

Peacefully situated down a country lane, in an Area of Outstanding Natural Beauty, this establishment offers stylish bedrooms in a converted dairy. The two rooms on the ground floor have direct access to their own terraces. Breakfast is served in the split-level dining room overlooking the wooded valley and fields, where there is a roaring log-burning stove in cooler months.

Rooms 3 en suite (2 GF) S £50; D £70-£80
Facilities FTV tea/coffee Cen ht **Parking** 3 **Notes** LB ⊗ No Children 12yrs Closed Dec & Jan

Courtmoor Farm *(ST207068)*
★★★★ FARMHOUSE

Upottery EX14 9QA
☎ 01404 861565   Mr & Mrs Buxton
e-mail: courtmoor.farm@btinternet.com
web: www.courtmoor.farm.btinternet.co.uk
dir: *4m NE of Honiton off A30*

This farmhouse is set in attractive grounds, with stunning views over the Otter Valley. All of the bedrooms share the views, and are spacious, comfortable and well equipped. Breakfast provides a tasty and substantial start to the day with local produce used whenever possible. Guests have access to the leisure room, gym and sauna. Self-catering cottages are also available.

Rooms 3 en suite (1 fmly) S £36-£38; D £59-£62*
Facilities FTV tea/coffee Cen ht Wi-fi Fishing Sauna Gymnasium Woodland nature trail **Parking** 20 **Notes** ⊗ Closed 20 Dec-1 Jan 17 acres non-working

Ridgeway Farm
★★★★ GUEST ACCOMMODATION

Awliscombe EX14 3PY
☎ 01404 841331 📠 01404 841119
e-mail: jessica@ridgewayfarm.co.uk
dir: *3m NW of Honiton. A30 onto A373, through Awliscombe to near end of 40mph area, right opp Godford Farm, farm 500mtrs up narrow lane, sign on entrance*

This 18th-century farmhouse has a peaceful location on the slopes of Hembury Hill, and is a good base for exploring nearby Honiton and the east Devon coast. Renovations have brought the cosy accommodation to a high standard and the atmosphere is relaxed and homely.

The proprietors and their family pets assure a warm welcome.

Rooms 2 en suite S £33-£37; D £56-£62 **Facilities** FTV TVL tea/coffee Dinner available Cen ht **Parking** 4 **Notes** LB ⊛

Threshays
★★★ BED AND BREAKFAST

Awliscombe EX14 3QB
☎ 01404 43551 & 07811 675800 📠 01404 43551
e-mail: threshays@btinternet.com
dir: *2.5m NW of Honiton on A373*

A converted threshing barn, situated on a non-working farm, Threshays has wonderful views over open countryside. With tea and cake offered on arrival, this family-run establishment provides comfortable accommodation in a friendly atmosphere. The lounge-dining room is a light and airy setting for the enjoyment of good breakfasts. Ample parking is a bonus.

Rooms 2 rms (1 fmly) S £28; D £50 **Facilities** TVL tea/coffee Cen ht Wi-fi **Parking** 6 **Notes** ⊗ Closed Sun-Tue ⊛

Cottage
★★★ GUEST ACCOMMODATION

TQ7 3HJ
☎ 01548 561555 📠 01548 561455
e-mail: info@hopecove.com
dir: *From Kingsbridge on A381 to Salcombe. 2nd right at Marlborough, left for Inner Hope*

Glorious sunsets can be seen over the attractive bay from this popular accommodation. Friendly and attentive service from the staff and management mean many guests return here. Bedrooms, many with sea views and some with balconies, are well equipped. The restaurant offers an enjoyable dining experience.

Rooms 34 rms (30 en suite) (5 fmly) (7 GF) S £45.30-£88.50; D £90.60-£177* (incl.dinner) **Facilities** FTV TV32B TVL tea/coffee Dinner available Direct Dial Licensed Wi-fi Table tennis **Conf** Max 70 Thtr 60 Class 60 Board 30 **Parking** 50 **Notes** LB Closed early Jan-early Feb

PREMIER COLLECTION

The Round House
★★★★★ GUEST HOUSE

EX39 5DN
☎ 01237 451687
e-mail: michael.m.clifford@btinternet.com
web: www.the-round-house.co.uk
dir: *1m W of Horns Cross on A39, 0.5m past Hoops Inn towards Bude*

This charming converted barn stands in landscaped gardens within easy reach of Clovelly. Guests receive a warm welcome and a complimentary cream tea on arrival, which may be served in the lounge with its exposed beams and inglenook fireplace. Bedrooms are comfortable with numerous thoughtful extra facilities. A varied choice is offered at breakfast.

Rooms 3 en suite (1 fmly) (1 GF) S £40; D £60-£65*
Facilities FTV TVL tea/coffee Cen ht **Parking** 8 **Notes** ⊗ No Children 12yrs

Strathmore
★★★★ GUEST ACCOMMODATION

57 St Brannock's Rd EX34 8EQ
☎ 01271 862248 📠 01271 862248
e-mail: peter@small6374.fsnet.co.uk
web: www.the-strathmore.co.uk
dir: *A361 from Barnstaple to Ilfracombe, Strathmore 1.5m from Mullacot Cross entering Ilfracombe*

Situated within walking distance of the town centre and beach, this charming Victorian property offers a very warm welcome. The attractive bedrooms are comfortably furnished, while public areas include a well-stocked bar,

continued

ILFRACOMBE *continued*

an attractive terraced garden, and an elegant breakfast room.

Rooms 8 en suite (3 fmly) S £32-£35; D £65-£76 **Facilities** tea/coffee Cen ht Licensed Wi-fi **Parking** 7 **Notes** LB

Collingdale Guest House

★★★★ GUEST HOUSE

13 Larkstone Ter EX34 9NU
☎ 01271 863770 📠 01271 863867
e-mail: stay@thecollingdale.co.uk
web: www.thecollingdale.co.uk
dir: Take A399 E through Ilfracombe, on left past B3230 turning

Built in 1869, this friendly establishment is within easy walking distance of the town centre and seafront. The well presented bedrooms, many with sweeping sea views, are equipped with modern facilities, and the comfortable lounge also has magnificent views over the sea. Dinner is available by arrangement and there is a cosy bar.

Rooms 9 rms (8 en suite) (1 pri facs) (3 fmly) S £40-£48; D £60-£80 **Facilities** FTV TVL tea/coffee Dinner available Licensed Wi-fi **Notes** LB ⊗ No Children 8yrs Closed Nov-Feb

Marine Court

★★★★ GUEST HOUSE

Hillsborough Rd EX34 9QQ
☎ 01271 862920
e-mail: marinecourthotel@btconnect.com
dir: M5 junct 27, A361 to Barnstaple, continue to Ilfracombe

This friendly and welcoming establishment offers comfortable and homely accommodation opposite the Old Thatched Inn. The well-presented bedrooms all provide good levels of comfort with thoughtful extras. Freshly prepared evening meals and breakfast are served in the spacious dining room which is next to the bar. On-site and adjacent parking is a bonus.

Rooms 8 en suite (2 fmly) S £37-£42; D £58-£64* **Facilities** tea/coffee Dinner available Cen ht Licensed **Parking** 3 **Notes** LB

Norbury House

★★★★ GUEST HOUSE

Torrs Park EX34 8AZ
☎ 01271 863888
e-mail: info@norburyhouse.co.uk
dir: From A399 to end of High St/Church St. At mini-rdbt after lights take 1st exit onto Church Rd. Bear left onto Osbourne Rd. At T-junct left onto Torrs Park. House at top of hill on right

This detached Victorian residence has a refreshingly different, contemporary style. The welcome is warm and genuine, allied with a helpful and attentive approach. A variety of bedrooms types are offered - all provide impressive levels of comfort and quality. An elegant lounge leads through to a conservatory which has an honesty bar. Outside, the terraced gardens offer a quiet spot to enjoy the lovely views. Cuisine is taken seriously here, with breakfast featuring quality, local produce.

Rooms 6 en suite (2 fmly); D £75-£95* **Facilities** STV FTV tea/coffee Cen ht Licensed Wi-fi **Conf** Max 18 Thtr 14 Class 14 Board 12 **Parking** 6 **Notes** LB ⊗

The Graystoke

★★★★ 🅰 GUEST HOUSE

58 St Brannocks Rd EX34 8EQ
☎ 01271 862328
e-mail: info@thegraystoke.co.uk
web: www.thegraystoke.co.uk
dir: 1.5m from rdbt at Mullacott Cross

Rooms 7 en suite S £28-£32; D £56-£64* **Facilities** FTV TVL tea/coffee Cen ht Licensed Wi-fi **Parking** 7 **Notes** LB ⊗ No Children Closed Dec-Feb

Avalon

★★★ GUEST HOUSE

6 Capstone Crescent EX34 9BT
☎ 01271 863325 📠 01271 866543
e-mail: avalon_ilfracombe@yahoo.co.uk
web: www.avalon-hotel.co.uk
dir: A361 to Ilfracombe, left at 1st lights, straight on 2nd lights, left at end of one-way system & left again

Conveniently located near the centre of Ilfracombe, this well-established guest house has magnificent sea views from the bedrooms and dining room. Avalon offers well-equipped bedrooms, one of which is located on the ground floor. Breakfast is served at separate tables in the well-appointed dining room and parking is available free of charge nearby.

Rooms 9 en suite (3 fmly) (1 GF) S £30-£34; D £54-£64 **Facilities** FTV tea/coffee Dinner available **Parking** 4 **Notes** LB ⊗ Closed Xmas & New Year

The Wayfarer Inn

★★★ INN

Lane End EX39 4LB
☎ 01271 860342
web: www.thewayfarerinstow.co.uk

Tucked away in a coastal village, this family-run pub offers a real West Country welcome. A number of the contemporary styled bedrooms have sea views, and a spacious suite is also available. The inn serves real ales from the barrel and a wide range of meals to suit all palates and pockets; the food is locally sourced and includes fresh fish caught from their own boat. A sun-trap beer garden is also available for alfresco eating, all within 20 yards of Instow's sandy beach and the Atlantic Ocean.

Rooms 6 en suite (2 fmly) **Facilities** tea/coffee Dinner available Cen ht Fishing **Notes** ⊗ No coaches

Orway Crescent Farm Bed & Breakfast

★★★★ BED AND BREAKFAST

Orway Crescent Farm, Orway EX15 2EX
☎ 01884 266876 & 0845 658 8472 📠 01884 266876
e-mail: orway.crescentfarm@btinternet.com
dir: M5 junct 28 onto A373 towards Honiton. After 5m Keepers Cottage pub on right, take next left for Sheldon - Broad Rd. 3rd on left to Orway, farm at bottom of hill

Located in a sleepy rural hamlet, this welcoming home has now been refurbished to an impressive standard and is just five miles from the M5. Bedrooms combine comfort and quality in equal measure with numerous useful extras which typify the caring and helpful approach here. The stylish modern bathrooms are simply superb, either for an invigorating shower or relaxing soak in the bath. The dining room is the venue for substantial breakfasts with lovely views across the fields to woodland beyond.

Rooms 3 en suite (1 fmly) (1 GF) S £32.50-£40; D £55-£60 **Facilities** STV FTV tea/coffee Cen ht Wi-fi **Parking** 3 **Notes** ⊗

KENTISBURY — Map 3 SS64

Night In Gails

★★★★ GUEST ACCOMMODATION

Kentisbury Mill EX31 4NF
☎ 01271 883545
e-mail: info@kentisburymill.co.uk
dir: M5 junct 27 onto A361 towards Barnstaple, then A399 to Blackmoor Gate. Turn left at Blackmoor Gate onto A39, then right onto B3229 at Kentisbury Ford, 1m on right

Originally consisting of an 18th-century cottage and mill, this relaxing hideaway has been sympathetically renovated to provide impressive levels of comfort, allied with caring hospitality. Bedrooms offer an appealing blend of old and new, with views over the extensive gardens. A guest lounge is also provided with plenty of local information for those wanting to explore the dramatic coast and countryside. Breakfast is Aga-cooked and includes superb eggs from the resident hens, together with wonderful local produce, a perfect start to the day.

Rooms 4 en suite S £28-£30; D £60-£65* **Facilities** FTV tea/coffee Cen ht Wi-fi **Parking** 6 **Notes** LB ⊗ Closed Xmas

LIFTON — Map 3 SX38

The Old Coach House

★★★★ BED AND BREAKFAST

The Thatched Cottage, Sprytown PL16 0AY
☎ 01566 784224 🖷 01566 784334
e-mail: tochsprytown@aol.com
web: www.theoldcoach-house.co.uk
dir: Off A30 through Lifton, 0.75m E to Sprytown x-rds, right to Thatched Cottage in 100yds

Set in a colourful cottage garden near the Cornwall border, the Old Coach House provides a warm welcome. The comfortable bedrooms have numerous extras, including a welcome basket. Hearty breakfasts, served in the beamed dining room of the adjacent Thatched Cottage, feature good local produce including vegetarian options.

Rooms 4 annexe en suite (3 fmly) (2 GF) **Facilities** tea/coffee Direct Dial **Parking** 6 **Notes** ⊗

Tinhay Mill Guest House and Restaurant

★★★★ ⚜ RESTAURANT WITH ROOMS

Tinhay PL16 0AJ
☎ 01566 784201 🖷 01566 784201
e-mail: tinhay.mill@talk21.com
web: www.tinhaymillrestaurant.co.uk
dir: A30/A388 approach Lifton, establishment at bottom of village on right

The former mill cottages are now a delightful restaurant with rooms of much charm. Beams and open fireplaces set the scene, with everything geared to ensure a relaxed and comfortable stay. Bedrooms are spacious and well equipped, with many thoughtful extras. Cuisine is taken seriously here, using the best of local produce.

Rooms 5 en suite (1 GF) S £55-£65; D £80-£90* **Facilities** FTV TVL Dinner available Cen ht Wi-fi **Parking** 19 **Notes** LB ⊗ No Children No coaches

LUSTLEIGH — Map 3 SX78

PREMIER COLLECTION

Eastwrey Barton

★★★★★ ⇔ GUEST ACCOMMODATION

Moretonhampstead Rd TQ13 9SN
☎ 01647 277338 🖷 01647 277133
e-mail: info@eastwreybarton.co.uk
web: www.eastwreybarton.co.uk
dir: On A382 between Bovey Tracey & Moretonhampstead, 6m from A38 (Drumbridges junct)

Warm hospitality and a genuine welcome are hallmarks at this family-run establishment, situated inside the Dartmoor National Park. Built in the 18th century, the house retains many original features and has views across the Wray Valley. Bedrooms are spacious and well equipped, while public areas include a snug lounge warmed by a crackling log fire. Breakfast and dinner showcase local produce with an impressive wine list to accompany the latter.

Rooms 5 en suite (1 fmly) S £65-£75; D £90-£110* **Facilities** FTV tea/coffee Dinner available Cen ht Licensed Wi-fi **Parking** 18 **Notes** ⊗ No Children 10yrs

PREMIER COLLECTION

Woodley House

★★★★★ GUEST ACCOMMODATION

Caseley Hill TQ13 9TN
☎ 01647 277214 🖷 01647 277126
dir: Off A382 into village, at T-junct right to Caseley, house 2nd on left

Set just a stroll from the village pub, church and tea room, Woodley House is a peaceful and tranquil retreat, with super views over the rolling countryside. A hearty breakfast, featuring as many as 12 home-made preserves, home-baked bread and a vast range of cooked breakfast options, can be enjoyed in the charming dining room. A good base for walkers, and dogs are welcome too.

Rooms 2 en suite; D £70-£72* **Facilities** FTV TVL tea/coffee Cen ht **Parking** 3 **Notes** No Children 10yrs ⊗

LYDFORD — Map 3 SX58

PREMIER COLLECTION

Moor View House

★★★★★ ⇔ GUEST ACCOMMODATION

Vale Down EX20 4BB
☎ 01822 820220 🖷 01822 820220
dir: 1m NE of Lydford on A386

Built around 1870, this charming house once changed hands over a game of cards. The elegant bedrooms are furnished with interesting pieces and retain many original features. Breakfast, and dinner by arrangement, are served house-party style at a large oak table. The two acres of moorland gardens give access to Dartmoor.

Rooms 4 en suite S £45-£50; D £70-£85* **Facilities** FTV TVL tea/coffee Dinner available Cen ht Licensed ⇔ **Parking** 15 **Notes** LB ⊗ No Children 12yrs ⊗

LYNMOUTH
Map 3 SS74

PREMIER COLLECTION

Sea View Villa
★★★★★ 🏠 ⊛ GUEST ACCOMMODATION

6 Summer House Path EX35 6ES
☎ 01598 753460 📄 01598 753496
e-mail: seaviewenquiries@aol.com
web: www.seaviewvilla.co.uk
dir: *A39 from Porlock, 1st left after bridge, Sea View Villa on right 20yds along path opp church*

This charming Georgian villa, built in 1721, has been appointed to a high standard by owners Steve Williams and Chris Bissex. Tucked away from the bustle of the main streets, the house provides elegant and peaceful accommodation. All bedrooms are equipped with thoughtful extras and have impressive views of the harbour and sea. The proprietors' genuine hospitality assures a relaxed and comfortable stay. Dinner and breakfast are not to be missed. Beauty therapies are available by prior arrangement.

Rooms 5 rms (3 en suite) (1 fmly) S £35-£40; D £110-£130* **Facilities** TVL tea/coffee Dinner available Cen ht Licensed Wi-fi **Notes** LB ⊗ No Children 14yrs Closed Jan RS 2wks Nov

PREMIER COLLECTION

Bonnicott House
★★★★★ 🏠 ⊛ GUEST HOUSE

10 Watersmeet Rd EX35 6EP
☎ 01598 753346
e-mail: stay@bonnicott.com
web: www.bonnicott.com
dir: *A39 from Minehead over East Lyn River Bridge, left onto Watersmeet Rd, 50yds on right opp church*

Bonnicott House is set in attractive gardens with spectacular views over the harbour towards the sea and cliffs. Bedrooms, most with sea views, are very well equipped, with comfortable furnishings and thoughtful extra facilities. Dinner offers fresh local produce, imaginatively presented, and at breakfast hearty portions are served fresh from being cooked on the Aga.

Rooms 8 rms (7 en suite) (1 pri facs) S £40-£86; D £45-£96* **Facilities** TVL tea/coffee Dinner available Cen ht Licensed Wi-fi **Conf** Max 16 Board 16fred **Notes** LB ⊗ No Children 14yrs

PREMIER COLLECTION

The Heatherville
★★★★★ 🏠 ⊛ GUEST ACCOMMODATION

Tors Park EX35 6NB
☎ 01598 752327 📄 01598 752634
web: www.heatherville.co.uk
dir: *Off A39 onto Tors Rd, 1st left fork into Tors Park*

With its secluded and elevated south-facing position, The Heatherville has splendid views over Lynmouth and surrounding woodland. Lovingly restored over the last few years to a very high standard, both the bedrooms and the lounge give a feeling of luxury, with the charm of a large country house. By arrangement, enjoyable evening meals, featuring organic and free-range produce whenever possible, are available. There is also an intimate bar.

Rooms 6 en suite; D £64-£90* **Facilities** tea/coffee Dinner available Cen ht Licensed **Parking** 7 **Notes** LB No Children 16yrs Closed Nov-Feb

Bay View House
★★★★ ⊛ GUEST HOUSE

Clooneavin Path EX35 6EE
☎ 01598 752270 📄 01598 752270
e-mail: enquiries@bayviewhouselynmouth.co.uk
dir: *Enter Lynmouth, cross bridge over Lyn River (do not turn left by Shelly's Hotel) continue up hill towards Lynton. Clooneavin Path 2nd right. (NB very sharp turning).*

Nestling in a peaceful, wooded location, yet within a couple of minutes walk of Lynmouth and the water-powered cliff railway to Lynton, this late Victorian house boasts stunning views over the harbour, sea and coastline. The bedrooms are very well equipped and all take full advantage of the views. Using the best of fresh, local ingredients, dinner is available by prior arrangement; although not licensed, guests may bring their own wine if required.

Rooms 3 en suite; D £62-£80 **Facilities** FTV tea/coffee Dinner available Cen ht **Parking** 3 **Notes** LB No Children 8yrs Closed Nov-Feb

Rock House
★★★★ GUEST ACCOMMODATION

Manor Grounds EX35 6EN
☎ 01598 753508 📄 0800 7566964
e-mail: enquiries@rock-house.co.uk
dir: *On A39, at foot of Countisbury Hill right onto drive, pass Manor green/play area to Rock House*

Located next to the river with wonderful views of the harbour and out to sea, this enchanting establishment dates back to the 18th century and has much to offer. Bedrooms are well appointed, and many have the benefit of wonderful views of the rolling waves. A choice of menus is offered, either in the spacious lounge/bar or in the smart dining room. The garden is a popular venue for cream teas in the summer.

Rooms 8 en suite (1 GF) S fr £45; D £93-£110* **Facilities** TVL tea/coffee Dinner available Cen ht Licensed Wi-fi 🕭 **Parking** 8 **Notes** LB Closed 24-25 Dec

River Lyn View
★★★ GUEST ACCOMMODATION

26 Watersmeet Rd EX35 6EP
☎ 01598 753501
e-mail: riverlynview@aol.com
dir: *On A39, 200yds past St John's church on right*

A warm welcome awaits you at the River Lyn View, just a stroll away from the picturesque harbour at Lynmouth. Exmoor National Park is a short drive away or you can enjoy a walk along the East Lyn's tranquil tree lined banks. Much of the accommodation overlooks the river, but all is comfortable and includes a good range of extras. There is a choice of lounges, and a hearty breakfast is served at individual tables in the open-plan dining area.

Rooms 4 en suite (2 fmly) S £30-£40; D £52-£60 **Facilities** FTV TVL tea/coffee Cen ht Wi-fi

LYNTON
Map 3 SS74

PREMIER COLLECTION

Victoria Lodge
★★★★★ 🏠 GUEST ACCOMMODATION

30-31 Lee Rd EX35 6BS
☎ 01598 753203
e-mail: info@victorialodge.co.uk
web: www.victorialodge.co.uk
dir: *Off A39 in village centre opp Post Office*

A warm welcome awaits you at this elegant villa, built in the 1880s and located in the heart of Lynton. Named after Queen Victoria's children and grandchildren, and reflecting the style of the period, bedrooms are decorated in rich colours and feature coronets, half-testers and a four-poster bed.

Rooms 8 en suite S £63.75-£119; D £75-£140* **Facilities** FTV tea/coffee Cen ht Wi-fi **Parking** 6 **Notes** ⊗ No Children 11yrs Closed Nov-23 Mar

PREMIER COLLECTION

Highcliffe House
★★★★★ GUEST ACCOMMODATION

Sinai Hill EX35 6AR
☎ 01598 752235
e-mail: info@highcliffehouse.co.uk
web: www.highcliffehouse.co.uk
dir: Off A39 into Lynton, signs for Old Village, at Crown pub up steep hill, house 150yds on left

Highcliffe House has stunning views of Exmoor and the coast, and across to South Wales. Built in the 1880s as a summer residence, this wonderful house is a good base for exploring the area. Bedrooms are spacious and elegant, likewise the lounges and conservatory dining room where wonderful breakfasts are accompanied by a spectacular outlook.

Rooms 7 en suite S £70-£90; D £85-£140*
Facilities FTV tea/coffee Cen ht Licensed Wi-fi
Parking 7 **Notes** LB ⊗ No Children 16yrs Closed Dec-mid Feb

North Walk House
★★★★ GUEST ACCOMMODATION

North Walk EX35 6HJ
☎ 01598 753372
e-mail: northwalkhouse@btinternet.com
web: www.northwalkhouse.co.uk
dir: In town centre. Off Castle Hill by church down North Walk Hill, on left

With fabulous views over the Bristol Channel to the Welsh coastline, North Walk House offers guests a friendly welcome. The contemporary bedrooms are comfortable and well equipped, with rooms featuring DVDs and ironing equipment. Evening meals, by arrangement, utilise organic produce whenever possible. The owners are happy to advise on local walks.

Rooms 6 en suite (1 GF) S £44.10; D £86-£116*
Facilities FTV tea/coffee Dinner available Cen ht Licensed Wi-fi **Conf** Max 12 Board 12 **Parking** 6 **Notes** LB ⊗ No Children 14yrs

St Vincent House & Restaurant
★★★★ ⊖ GUEST ACCOMMODATION

Castle Hill EX35 6JA
☎ 01598 752244 🖷 01598 752244
e-mail: welcome@st-vincent-hotel.co.uk
web: www.st-vincent-hotel.co.uk
dir: Off Lynmouth Hill onto Castle Hill, take left fork after NCP car park. 50mtrs on right, next to Exmoor museum

Expect a warm welcome at this attractive Grade II listed house. The individually furnished bedrooms are well equipped, and an open fire burns in the charming drawing room during cooler months, the venue for a pre-dinner drink. Exmoor produce is used in the restaurant alongside signature dishes such as Provençal Bouillabaisse and Noir de Noir Marquise together with classic Belgian beers.

Rooms 6 en suite; D £70-£75* **Facilities** STV FTV tea/coffee Dinner available Cen ht Licensed Wi-fi **Parking** 2 **Notes** LB ⊗ No Children 14yrs Closed Nov-Etr RS Mon & Tue eve (ex BH) Restaurant closed

Sinai House
★★★★ GUEST ACCOMMODATION

Lynway EX35 6AY
☎ 01598 753227 🖷 01598 752663
e-mail: enquiries@sinaihouse.co.uk
dir: A39 onto B3234 through town, pass church, house on right overlooking main car park

This Victorian residence has spectacular views over Lynton, Lynmouth and across the Bristol Channel. Guests are assured of a friendly welcome from the owners. Bedrooms are well furnished and the comfortable public rooms include a spacious, well-appointed lounge, a cosy bar and smartly presented dining room.

Rooms 8 rms (6 en suite) (2 pri facs) **Facilities** TVL tea/coffee Cen ht Licensed **Parking** 8 **Notes** ⊗ No Children 12yrs Closed 15 Nov-28 Dec & 3 Jan-15 Feb

Pine Lodge
Ⓤ

Lynway EX35 6AX
☎ 01598 753230
e-mail: info@pinelodgelynton.co.uk
web: www.pinelodgelynton.co.uk
dir: 500yds S of town centre off Lynbridge Rd opp Bridge Inn

Currently the rating for this establishment is not confirmed. This may be due to a change of ownership or because it has only recently joined the AA rating scheme. For up-to-date information see theAA.com

Rooms 4 en suite; D £60-£75* **Facilities** tea/coffee Cen ht **Parking** 6 **Notes** ⊗ No Children 12yrs

MARSH
Map 4 ST21

Cottage B & B
★★★★ GUEST ACCOMMODATION

EX14 9AJ
☎ 01460 234240
e-mail: buttonstephens@btopenworld.com
dir: A303 (Ilminster to Honiton), left off dual-carriageway, 1st right under bridge, 1st house on right

Set in the beautiful Blackdown Hills on the border of Devon and Somerset, this establishment has been appointed to a high standard. Bedrooms are at ground level, with walk-in shower rooms. Each room has its own entrance from the small courtyard where visitors, resident and non-resident, can sit in warmer weather and enjoy afternoon tea from the on-site tea-shop (seasonal afternoon opening times). Breakfast features local produce and eggs from the host's own chickens.

Rooms 4 en suite (4 GF) **Facilities** tea/coffee Cen ht **Parking** 4 **Notes** ⊛

MORETONHAMPSTEAD · Map 3 SX78

Moorcote Country Guest House

★★★★ GUEST HOUSE

Chagford Cross TQ13 8LS
☎ 01647 440966
e-mail: moorcote@smartone.co.uk
web: www.moorcotehouse.co.uk
dir: 500yds NW of village centre on A382, past hospital on right

Perched on a hill overlooking the town and surrounded by attractive mature country gardens, this Victorian house is a good base for exploring Dartmoor and only a short walk from the town centre. Friendly owners Pat and Paul Lambert extend a warm welcome to their guests, many of whom return on a regular basis.

Rooms 3 en suite (1 fmly) **Facilities** tea/coffee Cen ht **Parking** 6 **Notes** LB ✖ No Children 5yrs Closed Dec ✉

Great Sloncombe (SX737864)

★★★★ ▲ FARMHOUSE

TQ13 8QF
☎ 01647 440595 📠 01647 440595 Mrs T Merchant
e-mail: hmerchant@sloncombe.freeserve.co.uk
dir: A382 from Moretonhampstead towards Chagford, 1.5m left at sharp double bend & farm 0.5m up lane

Rooms 3 en suite **Facilities** tea/coffee Cen ht **Parking** 3 **Notes** No Children 8yrs 170 acres beef/horses

Great Wooston Farm (SX764890)

★★★★ ▲ FARMHOUSE

TQ13 8QA
☎ 01647 440367 📠 01647 440367 Mrs M Cuming
e-mail: info@greatwoostonfarm.com
web: www.greatwoostonfarm.com
dir: Onto Lime St (opp library) for 1.5m over cattle grid, fork left over 2nd cattle grid, 2nd house on right

Rooms 3 en suite S £35-£45; D £70-£80* **Facilities** FTV TVL tea/coffee Cen ht **Parking** 3 **Notes** LB ✖ 320 acres mixed

Cookshayes Country Guest House

★★★ GUEST HOUSE

33 Court St TQ13 8LG
☎ 01647 440374 📠 01647 440453
e-mail: cookshayes@aol.co.uk
web: www.cookshayes.co.uk
dir: A38 onto A382 to Moretonhampstead. Take B3212 towards Princetown. Cookshayes 400yds on left

A genuine welcome awaits at this secluded Victorian house, a perfect base for exploring the delights of Dartmoor. Bedrooms are comfortably furnished and well appointed, and one has a four-poster bed. The smart dining room is the venue for scrumptious breakfasts and excellent dinners, where local produce is cooked with skill and enthusiasm. Additional facilities include a cosy lounge, which overlooks the attractive garden.

Rooms 7 rms (5 en suite) (1 fmly) (1 GF) S £25; D £50-£55* **Facilities** TVL tea/coffee Dinner available Cen ht Licensed **Conf** Max 16 Class 10 Board 10 **Parking** 10 **Notes** LB No Children 5yrs

NEWTON ABBOT · Map 3 SX87

See also Widecombe in the Moor

Bulleigh Park (SX860660)

★★★★ 🏠 FARMHOUSE

Ipplepen TQ12 5UA
☎ 01803 872254 📠 01803 872254 Mrs A Dallyn
e-mail: bulleigh@lineone.net
dir: 3.5m S of Newton Abbot. Off A381 at Parkhill Cross by petrol station for Compton, continue 1m, signed

Bulleigh Park is a working farm, producing award-winning Aberdeen Angus beef. The owners have also won an award for green tourism by reducing the impact of the business on the environment. Expect a friendly welcome at this family home set in glorious countryside, where breakfasts are notable for the wealth of fresh, local and home-made produce, and the porridge is cooked using a secret recipe.

Rooms 2 en suite 1 annexe en suite (1 fmly) S £38-£42; D £68-£76 **Facilities** FTV TVL tea/coffee Cen ht Wi-fi **Parking** 6 **Notes** LB ✖ Closed Dec-1 Feb 60 acres beef/sheep/hens

Lyndale Bed and Breakfast

★★★★ BED AND BREAKFAST

Lyndale Leygreen, Teigngrace TQ12 6QW
☎ 01626 332491
e-mail: sue.haddy@btinternet.com
dir: Going S from Exeter on A38, pass Chudleigh exit, after 1.5m exit for Teigngrace. 1m on right

Peacefully located in the quiet village of Teigngrace, Lyndale is a modern detached bungalow surrounded by pleasant countryside views. The two well decorated and comfortably furnished bedrooms and bathrooms provide guests with plenty of space and comfort. Breakfast is taken in the bright conservatory overlooking the gardens and outdoor seating is available for sunnier days.

Rooms 2 en suite (2 GF) S £38.50-£40; D £57-£65* **Facilities** tea/coffee Cen ht **Parking** 4 **Notes** ✖ No Children ✉

Sampsons Farm & Restaurant

★★★★ ⊛ GUEST ACCOMMODATION

Preston TQ12 3PP
☎ 01626 354913 📠 01626 354913
e-mail: nigel@sampsonsfarm.com
web: www.sampsonsfarm.com
dir: A380 onto B3195 signed Kingsteignton. Pass Ten Tors Inn on left & 2nd right B3193 to Chudleigh. At rdbt 3rd exit, left after 1m

This attractive thatched 16th-century farmhouse stands in a quiet location. Accommodation is provided in the main house and in adjacent converted stables; all rooms are well-equipped and pleasantly appointed. The cuisine is notable and menus at dinner and breakfast feature fresh local produce and accomplished cooking.

Rooms 5 rms (2 en suite) 6 annexe en suite (2 fmly) S £60-£110; D £70-£160* **Facilities** FTV tea/coffee Dinner available Direct Dial Cen ht Licensed Wi-fi **Conf** Max 20 Class 20 Board 12 **Parking** 20 **Notes** LB ✖ No Children 8yrs

NEWTON POPPLEFORD — Map 3 SY08

Moores Restaurant & Rooms

★★★ ◎◎ RESTAURANT WITH ROOMS

6 Greenbank, High St EX10 0EB
☎ 01395 568100
e-mail: info.moores@btconnect.com
dir: On A3052 in village centre

Centrally located in the village, this small restaurant offers very comfortable, practically furnished bedrooms. Guests are assured of a friendly welcome and relaxed, efficient service. Good quality, locally sourced ingredients are used to produce imaginative dishes full of natural flavours.

Rooms 3 rms (1 en suite) (2 fmly) S £40-£50; D £50-£60 **Facilities** FTV tea/coffee Dinner available Cen ht **Conf** Max 12 Board 12fred **Notes** LB ⊗ Closed 1st 2wks Jan No coaches

OKEHAMPTON — Map 3 SX59

See also Holsworthy

Week Farm (SX519913)

★★★★ FARMHOUSE

Bridestowe EX20 4HZ
☎ 01837 861221 📠 01837 861221 Mrs Margaret Hockridge
e-mail: margaret@weekfarmonline.com
web: www.weekfarmonline.com
dir: 1m NE of Bridestowe. Off junct A30 & A386 towards Bridestowe, fork right, left at x-rds to Week Farm

A delicious complimentary cream tea awaits at this 17th-century farmhouse. Surrounded by undulating countryside, the farm also has three coarse fishing lakes, set in a conservation area. Traditional farmhouse breakfasts can be enjoyed in the dining room. The comfortable bedrooms are furnished in traditional style, and one ground-floor room has easier access.

Rooms 5 en suite (2 fmly) (1 GF) S £30-£35; D £60-£65* **Facilities** FTV TVL tea/coffee Cen ht ⚲ Fishing 3 Coarse fishing lakes **Conf** Max 12 **Parking** 10 **Notes** LB Closed 25 Dec 180 acres sheep/cattle

OTTERY ST MARY — Map 3 SY19

Fluxton Farm

★★ BED AND BREAKFAST

Fluxton EX11 1RJ
☎ 01404 812818 📠 01404 814843
web: www.fluxtonfarm.co.uk
dir: 2m SW of Ottery St Mary. B3174, W from Ottery over river, left, next left to Fluxton

A haven for cat lovers, Fluxton Farm offers comfortable accommodation with a choice of lounges and a large garden, complete with pond and ducks. Set in peaceful farmland four miles from the coast, this 16th-century longhouse has a wealth of beams and open fireplaces.

Rooms 7 en suite S fr £27.50; D fr £55* **Facilities** FTV TVL tea/coffee Cen ht **Parking** 15 **Notes** LB No Children 8yrs RS Nov-Apr pre-booked guests only, wknds only ⊗

PAIGNTON — Map 3 SX86

Aquamarine Guesthouse

★★★★ GUEST HOUSE

8 St Andrews Rd TQ4 6HA
☎ 01803 551193
e-mail: enquiries@aquamarine-hotel.co.uk
dir: Along Esplanade with sea on left, at mini-rdbt right onto Sands Rd, St Andrews Rd 2nd left

Located in a quiet road, just a short stroll from the town centre and the seafront, this smartly appointed establishment is well placed to explore Torbay. Bedrooms all provide good levels of comfort with spacious en suite facilities. Additional facilities include a choice of lounges, small bar and a lovely garden with decking.

Rooms 7 en suite (2 fmly) S £25-£28; D £50-£56* **Facilities** FTV TVL tea/coffee Dinner available Cen ht Licensed Wi-fi **Parking** 5 **Notes** LB ⊗

The Clydesdale

★★★★ GUEST HOUSE

5 Polsham Park TQ3 2AD
☎ 01803 558402
e-mail: theclydesdale@hotmail.co.uk
dir: Off A3022 Torquay Rd onto Lower Polsham Rd, 2nd right into Polsham Park

The friendly proprietors warmly welcome guests to their home with a splendid garden, just a short walk from the town centre and seafront. Two bedrooms are on the ground floor, and home-cooked evening meals are available by arrangement; the home-made cakes are a speciality.

Rooms 7 en suite (1 fmly) (2 GF) **Facilities** FTV TVL tea/coffee Dinner available Cen ht Wi-fi **Parking** 6 **Notes** LB Closed Xmas & New Year

The Commodore

★★★★ GUEST ACCOMMODATION

14 Esplanade Rd TQ4 6EB
☎ 01803 553107 📠 01803 557040
e-mail: info@commodorepaignton.com
web: www.commodorepaignton.com
dir: A379 to Paignton, A3022 to seafront. Pass multiplex cinema, property on right

With an excellent seafront location, all the popular attractions of the town including shopping, the harbour, cinema and restaurants, are all just a short stroll from this family-run accommodation. Bedrooms are generally spacious and well furnished and some enjoy sea views. Guests are welcome to use the lounge and a small downstairs bar is also available.

Rooms 11 en suite (2 fmly) (3 GF) S £25-£40; D £50-£70* **Facilities** FTV TVL tea/coffee Cen ht Licensed **Parking** 10 **Notes** LB

See advert on page 147

The Wentworth Guest House

★★★★ GUEST HOUSE

18 Youngs Park Rd, Goodrington TQ4 6BU
☎ 01803 557843
e-mail: enquiries@wentworthguesthouse.co.uk
dir: Through Paignton on A378, 1m left at rdbt, sharp right onto Roundham Rd, right & right again onto Youngs Park Rd

Within 200 yards of the beach, this Victorian house overlooks Goodrington Park and is convenient for many attractions and the town centre. The bedrooms are attractively decorated, well equipped, and feature many thoughtful extras. The traditional English breakfast is a tasty start to the day, and additional facilities include a comfortable bar and a spacious lounge.

Rooms 10 en suite (2 fmly) (1 GF) S £24-£29; D £48-£58* **Facilities** FTV TVL tea/coffee Cen ht Licensed Wi-fi **Parking** 4

PAIGNTON *continued*

Bay Cottage

★★★ GUEST ACCOMMODATION

4 Beach Rd TQ4 6AY
☎ 01803 525729
web: www.baycottagehotel.co.uk
dir: *Along B3201 Esplanade Rd past Paignton Pier, Beach Rd 2nd right*

Quietly located in a level terrace, the seafront, park, harbour and shops are all just a short stroll away. Run in a friendly and relaxed manner, Bay Cottage offers a range of bedrooms of various shapes and sizes, with a guest lounge also made available. Dinner is offered by prior arrangement and includes enjoyable home cooking in hearty portions.

Rooms 8 en suite (3 fmly) S £21-£24* **Facilities** FTV TVL tea/coffee Dinner available Cen ht Wi-fi **Notes** LB ⊗

The Park

★★★ GUEST ACCOMMODATION

Esplanade Rd TQ4 6BQ
☎ 01803 557856 ▤ 01803 555626
e-mail: stay@parkhotel.me.uk
web: www.theparkhotel.net
dir: *On Paignton seafront, nearly opp pier*

This large establishment has a prominent position on the seafront with excellent views of Torbay. The pleasant bedrooms are all spacious and available in a number of options, and several have sea views. Entertainment is provided on some evenings in the lounge. Dinner and breakfast are served in the spacious dining room, which overlooks the attractive front garden.

Rooms 47 en suite (5 fmly) (3 GF) **Facilities** tea/coffee Dinner available Cen ht Lift Licensed Wi-fi Pool Table Games room with 3/4 snooker table & table tennis **Conf** Max 120 Board 12 **Parking** 38

The Sealawn

★★★ GUEST HOUSE

Sea Front, 20 Esplanade Rd TQ4 6BE
☎ 01803 559031 ▤ 01803 666113
dir: *On seafront between pier & cinema*

With an ideal location right on the seafront, this traditional guest house is understandably popular. Bedrooms are comfortably decorated and furnished, and guests are also welcome to use the lounge and bar area. The large forecourt to the front of the accommodation includes some outdoor seating and much useful parking space.

Rooms 10 en suite (2 fmly) (2 GF) **Facilities** TVL tea/coffee Dinner available Cen ht Licensed **Parking** 12 **Notes** LB ⊗

Berkeley's of St James

★★★★ GUEST ACCOMMODATION

4 St James Place East, The Hoe PL1 3AS
☎ 01752 221654 ▤ 01752 221654
e-mail: enquiry@onthehoe.co.uk
dir: *Off A38 towards city centre, left at sign The Hoe, over 7 sets of lights, left onto Athenaeum St, right to Crescent Av, 1st left*

Located in a quiet square close to The Hoe and just a short walk from the city centre, this is a good choice for business and leisure. Bedrooms are comfortable, attractive and equipped with a number of thoughtful extras. An enjoyable breakfast using organic and local produce, whenever possible, is served in the dining room.

Rooms 5 en suite (1 fmly) (1 GF) S £40-£45; D £60-£70* **Facilities** FTV tea/coffee Cen ht **Parking** 3 **Notes** LB ⊗ Closed 23 Dec-1 Jan

Brittany Guest House

★★★★ GUEST ACCOMMODATION

28 Athenaeum St, The Hoe PL1 2RQ
☎ 01752 262247
e-mail: thebrittanyguesthouse@btconnect.com
dir: *A38/City Centre follow signs for Pavillions, bear left at mini-rdbt, turn left at lights onto Athenaeum St*

Situated in a pleasant street, within walking distance of Plymouth's many attractions, this well presented house offers comfortable and well-equipped accommodation. The proprietors provide friendly hospitality, and this is a popular choice, and many return frequently. Freshly cooked breakfast is served in the attractive dining room. Parking available.

Rooms 10 en suite (3 fmly) (1 GF) S £30-£40; D £46-£56* **Facilities** FTV TV9B tea/coffee Cen ht Wi-fi **Parking** 6 **Notes** ⊗ No Children 5yrs Closed 20 Dec-2 Jan

Jewell's

★★★★ GUEST ACCOMMODATION

220 Citadel Rd, The Hoe PL1 3BB
☎ 01752 254760 ▤ 01752 254760
dir: *A38 towards city centre, follow sign for Barbican, then The Hoe. Left at lights, right at top of road onto Citadel Rd. Jewell's 0.25m*

This smart, comfortable, family-run guest house is only a short walk from The Hoe and is convenient for the city centre and the Barbican. Bedrooms come with a wide range of extra facilities, and breakfast is served in the pleasant dining room. Some secure parking is available.

Rooms 10 rms (7 en suite) (5 fmly) (2 smoking) **Facilities** FTV tea/coffee Cen ht Wi-fi **Parking** 3 **Notes** ⊗

Ashgrove House

★★★ GUEST ACCOMMODATION

218 Citadel Rd, The Hoe PL1 3BB
☎ 01752 664046 ▤ 01752 252112
e-mail: ashgroveho@aol.com
dir: *Follow signs for The Hoe*

Conveniently situated within walking distance of all the city's attractions, this personally-run establishment offers well-presented accommodation; ideal for commercial visitors and also welcoming to children. Freshly-cooked breakfasts are provided and a comfortable lounge is available for guests.

Rooms 10 en suite (10 fmly) **Facilities** TVL tea/coffee Cen ht **Notes** ⊗ Closed mid Jan-mid Dec

The Cranbourne

★★★ GUEST ACCOMMODATION

278-282 Citadel Rd, The Hoe PL1 2PZ
☎ 01752 263858 & 224646 & 661400
▤ 01752 263858
e-mail: cran.hotel@virgin.net
web: www.cranbournehotel.co.uk
dir: *Behind the Promenade, Plymouth Hoe*

This attractive Georgian terrace house is located just a short walk from The Hoe, The Barbican and the city centre. Bedrooms are practically furnished and well equipped. Hearty breakfasts are served in the elegant dining room and there is also a cosy bar.

Rooms 40 rms (28 en suite) (5 fmly) (1 GF) S £25-£35; D £45-£60* **Facilities** FTV TVL tea/coffee Cen ht Licensed Wi-fi **Parking** 14

Devonshire

★★★ GUEST ACCOMMODATION

22 Lockyer Rd, Mannamead PL3 4RL
☎ 01752 220726 ▤ 01752 220766
e-mail: devonshiregh@blueyonder.co.uk
dir: At Hyde Park pub on traffic island turn left onto Wilderness Rd. After 60yds turn left onto Lockyer Rd

This comfortable Victorian house is located in a residential area close to Mutley Plain high street, from where there is a regular bus service to the city centre. The well-proportioned bedrooms are bright and attractive, and a comfy lounge is available. Parking is available.

Rooms 10 rms (5 en suite) (4 fmly) (3 GF) S £25-£40; D £46-£50* **Facilities** FTV TVL tea/coffee Cen ht Licensed Wi-fi **Parking** 6 **Notes** LB ⊗

The Lamplighter

★★★ GUEST ACCOMMODATION

103 Citadel Rd, The Hoe PL1 2RN
☎ 01752 663855 & 07793 360815 ▤ 01752 228139
e-mail: stay@lamplighterplymouth.co.uk
web: www.lamplighterplymouth.co.uk
dir: Near war memorial

With easy access to The Hoe, The Barbican and the city centre, this comfortable guest house provides a good base for leisure or business. Bedrooms, including family rooms, are light and airy and furnished to a consistent standard. Breakfast is served in the dining room, which has an adjoining lounge area.

Rooms 9 rms (7 en suite) (2 pri facs) (2 fmly) S £30-£35; D £50-£55* **Facilities** TVL tea/coffee Cen ht Wi-fi **Parking** 4

Rainbow Lodge Guest House

★★★ GUEST HOUSE

29 Athenaeum St, The Hoe PL1 2RQ
☎ 01752 229699 ▤ 01752 229357
e-mail: info@rainbowlodgeplymouth.co.uk
web: www.rainbowlodgeplymouth.co.uk
dir: A38 onto A374. Follow City Centre signs for 3m. Into left lane, follow signs to Pavillions mini rdbt. Left, through 6 sets of lights, turn left

Just a short stroll from the Hoe, this small and friendly establishment is well placed for exploring the city. Bedrooms are varied in size and style, some of which are suitable for family use. Substantial breakfasts are served in the homely dining room.

Rooms 11 rms (7 en suite) (1 pri facs) (2 fmly) (1 GF) S £25-£50; D £45-£65* **Facilities** tea/coffee Cen ht Wi-fi **Parking** 6 **Notes** LB ⊗ No Children 6yrs Closed 22 Dec-5 Jan

Riviera

★★★ GUEST HOUSE

8 Elliott St, The Hoe PL1 2PP
☎ 01752 667379 ▤ 01752 623318
e-mail: riviera-hoe@btconnect.com
dir: Follow signs to city centre, then The Hoe, located off Citadel Road

This late Victorian building retains many of the features typical of the period, and is only a short walk from Plymouth Hoe where Sir Francis Drake finished playing his game of bowls prior to defeating the approaching Spanish armada in 1588. Linda and Lester Wrench are committed to providing a highly personalised guest experience. Guests have use of a lounge and bar, and breakfast is served in the breakfast room.

Rooms 11 rms (8 en suite) S £33-£38; D £55-£56* **Facilities** FTV TVL tea/coffee Direct Dial Cen ht Licensed Wi-fi **Notes** ⊗ No Children 16yrs Closed mid Dec-early Jan

The Firs Guest Accommodation

★★ GUEST ACCOMMODATION

13 Pier St, West Hoe PL1 3BS
☎ 01752 262870 & 300010
e-mail: thefirsguesthouse@hotmail.co.uk

A well-located and-well established house on the West Hoe with convenient on-street parking. Friendly owners and comfortable rooms make it a popular destination.

Rooms 7 rms (2 en suite) (2 fmly) S £25-£30; D £45-£65* **Facilities** FTV tea/coffee Dinner available Cen ht **Notes** LB

3 Cherry Tree Close

★★★ BED AND BREAKFAST

EX5 2HF
☎ 01404 822047
dir: In village centre between bridge & church. 3.5m from M5 off old A30

Guests are assured of a warm welcome and a homely atmosphere at this spacious bungalow set in its own garden in the village of Rockbeare. 3 Cherry Tree Close is convenient for the M5, Exeter International Airport and Westpoint Arena, and is only a short drive from Dartmoor. One of the two bedrooms overlooks fields, and both come complete with tea- and coffee-making facilities. A TV lounge is available for guests, and breakfast is served in the dining room.

Rooms 2 rms (2 GF) **Facilities** TVL tea/coffee Cen ht **Parking** 3 **Notes** LB No Children Closed 23 Dec-4 Jan ⊛

Mariners

★★★★ 🛁 🍴 GUEST ACCOMMODATION

East Walk Esplanade EX12 2NP
☎ 01297 20560
dir: Off A3052 signed Seaton, Mariners on seafront

Located just yards from the beach and cliff paths, this comfortable accommodation has a friendly and relaxed atmosphere. Bedrooms, some having sea views, are well equipped, and public rooms are light and airy. The dining room is the venue for enjoyable breakfasts utilising quality local produce, and afternoon teas are also available on the seafront terrace.

Rooms 10 en suite (1 fmly) (2 GF) **Facilities** tea/coffee Dinner available Cen ht Licensed **Parking** 10 **Notes** ⊗ No Children 5yrs RS Nov-Jan Closed during periods in November to Jan

See Teignmouth

See also Ottery St Mary

The Salty Monk

★★★★★ ◎◎ 🍴 RESTAURANT WITH ROOMS

Church St, Sidford EX10 9QP
☎ 01395 513174
e-mail: saltymonk@btconnect.com
web: www.saltymonk.co.uk
dir: On A3052 opposite church

Set in the village of Sidford, this attractive property dates from the 16th century. Some of the well-presented bedrooms feature spa baths or special showers, and a ground-floor courtyard room has a king-size water bed. Meals are served in the restaurant, where the two owners both cook. Excellent local produce is used to create thoroughly enjoyable food of a high standard.

Rooms 5 en suite (3 GF) **Facilities** FTV tea/coffee Dinner available Cen ht Wi-fi **Conf** Max 14 Board 14 **Parking** 20 **Notes** Closed 2wks Nov & 3wks Jan No coaches

SIDMOUTH *continued*

Blue Ball Inn

★★★★ INN

Stevens Cross, Sidford EX10 9QL
☎ 01395 514062 📄 01395 519584
e-mail: rogernewton@blueballinn.net
dir: *On A3052, at Sidford straight over lights. Inn 600yds*

Ideally placed for exploring the many delights of East Devon, this long established inn has been overseen by five generations of the Newton family since 1912 and can trace its history back to 1385. After a devastating fire in 2006, the inn has been lovingly rebuilt and now provides impressive levels of comfort and quality. The bedrooms and stylish bathrooms provide an appealing blend of old and new with individuality and flair. The extensive bars have cosy nooks in which to enjoy the food and drink on offer, with an attractive garden also available.

Rooms 9 en suite (2 fmly) (1 GF) S £60; D £95
Facilities FTV tea/coffee Dinner available Cen ht Wi-fi
Conf Max 65 **Parking** 80 **Notes** LB ⊗

The Old Farmhouse

★★★★ GUEST ACCOMMODATION

Hillside Rd EX10 8JG
☎ 01395 512284
dir: *A3052 from Exeter to Sidmouth, right at Bowd x-rds, 2m left at rdbt, left at mini-rdbt, next right, over hump-back bridge, bear right on the corner*

This beautiful 16th-century thatched farmhouse, in a quiet residential area just a stroll from the Esplanade and shops, has been lovingly restored. Bedrooms are attractively decorated and the charming public rooms feature beams and an inglenook fireplace. The welcoming proprietors provide memorable dinners using traditional recipes and fresh local ingredients.

Rooms 3 en suite 3 annexe en suite (1 fmly) (1 GF)
S £29-£35; D £58-£70* **Facilities** TV3B TVL tea/coffee Dinner available Cen ht Licensed **Parking** 4 **Notes** LB No Children 12yrs Closed Nov-Feb ⊗

Dukes

★★★★ 🛏 INN

The Esplanade EX10 8AR
☎ 01395 513320 📄 01395 519318
e-mail: dukes@hotels-sidmouth.co.uk
web: www.hotels-sidmouth.co.uk
dir: *A3052, take 1st exit to Sidmouth on right, left onto Esplanade*

Situated in the heart of Sidmouth, this stylish inn offers a relaxed and convivial atmosphere with a great team of attentive staff. Bedrooms provide good levels of comfort with a number having the benefit of sea views. The menu employs the seasonable best from the area, with a choice of dining areas available, including the patio garden, perfect for soaking up the sun.

Rooms 13 en suite (5 fmly) S £35-£45; D £70-£120*
Facilities FTV tea/coffee Dinner available Cen ht Wi-fi
Parking 9 **Notes** LB RS 25 Dec Bar & rest for residents only

The Glendevon

★★★★ GUEST HOUSE

Cotmaton Rd EX10 8QX
☎ 01395 514028
e-mail: enquiries@glendevon-hotel.co.uk
web: www.glendevon-hotel.co.uk
dir: *A3052 onto B3176 to mini-rdbt. Right, house 100yds on right*

Located in a quiet residential area just a short walk from the town centre and beaches, this stylish Victorian house offers neat, comfortable bedrooms. Guests are assured of a warm welcome from the resident owners, who provide attentive service and wholesome home-cooked evening meals by arrangement. A lounge is also available.

Rooms 8 en suite **Facilities** FTV tea/coffee Dinner available Cen ht Licensed **Notes** LB ⊗ No Children ⊗

The Groveside

★★★★ GUEST HOUSE

Vicarage Rd EX10 8UQ
☎ 01395 513406
web: www.thegroveside.co.uk
dir: *0.5m N of seafront on A375*

Conveniently situated a short level walking distance from the town centre, the Groveside offers 'boutique-style' accommodation. A number of influences, such as Art Deco, have been used to impressive effect in bedrooms, while bathrooms also show individuality and flair. Guests are assured of attentive service and a relaxed and friendly atmosphere with every effort made to facilitate an enjoyable stay. Home-cooked evening meals are served by prior arrangement and on-site parking is an added bonus.

Rooms 9 rms (7 en suite) (2 pri facs) **Facilities** tea/coffee Dinner available Cen ht Licensed **Parking** 9 **Notes** ⊗ ⊗

Bramley Lodge Guest House

★★★ GUEST HOUSE

Vicarage Rd EX10 8UQ
☎ 01395 515710
e-mail: haslam@bramleylodge.fsnet.co.uk
dir: *0.5m N of seafront on A375*

Guests are assured of a warm and friendly welcome at this family-run, small guest house, located about a half mile from the sea. The neatly furnished bedrooms vary in size, and all are equipped to a good standard. Home-cooked evening meals are available, by prior arrangement, with special diets on request.

Rooms 6 rms (5 en suite) (1 fmly) S £28.50-£31; D £57-£64* **Facilities** FTV TVL tea/coffee Dinner available Cen ht **Parking** 6 **Notes** Closed Dec-Jan

Enstone

★★ GUEST HOUSE

Lennox Av EX10 8TX
☎ 01395 514444
e-mail: enstone1@hotmail.co.uk
dir: A375 Vicarage Rd into Sidmouth, left onto Lennox Av

Situated in colourful gardens at the end of a quiet cul de sac, this family-run guest house is just 200 yards from the town centre, and a short walk from the seafront. Bedrooms are neatly furnished with the best use made of the available space.

Rooms 4 rms (2 en suite) (1 fmly) (1 GF) S £25; D £42-£56* **Facilities** TVL tea/coffee Cen ht **Parking** 5 **Notes** LB No Children 2yrs Closed Oct-Mar

SOURTON   Map 3 SX59

Bearslake Inn

★★★★ INN

Lake EX20 4HQ
☎ 01837 861334   📠 01837 861108
e-mail: enquiries@bearslakeinn.com
dir: A30 from Exeter onto A386 signed Sourton/Tavistock, 2m on left from junct

Situated on the edge of the Dartmoor National Park, this thatched inn is believed to date back to the 13th century and was originally part of a working farm. There is character in abundance here with beams, flagstone floors and low ceilings, all of which contribute to an engaging atmosphere. Bedrooms have great individuality and provide period features combined with contemporary comforts. Local produce is very much in evidence on the menu with dinner served in the attractive Stable Restaurant. The beer garden is bordered by a moorland stream with wonderful views across open countryside.

Rooms 6 en suite (3 fmly) (1 GF) S £60; D £85* **Facilities** tea/coffee Dinner available Cen ht Wi-fi **Parking** 35 **Notes** RS Sun eve Bar & restaurant closed No coaches

---

SOUTH MOLTON   Map 3 SS72

PREMIER COLLECTION

Kerscott Farm (SS793255)

★★★★★ FARMHOUSE

Ash Mill EX36 4QG
☎ 01769 550262   📠 01769 550910   Mrs T Sampson
e-mail: kerscott.farm@virgin.net
dir: 6m E of S Molton. A361 onto B3227, signed 1.5m

Guests are assured of a genuinely warm welcome at this working beef and sheep farm on the edge of Exmoor National Park. Largely built in the 15th century, the property is full of character with original beams, sloping floors and inglenook fireplaces. Beautifully furnished throughout, the owners take great pride in their special corner of Devon. Dinner, by arrangement, uses home-grown produce whenever possible, and breakfast is equally hearty and memorable.

Rooms 3 en suite S £45; D £60-£65 **Facilities** FTV tea/coffee Dinner available Cen ht **Parking** 4 **Notes** LB No Children 18yrs Closed Xmas & New Year 110 acres beef/sheep

---

The Coaching Inn

★★★ INN

Queen St EX36 3BJ
☎ 01769 572526
dir: In town centre

This long established, former coaching inn, has been providing a warm welcome for weary travellers for many years. Situated in the heart of this bustling town, guests are assured of a relaxing stay with a genuine, family-run atmosphere. Bedrooms provide good levels of comfort with a number benefiting from recently refurbished bathrooms. An extensive menu is provided with an emphasis upon quality and value for money.

Rooms 10 en suite (2 fmly) S £35; D £60-£70* **Facilities** tea/coffee Dinner available Cen ht Wi-fi Pool Table **Conf** Max 100 Thtr 40 Class 40 Board 40 **Parking** 40 **Notes**

Stumbles

★★★ RESTAURANT WITH ROOMS

134 East St EX36 3BU
☎ 01769 574145   📠 01769 572558
e-mail: info@stumbles.co.uk
dir: M5 junct 27 to South Molton on A361. Establishment in town centre

Located in the centre of this bustling town, Stumbles is a charming place with a friendly and welcoming atmosphere. Bedrooms are individual in style with lots of character and good levels of comfort. A small conservatory area is available for guests. The restaurant is a popular venue for locals and visitors alike, with a varied menu on offer both at lunchtime and in the evenings.

Rooms 6 en suite 4 annexe en suite (1 fmly) (2 GF) S £40-£55; D £55-£70* **Facilities** FTV tea/coffee Dinner available Direct Dial Cen ht Wi-fi **Conf** Max 50 Thtr 30 Class 50 Board 50 **Parking** 25 **Notes** LB

STARCROSS   Map 3 SX98

The Croft Guest House

★★★★ 🅰 GUEST ACCOMMODATION

Cockwood Bridge EX6 8QY
☎ 01626 890282
e-mail: croftcockwood@aol.com
dir: M5 junct 30, follow signs for A379

Rooms 8 en suite (3 GF) S £40-£46; D £65-£70* **Facilities** FTV TVL tea/coffee Cen ht Licensed Wi-fi **Parking** 10 **Notes** LB No Children

STOWFORD   Map 3 SX48

Townleigh Farm

🆄

EX20 4DE
☎ 01566 783186
e-mail: mail@townleigh.com
dir: M5 jct 31, take A30 southbound Roadford, turn off left, left again, follow lane for approx 2m

Currently the rating for this establishment is not confirmed. This may be due to a change of ownership or because it has only recently joined the AA rating scheme.

Rooms 3 rms (2 en suite) (1 pri facs) **Facilities** TVL tea/coffee Dinner available Cen ht Wi-fi 🎣 Fishing **Parking** 8 **Notes** LB

PREMIER COLLECTION

Strete Barton House
★★★★★ GUEST HOUSE

Totnes Rd TQ6 0RU
☎ 01803 770364 🖻 01803 771182
e-mail: info@stretebarton.co.uk
web: www.stretebarton.co.uk
dir: Off A379 into village centre, just below church

This delightful 16th-century farmhouse has been refurbished to blend stylish accommodation with its original character. Bedrooms are very comfortably furnished and well equipped with useful extras. Breakfast utilises quality local produce and is served in the spacious dining room. Guests are also welcome to use the very comfortable lounge complete with real log burner for the cooler months. The village lies between Dartmouth and Kingsbridge and has easy access to the natural beauty of the South Hams as well as local pubs and restaurants.

Rooms 5 rms (4 en suite) (1 pri facs) 1 annexe en suite (1 GF); D £80-£120* **Facilities** FTV tea/coffee Cen ht Wi-fi **Parking** 4 **Notes** LB No Children 8yrs

See advert on page 129

PREMIER COLLECTION

Tor Cottage
★★★★★ GUEST ACCOMMODATION

PL16 0JE
☎ 01822 860248 🖻 01822 860126
e-mail: info@torcottage.co.uk
web: www.torcottage.co.uk

(For full entry see Chillaton)

The Coach House
★★★ GUEST ACCOMMODATION

PL19 8NS
☎ 01822 617515 🖻 01822 617515
e-mail: estevens255@aol.com
web: www.thecoachousehotel.co.uk
dir: 2.5m NW of Tavistock. A390 from Tavistock to Gulworthy Cross, at rdbt take 3rd exit towards Chipshop Inn turn right to Ottery, 1st building in village

Dating from 1857, this building was constructed for the Duke of Bedford and converted by the current owners. Some bedrooms are on the ground floor and in an adjacent barn conversion. Dinner is available in the cosy dining room or the restaurant, which leads onto the south-facing garden.

Rooms 6 en suite 3 annexe en suite (1 fmly) (4 GF) S £48; D £67* **Facilities** tea/coffee Dinner available Direct Dial Cen ht Licensed **Parking** 24 **Notes** LB No Children 5yrs

Sampford Manor
★★★ BED AND BREAKFAST

Sampford Spiney PL20 6LH
☎ 01822 853442
e-mail: manor@sampford-spiney.fsnet.co.uk
web: www.sampford-spiney.fsnet.co.uk
dir: B3357 towards Princetown, right at 1st x-rds. Next x-rds Warren Cross left for Sampford Spiney. 2nd right, house below church

Once owned by Sir Francis Drake, this manor house is tucked away in a tranquil corner of Dartmoor National Park. The family home is full of character, with exposed beams and slate floors, while outside, a herd of award winning alpacas graze in the fields. Genuine hospitality is assured together with scrumptious breakfasts featuring home-produced eggs. Children, horses (stabling available) and dogs are all equally welcome.

Rooms 3 rms (2 pri facs) (1 fmly) S £27-£35; D £50-£70* **Facilities** tea/coffee Cen ht **Parking** 3 **Notes** Closed Xmas

PREMIER COLLECTION

Thomas Luny House
★★★★★ GUEST ACCOMMODATION

Teign St TQ14 8EG
☎ 01626 772976
e-mail: alisonandjohn@thomas-luny-house.co.uk
dir: A381 to Teignmouth, at 3rd lights turn right to quay, 50yds turn left onto Teign St, after 60yds turn right through white archway

Built in the late 18th century by marine artist Thomas Luny, this charming house offers unique and comfortable accommodation in the old quarter of Teignmouth. Bedrooms are individually decorated and furnished, and all are well equipped with a good range of extras. An elegant drawing room with French windows leads into a walled garden with a terraced sitting area. A superb breakfast, featuring local produce, is served in the attractive dining room.

Rooms 4 en suite S £62-£70; D £75-£98* **Facilities** FTV tea/coffee Direct Dial Cen ht Licensed Wi-fi **Parking** 8 **Notes** LB ⊗ No Children 12yrs

Potters Mooring
★★★★ GUEST ACCOMMODATION

30 The Green, Shaldon TQ14 0DN
☎ 01626 873225 🖻 01626 872909
e-mail: mail@pottersmooring.co.uk
web: www.pottersmooring.co.uk
dir: A38 onto A380 signed Torquay, B3192 to Teignmouth & Shaldon, over river signs to Potters Mooring

A former sea captain's residence dating from 1625, Potters Mooring has been refurbished to provide charming accommodation of a very high standard, including a four-poster room. The friendly proprietors make every effort to ensure an enjoyable stay and the Captain Potter's breakfast features tasty local produce.

Rooms 5 rms (4 en suite) (1 pri facs) (1 fmly) **Facilities** FTV tea/coffee Cen ht Wi-fi **Parking** 8

The Minadab Cottage

★★★ BED AND BREAKFAST

60 Teignmouth Rd TQ14 8UT
☎ 01626 772044
e-mail: enquiries@minadab.co.uk
dir: M5 onto A380, 2nd left onto B3192, left at T-lights onto A379, cottage approx 1m

This unusual thatched building offers plenty of character and interest throughout. The friendly owners will be pleased to discuss the history of the property, including its unusual name. Bedrooms provide a range of shapes and sizes and include one on the ground floor. Enjoyable home-cooked dinners are usually available by prior arrangement.

Rooms 3 rms (2 en suite) (1 pri facs) (1 GF) S £50–£65; D £65–£70* **Facilities** tea/coffee Dinner available Cen ht DVD's & games available for use **Parking** 4 **Notes** ⊗ No Children 16yrs

THORVERTON   Map 3 SS90

Thorverton Arms

★★★ INN

EX5 5NS
☎ 01392 860205
e-mail: info@thethorvertonarms.co.uk
web: www.thethorvertonarms.co.uk
dir: Exit A396 at Ruffwell. 1m to centre of Thorverton. Thorverton Arms on left

Mid-way between Exeter and Tiverton, this 16th-century, former coaching inn is situated at the heart of a picturesque village. The open-plan bar is the hub of village life, offering a range of real ales, wines and spirits and a varied selection of locally sourced and freshly prepared meals. At the rear of the property, there's a patio and south-facing beer garden, featuring one of the oldest wisteria in Devon.

Rooms 6 en suite (1 fmly) S £50–£55; D £60–£68.50* **Facilities** FTV tea/coffee Dinner available Cen ht Pool Table **Parking** 15 **Notes** LB RS Mon-Fri Pub closes between 2.30-6pm

TIVERTON   Map 3 SS91

Hornhill Farmhouse (SS965117)

★★★★ 🏠 FARMHOUSE

Exeter Hill EX16 4PL
☎ 01884 253352 Mrs B Pugsley
e-mail: hornhill@tinyworld.co.uk
web: www.hornhill-farmhouse.co.uk
dir: Signs to Grand Western Canal, right fork up Exeter Hill. Farmhouse on left at top of hill

Hornhill has a peaceful hilltop setting with panoramic views of the town and the Exe Valley. Elegant decor and furnishings enhance the character of the farmhouse, which in part dates from the 18th century. Bedrooms are beautifully equipped with modern facilities and there is a lovely sitting room with a log fire. Breakfast is served at one large table in the spacious dining room.

Rooms 3 rms (1 en suite) (2 pri facs) (1 GF) S £35–£36; D £60–£63 **Facilities** tea/coffee 🍴 **Parking** 5 **Notes** ⊗ No Children 12yrs 🚗 75 acres beef/sheep

Quoit-At-Cross (ST923188)

★★★ FARMHOUSE

Stoodleigh EX16 9PJ
☎ 01398 351280 📠 01398 351351 Mrs L Hill
dir: M5 junct 27 for Tiverton. A396 N for Bampton, 3.5m left over bridge for Stoodleigh, farmhouse on junct

A friendly welcome is assured at this delightful stone-built property on a working farm; the house commands lovely views over rolling Devonshire countryside. The comfortable, attractive bedrooms are well furnished, and have many extra facilities. A lounge and pretty garden are available to guests.

Rooms 3 en suite (1 fmly); D £56–£60* **Facilities** TVL tea/coffee Cen ht **Parking** 3 **Notes** ⊗ Closed Xmas 🚗 160 acres organic/mixed

TORBAY

See Brixham, Paignton and Torquay

TORQUAY   Map 3 SX96

PREMIER COLLECTION

Linden House

★★★★★ 🍴 GUEST ACCOMMODATION

31 Bampfylde Rd TQ2 5AY
☎ 01803 212281
e-mail: lindenhouse.torquay@virgin.net
web: www.lindenhousetorquay.co.uk
dir: Onto A3022, 1st left opposite playing fields

This elegant Victorian building has been refurbished in a classic style with soft neutral colours providing charm and elegance. An especially warm welcome is provided by the enthusiastic proprietors. Bedrooms and bathrooms provide a range of welcome extras and include a garden room with its own patio. Delicious home-cooked dinners utilise fresh local produce and are available by prior arrangement. Gluten-free meals can be provided.

Rooms 7 en suite (1 GF) S £50–£60; D £65–£80* **Facilities** FTV TVL tea/coffee Dinner available Cen ht Wi-fi **Parking** 7 **Notes** LB ⊗ No Children

TORQUAY *continued*

PREMIER COLLECTION

The Marstan
★★★★★ GUEST HOUSE

Meadfoot Sea Rd TQ1 2LQ
☎ 01803 292837 📄 01803 299202
e-mail: enquiries@marstanhotel.co.uk
dir: *A3022 to seafront, left onto A379 Torbay Rd & Babbacombe Rd, right onto Meadfoot Rd, Marstan on right*

This elegant mid-19th-century villa provides high levels of comfort and quality throughout. The hospitality and service are excellent, and every effort is made to create a relaxed and enjoyable atmosphere. Public areas include an impressive dining room, a bar and a comfortable lounge. Outdoors guests can enjoy a heated swimming pool and hot tub in the pleasant garden.

Rooms 9 en suite (1 fmly) (2 GF) S £50-£65; D £79-£142* Facilities FTV tea/coffee Direct Dial Cen ht Licensed Wi-fi ⚡ Hot tub Conf Max 12 Thtr 12 Class 12 Board 12 Parking 8 Notes LB ⊗

The Colindale
★★★★ 🏠 GUEST ACCOMMODATION

20 Rathmore Rd, Chelston TQ2 6NY
☎ 01803 293947 📄 01803 251050
e-mail: rathmore@blueyonder.co.uk
web: www.colindalehotel.co.uk
dir: *From Torquay station 200yds on left in Rathmore Rd*

Having attractive, well-tended gardens, the Colindale is located in a quiet area close to the seafront. It is an elegant establishment and service is exemplary. Rooms, some with views over Torbay, are comfortable and attractively co-ordinated. Memorable breakfasts are enjoyed in the relaxing dining room.

Rooms 7 rms (6 en suite) (1 pri facs) S £40-£45; D £60-£75* Facilities FTV TVL tea/coffee Dinner available Cen ht Licensed Wi-fi Parking 6 Notes LB ⊗ No Children 12yrs Closed 20 Dec-3 Jan

Meadfoot Bay Guest House
★★★★ GUEST ACCOMMODATION

Meadfoot Sea Rd TQ1 2LQ
☎ 01803 294722 📄 01803 214473
e-mail: stay@meadfoot.com
dir: *A3022 to seafront, onto A379 & right onto Meadfoot Rd, 0.5m on right*

This detached Victorian Villa dates from 1850 and was originally a gentleman's residence. It's just a short stroll from Meadfoot Beach, the town and the harbour. A number of the smart bedrooms have private balconies or patios and ground floor rooms are also available. Public areas offer high levels of comfort and quality with a choice of lounges, and the elegant dining room where fresh local produce is utilised. Outside, there are four lovely decked areas for relaxing with a drink. Additional planned facilities include a fully equipped golfing studio.

Rooms 19 en suite (3 GF) S £49; D £98* Facilities FTV TVL tea/coffee Cen ht Licensed Wi-fi Access to nearby health club Parking 14 Notes LB ⊗ No Children 14yrs

Ashfield Guest House
★★★★ GUEST ACCOMMODATION

9 Scarborough Rd TQ2 5UJ
☎ 01803 293537
e-mail: enquiries@ashfieldguesthouse.co.uk
dir: *Torquay Seafront onto Belgrave Rd, 300mtrs turn right onto Scarborough Rd, 100mtrs on left*

On a quiet side street yet just a short walk from the bustling town centre, Ashfield Guest House offers comfortable bedrooms in a fine old mid-terrace property. The house has been sympathetically restored in recent years and guests have the sole use of the large lounge. Breakfasts are served at individual tables in the bright airy dining room.

Rooms 6 en suite (2 fmly) (2 GF) S £27.50-£30; D £55-£60 Facilities FTV TVL tea/coffee Cen ht Parking 3 Notes LB ⊗ Closed Dec-Mar

Aveland House
★★★★ GUEST ACCOMMODATION

Aveland Rd, Babbacombe TQ1 3PT
☎ 01803 326622 📄 01803 328940
e-mail: avelandhouse@aol.com
web: www.avelandhouse.co.uk
dir: *A3022 to Torquay, left onto B3199 Hele Rd onto Westhill Rd. Then Warbro Rd, 2nd left onto Aveland Rd*

Set in well-tended gardens in a peaceful area of Babbacombe, close to Cary Park, beaches, shops and attractions, Aveland House is within easy walking distance of Torquay harbour and town. This family-run house offers warm and attentive service. The attractive bedrooms are well equipped, and free Wi-fi is a feature. A pleasant bar and two comfortable lounges are available. Hearing-impaired visitors are especially welcome, as both

the proprietors are OCSL signers. Evening meals and bar snacks are available by arrangement.

Rooms 10 en suite (3 fmly) S £30-£36; D £60-£72* Facilities TVL tea/coffee Dinner available Cen ht Wi-fi Licensed bar Parking 10 Notes LB ⊗ RS Sun no evening meals

Barclay Court
★★★★ GUEST ACCOMMODATION

29 Castle Rd TQ1 3BB
☎ 01803 292791
e-mail: enquiries@barclaycourthotel.co.uk
dir: *M5 onto A38 then A380 to Torquay. A3022 Newton Rd left onto Upton Rd, right towards Lymington Rd. Right to Castle Circus, Castle Rd on left*

The delightful, personally run Barclay Court is within easy walking distance of Torquay's attractions and offers a friendly, relaxed atmosphere. Individually decorated rooms vary in size, but all are en suite and well equipped. There is a games room on the lower ground floor and the garden offers a quiet retreat for guests to relax in during the summer months.

Rooms 4 en suite 6 annexe en suite (1 fmly) (1 GF) S £25-£35; D £50-£70 Facilities FTV TVL tea/coffee Games room Parking 7 Notes ⊗ Closed 25 Dec & New Year RS Nov-Mar Limited rooms available 🛏

Berkeley House
★★★★ GUEST HOUSE

39 Babbacombe Downs Rd, Babbacombe TQ1 3LN
☎ 01803 322429
e-mail: reception@berkeleyhousetorquay.co.uk
dir: *A380 to Babbacombe, off Babbacombe Rd onto Princes St to seafront*

Warm and friendly hospitality awaits you at this very pleasant guest house, which is situated on the Babbacombe seafront. The bedrooms vary in size and style, but all are thoughtfully equipped. Three rooms have sea views. Separate tables are provided in the dining room, where hearty breakfasts are served.

Rooms 4 en suite S £40-£56; D £50-£66* Facilities tea/coffee Cen ht Licensed Wi-fi Parking 4 Notes ⊗ No Children 5yrs

Tel. 01803 553107

The Commodore

Relax in clean, comfortable surroundings, with friendly staff and fantastic views

www.commodorepaignton.com

14 Esplanade Road
Paignton
South
Devon
TQ4 6EB

Location, Location, Location

Free Parking, Family and Dog Friendly

Blue Conifer

★★★★ GUEST ACCOMMODATION

Higher Downs Rd, The Seafront, Babbacombe TQ1 3LD
☎ 01803 327637
dir: *Signs for Babbacombe & seafront, premises 500yds from model village, opp cliff railway*

Surrounded by neat gardens and having splendid views across beaches to the bay, this attractive property provides a relaxed and friendly atmosphere. Bedrooms, many with sea views, are well equipped and one is on the ground floor. A relaxing lounge and spacious car park are welcome additions.

Rooms 7 en suite (3 fmly) (1 GF) S £35-£41; D £54-£70*
Facilities tea/coffee Cen ht **Parking** 9 **Notes** LB Closed Nov-Feb ⊛

Brooklands

★★★★ GUEST HOUSE

5 Scarborough Rd TQ2 5UJ
☎ 01803 296696 📄 01803 296696
e-mail: enquiries@brooklandsguesthousetorquay.com
web: www.brooklandsguesthousetorquay.com
dir: *From seafront onto Belgrave Rd, Scarborough Rd 300mtrs on right*

This Victorian terraced property offers a convenient location for both the seafront and town centre, an ideal base for visiting the attractions of the English Riviera. It is a personally run guest house that provides friendly hospitality. Bedrooms offer good facilities with a thoughtful range of extras provided. The attractive breakfast room has separate tables for a hearty breakfast to start the day, and there's a separate lounge. Dinner is available during the summer season. Parking is available on-street, or to the rear on request.

Rooms 5 en suite (1 fmly) S £35-£45; D £50-£60*
Facilities FTV TVL tea/coffee Dinner available Cen ht Wi-fi
Parking 1 **Notes** LB

Court Prior

★★★★ GUEST HOUSE

St Lukes Road South TQ2 5NZ
☎ 01803 292766
e-mail: courtprior@btconnect.com
dir: *A380 to Torquay, at Halfords right at lights onto Avenue Rd to seafront, left at next lights up Sheddon Hill, 2nd lights onto St Lukes Rd*

Located in a quiet residential area within walking distance of the seafront and town centre, this charming house, built in 1860, offers comfortable accommodation. Rooms are spacious, well decorated and pleasantly furnished throughout. Traditional home-made dishes are served at dinner. There is also a large comfortable lounge.

Rooms 10 en suite (3 fmly) (2 GF) **Facilities** FTV TVL tea/coffee Dinner available Cen ht **Parking** 10 **Notes** ⊗ No Children 12yrs

Crown Lodge

★★★★ GUEST ACCOMMODATION

83 Avenue Rd TQ2 5LH
☎ 01803 298772 📄 01803 291155
e-mail: john@www.crownlodgehotel.co.uk
web: www.crownlodgehotel.co.uk
dir: *A380 through Kingskerswell, over rbt & 4 lights, right at Torre station, 200yds on left*

Located within walking distance of the harbour and seafront and close to the town centre, Crown Lodge offers stylish and comfortable accommodation. Bedrooms have been appointed to a high standard, each individually furnished with flair. The ground floor rooms are suitable for disabled guests. Well-cooked breakfasts are a delight.

Rooms 6 en suite (1 fmly) (2 GF); D £59-£79*
Facilities FTV tea/coffee Dinner available Cen ht Wi-fi
Parking 7 **Notes** LB ⊗ No Children 9yrs

Glenorleigh

★★★★ GUEST ACCOMMODATION

26 Cleveland Rd TQ2 5BE
☎ 01803 292135 📄 01803 213717
e-mail: glenorleighhotel@btinternet.com
web: www.glenorleigh.co.uk
dir: *A380 from Newton Abbot onto A3022, at Torre station lights right onto Avenue Rd & 1st left, across 1st junct, 200yds on right*

Located in a residential area, the Glenorleigh provides a range of smart bedrooms with some on the ground floor level. Facilities include a solarium, a heated outdoor pool with terrace, and a convivial bar, this family-run establishment is ideal for leisure or business guests. Breakfast provides a hearty start to the day and dinner is available with notice.

Rooms 15 rms (14 en suite) (6 fmly) (7 GF) **Facilities** TVL tea/coffee Dinner available Cen ht Licensed ⚲ Solarium Pool Table **Parking** 10 **Notes** ⊗

TORQUAY *continued*

Headland View

★★★★ 🏠 GUEST HOUSE

37 Babbacombe Seafront, Babbacombe TQ1 3LN
☎ **01803 312612**
e-mail: reception@headlandview.com
web: www.headlandview.com
dir: *A379 S to Babbacombe, off Babbacombe Rd left onto Portland Rd & Babbacombe Downs Rd & seafront*

There are spectacular views of the bay and the Downs from the lounge and many of the bedrooms of Headland View. The attentive proprietors offer a friendly welcome, and several of the attractive bedrooms have balconies. Breakfast is memorable for the well-cooked quality ingredients.

Rooms 6 rms (4 en suite) (2 pri facs) S £45-£50; D £64-£66* **Facilities** FTV TVL tea/coffee Cen ht Wi-fi **Parking** 4 **Notes** LB ⊗ No Children 5yrs Closed Nov-Mar ⊛

Kelvin House

★★★★ GUEST ACCOMMODATION

46 Bampfylde Rd TQ2 5AY
☎ **01803 209093** 📠 **01803 209093**
e-mail: kelvinhousehotel@hotmail.com
dir: *M5 take A3032 (Newton Rd) into Torquay. At lights at Torre Station turn right onto Avenue Rd. Bampfylde Rd is on left*

This attractive Victorian house was built in the 1880s and sits on a lovely tree-lined road. All rooms are en suite and have been refurbished to a high standard with many extras. A large elegant sitting room is available for guests and hearty breakfasts are served in the dining room or on the patio in good weather. This is a family-run property with a relaxed, friendly home-from-home atmosphere. Close to all travel links, it's an ideal base from which to tour the Torquay Riviera.

Rooms 8 en suite (1 fmly) (2 GF) S £46-£58; D £56-£68* **Facilities** FTV TVL tea/coffee Cen ht Licensed **Parking** 6 **Notes** LB ⊗

Kingsholm

★★★★ 🛏 GUEST HOUSE

539 Babbacombe Rd TQ1 1HQ
☎ **01803 297794** 📠 **0700 603 7426**
e-mail: enquiries@kingsholmhotel.co.uk
dir: *A3022 left onto Torquay seafront, left at clock tower rdbt, Kingsholm 400mtrs on left*

Guests will no doubt enjoy the friendly and welcoming atmosphere created here by the resident proprietors. A range of well furnished and decorated bedrooms and bathrooms provide guests with plenty of comfort and quality. A relaxing guest lounge, small bar area and car park to the rear are all welcome features. Dinner

featuring seasonal, home cooking is available by prior arrangement and should not be missed.

Rooms 9 en suite S £28-£33; D £56-£65* **Facilities** FTV tea/coffee Dinner available Cen ht Licensed Wi-fi **Parking** 4 **Notes** LB No Children 10yrs

Millbrook House

★★★★ GUEST ACCOMMODATION

1 Old Mill Rd, Chelston TQ2 6AP
☎ **01803 297394**
e-mail: marksj@sky.com

The delightful, personally run Millbrook House is within easy walking distance of Torquay's attractions and has a friendly and relaxed atmosphere. The well-maintained bedrooms provide many useful facilities; a king-size bed and a four-poster are available. There is a bar on the lower ground floor with pool and darts, and the garden has a summer house for guests to relax in on hotter days.

Rooms 10 en suite (1 fmly) (2 GF) S £30; D £50-£60* **Facilities** FTV TVL tea/coffee Cen ht Licensed Pool Table **Parking** 8 **Notes** ⊗ Closed Nov-Feb

Newton House

★★★★ GUEST ACCOMMODATION

31 Newton Rd, Torre TQ2 5DB
☎ **01803 297520** 📠 **01803 297520**
e-mail: newtonhouse_torquay@yahoo.com
web: www.newtonhouse-tq.co.uk
dir: *From Torre station bear left at lights, Newton House 40yds on left*

You are assured of a warm welcome at Newton House, which is close to the town centre and attractions. The comfortable bedrooms, some at ground level, have thoughtful extras, and a lounge is available. Breakfast is enjoyed in the pleasant dining room.

Rooms 9 en suite (3 fmly) (5 GF) S £25-£52; D £48-£64* **Facilities** FTV tea/coffee Cen ht Wi-fi Drying room for hikers **Parking** 15 **Notes** LB ⊗

Riviera Lodge

★★★★ GUEST ACCOMMODATION

26 Croft Rd TQ2 5UE
☎ **01803 209309** 📠 **0560 1136425**
e-mail: stay@rivieralodgehotel.co.uk

This establishment offers a relaxed atmosphere within walking distance of the promenade, shopping centre and the many attractions. Bedrooms vary in size, with the best use being made of available space; all rooms are well equipped. There is a spacious bar and lounge area and dinner, by arrangement, offers a choice of dishes.

Rooms 21 en suite (1 GF) S £41-£46; D £69-£76* **Facilities** FTV tea/coffee Dinner available Cen ht Licensed Wi-fi ↝ **Parking** 20 **Notes** LB ⊗ No Children 12yrs

Summerlands

★★★★ GUEST ACCOMMODATION

19 Belgrave Rd TQ2 5HU
☎ **01803 299844**
e-mail: summerlands@fsmail.net
web: www.summerlandsguesthousetorquay.co.uk
dir: *A3022 onto Newton Rd, towards seafront & town centre, onto Belgrave Rd. Summerlands on left just past lights*

Located just five minutes walk from the sea front, Summerlands offers a friendly and relaxed environment. There are six well equipped, modern, comfortable bedrooms, all of which are en suite. Breakfasts are served on the lower ground floor and provide a satisfying start to the day.

Rooms 6 en suite (2 fmly) (1 GF) S £35-£45; D £45-£60* **Facilities** FTV TVL tea/coffee Cen ht Wi-fi **Parking** 4 **Notes** ⊗ No Children 5yrs

Grosvenor House

★★★★ 🅰 GUEST HOUSE

Falkland Rd TQ2 5JP
☎ **01803 294110**
e-mail: aa@grosvenorhousehotel.co.uk
dir: *From Newton Abbot to Torquay, at Torre station right by Halfords, left at 2nd lights onto Falkland Rd*

Rooms 10 en suite (4 fmly) (3 GF) S fr £35; D fr £55* **Facilities** FTV TVL tea/coffee Dinner available Cen ht Licensed Wi-fi **Parking** 7 **Notes** LB ⊗ Closed Oct-Etr

Villa Marina

★★★★ Ⓐ GUEST HOUSE

Tor Park Rd TQ2 5BQ
☎ 01803 292187 🖷 01803 231177
e-mail: enquiries@villamarina-torquay.co.uk
dir: From M5 take A380 onto A3022, right at Torre Station, 200mtrs on left

Rooms 5 en suite (2 GF) S £42-£60; D £55-£80
Facilities FTV tea/coffee Cen ht Wi-fi Parking 5 Notes LB
Ⓧ No Children 12yrs

Walnut Lodge

★★★★ Ⓐ GUEST ACCOMMODATION

48 Bampfylde Rd TQ2 5AY
☎ 01803 200471 🖷 01803 200471
e-mail: stay@walnutlodgetorquay.co.uk
dir: M5 onto A3032 into Torquay, through lights at Torre Station, turn right signed sea front. After 1st of lights next left onto Bampfylde Rd

Rooms 6 en suite (1 fmly) (2 GF) S £40; D £64-£76*
Facilities FTV TVL tea/coffee Cen ht Wi-fi Parking 5
Notes LB Ⓧ

The Westgate

★★★★ Ⓐ GUEST ACCOMMODATION

Falkland Rd TQ2 5JP
☎ 01803 295350 🖷 01803 213710
e-mail: stay@westgatehotel.co.uk
dir: A380 to Torquay, at A3022 junct sharp left onto Falkland Rd, 300yds on left

Rooms 10 en suite (2 fmly) (1 GF) S £35.50-£46.50;
D £61-£89* Facilities FTV TVL tea/coffee Dinner available Cen ht Licensed Wi-fi Parking 10 Notes LB Ⓧ No Children 5yrs

Mariners Guest House

★★★ GUEST ACCOMMODATION

35 Belgrave Rd TQ2 5HX
☎ 01803 291604
e-mail: marinersguesthouse@btinternet.com
web: www.marinerstorquay.co.uk
dir: A380 onto A3022 to seafront, left onto Belgrave Rd, left at lights onto Lucius St, then 1st left

This personally run guest house provides friendly hospitality and willing service. It is within easy reach of the town centre, and the modern bedrooms are being refurbished to a good standard. Separate tables are provided in the attractive breakfast room.

Rooms 7 en suite (2 fmly) (2 GF) S £20-£35; D £40-£65*
Facilities FTV tea/coffee Cen ht Wi-fi Parking 4 Notes LB
Ⓧ

Stover Lodge

★★★ GUEST ACCOMMODATION

29 Newton Rd TQ2 5DB
☎ 01803 297287 🖷 01803 297287
e-mail: enquiries@stoverlodge.co.uk
web: www.stoverlodge.co.uk
dir: Follow signs to Torquay town centre, at station/Halfords left lane. Lodge on left after lights

Located close to the town centre, the family-run Stover Lodge is relaxed and friendly. Children and babies are welcome, and a cot and high chair can be provided on request. Hearty breakfasts, with a vegetarian option, are served in the dining room. There is a garden to enjoy in summer.

Rooms 9 rms (8 en suite) (1 pri facs) (3 fmly) (2 GF)
S £25-£40; D £50-£56* Facilities FTV tea/coffee Cen ht
Wi-fi Parking 10 Notes LB Ⓧ

Abberley House

★★★ GUEST ACCOMMODATION

100 Windsor Rd, Babbacombe TQ1 1SU
☎ 01803 392787
e-mail: stay@abberleyguesthouse.co.uk
web: www.abberleyguesthouse.co.uk
dir: A38, A380, B3199 to Plainmoor, turn onto Warbro Rd, right onto Hingston Rd, left onto Windsor Rd

Quietly located in a residential area, Abberley House is just a ten to fifteen minute walk from either the town centre or Babbacombe Downs. The friendly proprietors offer a warm welcome, alongside comfortable bedrooms in a variety of sizes with some ground floor rooms available. Carefully prepared, home-cooked dinners are offered by prior arrangement.

Rooms 7 en suite (1 fmly) (2 GF) Facilities FTV TVL tea/coffee Dinner available Cen ht Wi-fi Notes LB

Ashleigh House

★★★ GUEST HOUSE

61 Meadfoot Ln TQ1 2BP
☎ 01803 294660
e-mail: dawnsmale@btinternet.com
web: www.ashleighhousetorquay.co.uk

Quietly located in a residential area of Torquay, and only a five minute downhill walk from the town or harbour, this pleasant accommodation includes roadside permit parking. Relaxed and friendly hospitality is provided and guests are welcome to use the large, well furnished lounge. Bedrooms offer a range of shapes and sizes and include some useful extras. A carefully prepared breakfast is served in the bright, comfortable dining room.

Rooms 4 rms (3 en suite) (1 pri facs) (3 fmly) S £25-£35;
D £48-£54* Facilities TVL tea/coffee Dinner available Cen ht Notes LB Ⓢ

Atlantis

★★★ GUEST ACCOMMODATION

68 Belgrave Rd TQ2 5HY
☎ 01803 292917 🖷 01803 292917
e-mail: info@atlantis-torquay.co.uk
dir: Signs to Torquay seafront, turn left, left at lights onto Belgrave Rd, over next lights, premises on left

Convenient for the beach, theatre and conference centre, the Atlantis offers a thoughtfully equipped home-from-home. There is a well-stocked bar and a comfortable lounge, and the hearty breakfasts in the dining room are a tasty start to the day.

Rooms 10 rms (9 en suite) (7 fmly) S £20-£50;
D £40-£60 Facilities FTV TVL tea/coffee Cen ht Parking 3
Notes LB Ⓧ

TORQUAY *continued*

Briarfields

★★★ GUEST ACCOMMODATION

84-86 Avenue Rd TQ2 5LF
☎ **01803 297844**
e-mail: briarfields@aol.com
dir: *Exeter to Torquay on A380 on to A3022. Past Torre Station 400yds on right.*

Briarfields is conveniently located and is a short walk from the seafront and all the main tourist attractions. Bedrooms are comfortable, well equipped and thoughtfully furnished. Guests can also make use of the sun terrace at the rear of the property and soak up the early evening sun. Breakfasts are served at individual tables in the main dining room and a warm welcome is guaranteed.

Rooms 9 en suite (5 fmly) **Facilities** FTV tea/coffee Cen ht **Parking** 9

Burleigh House

★★★ GUEST ACCOMMODATION

25 Newton Rd TQ2 5DB
☎ **01803 291557**
e-mail: enquiry@burleigh-house.co.uk
dir: *A380, at Torre station, bear left at lights, 4th guest house on left*

This fine old house is a short walk from the town centre and the seafront boardwalk, and has the added bonus of secure parking at the rear of the property. The bedrooms vary in size and style with some large doubles and spacious single rooms available. All bedrooms are well equipped and Wi-fi is also available. Guests are assured of a warm welcome from the friendly owners.

Rooms 8 rms (6 en suite) (4 GF) S £20-£26; D £40-£54* **Facilities** FTV tea/coffee Cen ht Wi-fi **Parking** 8 **Notes** ⊗ No Children

Doogals

★★★ GUEST ACCOMMODATION

74 Belgrave Rd TQ2 5HY
☎ **01803 295966** 🖷 **01803 295966**
e-mail: skey@sky.com
dir: *Town centre signs, pass police station on right, through small shopping area, premises on right*

This privately-owned and personally run guest house is convenient for the town centre and attractions. It provides friendly hospitality and well equipped accommodation, which includes family rooms and bedrooms on the ground floor.

Rooms 7 en suite (2 fmly) (3 GF) S £20-£30; D £45-£65* **Facilities** FTV TVL tea/coffee Dinner available Cen ht **Parking** 4 **Notes** LB ⊗

Silverlands B & B

★★★ GUEST ACCOMMODATION

27 Newton Rd TQ2 5DB
☎ **01803 292013**
e-mail: enquiries@silverlandsguesthouse.co.uk
web: www.silverlandsguesthouse.co.uk
dir: *A380 onto A3022 for Torquay, premises on left after Torre station lights*

Convenient for the town centre and the beaches, this friendly establishment has a homely atmosphere. Some of the well-presented bedrooms are on the ground floor, and a hearty, freshly cooked breakfast is served in the dining room.

Rooms 9 rms (7 en suite) (2 pri facs) (2 fmly) (4 GF) S £20-£28; D £40-£56 **Facilities** FTV tea/coffee Dinner available Cen ht Wi-fi **Parking** 10 **Notes** LB ⊗

Tyndale

★★★ GUEST ACCOMMODATION

68 Avenue Rd TQ2 5LF
☎ **01803 380888**
dir: *A380 onto A3022, pass Torre station onto Avenue Rd, 1st lights right onto Old Mill Rd & right into car park*

Close to the seaside attractions and the town centre, this neatly presented house is only a short level walk from the railway station. Bedrooms are brightly decorated in a range of sizes. A comfortable lounge is provided and a freshly cooked, traditional British breakfast is served in the dining room.

Rooms 3 en suite (1 GF); D £38 **Facilities** FTV TVL tea/coffee Cen ht **Parking** 5 **Notes** LB ⊗ 🖾

Wayfarer Guest House

★★★ GUEST ACCOMMODATION

37 Belgrave Rd TQ2 5HX
☎ **01803 299138** 🖷 **01803 299138**
e-mail: wayfarertorquay@blueyonder.co.uk
web: www.wayfarertorquay.co.uk
dir: *A380 onto A3022 to seafront, left, onto Belgrave Rd, left at lights onto Lucious St, 1st left to car park*

The Wayfarer offers friendly accommodation, which is convenient for the town centre and the many seaside attractions. Bedrooms are smartly presented, well equipped and comfortable. Freshly prepared breakfasts are served at individual tables in the stylish dining room.

Rooms 6 en suite (2 fmly) (1 GF) S £23-£30; D £42-£58* **Facilities** FTV tea/coffee Cen ht Wi-fi **Parking** 3 **Notes** LB ⊗

Durant Arms

★★★★ 🍴 INN

Ashprington TQ9 7UP
☎ **01803 732240**
e-mail: info@thedurantarms.com
web: www.durantarms.co.uk
dir: *A381 from Totnes for Kingsbridge, 1m left for Ashprington*

This delightful inn, the focal point of the picturesque village of Ashprington, offers comfortable bedrooms in the main building or annexe, which are very well appointed and attractively decorated. A range of carefully prepared dishes from blackboard menus can be enjoyed in the character bar or dining room and local ales, juices and wines also feature.

Rooms 3 en suite 5 annexe en suite (2 GF) **Facilities** TV4B TVL tea/coffee Dinner available Cen ht **Conf** Max 20 Board 15 **Parking** 8 **Notes** LB No Children Closed 25-26 Dec evenings

The Old Forge at Totnes

★★★★ GUEST HOUSE

Seymour Place TQ9 5AY
☎ **01803 862174**
e-mail: enq@oldforgetotnes.com
dir: *From Totnes town centre cross river bridge & 2nd right*

Over 600 years old, this delightful property is close to the town centre and Steamer Quay. A range of bedroom styles is offered from spacious suites to cosy cottage-style. All are thoughtfully equipped with numerous extras. Public areas include a conservatory complete with hot tub, which overlooks the garden. Breakfast is a leisurely and enjoyable affair, served in the pleasantly appointed dining room.

Rooms 10 rms (9 en suite) (1 pri facs) (2 fmly) (2 GF) S £56-£81; D £72-£93 **Facilities** FTV tea/coffee Cen ht Licensed Wi-fi **Parking** 7 **Notes** LB ⊗

The Red Slipper

★★★★ GUEST ACCOMMODATION

Stoke Gabriel TQ9 6RU
☎ **01803 782315**
e-mail: enquiries@redslipper.co.uk
dir: Off A385 S to Stoke Gabriel. Opp Church House Inn

An ideal base for exploring the South Hams or just for a relaxing break, this delightful 1920s house is hidden away in the picturesque village of Stoke Gabriel. The bedrooms have many extra facilities. Well-cooked dinners are served by arrangement, and feature local produce.

Rooms 3 en suite **Facilities** TVL tea/coffee Dinner available Cen ht Licensed **Parking** 4

Steam Packet Inn

★★★★ 🍽 INN

St Peter's Quay TQ9 5EW
☎ **01803 863880** 📄 **01803 862754**
e-mail: steampacket@buccaneer.co.uk
web: www.steampacketinn.co.uk
dir: Off A38 at Totnes to Dartington & Totnes. Over 1st lights, pass railway station, signs for town centre at next rdbt. Over mini-rdbt, River Dart on left, inn 100yds on left

This friendly and popular riverside inn offers a warm welcome to visitors and locals alike. Complete with its own quay, the inn has a long history. Public areas offer open fires and a choice of dining options, including the heated, extensive waterside patio. Bedrooms are well equipped and comfortable and some have river views. Choices at lunch and dinner offer interesting and well-cooked dishes, while breakfast provides a satisfying start to the day.

Rooms 4 en suite (1 fmly) S £59.50; D £79.50*
Facilities tea/coffee Dinner available Cen ht Wi-fi Private moorings **Parking** 15 **Notes** LB No coaches

WESTWARD HO! Map 3 SS42

Culloden House

★★★ GUEST HOUSE

Fosketh Hill EX39 1UL
☎ **01237 479421**
e-mail: theAA@culloden-house.co.uk
web: www.culloden-house.co.uk
dir: S of town centre. Off B3236 Stanwell Hill onto Fosketh Hill

A warm welcome is assured in this family-friendly Victorian property which stands on a wooded hillside with sweeping views over the beach and coast. Guests can relax in the spacious lounge with its log-burning fire and enjoy the wonderful sea views.

Rooms 7 en suite (3 fmly) (1 GF) S £40-£50; D £60-£70*
Facilities FTV tea/coffee Cen ht **Parking** 4 **Notes** Closed Xmas & New Year RS Nov-Feb

WIDECOMBE IN THE MOOR Map 3 SX77

Manor Cottage

★★★ BED AND BREAKFAST

TQ13 7TB
☎ **01364 621218**
e-mail: di.richard@btinternet.com
dir: A382 to Bovey Tracey, left onto B3387 to Widecombe, cottage on right after old inn

Located in the centre of the historic village, this attractive cottage stands in a large and pleasant garden and has a lot of character. It offers friendly hospitality and spacious and comfortable bedrooms. Breakfast is served in the cosy dining room and features good home cooking using fresh local produce.

Rooms 3 rms (1 en suite); D £50-£60* **Facilities** TV2B tea/coffee Cen ht **Parking** 3 **Notes** ⊗ No Children 15yrs Closed Xmas 🐾

WOOLACOMBE Map 3 SS44

The Castle

★★★★ GUEST ACCOMMODATION

The Esplanade EX34 7DJ
☎ **01271 870788** 📄 **01271 870812**
e-mail: the.castlehotel@amserve.net
dir: A361 from Barnstaple to Ilfracombe, turn right at Woolacombe sign

Built in 1898 in the style of a castle, this Victorian stone folly has stunning views over the bay. The attractively decorated bedrooms are comfortable and well equipped. The lounge has a carved-wood ceiling and interesting panelling. There is also a lounge-bar, and breakfast is served in the elegant dining room.

Rooms 8 en suite (2 fmly) S £40; D £68-£74*
Facilities TVL tea/coffee Cen ht Licensed **Parking** 8 **Notes** ⊗ No Children 5yrs Closed Oct-Mar

YELVERTON Map 3 SX56

Harrabeer Country House

★★★★ GUEST ACCOMMODATION

Harrowbeer Ln PL20 6EA
☎ **01822 853302**
e-mail: reception@harrabeer.co.uk
web: www.harrabeer.co.uk
dir: In village. Off A386 Tavistock Rd onto Grange Rd, right onto Harrowbeer Ln

A warm welcome awaits you at this historic Devon longhouse situated on the edge of Dartmoor. Providing an excellent base for exploring this beautiful area, the accommodation has all the expected modern comforts with a lounge, bar and dining room overlooking the garden. There are also two self-catering units. Dinners are available by arrangement with special diets catered for.

Rooms 6 rms (5 en suite) (1 pri facs) (2 fmly) (1 GF) S £55-£80; D £65-£95* **Facilities** TVL tea/coffee Dinner available Direct Dial Cen ht Licensed Wi-fi **Conf** Max 20 Board 20 **Parking** 10 **Notes** Closed 3rd wk Dec, 2nd wk Jan

Overcombe House

★★★★ 🄰 GUEST HOUSE

Old Station Rd, Horrabridge PL20 7RA
☎ **01822 853501** 📄 **01822 853602**
e-mail: enquiries@overcombehotel.co.uk
web: www.overcombehotel.co.uk
dir: Signed 100yds off A386 at Horrabridge

Rooms 8 en suite (2 GF) S £45-£60; D £75-£90
Facilities tea/coffee Cen ht Licensed Wi-fi **Parking** 7 **Notes** ⊗ No Children 12yrs Closed 25 Dec

DORSET

ABBOTSBURY Map 4 SY58

East Farm House (SY578853)

★★★ FARMHOUSE

2 Rosemary Ln DT3 4JN
☎ 01305 871363 📠 01305 871363 Mrs W M Wood
e-mail: wendy@eastfarmhouse.co.uk
web: www.eastfarmhouse.co.uk
dir: B3157 W into Abbotsbury, Swan Inn on left, farmhouse 1st right onto Rosemary Ln

This unspoiled and charming farmhouse is in the centre of the pretty village and has been in the owner's family since 1729. The house has a homely atmosphere, traditionally furnished with much character, and filled with memorabilia. Hearty breakfasts are served in the lounge-dining room, where a log fire burns in winter.

Rooms 3 en suite Facilities tea/coffee Dinner available Cen ht Parking 3 Notes No Children 14yrs 20 acres horse stud/rare breed pigs

ASKERSWELL Map 4 SY59

The Spyway Inn

★★★★ INN♢

DT2 9EP
☎ 01308 485250 📠 01308 485250
e-mail: tim.wilkes@btconnect.com
dir: A35, turn signed Askerswell, follow Spyway Inn sign

Peacefully located in the rolling Dorset countryside, this family-run inn offers a warm and genuine welcome to all. Bedrooms are spacious and well appointed with a number of extras provided, including bath robes. Real ales are on tap in the bar, where locals congregate to put the world to rights. Menus feature home-cooked food with many dishes utilising local produce both at dinner and breakfast. The extensive beer garden is popular in summer with wonderful views a bonus.

Rooms 3 en suite (1 fmly) Facilities tea/coffee Dinner available Cen ht Parking 40 Notes ⊗

BEAMINSTER Map 4 ST40

Watermeadow House (ST535001)

★★★★★ 🅰 FARMHOUSE

Bridge Farm, Hooke DT8 3PD
☎ 01308 862619 📠 01308 862619 Mrs P M Wallbridge
e-mail: enquiries@watermeadowhouse.co.uk
web: www.watermeadowhouse.co.uk
dir: 3m E of Beaminster, in Hooke

Rooms 2 rms (1 en suite) (1 pri facs) (1 fmly) S £35-£45; D £60-£65* Facilities tea/coffee Cen ht Parking 6 Notes LB ⊗ Closed Nov-Mar 280 acres dairy/beef

BLANDFORD FORUM Map 4 ST80

PREMIER COLLECTION

Portman Lodge

★★★★★ BED AND BREAKFAST

Whitecliff Mill St DT11 7BP
☎ 01258 453727 📠 01258 453727
e-mail: enquiries@portmanlodge.co.uk
dir: On NW end of Blandford's one-way system, to access follow signs from town centre to Shaftesbury & hospital

Built in the Victorian period and once used as a music school, this house now provides elegant accommodation and a genuinely warm welcome. Carefully decorated and adorned with artefacts and pictures from the proprietors' extensive travels, the public rooms are spacious and inviting. A delicious breakfast is prepared with skill and served at a communal table. Dinner is available by prior arrangement.

Rooms 3 en suite S £45-£50; D £65-£70* Facilities tea/coffee Dinner available Cen ht Wi-fi Parking 6 Notes ⊗ No Children 10yrs

The Anvil Inn

★★★★ INN

Salisbury Rd, Pimperne DT11 8UQ
☎ 01258 453431 📠 01258 480182
e-mail: theanvil.inn@btconnect.com
dir: 2m NE of Blandford on A354 in Pimperne

Located in a village near Blandford, this 16th-century thatched inn provides a traditional country welcome. Bedrooms have been refurbished to high standards. Dinner is a varied selection of home-made dishes, plus there is a tempting variety of hand-pulled ales and wines by the glass.

Rooms 12 en suite Facilities STV tea/coffee Dinner available Direct Dial Cen ht Parking 18 Notes LB No coaches

St Martin's House

★★★★ BED AND BREAKFAST

Whitecliff Mill St DT11 7BP
☎ 01258 451245 & 07748 887719
e-mail: info@stmartinshouse.co.uk
dir: Off Market Pl onto Salisbury St & left onto White Cliff Mill St, on right before traffic island

Dating from 1866, this restored property was once part of the chorister's house for a local church. The bedrooms are comfortable and well equipped. The hosts offer warm hospitality and attentive service. Breakfast, which features local and home-made items, is enjoyed around a communal table.

Rooms 2 rms (2 pri facs) (1 fmly) S £45-£50; D £65-£70* Facilities tea/coffee Cen ht Wi-fi Parking 3 Notes Closed 22 Dec-6 Jan ⊛

The Old Bakery

★★★ BED AND BREAKFAST

Church Rd, Pimperne DT11 8UB
☎ 01258 455173 & 07799 853784
e-mail: jjtanners@hotmail.com
web: www.theoldbakerydorset.co.uk
dir: 2m NE of Blandford. Off A354 into Pimperne

Dating from 1890 and once, as the name suggests, the village bakery, this family home offers comfortable accommodation in a convenient location. Popular with business travellers, families can also be accommodated, with cots available. Substantial breakfasts featuring home-made bread and marmalade are served in the dining room.

Rooms 3 en suite (1 GF) Facilities TVL tea/coffee Dinner available Cen ht Parking 2 Notes ⊛

Pennhills Farmhouse (ST819101)

★★★ FARMHOUSE

Sandy Ln, Shillingstone DT11 0TF
☎ 01258 860491 Mrs Watts
dir: 6.5m NW of Blandford. Off A357 at Shillingstone Post Office onto Gunn Ln, bear right to T-junct, left onto Lanchard Ln, signed

Located in a quiet setting with views over the surrounding countryside, this delightful, family-run farmhouse provides spacious rooms. The substantial English breakfast consists of home-produced items, served house-party style around one large table in the lounge-dining room, where an open fire burns during the winter.

Rooms 2 en suite (1 fmly) (1 GF) Facilities TVL tea/coffee Cen ht Parking 4 Notes ⊛ Closed 22 Dec-3 Jan ⊛ 120 acres mixed

BOURNEMOUTH
Map 5 SZ09

PREMIER COLLECTION

The Balincourt
★★★★★ GUEST ACCOMMODATION

58 Christchurch Rd BH1 3PF
☎ 01202 552962 📄 01202 552962
e-mail: rooms@balincourt.co.uk
web: www.balincourt.co.uk
dir: On A35 between Lansdowne & Boscombe Gardens, opp Lynton Court pub

The friendly Balincourt offers high standards of accommodation within easy reach of the town centre and beaches. Bedrooms are individually decorated and equipped with a host of thoughtful extras. There is a lounge and bar, and freshly prepared evening meals are available in the attractive dining room.

Rooms 12 en suite S £40-£80; D £80-£100
Facilities TVL tea/coffee Dinner available Cen ht
Licensed **Conf** Max 20 **Parking** 11 **Notes** LB ⊗ No
Children 16yrs Closed Xmas

Fenn Lodge
★★★★ GUEST ACCOMMODATION

11 Rosemount Rd, Alum Chine BH4 8HB
☎ 01202 761273 📄 01202 761273
e-mail: fennlodge@btconnect.com
web: www.fennlodge.co.uk
dir: A338 into Poole, at rdbt onto B3065 signed Alum Chine & Sandbanks. Left at lights, right at rdbt onto Alumhurst Rd, 3rd left onto Rosemount Rd

Located within walking distance of Alum Chine and the beach, this stylish accommodation is friendly and relaxed. The hosts ensure their guests are well cared for and provide many thoughtful extras. Bournemouth and Poole are just a short drive away. Guests have use of an elegant comfortable lounge.

Rooms 11 rms (10 en suite) (1 pri facs) (1 fmly) (1 GF)
S £28-£32.50; D £51-£62* **Facilities** TVL tea/coffee
Cen ht Wi-fi **Parking** 6 **Notes** LB ⊗ Closed Nov-mid Mar

The Maples
★★★★ BED AND BREAKFAST

1 Library Rd, Winton BH9 2QH
☎ 01202 529820
e-mail: jeffreyhurrell@yahoo.co.uk
dir: 1.5m N of town centre. Off A3060 Castle Ln West onto Wimborne Rd, The Maples 1m on right after police station

A warm welcome awaits you at the Maples, which is just off Winton High Street. The atmosphere is friendly and bedrooms are quiet, comfortable and equipped with considerate extras. Breakfast is enjoyed in the pleasant dining room around a communal table.

Rooms 2 en suite (1 fmly) S £25-£30; D £50-£60
Facilities FTV tea/coffee Cen ht **Parking** 2 **Notes** ⊗ No
Children 7yrs 🚭

Newlands
★★★★ GUEST ACCOMMODATION

14 Rosemount Rd, Alum Chine BH4 8HB
☎ 01202 761922 📄 01202 769872
e-mail: newlandshotel@totalise.co.uk
web: www.newlandshotel.com
dir: A338/A35 to Liverpool Victoria rdb, exit for Alum Chine, left at lights, right at small rdbt onto Alumhurst Rd, 3rd left

An attractive and friendly Edwardian house, set in a quiet area near Alum Chine beach and within easy driving distance of Bournemouth and Poole centres, Newlands offers comfortable accommodation with Wi-fi and a guest lounge.

Rooms 8 en suite (3 fmly) **Facilities** tea/coffee Cen ht
Wi-fi **Parking** 8 **Notes** ⊗ Closed Dec & Jan

Rosscourt
★★★★ GUEST ACCOMMODATION

6 St Johns Rd, Boscombe BH5 1EL
☎ 01202 397537 📄 01202 397569
e-mail: enquiries@rosscourthotel.co.uk
dir: A3338 to Bournemouth & Boscombe, left at Christchurch Rd onto St Johns

Expect a warm welcome at this traditional family-run establishment in Boscombe Spa. Comfortable guest bedrooms provide the flexibility to suit all requirements. Hands-on proprietors aim to offer a great stay whether it is for business or pleasure. Situated in a prime location, they offer time to relax or a base for exploration.

Rooms 8 rms (7 en suite) (1 pri facs) (1 GF) S £45-£65;
D £60-£100* **Facilities** FTV TVL tea/coffee Cen ht Wi-fi
Parking 13 **Notes** LB ⊗ No Children 16yrs Closed Dec &
Jan

Thanet House
★★★★ GUEST ACCOMMODATION

2 Drury Rd, Alum Chine BH4 8HA
☎ 01202 761135
e-mail: stay@thanethouse.co.uk
dir: Signs for Alum Chine Beach. On corner of Alumhurst Rd & Drury Rd

A delightful Edwardian house, with a welcoming, friendly atmosphere; ideally located for the Jurassic Coast and the New Forest, and within walking distance of Westbourne and Alum Chine beaches. The bedrooms are filled with many homely extras and the whole house can be hired for a party or special event.

Rooms 8 rms (5 en suite) (3 pri facs) (2 fmly) S £30-£35;
D £60-£70* **Facilities** FTV tea/coffee Cen ht Licensed
Wi-fi **Parking** 5 **Notes** LB ⊗

Westcotes House
★★★★ GUEST HOUSE

9 Southbourne Overcliff Dr, Southbourne BH6 3TE
☎ 01202 428512 📄 01202 428512
web: www.westcoteshousehotel.co.uk
dir: 2m E of town centre. A35 onto B3059, into Grand Av, continue to end, right, house on right

The refurbished Westcotes House has spectacular views across Poole Bay. Situated on the quiet side of the town, it has well-equipped bedrooms, with one on the ground floor. There is a conservatory lounge, and enjoyable home-cooked dinners are available by arrangement.

Rooms 6 en suite (1 GF) S £45-£80; D £70-£80*
Facilities TVL tea/coffee Dinner available Cen ht
Parking 6 **Notes** ⊗ No Children 10yrs 🚭

BOURNEMOUTH *continued*

Wood Lodge

★★★★ GUEST ACCOMMODATION

10 Manor Rd, East Cliff BH1 3EY
☎ 01202 290891 📄 01202 290892
e-mail: enquiries@woodlodgehotel.co.uk
web: www.woodlodgehotel.co.uk
dir: *A338 to St Pauls rdbt, 1st exit left. Straight over next 2 rdbts, immediate left*

Expect a warm welcome from this family-run guest house. Set in beautiful gardens minutes from the seafront and a 10 minute walk from the town centre. Bedrooms, which vary in size, are well presented. Home-cooked evening meals and hearty breakfasts are served in the smart dining room.

Rooms 15 rms (14 en suite) (1 pri facs) (1 fmly) (4 GF) S £32-£60; D £64-£120 **Facilities** TVL tea/coffee Dinner available Cen ht Licensed Wi-fi ⇥ ⅃ Pool Table Use of pools, jacuzzi and sauna at nearby hotel **Conf** Max 30 Thtr 30 Class 30 Board 30 **Parking** 12 **Notes** LB

The Woodside

★★★★ GUEST HOUSE

29 Southern Rd BH6 3SR
☎ 01202 427213 📄 01202 427213
e-mail: enquiries@woodsidehotel.co.uk
dir: *Follow A35 from Bournemouth. Take B3059 at Pokesdown Station. Right at Boots. Straight on to Southern Rd*

Well located with some off street parking, The Woodside offers comfortable rooms and is run by friendly hosts. Dinner is available by prior arrangement and is served in a light and airy dining room.

Rooms 7 rms (6 en suite) (1 pri facs) (1 fmly) S £35-£45; D £55-£65 **Facilities** FTV tea/coffee Dinner available Cen ht Licensed Wi-fi **Parking** 4 **Notes** LB ⊗ No Children 16yrs

Blue Palms

★★★★ 🅰 BED AND BREAKFAST

26 Tregonwell Rd, West Cliff BH2 5NS
☎ 01202 554968 📄 01202 294197
e-mail: bluepalmshotel@btopenworld.com
web: www.bluepalmshotel.com
dir: *Off A338 at Bournemouth West rdbt signed town centre, Triangle, next rdbt onto Durley Chine Rd, at rdbt onto West Hill Rd, Tregonwell Rd 3rd left*

Rooms 10 en suite (2 fmly) (2 GF) S £35-£45; D £60-£84* **Facilities** FTV TVL tea/coffee Cen ht Licensed Wi-fi **Parking** 8 **Notes** LB ⊗

Carlton Lodge

★★★ GUEST ACCOMMODATION

12 Westby Rd, Boscombe BH5 1HD
☎ 01202 303650 📄 01202 303650
e-mail: enquiries@thecarltonlodge.com

This relaxing home-from-home, family run guest accommodation is only a five minute stroll from the beach and shopping centre at Boscombe. The en suite bedrooms are spacious and individually decorated. Hearty breakfasts feature homemade preserves and excellent locally sourced bacon and sausages. Bournemouth is a short drive away with Poole, Swanage and Christchurch on the doorstep.

Rooms 5 en suite (2 fmly) (2 GF) S £35-£45; D £50-£70 **Facilities** tea/coffee Cen ht **Parking** 6 **Notes** LB

Denewood

★★★ GUEST ACCOMMODATION

1 Percy Rd, Boscombe BH5 1JE
☎ 01202 394493 & 309913 📄 01202 391155
e-mail: info@denewood.co.uk
dir: *500yds NE of Boscombe Pier, signed*

Located within walking distance of the beach and Boscombe shopping centre, and close to Bournemouth centre, the Denewood offers individually decorated bedrooms. A full English breakfast is served at individual tables in the delightful dining room, and the beauty salon is perfect for a little indulgence.

Rooms 10 en suite (3 fmly) **Facilities** STV TVL tea/coffee Cen ht Solarium health & beauty salon **Parking** 14

The Hop Inn

★★★ INN

6 Westcliff Rd BH2 5EY
☎ 01202 244626
e-mail: thehopinn@btinternet.com

Centrally located on the West Cliff, The Hop Inn offers light, airy modern en suite accommodation in a contemporary style. The busy bar with big screens shows all major sporting events; there is a lively atmosphere and meals are available in the evening. Groups are welcome by arrangement.

Rooms 12 en suite S £25-£50; D £50-£90* **Facilities** STV tea/coffee Dinner available Cen ht Wi-fi **Parking** 3

Pinedale

★★★ GUEST ACCOMMODATION

40 Tregonwell Rd, West Cliff BH2 5NT
☎ 01202 553733 & 292702 📄 01202 553733
e-mail: thepinedalehotel@btconnect.com
dir: *A338 at Bournemouth West rdbt, signs to West Cliff, Tregonwell Rd 3rd left after passing Wessex Hotel*

This friendly guest accommodation is enthusiastically run by two generations of the same family, and offers comfortable accommodation within a short walk of the seafront and local attractions. The fresh-looking bedrooms are equipped with useful extras. There is also an attractive licensed bar and an airy dining room where you can enjoy wholesome home-cooked meals.

Rooms 15 rms (9 en suite) (1 fmly) **Facilities** TVL tea/coffee Dinner available Direct Dial Licensed Wi-fi **Parking** 15 **Notes** ⊗

Commodore

★★★ 🅰 INN

Overcliff Dr, Southbourne BH6 3TD
☎ 01202 423150 📄 01202 423519
e-mail: 7688@greeneking.co.uk
web: www.thecommodore.co.uk
dir: *1m E of town centre on seafront*

Rooms 9 en suite (1 fmly) **Facilities** tea/coffee Dinner available Cen ht Lift **Conf** Max 30 Thtr 30 Class 12 Board 20 **Parking** 12 **Notes** ⊗ No coaches

BRIDPORT   Map 4 SY49

See also Chideock

PREMIER COLLECTION

The Shave Cross Inn
★★★★★ ⬤ INN

Marshwood Vale DT6 6HW
☎ 01308 868358   📄 01308 867064
e-mail: roy.warburton@virgin.net
web: www.theshavecrossinn.co.uk
dir: *From B3165 turn at Birdsmoorgate and follow brown signs.*

This historic inn has been providing refreshment for weary travellers for centuries and continues to offer a warm and genuine welcome. The snug bar is dominated by a wonderful fireplace with crackling logs creating just the right atmosphere. Bedrooms are located in a separate Dorset flint and stone building. Quality is impressive throughout with wonderful stone floors and oak beams, combined with feature beds and luxurious bathrooms. Food has a distinct Caribbean and International slant with a number of authentic dishes incorporating excellent local produce.

Rooms 7 en suite (1 fmly) (3 GF) **Facilities** STV FTV tea/coffee Dinner available Direct Dial Cen ht Wi-fi Pool Table **Parking** 29 **Notes** No Children RS Mon (ex BH) Closed for lunch & dinner No coaches

PREMIER COLLECTION

The Roundham House
★★★★★ GUEST ACCOMMODATION

Roundham Gardens, West Bay Rd DT6 4BD
☎ 01308 422753   📄 01308 421500
e-mail: cyprencom@compuserve.com
dir: *A35 into Bridport, at Crown Inn rdbt take exit signed West Bay. House 400yds on left*

The hosts here are always on hand to welcome you to their lovely home, which comes complete with well-tended gardens and views to the nearby coast. Bedrooms are in a variety of sizes and are all filled with useful extras. Public areas include a comfortable lounge and well-appointed dining room.

Rooms 8 rms (7 en suite) (1 fmly) S £49-£57; D £85-£97* **Facilities** FTV tea/coffee Cen ht Licensed **Parking** 10 **Notes** No Children 6yrs Closed Dec-Feb

Britmead House
★★★★ GUEST ACCOMMODATION

West Bay Rd DT6 4EG
☎ 01308 422941   & 07973 725243
e-mail: britmead@talk21.com
web: www.britmeadhouse.co.uk
dir: *1m S of town centre, off A35 onto West Bay Rd*

Britmead House is located south of Bridport, within easy reach of the town centre and West Bay harbour. Family-run, the atmosphere is friendly and the accommodation well-appointed and comfortable. Suitable for business and leisure, many guests return regularly. A choice of breakfast is served in the light and airy dining room.

Rooms 8 en suite (2 fmly) (2 GF) S £40-£58; D £60-£76* **Facilities** TVL tea/coffee Cen ht **Parking** 12 **Notes** LB Closed 24-27 Dec

Oxbridge Farm (SY475977)
★★★★ FARMHOUSE

DT6 3UA
☎ 01308 488368 & 07766 086543   Mrs C Marshall
e-mail: jojokillin@hotmail.com
web: www.oxbridgefarm.co.uk
dir: *From A3066 Bridport to Beaminster. Take 1st right signed Oxbridge 1m*

Oxbridge Farm is nestled in the rolling hills of West Dorset in an Area of Outstanding Natural Beauty. The bedrooms are well equipped and offer a very good degree of comfort. A hearty breakfast is served in the attractive dining room overlooking the wonderful views.

Rooms 3 rms (2 en suite) (1 pri facs) **Facilities** TV1B TVL tea/coffee Dinner available Cen ht **Parking** 6 **Notes** ⊗ 🐾 40 acres sheep

CERNE ABBAS   Map 4 ST60

Abbots
★★★ GUEST ACCOMMODATION

7 Long St DT2 7JF
☎ 01300 341349   📄 01300 348090
e-mail: abbots@3lambs.com
dir: *From A352 follow signs to village centre, next to village stores opp New Inn public house*

It would be hard to imagine a more quintessentially English village, situated below the famous Cerne Abbas Giant on the hillside. Bedrooms here are above a quaint

tea-shop where genuinely friendly locals and visitors alike gather to enjoy home-made cakes and a refreshing brew! Quality produce is offered at breakfast, and in the evening a short stroll will reveal a choice of three pubs.

Rooms 5 en suite (1 fmly) S £35-£45; D £70-£80* **Facilities** tea/coffee Cen ht Licensed **Notes** 🐾

CHIDEOCK   Map 4 SY49

Betchworth House
★★★★ GUEST ACCOMMODATION

DT6 6JW
☎ 01297 489478   📄 01297 489932
e-mail: info@betchworthhouse.co.uk
web: www.betchworthhouse.co.uk
dir: *On A35 in village*

There is a warm welcome and thoughtful and attentive service at this Grade II listed 19th-century house. Bedrooms, including one on the ground floor, are attractive and all feature numerous extra touches. Breakfast is served in the comfortable dining room, where a good choice of hot and cold options is provided. Guests can unwind in the garden and off-road parking is available.

Rooms 5 rms (3 en suite) (2 pri facs) (1 fmly) (1 GF) S £35; D £50-£55* **Facilities** tea/coffee Cen ht **Parking** 5 **Notes** LB ⊗ No Children 8yrs Closed Xmas

Rose Cottage
★★★★ BED AND BREAKFAST

Main St DT6 6JQ
☎ 01297 489994   & 07980 400904
e-mail: enquiries@rosecottage-chideock.co.uk
dir: *On A35 in village centre, on left in W direction*

Located in the centre of a charming village, this 300-year-old cottage provides very well-appointed, attractive accommodation and a friendly welcome is assured. A delicious breakfast can be enjoyed in the renovated dining room which has many interesting features, and in finer weather guests can relax in the pretty garden.

Rooms 2 en suite S £45; D £60* **Facilities** FTV tea/coffee Cen ht Wi-fi **Parking** 2 **Notes** LB ⊗ Closed 31 Dec

CHIDEOCK *continued*

Warren House

★★★★ GUEST ACCOMMODATION

DT6 6JW
☎ 01297 489996
e-mail: kathy@warren-house.com
dir: *Off A35 in village centre signed North Chideock, parking signed 60yds*

Expect a friendly welcome on arriving at this thatched long house, built in the early 17th century, and situated in this picturesque Dorset village. Bedrooms, which are all named after local hills, are spacious and comfortable. Enjoy afternoon tea in the secluded garden. Private parking is available.

Rooms 4 en suite (2 fmly) S £35; D £55 **Facilities** FTV tea/coffee Cen ht Wi-fi **Parking** 5 **Notes** LB Closed Xmas ⊗

CHRISTCHURCH Map 5 SZ19

PREMIER COLLECTION

Druid House

★★★★★ GUEST ACCOMMODATION

26 Sopers Ln BH23 1JE
☎ 01202 485615 📠 01202 473484
e-mail: reservations@druid-house.co.uk
web: www.druid-house.co.uk
dir: *A35 exit Christchurch main rdbt onto Sopers Ln, establishment on left*

Overlooking the park, this delightful family-run establishment is just a stroll from High Street, the Priory and the Quay. Bedrooms, some with balconies, are very comfortably furnished, and the many welcome extras include CD players. There is a pleasant rear garden, patio and relaxing lounge and bar areas.

Rooms 8 en suite (3 fmly) (4 GF) **Facilities** STV tea/coffee Direct Dial Cen ht Licensed **Parking** 8 **Notes** ⊗

PREMIER COLLECTION

The Lord Bute & Restaurant

★★★★★ ◉◉ GUEST ACCOMMODATION

179-181 Lymington Rd, Highcliffe on Sea BH23 4JS
☎ 01425 278884 📠 01425 279258
e-mail: mail@lordbute.co.uk
web: www.lordbute.co.uk
dir: *A337 towards Highcliffe*

The elegant Lord Bute stands directly behind the original entrance lodges of Highcliffe Castle close to the beach and historic town of Christchurch. Bedrooms have been finished to a very high standard with many thoughtful extras including spa baths and satellite television. Excellent food is available in the smart restaurant, and conferences and weddings are catered for.

Rooms 9 en suite 4 annexe en suite (1 fmly) (6 GF) S £98; D £98-£225 **Facilities** FTV tea/coffee Dinner available Direct Dial Cen ht Licensed **Conf** Max 25 Thtr 25 Class 15 Board 18 **Parking** 40 **Notes** LB RS Mon Restaurant closed (open for breakfast)

PREMIER COLLECTION

Seawards

★★★★★ 🛏 BED AND BREAKFAST

13 Avon Run Close, Friars Cliff BH23 4DT
☎ 01425 273188 & 07811 934059
e-mail: seawards13@hotmail.com
web: www.seawards13.plus.com
dir: *A35 onto A337 towards Highcliffe, right towards Mudeford, down the Runway, onto Bure Ln, 2nd left onto Island Av, then 1st right, then right again*

Set in a peaceful cul-de-sac just a stroll from the beach, Seawards offers home-from-home comfort in thoughtfully equipped bedrooms. For those not wanting to go to the beach there is a pretty, well-tended garden and one of the rooms has a conservatory. Breakfast offers plenty of choice and quality ingredients.

Rooms 2 en suite (2 GF) **Facilities** STV FTV TVL tea/coffee Cen ht **Parking** 7 **Notes** ⊗ No Children 12yrs Closed 21 Dec-14 Jan ⊗

Mill Stream House

★★★★ BED AND BREAKFAST

6 Ducking Stool Walk, Off Ducking Stool Ln BH23 1GA
☎ 01202 480114 & 07733 477023
e-mail: hjewitt@btinternet.com
web: www.christchurchbedandbreakfast.co.uk
dir: *Follow signs to High St, left onto Millhams St then Ducking Stool Ln. Turn right just past tea rooms*

Located in the town centre, this property is ideally placed for the many restaurants and historic sites in Christchurch. Attractive boutique-style rooms have sumptuous beds, flat-screen TVs and free Wi-Fi. Delicious home cooked breakfasts are served in the open-plan kitchen/dining room at a communal table. Parking is gated and secure.

Rooms 2 en suite (1 GF) S £45-£60; D £60-£90 **Facilities** FTV TVL tea/coffee Cen ht **Parking** 2 **Notes** LB ⊗ No Children

---

Windy Willums

★★★★ BED AND BREAKFAST

38 Island View Av BH23 4DS
☎ 01425 277046 & 07973 235082
e-mail: enquiries@windywillums.co.uk
dir: *A35 Somerford rdbt take A337 for Highcliffe, mini-rdbt last exit 2nd left after Sandpiper pub*

Just a two minute walk from Mudeford beach, this establishment is an ideal base for windsurfing, sailing or for exploring the New Forest. The proprietor is passionate about gardening and has created a truly beautiful and peaceful outdoor space for guests to relax in.

Rooms 3 rms (2 en suite) (1 pri facs) (3 fmly) **Facilities** tea/coffee Cen ht Wi-fi **Parking** 3 **Notes** LB ⊗ No Children ⊗

Ashbourne

★★★★ GUEST ACCOMMODATION

47 Stour Rd BH23 1LN
☎ 01202 475574 📠 01202 482905
e-mail: ashcroftb@hotmail.com
dir: *A35 (Christchurch to Bournemouth), left at lights onto Stour Rd, over lights, 4th house on right*

Convenient for the historic market town of Christchurch, the scenic River Stour, the New Forest and nearby beaches, this delightful guest house provides a relaxed and friendly environment. Bedrooms and bathrooms are all neatly furnished and equipped with many extra facilities. Large cooked breakfasts are served in the bright dining room.

Rooms 7 rms (5 en suite) (1 fmly) S £45-£60; D £50-£60* **Facilities** STV tea/coffee Cen ht Wi-fi **Parking** 6 **Notes** ⊗ Closed Xmas & New Year ☺

Beautiful South

★★★★ BED AND BREAKFAST

87 Barrack Rd BH23 2AJ
☎ 01202 568183 & 07958 597686
e-mail: kevin.lovett1@ntlworld.com
web: www.christchurchbandb.co.uk
dir: 0.25m from Christchurch town centre on A35, opp Pizza Hut at Bailey Bridge

A convenient location near to the main road on the outskirts of Christchurch makes this friendly guest house a good choice for leisure and business. Totally refurbished throughout by the proprietor, public areas and bedrooms are bright and inviting, and hearty dinners can be enjoyed in the pleasantly appointed dining room.

Rooms 3 en suite (1 fmly) **Facilities** FTV tea/coffee Dinner available Cen ht **Parking** 4 **Notes** LB ⊗ ☺

The Beech Tree

★★★★ GUEST ACCOMMODATION

2 Stuart Rd, Highcliffe BH23 5JS
☎ 01425 272038 📠 01425 272038
e-mail: hkowalski@beechtree.info
web: www.beechtree.info

The Beech Tree is a superb family-run guest house in Highcliffe, with a very high standard of accommodation, cleanliness and facilities, offering an excellent full English breakfast and buffet. Situated on the edge of the New Forest, it is five minutes walk away from an award-winning village and beach, shop and restaurants. Activities close by include golf, walking, riding and sailing.

Rooms 7 en suite (2 GF) S £35-£45; D £56-£62* **Facilities** TVL tea/coffee Cen ht **Parking** 14 **Notes** LB ⊗

Bure Farmhouse

★★★★ BED AND BREAKFAST

107 Bure Ln, Friars Cliff BH23 4DN
☎ 01425 275498
e-mail: info@burefarmhouse.co.uk
dir: A35 & A337 E from Christchurch towards Highcliffe, 1st rdbt right onto The Runway. Bure Lane 3rd turn sharp right onto service road, farmhouse on left

A friendly welcome is assured at this family home. Individually decorated bedrooms offer comfort and provide useful extras. Hearty breakfasts are served

farmhouse style in the dining room overlooking the attractive gardens.

Rooms 3 rms (2 en suite) (1 pri facs) (1 fmly) S £30-£40; D £50-£68* **Facilities** tea/coffee Cen ht **Parking** 3 **Notes** LB ⊗ No Children 4yrs ☺

Grosvenor Lodge

★★★★ GUEST HOUSE

53 Stour Rd BH23 1LN
☎ 01202 499008 📠 01202 486041
e-mail: bookings@grosvenorlodge.co.uk
dir: A35 from Christchurch to Bournemouth, at 1st lights left onto Stour Rd, Lodge on right

A friendly and popular guest house near the centre of this historic town. The bedrooms are brightly and individually decorated and have lots of useful extras. Hearty breakfasts are served in the cheerful dining room, and there is an extensive selection of local restaurants for lunch and dinner.

Rooms 7 en suite (4 fmly) (1 GF) S £25-£50; D £50-£80 **Facilities** FTV tea/coffee Cen ht Wi-fi **Parking** 10 **Notes** LB ⊗

Riversmead

★★★★ GUEST ACCOMMODATION

61 Stour Rd BH23 1LN
☎ 01202 487195
e-mail: riversmead.dorset@googlemail.com
dir: A338 to Christchurch. Left turn to town centre, turn right over railway bridge

Ideally located close to the town centre, beaches and the New Forest with excellent access to all local transport, Riversmead is the perfect base for a short break or longer stay. This comfortable house offers a range of facilities including enclosed off-road parking, fridges in rooms and an excellent breakfast.

Rooms 3 en suite (1 fmly) S £40-£45; D £50-£60* **Facilities** FTV tea/coffee Cen ht Wi-fi **Parking** 9 **Notes** LB ⊗ No Children 3yrs ☺

The Rothesay

★★★★ GUEST ACCOMMODATION

175, Lymington Rd, Highcliffe BH23 4JS
☎ 01425 274172
e-mail: reservations@therothesayhotel.com
web: www.therothesayhotel.com
dir: A337 to Highcliffe towards The Castle, 1m on left

Set on the edge of Highcliffe village, the Rothesay is a great base for exploring the Dorset-Hampshire coast. Highcliffe Castle is just a 5 minute walk away, and there are clifftop walks and views to the Isle of Wight. The indoor pool is a real benefit, as are the pretty gardens and large car park.

Rooms 12 en suite 3 annexe en suite (1 fmly) (7 GF) S £48; D £75-£125* **Facilities** FTV TVL tea/coffee Cen ht Licensed Wi-fi 🔍 Sauna Pool Table **Conf** Max 30 Thtr 30 Class 30 Board 30 **Parking** 21 **Notes** LB ⊗ No Children 8yrs

The White House

★★★★ GUEST ACCOMMODATION

428 Lymington Rd, Highcliffe On Sea BH23 5HF
☎ 01425 271279 📠 01425 276900
e-mail: enquiries@thewhitehouse-christchurch.co.uk
web: www.thewhitehouse-christchurch.co.uk
dir: Off A35, signs to Highcliffe. After rdbt The White House 200yds on right

This charming Victorian house is just a short drive from Highcliffe beach, the New Forest and the historic town of Christchurch. Comfortable, well-appointed accommodation is provided, and a generous, freshly-cooked breakfast is served in the cosy dining room. Private car park.

Rooms 6 en suite S £29-£55; D £50-£76 **Facilities** tea/coffee Cen ht Wi-fi **Parking** 6 **Notes** LB ⊗

Brantwood Guest House

★★★ GUEST ACCOMMODATION

55 Stour Rd BH23 1LN
☎ 01202 473446 📠 01202 473446
e-mail: pam.brantwood@ntlworld.com
dir: A338 Bournemouth, 1st exit Christchurch right after railway bridge cross lights, 200yds on right

Relaxed and friendly guest house where the proprietors create a home-from-home atmosphere. Bedrooms and bathrooms are all well decorated and comfortably furnished. The town centre is just a stroll away and off-road parking is available.

Rooms 5 en suite (2 fmly) **Facilities** tea/coffee Cen ht **Parking** 5 **Notes** ⊗ ☺

CHRISTCHURCH *continued*

Seapoint

★★★ GUEST ACCOMMODATION

121 Mudeford BH23 4AF
☎ 01425 279541 📄 01425 279541
web: www.seapointb-b.com

Expect a friendly welcome at Seapoint, a pleasant white-painted house in a prime location at the entrance to Mudeford Quay, just a few minutes' walk from Christchurch Harbour. Enjoy the sea views while having your full English or Continental breakfast in the first floor breakfast room. The comfortable ground floor bedrooms include one with a four poster. Guests are welcome to make use of the colourful garden.

Rooms 4 rms (2 en suite) (2 pri facs) (2 fmly) (4 GF)
S £30-£70; D £50-£110* **Facilities** TVL tea/coffee Cen ht
Parking 4 **Notes** LB ⊗ 📶

Southern Comfort Guest House

★★★ GUEST ACCOMMODATION

51 Stour Rd BH23 1LN
☎ 01202 471373
e-mail: scomfortgh@aol.com
dir: A338 onto B3073 towards Christchurch, 2m onto B3059 (Stour Rd)

Convenient for Bournemouth, Christchurch and Southbourne, this practical and friendly guest house offers spacious bedrooms. Breakfast, served in the bright lounge-dining room, is a relaxed affair with a good choice of hot items.

Rooms 3 en suite (3 fmly) S £30; D £50-£60*
Facilities FTV TVL tea/coffee Cen ht **Parking** 4 **Notes** LB
⊗ 📶

Golfers Reach

Ⓤ

88 Lymington Rd, Highcliffe BH23 4JU
☎ 01425 272903
e-mail: golfersreach@yahoo.co.uk

Currently the rating for this establishment is not confirmed. This may be due to a change of ownership or because it has only recently joined the AA rating scheme.

Rooms 3 en suite S £35-£50; D £55-£65* **Notes** 📶

CORFE MULLEN
Map 4 SY99

Kenways

★★★ BED AND BREAKFAST

90a Wareham Rd BH21 3LQ
☎ 01202 694655
e-mail: eileen@kenways.com
web: www.kenways.com
dir: 2m SW of Wimborne. Off A31 to Corfe Mullen. Over B3074 rdbt, B&B 0.3m on right

Expect to be welcomed as one of the family at this homely guest house between Wimborne Minster and Poole. The spacious bedrooms are well provisioned with thoughtful extras, and breakfast is served in the pleasant conservatory overlooking the attractive gardens.

Rooms 3 rms (3 pri facs) (2 GF) S £30; D £60*
Facilities TVL tea/coffee Cen ht Wi-fi Table tennis Snooker table **Parking** 4 **Notes** 📶

CRANBORNE
Map 5 SU01

La Fosse at Cranborne

★★★★ ◉ RESTAURANT WITH ROOMS

London House, The Square BH21 5PR
☎ 01725 517604
e-mail: lafossemail@gmail.com
web: www.la-fosse.com
dir: M27(W) onto A31 to Ringwood, left onto B3081 to Verwood & Cranborne

This charming restaurant with rooms provides a home-from-home atmosphere. Family run by husband and wife team, Mark and Emmanuelle Hartstone, La Fosse provides charming accommodation and wonderful dinners using the best of local produce. On the edge of the New Forest which is ideal for exploring Wiltshire, Dorset and Hampshire. Wi-fi is available.

Rooms 6 rms (5 en suite) (1 pri facs) (2 fmly) S £49;
D £85* **Facilities** FTV tea/coffee Dinner available Direct Dial Cen ht Wi-fi **Notes** LB ⊗ Closed Xmas & New Year No coaches

---

DORCHESTER
Map 4 SY69

See also Sydling St Nicholas

PREMIER COLLECTION

Little Court

★★★★★ 🏠 GUEST ACCOMMODATION

5 Westleaze, Charminster DT2 9PZ
☎ 01305 261576 📄 01305 261359
e-mail: info@littlecourt.net
web: www.littlecourt.net
dir: A37 from Dorchester, 0.25m right at Loders Garage, Little Court 0.5m on right

Built in 1909 in the style of Lutyens, Little Court sits in over four acres of attractive grounds and gardens. The property has been refurbished to a very high standard and the friendly proprietors are on hand to ensure a pleasant stay. A delicious breakfast, including home-grown produce, can be enjoyed in the stylish dining room.

Rooms 8 en suite (1 fmly) S £69-£79; D £79-£89*
Facilities FTV tea/coffee Cen ht Licensed Wi-fi 🐾 🐕
Parking 10 **Notes** LB ⊗ Closed Xmas & New Year

The Casterbridge

★★★★ 🏠 GUEST ACCOMMODATION

49 High East St DT1 1HU
☎ 01305 264043 📄 01305 260884
e-mail: reception@thecasterbridgehotel.co.uk
dir: A35 onto B3150 at bottom of High East St

Conveniently located in the high street, this well established accommodation provides high quality bedrooms with a choice of traditional Georgian or more contemporary styles. There is an engaging period charm throughout the public areas with a lovely lounge and snug bar for a relaxing drink. Breakfast is something special with a wonderful choice of hot and cold items, all served in the elegant dining room or conservatory area with views of the courtyard garden.

Rooms 9 en suite 6 annexe en suite (1 fmly) (3 GF)
Facilities FTV tea/coffee Direct Dial Cen ht Licensed Wi-fi
Conf Max 15 Thtr 15 Class 15 Board 15 **Parking** 4
Notes ⊗ Closed 23-26 Dec

Baytree House Dorchester

★★★★ BED AND BREAKFAST

4 Athelstan Rd DT1 1NR
☎ 01305 263696
e-mail: info@baytreedorchester.com
dir: 0.5m SE of town centre

Friendly, family-run bed and breakfast situated in the heart of Dorchester, not far from the village of Higher Bockham - the birthplace of Thomas Hardy. Bedrooms are furnished in an appealing contemporary style and provide high levels of comfort. Breakfast is farmhouse style in the open plan kitchen/dining area. Parking is available.

Rooms 3 en suite S fr £35; D fr £65* **Facilities** FTV TVL tea/coffee Cen ht **Parking** 3 **Notes** LB ⊗ ⊜

Beggars Knap

★★★★ GUEST ACCOMMODATION

2 Weymouth Av DT1 1QS
☎ 01305 268191
e-mail: beggarsknap@hotmail.co.uk

Conveniently situated in the heart of the town, this renovated, detached Victorian property has connections with the local brewery and Thomas Hardy. Guest arrivals are handled with efficiency and warmth. Bedrooms are spacious, and furnished with a variety of styles of furnishings. The freshly-cooked breakfast features the best of locally sourced ingredients, with guests sitting around one large table. Off-street parking available.

Rooms 3 en suite (2 fmly) S £45-£59; D £60-£90* **Facilities** TVL tea/coffee Cen ht **Parking** 3 **Notes** RS Xmas & New Year open by reservation only ⊜

Higher Came Farmhouse

★★★★ GUEST ACCOMMODATION

Higher Came DT2 8NR
☎ 01305 268908 ▤ 01305 268908
e-mail: enquiries@highercame.co.uk
dir: From Dorchester bypass (A35) take A354 to Weymouth, 1st left to Winterbourne Herringston. At T-junct turn right after 1m golf course, next left to house

This farmhouse is situated deep in beautiful countryside yet only five minutes' drive from Dorchester and less than half an hour from the coastal town of Weymouth. Spacious bedrooms are attractively presented and a hearty breakfast is served family style in the bright dining room. There's a lounge with comfortable seating, and parking is a bonus.

Rooms 4 rms (1 en suite) (3 pri facs) (1 fmly) (1 GF) S £40-£50; D £75-£80* **Facilities** tea/coffee Cen ht Wi-fi **Parking** 6 **Notes** No Children 5yrs

Westwood House

★★★★ GUEST ACCOMMODATION

29 High West St DT1 1UP
☎ 01305 268018
e-mail: reservations@westwoodhouse.co.uk
web: www.westwoodhouse.co.uk
dir: On B2150 in town centre

Originally built in 1815, Westwood House is centrally located in the historic town of Dorchester and is ideal for leisure visitors to the area as well as the business traveller. This attractive property, run by a husband and wife team, offers well-appointed rooms with modern facilities in an informal, yet stylish environment.

Rooms 7 rms (5 en suite) (2 pri facs) (2 fmly) S £55-£65; D £75-£95* **Facilities** FTV tea/coffee Cen ht Wi-fi **Notes** ⊗

Yellowham Farmhouse

★★★★ GUEST ACCOMMODATION

Yellowham Wood DT2 8RW
☎ 01305 262892 ▤ 01305 848155
e-mail: mail@yellowham.freeserve.co.uk
web: www.yellowham.co.uk
dir: 1.5m NE of Dorchester, 500yds off A35

Located north-east of Dorchester in the heart of Hardy Country, the farm stands amid fields and the tranquil 130 acres of Yellowham Wood. There are spectacular views, and the comfortable bedrooms are all on the ground floor. Thomas Hardy's Cottage and Puddletown Heath are only half a mile to the south.

Rooms 4 en suite (1 fmly) (4 GF) S £48-£66; D £66-£80* **Facilities** tea/coffee Cen ht **Parking** 8 **Notes** LB No Children 4yrs

Bramlies

★★★ BED AND BREAKFAST

107 Briport Rd DT1 2NH
☎ 01305 265778
e-mail: bramlies@btinternet.com
web: www.bramlies.com
dir: On B3150 on W side of Dorchester

A traditional bed and breakfast operation on the outskirts of the town within easy walking distance of the centre and close to the hospital. The hospitality is excellent and the proprietors do all they can to make guests feel at home.

Rooms 1 en suite 2 annexe en suite (1 fmly) (2 GF) S £38-£45; D £64* **Facilities** FTV tea/coffee Cen ht Wi-fi **Parking** 5 **Notes** LB ⊗ No Children 12yrs ⊜

The Acorn Inn

★★★★ ◉ INN

DT2 0JW
☎ 01935 83228 ▤ 01935 83707
e-mail: stay@acorn-inn.co.uk
web: www.acorn-inn.co.uk
dir: 0.5m off A37 between Yeovil & Dorchester, signed Evershot & Holywell

This delightful 16th-century coaching inn is located at the heart of the village. Several of the bedrooms feature interesting four-poster beds, and all have been individually decorated and furnished. Public rooms retain many original features including oak panelling, open fires and stone-flagged floors. Fresh local produce is included on the varied menu.

Rooms 10 en suite (2 fmly) S £60-£75* **Facilities** STV TVL tea/coffee Dinner available Direct Dial Cen ht Wi-fi Pool Table **Conf** Max 60 Thtr 30 Class 60 Board 30 **Parking** 40 **Notes** LB

FARNHAM — Map 4 ST91

PREMIER COLLECTION

Farnham Farm House
★★★★★ GUEST ACCOMMODATION

DT11 8DG
☎ 01725 516254 📠 01725 516306
e-mail: info@farnhamfarmhouse.co.uk
dir: Off A354 Thickthorn x-rds into Farnham, continue
NW from village centre T-junct, 1m bear right at sign

Farnham Farm House is a country house in 350 acres of
arable farmland, offering a high level of quality,
comfort and service. The atmosphere is friendly and the
accommodation charming and spacious. In the winter,
a log fire burns in the attractive dining room, where a
delicious breakfast featuring local produce is served,
and views across the rolling countryside can be
enjoyed. Added features include the outdoor pool and
the Sarpenela Treatment room in the converted stable.

Rooms 3 en suite (1 fmly) S £60-£70; D £80*
Facilities FTV tea/coffee ⚡ 🍴 Holistic Therapies
Centre **Parking** 7 **Notes** ⊗ Closed 25-26 Dec

FERNDOWN — Map 5 SU00

City Lodge
★★★★ GUEST ACCOMMODATION

Ringwood Rd BH22 9AN
☎ 01202 578828
e-mail: bournemouth@citylodge.co.uk

Close to Bournemouth and the airport, City lodge provides
an ideal base for exploring the Dorset coastline. Situated
on the edge of the River Stour, many of the rooms have
the benefit of beautiful riverside views. Recently
refurbished, offering modern facilities such as en suite
bathrooms, LCD TVs and free Wi-fi. A large bar and
restaurant serve meals and snacks while parking is
gated and secure.

Rooms 45 en suite S £49-£69; D £49-£99 (room only)
Facilities FTV tea/coffee Dinner available Cen ht Licensed
Wi-fi **Conf** Max 120 **Parking** 300 **Notes** ⊗ Civ Wed 120

FIDDLEFORD — Map 4 ST81

The Fiddleford Inn
★★★★ INN

DT10 2BX
☎ 01258 472489
e-mail: fiddinn@hotmail.co.uk
dir: From Sturminster Newton take A357 to Blandford
Forum, 2m on left

Surrounded by beautiful Dorset countryside, this 18th-
century inn has much appeal and much to offer. Family
run, the welcome is always genuine whether you're
quaffing a quiet pint at the bar or sampling honest
traditional English cooking. Bedrooms combine style and
comfort with two suites available complete with separate
seating areas.

Rooms 3 en suite S £50-£90; D £85-£150 **Facilities** FTV
tea/coffee Dinner available Direct Dial Cen ht Wi-fi
Conf Max 20 Thtr 20 Class 16 Board 14 **Parking** 24
Notes LB No Children 9yrs Closed 25 Dec No coaches

FRAMPTON — Map 4 SY69

PREMIER COLLECTION

Frampton House
★★★★★ 🏠 🍴 GUEST ACCOMMODATION

DT2 9NH
☎ 01300 320308
e-mail: maynardryder@btconnect.com
dir: A356 into village, from green over bridge & left
onto driveway past houses

This quietly located, truly delightful Grade II listed
property is located close to Dorchester. The naturally
friendly owners ensure that guests feel immediately at
home. The bedrooms, drawing room and dining rooms
offer high standards of quality and comfort, and
dinner, served by arrangement, should not to be
missed.

Rooms 3 en suite S £75; D £95 **Facilities** FTV tea/
coffee Dinner available Cen ht Wi-fi 🌳 **Parking** 10
Notes No Children 6yrs ⊗

HENLEY — Map 4 ST60

Chapel House
★★★★ BED AND BREAKFAST

DT2 7BN
☎ 01300 345822 & 07814 705225
e-mail: enquiries@malcolmscholes.com
web: www.chapelhousebandb.com
dir: B3143 N of Dorchester. 1st left after Henley
Hillbillies, at x-rds turn left, continue 50yds

This sympathetically converted chapel offers easy access
to Dorchester and has high quality bedrooms, bathrooms
and public areas. Owner Malcolm Scholes has a relaxed,
informal style.

Rooms 3 rms (2 en suite) (1 pri facs); D £70-£95
Facilities tea/coffee Cen ht **Parking** 3 **Notes** LB ⊗ No
Children 7yrs Closed 20 Dec-20 Jan

HIGHCLIFFE

For accommodation details see Christchurch

LOWER ANSTY — Map 4 ST70

The Fox Inn
★★★★ INN

DT2 7PN
☎ 01258 880328 📠 01258 881440
e-mail: fox@anstyfoxinn.co.uk
web: www.anstyfoxinn.co.uk
dir: Off A354 at Millbourne St Andrew, follow brown signs
to Ansty

This popular inn has a long and interesting history
including strong links to the Hall and Woodhouse brewery.
Surrounded by beautiful Dorset countryside, this is a
great base for exploring the area. Bedrooms are smartly
appointed and offer generous levels of comfort. The
interesting menu focuses on excellent local produce, with
a choice of dining options including the oak-panelled
dining room. An extensive garden and patio area is also
available.

Rooms 11 en suite (7 fmly) S £45-£100; D £55-£105
Facilities TVL tea/coffee Dinner available Cen ht 🍴
Conf Max 60 Thtr 60 Class 40 Board 45 **Parking** 30
Notes LB

LYME REGIS — Map 4 SY39

See also Axminster (Devon)

Beech Grove House
★★★★★ 🅰 GUEST HOUSE

Rhode Ln, Uplyme DT7 3TX
☎ 01297 442723
e-mail: beechgroveuplyme@aol.com
Rooms 5 en suite; D £100-£130* **Facilities** FTV tea/
coffee Cen ht Wi-fi **Notes** LB ⊗ No Children Closed Dec-6
Feb

Old Lyme Guest House

★★★★ GUEST ACCOMMODATION

29 Coombe St DT7 3PP
☎ 01297 442929
e-mail: oldlyme.guesthouse@virgin.net
web: www.oldlymeguesthouse.co.uk
dir: In town centre. Off A3052 Church St onto Coombe St

Comfort is a high priority at this delightful 18th-century former post office, which is just a short walk from the seafront. Bedrooms, which vary in size, are all well equipped and include many thoughtful extras. A wide choice is offered at breakfast, served in the cheerful dining room.

Rooms 5 rms (4 en suite) (1 pri facs) (1 fmly);
D £72-£75* Facilities FTV TVL tea/coffee Cen ht Notes LB
⊗ No Children 5yrs ⊜

Albany

★★★ GUEST ACCOMMODATION

Charmouth Rd DT7 3DP
☎ 01297 443066
e-mail: albany@lymeregis.com
dir: 300yds NE of town centre on A3052

Situated on the outskirts of this popular town and within easy walking distance of the seafront, this attractive house provides comfortable accommodation and a home-from-home atmosphere. Bedrooms are comfortably furnished, the public rooms are inviting and guests are welcome to use the garden. Breakfast, featuring local ingredients, is served in the homely dining room.

Rooms 6 en suite (1 fmly) (1 GF) S fr £39; D fr £68*
Facilities TVL tea/coffee Cen ht Parking 6 Notes ⊗ No
Children 5yrs ⊜

The Orchard Country House

★★★★ GUEST HOUSE

Rousdon DT7 3XW
☎ 01297 442972 ☐ 01297 443670
e-mail: reception@orchardcountryhotel.com
web: www.orchardcountryhotel.com
dir: Take B3052 from Lyme Regis towards Sidmouth, on right after garage

Located in the peaceful village of Rousdon and set in attractive orchard gardens, this friendly and comfortable establishment is a good base for exploring the area. The hop-on hop-off bus stops just outside and is a handy way to visit many of the local attractions. There is a spacious lounge, and breakfast and dinner are served in the pleasant dining room.

Rooms 11 en suite (1 fmly) (1 GF) S £65-£75;
D £100-£120 Facilities FTV tea/coffee Dinner available
Cen ht Licensed Parking 25

The White House

★★★★ GUEST HOUSE

47 Silver St DT7 3HR
☎ 01297 443420
e-mail: whitehouselyme@btopenworld.com
dir: On B3165 (Axminster-Lyme Regis road) 50yds from A3052 junct

This charming guest house dates from 1770 and is located at the top of town, within walking distance of the beach and the harbour. The well-equipped bedrooms are cheerful and bright. Guests have use of a spacious lounge and an attractive dining room where hearty breakfasts are served.

Rooms 6 en suite; D £66-£70* Facilities TVL tea/coffee
Cen ht Parking 7 Notes LB ⊗ No Children 10yrs Closed
Xmas ⊜

Berrydown

★★★ BED AND BREAKFAST

Highcliff Rd DT7 3EW
☎ 01297 444448
dir: 0.5m W of town centre on A3052

Located at the top of Lyme Regis with pleasant views towards the sea, this welcoming establishment offers two comfortable bedrooms including one on the ground floor. Guests are encouraged to use the pleasant rear garden with terrace seating. A carefully prepared breakfast is served in the relaxing conservatory.

Rooms 2 rms (2 pri facs) (1 GF) S £35-£45; D £60-£65*
Facilities tea/coffee Cen ht Parking 4 Notes ⊗ ⊜

MILTON ABBAS   Map 4 ST80

Fishmore Hill Farm (ST799013)

★★★ FARMHOUSE

DT11 0DL
☎ 01258 881122 ☐ 01258 881122 Mr & Mrs N Clarke
e-mail: sarah@fishmorehillfarm.com
dir: Off A354 signed Milton Abbas, 3m left on sharp bend, up steep hill, 1st left

This working sheep farm and family home is surrounded by beautiful Dorset countryside, is close to historic Milton Abbey and only a short drive from the coast. Bedrooms, which vary in size, are comfortable and finished with considerate extras. The atmosphere is friendly and relaxed. Breakfast is served in the smart dining room around a communal table.

Rooms 3 en suite S £30-£35; D fr £70* Facilities TVL
tea/coffee Cen ht Parking 4 Notes Closed Xmas & New
Year ⊜ 50 acres sheep/horses

MOTCOMBE   Map 4 ST82

The Coppleridge Inn

★★★ ⚠ INN

SP7 9HW
☎ 01747 851980 ☐ 01747 851858
e-mail: thecoppleridgeinn@btinternet.com
web: www.coppleridge.com
dir: Off A350 to Motcombe, under railway bridge, 400yds right to Mere, inn 300yds on left

Rooms 10 en suite (2 fmly) (10 GF) S £45-£50;
D £80-£85* Facilities FTV TVL tea/coffee Dinner available
Direct Dial Cen ht Wi-fi ⊜ Pool Table Conf Max 60 Thtr 60
Class 60 Board 30 Parking 100 Notes LB Civ Wed 80

PIDDLEHINTON   Map 4 SY79

Longpuddle

★★★★ BED AND BREAKFAST

4 High St DT2 7TD
☎ 01300 348532
e-mail: ann@longpuddle.co.uk
dir: From Dorchester (A35) take B3143, after entering village 1st thatched house on left after village cross

This purpose-built annexed accommodation is perfectly located for exploring the delightful Dorset countryside and coast. Bedrooms are spacious, very well furnished and equipped with thoughtful extras such as mini fridges. Breakfast is served in the dining room of the main house, where a guest lounge is also located overlooking the lovely gardens.

Rooms 2 annexe en suite (2 fmly) S £50-£80; D £90-£110
Facilities TVL tea/coffee Wi-fi Parking 3 Notes RS
Dec-Jan Prior bookings only ⊜

PIDDLETRENTHIDE   Map 4 SY79

The Piddle Inn

★★★★ INN

DT2 7QF
☎ 01300 348468 ☐ 01300 348102
e-mail: piddleinn@aol.com
web: www.piddleinn.co.uk
dir: 7m N of Dorchester on B3143 in middle of Piddletrenthide

This inn is situated deep in the heart of the Dorset countryside in the Piddle Valley. Fresh flowers are put in each bedroom and most have lovely views. Dinner is served in the friendly bar downstairs, and the menu includes the fresh fish of the day. The gardens are perfect for alfresco dining.

Rooms 3 en suite (1 fmly) Facilities tea/coffee Dinner
available Direct Dial Cen ht Wi-fi Pool Table Parking 15
Notes No coaches

PIDDLETRENTHIDE *continued*

The Poachers

★★★★ INN

DT2 7QX
☎ **01300 348358** 📄 01300 348153
e-mail: info@thepoachersinn.co.uk
web: www.thepoachersinn.co.uk
dir: *N of Dorchester on B3143, inn on left*

This friendly, owner-run inn combines original 16th-century character with contemporary style in the bar and dining areas. Home-cooked meals are a feature, and the smart, en suite bedrooms open onto a courtyard. In fine weather guests can relax in the garden or beside the swimming pool.

Rooms 21 en suite (3 fmly) (12 GF) **Facilities** tea/coffee Dinner available Direct Dial Cen ht Wi-fi ⚡ **Conf** Class 20 **Parking** 42

POOLE	Map 4 SZ09

PREMIER COLLECTION

Luminiere Boutique Bed & Breakfast
★★★★★ BED AND BREAKFAST

78 Haven Rd BH13 7LZ
☎ **01202 707868**
e-mail: info@luminiere.co.uk

Situated a moment's walk from Sandbanks this quality bed and breakfast provides exquisite accommodation paired with a charming elegance in this beautifully designed house. Bedrooms are spacious and comfortably equipped with a range of thoughtful accessories. A hearty breakfast is served at individual tables in the bright and airy conservatory overlooking the landscaped front garden.

Rooms 6 rms (5 en suite) (1 pri facs) (1 fmly) (2 GF) S £95-£250; D £95-£250* **Facilities** FTV tea/coffee Cen ht Wi-fi **Parking** 5 **Notes** ⊗

Bees Knees Guest House

★★★★ 🏠 GUEST HOUSE

28 Davies Rd, Branksome BH12 2BB
☎ **01202 734509**
e-mail: bees.knees1@ntlworld.com
web: www.beesknees-guesthouse.co.uk

Situated just a short distance from the Sand Banks peninsula, close to the Jurassic Coast, between Bournemouth and Poole. Your hosts, Graham and Michelle, offer attentive service and warm, friendly hospitality. Rooms are well appointed, with excellent facilities, and are equipped with a good range of amenities. Both breakfast and dinner are served in the attractive conservatory, overlooking the garden. Michelle Elson was a finalist for the AA Friendliest Landlady of the Year 2009-2010 Award.

Rooms 3 en suite S £43-£45.50; D £75-£80* **Facilities** FTV TVL tea/coffee Dinner available Cen ht Licensed Wi-fi **Conf** Max 8 Thtr 8 Class 6 Board 8 **Parking** 2 **Notes** ⊗ No Children 18yrs

Acorns

★★★★ GUEST ACCOMMODATION

264 Wimborne Rd, Oakdale BH15 3EF
☎ **01202 672901** 📄 01202 672901
e-mail: enquiries@acornsguesthouse.co.uk
web: www.acornsguesthouse.co.uk
dir: *On A35, approx 1m from town centre, opp Texaco station*

A warm welcome is assured at Acorns, located with easy access to the town, ferry terminal, business parks and attractions. The bedrooms are furnished to a high standard, and an English breakfast is served in the charming dining room. There is also a quiet cosy lounge.

Rooms 4 en suite (1 GF); D £56-£65 **Facilities** FTV TVL tea/coffee Cen ht Wi-fi **Parking** 6 **Notes** LB ⊗ No Children 14yrs Closed 23 Dec-1 Jan

Blue Shutters

★★★★ GUEST ACCOMMODATION

109 North Rd, Parkstone BH14 0LU
☎ **01202 748129**
e-mail: stay@blueshutters.co.uk
web: www.blueshutters.co.uk
dir: *0.5m from Poole Park & Civic Centre buildings*

The friendly, family-run Blue Shutters is close to the civic centre and offers brightly decorated, well-equipped bedrooms. Sound, home-cooked breakfasts are served in the well-presented dining room overlooking the attractive garden. The guest lounge provides comfort and quiet.

Rooms 7 en suite (2 fmly) (1 GF) S £40-£50; D £70-£80* **Facilities** TVL tea/coffee Cen ht Wi-fi **Parking** 7 **Notes** ⊗ No Children 5yrs Closed 24 Dec-2 Jan

Towngate

★★★ GUEST HOUSE

58 Wimborne Rd BH15 2BY
☎ **01202 668552**
e-mail: ayoun19@ntlworld.com
dir: *B3093 from town centre, guest house on right*

Guests are assured of a warm welcome at this centrally located house, within walking distance of the town centre and harbour, and just a short drive from the ferry terminal. The well-equipped bedrooms are comfortable and nicely furnished.

Rooms 3 en suite S £45-£50; D £55-£60 **Facilities** tea/coffee Cen ht **Parking** 4 **Notes** ⊗ No Children 10yrs Closed mid Dec-mid Jan 🐾

The Burleigh

★★★ GUEST ACCOMMODATION

76 Wimborne Rd BH15 2BZ
☎ **01202 673889** 📄 01202 685283
dir: *Off A35 onto A349*

Suited to business and leisure, this well-kept guest house is close to the town centre and ferry terminal. The individually furnished and decorated bedrooms are of a good standard. Breakfast is served at separate tables and there is a small, attractive lounge.

Rooms 8 rms (4 en suite) (1 fmly) **Facilities** TVL tea/coffee Cen ht Wi-fi **Parking** 5

Centraltown

★★★ GUEST HOUSE

101 Wimborne Rd BH15 2BP
☎ **01202 674080** 📄 01202 674080
dir: *From town centre onto A3093, Barclays International building on left, guest house 500yds*

This friendly and well-maintained guest house is within easy access of the town centre, ferry terminals, speedway and many other attractions. Bedrooms are attractive and equipped with many useful extra facilities. A full English breakfast is served in the bright, cosy dining room.

Rooms 3 en suite **Facilities** tea/coffee Cen ht **Parking** 6 **Notes** ⊗ No Children 🐾

Seacourt

★★★ GUEST ACCOMMODATION

249 Blandford Rd, Hamworthy BH15 4AZ
☎ **01202 674995**
dir: *Off A3049/A35 signed to Hamworthy*

Within a short distance of the ferry port and town centre, this friendly establishment is well maintained and efficiently run. The comfortable bedrooms, some located on the ground floor, are all nicely decorated and equipped with useful extra facilities. Breakfast is served in the pleasant dining room at separate tables.

Rooms 5 en suite (1 fmly) (3 GF) (5 smoking) S £40-£56; D £56* **Facilities** tea/coffee Cen ht **Parking** 5 **Notes** ⊗ No Children 5yrs 🐾

Holly House

★★ GUEST ACCOMMODATION

97 Longfleet Rd BH15 2HP
☎ 01202 677839 📠 01202 461722
e-mail: maxine.curr@ntlworld.com
dir: Just off A35

Holly House is across the road from Poole Hospital and is well situated for the town centre and the ferry terminal. It has a friendly and relaxed atmosphere. The comfortable bedrooms are simply furnished and are ideal for business or leisure.

Rooms 4 en suite (3 fmly) S fr £35; D fr £48* **Facilities** TVL tea/coffee Cen ht **Parking** 7 **Notes** ⊗ Closed 20 Dec-5 Jan RS 6 Jan 🐾

Queen Anne House

★★★★ GUEST ACCOMMODATION

2/4 Fortuneswell DT5 1LP
☎ 01305 820028
e-mail: margaretdunlop@tiscali.co.uk
dir: A354 to Portland then Fortuneswell. House on left 200yds past Royal Portland Arms

This delightful Grade II listed building is a charming and comfortable place to stay; particularly delightful are the Italianate gardens to the rear. Ideal for business and for leisure, Queen Anne House is close to the famous Chesil Beach, Portland Bill and Weymouth. Bedrooms are particularly attractive and pleasantly furnished. At breakfast, where guests are seated at one large table, there is a wide choice of options.

Rooms 3 en suite S £42.50-£44; D £65-£68* **Facilities** FTV TVL tea/coffee Cen ht Wi-fi **Parking** 4 **Notes** ⊗ 🐾 🐾

Beach House

★★★ GUEST HOUSE

51 Chiswell DT5 1AW
☎ 01305 821155
e-mail: roy@beach-house-bandb.co.uk
dir: A354, after causeway take right lane to Victoria Square & into Chiswell. 150mtrs on right

Dating back to the early 19th century, this grand building was formerly a public house, but more recently has been providing relaxed and welcoming accommodation. Situated at the side of the stunning sweep of Chesil

Beach, this establishment is also handy for the sailing academy. Bedrooms provide good levels of comfort and quality, many having stripped wooden floors and simple, stylish decor. A lounge and bar are also available, together with a light and airy breakfast room.

Rooms 6 rms (5 en suite) (1 pri facs) (2 fmly) S £30-£44; D £50-£70* **Facilities** FTV tea/coffee Cen ht Licensed Wi-fi **Parking** 8 **Notes** LB ⊗

Portland Lodge

★★★ GUEST ACCOMMODATION

Easton Ln DT5 1BW
☎ 01305 820265 📠 01305 860359
e-mail: info@portlandlodge.com
dir: Signs to Easton/Portland Bill, rdbt at Portland Heights Hotel 1st right. Portland Lodge 200yds

Situated on the fascinating island of Portland, this modern, lodge-style establishment provides comfortable accommodation including a number of ground-floor bedrooms. Breakfast is served in the spacious dining room with a friendly team of staff on hand. This is an ideal location for those wishing to explore the World Heritage coastline.

Rooms 30 annexe en suite (15 fmly) (7 GF) S £38-£48; D £48-£58 (room only)* **Facilities** tea/coffee Cen ht **Parking** 50 **Notes** LB ⊗

Offley Bed & Breakfast

★★★★ GUEST ACCOMMODATION

Looke Ln DT2 9BD
☎ 01308 897044 & 07792 624977
dir: Off B3157 into village centre

With magnificent views over the Bride Valley, this village house provides comfortable, quality accommodation. Guests are assured of a warm, friendly welcome; an ideal venue to enjoy the numerous local attractions. There are several local inns, one in the village, just a gentle stroll away.

Rooms 3 rms (2 en suite) **Facilities** TV2B TVL tea/coffee Cen ht **Parking** 3 **Notes** 🐾

La Fleur de Lys Restaurant with Rooms

★★★★ ⑩⑩ RESTAURANT WITH ROOMS

Bleke St SP7 8AW
☎ 01747 853717 📠 01747 853130
e-mail: info@lafleurdelys.co.uk
web: www.lafleurdelys.co.uk
dir: 0.25m off junct of A30 with A350 at Shaftesbury towards town centre

Located just a few minutes' walk from the famous Gold Hill, this light and airy restaurant with rooms combines efficient service in a relaxed and friendly atmosphere. Bedrooms, which are suitable for both business and

leisure guests, vary in size but all are well equipped, comfortable and tastefully furnished. A relaxing guest lounge and courtyard are available for afternoon tea or pre-dinner drinks.

Rooms 7 en suite (2 fmly) (1 GF) S £75-£90; D £100-£155* **Facilities** FTV TVL tea/coffee Dinner available Direct Dial Cen ht Wi-fi **Conf** Max 12 Board 10 **Parking** 10 **Notes** LB ⊗ Closed 3rd wk Jan No coaches

Avalon Townhouse

★★★★ BED AND BREAKFAST

South St DT9 3LZ
☎ 01935 814748
e-mail: enquiries@avalontownhouse.co.uk
web: www.avalontownhouse.co.uk
dir: A30 from Shaftesbury, towards Sherborne town centre, left onto South St

Avalon is a spacious and comfortable Edwardian townhouse in the heart of historic Sherborne. The building was recently refurbished to a high standard, and the husband and wife team provide a warm welcome and fine, freshly prepared food using local produce.

Rooms 3 en suite S £70-£80; D £80-£90* **Facilities** FTV TVL tea/coffee Cen ht Wi-fi **Notes** ⊗ No Children 18yrs

Thorn Bank

★★★★ BED AND BREAKFAST

Long St DT9 3BS
☎ 01935 813795
e-mail: savileplatt@hotmail.com
dir: A30 onto North Rd, then St Swithin's Rd. Right onto Long St, 75yds on right

Located just a short walk from the centre of town and the Abbey, this elegantly appointed Grade II listed Georgian townhouse is a perfect base from which to explore this delightful area. Attentive service is a hallmark here with every effort made to ensure an enjoyable and relaxing stay. The spacious bedrooms provide impressive quality and comfort with lovely views over the garden. Breakfast makes use of local Dorset produce and in summer months guests are welcome to eat al fresco on the lovely patio.

Rooms 2 en suite 1 annexe en suite S £50-£65; D £70-£95* **Facilities** FTV tea/coffee Cen ht 🍴 **Parking** 3 **Notes** LB ⊗ No Children 18yrs

SHERBORNE *continued*

The Alders

★★★★ BED AND BREAKFAST

Sandford Orcas DT9 4SB
☎ 01963 220666 📄 01963 220666
e-mail: jonsue@btinternet.com
web: www.thealdersbb.com
dir: *3m N of Sherborne. Off B3148 signed Sandford Orcas, near Manor House in village*

Located in the charming conservation area of Sandford Orcas and set in a lovely walled garden, this delightful property offers attractive, well-equipped bedrooms. A huge inglenook with a wood-burning fire can be found in the comfortable sitting room, which also features the owner's watercolours.

Rooms 3 en suite (1 fmly); D £50-£68 **Facilities** TVL tea/coffee Cen ht Wi-fi **Parking** 4 **Notes** ⊗ ⊜

Stowell Farm (ST686223)

★★★★ FARMHOUSE

Stowell DT9 4PE
☎ 01963 370200 Mrs E Kingman
e-mail: stowellfarm@btconnect.com
dir: *5m NE of Sherborne. Off A357 to Stowell, farm next to church*

This 15th-century property on a working dairy farm is situated in rolling countryside five miles from Sherborne and handy for the main roads. Guests receive a friendly welcome and can look forward to a peaceful stay. Bedrooms are attractively decorated and have comfortable beds and good views. The spacious bathrooms are equipped with both showers and baths.

Rooms 2 rms (2 pri facs) S £40-£50; D £60-£62* **Facilities** TVL tea/coffee Riding **Parking** 5 **Notes** ⊗ Closed Dec-Jan ⊜ 220 acres dairy/beef

Longbar Farm

★★★ BED AND BREAKFAST

Level Ln, Charlton Horethorne DT9 4NN
☎ 01963 220266
e-mail: enquiries@longbarfarm.co.uk
dir: *Take B3145 from A30 or A303 to Charlton Horethorne. Turn opp church onto Cowpath Ln, then 2nd right onto Level Ln*

This peacefully located establishment is located midway between Wincanton and Sherborne in the heart of an engaging village. Tea and cake are always on offer for guests, typifying the warm and genuine approach of the owners. Bedrooms provide good levels of comfort with all the expected necessities. Breakfast is a tasty and substantial start to the day, served in the comfort of the dining room which adjoins the spacious guest lounge. The local pub is just a short stroll away or alternatively, a number of other pubs and restaurants are within easy reach.

Rooms 2 en suite (1 fmly) S £30-£35; D £52-£55* **Facilities** FTV TVL tea/coffee Cen ht Wi-fi **Parking** 5 **Notes** ⊗ Closed 24-30 Dec ⊜

Venn (ST684183)

★★★ FARMHOUSE

Milborne Port DT9 5RA
☎ 01963 250598 📄 01963 250598 Mrs Pauline Tizzard
e-mail: info@colintizzard.co.uk
dir: *3m E of Sherborne on A30 on edge of Milborne Port*

Expect a friendly welcome at this farmhouse, set in a good location for exploring west Dorset, which specialises in training National Hunt racehorses. The individually furnished bedrooms are comfortable and bathrooms are fitted with power showers. Downstairs a farmhouse breakfast is served in the lounge-dining room.

Rooms 3 en suite S fr £30; D fr £52* **Facilities** TVL tea/coffee Cen ht Fishing **Parking** 6 **Notes** Closed Xmas ⊜ 375 acres dairy/mixed/race horses

STURMINSTER NEWTON	Map 4 ST71

PREMIER COLLECTION

The Crown Inn

★★★★★ 🛏🍴 INN

Marnhull DT10 1LN
☎ 01258 820224 📄 01258 821272
e-mail: info@thecrownatmarnhull.co.uk
dir: *3m N of Sturminster Newton. On B3092 in Marnhull*

Dating back to the 16th century, this inn has strong connections with Thomas Hardy and was even featured in *Tess of the D'Urbervilles* where it was known as The Pure Drop Inn. Bedrooms provide sumptuous levels of comfort and quality, with a host of additional facilities such as Egyptian cotton bed linen, CD players and mini-bars. Bathrooms are equally impressive, complete with free standing baths, quality toiletries, bath robes and fluffy towels. Roaring logs fires, beams and original features contribute to an atmosphere in which to enjoy a showcase of local produce at both dinner and breakfast.

Rooms 5 en suite (2 fmly) (1 GF) **Facilities** FTV tea/coffee Dinner available Direct Dial Cen ht Wi-fi **Conf** Max 14 **Parking** 40 **Notes** No coaches

Skylands

★★★★ BED AND BREAKFAST

Lower Rd, Stalbridge DT10 2SW
☎ 01963 362392
e-mail: alison@skylands.co.uk
dir: *A357 in village, onto Lower Rd signed Marnhill/village hall. After 0.75m Skylands sign, drive on left before x-rds*

Located on the edge of the Blackmore Vale, this 17th-century farmhouse provides well-presented accommodation. The two bedrooms have private facilities. Guests can bring their own horses, and there is a British Horse Society instructor on site.

Rooms 2 rms (2 pri facs) **Facilities** TVL tea/coffee Cen ht Wi-fi Fishing Stables **Parking** 20 **Notes** ⊗ No Children 12yrs ⊜

Stourcastle Lodge

★★★★ GUEST HOUSE

Goughs Close DT10 1BU
☎ 01258 472320
e-mail: enquiries@stourcastle-lodge.co.uk
dir: *Off town square opp cross*

Tucked away off the market square, this charming 18th-century house is set in delightful gardens and offers warm hospitality. Bedrooms are spacious, well presented and comfortably appointed. A lounge, complete with crackling log fire, is also available. Satisfying, Aga-cooked meals are served at dinner and breakfast in the attractive dining room.

Rooms 5 en suite S £53-£60; D £88-£102 **Facilities** FTV tea/coffee Dinner available Direct Dial Cen ht Wi-fi **Parking** 8 **Notes** LB ⊗ No Children 18yrs

SWANAGE	Map 5 SZ07

Swanage Haven

★★★★ GUEST HOUSE

3 Victoria Rd BH19 1LY
☎ 01929 423088 📄 01929 421912
e-mail: info@swanagehaven.com
web: www.swanagehaven.com

A boutique style guest house close to Swanage Beach and coastal path. Exclusively for adults, the accommodation is modern and contemporary with many extras such as fluffy robes, slippers, Wi-fi and a hot tub. Hands-on owners provide excellent hospitality with relaxed and friendly service. Breakfasts are superb; top quality organic and local produce feature on the extensive menu.

Rooms 8 en suite S £40-£45; D £60-£70* **Facilities** FTV TVL tea/coffee Cen ht Licensed Hot tub **Parking** 8 **Notes** LB ⊗ No Children

Railway Cottage
★★★ GUEST ACCOMMODATION

26 Victoria Av BH19 1AP
☎ 01929 425542
e-mail: enquiries@railway-cottage.co.uk

This friendly and relaxed family home provides a warm welcome for guests visiting Swanage. Less than 5 minutes' walk from the beach and the famous Swanage steam railway; guests can be assured of a comfortable stay and a good breakfast. A ground floor room is available.

Rooms 6 en suite (1 fmly) (1 GF) **Facilities** tea/coffee Dinner available Cen ht **Parking** 5 **Notes**

SYDLING ST NICHOLAS   Map 4 SY69

Greyhound Inn
★★★★ INN

26 High St DT2 9PD
☎ 01300 341303
e-mail: info@thegreyhounddorset.co.uk
dir: Off A37 into village centre

Situated in this traditional English village complete with stream, this inn is well located for exploring Hardy Country. The stylish, well-equipped rooms include three at ground-floor level. Flagstone floors and attractive, relaxed surroundings make this inn a popular place for dining. An interesting and wide range of meals is offered in either the restaurant, bar or conservatory.

Rooms 6 en suite (3 fmly) (3 GF) **Facilities** tea/coffee Dinner available Cen ht Wi-fi **Parking** 30 **Notes** Closed Sun eve

---

TARRANT MONKTON   Map 4 ST90

The Langton Arms
★★★★ ⊛ INN

DT11 8RX
☎ 01258 830225   🖷 01258 830053
e-mail: info@thelangtonarms.co.uk
dir: Off A354 in Tarrant Hinton to Tarrant Monkton, through ford, Langton Arms opp

Tucked away in this sleepy Dorset village, the Langton Arms offers stylish, light and airy accommodation and is a good base for touring this attractive area. Bedrooms, all situated at ground level in the modern annexe, are very well equipped and comfortable. There is a choice of dining options, the relaxed bar-restaurant or the more formal Stables restaurant (open Wednesday to Saturday evenings and Sunday lunch), offering innovative and appetising dishes. Breakfast is served in the conservatory dining room just a few steps through the pretty courtyard.

Rooms 6 annexe en suite (6 fmly) (6 GF) S £70; D £90* **Facilities** tea/coffee Dinner available Direct Dial Cen ht **Conf** Max 70 Thtr 70 Class 70 Board 70 **Parking** 100 **Notes** Civ Wed 60

VERWOOD   Map 5 SU00

Farleigh
★★★★ BED AND BREAKFAST

38 Dewlands Rd BH31 6PN
☎ 01202 826424   🖷 01202 826424
e-mail: jeanettehamp@waitrose.com
dir: A31 onto B3081, 3m from A31 into Verwood, pass fire station, over rdbt, 1st left

There is a warm welcome at this dormer bungalow in the peaceful village; the New Forest, Bournemouth and the coast are all within easy reach. The attractive bedrooms are thoughtfully equipped and have stylish modern en suites, and a hearty breakfast is served in the smart dining room.

Rooms 2 en suite S £30-£43; D £45-£63* **Facilities** tea/coffee Cen ht **Parking** 3 **Notes** LB ⊗ ⊜

WAREHAM   Map 4 SY98

PREMIER COLLECTION

Kemps Country House
★★★★★ ⊛ GUEST ACCOMMODATION

East Stoke BH20 6AL
☎ 0845 8620315   🖷 0845 8620316
e-mail: info@kempscountryhouse.co.uk
web: www.kempshotel.com
dir: Follow A352 W from Wareham, 3m on right in village of East Stoke

Located within easy reach of the Dorset coastline, this former rectory provides a calming, friendly atmosphere and is the perfect base for touring the area. The refurbished bedrooms are spacious and well appointed, and benefit from plenty of modern extras; super king-size beds, flat screen TV and power showers. Breakfast and dinner are served in the elegant dining room and offer an imaginative choice of modern British cuisine.

Rooms 4 en suite 12 annexe en suite (2 fmly) (6 GF) **Facilities** FTV tea/coffee Dinner available Direct Dial Cen ht Licensed Wi-fi **Parking** 24 **Notes** LB ⊗

Purbeck Vineyard
★★★★ 🏠 ⊜ GUEST ACCOMMODATION

Valley Rd, Harmans Cross BH20 5HU
☎ 01929 481525   & 07780 614050
e-mail: theresa@vineyard.uk.com
dir: On A351 in Harmans Cross, on right

This unique establishment situated on a working vineyard benefits from several bedrooms which overlook the stunning countryside and is only a few minutes' drive from the equally scenic south coast. Accommodation is comfortable and furnished to a very high standard; bathrooms have powerful showers with generously sized fluffy towels. Enjoy a freshly prepared dinner made using a number of locally sourced ingredients and try a glass of the delicious house wine from the vineyard. Breakfast is heartily substantial, creating a fabulous start to the day.

Rooms 6 en suite (1 fmly) (1 GF) S £85; D £99* **Facilities** FTV tea/coffee Dinner available Direct Dial Cen ht Licensed Wi-fi **Conf** Max 24 Thtr 12 Class 12 Board 12 **Parking** 8 **Notes** LB ⊗

WAREHAM *continued*

Hyde Cottage Bed & Breakfast

★★★★ BED AND BREAKFAST

Furzebrook Rd, Stoborough BH20 5AX
☎ 01929 553344
e-mail: hydecottbb@yahoo.co.uk
dir: *2m S of Wareham. Off A351 rdbt for Furzebrook/Blue Pool, premises on right*

Easy to find, on the Corfe Castle side of Wareham, this friendly guest house has a great location. Bedrooms are all large, with lounge seating, and some are suitable for families. All are well equipped with extras such as fridges. Meals are served *en famille* in the dining area downstairs.

Rooms 3 en suite (2 fmly) (1 GF) S £30-£35; D £56-£64*
Facilities FTV tea/coffee Dinner available Cen ht
Parking 4 **Notes** LB ⊗ Closed 24-27 Dec ⊗

The Old Granary (SY886858)

★★★★ FARMHOUSE

West Holme Farm BH20 6AQ
☎ 01929 552972   Mrs Venn Goldsack
e-mail: venngoldsack@lineone.net
web: www.theoldgranarybandb.co.uk
dir: *A352 from Wareham onto B3090, turn into Holme Nurseries, house on right*

A friendly, well run bed and breakfast with an experienced host, this is a former granary to the working farm, architect-designed with high ceilings and lots of light. Rooms are comfortable and well maintained and the hearty breakfast is a great start to the day.

Rooms 2 en suite (1 GF) **Facilities** tea/coffee Cen ht
Parking 2 **Notes** ⊗ No Children 16yrs Closed 19 Dec-3 Jan 50 acres horticultural

Luckford Wood House

★★★ GUEST ACCOMMODATION

East Stoke BH20 6AW
☎ 01929 463098   & 07888 719002
e-mail: luckfordleisure@hotmail.co.uk
web: www.luckfordleisure.co.uk
dir: *3m W of Wareham. Off A352, take B3070 to Lulworth, turn right onto Holme Ln. 1m right onto Church Ln*

Rurally situated about three miles west of Wareham, this family home offers comfortable accommodation. Situated on the edge of woodland, there is abundant wildlife to

see. Guests can be assured of a friendly welcome and an extensive choice at breakfast.

Rooms 6 rms (3 en suite) (1 pri facs) (3 fmly) (1 GF)
S £30-£55; D £50-£75* **Facilities** FTV TVL tea/coffee
Cen ht Wi-fi **Parking** 6 **Notes** LB

WEYMOUTH	Map 4 SY67

See also Portland

The Pebbles

★★★★ GUEST ACCOMMODATION

18 Kirtleton Av DT4 7PT
☎ 01305 784331   📄 01305 784335
e-mail: info@thepebbles.co.uk
web: www.thepebbles.co.uk
dir: *On A354, take 2nd exit at Manor rdbt onto Dorchester Rd South. After 1m, turn right at brown sign onto Carlton Rd North, then 1st left*

Situated in a quiet residential avenue and just a short walk from the seafront, this Victorian establishment is an excellent base for all the local attractions. A warm welcome is assured, and every effort is made to ensure an enjoyable and relaxing stay. Stylish bedrooms are smartly presented with thoughtful extras provided - a ground floor room is also available. The refurbished dining room is the venue for satisfying breakfasts featuring local Dorset produce.

Rooms 6 en suite (1 GF) S £45-£55; D £60-£95*
Facilities FTV tea/coffee Cen ht Wi-fi **Parking** 8 **Notes** LB
⊗ No Children 5yrs

Channel View

★★★★ GUEST HOUSE

10 Brunswick Ter, The Esplanade DT4 7RW
☎ 01305 782527
e-mail: leggchannelview@aol.com
dir: *Off A353 The Esplanade onto Dorchester Rd, right onto Westerall Rd, 1st left at lights to Brunswick Ter*

Just off The Esplanade, this guest house is in a superb spot close to the beach and within walking distance of the attractions. Bedrooms are on three floors and vary in size. Some have lovely views over the bay and all offer good levels of comfort and decor. Guests receive a warm welcome and breakfast is served in the well-appointed dining room.

Rooms 7 rms (6 en suite) (1 fmly) **Facilities** TVL tea/coffee Cen ht **Notes** ⊗

The Esplanade

★★★★ GUEST ACCOMMODATION

141 The Esplanade DT4 7NJ
☎ 01305 783129   📄 01305 783129
e-mail: stay@theesplanadehotel.co.uk
web: www.theesplanadehotel.co.uk
dir: *On seafront, between Jubilee Clock & pier bandstand*

Dating from 1835, this attractive Georgian property has public rooms, including a first-floor lounge, that all enjoy splendid sea views. A warm welcome is assured from the friendly owners. Bedrooms, some with sea views, are well furnished and nicely decorated and include many thoughtful extras.

Rooms 11 en suite (2 fmly) (2 GF) S £45-£60;
D £70-£110 **Facilities** FTV TVL tea/coffee Cen ht Licensed
Wi-fi **Parking** 9 **Notes** LB ⊗ Closed Nov-Feb

The Heritage Restaurant with Rooms

★★★★ 🍴 RESTAURANT WITH ROOMS

8 East St, Chickerell DT3 4DS
☎ 01305 783093   📄 01305 786668
e-mail: mail@the-heritage.co.uk
dir: *In village centre*

Located just three miles from Weymouth and less than a mile from the spectacular Chesil Beach, this building dates back to 1769. Attentive service and a friendly, caring approach are hallmarks here, with every effort made to ensure a relaxing stay. Excellent Dorset produce is featured on the menus that are offered in the elegant restaurant. After dinner, the comfortable bedrooms await, each individually styled and well appointed.

Rooms 6 en suite (1 fmly) S fr £65; D fr £96*
Facilities tea/coffee Dinner available Direct Dial Cen ht
Wi-fi **Conf** Max 14 Board 14 **Parking** 10 **Notes** LB No coaches

Letchworth Guest House

★★★★ GUEST HOUSE

5 Waterloo Place, The Esplanade DT4 7NY
☎ 01305 786663 📠 01305 759203
e-mail: letchworth.hotel@virgin.net
web: www.letchworthweymouth.co.uk
dir: *Off A31 at Bere Regis to Weymouth, signs to seafront & The Esplanade*

Expect a warm welcome at this well-maintained, licensed guest house on the seafront. The bedrooms are brightly decorated and thoughtfully equipped with many useful extras, and there is also a cosy lounge.

Rooms 6 rms (4 en suite) (2 fmly) S £30-£35;
D £60-£70* **Facilities** FTV TVL tea/coffee Licensed
Parking 6 **Notes** LB ⊗ No Children 5yrs

St John's Guest House

★★★★ GUEST ACCOMMODATION

7 Dorchester Rd DT4 7JR
☎ 01305 775523
e-mail: stjohnsguesthouse@googlemail.com
dir: *Opp St John's Church, 60yds from beach*

Located just 70 yards from the beach, this elegant Victorian property was built around 1880. Hospitality here is warm and genuine; and the refurbishment, which has resulted in an appealing, uncluttered style, means that standards are high throughout. Bedrooms are all well equipped with such extras as DVD players, Wi-fi access and comfy beds. Breakfast is served in the light and airy dining room with a lounge area also available for guests.

Rooms 7 en suite (2 fmly) (3 GF) S £28-£34.50;
D £56-£69* **Facilities** FTV tea/coffee Cen ht Wi-fi
Parking 10 **Notes** LB ⊗ No Children 4yrs

The Seaham

★★★★ GUEST HOUSE

3 Waterloo Place DT4 7NU
☎ 01305 782010
e-mail: seanhourigan2001@yahoo.co.uk
dir: *500yds N of town centre off A353 The Esplanade*

This well-presented establishment stands on the seafront close to the town centre. It is a good base for exploring the area, and offers attractive bedrooms with many useful extras. Generous breakfasts are served in the well-appointed dining room, which has an adjoining lounge.

Rooms 5 en suite **Facilities** TVL tea/coffee **Notes** ⊗ No Children Closed Jan 🚭

Wenlock House

★★★★ GUEST ACCOMMODATION

107 The Esplanade DT4 7EE
☎ 01305 786674
e-mail: stay@wenlockweymouth.co.uk
dir: *On A353 (The Esplanade) King St junct*

Wenlock House offers a good standard of accommodation and a friendly atmosphere on the seafront, just a short walk from the station and town centre. The hosts are very attentive and always happy to help. The attractive bedrooms are well equipped and many have excellent views.

Rooms 11 rms (8 en suite) (3 fmly) S £40; D £80*
Facilities FTV tea/coffee Cen ht Wi-fi **Parking** 10
Notes LB ⊗ No Children 5yrs Closed 30 Nov-Dec

The Alendale Guest House

★★★ GUEST HOUSE

4 Waterloo Place DT4 7NX
☎ 01305 788817
e-mail: bowie538@aol.com
dir: *Turn left at clock tower, through 2nd set of lights, Alendale 20mtrs on left*

This friendly property is located just 50 yards from the beach, and provides a warm, homely environment with easy access to the town centre and ferry terminals. Bedrooms are light and airy with an uncluttered contemporary style and come equipped with useful extras. The attractive dining room is the venue for excellent local Dorset produce which is utilised in the imaginative and extensive breakfast menu, including both full English and Scottish options. Ample off-road parking is also a bonus here.

Rooms 5 en suite (3 fmly) S £34-£44; D £60-£68*
Facilities FTV TVL tea/coffee Cen ht Wi-fi **Parking** 6
Notes LB ⊗

Kimberley Guest House

★★★ GUEST HOUSE

16 Kirtleton Av DT4 7PT
☎ 01305 783333 📠 01305 839603
e-mail: kenneth.jones@btconnect.com
dir: *Off A384 Weymouth road right onto Carlton Rd North, opp Rembrandt Hotel, Kirtleton Av on left*

This friendly guest house is in a quiet residential area near the seafront. Bedrooms are well presented, and in addition to a hearty breakfast, traditional home-cooked meals using fresh local and seasonal produce are served by arrangement.

Rooms 11 rms (7 en suite) (2 fmly) (1 GF) S £21-£23;
D £43-£50* **Facilities** tea/coffee Dinner available Cen ht
Parking 8 **Notes** LB ⊗ Closed 1-29 Dec 🚭

Bedford House

★★★ GUEST ACCOMMODATION

17 The Esplanade DT4 8DT
☎ 01305 786995 📠 01305 786995
dir: *Along The Esplanade W towards harbour, turn right around amusement gardens (one-way), Bedford House on left*

Known locally as the Bear House, because of the ever-growing collection of bears of every shape and description, Bedford House offers comfortable accommodation. Guests are assured of a friendly welcome and a relaxed atmosphere. Bedrooms are stylishly decorated. The front-facing rooms are popular for their views over the bay, while rear-facing rooms look to the harbour.

Rooms 9 en suite (3 fmly) S £32-£38; D £54-£68*
Facilities TVL tea/coffee Cen ht Licensed Wi-fi **Notes** LB
⊗ Closed mid Nov-mid Feb 🚭

WEYMOUTH *continued*

Molyneux Guest House

★★★ GUEST HOUSE

9 Waterloo Place, The Esplanade DT4 7PD
☎ 01305 774623 & 07947 883235
e-mail: stay@molyneuxguesthouse.co.uk
web: www.molyneuxguesthouse.co.uk
dir: *A354 to Weymouth seafront, onto The Esplanade, The Molyneux on right*

Located close to the seafront and beautiful beaches of Weymouth, this guest house offers a genuine warm welcome. Bedrooms are brightly decorated and comfortable and there is also a lounge. Breakfast is enjoyed in the smart dining room. Off-road parking to the rear is a bonus.

Rooms 6 rms (5 en suite) (1 pri facs) (2 fmly) (1 GF) S £25-£40; D £45-£68* **Facilities** FTV TVL tea/coffee Cen ht Licensed **Parking** 6 **Notes** LB ⊗

Tara

★★★ GUEST HOUSE

10 Market St DT4 8DD
☎ 01305 766235
dir: *From Alexandra Gardens on The Esplanade right onto Belle Vue, right & left onto Market St*

Neatly presented, this welcoming establishment is set just back from the seafront at the harbour end of town. Strictly non-smoking, the guest house provides a relaxed and friendly atmosphere. Bedrooms offer good levels of comfort. Home-cooked evening meals are served every day except Sundays.

Rooms 6 en suite (1 fmly) S £25-£30; D £50-£60* **Facilities** tea/coffee Dinner available Cen ht **Notes** LB ⊗ No Children 14yrs ☺

The Trelawney

★★★ GUEST ACCOMMODATION

1 Old Castle Rd DT4 8QB
☎ 01305 783188 📄 01305 783181
e-mail: trelawney-hotel@freeuk.com
dir: *From Harbourside follow Portland signs, Trelawney 700yds on left*

This charming Victorian house stands amid attractive gardens in a quiet residential area a short walk from the town centre and beach. The friendly proprietors provide a comfortable environment, and many guests return regularly. Generous English breakfasts are offered in the light and airy dining room, and a comfortable lounge is available.

Rooms 8 en suite (3 fmly) S £45-£60; D £72-£80 **Facilities** TVL tea/coffee Cen ht Licensed ♨ **Parking** 13 **Notes** LB ⊗ No Children 5yrs Closed Oct-Apr

Wadham Guesthouse

★★★ GUEST ACCOMMODATION

22 East St DT4 8BN
☎ 01305 779640
dir: *Off S end of A353 The Esplanade*

The pleasant guest house offers a range of rooms in the town centre, and is a good base for touring or for a short stay. The comfortable bedrooms are attractively decorated, and home-cooked breakfasts are served in the ground-floor dining room. Parking permits available.

Rooms 9 en suite (3 fmly) (1 GF) S £26-£30; D £52-£60 **Facilities** TVL tea/coffee Cen ht **Notes** LB ⊗ No Children 4yrs Closed Xmas ☺

Field Barn House

★★ GUEST ACCOMMODATION

44 Fieldbarn Dr, Southill DT4 0EE
☎ 01305 779140 & 07955 180934
dir: *1m NW of town centre. Off A354 Weymouth Way rdbt onto Fieldbarn Dr (Southill), 300yds on right*

Located on a residential estate on the outskirts of the town, yet only a short drive from the sandy beaches and town centre, this modern home is family run and provides guests with comfortable accommodation. A full English breakfast is taken at a communal table overlooking the well-tended rear garden.

Rooms 3 rms (1 fmly) S £22-£26; D £44-£52* **Facilities** FTV tea/coffee Cen ht **Parking** 4 **Notes** LB ⊗ No Children 3yrs Closed 15-31 Dec ☺

WIMBORNE MINSTER   Map 5 SZ09

PREMIER COLLECTION

Les Bouviers Restaurant with Rooms

★★★★★ ⊛⊛ RESTAURANT WITH ROOMS

Arrowsmith Rd, Canford Magna BH21 3BD
☎ 01202 889555 📄 01202 639428
e-mail: info@lesbouviers.co.uk
web: www.lesbouviers.co.uk
dir: *A31 onto A349. In 0.6m turn left. In approx 1m right onto Arrowsmith Rd. Establishment approx 100yds on right*

An excellent restaurant with rooms in a great location, set in six acres of grounds. Food is a highlight of any stay here as is the friendly, attentive service. The beautiful bedrooms have supremely comfortable beds and are extremely well equipped, with great bathrooms. One has a balcony and all have been carefully designed and furnished in contemporary style.

Rooms 6 en suite (4 fmly) S fr £90; D £100-£180 **Facilities** FTV tea/coffee Dinner available Direct Dial Cen ht Wi-fi All bathrooms have steam showers or air baths **Conf** Max 120 Thtr 100 Class 100 Board 100 **Parking** 50 **Notes** LB RS Sun eve restricted opening & restaurant closed Civ Wed 120

Ashton Lodge

★★★★ GUEST ACCOMMODATION

10 Oakley Hill BH21 1QH
☎ 01202 883423 📄 01202 883423
e-mail: ashtonlodge@tiscali.co.uk
web: www.ashton-lodge.co.uk
dir: *Off A31 S of Wimborne onto A349 for Poole, left next rdbt signed Wimborne/Canford Magna, house 200yds on right*

A warm welcome is assured at this delightful modern home, which provides comfortable bedrooms, stylishly furnished with attractively co-ordinated decor and fabrics. All rooms are well equipped, with many extra facilities provided. Hearty breakfasts are served in the spacious dining room, which overlooks the well-maintained garden.

Rooms 5 rms (2 en suite) (1 pri facs) (2 fmly) S £37; D £66-£68* **Facilities** FTV TVL tea/coffee Cen ht Wi-fi **Parking** 4 **Notes** LB ⊗ ☺

WINFRITH NEWBURGH — Map 4 SY88

The Red Lion

★★★ INN

DT2 8LE
☎ 01305 852814 📠 01305 851768
dir: *On A352, N of village*

Situated between Dorchester and Wareham, this traditional longhouse is surrounded by rolling countryside and is a good centre for touring the numerous attractions in the area. The character public areas offer an extensive range of dishes, and booking is essential at weekends. The comfortable bedrooms are well equipped.

Rooms 3 en suite S £50; D £70-£80* **Facilities** tea/coffee Dinner available Cen ht **Parking** 70 **Notes** LB ⊗ No Children 12yrs No coaches

WINTERBORNE WHITECHURCH — Map 4 ST80

Shalom

★★★★ BED AND BREAKFAST

Blandford Hill DT11 0AA
☎ 01258 881299
e-mail: tranquillity@shalom2414.freeserve.co.uk
dir: *On A354 5m SW from Blandford*

A warm welcome awaits guests to Shalom, situated in a village on the edge of an Area of Outstanding Natural Beauty. The comfortable modern house has attractive bedrooms enhanced with thoughtful extras. A delicious breakfast featuring organic and local produce is enjoyed in the dining room. Walkers and cyclists are welcome (there is a garage available for bikes).

Rooms 2 en suite; D £66-£70* **Facilities** tea/coffee Cen ht **Parking** 3 **Notes** ⊗ No Children Closed Xmas & New Year 🖼

WINTERBOURNE ABBAS — Map 4 SY69

The Coach & Horses

★★★ INN

DT2 9LU
☎ 01305 889340 📠 01305 889766
e-mail: info@thecoachandhorsesdorset.co.uk
dir: *On A35 between Dorchester & Bridport*

This former coaching inn dates back to the 1800s and provides an ideal place for exploring the wonderful Dorset countryside or perhaps as a stopover on the journey further into the West Country. The welcome is warm and genuine with caring staff making every effort to ensure a relaxing and memorable stay. An extensive menu is offered, along with a popular carvery and a choice of local beers. Bedrooms offer good levels of space and comfort for a restful night's sleep.

Rooms 5 en suite S £45; D £65* **Facilities** tea/coffee Dinner available Cen ht **Parking** 45 **Notes** ⊗ Closed 24 Dec-1 Jan

CO DURHAM

BARNARD CASTLE — Map 19 NZ01

PREMIER COLLECTION

Greta House

★★★★★ 🏠 BED AND BREAKFAST

89 Galgate DL12 8ES
☎ 01833 631193 📠 01833 631193
e-mail: kathchesman@btinternet.com
dir: *400yds NE of town centre on A67*

Expect very warm hospitality at this spacious Victorian villa built in 1870. Greta House is convenient for the Bowes Museum, local antiques shops, High Force and Raby Castle, and is a truly comfortable home from home. Bedrooms come with a wealth of thoughtful extras, and memorable breakfasts are served in the elegant dining room.

Rooms 3 en suite; D £68-£70* **Facilities** FTV tea/coffee Cen ht **Notes** ⊗ No Children 5yrs 🖼

PREMIER COLLECTION

Number 34

★★★★★ GUEST ACCOMMODATION

34 The Bank DL12 8PN
☎ 01833 631304
e-mail: evasreid@aol.com
dir: *3m from A66, on left after Butter Market rdbt*

This delightful house has its share of history: the regal dining room dates back to Elizabethan times. A warm welcome is always guaranteed, and bedrooms are generally spacious, well equipped and very stylishly furnished. One room is en suite and two have private facilities. Guests can relax in the lounge or use the garden in the warmer weather. Breakfasts are a treat with homemade and local produce a feature.

Rooms 3 rms (1 en suite) (2 pri facs) S £45-£55; D £60-£85* **Facilities** tea/coffee Cen ht **Notes** LB ⊗ No Children 12yrs 🖼

Homelands

★★★★ 🏠 GUEST ACCOMMODATION

85 Galgate DL12 8ES
☎ 01833 638757
e-mail: enquiries@homelandsguesthouse.co.uk
web: www.homelandsguesthouse.co.uk
dir: *400yds NE of town centre on A67*

A warm welcome awaits you at this Victorian property, which has been renovated to provide attractive and well-equipped bedrooms. A hearty breakfast using local and home-made produce is served in the elegant dining room overlooking the garden. Light snacks are available in the stylish lounge.

Rooms 4 rms (3 en suite) (1 pri facs) 1 annexe en suite (1 GF) S £40-£48; D £65-£70 **Facilities** tea/coffee Cen ht Licensed **Notes** ⊗ No Children 5yrs Closed 23 Dec-2 Jan

Wilson House (NZ081124)

★★★★ 🏠 FARMHOUSE

Barningham DL11 7EB
☎ 01833 621218 Mrs H Lowes
e-mail: helowes@tiscali.co.uk
dir: *5m SE of Barnard Castle. S off A66 at Greta Bridge to Barningham, 2nd farm on right*

The attractive farmhouse, set in 475 acres among superb Pennine scenery, is an ideal retreat for a relaxing break. You can expect good home cooking, flexible bedrooms, and guests can wander around the farm and enjoy the spectacular views.

Rooms 4 rms (2 en suite) (2 GF) S £28-£40; D £56-£70* **Facilities** tea/coffee Dinner available Cen ht **Parking** 5 **Notes** LB ⊗ No Children 5yrs Closed 30 Nov-1 Mar 🖼 475 acres mixed/livestock

COWSHILL — Map 18 NY84

Low Cornriggs Farm (NY845413)

★★★★ 🏠 🍴 FARMHOUSE

Cowshill-in-Weardale DL13 1AQ
☎ **01388 537600 & 07818 843159   Mrs J Elliott**
e-mail: cornriggsfarm@btconnect.com
web: www.britnett.net/lowcornriggsfarm
dir: *0.6m NW of Cowshill on A689*

Situated in the heart of Weardale yet also close to Cumbria, this delightful farmhouse has stunning views. Original stone and stripped pine are combined to provide a house with real character. Excellent home-cooked dinners are offered along with charming hospitality. Bedrooms are attractive and thoughtfully equipped with many homely extras. There is a riding stable available on the farm.

Rooms 3 en suite 2 annexe en suite (1 fmly) (2 GF) S £38-£40; D £58-£60 **Facilities** TVL tea/coffee Dinner available Cen ht **Parking** 6 **Notes** LB ⊗ No Children 8yrs 42 acres beef

DARLINGTON

See Aldbrough St John (Yorkshire, North)

DURHAM — Map 19 NZ24

The Old Mill

★★★★ INN

Thinford Rd, Metal Bridge DH6 5NX
☎ **01740 652928** 📠 **01740 657230**
e-mail: office@theoldmill.uk.com
web: www.theoldmill.uk.com
dir: *5m S of Durham. A1(M) junct 61, onto A688 S for 1.5m, left at rdbt & sharp right*

This traditional, family-owned inn offers a friendly welcome. The stylish bedrooms are very well equipped, and the bar offers a comprehensive list of wines and beer, and a very good selection of meals.

Rooms 8 en suite **Facilities** STV tea/coffee Dinner available Direct Dial Cen ht Jacuzzi/Spa **Conf** Max 40 Thtr 40 Class 40 Board 25 **Parking** 40 **Notes** ⊗ Closed 26 Dec RS 25 Dec

The Bay Horse

Ⓤ

Brandon Village DH7 8ST
☎ **0191 378 0498**

Currently the rating for this establishment is not confirmed. This may be due to a change of ownership or because it has only recently joined the AA rating scheme.

Rooms 10 en suite (1 fmly) S £40-£50; D £50-£80* **Facilities** TVL Dinner available Cen ht Licensed **Parking** 20

HASWELL PLOUGH — Map 19 NZ34

The Gables

★★★ Ⓐ GUEST ACCOMMODATION

Front St DH6 2EW
☎ **0191 526 2982** 📠 **0191 526 2982**
e-mail: jmgables@aol.com
web: www.thegables.co.uk
dir: *On B1283 in village centre*

Rooms 5 en suite (1 fmly) S £48-£56; D £64-£72* **Facilities** STV FTV TVL tea/coffee Dinner available Cen ht Licensed Wi-fi **Parking** 30

MIDDLETON-IN-TEESDALE — Map 18 NY92

Brunswick House

★★★★ Ⓐ GUEST HOUSE

55 Market Place DL12 0QH
☎ **01833 640393**
e-mail: enquiries@brunswickhouse.net
dir: *In town centre on B6277 opp St Mary's Church*

Rooms 5 en suite S £40; D £60-£65* **Facilities** tea/coffee Dinner available Cen ht Licensed **Parking** 5 **Notes** LB ⊗

STANLEY — Map 19 NZ15

Bush Blades Farm (NZ168533)

★★★ FARMHOUSE

Harperley DH9 9UA
☎ **01207 232722   Mrs P Gibson**
e-mail: bushbladesfarm@hotmail.com
dir: *2m W of Stanley. A693 W from Stanley for Consett, 0.5m right to Harperley, farm 0.5m on right up hill from x-rds*

A warm welcome awaits you at this traditional farmhouse. Set in a peaceful location conveniently placed for visiting Beamish and Durham, Bush Blades offers a friendly and relaxed atmosphere, and spacious, traditionally furnished bedrooms, one on the ground floor.

Rooms 2 en suite (1 GF) (2 smoking) **Facilities** TVL tea/coffee Cen ht **Parking** 4 **Notes** ⊗ No Children 12yrs Closed 20 Dec-2 Jan 🐑 50 acres sheep

STOCKTON-ON-TEES — Map 19 NZ41

The Parkwood Inn

★★★ INN

64-66 Darlington Rd, Hartburn TS18 5ER
☎ **01642 587933**
e-mail: theparkwoodhotel@aol.com
web: www.theparkwoodhotel.com
dir: *1.5m SW of town centre. A66 onto A137 signed Yarm & Stockton West, left at lights onto A1027, left onto Darlington Rd*

Expect a friendly welcome at this family-run establishment. The well-equipped en suite bedrooms come with many homely extras and a range of professionally prepared meals are served in the cosy bar lounge, conservatory, or the attractive dining room.

Rooms 6 en suite S £45; D £59* **Facilities** tea/coffee Dinner available Cen ht **Parking** 36 **Notes** No coaches

ESSEX

CHIPPING ONGAR — Map 6 TL50

PREMIER COLLECTION

Diggins Farm *(TL582082)*
★★★★★ FARMHOUSE

Fyfield CM5 0PP
☎ 01277 899303 📄 01277 899015 **Mrs M Frost**
dir: *B184 N from Fyfield, right after Black Bull pub, farm 0.75m on left*

This delightful Grade II listed 16th-century farmhouse is set amid open farmland in the Roding Valley, and is only a short drive from Stansted Airport. The spacious bedrooms are attractively decorated, carefully furnished and well equipped. Margaret Frost was the AA Friendliest Landlady of the Year 2008-2009.

Rooms 2 rms (1 en suite) (1 pri facs) S £35; D £70*
Facilities tea/coffee Cen ht **Parking** 20 **Notes** ⊗ No Children 12yrs Closed 15 Dec-3 Jan 🐾 440 acres arable

CLACTON-ON-SEA — Map 7 TM11

The Chudleigh
★★★★ GUEST ACCOMMODATION

13 Agate Rd, Marine Parade West CO15 1RA
☎ 01255 425407 📄 01255 470280
e-mail: chudleighhotel@btconnect.com
dir: *With sea on left, cross lights at pier, turn onto Agate Rd*

Conveniently situated for the seafront and shops, this immaculate property has been run by the friendly owners Peter and Carol Oleggini for the last 30 years. Bedrooms are most attractive with co-ordinating décor and well chosen fabrics. Breakfast is served in the smart dining room and there is a cosy lounge with comfortable seating.

Rooms 10 en suite (2 fmly) (2 GF) S £48-£50; D £75-£78
Facilities TVL tea/coffee Direct Dial Cen ht Licensed **Parking** 7 **Notes** No Children 1yr RS Oct-Mar Closed for 2 wks, some wknds B&B only

The Sandrock
★★★★ GUEST ACCOMMODATION

1 Penfold Rd, Marine Parade West CO15 1JN
☎ 01255 428215
e-mail: thesandrock@btinternet.com
web: www.thesandrock.co.uk
dir: *A133 to seafront, turn right, pass lights at pier, then take 2nd right*

A warm welcome is offered at this Victorian property, just off the seafront and within easy walking distance of the town centre. The attractive bedrooms vary in size and style, are thoughtfully equipped, and some have sea

views. Breakfast is served in the smart bar-restaurant and there is also a cosy lounge.

Rooms 9 en suite (1 fmly) (1 GF) S £40-£43; D £60-£63*
Facilities TVL tea/coffee Cen ht Wi-fi **Parking** 5 **Notes** LB

The Beeches Guest Accommodation
★★★ GUEST ACCOMMODATION

12/14 Ellis Rd CO15 1ER
☎ 01255 421713 & 07947 259048 📄 01255 421713
e-mail: info@thebeechesclacton.co.uk
web: www.thebeechesclacton.co.uk

The Beeches is ideally located for an easy reach of the beach, pier and shopping area. The husband and wife team welcome you to their home, where the service is attentive, hospitality genuine and rooms nicely decorated and comfortable. The attractive dining room provides the perfect venue for a hearty breakfast

Rooms 13 rms (10 en suite) (4 fmly) (4 GF) **Facilities** tea/coffee **Parking** 7

COLCHESTER — Map 13 TL92

See also Nayland (Suffolk)

Fridaywood Farm *(TL985213)*
★★★★ FARMHOUSE

Bounstead Rd CO2 0DF
☎ 01206 573595 📄 01206 547011 **Mrs J Lochore**
e-mail: lochorem8@aol.com
dir: *3m S of Colchester, from A12 follow signs for zoo to Mersea, cross B1026. At Maypole pub, right for Bounstead Rd*

A traditional farmhouse surrounded by wooded countryside. Bedrooms are generally quite spacious, and each one is carefully decorated, furnished with well-chosen pieces, and equipped with many thoughtful touches. Public rooms include an elegant dining room where breakfast is served at a large communal table, and a cosy sitting room.

Rooms 2 en suite S £45-£60; D £65-£80 **Facilities** tea/coffee Cen ht Wi-fi 🐾 **Parking** 6 **Notes** ⊗ No Children 12yrs 🐾 500 acres sheep/arable

Old Manse
★★★★ GUEST ACCOMMODATION

15 Roman Rd CO1 1UR
☎ 01206 545154 📄 01206 545153
e-mail: wendyanderson15@hotmail.com
web: www.theoldmanse.uk.com
dir: *In town centre, 250yds E of castle. Off High St-East Hill onto Roman Rd*

Expect a warm welcome from the caring host at this Victorian house, situated just a short walk from the castle and High Street. Bedrooms are carefully decorated with co-ordinated soft furnishings and equipped with many thoughtful touches. Breakfast is served seated at a large communal table in the attractive dining room and there is a comfortable lounge.

Rooms 3 rms (2 en suite) (1 pri facs) S £45-£60; D £65-£75 **Facilities** tea/coffee Cen ht Wi-fi **Parking** 1 **Notes** ⊗ No Children 8yrs Closed 23-31 Dec 🐾

DEDHAM — Map 13 TM03

The Sun Inn
★★★★ @ 🏠 INN

High St CO7 6DF
☎ 01206 323351 📄 01206 323964
e-mail: office@thesuninndedham.com
dir: *In village centre opp church*

A charming 15th-century coaching inn situated in the centre of Dedham opposite the church. The carefully decorated bedrooms have many features that include four-poster and half tester beds, along with many thoughtful touches. The open-plan public rooms have a wealth of character with inglenook fires, oak beams and fine oak panelling.

Rooms 5 en suite **Facilities** tea/coffee Dinner available Cen ht **Parking** 15 **Notes** Closed 25-28 Dec Civ Wed 100

FRINTON-ON-SEA — Map 7 TM22

Uplands
★★★ GUEST ACCOMMODATION

41 Hadleigh Rd CO13 9HQ
☎ 01255 674889 📄 01255 674889
e-mail: info@uplandsguesthouse.co.uk
web: www.uplandsguesthouse.com
dir: *B1033 into Frinton, over level crossing, Hadleigh Rd 3rd left, Uplands 250yds on left*

This large Edwardian house stands in a peaceful side road just a short walk from the shops and seafront. Bedrooms are pleasantly decorated and thoughtfully equipped with a good range of useful extras. Public rooms include a large lounge-dining room where breakfast is served at individual tables.

Rooms 5 rms (4 en suite) (1 fmly) S £25-£30; D £54-£60* **Facilities** TVL tea/coffee Dinner available Cen ht Wi-fi **Parking** 4 **Notes** LB ⊗

GREAT DUNMOW   Map 6 TL62

Homelye Farm

★★★★ GUEST ACCOMMODATION

Homelye Chase, Braintree Rd CM6 3AW
☎ 01371 872127   📠 01371 876428
e-mail: homelyebandb@btconnect.com
web: www.homelyefarm.com
dir: 1.5m E of Great Dunmow. Off B1256 at water tower

Expect a warm welcome at this working farm situated in a peaceful rural location just a short drive from the town centre. The spacious bedrooms are in converted outbuildings; each one features exposed beams, co-ordinated fabrics and attractive pine furnishings. Breakfast is taken at individual tables in the original farmhouse.

Rooms 13 annexe en suite (1 fmly) (13 GF) S £50-£55; D £65-£85* **Facilities** FTV tea/coffee Cen ht Wi-fi **Parking** 16 **Notes** ⊗ Closed 24-27 Dec

---

Puttocks Farm B&B

★★★★ 🄰 BED AND BREAKFAST

Philpot End CM6 1JQ
☎ 01371 872377   📠 01371 876566
e-mail: roger@puttocksfarm.com
dir: A120 Dunmow S junct onto B184 to Ongar & Rodings. Left after bridge over A120

Rooms 4 annexe en suite (1 fmly) (4 GF) S £35-£40; D £55-£60* **Facilities** FTV tea/coffee Cen ht Wi-fi **Parking** 10 **Notes** LB ⊗ ⊜

GREAT YELDHAM   Map 13 TL73

The White Hart

★★★★ ◉ RESTAURANT WITH ROOMS

Poole St CO9 4HJ
☎ 01787 237250   📠 01787 238044
e-mail: mjwmason@yahoo.co.uk
dir: On A1017 in village

A large timber-framed character building houses the main restaurant and bar areas whilst the bedrooms are located in the converted coach house; all are smartly appointed and well equipped with many thoughtful extras. A comfortable lounge-bar area and beautifully landscaped gardens provide areas for relaxation. Locally sourced produce is used in the main house restaurant, popular with local residents and guests alike.

Rooms 11 en suite (2 fmly) (5 GF) S £49.95; D £69.95-£120 (room only)* **Facilities** FTV tea/coffee Dinner available Direct Dial Cen ht Wi-fi **Conf** Max 200 Thtr 200 Class 200 Board 50 **Parking** 80 **Notes** LB Civ Wed 85

HATFIELD HEATH   Map 6 TL51

Lancasters Farm *(TL544149)*

★★★★ FARMHOUSE

Chelmsford Rd CM22 7BB
☎ 01279 730220   📠 01279 730220   Mrs M Hunt
dir: A1060 from Hatfield Heath for Chelmsford, 1m left on sharp right bend, through white gates

Guests are made to feel at home at this delightfully spacious house, which is the heart of this large working arable farm close to Stansted Airport. Bedrooms vary in size and style but all are smartly decorated and thoughtfully equipped. Garaging can be arranged, as can transport to and from the airport.

Rooms 4 rms (2 en suite) (2 pri facs) S fr £35; D £70-£80* **Facilities** tea/coffee Cen ht **Parking** 6 **Notes** ⊗ No Children 12yrs Closed 14 Dec-4 Jan ⊜ 260 acres arable

---

LATCHINGDON   Map 7 TL80

Crouch Valley Lodge & Blue Toad Restaurant

★★★ GUEST ACCOMMODATION

Burnham Rd CM3 6EX
☎ 01621 740770   📠 01621 743355
e-mail: info@crouchvalley.com
web: www.crouchvalley.com
dir: B1018 through village, at mini rdbt turn right, lodge 300yds on right

Situated in rural Essex, this modern establishment offers comfortable, well-equipped chalet-style accommodation, with two rooms having easier access. Breakfast is served in the adjoining restaurant, and an interesting choice of dishes is available for dinner.

Rooms 10 en suite (8 fmly) (10 GF) S £30-£60; D £50-£80 (room only) **Facilities** STV FTV tea/coffee Dinner available Cen ht Licensed Wi-fi **Parking** 50 **Notes** LB

LITTLE HALLINGBURY   Map 6 TL51

Homesdale

★★★ GUEST HOUSE

Lower Rd CM22 7QY
☎ 01279 600647   📠 01279 600647
e-mail: info@homesdale.net
web: www.homesdale.net
dir: A1060 through village, 200yds past sign to Wrights Green

Conveniently situated near Stansted Airport, this charming guest house provides ideal accommodation for a short stopover or a weekend break in the Bishop's Stortford area. The atmosphere is homely, dinner can be arranged and breakfast is served in the dining room overlooking the garden. The pool is a refreshing bonus for the warmer summer months.

Rooms 4 en suite (1 fmly) (1 GF) (1 smoking) **Facilities** STV FTV tea/coffee Dinner available Cen ht Wi-fi ⊰ **Parking** 5

MANNINGTREE   Map 13 TM13

PREMIER COLLECTION

Dairy House *(TM148293)*

★★★★★ FARMHOUSE

Bradfield Rd CO11 2SR
☎ 01255 870322   Mrs B Whitworth
e-mail: bridgetwhitworth@btinternet.com

(For full entry see Wix)

SAFFRON WALDEN   Map 12 TL53

Warner's Farm

★★★★ BED AND BREAKFAST

Top Rd, Wimbish Green CB10 2XJ
☎ 01799 599525
e-mail: info@warnersfarm.co.uk
web: www.warnersfarm.co.uk
dir: 4m SE of Saffron Walden. Off B184 to Wimbish Green

Expect a warm welcome at this delightful property set in five acres of grounds and surrounded by open countryside. The comfortable bedrooms have a wealth of character; each one has co-ordinated fabrics and many thoughtful touches. Breakfast is taken in the smart

---

dining room and guests have the use of a lounge with an open fireplace.

Rooms 4 rms (3 en suite) (1 pri facs) (2 fmly) S £35–£50; D £60–£80* **Facilities** FTV TVL tea/coffee Cen ht Wi-fi ⚲ **Parking** 15 **Notes** LB ⊗ No Children 1–10yrs Closed 22 Dec–4 Jan ⊜

See advert on this page

SOUTHEND-ON-SEA Map 7 TQ88

Ilfracombe House

★★★★ GUEST ACCOMMODATION

9–13 Wilson Rd SS1 1HG
☎ 01702 351000 📠 01702 393989
e-mail: info@ilfracombehotel.co.uk
web: www.ilfracombehotel.co.uk
dir: *500yds W of town centre. Off A13 at Cricketers pub onto Milton Rd, 3rd left onto Cambridge Rd, 4th right, car park in Alexandra Rd*

Ilfracombe House lies in Southend's conservation area, just a short walk from the cliffs, gardens and the beach. The public rooms include a dining room, lounge and a cosy bar, and the well-equipped bedrooms include deluxe options and two four-poster rooms.

Rooms 20 en suite (3 fmly) (2 GF) **Facilities** STV FTV TVL tea/coffee Dinner available Direct Dial Cen ht Licensed **Parking** 9

Terrace Guest House

★★★ GUEST ACCOMMODATION

8 Royal Ter SS1 1DY
☎ 01702 348143 📠 01702 348143
e-mail: info@terraceguesthouse.co.uk
dir: *From pier up Pier Hill onto Royal Terrace*

Set on a terrace above the Western Esplanade, this comfortable guest house has an informal atmosphere.

There is a cosy bar, and an elegant sitting room and breakfast room. The spacious, well-planned bedrooms consist of four en suite front and rear-facing rooms, and several front-facing rooms that share two bathrooms.

Rooms 9 rms (6 en suite) (2 fmly) S fr £35; D fr £55* **Facilities** TVL tea/coffee Cen ht Wi-fi **Notes** LB Closed 21 Dec–4 Jan

STANSTED AIRPORT Map 6 TL52

See also Bishop's Stortford (Hertfordshire)

The White House

★★★★ GUEST ACCOMMODATION

Smiths Green CM22 6NR
☎ 01279 870257 📠 01279 870423
e-mail: enquiries@whitehousestansted.co.uk
web: www.whitehousestansted.co.uk
dir: *M11 junct 8, B1256 towards Takeley. Through lights at Four Ashes x-rds. 400yds, corner of B1256 & Smiths Green*

The White House is a delightful 16th-century property situated close to Stansted Airport (but not on the flight path). The stylish bedrooms feature superb beds, luxurious bathrooms and many thoughtful touches. Traditional breakfasts are served in the farmhouse-style kitchen, using local ingredients. Evening meals are available at the Lion and Lamb, a nearby pub/restaurant

owned by the proprietors, who can usually provide transport.

Rooms 3 rms (2 en suite) (1 pri facs) (3 fmly) S £60; D £65* **Facilities** tea/coffee Dinner available Cen ht Wi-fi **Parking** 6 **Notes** ⊗ Closed 24-25, 31 Dec & 1 Jan

Little Bullocks Farm

★★★★ GUEST ACCOMMODATION

Hope End CM22 6TA
☎ 01279 870464 📠 01279 871430
e-mail: julie@waterman-farm.demon.co.uk
web: www.littlebullocksfarm.co.uk
dir: *M11 junct 8, B1256 to Takeley, over lights, 1st right to Hope End, left at triangle island, on left at bottom of lane*

Expect a friendly welcome at this pleasant, family-run guest house, which is situated in a peaceful rural location just a short drive from the M11 and Stansted Airport. The bedrooms are cheerfully decorated, with co-ordinated soft furnishings and many thoughtful touches. Breakfast is served at individual tables in the smart dining room.

Rooms 4 en suite (2 fmly) (4 GF) **Facilities** TVL tea/coffee Cen ht **Parking** 15 **Notes** ⊗ ⊜

Warner's Farm

Saffron Walden Tourist Information Office have selected Warner's Farm for the Best B&B Guesthouse in Essex Award for 2009

Wimbish Green, Saffron Walden, Essex CB10 2XJ
Tel: 01799 599 525   Mobile: 07989562316
Email: info@warnersfarm.co.uk
Website: www.warnersfarm.co.uk

Stay in style in a luxury 15th C farmhouse in beautiful peaceful countryside, close to Saffron Walden, Audley End House, Thaxted, Duxford Imperial War Museum, based between Cambridge and Stansted, this is an ideal base for touring this lovely historic area.

All ensuite rooms: King, double or twin.
Ground floor Garden rooms with ramps and wet-rooms.
Whole house hire for groups of up to 18.
Outdoor heated swimming pool (May–Oct)

Our lovely, unique home offers a memorable experience in luxury B&B

Thaxted Bed & Breakfast

★★★★ GUEST ACCOMMODATION

Totmans Farm, Dunmow Rd CM6 2LU
☎ 01371 830233 ▤ 01371 831545
e-mail: stay@thaxtedandstanstedbandb.co.uk
web: www.thaxtedandstanstedbandb.co.uk
dir: On brow of B184 at S end of Thaxted

There is a warm welcome at this charming property situated just a short drive from Stansted airport and close to major roads. The spacious, thoughtfully equipped bedrooms are in a converted outbuilding. Each room has a separate lounge-dining area and a door to the communal west-facing conservatory.

Rooms 5 en suite (1 fmly) (1 GF) **Facilities** TVL tea/coffee Cen ht **Parking** 5 **Notes** ⊗

The Farmhouse Inn

★★★ INN

Monk Street CM6 2NR
☎ 01371 830864 ▤ 01371 831196
e-mail: info@farmhouseinn.org
web: www.farmhouseinn.org
dir: M11 to A120 to B184, 1m from Thaxted, between Thaxted & Great Dunmow

This 16th-century inn overlooks the Chelmer Valley, and is surrounded by open countryside. The property is ideally situated in the quiet hamlet of Monk Street about two miles from the historic town of Thaxted. Bedrooms are pleasantly decorated and equipped with modern facilities. Public rooms include a cosy lounge bar and a large smartly appointed restaurant.

Rooms 11 annexe en suite **Facilities** FTV tea/coffee Dinner available Cen ht Wi-fi **Conf** Max 80 Thtr 80 Class 60 Board 50 **Parking** 35

See Southend-on-Sea

Ollivers Farm

★★★ BED AND BREAKFAST

CO9 4LS
☎ 01787 237642 ▤ 01787 237602
e-mail: bandbolliversfarm@tesco.net
web: www.essex-bed-breakfast.co.uk
dir: 500yds SE of village centre. Off A1017 in Great Yeldham to Toppesfield, farm 1m on left before T-junct to village

Impressive 16th-century farmhouse full of charm and character set amid pretty landscaped gardens in a peaceful rural location. Bedrooms are pleasantly decorated and thoughtfully equipped. Public rooms have

a wealth of original features including exposed beams and a huge open fireplace in the reception hall.

Rooms 3 rms (1 en suite) (1 pri facs) S £45-£50; D £75-£80* **Facilities** tea/coffee Shed for bikes **Parking** 4 **Notes** ⊗ No Children 10yrs Closed 23 Dec-1 Jan ⊛

See also Southend-on-Sea

The Trinity

★★★ GUEST ACCOMMODATION

3 Trinity Av SS0 7PU
☎ 01702 342282
e-mail: enquiries@thetrinityhotel.co.uk
dir: A13 to Milton Rd, at lights turn right towards Cliffs pavilion, left onto Cambridge Rd and right onto Trinity Av

New life has been injected in this property, a contemporary establishment with en suite accommodation within a short distance of the Westcliff sea front. All rooms are beautifully appointed and comfortably equipped. A freshly prepared breakfast is taken at the communal table in the attractive breakfast room.

Rooms 7 en suite (1 fmly) S £35-£45; D £55-£75* **Facilities** FTV tea/coffee Cen ht **Notes** ⊗

PREMIER COLLECTION

Dairy House *(TM148293)*

★★★★★ FARMHOUSE

Bradfield Rd CO11 2SR
☎ 01255 870322 **Mrs B Whitworth**
e-mail: bridgetwhitworth@btinternet.com
web: www.dairyhousefarm.info
dir: Off A120 into Wix, turn at x-rds to Bradfield, farm 1m on left

This Georgian house stands amid 700 acres of arable land, with stunning views of the surrounding countryside. Extensively renovated in the Victorian style, it still retains original decorative tiled floors, moulded cornices and marble fireplaces. The spacious bedrooms are carefully furnished and equipped with many thoughtful touches. Breakfast is served in the elegant antique-furnished dining room and there is a cosy lounge.

Rooms 2 en suite S £42-£46; D £60-£70 **Facilities** FTV TVL tea/coffee Cen ht Wi-fi ⏋ Farm reservoir fishing **Parking** 8 **Notes** ⊗ No Children 12yrs ⊛ 700 acres arable/fruit

Tally Ho Bed & Breakfast

★★★★ BED AND BREAKFAST

20 Beckford Rd GL20 8NL
☎ 01242 621482
e-mail: tallyhobb@aol.com
dir: M5 junct 9, A46 signed Evesham, through Ashchurch. Take B4077 signed Stow-on-the-Wold & Alderton. Left in 1.5m opp garage signed Alderton

Convenient for the M5, this friendly establishment stands in a delightful quiet village. Bedrooms, including two on the ground floor, offer modern comforts and attractive co-ordinated furnishings. Breakfast is served in the stylish dining room, and for dinner, the village pub is just a stroll away.

Rooms 3 en suite (1 fmly) (2 GF) S £40-£45; D £60-£65* **Facilities** tea/coffee Cen ht Wi-fi **Parking** 3 **Notes** LB

See advert on opposite page

The Old Passage Inn

★★★★ ⊛⊛ 🛏 RESTAURANT WITH ROOMS

Passage Rd GL2 7JR
☎ 01452 740547 ▤ 01452 741871
e-mail: oldpassage@ukonline.co.uk
dir: A38 onto B4071 through Arlingham. House by river

Delightfully located on the very edge of the River Severn, this relaxing restaurant with rooms combines high quality food with an air of tranquillity. An outdoor terrace is available in warmer months. The menu offers a wide range of seafood and shellfish dishes including crab, oysters and lobsters from Cornwall (kept alive in seawater tanks). Bedrooms and bathrooms are decorated in a modern style and include a range of welcome extras such as air conditioning and a well-stocked mini-bar.

Rooms 3 en suite S £70-£130; D £90-£130* **Facilities** STV tea/coffee Dinner available Cen ht Wi-fi **Parking** 30 **Notes** Closed 24-31 Dec No coaches

BERKELEY — Map 4 ST69

The Malt House

★★★ INN

22 Marybrook St GL13 9BA
☎ 01453 511177 · 01453 810257
e-mail: the-malthouse@btconnect.com
web: www.themalthouse.uk.com
dir: *A38 into Berkeley, at town hall follow road to right, premises on right past hospital & opposite school*

Well located for business and leisure, this family-run inn has a convivial atmosphere. Bedrooms are soundly appointed while public areas include a choice of bars, a skittle alley and an attractive restaurant area. Local attractions include Berkeley Castle, and the Wildfowl & Wetlands Trust at Slimbridge.

Rooms 10 rms (9 en suite) (2 fmly) **Facilities** FTV tea/coffee Dinner available Cen ht Pool Table Skittle Alley **Parking** 30 **Notes** ⊗

BIBURY — Map 5 SP10

Cotteswold House

★★★★ BED AND BREAKFAST

Arlington GL7 5ND
☎ 01285 740609 · 01285 740609
e-mail: enquiries@cotteswoldhouse.net
web: www.cotteswoldhouse.net
dir: *On B4425, 500yds W of village centre*

Convenient for exploring the Cotswolds, Cotteswold House offers a warm welcome together with high levels of comfort and quality. Spacious bedrooms are equipped with thoughtful extras, and there is a cosy lounge with useful local information.

Rooms 3 en suite S fr £48; D fr £68* **Facilities** tea/coffee Cen ht **Parking** 3 **Notes** LB ⊗

BLOCKLEY — Map 10 SP13

PREMIER COLLECTION

Lower Brook House

★★★★★ 🍴 🛏 GUEST ACCOMMODATION

Lower St GL56 9DS
☎ 01386 700286 · 01386 701400
e-mail: info@lowerbrookhouse.com
web: www.lowerbrookhouse.com
dir: *In village centre*

Dating from the 17th century, this enchanting house is the perfect place to relax. Genuine hospitality and attentive service are hallmarks here, and bedrooms come in all shapes and sizes. There's a lot of character in the public areas, with beams, flagstone floors, huge fireplace and deep stone walls. Enjoy a delicious breakfast and an aperitif in the garden, but leave room for the skilfully prepared dinner.

Rooms 6 en suite S £80-£185; D £80-£185* **Facilities** tea/coffee Dinner available Cen ht Licensed Wi-fi **Parking** 8 **Notes** ⊗ No Children 10yrs

BOURTON-ON-THE-WATER — Map 10 SP12

Coombe House

★★★★ GUEST ACCOMMODATION

Rissington Rd GL54 2DT
☎ 01451 821966 · 01451 810477
e-mail: info@coombehouse.net
dir: *Off A429 through village, past Birdland on right, 300yds on left just past Bridle Cl*

A warm welcome is assured at this immaculately presented house, set in a mature garden. Bedrooms are equipped with a wealth of homely extras and ground-floor rooms are available. Facilities include a comfortable lounge and sun terrace, and breakfast is served in the attractive breakfast room overlooking the flower-filled garden.

Rooms 6 en suite (2 GF) S £50-£65; D £65-£85* **Facilities** TVL tea/coffee Cen ht **Parking** 6 **Notes** ⊗ No Children 12yrs RS Nov-Feb Usually wknd opening

Larks Rise

★★★★ BED AND BREAKFAST

Old Gloucester Rd GL54 3BH
☎ 01451 822613 & 07884 438498
e-mail: larks.rise@virgin.net
web: www.larksrisehouse.co.uk
dir: *0.5m W of village. A249 onto A436, 1st driveway on left*

A relaxed and welcoming establishment that sits in an acre of gardens on the edge of the village. Comfort and style are of paramount importance at this delightful property where the proprietors offer a very warm welcome. The bedrooms are really comfortable with cotton sheets on pocket sprung mattresses and high quality en suite facilities. Breakfasts feature locally sourced produce; there is ample parking.

Rooms 3 rms (2 en suite) (1 pri facs) (1 GF) S £60-£75; D £60-£85* **Facilities** tea/coffee Cen ht Wi-fi **Parking** 6 **Notes** ⊗ No Children 12yrs

Tally Ho
Bed and Breakfast

20 Beckford Rd, Alderton, Cheltenham, Glos GL20 8NL
Tel: 01242 621482   Email: tallyhobb@aol.com
www.cotswolds-bedandbreakfast.co.uk

A warm welcome awaits you at the Tally Ho, a delightful establishment set right in the heart of the picturesque village of Alderton in the English Cotswolds. Commended for its outstanding facilities, Tally Ho provides for your every need. It is also commended for the standard of food, comfort and personal service which every guest is treated to.

Bed and Breakfast is catered for in luxurious ensuite double, twin and family bedrooms. Ground floor ensuite rooms available for easy access. Private parking.

Book online: www.cotswolds-bedandbreakfast.co.uk

BOURTON-ON-THE-WATER *continued*

The Cotswold House

★★★ BED AND BREAKFAST

Lansdowne GL54 2AR
☎ 01451 822373
e-mail: meadowscotswoldhouse@btinternet.com
dir: *Off A429 into Lansdowne, continue 0.5m to Cotswold House on right opp Paragon Garage*

A warm welcome is assured at this well maintained, mellow-stone house. Just a short walk from the church and the many attractions of this popular village, this is a great base for touring the Cotswolds. Bedrooms are comfortably furnished, and one is a self-contained conversion of the former village telephone exchange, set within immaculate gardens.

Rooms 3 en suite 1 annexe en suite (2 fmly) (1 GF) S £30-£50; D £55-£70* **Facilities** TVL tea/coffee Cen ht **Parking** 5 **Notes** LB ⊗ ⊛

Strathspey

★★★ BED AND BREAKFAST

Lansdowne GL54 2AR
☎ 01451 810321 & 07889 491993
e-mail: information@strathspey.org.uk
web: www.strathspey.org.uk
dir: *Off A429 into Lansdowne, 200yds on right*

This friendly Edwardian-style cottage is just a short riverside walk from the charming village centre, the perfume factory and the famous model village. Bedrooms, (including one at ground floor level with its own front door) are well presented with many useful extras, and substantial breakfasts are part of the caring hospitality.

Rooms 2 en suite 1 annexe en suite (1 fmly) (1 GF) S fr £45; D fr £58 **Facilities** TVL tea/coffee Cen ht **Parking** 4 **Notes** LB ⊛

| CHELTENHAM | Map 10 SO92 |

PREMIER COLLECTION

Beaumont House

★★★★★ GUEST ACCOMMODATION

56 Shurdington Rd GL53 0JE
☎ 01242 223311   🖹 01242 520044
e-mail: reservations@bhhotel.co.uk
web: www.bhhotel.co.uk
dir: *S side of town on A46 to Stroud*

Built as a private residence, this popular establishment exudes genteel charm. Public areas include a large lounge and an elegant dining room which overlooks the garden. Many improvements have taken place recently and include new studio bedrooms on the top floor. These complement the already completed 'Out of Asia' and 'Out of Africa' bedrooms, which are luxuriously furnished and very well equipped. Bedrooms situated to the rear of the building have views over Leckhampton Hill and there are also bedrooms on the lower ground floor.

Rooms 16 en suite (3 fmly) S £65-£78; D £88-£233* **Facilities** STV FTV tea/coffee Dinner available Direct Dial Cen ht Licensed Wi-fi **Parking** 16 **Notes** LB ⊗ No Children 5yrs

PREMIER COLLECTION

Cleeve Hill House

★★★★★ GUEST ACCOMMODATION

Cleeve Hill GL52 3PR
☎ 01242 672052   🖹 01242 679969
e-mail: info@cleevehill-hotel.co.uk
dir: *3m N of Cheltenham on B4632*

This large detached property was built in Edwardian times and both the lounge and many of the bedrooms have spectacular views across to the Malvern Hills. Room shapes and sizes vary but all are comfortably furnished with many welcome extras; some have four-poster beds. In addition to the relaxing guest lounge, an honesty bar is in place. Breakfast, served in the pleasant conservatory, offers a good selection of carefully presented hot and cold items.

Rooms 10 en suite (1 GF) **Facilities** STV FTV tea/coffee Direct Dial Cen ht Licensed Wi-fi **Parking** 11 **Notes** ⊗ No Children 8yrs

---

PREMIER COLLECTION

Georgian House

★★★★★ BED AND BREAKFAST

77 Montpellier Ter GL50 1XA
☎ 01242 515577   🖹 01242 545929
e-mail: penny@georgianhouse.net
web: www.georgianhouse.net
dir: *M5 junct 11, A40 into town centre & onto Montpellier Ter, Georgian House on right after park*

Dating from 1807, this elegant Georgian house is located in the fashionable area of Montpellier. Renovation has resulted in delightful accommodation with quality and comfort throughout. Bedrooms are individually styled, with contemporary comforts cleverly interwoven with period furnishings to great effect. Warm hospitality and attentive service ensure a memorable stay.

Rooms 3 en suite S £65-£80; D £80-£105* **Facilities** FTV tea/coffee Cen ht Wi-fi **Parking** 2 **Notes** ⊗ No Children 16yrs Closed Xmas & New Year

PREMIER COLLECTION

Lypiatt House

★★★★★ GUEST ACCOMMODATION

Lypiatt Rd GL50 2QW
☎ 01242 224994   🖹 01242 224996
e-mail: stay@lypiatt.co.uk
dir: *M5 junct 11 to town centre. At Texaco petrol station mini-rdbt take exit signed Stroud. Fork right, pass shops, turn sharp left onto Lypiatt Rd*

Close to the fashionable area of Montpellier, set in its own grounds, with ample parking, Lypiatt House is built in typical Victorian style. Contemporary decor enhances the traditional features of the building. Bedrooms and bathrooms offer a range of shapes and sizes with all rooms decorated and maintained to high standards and including a range of welcome extras. Guests may use the elegant drawing room and the conservatory, which has an honesty bar.

Rooms 10 en suite (2 GF) S £70-£90; D £80-£110* **Facilities** FTV tea/coffee Direct Dial Cen ht Licensed Wi-fi **Conf** Max 10 Board 10 **Parking** 10 **Notes** LB ⊗ No Children 10yrs

Badger Towers

★★★★ GUEST ACCOMMODATION

133 Hales Rd GL52 6ST
☎ 01242 522583 📄 01242 574800
e-mail: mrbadger@badgertowers.co.uk
web: www.badgertowers.co.uk
dir: *Off A40 (London Rd) onto Hales Rd, 0.5m on right towards Prestbury & race course*

Located in the residential area of Battledown, close to the racecourse, town centre and GCHQ, this elegant Victorian house offers thoughtfully furnished bedrooms, a light and airy breakfast room, and a spacious lounge complete with piano. The well-cooked breakfasts, with an emphasis on local produce, are a satisfying start to the day.

Rooms 7 en suite (2 GF) S £50-£65; D £70-£105*
Facilities FTV tea/coffee Cen ht Wi-fi **Parking** 7 **Notes** LB
Closed Xmas & New Year

The Battledown

★★★★ GUEST HOUSE

125 Hales Rd GL52 6ST
☎ 01242 233881
e-mail: battledown125@hotmail.com
dir: *0.5m E of town centre. A40 onto B4075, 0.5m on right*

This elegant and well-proportioned Grade II listed house offers comfortable accommodation close to the town centre and racecourse. The refurbished bedrooms and bathrooms provide plenty of quality and comfort with some welcome extras, while the smart dining room is an attractive setting for breakfast.

Rooms 7 en suite (2 fmly) S £45-£55; D £68-£70*
Facilities tea/coffee Cen ht Wi-fi **Parking** 7 **Notes** LB ⊗
Closed Xmas

Clarence Court

★★★★ GUEST ACCOMMODATION

Clarence Square GL50 4JR
☎ 01242 580411 📄 01242 224609
e-mail: enquiries@clarencecourthotel.co.uk
web: www.clarencecourthotel.com
dir: *Situated in an attractive, tree-lined Georgian square, this property was once owned by the Duke of Wellington. Sensitive refurbishment is now returning the building to its former glory with elegant public rooms reflecting the*

grace of a bygone age. Spacious bedrooms offer ample comfort and quality, with many original features retained. This peaceful location is only a five-minute stroll from the town centre.

Rooms 21 rms (19 en suite) (3 fmly) (7 GF) **Facilities** tea/coffee Direct Dial Cen ht Licensed **Parking** 21

Hope Orchard

★★★★ GUEST ACCOMMODATION

Gloucester Rd, Staverton GL51 0TF
☎ 01452 855556 📄 01452 530037
e-mail: info@hopeorchard.com
web: www.hopeorchard.com
dir: *A40 onto B4063 at Arlecourt rdbt, Hope Orchard 1.25m on right*

Situated midway between Gloucester and Cheltenham, this is a good base for exploring the area. The comfortable bedrooms are next to the main house, and all are on the ground floor and have their own separate entrances. There is a large garden, and ample off-road parking is available.

Rooms 8 en suite (8 GF) **Facilities** FTV tea/coffee Direct Dial Cen ht Wi-fi **Parking** 10

The Prestbury House

★★★★ GUEST ACCOMMODATION

The Burgage, Prestbury GL52 3DN
☎ 01242 529533 📄 01242 227076
e-mail: enquiries@prestburyhouse.co.uk
web: www.prestburyhouse.co.uk
dir: *1m NE of Cheltenham. Follow all signs for racecourse, Evesham (A435) & Prestbury (B4632) From racecourse follow Prestbury signs. 2nd left signed Prestbury House, 500yds from racecourse entrance*

Standing its own grounds, this impressive house offers a wealth of history along with spacious and comfortable accommodation. Bedrooms are divided between the larger rooms of the main house and an adjacent former coach house. The public areas are full of character and include a comfy bar, traditional breakfast room and delightful surrounding gardens.

Rooms 7 en suite 7 annexe en suite (1 fmly) (3 GF) S £50-£88; D £50-£135 **Facilities** STV TVL tea/coffee Direct Dial Cen ht Licensed Wi-fi ⚓ Gymnasium Archery, Bike hire, Trim trail **Conf** Max 40 Thtr 40 Class 25 Board 20 **Parking** 40 **Notes** LB ⊗ Civ Wed 60

33 Montpellier

★★★★ GUEST ACCOMMODATION

33 Montpellier Ter GL50 1UX
☎ 01242 526009
e-mail: montpellierhotel@btopenworld.com
dir: *M5 junct 11, A40 to rdbt at Montpellier, over rdbt & 100yds on right*

The friendly and welcoming Montpellier forms part of an elegant Georgian terrace overlooking the municipal gardens in a fashionable area of town convenient for shops, restaurants and amenities. Bedrooms are light, airy and well equipped with a range of practical extras and thoughtful touches. Breakfast is served in the lower ground floor dining room.

Rooms 7 en suite (5 fmly) S fr £35; D fr £55 (room only)*
Facilities FTV TVL tea/coffee Cen ht Licensed Wi-fi
Notes LB ⊗ ⊜

White Lodge

★★★★ GUEST ACCOMMODATION

Hatherley Ln GL51 6SH
☎ 01242 242347 📄 01242 242347
e-mail: pamela@whitelodgebandb.wanadoo.co.uk
dir: *M5 junct 11, A40 to Cheltenham, 1st rdbt 4th exit Hatherley Ln, White Lodge 1st on right*

Built around 1900, this well cared for, smart and friendly establishment is convenient for access to the M5. Bedrooms, of varied size, offer quality and many extra facilities, including fridges and Wi-fi. The very comfortable dining room, where breakfast is served around a grand table, looks out across the pleasant backdrop of White Lodge's extensive gardens.

Rooms 4 en suite (1 GF) S £42-£45; D £60-£65
Facilities FTV tea/coffee Cen ht Wi-fi **Parking** 6 **Notes** ⊜

Wishmoor House

★★★★ GUEST ACCOMMODATION

147 Hales Rd GL52 6TD
☎ 01242 238504 📄 01242 226090
e-mail: wishmoor@hotmail.co.uk
dir: *A40 onto B4075 Hales Rd signed Prestbury, racecourse, crematorium, 0.5m on right*

Wishmoor House is an elegantly modernised spacious Victorian residence, situated between the town centre and racecourse with easy access from all major roads and ample parking. Inside you can expect charming period features, wonderful views and a warm welcome. Free Wi-fi is available.

Rooms 10 rms (9 en suite) (1 pri facs) (2 fmly)
Facilities tea/coffee Cen ht Wi-fi **Conf** Max 10 Thtr 10 Class 10 Board 10 **Parking** 9 **Notes** ⊗

CHELTENHAM *continued*

The Beaufort Arms

★★★ INN

184 London Rd GL52 6HJ
☎ 01242 526038 🖶 01242 526038
e-mail: beaufort.arms@blueyonder.co.uk
dir: *On A40*

Located on the main road, just outside of the town centre, this traditional inn offers a friendly welcome and a relaxed style of service and hospitality. Bedrooms, some with en suite and some sharing bathrooms, have been refurbished to provide sound standards throughout. A range of home cooked meals and a selection of real ales are available.

Rooms 5 rms (2 en suite) (1 fmly) S £30-£35; D £50-£56
Facilities FTV TVL tea/coffee Dinner available Cen ht Wi-fi Pool Table **Parking** 5 **Notes** ⊗

Cheltenham Guest House

★★★ GUEST HOUSE

145 Hewlett Rd GL52 6TS
☎ 01242 521726
e-mail: info@cheltenhamguesthouse.biz
dir: *A40 London Rd into town, follow GH signs to hospital, Hewlett Rd on right after A&E*

This quietly located guest house is just outside the main town, yet within easy walking distance of it. Bedrooms and bathrooms come in a variety of shapes and sizes; all are well equipped. The bright and comfortable breakfast room provides an ideal setting for carefully prepared breakfasts including some extra options such as omelettes.

Rooms 9 rms (7 en suite) (1 fmly) S £38-£50; D £55-£70* **Facilities** FTV tea/coffee Cen ht Wi-fi **Parking** 6 **Notes** ⊗

CHIPPING CAMPDEN — Map 10 SP13

See also Blockley

PREMIER COLLECTION

The Malt House

★★★★★ GUEST HOUSE

Broad Campden GL55 6UU
☎ 01386 840295 🖶 01386 841334
e-mail: info@malt-house.co.uk
web: www.malt-house.co.uk
dir: *0.8m SE of Chipping Campden in Broad Campden, by church*

Formed from the village malt house and adjacent cottages, this beguiling house dates from the 16th century. Original features are mixed with contemporary comforts, and bedrooms have quality soft fabrics and period furniture. There is a choice of lounges, an elegant breakfast room, and a wonderful garden with croquet lawn and relaxing seating.

Rooms 4 en suite 3 annexe en suite (3 fmly) (1 GF) S £85; D £140* **Facilities** FTV TVL tea/coffee Cen ht Licensed Wi-fi **Conf** Max 8 Board 8 **Parking** 10 **Notes** ⊗ Closed 22-28 Dec

PREMIER COLLECTION

Staddlestones

★★★★★ BED AND BREAKFAST

7 Aston Rd GL55 6HR
☎ 01386 849288
e-mail: info@staddle-stones.com
web: www.staddle-stones.com
dir: *B4081 signed to Mickleton, out of Chipping Campden 200mtrs. House on right opp gravel lane*

A warm welcome can be expected from host Pauline Kirton at this delightful property, situated just a short walk from the Cotswold village of Chipping Campden and an ideal base for walking, cycling, golf or just relaxing. There are three bedrooms offering quality and comfort plus some thoughtful extras. A hearty breakfast is served in the dining room around the communal table, and there's a good choice of mostly organic produce sourced from local farms. Dinner can be provided by arrangement.

Rooms 2 en suite 1 annexe en suite (1 fmly); D £65-£85* **Facilities** FTV tea/coffee Dinner available Cen ht Wi-fi **Parking** 6 **Notes** No Children 12yrs ☏

Bramley House

★★★★ BED AND BREAKFAST

6 Aston Rd GL55 6HR
☎ 01386 840066 & 07855 760113
e-mail: povey@bramleyhouse.co.uk
dir: *Off High St onto B4081 towards Mickleton, house 0.5m opp cul-de-sac Grevel Ln & post box*

A warm welcome and refreshments on arrival await at Bramley House. With ample off-road parking and situated just a stroll from the centre of the popular market town, this friendly, family home offers attractively co-ordinated accommodation, with many thoughtful extras. The tranquil rear room offers superb field views. A delicious breakfast, featuring organic produce whenever possible, is served in the smart dining room around a large communal table.

Rooms 2 en suite S £50-£55; D £63-£68* **Facilities** tea/coffee Cen ht Wi-fi **Parking** 3 **Notes** ⊗ No Children 12yrs Closed 16 Dec-Jan ☏

The Kings

★★★★ ⚜ RESTAURANT WITH ROOMS

The Square GL55 6AW
☎ 01386 840256 & 841056 🖶 01386 841598
e-mail: info@kingscampden.co.uk
dir: *In centre of town square*

Located in the centre of a delightful Cotswold town, this establishment effortlessly blends a relaxed and friendly welcome with efficient service. Bedrooms and bathrooms come in a range of shapes and sizes but all are appointed to high levels of quality and comfort. Dining options, whether in the main restaurant or the comfortable bar area, include a tempting menu to suit all tastes from lighter salads and pasta to local meats and fish dishes. Five annexe rooms are due to open summer 2009.

Rooms 14 en suite (2 fmly) S fr £89; D £100-£195* **Facilities** FTV tea/coffee Dinner available Direct Dial Cen ht Wi-fi **Conf** Thtr 30 Class 20 Board 20 **Parking** 8 **Notes** LB Civ Wed 60

Poppy Bank

★ ★ ★ ★ BED AND BREAKFAST

4 Aston Rd GL55 6HR
☎ 01386 840424
e-mail: stay@poppybank.co.uk
dir: *A44 onto B4081 through Chipping Campden towards Mickleton House, 0.25m from village centre on right*

Just a few minutes easy walk away from the village centre, this recently developed accommodation is well equipped, light and airy. Bedrooms are spacious with comfortable seating, and one room has French doors overlooking the pretty rear garden and open farm land. Breakfast is taken in the cosy dining room/lounge at separate tables.

Rooms 2 en suite (1 fmly) **Facilities** tea/coffee Cen ht Wi-fi **Parking** 6 **Notes** ⊗ RS Xmas wk ⊛

Catbrook House

★ ★ ★ ★ BED AND BREAKFAST

Catbrook GL55 6DE
☎ 01386 841499
e-mail: m.klein@virgin.net
dir: *B4081 into Chipping Campden, signs for Broad Campden until Catbrook House on right*

Along with stunning rural views and close proximity to the town centre, this mellow stone house provides comfortable, homely bedrooms. The attentive hosts extend a friendly welcome. A traditional English breakfast is served in the comfortably furnished dining room.

Rooms 3 rms (1 en suite) (2 pri facs) S fr £43; D fr £53* **Facilities** TV2B tea/coffee Cen ht **Parking** 3 **Notes** ⊗ No Children 9yrs Closed Xmas ⊛

The Chance

★ ★ ★ ★ ⌂ BED AND BREAKFAST

1 Aston Rd GL55 6HR
☎ 01386 849079
e-mail: enquiries@the-chance.co.uk
web: www.the-chance.co.uk
dir: *B4081 towards Mickleton from Chipping Campden, signed on right hand side*

Located just a short stroll from the pleasant town of Chipping Campden, The Chance offers two well decorated and well maintained bedrooms where a range of welcome extras are helpfully provided for guests. A friendly welcome from the resident proprietor may well include the offer of tea and homemade cakes. Breakfast is a real treat with a varied menu utilising fresh local produce with something to suit all tastes.

Rooms 2 en suite; D £65-£75* **Facilities** tea/coffee Dinner available Cen ht Wi-fi Hot tub, Hydro therapy spa **Parking** 6 **Notes** LB ⊗ No Children 12yrs Closed 24-26 Dec ⊛

Holly House

★ ★ ★ ★ BED AND BREAKFAST

Ebrington GL55 6NL
☎ 01386 593213
e-mail: hutsbybandb@aol.com
web: www.hollyhousebandb.co.uk
dir: *B4035 from Chipping Campden towards Shipston on Stour, 0.5m left to Ebrington & signed*

Set in the heart of the pretty Cotswold village of Ebrington, this late Victorian house offers thoughtfully equipped accommodation. Bedrooms are housed in buildings that were formerly used by the local wheelwright, and offer level access, seclusion and privacy. Quality English breakfasts are served in the light and airy dining room. For other meals, the village pub is just a short walk away.

Rooms 2 en suite 1 annexe en suite (1 fmly) (3 GF) S £45-£60; D £65-£70* **Facilities** tea/coffee Cen ht **Parking** 5 **Notes** ⊗ Closed Xmas ⊛

Manor Farm *(SP124412)*

★ ★ ★ ★ FARMHOUSE

Weston Subedge GL55 6QH
☎ 01386 840390 & 07889 108812
▤ 0870 1640638 Mrs L King
e-mail: lucy@manorfarmbnb.demon.co.uk
web: www.manorfarmbnb.demon.co.uk
dir: *2m NW of Chipping Campden. On B4632 in Weston Subedge*

A genuine welcome is extended at this 17th-century mellow Cotswold-stone farmhouse. The welcome also extends to pets, and stabling is available by arrangement. Bedrooms are comfortable and homely with thoughtful extras. Facilities include a lounge with a wood-burning stove, and an elegant dining room where mouth-watering breakfasts are served.

Rooms 3 en suite **Facilities** TVL tea/coffee Cen ht **Parking** 8 **Notes** LB ⊗ 800 acres arable/cattle/horses/sheep

Myrtle House

★ ★ ★ ★ BED AND BREAKFAST

High St, Mickleton GL55 6SA
☎ 01386 430032
e-mail: louanne@myrtlehouse.co.uk
dir: *A46 onto B4632 towards Broadway. In Mickleton, on left opp Three Ways House*

Myrtle House stands on the high street of this pleasant Cotswold village. Bedrooms are spacious and well equipped with a range of useful extras and information. The ambience created here by the resident proprietors is relaxed and welcoming. Breakfast is a highlight with a selection of carefully prepared local produce, fresh fruits and home-cooked cakes and croissants. In the evening,

there is a good selection of dining options just a short stroll away.

Rooms 5 en suite (2 fmly) S £45-£60; D £65-£80 **Facilities** tea/coffee Dinner available Cen ht Wi-fi **Parking** 2 **Notes** LB

Stonecroft Bed & Breakfast

★ ★ ★ ★ BED AND BREAKFAST

Stonecroft, George Ln GL55 6DA
☎ 01386 840486
e-mail: info@stonecroft-chippingcampden.co.uk

Quietly located in a residential area just a stroll from the High Street, this well-maintained property offers relaxing accommodation. Guests have the key to their own entrance and can come and go as they please. Breakfast is served around one large table in the compact but well-furnished dining room.

Rooms 2 en suite S £50-£55; D £65* **Facilities** FTV tea/coffee Cen ht **Parking** 2 **Notes** ⊗ No Children 12yrs ⊛

CHIPPING SODBURY Map 4 ST78

The Moda House

★ ★ ★ ★ GUEST ACCOMMODATION

1 High St BS37 6BA
☎ 01454 312135 ▤ 01454 850090
e-mail: enquiries@modahouse.co.uk
web: www.modahouse.co.uk
dir: *In town centre*

This popular Grade II listed Georgian house has an imposing position at the top of the High Street. It has been refurbished to provide modern bedrooms of varying shapes and sizes and comfortable public areas, while retaining many original features. Room facilities include satellite television and phones.

Rooms 7 en suite 3 annexe en suite (1 fmly) (3 GF) S £65; D £82-£95* **Facilities** STV TVL tea/coffee Direct Dial Cen ht Licensed Wi-fi **Conf** Max 20 Thtr 10 Board 10

COLEFORD   Map 4 SO51

Chapel Cottage

★★★★ GUEST ACCOMMODATION

3 Chapel Rd, Berry Hill GL16 7QY
☎ 01594 836547
e-mail: chapelcottagefod@btinternet.com
dir: Off A4136 at Five Acres onto Park Rd. 1st left, 200yds on left

This lovely 19th-century cottage is well situated for exploring the Forest of Dean. The welcome here is genuine and every effort is made to ensure a relaxing and comfortable stay. Bedrooms are attractively styled to a high standard with a host of thoughtful extras, and the contemporary bathrooms are of a high quality. Breakfast is a tasty and satisfying feast, served in the light and airy dining room.

Rooms 3 en suite **Facilities** tea/coffee Dinner available Cen ht **Parking** 3 **Notes** ⊗ 🐾

Dryslade Farm *(SO581147)*

★★★★ FARMHOUSE

English Bicknor GL16 7PA
☎ 01594 860259 📠 01594 860259   Mrs D Gwilliam
e-mail: daphne@drysladefarm.co.uk
web: www.drysladefarm.co.uk
dir: 3m N of Coleford. Off A4136 onto B4432, right towards English Bicknor, farm 1m

Visitors are warmly welcomed at this 184-acre working farm, which dates from 1780 and has been in the same family for almost 100 years. The en suite bedrooms are attractively furnished in natural pine and are well equipped. The lounge leads onto a conservatory where hearty breakfasts are served.

Rooms 3 en suite (1 GF) S £40-£45; D £60-£70
Facilities TVL tea/coffee Cen ht **Parking** 6 **Notes** LB 🐾
184 acres beef

Cor Unum

★★★ BED AND BREAKFAST

Monmouth Rd, Edge-End GL16 7HB
☎ 01594 837960
e-mail: antony@jones3649.freeserve.co.uk
dir: On A4136 in village of Edge End

A genuine welcome is assured at this comfortably-appointed bungalow which is located in the heart of the Forest of Dean. Bedrooms are neatly furnished, and the lounge has wonderful views across the garden to the Welsh mountains. Breakfast, served in the cosy dining room, is a tasty and fulfilling start to the day.

Rooms 3 rms (2 en suite) (3 GF) S £20-£35; D £50-£70*
Facilities FTV TVL tea/coffee Cen ht **Parking** 1 **Notes** LB No Children Closed 20-30 Dec 🐾

COWLEY   Map 10 SO91

The Green Dragon

★★★★ ⊜ INN

Cockleford GL53 9NW
☎ 01242 870271
e-mail: green-dragon@buccaneer.co.uk

This establishment offers all the charm and character of an English country pub combined with a relaxed atmosphere and carefully prepared food made from local produce. Bedrooms, some at ground floor level, are located in an annexe and vary in size. There is a terrace to the front where guests may enjoy a drink on warm sunny days.

Rooms 9 en suite (4 GF) S £70; D £95-£150*
Facilities tea/coffee Dinner available Direct Dial Cen ht Wi-fi **Conf** Max 65 Thtr 65 Class 65 Board 65 **Parking** 11 **Notes** LB

EBRINGTON   Map 10 SP14

The Ebrington Arms

★★★★ 🍴 INN

GL55 6NH
☎ 01386 593223
e-mail: info@theebringtonarms.co.uk
web: www.theebringtonarms.co.uk
dir: From Chipping Campden take B4035 towards Shipston-on-Stour, left to Ebrington

Located in the quiet, unspoilt village of Ebrington, just a couple of miles from Chipping Campden, this 17th-century inn provides an excellent selection of real ales, fine wines and really enjoyable homemade dishes utilising the finest of produce. Food is served in the traditional ambience of the bar or the cosy dining room with roaring open fire. Bedrooms are full of character and include some welcome extras. A large beer garden and car park are also available.

Rooms 3 en suite **Facilities** FTV tea/coffee Dinner available Cen ht **Conf** Max 32 Thtr 32 Class 32 Board 25 **Parking** 10

FORD   Map 10 SP02

The Plough Inn

★★★★ INN

GL54 5RU
☎ 01386 584215 📠 01386 584042
e-mail: info@theploughinnatford.co.uk
web: www.theploughinnatford.co.uk
dir: On B4077 in village

Popular with locals and the racing fraternity, this charming 16th-century inn retains many original features such as Cotswold stone walls, open fires and beamed ceilings. Cheltenham, Tewkesbury and many popular Cotswold towns and villages are in close proximity. Home-cooked food featuring local produce is a highlight. Bedrooms are situated in a restored stable block across a courtyard, adjacent to the delightful beer garden.

Rooms 3 annexe en suite (2 fmly) **Facilities** FTV tea/coffee Dinner available Cen ht **Conf** Max 30 **Parking** 50 **Notes** LB ⊗

The Inn at Fossebridge

★★★★ 🍽 INN

GL54 3JS
☎ 01285 720721 📠 01285 720793
e-mail: info@fossebridgeinn.co.uk
dir: on A429, 3m S of A40 & 6m N of Cirencester

Located not too far from Stratford-upon-Avon, Cheltenham and Cirencester this inn is around 300 years old, and was once a coaching inn on the old Fosse Way. Today it is a beautiful Cotswold retreat with wonderful accommodation and grounds. Fine food is served in the character bar and dining areas, and a warm welcome awaits all visitors.

Rooms 8 en suite (1 fmly) S £110-£120; D £110-£160*
Facilities STV TVL tea/coffee Dinner available Cen ht
Fishing **Conf** Max 70 Thtr 40 Class 40 Board 12
Parking 30 **Notes** LB No coaches Civ Wed 70

The Crown Inn

★★★★ INN

GL6 8JG
☎ 01285 760601
e-mail: enquiries@thecrowninn-cotswolds.co.uk
dir: Off A419 signed Frampton Mansell, 0.75m at village centre

This establishment was a cider house in the 17th century, and guests will now find that roaring log fires, locally brewed ales and traditional, home-cooked food are on offer. The bedrooms are in an annexe, and ample parking is available.

Rooms 12 en suite (1 fmly) (4 GF) S £65-£85; D £85-£100* **Facilities** tea/coffee Dinner available Cen ht Wi-fi **Conf** Max 40 **Parking** 35 **Notes** LB

Brookthorpe Lodge

★★★ 🅰 GUEST HOUSE

Stroud Rd, Brookthorpe GL4 0UQ
☎ 01452 812645 📠 01452 812645
e-mail: enq@brookthorpelodge.demon.co.uk
dir: 3m S of Gloucester on A4173

Rooms 10 rms (6 en suite) (1 fmly) (3 GF) S £30-£50; D £60-£70* **Facilities** tea/coffee Cen ht Licensed Wi-fi **Parking** 15 **Notes** LB ⊗ Closed Xmas & New Year

---

Guiting Guest House

★ ★ ★ ★ GUEST HOUSE

Post Office Ln GL54 5TZ
☎ 01451 850470
e-mail: info@guitingguesthouse.com
web: www.guitingguesthouse.com
dir: In village centre

In keeping with all the surrounding houses, this engaging family home is built of mellow Cotswold stone. Charming and comfortable bedrooms offer both individuality and character, as do the public rooms, which include the stylish dining room and snug lounge. Breakfast (and dinner by arrangement) use excellent local produce whenever possible.

Rooms 2 en suite 4 annexe rms 3 annexe en suite (1 pri facs) (2 GF) S fr £45; D fr £85* **Facilities** tea/coffee Dinner available Cen ht Wi-fi **Parking** 3 **Notes** LB

Leasow House

★★★★ GUEST ACCOMMODATION

Laverton Meadows WR12 7NA
☎ 01386 584526 📠 01386 584596
e-mail: leasow@hotmail.com
dir: 2m SW of Broadway. Off B4632 towards Wormington, 500yds on right

Located in the countryside to the south-west of Broadway, this 16th-century former farmhouse has been restored to provide high standards of comfort. Bedrooms have a wealth of extras and the attractive dining room is the setting for comprehensive breakfasts. There is also an elegant library lounge and a warm welcome is assured.

Rooms 5 en suite 2 annexe en suite (2 fmly) (1 GF)
Facilities tea/coffee Direct Dial Cen ht **Parking** 10
Notes No Children 8yrs Closed Xmas & New Year

Cambrai Lodge

★★★★ GUEST ACCOMMODATION

Oak St GL7 3AY
☎ 01367 253173 & 07860 150467
e-mail: info@cambrailodgeguesthouse.co.uk
web: www.cambrailodgeguesthouse.co.uk
dir: In town centre, off High St onto A361 Oak St

This delightful house is just a stroll from the centre of the historic market town with its many pubs serving meals. Individually styled bedrooms, some in a pretty cottage across the garden, include a four-poster room and two ground-floor bedrooms. Breakfast is served in the conservatory overlooking the gardens.

Rooms 2 en suite 3 annexe en suite (1 fmly) (2 GF)
S £45-£65; D £55-£75 **Facilities** FTV tea/coffee Cen ht
Parking 12 **Notes** ⊛

New House Farm B&B *(SO685229)*

★★★★ FARMHOUSE

Barrel Ln, Aston Ingham GL17 0LS
☎ 01452 830484 & 07768 354922
📠 01452 830484 Ms R Smith
e-mail: scaldbrain@btinternet.com
dir: A40 onto B4222, Barrel Ln on right before Aston Ingham

Located in tranquil wooded countryside, this working farm is a good touring base on the Gloucestershire-Herefordshire border. Set in 65 acres, the welcoming farmhouse will certainly appeal to nature lovers, and there is a comfortable lounge and bar. Breakfast consists of a good selection of carefully prepared local produce.

Rooms 3 en suite (1 fmly) S £35-£45; D £60-£78*
Facilities TVL tea/coffee Cen ht Wi-fi 🐾 **Conf** Max 15
Parking 10 **Notes** LB ⊗ No Children 10yrs 65 acres sheep/woodland

MARSHFIELD — Map 4 ST77

Lord Nelson Inn

★★★ INN

SN14 8LP

☎ 01225 891820

e-mail: thelordnelsoninn@btinternet.com

web: www.thelordnelsoninn.info

dir: *M4 junct 18 onto A46 towards Bath. Left at Cold Ashton rdbt towards Marshfield*

Located at one end of the pleasant village of Marshfield, the Lord Nelson is a traditional coaching inn with a pleasant ambience. The spacious bar provides a good opportunity to mix with the locals, while the candlelit restaurant offers a quieter environment in which to enjoy the excellent selection of carefully prepared homemade dishes. Bedrooms and bathrooms are all well decorated and furnished.

Rooms 3 en suite S £25-£37.50; D £50-£67.50* **Facilities** tea/coffee Dinner available Cen ht **Conf** Max 80 Thtr 40 Class 30 Board 30 **Notes** LB

MORETON-IN-MARSH — Map 10 SP23

Hoggs Barn

★★★★ BED AND BREAKFAST

Chastleton GL56 0SL

☎ 01608 674343 ⓘ 01608 674626

e-mail: mp.allen@btconnect.com

dir: *From Moreton-in-Marsh, A44 towards Chipping Norton. Take 2nd sign for Chastleton*

Peacefully located in the Cotswold countryside, this charming "barn" offers pleasant views in all directions. Bedrooms and bathrooms offer high levels of quality and comfort and a range of welcome extras are helpfully included. The large lounge is solely for guest use and is especially comfortable when the roaring log fire is lit. Breakfast is a highlight with a good selection of carefully prepared homemade and local produce.

Rooms 2 en suite S £50; D £75* **Facilities** tea/coffee Cen ht Wi-fi **Conf** Max 20 Thtr 20 Class 20 Board 20 **Parking** 20 **Notes** LB ⊗ No Children 10yrs ⊜

NAILSWORTH — Map 4 ST89

Hazelwood

★★★★ BED AND BREAKFAST

Church St GL6 0BP

☎ 01453 839304

e-mail: stay@hazelwood.me.uk

web: www.hazelwood.me.uk

dir: *Off A46 in town centre onto A4014 (Avening Rd), 1st right*

Quietly located just a stroll from the centre of this interesting town, Hazelwood offers a comfortable and relaxing base for exploring the Cotswolds. The spacious

bedrooms have many thoughtful extras, and the pleasant garden and off-road parking are welcome benefits.

Rooms 3 rms (2 en suite) (1 pri facs) S £35-£40; D £50-£60* **Facilities** tea/coffee Cen ht Wi-fi **Parking** 3 **Notes** ⊗ No Children 12yrs ⊜

Heavens Above

★★★★ ⓜⓜ RESTAURANT WITH ROOMS

3 Cossack Square GL6 0DB

☎ 01453 832615

e-mail: info@wild-garlic.co.uk

dir: *M4 junct 18. A46 towards Stroud. Enter Nailsworth, turn left at rdbt and then an immediate left. Restaurant opposite Britannia Pub*

Situated in a quiet corner of this charming Cotswold town, this restaurant with rooms offers a delightful combination of welcoming and relaxed hospitality with high quality cuisine. Bedrooms are located above the restaurant and are spacious and well equipped. A small and friendly team of staff ensure guests are very well looked after throughout their stay.

Rooms 3 rms (1 en suite) (2 fmly) S £65-£85; D £65-£85* **Facilities** tea/coffee Dinner available Cen ht Wi-fi Golf **Notes** ⊗ No coaches

Highlands

★★★★ BED AND BREAKFAST

Shortwood GL6 0SJ

☎ 01453 832591 ⓘ 01453 833590

e-mail: anne@nailsworthbandb.co.uk

dir: *Off A46 rdbt in Nailsworth onto Nympsfield road, turn left, pass bus station, fork left at Britannia Inn, follow signs for Wallow Green, Highlands opp church*

This friendly guest house occupies a quiet elevated position on the outskirts of Nailsworth. The homely bedrooms are filled with stylish furniture and accessories, and there is a comfortable conservatory-lounge and an attractive breakfast dining room.

Rooms 3 en suite (1 GF) S £35-£40; D £60-£65* **Facilities** TVL tea/coffee Cen ht Wi-fi **Parking** 3 **Notes** LB ⊗ No Children 8yrs

NAUNTON — Map 10 SP12

Mill View

★★★★ GUEST HOUSE

2 Mill View GL54 3AF

☎ 01451 850586 ⓘ 01451 850970

e-mail: ralph.boult@care4free.net

web: www.millviewguesthousecotswolds.com

dir: *Gff B4068 to E end of village*

Lying opposite a historic watermill, this former family home has been extended and modernised to provide every comfort. A warm welcome and attentive care is assured in this non-smoking house, which has one bedroom equipped for easier access. The accommodation provides a good base for walkers or for touring Gloucestershire.

Rooms 3 en suite (1 GF) S £45-£55; D £65-£75* **Facilities** TVL tea/coffee Dinner available Cen ht **Parking** 4 **Notes** LB ⊗ ⊜

NEWENT — Map 10 SO72

Three Choirs Vineyards

★★★★ ⓜⓜ RESTAURANT WITH ROOMS

GL18 1LS

☎ 01531 890223 ⓘ 01531 890877

e-mail: info@threechoirs.com

web: www.threechoirs.com

dir: *On B4215 N of Newent, follow brown tourist signs*

This thriving vineyard continues to go from strength to strength and provides a wonderfully different place to stay. The restaurant, which overlooks the 100-acre estate, enjoys a popular following thanks to well-executed dishes that make good use of local produce. Spacious, high quality bedrooms are equipped with many extras, and each opens on to a private patio area from where wonderful views can be enjoyed.

Rooms 11 annexe en suite (1 fmly) (11 GF); D £115-£165* **Facilities** FTV tea/coffee Dinner available Direct Dial Cen ht Wine tasting Vineyard Tours **Conf** Max 20 Thtr 20 Class 15 Board 20 **Parking** 11 **Notes** LB Closed 24-27 Dec No coaches

Malswick Mill B&B

★★★ BED AND BREAKFAST

Malswick Mill, Malswick GL18 1HF
☎ 01452 790680
web: www.malswickmill.co.uk
dir: N from Mailswick Mill on A40, on right 1m after petrol station

Malswick Mill is a family-run B&B with a small, high quality fishery, located on the outskirts of The Forest of Dean. Bedrooms are located in a newly refurbished annexe building, while a separate converted barn provides an ideal area in which to enjoy breakfast or a drink from the bar in the evening. In addition to fishing, guests can enjoy the delightful surrounding grounds or simply sit by the lake and relax.

Rooms 3 en suite (1 fmly) (3 GF) **Facilities** TVL tea/coffee Cen ht Licensed Fishing **Parking** 20 **Notes** ⊗ Closed 22 Dec-3 Jan ⊕

Northfield Guest House

★★★★ GUEST ACCOMMODATION

Cirencester Rd GL54 3JL
☎ 01451 860427 🖹 01451 860427
e-mail: p.loving@sky.com
dir: Signed off A429 (Northleach-Cirencester road), 1m from Northleach lights

Located south of the historic town, this Cotswold stone house offers homely bedrooms, two of which have direct access to the immaculate gardens. Tasty eggs from the contented resident hens feature at breakfast, served in the elegant dining room. A comfortable lounge is also provided.

Rooms 2 en suite 1 annexe en suite (1 fmly) (3 GF) **Facilities** TVL tea/coffee Cen ht **Parking** 10 **Notes** ⊗ Closed Dec-Feb

The Puesdown Inn

★★★★ ⊚⊚ INN

Compton Abdale GL54 4DN
☎ 01451 860262 🖹 01451 861262
e-mail: inn4food@btopenworld.com
web: www.puesdown.cotswoldinns.com
dir: 3m W from Northleach on A40

A friendly welcome awaits at this long-established inn, a popular stop-off between Cheltenham and Oxford. The stylish modern restaurant provides an enjoyable and informal environment for sampling accomplished cuisine. Individually designed bedrooms, which are accessed externally, have great appeal and offer high standards of contemporary quality.

Rooms 3 en suite (1 fmly) (3 GF) S £50-£79.50; D £79.50-£89.50 (room only)* **Facilities** tea/coffee Dinner available Cen ht Wi-fi **Conf** Max 50 Thtr 50 Class 20 Board 20 **Parking** 80 **Notes** LB Closed 1 wk Jan RS Sun eve Restaurant & bar closed

The Sodbury House

★★★ GUEST HOUSE

Badminton Rd BS37 6LU
☎ 01454 312847 🖹 01454 273105
e-mail: info@sodburyhouse.co.uk
web: www.sodburyhouse.co.uk
dir: M4 junct 18, A46 N, 2m left onto A432 to Chipping Sodbury, house 1m on left

This comfortably furnished 19th-century farmhouse stands in six acres of grounds. The bedrooms, many located on the ground floor and in buildings adjacent to the main house, have many extra facilities. Breakfast is a varied choice served in the spacious breakfast room.

Rooms 6 en suite 9 annexe en suite (2 fmly) (7 GF) S £59; D £85* **Facilities** TVL tea/coffee Direct Dial Cen ht Wi-fi ⛵ **Conf** Thtr 40 Class 25 Board 20 **Parking** 30 **Notes** ⊗ Closed 24 Dec-3 Jan

PREMIER COLLECTION

Prospect Cottage

★★★★★ GUEST ACCOMMODATION

Lower Wye Valley Rd, Bigsweir GL15 6RR
☎ 01594 530566 🖹 01594 530566
e-mail: enquiries@prospectcottage.com
dir: 1m W of St Briavels. Off A466 onto track adjoining Bigsweir Bridge lights, continue 1m

With a peaceful riverside location, this pretty house will have special appeal to guests with an interest in wildlife. A variety of birds can be observed from the comfortable balcony and guests also have use of a well-furnished lounge. Although some 200 years old, the house has contemporary styling throughout that creates a calm and relaxing environment. Friendly and attentive service is a highlight of any stay here, as are the carefully prepared, delicious home-cooked dinners.

Rooms 2 rms (2 pri facs) S £55-£65; D £80-£90* **Facilities** STV TVL tea/coffee Dinner available Cen ht Fishing **Parking** 8 **Notes** LB ⊗ No Children 11yrs ⊕

The Florence

★★★★ GUEST ACCOMMODATION

Bigsweir GL15 6QQ
☎ 01594 530830 🖹 01594 530830
e-mail: enquiries@florencehotel.co.uk
dir: On A466 between Monmouth & Chepstow

Located on the Wye Valley road, The Florence has delightful views across the river and stands in over five acres of gardens with woodland walks. Bedrooms, some in the main house and the others in an adjacent cottage, come in a range of sizes and styles. Guests can enjoy cream teas in the garden, a drink in the snug, and choose from a wide selection of carefully prepared dishes at both lunch and dinner.

Rooms 4 en suite 4 annexe en suite (1 fmly) (2 GF) S £35-£37.50; D £70-£75* **Facilities** tea/coffee Dinner available Cen ht Licensed Fishing **Conf** Max 12 Thtr 12 Class 12 Board 12 **Parking** 30 **Notes** LB ⊗ No Children 5yrs

Aston House

★★★★ BED AND BREAKFAST

Broadwell GL56 0TJ
☎ 01451 830475
e-mail: fja@astonhouse.net
dir: *A429 from Stow-on-the-Wold towards Moreton-in-Marsh, 1m right at x-rds to Broadwell, Aston House 0.5m on left*

Peacefully located on the edge of the village of Broadwell, this is an ideal base from which to explore the charming delights of the Cotswolds. A warm and genuine welcome is assured and every effort is made to ensure a relaxed and enjoyable stay. Great care and attention are hallmarks here, and bedrooms come equipped with many thoughtful extras such as electric blankets.

Rooms 3 rms (2 en suite) (1 pri facs) (1 GF) D £62-£70 **Facilities** tea/coffee Cen ht stairlift **Parking** 3 **Notes** ⊗ No Children 10yrs Closed Nov-Feb ⊛

Kings Head Inn & Restaurant

★★★★ ⊛ INN

The Green, Bledington OX7 6XQ
☎ 01608 658365 📠 01608 658902
e-mail: kingshead@orr-ewing.com
web: www.kingsheadinn.net
dir: *4m SE off B4450*

Located on the delightful village green near the river, this 16th-century inn has spacious public areas with open fires, wobbly floors, beams and wood furnishings. The comfortable restaurant offers excellent dining and the bedrooms have been creatively decorated and well furnished; some rooms are in a converted annexe.

Rooms 6 en suite 6 annexe en suite (3 GF) **Facilities** FTV TVL tea/coffee Dinner available Direct Dial Cen ht Wi-fi **Parking** 24 **Notes** ⊗ Closed 25-26 Dec No coaches

Woodlands Guest House

★★★★ GUEST ACCOMMODATION

Upper Swell GL54 1EW
☎ 01451 832346
e-mail: amandak247@talktalk.net
dir: *Upper Swell 1m from Stow-on-the-Wold, take B4077 (Tewkesbury Road)*

Situated in the small hamlet of Upper Swell, Woodlands provides an ideal base for exploring many charming nearby villages. This establishment enjoys delightful rural views and has comfortably appointed bedrooms with a good range of extra accessories. Breakfast is served in the welcoming dining room around the communal dining table. Off-road parking is available.

Rooms 5 en suite (2 GF) **Facilities** FTV TV4B tea/coffee Cen ht Wi-fi **Parking** 8 **Notes** LB ⊗ ⊛

Corsham Field Farmhouse *(SP217249)*

★★★ FARMHOUSE

Bledington Rd GL54 1JH
☎ 01451 831750 📄 01451 832247 Mr R Smith
e-mail: farmhouse@corshamfield.co.uk
dir: *2m SE of Stow on B4450*

This establishment, which has views of the surrounding countryside from its elevated position, is a popular choice with walking groups and families. The modern bedrooms are practically equipped and located in two separate houses. Enjoyable breakfasts are taken in the spacious dining room, which also provides a lounge. The local pub is just a short walk away and has a reputation for good food.

Rooms 7 rms (5 en suite) (3 fmly) (2 GF) S £35-£45; D £50-£65* **Facilities** tea/coffee Cen ht Wi-fi **Parking** 10 **Notes** LB ⊗ ⊛ 100 acres arable

Limes

★★★ GUEST ACCOMMODATION

Evesham Rd GL54 1EJ
☎ 01451 830034 📄 01451 830034
e-mail: thelimes@zoom.co.uk
dir: *500yds from village centre on A424*

Just a short walk from the village centre, this Victorian house provides a comfortable base from which to explore this beautiful area. Bedroom styles vary, with four-poster and ground-floor rooms offered. A warm and genuine welcome is extended, and many guests return on a regular basis. A spacious lounge is available and breakfast is served in the light and airy dining room.

Rooms 5 en suite 2 annexe en suite (2 fmly) (2 GF) S £30-£53; D £52-£65* **Facilities** STV TVL tea/coffee Cen ht **Parking** 4 **Notes** Closed Xmas ⊛

1 Woodchester Lodge

★★★★ BED AND BREAKFAST

Southfield Rd, North Woodchester GL5 5PA
☎ 01453 872586
e-mail: anne@woodchesterlodge.co.uk
dir: *A46 onto Selsley Rd, take 2nd left, 200yds on left*

Close to the newly re-routed Cotswold Way, this late Victorian former timber merchant's house is set in the peaceful village of North Woodchester and is just a short drive from Stroud. In its own landscaped gardens, this large house has spacious, sympathetically restored bedrooms and a comfortable lounge. Evening meals and freshly prepared breakfasts are not to be missed.

Rooms 2 rms (1 en suite) (1 pri facs) (1 fmly) S £40-£45; D £60-£65* **Facilities** TVL tea/coffee Dinner available Cen ht Wi-fi ⛳ Golf 18 Squash Riding **Parking** 4 **Notes** ⊗ Closed Xmas & Etr

Hyde Crest

★★★★ BED AND BREAKFAST

Cirencester Rd GL6 8PE
☎ 01453 731631
e-mail: anthea@hydecrest.demon.co.uk
web: www.hydecrest.co.uk
dir: *Off A419, 5m E of Stroud, signed Minchinhampton & Aston Down, house 3rd right opp Ragged Cot pub*

Hyde Crest lies on the edge of the picturesque Cotswold village of Minchinhampton. Bedrooms are located at ground floor level, each with a private patio where welcome refreshments are enjoyed upon arrival (weather permitting). Guests are attentively cared for and scrumptious breakfasts are served in the small lounge-dining room around a communal table.

Rooms 3 en suite (3 GF) **Facilities** TVL tea/coffee Cen ht Wi-fi **Parking** 6 **Notes** No Children 10yrs RS Xmas & New Year (no meals available) 🐾

TETBURY — Map 4 ST89

PREMIER COLLECTION

Beaufort House
★★★★ BED AND BREAKFAST

Willesley GL8 8QU
☎ 01666 880444 📠 01666 880079
e-mail: beauforthouseuk@aol.com
dir: *4m SW of Tetbury. A433 to Willesley, House set back from road*

Within easy reach of Bath and Bristol, this former staging post and inn built of beautiful local stone, dates back to the 17th century. Bedrooms, all with spacious en suites, are thoughtfully equipped and elegantly furnished. There is also a deeply comfortable guest lounge. Breakfast, featuring organic items (when available), is served in the dining room around one grand table. A delightful walled garden may be enjoyed in warmer weather.

Rooms 4 en suite S £75; D £89 **Facilities** FTV TVL tea/coffee Cen ht Wi-fi **Parking** 4 **Notes** ⊗ No Children 10yrs

See advert on this page

Folly Farm B&B & Cottages
★★★ GUEST ACCOMMODATION

Folly Farm, Long Newton GL8 8XA
☎ 01666 502475 📠 01666 502358
e-mail: info@gtb.co.uk
web: www.gtb.co.uk
dir: *M4 junct 17, B4014 signed Tetbury, on right after Welcome to Tetbury sign*

Folly Farm is located among rolling countryside just a 10-minute walk from Tetbury. The well-equipped bedrooms are next to a huge tithe barn with pleasant surrounding grounds, making this a popular venue for weddings. Breakfast is continental only, to be taken at guests' leisure in the bedroom where a refrigerator and dining table are provided.

Rooms 12 en suite (2 fmly) (6 GF) S fr £50; D £60-£100* **Facilities** tea/coffee Cen ht 🛁 **Conf** Max 180 Thtr 100 Class 64 Board 65 **Parking** 100 **Notes** ⊗ Civ Wed 180

TEWKESBURY — Map 10 SO83

Willow Cottages
★★★ GUEST ACCOMMODATION

Shuthonger Common GL20 6ED
☎ 01684 298599 📠 01684 298599
e-mail: RobBrd1@aol.com
dir: *1m N of Tewkesbury, on A38, house on right; or 1m S of M50 junct 1, on A38 house on left*

Located to the north of Tewkesbury in pretty rural surroundings, this welcoming house offers comfortable homely bedrooms with efficient modern bathrooms and a cosy, pine furnished breakfast room. This establishment makes an excellent base for those visiting this picturesque area whether for work or pleasure.

Rooms 3 en suite (1 fmly) S £20-£32; D £40-£56* **Facilities** tea/coffee Dinner available Cen ht **Parking** 6 **Notes** LB 🐾

WILLERSEY — Map 10 SP13

Lowerfield Farm *(SP098406)*
★★★★ Ⓜ FARMHOUSE

WR11 7HF
☎ 01386 858273 📠 01386 854608 Mr & Mrs Atkinson
e-mail: info@lowerfieldfarm.com
dir: *At mini rdbt in Willersey, take Badsey Ln. On right after 0.75m*

Rooms 6 en suite (2 fmly) (2 GF) **Facilities** FTV TVL tea/coffee Dinner available Cen ht Licensed Wi-fi **Parking** 10 **Notes** 6 acres mixed

Beaufort House

Believed to have been a Coaching Inn dating back to the 17th century, Beaufort House is now a luxurious family home where the emphasis is placed firmly on comfort, stylish surroundings and personal service.

The house overlooks Silk Wood, part of the world famous Westonbirt National Arboretum, to which their is direct access from a gate in the field opposite. For the less energetic, afternoon tea or a glass of wine in the evening can be enjoyed in the gazebo in the peaceful surroundings of the walled garden.

The guests' sitting room is very comfortably furnished and has an open fire at colder times of the year.

Breakfast is served around the beautiful magogany table in the family dining room.

Willesley, Tetbury,
Gloucestershire GL8 8QU
Contact: John Prescott
Tel: 01666 880444
Email: beauforthouseuk@aol.com

WINCHCOMBE — Map 10 SP02

Sudeley Hill Farm *(SP038276)*

★★★★ FARMHOUSE

GL54 5JB
☎ 01242 602344 📠 01242 602344 Mrs B Scudamore
e-mail: scudamore4@aol.com
dir: *Off B4632 in Winchcombe onto Castle St, White Hart Inn on corner, farm 0.75m on left*

Located on an 800-acre mixed arable and sheep farm, this 15th-century mellow stone farmhouse is full of original features including fires and exposed beams. Genuine hospitality is always on offer here with a relaxed and welcoming atmosphere. The comfortable bedrooms are filled with thoughtful extras, and memorable breakfasts are served in the elegant dining room overlooking immaculate gardens.

Rooms 3 en suite (1 fmly) S £30-£45; D £70-£75*
Facilities TVL tea/coffee Cen ht **Parking** 10 **Notes** ⊗
Closed Xmas ⊗ 800 acres sheep/arable

Wesley House

★★★★ ⊕⊕ 🏠 RESTAURANT WITH ROOMS

High St GL54 5LJ
☎ 01242 602366 📠 01242 609046
e-mail: enquiries@wesleyhouse.co.uk
web: www.wesleyhouse.co.uk
dir: *In town centre*

This 15th-century, half-timbered property is named after John Wesley, founder of the Methodist Church, who stayed here while preaching in the town. Bedrooms are small but full of character. In the rear dining room, a unique lighting system changes colour to suit the mood required, and to highlight the various floral creations by a world-renowned flower arranger. A glass atrium covers the outside terrace.

Rooms 5 en suite S £70-£75; D £85-£100 **Facilities** tea/coffee Dinner available Cen ht Wi-fi **Conf** Thtr 30 Class 40 **Notes** LB ⊗ RS Sun eve Restaurant closed Civ Wed 60

GREATER MANCHESTER

ALTRINCHAM — Map 15 SJ78

Rostherne Country House

★★★★ GUEST ACCOMMODATION

Rostherne Ln, Rostherne WA16 6RY
☎ 01565 832628
e-mail: info@rosthernehouse.co.uk

(For full entry see Knutsford (Cheshire))

BOLTON — Map 15 SD70

Broomfield House

★★★ GUEST HOUSE

33-35 Wigan Rd, Deane BL3 5PX
☎ 01204 61570 📠 01204 650932
e-mail: chris@broomfield.force9.net
dir: *M61 junct 5, A58 to 1st lights, straight onto A676, premises on right*

A friendly relaxed atmosphere prevails at Broomfield House, close to the motorway and west of the town centre. There is a comfy lounge and separate bar area. Hearty breakfasts are served in the dining room.

Rooms 20 en suite (2 fmly) (2 GF) (9 smoking) S £42; D £55 **Facilities** TVL tea/coffee Cen ht Licensed Wi-fi **Parking** 12

DELPH — Map 16 SD90

Wellcroft House

★★★★ GUEST ACCOMMODATION

Bleak Hey Nook OL3 5LY
☎ 01457 875017
e-mail: wellcrofthouse@hotmail.co.uk
web: www.wellcrofthouse.co.uk
dir: *Off A62 on Standedge Foot Rd near A670 junct*

Commanding superb views down the valley below this former weaver's cottage offers warm traditional hospitality to walkers on the Pennine Way and those simply touring the Pennine towns and villages. Modern comforts in all bedrooms and transport from local railway or walks is routinely provided by the friendly proprietors.

Rooms 3 rms (2 en suite) (1 GF) S £30-£35; D £50-£60* **Facilities** TVL tea/coffee Dinner available Cen ht Pool Table **Parking** 1 **Notes** LB ⊗

DIGGLE — Map 16 SE00

Sunfield Accommodation

★★ GUEST ACCOMMODATION

Diglea OL3 5LA
☎ 01457 874030
e-mail: info@sunfieldaccom.co.uk
dir: *Off A670 to Diggle, off Huddersfield Rd onto Sam Rd to Diggle Hotel & signs for Diggle Ranges*

This friendly, family-run operation is located within easy reach of Manchester and the M62, and affords wonderful views over the Pennines; bedrooms are on the ground floor and pets are made welcome. Breakfast is served at one large table and a couple of good pubs serving food are located at the bottom of the lane.

Rooms 4 en suite (1 fmly) (4 GF) S £30-£40; D £50-£55* **Facilities** FTV TVL tea/coffee Cen ht **Parking** 11 **Notes** ⊗

LITTLEBOROUGH — Map 16 SD91

Hollingworth Lake Bed & Breakfast

★★★★★ 🅰 GUEST ACCOMMODATION

164 Smithy Bridge Rd OL15 0DB
☎ 01706 376583 📠 01706 374054
dir: *M62 junct 21, take A640N brown signs to Hollingworth Lake Country Park, at T-junct onto small rdbt, right onto Smithy Bridge Rd, 50yds on right*

Rooms 3 en suite 2 annexe en suite (1 fmly) (2 GF) S £37.50; D £50 **Facilities** STV FTV tea/coffee Cen ht Wi-fi **Conf** Max 10 **Parking** 8 **Notes** RS 25-26 Dec & 1 Jan No breakfast

MANCHESTER — Map 15 SJ89

The Ascott

★★★★ GUEST ACCOMMODATION

6 Half Edge Ln, Ellesmere Park, Eccles M30 9GJ
☎ 0161 950 2453 📠 0161 661 7063
e-mail: ascottmanchester@talk21.com
web: www.ascotthotel.co.uk
dir: *M602 junct 2, left onto Wellington Rd, 0.25m right onto Abbey Grove & left onto Half Edge Ln*

Set in a mainly residential area close to major routes, this early Victorian house, once the home of the mayor of Eccles, has been renovated to provide thoughtfully furnished bedrooms with smart modern bathrooms. A choice of breakfast rooms is available and there is an elegant lounge.

Rooms 14 rms (13 en suite) (1 pri facs) (1 fmly) (4 GF) **Facilities** TVL tea/coffee Direct Dial Cen ht Wi-fi **Parking** 12 **Notes** ⊗ Closed 22 Dec-2 Jan RS Sun Closed 1-5pm

New Central Guest House

★★★ GUEST ACCOMMODATION

144-146 Heywood St, Off Cheetham Hill Rd M8 0DF
☎ 0161 205 2169 📄 0161 211 9299
e-mail: info@newcentralhotel.com
dir: 1.5m N of city centre. Off A665 Cheetham Hill Rd opp Esso station onto Heywood St

Located within easy reach of the city, this refurbished property offers very good hospitality and modern bedrooms. There is a cosy lounge and secure parking, and ample breakfasts are served in the spacious dining room.

Rooms 9 rms (5 en suite) (3 fmly) Facilities TVL tea/coffee Cen ht Wi-fi Parking 2 Notes ⊗ No Children 5yrs

Thistlewood

★★★ GUEST HOUSE

203 Urmston Ln, Stretford M32 9EF
☎ 0161 865 3611 📄 0161 866 8133
e-mail: iain.campbell30@ntlworld.com
dir: M60 junct 7, A56 towards Stretford, left onto A5181 & Sandy Ln, left onto A5213

This grand Victorian house is set in attractive grounds in a residential area close to the M60. Within easy reach are Old Trafford football and cricket grounds, and the airport. The bedrooms are well equipped, and the public rooms, including a lounge, are spacious and comfortable.

Rooms 9 en suite S fr £40; D fr £54* Facilities TVL tea/coffee Cen ht Licensed Wi-fi Parking 12 Notes ⊗

Luther King House

★★★ 🄰 GUEST ACCOMMODATION

Brighton Grove, Off Wilmslow Rd M14 5JP
☎ 0161 224 6404 📄 0161 248 9201
e-mail: reception@lkh.co.uk
web: www.lkh.co.uk
dir: S of city centre opp Platt Fields park

Rooms 46 en suite (7 fmly) (6 GF) Facilities STV tea/coffee Dinner available Direct Dial Cen ht Licensed Pool Table Conf Max 125 Thtr 70 Class 70 Board 54 Parking 45 Notes Closed 24 Dec-2 Jan Civ Wed 125

MANCHESTER AIRPORT   Map 15 SJ88

Rylands Farm Guest House

★★★ GUEST ACCOMMODATION

Altrincham Rd SK9 4LT
☎ 01625 535646 & 548041 📄 01625 255256
e-mail: info@rylandsfarm.com
web: www.rylandsfarm.com
dir: M56 junct 6, A538 towards Wilmslow, house 1.5m on left after Wilmslow Moat House

Situated in pretty gardens and convenient for Manchester Airport, this property provides a range of bedrooms, some of which are well furnished and located in a separate building. Breakfast is taken in an attractive conservatory dining room, which also contains a comfortable lounge area with honesty bar.

Rooms 3 en suite 6 annexe en suite (3 fmly) (3 GF) Facilities TVL tea/coffee Dinner available Cen ht Licensed Conf Max 30 Class 30 Parking 15 Notes Closed 24-25 Dec & 31 Dec-1 Jan

MELLOR   Map 16 SJ98

The Moorfield Arms

★★★★ INN

Shiloh Rd SK6 5NE
☎ 0161 427 1580 📄 0161 427 1582
e-mail: info@moorfieldarms.co.uk
dir: 1m NE of Mellor. Off A6015 towards Mellor, right onto Shiloh Rd, 0.3m on left

Located in an elevated position with stunning views of the surrounding countryside including Kinder Scout, this 400-year-old property has been renovated and extended to provide spacious, comfortable public areas and tastefully furnished modern bedrooms in a sympathetic barn conversion.

Rooms 4 annexe en suite (1 fmly) (3 GF) S £60; D £70-£90* Facilities tea/coffee Dinner available Cen ht Conf Max 90 Class 40 Board 25 Parking 100 Notes LB ⊗

SALE   Map 15 SJ79

Brooklands Lodge

★★★★ GUEST HOUSE

208 Marsland Rd M33 3NE
☎ 0161 973 3283
e-mail: enquiries@brooklandslodge.co.uk
web: www.brooklandslodge.co.uk
dir: M60 junct 6, 1m on A6144 Marsland Rd

This long established, privately run guest house is well located for Manchester Airport, the city centre, Old Trafford and the Trafford Centre. The comfortably furnished accommodation includes thoughtful extras to provide a home from home. Breakfast can be taken either in your room or in the attractive dining room.

Rooms 8 rms (7 en suite) (1 pri facs) (3 fmly) (5 GF) S £40-£45; D £55-£70* Facilities FTV TVL tea/coffee Dinner available Cen ht Wi-fi Conf Max 16 Thtr 16 Class 16 Board 16 Parking 9 Notes LB No Children 5yrs

WIGAN   Map 15 SD50

The Beeches

★★★ RESTAURANT WITH ROOMS

School Ln, Standish WN6 0TD
☎ 01257 426432 & 421316 📄 01257 427503
e-mail: mail@beecheshotel.co.uk
dir: M6 junct 27, A5209 into Standish on School Ln

Located a short drive from M6, this elegant Victorian house has been renovated to provide high standards of comfort. Bedrooms are equipped with practical and homely extras, and public areas include spacious lounges, a popular brasserie, and a self-contained function suite.

Rooms 10 en suite (4 fmly) S £35-£40; D £45-£50* Facilities FTV tea/coffee Dinner available Cen ht Conf Max 120 Thtr 100 Board 40 Parking 120 Notes LB ⊗ Civ Wed 60

HAMPSHIRE

ALRESFORD

See New Alresford

ALTON   Map 5 SU73

Beech Barns Guest House

★★★★ GUEST ACCOMMODATION

61 Wellhouse Rd, Beech GU34 4AQ
☎ 01420 85575 & 07759 723112 📄 01420 85575
e-mail: timsiggs@yahoo.com
dir: 1.5m W of Alton. Off A339 towards Beech, 2nd right onto Wellhouse Rd, 0.5m left

This well-appointed property has easy access to the motorway system. Set on the outskirts of Alton in its own grounds at the end of a quiet lane, there is no shortage of walking and cycling around this picturesque village. The proprietors are welcoming and friendly, and bedrooms are smartly appointed in contemporary style to provide a good range of facilities. A separate lounge is available for guest use, and dinner can be offered on request.

Rooms 9 en suite (2 fmly) (6 GF) Facilities TVL tea/coffee Dinner available Cen ht ⌂ Conf Max 18 Class 18 Parking 12

The Granary (SU770397)

★★★★ 🅰 FARMHOUSE

Stubbs Farm, Kingsley GU35 9NR
☎ 01420 474906 📄 01420 474906 Mrs J Stephens
e-mail: info@stubbsfarm.co.uk
web: www.stubbsfarm.co.uk
dir: A31 onto B3004, after 5m turn left to South Hay. 1m left to Stubbs Farm - no through road

Rooms 3 en suite S fr £55; D fr £80 Facilities tea/coffee Cen ht Fishing Parking 3 Notes ⊗ No Children 12yrs Closed 14 Dec-5 Jan 600 acres arable/beef

ANDOVER   Map 5 SU34

The Barn House B&B

★★★★★ 🅰 BED AND BREAKFAST

Forton SP11 6NU
☎ 01264 720544
e-mail: hello@thebarnhousebandb.co.uk
web: www.thebarnhousebandb.co.uk
dir: M3 junct 8 onto A303, onto B3048 to Longparish. Right to Forton, 2nd drive on left

Rooms 2 en suite S £60-£75; D £80-£105 Facilities FTV tea/coffee Cen ht Parking 4 Notes ⊗

See advert on opposite page

Forest Edge

★★★★ BED AND BREAKFAST

Andover Down SP11 6LJ
☎ 01264 364526
e-mail: david@forest-edge.co.uk
web: www.forest-edge.co.uk
dir: 1.5m E of Andover. A303 onto A3093 & B3400, 1m on right

Forest Edge is situated in the beautiful Hampshire countryside, a few miles from Andover and within easy reach of the A303, M3, Basingstoke, Winchester and Salisbury. The property is set in over an acre of landscaped and eco-friendly gardens where guests can relax or walk at their leisure.

Rooms 4 en suite (4 GF) S £40-£45; D £60-£65* Facilities FTV tea/coffee Dinner available Cen ht Wi-fi 🏊 ⌂ Gymnasium Conf Max 8 Parking 6 Notes ⊗

May Cottage

★★★★ BED AND BREAKFAST

SP11 8LZ
☎ 01264 771241 & 07768 242166 📄 01264 771770
e-mail: info@maycottage-thruxton.co.uk
web: www.maycottage-thruxton.co.uk
dir: 3.5m W of Andover. Off A303 signed Thruxton (Village Only), opp George Inn

Excellent customer care is assured at this 18th-century, part-thatched house, which stands in pretty gardens in the heart of the village. Fine art and furnishings enhance the original features, and bedrooms are filled with a wealth of thoughtful extras. Comprehensive breakfasts are served in the attractive dining room.

Rooms 3 en suite S £45-£65; D £65-£90* Facilities STV TVL tea/coffee Cen ht Parking 5 Notes LB ⊗ 🐾

ASHURST   Map 5 SU31

Forest Gate Lodge

★★★★ 🅰 GUEST HOUSE

161 Lyndhurst Rd SO40 7AW
☎ 023 8029 3026 📄 023 8029 3026
dir: On A35 in village

Rooms 4 en suite (1 fmly) S £15-£35; D £30-£70* Facilities FTV tea/coffee Cen ht Parking 6 Notes LB ⊗ No Children 5yrs 🐾

BARTON-ON-SEA   Map 5 SZ29

Pebble Beach

★★★★ RESTAURANT WITH ROOMS

Marine Dr BH25 7DZ
☎ 01425 627777 📄 01425 610689
e-mail: mail@pebblebeach.uk.com
dir: Follow A35 from Southampton onto A337 to New Milton, turn left onto Barton Court Av to clifftop

Situated on the cliff top the restaurant at this establishment boasts stunning views towards The Needles. Bedrooms and bathrooms, situated above the restaurant, are well equipped and provide a range of accessories to enhance guest comfort. A freshly cooked breakfast is served in the main restaurant.

Rooms 3 en suite S £69.95; D £89.95-£99.95* Facilities FTV tea/coffee Dinner available Cen ht Parking 20 Notes ⊗ RS 25 Dec & 1 Jan dinner not available No coaches

BENTLEY   Map 5 SU74

PREMIER COLLECTION

Bentley Green Farm

★★★★★ 🅰 BED AND BREAKFAST

The Drift GU10 5JX
☎ 01420 23246 & 07711 981614
e-mail: enquiries@bentleygreenfarm.co.uk
web: www.bentleygreenfarm.co.uk
dir: 500yds S of village. Off A31 Farnham-Alton signed Bentley, left at T-junct & 1st right

Situated just off the A31, a short drive from the village centre, this Grade II listed farm offers outstanding luxury. The first floor smaller double in the main house boasts a private bathroom and wet room shower. A separate ground floor private lounge with fireplace is the ideal place to sample owners Glenda and Chris Powell's excellent hospitality. The annexe suite of rooms includes lounge, dining and kitchen area overlooking the gardens and swimming pool. A total of 39 acres surrounds the house boasting a tennis court, spa pool and its own private fishing. Breakfast is served in the dining room around a big oak table.

Rooms 1 rms (1 pri facs) 1 annexe en suite (1 fmly) (1 GF) S £85; D £95-£115* Facilities STV FTV TVL tea/coffee Cen ht 🐾 🎣 Fishing Trampolines, tree house, hot tub Parking 13 Notes ⊗ 🐾

BRANSGORE
Map 5 SZ19

Tothill House

★★★★ BED AND BREAKFAST

Black Ln, off Forest Rd BH23 8EA
☎ 01425 674414 📄 01425 672235
dir: M27 onto A31 or A35, house is 0.75m NE of Bransgore centre

Built for an admiral in 1908, Tothill House is located in the southern part of the New Forest. The garden backs on to the forest, where deer, ponies and other wildlife are frequent visitors. The spacious bedrooms are furnished to a high standard, reflecting the character of the house. There is an elegant library, and a generous breakfast is served in the dining room.

Rooms 3 rms (2 en suite) (1 pri facs) S £40; D £70-£80*
Facilities tea/coffee Cen ht **Parking** 6 **Notes** ⊗ No Children 16yrs Closed Nov-Feb 🐾

BROCKENHURST
Map 5 SU30

PREMIER COLLECTION

The Cottage Lodge

★★★★★ GUEST ACCOMMODATION

Sway Rd SO42 7SH
☎ 01590 622296 📄 01590 623014
e-mail: enquiries@cottagelodge.co.uk
web: www.cottagelodge.co.uk
dir: Off A337 opp Careys Manor Hotel onto Grigg Ln, 0.25m over x-rds, cottage next to war memorial

This 17th-century forester's cottage in the town centre is a good base for exploring the New Forest. The comfortable bedrooms are individually furnished and thoughtfully equipped. There is a cosy bar lounge with a fire, where tea can be served and a small selection of drinks is available.

Rooms 9 en suite 3 annexe en suite (6 GF) S £50-£120; D £55-£160 **Facilities** tea/coffee Cen ht Licensed Wi-fi **Parking** 14 **Notes** LB No Children 10yrs Closed Xmas & New Year

Little Heathers Guest House

★★★★ GUEST ACCOMMODATION

13 Whitemoor Rd SO42 7QG
☎ 01590 623512
e-mail: littleheathers@msn.com
dir: M27 junct 1 onto A337 through Lyndhurst. Right onto Meerut Rd, right again onto Rhinefield Rd. Left onto Oberfield Rd, left onto Whitemoor Rd

Set in a quiet cul-de-sac on the outskirts of the village, this modern guest house offers well-appointed and comfortable ground floor accommodation. A well-prepared and hearty breakfast can be enjoyed overlooking the gardens, and is the perfect start to a day perhaps spent exploring the New Forest and other nearby attractions.

Rooms 3 en suite (1 fmly) (3 GF) S £45-£55; D £70-£80*
Facilities tea/coffee Cen ht **Parking** 4 **Notes** ⊗ 🐾

Seraya

★★★ BED AND BREAKFAST

8 Grigg Ln SO42 7RE
☎ 01590 622426
e-mail: edwin.ward@btinternet.com
web: www.serayanewforest.co.uk
dir: Off A337 opp Careys Manor Hotel onto Grigg Ln, 500yds on corner Horlock Rd

Well placed for visiting the New Forest, and close to the centre of town with its good eating options, this delightful guest house offers attractive rooms with a broad selection of extra facilities. A hearty breakfast is served around the communal dining table.

Rooms 3 rms (1 en suite); D £52-£65* **Facilities** tea/coffee Cen ht **Parking** 3 **Notes** LB 🐾

The Barn House
bed and breakfast

AA Associate Bed & Breakfast

enjoyEngland.com ★★★★★ BED & BREAKFAST

Silver

A luxury Five Star B&B
accommodation in Hampshire's picturesque Test Valley.

During your stay with us you can enjoy the Hampshire countryside, explore the surrounding pretty villages with their thatched cottages and country pubs, stroll beside the River Test, or discover the many places of interest nearby.

We provide the highest standards of accommodation, food and hospitality to make your stay as comfortable as possible.

Tel: +44 (0)1264 720544
www.thebarnhousebandb.co.uk

BURGHCLERE | Map 5 SU46

Carnarvon Arms

Ⓤ

Winchester Rd, Whitway RG20 9LE
☎ 01635 278222
e-mail: info@carnarvonarms.com
dir: From A34 take road signed Highclere Castle & Tothill Svcs

Currently the rating for this establishment is not confirmed. This may be due to a change of ownership or because it has only recently joined the AA rating scheme. For up-to-date information please see the AA website: theAA.com.

Rooms 7 en suite 16 annexe en suite (16 GF) S £69-£89; D £79-£95* **Facilities** FTV TVL tea/coffee Dinner available Direct Dial Cen ht Licensed Wi-fi **Conf** Max 50 Thtr 50 Class 32 Board 26 **Parking** 40

CADNAM | Map 5 SU31

Walnut Cottage

★★★★ BED AND BREAKFAST

Old Romsey Rd SO40 2NP
☎ 023 8081 2275
dir: M27 junct 1, Cadnam rdbt onto A3090, Old Romsey Rd 1st left

This charming, mid 19th-century cottage is convenient for the New Forest or nearby business areas. The comfortable bedrooms are brightly decorated. An inviting lounge is available, and hearty English breakfasts are enjoyed around a large table in the cosy dining room.

Rooms 3 rms (2 en suite) (1 pri facs) (1 GF) S £44; D £59 **Facilities** TVL tea/coffee Cen ht **Parking** 3 **Notes** ⊗ No Children 14yrs Closed 24-26 Dec ⊛

DUMMER | Map 5 SU54

Tower Hill House

★★★ BED AND BREAKFAST

Tower Hill, Winchester Rd RG25 2AL
☎ 01256 398340 ▤ 01256 398340
e-mail: martin.hyndman@virgin.net
web: www.towerhill-guesthouse.co.uk
dir: In village. M3 junct 7, onto A30 towards Winchester, 2nd left, opp sign for North Waltham

Ideally situated for access to the M3 and A30, while overlooking fields and countryside, this family-run bed and breakfast is in the pretty village of Dummer, just 10 minutes away from the centre of Basingstoke. Bedrooms are simply, but comfortably furnished and a well-prepared breakfast is served in the cheerful dining room.

Rooms 4 rms S £25-£30; D £45-£55* **Facilities** tea/coffee Cen ht Wi-fi **Parking** 6

EASTON | Map 5 SU53

The Cricketers Inn

★★★ INN

SO21 1EJ
☎ 01962 779353
e-mail: robbo1506@btconnect.com
web: www.brilliantpub.co.uk/cricketersinnhampshire
dir: Off B3047 in village centre

Located in the heart of the village and just a short drive from Winchester, this inn combines a friendly village pub atmosphere with three attractive, comfortable and well-equipped bedrooms. The traditional bar and restaurant serve good, home-prepared meals and snacks.

Rooms 3 en suite (1 fmly) S £45-£60; D £50-£65* **Facilities** FTV tea/coffee Dinner available Cen ht Wi-fi **Parking** 12 **Notes** RS Mon-Thu 3-6pm pub only

---

EAST TYTHERLEY | Map 5 SU22

The Star Inn

★★★★ ◉◉ INN

SO51 0LW
☎ 01794 340225
e-mail: info@starinn.co.uk
dir: 1m S of East Tytherley

This charming coaching inn offers bedrooms in a purpose-built annexe, separate from the main pub. The spacious rooms have high levels of quality and comfort, and an outdoor children's play area is available. The inn has a loyal following of locals and visitors, drawn especially by the excellent food.

Rooms 3 annexe en suite (3 GF) S £55-£70; D fr £80* **Facilities** FTV tea/coffee Dinner available Wi-fi **Conf** Max 30 Thtr 24 Class 24 Board 30 **Parking** 50 **Notes** LB RS Sun eve & Mon

---

EMSWORTH | Map 5 SU70

36 on the Quay

★★★★ ◉◉◉ RESTAURANT WITH ROOMS

47 South St PO10 7EG
☎ 01243 375592 & 372257

Occupying a prime position with far reaching views over the estuary, this 16th-century house is the scene for some accomplished and exciting cuisine. The elegant restaurant occupies centre stage with peaceful pastel shades, local art and crisp napery together with glimpses of the bustling harbour outside. The contemporary bedrooms offer style, comfort and thoughtful extras.

Rooms 5 en suite **Facilities** tea/coffee Dinner available Cen ht **Parking** 6 **Notes** LB Closed 3wks Jan, 1wk late May & 1wk late Oct

---

Hollybank House

★★★★ BED AND BREAKFAST

Hollybank Ln PO10 7UN
☎ 01243 375502 ▤ 01243 378118
e-mail: anna@hollybankhouse.com
web: www.hollybankhouse.com
dir: 1m N of town centre. A259 onto B2148, 1m right onto Southleigh Rd, 3rd left onto Hollybank Ln, house at top

This beautiful Georgian country house stands in a 10-acre woodland garden with a tennis court, on the outskirts of Emsworth, and looks out to Chichester Harbour. All the bedrooms are spacious. Emsworth has a variety of restaurants, pubs and harbour walks.

Rooms 4 rms (3 en suite) (1 pri facs) (1 fmly) S £45-£55; D fr £70 **Facilities** tea/coffee Cen ht Wi-fi ➃ ➄ **Parking** 8

Jingles

★★★★ GUEST ACCOMMODATION

77 Horndean Rd PO10 7PU
☎ 01243 373755
e-mail: info@thejingles.co.uk
dir: A3 (M, junct 2, follow signs for Emsworth, 4m, 1st building in Emsworth

Jingles is a family-run business, located in the charming maritime village of Emsworth. Situated adjacent to open farmland, it's a great location for visiting both Portsmouth and Chichester. All bedrooms are en suite and decorated to a high standard. The dining room is the setting for a cooked English breakfast, and a drawing room is available for relaxing in. Wi-fi is available, and guests have complimentary use of the health and fitness club which is only one and a half miles away.

Rooms 28 en suite (2 fmly) (7 GF) **Facilities** FTV tea/coffee Cen ht Wi-fi **Parking** 24 **Notes** ⊗

FAREHAM — Map 5 SU50

Wisteria House

★★★★ BED AND BREAKFAST

14 Mays Ln, Stubbington PO14 2EP
☎ **01329 511940**
e-mail: info@wisteria-house.co.uk
dir: M27 junct 9, take A27 to Fareham. Right onto B3334, at rdbt left onto Mays Ln

Wisteria House is located on the edge of the village of Stubbington, just a short walk from local amenities, and only one mile from the beach at Lee-on-the-Solent. The charming and comfortable bedrooms have en suite bathrooms, are all located on the ground floor, and also now have Wi-fi. Off-road parking is available.

Rooms 2 en suite (2 GF) S £47; D £62* **Facilities** FTV tea/coffee Cen ht Wi-fi **Parking** 2 **Notes** ⊗ No Children 8yrs

Travelrest - Solent Gateway

★★★ GUEST ACCOMMODATION

22 The Avenue PO14 1NS
☎ **01329 232175** ▤ **01329 232196**
e-mail: solentreservations@travelrest.co.uk
web: www.travelrest.co.uk
dir: 0.5m from town centre on A27. 0.25m from railway station

Situated just west of the town centre, this well-presented accommodation is convenient for the ferry terminals and naval heritage sites. The comfortable bedrooms are spacious and well equipped, and one has a four-poster bed. Breakfast is served in the cosy conservatory-dining room and conference rooms are available.

Rooms 19 en suite (3 fmly) (6 GF) S £50–£75; D £50–£75 (room only)* **Facilities** FTV tea/coffee Dinner available Direct Dial Cen ht Wi-fi **Parking** 27

Catisfield Cottage

★★ Ⓐ BED AND BREAKFAST

1 Catisfield Ln PO15 5NW
☎ **01329 843301**
dir: Off A27 at Highlands Rd lights, Catisfield Ln 2nd left

Rooms 6 rms (3 en suite) (1 fmly) S £26–£40; D £53–£65* **Facilities** FTV TVL tea/coffee Cen ht **Parking** 6 **Notes** Closed 24 Dec-5 Jan

FARNBOROUGH — Map 5 SU85

Tudorwood Guest House

★★★★ GUEST HOUSE

164 Farnborough Rd GU14 7JJ
☎ **01252 541123**
e-mail: pshutak@btinternet.com
dir: Off A325 (Farnborough Rd) left onto Sycamore Rd, left onto Salisbury Rd, left onto Cedar Rd & right onto Old Farnborough Rd

A delightful Tudor-style house located just a few minutes from the town centre. Individually decorated bedrooms are well appointed with a range of useful facilities. Public areas include a pleasant conservatory lounge and intimate dining room where home-cooked dinners are available. Ample parking is provided to the front of the property.

Rooms 2 en suite 4 annexe en suite (1 fmly) (4 GF) S £40–£55; D £55–£70 **Facilities** TVL tea/coffee Dinner available Cen ht Wi-fi DVD library **Conf** Max 20 Thtr 20 Class 16 Board 16 **Parking** 7 **Notes** ⊗ Closed 24-29 Dec

GOSPORT — Map 5 SZ69

Thirty Three A

★★★★ ▤ BED AND BREAKFAST

33a Anglesey Rd, Alverstoke PO12 2EG
☎ **023 9251 0119** & **07866 400700** ▤ **023 9251 0119**
e-mail: rob.turnerchina@ntlworld.com
dir: 1m W of town centre. Off B3333 onto Anglesey Rd

Close to Alverstoke church, the house is tucked away in its secluded garden. The friendly proprietors have made the two bedrooms stylish and comfortable, both have flat-screen TVs. Breakfast is a gourmet treat that is served in the open-plan kitchen/lounge that overlooks the garden.

Rooms 2 en suite (1 fmly) (2 GF) S £65–£69; D £85–£89* **Facilities** FTV tea/coffee Cen ht Wi-fi **Parking** 2

HAWKLEY — Map 5 SU72

The Hawkley Inn

★★★ INN

Pococks Ln GU33 6NE
☎ **01730 827205** ▤ **01730 827954**
e-mail: info@hawkleyinn.co.uk
dir: A3 Liss rdbt towards Liss B3006. Right at Spread Eagle 2.5m turn left at Pococks Ln

This inn is conveniently situated just off the A3 and is a perfect base for ramblers, and leisure and business guests alike. The rustic bar areas contrast hugely in style from the contemporary, thoughtfully-equipped bedrooms; the bathrooms have powerful showers. Delicious home-made 'comfort food' is on offer at lunchtime and in the evenings, and breakfast provides a great start to the day.

Rooms 5 en suite (1 fmly) (1 GF) **Facilities** FTV tea/coffee Dinner available Cen ht **Parking** 2 **Notes** ⊗ No coaches

HAYLING ISLAND — Map 5 SU70

Ravensdale

★★★★ BED AND BREAKFAST

19 St Catherines Rd PO11 0HF
☎ **023 9246 3203** & **07802 188259** ▤ **023 9246 3203**
e-mail: phil.taylor@tayloredprint.co.uk
web: www.ravensdale-hayling.co.uk
dir: A27 onto A3023 at Langstone, cross Hayling Bridge, 3m to mini rdbt, right into Manor Rd 1m. Right at Barley Mow into Station Rd, 3rd left into St Catherines Rd

A warm welcome awaits you to this comfortable home, quietly situated near the beach and golf course. Bedrooms are attractive, very comfortable and enhanced with numerous thoughtful extras. Home cooking can be enjoyed at breakfast (and dinner by arrangement) in the dining room, and there is also a lounge area.

Rooms 3 rms (2 en suite) (1 pri facs) S £40–£42; D £66–£68 **Facilities** TVL tea/coffee Dinner available Cen ht **Parking** 4 **Notes** ⊗ No Children 8yrs Closed last 2wks Dec ⊠

HAYLING ISLAND continued

Redwalls

★★ BED AND BREAKFAST

66 Staunton Av PO11 0EW

☎ 023 9246 6109

e-mail: daphne@redwalls.co.uk

dir: A3023 to South Hayling seafront, right along seafront & 4th right

Built around the turn of the 20th century, the characterful home of Daphne and Noel Grover offers a peaceful retreat close to the seafront and local attractions. The bedrooms and public areas enjoy a homely ambience and there is a garden and conservatory lounge for guests to use.

Rooms 3 en suite S £35; D £50 Facilities TVL tea/coffee Cen ht Parking 4 Notes ⊗ No Children Closed Xmas & New Year ⊜

HOOK   Map 5 SU75

Oaklea Guest House

★★★★ GUEST HOUSE

London Rd RG27 9LA

☎ 01256 762673   📠 01256 762150

e-mail: reception@oakleaguesthouse.co.uk

dir: From village centre, 500yds on right on A30 towards Basingstoke

You can be sure of a warm welcome at this Victorian house located just a short drive from the M3. Bedrooms are well appointed with modern facilities. There is a comfortable lounge, and the large dining room has a bar.

Rooms 15 en suite (2 fmly) (1 GF) S £45-£52; D £60-£65* Facilities TVL tea/coffee Cen ht Licensed Wi-fi Parking 15 Notes Closed Xmas & New Year

Cherry Lodge Guest House

★★★ GUEST ACCOMMODATION

Reading Rd RG27 9DB

☎ 01256 762532   📠 01256 766068

e-mail: cherrylodge@btinternet.com

dir: On B3349 (Reading Rd), next to Hook garden centre

This pleasant bungalow is peacefully set back from the road, and is convenient for the M3. It provides extremely friendly hospitality and is popular with business guests. Breakfast is served from 6.30am. A spacious lounge is provided and bedrooms are well equipped.

Rooms 10 en suite (1 fmly) (10 GF) S fr £35; D fr £50* Facilities STV TVL tea/coffee Direct Dial Cen ht Wi-fi Parking 20 Notes ⊗ Closed Xmas-New Year

HYTHE   Map 5 SU40

Four Seasons B&B

★★★★ BED AND BREAKFAST

Hamilton Rd SO45 3PD

☎ 023 8084 5151   📠 023 8084 6285

e-mail: fourseasonshythe@btconnect.com

web: www.the-four-seasons.co.uk

dir: M27 junct 2 onto A326. Exit at Holbury/Hardley, 1st left then next left

Set in a quiet residential area close to good transport links across the south. Bedrooms are well presented, very comfortable and are enhanced by many thoughtful extras. There is a comfortable lounge, and a traditional English breakfast is served in the attractive dining room. Ample car parking is available.

Rooms 12 rms (7 en suite) (4 fmly) (2 GF) S £30-£45; D £65-£80* Facilities FTV TVL tea/coffee Cen ht Wi-fi Parking 11 Notes LB ⊗

ISLE OF WIGHT

See Wight, Isle of

LEE-ON-THE-SOLENT   Map 5 SU50

West Wind Guest House

★★★★ GUEST ACCOMMODATION

197 Portsmouth Rd PO13 9AA

☎ 023 9255 2550

e-mail: maggie@west-wind.co.uk

dir: M27 junct 11, A32, then B3385 for Lee-on-the-Solent, left at beach, 800mtrs on left

This well cared for white-painted house is situated just a short walk from the seafront and imposing views across the Solent, and offers good comfortable standards in bedrooms and bathrooms. The freshly-cooked breakfasts include locally-made sausages.

Rooms 6 en suite (1 GF) Facilities FTV tea/coffee Cen ht Wi-fi Parking 6 Notes ⊗ No Children 10yrs Closed Xmas & New Year

Apple Tree Cottage B&B

★★★ BED AND BREAKFAST

159 Portsmouth Rd PO13 9AD

☎ 023 9255 1176   📠 023 9235 2492

e-mail: appletreecottage@ntlworld.com

web: www.leeonthesolentbedandbreakfast.com

dir: From Marine Pde pass Old Ship public house onto Portsmouth Rd. Pass Inn by sea on right, 4th house along

This is a small, family-run establishment that offers a warm welcome and is just 50 yards from the seafront and Sailing Club; there is easy access to Southampton and Portsmouth. Both rooms, with views of the Solent, have a maritime theme and enjoy a wide range of useful facilities including DVD players and Wi-fi. Rooms are decorated and furnished to a high standard with high

quality linen and towels; the Lighthouse Room has a four-poster. Breakfast is served in the pretty dining room.

Rooms 2 en suite (1 fmly) S £40-£45; D £50-£55* Facilities FTV tea/coffee Cen ht Wi-fi Parking 3 Notes ⊗ No Children 6yrs ⊜

LYMINGTON   Map 5 SZ39

See also Milford-on-Sea & Sway

PREMIER COLLECTION

The Olde Barn

★★★★★ BED AND BREAKFAST

Christchurch Rd, Downton SO41 0LA

☎ 01590 644939   & 07813 679757

📠 01590 644939

e-mail: julie@theoldebarn.co.uk

dir: On A337 3m W of Lymington, in Downton

A 17th-century barn and associated buildings have been restored to provide stylish accommodation. Bedrooms are smartly decorated and furnished, and the spacious bathrooms have power showers. There is a comfortable lounge, and a traditional English breakfast is served around a farmhouse table in the attractive dining room.

Rooms 3 en suite (1 fmly) (3 GF) S £50-£70; D £60-£75* Facilities STV TVL tea/coffee Cen ht Parking 6 Notes ⊗ No Children 10yrs

Auplands

★★★★ BED AND BREAKFAST

22 Southampton Rd SO41 9GG

☎ 01590 675944

e-mail: sue@auplands.com

web: www.auplands.com

dir: On A337 before town centre, almost opp supermarket

Located just a short walk from High Street, this friendly family-run establishment provides comfortable, neatly decorated and well-equipped bedrooms. Hearty English breakfasts are served at individual tables in the attractive dining room. Off-road parking.

Rooms 3 en suite Facilities tea/coffee Cen ht Wi-fi Parking 8 Notes LB ⊗ No Children 5yrs ⊜

Harts Lodge

★★★★ BED AND BREAKFAST

242 Everton Rd, Everton SO41 0HE

☎ 01590 645902

dir: From Lymington 2.5m W to Everton, off A337 onto Everton Rd, 0.5m on left

This attractive bungalow is situated in 3 acres of peaceful gardens and paddocks. The bedrooms are furnished to a high standard and feature many thoughtful touches; one room has outside access. Public areas include a lounge and a pleasant breakfast room, with views of the garden and a small pond.

Rooms 3 en suite (1 fmly) (3 GF) S £35-£45; D £55-£65* **Facilities** tea/coffee Cen ht **Parking** 6 **Notes** LB ⊗ No Children 8yrs ⊛

Glenhurst
★★★★ 🅐 BED AND BREAKFAST

86 Wainsford Rd, Everton SO41 0UD
☎ 01590 644256 & 07763 322519 📠 01590 644256
e-mail: newforestrose@btinternet.com
web: www.newforest-bedbreakfast.co.uk
dir: 2m W of Lymington. Off A337 into Everton, off Old Christchurch Rd onto Wainsford Rd, Glenhurst 0.25m

Rooms 2 en suite 1 annexe rms (1 annexe pri facs) (3 GF) S £30-£45; D £55-£75* **Facilities** STV FTV tea/coffee Dinner available Cen ht Wi-fi **Parking** 4 **Notes** LB

Gorse Meadow Country House
★★★ GUEST HOUSE

Sway Rd SO41 8LR
☎ 01590 673354 📠 01590 673336
e-mail: gorsemeadow@btconnect.com
web: www.gorsemeadowguesthouse.co.uk
dir: Off A337 from Brockenhurst, right onto Sway Rd before Toll House pub, Gorse Meadow 1.5m on right

This imposing Edwardian house is situated in 14 acres of grounds, and most of the bedrooms enjoy views across the gardens and paddocks. Situated just one mile from Lymington, this is an excellent base to enjoy the many leisure pursuits that the New Forest has to offer. Meals are also available here, and Mrs Tee often uses the local wild mushrooms in her dishes.

Rooms 5 en suite (2 fmly) (2 GF) D £90-£120 **Facilities** tea/coffee Dinner available Cen ht Licensed Wi-fi Health Club Membership **Conf** Max 12 Board 12 **Parking** 20

Passford Farm
★★★ BED AND BREAKFAST

Southampton Rd SO41 8ND
☎ 01590 674103 📠 01590 677074
dir: Opp Welcome to Lymington sign

Set in five acres with delightful gardens and a pond, parts of this charming thatched cottage date back 700 years. With its wealth of beams and fireplaces, Passford Farm is full of character. The proprietors adopt a relaxed and friendly approach, and ensure you enjoy the comfortable facilities.

Rooms 3 en suite (1 fmly) **Facilities** STV TVL tea/coffee Cen ht **Parking** 20 **Notes** LB ⊗ No Children 12yrs ⊛

Rosewood B&B
★★★ BED AND BREAKFAST

45 Ramley Rd SO41 8GZ
☎ 01590 677970
dir: M27 to Lyndhurst then A337 to Lymington. Continue towards Christchurch, right before shops at Pennington into South St, past church into Ramley Rd. Rosewood 0.5m on right

Expect a warm welcome with an African theme at this family-run establishment. Located opposite Pennington Common on the edge of Lymington, this is an ideal area for exploring the area around the New Forest. Breakfast is served in the dining room which leads into a large conservatory.

Rooms 3 rms (1 en suite) (1 pri facs) S £30-£50; D £50-£60* **Facilities** tea/coffee Cen ht **Parking** 2 **Notes** LB Closed Xmas ⊛

LYNDHURST   Map 5 SU30

Temple Lodge
★★★★ 🔔 GUEST ACCOMMODATION

2 Queens Rd SO43 7BR
☎ 023 8028 2392 📠 023 8028 4910
e-mail: templelodge@btinternet.com
web: www.templelodge-guesthouse.com
dir: M27 junct 2/3 onto A35 to Ashurst/Lyndhurst, Temple Lodge on 2nd corner on right, opposite forest

Temple Lodge is a well appointed Victorian house with very friendly hosts. Guests will enjoy easy access to the New Forest and Lyndhurst town centre, with good off-road parking. The bedrooms feature lots of thoughtful extras including mini bars. The breakfasts should not be missed.

Rooms 6 en suite (2 fmly); D £60-£110 **Facilities** FTV TVL tea/coffee Cen ht Wi-fi **Parking** 6 **Notes** LB ⊗ No Children 12yrs

Whitemoor House
★★★★ 🔔 GUEST ACCOMMODATION

Southampton Rd SO43 7BU
☎ 023 8028 3043
e-mail: whitemoor@tiscali.co.uk
dir: 0.5m NE of town centre on A35

A warm welcome is assured at this well-run establishment in the New Forest. The comfortable bedrooms are brightly decorated and well equipped. A full

English breakfast is served with homemade preserves in the tastefully appointed breakfast room.

Rooms 6 en suite (1 fmly) S £40-£65; D £65-£80 **Facilities** FTV TVL tea/coffee Cen ht Licensed Wi-fi **Parking** 6 **Notes** ⊗ No Children 10yrs Closed 27 Dec-15 Jan ⊛

Clayhill House
★★★★ BED AND BREAKFAST

SO43 7DE
☎ 023 8028 2304 📠 023 8028 2093
e-mail: clayhillhouse@tinyworld.co.uk
web: www.clayhillhouse.co.uk
dir: Exit M27 junct 2. A35 to Lyndhurst then A337 signed Brockenhurst, 0.75m from village

Set at the edge of this attractive town, and convenient for visiting the New Forest and coastal attractions nearby, Clayhill House is a well-appointed property, which offers friendly service and comfortable accommodation. The bedrooms are particularly well equipped with thoughtful extras. Freshly-cooked breakfasts are served in the dining room.

Rooms 3 en suite (1 fmly) S £45-£60; D £65-£70 **Facilities** FTV tea/coffee Cen ht Wi-fi **Parking** 6 **Notes** LB ⊗ No Children 7yrs Closed 22 Dec-4 Jan

The Rufus House
★★★★ GUEST ACCOMMODATION

Southampton Rd SO43 7BQ
☎ 023 8028 2930
e-mail: stay@rufushouse.co.uk
web: www.rufushouse.com
dir: From Lyndhurst centre onto A35 (Southampton Rd), 300yds on left

Located on the edge of town, this delightful family-run Victorian property is well situated for exploring the New Forest. The brightly decorated bedrooms are appointed to a high standard, while the turret lounge and the garden terrace are great spots for relaxing.

Rooms 11 en suite (1 fmly) (2 GF) **Facilities** TVL tea/coffee Cen ht **Parking** 12 **Notes** ⊗ No Children 5yrs

LYNDHURST *continued*

Burwood Lodge

★★★★ 🄰 GUEST ACCOMMODATION

27 Romsey Rd SO43 7AA
☎ 023 8028 2445 📄 023 8028 4722
e-mail: burwoodlodge@yahoo.co.uk
Rooms 7 en suite (2 fmly) (1 GF) S £40-£55; D £70-£76*
Facilities FTV TVL tea/coffee Cen ht Wi-fi Parking 10
Notes LB ⊗ No Children 6yrs ♿

Heather House

★★★ GUEST ACCOMMODATION

Southampton Rd SO43 7BQ
☎ 023 8028 4409 📄 023 8028 4431
e-mail: enquiries@heatherhouse.co.uk
web: www.heatherhouse.co.uk
dir: *M27 junct 1, A337 to Lyndhurst. At lights in centre turn left, establishment 800yds on left*

This impressive double-fronted Edwardian house stands in attractive gardens on the edge of town with views of the New Forest. Bedrooms are comfortably appointed with some suitable for families. Breakfast is served in the pleasant dining room.

Rooms 10 en suite (1 fmly) (1 GF) S £24-£40;
D £55-£80* Facilities FTV TVL tea/coffee Cen ht Licensed Wi-fi Parking 12 Notes LB ⊗ No Children 7yrs Closed 23 Dec-2 Jan

Little Hayes

★★★ BED AND BREAKFAST

43 Romsey Rd SO43 7AR
☎ 023 8028 3816
e-mail: wendy@littlehayes.co.uk
dir: *M27 junct 1 onto A337. On entering Lyndhurst, 200yds on right*

A friendly, well run bed and breakfast located a few moments walk of the town centre, pubs and restaurants. Breakfast featuring local produce is served in the cosy dining room. Little Hayes provides an ideal base for touring the New Forest National Park, and benefits from off-road parking.

Rooms 3 en suite; D £70-£80* Facilities FTV tea/coffee Cen ht Wi-fi Parking 6 Notes ⊗ No Children

The Willows

★★★ BED AND BREAKFAST

72 Lyndhurst Rd, Ashurst SO40 7BE
☎ 023 8029 2745 📄 023 8029 2745
e-mail: the_willows_ashurst@hotmail.com
dir: *3m NE of Lyndhurst on A35 in Ashurst*

Located north-east of Lyndhurst, this delightful property has good access to Southampton, the New Forest and

numerous places of interest. Rooms are comfortable and well equipped. A full English breakfast or alternative choices are served at individual tables in the cosy and light dining room.

Rooms 3 rms (2 en suite) (1 fmly) S £28-£35;
D £60-£70* Facilities TVL tea/coffee Cen ht Parking 4
Notes LB ⊗ No Children 10yrs

| MILFORD ON SEA | Map 5 SZ29 |

PREMIER COLLECTION

Ha'penny House

★★★★★ 🄱 GUEST ACCOMMODATION

16 Whitby Rd SO41 0ND
☎ 01590 641210
e-mail: info@hapennyhouse.co.uk
web: www.hapennyhouse.co.uk
dir: *A337 at Everton onto B3058, through village onto Cliff Rd, right onto Cornwallis Rd, right at T-junct onto Whitby Rd, house 50yds on left*

This delightful house is in a peaceful residential area close to the clifftop with its stunning views towards the Isle of Wight. Individually styled bedrooms are beautifully appointed and equipped with a host of thoughtful extras. There is a stylish lounge, and an elegant dining room where superb breakfasts are served.

Rooms 4 en suite S £46-£55; D £66-£85*
Facilities FTV TVL tea/coffee Cen ht Wi-fi Parking 7
Notes LB ⊗ No Children 12yrs

Alma Mater

★★★★ BED AND BREAKFAST

4 Knowland Dr SO41 0RH
☎ 01590 642811
e-mail: bandbalmamater@vwclub.net
web: www.almamaternewforest.co.uk
dir: *A337 at Everton onto B3058 to Milford on Sea. Pass South Lawn Hotel, right onto Manor Rd, 1st left onto Knowland Dr, 3rd bungalow on right*

Alma Mater is in a quiet residential area within walking distance of the village centre and beaches. The comfortable bedrooms are all well appointed with many thoughtful touches including digital TV and toiletries. One room is on the ground floor and has twin beds, and the elegant dining room also has a conservatory where a wide choice of breakfasts can be enjoyed.

Rooms 3 en suite (1 GF) S £40-£50; D £70-£80*
Facilities TVL tea/coffee Cen ht Parking 4 Notes LB ⊗
No Children 15yrs ♿

Pilgrims Rest

★★★★ GUEST ACCOMMODATION

Westover Rd SO41 0PW
☎ 01590 641167
e-mail: pilgrimsrestbandb@yahoo.co.uk
dir: *From Lymington follow New Milton signs, in 2m left onto B3058 through village, 2nd left*

A traditional bed and breakfast with friendly hosts, very well appointed rooms and a breakfast that is a great start to the day. Pilgrims Rest lies within walking distance of the beach and the town of Milford on Sea. All rooms are en suite.

Rooms 4 en suite S £35-£45; D £70* Facilities FTV tea/coffee Cen ht Parking 6 Notes LB ⊗ No Children 5yrs ♿

NEW ALRESFORD — Map 5 SU53

Haygarth

★★★ Ⓐ BED AND BREAKFAST

82 Jack Lyns Ln SO24 9LJ
☎ 01962 732715 & 07986 372895
e-mail: valramshaw@aol.com
dir: B3046 from New Alresford centre for Cheriton,
Haygarth 0.5m on right

Rooms 3 rms (2 en suite) (1 pri facs) (3 GF) S £35; D £65
Facilities TVL tea/coffee Cen ht Parking 7 Notes LB ⊗
♨

PETERSFIELD — Map 5 SU72

See also Rogate (West Sussex)

The Flying Bull Inn

★★★★ INN

London Rd, Rake, Liss GU33 7JB
☎ 01730 892285 ▤ 01730 892282
e-mail: info@theflyingbull.co.uk
dir: From A3 Sbound, take exit for Liphook & follow signs
for B2070. In Rake on right

Conveniently located in the delightful village of Rake.
Bedrooms take their name from English Counties, all of
which are smartly appointed and well equipped with
many thoughtful extras. The comfortable main bar and
restaurant areas are open for both lunch and dinner and
offer a good range of home-cooked meals. After a restful
night's sleep a hearty breakfast or lighter continental
option is served in the restaurant.

Rooms 7 en suite (1 fmly) (5 GF); D £60-£75 (room only)*
Facilities FTV tea/coffee Dinner available Cen ht
Parking 35 Notes No coaches

PORTSMOUTH & SOUTHSEA — Map 5 SU60

St Margaret's Lodge

★★★★ GUEST HOUSE

3 Craneswater Gate PO4 0NZ
☎ 023 9282 0097 ▤ 023 9282 0097
e-mail: enquiries@stmargarets-southsea.co.uk
web: www.stmargarets-southsea.co.uk
dir: From South Parade Pier E along A288 St Helens
Parade, 2nd left

This establishment is in a quiet residential area close to
the seafront and town centre. The attractive bedrooms
have co-ordinated soft furnishings and many thoughtful
extras. Breakfast is served in the smart dining room and
there are two lounges and a cosy bar.

Rooms 14 en suite (1 fmly) S fr £35; D fr £58*
Facilities TVL tea/coffee Cen ht Wi-fi Parking 5 Notes ⊗
Closed 21 Dec-2 Jan

Upper Mount House

★★★★ GUEST ACCOMMODATION

The Vale, Off Clarendon Rd, Southsea PO5 2EQ
☎ 023 9282 0456 ▤ 023 9282 0456
e-mail: uppermountportsmouth@btconnect.com
dir: Off M275 for D-Day Museum onto road opposite
Museum, over x-rds, right at T-junct, right again

This impressive Victorian villa retains many original
features and is peacefully located in a residential cul-de-
sac. Public areas include a comfortable lounge and an
attractive dining room where a fine collection of Venetian
glassware is displayed. The bedrooms are spacious and
well equipped, and come in a variety of styles.

Rooms 16 en suite (3 fmly) (7 GF) Facilities FTV TVL tea/
coffee Direct Dial Cen ht Wi-fi Parking 17 Notes ⊗
Closed 2wks Xmas

Victoria Court

★★★★ Ⓐ GUEST ACCOMMODATION

29 Victoria Road North, Southsea PO5 1PL
☎ 023 9282 0305
e-mail: stay@victoriacourt.co.uk
web: www.victoriacourt.co.uk
dir: M275 junct 12, A3 into Portsmouth, onto A2030, 2nd
rdbt right onto A2151, Victoria Rd North

Rooms 6 en suite (2 fmly) (1 GF) Facilities FTV tea/coffee
Cen ht Wi-fi Parking 2 Notes ⊗

The Festing Grove

★★★ GUEST ACCOMMODATION

8 Festing Grove, Southsea PO4 9QA
☎ 023 9273 5239
e-mail: thefestinggrove@ntlworld.com
dir: E along seafront to South Parade Pier, after pier
sharp left, around lake, 3rd left & 2nd right

A well-presented property situated within easy walking
distance of the seafront and pier. A continual programme
of upgrading ensures that the rooms enjoy a high
standard of decor and comfort. Breakfast is served in the
homely dining room, and there is a well-appointed
lounge.

Rooms 6 rms (1 en suite) (2 fmly) Facilities TVL tea/
coffee Cen ht Notes ⊗

Abbey Lodge

★★★ GUEST HOUSE

30 Waverley Rd, Southsea PO5 2PW
☎ 023 9282 8285 ▤ 023 9287 2943
e-mail: linda@abbeylodge.co.uk
dir: Off A288 South Parade near pier onto B2155
Clarendon Rd & Waverley Rd

A warm welcome awaits you at this attractive property
close to the seafront and within walking distance of the
shops. It offers well-equipped bedrooms, and breakfast is
served in a cosy dining room at individual tables.

Rooms 9 rms (3 en suite) (2 fmly) Facilities tea/coffee
Cen ht Wi-fi Notes ⊗ No Children 5yrs Closed Xmas &
New Year

Amberley Court

★★★ GUEST ACCOMMODATION

97 Waverley Rd, Southsea PO5 2PL
☎ 023 9273 7473 ▤ 023 9275 2343
e-mail: mail@amberleycourt.co.uk
dir: Off A288 South Parade near pier onto B2155
Clarendon Rd & Waverley Rd

Amberley Court has a convenient location less than half a
mile from the seafront and its attractions. The
comfortable bedrooms have bright modern co-ordinated
fabrics, and come with good facilities. Some rooms and a
smart conservatory-dining room are in a second house
nearby.

Rooms 9 en suite (4 fmly) S £25-£75; D £45-£95*
Facilities TVL tea/coffee Cen ht Wi-fi Parking 4 Notes LB
⊗

Norfolk House

★★★ GUEST ACCOMMODATION

25 Granada Rd, Southsea PO4 0RD
☎ 023 9282 4162
e-mail: jbpnorfolk@ntlworld.com
web: www.thenorfolksouthsea.com
dir: From South Parade Pier E along A288 St Helens
Parade, 1st left

Situated within walking distance of Southsea's
attractions, Norfolk House is suited for both business and
leisure guests. The attractive rooms come with a range of
useful extras, and some include a workspace. A lounge is
also available.

Rooms 8 en suite (2 fmly) S £29-£32; D £46-£58*
Facilities FTV tea/coffee Cen ht Parking 5 Notes ⊗
Closed Xmas

RINGWOOD   Map 5 SU10

Moortown Lodge

★★★★ GUEST ACCOMMODATION

244 Christchurch Rd BH24 3AS
☎ 01425 471404 📠 01425 476527
e-mail: enquiries@moortownlodge.co.uk
web: www.moortownlodge.co.uk
dir: 1m S of Ringwood. Off A31 at Ringwood onto B3347, follow signs to Sopley. Lodge next to David Lloyds Leisure Club

The light and airy accommodation is finished to a very high standard, with digital TV and broadband available in each room. Two of the well-equipped bedrooms are on ground level and another features a four-poster bed. Breakfast is served in the smart lounge-dining room at separate tables.

Rooms 7 en suite (3 fmly) (2 GF); D £84-£94*
Facilities FTV tea/coffee Direct Dial Cen ht Wi-fi Access to facilities of adjoining leisure club **Parking** 9 **Notes** LB

Amberwood

★★★★ GUEST ACCOMMODATION

3/5 Top Ln BH24 1LF
☎ 01425 476615 📠 01425 476615
e-mail: maynsing@aol.com
web: www.amberwoodbandb.co.uk
dir: A31 onto B3347, over rdbt, left onto School Ln, left onto Top Ln

This delightful Victorian home is situated in a quiet residential area within easy walking distance of the town centre. Bedrooms are attractively furnished and decorated, with many thoughtful extras. A substantial breakfast is served around one large table in the

conservatory, which overlooks the well-tended garden. A lounge is also available.

Rooms 2 en suite (1 fmly) S £35-£40; D £60*
Facilities FTV TVL tea/coffee Direct Dial Cen ht Wi-fi
Parking 2 **Notes** LB ⊗ No Children 12yrs Closed Xmas & New Year ☻

Little Forest Lodge

★★★★ GUEST HOUSE

Poulner Hill BH24 3HS
☎ 01425 478848 📠 01425 473564
dir: 1.5m E of Ringwood on A31

A warm welcome is given to you and your pets, at this charming Edwardian house set in two acres of woodland. Bedrooms are pleasantly decorated and equipped with thoughtful extras. Both the attractive wood-panelled dining room and the delightful lounge, with bar and wood-burning fire, overlook the gardens.

Rooms 6 en suite (3 fmly) (1 GF) S £45-£50; D £70*
Facilities tea/coffee Cen ht Licensed ⚓ **Parking** 10

Old Stacks

★★★★ GUEST ACCOMMODATION

154 Hightown Rd BH24 1NP
☎ 01425 473840
e-mail: oldstacksbandb@aol.com
dir: Off A31 1m E of Ringwood signed Hightown, left onto Eastfield Ln, 0.5m right

This delightful bungalow is set in charming gardens. Of the two bedrooms, the twin bedroom has an en suite and its own garden entrance, while the double room has an adjoining bathroom. There is a comfortable lounge for guests' use and a hearty breakfast is served around a large table in the dining room.

Rooms 2 rms (1 en suite) (1 pri facs) (2 GF); D £60-£70
Facilities TVL tea/coffee Cen ht **Parking** 4 **Notes** LB ⊗ No Children 12yrs Closed Xmas & New Year ☻

Picket Hill House

★★★★ 🏠 BED AND BREAKFAST

Picket Hill BH24 3HH
☎ 01425 476173 📠 01425 470022
e-mail: b+b@pickethill.freeserve.co.uk
dir: From Burley junct/services 2m E of Ringwood, off A31 to Ringwood, 250yds left to Hightown & Crow

This is a good choice as a base for exploring the beautiful New Forest, where guests will be assured of a warm welcome. The comfortable bedrooms are well furnished and equipped with many extra facilities, and there is a spacious and comfortable first-floor lounge overlooking the delightful gardens. Delicious breakfasts are enjoyed at one large table in the dining room.

Rooms 3 en suite; D £64-£72* **Facilities** TVL tea/coffee Cen ht Wi-fi Golf **Parking** 6 **Notes** LB ⊗ No Children 12yrs Closed 23 Dec-2 Jan

Valley View

★★★★ BED AND BREAKFAST

Cowpits Ln, North Poulner BH24 3JX
☎ 01425 475855 & 07930 463134 📠 01425 472542
e-mail: es-brown@tiscali.co.uk
dir: A31 E 0.75m, E of Ringwood. Left to Hangelsley, 1st right 0.5m to x-rds, 75yds on right

This establishment is set in a peaceful location with easy access to the New Forest, the Dorset coast and Salisbury. The bedroom has many considerate extras, and breakfast, featuring home-made preserves, is served in the family dining room. A home-cooked dinner is available by arrangement.

Rooms 2 rms (2 pri facs) S £30-£32; D £60-£64*
Facilities tea/coffee Dinner available Cen ht **Parking** 5
Notes LB ⊗ ☻

Fraser House

★★★★ 🅰 BED AND BREAKFAST

Salisbury Rd, Blashford BH24 3PB
☎ 01425 473958 📄 01425 473958
e-mail: mail@fraserhouse.net
dir: Off A31 at Ringwood onto A338 Salisbury Rd, house 1m on right

Rooms 6 en suite (1 fmly) S £48–£55; D £70–£80*
Facilities FTV TVL tea/coffee Cen ht Wi-fi Parking 6
Notes No Children 12yrs

Candlesticks Inn

★★★ GUEST HOUSE

136 Christchurch Rd BH24 3AP
☎ 01425 472587 📄 01425 471600
e-mail: info@hotelnewforest.co.uk
web: www.hotelnewforest.co.uk
dir: 0.5m SE of town centre on B3347

This 15th-century thatched property on the edge of town offers accommodation with a restaurant; it is conveniently located for Bournemouth and the New Forest National Park. Ample parking is available.

Rooms 8 annexe en suite (1 fmly) (4 GF) S £45–£60;
D £50–£75* Facilities tea/coffee Dinner available Direct Dial Cen ht Licensed Wi-fi Sauna (sauna also available for wheelchair users) Parking 30 Notes LB ⊗ Closed 23 Dec–10 Jan

Lochend

★★★ BED AND BREAKFAST

Hurst Corner, Salisbury Rd BH24 1AX
☎ 01425 473836
e-mail: kenburnsbrown@btinternet.com
dir: A31 onto A338 towards Fordingbridge, 0.25m right onto Hurst Rd

Located on the north side of town with easy access to the shops, the New Forest and various places of interest, this delightful property has both of its spacious, comfortable bedrooms on the ground floor. A charming garden is also available to guests, and English breakfasts are served at one large table.

Rooms 2 rms (1 en suite) (1 pri facs) (1 fmly) (2 GF)
S £30–£35; D £50* Facilities tea/coffee Cen ht Parking 4
Notes LB Closed 20 Dec–3 Jan 🐾

ROMSEY   Map 5 SU32

See also East Tytherley

Greenvale Farm

★★★★ BED AND BREAKFAST

Melchet Park, Sherfield English SO51 6FS
☎ 01794 884858
e-mail: suebrown@greenvalefarm.com
web: www.greenvalefarm.com
dir: 5m W of Romsey. On S side of A27 through red-brick archway for Melchet Court, Greenvale Farm 150yds on left, left at slatted barn

Located four miles from the New Forest and within easy reach of Winchester and Salisbury, this self-contained establishment has plenty of facilities. With a working farm next door, don't be surprised if you are woken by a cockerel crowing in the morning, or you hear guinea fowl 'chattering' at night. The hearty breakfast, with freshly laid eggs if possible, will set you up for the day.

Rooms 1 annexe en suite (1 GF) Facilities tea/coffee Cen ht Wi-fi Parking 10 Notes LB ⊗ No Children 14yrs 🐾

Country Accommodation Guest House

★★★★ BED AND BREAKFAST

The Old Post Office, New Rd, Michelmersh SO51 0NL
☎ 01794 368739
e-mail: oldpodingo@aol.com
dir: 3m N of Romsey, off A3057 onto New Rd into Michelmersh

This attractive guest house is decorated with country memorabilia that reflect the history of this delightful property. The comfortable bedrooms have excellent facilities and many useful extras. This is a good location

---

for business guests and for those touring this beautiful part of Hampshire.

Rooms 3 annexe en suite (1 fmly) (3 GF) S £35; D £60
Facilities tea/coffee Cen ht Parking 5 Notes ⊗ No Children 12yrs

The Courtyard

★★★ BED AND BREAKFAST

49 The Hundred SO51 8GE
☎ 01794 516434 & 07879 000000
e-mail: babidge@btinternet.com
dir: From A27 follow signs to town centre. Follow one-way system, past bus station, to rdbt, turn right

Centrally located in the village, this property offers en suite bedrooms located above a traditional and charming tea room. The bedrooms are fresh and contemporary. Staff are friendly and attentive, and a hearty breakfast utilises top notch ingredients.

Rooms 3 en suite S fr £45; D fr £70* Facilities tea/coffee Cen ht Conf Max 20 Thtr 20 Board 20 Parking 3
Notes Closed 23 Dec–5 Jan 🐾

SOUTHAMPTON   Map 5 SU41

PREMIER COLLECTION

Riverside Bed & Breakfast

★★★★★ BED AND BREAKFAST

4 Tides Reach, 53 Whitworth Rd SO18 1GE
☎ 023 8063 0315 📄 023 8063 0315
e-mail: gordon-funnelle@supanet.com
dir: 2m NE of city centre. M27 junct 5, A335 onto Thomas Lewis Way, left onto A3035 over river, sharp right onto Whitworth Crescent & Whitworth Rd

Located in a quieter part of Southampton, just five minutes walk away from public transport links and a ten-minute drive from the airport, this small and homely house has wonderful river views. Bedrooms have many thoughtful touches and guests have their own comfortable lounge. A wonderful continental breakfast is served in the dining room or on the balcony in warmer weather.

Rooms 2 rms (2 pri facs) S £35–£45; D £60–£65*
Facilities FTV tea/coffee Cen ht Parking 1 Notes ⊗ No Children 14yrs 🐾

SOUTHAMPTON *continued*

White Star Tavern, Dining and Rooms

★★★★ ⚘ INN

28 Oxford St SO14 3DJ
☎ 023 8082 1990 🖨 023 8090 4982
e-mail: reservations@whitestartavern.co.uk
web: www.whitestartavern.co.uk
dir: *M3 junct 14 onto A33, towards Ocean Village*

This stylish tavern is conveniently located in the popular Oxford Street area, a moment's walk to the city centre. Bedrooms take their name from the ships of the White Star line, and are smartly appointed and well equipped with many thoughtful extras. The main bar and restaurant areas provide comfortable seating in well styled surroundings. Award-winning cuisine is served in the White Star restaurant whilst in the morning an à la carte breakfast is served in the bar area. Private meeting space is also available.

Rooms 13 en suite S £89-£179; D £99-£179 (room only)*
Facilities FTV TVL tea/coffee Dinner available Direct Dial Cen ht Wi-fi Conf Max 12 Board 12 Notes LB ⊗

Alcantara Guest House

★★★★ GUEST ACCOMMODATION

20 Howard Rd, Shirley SO15 5BN
☎ 023 8033 2966 🖨 023 8049 6163
e-mail: alcantaraguesthouse@sky.com
dir: *0.5m NW of city centre. Off A3057 onto Howard Rd*

A warm welcome is assured at this Victorian property, named after the ocean liner to reflect the establishment's shipping connections and location close to the city centre. Bedrooms are comfortable and well decorated and have many thoughtful extras. An appetising breakfast can be served in the bright and airy dining room. Secure off-road parking is available.

Rooms 9 rms (6 en suite) (3 fmly) (2 GF) S £32-£42; D £65* Facilities FTV tea/coffee Cen ht Wi-fi Parking 7 Notes ⊗ No Children 12yrs RS 2wks Xmas

Eversley Guest House

★★★★ GUEST ACCOMMODATION

Eversley, Kanes Hill, West End SO19 6AJ
☎ 023 8046 4546
e-mail: info@eversleyguesthouse.org.uk
web: www.eversleyguesthouse.org.uk
dir: *M27 junct 7, take A334 towards Southampton. At rdbt, 2nd exit onto A27, 0.5m on right*

Within easy driving distance of Southampton city centre, Eversley offers a quiet retreat where a friendly welcome awaits you. Bedrooms are comfortable, thoughtfully equipped and are complemented by smart en suite facilities. Memorable breakfasts are served in an attractive dining room, and Wi-fi is a bonus.

Rooms 5 en suite (1 fmly) S £45-£50; D £60-£65*
Facilities FTV tea/coffee Cen ht Wi-fi Parking 5 Notes ⊗

Hunters Lodge

★★★★ GUEST ACCOMMODATION

25 Landguard Rd, Shirley SO15 5DL
☎ 023 8022 7919
e-mail: hunterslodge.hotel@virgin.net
web: www.hunterslodgehotel.net
dir: *500yds NW of Southampton Central station. Off A3057 Shirley Rd onto Languard Rd*

Located in a leafy residential area close to the city centre and convenient for the docks, ferry terminal, university and hospital, this double-fronted Victorian house provides business and leisure guests with comfortable, well-equipped bedrooms. Full English breakfast is served at shared tables in the elegant dining room. There is also a television lounge and a well-stocked bar.

Rooms 14 en suite (1 fmly) (1 GF) S £46-£55; D £75-£80* Facilities TVL tea/coffee Direct Dial Cen ht Licensed Wi-fi Parking 16 Notes ⊗

Landguard Lodge

★★★ GUEST HOUSE

21 Landguard Rd SO15 5DL
☎ 023 8063 6904 🖨 023 8063 2258
e-mail: info@landguardlodge.co.uk
web: www.landguardlodge.co.uk
dir: *500yds NW of Southampton Central station. Off A3057 Shirley Rd onto Landguard Rd*

This Victorian house is in a quiet residential area a short walk from the railway station. The bedrooms are bright, comfortable and well equipped with many thoughtful extras.

Rooms 11 en suite (1 fmly) (2 GF) S fr £40; D fr £60* Facilities tea/coffee Cen ht Wi-fi Parking 3 Notes ⊗ No Children 5yrs

Mayview

★★★ Ⓐ GUEST HOUSE

30 The Polygon SO15 2BN
☎ 023 8022 0907 & 07973 874194 🖨 07977 017921
e-mail: info@mayview.co.uk
web: www.mayview.co.uk
Rooms 9 rms (1 en suite) (1 fmly) (1 GF) Facilities tea/coffee Cen ht Notes ⊗ Closed 25 Dec

The Brimar

★★ GUEST ACCOMMODATION

10-14 High St, Totton SO40 9HN
☎ 023 8086 2950 🖨 023 8086 1301
e-mail: info@brimar-guesthouse.co.uk
dir: *3m W of city centre, off A35 in Totton High St*

This guest house offers practical, comfortable accommodation at reasonable prices. Not all rooms are en suite but bathrooms are well situated. Breakfast is served in the dining room or as a take-away option. The

Brimar is well placed for the M27 and Southampton docks, and off-road parking is available.

Rooms 21 rms (8 en suite) (2 fmly) (8 GF) (3 smoking) S £30-£35; D £60-£70* Facilities Cen ht Wi-fi Parking 20 Notes ⊗

SOUTHSEA

See Portsmouth & Southsea

STEEP   Map 5 SU72

The Cricketers Inn

★★★ INN

1 Church Rd GU32 2DW
☎ 01730 261035 🖨 01730 261035
e-mail: thecricketerssteep@btconnect.com
dir: *A3 junct with A272, follow signs to Petersfield. At next rdbt, 1st exit signed Steep, 1.5m on right*

Situated close to Petersfield in the village of Steep, this is a popular village inn offering quality, comfortable accommodation equipped with many thoughtful extras. The comfortable, traditional bar and restaurant area is popular for residents and locals alike. Ample on-site parking is available.

Rooms 6 en suite (2 fmly) (2 GF) S £69; D £79*
Facilities tea/coffee Dinner available Cen ht Wi-fi Parking 32 Notes LB

STOCKBRIDGE   Map 5 SU33

Old Drapery Guesthouse

★★★★ GUEST HOUSE

Middle Wallop SO20 8HN
☎ 01264 781301 🖨 01264 781301
e-mail: amanda@olddraperyguesthouse.co.uk
web: www.olddraperyguesthouse.co.uk
dir: *A303 onto A343, turn right at x-rds by George Inn, 2nd on left*

A Georgian family home in the Wallops, close to Stockbridge and set just off the main road in mature gardens. A warm welcome and attentive service awaits guests and accommodation provides good levels of comfort throughout. Off-street parking is available.

Rooms 4 en suite S £35-£45; D £70-£90* Facilities FTV tea/coffee Dinner available Cen ht Wi-fi Parking 5 Notes ⊗ No Children 12yrs Closed 24-26 & 31 Dec-1 Jan

York Lodge

★★★★ BED AND BREAKFAST

Five Bells Ln, Nether Wallop SO20 8HE
☎ 01264 781313
e-mail: bradley@york-lodge.co.uk
web: www.york-lodge.co.uk
dir: *Turn off A30 or A343 onto B3084, turn onto Hosketts Ln, fork left, 1st house on right*

Located in the picturesque village famous for Agatha Christie's *Miss Marple* series, this charming house has comfortable accommodation in a self-contained wing. Bedrooms are stylishly presented with many thoughtful extra facilities. The dining room overlooks peaceful gardens, and delicious dinners are available by arrangement.

Rooms 2 en suite (2 GF) S £40-£60; D £60-£75*
Facilities FTV tea/coffee Cen ht Wi-fi **Parking** 4 **Notes** No Children 8yrs ⊗

The Three Cups Inn

★★★ INN

High St SO20 6HB
☎ 01264 810527 📠 08708 913158
e-mail: manager@the3cups.co.uk

A former coaching inn on the high street in a popular town, with its own parking. Rooms are comfortable and well equipped, and food is available every evening.

Rooms 8 en suite (3 fmly) S £65-£72; D £79-£85*
Facilities tea/coffee Dinner available Cen ht Wi-fi Fishing **Parking** 15

The Nurse's Cottage Restaurant with Rooms

★★★★ 🛏 🍽 GUEST ACCOMMODATION

Station Rd SO41 6BA
☎ 01590 683402
e-mail: nurses.cottage@lineone.net
web: www.nursescottage.co.uk
dir: *Off B3055 in village centre, close to shops*

Enjoying a prominent position in the New Forest village of Sway, the Nurse's Cottage is the recipient of numerous hospitality awards. Quality is paramount in each of the individually styled bedrooms and each room offers a host of thoughtful extras including flat-screen TVs, DVDs, complimentary soft drinks, Wi-fi and delicious handmade chocolates. The conservatory restaurant overlooks the neat garden and the seasonally changing dinner menu features the best in local produce. A wide ranging choice of hot and cold dishes at breakfast guarantees a good start to the day.

Rooms 5 en suite (5 GF) S £90-£95; D £190-£210 (incl. dinner) **Facilities** FTV tea/coffee Dinner available Direct Dial Cen ht Licensed Wi-fi **Parking** 5 **Notes** LB No Children 10yrs Closed Feb-Mar & Nov (3wks)

Acorn Shetland Pony Stud

★★★★ BED AND BREAKFAST

Meadows Cottage, Arnewood Bridge Rd SO41 6DA
☎ 01590 682000
e-mail: meadows.cottage@virgin.net
dir: *M27 junct 1, A337 to Brockenhurst, B3055 to Sway, pass Birchy Hill Nursing Home, over x-rds, 2nd entrance left*

Located on the outskirts of Sway, this comfortable establishment is set in over six acres of pony paddocks and a water garden. The ground-floor bedrooms are well furnished and have direct access onto patios. The enjoyable, freshly cooked breakfasts use a range of fine produce including delicious home-made bread.

Rooms 3 en suite (1 fmly) (3 GF) **Facilities** tea/coffee Cen ht Carriage driving with Shetland ponies **Parking** 30 **Notes** ⊗

PREMIER COLLECTION

Giffard House

★★★★★ GUEST HOUSE

50 Christchurch Rd SO23 9SU
☎ 01962 852628 📠 01962 856722
e-mail: giffardhotel@aol.com
dir: *M3 junct 11, at rdbt 3rd exit onto A333 St Cross road for 1m. Pass BP garage on right, take next left then 2nd right. 150mtrs on left*

A warm welcome awaits you here at this stunning 19th-century Victorian house. The accommodation is luxurious, comfortable and well equipped for both the business and leisure traveller. There is also a fully licensed bar set in the elegant conservatory.

Rooms 13 en suite (1 fmly) (4 GF) S £69; D £89-£125*
Facilities STV FTV tea/coffee Direct Dial Cen ht Licensed Wi-fi **Conf** Max 15 Thtr 15 Class 15 Board 13 **Parking** 13 **Notes** ⊗ Closed 24 Dec-2 Jan

PREMIER COLLECTION

Orchard House

★★★★★ BED AND BREAKFAST

3 Christchurch Gardens, St Cross SO23 9TH
☎ 01962 861544 📠 01962 861988
e-mail: hopefamily@hotmail.co.uk
dir: *B3335 to Winchester & St Cross, after 2nd lights left into Barnes Close, right into Christchurch Rd, right into Christchurch Gdns, last house on right*

This friendly, family-run B&B is in a peaceful cul-de-sac, close to Winchester and the famous college, yet within easy reach of the M3. It offers a relaxed atmosphere, professional service and warm hospitality. The bedroom is spacious, comfortable and very well equipped for either the business or leisure guest alike. Gardens are well tended, and the balcony overlooking the rear garden can be used for breakfast on warmer summer mornings, and there is also ample parking available.

Rooms 1 en suite S £50-£60; D £80-£90*
Facilities STV TVL tea/coffee Cen ht **Parking** 2 **Notes** ⊗ No Children 6yrs ⊗

WINCHESTER *continued*

The Grange

★★★★ GUEST ACCOMMODATION

Sleeper Hill SO22 4NA
☎ **01962 851419   & 07771 927012** 📠 01962 851419
e-mail: jeannesaywell@aol.com
dir: *From Romsey Rd onto Sleepers Hill, 1st lane on left to The Grange*

A large family house within minutes of the city centre, its cathedral, and shopping centre. The hosts are friendly and welcoming, rooms are very comfortable and well equipped, and the freshly cooked breakfast is a great start to the day.

Rooms 3 en suite (3 fmly) **Facilities** FTV TVL tea/coffee Cen ht Gym outdoor Jacuzzi **Parking** 8 **Notes** ⊗ No Children 12yrs Closed Xmas & New Year

Heybridge

★★★★ BED AND BREAKFAST

Clifton Rd SO22 5BP
☎ **01962 865007   & 07779 436305**
e-mail: jacquiekennedy@yahoo.co.uk
dir: *500yds W of city centre. Off A3040 Romsey Rd onto Clifton Rd*

Close to the town centre in a quiet suburb, overlooking the park, Heybridge offers a quiet location with very comfortable accommodation. The two bedrooms are both en suite, comfortable and very smartly appointed. A substantial breakfast is served in the spacious dining room.

Rooms 2 en suite S £50-£55; D £75-£80* **Facilities** tea/coffee Cen ht **Parking** 1 **Notes** ⊗ 🖾

The Old Vine

★★★★ INN

8 Great Minster St SO23 9HA
☎ **01962 854616**
e-mail: reservations@oldvinewinchester.com
web: www.oldvinewinchester.com
dir: *M3 junct 11 towards St Cross, turn right at Green Man Pub, left onto Symonds St, left onto Little Minster St*

Extensively and sympathetically restored and updated over the years this inn looks out onto the cathedral. Bedrooms are named and themed after various designers, and food is served in the restaurant and bar downstairs. Permit parking is available.

Rooms 5 en suite (1 fmly) S £90-£160; D £100-£170* **Facilities** FTV tea/coffee Dinner available Cen ht **Notes** ⊗ No coaches

The Running Horse

★★★★ 🏵 INN

88 Main Rd, Littleton SO22 6QS
☎ **01962 880218** 📠 01962 886596
e-mail: runninghorseinn@btconnect.com
dir: *B3049 out of Winchester 1.5m, turn right into Littleton after 1m, Running Horse on right*

Situated in a pretty rural location, yet with easy access to the M3, this is a great location for business and leisure travellers visiting Hampshire. Offering quality accommodation, the Running Horse is minimalist in its design, and provides comfortable beds and a small workstation area. Highlights of a stay here are a meal in the smart restaurant or a drink in the bar.

Rooms 9 annexe en suite (1 fmly) (9 GF) S £65; D £85-£110* **Facilities** tea/coffee Dinner available Cen ht Wi-fi **Parking** 70 **Notes** No coaches

The Green Man Inn

★★★ INN

53 Southgate St SO23 9EH
☎ **01962 890074   & 07738 434531**
e-mail: nickwhite140@msn.com
dir: *M3 junct 11, 3rd exit from 2nd rdbt onto Saint Cross St then Southgate St, opp cinema*

A traditional inn located in the historic city of Winchester. Comfortable en suite bedrooms are tastefully appointed and located on the top two floors of this three storey building. The popular bar and dining area features a range of real ales and a regularly changing specials board.

Rooms 4 en suite (1 fmly) S fr £35; D £75-£85* **Facilities** FTV tea/coffee Dinner available Cen ht Wi-fi **Conf** Thtr 10 Class 10 Board 10 **Notes** No coaches

24 Clifton Road

★★★ BED AND BREAKFAST

SO22 5BU
☎ **01962 851620**
e-mail: a.williams1997@btinternet.com
dir: *500yds NW of city centre. B3040 Romsey Rd W from city centre, Clifton Rd 2nd right*

This delightful house is in a quiet residential area close to the railway station and High Street. It combines townhouse elegance with a homely cottage charm, and is handy for local walks. The bedroom is comfortably furnished and the bathroom has a deep claw-foot bath. There is a lounge and a dining room.

Rooms 1 rms (1 pri facs) S £35; D £55 **Facilities** TVL tea/coffee Cen ht **Parking** 2 **Notes** ⊗ No Children 6yrs 🖾

The Westgate Inn

★★★ INN

2 Romsey Rd SO23 8TP
☎ **01962 820222** 📠 01962 820222
e-mail: wghguy@yahoo.co.uk
dir: *M3 junct 9 follow signs to city centre, on corner of Romsey Rd & Upper High St*

The Westgate Inn is well placed at the west end of the city near the castle. A popular restaurant serves good, home-prepared Indian meals and snacks. The traditional bar is always busy. The attractive and good-sized bedrooms on two floors are well equipped.

Rooms 8 rms (6 en suite) (8 smoking); D £70-£85* **Facilities** FTV tea/coffee Dinner available Direct Dial Cen ht Wi-fi **Conf** Max 12 Board 12 **Notes** No Children No coaches

ABBEY DORE   **Map 9 SO33**

Old Rectory

★★★★ BED AND BREAKFAST

HR2 0AA
☎ **01981 240311**
e-mail: howesdore@btinternet.com
web: www.bedandbreakfastoldrectory.co.uk

A warm welcome is offered at the Old Rectory which has been a private residence since 1958 and sits just a very short distance from the restored Abbey Dore Abbey, now the parish church. Set in some wonderful grounds this Georgian property provides two comfortable and spacious bedrooms which offer useful guest extras and have fabulous views. There is a cosy lounge with log fire for the colder days, and an elegant dining room set with a communal table for the hearty breakfasts served by the friendly and charming hosts.

Rooms 2 en suite (2 fmly) S £35-£40; D £60-£70* **Facilities** TV1B TVL tea/coffee ♨ **Parking** 3 **Notes** LB ⊕

ADFORTON
Map 9 S047

Brick House Farm

★★★★ 🏠 ⊜ BED AND BREAKFAST

SY7 0NF
☎ 01568 770870
e-mail: info@adforton.com
web: www.adforton.com
dir: On A4110 in Adforton opposite St Andrew's Church

Located at the heart of the village community, this 16th-century longhouse has been sympathetically renovated to provide high standards of comfort and facilities. Superb beds are just one feature of the thoughtfully furnished accommodation, and smart modern private bathrooms are an additional benefit. Comprehensive breakfasts and imaginative set dinners featuring locally-sourced produce including home grown items are served in a cosy combined sitting/dining room. A warm welcome is assured.

Rooms 2 rms (2 pri facs); D £75 **Facilities** STV FTV TVL tea/coffee Dinner available Cen ht Riding **Conf** Max 16 Thtr 16 Class 16 Board 16 **Parking** 4 **Notes** No Children 12yrs

---

BROCKHAMPTON
Map 10 S053

Ladyridge Farm

★★★★ ⊜ GUEST HOUSE

HR1 4SE
☎ 01989 740220 📠 01989 740220
e-mail: carolgrant@ladyridgefarm.fsworld.co.uk
dir: Off B4224 signed Brockhampton Church between How Caple & Townhope. 400yds on right after thatched church

This working farm, set in delightful countryside, provides a peaceful haven and is also home to rare breed ducks, poultry and sheep. Bedrooms are spacious, traditional

and thoughtfully equipped. Meals are served family-style in the attractive dining room, using local fresh ingredients and home-produced free-range eggs.

Rooms 3 rms (2 pri facs) (1 fmly) S £28-£30; D £52-£56* **Facilities** tea/coffee Dinner available Cen ht **Parking** 6 **Notes** LB ⊕ ⊕

BROMYARD
Map 10 S065

Linton Brook Farm (S0676538)

★★★★ FARMHOUSE

Malvern Rd, Bringsty WR6 5TR
☎ 01885 488875 📠 01885 488875 Mrs S Steeds
dir: Off A44 1.5m E of Bromyard onto B4220 signed Malvern. Farm 0.5m on left

Dating back some 400 years, this large house has a wealth of character and has been renovated to provide modern comforts. Accommodation is spacious and there is a comfortable sitting room with a welcoming wood-burning stove. The breakfast room has exposed beams, antique furniture and an inglenook fireplace.

Rooms 3 rms (2 en suite) (1 pri facs) **Facilities** TVL tea/coffee Dinner available Cen ht **Parking** 12 **Notes** ⊕ Closed Xmas & New Year RS end Oct-end Apr No single person single night bookings ⊕ 68 acres grassland

---

Little Hegdon Farm House

★★★★ BED AND BREAKFAST

Hegdon Hill, Pencombe HR7 4SL
☎ 01885 400263 & 07779 595445
e-mail: howardcolegrave@hotmail.com
web: www.littlehegdonfarmhouse.co.uk
dir: 4m SW of Bromyard. From Bromyard to Pencombe, 1.5m towards Risbury, at top of Hegdon Hill down farm lane for 500yds

Located in a pretty hamlet, this traditional house has been renovated to provide high standards of comfort. Original features include exposed beams and open fires, and the bedrooms are equipped with lots of thoughtful extras. They also enjoy stunning views of the countryside.

Rooms 2 en suite S £35; D £60 **Facilities** TVL tea/coffee Cen ht ♨ Riding Pool Table **Parking** 4 **Notes** ⊕

GOODRICH
Map 10 S051

Granton House B&B

★★★★ BED AND BREAKFAST

HR9 6JE
☎ 01600 890277
e-mail: info@grantonhouse.co.uk
web: www.grantonhouse.co.uk
dir: A40 S from Ross-on-Wye, 2nd Goodrich exit into village, pass Cross Keys continue straight for approx 0.5m

A genuinely warm and friendly welcome awaits at Granton House, parts of which date back to the late 18th century. It is situated in extensive grounds and gardens, in a picturesque rural area on the edge of Goodrich village. The house, which was once the home of Victorian artist Joshua Cristall, has been extensively and tastefully renovated to provide high quality, thoughtfully equipped accommodation.

Rooms 3 en suite (1 fmly); D £80-£95* **Facilities** tea/coffee Cen ht Wi-fi **Parking** 4 **Notes** LB ⊕ No Children 12yrs Closed 18 Dec-2 Jan

---

HEREFORD
Map 10 S053

See also Little Dewchurch & Moccas

PREMIER COLLECTION

Somerville House

★★★★★ GUEST ACCOMMODATION

12 Bodenham Rd HR1 2TS
☎ 01432 273991 📠 01432 268719
e-mail: enquiries@somervillehouse.net
web: www.somervillehouse.net
dir: A465, at Aylestone Hill rdbt towards city centre, left at Southbank Rd, leading to Bodenham Rd

A detached late-Victorian villa situated in a quiet tree-lined residential road, offering a boutique-style bed and breakfast experience. Expect a warm and friendly welcome from Rosie and Bill who offer quality accommodation with high standards of luxury and comfort. All bedrooms are spacious and provide a good range of quality extras. Breakfast is served in the light and contemporary dining room at individual tables. There is a terraced garden to the rear where guests can sit and relax, or indoors, they can make use of the comfortable lounge. There is ample parking.

Rooms 12 en suite (2 fmly) (1 GF) S £50-£55; D £65-£99 **Facilities** FTV tea/coffee Cen ht Licensed Wi-fi Arrangement with health spa **Conf** Max 10 Thtr 10 Class 10 Board 10 **Parking** 10 **Notes** LB ⊕

HEREFORDSHIRE *continued*

Bay Horse Inn

★★★★ INN

236 Kings Acre Rd HR4 0SD
☎ 01432 273351
e-mail: info@thebayhorsehereford.co.uk
dir: *On A438, pass Wyevale, 1000yds on left*

The friendly and courteous staff at this delightful inn on the outskirts of Hereford, extend a warm welcome to all. Some of the bedrooms are purpose built and on the ground floor; one has wheelchair access with a wet room shower facility. There are further second-floor bedrooms, two of which are suitable for families; all bedrooms are spacious and tastefully decorated. A good menu choice of quality dishes is offered at dinner, and also at breakfast which served at separate tables.

Rooms 8 annexe en suite (1 fmly) (4 GF) S £55-£65; D £65-£95* **Facilities** FTV TVL tea/coffee Dinner available Direct Dial Cen ht Wi-fi **Conf** Max 40 Thtr 40 Class 40 Board 32 **Parking** 30 **Notes** LB ⊗ No Children 12yrs

Holly House Farm (SO456367)

★★★★ FARMHOUSE

Allensmore HR2 9BH
☎ 01432 277294 & 07889 830223
📄 01432 261285 Mrs D Sinclair
e-mail: hollyhousefarm@aol.com
web: www.hollyhousefarm.org.uk
dir: *A465 S to Allensmore, right signed Cobhall Common, at small x-rds right into lane, house on right*

Surrounded by open countryside, this spacious farmhouse is a relaxing base for those visiting this beautiful area. The homely and comfortable bedrooms offer lovely views over the fields. Breakfast makes use of local produce together with home-made jams and marmalade. Pets are very welcome here and the proprietor is happy to look after them during the day if required.

Rooms 2 rms (1 en suite) (1 pri facs) **Facilities** tea/coffee Cen ht **Parking** 32 **Notes** Closed 25-26, 31 Dec & 1 Jan ⊛ 11 acres horses

Norfolk House

★★★★ GUEST ACCOMMODATION

23 Saint Martin St HR2 7RD
☎ 01432 340900
e-mail: info@norfolkhousehereford.co.uk
web: www.norfolkhousehereford.co.uk

Norfolk House is a large mid-terraced Georgian property situated south of the River Wye in Hereford, only 100 metres from the city's old bridge and the Left Bank Village. An ideal location for exploring the nearby towns of Leominster, Ludlow, Ledbury, Kington, Ross-on-Wye and Worcester. The accommodation provides five comfortable en suite bedrooms and include doubles (with king-sized beds) and twin rooms. In the welcoming dining room a hearty breakfast, made from fresh local produce, is provided. Wi-fi is available.

Rooms 5 en suite (1 fmly) **Facilities** FTV tea/coffee Cen ht Wi-fi **Parking** 3 **Notes** ⊗ No Children 5yrs

Sink Green (SO542377)

★★★★ FARMHOUSE

Rotherwas HR2 6LE
☎ 01432 870223 📄 01432 870223 Mr D E Jones
e-mail: enquiries@sinkgreenfarm.co.uk
web: www.sinkgreenfarm.co.uk
dir: *3m SE of city centre. Off A49 onto B4399 for 2m*

This charming 16th-century farmhouse stands in attractive countryside and has many original features, including flagstone floors, exposed beams and open fireplaces. Bedrooms are traditionally furnished and one has a four-poster bed. The pleasant garden has a comfortable summer house, hot tub and barbecue.

Rooms 3 en suite S £35-£55; D £70-£80 **Facilities** FTV TVL tea/coffee Cen ht Wi-fi Fishing Hot tub **Parking** 10 **Notes** LB ⊛ 180 acres beef

Charades Guest House

★★★★ 🅰 GUEST HOUSE

34 Southbank Rd HR1 2TJ
☎ 01432 269444 📄 01432 269444
e-mail: stay@charadeshereford.co.uk
web: www.charadeshereford.co.uk
dir: *Off A4103 Ayelstone Hill, right onto Southbank Rd, 500yds on right*

Rooms 14 en suite (5 fmly) (3 GF) S £45; D £65-£75 **Facilities** TVL tea/coffee Cen ht Wi-fi **Parking** 16 **Notes** LB ⊗

Heron House

★★★ 🅰 BED AND BREAKFAST

Canon Pyon Rd, Portway HR4 8NG
☎ 01432 761111 📄 01432 760603
e-mail: info@theheronhouse.com
web: www.theheronhouse.com
dir: *A4103 onto A4110 until Portway x-rds, Heron House 200yds on left*

Rooms 2 rms (1 en suite) S £27; D £30-£60* **Facilities** tea/coffee Cen ht **Parking** 5 **Notes** ⊗ No Children 10yrs ⊛

LEDBURY Map 10 SO73

Bodenham Farm (SO653318)

★★★★ FARMHOUSE

Much Marcle HR8 2NJ
☎ 01531 660222 & 07754 415604 Mrs L Morgan
e-mail: stay@bodenhamfarm.co.uk
web: www.bodenhamfarm.co.uk
dir: *5m SW of Ledbury. 0.5m S of Much Marcle on A449*

Set in well-tended gardens, this impressive and attractive Grade II listed house dates from the 18th century. Full of character, the comfortable accommodation retains many original features including exposed beams and four-poster beds, along with modern facilities. The welcoming proprietors make you feel very much at home.

Rooms 3 en suite S £45-£85; D £70-£85 **Facilities** TVL tea/coffee Cen ht Wi-fi **Parking** 8 **Notes** ⊗ No Children 12yrs ⊛ 5 acres highland cattle/chickens

Moor Court Farm (SO639447)

★★★★ FARMHOUSE

Stretton, Grandison HR8 2TP
☎ 01531 670408 🖨 01531 670408 Mrs E Godsall
dir: 1.5m E of A417 at Upper Eggleton

This 15th-century house is situated on a mixed farm with working oast houses where hops are dried. Bedrooms are thoughtfully equipped and furnished, and one has a four-poster. Public areas include a comfortable lounge with an impressive stone fireplace and a dining room, where breakfast includes local produce and eggs from the farm.

Rooms 3 en suite Facilities tea/coffee Dinner available Cen ht Licensed Fishing Parking 5 Notes ⊗ No Children 8yrs ⊜ 200 acres mixed/livestock/hops

Wall Hills House

★★★★ GUEST ACCOMMODATION

Hereford Rd HR8 2PR
☎ 01531 632833
e-mail: wallhills@btinternet.com
dir: Leave Ledbury on A438, entrance to drive within 200yds on left after rdbt

Expect a friendly welcome at Wall Hills House, which is set amongst fields and woodland half a mile from the main road and close to the old market town of Ledbury. The area is ideal for walkers, with the wonderful scenery of the Malvern Hills nearby. Bedrooms are spacious, reflecting the Georgian era in which the house was built, and the front-facing rooms command views over rural Herefordshire. Dinner is freshly prepared using fresh, local ingredients with vegetables usually picked from the owner's garden, and served in the cosy dining room at individually set tables.

Rooms 3 rms (2 en suite) (1 pri facs) S £58-£75; D £79-£85* Facilities tea/coffee Dinner available Cen ht Licensed Wi-fi Parking 6 Notes LB ⊗ Closed Xmas & New Year

---

LEOMINSTER — Map 10 SO45

PREMIER COLLECTION

Hills Farm (SO564638)

★★★★★ FARMHOUSE

Leysters HR6 0HP
☎ 01568 750205 Mrs J Conolly
e-mail: j.conolly@btconnect.com
web: www.thehillsfarm.co.uk
dir: Off A4112 (Leominster to Tenbury Wells), on outskirts of Leysters

Set in a peaceful location with views of the surrounding countryside, this property dates in part from the 16th century. The friendly, attentive proprietors provide a relaxing and homely atmosphere. The attractive bedrooms, in the converted barns, are spacious and comfortable. Breakfasts, served in the dining room and conservatory, feature fresh local produce.

Rooms 3 annexe en suite (1 GF) S £38-£40; D £76-£80* Facilities FTV tea/coffee Cen ht Parking 8 Notes ⊗ No Children 12yrs Closed Dec & Jan 120 acres arable

---

LITTLE DEWCHURCH — Map 10 SO53

Cwm Craig (SO535322)

★★★★ FARMHOUSE

HR2 6PS
☎ 01432 840250 🖨 01432 840250 Mrs G Lee
e-mail: leead@btconnect.com
dir: Off A49 into Little Dewchurch, turn right in village, Cwm Craig 1st farm on left

This Georgian farmhouse is situated on the outskirts of the village in glorious countryside and offers spacious accommodation. Bedrooms are carefully furnished and public areas consist of a comfortable lounge, games room and dining rooms, one of which is offered for the use of families. A hearty breakfast is supplemented by eggs from the farm's hens.

Rooms 3 en suite (1 fmly) Facilities TVL tea/coffee Cen ht Pool Table Parking 6 Notes ⊗ ⊜ 190 acres organic arable

---

MOCCAS — Map 9 SO34

PREMIER COLLECTION

Moccas Court

★★★★★ 🏠 🍽 GUEST ACCOMMODATION

HR2 9LH
☎ 01981 500019 🖨 01981 500095
e-mail: bencmaster@btconnect.com
dir: A438, in 10m right to Bredwardine, right at T-junct approx 2.5m left to Moccas Court

This memorable Grade I listed Georgian family home is of such historic interest that it is open to the public as a stately home. You can dwell in the lap of luxury, attended to by the most charming and genial hosts. A delicious dinner, served around a large circular table in the splendid dining room, should not be missed. Ben and Mimi Chester-Master were finalists in the AA Friendliest Landlady of the Year 2009-2010 Award.

Rooms 5 rms (4 en suite) (1 pri facs); D £137-£219* Facilities FTV tea/coffee Dinner available Cen ht Licensed Wi-fi 🎣 Fishing Parking 35 Notes LB ⊗ No Children 16yrs Closed Jan-Apr RS Sun-Wed Civ Wed 60

PETERCHURCH — Map 9 SO33

Hinton Green Country House B&B

★★★ BED AND BREAKFAST

Hinton Green HR2 0SH
☎ 01981 550135
e-mail: info@hintongreen.com
web: www.hintongreen.com
dir: B4348 to Peterchurch, turn left at Nags Head, 3rd house on right

A warm and friendly welcome awaits guests at this fine 16th-century property which has been lovingly restored by the present proprietors, Pat and Sandy, who have created three guest bedrooms that have quality fittings. Bedrooms are comfortable and offer a good range of extras. Peterchurch is in the centre of the Golden Valley with many local walks. Hinton Green is within easy walking distance of the village centre with shops, restaurants and pubs.

Rooms 3 en suite (1 fmly) Facilities TVL tea/coffee Cen ht Conf Max 8 Parking 4 Notes LB ⊗ ⊜

See also Goodrich

Brookfield House

★★★★ GUEST ACCOMMODATION

Over Ross St HR9 7AT
☎ 01989 562188
e-mail: info@brookfield-house.co.uk
web: www.brookfield-house.co.uk
dir: *500yds N of town centre. Off B4234 Over Ross St onto Brookmead & up driveway*

Dating from the 18th century, this large detached house lies just north of the town centre. Refurbished to a high standard throughout, the bedrooms are spacious, comfortably appointed and well equipped. Breakfast is served in the light and airy dining room. A relaxing lounge is also available for guest use, as are the attractive gardens.

Rooms 3 en suite (1 fmly); D £64-£72* **Facilities** tea/coffee Cen ht Wi-fi **Parking** 12 **Notes** ⊗ No Children 12yrs

The Bridge at Wilton

★★★★ ⊚⊚ RESTAURANT WITH ROOMS

Wilton HR9 6AA
☎ 01989 562655   📠 01989 567652
e-mail: info@bridge-house-hotel.com
web: www.bridge-house-hotel.com
dir: *Off junct A40 & A49 into Ross-on-Wye, 300yds on left*

Built about 1740, this elegant house is just a stroll across the bridge from delightful Ross-on-Wye. Standards here are impressive and bedrooms offer ample space, comfort and genuine quality. Period features in the public areas add to the stylish ambience, and the gardens run down to the river. The restaurant serves accomplished cuisine.

Rooms 9 en suite S £75-£80; D £100-£120*
Facilities tea/coffee Dinner available Direct Dial Cen ht Wi-Fi Fishing **Conf** Max 12 **Parking** 30 **Notes** LB ⊗ No Children 14yrs No coaches

Lea House

★★★★ ☕ ⊜ GUEST ACCOMMODATION

Lea HR9 7JZ
☎ 01989 750652   📠 01989 750652
e-mail: enquiries@leahouse.co.uk
web: www.leahouse.co.uk
dir: *4m SE of Ross on A40 towards Gloucester, in Lea village*

This former coaching inn near Ross is a good base for exploring the Forest of Dean and the Wye Valley. The individually furnished bedrooms are thoughtfully equipped and very homely. The atmosphere is relaxed and comfortable. Home cooked dinner can be taken by prior arrangement. Breakfast in the oak-beamed dining room is an experience with home-made breads, freshly

squeezed juice, fresh fruit platters, local sausages and a choice of fish.

Rooms 3 rms (2 en suite) (1 pri facs) (1 fmly)
S £37.50-£45; D £65-£75* **Facilities** TVL tea/coffee Dinner available Cen ht Wi-fi **Parking** 4 **Notes** LB

Lumleys

★★★★ BED AND BREAKFAST

Kern Bridge, Bishopswood HR9 5QT
☎ 01600 890040   📠 0870 706 2378
e-mail: helen@lumleys.force9.co.uk
web: www.thelumleys.co.uk
dir: *Off A40 onto B4229 at Goodrich, over Kern Bridge, right at Inn On The Wye, 400yds opp picnic ground*

This pleasant and friendly guest house overlooks the River Wye, and has been a hostelry since Victorian times. It offers the character of a bygone era combined with modern comforts and facilities. Bedrooms are individually and carefully furnished and one has a four-poster bed and its own patio. Comfortable public areas include a choice of sitting rooms.

Rooms 3 en suite; D £60-£70* **Facilities** STV FTV TVL tea/coffee Dinner available Direct Dial Cen ht Wi-fi **Parking** 15 **Notes** ⊚

Orles Barn

★★★★ ⊜ RESTAURANT WITH ROOMS

Wilton HR9 6AE
☎ 01989 562155   📠 01989 768470
e-mail: reservations@orles-barn.co.uk
web: www.orles-barn.co.uk
dir: *A49/A40 rdbt outside Ross-on-Wye, take slip road between petrol station & A40 to Monmouth. 100yds on left*

Kelly and Richard Bailey offer a warm welcome to all guests at their property that dates from the 14th and 17th centuries when it was a farmhouse and barn. The bedrooms are comfortable, and public areas include a smart cosy lounge with a bar plus a spacious restaurant. Here, dinners and Sunday lunches are served from a balanced menu of fresh local and seasonal ingredients. Breakfast provides some quality local items and a good start to the day.

Rooms 8 rms (7 en suite) (1 pri facs) (1 fmly) (1 GF)
S £49-£75; D £59-£105* **Facilities** tea/coffee Dinner available Cen ht Wi-fi ⊜ **Conf** Max 100 Thtr 100 Class 50 Board 40 **Parking** 20 **Notes** LB Civ Wed 100

Thatch Close

★★★★ GUEST ACCOMMODATION

Llangrove HR9 6EL
☎ 01989 770300
e-mail: info@thatchclose.co.uk
web: www.thatchclose.co.uk
dir: *Off A40 at Symonds Yat West/Whitchurch junct to Llangrove, right at x-rds after Post Office & before school. Thatch Close 0.6m on left*

Standing in 13 acres, this sturdy 18th-century farmhouse is full of character. Expect a wonderfully warm atmosphere with a genuine welcome from your hosts. The homely bedrooms are equipped for comfort with many thoughtful extras. Breakfast and dinner are served in the elegant dining room, and a lounge is available. The extensive patios and gardens are popular in summer, providing plenty of space to find a quiet corner and relax with a good book.

Rooms 3 en suite S fr £35; D fr £58* **Facilities** TVL tea/coffee Dinner available Cen ht **Parking** 8 **Notes** LB ⊚

Nature's Choice

★★★ GUEST HOUSE

Raglan House, 17 Broad St HR9 7EA
☎ 01989 763454   📠 01989 763064
e-mail: deanclarke@surfree.co.uk
dir: *Market Place onto Broad St, 100yds on left*

Under the new ownership of Anna and Dean Clarke there is a friendly welcome awaiting all guests along with a comfortable stay in the well presented bedrooms. This Grade II listed Queen Anne property is located in the town centre, close to all amenities and as the name suggests, the emphasis here is on healthy food with vegetarian and gluten-free options in the café part of the guest house where food is available all day. Guests have the option of discounted meals. Anna's speciality is Russian style cooking.

Rooms 4 en suite S £35-£39.50; D £55-£59.50
Facilities FTV Dinner available Cen ht Licensed Wi-fi **Notes** ⊗

SHOBDON Map 9 SO46

The Bateman Arms

★★★★ INN

HR6 9LX
☎ 01568 708374   🖹 08701 236418
e-mail: diana@batemanarms.co.uk
web: www.batemanarms.co.uk
dir: On B4362 in Shobdon

Located in the village, parts of this refurbished inn date back over 400 years. Now under the new ownership of Bill and Diana Mahood who offer a warm welcome to all their guests. The accommodation comprises six modern bedrooms located in the separate building, and three bedrooms in the main house; all are comfortable and well appointed. Much character has been retained with plenty of oak beams and a large log fire adding to the warm ambience of the public areas. In addition to the friendly welcome, the food, using carefully prepared local produce, is a key feature.

Rooms 3 en suite 6 annexe en suite (2 fmly) (3 GF) S £55-£65; D £85-£95 Facilities FTV tea/coffee Dinner available Cen ht Wi-fi Pool Table Games room Parking 40 Notes LB

SYMONDS YAT (EAST) Map 10 SO51

Garth Cottage

★★★★ GUEST ACCOMMODATION

HR9 6JL
☎ 01600 890364
e-mail: val.eden@virgin.net
web: www.garthcottage-symondsyat.com
dir: Off A40 onto B4229, signs for Symonds Yat East

The Eden family's warm hospitality and attention to guest comfort is evident in this attractive and impeccably maintained 18th-century house. The bedrooms are well equipped, and breakfast and dinner are served in the conservatory-dining room overlooking the River Wye. There is also a cosy bar and a choice of lounges, including a sun lounge that also looks over the river.

Rooms 4 en suite S £35; D £74* Facilities TVL tea/coffee Dinner available Cen ht Licensed Fishing Parking 9 Notes ⊗ No Children 12yrs Closed Nov-Mar

Saracens Head Inn

★★★★ INN

HR9 6JL
☎ 01600 890435   🖹 01600 890034
e-mail: contact@saracensheadinn.co.uk
web: www.saracensheadinn.co.uk
dir: Off A40 at Little Chef, signed Symonds Yat East, 3m

Dating from the 16th century, the friendly, family-run Saracens Head faces the River Wye and has wonderful views. The well-equipped bedrooms are decorated in a cottage style, and there is a cosy lounge, an attractive dining room, and a popular public bar with a riverside patio. All meals are offered from a comprehensive menu changed regularly, and include locally-sourced produce.

Rooms 8 en suite 2 annexe en suite (1 fmly) (1 GF) S £50-£70; D £79-£130* Facilities FTV TVL tea/coffee Dinner available Direct Dial Cen ht Wi-fi Fishing Pool Table Conf Max 25 Thtr 25 Class 25 Board 25 Parking 35 Notes LB No Children 7yrs No coaches

The Royal Lodge

★★★ GUEST ACCOMMODATION

HR9 6JL
☎ 01600 890238   🖹 01600 891425
e-mail: info@royalhotel-symondsyat.com
web: www.royallodgesymondsyat.co.uk
dir: Midway between Ross and Monmouth. Turn off at signs for Goodich B4229 to Symonds Yat East

The Royal Lodge is under new ownership and stands at the top end of the village overlooking the River Wye. Bedrooms are spacious and comfortable and there is a cosy lounge with an open fireplace, along with a television. The bedrooms do not have TVs, as the Lodge operates a quiet policy. Meals are offered in the welcoming restaurant which provides carefully prepared fresh and local ingredients. Staff are pleasant and friendly.

Rooms 20 en suite (5 fmly) Facilities TVL tea/coffee Dinner available Direct Dial Cen ht Licensed Wi-fi Conf Max 70 Thtr 70 Class 20 Board 30 Parking 150

SYMONDS YAT (WEST) Map 10 SO51

Norton House

★★★★ 🛏 🍽 GUEST ACCOMMODATION

Whitchurch HR9 6DJ
☎ 01600 890046   🖹 01600 890045
e-mail: su@norton.wyenet.co.uk
web: www.norton-house.com
dir: 0.5m N of Symonds Yat West. Off A40 into Whitchurch, left onto Old Monmouth Rd

Built as a farmhouse, Norton House dates back 300 years and retains much character through features such as flagstone floors and beamed ceilings. The bedrooms, including a four-poster room, are individually styled and furnished for maximum comfort. Excellent local produce is used to create an imaginative range of breakfast and dinner options. The charming public areas include a snug lounge, with a wood-burning stove. Self-catering cottages are also available.

Rooms 3 en suite S £45-£50; D £70-£90 Facilities TVL tea/coffee Dinner available Cen ht Parking 5 Notes No Children 12yrs Closed 25-26 Dec

VOWCHURCH Map 9 SO33

Yew Tree House

★★★★ 🅰 BED AND BREAKFAST

Bacho Hill HR2 9PF
☎ 01981 251195   🖹 01981 251195
e-mail: enquiries@yewtreehouse-hereford.co.uk
web: www.yewtreehouse-hereford.co.uk
dir: On B4348 between Kingstone & Vowchurch

Rooms 3 en suite (2 fmly) S £45-£55; D £70-£75* Facilities TVL tea/coffee Dinner available Cen ht Wi-fi Parking 4 Notes LB ⊛

WHITCHURCH Map 10 SO51

Portland House Guest House

★★★★ GUEST ACCOMMODATION

HR9 6DB
☎ 01600 890757
e-mail: info@portlandguesthouse.co.uk
web: www.portlandguesthouse.co.uk
dir: Off A40 between Monmouth & Ross on Wye. Take turn for Whitchurch/Symonds Yat West

Portland House is an impressive dwelling, dating in part to the 17th century. Comfortable bedrooms include a
continued

WHITCHURCH *continued*

large family room, an accessible bedroom on the ground floor, and a four-poster suite. All have a thoughtful range of extras. Walkers can use the Boot Room and guests have use of the laundry, the terrace garden area, and the attractive lounge. Breakfast, with home-made bread and up to eight kinds of home-made preserve, is served around the shared dining table, or at a separate table in the cosy elegant dining room. With prior arrangement, evening meals can be provided.

Portland House Guest House

Rooms 6 en suite (2 fmly) (1 GF) S £48-£55; D £70-£105* **Facilities** TVL tea/coffee Dinner available Cen ht Licensed Wi-fi **Parking** 6 **Notes** LB ⊗ Closed 25-26 Dec & Jan

| **WHITNEY-ON-WYE** | Map 9 SO24 |

The Rhydspence Inn

★★★★ INN

HR3 6EU
☎ 01497 831262 📄 01497 831751
e-mail: info@rhydspence-inn.co.uk
dir: *N side of A438 1m W of Whitney*

Dating back to the 14th century this large, privately owned and personally run hostelry is three miles north of Hay-on-Wye. Surrounded by attractive gardens and with a stream that forms part of the boundary between England and Wales, the inn provides modern accommodation, and public rooms that include a very attractive restaurant and two quaint bars with low beamed ceilings and log fires.

Rooms 7 en suite **Facilities** tea/coffee Dinner available Cen ht **Parking** 60 **Notes** ⊗ No coaches

| **YARKHILL** | Map 10 SO64 |

Garford Farm *(SO600435)*

★★★★ FARMHOUSE

HR1 3ST
☎ 01432 890226 📄 01432 890707 Mrs H Parker
e-mail: garfordfarm@btconnect.com
dir: *Off A417 at Newtown x-rds onto A4103 for Hereford, farm 1.5m on left*

This black and white timber-framed farmhouse, set on a large arable holding, dates from the 17th century. Its

character is enhanced by period furnishings, and fires burn in the comfortable lounge during colder weather. The traditionally furnished bedrooms, including a family room, have modern facilities.

Rooms 2 en suite (1 fmly); D fr £60* **Facilities** tea/coffee Cen ht 🎣 Fishing **Parking** 6 **Notes** No Children 2yrs Closed 25-26 Dec ⊛ 700 acres arable

HERTFORDSHIRE

| **BENINGTON** | Map 6 TL22 |

Meadow House

★★★★ BED AND BREAKFAST

88 Whempstead Rd SG2 7DE
☎ 01438 869123
e-mail: pam@focuscorp.co.uk
dir: *Exit A10 at Ware onto A602. At top of 2nd hill, right signed Benington. 2.3m, Meadow House on left*

A beautiful family house with a large garden, ample parking space, comfortable sitting room and two well-appointed bedrooms, one en suite and one with private bathroom, now refurbished, which offer comfortable beds, Freeview channels and free Wi-fi. Breakfast is served at the large table in the dining room and the menu offer good quality produce, locally sourced.

Rooms 2 rms (1 en suite) (1 pri facs) S £35-£50; D £65-£75 **Facilities** FTV tea/coffee Cen ht Wi-fi Gymnasium **Parking** 10 **Notes** ⊗ No Children 12yrs ⊛

| **BISHOP'S STORTFORD** | Map 6 TL42 |

Broadleaf Guest House

★★★ BED AND BREAKFAST

38 Broadleaf Av CM23 4JY
☎ 01279 835467
e-mail: b-tcannon@tiscali.co.uk
dir: *1m SW of town centre. Off B1383 onto Whittinton Way & Friedburge Av, Broadleaf Av 6th left*

A delightful detached house situated in a peaceful residential area close to the town centre, and within easy striking distance of the M11 and Stansted Airport. The pleasantly decorated bedrooms are carefully furnished and equipped with many thoughtful touches. Breakfast is served in the smart dining room, which overlooks the pretty garden.

Rooms 2 rms (1 fmly) **Facilities** tea/coffee Cen ht **Parking** 2 **Notes** ⊛

Pearse House

★★★ GUEST ACCOMMODATION

Parsonage Ln CM23 5BQ
☎ 01279 757400 📄 01279 506591
e-mail: enquiries@pearsehouse.co.uk
dir: *M11 junct 8, A120, A1250 into Bishop's Stortford. Right at rdbt onto Parsonage Ln, house 1st on left*

An imposing, half-timbered Victorian house situated on the edge of town and just a short drive from Stansted Airport. Bedrooms are smartly appointed and equipped with modern facilities. The spacious public areas include a bar, lounge, dining room and conference facilities.

Rooms 13 en suite 24 annexe en suite (2 fmly) (1 GF) S £75; D £85* **Facilities** TVL tea/coffee Dinner available Direct Dial Cen ht Wi-fi Small fitness room **Conf** Max 300 Thtr 150 Class 60 Board 30 **Parking** 100 **Notes** LB ⊗ Closed Xmas & New Year Civ Wed 60

Hallingbury House

Ⓤ

Tilekiln Green, Great Hallingbury CM22 7TS
e-mail: ludo@ttg.co.uk

Currently the rating for this establishment is not confirmed. This may be due to a change of ownership or because it has only recently joined the AA rating scheme. For up-to-date information please see the AA website: theAA.com

Rooms 16 en suite S £53-£85; D £60-£100*

| **BUNTINGFORD** | Map 12 TL32 |

Sword Inn Hand

★★★★ INN

Westmill SG9 9LQ
☎ 01763 271356
e-mail: welcome@theswordinnhand.co.uk
web: www.theswordinnhand.co.uk
dir: *In Westmill, off A10 S of Buntingford*

Set in the peaceful village of Westmill amid rolling countryside, this charming 14th-century inn offers excellent accommodation and a friendly and relaxed atmosphere. Purpose-built ground-floor bedrooms are located just off the rear gardens; these very well-equipped and carefully appointed rooms have their own access. Character public rooms include a choice of restaurant and bar dining options, along with a choice of draught ales.

Rooms 4 en suite (4 GF) **Facilities** STV FTV TVL tea/coffee Dinner available Cen ht Wi-fi **Parking** 25 **Notes** ⊗

DATCHWORTH — Map 6 TL21

PREMIER COLLECTION

Farmhouse B&B
★★★★★ BED AND BREAKFAST

Hawkins Grange Farm, Hawkins Hall Ln SG3 6TF
☎ 01438 813369 📠 01438 813369
e-mail: mail@hawkinsgrangefarm.com
web: www.hawkinsgrangefarm.com
dir: *A1(M) junct 7 onto A602 (Hertford). From Bragbury End onto Bragbury Ln, 2m on left after phone box*

This detached property is set in several acres of grassland on the edge of the pretty village of Datchworth. A warm and professional welcome is provided by your host Jane. Bedrooms are comfortably furnished with an abundance of accessories. Full English or continental breakfast is served, including organic, local produce and home-made items.

Rooms 3 rms (2 en suite) (1 pri facs) S £35-£45; D £70 **Facilities** FTV tea/coffee Cen ht Wi-fi **Parking** 8 **Notes** ⊗

HARPENDEN — Map 6 TL11

The Silver Cup
★★★★ INN

5 St Albans Rd AL5 2JF
☎ 01582 713095 📠 01582 469713
e-mail: info@silvercup.co.uk
web: www.silvercup.co.uk
dir: *200yds SW of Harpenden station on A1081 St Albans Rd*

Located south of Harpenden high street opposite the common, this small family-owned inn offers comfortable,

well equipped rooms with many additional extras such as an honesty bar and home-made biscuits. Public areas are stylish and well presented and the attractive restaurant serves a superior quality menu complemented by real ales and a good wine list. Service is friendly and helpful.

Rooms 6 en suite (1 fmly) **Facilities** TVL tea/coffee Dinner available Cen ht Wi-fi **Parking** 7 **Notes** ⊗ No coaches

See advert on this page

HEMEL HEMPSTEAD — Map 6 TL00

Alexandra
★★ GUEST ACCOMMODATION

40/42 Alexandra Rd HP2 5BP
☎ 01442 242897 📠 01442 211829
e-mail: alexhous@aol.com
dir: *Off B487 Queensway in town centre*

This well-managed guest house has a regular business clientele and provides well-equipped bedrooms with practical extras. Breakfast is served in the ground-floor dining room, which also contains a lounge area. There is a good selection of tourist information.

Rooms 18 rms (12 en suite) (6 pri facs) (3 fmly) (3 GF) (6 smoking) S £38-£48; D £50-£60* **Facilities** STV TVL tea/coffee Cen ht Wi-fi **Parking** 6 **Notes** ⊗ No Children 2yrs Closed 23 Dec-2 Jan

HERTFORD — Map 6 TL31

Mulberry Lodge
★★★★ GUEST ACCOMMODATION

Newgate St SG13 8NQ
☎ 01707 879652 📠 01707 879653
e-mail: bookings@mulberrylodge.org.uk
web: www.mulberrylodge.org.uk
dir: *M25 junct 25, signs for Paradise Wildlife Park, left at T-junct, Lodge on left*

Mulberry Lodge offers carefully furnished accommodation in a smart barn conversion in peaceful rural surroundings at Epping Green. The spacious bedrooms have king-size doubles (or twins) and are very well equipped for business travellers, providing safes, direct dial telephones with modem points, and modern bathrooms. Freshly cooked breakfasts are served in the open-plan diner, which has an adjacent small lounge area and a 24-hour manned reception desk. Secure parking is a bonus.

Rooms 12 en suite (12 GF) S £49.50-£65; D £49.50-£69* **Facilities** TVL tea/coffee Direct Dial Cen ht Licensed **Parking** 15 **Notes** Closed 24-26, 31 Dec & 1 Jan

The Silver Cup

cask Marque standard ale • extensive wine selection • bespoke menus • in-house functions • large parties & outside catering a speciality • separate pub/restaurant areas • sky sports • free broadband • friendly, helpful staff • quality of service guaranteed

We are a family run, traditional coaching inn situated on the idyllic Harpenden common. We are within easy reach of the M1 & the M25, the town's train service runs into London every half hour & we are only 20 minutes from Luton Airport. Our popular accommodation is tastefully decorated with plenty of space to catch up on work or simply relax while taking advantage of the mini bar provided. Downstairs our elegant & atmospheric restaurant serves up a range of affordable dishes made using fresh, quality ingredients.
After dinner you can retire next door to our bar for a crisp cold lager or perhaps one of our exceptional real ales. With 4 TVs & the ability to show up to 3 different events at the same time we enjoy a great following from sports fans who appreciate the friendly atmosphere we have created to relax & enjoy the match.
Liz, the boys & all the staff look forward to welcoming you soon!

5 St. Albans Road, Harpenden, AL5 2JF
www.silvercup.co.uk
info@silvercup.co.uk
01582 713095

HERTFORD *continued*

Orchard Cottage
★★★★ GUEST ACCOMMODATION

East End Green SG14 2PD
☎ **01992 583494** & **07885 747000**
e-mail: looadams@sky-mail.net
dir: *2m SW of Hertford. Off A414 at East End Green sign, 5th drive left on gravel road*

A friendly welcome awaits at Orchard Cottage, set in a peaceful rural location yet only five minutes from Hertford. This large cottage sits in lovely gardens and has views of the countryside. Bedrooms, with beamed ceilings, offer comfortable accommodation.

Rooms 4 rms (2 en suite) (2 pri facs) (1 fmly) S £35-£40; D £60-£70* **Facilities** FTV TVL tea/coffee Cen ht Wi-fi **Parking** 6 **Notes** ⊗ Closed Xmas & New Year ⊛

HERTFORD HEATH Map 6 TL31

PREMIER COLLECTION

Brides Farm
★★★★★ BED AND BREAKFAST

The Roundings SG13 7PY
☎ **01992 466687** & **463315** 🖷 **01992 478776**
e-mail: rjbartington@btinternet.com
dir: *B1197 to Hertford Heath. Right at College Arms into The Roundings. Left to Brides Farm*

This is an elegant country house in a parkland setting with quiet gardens for guests to enjoy. The accommodation is very comfortable and well equipped. There is a large sitting room overlooking the gardens and a formal dining room where continental and English breakfasts are served. Ample parking is available.

Rooms 3 en suite S £40; D £60* **Facilities** tea/coffee Cen ht **Parking** 10 **Notes** LB

PREMIER COLLECTION

Rushen
★★★★★ BED AND BREAKFAST

Mount Pleasant SG13 7QY
☎ **01992 581254** 🖷 **01992 534737**
e-mail: wilsonamwell@btinternet.com
dir: *From A10 exit at Hertford slip road, 1st left onto B1502. 1st right at top of lane, bear left at village green. Rushen on left at end of green*

You will find a warm welcome at Rushen, which is situated at the end of the village green in Hertford Heath. Rooms are comfortable and well appointed. Breakfast offers a good range of choice using local and organic produce when possible.

Rooms 2 rms (1 en suite) (1 pri facs) S £35-£40; D £70-£80* **Facilities** FTV tea/coffee Cen ht Wi-fi **Parking** 3 **Notes** ⊗ Closed 22 Dec-3 Jan

HITCHIN Map 12 TL12

The Greyhound
★★★ INN

London Rd, St Ippollitts SG4 7NL
☎ **01462 440989**
e-mail: greyhound@freenet.co.uk
dir: *On B656, 1m S of Hitchin*

A popular inn situated on the outskirts of town amid open farmland. Service is friendly and helpful, and a range of interesting meals is readily available in the bar and dining area. Bedrooms are well equipped and have cheerful colour schemes.

Rooms 5 en suite (1 fmly) **Facilities** tea/coffee Dinner available Cen ht **Conf** Max 30 **Parking** 25

See advert on opposite page

MUCH HADHAM Map 6 TL41

High Hedges Bed & Breakfast
★★★★ BED AND BREAKFAST

High Hedges, Green Tye SG10 6JP
☎ **01279 842505**
e-mail: info@high-hedges.co.uk
dir: *From B1004 turn off to Green Tye at Prince of Wales pub, turn into private road, 1st on right*

Expect a warm welcome at High Hedges. Bedrooms are well presented and comfortable, and come with many thoughtful extra touches. A substantial breakfast is served in the comfortable dining room. Half Moon Holistic Therapies is part of the B&B, and offers a range of massages and other treatments.

Rooms 3 rms (2 en suite) (1 pri facs) (1 GF) S £35-£40; D £60-£65 **Facilities** FTV tea/coffee Cen ht Wi-fi Holistic therapies **Parking** 3 **Notes** ⊗ Closed 25-26 Dec & 31 Dec-1 Jan ⊛

NUTHAMPSTEAD Map 12 TL43

The Woodman Inn
★★★ INN

SG8 8NB
☎ **01763 848328** 🖷 **01763 848328**
e-mail: woodman.inn@virgin.net
dir: *A505 to Royston, take right onto B1368 to Barkway, 1st left past Tally Ho, in 2m turn right. Inn on left*

This 17th-century inn has many fine features, and is close to the Duxford Imperial War Museum. The practical bedrooms are decorated in a traditional style. The kitchen offers a good range of British meals, plus a generous breakfast.

Rooms 4 en suite (2 GF) **Facilities** TV2B TVL tea/coffee Dinner available Cen ht Pool Table **Parking** 30 **Notes** ⊗ RS Sun eve Bar & Restaurant closed

ST ALBANS
Map 6 TL10

Fern Cottage
★★★★ 🅰 BED AND BREAKFAST

116 Old London Rd AL1 1PU
☎ 01727 834200
e-mail: bookinginfo@ferncottage.uk.net
dir: M25 junct 22, A1081 to St Albans, 3rd exit off London Coney rdbt for 1m, under railway bridge, over mini-rdbt & 2nd left onto Old London Rd. Fern Cottage 400yds on left

Rooms 3 en suite (1 GF) S £35-£50; D £50-£68*
Facilities tea/coffee Cen ht Wi-fi Parking 3 Notes ⊛

Tresco
★★★ 🅰 BED AND BREAKFAST

76 Clarence Rd AL1 4NG
☎ 01727 864880
e-mail: pat_leggatt@hotmail.com
dir: Off A1057 (Hatfield Rd) onto Clarence Rd at Crown pub, B&B 300yds on right

Rooms 2 rms Facilities FTV tea/coffee Cen ht Parking 1 Notes ⊛ No Children 10yrs ⊛

STAPLEFORD
Map 6 TL31

Papillon Woodhall Arms
★★★ INN

17 High Rd SG14 3NW
☎ 01992 535123   📠 01992 587030
e-mail: papillonwoodhall@aol.com
web: www.papillon-woodhallarms.co.uk
dir: 2.5m from Hertford town (A414)

Located in the village centre, this Victorian house has been sympathetically renovated and extended to provide good standards of comfort and facilities. Bedrooms are equipped with both practical and thoughtful extras and public areas include a spacious restaurant offering a wide range of international dishes.

Rooms 10 en suite (1 fmly) S £27-£40; D £42-£64
Facilities TVL tea/coffee Dinner available Cen ht
Conf Max 50 Thtr 50 Class 30 Board 20 Parking 33
Notes ⊛

WARE
Map 6 TL31

Chapmore End Farm
★★★★ BED AND BREAKFAST

Chapmore End SG12 0HF
☎ 01920 463506
e-mail: chapmorefarm@live.com
dir: A602 onto B158, in 1m at top of hill turn right

This attractive 'old barn' has been rebuilt to accommodate the needs of families together with the needs of the modern traveller. Rooms are spacious and well appointed; English breakfast is cooked on the traditional Aga and is served at the communal table in the charming conservatory. The house is located in the heart of tranquil village.

Rooms 3 rms (1 en suite) (2 pri facs) (1 fmly) (1 GF) S £50-£55; D £65-£95* Facilities tea/coffee Cen ht Wi-fi Parking 6 Notes ⊛ Closed 20 Dec-2 Jan

WATFORD
Map 6 TQ19

Travel Stop Inn
★★★ GUEST ACCOMMODATION

26-28 Upton Rd WD18 0JF
☎ 01923 224298   📠 01923 253553
e-mail: info@travelstopinn.com
web: www.travelstopinn.com
dir: M1 junct 5, A4008 to Watford centre. On ring road stay in centre lane, past lights at Market St, bus stop on left. Left into Upton Rd

Located within easy walking distance of the town centre, this renovation of two Edwardian houses provides a range of bedrooms equipped with lots of homely extras. There is a cocktail bar and restaurant in the White House Hotel opposite, which is under the same ownership; it is here that guests check in and take breakfast.

Rooms 26 annexe en suite (1 fmly) (7 GF) S £54.95; D £59.95 (room only)* Facilities STV TVL tea/coffee Dinner available Direct Dial Cen ht Licensed Complimentay use of local gym Conf Max 200 Thtr 200 Class 80 Board 60 Parking 35 Notes ⊛ RS Xmas/New Year Reduced restaurant service Civ Wed 120

The Greyhound Inn
An Independent Inn offering the best British hospitality

London Road, St. Ippolyts, Herts. SG4 7NL
Email greyhound@freenet.co.uk
Prop. Roy Pearce F.B.I.I.   01462 440989

Situated in the beautiful rural countryside of Hertfordshire 2km. south of the historic market town of Hitchin with easy access to the A1(M) and M1 and close to Baldock, Letchworth, Luton, Luton Airport, Welwyn Garden City and Stevenage. This makes us an ideal place to stay for business travellers and visitors. The fast (25mins) train service makes visiting London or Cambridge easy and cheap. We have an excellent reputation for food, hospitality and beer. An Inn existed on this site 300 years ago, it was rebuilt in 1900 and more recently extended by us. We hope it retains its warm welcome and that you enjoy being here in what really is our home. Traditional Sunday roast served every Sunday lunchtime.

The Fairway Tavern

★★★ GUEST ACCOMMODATION

Old Herns Ln AL7 2ED
☎ 01707 336007 & 339349   📠 01707 376154
e-mail: info@fairwaytavern.co.uk
web: www.fairwaytavern.co.uk
dir: *Exit A1 junct 6, B1000 through Digswell for 2m,
follow golf complex signs*

Enjoying a picturesque location, this property is located
on Panshanger Golf Complex, with lodge style bedrooms
opening out onto views of the golf course and rolling
countryside. Bedrooms are smartly presented and are well
equipped for business and leisure guests. Breakfast and
meals up to 5pm are served by the friendly staff in the
adjacent pub. A large peaceful garden and a function
room for private hire are available.

Rooms 7 en suite (2 fmly) (7 GF) S £45-£55; D £55-£70
(room only)* **Facilities** tea/coffee Dinner available Direct
Dial Cen ht Lift Licensed Wi-fi Golf 18 ⅃ Squash Pool
Table **Conf** Thtr 120 Class 80 Board 25 **Parking** 200
Notes ⊗

KENT

ASHFORD   Map 7 TR04

The Croft

★★★ GUEST ACCOMMODATION

Canterbury Rd, Kennington TN25 4DU
☎ 01233 622140   📠 01233 635271
e-mail: info@thecroft.biz
dir: *M20 junct 10, 2m on A28 signed Canterbury*

An attractive red-brick house situated in two acres of
landscaped grounds just a short drive from Ashford
railway station. The generously proportioned bedrooms
are in the main house and in pretty cottages; all are
pleasantly decorated and thoughtfully equipped. Public
rooms include a smart Italian restaurant, a bar, and a
cosy lounge.

Rooms 14 en suite (4 GF) S £45-£50; D £58-£68*
Facilities tea/coffee Dinner available Direct Dial Cen ht
Licensed Wi-fi **Conf** Max 40 Thtr 40 Class 20 Board 22
Parking 30 **Notes** LB Civ Wed 40

Ashford Warren Cottage

★★ GUEST ACCOMMODATION

136 The Street, Willesborough TN24 0NB
☎ 01233 621905   📠 01233 633587
e-mail: carol@warrencottage.co.uk
web: www.warrencottage.com
dir: *M20 junct 10, B2164 (Kennington Rd) towards
Canterbury. Right onto The Street, house on left*

This property is over 300 years old and full of character
with original oak beams and fireplaces that add to the
cosy, friendly atmosphere. It is in close proximity to the
M20 and the Channel Tunnel, and nearby places of
interest include Dover Castle, Leeds Castle, Canterbury,
Tenterden and Rye.

Rooms 4 en suite 3 annexe en suite (3 fmly) (3 GF)
S £45-£60; D £50-£80 (room only) **Facilities** tea/coffee
Cen ht Licensed **Parking** 20 **Notes** ⊗

AYLESFORD   Map 6 TQ75

Wickham Lodge

★★★★★ Ⓐ GUEST ACCOMMODATION

The Quay, 73 High St ME20 7AY
☎ 01622 717267   📠 01622 792855
e-mail: wickhamlodge@aol.com
web: www.wickhamlodge.co.uk
dir: *M20 junct 5, signs to Aylesford. The Quay on small
road beside Chequers pub*

Rooms 3 rms (2 en suite) (1 pri facs) (1 fmly) (1 GF)
S £45; D £90* **Facilities** FTV tea/coffee Cen ht Wi-fi
Parking 4

BENENDEN   Map 7 TQ83

Apple Trees B&B

★★★★ BED AND BREAKFAST

Goddards Green TN17 4AR
☎ 01580 240622
e-mail: garryblanch@aol.com
web: www.appletreesbandb.co.uk
dir: *3m E of Cranbrook. Off A262 at Sissinghurst S onto
Chaple Ln, over x-rds, 2m left to Goddards Green, 1m
on right*

This spacious rural cottage is situated in the heart of the
Kentish countryside, and is convenient for those visiting
Sissinghurst Castle and Great Dixter House. Bedrooms
are attractively appointed and include plenty of
thoughtful extras. TV can be watched in the comfortable
lounge, and breakfast is served in the rustic dining room
with picturesque views of the garden.

Rooms 3 rms (1 en suite) (2 pri facs) (3 GF) S £40-£60;
D £55-£70* **Facilities** TVL tea/coffee Cen ht Wi-fi
Parking 6 **Notes** ⊗ ⊜

BIDDENDEN   Map 7 TQ83

Heron Cottage

★★★★ GUEST ACCOMMODATION

TN27 8HH
☎ 01580 291358   📠 01580 291358
e-mail: susantwort@hotmail.com
web: www.heroncottage.info
dir: *1m NW of Biddenden. A262 W from Biddenden, 1st
right, 0.25m across sharp left bend through stone pillars,
left onto unmade road*

Expect a warm welcome at this picturesque, extended
cottage, set in immaculate, mature gardens in peaceful
Kent countryside. The bedrooms are thoughtfully equipped
and have co-ordinated soft furnishings. Breakfast is
served in the smart dining room, and the cosy sitting
room has an open fireplace.

Rooms 7 rms (6 en suite) (2 fmly) (1 GF) S £50-£65;
D £55-£75 **Facilities** TVL tea/coffee Dinner available
Cen ht ⅃ Fishing **Conf** Max 20 Board 20 **Parking** 8
Notes Closed Dec-Feb ⊜

BROADSTAIRS   Map 7 TR36

Bay Tree Broadstairs

★★★★ GUEST ACCOMMODATION

12 Eastern Esplanade CT10 1DR
☎ 01843 862502   📠 01843 860589
dir: *A255 onto Rectory Rd & Eastern Esplanade*

Expect a warm welcome at this family-run establishment,
situated on an elevated position overlooking East Cliff.
The attractive bedrooms are well equipped and some
have a balcony with a sea view. There is a comfortable
lounge bar, and a good breakfast and dinner menu is
offered in the dining room.

Rooms 10 en suite (1 GF) S £42-£72; D £84-£94*
Facilities TVL tea/coffee Dinner available Cen ht Licensed
Parking 11 **Notes** LB ⊗ No Children 10yrs Closed Xmas
& New Year

CANTERBURY — Map 7 TR15

PREMIER COLLECTION

Magnolia House
★★★★★ GUEST ACCOMMODATION

36 St Dunstan's Ter CT2 8AX
☎ 01227 765121 & 07776 236459
📠 01227 765121
e-mail: info@magnoliahousecanterbury.co.uk
web: www.magnoliahousecanterbury.co.uk
dir: A2 E onto A2050 for city centre, 1st rdbt left signed University of Kent. St Dunstan's Ter 3rd right

This charming property combines a warm welcome with superbly appointed bedrooms, equipped with lots of extra amenities including internet access. Evening meals (by arrangement from November to February) are delightful, served in the dining room overlooking the attractive walled garden. A wide range of items are offered at breakfast.

Rooms 7 en suite (1 GF) S £55-£65; D £95-£125*
Facilities FTV tea/coffee Dinner available Cen ht Wi-fi Parking 5 Notes ⊗ No Children 12yrs

PREMIER COLLECTION

Yorke Lodge
★★★★★ GUEST ACCOMMODATION

50 London Rd CT2 8LF
☎ 01227 451243 📠 01227 462006
e-mail: info@yorkelodge.com
web: www.yorkelodge.com
dir: From London M2/A2, 1st exit signed Canterbury. At 1st rdbt left onto London Rd

The charming Victorian property stands in a tree-lined road just ten minutes walk from the town centre and railway station. The spacious bedrooms are thoughtfully equipped and carefully decorated; some rooms have four-poster beds. The stylish dining room leads to a conservatory-lounge, which opens onto a superb terrace.

Rooms 8 en suite (1 fmly) S £50-£55; D £90-£120*
Facilities FTV tea/coffee Cen ht Wi-fi Parking 5 Notes LB

Chislet Court Farm (TR224644)
★★★★ FARMHOUSE

Chislet CT3 4DU
☎ 01227 860309 📠 01227 860444 Mr & Mrs M Wilkinson
e-mail: kathy@chisletcourtfarm.com
web: www.chisletcourtfarm.com
dir: Off A28 in Upstreet, farm on right 100yds past church

This delightful 18th-century house is situated in a pretty village six miles from Canterbury. The house is smartly maintained and set in delightful grounds. The en suite bedrooms are extremely spacious, well appointed, and have smart modern bathrooms. A hearty Aga-cooked breakfast is served in the charming conservatory overlooking the garden.

Rooms 2 en suite S £50; D £80 Facilities FTV tea/coffee Cen ht Wi-fi Parking 4 Notes ⊗ No Children 12yrs Closed Xmas ⊛ 800 acres arable

House of Agnes
★★★★ GUEST ACCOMMODATION

71 Saint Dunstans St CT2 8BN
☎ 01227 472185 📠 01227 470478
e-mail: info@houseofagnes.co.uk
dir: On A290 between London Rd & Orchard St, 300mtrs from West Gate

This historic 14th-century property has been refurbished to create a luxury bed and breakfast that offers individually themed rooms, ranging from the traditional to the more exotic. All rooms have a nice range of amenities such as flat-screen TVs and Wi-fi. This establishment is also licensed for weddings.

Rooms 8 en suite (1 fmly) S £40-£85; D £70-£130*
Facilities FTV tea/coffee Cen ht Licensed Wi-fi 🥾 Boules Conf Thtr 30 Class 12 Board 20 Parking 20 Notes LB ⊗ No Children 5yrs Closed 24-25 Dec Civ Wed 60

The White House
★★★★ GUEST ACCOMMODATION

6 St Peters Ln CT1 2BP
☎ 01227 761836
e-mail: info@whitehousecanterbury.co.uk
dir: A290 into city, through Westgate, sharp left onto Pound Ln, 1st right into St Peters Lane

This attractive Regency house is in a quiet road close to the High Street and next to the Marlowe Theatre. Whether contemporary and traditional in design, all the bedrooms are comfortably furnished and provide an abundance of thoughtful extras. Fresh quality produce is offered at breakfast which is served in the smart dining room. This is a non-smoking establishment.

Rooms 7 en suite S £55; D £80-£105* Facilities tea/coffee Cen ht Wi-fi Notes ⊗ No Children 16yrs

Beech Bank
★★★★ GUEST ACCOMMODATION

Duckpit Ln, Waltham CT4 5QA
☎ 01227 700302 📠 01227 700302
e-mail: grandbeech@hotmail.com
dir: 5.5m S of Canterbury. Off B2068 through Petham, left by telephone onto Duckpit Ln, 2m on left

A 15th-century coach house set in landscaped grounds with magnificent views of the surrounding countryside. Original features include a minstrels' gallery, oak beams and exposed brickwork. Bedrooms are carefully decorated and thoughtfully equipped, and one room has a four-poster bed. Breakfast is served in the elegant Victorian conservatory.

Rooms 3 rms (2 en suite) (1 pri facs) (1 fmly) (2 GF) Facilities tea/coffee Cen ht 🌳🌳 Parking 10 Notes ⊗ No Children 4yrs Closed 20 Dec-5 Jan ⊛

Castle House
★★★★ GUEST ACCOMMODATION

28 Castle St CT1 2PT
☎ 01227 761897
e-mail: enquiries@castlehousehotel.co.uk
web: www.castlehousehotel.co.uk
dir: Opposite Canterbury Castle ruins, off A28 ring road

Conveniently located in the city centre opposite the imposing ruins of the ancient Norman castle; part of the building dates back to 1730s. Bedrooms are spacious, all

continued

CANTERBURY *continued*

with en suite facilities and many little extras such as Wi-fi. There is a walled garden in which to relax during the warmer months.

Rooms 7 en suite 5 annexe en suite (4 fmly) (2 GF) S £65; D £75* **Facilities** TVL tea/coffee Dinner available Cen ht Wi-fi **Conf** Max 35 **Parking** 12 **Notes** LB ⊗

Ersham Lodge

★★★ GUEST ACCOMMODATION

12 New Dover Rd CT1 3AP
☎ 01227 463174
e-mail: info@ersham-lodge.co.uk
dir: From Canterbury ring road signs for Dover, premises on right just after lights by Blockbuster Video

This attractive twin-gabled Victorian house is just a short walk from the college, cathedral and the city's attractions. Bedrooms are smartly decorated and comfortable, and there is a cosy lounge and a spacious breakfast room which looks out onto the well-kept patio and garden. Free guest parking is available.

Rooms 10 en suite (1 fmly) (5 GF) S fr £45; D fr £80* **Facilities** tea/coffee Cen ht Wi-fi **Conf** Max 30 Class 30 Board 20 **Parking** 10 **Notes** LB ⊗

Canterbury Pilgrims

★★★ INN

18 The Friars CT1 2AS
☎ 01227 464531 🖷 01227 762514
e-mail: pilgrimshotel@aol.com
web: www.pilgrimshotel.com
dir: Signs for Marlowe Theatre, establishment opp

Situated in the centre of historic Canterbury opposite the Marlowe Theatre, parts of the Pilgrims date back some 350 years. Bedrooms are comfortably appointed and well equipped. The public rooms include a spacious bar, a smart meeting room and a contemporary style restaurant, where a good selection of dishes is available.

Rooms 15 en suite (1 fmly) **Facilities** tea/coffee Dinner available Direct Dial Cen ht **Conf** Max 30 Thtr 25 Class 25 Board 20 **Parking** 10 **Notes** ⊗

Cathedral Gate

★★★ GUEST ACCOMMODATION

36 Burgate CT1 2HA
☎ 01227 464381 🖷 01227 462800
e-mail: cgate@cgate.demon.co.uk
dir: In city centre. Next to main gateway into cathedral precincts

Dating from 1438, this house has an enviable central location next to the cathedral. Old beams and winding corridors are part of the character of the property. Bedrooms are traditionally furnished, equipped to modern standards and many have cathedral views. Luggage can be unloaded at reception before parking in a nearby car park.

Rooms 13 rms (2 en suite) 12 annexe rms 10 annexe en suite (5 fmly) S £32.50–£105; D £62–£105 **Facilities** tea/coffee Dinner available Direct Dial Cen ht Licensed Wi-fi **Notes** LB

Anns House

★★★ 🅰 GUEST HOUSE

63 London Rd CT2 8JZ
☎ 01227 768767 🖷 01227 768172
e-mail: info@annshousecanterbury.co.uk
web: www.annshousecanterbury.co.uk
dir: M2 onto A2, 1st exit signed Canterbury. At 1st rdbt, left onto London Rd

Rooms 8 en suite (2 fmly) S £45–£60; D £65–£75 **Facilities** FTV TVL tea/coffee Cen ht Wi-fi **Parking** 10 **Notes** LB

DARTFORD Map 6 TQ57

Rising Sun

★★★ INN

Fawkham Green DA3 8NL
☎ 01474 872291 🖷 01474 872779
dir: M25 junct 3, A20 Brands Hatch. Turn onto Scratchers Ln until sign for Fawkham. Left onto Brandshatch Rd, inn on left

This popular inn overlooks the village green just a short drive from Brands Hatch. All the en suite bedrooms are spacious, pleasantly decorated and comfortable. There is a busy character bar, restaurant, and a patio for alfresco dining in warmer weather.

Rooms 5 en suite (1 fmly) (2 GF) S £50–£55; D £65–£75* **Facilities** tea/coffee Dinner available Cen ht Wi-fi **Parking** 20 **Notes** ⊗ No coaches

See advert on opposite page

DEAL Map 7 TR35

PREMIER COLLECTION

Sutherland House

★★★★★ GUEST ACCOMMODATION

186 London Rd CT14 9PT
☎ 01304 362853 🖷 01304 381146
e-mail: info@sutherlandhouse.fsnet.co.uk
dir: 0.5m W of town centre/seafront on A258

This stylish accommodation demonstrates impeccable taste with its charming, well-equipped bedrooms and a comfortable lounge. A fully stocked bar, books, free Wi-fi, Freeview TV and radio are some of the many amenities offered. The elegant dining room is the venue for a hearty breakfast and dinner is available by prior arrangement.

Rooms 4 en suite (1 GF) S £57–£65; D £67–£75* **Facilities** FTV tea/coffee Dinner available Direct Dial Cen ht Licensed Wi-fi **Conf** Max 12 Thtr 12 Class 12 Board 12 **Parking** 7 **Notes** LB No Children 5yrs

The Plough Inn

★★★★ INN

Church Ln, Ripple CT14 8JH
☎ 01304 360209
e-mail: plough@sutton-vale.co.uk

This charming country inn in the rural village of Ripple is ideally located for easy access to Dover and Deal. Bedrooms are attractively decorated, bright and spacious with plenty of thoughtful extras for guest comfort. Home-cooked food and real ale are served at lunch and dinner, as well as a hearty breakfast to start the day.

Rooms 3 en suite (1 fmly) **Facilities** FTV TVL tea/coffee Dinner available Cen ht Wi-fi ⚄ Golf 18 Fishing Squash Riding Pool Table **Parking** 31

Sondes Lodge

★★★ GUEST ACCOMMODATION

14 Sondes Rd CT14 7BW
☎ 01304 368741
e-mail: sondes.lodge@tiscali.co.uk
web: www.sondeslodge.co.uk
dir: From Dover take A258 to Deal, pass Deal Castle, towards town centre. 4th right onto Sondes Rd. Lodge on right

Expect a warm welcome at this smart guest house situated in a side road just off the seafront and a short walk from the town centre. The pleasant bedrooms have co-ordinated fabrics and many thoughtful touches. Breakfast is served at individual tables in the lower ground-floor dining room.

Rooms 3 en suite (1 fmly) (1 GF) **Facilities** FTV tea/coffee Dinner available Cen ht Wi-fi **Notes** ⊛

DODDINGTON   Map 7 TQ95

PREMIER COLLECTION

The Old Vicarage
★★★★★ GUEST ACCOMMODATION

Church Hill ME9 0BD
☎ 01795 886136   🖹 01795 886136
e-mail: claire@oldvicaragedoddington.co.uk
dir: From A2 take Faversham Rd signed Doddington for 4.4m. Turn right towards church

A stunning Grade II listed property situated at the edge of the village beside the old church. Spacious rooms with flat-screen TVs, and special touches such as binoculars and bird reference books. Guests can relax in the elegant lounge, and a bountiful breakfast is served in the stylish dining room overlooking endless green fields. Claire Finlay was a finalist in the AA Friendliest Landlady of the Year 2009-2010 Award.

Rooms 3 en suite (1 fmly) S fr £55; D fr £75*
Facilities FTV tea/coffee Cen ht Wi-fi ⚄ Pool Table **Parking** 6 **Notes** ⊛ No Children 3yrs Closed 25 Dec-2 Jan

---

DOVER   Map 7 TR34

PREMIER COLLECTION

The Marquis at Alkham
★★★★★ ◉◉ RESTAURANT WITH ROOMS

Alkham Valley Rd, Alkham CT15 7DF
☎ 01304 873410   🖹 01304 873418
e-mail: info@themarquisatalkham.co.uk
web: www.themarquisatalkham.co.uk
dir: From Dover take A256, at rdbt 1st exit onto London Rd, then left onto Alkham Rd, then Alkham Valley Rd. 1.5m after sharp bend

Located between Dover and Folkestone, this modern, contemporary restaurant with rooms offers luxury accommodation with modern features - flat-screen TV, Wi-fi, power showers and bath robes to name but a few. All bedrooms are individually designed and stylish with fantastic views of the Kent Downs. The award-winning restaurant, open for lunch and dinner, serves modern British cuisine. Continental and a choice of cooked breakfasts are offered.

Rooms 5 en suite (1 fmly) S £65-£185; D £75-£195*
Facilities FTV TVL Dinner available Cen ht Wi-fi
Conf Max 20 Thtr 20 Class 20 Board 16 **Parking** 22
Notes LB ⊛

The Rising Sun Inn & Inglenooks Restaurant

Fawkham Green, Longfield   Tel: 01474 872291

A pub since 1702. The Rising Sun Inn stands behind a picturesque village green not far from Brands Hatch. With a 40 seater restaurant, cosy bar & large inglenook fireplace. Offering a very wide range of food from traditional house special, full à-la-carte & extensive bar menu.

Open 7 days a week

Food served all day everyday

Quality Bed & Breakfast available – 4 posters & twin rooms from The Rising Sun

AA & Tourist Board rated 3 stars

DOVER *continued*

Beulah House

★★★★ GUEST ACCOMMODATION

94 Crabble Hill, London Rd CT17 0SA
☎ 01304 824615 📠 01304 828850
e-mail: owen@beulahhouse94.freeserve.co.uk
web: www.beulahguesthouse.co.uk
dir: *On A256*

An impressive Victorian house located just a stroll from the town centre and close to the ferry port. The spacious bedrooms are pleasantly decorated and thoughtfully equipped. Public rooms include two conservatories and a comfortable lounge. The impressive garden has an interesting display of topiary and a small menagerie.

Rooms 8 en suite S £55-£65; D £72-£78* **Facilities** TVL tea/coffee Cen ht Wi-fi **Parking** 8 **Notes** LB ⊗ No Children 12yrs

Hubert House Guesthouse & Bistro

★★★★ GUEST HOUSE

9 Castle Hill Rd CT16 1QW
☎ 01304 202253 📠 01304 210142
e-mail: stay@huberthouse.co.uk
web: www.huberthouse.co.uk
dir: *On A258 by Dover Castle*

This charming Georgian house is within walking distance of the ferry port and the town centre. Bedrooms are sumptuously decorated and furnished with an abundance of practical extras. Breakfast, including full English and healthy options, is served in the smart coffee house, which is open all day. Families are especially welcome.

Rooms 6 en suite (4 fmly) S £45-£65; D £55-£85* **Facilities** STV FTV tea/coffee Dinner available Cen ht Licensed Wi-fi **Parking** 6 **Notes** LB

Bleriot's

★★★ GUEST ACCOMMODATION

Belper House, 47 Park Av CT16 1HE
☎ 01304 211394
e-mail: info@bleriots.net
web: www.bleriots.net
dir: *A20 to Dover, left onto York St, right at lights into Ladywell. Left at next lights onto Park Ave*

This large, family-run Victorian property is convenient for the ferry port and town centre. Guests receive a warm welcome and can enjoy a range of comfortable, spacious

en suite bedrooms. The attractive dining room is the venue for a wholesome breakfast to start the day.

Rooms 8 en suite (2 fmly) S £30-£50; D £48-£62 **Facilities** tea/coffee Cen ht **Parking** 8 **Notes** LB ⊗

Ardmore Guest House

★★★ GUEST ACCOMMODATION

18 Castle Hill Rd CT16 1QW
☎ 01304 205895 📠 01304 208229
e-mail: res@ardmoreph.co.uk
web: www.ardmoreph.co.uk
dir: *On A258 by Dover Castle*

Dating from 1796, this delightful house is adjacent to Dover Castle. Convenient for the town centre and ferry port, the Ardmore offers comfortable accommodation and friendly hospitality. The non-smoking bedrooms are spacious and airy. Public rooms include a comfortable lounge and a well-appointed breakfast room.

Rooms 4 en suite (1 fmly); D £48-£65* **Facilities** tea/coffee Cen ht **Notes** ⊗ Closed Xmas

Kernow

★★★ GUEST ACCOMMODATION

189 Folkestone Rd CT17 9SJ
☎ 01304 207797
dir: *B2011 W from town centre onto Folkestone Rd*

This welcoming guest house is convenient for the ferries and railway station. The neat accommodation is well maintained, and two bathrooms are available. There is adequate parking at the front of the property, and breakfast can be arranged to suit your travel arrangements.

Rooms 3 rms **Facilities** TVL tea/coffee Cen ht **Parking** 4 **Notes** ⊛

Peverell House

★★★ GUEST ACCOMMODATION

28 Park Av CT16 1HD
☎ 01304 202573
e-mail: info@peverellhouse.co.uk
web: www.peverellhouse.co.uk
dir: *From A2 rdbt turn right towards Dover Castle, 2nd right onto Connaught Rd, 1st left*

This hilltop Victorian house has bright spacious rooms; some overlooking the town others with views of Dover Castle. A hearty English breakfast is served in the comfortable dining room and guests may relax in the cosy lounge.

Rooms 7 rms (3 en suite) (1 pri facs) (3 fmly) S £33-£50; D £48-£62* **Facilities** tea/coffee Cen ht **Parking** 7 **Notes** ⊗

St Martins

★★★ GUEST ACCOMMODATION

17 Castle Hill Rd CT16 1QW
☎ 01304 205938 📠 01304 208229
e-mail: res@stmartinsgh.co.uk
web: www.stmartinsgh.co.uk
dir: *On A258 by Dover Castle*

Located close to the castle, ferry port and town centre, this smart guest house offers a friendly welcome. The thoughtfully equipped en suite bedrooms are attractively decorated, and most rooms enjoy a sunny aspect. Breakfast is served in the pine-furnished dining room, and there is also a comfortable lounge.

Rooms 6 en suite (3 fmly); D £48-£55* **Facilities** tea/coffee Cen ht **Notes** ⊗ Closed Xmas

The Swingate Inn

★★★ INN

Deal Rd CT15 5DP
☎ 01304 204043 📠 01304 204043
e-mail: info@swingate.com
dir: *Dover Eastern Docks. Turn right at rdbt up Jubilee Way for 1m, at rdbt turn right onto A258 to Deal*

Situated in a convenient location on the outskirts of Dover and very convenient for the ferries. Bedrooms are traditionally decorated and offer comfortable accommodation. The bar is spacious and offers an informal, friendly atmosphere. There is an outside bar and garden and plenty of parking spaces. Cooked or continental breakfasts are available.

Rooms 10 en suite (2 fmly) **Facilities** tea/coffee Dinner available Cen ht Wi-fi **Conf** Max 30 Thtr 30 Class 30 Board 20 **Parking** 60 **Notes** ⊗ Civ Wed 120

Waterside

★★★★ GUEST ACCOMMODATION

15 Hythe Rd TN29 0LN
☎ 01303 872253 📠 01303 872253
e-mail: info@watersideguesthouse.co.uk
dir: *M20 junct 11 onto A259 follow signs for Hythe then Dymchurch, 0.5m past village sign*

Waterside is located overlooking a picturesque stream, and sandy beaches are a few minutes away. Bedrooms are comfortably appointed and have sparkling en suite bathrooms. Breakfast is served in the cosy dining room and a small bar and lounge is provided for added guest comfort. Parking is available.

Rooms 5 en suite (1 fmly) S £40-£63; D £58-£63* **Facilities** TVL tea/coffee Dinner available Cen ht Licensed Wi-fi **Parking** 6 **Notes** LB ⊗

FARNINGHAM — Map 6 TQ56

PREMIER COLLECTION

Beesfield Farm *(TQ554660)*
★★★★★ FARMHOUSE

Beesfield Ln DA4 0LA
☎ 01322 863900 📠 01322 863900 Mr & Mrs D Vingoe
e-mail: kim.vingoe@btinternet.com
dir: *From village centre S onto Beesfield Ln, farm 0.5m on left*

Set amid mature gardens and surrounded by open farmland, this attractive house is close to major roads, Brands Hatch and Bluewater Shopping Centre. Individually decorated bedrooms and bathrooms are beautifully appointed and have many thoughtful touches. Breakfast is served at a large polished table in the elegant dining room, and there is a stylish lounge with plush furnishings.

Rooms 3 en suite S £55-£70; D £80-£90*
Facilities FTV TVL tea/coffee Cen ht Wi-fi **Parking** 10 **Notes** LB ⊗ No Children 12yrs Closed 8 Dec-Jan 🌐 400 acres arable/dairy/mixed

FAVERSHAM — Map 7 TR06

Court Lodge B&B

★★★★ GUEST ACCOMMODATION

Court Lodge, Church Rd, Oare ME13 0QB
☎ 01795 591543 📠 01795 591543
e-mail: d.wheeldon@btconnect.com
dir: *A2 onto B2045, left onto The Street, right onto Church Rd, 0.25m on left*

Surround by arable land, and commanding fabulous views, this charming farmhouse has been restored to a very high standard. Inside is a mini museum of antique furniture and Victorian fittings include restored bathtubs, sinks and kitchen appliances. Modern additions such as free Wi-fi are provided. Home-made cakes and jams and the warm hospitality of owners Dennise and John guarantee a memorable stay.

Rooms 2 rms (1 en suite) (1 pri facs) S £50; D £70
Facilities tea/coffee Cen ht Wi-fi **Parking** 10 **Notes** ⊗ 🌐

FOLKESTONE — Map 7 TR23

PREMIER COLLECTION

The Relish
★★★★★ GUEST ACCOMMODATION

4 Augusta Gardens CT20 2RR
☎ 01303 850952 📠 01303 850958
e-mail: reservations@hotelrelish.co.uk
web: www.hotelrelish.co.uk
dir: *Off A2033 (Sandgate Rd)*

Expect a warm welcome at this impressive Victorian terrace property, which overlooks Augusta Gardens in the fashionable West End of town. The bedrooms feature beautiful contemporary natural-wood furniture, lovely co-ordinated fabrics and many thoughtful extras like DVD players and free Broadband access. Public rooms include a modern lounge-dining room, and a sun terrace where breakfast is served in the summer.

Rooms 10 en suite (2 fmly) S £65; D £90-£140*
Facilities FTV Direct Dial Cen ht Wi-fi **Conf** Max 20 Thtr 20 Class 10 Board 20 **Notes** ⊗ Closed 22 Dec-2 Jan

Chandos Guest House

★★★ GUEST ACCOMMODATION

77 Cheriton Rd CT20 1DG
☎ 01303 851202 & 07799 886297
e-mail: froggydon@aol.com
web: www.chandosguesthouse.co.uk
dir: *M20 junct 13. Right towards Folkestone. At 2nd set of lights, middle lane. Continue for 1m, straight over rdbt, premises located 0.25m on right*

Close to the town centre and only a five minute drive from the Eurotunnel, this pleasant guest house is ideal for continental travellers. Bedrooms and bathrooms are well equipped, bright and comfortable. Free Wi-fi is available. A hearty breakfast is served in the spacious ground-floor dining room. Early morning departures are catered for.

Rooms 10 rms (6 en suite) (4 pri facs) (4 fmly) S £25-£27.50; D £50-£55 **Facilities** FTV tea/coffee Cen ht Wi-fi **Parking** 6 **Notes** LB ⊗

Langhorne Garden
★★★ GUEST ACCOMMODATION

10-12 Langhorne Gardens CT20 2EA
☎ 01303 257233 📠 01303 242760
e-mail: info@langhorne.co.uk
web: www.langhorne.co.uk
dir: *Exit M20 junct 13, follow signs for The Leas, 2m*

Once a Victorian villa, Langhorne Garden is close to the seafront, shops and restaurants. Bright spacious bedrooms are traditionally decorated with plenty of original charm. Public rooms include a choice of comfortable lounges and a bar, a spacious dining room and a popular local bar in the basement with billiards, darts and table football.

Rooms 29 en suite (8 fmly) **Facilities** STV FTV tea/coffee Dinner available Direct Dial Cen ht Lift Licensed Wi-fi Pool Table **Conf** Thtr 40 Class 20 Board 20 **Notes** Closed Xmas RS Jan-Etr no evening meal

GOUDHURST — Map 6 TQ73

The Star & Eagle
★★★★ ⊜ INN

High St TN17 1AL
☎ 01580 211512 📠 01580 212444
e-mail: starandeagle@btconnect.com
web: www.starandeagle.co.uk
dir: *Off A21 to Hastings rd, take A262, inn at top of village next to church*

A hearty welcome is assured at this 15th-century inn located in the heart of a delightful village. Within easy reach of Royal Tunbridge Wells and The Weald this is a great base for walkers. Both bedrooms and public areas boast original features and much character. A wide range of delicious home-made dishes is available in the restaurant and bar.

Rooms 10 rms (8 en suite) S £65-£130; D £75-£130*
Facilities FTV Dinner available Direct Dial Cen ht Wi-fi **Conf** Max 30 Thtr 30 Class 15 Board 12 **Parking** 20 **Notes** ⊗ RS 24-26 Dec. Closed 25-26 Dec eve Civ Wed 50

HAWKHURST — Map 7 TQ73

PREMIER COLLECTION

Southgate-Little Fowlers
★★★★★ GUEST ACCOMMODATION

Rye Rd TN18 5DA
☎ 01580 752526 📠 01580 752526
e-mail: susan.woodard@southgate.uk.net
dir: 0.25m E of Hawkhurst on A268

A warm welcome is assured at this wonderful 300-year-old former dower house. Set in immaculate mature gardens, the renovated property provides attractive accommodation throughout. Spacious bedrooms are carefully decorated and equipped with many thoughtful extras. A hearty breakfast is served at individual tables in the delightful Victorian conservatory.

Rooms 2 en suite (1 fmly) S £60-£65; D £70-£90
Facilities TVL tea/coffee Cen ht Wi-fi Parking 5
Notes ⊗ No Children 8yrs Closed Nov-Feb ⊜

HYTHE — Map 7 TR13

Seabrook House
★★★★ GUEST ACCOMMODATION

81 Seabrook Rd CT21 5QW
☎ 01303 269282 📠 01303 237822
e-mail: seabrookhouse@hotmail.co.uk
web: www.seabrook-house.co.uk
dir: 0.9m E of Hythe on A259

A stunning Victorian house situated just a few miles from the M20 and Eurotunnel. The property is set in pretty gardens and within easy walking distance of the beach. The attractive bedrooms are carefully furnished and thoughtfully equipped. Public rooms include an elegant lounge, where tea and coffee are served in the evening, a sunny conservatory and large dining room.

Rooms 13 en suite (4 fmly) (4 GF) Facilities TVL tea/coffee Cen ht Parking 13 Notes ⊗

IVYCHURCH — Map 7 TR02

PREMIER COLLECTION

Olde Moat House
★★★★★ ⊜ GUEST ACCOMMODATION

TN29 0AZ
☎ 01797 344700 📠 01797 343919
e-mail: oldemoathouse@hotmail.com
web: www.oldemoathouse.co.uk
dir: Off junct A2070 & A259 into Ivychurch, left & 0.75m on left

Situated eight miles north-east of Rye this charming character property sits peacefully amongst carefully tended gardens. Spacious bedrooms are elegantly furnished and an abundance of accessories are provided for guest comfort. The elegant dining room overlooks the gardens, and a cosy lounge with oak beams and open fireplace is furnished with comfortable sofas. Dianna Epton was a finalist for the AA Friendliest Landlady of the Year 2009-2010 Award.

Rooms 3 en suite Facilities TVL tea/coffee Dinner available Cen ht Parking 10 Notes ⊗ No Children 16yrs

MAIDSTONE — Map 7 TQ75

See also Marden

The Black Horse Inn
★★★★ INN

Pilgrims Way, Thurnham ME14 3LD
☎ 01622 737185 & 630830 📠 01622 739170
e-mail: info@wellieboot.net
web: www.wellieboot.net/home_blackhorse.htm
dir: M20 junct 7, N onto A249. Right into Detling, opp pub onto Pilgrims Way for 1m

This charming inn dates from the 17th century, and the public areas have a wealth of oak beams, exposed brickwork and open fireplaces. The stylish bedrooms are in a series of cosy cabins behind the premises; each one is attractively furnished and thoughtfully equipped.

Rooms 30 annexe en suite (8 fmly) (30 GF) S £60-£70; D £70-£95* Facilities FTV tea/coffee Dinner available Cen ht Wi-fi Parking 40 Notes LB No coaches Civ Wed 40

Aylesbury House
★★★★ GUEST ACCOMMODATION

56-58 London Rd ME16 8QL
☎ 01622 762100 📠 01622 664673
e-mail: mail@aylesburyhouse.co.uk
dir: M20 junct 5 on A20 to Maidstone. Aylesbury House on left before town centre

Located just a short walk from the town centre, this smartly maintained establishment offers a genuine welcome. The carefully decorated bedrooms have co-ordinated soft fabrics and many thoughtful touches. Breakfast is served in the smart dining room overlooking a walled garden.

Rooms 8 en suite S £50-£60; D £65-£75 Facilities FTV tea/coffee Cen ht Wi-fi Parking 8

Conway House
★★★★ GUEST ACCOMMODATION

12 Conway Rd ME16 0HD
☎ 01622 688287 📠 01622 726323
e-mail: t.griffiths295@btinternet.com
dir: M20 junct 5, A20 to Maidstone 0.5m, right at BP garage

This large, modern, family house is a short drive from the M20 and Maidstone town centre. Bedrooms are beautifully furnished and have spacious en suite bathrooms. Plentiful amenities and warm hospitality make this a perfect choice for business and leisure guests.

Rooms 2 en suite S £45; D £60 Facilities FTV tea/coffee Cen ht Wi-fi Parking 2 Notes ⊗ Closed Xmas

Langley Oast
★★★★ GUEST ACCOMMODATION

Langley Park, Langley ME17 3NQ
☎ 01622 863523 📠 01622 863523
e-mail: margaret@langleyoast.freeserve.co.uk
dir: 2.5m SE of Maidstone off A274. After Parkwood Business Estate lane signed Maidstone Golf Centre

This traditional Kent oast house is a short drive from the town centre and has views of the surrounding countryside. Bedrooms are spacious and well appointed. Two are in the 24-foot diameter towers and one has a jacuzzi bath. Breakfast is served in an elegant dining room around one large table, and an attractive garden is an additional bonus.

Rooms 3 rms (2 en suite) (1 fmly) S £40-£60; D £55-£95 Facilities tea/coffee Cen ht Jacuzzi in 1 bedroom Parking 5 Notes ⊗ Closed Xmas ⊜

Roslin Villa

★★★★ GUEST HOUSE

11 St Michaels Rd ME16 8BS
☎ 01622 758301 📠 01622 761459
e-mail: info@roslinvillaguesthouse.com
web: www.roslinvillaguesthouse.com
dir: 0.6m W of town centre. Off A26 Tonbridge Rd, brown tourist signs to Roslin Villa

Expect a warm welcome from the caring hosts at this delightful detached Victorian house, which is within easy walking distance of the town centre and only a short drive from the M20. The smart bedrooms are carefully furnished and equipped with many thoughtful touches. Public rooms include a cosy lounge and an elegant dining room.

Rooms 5 en suite (1 fmly) **Facilities** TVL tea/coffee Cen ht Wi-fi **Conf** Max 15 Class 15 Board 15 **Parking** 10 **Notes** No Children 12yrs

Stone Court

★★★★ ⊛ GUEST ACCOMMODATION

28 Lower St ME15 6LX
☎ 01622 769769 📠 01622 769888
e-mail: stonecourt@ohiml.com
web: www.oxfordhotelsandinns.com
dir: M20 junct 6, 2nd exit at next 2 rdbts onto A229 towards Hastings. Remain in right lane at lights. Stone Court just past police station

This former judiciary chambers is a listed building and contrary to its contemporary façade has many interesting interior features. The popular fine-dining restaurant boasts an impressive menu selection and wine list. Bedrooms are spacious and comfortably appointed.

Rooms 16 en suite (2 fmly) **Facilities** tea/coffee Direct Dial Wi-fi **Parking** 12 **Notes** Civ Wed 60

Rock House Bed & Breakfast

★★★ GUEST ACCOMMODATION

102 Tonbridge Rd ME16 8SL
☎ 01622 751616 📠 01622 756119
e-mail: rock.house@btconnect.com
dir: On A26, 0.5m from town centre

This friendly, family-run guest house is just a short walk from the town centre. Breakfast is served in the conservatory dining room that overlooks the attractive

walled garden. Bedrooms are brightly decorated and equipped with modern facilities.

Rooms 14 rms (8 en suite) (4 fmly) S £40-£49; D £49-£59* **Facilities** FTV TVL tea/coffee Cen ht Wi-fi **Parking** 7

Maidstone Lodge

★★★ Ⓐ GUEST ACCOMMODATION

22/24 London Rd ME16 8QL
☎ 01622 758778 📠 01622 609984
e-mail: maidstonelodge@btinternet.com
dir: 400yds W of town centre on A20

Rooms 14 rms (1 GF) (7 smoking) S £40; D £60* **Facilities** TVL tea/coffee Cen ht Licensed **Parking** 15 **Notes** ⊗ Closed 24 Dec-1 Jan

PREMIER COLLECTION

Merzie Meadows

★★★★★ BED AND BREAKFAST

Hunton Rd TN12 9SL
☎ 01622 820500 📠 01622 820500
e-mail: pamela@merziemeadows.co.uk
dir: A229 onto B2079 for Marden, 1st right onto Underlyn Ln, 2.5m large Chainhurst sign, right onto drive

A detached property set in 20 acres of mature gardens in the Kent countryside. The generously proportioned bedrooms are housed in two wings, which overlook a terrace; each room is carefully decorated, thoughtfully equipped and furnished with well-chosen pieces. The attractive breakfast room has an Italian tiled floor and superb views of the garden.

Rooms 2 en suite (1 fmly) (2 GF) S £80; D £85-£95* **Facilities** STV FTV TVL tea/coffee Cen ht Wi-fi **Parking** 4 **Notes** ⊗ No Children 15yrs Closed mid Dec-mid Feb ⊛

Honeychild Manor Farmhouse *(TR062276)*

★★★★ ⌂ FARMHOUSE

St Mary In The Marsh TN29 0DB
☎ 01797 366180 & 07951 237821
📠 01797 366925 Mrs V Furnival
e-mail: honeychild@farming.co.uk
dir: 2m N of New Romney off A259. S of village centre

This imposing Georgian farmhouse is part of a working dairy farm on Romney Marsh. Walkers and dreamers alike will enjoy the stunning views and can relax in the beautifully landscaped gardens or play tennis on the full-sized court. A hearty breakfast is served in the elegant dining room and features quality local produce. Bedrooms are pleasantly decorated, well furnished and thoughtfully equipped. This establishment is pet friendly.

Rooms 3 rms (1 en suite) (2 pri facs) (1 fmly) S £25-£30; D £50-£70* **Facilities** tea/coffee Dinner available Cen ht Wi-fi ⛳ **Parking** 10 **Notes** LB ⊛ 1500 acres arable/dairy

The Vicarage B&B

★★★ GUEST ACCOMMODATION

Maytham Rd TN17 4ND
☎ 01580 241235 📠 01580 241235
e-mail: vicarage1965@btinternet.com
dir: A28 through Rolvenden. Left at church into Matham Rd. 1st drive on right after 150mtrs

White-painted vicarage nestled next to the handsome village church. Bedrooms are fresh and bright with lush garden views. A hearty breakfast provides the perfect start to the day. The village of Tenterden and celebrated English vineyards are located nearby.

Rooms 2 rms S £30-£40; D £55-£65* **Facilities** tea/coffee Cen ht Wi-fi **Parking** 3 **Notes** LB ⊗ Closed Xmas & Etr ⊛

SANDWICH Map 7 TR35

The New Inn
★★★ INN

2 Harnet St CT13 9ES
☎ 01304 612335 📠 01304 619133
e-mail: new.inn@thorleytaverns.com
dir: Off A256, one-way system into town centre, inn on right

A popular inn situated in the heart of this busy historic town. The large open-plan lounge bar offers an extensive range of beers and an interesting choice of home-made dishes. Bedrooms are furnished in pine and have many useful extras.

Rooms 5 en suite (3 fmly) (2 smoking) **Facilities** STV tea/coffee Dinner available Direct Dial Cen ht **Parking** 17 **Notes** ⊗ No coaches

SEVENOAKS Map 6 TQ55

See also Farningham

The Studio at Double Dance
★★★★ GUEST ACCOMMODATION

Tonbridge Rd, Ightham TN15 9AT
☎ 01732 884198 & 07811 066253
e-mail: pennycracknell@doubledance.co.uk
dir: A227 S from Ightham towards Tonbridge, 1st left onto Mill Ln, driveway 1st right

Close to Sevenoaks this delightful contemporary annexe sits in peaceful gardens, and enjoys impressive views of the North Downs. Comfortable accommodation is self-contained with private access and a wide range of facilities. An ample continental breakfast is provided, and home-made cakes and pastries are a speciality.

Rooms 1 annexe en suite S £50-£60; D £55-£65* **Facilities** tea/coffee Cen ht Wi-fi 🏊 **Parking** 2 **Notes** ⊗ No Children 9yrs 🐾

Yew Tree Barn
★★★★ GUEST ACCOMMODATION

Long Mill Ln, Crouch, Borough Green TN15 8QB
☎ 01732 780461
e-mail: bartonje@hotmail.com
web: www.yewtreebarn.com
dir: A25 (Maidstone Rd) turn left after Esso garage. Crouch Lane 1m, right to Crouch. Yew Tree Barn on left

Situated in the picturesque village of Crouch this attractively converted barn is in an ideal position from which to explore the beautiful Kent countryside. Brands Hatch racing circuit and The London Golf Club are just a short drive away as well as Leeds and Lullingstone Castles. Welcoming hosts Tricia and James offer spaciously comfortable bedrooms with free Wi-fi. The charming dining room and guest lounge overlook the well-tended gardens.

Rooms 2 en suite (2 fmly) (1 GF) S £40-£50; D £60-£70* **Facilities** TVL tea/coffee Cen ht Wi-fi **Parking** 5 **Notes** ⊗ Closed 21 Dec-7 Jan 🐾

SITTINGBOURNE Map 7 TQ96

The Beaumont
★★★★ GUEST ACCOMMODATION

74 London Rd ME10 1NS
☎ 01795 472536 📠 01795 425921
e-mail: info@thebeaumont.co.uk
web: www.thebeaumont.co.uk
dir: From M2 or M20 take A249 N. Exit at A2, 1m on left towards Sittingbourne

This Georgian farmhouse, a charming family-run property, offers the best of hospitality and service. Comfortable bedrooms and bathrooms are well equipped for business and leisure guests. Breakfast in the bright, spacious conservatory makes good use of local produce and homemade preserves. Off-road parking is available.

Rooms 9 rms (6 en suite) (3 pri facs) (3 GF) S £40-£70; D £70-£80 **Facilities** STV TVL tea/coffee Direct Dial Cen ht Wi-fi **Conf** Max 12 Thtr 12 Class 12 Board 12 **Parking** 9 **Notes** Closed 24 Dec-1 Jan

Sandhurst Farm Forge
★★★ GUEST ACCOMMODATION

Seed Rd, Newnham ME9 0NE
☎ 01795 886854
e-mail: rooms.forge@btinternet.com
dir: Off A2 into Newnham, onto Seed Rd by church, establishment 1m on right

A warm welcome is assured at this peaceful location, which also features a working forge. The spacious bedrooms are in a converted stable block and provide smartly furnished accommodation. Breakfast is served in the dining room adjoining the bedrooms. The owner has won an award for green tourism by reducing the impact of the bus ness on the environment.

Rooms 2 en suite (2 GF) S £35; D £65* **Facilities** tea/coffee Cen ht Wi-fi **Parking** 6 **Notes** No Children 12yrs Closed 23 Dec-1 Jan

SUTTON Map 7 TR34

Sutton Vale Country Club
★★★ GUEST ACCOMMODATION

Vale Rd CT15 5DH
☎ 01304 366233 & 374155 📠 01304 381132
e-mail: office@sutton-vale.co.uk
dir: In village centre

Surrounded by countryside yet only a short distance from the historical town of Dover, Sutton Vale provides a wealth of activities including an indoor pool. Comfortable bedrooms in the main house are stylishly decorated and annexe rooms have private terraces. Breakfast is served in the dining room and evening entertainment is available in high season.

Rooms 4 en suite **Facilities** TVL tea/coffee Dinner available Cen ht 🏊 Pool Table **Conf** Max 100 Thtr 100 Class 60 Board 50 **Parking** 50 **Notes** LB ⊗

TENTERDEN Map 7 TQ83

Collina House
★★★★ GUEST ACCOMMODATION

5 East Hill TN30 6RL
☎ 01580 764852 & 764004 📠 01580 762224
e-mail: enquiries@collinahousehotel.co.uk
web: www.collinahousehotel.co.uk
dir: Off High St, E onto B2067 Oaks Rd, property on left opp orchard

This attractive, restored half-timbered Edwardian house has a peaceful location just a short walk from the town centre. The smart en suite bedrooms are spacious and thoughtfully equipped. Public areas include a formal bar and an elegant restaurant offering imaginative home-made dishes.

Rooms 12 en suite 3 annexe en suite (8 fmly) **Facilities** tea/coffee Dinner available Direct Dial Cen ht Licensed **Parking** 15 **Notes** LB ⊗ Closed 21 Dec-11 Jan

TUNBRIDGE WELLS (ROYAL)　　Map 6 TQ53

PREMIER COLLECTION

Danehurst House
★★★★★ BED AND BREAKFAST

41 Lower Green Rd, Rusthall TN4 8TW
☎ 01892 527739　📄 01892 514804
e-mail: info@danehurst.net
web: www.danehurst.net
dir: 1.5m W of Tunbridge Wells in Rusthall. Off A264 onto Coach Rd & Lower Green Rd

Situated in pretty gardens in a quiet residential area, this Victorian gabled house is located to the west of the historic spa town. The house retains many original features and is attractively decorated throughout. Public areas include a comfortable lounge with a small bar. The homely bedrooms come with a wealth of thoughtful extras, and excellent breakfasts are served in the conservatory.

Rooms 4 en suite (1 fmly) S £59.50–£79.50;
D £69.50–£99.50* Facilities TVL tea/coffee Cen ht Licensed Parking 6 Notes ⊗ No Children 8yrs Closed Xmas & 1st 2wks Feb

The Beacon
★★★★ INN

Tea Garden Ln, Rusthall TN3 9JH
☎ 01892 524252　📄 01892 534288
e-mail: beaconhotel@btopenworld.com
web: www.the-beacon.co.uk
dir: 1.5m W of Tunbridge Wells. Signed off A264 onto Tea Garden Ln

This charming 18th-century inn is situated on an elevated position amid 16 acres of land and surrounded by open countryside. The open-plan public areas are full of character and include ornate fireplaces and stained glass windows. The spacious bedrooms are attractively decorated, comfortably furnished and have many thoughtful touches.

Rooms 3 en suite S £68.50; D £97* Facilities TV2B tea/coffee Dinner available Direct Dial Cen ht Wi-fi Fishing Conf Thtr 50 Class 40 Board 30 Parking 42 Notes Civ Wed 100

Bentham Hill Stables
★★★★ GUEST ACCOMMODATION

Stockland Green Rd TN3 0TJ
☎ 01892 516602
e-mail: d-waddell@sky.com
dir: 2m NW of Tunbridge Wells. Off A26 signed Salomons/ Speldhurst, 1m right onto Bentham Hill/Stockland Green Rd, sharp right again

This converted stable block with its sunny French-style courtyard is located in peaceful woodlands only a short drive from the town. Bedrooms are light and airy with exposed brick walls and shuttered windows and some rooms have small private terraces. A freshly cooked breakfast is served in the delightful dining room.

Rooms 3 en suite (3 GF) S £45–£55; D £65–£75*
Facilities tea/coffee Cen ht Parking 3 Notes ⊗ No Children 8yrs Closed 23-27 Dec 🐾

WESTERHAM　　Map 6 TQ45

Corner Cottage
★★★★ GUEST ACCOMMODATION

Toys Hill TN16 1PY
☎ 01732 750362　📄 01732 750754
e-mail: szeman@jshmanco.com
dir: A25 to Brasted, onto Chart Ln signed Fox & Hounds. Turn right onto Puddledock Ln, 1st house on left

Settled in a charming village this spacious, well-equipped annexe is comfortably furnished and includes many thoughtful touches. In the main cottage a hearty Aga-cooked breakfast is served in the rustic dining room with stunning views of the countryside.

Rooms 1 annexe en suite (1 fmly) S £55; D £75–£80*
Facilities tea/coffee Dinner available Cen ht Wi-fi
Parking 2 Notes 🐾

WROTHAM HEATH　　Map 6 TQ65

Pretty Maid House B&B
★★★★ GUEST ACCOMMODATION

London Rd TN15 7RU
☎ 01732 886445　📄 01732 886439
e-mail: stay@prettymaid.co.uk
dir: M26 junct 2A towards Maidstone on A20, through lights, 300mtrs on left

Situated close to Brands Hatch Circuit, and within easy reach of the Bluewater Shopping Centre and Lullingstone Castle, this family home has been carefully designed to offer spacious, comfortable accommodation. Well-appointed bedrooms vary in size and provide many thoughtful extras including free Wi-fi. Breakfast is served in the large, bright dining room or can be offered as room service. Seasonal rates are available.

Rooms 7 rms (6 en suite) (1 pri facs) (2 fmly) (2 GF)
S £49.50–£55; D £59.50–£75 (room only)* Facilities FTV tea/coffee Cen ht Wi-fi Parking 7 Notes Closed 24 Dec-4 Jan

LANCASHIRE

ACCRINGTON　　Map 18 SD72

The Maple Lodge
★★★★ GUEST ACCOMMODATION

70 Blackburn Rd, Clayton-le-Moors BB5 5JH
☎ 01254 301284　📄 0560 112 5380
e-mail: info@stayatmaplelodge.co.uk
dir: M65 junct 7, signs for Clayton-le-Moors, right at T-junct onto Blackburn Rd

This welcoming house is convenient for the M65, and provides comfortable, well-equipped bedrooms. There is an inviting lounge with well-stocked bar, and freshly cooked dinners (by arrangement) and hearty breakfasts are served in the attractive dining room.

Rooms 4 en suite 4 annexe en suite (1 fmly) (4 GF)
Facilities FTV TVL tea/coffee Dinner available Direct Dial Cen ht Licensed Wi-fi Parking 6 Notes LB

Pilkington's Guest House
★★★ GUEST HOUSE

135 Blackburn Rd BB5 0AA
☎ 01254 237032　📄 01254 237032
e-mail: pilkybuses@hotmail.com

Located close to the railway station, this family-run property has two comfortable bedrooms in the main house and four further bedrooms in the carefully refurbished terrace a short way along the street. Home cooked breakfasts are served in the main house.

Rooms 2 rms (2 pri facs) 4 annexe rms (2 fmly) (2 GF) S fr £30; D £60* Facilities FTV tea/coffee Cen ht Snooker Pool Table Conf Max 100 Thtr 100 Class 100 Board 100 Parking 6 Notes ⊗ 🐾

BLACKBURN　　Map 18 SD62

Fernhurst
★★★★ INN

466 Bolton Rd BB2 4JP
☎ 01254 693541
e-mail: info@thefernhurst.co.uk
dir: M65 junct 4, A666 to Blackburn

Situated close to the town centre opposite Ewood Park, home of Blackburn Rovers Football Club; Fernhurst is the official away supporters' pub on match days. Guests can enjoy the big match atmosphere and watch Sky sport channels in the pub on large screens. Comfortable bedrooms are situated adjacent to the main building - all are contemporary in style.

Rooms 30 annexe en suite (15 GF) S £55–£59.50;
D £55–£59.50 (room only)* Facilities FTV Cen ht Wi-fi Parking 60 Notes ⊗

BLACKPOOL — Map 18 SD33

Bona Vista

★★★★ GUEST ACCOMMODATION

104-106 Queens Promenade FY2 9NX
☎ 01253 351396   📄 01253 594985
e-mail: enquires@bonavistahotel.com
dir: 0.25m N of Uncle Toms Cabin & Castle Casino

The Bona Vista has a peaceful seafront location on North Shore within reach of the town's amenities. Its attractive bedrooms are well equipped and some have sea views. There is a spacious dining room and a comfortable bar and lounges. Sixteen parking spaces are available, a boon in busy Blackpool.

Rooms 19 rms (17 en suite) (4 fmly) **Facilities** TVL tea/coffee Dinner available Cen ht Licensed Pool Table **Conf** Max 50 Thtr 50 Class 50 Board 50 **Parking** 16

The Craigmore

★★★★ GUEST HOUSE

8 Willshaw Rd, Gynn Square FY2 9SH
☎ 01253 355098
e-mail: enquiries@thecraigmore.com
dir: 1m N of Tower. A584 N over Gynn rdbt, 1st right onto Willshaw Rd. The Craigmore 3rd on left

This well-maintained property is in an attractive location overlooking Gynn Square gardens, with the Promenade and tram stops just yards away. Several of the smart modern bedrooms are suitable for families. There is a comfortable lounge, a sun lounge and patio, and the pretty dining room has a small bar.

Rooms 8 en suite (4 fmly) S £31-£41; D £50-£58* **Facilities** FTV TVL tea/coffee Dinner available Cen ht Licensed **Notes** LB ⊗ Closed Dec-Feb RS Feb-Mar Open on wknds & BHs

The Ramsay

★★★★ GUEST ACCOMMODATION

90-92 Queen Promenade FY2 9NS
☎ 01253 352777   📄 01253 351207
e-mail: enquiries@theramsayhotel.co.uk

On Blackpool's North Shore and within easy reach of the town centre, this friendly establishment offers comfortable, well-equipped bedrooms, many with sea views. Meals are served in the attractive dining room and lighter snacks are also available in the bar.

Rooms 20 en suite (2 fmly) S £25-£37.50; D £50-£80* **Facilities** TVL tea/coffee Dinner available Cen ht Lift Licensed **Parking** 10 **Notes** ⊗ Closed Nov-Mar

Sunny Cliff

★★★★ GUEST ACCOMMODATION

98 Queens Promenade, Northshore FY2 9NS
☎ 01253 351155
dir: On A584, 1.5m N of Blackpool Tower, just past Sheraton Hotel

Under the same ownership for four decades, this friendly guest house overlooking the seafront offers a genuine home-from-home atmosphere. The pretty bedrooms, some with sea views, are neatly furnished. There is a cosy bar, a sun lounge, a comfortable lounge, and a smart dining room where good home cooking features.

Rooms 9 en suite (3 fmly) (2 smoking) S £25-£28; D £50-£56* **Facilities** TVL tea/coffee Dinner available Cen ht Licensed **Parking** 6 **Notes** LB ⊗ Closed 9 Nov-Etr ⊠

The Baron

★★★★ 🄰 GUEST ACCOMMODATION

296 North Promenade FY1 2EY
☎ 01253 622729   📄 0161 297 0464
e-mail: baronhotel@f2s.com
web: www.baronhotel.co.uk
Rooms 21 en suite (1 fmly) (3 GF) (2 smoking) S £25-£40; D £50-£80* **Facilities** FTV tea/coffee Dinner available Cen ht Lift Licensed Wi-fi **Conf** Max 20 Thtr 20 Class 20 Board 20 **Parking** 16 **Notes** LB ⊗ No Children 12yrs

Hartshead

★★★ GUEST ACCOMMODATION

17 King Edward Av, North Shore FY2 9TA
☎ 01253 353133 & 357111
e-mail: info@hartshead-hotel.co.uk
dir: M55 junct 4, A583 & A584 to North Shore, off Queens Promenade onto King Edward Av

Popular for its location near the seafront, this enthusiastically run establishment has modern bedrooms of various sizes, equipped with a good range of practical extras. A veranda-sitting room is available, in addition to a comfortable lounge bar, and breakfast and pre-theatre dinners are served in the attractive dining room.

Rooms 10 en suite (3 fmly) S £21-£35; D £42-£60* **Facilities** FTV TVL tea/coffee Dinner available Cen ht Licensed **Parking** 6 **Notes** LB ⊗

Denely

★★★ GUEST HOUSE

15 King Edward Av FY2 9TA
☎ 01253 352757
e-mail: denely@tesco.net
dir: 1m N of Blackpool Tower

Just a stroll from this Promenade and Gynn Square gardens, the welcoming guest house offers a spacious lounge and a bright dining room along with simply furnished bedrooms. The friendly resident owners provide attentive service, and evening meals are available by arrangement.

Rooms 9 en suite (3 fmly); D £40-£50* **Facilities** FTV TVL tea/coffee Dinner available Cen ht **Parking** 6 **Notes** LB ⊗ Closed Dec-Jan

Derby Lodge

★★★ GUEST ACCOMMODATION

8 Derby Rd FY1 2JF
☎ 01253 753444   📄 01253 753444
e-mail: derbylodgehotel@btconnect.com
web: www.derbylodgehotelandrestaurant.com
dir: From M55 follow signs for Promenade, north (with sea on left), right onto Derby Rd, located on right

Located close to the seafront and the town centre, Derby Lodge offers spacious well-equipped accommodation in a friendly atmosphere. Dinner is available in the attractive restaurant and there is a small bar.

Rooms 7 en suite (3 fmly) **Facilities** FTV tea/coffee Dinner available Licensed Wi-fi **Conf** Max 24 Thtr 24 Class 24 Board 20 **Parking** 4 **Notes** ⊗

Funky Towers

★★★ GUEST ACCOMMODATION

297 The Promenade FY1 6AL
☎ **01253 400123**
e-mail: stay@funkytowers.com
web: www.funkytowers.com
dir: *On seafront promenade halfway between The Tower & Pleasure Beach*

The friendly, family-run guest house has a prime location facing the sea, between the Pleasure Beach and Central Pier. There is a spacious bar and a modern café with direct access to seafront. The bedrooms are equipped with lots of extras; some feature four-posters and others have great sea views.

Rooms 14 en suite (5 fmly) (1 GF) S £45; D £70-£99*
Facilities TVL tea/coffee Cen ht Licensed Wi-fi Pool Table **Parking** 3 **Notes** ⊗

Lancaster House

★★★ GUEST ACCOMMODATION

170 - 274 Central Dr FY1 5JB
☎ **01253 341928** 📄 **01253 402878**
e-mail: maria@lancasterhousehotel.co.uk

A short walk from the town centre and the seafront, Lancaster House is a family-run establishment which makes a good base for either business or leisure guests. There is an attractive bar, and meals are served in the popular Oliver's Bistro where a large selection of interesting dishes is available.

Rooms 11 en suite (2 fmly) **Facilities** FTV TVL Dinner available Cen ht Licensed Wi-fi **Parking** 11 **Notes** ⊗ Closed Jan

The Sandalwood

★★★ GUEST HOUSE

3 Gynn Av FY1 2LD
☎ **01253 351795** 📄 **01253 351795**
e-mail: peter.gerald@btconnect.com
web: www.sandalwoodhotel.co.uk
dir: *North of tower along promenade. 1st right, then 1st left after Hilton Hotel*

Situated on Blackpool's North Shore, The Sandalwood offers a friendly atmosphere and attractive, well-equipped accommodation. There is a comfortable lounge, and dinner or lighter snacks are available by arrangement.

Rooms 9 rms (7 en suite) (2 fmly) **Facilities** TVL tea/coffee Dinner available Cen ht Licensed **Parking** 2 **Notes** ⊗ Closed 20-30 Dec

Wilmar

★★★ GUEST HOUSE

42 Osborne Rd FY4 1HQ
☎ **01253 346229** 📄 **01253 200343**
e-mail: info@thehotelwilmar.co.uk
dir: *From M55 follow Main Parking Area, right at Waterloo Rd exit, left at lights, left at 2nd lights, bear right at Grand Hotel & right again*

This friendly, family-run guest house has a convenient location close to the Pleasure Beach, Sandcastles and all the resort's major South Promenade attractions. Bedrooms are brightly appointed, smartly maintained and include a family suite. A cosy lounge and bar are available and dinner is served by arrangement.

Rooms 7 rms (6 en suite) (1 pri facs) (1 fmly) S £20-£25; D £40-£50* **Facilities** FTV TVL tea/coffee Dinner available Cen ht Licensed Wi-fi **Notes** LB ⊗

The Montclair

★★★ 🄰 GUEST HOUSE

95 Albert Rd FY1 4PW
☎ **01253 625860**
e-mail: chrissbowen@aol.com
Rooms 15 en suite (4 fmly) S £25-£30; D £46-£60
Facilities FTV TVL Dinner available Cen ht Licensed
Parking 7 **Notes** LB ⊗

The Vidella

★★★ 🄰 GUEST ACCOMMODATION

80-82 Dickson Rd FY1 2BU
☎ **01253 621201** 📄 **01253 620319**
e-mail: info@videllahotel.com
web: www.videllahotel.com
dir: *N from North Pier on A584, right onto Cocker St, left at x-rds*

Rooms 29 en suite (6 fmly) (3 GF) (9 smoking)
S £20-£37.50; D £40-£75* **Facilities** FTV tea/coffee Dinner available Cen ht Licensed Wi-fi Pool Table
Conf Max 50 Thtr 50 Class 50 Board 50 **Parking** 5
Notes LB

Briny View

★★ 🄰 GUEST ACCOMMODATION

2 Woodfield Rd FY1 6AX
☎ **01253 346584**
e-mail: brinyviewhotel@aol.com
dir: *Off A584 Promenade between Central Pier & South Pier, opposite St Chads headland*

Rooms 11 rms (7 en suite) (1 pri facs) (4 fmly)
S £25-£30; D £45-£55* **Facilities** FTV TVL tea/coffee Cen ht Licensed **Notes** LB ⊗ Closed Dec 🛏

BOLTON-BY-BOWLAND Map 18 SD74

Middle Flass Lodge

★★★★ 🍽 GUEST HOUSE

Settle Rd BB7 4NY
☎ **01200 447259** 📄 **01200 447300**
e-mail: middleflasslodge@btconnect.com
web: www.middleflasslodge.co.uk
dir: *2m N of Bolton by Bowland. Off A59 for Sawley, N to Forest Becks, over bridge, 1m on right*

Set in peaceful countryside in the Forest of Bowland, this smart house provides a warm welcome. Stylishly converted from farm outbuildings, exposed timbers feature throughout, including the attractive restaurant and cosy lounge. The modern bedrooms include a family room. Thanks to the accomplished chef, the restaurant is also popular with non-residents.

Rooms 5 en suite 2 annexe en suite (1 fmly) S £32-£50;
D £62-£75 **Facilities** FTV TVL tea/coffee Dinner available Cen ht Licensed Wi-fi **Parking** 14 **Notes** LB ⊗

BURNLEY Map 18 SD83

Ormerod House

★★★ GUEST ACCOMMODATION

121/123 Ormerod Rd BB11 3QW
☎ 01282 423255
dir: *Burnley centre onto A682, 200yds N after rdbt right onto Ormerod Rd, pass Burnley College, 300yds on right*

The welcoming guest house is a short walk from the town centre and is handy for Queens Park, Thompson's Park and Burnley FC. The bright modern bedrooms are well equipped and there is a comfortable lounge. Separate tables are provided in the smart breakfast room.

Rooms 9 en suite (2 fmly) **Facilities** TVL tea/coffee Cen ht **Parking** 8 **Notes** ⊗

CARNFORTH Map 18 SD47

Longlands Inn & Restaurant

★★★★ 🅰 INN

Witfield LA6 1JH
☎ 01524 781256 📠 01524 781004
e-mail: info@longlandshotel.co.uk
dir: *M6 junct 35, M601 towards Kendal. At rdbt, 2nd exit (A6) to Milnthorpe, next rdbt 2nd exit (A6070) to Burton-in-Kendal. Over motorway, inn on right*

Rooms 11 en suite (1 fmly) S £55-£60; D £80-£85* **Facilities** FTV TVL tea/coffee Dinner available Direct Dial Cen ht Wi-fi Pool Table **Conf** Max 70 Thtr 70 **Notes** LB

CHORLEY

See Eccleston

ECCLESTON Map 15 SD51

Parr Hall Farm

★★★★ GUEST ACCOMMODATION

8 Parr Ln PR7 5SL
☎ 01257 451917 📠 01257 453749
e-mail: enquiries@parrhallfarm.com
dir: *Off B5250 at the Green/Towngate junct turn into Parr Ln, 1st property on left*

This attractive well-maintained farmhouse, located in a quiet corner of the village, yet close to the M6, dates back to the 18th century. The majority of bedrooms are located in a barn conversion and include luxury en suite bathrooms and lots of thoughtful extras. A comprehensive continental breakfast is included in the room price.

Rooms 9 annexe en suite (1 fmly) (5 GF) S £40-£45; D £70-£80* **Facilities** tea/coffee Cen ht Wi-fi 🦌 Guided Walks **Conf** Class 15 Board 10 **Parking** 20 **Notes** ⊗

FLEETWOOD Map 18 SD34

Normandy

★★★ GUEST HOUSE

100 Promenade Rd FY7 6RF
☎ 01253 872961 📠 01253 872961
e-mail: normandy-house@btconnect.com
dir: *From A585, Marine Hall on right, left onto Mount Rd & Promenade Rd*

This friendly family-run guest house is close to the town centre and the beach and its attractions. Bedrooms are comfortable and carefully decorated and well equipped, There is also a small lounge and dinner is served by arrangement in the dining room which has a small bar.

Rooms 3 en suite (1 fmly) S £25; D £50* **Facilities** FTV tea/coffee Dinner available Cen ht Licensed **Notes** LB ⊗ Closed 24 Dec-5 Jan 🚭

GARSTANG Map 18 SD44

The Crofters Inn

★★★★ INN

New Rd, A6 Cabus PR3 1PH
☎ 01995 604128 📠 01772 289347
e-mail: bookings@croftershotel.co.uk
dir: *On A6, midway between junct 32 & 33 of M6*

This is an attractive inn close to the charming market town of Garstang. Bedrooms are spacious and well equipped, and meals are available either in the Crofter's Brasserie or the Tavern Bar. There are also extensive function facilities.

Rooms 19 en suite (2 fmly) S £49-£59; D £60-£85* **Facilities** FTV TVL tea/coffee Dinner available Direct Dial Cen ht Wi-fi **Conf** Max 270 Thtr 270 Class 150 Board 80 **Parking** 200 **Notes** LB ⊗ Civ Wed 270

LANCASTER Map 18 SD46

Lancaster Town House

★★★ 🅰 GUEST ACCOMMODATION

11/12 Newton Ter, Caton Rd LA1 3PB
☎ 01524 65527 📠 01524 383148
e-mail: hedge-holmes@talk21.com
dir: *M6 junct 34, 1m towards Lancaster, house on right*

Rooms 7 en suite (1 fmly) S £37-£40; D £60-£65* **Facilities** FTV TVL tea/coffee Cen ht Wi-fi **Notes** ⊗

Penny Street Bridge

🆄

Penny St LA1 1XT
☎ 01524 599900 📠 01524 599901
e-mail: info@pennystreetbridge.co.uk

Currently the rating for this establishment is not confirmed. This may be due to a change of ownership or because it has only recently joined the AA rating scheme. For up-to-date information please see the AA website: theAA.com

Rooms 28 en suite (2 fmly) S £85; D £85* **Facilities** FTV tea/coffee D nner available Cen ht Lift Licensed Wi-fi **Conf** Max 20 Thtr 20 Board 20 **Parking** 4 **Notes** LB ⊗

LEYLAND Map 15 SD52

Sleepyhollow

★★★★ BED AND BREAKFAST

458 Croston Rd, Farington Moss PR26 6PJ
☎ 01772 424244 & 07788 178555
e-mail: sleepyhollow103@aol.com
web: www.sleepyhollow-uk.co.uk
dir: *M6 junct 29 straight over 3 rdbts, next rdbt bear left onto Croston Rd, 1m on right*

Situated just five minutes from the M6 and M65 and set in half an acre of land, Sleepyhollow offers accommodation in two well appointed bedrooms. The hearty breakfast will set you up for the day.

Rooms 2 en suite S £35-£40; D £50-£55* **Facilities** FTV TVL tea/coffee Cen ht Wi-fi **Parking** 5 **Notes** ⊗ No Children 15yrs Closed 25-26 Dec

LYTHAM ST ANNES Map 18 SD32

Strathmore

★★★ GUEST ACCOMMODATION

305 Clifton Drive South FY8 1HN
☎ 01253 725478
dir: *In centre of St Annes opp Post Office*

This friendly, family-run property has a central location close to the promenade. The long-established Strathmore offers smartly furnished and well-equipped bedrooms. There is an elegant lounge where you can enjoy a relaxing drink, and a smart dining room.

Rooms 8 rms (5 en suite) S £23-£29; D £46-£58 **Facilities** tea/coffee Cen ht **Parking** 10 **Notes** LB ⊗ No Children 9yrs 🚭

MORECAMBE   Map 18 SD46

Morecambe Bay Guest House

★★★★ GUEST HOUSE

35 Marine Road West LA3 1BZ
☎ 01524 426593
e-mail: info@morecambebayguesthouse.co.uk

This friendly family-run house has a stunning outlook
over Morecambe Bay. The contemporary bedrooms,
including a ground floor room, are spacious and well
furnished with good quality en suites. Breakfast is served
in the pleasant downstairs dining room, and there is also
a lounge area.

Rooms 4 en suite (1 GF) **Facilities** FTV tea/coffee Cen ht
Wi-fi **Notes** LB ⊗

Beach Mount

★★★ GUEST ACCOMMODATION

395 Marine Road East LA4 5AN
☎ 01524 420753
e-mail: beachmounthotel@aol.com
dir: M6 junct 34/35, follow signs to Morecambe. Beach
Mount 0.5m from town centre on E Promenade

This spacious property overlooks the bay and features a
range of room styles that includes a family room and a
junior suite. Guests have use of a comfortable lounge
with fully licensed bar, and breakfasts are served in a
pleasant separate dining room.

Rooms 10 en suite (1 GF) (10 smoking) S £28-£46.50;
D £51-£58* **Facilities** FTV tea/coffee Cen ht Licensed
Notes LB Closed Nov-Mar

Belle Vue

★★★ GUEST ACCOMMODATION

330 Marine Rd LA4 5AA
☎ 01524 411375 📠 01524 411375
dir: On seafront between lifeboat house & bingo hall

With fine views over the promenade and Morecambe Bay,
the Belle Vue provides a range of bedrooms styles on
three floors; most are accessible by lift. There are
comfortable lounges and a spacious lounge bar where

entertainment is provided at peak times. A choice of
dishes is available in the large dining room.

Rooms 41 rms (34 en suite) (3 fmly) S £32; D £60
Facilities TVL tea/coffee Dinner available Cen ht Lift
Licensed **Parking** 3 **Notes** LB ⊗ No Children 14yrs Closed
Jan-Mar

The Craigwell

★★★ GUEST HOUSE

372 Marine Road East LA4 5AH
☎ 01524 410095
e-mail: craigwellhotel@tiscali.co.uk
web: www.craigwellhotel.co.uk
dir: A589 to seafront, left, Craigwell 400yds

This house is part of a Victorian terrace and looks out
over Morecambe Bay to the distant Cumbrian hills. There
is a stylish lounge with fine views and a spacious
breakfast room to the rear. Bedrooms are pleasantly
decorated, and have all the expected facilities; six enjoy
views of the bay. There is a private car park at the rear.

Rooms 12 en suite (1 fmly) S £28-£35; D £56-£65*
Facilities FTV TVL tea/coffee Cen ht Wi-fi **Conf** Thtr 30
Class 15 Board 20 **Parking** 4 **Notes** LB

The Sea Lynn Guest House

★★★ GUEST ACCOMMODATION

29 West End Rd LA4 4DJ
☎ 01524 411340
e-mail: thesealynn@hotmail.com
dir: Follow signs for West End seafront, turn right, then
3rd right, 50yds on right

Set just back from the promenade and near the tourist
attractions, this terrace house with a tidy front patio
area, and offers accommodation on four floors. Guests
have use of a cosy lounge on the ground floor and a
comfortable breakfast room on the first floor. Bedrooms
are fresh in design, with all the expected facilities. All
guests will receive a warm welcome.

Rooms 12 rms (3 en suite) (1 fmly) (3 GF) S £23-£26;
D £46-£58* **Facilities** FTV TVL tea/coffee Cen ht Wi-fi
Notes LB ⊗

The Trevelyan

★★★ GUEST ACCOMMODATION

27 West End Rd LA4 4DJ
☎ 01524 412013
e-mail: contact@thetrevelyanhotel.co.uk
dir: M6 junct 34, signed Morecambe, then West End. At
seafront right, 3rd right into West End Rd, house 50yds
on right

You are assured of a warm welcome at The Trevelyan, a
family-run guest house which is situated just 50 yards
from the seafront, and is well located for Morecambe's
attractions. Bedrooms are comfortably proportioned and
well equipped, and there is an inviting lounge, a cosy bar,
and a bright airy dining room where delicious freshly
cooked evening meals (by arrangement), and traditional
English breakfasts, are served at individual tables.

Rooms 10 rms (2 en suite) (1 fmly) (2 GF) **Facilities** FTV
TVL tea/coffee Dinner available Cen ht Licensed Wi-fi
Notes ⊗

Yacht Bay View

★★★ GUEST HOUSE

359 Marine Road East LA4 5AQ
☎ 01524 414481
e-mail: yachtbayview@hotmail.com
dir: 0.5m NE of town centre on seafront promenade

Overlooking Morecambe Bay, this family-run property
offers comfortable bedrooms, some with impressive
views, and all with en suite shower rooms. Guests are
given a warm welcome and breakfast is served in the
dining room, which also has a lounge area.

Rooms 7 en suite (1 fmly) S £25-£32; D £50-£64*
Facilities FTV TVL tea/coffee Dinner available Wi-fi
Notes LB ⊗

PRESTON
Map 18 SD52

See also Blackburn

PREMIER COLLECTION

Whitestake Farm
★★★★★ BED AND BREAKFAST

Pope Ln, Whitestake PR4 4JR
☎ 01772 619392 🖷 01772 611146
e-mail: enquiries@gardenofedenspa.co.uk
web: www.gardenofedenspa.co.uk
dir: M6 junct 29, A582 Lytham St Annes, Penwortham
Way, left onto Chain House Ln, right onto Pope Ln.
Whitestake Farm on right

A warm welcome is assured at this attractive white
farmhouse, peacefully located just minutes from
Preston and the M6, within easy reach of Southport and
Lytham. Beautifully appointed bedrooms and
bathrooms are spacious and thoughtfully equipped.
Carefully prepared, substantial breakfasts are taken
around a large table in an elegant dining room and
spacious sumptuous lounges are also a feature. Guests
can also make use of the indoor swimming pool and
rejuvenating and relaxing spa treatments are
available.

Rooms 2 en suite S £60; D £120* Facilities STV FTV
TVL tea/coffee Dinner available Cen ht Licensed Wi-fi
🏊 Parking 6 Notes ⊗

Willow Cottage B&B
★★★★ 🅰 BED AND BREAKFAST

Thropps Ln, Longton PR4 5SW
☎ 01772 617570
e-mail: willow.cottage@btconnect.com
Rooms 2 en suite (1 fmly) S fr £40; D fr £60*
Facilities FTV TVL tea/coffee Cen ht 🍴 Parking 12
Notes ⊗ No Children 12yrs ⊛

Birch Croft Bed & Breakfast
★★★ BED AND BREAKFAST

Gill Ln, Longton PR4 4SS
☎ 01772 613174 🖷 01772 613174
e-mail: johnsuts@btinternet.com
web: www.birchcroftbandb.co.uk
dir: From A59 right at rdbt to Midge Hall. Premises 4th
on left

Located only 10 minutes away from major motorway links
(M6, M65, M61) this establishment is on the doorstep of
many nearby attractions and close to Southport, Preston
and Blackpool. This is a friendly, family run business
which offers comfortable accommodation in a very
peaceful location.

Rooms 3 en suite (1 fmly) Facilities TVL tea/coffee Cen ht
Wi-fi Parking 11 Notes LB ⊗ ⊛

Ashton Lodge Guest House
★★ GUEST ACCOMMODATION

37 Victoria Pde, Ashton PR2 1DT
☎ 01772 728414 🖷 01772 720580
e-mail: greathospitality@btconnect.com
dir: M6 junct 31, A59 onto A5085, 3.3m onto A5072
Tulketh Rd, 0.3m onto Victoria Pde

This detached Victorian guest house offers good value
accommodation. Bedrooms vary in size, with some on the
ground floor. The dining room is the setting for hearty
traditional breakfasts served at individual tables.

Rooms 8 rms (6 en suite) (5 fmly) (3 GF) S £28-£35;
D £40-£48* Facilities FTV TVL tea/coffee Cen ht Wi-fi
Notes ⊗

WHITEWELL
Map 18 SD64

PREMIER COLLECTION

The Inn at Whitewell
★★★★★ ⊛ INN

Forest of Bowland, Clitheroe BB7 3AT
☎ 01200 448222 🖷 01200 448298
e-mail: reception@innatwhitewell.com
dir: M6 junct 31a, B6243 to Longridge. Left at mini-
rdbt. After 3 rdbts leave Longridge. Approx 3m, sharp
left bend (with white railings), then right. Approx 1m
left, right at T-junct. Next left, 3m to Whitewell

This long-established culinary destination is hidden
away in quintessential Lancashire countryside just 20
minutes from the M6. The fine dining restaurant is
complemented by two historic and cosy bars with
roaring fires, real ales and polished service. Bedrooms
are richly furnished with antiques and eye-catching
bijouterie, while many of the bathrooms have Victorian
brass showers.

Rooms 19 en suite 4 annexe en suite (1 fmly) (1 GF)
S £77-£165; D £105-£203* Facilities STV FTV tea/
coffee Dinner available Direct Dial Cen ht Wi-fi Fishing
Conf Max 45 Thtr 45 Board 35 Parking 60 Notes No
coaches Civ Wed 80

LEICESTERSHIRE

ASHBY-DE-LA-ZOUCH

See Coalville

BARKESTONE-LE-VALE
Map 11 SK73

Woodside Farm
★★★★ BED AND BREAKFAST

Long Ln NG13 0HQ
☎ 01476 870336 & 07703 299291
e-mail: hickling-woodside@supanet.com
dir: 1m SE of Barkestone. Off A52 at Bottesford for Harby
& Belvoir Castle, after Redmile x-rds, left onto lane,
farm 0.5m

A warm welcome awaits at this friendly farm, located on
the Belvoir Castle estate in the peaceful Vale of Belvoir
within easy reach of Nottingham and Grantham. The
smart bedrooms have beautiful views over open
countryside, and hearty breakfasts are served in the
lounge-dining room. Packed lunches are available on
request.

Rooms 2 en suite (1 fmly) (1 GF) S £45-£55; D £65-£75
Facilities tea/coffee Cen ht Golf Fishing Riding Parking 5
Notes LB ⊗ RS mid Sep-mid May advance bookings only
⊛

BARROW UPON SOAR
Map 11 SK51

The Hunting Lodge
★★★★ INN

38 South St LE12 8LZ
☎ 01509 412337 🖷 01509 410838
web: www.thehuntinglodgebarrowonsoar.co.uk

The themed bedrooms at this modern inn include a Fagin
room, a Chopin room and a Dali room; all are well
equipped and have good facilities. There is a popular bar
and a good range of interesting food is served in the
brasserie.

Rooms 6 en suite (2 fmly) S £90; D £90-£140*
Facilities tea/coffee Dinner available Direct Dial Cen ht
Wi-fi Conf Max 50 Thtr 50 Class 50 Board 30 Parking 60
Notes ⊗

BELTON
Map 11 SK42

The Queen's Head
★★★★ ◉◉ 🏠 RESTAURANT WITH ROOMS

2 Long St LE12 9TP
☎ 01530 222359 📠 01530 224680
e-mail: enquiries@thequeenshead.org
web: www.thequeenshead.org
dir: From Loughborough turn left onto B5324, 3m into Belton

This well furnished establishment is found in the village centre and has public rooms with a modern feel. The individually designed bedrooms feature crisp white linen, fluffy duvets and pillows, 19-inch LCD TVs with Freeview and DVD players. The restaurant has earned a well deserved reputation for its award-winning cuisine; the menus are based on the freshest, locally sourced produce quality.

Rooms 6 en suite (2 fmly) S £65; D £80-£100
Facilities FTV TVL tea/coffee Dinner available Cen ht Wi-fi
Conf Max 40 Thtr 40 Class 18 Board 30 Parking 20
Notes Civ Wed 50

CASTLE DONINGTON
See East Midlands Airport

COALVILLE
Map 11 SK41

Ravenstone Guesthouse
★★★★ 🏠 GUEST HOUSE

Ravenstone LE67 2AE
☎ 01530 810536
e-mail: annthorne@ravenstone-guesthouse.co.uk
web: www.ravenstone-guesthouse.co.uk
dir: 1.5m W of Coalville. Off A447 onto Church Ln for Ravenstone, 2nd house on left

Situated in the heart of Ravenstone village, this early 18th-century house is full of character. The bedrooms are individually decorated and feature period furniture, and local produce is used for dinner and in the extensive breakfast menu. The beamed dining room has an honesty bar and there is also a cosy lounge.

Rooms 3 en suite Facilities FTV TVL tea/coffee Dinner available Cen ht Licensed Wi-fi Painting tuition Parking 6
Notes No Children 18yrs Closed 23-30 Dec & 1 Jan RS 31 Dec-1 Jan No breakfast on 1 Jan

EAST MIDLANDS AIRPORT
Map 11 SK42

PREMIER COLLECTION

Kegworth House
★★★★★ GUEST HOUSE

42 High St DE74 2DA
☎ 01509 672575 📠 01509 670645
e-mail: info@kegworthhouse.co.uk
web: www.kegworthhouse.co.uk
dir: M1 junct 24, A6 to Loughborough. 0.5m 1st right onto Packington Hill. Left at junct, Kegworth House 50yds on left

Convenient for major roads and East Midlands Airport, this impressive Georgian house with an immaculate walled garden has been lovingly restored. The individually styled bedrooms are luxuriously appointed and equipped with a wealth of thoughtful extras. The elegant dining room is the setting for memorable dinners by arrangement, and wholesome breakfasts featuring local produce are served in the attractive kitchen.

Rooms 11 en suite (2 fmly) (2 GF) S £50-£135; D £60-£195* Facilities TVL tea/coffee Direct Dial Cen ht Licensed Wi-fi Access to health club Conf Max 12 Board 12 Parking 25 Notes ⊗

HUSBANDS BOSWORTH
Map 11 SP68

Croft Farm B&B (SP634860)
★★★★ FARMHOUSE

Leicester Rd LE17 6NW
☎ 01858 880679 Mrs Smith
e-mail: janesmith06@aol.com
web: www.croftfarm.org.uk
dir: Take A5199 from Husbands Bosworth towards Leicester, Croft Farm 0.25m on left

This very spacious and delightfully furnished house stands on the edge of the village in very well cared for grounds. Bedrooms are thoughtfully equipped and there is a very comfortable guests' lounge. Expect a substantial breakfast together with friendly and attentive service.

Rooms 4 en suite (2 fmly) Facilities TVL tea/coffee Cen ht Wi-fi Parking 15 Notes ⊗ 🐾 350 acres sheep/arable/beef/mixed

KEGWORTH
See East Midlands Airport

KNIPTON
Map 11 SK83

The Manners Arms
★★★★ ◉ RESTAURANT WITH ROOMS

Croxton Rd NG32 1RH
☎ 01476 879222 📠 01476 879228
e-mail: info@mannersarms.com
web: www.mannersarms.com
dir: Off A607 into Knipton

Part of the Rutland Estate and built as a hunting lodge for the 6th Duke, the Manners Arms has been renovated to provide thoughtfully furnished bedrooms designed by the present Duchess. Public areas include the intimate themed Beater's Bar and attractive Red Coats Restaurant, popular for imaginative dining.

Rooms 10 en suite (1 fmly) Facilities TVL tea/coffee Dinner available Direct Dial Cen ht Wi-fi Conf Max 50 Thtr 50 Class 25 Board 20 Parking 60 Notes No coaches Civ Wed 50

| **LEICESTER** | Map 11 SK50 |

Stoney Croft

★★★ GUEST ACCOMMODATION

5-7 Elmfield Av, Off London Rd LE2 1RB
☎ 0116 270 7605 ▤ 0116 270 6067
e-mail: reception@stoneycrofthotel.co.uk
web: www.stoneycrofthotel.co.uk
dir: *Near city centre on A6 to Market Harborough*

Stoney Croft provides comfortable accommodation and helpful service. Public rooms include a foyer-lounge area, breakfast room and conference facilities. There is also a large restaurant-bar where a good selection of freshly cooked dishes is available. The modern bedrooms come with desks.

Rooms 41 en suite (4 fmly) (6 GF) S £48-£55; D £65-£100 **Facilities** TVL tea/coffee Dinner available Direct Dial Cen ht Licensed Wi-fi Pool Table **Conf** Max 150 Thtr 150 Class 20 Board 30 **Parking** 30 **Notes** LB Civ Wed 120

Abinger Guest House

★★★ Ⓐ GUEST HOUSE

175 Hinckley Rd LE3 0TF
☎ 0116 255 4674 ▤ 0116 271 5202
e-mail: abinger@btinternet.com
web: www.leicesterguest.co.uk
dir: *0.5m W of city centre, off A47 or A5460*

Rooms 8 rms (2 fmly) (2 GF) S £28-£33; D £39-£48* **Facilities** FTV tea/coffee Cen ht Wi-fi **Notes** ⊗ Closed Xmas

---

| **LOUGHBOROUGH** | Map 11 SK51 |

The Falcon Inn

★★★ INN

64 Main St, Long Whatton LE12 5DG
☎ 01509 842416 ▤ 01509 646802
e-mail: enquiries@thefalconinnlongwhatton.com
dir: *M1 junct 23 N or junct 24 S, follow signs to Airport. After lights 1st left to Diseworth, left at T-junct, left towards Long Whatton, on right*

This late 18th-century traditional country pub sits in the quiet village of Long Whatton. Inside, the relaxed and friendly atmosphere is complemented by a good choice of freshly made meals, real ales and efficient service. Smartly appointed bedrooms are housed in a converted former school house and stable block at the rear of the main inn. Ample private parking is provided.

Rooms 11 annexe en suite (5 GF) **Facilities** FTV tea/coffee Dinner available Cen ht Wi-fi petanque pitch **Conf** Max 30 Thtr 20 Class 20 Board 20 **Parking** 46 **Notes** ⊗

| **MARKET BOSWORTH** | Map 11 SK40 |

Softleys

★★★ GUEST ACCOMMODATION

2 Market Place CV13 0LE
☎ 01455 290464
e-mail: softleysrestaurant@tiscali.co.uk
dir: *On B585 in Market Place*

Softleys is a Grade II listed building dating back to 1794. The bedrooms are en suite set on the third floor offering picturesque views over Market Bosworth. Quality food is served using locally sourced ingredients.

Rooms 3 en suite S £49-£65; D £59-£75* **Facilities** tea/coffee Dinner available Direct Dial Cen ht Licensed Wi-fi **Conf** Max 24 Thtr 24 Class 24 Board 24 **Notes** RS Sun eve & Mon No food available

---

| **MARKET HARBOROUGH** | Map 11 SP78 |

See also Medbourne

Hunters Lodge

★★★★ Ⓐ BED AND BREAKFAST

By Foxton Locks, Gumley LE16 7RT
☎ 0116 279 3744 ▤ 0116 279 3855
e-mail: info@hunterslodgefoxton.co.uk
dir: *M1 junct 20, A4304 for Market Harborough, after 8m in Lubenham 2nd left signed Foxton. Next left signed Laughton, pass village hall, 1.5m over hump backed bridge. Next right Gumley in 200yds right, signed Foxton*

Rooms 2 en suite (1 fmly) (2 GF) S £38-£40; D £60* **Facilities** STV TVL tea/coffee Cen ht Wi-fi **Parking** 5

| **MEDBOURNE** | Map 11 SP89 |

The Horse & Trumpet

★★★★ ◉◉ RESTAURANT WITH ROOMS

Old Green LE16 8DX
☎ 01858 565000 ▤ 01858 565551
e-mail: info@horseandtrumpet.com
dir: *In village centre, opposite church*

Tucked away behind the village bowling green, this carefully restored and re-thatched former farmhouse and pub now offers fine dining and quality accommodation. The golden stone three-storey building hosts three dining rooms, in which chef Gary Maganani and his team provides imaginative food from high quality produce;

---

service is both professional and friendly. The smartly appointed bedrooms are located to the rear of the building in a barn conversion; attractively furnished and thoughtfully equipped for modern travellers.

Rooms 4 annexe en suite (2 GF) **Facilities** tea/coffee Dinner available Direct Dial Cen ht **Conf** Max 25 **Notes** ⊗ No Children 5yrs RS Sun eve & Mon restaurant closed No coaches

Medbourne Grange (SP815945)

★★★★ FARMHOUSE

LE16 8EF
☎ 01858 565249 & 07730 956116
▤ 01858 565257 **Mrs S Beaty**
dir: *2m NE of Medbourne. Between Market Harborough & Uppingham off B664*

This 150-year-old working farm has unrivalled views of the Welland Valley and is well situated for Rutland Water, Uppingham or Market Harborough. Mrs Beaty is a natural host, ensuring that guests receive a warm welcome and friendly service. Individually furnished bedrooms are complemented by comfortable day rooms, and freshly prepared breakfasts are served in the smart dining room.

Rooms 3 en suite **Facilities** TVL tea/coffee Cen ht ⚡ **Parking** 6 **Notes** ⊗ ⊜ 500 acres arable

The Nevill Arms

★★★★ INN

12 Waterfall Way LE16 8EE
☎ 01858 565288 ▤ 01858 565509
e-mail: info@thenevillarms.net
web: www.thenevillarms.net
dir: *From Uppingham follow B664 SW for 7m. From Market Harborough follow B664 NE for 5m*

An 18th-century, Tudor-style, Grade II listed inn which has been sympathetically refurbished to retain its original character and features such as a large studded oak door, oak beamed ceilings, stone inglenook fireplace and leaded stone mullion windows. Public rooms include a stylish restaurant, a conservatory and a lounge bar. Bedrooms are tastefully appointed and well equipped.

Rooms 11 en suite (1 fmly) S £69-£89; D £89-£99* **Facilities** FTV tea/coffee Dinner available Cen ht Wi-fi **Conf** Max 30 Thtr 18 Class 30 Board 30 **Parking** 25 **Notes** ⊗

MELTON MOWBRAY Map 11 SK71

Bryn Barn

★★★★ GUEST ACCOMMODATION

38 High St, Waltham-on-the-Wolds LE14 4AH
☎ 01664 464783 & 07791 215614
e-mail: glenarowlands@onetel.com
web: www.brynbarn.co.uk
dir: 4.5m NE of Melton. Off A607, in Waltham-on-the-Wolds centre

A warm welcome awaits at this attractive, peacefully located cottage within easy reach of Melton Mowbray, Grantham, Rutland Water and Belvoir Castle. Bedrooms are smartly appointed and comfortably furnished, while public rooms include an inviting lounge overlooking a wonderful courtyard garden. Meals are available at one of the nearby village pubs.

Rooms 4 rms (3 en suite) (1 pri facs) (2 fmly) (1 GF) S £30-£40; D £55-£65* Facilities FTV TVL tea/coffee Cen ht Wi-fi Parking 4 Notes LB Closed 21 Dec-4 Jan

Noels Arms

★★ INN

31 Burton St LE13 1AE
☎ 01664 562363
dir: On A606, S of town centre at Mill St junct

The traditional inn lies close to the town centre. The bar is the focal point of the inn, where breakfast is served and staff and locals generate a relaxed and friendly atmosphere. Bedrooms come in a variety of co-ordinated styles and sizes, each furnished in pine.

Rooms 6 rms (4 en suite) (2 fmly) S fr £28; D fr £52* Facilities STV tea/coffee Cen ht Pool Table Notes ⊛

MOUNTSORREL Map 11 SK51

The Swan Inn

★★★★ INN

10 Loughborough Rd LE12 7AT
☎ 0116 230 2340   0116 237 6115
e-mail: office@swaninn.eu
web: www.the-swan-inn.eu
dir: In village centre

This traditional 17th-century inn is in the centre of the village and offers well produced meals in the bar, together with a wide range of real ales. The accommodation consists of a luxury suite which includes a double bedroom, a lounge, a large bathroom and an office. Continental breakfast is available in the suite.

Rooms 1 en suite S £70-£98; D £70-£98* Facilities FTV TVL tea/coffee Dinner available Direct Dial Cen ht Wi-fi Parking 12 Notes No coaches

NARBOROUGH Map 11 SP59

Fossebrook

★★★★ GUEST ACCOMMODATION

Coventry Rd, Croft LE9 3GP
☎ 01455 283517   01455 283517
dir: 0.6m SE of village centre on B4114

This friendly guest house stands in a quiet rural location with good access to major roads. Bedrooms are spacious, very comfortable and offer an excellent range of facilities including videos in all rooms. Breakfast is served in the bright dining room, which overlooks pleasant gardens and grounds.

Rooms 4 en suite (4 GF) S £40; D £40* Facilities tea/coffee Cen ht Parking 16 Notes ⊛ Closed 24 Dec-2 Jan

REDMILE Map 11 SK73

The Peacock Inn

★★★★ INN

Main St NG13 0GA
☎ 01949 842554
e-mail: reservations@thepeacockinnredmile.co.uk
dir: Off A52 between Bingham & Bottesford, follow signs for Belvoir Castle, then Redmile

Between Nottingham and Grantham in a peaceful village, this period inn provides well-equipped bedrooms, which are named after wild animals, and all have efficient bathrooms. Public areas retain many fine original features and in addition to a wide range of bar meals, a carte menu is available in a formal restaurant on two weekend evenings.

Rooms 10 en suite (1 fmly) Facilities tea/coffee Dinner available Direct Dial Cen ht Conf Max 50 Thtr 40 Class 50 Board 40 Parking 40

SHEPSHED Map 11 SK41

PREMIER COLLECTION

The Grange Courtyard
★★★★★ GUEST ACCOMMODATION

Forest St LE12 9DA
☎ 01509 600189   01509 603834
e-mail: linda.lawrence@thegrangecourtyard.co.uk
web: www.thegrangecourtyard.co.uk
dir: M1 junct 23, right at lights onto Leicester road, over mini rdbt onto Forest St

Dating from 18th century, this Grade II listed building, set in attractive mature gardens and grounds, with the added bonus of secure private parking. The accommodation is housed in individually appointed cottage bedrooms, each immaculately presented and extensively equipped. Guests also have access to fully equipped kitchens. Attentive personal service from the charming proprietor and her helpful team makes a stay here a home-from-home experience.

Rooms 20 en suite (1 fmly) (12 GF) S fr £69; D fr £80.50* Facilities tea/coffee Direct Dial Cen ht Licensed Wi-fi Conf Max 12 Class 12 Board 12 Parking 15 Notes RS Xmas & Etr self-catering

WIGSTON Map 11 SP69

Plough Inn

★★★★ INN

44 Bushloe Rd LE18 2BA
☎ 0116 281 0078   0116 210 0674
e-mail: theploughwigston@ntlworld.com
dir: Just off A599 (old A50), next to All Saints church

Located within easy travelling distance from Leicester, this half timbered and red brick inn provides a range of thoughtfully furnished bedrooms located in a separate accommodation wing, ensuring a peaceful night's sleep. A wide range of food and ales is available in the spacious public areas and hospitality is natural and caring.

Rooms 7 annexe en suite (1 fmly) (7 GF) S fr £45; D fr £65* Facilities tea/coffee Dinner available Cen ht Parking 32 Notes ⊛ No coaches

WOODHOUSE EAVES — Map 11 SK51

The Wheatsheaf Inn

★★★ INN

90 Brand Hill LE12 8SS
☎ 01509 890320
e-mail: richard@wheatsheafinn.net
web: www.wheatsheafinn.net

Originally built around 1800 by the local miners of Swithland slate mines, this charming inn offers a friendly service, good food and modern accommodation in the adjacent self-contained cottage. The first-floor restaurant proves very popular with locals, offering Specials and Bistro menus that include traditional English fayre, plus fresh fish dishes appear as blackboard specials.

Rooms 3 annexe en suite (1 GF) S fr £60; D fr £80* **Facilities** FTV TVL tea/coffee Dinner available Cen ht Wi-fi **Conf** Thtr 18 Class 12 Board 14 **Parking** 70 **Notes** No coaches

LINCOLNSHIRE

BOSTON — Map 12 TF34

Palethorpe House

★★★★ GUEST ACCOMMODATION

138 Spilsby Rd PE21 9PE
☎ 01205 359000 & 07888 758608 📠 01205 359000
dir: 0.5m from town centre on left, 200yds from Pilgrim Hospital

Friendly and welcoming, this Grade II listed Victorian villa, built by John Palethorpe in 1853, stands in a conservation area within easy walking distance of the town centre. The house is appointed to a very good standard, offering carefully furnished day rooms that include a lounge with satellite TV and a pleasant breakfast room. A continental breakfast only is available during the week, with cooked options at the weekend. Bedrooms are thoughtfully equipped, have quality beds and well-appointed bathrooms.

Rooms 2 en suite (2 fmly) **Facilities** STV TVL tea/coffee Cen ht **Parking** 3 **Notes** ⊗ 📧

BRIGG — Map 17 TA00

The Queens Head

★★★ INN

Station Rd, North Kelsey Moor LN7 6HD
☎ 01652 678055 📠 01652 678954
e-mail: info@queens-head.biz
web: www.queens-head.biz
dir: 6m SE of Brigg. Off B1434 to North Kelsey Moor

A small and friendly family-run inn with purpose-built en suite bedrooms. The rear car park overlooks a small garden. A wide range of ales and wines is available in the locals' bar, and an extensive menu can be enjoyed either in the bar or popular restaurant.

Rooms 5 en suite (5 GF) **Facilities** tea/coffee Dinner available Cen ht **Conf** Max 50 Thtr 50 Class 50 Board 50 **Parking** 50 **Notes** ⊗

CLEETHORPES — Map 17 TA30

Adelaide

★★★★ GUEST ACCOMMODATION

41 Isaac's Hill DN35 8JT
☎ 01472 693594 📠 01472 329717
e-mail: adelaide.hotel@ntlworld.com
dir: 500yds W of seafront. Junct A180 & A46 onto A1098 Isaac's Hill, on right at bottom of hill

This beautifully presented house offers well-equipped bedrooms and comfortable public rooms, and hospitality is a major strength. Good home cooking is provided and there is a small lounge with a bar. Secure parking is available.

Rooms 5 rms (3 en suite) (1 fmly) **Facilities** STV TVL tea/coffee Dinner available Cen ht Licensed **Notes** ⊗ No Children 4yrs

The Comat

★★★★ GUEST ACCOMMODATION

26 Yarra Rd DN35 8LS
☎ 01472 694791 & 591861 📠 01472 694791
e-mail: comat-hotel@ntlworld.com
web: www.comat-hotel.co.uk
dir: Off A1098 (Alexandra Rd), on left of library

A short walk from the shops and seafront, the welcoming Comat offers cosy, well-equipped bedrooms, one with a four-poster bed. Tasty English breakfasts are served in the bright dining room, and a quiet sitting room and bar overlook the colourful flower terrace.

Rooms 6 en suite (2 fmly) (2 GF) S £45-£58; D £60-£75 **Facilities** TVL tea/coffee Cen ht Licensed Wi-fi **Notes** LB ⊗ No Children 3yrs

Sherwood Guest House

★★★★ GUEST ACCOMMODATION

15 Kingsway DN35 8QU
☎ 01472 692020 📠 01472 239177
e-mail: sherwood.guesthouse@ntlworld.com
dir: On A1098 (seafront road), 3m from A180

This non-smoking Victorian house stands on the seafront overlooking the promenade and the beach, and is a short walk the town centre. Bedrooms are immaculate and the hearty breakfast comes with attentive service. There is a lounge, and limited off-road parking is available.

Rooms 6 rms (3 en suite) **Facilities** tea/coffee Cen ht Wi-fi **Parking** 2 **Notes** LB ⊗ No Children

Tudor Terrace

★★★★ GUEST HOUSE

11 Bradford Av DN35 0BB
☎ 01472 600800 📠 01472 501395
e-mail: tudor.terrace@ntlworld.com
dir: Off seafront onto Bradford Ave

This guest house offers attractive bedrooms that are thoughtfully designed and furnished to a high standard. Guests can relax in the lounge, or outside on the patio in the well-maintained garden. Very caring and friendly service is provided, and the house is non-smoking except in the garden. Mobility scooter rental is available.

Rooms 6 en suite (1 GF) **Facilities** TVL tea/coffee Dinner available Cen ht **Parking** 3 **Notes** No Children

Alpine House

★★★ GUEST ACCOMMODATION

55 Clee Rd DN35 8AD
☎ 01472 690804
e-mail: nw.sanderson@ntlworld.com
dir: On A46 before junct A180 & A1098 Isaac's Hill rdbt

Carefully run by the resident owners, and convenient for the town centre and attractions, this friendly guest house offers compact, well-equipped bedrooms and a comfortable lounge.

Rooms 5 rms (2 fmly) S £20-£25; D £38-£45 (room only)* **Facilities** FTV TVL tea/coffee Cen ht **Parking** 3 **Notes** LB ⊗ No Children 2yrs 📧

Brier Park Guest House

★★★ GUEST ACCOMMODATION

27 Clee Rd DN35 8AD
☎ 01472 605591
e-mail: graham.sherwood2@ntlworld.com
dir: Left at bottom of Isaac's Hill, 150yds on left

A private house personally managed by the owner offering a friendly atmosphere and comfortable compact bedrooms that are brightly decorated. Breakfast is freshly cooked to order, and convenient parking in front is a bonus.

Rooms 6 rms (3 en suite) (1 fmly) (2 GF) S £20-£25; D £50-£60 (room only)* **Facilities** FTV TVL tea/coffee Cen ht Wi-fi **Parking** 2 **Notes** LB ⊗ No Children 5yrs ⊜

Holmhirst

★★★ GUEST ACCOMMODATION

3 Alexandra Rd DN35 8LQ
☎ 01472 692656 📄 01472 692656

Overlooking the sea and the pier, this Victorian terrace house offers comfortable well-equipped bedrooms, many with showers en suite. Tasty English breakfasts and a range of lunchtime and evening meals are available. There is a well-stocked bar, and the resident owners are fluent in several languages.

Rooms 8 rms (5 en suite) **Facilities** TV7B TVL tea/coffee Dinner available Cen ht Licensed **Notes** ⊗ No Children 4yrs

Ginnies

★★★ 🅰 GUEST ACCOMMODATION

27 Queens Pde DN35 0DF
☎ 01472 694997 📄 01472 593153
e-mail: enquiries@ginnies.co.uk
dir: On A1098 Queens Parade, off seafront Kingsway

Rooms 7 rms (5 en suite) (2 pri facs) (3 fmly) (1 GF); D £40-£70* **Facilities** FTV TVL tea/coffee Cen ht Wi-fi **Parking** 4 **Notes** LB ⊗ RS 24 Dec-2 Jan. Room only 24, 25 & 31 Dec

DONINGTON ON BAIN — Map 17 TF28

The Black Horse Inn

★★★ INN

Main Rd LN11 9TJ
☎ 01507 343640 📄 01507 343640
e-mail: barrett@blackhorse1125.freeserve.co.uk
dir: In village centre

An ideal touring base for the Viking Way, Cadwell Park, and the market towns of Market Rasen and Louth. A wide range of food and beers is available in this popular inn,

and the spacious bedrooms are comfortable and all are en suite.

Rooms 8 en suite (4 GF) **Facilities** tea/coffee Dinner available Cen ht Pool Table **Parking** 60

EPWORTH — Map 17 SE70

Wesley Guest House

★★★★ GUEST ACCOMMODATION

16 Queen St DN9 1HG
☎ 01427 874512 📄 01427 874592
e-mail: enquiries@wesleyguesthouse.com
web: www.wesleyguesthouse.com
dir: In town centre, 200yds off Market Place

Situated near the Market Cross and close to The Old Rectory, this detached guest house offers a friendly welcome, modern, non-smoking en suite rooms, and secure off-road parking. Finningley airport is close by.

Rooms 4 en suite 2 annexe en suite (1 fmly) (1 GF) **Facilities** FTV tea/coffee Cen ht Wi-fi **Parking** 5 **Notes** ⊗

GAINSBOROUGH — Map 17 SK88

See also Marton

Eastbourne House

★★★★ GUEST HOUSE

81 Trinity St DN21 1JF
☎ 01427 679511 📄 01427 679511
e-mail: info@eastbournehouse.co.uk
dir: In town centre. Off A631 onto A159 Trinity St

Located in a residential area west of the town centre, this impressive Victorian house has been restored to provide high standards of comfort and facilities. Bedrooms are thoughtfully furnished and the comprehensive breakfast uses quality local produce.

Rooms 5 rms (3 en suite) (2 pri facs) (1 fmly) S £38-£50; D £50-£70* **Facilities** FTV tea/coffee Cen ht Wi-fi **Parking** 1 **Notes** ⊗

GRANTHAM — Map 11 SK93

PREMIER COLLECTION

La Casita

★★★★★ 🏠 BED AND BREAKFAST

Frith House, Main St NG32 3BH
☎ 01400 250302 & 07836 695282
📄 01400 250302
e-mail: jackiegonzalez@btinternet.com

(For full entry see Normanton)

Belvoir Vale Cottage

★★★★ 🏠 GUEST ACCOMMODATION

Stenwith, Woolsthorpe-By-Belvoir NG32 2HE
☎ 01949 842434
e-mail: reservations@belvoirvale-cottage.co.uk
web: www.belvoirvale-cottage.co.uk
dir: A1/A52 junct towards Nottingham, at Sedgebrook S to Stenwith & Woolsthorpe for 1.5m, immediately past T-junct

This pair of early Victorian cottages is located on the edge of the beautiful Vale of Belvoir with views of the castle. Fully modernised and extended, the cottages retain their character and offer well-appointed accommodation, with crisp cotton sheets, powerful showers and freshly cooked and tasty breakfasts.

Rooms 3 en suite (1 GF) S £50-£75; D £70-£95 **Facilities** tea/coffee Dinner available Cen ht Wi-fi **Parking** 6 **Notes** LB ⊗ No Children 12yrs ⊜

Beechleigh Guest House

★★★★ GUEST HOUSE

55 North Pde NG31 8AT
☎ 01476 572213 📄 01476 566058
e-mail: info@beechleigh.co.uk
web: www.beechleigh.co.uk
dir: 0.5m N of town centre. A52 onto B1174 by Asda, 200yds on left

This Edwardian house sits just a short walk from the town centre on the northern approach. Offering comfortably appointed bedrooms that are equipped with many thoughtful extras including Wi-fi. Freshly cooked breakfasts are taken in the pleasant dining room, and off-road parking is available.

Rooms 3 rms (1 fmly) **Facilities** STV tea/coffee Dinner available Cen ht **Parking** 5 **Notes** No Children 5yrs

The Welby Arms

★★★★ INN

The Green, Allington NG32 2EA
☎ 01400 281361 📄 01400 281361
dir: 4m NW of Grantham. Off A52 into Allington

Set in the pleasant village of Allington, The Welby Arms is just off the busy A1, handy for Grantham but deep in the countryside. There are three purpose built en suite

continued

GRANTHAM *continued*

bedrooms in a former byre behind the village inn. The inn serves a wide range of real ales and an extensive menu that is very popular with locals.

Rooms 3 annexe en suite S £48; D £70* **Facilities** FTV Dinner available Cen ht **Parking** 30 **Notes** ⊗

HEMSWELL   Map 17 SK99

PREMIER COLLECTION

Hemswell Court
★★★★★ ⚑ GUEST ACCOMMODATION

Lancaster Green, Hemswell Cliff DN21 5TQ
☎ 01427 668508 📠 01427 667335
e-mail: function@hemswellcourt.com
dir: *1.5m SE of Hemswell on A631 in Hemswell Cliff*

Originally an officers' mess, Hemswell Court is now a venue for conferences, weddings or private gatherings. The modern bedrooms and many suites are ideal for families or groups of friends, and all rooms are well equipped. The lounges and dining rooms are enhanced by many antique pieces.

Rooms 23 en suite (2 fmly) (4 GF) **Facilities** TV4B TVL tea/coffee Dinner available Cen ht Licensed Wi-fi 🕹️ 🛥️ **Conf** Max 200 Thtr 200 Class 150 Board 150 **Parking** 150 **Notes** ⊗ Closed Xmas & New Year Civ Wed 200

HOLBEACH   Map 12 TF32

The Mansion House
★★★★ GUEST HOUSE

45 High St PE12 7DY
☎ 01406 426919 & 425270 📠 01406 426848
e-mail: rickerby3@aol.com
web: www.holbeachhotels.com
dir: *A17 into Holbeach, at rdbt turn left along High St, on left past church opposite health food shop*

Expect a warm welcome at this delightful period property which dates back to the 16th century. This historic building has been sympathetically restored and retains much of its original character; public rooms include a choice of dining rooms, a cosy lounge and a smart bar. The bedrooms have co-ordinated soft furnishings, stripped pine furniture and modern facilities.

Rooms 8 en suite 1 annexe en suite (3 fmly) (1 GF) S £65-£80; D £77.50-£100* **Facilities** FTV TVL tea/coffee Dinner available Cen ht Licensed Wi-fi Small fitness room **Conf** Max 20 Thtr 20 Class 16 Board 16 **Parking** 5 **Notes** LB RS Xmas-New Year No rest/bar, continental breakfast only

HORNCASTLE   Map 17 TF26

Greenfield Farm *(TF175745)*
★★★★ FARMHOUSE

Mill Ln/Cow Ln, Minting LN9 5PJ
☎ 01507 578457 & 07768 368829
📠 01507 578457 Mrs J Bankes Price
e-mail: info@greenfieldfarm.net
web: www.greenfieldfarm.net
dir: *A158 NW from Horncastle. 5m left at The New Midge pub, farm 1m on right*

Located on the outskirts of Minting village, this impressive red-brick farmhouse has fine views over its gardens across the Lincolnshire countryside. The spacious house offers comfortable en suite bedrooms and a cosy lounge.

Rooms 3 en suite S £38; D £56-£62* **Facilities** TVL tea/coffee Cen ht Wi-fi **Parking** 12 **Notes** LB ⊗ No Children 10yrs Closed Xmas & New Year ⊗ 387 acres arable

HOUGH-ON-THE-HILL   Map 11 SK94

PREMIER COLLECTION

The Brownlow Arms
★★★★★ ⚑ INN

High Rd NG32 2AZ
☎ 01400 250234 📠 01400 271193
e-mail: paulandlorraine@thebrownlowarms.com
web: www.thebrownlowarms.com

This beautiful 16th-century property enjoys a peaceful location in the picturesque village, located between Newark and Grantham. Tastefully appointed and spacious public areas have many original features and include a choice of luxurious lounges and an elegant restaurant offering imaginative cuisine. The bedrooms are stylish, comfortable and particularly well equipped.

Rooms 4 en suite S fr £65; D fr £96 **Facilities** tea/coffee Dinner available Direct Dial **Parking** 20 **Notes** ⊗ No Children 12yrs Closed 25-27 Dec & 31 Dec-20 Jan No coaches

LINCOLN   Map 17 SK97

See also Horncastle, Marton & Swinderby

PREMIER COLLECTION

Bailhouse & Mews
★★★★★ GUEST ACCOMMODATION

34 Bailgate LN1 3AP
☎ 01522 520883 & 07976 112233
📠 01522 521829
e-mail: info@bailhouse.co.uk
dir: *100yds W of cathedral*

This renovated 18th-century building in the cathedral quarter offers high levels of modern comfort. One room has an exposed cruck beam of a surviving 14th-century hall. A private car park surrounds an old chapel, and customer care is of the highest standard.

Rooms 10 en suite (1 fmly) (3 GF) **Facilities** TVL tea/coffee Direct Dial Cen ht Licensed Wi-fi ⚡ **Conf** Max 20 Board 20 **Parking** 15 **Notes** LB ⊗

PREMIER COLLECTION

Charlotte House
★★★★★ GUEST ACCOMMODATION

The Lawn, Union Rd LN1 3BJ
☎ 01522 541000 📠 08718 724396
e-mail: info@charlottehouselincoln.com
web: www.charlottehouselincoln.com

Expect a warm welcome at this 1930s Art Deco building, situated in the cathedral quarter opposite Lincoln Castle. The property has been appointed to a very high standard, and the individually decorated bedrooms are tastefully appointed and thoughtfully equipped. Public areas include an impressive south facing lounge and a large period bar.

Rooms 14 en suite **Facilities** FTV TVL Direct Dial Cen ht Licensed Wi-fi **Conf** Max 100 Thtr 100 Class 60 Board 50 **Parking** 10

PREMIER COLLECTION

Minster Lodge
★★★★★ GUEST ACCOMMODATION

3 Church Ln LN2 1QJ
☎ 01522 513220   📠 01522 513220
e-mail: info@minsterlodge.co.uk
dir: 400yds N of cathedral

A charming house located in a convenient location close to the Cathedral and Castle. Spacious bedrooms are enhanced by newly refurbished bathrooms and are full of thoughtful extras. A large comfortable sitting room with deep sofas and an attractive dining room where enjoyable Aga-cooked breakfasts ensure guests have an memorable stay.

Rooms 6 en suite (3 fmly) S £65-£120; D £75-£120*
Facilities TVL tea/coffee Direct Dial Cen ht Wi-fi
Parking 11 **Notes** LB

See advert on this page

6 Lee Road
★★★★ GUEST ACCOMMODATION

LN2 4BH
☎ 01522 522577
e-mail: carolemann@gmail.com
dir: 0.5m NE of cathedral. Off A15 onto Lee Rd

A private house in a residential suburb, in the cathedral quarter of the city that offers a high level of comfort and careful hospitality. There is off-road parking, and the landscaped gardens offer an oasis of tranquillity, but all the delights of the city are close by.

Rooms 1 en suite; D £60-£90* **Facilities** FTV tea/coffee Cen ht **Parking** 2 **Notes** ⊗ No Children ⊗

Carholme Guest House
★★★★ GUEST HOUSE

175 Carholme Rd LN1 1RU
☎ 01522 531059
e-mail: root@carholmeguesthouse.com
dir: From A1 take A57. From A46 take A57, 0.5m on left after racecourse

Situated a short walk from Lincoln Marina and the university, this small family-run guest house provides well appointed accommodation that is attractively decorated and well maintained, equipped with many useful extras; a ground floor bedroom is available. A freshly cooked breakfast is served in a pleasant dining area and guests have use of a comfortable ground floor lounge.

Rooms 5 rms (4 en suite) (1 pri facs) (1 fmly) (1 GF) S £32-£45; D £52-£65* **Facilities** TVL tea/coffee Cen ht **Parking** 3 **Notes** ⊗ Closed 23 Dec-2 Jan

Carline
★★★★ GUEST HOUSE

1-3 Carline Rd LN1 1HL
☎ 01522 530422   📠 01522 530422
e-mail: sales@carlineguesthouse.co.uk
dir: Left off A1102, A15 N. Premises 1m from A46 bypass & A57 into city

This smart double-fronted Edwardian house is within easy walking distance of the castle and the cathedral. Bedrooms are particularly smartly appointed and have a host of useful extras. Breakfast is served at individual tables in the spacious dining room.

Rooms 9 en suite (1 fmly) (3 GF) S £38-£40; D £58-£60 **Facilities** tea/coffee Cen ht Wi-fi **Parking** 6 **Notes** LB ⊗ No Children 3yrs Closed Xmas & New Year ⊗

Eagles Guest House
★★★★ GUEST ACCOMMODATION

552A Newark Rd, North Hykeham LN6 9NG
☎ 01522 686346
e-mail: eaglesguesthouse@yahoo.co.uk
dir: A46 onto A1434, signed Lincoln south, North Hykeham, South Hykeham, 0.5m on right

This large, modern detached house is situated within easy access of the A46 and the historic city of Lincoln. The smartly appointed, thoughtfully equipped bedrooms are bright and fresh in appearance. A substantial breakfast is served in the pleasant dining room, and free Wi-fi is available throughout the property.

Rooms 5 en suite (1 fmly) (1 GF) S £30-£40; D £45-£62* **Facilities** FTV tea/coffee Cen ht Wi-fi **Parking** 6 **Notes** ⊗ No Children 9yrs

The Loudor
★★★★ GUEST ACCOMMODATION

37 Newark Rd, North Hykeham LN6 8RB
☎ 01522 680333   📠 01522 680403
e-mail: info@loudorhotel.co.uk
dir: 3m from city centre. A46 onto A1434 for 2m, on left opp shopping centre

Originally a private residence, The Loudor offers high quality en suite accommodation in a friendly relaxing atmosphere. With ample parking it is located three miles from Lincoln centre and is within walking distance of shops, pubs and restaurants.

Rooms 9 en suite (1 fmly) S £37; D £52-£54* **Facilities** tea/coffee Cen ht **Parking** 9 **Notes** ⊗ Closed 2wks Xmas & New Year

Minster Lodge
3 Church Lane, Lincoln, LN2 1QJ

Minster Lodge offers high quality facilities, managing to maintain the superb character and charm of the building with all the comforts and conveniences of modern living and personal attention and service.

Set in a fabulous location, just a few steps away from the famous Bailgate and in view of the magnificent Lincoln Cathedral, Minster Lodge is ideally positioned allowing guests instant and easy access to the city centre. An array of quality and unique shops as well as historic buildings and fabulous restaurants are on it's doorstep.

A traditional or continental breakfast is provided; all produce sourced using the finest local producers and the eggs that are laid by our own hens in the garden.

Our 6 en-suite bedrooms, offer high quality beds and bedding for a restful nights sleep. Three offering twin or family occupation.

A luxurious guest lounge is always available as our aim is your complete satisfaction and for you to be delighted with your stay.

So, if you plan to visit Lincoln, please don't hesitate to call Minster Lodge to check on our availability.

The whole lodge is internet/WIFI enabled.

Tel: 01522 513220
Email: info@minsterlodge.co.uk
Website: www.minsterlodge.co.uk

LINCOLN *continued*

The Old Bakery

★★★★ ◉◉ RESTAURANT WITH ROOMS

26/28 Burton Rd LN1 3LB
☎ 01522 576057
e-mail: enquiries@theold-bakery.co.uk
dir: *Exit A46 at Lincoln North follow signs for cathedral. 3rd exit at 1st rdbt, 1st exit at next rdbt*

Situated close to the castle at the top of the town, this converted bakery offers well-equipped bedrooms and a delightful dining operation. The cooking is international and uses much local produce. Expect good friendly service from a dedicated staff.

Rooms 4 rms (2 en suite) (2 pri facs) (1 fmly) S £50; D £53–£63* **Facilities** FTV tea/coffee Dinner available Cen ht Wi-fi **Notes** ⊗

Orchard House

★★★★ GUEST ACCOMMODATION

119 Yarborough Rd LN1 1HR
☎ 01522 528795
e-mail: enquiries@guesthouselincoln.com
dir: *A1 onto A57 into Lincoln, just off A46 bypass*

Close to the shopping centre and cathedral, this detached Edwardian house is situated in immaculate gardens complete with an apple orchard. Bedrooms are well equipped and homely, and the bright, attractive dining room has views out over the valley.

Rooms 5 rms (3 en suite) (2 pri facs) (1 fmly) **Facilities** FTV tea/coffee Cen ht **Parking** 6 **Notes** ⊗ ⊜

St Clements Lodge

★★★★ GUEST ACCOMMODATION

21 Langworth Gate LN2 4AD
☎ 01522 521532   01522 521532
e-mail: enquiries@stclementslodge.co.uk
dir: *350yds E of cathedral, down Eastgate onto Langworth Gate*

An attractive house that is in an ideal location for exploring the cathedral, castle and the exclusive shops. A warm welcome can be expected from hospitable owners. The attractive bedrooms are well equipped with good sized bathrooms. Hearty breakfasts are served in the charming dining room, where you can discuss the day's plans with the helpful proprietors.

Rooms 3 rms (2 en suite) (1 pri facs) (1 fmly) S fr £48; D fr £65 **Facilities** FTV tea/coffee Cen ht Wi-fi **Parking** 3 **Notes** ⊗ ⊜

South Park Guest House

★★★★ GUEST HOUSE

11 South Park LN5 8EN
☎ 01522 887136   01522 887136
e-mail: enquiry@southparkguesthouse.co.uk
dir: *1m S of city centre on A15*

A Victorian house situated on the inner ring road facing South Park. The staff are friendly and attentive, and bedrooms, though compact, are well equipped. Breakfast is served in a modern dining room overlooking the park.

Rooms 6 en suite 1 annexe en suite (2 fmly) (1 GF) S £30–£40; D £48–£55* **Facilities** FTV tea/coffee Dinner available Cen ht Wi-fi **Parking** 7 **Notes** LB ⊗

Stables B&B

★★★★ BED AND BREAKFAST

32 Saxon St LN1 3HQ
☎ 01522 851750
e-mail: info@stablesbandb.com
dir: *A46/A15 to Cathedral, right onto Rasen Ln, 2nd right on Saxon St, then Saint Nicholas St*

A converted Victorian stable in a quiet location with courtyard parking. Near the Cathedral Quarter and restaurants, it makes an ideal choice for relaxing breaks and business visits to Lincoln. Stables offers modern

comfortable bedrooms with Wi-fi. Breakfasts, using local produce, are freshly prepared to order.

Rooms 3 en suite (1 GF) S £40–£85; D £60–£100* **Facilities** tea/coffee Cen ht Wi-fi **Parking** 3 **Notes** ⊗ No Children 10yrs

The Tennyson

★★★★ GUEST HOUSE

7 South Park LN5 8EN
☎ 01522 521624   01522 521355
e-mail: enquiries@thetennyson.com
web: www.thetennyson.com
dir: *S of city centre on A15, near South Park Common*

This smart house is just one mile from the city centre, situated on the ring road overlooking South Park. Bedrooms are attractively appointed and have a host of thoughtful extras. There is a modern lounge and a smart dining room where impressive breakfasts are served.

Rooms 8 en suite S fr £45; D £55* **Facilities** tea/coffee Cen ht Wi-fi **Parking** 8 **Notes** LB ⊗ Closed 24-31 Dec

Westlyn Guest House

★★★★ GUEST HOUSE

67 Carholme Rd LN1 1RT
☎ 01522 537468   01522 537468
e-mail: westlynbblincoln@hotmail.com
dir: *A46 onto A57 to city, Westlyn 1m on left*

This friendly guest house is within easy walking distance of the city centre. The smart bedrooms are comfortably furnished, and public areas include a cosy lounge, a conservatory, and a pleasant dining room where hearty breakfasts are served.

Rooms 4 en suite (3 fmly) S £28–£32; D £48–£52* **Facilities** tea/coffee Cen ht Wi-fi **Parking** 5 **Notes** ⊗ No Children 12yrs ⊜

Newport

★★★ GUEST HOUSE

26-28 Newport Rd LN1 3DF
☎ 01522 528590   01522 542868
e-mail: info@newportguesthouse.com
web: www.newportguesthouse.com
dir: *600mtrs N of cathedral*

Situated in the quieter upper part of the city and just a few minutes' walk from the cathedral, this double-fronted terrace house offers well-equipped and comfortable bedrooms with broadband access. The pleasing public areas include a very comfortable sitting room and a bright and attractive breakfast room.

Rooms 9 en suite (2 GF) S £37–£40; D £55–£60 **Facilities** FTV TVL tea/coffee Cen ht Wi-fi **Parking** 4

Jaymar

★★ GUEST ACCOMMODATION

31 Newland St West LN1 1QQ
☎ 01522 532934 🖷 01522 820182
e-mail: ward.jaymar4@ntlworld.com
dir: A46 onto A57 to city, 1st lights left onto Gresham St, then 2nd right, 500yds on left

Situated within easy walking distance of the city, this small, friendly guest house has two well-equipped bedrooms. A full English breakfast, with vegetarian options, is served in the cosy dining room, and an early breakfast, from 5am onwards, is available on request. Children and pets are welcome, and guests can be collected from the bus or railway stations if required.

Rooms 2 rms (1 fmly) **Facilities** tea/coffee **Notes** 🖸

LOUTH — Map 17 TF38

The Manse B&B

★★★ BED AND BREAKFAST

Middlesykes Ln, Grimoldby LN11 8TE
☎ 01507 327495
e-mail: knowles578@btinternet.com
dir: Grimoldby 4m from Louth on B1200 onto Tinkle St, turn right onto Middlesykes Ln

Located in a quiet country lane, this pleasantly appointed house offers comfortable accommodation and a warm welcome. The enthusiastic and helpful proprietors make every effort to ensure guests feel welcome at their home; freshly cooked evening meals are available by prior arrangement. This makes an ideal location for exploring the delights of The Wolds.

Rooms 4 rms (3 en suite) (1 pri facs) (1 fmly) (1 GF)
S £40-£45; D £55-£65* **Facilities** TVL tea/coffee Dinner available Cen ht Wi-fi **Parking** 5 **Notes** LB 🖾 No Children 5yrs Closed 25 Dec 🖸

MABLETHORPE — Map 17 TF58

Park View Guest House

★★★ GUEST HOUSE

48 Gibraltar Rd LN12 2AT
☎ 01507 477267 🖷 01507 477267
e-mail: malcolm@pvgh.freeserve.co.uk
dir: Take A1104, at beach turn right onto Gibraltar Rd

This well-established guest house is ideally situated just beside Mablethorpe's golden beach and the Queens Park, and also within easy walking distance of the main town centre amenities. Service is both helpful and friendly, provided by the resident proprietors, Debbie and Malcolm. The accommodation is soundly presented and of varying sizes, the ground-floor bedrooms proving particularly popular.

Rooms 5 rms (2 en suite) (1 fmly) (3 GF) S £22.50; D £45-£50* **Facilities** TVL tea/coffee Dinner available Cen ht Licensed **Parking** 6 **Notes** LB 🖸

MARKET RASEN — Map 17 TF18

PREMIER COLLECTION

Blaven

★★★★★ BED AND BREAKFAST

Walesby Hill, Walesby LN8 3UW
☎ 01673 838352
e-mail: blavenhouse@hotmail.com
dir: A46 Market Rasen to Grimsby, right at junct with A1103, left at T-junct, Blaven 100yds on right

On the edge of the village of Walesby, this smart house offers warm hospitality and comfortable en suite bedrooms. Freshly prepared breakfasts are served around one table in the dining room, while a large conservatory-lounge overlooks immaculate gardens.

Rooms 3 rms (2 en suite) (1 pri facs) S £45; D £60* **Facilities** TVL tea/coffee Cen ht **Parking** 4 **Notes** 🖾 No Children 10yrs Closed Xmas & New Year 🖸

Chuck Hatch

★★★★ BED AND BREAKFAST

Kingerby Rd, West Rasen LN8 3NB
☎ 01673 842947 & 07745 288463 🖷 01673 842947
e-mail: info@chuckhatch.co.uk
dir: A631 West Rasen follow signs Osgodby & North Owersby, house 0.5m on left

Built in 1780, Chuck Hatch stands in grounds in peaceful open countryside. The en suite bedrooms are individually styled and well equipped. Public rooms include a lounge and a delightful breakfast room, which looks out over the lake and grounds beyond. Smoking is not permitted in the house.

Rooms 4 en suite S £40-£70; D £70-£80* **Facilities** TVL tea/coffee Cen ht Fishing **Parking** 6 **Notes** LB 🖾 No Children 16yrs 🖸

Wold View House B&B

★★★ BED AND BREAKFAST

Bully Hill Top, Tealby LN8 6JA
☎ 01673 838226 🖷 01673 838226
e-mail: irene@woldviewhouse.co.uk
dir: A46 onto B1225 towards Horncastle, after 7m Wold View House at x-rds

Situated at the top of Bully Hill with expansive views across The Wold, this smart teashop with guest house offers modern bedrooms and warm hospitality. Ideal for walking, riding, or touring the charming nearby villages and coastline, the house is also only a short drive from Lincoln.

Rooms 3 rms (1 en suite) S £35-£40; D £65-£68* **Facilities** TVL tea/coffee Dinner available Cen ht Licensed Wi-fi **Parking** 15 **Notes** LB 🖸

MARTON (VILLAGE) — Map 17 SK88

Black Swan Guest House

★★★★ GUEST ACCOMMODATION

21 High St DN21 5AH
☎ 01427 718878
e-mail: info@blackswanguesthouse.co.uk
web: www.blackswanguesthouse.co.uk
dir: On A156 in village centre at junct A1500

Centrally located in the village, this 18th-century former coaching inn retains many original features, and offers good hospitality and homely bedrooms with modern facilities. Tasty breakfasts are served in the cosy dining room and a comfortable lounge with Wi-fi access is available. Transport to nearby pubs and restaurants can be provided.

Rooms 6 en suite 4 annexe en suite (3 fmly) (4 GF) S £45; D £68 **Facilities** FTV TVL tea/coffee Cen ht Licensed Wi-fi **Parking** 10 **Notes** LB

NORMANTON | Map 11 SK94

PREMIER COLLECTION

La Casita
★★★★★ BED AND BREAKFAST

Frith House, Main St NG32 3BH
☎ 01400 250302 & 07836 695282
📠 01400 250302
e-mail: jackiegonzalez@btinternet.com
web: www.lacasitabandb.co.uk
dir: In village centre on A607

A self-contained one bedroom family suite (can sleep four) built in the gated gardens of the owners' house. Furnished to a high standard and with many extras offering both comfort and luxury, the owners give careful service.

Rooms 1 annexe en suite (1 fmly) (1 GF) S £95; D £125 **Facilities** STV FTV TVL tea/coffee Direct Dial Cen ht Wi-fi **Parking** 3 **Notes** LB ⊗

SKEGNESS | Map 17 TF56

Sunnyside B&B
★★★ GUEST ACCOMMODATION

34 Scarborough Ave PE25 2TA
☎ 01754 765119
e-mail: form@skegness-accommodation.co.uk
dir: From A52 or A158 follow signs for seafront. Scarborough Ave opposite pier, Sunnyside on left before church

Ideally situated in a quiet avenue that is close to Skegness Pier and the northern promenade. The bedrooms are pleasantly decorated and have a good range of useful facilities such as fridges, freeview TV and DVD players. Breakfast is served at individual tables in the breakfast room and guests also have the use of a conservatory.

Rooms 8 en suite (2 fmly) (1 GF) S £25-£30; D £50* **Facilities** FTV TVL tea/coffee Cen ht **Parking** 4 **Notes** LB ⊗ RS Nov-Feb (ex New Year) open wknds only

The Cottage Restaurant
★★★ ⓐ GUEST ACCOMMODATION

Croft Bank PE24 4RE
☎ 01754 762890
e-mail: info@thecottageghcroft.co.uk
Rooms 2 en suite S £40-£60; D £50-£70 **Facilities** tea/coffee Dinner available Cen ht Licensed Wi-fi **Parking** 30 **Notes** ⊗

SKILLINGTON | Map 11 SK82

The Cross Swords Inn
★★★ INN

The Square NG33 5HB
☎ 01476 861132
e-mail: harold@thecross-swordsinn.co.uk
dir: Between Grantham & Stamford, W off A1 at Colsterworth rdbt

Located at the crossroads at the centre of the award-winning village of Skillington, and very popular with the local community, this traditional inn offers three modern, well-equipped bedrooms that are housed in an attractive cottage at the top of the courtyard, and named in keeping with the history of the village. All are very comfortable and have smart modern bathrooms. The inn provides imaginative food and a range of real ales in a rustic period atmosphere.

Rooms 3 annexe en suite (3 GF) S £45-£60; D £58-£78 **Facilities** FTV tea/coffee Dinner available Cen ht **Parking** 12 **Notes** ⊗ No Children 10yrs RS Sun & Mon bar and restaurant closed

STAMFORD | Map 11 TF00

PREMIER COLLECTION

Rock Lodge
★★★★★ GUEST ACCOMMODATION

1 Empingham Rd PE9 2RH
☎ 01780 481758 📠 01780 481757
e-mail: rocklodge@innpro.co.uk
dir: Off A1 at A606 signed Oakham, into Stamford, Rock Lodge 1.25m on left

Philip and Jane Sagar have considerable experience in managing luxury hotels and offer a warm welcome to their imposing 1900 house near the town centre. The attractive bedrooms are individually furnished and have a good range of facilities. Character public rooms include the oak-panelled drawing room with mullion windows. Breakfast is served in a sunny room overlooking the gardens.

Rooms 6 en suite (1 fmly) (2 GF) S £68-£82; D £84-£100* **Facilities** STV FTV TVL tea/coffee Cen ht Wi-fi **Parking** 7 **Notes** ⊗

Candlesticks
★★★ RESTAURANT WITH ROOMS

1 Church Ln PE9 2JU
☎ 01780 764033 📠 01780 756071
e-mail: info@candlestickshotel.co.uk
dir: On B1081 High Street St Martins. Church Ln opposite St Martin Church

A 17th-century property situated in a quite lane in the oldest part of Stamford just a short walk from the centre of town. The bedrooms are pleasantly decorated and equipped with a good range of useful extras. Public rooms feature Candlesticks restaurant, a small lounge and a cosy bar.

Rooms 8 en suite S £50-£75; D £65-£85* **Facilities** STV FTV tea/coffee Dinner available Direct Dial Cen ht **Parking** 8 **Notes** LB ⊗ RS No restaurant or bar service Mon No coaches

SUTTON ON SEA | Map 17 TF58

Athelstone Lodge
★★★ GUEST ACCOMMODATION

25 Trusthorpe Rd LN12 2LR
☎ 01507 441521
dir: On A52, N of village

Situated between Mablethorpe and Skegness and close to the promenade, Athelstone Lodge has pleasant, soundly maintained bedrooms equipped with many useful extras. Breakfast is served in the dining room and a bar and a lounge are also available. A variety of enjoyable home-cooked dinners is served.

Rooms 6 rms (5 en suite) (1 fmly) S £28-£30; D £56-£60* **Facilities** TVL tea/coffee Dinner available Cen ht Licensed **Parking** 6 **Notes** LB Closed Nov-Feb

SWINDERBY | Map 17 SK86

Halfway Farm Motel
★★★ GUEST ACCOMMODATION

Newark Road (A46) LN6 9HN
☎ 01522 868749 📠 01522 868082
e-mail: halfwayfarmmotel@hotmail.com
web: www.halfway-farm-motel.co.uk
dir: On A46 opp Swinderby rbt

This 300-year-old farmhouse is set back from the A46, midway between Lincoln and Newark. Spacious bedrooms are traditional in the main house, while motel-style rooms are located around a courtyard to the rear. There is a bright, airy dining room and comfortable lounge. A good base for touring or antique hunting.

Rooms 6 rms (5 en suite) 10 annexe en suite (1 fmly) (13 GF) **Facilities** tea/coffee Direct Dial Cen ht **Conf** Max 30 **Parking** 25 **Notes** ⊗ RS Dec-Jan

TIMBERLAND   Map 17 TF15

The Penny Farthing

★★★★ INN

Station Rd LN4 3SA
☎ 01526 378359
e-mail: pennyfarthing@talktalkbusiness.net
dir: Junct of B1191 & B1189, signed 1m to Timberland

A warm welcome awaits at this charming inn situated in the heart of a delightful Lincolnshire village. Public areas include a large open plan lounge/bar/dining area as well as an additional restaurant to the front of the property. The bedrooms are tastefully decorated and thoughtfully equipped with a good range of useful facilities.

Rooms 7 en suite (1 fmly) S £55; D £70* **Facilities** FTV tea/coffee Dinner available Cen ht Wi-fi **Parking** 12

WHAPLODE   Map 12 TF32

Westgate House & Barn

★★★★ BED AND BREAKFAST

Little Ln PE12 6RU
☎ 01406 370546
e-mail: enquiries@westgatehousebandb.co.uk
web: www.westgatehousebandb.co.uk
dir: Follow brown signs in Whaplode (on A151)

Located in a peaceful rural location, in well-established cottage gardens and grounds, Westgate House offers comfortably appointed accommodation in a delightful barn conversion. Breakfast is taken in the main house, in a charming room with wood-burning stove and garden views. The freshly cooked breakfast includes good locally sourced ingredients and homemade preserves.

Rooms 2 annexe en suite **Facilities** tea/coffee Cen ht **Parking** 2 **Notes** LB ⊗ ⊠

WINTERINGHAM   Map 17 SE92

PREMIER COLLECTION

Winteringham Fields
★★★★★ ◉◉◉ RESTAURANT WITH ROOMS

DN15 9PF
☎ 01724 733096   📠 01724 733898
e-mail: wintfields@aol.com
dir: In village centre at x-rds

This highly regarded restaurant with rooms, located deep in the countryside in Winteringham village, is six miles west of the Humber Bridge. Public rooms and bedrooms, some of which are housed in renovated barns and cottages, are delightfully cosseting. Award-winning food is available in the restaurant.

Rooms 4 en suite 6 annexe en suite (3 GF) **Facilities** tea/coffee Dinner available Direct Dial Cen ht courtyard bedrooms recommended **Conf** Max 50 Thtr 50 Class 50 Board 50 **Parking** 14 **Notes** LB Closed 25 Dec for 2 wks, last wk Oct, 2 wks Aug No coaches

WOODHALL SPA   Map 17 TF16

Claremont Guest House

Ⓤ

9/11 Witham Rd LN10 6RW
☎ 01526 352000
web:
www.woodhall-spa-guesthouse-bedandbreakfast.co.uk
dir: In town centre on B1191 near mini-rdbt

Currently the rating for this establishment is not confirmed. This may be due to a change of ownership or because it has only recently joined the AA rating scheme.

Rooms 11 rms (5 en suite) (4 pri facs) (5 fmly) (2 GF) S fr £30; D fr £60* **Facilities** FTV tea/coffee Wi-fi 🏊 **Parking** 5 **Notes** LB

WOOLSTHORPE   Map 11 SK83

The Chequers Inn

★★★★ ◉ INN

Main St NG32 1LU
☎ 01476 870701   📠 01476 870085
e-mail: justinnabar@yahoo.co.uk
dir: In village opp Post Office

A 17th-century coaching inn set in the lee of Belvoir Castle next to the village cricket pitch and having its own pétanque pitch. Exposed beams, open fireplaces and original stone and brickwork, with 24 wines by the glass, a gastro menu, and real ales. Comfortable bedrooms are in the former stable block.

Rooms 4 annexe en suite (1 fmly) (3 GF) **Facilities** TVL tea/coffee Dinner available Cen ht **Conf** Max 80 Thtr 80 Class 50 Board 25 **Parking** 40

LONDON

N1

Kandara PLAN 1 F4

★★★ 🅰 BED AND BREAKFAST

68 Ockendon Rd N1 3NW
☎ 020 7226 5721   📠 020 7226 3379
e-mail: admin@kandara.co.uk
dir: At Highbury corner rdbt on A1 onto St Pauls Rd for 0.5m, right at junct onto Essex Rd, Ockendon Rd 5th left

Rooms 10 rms 2 annexe rms (4 fmly) (2 GF) S £47-£63; D £67-£83* **Facilities** FTV tea/coffee Cen ht **Notes** ⊗ Closed 23-27 Dec

N4

Mount View PLAN 1 F5

★★★★ GUEST HOUSE

31 Mount View Rd N4 4SS
☎ 020 8340 9222
e-mail: info@mountviewguesthouse.com
dir: Off A1201 Crouch Hill in Crouch End

This delightful Victorian house is in a quiet, tree-lined residential area with good transport links to the City and the West End. The bedrooms and public areas are carefully furnished and facilities include a washing machine and access to the internet. Well-prepared breakfasts are served at a large communal table and the resident owners provide very friendly hospitality.

Rooms 3 rms (2 en suite) **Facilities** tea/coffee Cen ht Wi-fi **Notes** ⊗

N4 *continued*

Ossian House PLAN 1 F5

★★★ BED AND BREAKFAST

20 Ossian Rd N4 4EA
☎ 020 8340 4331 📄 020 8340 4331
e-mail: ann@ossianguesthouse.co.uk
web: www.ossianguesthouse.co.uk
dir: *Off A1201 Crouch Hill onto Mount View Rd, 1st right down hill, 1st left*

This pleasant guest house is in a quiet location north of the city. Bedrooms are stylishly furnished, with a very good range of facilities and accessories. Breakfast is served round one large table in the attractive dining room.

Rooms 3 en suite Facilities TVL tea/coffee Cen ht Notes ✪ ➡

N8

White Lodge PLAN 1 F5

★★★ GUEST ACCOMMODATION

1 Church Ln, Hornsey N8 7BU
☎ 020 8348 9765 📄 020 8340 7851
e-mail: info@whitelodgehornsey.co.uk
web: www.whitelodgehornsey.co.uk
dir: *A406 to Bounds Green, Hornsey High Rd & Church Ln*

This well-maintained, friendly guest house is in a convenient location close to shops and restaurants. Bedrooms are traditionally appointed and airy public areas include an attractive lounge and spacious dining room where continental breakfast is served.

Rooms 16 rms (8 en suite) (5 fmly) (1 GF) Facilities tea/coffee Cen ht Wi-fi Notes ✪

N12

Glenlyn Guest House PLAN 1 E6

★★★ GUEST ACCOMMODATION

6 Woodside Park Rd N12 8RP
☎ 020 8445 0440 📄 020 8446 2902
e-mail: contactus@glenlynhotel.com
web: www.glenlynhotel.com
dir: *M25 junct 23 towards High Barnet, A1000 into North Finchley on right after Sainsburys*

Located in the heart of Finchley and set in four large Victorian terraced houses, the Glenlyn offers a choice of rooms spanning from cosy loft rooms to interconnecting

family rooms. Guests can relax in the private bar or unwind in the garden. Breakfast is served in the airy conservatory.

Glenlyn Guest House

Rooms 27 en suite (4 fmly) (3 GF) S £65; D £75*
Facilities FTV TVL tea/coffee Direct Dial Cen ht Licensed Wi-fi Parking 14 Notes ✪

NW1

MIC Conferences and Accommodation

PLAN 2 D5

★★★★ 🍴 GUEST ACCOMMODATION

81-103 Euston St NW1 2EZ
☎ 020 7380 0001 📄 020 7387 5300
e-mail: sales@micentre.com
web: www.micentre.com
dir: *Euston Rd left at lights onto Melton St, 1st left onto Euston St, MIC 100yds on left*

Located within walking distance of Euston station, this smart property is convenient for central London. Stylish air-conditioned bedrooms are thoughtfully equipped for business and leisure. The airy Atrium Bar and Restaurant offers drinks, light snacks and an evening menu. Extensive conference and meeting facilities are available.

Rooms 28 en suite (2 fmly) S £93-£150;
D £105.50-£150* Facilities STV TVL tea/coffee Dinner available Direct Dial Cen ht Lift Licensed Wi-fi Conf Max 150 Thtr 150 Class 50 Board 45 Notes LB ✪

Euston Square PLAN 2 C5

★★★ GUEST ACCOMMODATION

152-156 North Gower St NW1 2LU
☎ 020 7388 0099 📄 020 7788 9699
e-mail: reservations@euston-square-hotel.com
web: www.euston-square-hotel.com
dir: *On junct Euston Rd, next to Euston Sq tube station*

Over the tube station, this property is ideal for both the business and leisure markets. The smart compact bedrooms and en suite bathrooms are well designed. Small conference facilities and a modern reception area are available. Breakfast and light meals are served in the bar lounge area, FAB.

Rooms 75 en suite (4 GF) Facilities STV TVL tea/coffee Dinner available Direct Dial Cen ht Lift Licensed Wi-fi Conf Thtr 120 Class 50 Board 50 Notes LB ✪

NW3

The Langorf PLAN 2 E5

★★★★ GUEST ACCOMMODATION

20 Frognal, Hampstead NW3 6AG
☎ 020 7794 4483 📄 020 7435 9055
e-mail: info@langorfhotel.com
web: www.langorfhotel.com
dir: *Off A41 (Finchley Rd), near Finchley Rd tube station*

Located on a leafy and mainly residential avenue within easy walking distance of shops and restaurants, this elegant Edwardian property has been appointed to provide high standards of comfort and facilities. Bedrooms are furnished with flair and a warm welcome is assured.

Rooms 31 en suite (4 fmly) (3 GF) S £55-£82;
D £59-£110* Facilities STV TVL tea/coffee Direct Dial Cen ht Lift Licensed Wi-fi Conf Max 30 Thtr 30 Class 20 Board 15 Parking Notes LB ✪

La Gaffe PLAN 2 E5

★★★ GUEST ACCOMMODATION

107-111 Heath St NW3 6SS
☎ 020 7435 4941 & 7435 8965 📄 020 7794 7592
e-mail: info@lagaffe.co.uk
dir: On A502, 250yds N of Hampstead tube station

This family owned and run guest house, just north of Hampstead High Street, offers charm and warm hospitality. The Italian restaurant, which is open most lunchtimes for dinner, is popular with locals. Bedrooms are compact, but all are en suite.

Rooms 11 en suite 7 annexe en suite (2 fmly) (2 GF) S £70-£100; D £95-£125* **Facilities** FTV tea/coffee Dinner available Direct Dial Cen ht Licensed Wi-fi **Conf** Max 10 Board 10 **Notes** ⊗ RS 26 Dec Restaurant closed

NW8

The New Inn PLAN 1 E4

★★★ INN

2 Allitsen Rd, St Johns Wood NW8 6LA
☎ 020 7722 0726 📄 020 7722 0653
e-mail: thenewinn@gmail.com
web: www.newinnlondon.co.uk
dir: Off A41 by St Johns Wood tube station onto Acacia Rd, last right, to end on corner

Built in 1810, this popular inn is in a leafy suburb only a stroll from Regents Park. Bedrooms are appointed to a high standard, while Thai cuisine and traditional fare are offered in the atmospheric bar lounge.

Rooms 5 en suite S £80; D £80 (room only) **Facilities** FTV tea/coffee Dinner available Cen ht Wi-fi **Notes** ⊗ No coaches

NW9

Kingsland PLAN 1 C5

★★★ GUEST ACCOMMODATION

Kingsbury Circle, Kingsbury NW9 9RR
☎ 020 8206 0666 📄 020 8206 0555
e-mail: stay@kingslandhotel.co.uk
web: www.kingslandhotel.co.uk
dir: Kingsbury Circle junct A4006 & A4140

Located at the roundabout near Kingsbury Station, shops, restaurants and Wembley complex, the Kingsland provides modern bedrooms with smart bathrooms en suite. A continental breakfast is supplied, and a passenger lift and car park are available.

Rooms 28 en suite (5 fmly) (6 GF) S £50-£55; D £55-£65 **Facilities** STV tea/coffee Direct Dial Cen ht Lift Wi-fi **Parking** 30 **Notes** ⊗

SW1

Best Western Corona PLAN 2 D1

★★★★ GUEST ACCOMMODATION

87-89 Belgrave Rd SW1V 2BQ
☎ 020 7828 9279 📄 020 7931 8576
e-mail: info@coronahotel.co.uk
dir: From Pimlico St take exit 2 onto Tachbrook St. Make 1st left, 1st right onto Belgrave Rd

Centrally located, this elegant Victorian property is appointed to a high standard. The smart, well-equipped bedrooms offer comfortable, modern accommodation. A continental breakfast is served in the basement dining room, and room service is also available.

Rooms 51 en suite (8 fmly) (7 GF) S £65-£105; D £75-£125 **Facilities** STV tea/coffee Direct Dial Lift Wi-fi **Notes** LB ⊗

Sidney London-Victoria PLAN 2 C1

★★★★ GUEST ACCOMMODATION

68-76 Belgrave Rd SW1V 2BP
☎ 020 7834 2738 📄 020 7630 0973
e-mail: reservations@sidneyhotel.com
web: www.sidneyhotel.com
dir: A202 (Vauxhall Bridge Rd) onto Charlwood St & junct with Belgrave Rd

This smart property near Pimlico offers brightly decorated bedrooms that are well equipped for business use, while several rooms are suitable for families. Public areas include a bar lounge and an airy breakfast room.

Rooms 82 en suite (13 fmly) (9 GF) **Facilities** STV TVL tea/coffee Direct Dial Cen ht Lift Licensed Wi-fi **Conf** Thtr 30 Class 25 Board 14 **Notes** ⊗

See advert on page 239

The Windermere PLAN 2 C1

★★★★ GUEST ACCOMMODATION

142/144 Warwick Way, Victoria SW1V 4JE
☎ 020 7834 5163 📄 020 7630 8831
e-mail: reservations@windermere-hotel.co.uk
web: www.windermere-hotel.co.uk
dir: On B324 off Buckingham Palace Rd, at junct with Alderney St

The Windermere is a relaxed, informal and family-run establishment within easy reach of Victoria Station and many of the capital's attractions. Bedrooms, although varying in size, are stylish, comfortable and well equipped. The Pimlico restaurant serves delicious evening meals and hearty cooked breakfasts.

Rooms 20 en suite (3 fmly) (3 GF) S £99; D £124-£155* **Facilities** FTV TVL tea/coffee Dinner available Direct Dial Cen ht Licensed Wi-fi **Conf** Max 20 **Notes** ⊗

Best Western Victoria Palace PLAN 2 C1

★★★ GUEST ACCOMMODATION

60-64 Warwick Way SW1V 1SA
☎ 020 7821 7113 📄 020 7630 0806
e-mail: info@bestwesternvictoriapalace.co.uk
web: www.bestwesternvictoriapalace.co.uk

An elegant, 19th-century building located in the heart of London, near to Belgravia and a five minute walk from Victoria rail, underground and coach stations. The bedrooms, have en suite shower rooms. A buffet-style breakfast is served in the basement dining room.

Rooms 50 en suite (4 fmly) (4 GF) **Facilities** STV TVL tea/coffee Direct Dial Cen ht Lift **Notes** ⊗

SW1 *continued*

Central House PLAN 2 D1

★★★ GUEST ACCOMMODATION

39 Belgrave Rd SW1V 2BB
☎ 020 7834 8036 📠 020 7834 1854
e-mail: info@centralhousehotel.co.uk
dir: *Near Victoria station*

Located a short walk from Victoria station, the Central House offers sound accommodation. Bedroom sizes vary, and each room is suitably appointed, with en suite, compact, modular shower rooms. A self-service continental breakfast is offered in the lower ground-floor dining room.

Rooms 54 en suite (4 fmly) **Facilities** TVL tea/coffee Direct Dial Cen ht Lift

Comfort Inn PLAN 2 C1

★★★ GUEST ACCOMMODATION

8-12 St Georges Dr SW1V 4BJ
☎ 020 7834 2988 📠 020 7821 5814
e-mail: info@comfortinnbuckinghampalacerd.co.uk
dir: *Off Buckingham Palace Rd onto Elizabeth Bridge & St Georges Dr*

Located just a short walk south from Victoria station, this establishment is a good base for visiting the capital's attractions. All bedrooms and public areas are smartly appointed and offer very good levels of comfort. An extensive continental breakfast is served.

Rooms 51 en suite (4 fmly) (7 GF) **Facilities** STV TVL tea/coffee Direct Dial Cen ht Lift **Conf** Max 20 Thtr 20 Class 20 Board 20 **Notes** ⊗

Comfort Inn Victoria PLAN 2 C1

★★★ GUEST ACCOMMODATION

18-24 Belgrave Rd, Victoria SW1V 1QF
☎ 020 7233 6636 📠 020 7932 0538
e-mail: stay@comfortinnvictoria.co.uk

Having a prime location close to Victoria station, this property offers brightly appointed en suite accommodation that is thoughtfully equipped for

business and leisure guests. A continental breakfast is offered in the basement dining room.

Rooms 48 en suite (16 fmly) (9 GF) S £49-£159; D £59-£179* **Facilities** STV FTV TVL tea/coffee Direct Dial Cen ht Lift Wi-fi **Notes** ⊗

Elizabeth PLAN 2 C1

★★★ GUEST ACCOMMODATION

37 Eccleston Square SW1V 1PB
☎ 020 7828 6812 📠 020 7828 6814
e-mail: info@elizabethhotel.com
web: www.elizabethhotel.com
dir: *500yds S of Victoria station. Off A3213 Belgrave Rd onto Eccleston Sq*

This friendly, well-run property is just a short walk from Victoria Station and within easy reach of central London attractions. The well-equipped bedrooms include some spacious apartments ideal for families.

Rooms 43 rms (39 en suite) (10 fmly) (4 GF) S £79-£99; D £99-£129* **Facilities** tea/coffee Direct Dial Cen ht Lift Wi-fi **Notes** ⊗

Victoria Inn PLAN 2 C1

★★★ GUEST HOUSE

65-67 Belgrave Rd, Victoria SW1V 2BG
☎ 020 7834 6721 & 7834 0182 📠 020 7931 0201
e-mail: welcome@victoriainn.co.uk
web: www.victoriainn.co.uk
dir: *On A3213, 0.4m SE of Victoria station, near Pimlico tube station*

A short walk from Victoria station, this Victorian property offers modern, well-equipped accommodation for business and leisure guests. There is a comfortable reception lounge, and a limited self-service buffet breakfast is available in the basement breakfast room.

Rooms 43 en suite (7 fmly) S £49-£69; D £59-£89 **Facilities** STV tea/coffee Direct Dial Cen ht Lift Wi-fi **Notes** LB ⊗

Winchester PLAN 2 C1

★★★ GUEST ACCOMMODATION

17 Belgrave Rd SW1V 1RB
☎ 020 7828 2972 📠 020 7828 5191
e-mail: info@winchester-hotel.net
web: www.winchester-hotel.net
dir: *On A3213, 300yds SE of Victoria station*

Conveniently located close to Victoria this welcoming, well maintained house provides an ideal base for tourists. Bedrooms vary in size and style but all are well equipped, decorated in bright colours and boast comfortable modern beds. Freshly cooked breakfasts are served in the traditionally styled dining room. Staff are friendly and keen to please.

Rooms 19 en suite (2 fmly) (2 GF) **Facilities** STV tea/coffee Direct Dial Cen ht **Notes** ⊗ No Children 5yrs

Stanley House PLAN 2 C1

★★ 🅰 BED AND BREAKFAST

19-21 Belgrave Rd, Victoria SW1V 1RB
☎ 020 7834 5042 & 7834 7292 📠 020 7834 8439
e-mail: cmahotel@aol.com
web: www.londonbudgethotels.co.uk
dir: *Near Victoria station*

Rooms 44 rms (41 en suite) (7 fmly) (8 GF) S £45-£55; D £55-£65 **Facilities** FTV TVL Direct Dial Cen ht Wi-fi **Notes** LB ⊗ No Children 5yrs

---

SW3

PREMIER COLLECTION

San Domenico House PLAN 2 B1

★★★★★ GUEST ACCOMMODATION

29-31 Draycott Place SW3 2SH
☎ 020 7581 5757 📠 020 7584 1348
e-mail: info@sandomenicohouse.com

This stunning property in the heart of Chelsea offers beautifully individually styled bedrooms, all with antique and period pieces, and well appointed en suites complete with Italian Spa toiletries. A sumptuous drawing room with wonderful works of art is available for guests to relax in or maybe to enjoy afternoon tea. Breakfast is served either to guests' bedrooms or in the lower ground floor elegant dining room. Staff are friendly and attentive. San Domenico House was the winner of the AA London B&B of the Year 2008-2009.

Rooms 15 en suite (9 smoking) S £210-£360; D £235-£360 (room only)* **Facilities** STV Direct Dial Cen ht Lift Licensed **Notes** ⊗

Sidney
— LONDON-VICTORIA —

YOUR ADDRESS IN LONDON

Formed from the amalgamation of five, six storey townhouses, an elegant grade II listed Victorian structure is a favourite haunt of tourists from both home & abroad & a preferred base for business men & women with reasonably priced accommodation which ensures that many guests return on a regular basis.

Within a small radius, London's historical landmarks such as Big Ben and The Houses of Parliament jostle with modern day celebrated attractions like the London Eye and London Aquarium whilst the theatre district of the 'West-End' is just a short distance away.

Ideal central location (close to Victoria & Pimlico Coach, Rail & Underground Station(s), the London Waterloo (Eurostar) International Terminal & all major international airports provides a direct link to central London, the UK, Europe & rest of the World.

♦ 82 comfortable ensuite bedrooms with modern amenities
♦ Non-smoking rooms (available upon request)
♦ Complimentary full English buffet breakfast
♦ Two passenger elevators
♦ Refurbished Reception, Lounge & Bar
♦ Refurbished Brasserie (breakfast service only)

♦ Limited business services & high speed internet access
♦ Newly refurbished small Business Centre
♦ Newly refurbished Conference/Meeting rooms & facilities
♦ Enticing array of restaurants within minutes walking distance
♦ Easy access to public transportation
♦ Assistance with arrangements / tickets / tours / excursions / travel

68-76 Belgrave Road | Victoria | London SW1V 2BP | United Kingdom | **W** http://www.SidneyHotel.com
T +44 (0)20 7834-2738 | **F** +44 (0)20 7630-0973 | **E** info@SidneyHotel.com

Best Western
The Boltons

The newly refurbished Best Western The Boltons is located in the heart of London's fashionable Earls Court and is within walking distance of the Earls Court Exhibition Centre, Olympia Exhibition Centre and the Commonwealth Institute. By tube, the hotel is minutes away from the West End, Knightsbridge and London's vibrant nightlife. The Best Western The Boltons boasts 57 fully air-conditioned rooms with flat screen televisions, freeview, Wi-Fi internet access and 24 hour room service.

19–21 Penywern Road, Earls Court,
London, SW5 9TT
Telephone: +44 (0) 207 373 8900
Fax: +44 (0) 207 244 6835
Email: reservations@theboltonshotel.co.uk
Web: www.theboltonshotel.co.uk

SW5

Best Western The Boltons PLAN 1 D3

★★★★ GUEST ACCOMMODATION

19-21 Penywren Rd, Earls Court SW5 9TT
☎ 020 7373 8900 ▤ 020 7244 8835
e-mail: reservations@theboltonshotel.co.uk
dir: A3220 from Cromwell Rd, follow road past Earls Court station, 1st right into Penywern Rd. Located on left

This smart, newly renovated property boasts an excellent location, just seconds walk from Earls Court tube station and exhibition centre, and with easy reach of museums and major shopping areas. Both public areas and bedrooms have an airy contemporary feel with stylish furnishings and fittings. En suite bedrooms have comfy beds, flat-screen satellite TV and Wi-fi. 24-hour room service and buffet breakfast are available.

Rooms 57 en suite (5 fmly) (5 GF) Facilities STV FTV tea/coffee Direct Dial Lift Wi-fi Notes ⊗

See advert on page 239

Best Western Shaftesbury Kensington

PLAN 1 D3

★★★★ GUEST ACCOMMODATION

33-37 Hogarth Rd, Kensington SW5 0QQ
☎ 020 7370 6831 ▤ 020 7373 6179

Well appointed to a high standard, this property has a smart modern feel and is conveniently located for the exhibition centre, the West End and local transport links. Bedrooms are furnished and decorated to a very high standard, offering guests a comprehensive range of modern facilities and amenities.

Rooms 133 en suite (7 GF) Facilities STV tea/coffee Direct Dial Cen ht Lift Licensed Gymnasium Conf Max 15 Board 15 Notes ⊗

The Mayflower PLAN 1 D3

★★★★ GUEST ACCOMMODATION

26-28 Trebovir Rd SW5 9NJ
☎ 020 7370 0991 ▤ 020 7370 0994
e-mail: info@mayflower-group.co.uk
web: www.mayflowerhotel.co.uk
dir: Left from Earls Court tube station & 1st left into Trebovir Rd, premises on left

This smart guest house is a short walk from Earls Court, and close to Olympia and West London's museums and attractions. Stylish, individually designed bedrooms vary in size but all are extremely well equipped and have smart, modern en suites. There is a comfortable, stylish lounge and an airy dining room where breakfast is served.

Rooms 47 en suite (4 fmly) (5 GF) Facilities STV FTV tea/coffee Direct Dial Cen ht Lift Wi-fi Conf Max 25 Class 25 Board 25 Parking 4 Notes LB ⊗

See advert on this page

Quality Crown Kensington PLAN 1 D3

★★★★ GUEST ACCOMMODATION

162 Cromwell Rd, Kensington SW5 0TT
☎ 020 7244 2400 ▤ 020 7244 2500
e-mail: stay@qualitycrown.com

This delightful property enjoys a prime location adjacent to the famous Cromwell Road Hospital, within easy reach of the V&A Museum and the chic shops of Knightsbridge and South Kensington. Bedrooms are extremely well equipped and along with the comfortable public areas have a stylish, contemporary feel. The popular smart bar is a feature.

Rooms 82 en suite Facilities STV TVL tea/coffee Dinner available Direct Dial Cen ht Lift Licensed Parking Notes ⊗

My Place PLAN 1 D3

★★★ GUEST ACCOMMODATION

1-3 Trebovir Rd SW5 9LS
☎ 020 7373 0833 ▤ 020 7373 9998
e-mail: info@myplacehotel.co.uk
web: www.myplacehotel.co.uk
dir: A4 West Cromwell Rd onto Earls Court Rd, 3rd right

This Victorian house is in a quiet residential street close to Earls Court station with easy access to the West End. The smart bedrooms vary in size and have an extremely good range of modern facilities. Breakfast is served in the dining room overlooking a spacious garden. Free entry to the on-site nightclub is included.

Rooms 50 en suite (6 fmly) S £55-£65; D £70-£85 Facilities FTV TVL Direct Dial Cen ht Lift Licensed Wi-fi Night Club Conf Max 100 Thtr 100 Class 100 Board 20 Notes LB ⊗

THE MAYFLOWER

Recently renovated, the Mayflower offers 48 individually designed and decorated bedrooms complemented by marble walk-in bath/shower rooms with all amenities.

"Providing comfort and relaxation whether rooms standard, executive or luxury . . ."

26–28 Trebovir Road, Earls Court, London, SW5 9NJ   Tel: +44 (0)207 370 0991

A part of the Mayflower Collection: www.themayflowercollection.com

The Trebovir PLAN 1 D3

★★★ GUEST ACCOMMODATION

18-20 Trebovir Rd SW5 9NH
☎ **020 7373 6625** 📄 **020 7244 6525**
e-mail: info@trebovirhotel.com

The Trebovir occupies two adjoining west London townhouses within easy reach of excellent transport links, the Earl's Court arena and the Olympia Exhibition centre. The newly refurbished rooms are well equipped with many thoughtful extras such as flat-screen TV and Wi-fi. Breakfast is served in the attractive and cosy dining room.

Rooms 62 en suite (3 fmly) (9 GF) S £50-£75; D £75-£105 **Facilities** FTV tea/coffee Direct Dial Cen ht Lift Wi-fi **Notes** ⊗

SW7

Ashburn PLAN 2 A1

★★★★ GUEST ACCOMMODATION

111 Cromwell Rd SW7 4DP
☎ **020 7244 1999** 📄 **020 7244 1998**
e-mail: reservations@ashburn-hotel.co.uk
dir: On Cromwell Rd, near junct with Gloucester Rd

This stunning establishment benefits from a great location in a peaceful Kensington side street which is less than a five minute walk from Gloucester Road Underground. All areas including the guest lounge, bar, dining room and accommodation have been stylishly renovated to a very high standard with guest comfort a priority. Light hot and cold snacks are available during the day and evening. A Continental or full English breakfast is served in the attractive dining room located on the lower ground floor.

Rooms 38 en suite (3 GF) (3 smoking) S £120-£170; D £139-£215* **Facilities** STV FTV TVL tea/coffee Dinner available Direct Dial Cen ht Lift Wi-fi **Notes** ⊗

The Gallery PLAN 2 A1

★★★★ GUEST ACCOMMODATION

8-10 Queensberry Place, South Kensington SW7 2EA
☎ **020 7915 0000** 📄 **020 7970 1805**
e-mail: reservations@eeh.co.uk
web: www.eeh.co.uk
dir: Off A4 Cromwell Rd opp Natural History Museum, near South Kensington tube station

This stylish property, close to Kensington and Knightsbridge, offers friendly hospitality, attentive service and sumptuously furnished bedrooms, some with a private terrace. Public areas include a choice of lounges (one with internet access) and an elegant bar. There is an option of English or continental breakfast, and 24-hour room service is available.

Rooms 36 en suite S £120-£141; D £141-£211.50 (room only) **Facilities** STV tea/coffee Dinner available Direct Dial Cen ht Lift Licensed Wi-fi **Conf** Max 40 Thtr 40 Board 30 **Notes** ⊗

The Gainsborough PLAN 2 A1

★★★★ GUEST ACCOMMODATION

7-11 Queensberry Place, South Kensington SW7 2DL
☎ **020 7957 0000** 📄 **020 7970 1805**
e-mail: reservations@eeh.co.uk
web: www.eeh.co.uk
dir: Off A4 Cromwell Rd opp Natural History Museum, near South Kensington tube station

This smart Georgian house is in a quiet street near South Kensington's museums. Bedrooms are individually designed with fine fabrics, quality furnishings and co-ordinated colours. A choice of breakfasts is offered in the attractive dining room. There is also a delightful lobby lounge and 24-hour room service is available.

Rooms 48 en suite (5 fmly) **Facilities** STV tea/coffee Dinner available Direct Dial Cen ht Lift Licensed Wi-fi **Conf** Max 40 Class 40 Board 30 **Notes** ⊗

W1

AA GUEST ACCOMODATION OF THE YEAR FOR LONDON

The Sumner PLAN 2 B4

★★★★ GUEST ACCOMMODATION

54 Upper Berkeley St, Marble Arch W1H 7QR
☎ 020 7723 2244 📄 020 7705 8767
e-mail: hotel@thesumner.com

Centrally located just five minutes walk from Marble Arch, The Sumner is part of a Georgian terrace. Refurbished throughout to a very high standard, this delightful property combines much of the original character of the building with modern comfort. Air-conditioned rooms have all been designer decorated and feature widescreen LCD TVs, free Broadband, as well as a range of traditional amenities. The breakfast buffet is included in the rate and there is also an elegant lounge for guests to relax in. The Sumner is the winner of the AA Guest Accommodation of the Year for London 2009-2010 Award.

Rooms 20 en suite S £150-£190; D £150-£190*
Facilities FTV Direct Dial Cen ht Lift Licensed Wi-fi
Notes ⊗ No Children 5yrs

Best Western Premier Shaftesbury PLAN 2 D3

★★★★ GUEST ACCOMMODATION

65-73 Shaftesbury Av W1D 6EX
☎ 020 7871 6000
e-mail: reservations@shaftesburyhotel.co.uk
dir: From Piccadilly Circus 300yds up Shaftesbury Ave, at junct with Dean St

In the centre of the West End, this boutique property offers plenty of warm, traditional hospitality. The Shaftesbury is next to two major underground stations, with comfortably sized public areas, a refreshment lounge, the Premier Bar, restaurants, conference facilities, and a fitness room.

Rooms 67 en suite (2 fmly) **Facilities** STV tea/coffee Direct Dial Lift Licensed Gymnasium **Conf** Max 12 Board 12 **Notes** ⊗

Hart House PLAN 2 B4

★★★★ GUEST ACCOMMODATION

51 Gloucester Place, Portman Sq W1U 8JF
☎ 020 7935 2288 📄 020 7935 8516
e-mail: reservations@harthouse.co.uk
web: www.harthouse.co.uk
dir: Off Oxford St behind Selfridges, near Baker St & Marble Arch tube stations

This elegant Georgian house is only a short walk from Oxford Street, Selfridges and Madame Tussaud's. Bedrooms and public areas are smartly furnished, stylishly decorated and have been carefully restored to retain much of the house's original character. English breakfast is served in the stylish dining room.

Rooms 15 en suite (4 fmly) (4 GF) S £89-£95; D £98-£135 **Facilities** FTV tea/coffee Direct Dial Cen ht Wi-fi **Notes** ⊗

See advert on opposite page

The St George PLAN 2 B4

★★★★ GUEST ACCOMMODATION

49 Gloucester Place W1U 8JE
☎ 020 7486 8586 📄 020 7486 6567
e-mail: reservations@stgeorge-hotel.net
dir: Off Marylebone Rd, between Marble Arch & Baker St tube stations

This attractive, Grade II listed house is in the heart of the West End near Oxford St. Bedrooms are furnished to a high standard and offer many facilities such as modem points, safes, hairdryers and mini-fridges. There is a smart breakfast room and the friendly staff offer a very warm welcome.

Rooms 19 en suite (3 fmly) (3 GF) S £85-£105; D £110-£150 **Facilities** STV FTV TVL tea/coffee Direct Dial Cen ht Wi-fi **Conf** Max 20 Thtr 15 Class 20 Board 20 **Notes** LB ⊗

The Regency PLAN 2 C4

★★★ GUEST ACCOMMODATION

19 Nottingham Place W1U 5LQ
☎ 020 7486 5347 📄 020 7224 6057
e-mail: enquiries@regencyhotelwestend.co.uk
web: www.regencyhotelwestend.co.uk
dir: A501 Marylebone Rd S onto Baker St, left onto Paddington St, left onto Nottingham Place

The Regency, a converted mansion, is close to Baker Street tube station, Madame Tussaud's, West End shops and Harley Street. Bedrooms are well equipped and some rooms are suitable for families. Breakfast is served in the brightly appointed basement breakfast room. Free Wi-fi is available.

Rooms 20 en suite (2 fmly) (5 smoking) **Facilities** STV TVL tea/coffee Dinner available Direct Dial Cen ht Lift Wi-fi **Notes** LB ⊗

Lincoln House PLAN 2 B4

★★ GUEST ACCOMMODATION

33 Gloucester Place W1U 8HY
☎ 020 7486 7630 📄 020 7486 0166
e-mail: reservations@lincoln-house-hotel.co.uk
web: www.lincoln-house-hotel.co.uk
dir: Walking from Marble Arch Station, left onto Oxford St, left onto Portman St, continues onto Gloucester Place

This impressive Georgian property, located close to Oxford Street, is a friendly, family-run establishment. Comfortable bedrooms vary in size and many benefit from air conditioning. Public areas are decorated to a high standard with a cottage-style breakfast room on the lower ground floor.

Rooms 24 en suite (5 fmly) (6 GF) **Facilities** STV tea/coffee Direct Dial Wi-fi **Parking** 10 **Notes** LB ⊗

Mermaid Suite PLAN 2 C4

★★ GUEST ACCOMMODATION

3-4 Blenheim St W1S 1LA
☎ 020 7629 1875 📄 020 7499 9475
e-mail: info@mermaidsuite.com
dir: Off New Bond St near Bond St tube station

Located just off Oxford St, the Mermaid Suite provides excellent accommodation in one of London's best-known shopping areas. Bedrooms, on several floors and different buildings, are all smartly presented and well equipped. There is also a popular Italian restaurant, which is open all day.

Rooms 30 rms (29 en suite) (4 fmly) (2 smoking) **Facilities** STV tea/coffee Dinner available Direct Dial Cen ht **Notes** ⊗ Closed 23 Dec RS 28 Dec

W2

Best Western Mornington PLAN 2 A3

★★★★ GUEST ACCOMMODATION

12 Lancaster Gate W2 3LG
☎ 020 7262 7361 📠 020 7706 1028
e-mail: london@mornington.co.uk
dir: N of Hyde Park, off A402 Bayswater Rd

This fine Victorian building is located in a quiet road close to Lancaster Gate station for easy access to the West End. The bedrooms have been appointed to provide comfortable, stylish accommodation. There is a lounge/bar and an attractive dining room where an extensive Scandinavian-style breakfast is served.

Rooms 66 en suite (9 fmly) (2 GF) (20 smoking)
Facilities STV tea/coffee Direct Dial Cen ht Lift Licensed Wi-fi **Conf** Max 14 Thtr 14 Class 14 Board 14

Best Western Shaftesbury Paddington Court London PLAN 2 A3

★★★★ GUEST ACCOMMODATION

27 Devonshire Ter W2 3DP
☎ 020 7745 1200 📠 020 7745 1221
e-mail: info@paddingtoncourt.com
web: www.paddingtoncourt.com
dir: From A40 take exit before Paddington flyover, follow Paddington Station signs. Devonshire Ter is off Craven Rd

This establishment benefits from its convenient location close to Paddington mainline train station including links to the underground stations and the Heathrow Express terminal. Situated next to Hyde Park and Kensington Palace Gardens this establishment offers smart and comfortable guest accommodation and a guaranteed substantial breakfast. Club Rooms are also available with additional extras including the exclusive use of the Club Lounge. A room is available for small meetings by prior arrangement.

Rooms 165 en suite 35 annexe en suite (43 fmly)
Facilities STV TVL tea/coffee Direct Dial Lift Licensed

Hyde Park Radnor PLAN 2 A5

★★★★ GUEST ACCOMMODATION

7-9 Sussex Place, Hyde Park W2 2SX
☎ 020 7723 5969 📠 020 7262 8955
e-mail: hydeparkradnor@btconnect.com
web: www.hydeparkradnor.com
dir: Off A402 Bayswater Rd onto Lancaster Ter & Sussex Gardens, right onto Sussex Place

This smart property is within walking distance of Paddington station and close to all London's central attractions. The smart bedrooms are brightly appointed, well equipped and have modern en suites. English breakfast is served in the lower ground-floor dining room.

Rooms 36 en suite (10 fmly) (5 GF) **Facilities** STV TVL tea/coffee Direct Dial Cen ht Lift **Parking** 2 **Notes** ⊗

The New Linden PLAN 1 D4

★★★★ GUEST ACCOMMODATION

59 Leinster Square, Notting Hill W2 4PS
☎ 020 7221 4321 📠 020 7727 3156
e-mail: newlindenhotel@mayflower-group.co.uk
dir: Off A402, Bayswater Rd

The friendly New Linden has a good location north of Kensington Gardens. Its stylish en suite bedrooms are richly furnished and thoughtfully equipped with CD players and safes. A good continental breakfast is served in the basement dining room.

Rooms 50 en suite **Facilities** STV tea/coffee Direct Dial Cen ht Lift Wi-fi **Notes** ⊗

See advert on page 244

Hart House

51 Gloucester Place, London W1U 8JF

Tel: +44 (020) 7935 2288 Fax: +44 (020) 7935 8516

Email: reservations@harthouse.co.uk

www.harthouse.co.uk

AA ★★★★ Guest Accommodation

One of London's Best B&B Townhouses

Centrally located in the heart of London's West End

Clean & Comfortable Fully Refurbished Bedrooms

Reasonable Rates

W2 *continued*

Quality Crown Hyde Park PLAN 2 A3

★★★★ GUEST ACCOMMODATION

8-14 Talbot Square W2 1TS
☎ 020 7262 6699   🖹 020 7723 3233
e-mail: res.hydepark@lth-hotels.com
dir: *SE of Paddington station off Sussex Gardens*

This well-presented property is convenient for Hyde Park, Paddington and Marble Arch. The modern bedrooms are furnished to a good standard and the executive rooms are particularly impressive. Public areas include a compact but stylish bar and lounge, and a basement restaurant where hearty breakfasts are served.

Rooms 75 en suite (8 fmly) (8 GF) Facilities FTV TVL tea/coffee Direct Dial Cen ht Lift Licensed Wi-fi Notes LB ⊗

Quality Crown Paddington PLAN 2 A4

★★★★ GUEST ACCOMMODATION

144 Praed St, Paddington W2 1HU
☎ 020 7706 8888   🖹 020 7706 8800
e-mail: seay@qualitycrown.com

This contemporary, stylish property enjoys a central location, adjacent to Paddington Station. Bedrooms and en suites vary in size but all are extremely smartly appointed and boast a host of extra facilities including CD players, flat-screen TVs, room safes and internet access. A small gym, stylish lounge and meeting rooms are also available.

Rooms 83 en suite Facilities STV TVL tea/coffee Dinner available Direct Dial Cen ht Lift Licensed Conf Max 22 Board 22 Notes ⊗

The Shaftesbury Premier London Hyde Park PLAN 2 A4

★★★★ GUEST ACCOMMODATION

78-82 Westbourne Ter, Paddington W2 6QA
☎ 020 7262 4521   🖹 020 7262 7610
e-mail: reservations@londonpremierhotels.co.uk
dir: *Off A40 onto Lancaster Ter, at crossing left onto slip road*

This attractive property enjoys a central location within easy reach of central London shops and attractions. The en suite bedrooms and public areas have a smart contemporary feel. Although rooms vary in size, all boast many useful facilities such as free internet access, mini-fridges and irons.

Rooms 119 en suite (2 GF) S £99-£350; D £109-£395 (room only)* Facilities STV tea/coffee Direct Dial Lift Licensed Wi-fi Parking 12 Notes ⊗

Shaftesbury Premier Paddington PLAN 2 A3

★★★★ GUEST ACCOMMODATION

55-61 Westbourne Ter W2 6QA
☎ 020 7723 3434   🖹 020 7402 0433
dir: *Off A40 onto Lancaster Ter*

This smart property enjoys a convenient location within walking distance of Hyde Park and of many of London's major shops and attractions. Bedrooms are smartly appointed and boast modern technology. A hearty breakfast is served in the airy dining room. Limited off-street parking (chargable) is a bonus. The staff are friendly and attentive.

Rooms 118 en suite (2 GF) S £99-£350; D £109-£395 (room only)* Facilities STV tea/coffee Dinner available Direct Dial Cen ht Lift Licensed Wi-fi Parking 10 Notes ⊗

Princes Square PLAN 2 A3

★★★ GUEST ACCOMMODATION

23-25 Princes Square, off Ilchester Gardens, Bayswater W2 4NJ
☎ 020 7229 9876   🖹 020 7229 4664
e-mail: info@princessquarehotel.co.uk
dir: *From Bayswater 1st left onto Moscow Rd, then 3rd right into Ilchester Gardens*

This fine building is in a quiet road close to tube stations for easy access to the West End. The comfortable bedrooms provide stylish accommodation, and there is a small bar and an attractive dining room where a continental breakfast is served.

Rooms 50 en suite (3 fmly) (6 GF) S £55-£115; D £75-£150* Facilities STV tea/coffee Direct Dial Cen ht Lift Wi-fi Notes LB ⊗

Admiral PLAN 2 A3

★★★ GUEST ACCOMMODATION

143 Sussex Gardens, Hyde Park W2 2RY
☎ 020 7723 7309   🖹 020 7723 8731
e-mail: enquiries@admiral-hotel.com

The Admiral is a short walk from Paddington station and is convenient for Hyde Park and the West End. The smart

NEW LINDEN

THE NEW LINDEN

As London's newest townhouse accommodation, it offers 50 individually designed bedrooms with striking interiors and colours providing the setting for elegant, hand-made furnishing and marble en-suite bathrooms.

"Redefining service"

59 Leinster Square, London, W2 4PS   Tel: +44 (0)207 221 4321

A part of the Mayflower Collection: www.themayflowercollection.com

bedrooms are enhanced with attractive artworks, and a full English breakfast is provided.

Rooms 21 en suite (12 fmly) (1 GF) S £49-£70; D £68-£95* **Facilities** STV FTV TVL tea/coffee Dinner available Direct Dial Cen ht Licensed Wi-fi **Conf** Max 30 Class 25 Board 25 **Parking** 3 **Notes** LB ⊗

Kingsway Park Guest Accommodation
PLAN 2 A4

★★★ GUEST ACCOMMODATION

139 Sussex Gardens W2 2RX
☎ 020 7723 5677 & 7724 9346 ▤ 020 7402 4352
e-mail: info@kingswaypark-hotel.com
web: www.kingswaypark-hotel.com

This Victorian property has a central location within walking distance of Marble Arch, Hyde Park and Paddington. Bedrooms offer well-equipped value accommodation. Public areas include a reception lounge and a basement breakfast room adorned with interesting artwork. A limited number of parking spaces is available.

Rooms 22 en suite (5 fmly) (2 GF) **Facilities** STV FTV TVL tea/coffee Dinner available Direct Dial Cen ht Licensed **Conf** Max 30 **Parking** 3 **Notes** LB ⊗

Park Lodge PLAN 2 A3

★★★ GUEST ACCOMMODATION

73 Queensborough Ter, Bayswater W2 3SU
☎ 020 7229 6424 ▤ 020 7221 4772
e-mail: info@hotelparklodge.com
dir: Off Bayswater Rd near Queensway tube station

A short walk from Kensington Gardens and fashionable Queensway, this former house has been converted to provide good, practically equipped bedrooms. Bathrooms are bright and well appointed. Breakfast is served in the basement dining room.

Rooms 29 en suite (1 fmly) (3 GF) **Facilities** STV FTV tea/coffee Direct Dial Cen ht Lift **Notes** ⊗

Soroptimist Residential Club PLAN 2 A3

★★★ GUEST ACCOMMODATION

63 Baywater Rd W2 3PH
☎ 020 7723 8575 ▤ 020 7723 1061
e-mail: soropclub.63@virgin.net

This friendly establishment offers a surprisingly tranquil environment, located less than one minute's walk from Lancaster Gate tube station and directly opposite Hyde Park. All bedrooms are comfortable with en suite facilities and comprise a range of singles and twins; there is also a room which can accommodate three guests. Hot snacks are available throughout the afternoon and evening by prior arrangement and a good continental breakfast is served in the mornings. A room is available for meetings and private functions.

Rooms 17 en suite (1 fmly) S £60; D £100* **Facilities** tea/coffee Lift Wi-fi **Conf** Max 40 Class 40 Board 20 **Notes** ⊗ Closed 21-31 Dec

Barry House PLAN 2 A4

★★★ Ⓐ BED AND BREAKFAST

12 Sussex Place, Hyde Park W2 2TP
☎ 020 7723 7340 ▤ 020 7723 9775
e-mail: hotel@barryhouse.co.uk
web: www.barryhouse.co.uk
dir: 300yds SE of Paddington station

Rooms 18 rms (15 en suite) (5 fmly) (2 GF) S £42-£59; D £75-£99 **Facilities** FTV tea/coffee Direct Dial Cen ht Wi-fi **Notes** ⊗

Parkwood at Marble Arch PLAN 2 B3

★★ GUEST ACCOMMODATION

4 Stanhope Place, Marble Arch W2 2HB
☎ 020 7402 2241 ▤ 020 7402 1574
e-mail: reception@parkwoodhotel.com
web: www.parkwoodhotel.com
dir: Near Marble Arch tube station

Located in a quiet residential street next to Marble Arch and Oxford Street, the friendly Parkwood provides a central base for budget-conscious shoppers and tourists. Family rooms are available, and a freshly cooked breakfast is served in the attractive basement dining room.

Rooms 16 rms (12 en suite) (1 fmly) (2 GF) **Facilities** STV TVL tea/coffee Direct Dial Cen ht **Notes** ⊗

W6

Orlando PLAN 1 D3

★★ GUEST ACCOMMODATION

83 Shepherds Bush Rd W6 7LR
☎ 020 7603 4890 ▤ 020 7603 4890
e-mail: hotelorlando@btconnect.com
web: www.hotelorlando.co.uk
dir: On A219 between Hammersmith & Shepherd's Bush tube stations

The Orlando is part of a Victorian terrace within easy walking distance of tube stations. Bedrooms, varying in size and style, are soundly furnished and well maintained. Breakfast is served at individual tables in the smart basement dining room.

Rooms 14 en suite (3 fmly) **Facilities** tea/coffee Direct Dial Cen ht **Notes** ⊗

W7

Hanwell Bed and Breakfast PLAN 1 B4

★★ BED AND BREAKFAST

110A Grove Av, Hanwell W7 3ES
☎ 020 8567 5015
e-mail: tassanimation@aol.com
web: www.ealing-hanwell-bed-and-breakfast.co.uk
dir: 1.5m from Greenford Rd

Hanwell Bed and Breakfast occupies a convenient and peaceful location close to regular bus routes and within walking distance of Ealing Hospital and near to Ealing golf course. An array of restaurants offering menus to suit all palates is available within minutes. The accommodation is comfortable and the top floor en suite bedroom is available for longer term stays (minimum seven nights). Breakfast provides an excellent start to the day.

Rooms 2 rms (1 en suite) (1 pri facs) (2 fmly) **Facilities** tea/coffee Dinner available Cen ht Wi-fi **Parking** 2 **Notes** LB ⊗ Closed 25 Dec ⊛

W14

Avonmore PLAN 1 D3

★★★ GUEST ACCOMMODATION

66 Avonmore Rd W14 8RS
☎ 020 7603 4296 & 7603 3121 📠 056 0153 5230
e-mail: reservations@avonmorehotel.co.uk
web: www.avonmorehotel.co.uk
dir: *Off Hammersmith Rd opp Olympia Exhibition Centre*

Avonmore occupies a convenient location only a few minutes walk from Kensington Olympia and one stop on the District Line underground from Earls Court. The accommodation is comfortable and bedrooms are equipped with mini bars and fans. Wi-fi is available throughout the establishment. The team at Avonmore are friendly and guest focused.

Rooms 9 rms (7 en suite) (2 pri facs) (3 fmly) (2 GF) S £40–£50; D £60–£100 **Facilities** TVL tea/coffee Direct Dial Cen ht Licensed Wi-fi **Notes** LB ⊗

WC1

Euro PLAN 2 D5

★★★ GUEST ACCOMMODATION

51-53 Cartwright Gardens, Russell Square WC1H 9EL
☎ 020 7387 4321 📠 020 7383 5044
e-mail: reception@eurohotel.co.uk
dir: *Off Euston Rd onto Judd St, right onto Leigh St & Cartwright Gardens. Near Euston tube station*

This friendly guest house is in a leafy Georgian crescent only a short walk from Russell Square tube station with its direct link to Heathrow, as well as Euston. Bedrooms are well equipped and many have en suite bathrooms. Breakfast is served at individual tables in the attractive dining room.

Rooms 31 rms (23 en suite) (6 pri facs) (9 fmly) (4 GF) **Facilities** STV tea/coffee Direct Dial Cen ht Wi-fi 🛎 **Notes** ⊗

The George PLAN 2 D5

★★★ GUEST ACCOMMODATION

58-60 Cartwright Gardens WC1H 9EL
☎ 020 7387 8777 📠 020 7387 8666
e-mail: ghotel@aol.com
web: www.georgehotel.com
dir: *From St Pancras 2nd left onto Marchmont St & 1st left onto Cartwright Gardens*

The George is within walking distance of Russell Square and the tube, and convenient for London's central attractions. The brightly appointed bedrooms vary in size, many have en suites, and some rooms are suitable for families. A substantial breakfast is served in the attractive ground-floor dining room.

Rooms 40 rms (14 en suite) (14 fmly) (4 GF) **Facilities** STV TVL tea/coffee Direct Dial Cen ht 🛎 Free Internet access **Notes** ⊗

The Jesmond Dene PLAN 2 D5

★★★ GUEST ACCOMMODATION

27 Argyle St, Kings Cross WC1H 8EP
☎ 020 7837 4654 📠 020 7833 1633
e-mail: info@jesmonddenehotel.co.uk
web: www.jesmonddenehotel.co.uk

Less than five minutes walk from the mainline and underground station of Kings Cross is The Jesmond Dene. Accommodation comprises comfortable bedrooms most of which benefit from their own en suite facilities; some bathroom facilities are shared. Warm service and hospitality is provided along with a well cooked breakfast served in the bright dining room.

Rooms 22 rms (11 en suite) (4 fmly) (5 GF) S £40–£90; D £50–£110* **Facilities** STV FTV tea/coffee Cen ht Wi-fi **Parking** 6 **Notes** ⊗

LONDON, GREATER

BARNET   Map 6 TQ29

Savoro Restaurant with Rooms

★★★ ⚛ RESTAURANT WITH ROOMS

206 High St EN5 5SZ
☎ 020 8449 9888 📠 020 8449 7444
e-mail: savoro@savoro.co.uk
web: www.savoro.co.uk
dir: *M25 junct 23 on A1000 in crescent behind Hadley Green Jaguar Garage*

Set back from the main high street, the traditional frontage of this establishment belies the stylishly modern bedrooms and well designed bathrooms within. The award-winning restaurant is an additional bonus.

Rooms 11 rms (9 en suite) (2 pri facs) (2 fmly) (3 GF) S £40–£65; D £70–£120 (room only)* **Facilities** FTV tea/coffee Dinner available Cen ht Wi-fi **Parking** 9 **Notes** LB ⊗ No coaches

BRENTFORD

See London Plan 1 C3

Primrose House

★★★★ GUEST ACCOMMODATION

56 Boston Gardens TW8 9LP
☎ 020 8568 5573
e-mail: information@primrosehouse.com
web: www.primrosehouse.com
dir: *Off A3002 Boston Manor Rd near Boston Manor tube station*

A warm welcome is assured at this delightful guest house, set in a quiet residential area convenient for central London and Heathrow by tube or road. The individually styled bedrooms are carefully appointed and feature numerous thoughtful extras. A continental breakfast is served in the dining room overlooking the garden.

Rooms 4 rms (2 en suite) S £43–£53; D £58–£68 **Facilities** FTV TVL tea/coffee Cen ht Wi-fi **Parking** 2 **Notes** ⊗

CRANFORD

See London Plan 1 A3 For accommodation details see Heathrow Airport

CROYDON

See London plan 1 F1

Kirkdale

★★★ GUEST ACCOMMODATION

22 St Peters Rd CR0 1HD
☎ 020 8688 5898 📠 020 8680 6001
e-mail: reservations@kirkdalehotel.co.uk
dir: *A23 onto A232 W & A212 Lower Coombe St, 500yds right*

Close to the town centre, this Victorian property retains many original features. Public areas include a small lounge bar and an attractive breakfast room, and the bedrooms have good facilities. There is a sheltered patio for the summer.

Rooms 19 en suite (6 GF) S £50–£65; D £60–£75* **Facilities** TVL tea/coffee Direct Dial Cen ht Licensed Wi-fi **Parking** 12 **Notes** ⊗

FELTHAM

See London Plan 1 A2 For accommodation details see Heathrow Airport

HARROW ON THE HILL

See London Plan 1 B5

Old Etonian

★★★ GUEST ACCOMMODATION

36-38 High St HA1 3LL
☎ 020 8423 3854 & 8422 8482 📄 020 8423 1225
e-mail: info@oldetonian.com
web: www.oldetonian.com
dir: In town centre. On B458 opp Harrow School

In the heart of this historic part of London and opposite the prestigious school, this friendly guest house is a delight. Recently redecorated bedrooms are attractive, well appointed and comfortable. A continental breakfast is served in the dining room, which in the evening is home to a lively restaurant. On-road parking available.

Rooms 9 en suite (1 GF) S £67.50; D £75* **Facilities** FTV TVL tea/coffee Dinner available Direct Dial Cen ht Licensed **Conf** Max 30 Thtr 20 Class 20 Board 20 **Parking** 3 **Notes** ⊗

HEATHROW AIRPORT

See London plan 1 A3

The Cottage PLAN 1 B2

★★★★ GUEST ACCOMMODATION

150-152 High St TW5 9WB
☎ 020 8897 1815
e-mail: info@the-cottage.eu
dir: M4 junct 3, A312 towards Feltham, left at lights, left after 1st pub on left

This beautiful property is a peacefully situated oasis, family run within five minutes of Heathrow Airport. It offers comfortable tastefully decorated and spacious accommodation in the main house, and six new bedrooms located at the rear of the garden, connected to the main

building by a covered walkway overlooking the stunning courtyard.

Rooms 14 en suite 6 annexe en suite (4 fmly) (12 GF) S £55-£65; D £75-£85 **Facilities** tea/coffee Cen ht Wi-fi **Parking** 20 **Notes** ⊗ Closed 24-26 Dec & 31 Dec-1 Jan

Crompton Guest House

★★★★ GUEST HOUSE

49 Lampton Rd TW3 1JG
☎ 020 8570 7090 📄 020 8577 1975
e-mail: cromptonguesthouse@btinternet.com
dir: M4 junct 3, follow signs for Hounslow. Turn onto Bath Rd (A3005), left at Yates pub. 200yds on right just before bridge

Located just a moment's walk away from Hounslow underground station this accommodation is popular with both business and leisure travellers. Bedrooms and bathrooms are comfortable and well equipped with good facilities. Breakfast is served in the intimate dining room where a freshly prepared breakfast is served. Ample off street parking is an additional plus.

Rooms 11 en suite (5 fmly) (2 GF) S £60-£100; D £75-£120 **Facilities** STV FTV tea/coffee Dinner available Direct Dial Cen ht Wi-fi **Parking** 12 **Notes** LB ⊗

HOUNSLOW

See London Plan 1 B2 For accommodation details see under Heathrow Airport

ILFORD

See London Plan 1 H5

Cranbrook

★★ Ⓐ GUEST ACCOMMODATION

22-24 Coventry Rd IG1 4QR
☎ 020 8554 6544 📄 020 8518 1463
e-mail: manager@expresslodging.co.uk
dir: From M25 to A406 east, exit at junct A123 past Ilford station, on right

Rooms 45 rms (25 en suite) 15 annexe en suite (4 fmly) (17 GF) **Facilities** STV FTV tea/coffee **Conf** Max 30 Thtr 30 Class 30 Board 30 **Parking** 35 **Notes** ⊗

The Park

★★ Ⓐ GUEST ACCOMMODATION

327 Cranbrook Rd IG1 4UE
☎ 020 8554 9616 📄 020 8518 2700
e-mail: manager@expresslodging.co.uk
web: www.parkhotelilford.com
dir: Exit A406 onto A123, pass Ilford station, Macdonalds and Pizza Hut, located on left

Rooms 30 rms (25 en suite) (2 fmly) (11 GF) **Facilities** STV FTV tea/coffee **Conf** Max 50 Thtr 50 Class 50 Board 50 **Parking** 30 **Notes** ⊗

KINGSTON UPON THAMES

See London Plan 1 C1

Chase Lodge House

★★★ GUEST ACCOMMODATION

10 Park Rd, Hampton Wick KT1 4AS
☎ 020 8943 1862 📄 020 8943 9363
e-mail: info@chaselodgehotel.com
web: www.chaselodgehotel.com
dir: A308 onto A310 signed Twickenham, 1st left onto Park Rd

This delightful guest house is set in a quiet residential area, a short walk from Kingston Bridge. The individually decorated rooms vary in size and are all well-appointed and feature a range of useful extras. An attractive lounge-bar-restaurant is provided where breakfast, snacks and dinner by pre-arrangement are served. On-road parking is available.

Rooms 10 en suite S £55-£78; D £71-£185* **Facilities** FTV Direct Dial Wi-fi **Conf** Max 65 Thtr 50 Class 65 Board 30 **Notes** LB

RICHMOND (UPON THAMES)

See London Plan 1 C2

Hobart Hall

★★★ GUEST ACCOMMODATION

43-47 Petersham Rd TW10 6UL
☎ 020 8940 0435 📄 020 8332 2996
e-mail: hobarthall@aol.com
dir: 200yds S of Richmond Bridge on A307

Built around 1690, this impressive yet friendly establishment stands beside the River Thames close to Richmond Bridge. Many of the spacious bedrooms have river views and a good range of modern facilities. There is a comfortable lounge, an attractive breakfast room, and a meeting room that overlooks the river.

Rooms 33 rms (18 en suite) (5 fmly) (3 GF) S £50-£75; D £75-£100* **Facilities** TVL tea/coffee Direct Dial Cen ht Wi-fi **Parking** 14 **Notes** ✪ RS 25-26 Dec & 1 Jan

SUTTON Map 6 TQ26

Ashling Tara

★★★ GUEST ACCOMMODATION

50 Rosehill SM1 3EU
☎ 020 8641 6142 & 8296 9866 📄 020 8644 7872
e-mail: info@ashlingtarahotel.com
web: www.ashlingtarahotel.com

Situated only a few minutes away from Sutton station, and a short walk from the town centre, this is a handy location for business travellers requiring access to the City. Bedrooms are generally spacious with comfortable easy chairs and the landing has a communal seating area for people travelling together.

Rooms 9 en suite (2 fmly) (4 GF) **Facilities** tea/coffee Cen ht **Parking** 10 **Notes** ✪

MERSEYSIDE

BIRKENHEAD Map 15 SJ38

Shrewsbury Lodge

★★★ Ⓐ GUEST ACCOMMODATION

31 Shrewsbury Rd, Oxton CH43 2JB
☎ 0151 652 4029 📄 0151 653 3593
e-mail: info@shrewsbury-hotel.com
web: www.shrewsbury-hotel.com

Rooms 16 en suite (3 fmly) (5 GF) S £30-£48; D £65-£98 (room only) **Facilities** TVL tea/coffee Dinner available Cen ht Licensed Wi-fi **Conf** Max 25 Thtr 25 Class 25 Board 25 **Parking** 12

BROMBOROUGH Map 15 SJ38

The Dibbinsdale

Ⓤ

Dibbinsdale Rd CH63 0HQ
☎ 0151 334 9818
e-mail: info@thedibbinsdale.co.uk
dir: M53 junct 4 towards Bebbington. Right at 1st lights, after 1.8m on this road

Currently the rating for this establishment is not confirmed. This may be due to a change of ownership or because it has only recently joined the AA rating scheme. For up-to-date information please see the AA website: theAA.com

Rooms 13 en suite S £40-£75; D £60-£80* **Facilities** FTV tea/coffee Dinner available Cen ht Licensed **Parking** 20 **Notes** ✪ No Children

SOUTHPORT Map 15 SD31

Bay Tree House B&B

★★★★ 🏠 GUEST ACCOMMODATION

No1 Irving St, Marine Gate PR9 0HD
☎ 01704 510555 📄 0870 753 6318
e-mail: baytreehouseuk@aol.com
web: www.baytreehousesouthport.co.uk
dir: Off Leicester St

A warm welcome is assured at this immaculately maintained house, located a short walk from promenade and central attractions. Bedrooms are equipped with a wealth of thoughtful extras, and delicious imaginative breakfasts are served in an attractive dining room overlooking the pretty front patio garden.

Rooms 6 en suite S £45-£70; D £70-£110 **Facilities** FTV tea/coffee Dinner available Direct Dial Cen ht Licensed Wi-fi **Parking** 2 **Notes** LB Closed 14 Dec-1 Feb

The Baytrees

★★★★ GUEST ACCOMMODATION

4 Queens Rd PR9 9HN
☎ 01704 536513 📄 01704 536513
e-mail: stay@baytreeshotel.freeserve.co.uk
web: www.baytreeshotel.co.uk
dir: From B565 (Lord St) towards fire station, right at rdbt onto Manchester Rd, left at lights, 200yds on right

Located a short walk from Lord Street, this elegant late Victorian house has been appointed to provide thoughtfully furnished bedrooms with smart modern en suite bathrooms. Breakfast is served in the attractive dining room overlooking the pretty rear garden, and a lounge is also available.

Rooms 12 en suite (5 fmly) (2 GF) S £32.50-£35; D £59-£62.50* **Facilities** TVL tea/coffee Cen ht **Parking** 11 **Notes** ✪ Closed Xmas

Bowden Lodge

★★★★ GUEST ACCOMMODATION

18 Albert Rd PR9 0LE
☎ 01704 543531 📄 01704 539112
e-mail: stay@bowdenlodge.co.uk
web: www.bowdenlodge.co.uk
dir: A565 N from town centre, over rdbt, 150yds on right

This stylish house is in a quiet residential area just a stroll from Lord Street and the town's attractions. Bedrooms, many suitable for families, are smartly furnished and well equipped. Day rooms include a lounge with deep sofas, and a bright dining room where hearty cooked breakfasts are served. Value for money and a friendly welcome are assured.

Rooms 10 en suite (3 fmly) S £32-£45; D £60-£100* **Facilities** FTV TVL tea/coffee Dinner available Cen ht Licensed Wi-fi **Parking** 10 **Notes** LB ✪

Rosedale

★★★★ GUEST ACCOMMODATION

11 Talbot St PR8 1HP
☎ 01704 530604 📄 01704 530604
e-mail: info@rosedale-hotel.co.uk
dir: A570 into Southport, left onto Talbot St

The smart and friendly Rosedale stands in a quiet street only a short walk from the town's attractions. The bright bedrooms are thoughtfully equipped, and there is a comfortable lounge, a cosy bar and a lovely garden.

Rooms 9 rms (8 en suite) (1 pri facs) (2 fmly) **Facilities** TVL tea/coffee Dinner available Cen ht Licensed **Parking** 6 **Notes** ✪ Closed 21 Dec-3 Jan

The White Lodge

★★★★ GUEST ACCOMMODATION

12 Talbot St PR8 1HP
☎ 01704 536320 📄 01704 536320
dir: *In town centre. Off A570 Eastbank St onto Talbot St, 100yds on right*

Expect a genuine welcome at this family-run, non-smoking guest house, just a stroll from the town centre. Bedrooms, including one on the ground floor, are thoughtfully equipped, and the public areas feature a comfy lounge and a cosy cellar bar. Evening meals are available by arrangement.

Rooms 8 rms (6 en suite) (2 fmly) (1 GF) S £35-£50; D £70-£85* **Facilities** tea/coffee Dinner available Cen ht Licensed **Parking** 6 **Notes** LB ⊗ ☺

Whitworth Falls

★★★★ GUEST ACCOMMODATION

16 Lathom Rd PR9 0JH
☎ 01704 530074
e-mail: whitworthfalls@rapid.co.uk
dir: *A565 N from town centre, over rdbt, 2nd left onto Alexandra Rd, 4th right*

Located on a mainly residential avenue within easy walking distance of seafront and Lord Street shops, this Victorian house has been renovated to provide a range of practical but homely bedrooms. Breakfasts and pre-theatre dinners are served in the attractive dining room, and a comfortable sitting room and lounge bar are also available.

Rooms 12 en suite (2 fmly) (1 GF) **Facilities** TVL tea/coffee Dinner available Direct Dial Cen ht Licensed **Parking** 8

Lyndhurst

★★ GUEST HOUSE

101 King St PR8 1LQ
☎ 01704 537520 & 07759 526864 📄 01704 537520
dir: *Off A570 Eastbank St at McDonalds onto King St*

This well maintained friendly guest house is situated just a short walk from Lord Street and the town's main attractions. It offers brightly decorated, comfortable accommodation. Public areas include a cosy lounge that leads onto the breakfast room.

Rooms 6 rms **Facilities** TVL tea/coffee Cen ht **Parking** 2 **Notes** LB No Children 12yrs Closed Xmas & New Year ☺

ALBURGH Map 13 TM28

The Dove Restaurant with Rooms

★★★★ ⑧⑧ RESTAURANT WITH ROOMS

Holbrook Hill IP20 0EP
☎ 01986 788315 📄 01986 788315
e-mail: thedovenorfolk@freeola.com
dir: *Between Harleston & Bungay at junct A143 & B1062*

A warm welcome awaits at this restaurant with rooms. Bedrooms are pleasantly decorated, furnished with pine pieces and have modern facilities. Public rooms include a lounge area with a small bar, and a smart restaurant with well-spaced tables.

Rooms 2 rms (1 en suite) (1 pri facs) (1 fmly) S £38; D £58* **Facilities** tea/coffee Dinner available Cen ht Wi-fi **Parking** 20 **Notes** ⊗ No coaches

ALDBOROUGH Map 13 TG13

PREMIER COLLECTION

Aldborough Hall
★★★★★ BED AND BREAKFAST

NR11 7HU
☎ 01263 570200 📄 01263 577848
e-mail: contact@aldboroughhall.co.uk
dir: *Off A140, past Aldborough*

This superb Georgian country house is situated in a peaceful rural location amidst pretty landscaped grounds. The tastefully appointed bedrooms are individually decorated and have plush soft furnishings along with many thoughtful touches to enhance guests comfort. The stylish public rooms offer a high degree of comfort; they include a lounge, a dining room and a smart breakfast room with individual tables.

Rooms 4 en suite; D £85-£140* **Facilities** STV tea/coffee Cen ht Licensed Wi-fi ⌣ **Conf** Max 30 Thtr 30 Class 20 Board 20 **Parking** 12 **Notes** LB ⊗ No Children 12yrs Civ Wed 50

ATTLEBOROUGH Map 13 TM09

Sherbourne House

★★★★ ⑧ RESTAURANT WITH ROOMS

8 Norwich Rd NR17 2JX
☎ 01953 454363
e-mail: stay@sherbourne-house.co.uk
web: www.sherbourne-house.co.uk
dir: *Off B1077*

Expect a warm welcome from the caring hosts at this delightful 17th-century property situated just a short walk from the centre of a historic market town. Public rooms include a choice of lounges, a sunny conservatory/lounge bar and a restaurant that serves dishes based on the highest quality, locally sourced produce. The individually decorated bedrooms are smartly appointed and have many thoughtful touches.

Rooms 8 en suite (1 fmly) (1 GF) **Facilities** FTV tea/coffee Dinner available Cen ht Wi-fi **Conf** Max 30 Thtr 30 Class 16 Board 20 **Parking** 30 **Notes** No coaches Civ Wed 40

Rylstone B&B

★★★★ BED AND BREAKFAST

Bell Rd, Rockland St Peter NR17 1UL
☎ 01953 488199 📄 0870 1320816
e-mail: margaret@hneale.f9.co.uk
dir: *4m W of Attleborough. B1077 to Rockland St Peter, at x-rds onto Chapel St & Bell Rd*

A delightful detached property situated in a peaceful rural location on the edge of the village. The pleasantly decorated bedrooms have co-ordinated fabrics and many thoughtful touches. Public rooms include a large lounge with a log burner and a conservatory, which has views of the surrounding countryside.

Rooms 3 rms (2 en suite) (1 pri facs) S £30-£35; D £65-£70 **Facilities** tea/coffee Cen ht **Parking** 3 **Notes** LB ⊗ ☺

BACTON Map 13 TG33

Grange Cottage B&B

★★ BED AND BREAKFAST

1 Grange Cottage, Pollard St NR12 0LH
☎ 01692 652219
e-mail: grangecottage1@yahoo.co.uk
dir: *North Walsham to Edingthorpe on B1150. Continue to Pollard St, B&B sign on right*

Expect a warm welcome from the caring hosts at this delightful cottage situated in a peaceful rural location surrounded by open countryside. Bedrooms are smartly decorated and equipped with a good range of thoughtful touches. Breakfast is served at a large communal table in the cheerful dining room which overlooks the garden.

Rooms 3 rms (1 en suite) S £30; D £50-£58* **Facilities** tea/coffee Cen ht **Parking** 3 **Notes** ⊗ Closed 24-26 Dec ☺

BARNEY
Map 13 TF93

The Old Brick Kilns
★★★★ BED AND BREAKFAST

Little Barney Ln NR21 0NL
☎ 01328 878305 📠 01328 878948
e-mail: enquiries@old-brick-kilns.co.uk
web: www.old-brick-kilns.co.uk
dir: Off B1354 to Barney, 0.3m left onto Little Barney Ln, B&B 0.75m at end

This delightful country house, originally three separate cottages, provides attractive accommodation in peaceful grounds. Breakfasts are served at a communal table in the lounge-dining room. Due to the narrow access road, no arrivals can be accepted until after 1pm.

Rooms 3 en suite S £35; D £65 **Facilities** TVL tea/coffee Cen ht Wi-fi Fishing Pool Table **Parking** 20 **Notes** ⊗ No Children 16yrs

BARTON BENDISH
Map 12 TF70

Spread Eagle Inn
★★★★ ⊛ INN

Church Rd PE33 9GF
☎ 01366 347995 📠 0871 9005576
e-mail: info@spreadeaglenorfolk.co.uk
web: www.spreadeaglenorfolk.co.uk
dir: A1122 turn off at sign for Barton Bendish, 1m turn left onto Church Rd

Set in the delightfully quiet village of Barton Bendish, this traditional village inn offers tastefully appointed public areas with many original features. A good selection of real ales and enjoyable dining offering imaginative cuisine. The newly converted bedrooms are stylish, comfortable and particularly well equipped and are situated in the stable block.

Rooms 5 annexe en suite (1 fmly) (5 GF); D £70-£200* **Facilities** FTV tea/coffee Dinner available Cen ht Wi-fi **Parking** 30 **Notes** LB RS Mon-Wed closed lunchtimes No coaches

BLAKENEY
Map 13 TG04

PREMIER COLLECTION

Blakeney House
★★★★★ GUEST HOUSE

High St NR25 7NX
☎ 01263 740561 📠 01263 741750
e-mail: admin@blakeneyhouse.com
web: www.blakeneyhouse.com
dir: In village centre

A stunning Victorian manor house set amid two acres of attractive landscaped grounds just a short walk from the quay and town centre. The stylish, individually decorated bedrooms have co-ordinated fabrics and many thoughtful touches. Breakfast is served at individual tables in the smart dining room, which overlooks the well-stocked front garden.

Rooms 8 rms (7 en suite) (1 pri facs) (1 fmly) S £50-£90; D £70-£140 (room only)* **Facilities** tea/coffee Cen ht Wi-fi **Parking** 8 **Notes** ⊗ No Children 12yrs

BRISLEY
Map 13 TF92

The Brisley Bell Inn & Restaurant
★★★ INN

The Green NR20 5DW
☎ 01362 668686
e-mail: info@brisleybell-inn.co.uk
web: www.brisleybell-inn.co.uk
dir: Between Fakenham & East Dereham on B1145

Delightful village inn situated in a peaceful location just a short drive from the town centre. The bedrooms are generally quite spacious, each one is smartly appointed with modern furniture and co-ordinated soft furnishings. Public rooms include a beamed bar and a cosy restaurant serving an interesting choice of dishes.

Rooms 3 rms (1 en suite) (1 fmly) S £40-£58; D £50-£64* **Facilities** FTV tea/coffee Dinner available Cen ht Wi-fi **Conf** Max 40 Thtr 40 Class 36 Board 20 **Parking** 30 **Notes** ⊗

BROOKE
Map 13 TM29

Old Vicarage
★★★★ BED AND BREAKFAST

48 The Street NR15 1JU
☎ 01508 558329
dir: Off B1332 in village centre near church

Set in mature gardens in a peaceful village, this charming house is within easy driving distance of Norwich. The individually decorated bedrooms are thoughtfully furnished and equipped, and one room has a lovely four-poster bed. There is an elegant dining room and a cosy lounge, and dinner is available by arrangement. Service is genuinely helpful, provided in a relaxed and friendly manner.

Rooms 2 en suite S £40; D £60 **Facilities** TVL tea/coffee Dinner available Cen ht **Parking** 4 **Notes** LB ⊗ No Children 15yrs ⊛

BURNHAM MARKET
Map 13 TF84

See also Wells-next-the-Sea

Whitehall Farm (TF856412)
★★★★ FARMHOUSE

Burnham Thorpe PE31 8HN
☎ 01328 738416 & 07050 247390
📠 01328 730937 Mrs V Southerland
e-mail: barrysoutherland@aol.com
web: www.whitehallfarm-accommodation.com
dir: From Lord Nelson pub in Burnham towards Holkham/Wells, last building on right leaving village

The large farmhouse forms part of a working arable farm. The property stands in large landscaped gardens with a menagerie of animals and offers a relaxing and informal atmosphere. Bedrooms are spacious, comfortable and equipped with DVDs, televisions and many extras. Communal hearty breakfasts are served in the cosy dining room.

Rooms 3 en suite (1 fmly) S £40-£45; D fr £75* **Facilities** FTV tea/coffee Cen ht Wi-fi **Parking** 7 **Notes** LB Closed 23-27 Dec 560 acres arable

CLEY NEXT THE SEA | Map 13 TG04

PREMIER COLLECTION

Old Town Hall House
★★★★★ BED AND BREAKFAST

Coast Rd NR25 7RB
☎ 01263 740284
web: www.oldtownhallhouse.co.uk
dir: On A149 in centre of Cley. Opposite old red phone box

Expect a warm welcome from the caring hosts at this delightful detached property situated in the heart of a bustling North Norfolk village, which has been designated as an Area of Outstanding Natural Beauty, and has a superb bird watching reserve on its outskirts. The tastefully appointed bedrooms have lovely co-ordinated soft fabrics and many thoughtful touches. Breakfast, using locally sourced produce, is served at individual tables in the stylish dining room.

Rooms 3 en suite; D £75-£95* Facilities tea/coffee Cen ht Notes ⊗ No Children Closed Xmas & Jan

COLTISHALL | Map 13 TG21

The Hedges
★★★★ GUEST ACCOMMODATION

Tunstead Rd NR12 7AL
☎ 01603 738361 📄 01603 738983
e-mail: info@hedgesbandb.co.uk
web: www.hedgesbandb.co.uk
dir: Off B1354 onto White Lion Rd & right fork

A delightful family-run guest house situated close to the Norfolk Broads. The spacious bedrooms have co-ordinated fabrics and many thoughtful touches; most rooms have lovely views of the surrounding countryside. Breakfast is served in the dining room and guests have the use of a smart conservatory which overlooks the garden.

Rooms 5 en suite (2 fmly) (2 GF) S £35-£45; D £55-£59 Facilities TVL tea/coffee Cen ht Parking 5 Notes LB ⊗ Closed 23-28 Dec

COLTON | Map 13 TG10

The Ugly Bug Inn
★★★ INN

High House Farm Ln NR9 5DG
☎ 01603 880794
e-mail: john_lainchbury@hotmail.com
dir: A47 New Mattishall/Honningham rdbt, take only exit then 2nd left, inn on right

A popular inn situated in a tranquil rural location on the edge of the village just off the main A47 with its links to Norwich and the surrounding areas. Dinner and breakfast are served in the conservatory dining room, which overlooks the garden. The bedrooms are pleasantly appointed with co-ordinated fabrics and a good range of useful extras.

Rooms 4 en suite (1 GF) S £35-£60; D £60-£90* Facilities tea/coffee Dinner available Cen ht Wi-fi Fishing Conf Max 40 Thtr 40 Class 40 Board 24 Parking 40 Notes LB

CROMER | Map 13 TG24

See also Sheringham

PREMIER COLLECTION

Incleborough House
★★★★★ BED AND BREAKFAST

Lower Common, East Runton NR27 9PG
☎ 01263 515939
e-mail: enquiries@incleboroughhouse.co.uk
web: www.incleboroughhouse.co.uk
dir: On A149 turn left onto Felbrigg road, 150mtrs on left

Guests can look forward to tea and home-made cake on arrival at this large, award-winning, 16th-century property which has been lovingly restored by the current owners. The attractively decorated bedrooms are carefully furnished throughout and plenty of useful extras. The spacious public areas include a luxurious drawing room with leather sofas and an open fireplace. Breakfast is served at individual tables in the large open-plan conservatory which has a lush indoor tropical garden.

Rooms 4 en suite (1 GF) S £112.50-£146.25; D £150-£195* Facilities STV FTV TVL tea/coffee Dinner available Cen ht Wi-fi Pool Table Parking 7 Notes LB No Children 14yrs

Shrublands Farm (TG246393)
★★★★ FARMHOUSE

Church St, Northrepps NR27 0AA
☎ 01263 579297 📄 01263 579297 Mrs A Youngman
e-mail: youngman@farming.co.uk
web: www.shrublandsfarm.com
dir: Off A149 to Northrepps, through village, past Foundry Arms, cream house 50yds on left

Expect a warm welcome from the caring host at this delightful 18th-century farmhouse, set in landscaped grounds and surrounded by 300 acres of arable farmland. Public areas include a cosy lounge with a wood-burning stove, and breakfast is served at a communal table in the elegant dining room.

Rooms 3 rms (1 en suite) (2 pri facs) S £42-£46; D £64-£72* Facilities FTV TVL tea/coffee Cen ht Parking 5 Notes LB ⊗ No Children 12yrs 300 acres arable

White Horse
★★★★ ⑥ INN

34 High St, Overstrand NR27 0AB
☎ 01263 579237
e-mail: reservations@whitehorseoverstrand.co.uk
dir: From A140, before Cromer, turn right onto Mill Rd. At bottom turn right onto Station Rd. After 2m, bear left onto High St, White Horse on left

A smartly appointed inn ideally situated in the heart of this popular village on the north Norfolk coastline. The modern bedrooms are tastefully appointed and equipped with a good range of useful extras. Public rooms include a large open plan lounge bar with comfortable seating and a relaxed dining area.

Rooms 7 en suite (1 fmly) S £65-£79; D £72-£99 Facilities TVL tea/coffee Dinner available Cen ht Wi-fi Pool Table Parking 6 Notes LB

Beachcomber Guest House
★★★★ GUEST HOUSE

17 Macdonald Rd NR27 9AP
☎ 01263 513398
e-mail: info@beachcomber-guesthouse.co.uk
dir: Off A149 Runton Rd, 500yds W of pier

A smartly maintained Edwardian house situated in a peaceful side road close to the seafront and town centre.

continued

CROMER *continued*

The pleasant bedrooms are carefully furnished and equipped with many thoughtful touches. Breakfast is served in the smart dining room and there is a comfortable lounge.

Rooms 5 rms (4 en suite) (1 pri facs) (1 fmly) S £35-£50; D £60-£64* **Facilities** TVL tea/coffee Cen ht **Notes** LB ⊗ No Children 8yrs ⌾

Bon Vista
★★★★ GUEST ACCOMMODATION

12 Alfred Rd NR27 9AN
☎ 01263 511818
e-mail: jim@bonvista-cromer.co.uk
web: www.bonvista-cromer.co.uk
dir: *From pier onto A148 (coast road), in 400yds left onto Alfred Rd*

This delightful Victorian terrace house, situated in a peaceful side road adjacent to the seafront and just a short walk from the town centre extends a warm welcome. The individually decorated bedrooms have co-ordinated soft fabrics and public rooms include an attractive dining room and a spacious first floor lounge.

Rooms 5 en suite (2 fmly); D £60-£72* **Facilities** TVL tea/coffee Cen ht **Parking** 2 **Notes** LB ⊗ ⌾

Cliff Lane House
★★★★ BED AND BREAKFAST

NR27 0AL
☎ 01263 519139
e-mail: clifflanehouse@fsmail.net

A delightful detached property situated just a short walk from the seafront and the town centre. Bedrooms are tastefully appointed lots of useful touches to add to guests' comfort. Public rooms include a smart lounge with plush sofas, and breakfast is served at individual tables in the dining room.

Rooms 3 en suite (1 GF) S £55-£60; D £70-£80* **Facilities** Cen ht Wi-fi **Notes** ⊗ No Children

Corner House
★★★★ BED AND BREAKFAST

2 Station Rd NR27 9QD
☎ 01263 838540   & 07769 800831   ▤ 01263 838540
e-mail: linjimhoward@btinternet.com

(For full entry see West Runton)

Homefield Guest House
★★★★ GUEST HOUSE

48 Cromer Rd, West Runton NR27 9AD
☎ 01263 837337
e-mail: homefield@hotmail.co.uk
web: www.homefieldguesthouse.co.uk
dir: *On A149 (coast road) between Sheringham & Cromer*

This large Victorian house was previously owned by the Canon of Cromer and is situated in the peaceful village of West Runton between Cromer and Sheringham. The pleasantly co-ordinated bedrooms have many useful extras. Breakfast, which includes locally sourced produce, is served at individual tables in the smart dining room.

Rooms 6 en suite S £40-£60; D £60-£80* **Facilities** TVL tea/coffee Cen ht Wi-fi **Parking** 8 **Notes** LB ⊗ No Children 14yrs

Morden House
★★★ GUEST HOUSE

20 Cliff Av NR27 0AN
☎ 01263 513396   ▤ 01263 513396
e-mail: rosevotier@hotmail.co.uk
dir: *Off A140 (Norwich to Cromer road), 50yds on right before traffic lights*

This charming, detached, late Victorian residence, built at the turn of the century. Decorated and furnished tastefully throughout, the house is ideally situated on a quiet avenue in Cromer; only a few minutes walk from the beach and town centre. Bedrooms are traditional and well equipped. Day rooms include the lounge, attractive dining room and real fires in the cooler months. Dinners are available by prior arrangement.

Rooms 4 en suite S £35-£47.50; D £70-£72* **Facilities** TVL tea/coffee Dinner available Cen ht **Parking** 3 **Notes** LB ⊗ ⌾

Glendale
★★★ GUEST HOUSE

33 Macdonald Rd NR27 9AP
☎ 01263 513278
e-mail: glendalecromer@aol.com
dir: *A149 (coast road) from Cromer centre, 4th left*

Victorian property situated in a peaceful side road adjacent to the seafront and just a short walk from the town centre. Bedrooms are pleasantly decorated, well maintained and equipped with a good range of useful extras. Breakfast is served at individual tables in the smart dining room.

Rooms 5 rms (1 en suite) S £23-£32; D £46-£64 **Facilities** tea/coffee **Parking** 2 **Notes** LB Closed 20 Oct-1 Apr

The Sandcliff
★★★ GUEST HOUSE

Runton Rd NR27 9AS
☎ 01263 512888   ▤ 01263 512888
e-mail: bookings@sandcliffcromer.co.uk
dir: *50yds W of town centre on A149*

Ideally situated on the seafront overlooking the beach and sea just a short walk from the town centre, many improvements have taken place to this popular establishment in recent years. Public rooms include a large lounge bar with comfortable seating and a spacious dining room where breakfast and dinner are served. The bedrooms are pleasantly decorated, thoughtfully equipped and some have superb sea views.

Rooms 22 rms (16 en suite) (10 fmly) (3 GF) **Facilities** TVL tea/coffee Dinner available Licensed **Conf** Max 50 Thtr 50 Class 50 Board 50 **Parking** 10

Westgate Lodge B&B
★★★ BED AND BREAKFAST

10 MacDonald Rd NR27 9AP
☎ 01263 512840
e-mail: westgatelodge@mail.com
dir: *Along seafront & left after the Cliftonville Hotel, Westgate Lodge 50yds on right*

Situated in a peaceful side road next to the seafront and just a short walk from the centre of town. Bedrooms vary in size and style; each one is pleasantly decorated and has many thoughtful touches. Breakfast is served in the smart dining room and there is a cosy lounge.

Rooms 3 en suite; D £50-£62* **Facilities** tea/coffee Cen ht **Parking** 5 **Notes** LB ⊗ No Children 3yrs Closed Xmas & New Year ⌾

DEREHAM   Map 13 TF91

Orchard Cottage

★★★★ BED AND BREAKFAST

The Drift, Gressenhall NR20 4EH
☎ 01362 860265 📠 01362 689265
e-mail: ann@walkers-norfolk.co.uk
dir: 2m NE of Dereham. Off B1146 in Beetley to
Gressenhall, right at x-rds onto Bittering St, right at
x-rds, 2nd right.

Orchard Cottage is an attractive newly-built Norfolk flint
building situated in the historic rural village of
Gressenhall near Dereham. The comfortable country style
bedrooms are smartly decorated and situated on the
ground floor; one of the rooms has a superb wet room.
Public rooms include a lounge, a dining room and a
study. Dinner is available by arrangement.

Rooms 2 en suite (2 GF) S £48-£54; D £58-£64
Facilities FTV TVL tea/coffee Dinner available Cen ht Wi-fi
Parking 2 Notes LB ⊛

The Yaxham Mill

★★★★ INN

Norwich Rd, Yaxham NR19 1RP
☎ 01362 851182 📠 01362 691482
e-mail: yaxhammill@hotmail.co.uk
web: www.yaxhammill.co.uk
dir: 1.5m S of Dereham. B1135 into Yaxham, at E end
of village

This popular inn is situated in a peaceful rural location
just a short drive from the market town of Dereham. The
comfortable lounge bar and smart restaurant offer a good
choice of dishes. The bedrooms are housed in two wings
adjacent to the main building; each one has attractive
pine furnishings and many thoughtful touches.

Rooms 6 en suite 6 annexe en suite (5 fmly) (7 GF)
Facilities tea/coffee Dinner available Cen ht Parking 45
Notes ⊛ No coaches

DOCKING   Map 13 TF73

Jubilee Lodge

★★★★ GUEST ACCOMMODATION

Station Rd PE31 8LS
☎ 01485 518473 📠 01485 518473
e-mail: eghoward62@hotmail.com
web: www.jubilee-lodge.com
dir: 400yds N of village centre on B1153

Ideally placed for touring the North Norfolk coast, with
Sandringham, Hunstanton, Burnham Market and
Fakenham within easy striking distance. Bedrooms are
pleasantly decorated, thoughtfully equipped and come
with en suite facilities. Public rooms include a cosy guest

lounge and breakfast is served at individual tables in the
smart dining room.

Rooms 3 en suite S £30; D £50* Facilities TVL tea/coffee
Cen ht Fishing Parking 3 Notes LB ⊛ No Children 16yrs
⊛

DOWNHAM MARKET   Map 12 TF60

Crosskeys Riverside House

★★★ BED AND BREAKFAST

Bridge St, Hilgay PE38 0LD
☎ 01366 387777 📠 01366 387777
e-mail: crosskeyshouse@aol.com
web: www.crosskeys.info
dir: 2m S of Downham Market. Off A10 into Hilgay,
Crosskeys on bridge

Situated in the small village of Hilgay on the banks of the
River Wissey, this former coaching inn offers comfortable
accommodation that includes a number of four-poster
bedrooms; many rooms have river views. Public rooms
include a dining room with oak beams and inglenook
fireplace, plus a rustic residents' bar lounge.

Rooms 4 en suite (1 fmly) (2 GF) S £30-£55; D £55*
Facilities tea/coffee Cen ht Fishing Rowing boat for
guests use Parking 10

FAKENHAM   Map 13 TF92

See also Barney

White Horse

★★★★ INN

Fakenham Rd, East Barsham NR21 0LH
☎ 01328 820645 📠 01328 821079
dir: A148 onto B1105 towards Walsingham, inn 2m on
left just before Barsham Manor

Delightful inn situated in a peaceful, rural location just to
the north of Fakenham town centre, in the small village of
East Barsham. The smart bedrooms are carefully
furnished and well equipped. An interesting choice of
dishes is served in the public areas, which include a
small dining room and a cosy, well-stocked lounge bar.

Rooms 3 en suite (1 fmly) Facilities tea/coffee Dinner
available Cen ht Organised bird watching tours
Parking 50 Notes ⊛

Abbott Farm (TF975390)

★★★ FARMHOUSE

Walsingham Rd, Binham NR21 0AW
☎ 01328 830519 📠 01328 830519 Mrs E Brown
e-mail: abbot.farm@btinternet.com
web: www.abbottfarm.co.uk
dir: NE of Fakenham. From Binham SW onto Walsingham
Rd, farm 0.6m on left

A detached red-brick farmhouse set amidst 190 acres of
arable farmland and surrounded by open countryside. The
spacious bedrooms are pleasantly decorated and
thoughtfully equipped; they include a ground-floor room
with a large en suite shower. Breakfast is served in the
attractive conservatory, which has superb views of the
countryside.

Rooms 3 en suite (2 GF) Facilities TVL tea/coffee Cen ht
Parking 20 Notes Closed 24-26 Dec ⊛ 190 acres arable

Fieldview Guest House

★★★ GUEST HOUSE

West Barsham Rd, East Barsham NR21 0AR
☎ 01328 820083
e-mail: info@fieldview.net
dir: From A148 at Fakenham take B1105 to E Barsham,
1st left after village sign

Delightful detached Norfolk flint property ideally situated
for touring the North Norfolk coast. Breakfast is served at
individual pine tables in the dining room which has
superb views of the surrounding countryside. Bedrooms
are pleasantly decorated and equipped with a good range
of useful extras.

Rooms 5 rms (2 en suite) (1 fmly) (1 GF) Facilities TVL
tea/coffee Cen ht Parking 5 Notes ⊛ No Children 7yrs ⊛

GORLESTON ON SEA   Map 13 TG50

Avalon

★★★★ GUEST ACCOMMODATION

54 Clarence Rd NR31 6DR
☎ 01493 662114 📠 01493 668528
e-mail: info@avalon-gorleston.co.uk
web: www.avalon-gorleston.co.uk
dir: A12 past James Paget Hospital. Take 2nd exit at rdbt
towards Gorleston. Next rdbt 2nd exit, 1st right

This Edwardian terrace house is just a short walk from
the promenade and beach. Breakfast and evening meals
are served in the smart dining room and there is a cosy
lounge bar; service is both helpful and friendly. Bedrooms
are pleasantly appointed, each thoughtfully equipped and
well furnished.

Rooms 10 en suite (6 fmly) (1 GF) Facilities TVL tea/
coffee Dinner available Cen ht Licensed Wi-fi Notes ⊛

GORLESTON ON SEA *continued*

Jennis Lodge

★★★ GUEST HOUSE

63 Avondale Rd NR31 6DJ
☎ 01493 662840
e-mail: bookings@jennis-lodge.co.uk
dir: *A12, past James Paget Hosp, rdbt 2nd exit, next rdbt 2nd exit, left & 2nd right*

A friendly, family run guest house situated close to the seafront, marine gardens and town centre. The smartly decorated bedrooms have pine furniture and many thoughtful touches that include TV, DVD or video plus broadband connection. Breakfast and dinner are served in the smart dining room and guests have the use of a cosy lounge with comfy sofas.

Rooms 7 rms (6 en suite) (1 pri facs) (2 fmly) S £25–£28; D £46–£50* **Facilities** FTV TVL tea/coffee Dinner available Cen ht **Notes** LB

GREAT ELLINGHAM   Map 13 TM09

Aldercarr Hall

★★★★ GUEST ACCOMMODATION

Attleborough Rd NR17 1LQ
☎ 01953 455766 & 07710 752213 📠 01953 457993
e-mail: bedandbreakfast@aldercarr-limited.com
dir: *On B1077 500yds SE of village*

Situated amidst extensive grounds and surrounded by open countryside on the edge of Great Ellingham. Public rooms include a comfortably appointed conservatory and a delightful dining room where breakfast is served around a large table. The excellent facilities include a health, beauty and hairdressing studio, an indoor swimming pool, a Jacuzzi and a large function suite.

Rooms 3 annexe en suite (1 fmly) (3 GF) **Facilities** TVL tea/coffee Cen ht 🏌 Golf Fishing Riding Snooker Sauna Pool Table **Conf** Max 125 Board 9 **Parking** 200 **Notes** ⊗

GREAT YARMOUTH   Map 13 TG50

PREMIER COLLECTION

Andover House

★★★★★ 🍽 RESTAURANT WITH ROOMS

28-30 Camperdown NR30 3JB
☎ 01493 843490 📠 01493 852546
e-mail: info@andoverhouse.co.uk
web: www.andoverhouse.co.uk
dir: *Opposite Wellington Pier, turn onto Shadingfield Close, right onto Kimberley Terrace, follow onto Camperdown. Property on left*

This lovely Victorian house has been totally transformed by the current owners, following a complete internal renovation. The property features a series of contemporary spaces that include a large open-plan lounge bar, a brasserie-style restaurant, a cosy lounge and a smart sun terrace. Bedrooms are tastefully appointed with co-ordinated soft furnishings and have many thoughtful touches.

Rooms 20 en suite S £79; D £98–£148* **Facilities** STV FTV TVL tea/coffee Dinner available Direct Dial Cen ht Wi-fi **Conf** Max 100 Thtr 40 Class 60 Board 14 **Notes** ⊗ No Children 16yrs No coaches

---

Barnard House

★★★★ BED AND BREAKFAST

2 Barnard Crescent NR30 4DR
☎ 01493 855139
e-mail: enquiries@barnardhouse.com
dir: *0.5m N of town centre. Off A149 onto Barnard Crescent*

A friendly, family-run guest house, set in mature landscaped gardens in a residential area. The smartly decorated bedrooms are thoughtfully equipped. Breakfast is served in the stylish dining room and there is an elegant lounge with comfy sofas. A warm welcome is assured.

Rooms 3 rms (2 en suite) (1 pri facs) S £40; D £60–£65* **Facilities** FTV TVL tea/coffee Cen ht Wi-fi **Parking** 3 **Notes** LB Closed Xmas & New Year

---

The Classic Lodge

★★★★ BED AND BREAKFAST

13 Euston Rd NR30 1DY
☎ 01493 852851 📠 01493 852851
web: www.classiclodge.com
dir: *A12 to A47, follow signs for seafront. Turn left Sainsbury's, ahead at lights 200mtrs on right, 100mtrs from seafront*

An impressive Victorian villa situated just a short stroll from the seafront and town centre. Breakfast is served at individual tables in the large lounge-dining room, and the spacious bedrooms are carefully furnished and

---

equipped with a very good range of facilities. Secure parking is provided at the rear of the property.

Rooms 3 en suite S £25–£50; D £50–£60 **Facilities** FTV TVL tea/coffee Cen ht Wi-fi **Parking** 7 **Notes** LB ⊗ No Children 18yrs Closed Nov-Apr 🐾

---

3 Norfolk Square

★★★★ GUEST HOUSE

3 Norfolk Square NR30 1EE
☎ 01493 843042 📠 01493 857276
e-mail: info@3norfolksquare.co.uk
web: www.3norfolksquare.co.uk
dir: *From Britannia Pier, 200yds N along seafront, left onto Albemarle Rd*

Delightful refurbished property situated in a peaceful side road just a short walk from the seafront and town centre. The bedrooms are smartly decorated, have co-ordinated soft furnishings and many thoughtful touches. Breakfast and dinner are served in the lower ground floor dining room/bar, and guests also have the use of a large lounge.

Rooms 8 en suite (2 GF) S £30–£50; D £40–£100* **Facilities** FTV TVL tea/coffee Dinner available Cen ht Licensed Wi-fi **Conf** Max 20 Class 20 Board 20 **Parking** 3 **Notes** LB ⊗ No Children 18yrs

---

All Seasons Guest House

★★★★ GUEST HOUSE

10 Nelson Road South NR30 3JL
☎ 01493 852713
e-mail: m kenmore@sky.com
dir: *From seafront (with sea on left) turn onto Kings Rd, Nelson Rd South, 150yds on right*

A well maintained terrace property situated just a short walk from the beach and town centre. Bedrooms are pleasantly decorated with co-ordinated fabrics and have a good range of useful facilities. Breakfast is served at individual tables in the dining room and guests have the use of a comfy lounge.

Rooms 8 en suite (2 fmly) (1 GF) **Facilities** STV TVL tea/coffee Dinner available Cen ht Wi-fi **Conf** Max 16 Thtr 16 Class 16 Board 16 **Notes** LB ⊗

The Chequers

★★★★ GUEST HOUSE

27 Nelson Road South NR30 3JA
☎ 01493 853091
e-mail: mitchellsatchequers@hotmail.co.uk
dir: *Off A47 signed Seafront, right onto Marine Parade & Kings Rd, 1st right*

Guests will receive a warm welcome from the caring hosts at this privately run establishment situated just a short walk from Wellington pier and the beach. Public rooms include a cosy bar, residents' lounge and a smart dining room. Bedrooms are cheerfully decorated and well-equipped.

Rooms 8 rms (7 en suite) (1 pri facs) (2 fmly) **Facilities** FTV TVL tea/coffee Dinner available Cen ht Licensed Wi-fi **Notes** ✿

Knights Court

★★★★ GUEST ACCOMMODATION

22 North Dr NR30 4EW
☎ 01493 843089 📠 01493 850780
e-mail: enquiries@knights-court.co.uk
dir: 600yds N of Britannia Pier, opp Waterways & Gardens

Knights Court stands on the seafront overlooking the Venetian Waterways and the beach. The spacious bedrooms are carefully decorated and equipped with many thoughtful touches, and most rooms have lovely sea views. Breakfast and dinner are served in the smart dining room and there is a cosy lounge bar.

Rooms 14 en suite 6 annexe en suite (5 fmly) (6 GF) S £34-£46; D £60-£79* **Facilities** FTV tea/coffee Dinner available Direct Dial Cen ht Licensed Wi-fi **Parking** 21 **Notes** LB ✿ Closed 31 Oct-20 Mar

Marine Lodge

★★★★ GUEST ACCOMMODATION

19-20 Euston Rd NR30 1DY
☎ 01493 331120
e-mail: res@marinelodge.co.uk

This establishment's enviable seafront position has panoramic views of the bowling greens and beach, and is within easy walking distance of Britannia Pier. Bright modern bedrooms are complemented by smart public areas that include a bar area where light snacks are available during the evening. Guests also have complimentary use of the indoor swimming pool at the sister Palm Court Hotel.

Rooms 40 en suite (5 fmly) (5 GF) **Facilities** FTV TVL tea/coffee Cen ht Lift Licensed Wi-fi **Conf** Thtr 50 Class 35 Board 25 **Parking** 38 **Notes** LB ✿

The Winchester

★★★★ GUEST ACCOMMODATION

12 Euston Rd NR30 1DY
☎ 01493 843950
e-mail: enquiries@winchesterprivatehotel.com
dir: A12 onto A47, signs for seafront, left at Sainsbury's over lights, premises 400yds on right

The friendly hosts at The Winchester give a warm welcome at this guest house just off the seafront. The pleasant bedrooms vary in size and style and are thoughtfully equipped. Public rooms include a large lower ground-floor dining room, a small conservatory and a foyer with plush sofas.

Rooms 14 en suite (2 fmly) (5 GF) S £25-£30; D £50-£60* **Facilities** TVL tea/coffee Dinner available Cen ht Wi-fi **Parking** 10 **Notes** LB ✿ No Children 12yrs Closed Dec-Jan RS Oct-Etr No evening meals ✿

Blenheim

★★★ GUEST HOUSE

58 Apsley Rd NR30 2HG
☎ 01493 856469 📠 01493 856469
e-mail: densimp@aol.com
web: www.theblenheimhotel.co.uk
dir: Near Britannia Pier

This friendly, family-run property lies in a residential side street just a 2-minute walk from the Golden Mile beach, theatre and Britannia Pier. Public rooms include a comfortable lounge bar with a large-screen television and a pleasant dining room. Bedrooms vary in style and size, and a number have en suites.

Rooms 12 rms (8 en suite) (1 fmly) S fr £25; D £50-£100* **Facilities** TVL tea/coffee Dinner available Cen ht Licensed Pool Table **Notes** LB

The Elmfield

★★★ GUEST HOUSE

38 Wellesley Rd NR30 1EU
☎ 01493 859827
e-mail: stay@theelmfield.co.uk
web: www.theelmfield.co.uk

Expect a warm welcome at this family-run guest house situated just a short walk from the beach and shops. Bedrooms are pleasantly decorated with matching soft furnishings and have a range of useful extras; some rooms have sea views. Public rooms include a cosy lounge bar with a large-screen TV and breakfast is served in the smart dining room.

Rooms 9 en suite (3 fmly) **Facilities** TVL tea/coffee Cen ht Licensed Wi-fi **Parking** 5 **Notes** ✿

Harbour

★★★ GUEST HOUSE

20 Pavilion Rd, Gorleston on Sea NR31 6BY
☎ 01493 661031 📠 01493 661031
e-mail: jeffchambers@harbourhotel.freeserve.co.uk
dir: A12 into Gorleston on Sea centre & signs to beach, premises near lighthouse

Ideally situated close to the seafront within easy walking distance of the town centre. The pleasant, well-equipped bedrooms vary in size and style, and some rooms have lovely sea views. Breakfast is served in the spacious dining room, and evening snacks are available in the lounge bar.

Rooms 8 rms (4 en suite) (6 fmly) S £36-£40; D £54-£56* **Facilities** TVL tea/coffee Cen ht Licensed **Parking** 3 **Notes** LB ✿ ✉

Haydee

★★★ GUEST HOUSE

27 Princes Rd NR30 2DG
☎ 01493 844580 📠 01493 844580
e-mail: info@haydee.co.uk
web: www.haydee.co.uk
dir: Off A47 to seafront, Princes Rd opp Britannia Pier

The Haydee is in a side road just a stroll from the seafront, pier and town centre. The pleasant bedrooms vary in size and style, but all are well equipped. Breakfast is served in the smart dining room and there is a cosy lounge bar.

Rooms 8 en suite (2 fmly) (2 smoking) S £20-£25; D £40-£50* **Facilities** TVL tea/coffee Cen ht Licensed **Notes** LB ✿

Senglea Lodge

★★★ GUEST ACCOMMODATION

7 Euston Rd NR30 1DX
☎ 01493 859632
e-mail: senglealodge@fsmail.net
dir: From A4 straight over 1st 2 rdbts. At lights left towards seafront. Through next lights, Lodge on right

Delightful terrace property situated just off the seafront and very close to the town centre. Bedrooms are pleasantly decorated and offer a good range of extras. Breakfast is served at individual tables in the smart open-plan lounge/dining room.

Rooms 6 rms (4 en suite) (2 fmly) (2 smoking) S £20-£22; D £40-£44* **Facilities** FTV TVL tea/coffee Cen ht **Notes** LB ✿ Closed 23 Dec-2 Jan

GREAT YARMOUTH *continued*

Shemara Guest House

★★★ GUEST HOUSE

11 Wellesley Rd NR30 2AR
☎ 01493 844054
e-mail: info@shemaraguesthouse.co.uk
dir: *A47 to Great Yarmouth, follow signs for seafront, take 4th right, Shemara on right*

Shemara is ideally situated in the heart of this busy resort, as it is just a short walk from the town centre and seafront. Bedrooms come in a variety of sizes and styles, each one is pleasantly decorated and well equipped. Breakfast is served at individual tables in the open-plan lounge/dining room.

Rooms 7 en suite (2 fmly) S £18-£25; D £36-£50
Facilities TVL tea/coffee Dinner available Cen ht
Notes LB ⊗ ⊜

Swiss Cottage B&B Just for Non Smokers

★★★ GUEST ACCOMMODATION

31 North Dr NR30 4EW
☎ 01493 855742 & 08450 943949 📱 01493 843547
e-mail: info@swiss-cottage.info
web: www.swisscottagebedandbreakfast.co.uk
dir: *0.5m N of town centre. Off A47 or A12 to to seafront, 750yds N of pier. Turn left at Britannia Pier. Swiss Cottage on left opposite Water Gardens*

A charming detached property situated in the peaceful part of town overlooking the Venetian waterways and the sea beyond. The comfortable co-ordinated bedrooms are pleasantly decorated and equipped with useful extras. Breakfast is served in the smart dining room and guests have use of an open-plan lounge area.

Rooms 8 en suite 1 annexe en suite (2 GF) S £30-£38; D £50-£75* **Facilities** FTV tea/coffee Cen ht Wi-fi
Parking 9 **Notes** LB No Children 11yrs Closed Nov-Feb

Victoria

★★★ GUEST ACCOMMODATION

2 Kings Rd NR30 3JW
☎ 01493 843872 & 842132 📱 01493 843872
e-mail: jhemsley@ukonline.co.uk
web: www.hotelvictoria.org.uk
dir: *Off seafront, opposite model village*

Large detached property situated just off the seafront close to Wellington Pier and the town centre. Bedrooms come in a variety of sizes and styles; each one is pleasantly decorated and thoughtfully equipped. Dinner and breakfast are served in the open plan lounge/dining room. The Victoria also has a smart outdoor swimming pool.

Rooms 36 en suite (12 fmly) (2 GF) S £25-£30; D £45-£60* **Facilities** FTV TVL tea/coffee Dinner available Cen ht Lift Licensed Wi-fi ↗ Pool Table **Conf** Max 50 Thtr 50 Class 50 Board 30 **Parking** 20 **Notes** LB ⊗

Rhonadean

★★ GUEST HOUSE

110-111 Wellesley Rd NR30 2AR
☎ 01493 842004
e-mail: barbara@6wheeler0.wanadoo.co.uk
dir: *500yds N of town centre. Off A47 onto B1141 Fuller's Hill towards seafront, onto St Nicholas Rd & 3rd right*

Rhonadean is situated in a side road adjacent to the seafront and just a short walk from the town centre. Public rooms include a small lounge bar and a dining room where breakfast and dinner are served at individual tables. Bedrooms vary in size and style; each one is pleasantly decorated and well equipped.

Rooms 18 rms (17 en suite) (1 pri facs) (7 fmly) (8 GF)
Facilities TVL tea/coffee Dinner available Cen ht Licensed Pool Table **Notes** ⊗ Closed 24-26 Dec

Amber Lodge

Ⓤ

21 Princes Rd NR30 2DG
☎ 01493 843371
e-mail: paul@amberlodgehotel.co.uk
dir: *From A47 follow signs to seafront, turn right onto Wellesley Rd, 2nd left onto Princes Rd*

Currently the rating for this establishment is not confirmed. This may be due to a change of ownership or because it has only recently joined the AA rating scheme.

Rooms 10 rms (8 en suite) (2 fmly) **Facilities** TVL tea/coffee Dinner available Cen ht Licensed **Notes** ⊗ ⊜

HARLESTON   Map 13 TM28

Heath Farmhouse

★★★★ BED AND BREAKFAST

Homersfield IP20 0EX
☎ 01986 788417
e-mail: julia.john.hunt@googlemail.com
dir: *A143 onto B1062 towards Flixton, over bridge past Suffolk sign & 2nd farm entrance on left at AA sign*

A charming 16th-century farmhouse set amid attractive landscaped grounds that include a croquet lawn. The property retains much of its original character with exposed beams, open fireplaces and wood-burning stoves. The pleasant bedrooms are carefully furnished and have many thoughtful touches. Breakfast and dinner are served in the smart dining room overlooking the garden.

Rooms 2 rms (1 fmly) S £30; D £55* **Facilities** TVL tea/coffee Dinner available Cen ht ⛳ Table tennis **Parking** 8 **Notes** ⊗ ⊜

HEVINGHAM   Map 13 TG12

Marsham Arms Inn

★★★★ ⒶINN

Holt Rd NR10 5NP
☎ 01603 754268
e-mail: nigelbradley@marshamarms.co.uk
web: www.marshamarms.co.uk
dir: *N of Norwich. Off A140 near Norwich Airport onto B1149, through Horsford, establishment 2m on right*

Rooms 11 annexe en suite (8 fmly) (11 GF) S £58.50-£70; D £60-£100* **Facilities** FTV tea/coffee Dinner available Direct Dial Cen ht Wi-fi **Conf** Max 50 Thtr 50 Class 30 Board 30 **Parking** 100 **Notes** LB

HINDRINGHAM

Map 13 TF93

PREMIER COLLECTION

Field House
★★★★★ ≋ BED AND BREAKFAST

Moorgate Rd NR21 0PT
☎ 01328 878726
e-mail: stay@fieldhousehindringham.co.uk
web: www.fieldhousehindringham.co.uk
dir: *Off A148 to Hindringham, onto Moorgate Rd at Lower Green, Field House on left*

A warm friendly welcome and genuine hospitality are to be expected from the caring hosts at this delightful property. Field House is situated in a peaceful rural location amid pretty landscaped gardens. The individually decorated bedrooms are tastefully furnished and have co-ordinated soft fabrics as well as many thoughtful touches. Breakfast is served in the lounge-dining room and features quality, locally sourced produce.

Rooms 2 en suite 1 annexe en suite S £70-£75; D £90-£110 **Facilities** FTV tea/coffee Cen ht Wi-fi 🏊 **Parking** 3 **Notes** LB ⊗ No Children 10yrs Closed 25-26 Dec 🖃

HOLT

Map 13 TG03

See also Thurning

PREMIER COLLECTION

Plantation House
★★★★★ GUEST HOUSE

Ashburn, Old Cromer Rd, High Kelling NR25 6AJ
☎ 01263 710121
e-mail: info@plantation-house.net
web: www.plantation-house.net
dir: *Signs for Kelling Hospital on A148, 1st left & sharp right, 1st house*

A charming property situated on the outskirts of Holt in the wooded village of High Kelling. The property has been lovingly restored by the current owners and provides stylish accommodation throughout. Public rooms feature a colonial-style lounge-dining room with darkwood tables and a leather Chesterfield. The elegant bedrooms have a bright and airy feel; each one has attractive solid wood furniture, co-ordinated fabrics and many thoughtful touches.

Rooms 4 en suite S £55-£75; D £80-£95* **Facilities** tea/coffee Cen ht Wi-fi **Parking** 5 **Notes** LB ⊗ No Children 12yrs

The Lawns Wine Bar
★★★★ ⊛ RESTAURANT WITH ROOMS

26 Station Rd NR25 6BS
☎ 01263 713390
e-mail: mail@lawnsatholt.co.uk
dir: *A148 (Cromer road). 0.25m from Holt rdbt, turn left, 400yds along Station Rd*

A superb Georgian house situated in the centre of this delightful north Norfolk market town. The open-plan public areas include a large wine bar with plush sofas, a conservatory and a smart restaurant. The spacious bedrooms are tastefully appointed with co-ordinated soft furnishings and have many thoughtful touches.

Rooms 8 en suite; D £85-£110* **Facilities** FTV tea/coffee Dinner available Cen ht Wi-fi **Parking** 14 **Notes** LB

The Old Telephone Exchange Bed & Breakfast
★★★★ BED AND BREAKFAST

37 New St NR25 6JH
☎ 01263 712992
e-mail: christopher.manders@btinternet.com
dir: *Off High St onto New St, establishment 200yds on left*

Expect a warm welcome at this small, family-run bed and breakfast situated in a quiet side road close to the town centre. The immaculate bedrooms are tastefully appointed and equipped with many thoughtful touches. Public rooms feature a comfortable lounge-dining area with a wide-screen television, plush sofas, books and games.

Rooms 3 en suite (3 GF) S £55-£70; D £60-£75 **Facilities** TVL tea/coffee Cen ht **Parking** 2 **Notes** LB ⊗ No Children 10yrs 🖃

White Cottage B&B
★★★★ GUEST ACCOMMODATION

Norwich Rd NR25 6SW
☎ 01263 713353
e-mail: enquiries@whitecottageholt.co.uk
dir: *From A148 from Holt take B1149, 0.5m on left after police station*

A delightful detached cottage situated just a short walk from this busy town centre. Breakfast is served at individual tables in the smart dining room and guests have the use of a cosy lounge with comfy sofas. The bedrooms are pleasantly decorated and equipped with a good range of useful extras.

Rooms 2 en suite; D £60-£70* **Facilities** tea/coffee Cen ht **Notes** LB ⊗ No Children 10yrs Closed 21 Dec-7 Jan 🖃

HUNSTANTON

Map 12 TF64

Claremont
★★★★ GUEST HOUSE

35 Greevegate PE36 6AF
☎ 01485 533171
e-mail: claremontgh@tiscali.co.uk
dir: *Off A149 onto Greevegate, house before St Edmund's Church*

This Victorian guest house, close to the shops, beach and gardens, has individually decorated bedrooms with a good range of useful extras. There is also a ground-floor room as well as two feature rooms, one with a four-poster, and another with a canopied bed.

Rooms 7 en suite (1 fmly) (1 GF) **Facilities** TVL tea/coffee Cen ht **Parking** 4 **Notes** No Children 5yrs Closed 15 Nov-15 Mar 🖃

HUNSTANTON *continued*

The Lodge

★★★★ INN

Old Hunstanton Rd PE36 6HX
☎ 01485 532896 📠 01485 535007
e-mail: thelodge@norfolk-hotels.co.uk
web: www.norfolk-hotels.co.uk
dir: On A149 (coast road) from King's Lynn or Cromer

The Lodge is ideally situated in the picturesque village of Old Hunstanton on the beautiful North Norfolk Coast just 400 yards from the beach. The contemporary open plan public rooms include a large lounge bar/dining area and an intimate restaurant. Bedrooms have recently been refurbished with modern décor and smart solid wood furniture.

Rooms 13 en suite 1 annexe en suite (2 GF) S £45–£75; D £80–£140 (incl.dinner) **Facilities** FTV tea/coffee Dinner available Direct Dial Cen ht Wi-fi Pool Table **Parking** 25 **Notes** LB No coaches

The Neptune Restaurant with Rooms

★★★★ ◉◉◉ RESTAURANT WITH ROOMS

85 Old Hunstanton Rd, Old Hunstanton PE36 6HZ
☎ 01485 532122
e-mail: reservations@theneptune.co.uk
web: www.theneptune.co.uk
dir: On A149, past Hunstanton, 200mtrs on left after post office

This charming 18th-century coaching inn, now a restaurant with rooms, is ideally situated for touring the Norfolk coastline. The smartly appointed bedrooms are brightly finished with co-ordinated fabrics and handmade New England furniture. Public rooms feature white clapboard walls, polished dark wood floors, fresh flowers and Lloyd Loom furniture. The food is very much a draw here with the carefully prepared, award-winning cuisine utilising excellent local produce, from oysters and mussels from Thornham to quinces grown on a neighbouring farm.

Rooms 7 en suite **Facilities** FTV tea/coffee Dinner available Direct Dial Cen ht **Parking** 6 **Notes** ⊗ No Children 10yrs Closed last 2wks in Jan RS Oct-Apr Closed Mon No coaches

The King William IV, Country Inn & Restaurant

★★★★ A INN

Heacham Rd, Sedgeford PE36 5LU
☎ 01485 571765 📠 01485 571743
e-mail: info@thekingwilliamsedgeford.co.uk
web: www.thekingwilliamsedgeford.co.uk
dir: A149 to Hunstanton, right at Norfolk Lavender in Heacham onto B1454, signed Docking. 2m to Sedgeford

Rooms 9 en suite (4 fmly) S £50–£65; D £85–£90* **Facilities** tea/coffee Dinner available Cen ht Wi-fi Golf Leisure/Tennis centre 0.5m **Parking** 50 **Notes** LB RS 24-25 Dec no accommodation No coaches

Rosamaly

★★★★ A GUEST ACCOMMODATION

14 Glebe Av PE36 6BS
☎ 01485 534187 & 07775 724484
e-mail: vacancies@rosamaly.co.uk
dir: A149 to Hunstanton. At rdbt take 3rd exit staying on A149 towards Cromer. In 1m church on left, Glebe Av 2nd left, Rosamaly 50yds on left

Rooms 6 en suite (2 fmly) (1 GF) S £35–£62; D £58–£62* **Facilities** TVL tea/coffee Dinner available Cen ht **Notes** LB Closed 24 Dec-1 Jan ◉

Richmond House Bed & Breakfast

★★★ GUEST HOUSE

6-8 Westgate PE36 5AL
☎ 01485 532601
e-mail: richmondhousehotel@xln.co.uk
dir: Off A149 onto Westgate

This well-maintained house is well situated for the seafront and town centre. Its pleasant bedrooms vary in size and style, but all are well equipped and some rooms have superb sea views. Public rooms feature a smart restaurant and a cosy lounge bar.

Rooms 14 rms (10 en suite) (5 GF) S £30–£35; D £50–£55* **Facilities** tea/coffee Dinner available Cen ht Lift Licensed **Notes** ⊗ No Children 18yrs Closed Nov-Etr ◉

The White Cottage

★★★ GUEST ACCOMMODATION

19 Wodehouse Rd PE36 6JW
☎ 01485 532380

A charming cottage situated in a quiet side road in Old Hunstanton. The property has been owned and run by Mrs Burton for over 25 years. The spacious bedrooms are attractively decorated, and some have lovely sea views. Dinner is served in the smart dining room and there is a cosy sitting room with a television.

Rooms 3 rms (1 en suite) **Facilities** TV1B TVL Dinner available Cen ht **Parking** 11 **Notes** LB No Children 3yrs ◉

Fairlight Lodge

★★★★ GUEST ACCOMMODATION

79 Goodwins Rd PE30 5PE
☎ 01553 762234 📠 01553 770280
e-mail: enquiries@fairlightlodge.co.uk
dir: Off A17/A47 onto A148 into town, over rdbt onto B1144 Vancouver Av, straight onto Goodwins Rd

This well-maintained Victorian house stands in attractive gardens on the outskirts of town. The friendly proprietors ensure that good standards are maintained, and the bedrooms and bathrooms are smartly appointed and attractively co-ordinated. Some delightful ground-floor annexe rooms are available and open on-to the garden. A hearty breakfast is served in the bright, cosy dining room.

Rooms 5 rms (4 en suite) (1 pri facs) 2 annexe en suite (1 fmly) (4 GF) S £34–£36; D £51–£53* **Facilities** FTV tea/coffee Cen ht Wi-fi **Parking** 6 **Notes** ⊗ Closed 24 Dec-2 Jan

Guanock

★★★ GUEST ACCOMMODATION

10-11 Guanock Place PE30 5QJ
☎ 01553 772959 📠 01553 772959
dir: Signs to town centre, premises on right of South Gates

Located within easy walking distance of the town centre, this friendly, family-run guest house offers comfortable, practical accommodation. Public areas include a lounge bar, pool room, and a bright dining room where breakfast is served at individual tables. There is also a delightful little roof garden.

Rooms 17 rms (5 fmly) (1 GF) S £28–£32; D fr £50* **Facilities** STV tea/coffee Dinner available Cen ht Licensed Pool Table **Parking** 8 **Notes** ⊗ Closed 24 Dec-3 Jan

Bramley

★★★★ BED AND BREAKFAST

Weasenham Rd PE32 2QT
☎ 01328 701592 📠 01328 701592
e-mail: bramleybandb@hotmail.co.uk
web: www.bramley-litcham.co.uk
dir: A1065 onto B1145. Left at x-rds, left at school, 4th house on left

A warm welcome awaits at this delightful detached house, set in a peaceful location on the village fringe, with ample safe parking in generous grounds. The mostly spacious bedrooms are thoughtfully furnished to ensure guest comfort and have smartly appointed en suite shower rooms. A hearty, freshly-cooked breakfast is served at individual tables in the separate elegant dining room.

Rooms 3 en suite (1 fmly) **Facilities** tea/coffee Cen ht **Parking** 3 **Notes** LB ⊗ ◉

LITTLE WALSINGHAM — Map 13 TF93

The Old Bakehouse Tea Room & Guest House

★★★ GUEST HOUSE

33 High St NR22 6BZ
☎ 01328 820454 📄 01328 820454
e-mail: theoldbakehouseguesthouse@yahoo.co.uk
dir: Exit A148 (Fakenham Bypass) to Wells & Walsingham (B1105). Do not turn left at x-rds, continue straight ahead into Walsingham. Next to post office

Ideally situated in the heart of the historical shrine village of Little Walsingham, The Old Bakehouse offers spacious bedrooms with pine furniture, co-ordinated soft furnishings and many thoughtful touches. Breakfast is served in the large dining room, which is now a traditional tea room during the day.

Rooms 3 en suite S £40-£50; D £70-£80* **Facilities** tea/coffee Dinner available Cen ht Wi-fi **Notes** ⊗

NEATISHEAD — Map 13 TG32

Regency

★★★★ GUEST HOUSE

The Street NR12 8AD
☎ 01692 630233 📄 01692 630233
e-mail: regencywrigley@btinternet.com
dir: 3m from Wroxham. Village 1m from A1151

A charming 17th-century property, situated in a picturesque village close to the Norfolk Broads. The well-equipped and attractive bedrooms have co-ordinated soft furnishings. Breakfast is served in the smart dining room and there are two comfortable lounges with sofas.

Rooms 3 en suite (1 fmly) S fr £40; D £76-£80* **Facilities** tea/coffee Dinner available **Parking** 6 **Notes** LB ☎

NORTH WALSHAM — Map 13 TG23

PREMIER COLLECTION

White House Farm

★★★★★ GUEST ACCOMMODATION

Knapton NR28 0RX
☎ 01263 721344 & 07879 475220
e-mail: info@whitehousefarmnorfolk.co.uk

The caring hosts at this delightful Grade II listed 18th-century flint cottage are particularly welcoming. The property is surrounded by open farmland and has been restored to retain many of its original features. Bedrooms are attractively decorated, tastefully furnished and equipped with many thoughtful touches. Breakfast is served in the smart dining room and guests have the use of a cosy lounge.

Rooms 3 en suite (1 fmly) **Facilities** FTV TVL tea/coffee Cen ht Wi-fi **Parking** 8 **Notes** ⊗ No Children 12yrs

Chimneys

★★★★ BED AND BREAKFAST

51 Cromer Rd NR28 0HB
☎ 01692 406172 & 07952 117701
e-mail: jenny.harmer@8virgin.net
dir: 0.5m NW of town centre on A149

A delightful Edwardian-style town house set amidst mature secluded grounds close to the town centre. Bedrooms are tastefully furnished and thoughtfully equipped, the superior room has a Jacuzzi bath. Breakfast is served in the smart dining room and guests are welcome to sit on the balcony, which overlooks the garden. Dinner is available by prior arrangement.

Rooms 3 en suite (1 fmly) S £40-£45; D £60-£75 **Facilities** FTV tea/coffee Dinner available Cen ht Wi-fi Pool Table **Parking** 5 **Notes** ☎

The Scarborough Hill Country Inn

★★★★ INN

Old Yarmouth Rd NR28 9NA
☎ 01692 402151 📄 01692 406686
e-mail: scarboroughhill@nascr.net
web: www.arlingtonhotel.co.uk
dir: From Norwich B1150, straight through lights, across mini-rdbt, right at next rdbt, 1m on right

A delightful inn with a country house feel situated on the outskirts of town, in a peaceful location amidst landscaped grounds. Public rooms include a smart lounge bar with plush sofas, an intimate dining room and a large conservatory. Bedrooms are generally quite spacious; each one is pleasantly furnished and thoughtfully equipped.

Rooms 8 en suite 1 annexe en suite (1 fmly) (1 GF) S fr £57.50; D fr £70* **Facilities** FTV TVL tea/coffee Dinner available Direct Dial Cen ht Wi-fi **Parking** 80 **Notes** ⊗ Civ Wed

Kings Arms

★★★ INN

Kings Arms St NR28 9JX
☎ 01692 403054 📄 01692 500095
dir: In town centre

A former coaching inn situated in the heart of this bustling market town. The spacious public areas include a public bar, lounge bar and a popular restaurant. The bedrooms are pleasantly decorated and equipped with a good range of useful extras.

Rooms 7 en suite **Facilities** tea/coffee Dinner available Cen ht Pool Table **Conf** Max 100 **Parking** 15 **Notes** ⊗

NORWICH — Map 13 TG20

Gothic House Bed & Breakfast

★★★★ GUEST ACCOMMODATION

King's Head Yard, Magdalen St NR3 1JE
☎ 01603 631879
e-mail: charvey649@aol.com
dir: Follow signs for A147, turn off at rdbt past flyover into Whitefriars. Right again onto Fishergate, at end, right onto Magdalen St

This bed and breakfast establishment is an elegant Grade II listed Regency townhouse set in a quiet courtyard in the heart of Norwich. The property has been lovingly restored and retains much of its original character. The spacious bedrooms are individually decorated and have many thoughtful touches. Breakfast, which includes locally sourced produce, is served in the elegant dining room.

Rooms 2 rms (2 pri facs) S £65; D £95* **Facilities** STV FTV tea/coffee Cen ht Wi-fi **Parking** 2 **Notes** ⊗ No Children 18yrs Closed Feb ☎

NORWICH *continued*

Old Thorn Barn

★★★★ GUEST ACCOMMODATION

Corporation Farm, Wymondham Rd, Hethel NR14 8EU
☎ 01953 607785 & 07726 961530 🖹 01953 601909
e-mail: enquires@oldthornbarn.co.uk
dir: *6m SW of Norwich. Follow signs for Lotus Cars from A11or B1113, on Wymondham Rd*

A delightful Grade II listed barn situated in a peaceful rural location just a short drive from the city centre. The property has stylish, thoughtfully equipped bedrooms with polished wood floors and antique pine furniture. Breakfast is served in the open-plan barn, which also has a wood-burning stove and a cosy lounge area.

Rooms 5 en suite 2 annexe en suite (7 GF) S £34-£40; D £56-£60 **Facilities** FTV TVL tea/coffee Cen ht Wi-fi **Parking** 14 **Notes** ⊗

Church Farm

★★★★ GUEST ACCOMMODATION

Church St, Horsford NR10 3DB
☎ 01603 898020 🖹 01603 891649
e-mail: churchfarmguesthouse@btopenworld.co.uk
dir: *5m NW of city centre. A140 onto B1149, right at x-rds*

Set in a peaceful rural location just a short drive from Norwich airport and the city centre. The spacious bedrooms are smartly decorated, pleasantly furnished and have many thoughtful touches. Breakfast is served at individual tables in the conservatory-style lounge-dining room, which overlooks the garden and sun terrace.

Rooms 10 en suite (1 fmly) (3 GF) **Facilities** FTV TVL tea/coffee Cen ht **Parking** 20 **Notes** ⊗

Cringleford Guest House

★★★★ GUEST HOUSE

1 Gurney Ln, Cringleford NR4 7SB
☎ 01603 451349 & 07775 725933
e-mail: robandkate@cringlefordguesthouse.co.uk
web: www.cringlefordguesthouse.co.uk
dir: *From A11/A47 Thickthorn rdbt signs to Norwich, 0.25m slip road to Cringleford, left at junct onto Colney Ln, Gurney Ln 5th on right*

A delightful property, situated just a short drive from the hospital, University of East Anglia and major roads. The pleasant, well-equipped bedrooms have co-ordinated fabrics and pine furniture. Breakfast is served at individual tables in the smart dining room.

Rooms 5 en suite (3 fmly) (1 GF) S £40-£45; D £60-£65* **Facilities** TVL tea/coffee Cen ht Wi-fi **Parking** 5 **Notes** LB ⊗ Closed 2wks Xmas

Wensum Guest House

★★★★ GUEST HOUSE

225 Dereham Rd NR2 3TF
☎ 01603 621069 🖹 01603 618445
e-mail: info@wensumguesthouse.co.uk
dir: *From A47 1st exit into Norwich A1074 Dereham Rd*

Expect a warm welcome at this modern refurbished guest house situated just a short walk from the city centre. Public rooms include a smart open-plan dining room and a cosy lounge with flat screen TV and plush leather sofas. The contemporary style bedrooms are pleasantly decorated and thoughtfully equipped.

Rooms 9 rms (5 en suite) (4 pri facs) 9 annexe rms 7 annexe en suite (2 annexe pri facs) (4 fmly) (8 GF) **Facilities** FTV tea/coffee Cen ht Wi-fi **Parking** 16 **Notes** ⊗ Closed 24 Dec-3 Jan

Edmar Lodge

★★★ GUEST ACCOMMODATION

64 Earlham Rd NR2 3DF
☎ 01603 615599 🖹 01603 495599
e-mail: mail@edmarlodge.co.uk
web: www.edmarlodge.co.uk
dir: *Off A47 S bypass onto B1108 Earlham Rd, follow university and hospital signs*

Located just a ten minute walk from the city centre, this friendly family-run guest house offers a convenient

location and ample private parking. Individually decorated bedrooms are smartly appointed and well equipped. Freshly prepared breakfasts are served in the cosy dining room; a microwave and a refrigerator are also available.

Edmar Lodge

Rooms 5 en suite (1 fmly) S £38-£43; D £45-£50 **Facilities** FTV tea/coffee Cen ht Wi-fi **Parking** 6

The Larches

★★★ GUEST ACCOMMODATION

345 Aylsham Rd NR3 2RU
☎ 01603 415420 🖹 01603 465340
e-mail: lynda@thelarches.com
web: www.thelarches.com
dir: *On A140, 500yds past ring road, on left adjacent to Lloyds Bank*

A modern, detached property situated only a short drive from the city centre and airport. The spacious, well-equipped bedrooms are brightly decorated, pleasantly furnished and have co-ordinated soft fabrics. Breakfast is served at individual tables in the smart lounge-dining room.

Rooms 7 en suite (2 fmly) (1 GF) S £32; D £55* **Facilities** STV FTV TVL tea/coffee Cen ht Wi-fi **Parking** 10

Marlborough House

★★★ GUEST HOUSE

22 Stracey Rd, Thorpe Rd NR1 1EZ
☎ 01603 628005 🖹 01603 628005
e-mail: marlbhouse@btconnect.com
dir: *Off A!242 0.5m E of city centre*

A friendly family-run property situated close to the railway station, football ground and just a short walk from the city centre. Its pleasant bedrooms have modern facilities, and the public rooms include a cosy lounge bar and a traditionally furnished breakfast room with separate tables.

Rooms 12 rms (7 en suite) (1 pri facs) (2 fmly) (1 GF) S £30-£44; D £54-£58 **Facilities** TVL tea/coffee Cen ht Licensed **Parking** 5 **Notes** LB ⊗ Closed 25-30 Dec 🖭

OXBOROUGH — Map 12 TF70

Bedingfeld Arms
★★★ INN

PE33 9PS
☎ 01366 328300
e-mail: sam.clark@tiscali.co.uk
web: www.bedingfeldarms.com

This establishment provides five annexe rooms in a newly refurbished stable block adjacent to the Bedingfeld Arms. The rooms are spacious, smartly presented with en suite facilities. This is a family run, traditional English pub offering friendly hospitality and home-made pub food including a selection of specials plus a range of locally produced ales.

Rooms en suite 5 annexe en suite (1 fmly) (5 GF) S fr £35; D fr £55* **Facilities** TVL tea/coffee Dinner available Cen ht **Parking** 5

RINGSTEAD — Map 12 TF74

The Gin Trap Inn
★★★★ ⑧ INN

6 High St PE36 5JU
☎ 01485 525264
e-mail: thegintrap@hotmail.co.uk
dir: A149 from Kings Lynn towards Hunstanton. In 15m turn right at Heacham for Ringstead into village centre

This delightful 17th-century inn is in a quiet village just a short drive from the coast. The public rooms include a large open-plan bar and a cosy restaurant. The accommodation is luxurious. Each individually appointed bedroom has been carefully decorated and thoughtfully equipped.

Rooms 3 en suite S £49-£80; D £78-£140* **Facilities** tea/coffee Dinner available Cen ht Wi-fi **Parking** 20 **Notes** No Children No coaches

SHERINGHAM — Map 13 TG14

See also Cromer

PREMIER COLLECTION

The Eight Acres
★★★★★ 🛏 BED AND BREAKFAST

Glebe Farm, Holt Rd, Aylmerton NR11 8QA
☎ 01263 838094 📠 01263 838094
dir: On A148 3m from Cromer, 6m from Holt

A warm welcome is assured at this modern detached farmhouse, which is set amid open countryside just off the A148. Bedrooms are smartly decorated with co-ordinated soft furnishings, lovely pine furniture and many thoughtful extras such as flat-screen digital TVs with built-in DVD. Public rooms feature a large open-plan lounge/dining room.

Rooms 2 en suite S £50-£55; D £60-£65* **Facilities** FTV tea/coffee Cen ht Wi-fi DVD players available in rooms **Parking** 2 **Notes** ⊗ No Children 16yrs Closed Nov-Feb ✉

PREMIER COLLECTION

Fairlawns
★★★★★ GUEST HOUSE

26 Hooks Hill Rd NR26 8NL
☎ 01263 824717
e-mail: info@fairlawns-sheringham.co.uk
web: www.fairlawns-sheringham.com
dir: A148 (King's Lynn to Cromer), exit A1082. Left at 1st rdbt, next left into Holt Rd, left into Vicarage Rd, right into Hooks Hill Rd

A lovely Victorian property which is situated just a few minutes' walk from the town centre and beach. The attractively decorated bedrooms are tastefully furnished and equipped with many thoughtful touches. The stylish public areas include a comfortable lounge with a small corner bar, a conservatory dining room and a lovely garden with croquet pitch.

Rooms 5 en suite (1 fmly) S £65-£70; D £90-£110 **Facilities** TVL tea/coffee Direct Dial Cen ht Licensed ⌣ ⌁ **Notes** ⊗ ✉

PREMIER COLLECTION

Ashbourne House
★★★★★ 🛏 GUEST ACCOMMODATION

1 Nelson Rd NR26 8BT
☎ 01263 821555 📠 01263 821555
e-mail: nailligill@yahoo.co.uk
dir: Take A149 Cromer road towards Cromer, turn left over Beeston Common. Under bridge, at top of Curtis Ln turn left, situated on right

This superb detached property has been tastefully refurbished to a very high standard by the current owners. The smartly appointed bedrooms have lovely soft furnishings and are full of thoughtful touches. Public rooms include a large entrance hall, a guest lounge and a snooker room on the second floor. Breakfast is served in the stylish panelled dining room, which overlooks the smart landscaped gardens that slope upwards to the cliff top.

Rooms 3 en suite S £45-£50; D £60-£65* **Facilities** TVL tea/coffee Cen ht 3/4 size snooker table **Parking** 3 **Notes** ⊗ No Children 12yrs ✉

PREMIER COLLECTION

The Eiders Bed & Breakfast
★★★★★ BED AND BREAKFAST

Holt Rd, Aylmerton NR11 8QA
☎ 01263 837280
e-mail: enquiries@eiders.co.uk
web: www.eiders.co.uk
dir: From Cromer on A148, enter Aylmerton, pass garage on left. After x-rds, 2nd entrance on right

The Eiders is situated just a short drive from the centre of town and is ideally placed for touring the north Norfolk coast. The tastefully appointed bedrooms have lovely co-ordinated fabrics and many thoughtful touches. Breakfast is served at individual tables in the conservatory which overlooks the gardens and duck pond. Guests have the use of a heated swimming pool which is open from May to September.

Rooms 6 en suite (2 fmly) (6 GF) S £60-£70; D £80-£110* **Facilities** FTV TVL tea/coffee Cen ht Wi-fi ⌁ **Parking** 7 **Notes** LB ⊗ ✉

SHERINGHAM *continued*

At Knollside

★★★★ BED AND BREAKFAST

43 Cliff Rd NR26 8BJ
☎ 01263 823320 & 07771 631980 📄 01263 823320
e-mail: avril@at-knollside.co.uk
web: www.at-knollside.co.uk
dir: *250yds E of town centre. A1082 to High St, onto Wyndham St & Cliff Rd*

Expect a warm welcome from the caring hosts at this delightful Victorian house overlooking the beach and sea. Bedrooms are tastefully furnished, have co-ordinated fabrics and enjoy many thoughtful touches. Breakfast is served in the elegant dining room and features local produce. Guests also have the use of a comfortable lounge.

Rooms 3 en suite; D £69-£80 **Facilities** tea/coffee Cen ht ♿ **Parking** 3 **Notes** LB ⊗ No Children 3yrs ⊛

Bay Leaf Guest House

★★★★ BED AND BREAKFAST

10 St Peters Rd NR26 8QY
☎ 01263 823779
e-mail: bayleafgh@aol.com
dir: *A149 (Weybourne Rd) onto Church St, 2nd right*

A lovely Victorian property situated just a short walk from the golf course, steam railway and town centre. There is a smart lounge bar, and breakfast is served in the conservatory-dining room which overlooks the patio.

Rooms 7 en suite (2 fmly) (2 GF) S £38-£50; D £52-£72* **Facilities** tea/coffee Cen ht Licensed **Parking** 5 **Notes** LB ⊗ No Children 8yrs ⊛

Brambles Bed & Breakfast

★★★★ GUEST ACCOMMODATION

5 Nelson Rd NR26 8BT
☎ 01263 825567 📄 01263 825567
e-mail: enquiries@stayatbrambles.co.uk
dir: *Leave A148 into Sheringham across rdbt, right at Lobster pub. Left onto Cliff Rd, right onto Nelson Rd*

A warm welcome is offered by the caring hosts at this delightful detached property situated just a short walk from the seafront and town centre. The well-equipped bedrooms bedrooms are pleasantly decorated and breakfast is served in the smart dining room.

Rooms 3 en suite (1 fmly) (1 GF) S £50-£60; D £60-£70* **Facilities** tea/coffee Cen ht **Parking** 6 **Notes** LB ⊗ ⊛

Highfield

★★★★ GUEST HOUSE

5 Montague Rd NR26 8LN
☎ 01263 825524 & 07769 628817
e-mail: gmcaldwell@aol.com
dir: *Off A148, left at mini rdbt, 1st right. Left at church, left onto South St & Montague Rd*

This delightful guest house is situated in a peaceful side road within easy walking distance of the shops and beach. It offers smart, thoughtfully equipped bedrooms, and breakfast is served at individual tables in the attractive dining room.

Rooms 6 rms (5 en suite) (1 pri facs) (2 fmly) **Facilities** TVL tea/coffee Cen ht **Conf** Max 20 Board 20 **Parking** 2 **Notes** ⊗ No Children 8yrs Closed 22 Dec-1 Feb ⊛

Magnolia Cottage

★★★★ BED AND BREAKFAST

8 Holt Rd NR26 8NA
☎ 01263 824635
e-mail: abolderstone@btinternet.com
dir: *A148 onto A1082, at rdbt left onto A149. 1st left onto Holt Rd, 200yds on right*

Delightful detached cottage set in pretty landscaped grounds in a peaceful residential area just a short walk from the centre of town. The thoughtfully-equipped bedrooms are tastefully decorated. Breakfast is served at individual tables in the smart conservatory which overlooks the neat gardens.

Rooms 2 rms (1 en suite) (1 pri facs) D £50-£70* **Facilities** FTV TVL tea/coffee Cen ht Golf 18 **Parking** 2 **Notes** ⊗ No Children 14yrs ⊛

The Old Barn

★★★★ Ⓐ GUEST ACCOMMODATION

Cromer Rd, West Runton NR27 9QT
☎ 01263 838285
dir: *A149 from Cromer to West Runton, 2m opp church*

Rooms 3 rms (2 en suite) (1 pri facs) (1 GF) S fr £45; D £64-£70* **Facilities** TVL tea/coffee Cen ht **Parking** 6 **Notes** ⊗ No Children 18yrs ⊛

SWAFFHAM Map 13 TF80

Red Lion Motel

★★ INN

87 Market Place PE37 7AQ
☎ 01760 721022 📄 01760 720664
e-mail: gwhoare@aol.com
dir: *In town centre*

Located in the central Market Place, this popular inn offers a range of real ales, meals and snacks in the lounge bar. Accommodation is in a motel-style block across the rear courtyard and includes bedrooms with modern facilities and some rooms suitable for families.

Rooms 9 annexe en suite (9 GF) **Facilities** tea/coffee Dinner available Cen ht **Parking** 8 **Notes** ⊗

THOMPSON Map 13 TL99

The Chequers Inn

★★★★ Ⓐ INN

Griston Rd IP24 1PX
☎ 01953 483360 📄 01953 488092
e-mail: richard@thompsonchequers.co.uk
dir: *NE of Thetford. Off A1075 to Thompson village x-rds*

Rooms 3 annexe en suite (1 fmly) (3 GF) S £45; D £65* **Facilities** FTV tea/coffee Dinner available Direct Dial Cen ht Fishing **Parking** 35

THURNING Map 13 TG02

Rookery Farm *(TG78307)*

★★ FARMHOUSE

NR24 2JP
☎ 01263 860357 Mrs A M Fisher
dir: *Off B1354 S through Briston, left at x-rds signed Saxthorpe, farm 0.6m on left*

A delightful 300-year-old red-brick farmhouse, set amid landscaped grounds in peaceful countryside. The spacious bedrooms are pleasantly decorated and well equipped. Breakfast is served at a large table in the dining room, which doubles as a sitting room.

Rooms 2 rms (1 en suite) (1 fmly) **Facilities** TVL tea/coffee Dinner available **Notes** ⊗ Closed Dec-Jan ⊛ 400 acres arable

THURSFORD Map 13 TF93

PREMIER COLLECTION

Holly Lodge
★★★★★ ⬤ BED AND BREAKFAST

The Street NR21 0AS
☎ 01328 878465 ▤ 01328 878465
e-mail: info@hollylodgeguesthouse.co.uk
dir: Off A148 into Thursford, village green on left. 2nd driveway on left past green

An award-winning 18th-century property situated in a picturesque location surrounded by open farmland. The stylish cottage bedrooms are in a converted stable block, each room individually decorated, beautifully furnished and equipped with many useful extras. The attractive public rooms have a wealth of character, with flagstone floors, oak beams and open fireplaces. There are also superb landscaped grounds to enjoy.

Rooms 3 en suite (3 GF) S £60-£90; D £80-£110*
Facilities TVL tea/coffee Dinner available Cen ht Wi-fi
Parking 6 **Notes** LB ⊗ No Children 14yrs Closed Jan

The Old Forge Seafood Restaurant
★★★ ⬤ RESTAURANT WITH ROOMS

Seafood Restaurant, Fakenham Rd NR21 0BD
☎ 01328 878345
e-mail: sarah.goldspink@btconnect.com
dir: On A148 (Fakenham to Holt road), next to garage at Thursford

Expect a warm welcome at this delightful relaxed restaurant with rooms. The open-plan public areas include a lounge bar area with comfy sofas, and a intimate restaurant with pine tables. Bedrooms are pleasantly decorated and equipped with a good range of useful facilities.

Rooms 2 en suite S £30; D £60 **Facilities** FTV tea/coffee Dinner available **Conf** Max 28 Class 28 **Parking** 10
Notes No coaches

WELLS-NEXT-THE-SEA Map 13 TF94

Branthill Farm (TF900407)
★★★ FARMHOUSE

NR23 1SB
☎ 01328 710246 ▤ 01328 711524 Mrs Maufe
e-mail: branthill.farms@unicombox.co.uk
web: www.therealaleshop.com
dir: 1.5m SW of Wells off B1105

Branthill is a friendly family-run farmhouse situated in peaceful countryside just a short drive from the north Norfolk coast. A hearty breakfast is served at the large communal table in the attractive dining room. The one bedroom is equipped with many useful extras and offers a good degree of comfort. A real ale shop is a successful addition to the farm.

Rooms 1 en suite **Facilities** tea/coffee Cen ht ⌇ ⬤
Parking 2 **Notes** LB ⊗ No Children 1mth ⬤ 1000 acres arable

Kilcoroon
★★★ BED AND BREAKFAST

Chancery Ln NR23 1ER
☎ 01328 710270
e-mail: terry@kilcoroon.co.uk
dir: Exit B1105 onto Mill Rd. 3rd right onto Buttlands. Left of Crown Hotel

Delightful detached period property situated by the green, just off the Buttlands and a short walk from the town centre. The spacious bedrooms are pleasantly decorated with co-ordinated fabrics and equipped with modern facilities. Breakfast is served at a large communal table in the elegant dining room.

Rooms 3 rms (1 en suite) S £55-£65; D £70-£80*
Facilities tea/coffee Cen ht **Notes** ⊗ No Children 10yrs Closed 23-31 Dec ⬤

WEST RUNTON Map 13 TG14

Corner House
★★★★ BED AND BREAKFAST

2 Station Rd NR27 9QD
☎ 01263 838540 & 07769 800831 ▤ 01263 838540
e-mail: linjimhoward@btinternet.com
web: www.cornerhousenorfolk.com
dir: Station Rd, N off A149, in villlage centre, B&B 1st on right

A warm welcome is to be expected from the caring hosts at this delightful property situated just off the main coast road on the outskirts of Sheringham. Bedrooms are cheerfully decorated, have co-ordinated fabrics, and benefit from many thoughtful touches. Public areas include a large breakfast room and a cosy TV lounge.

Rooms 3 rms (1 en suite) (2 pri facs) S £40; D £60-£66*
Facilities TVL tea/coffee Cen ht **Notes** ⊗ No Children 8yrs ⬤

WORSTEAD Map 13 TG32

The Ollands
★★★★ ⬤ GUEST HOUSE

Swanns Yard NR28 9RP
☎ 01692 535150 ▤ 01692 535150
e-mail: theollands@btinternet.com
dir: Off A149 to village x-rds, off Back St

This charming detached property is set in the heart of the picturesque village of Worstead. The well-equipped bedrooms are pleasantly decorated and carefully

furnished, and breakfast served in the elegant dining room features local produce.

Rooms 3 en suite (1 GF) S £37.50-£39.50; D £60-£64*
Facilities TVL tea/coffee Dinner available Cen ht Wi-fi
Parking 8 **Notes** LB

WORTWELL Map 13 TM28

Fourwinds Cottage
[U]

Tunbeck Rd IP20 0HP
☎ 01986 788418
e-mail: fourwindstunbeck@aol.com
dir: A143 from Harleston turn left before Dove public house

Currently the rating for this establishment is not confirmed. This may be due to a change of ownership or because it has only recently joined the AA rating scheme.

Rooms 2 en suite 1 annexe en suite (3 GF) S £35; D £60*
Facilities STV tea/coffee Cen ht **Parking** 3 **Notes** LB ⊗ No Children 5yrs ⬤

WROXHAM Map 13 TG31

Wroxham Park Lodge Guest House
★★★★ Ⓐ BED AND BREAKFAST

142 Norwich Rd NR12 8SA
☎ 01603 782991
e-mail: parklodge@computer-assist.net
dir: On A1151 in village centre

Rooms 3 en suite S £38-£42; D £58-£62* **Facilities** tea/coffee Cen ht Golf **Parking** 4 **Notes** LB ⊗ No Children ⬤

Beech Tree House
★★★ BED AND BREAKFAST

Wroxham Rd, Rackheath NR13 6NQ
☎ 01603 781419 & 07889 152063 ▤ 01603 781419
e-mail: beechtree@talk21.com
dir: 1.5m SW of Wroxham on A1151 opp Green Man pub

This detached property, set amid pretty landscaped grounds and surrounded by farmland, is just a short drive from Norwich and Wroxham Broads. The spacious, thoughtfully-equipped bedrooms are pleasantly decorated with co-ordinated soft furnishings. Breakfast is served in the conservatory-lounge that overlooks the garden.

Rooms 3 rms (1 en suite) (3 fmly) D £55-£65*
Facilities FTV TVL tea/coffee Cen ht ⬤ Golf **Parking** 5
Notes LB Closed 23 Dec-1 Jan ⬤

NORTHAMPTONSHIRE

COLLYWESTON — Map 11 SK90

The Collyweston Slater
★★★★ ◉◉ INN

87 Main Rd PE9 3PQ
☎ 01780 444288
e-mail: info@thecollywestonslater.co.uk
dir: 4m SW of Stamford on A43

This pleasant village inn is appointed to a smart, modern standard throughout. Individually designed bedrooms are stylish and well equipped, while the ground floor public areas are given over to a stylish brasserie. The modern British food is worthy of note, with monthly changing menus supplemented by daily specials.

Rooms 5 en suite (1 fmly) Facilities tea/coffee Dinner available Cen ht Wi-fi Petanque Piste Conf Max 12 Thtr 12 Class 6 Board 10 Parking 30 Notes ⊗

ECTON — Map 11 SP86

The World's End
★★★ INN

Main St NN6 0QN
☎ 01604 414521 📠 01604 400334
e-mail: info@theworldsend.org
dir: On A4500 on outskirts of Ecton. A45 for Cogenhoe/ Great Billing, follow Ecton signs

A modern inn with striking interior, wooden floors, leather sofas, mirrors and downlighters. Smart, well appointed, boutique-style bedrooms have flat-screen TVs, broadband and power showers along with all the expected amenities. The restaurant offers plenty of choice to suit all appetites.

Rooms 20 en suite (9 GF) S £65-£85; D £65-£85* Facilities tea/coffee Direct Dial Cen ht Lift Wi-fi Conf Max 35 Thtr 35 Class 16 Board 16 Parking 50 Notes ⊗

KILSBY — Map 11 SP57

Hunt House Quarters
★★★★ GUEST ACCOMMODATION

Main Rd CV23 8XR
☎ 01788 823282
e-mail: luluharris@hunthouse.fsbusiness.co.uk
web: www.hunthousekilsby.com
dir: On B3048 in village

This thatched 17th-century hunting lodge has been renovated to provide quality bedrooms with smart modern bathrooms in a converted stable block. Comprehensive breakfasts are served in the adjacent courtyard building.

Rooms 4 en suite (1 fmly) (4 GF) S £59.95-£75; D £75-£85 Facilities tea/coffee Cen ht Licensed Wi-fi Parking 8 Notes LB ⊗

OLD STRATFORD — Map 11 SP74

The Lodge
★★★ BED AND BREAKFAST

Furtho Manor Farm MK19 6NR
☎ 01908 543765
e-mail: dsansome@talktalk.net
dir: Just off A5, on A508 towards Northampton

Situated on a dairy farm, bedrooms in this family bungalow overlook countryside. There are three bedrooms, one of which has self-catering facilities. Breakfast is served farmhouse style in the open-plan kitchen/dining room.

Rooms 3 rms (2 en suite) (1 pri facs) (3 GF) S £30-£40; D £55-£65* Facilities FTV tea/coffee Cen ht Wi-fi 🎣 Fishing Parking 6 Notes ⊗ RS 24 Dec-1 Jan Accommodation only ✉

OUNDLE — Map 11 TL08

Bridge Cottage Bed & Breakfast
★★★★ BED AND BREAKFAST

Oundle Rd, Woodnewton PE8 5EG
☎ 01780 470779 & 07979 644864 📠 01780 470860
e-mail: enquiries@bridgecottage.net
dir: A1 onto A605, right at 1st rdbt, through Fortheringham towards Woodnewtown. 1st house on left entering village

A delightful and peaceful location on the periphery of the village of Woodnewton (next to the bridge) and bordered by open countryside, this lovely B&B offers real home-from-home comforts with tastefully appointed accommodation. A warm welcome and a tasty, freshly cooked breakfast ensure that guests return time and again. Breakfast is taken in the open-plan kitchen, which overlooks lovely garden that has summerhouse, bubbling brook and an abundance of birdlife (spot the Kingfisher).

Rooms 3 rms (2 en suite) (1 pri facs) S £40-£55; D £80-£90 Facilities tea/coffee Cen ht Parking 3 Notes RS 24-26 Dec ✉

STANWICK — Map 11 SP97

PREMIER COLLECTION

The Courtyard Luxury Lodge
★★★★★ GUEST ACCOMMODATION

Rutland Lodge, West St NN9 6QY
☎ 01933 622233 📠 01933 622276
e-mail: bookings@thecourtyard.me.uk
web: www.thecourtyard.me.uk
dir: A45 rdbt to Stanwick, entrance immediately on right

Standing in extensive and delightful gardens and on the edge of the village, this very well-furnished detached house offers guests every possible comfort, and the lounge is especially relaxing. Quality breakfasts are served around a large oak table and hospitality is really special.

Rooms 12 en suite (10 GF) S £59-£65; D £75-£85* Facilities FTV TVL tea/coffee Dinner available Cen ht Licensed Wi-fi Conf Max 30 Thtr 30 Class 20 Board 20 Parking 50 Notes LB Civ Wed 100

NORTHUMBERLAND

ALNWICK — Map 21 NU11

Bondgate House
★★★★ 🏠 GUEST HOUSE

20 Bondgate Without NE66 1PN
☎ 01665 602025
e-mail: enquiries@bondgatehouse.co.uk
web: www.bondgatehouse.co.uk
dir: A1 onto B6346 into town centre, 200yds past war memorial on right

Originally a doctor's house, this Georgian building stands close to the historic gateway into the town centre. Friendly service complements an attractive breakfast room, memorable breakfasts and the cosy lounge. Bedrooms are all well equipped and thoughtfully furnished and include three rooms in converted stables set in a secluded garden behind the house. Anne and Stephen Larvin were finalists for the AA Friendliest Landlady of the Year 2009-2010 Award.

Rooms 3 en suite 3 annexe en suite (1 fmly) (1 GF); D £80-£85* Facilities TVL tea/coffee Cen ht Aromatherapy massage Parking 8 Notes ⊗ No Children 5yrs Closed Xmas ✉

BARDON MILL   Map 21 NY76

Gibbs Hill Farm B&B *(NY749693)*

★★★★ 🅐 FARMHOUSE

NE47 7AP
☎ **01434 344030** 🖷 01434 344030 Mrs V Gibson
e-mail: val@gibbshillfarm.co.uk
dir: *Off A69 at Bardon Mill, signs to Oncebrewed, over B6318, up hill, 1m right at sign to Gibbs Hill*

Rooms 3 en suite (1 fmly) S £45-£55; D £65-£70*
Facilities FTV TVL tea/coffee Dinner available Cen ht
Fishing Riding **Parking** 10 **Notes** LB ⊗ No Children 10yrs
Closed Nov-Apr 750 acres mixed

BELFORD   Map 21 NU13

PREMIER COLLECTION

Market Cross

★★★★★ 🛏 GUEST ACCOMMODATION

1 Church St NE70 7LS
☎ **01668 213013**
e-mail: info@marketcross.net
web: www.marketcross.net
dir: *Off A1 into village, opp church*

Lying in the heart of the village, this Grade II listed building offers delightful, individually styled and thoughtfully equipped bedrooms. A friendly welcome awaits you, and breakfast is also a real treat, an extensive and impressive range of delicious cooked dishes using local produce.

Rooms 3 en suite (1 fmly); D £70-£120* **Facilities** FTV
TVL tea/coffee Cen ht Wi-fi **Parking** 3 **Notes** LB

BERWICK-UPON-TWEED   Map 21 NT95

PREMIER COLLECTION

West Coates

★★★★★ 🛏 🍽 BED AND BREAKFAST

30 Castle Ter TD15 1NZ
☎ **01289 309666** 🖷 01289 309666
e-mail: karenbrownwestcoates@yahoo.com
dir: *A6105 into Berwick-upon-Tweed onto Castle Terrace, half-way down on left*

This impressive family house is set in mature gardens and all guests are given a warm welcome. The spacious bedrooms are beautifully appointed with a wide range of thoughtful extras. Facilities also include a swimming pool and hot tub. Delicious meals made using fresh local produce are served in the dining room, which also has a comfortable lounge area.

Rooms 3 rms (2 en suite) (1 pri facs) S £60-£70;
D £90-£120* **Facilities** FTV tea/coffee Dinner available
Cen ht Wi-fi 🏊 ⛲ Hot tub **Parking** 3 **Notes** LB ⊗ No
Children Closed Xmas & New Year

Lindisfarne Inn

★★★ INN

Beal TD15 2PD
☎ **01289 381223** 🖷 01289 381223
e-mail: enquiries@lindisfarneinn.co.uk
dir: *On A1, turn off for Holy Island*

The Lindisfarne Inn stands on the site of the old "Plough Hotel" at Beal, on the road leading to Holy Island. Now totally refurbished and re-opened with a traditional bar, rustic style restaurant and comfortably equipped courtyard bedrooms in the adjacent wing. Food is available all day.

Rooms 21 annexe en suite (20 fmly) (10 GF)
Facilities FTV TVL tea/coffee Dinner available Cen ht
Parking 25

CHATTON   Map 21 NU02

AA GUEST ACCOMMODATION OF THE YEAR FOR ENGLAND

PREMIER COLLECTION

Chatton Park House

★★★★★ 🛏 BED AND BREAKFAST

NE66 5RA
☎ **01668 215507** 🖷 01668 215507
e-mail: enquiries@chattonpark.com
web: www.chattonpark.com
dir: *A1 N onto B6348 for 4m, on right*

This charming Georgian house is nestled in 4 acres of gardens, with views out to the Northumberland countryside and Cheviots hills. Once the former home of the current Duke of Northumberland, whose family seat is Alnwick Castle. Spacious bedrooms are very elegantly furnished, one is a suite. The dining room and drawing room overlook the gardens and both have open fires. A warm welcome is guaranteed, as Chatton Park House is the winner of the AA's Guest Accommodation of the Year for England 2009-2010 Award.

Rooms 3 en suite; D £100-£140* **Facilities** FTV tea/coffee Cen ht Wi-fi 🏌 **Parking** 3 **Notes** ⊗ No Children 12yrs

---

CORNHILL-ON-TWEED   Map 21 NT83

PREMIER COLLECTION

Ivy Cottage

★★★★★ 🛏 GUEST ACCOMMODATION

1 Croft Gardens, Crookham TD12 4ST
☎ **01890 820667** 🖷 01890 820667
e-mail: ajoh540455@aol.com
web: www.ivycottagecrookham.co.uk
dir: *4m E of Cornhill. Off A697 onto B6353 into Crookham*

Hospitality is second to none at this pristine modern house set in delightful gardens in a quiet village. Three rooms are available, and all are thoughtfully furnished with either a super private bathroom or full en suite. Delicious Aga-cooked breakfasts are served either in the farmhouse-style kitchen or the cosy dining room, and dinners are available by arrangement. Guests can enjoy tea in the spacious lounge or charming summerhouse.

Rooms 3 rms (1 en suite) (2 pri facs) (1 GF)
S £45-£50* **Facilities** FTV TVL tea/coffee Dinner
available Cen ht **Parking** 2 **Notes** LB No Children 5yrs
🍽

FALSTONE — Map 21 NY78

Pheasant Inn

★★★★ INN

Stannersburn NE48 1DD
☎ 01434 240382 📠 01434 240382
e-mail: enquiries@thepheasantinn.com
web: www.thepheasantinn.com
dir: 1m S of Falstone. Off B6320 to Kielder Water, via
Bellingham or via Hexham A69 onto B6320 via Wall-
Wark-Bellingham

This charming establishment epitomises the traditional
country inn; it has character, good food and warm
hospitality. Bright modern bedrooms, some with their own
entrances, are all contained in stone buildings adjoining
the inn. Delicious home-cooked meals are served in the
bar with its low-beamed ceilings and exposed stone
walls, or in the attractive dining room.

Rooms 8 annexe en suite (1 fmly) (5 GF) S £50-£55;
D £85-£90 **Facilities** tea/coffee Dinner available Cen ht
Parking 40 **Notes** LB Closed Xmas RS Nov-Mar (closed
Mon/Tue) No coaches

The Blackcock Inn

★★★ INN

NE48 1AA
☎ 01434 240200
e-mail: thebcinn@yahoo.co.uk
dir: From Hexham take A6079 to Bellingham, then left at
church. In village centre, towards Kielder Water

This traditional family-run village inn lies close to Kielder
Water. A cosy pub, it has a very homely atmosphere, with
welcoming fires in the colder weather. The bedrooms are
very comfortable and well equipped, with family rooms
available. Evening meals are served here or in the cosy
restaurant. The inn is closed during the day on Tuesdays
throughout winter.

Rooms 6 rms (4 en suite) (2 pri facs) (1 fmly) S £35-£60;
D £70-£80* **Facilities** tea/coffee Dinner available Cen ht
Wi-fi Fishing Pool Table Children's play area **Parking** 15
Notes LB RS Tue Closed during low season

FELTON — Map 21 NU10

Birchwood House

★★★ GUEST ACCOMMODATION

Kitswell Dene NE65 9NZ
☎ 01670 787828 📠 01670 787828
e-mail: gbblewitt@btinternet.com
web: www.gbblewitt.co.uk
dir: Just off A1. Take Swarland exit, bear left, left again

Conveniently situated close to the A1, this smart house
offers warm hospitality and spacious, well-equipped en
suite bedrooms. Freshly prepared, hearty breakfasts are
served in the dining room and guests can also enjoy the
separate lounge. Bedrooms are all on the ground floor.

Rooms 4 en suite (1 fmly) (4 GF) S £30-£35; D £60-£70
Facilities FTV TVL tea/coffee Cen ht Wi-fi **Parking** 10
Notes ⊗ Closed 24 Dec-1 Mar RS Nov-23 Dec & 2 Mar-
Apr ⊗

GILSLAND — Map 21 NY66

Bush Nook

★★★★ GUEST HOUSE

Upper Denton CA8 7AF
☎ 016977 47194 📠 016977 47194
e-mail: info@bushnook.co.uk
web: www.bushnook.co.uk
dir: Halfway between Brampton & Haltwhistle. Off A69
signed Spadeadam, Birdoswald, Bush Nook

Located in open countryside, this converted farmhouse
offers comfortable bedrooms, split between the main
house and the barn, with many original features. Other
guest areas include the spacious breakfast room, cosy
lounge and impressive conservatory leading out to a
large, well maintained garden. Particularly popular with
walkers and cyclists, although a warm welcome is given
to all.

Rooms 7 en suite (1 GF) S £40; D £72-£100 **Facilities** FTV
tea/coffee Dinner available Cen ht Licensed Wi-fi
Parking 6 **Notes** LB ⊗ Closed Xmas & New Year

HALTWHISTLE — Map 21 NY76

See also Brampton (Cumbria)

Vallum Lodge

★★★★ GUEST HOUSE

Military Rd, Twice Brewed NE47 7AN
☎ 01434 344248 📠 01434 344488
e-mail: stay@vallum-lodge.co.uk
web: www.vallum-lodge.co.uk
dir: On B6318, 400yds W of Once Brewed National Park
visitors' centre

Set in the Northumberland National Park, a real home-
from-home atmosphere is found at this well-equipped
roadside guest house, which provides easy access to
Hadrian's Wall. The en suite bedrooms feature homely
extras. Breakfast is served in the smart dining room and
there is a cosy lounge. The Lodge is licensed and all
accommodation is on the ground floor.

Rooms 6 en suite (1 fmly) (6 GF); D £75-£80*
Facilities FTV TVL tea/coffee Cen ht Licensed Wi-fi
Parking 15 **Notes** ⊗

HEXHAM — Map 21 NY96

Peth Head Cottage

★★★★ BED AND BREAKFAST

Juniper NE47 0LA
☎ 01434 673286 📠 01434 673038
e-mail: peth_head@btopenworld.com
web: www.peth-head-cottage.co.uk
dir: B6306 S from Hexham, 200yds fork right, next left.
Continue 3.5m, house 400yds on right after Juniper sign

Warm and caring hospitality is assured at this lovely
sandstone cottage located in the peaceful hamlet of
Juniper. Guests can enjoy home-made biscuits on arrival
and home-baked bread and preserves at breakfast. The
attractive bedrooms are equipped with lots of thoughtful

extras and day rooms feature a cosy lounge-breakfast room. Self-catering is also available.

Rooms 2 en suite S £29; D £58 **Facilities** TVL tea/coffee Cen ht **Parking** 2 **Notes** LB ⊗

NEWTON-ON-THE-MOOR   Map 21 NU10

The Cook and Barker Inn

★★★★ 🍽 INN

NE65 9JY
☎ 01665 575234   📄 01665 575234
dir: *North on A1, pass Morpeth. A1 becomes single carriageway for 8m, then dual carriageway. Up slight incline 3m, follow signs on left to Newton-on-the-Moor*

Set in the heart of a quiet village, this inn is popular with visitors and locals. The emphasis is on food here with interesting home-made dishes offered in the restaurant and bar areas. Bedrooms are smartly furnished and well equipped and are split between the main house and the adjacent annexe.

Rooms 4 en suite 14 annexe en suite (2 fmly) (7 GF) **Facilities** tea/coffee Dinner available Cen ht **Conf** Max 50 Thtr 50 Class 50 Board 25 **Parking** 64 **Notes** ⊗

ROTHBURY   Map 21 NU00

PREMIER COLLECTION

The Orchard House

★★★★★ 🛏 GUEST ACCOMMODATION

High St NE65 7TL
☎ 01669 620684
e-mail: graham@orchardhouserothbury.com
web: www.orchardhouserothbury.com
dir: *In village centre*

This delightful accommodation is located in an attractive Georgian period house within easy walking distance of the village amenities. Full of character, the restful atmosphere is enhanced by genuinely friendly service and hospitality. Individually styled bedrooms are all finished to a high standard and are very well equipped. The elegant lounge is richly styled and very comfortable, the elegant dining room has an honesty bar and interesting breakfasts featuring the best of local and organic produce are served here.

Rooms 5 en suite (1 fmly) **Facilities** tea/coffee Cen ht Licensed Golf 18 **Notes** ⊗ Closed Xmas & New Year

---

SEAHOUSES   Map 21 NU23

Bamburgh Castle Inn

★★★ INN

NE68 7SQ
☎ 01665 720283   📄 01665 720284
e-mail: enquiries@bamburghcastleinn.co.uk
web: www.bamburghcastleinn.co.uk
dir: *A1 onto B1341to Bamburgh, B1340 to Seahouses, follow signs to harbour*

Situated in a prime location on the quayside in the popular coastal resort of Seahouses, this establishment has arguably the best viewpoint along the coast. Dating back to the 18th century, the inn has been transformed in recent years and has superb dining and bar areas, with outside seating available in warmer weather. There are smart, comfortable bedrooms, many with views of the Farne Islands and the inn's famous namesake Bamburgh Castle.

Rooms 27 en suite 2 annexe en suite (6 fmly) (8 GF) S £37.50-£90; D £75-£90* **Facilities** FTV TVL tea/coffee Dinner available Cen ht Sauna Solarium Gymnasium Access to Ocean Club Spa **Conf** Max 50 **Parking** 35 **Notes** LB

SLAGGYFORD   Map 18 NY65

Yew Tree Chapel

★★★★ 🅰 GUEST ACCOMMODATION

CA8 7NH
☎ 01434 382525
e-mail: info@yewtreechapel.co.uk
dir: *A686 Alston to Brampton road, take only turning in village*

Rooms 3 en suite S £35-£39; D £60-£68* **Facilities** STV FTV TVL Dinner available Cen ht Licensed Wi-fi **Conf** Max 12 Thtr 12 Class 6 Board 6 **Parking** 3

WOOLER   Map 21 NT92

PREMIER COLLECTION

The Old Manse

★★★★★ 🛏 GUEST ACCOMMODATION

New Rd, Chatton NE66 5PU
☎ 01668 215343
e-mail: chattonbb@aol.com
web: www.oldmansechatton.co.uk
dir: *4m E of Wooler. On B6348 in Chatton*

Built in 1875, this elegant former manse is located on the edge of the village convenient for St Cuthbert's Way. There is a four-poster and double room upstairs, and a ground-floor room with its own entrance, sitting room and patio; all are thoughtfully equipped with a wealth of thoughtful extras including fridge with fruit, CD player, juices and biscuits. Sumptuous day rooms include wood-burning stoves. Impressive breakfasts are served in a conservatory overlooking the pretty gardens and a warm welcome is assured.

Rooms 3 en suite (1 GF) S £50-£90; D £80-£100* **Facilities** TVL tea/coffee Cen ht **Parking** 4 **Notes** ⊗ No Children 14yrs Closed Nov-Feb ✉

Winton House

★★★ BED AND BREAKFAST

39 Glendale Rd NE71 6DL
☎ 01668 281362
e-mail: enquiries@wintonhousebandb.co.uk
dir: *Off A697 into Wooler, Glendale Rd off High St, 150mtrs on left*

Located on a quiet residential avenue close to town centre, this elegant Edwardian house is popular with cyclists and walkers for St. Cuthbert's Way, providing comfortable bedrooms equipped with thoughtful extras. Breakfast, featuring the best of local produce is taken in an attractive dining room and a warm welcome is assured.

Rooms 3 rms (2 en suite); D £57-£65* **Facilities** tea/coffee Cen ht **Notes** LB ⊗ No Children 16yrs Closed Nov-Feb

NOTTINGHAMSHIRE

BINGHAM
Map 11 SK73

Yeung Sing

★★★ GUEST ACCOMMODATION

15 Market St NG13 8AB
☎ **01949 831831 & 831222** 🖨 **01949 838833**
e-mail: manager@yeung-sing.co.uk
dir: Off junct A52 & A46

This family-run guest house is in the centre of the market town. The smart ground-floor public rooms include a bar and the highly successful Yeung Sing restaurant, which serves a fine selection of Cantonese and regional Chinese dishes. The bedrooms are well equipped and have modern en suites.

Rooms 15 en suite (2 fmly) **Facilities** TVL tea/coffee Dinner available Direct Dial Cen ht Lift **Conf** Max 100 Thtr 100 Class 30 Board 30 **Parking** 30 **Notes** LB ⊗ Closed 25-26 Dec

COTGRAVE
Map 11 SK63

Jerico Farm (SK654307)

★★★★ 🏠 FARMHOUSE

Fosse Way NG12 3HG
☎ **01949 81733   Mrs S Herrick**
e-mail: info@jericofarm.co.uk
web: www.jericofarm.co.uk
dir: Farm driveway off A46, 1m N of junct A46 & A606

A friendly relaxed atmosphere is offered at this attractive farmhouse, which stands in peaceful extensive grounds just off the A46, close to Nottingham, Melton Mowbray and the Vale of Belvoir. Day rooms include a comfortable lounge and a separate dining room overlooking the gardens, in which substantial tasty breakfasts are served. Spacious bedrooms are beautifully appointed and thoughtfully equipped.

Rooms 3 en suite **Facilities** TVL tea/coffee Cen ht Wi-fi Fishing **Conf** Max 6 **Parking** 4 **Notes** ⊗ No Children 10yrs Closed 24 Dec-2 Jan 150 acres mixed

EDWINSTOWE
Map 16 SK66

The Forest Lodge

★★★★ INN

Church St NG21 9QA
☎ **01623 824443** 🖨 **01623 824686**
e-mail: audrey@forestlodgehotel.co.uk
dir: A614 into Edwinstowe. On B6034, opp St Mary's church

Situated in the heart of Sherwood Forest, The Forest Lodge is a 17th-century coaching inn, lovingly restored and refurbished to provide the visitor with a warm and homely base from which to explore the unique attractions of this fascinating and historic area. The rooms have been tastefully modernised and the bar provides home comforts and good company. Food is served in the bar or in the restaurant.

Rooms 8 en suite 5 annexe en suite (2 fmly) (5 GF) S £59; D £74* **Facilities** tea/coffee Dinner available Cen ht Wi-fi **Conf** Max 75 Thtr 75 Class 45 Board 50 **Parking** 35

ELTON
Map 11 SK73

PREMIER COLLECTION

The Grange

★★★★★ 🛏 BED AND BREAKFAST

Sutton Ln NG13 9LA
☎ **07887 952181**
e-mail: d.bmasson@btinternet.com
web: www.thegrangebedandbreakfastnotts.co.uk
dir: From Grantham A1 onto A52 to Elton x-rds, left 200yds, B&B on right

Parts of this lovely house date back to the early 17th century and the rooms command fine views across the gardens and rolling open countryside. Bedrooms contain many thoughtful extras and fine hospitality is assured from the proprietors.

Rooms 3 en suite S £40-£49; D £65-£69* **Facilities** FTV TVL tea/coffee Cen ht Wi-fi **Parking** 8 **Notes** ⊗ 🚭

HOLBECK
Map 16 SK57

PREMIER COLLECTION

Browns

★★★★★ 🛏 BED AND BREAKFAST

The Old Orchard Cottage, Holbeck Ln S80 3NF
☎ **01909 720659** 🖨 **01909 720659**
e-mail: browns.holbeck@btconnect.com
dir: 0.5m off A616 Sheffield-Newark road, turn for Holbeck at x-rds

Set amid beautifully tended gardens with lily-ponds and extensive lawns, this mid 18th-century cottage is a tranquil rural hideaway. Breakfasts are served in the Regency-style dining room, and the elegant bedrooms have four-poster beds and many extras. The friendly owners provide attentive service, including courtesy transport to nearby restaurants if required.

Rooms 3 annexe en suite (3 GF) S £57-£65; D £74-£84* **Facilities** tea/coffee Cen ht **Parking** 3 **Notes** ⊗ No Children 15yrs Closed Xmas wk 🚭

HOLME PIERREPONT
Map 11 SK63

Holme Grange Cottage

★★★ GUEST ACCOMMODATION

Adbolton Ln NG12 2LU
☎ **0115 981 0413**
e-mail: jean.colinwightman@talk21.com
dir: Off A52 SE of Nottingham, opp National Water Sports Centre

A stone's throw from the National Water Sports Centre, this establishment with its own all-weather tennis court is ideal for the active guest. Indeed, when not providing warm hospitality and freshly cooked breakfasts, the proprietor is usually on the golf course.

Rooms 3 rms (1 en suite) (1 fmly) S £32-£36; D £52-£56 **Facilities** TVL tea/coffee Cen ht 🏊 **Parking** 6 **Notes** LB Closed Xmas 🚭

MANSFIELD
Map 16 SK56

Bridleways Holiday Homes & Guest House

★★★ GUEST HOUSE

Newlands Rd, Forest Town NG19 0HU
☎ **01623 635725** 🖨 **01623 635725**
e-mail: bridleways@webnet2000.net
web: www.stayatbridleways.co.uk
dir: Off B6030

Beside a quiet bridleway that leads to Vicar Water Country Park and Sherwood Pines Forest Park this friendly guest house is a good touring base for walkers, cyclists or sightseeing. The new double, twin and family bedrooms are particularly spacious and all bedrooms are en suite. Lovely breakfasts are served in a cottage style dining room.

Rooms 9 en suite (1 fmly) (2 GF) S £36; D £68* **Facilities** tea/coffee Wi-fi **Parking** 14 **Notes** ⊗

NEWARK-ON-TRENT
Map 17 SK75

Compton House
★★★★ GUEST HOUSE

117 Baldertongate NG24 1RY
☎ 01636 708670
e-mail: info@comptonhousenewark.com
web: www.comptonhousenewark.com
dir: 500yds SE of town centre. Off B6326 onto Sherwood
Av, 1st right onto Baldertongate

Located a short walk from the central attractions, this
elegant period house has been renovated to provide high
standards of comfort. Individually themed bedrooms
come with a wealth of thoughtful extras and smart
modern bathrooms. Comprehensive breakfasts, and
wholesome dinners by arrangement, are served in the
attractive dining room and a lounge is available.

Rooms 7 rms (6 en suite) (1 pri facs) (1 fmly) (1 GF)
S £45-£65.50; D £85-£110* Facilities FTV tea/coffee
Dinner available Cen ht Wi-fi Conf Max 10 Thtr 10 Class
10 Board 10 Parking 2 Notes ⊗

Greystones Guest Accommodation
★★★★ BED AND BREAKFAST

Main St, South Scarle NG23 7JH
☎ 01636 893969 📄 01636 893969
e-mail: sheenafowkes@greystonesguests.co.uk
web: www.greystonesguests.co.uk
dir: A1 onto A46. A1133 to Collingham, signed to South
Scarle

Service is both friendly and helpful at the Greystones, a
tranquil 400-year-old Grade II-listed former farmhouse,
which sits in the conservation village of South Scarle. The
building has been sympathetically renovated to retain
much of the original character (this includes the quirky
uneven floors and walls). Bedrooms are individually
appointed, comfortable and well equipped.

Rooms 5 rms (4 en suite) (1 pri facs) (1 fmly) (2 GF)
S £45-£50; D £60-£70 Facilities FTV tea/coffee Dinner
available Cen ht Wi-fi Parking 3 Notes LB ⊗ No Children
⊗

NOTTINGHAM
Map 11 SK53

See also Barkestone-le-Vale (Leics) & Cotgrave

PREMIER COLLECTION

Restaurant Sat Bains with Rooms
★★★★★ ◉◉◉◉ ▥ RESTAURANT WITH ROOMS

Trentside, Lenton Ln NG7 2SA
☎ 0115 986 6566 📄 0115 986 0343
e-mail: info@restaurantsatbains.net
dir: M1 junct 24 take A453 Nottingham S. Over River
Trent in central lane to rdbt. Left then left again
towards river. Establishment on left after bend

This charming restaurant with rooms, a stylish
conversion of Victorian farm buildings, is situated on
the river and close to the industrial area of
Nottingham. The bedrooms create a warmth and magic
by using quality soft furnishings and antique and
period furniture; suites and four-poster rooms are
available. Public areas are chic and cosy, and the
delightful restaurant complements the outstanding
cuisine on offer.

Rooms 4 en suite 4 annexe en suite (6 GF) S £90-£129;
D £129-£265* Facilities STV Dinner available Direct
Dial Cen ht Parking 22 Notes ⊗ Closed 1st wk Jan &
2wks mid Aug RS Sun & Mon Rooms & Restaurant
closed

PREMIER COLLECTION

Greenwood Lodge City Guest House
★★★★★ GUEST HOUSE

5 Third Av, Sherwood Rise NG7 6JH
☎ 0115 962 1206 📄 0115 962 1206
e-mail: pdouglas71@aol.com
web: www.greenwoodlodgecityguesthouse.co.uk
dir: A60 (Mansfield Rd) from city, 1st rdbt onto 1st
exit to small rdbt, 2nd exit onto A692 Sherwood Rise,
3rd left

A warm welcome is assured at this fine house, built in
1834, located in a quiet residential area one mile from
the city centre. Day rooms include an elegant drawing
room and a conservatory-dining room overlooking the
secluded garden. Individually furnished bedrooms,
equipped with many thoughtful extras, are decorated in
a traditional style, complementing the antique
furniture. Off-road parking is a bonus.

Rooms 6 en suite S £47.50; D £80-£95* Facilities tea/
coffee Cen ht Licensed Wi-fi Parking 6 Notes ⊗ No
Children 10yrs Closed 24-28 Dec

Cockliffe Country House
★★★★ ◉ RESTAURANT WITH ROOMS

Burntstump Country Park, Burntstump Hill, Arnold
NG5 8PQ
☎ 0115 968 0179 📄 0115 968 0623
e-mail: enquiries@cockliffehouse.co.uk

Expect a warm welcome at this delightful property
situated in a peaceful rural location amidst neat
landscaped grounds, close to Sherwood Forest. Public
areas include a smart breakfast room, a tastefully
appointed restaurant and a cosy lounge bar. The
individually decorated bedrooms have co-ordinated soft
furnishings and many thoughtful touches.

Rooms 7 en suite 4 annexe en suite (5 GF) S £85-£95;
D £105-£150* Facilities STV FTV tea/coffee Dinner
available Direct Dial Cen ht Wi-fi ◗ Conf Max 30 Thtr 30
Class 25 Board 30 Parking 60 Notes No coaches Civ Wed
60

Beech Lodge
★★★★ GUEST ACCOMMODATION

222 Porchester Rd NG3 6HG
☎ 0115 952 3314
web: www.beechlodgeguesthouse.com
dir: Off A684 onto Porchester Rd, 8th left, Punchbowl pub
on right corner, Beech Lodge on left corner

A friendly welcome is assured at Beech Lodge and the
modern accommodation is well presented and suitably
equipped. The ground-floor lounge is particularly
comfortable, and there is a small conservatory. Breakfast
is a good choice of freshly cooked and carefully presented
fare served in the dining area next to the lounge.

Rooms 4 en suite (1 fmly) S £35; D £60* Facilities FTV
TVL tea/coffee Cen ht Wi-fi Parking 4 Notes LB ⊗ No
Children 8yrs

The Yellow House
★★★★ GUEST ACCOMMODATION

7 Littlegreen Rd, Woodthorpe NG5 4LE
☎ 0115 926 2280
e-mail: suzanne.prewsmith1@btinternet.com
web: www.bandb-nottingham.co.uk
dir: Off A60 Mansfield Rd N from city centre onto A6211,
over rdbt, 1st right to x-rds, left, house on left

A semi-detached private house in a quiet residential
suburb to the north-east of the city, with easy access. A
warm welcome is assured; the one purpose-built bedroom
contains many thoughtful extras, and the family pet dog
is also very friendly.

Rooms 1 en suite S fr £45; D fr £65* Facilities TVL tea/
coffee Cen ht Parking 1 Notes ⊗ No Children Closed
Xmas & New Year ⊗

NOTTINGHAM *continued*

The Acorn

★★★ GUEST HOUSE

4 Radcliffe Rd, West Bridgford NG2 5FW
☎ **0115 981 1297** 📄 **0115 981 7654**
e-mail: reservations@acorn-hotel.co.uk
dir: *A6011 onto A6520, next to Trent Bridge Cricket Ground*

Located a short walking distance from the county cricket ground and football stadia, this property provides a range of bedrooms with en suite facilities. Breakfast is taken in a pine-furnished dining room. Car parking and a guest lounge are additional benefits.

Rooms 12 en suite (2 fmly) (1 GF) S £25–£40; D £46–£55* **Facilities** TVL tea/coffee Cen ht Wi-fi **Parking** 12 **Notes** ⊗

Andrews

★★★ GUEST ACCOMMODATION

310 Queens Rd, Beeston NG9 1AJ
☎ **0115 925 4902**
e-mail: andrews.hotel@ntlworld.com
dir: *A52 onto B6006 to Beeston, right at 4th lights onto Queens Rd, 200yds on right*

This pleasant establishment is close to the shops and park in Beeston, and is popular with business people and tourists alike. Guests have the use of a comfortable lounge and a separate dining room. Bedrooms, which vary in size, are well presented and suitably equipped.

Rooms 10 rms (3 en suite) (1 fmly) (1 GF) S £27–£38; D £50–£55* **Facilities** TVL tea/coffee Cen ht Wi-fi **Parking** 6 **Notes** LB 📷

Hall Farm House

★★★ GUEST ACCOMMODATION

Gonalston NG14 7JA
☎ **0115 966 3112**
web: www.hallfarmhousebandb.com
dir: *NE of Nottingham. Off A612 x-rds into Gonalston, 1st right after post box*

This charming 17th-century former farmhouse is tucked away behind trees in the pretty village of Gonalston. Bedrooms are comfortable, and the beamed living rooms are full of character. There are extensive grounds, and there is a good choice of pubs for evening meals nearby.

Rooms 4 rms (2 en suite) (1 fmly) S £40–£45; D £60–£65* **Facilities** TV3B TVL tea/coffee Cen ht 🐾 🐕 Table tennis **Parking** 5 **Notes** LB ⊗ Closed 20 Dec–2 Jan 📷

Old Rectory Farm B&B

★★★ BED AND BREAKFAST

Main St, Strelley Village NG8 6PE
☎ **0115 929 8838**
e-mail: enq@oldrectoryfarm.com
web: www.oldrectoryfarm.com
dir: *M1 junct 26 onto A6002, after 1m turn right to Strelley village, 0.5m opp church*

Located in the pretty village of Strelley opposite the notable All Saints parish church, this period property has been sympathetically restored to provide modern comfort in a home-from-home atmosphere. Bedrooms are equipped with lots of thoughtful extras and memorable breakfasts feature eggs from the farm's own chickens, along with home-made preserves.

Rooms 4 rms (2 en suite) (1 fmly) (1 GF) **Facilities** TVL tea/coffee Cen ht Wi-fi **Parking** 6 **Notes** 📷

Tree Tops Guest House

🅄

101–103 Castle Boulevard NG7 1FE
☎ **07890 104343**
e-mail: alice@burtbros.co.uk
dir: *From Nottingham Castle, Canal St merges into Castle Bld, turn left onto Haslam St, Treetops at side of Cafe 101*

Currently the rating for this establishment is not confirmed. This may be due to a change of ownership or because it has only recently joined the AA rating scheme.

Rooms 7 rms (1 en suite) (1 pri facs) (1 fmly) S £35; D £40 **Facilities** TVL Cen ht **Parking** 3 **Notes** ⊗ Closed 25 & 31 Dec 📷

See advert on this page

The Old Forge

★★★ GUEST HOUSE

Burgage Ln NG25 0ER
☎ **01636 812809** 📄 **01636 816302**
e-mail: theoldforgesouthwell@yahoo.co.uk
dir: *Off A612 past Minster, Church St, left onto Newark Rd, 2nd left onto Burgage Ln*

An interesting house packed with pictures and antique furniture, the Old Forge is central and handy for the Minster, while its own parking also makes this a good touring base. Bedrooms are comfortable and a secluded conservatory-lounge and spacious breakfast room are available.

Rooms 3 en suite 1 annexe en suite (1 GF) S £48–£60; D £78* **Facilities** tea/coffee Direct Dial Cen ht **Parking** 4

Tree Tops B&B

101–103 Castle Boulevard, Nottingham NG7 1FE

Located just 5 minutes walk from Nottingham's city centre in the shadows of Nottingham Castle, Tree Tops is a clean and modern guesthouse.

Everything the city has to offer including stylish bars, restaurants and a vibrant nightlife is a stones throw away. With single, twin, double, triple and family rooms at affordable rates. We are also the ideal accommodation choice for visitors to The QMC hospital, Nottingham Uni, Trent cricket and Forest Grounds.

Our lounge room with TV and kitchen is a welcome haven for our guests. A hearty breakfast is also included to set you up for the day and we have a cafe open between Monday and Saturday.

Tel: 07890 104343
Email: alice@burtbros.co.uk
Book online: www.treetopsnottingham.co.uk

WELLOW — Map 17 SK66

Scotts Farm B & B

★★★ BED AND BREAKFAST

Wellow Park Stables, Rufford Ln NG22 0EQ
☎ 01623 861040 & 07860 869378 📄 01623 835292
e-mail: judithcadman1973@aol.com
web: www.wellowpark.co.uk
dir: A616 SE from New Ollerton, 1m right onto Rufford Ln

Scotts Farm is a part of Wellow Park Stables, a family equestrian centre located on the quiet outskirts of Wellow in Sherwood Forest. The resident proprietors provide helpful service, and well-proportioned bedrooms that share a bathroom. Breakfast is served in the kitchen. Stabling, dressage instruction, show jumping and cross-country rides are available by arrangement.

Rooms 3 rms (1 en suite) (3 fmly) **Facilities** tea/coffee Cen ht Riding **Parking** 6 **Notes** ⊗

WORKSOP — Map 16 SK57

Acorn Lodge

★★★★ GUEST ACCOMMODATION

85 Potter St S80 2HL
☎ 01909 478383 📄 01909 478383
e-mail: info@acornlodgeworksop.co.uk
dir: A1 onto A57. Take B6040 (town centre) through Manton, Lodge on right, 100mtrs past Priory

Originally part of the community house of the Priory Church, this property has been modernised to offer comfortable, well-appointed accommodation. Good breakfasts are served in the pleasant breakfast room and ample private parking is available at the rear.

Rooms 7 en suite (2 fmly) S fr £35; D fr £45 (room only)* **Facilities** FTV tea/coffee Cen ht Wi-fi **Parking** 15 **Notes** ⊗

OXFORDSHIRE

ABINGDON — Map 5 SU49

PREMIER COLLECTION

B&B Rafters

★★★★★ BED AND BREAKFAST

Abingdon Rd OX13 6NU
☎ 01865 391298 📄 01865 391173
e-mail: enquiries@bnb-rafters.co.uk
web: www.bnb-rafters.co.uk
dir: A34 onto A415 towards Witney, Rafters on A415 in Marcham next to pedestrian crossing, on the right

Set amid immaculate gardens, this modern house is built in a half-timbered style and offers spacious accommodation together with a warm welcome. Bedrooms are stylishly furnished and equipped with a range of homely extras. Comprehensive breakfasts feature local and organic produce when possible.

Rooms 4 rms (2 en suite) (2 pri facs) S £45-£75; D £79-£99* **Facilities** FTV tea/coffee Cen ht Wi-fi **Parking** 9 **Notes** ⊗

ARDINGTON — Map 5 SU48

The Boar's Head

★★★★ 🟢🟢 INN

Church St OX12 8QA
☎ 01235 833254 📄 01235 833254
e-mail: info@boarsheadardington.co.uk
dir: In village next to church

This characterful inn has been serving the local community for over 150 years and is set in a beautiful and seemingly timeless village. Great care has gone into creating a stylish and welcoming ambience in the comfortable bedrooms and the welcoming bar and restaurant where Bruce Buchan's accomplished cuisine can be enjoyed.

Rooms 3 en suite (1 fmly) **Facilities** tea/coffee Dinner available Direct Dial Cen ht Wi-fi **Parking** 20 **Notes** No coaches

ASTON ROWANT — Map 5 SU79

Lambert Arms

★★★★ 🟢 🏨 INN

London Rd OX49 5SB
☎ 0845 4593736 📄 01844 351893
e-mail: info@lambertarms.com
dir: M40 junct 6, follow signs to Chinnor (B4009) then left to Thame (A40)

Completely transformed inside, yet retaining its original, historical features, this lovely coaching inn has been caringly restored to its former glory, with a modern twist. You'll find a comfortable and friendly bar with open log fires, real ales and a mouth-watering array of food, including favourite pub classics using fresh, seasonal locally sourced produce.

Rooms 9 rms (8 en suite) (1 pri facs) 35 annexe en suite (13 fmly) (16 GF); D £70-£110* **Facilities** STV FTV tea/coffee Dinner available Direct Dial Cen ht Lift Wi-fi Golf Gymnasium Ella Bache Treatment rooms **Conf** Max 140 Thtr 120 Class 62 Board 38 **Parking** 75 **Notes** Civ Wed 120

BAMPTON — Map 5 SP30

Upham House Bed & Breakfast

★★★★ BED AND BREAKFAST

The Lanes OX18 2JG
☎ 01993 852703 & 07946 625563 📄 01993 852703
e-mail: pat@uphamhouse.co.uk
web: www.uphamhouse.co.uk
dir: A4095 between Faringdon & Brize Norton

A delightful stone-built house in a traditional country style, Upham House provides well-appointed and tastefully decorated accommodation, with a welcoming atmosphere; quality linens and towels, comfortable beds, fresh flowers and local produce used wherever possible. Situated in part of the Conservation Area of Bampton, with no passing traffic, yet only five minutes' walk from the village centre, it also benefits from being just a short drive from the River Thames and Kelmscott Manor - home of William Morris. Bampton is just eight miles from Burford, 'the gateway to the Cotswolds.'

Rooms 2 rms (1 en suite) (1 pri facs); D £60-£70* **Facilities** TVL tea/coffee Cen ht Wi-fi **Parking** 2 **Notes** ⊗ No Children 6yrs Closed 23 Dec-5 Jan 🍴

BANBURY
Map 11 SP44

The Mill House Country Guest House

★★★★ GUEST ACCOMMODATION

North Newington Rd OX15 6AA
☎ 01295 730212 📄 01295 730363
e-mail: lamadonett@aol.com
web: www.themillhousebanbury.com
dir: M40 junct 11, signs to Banbury Cross, onto B4035
(Shipston-on-Stour), 2m right for Newington

This 17th-century miller's house belongs to the paper mill
first mentioned in Shakespeare's Henry VI. It stands in
peaceful gardens not far from the Banbury Cross. There
are individually styled bedrooms in the main house or
refurbished cottages across the courtyard with lounge-
kitchens and en suite bedrooms. There are also a
pleasant lounge-bar and meeting facilities in the main
house.

Rooms 3 en suite 4 annexe en suite (2 fmly) S £69-£79;
D £85-£125 **Facilities** FTV TVL tea/coffee Direct Dial
Cen ht Wi-fi **Conf** Max 12 Board 12 **Parking** 20 **Notes** LB
⊗ Closed 2wks Xmas

The Blinking Owl

★★★ INN

Main St, North Newington OX15 6AE
☎ 01295 730650
e-mail: theblinkingowl@btinternet.com
dir: B4035 from Banbury, 2m sharp bend, right to North
Newington, inn opp green

An important part of the community in the pretty village
of North Newington, this former 17th-century inn retains
many original features including impressive open fires.
Straight forward food and a range of real ales are served
in the beamed bar-lounges. The converted barn houses
the three bedrooms and the restaurant, which is open at
weekends.

Rooms 3 en suite S £50-£60; D £65-£75* **Facilities** tea/
coffee Dinner available Cen ht **Parking** 14 **Notes** ⊗ ⊛

Fairlawns

★★★ GUEST ACCOMMODATION

60 Oxford Rd OX16 9AN
☎ 01295 262461 & 07831 330220 📄 01295 261296
e-mail: fairlawnsgh@aol.com
dir: 0.5m S of town centre on A4260 near hospital

This extended Edwardian house retains many original
features and has a convenient location. Bedrooms are
mixed in size, and all are neatly furnished, some with
direct access to the car park. A comprehensive breakfast
is served in the traditional dining room and a selection of
soft drinks and snacks is also available.

Rooms 11 rms (10 en suite) 6 annexe en suite (5 fmly) (9
GF) S £30-£49; D £45-£60* **Facilities** tea/coffee Direct
Dial Cen ht Wi-fi **Parking** 17

Lampet Arms

★★★ GUEST ACCOMMODATION

Main St, Tadmarton OX15 5TB
☎ 01295 780070 📄 01295 788066
dir: 4m W of Banbury on B4035 in Tadmarton, opp church

Located between Banbury and Shipston on Stour, this
well-proportioned Victorian property provides warm and
inviting open-plan public areas, the setting for home-
cooked food and fine wines. The spacious, thoughtfully
equipped bedrooms are in a converted coach house.

Rooms 4 annexe en suite (3 fmly) (2 GF) S fr £50;
D £70-£73* **Facilities** tea/coffee Dinner available Direct
Dial Cen ht Licensed Pool Table **Conf** Board 20
Parking 15 **Notes** Closed Sun in winter

BICESTER
Map 11 SP52

Manor Farm B&B

★★★★ BED AND BREAKFAST

Hethe OX27 8ES
☎ 01869 277602
e-mail: chrmanor@aol.com
web: www.freewebs.com/manorfarm
dir: Off B4100 signed Hardwick, after 2m village of
Hethe, 1st house after church

Guests are warmly welcomed at this delightful stone
farmhouse in the peaceful village of Hethe, close to the
M40 and Bicester, and a short drive from Oxford. The
property retains many original features such as Georgian
beams and open fireplaces, and offers comfortable
spacious accommodation with beautiful stylish
bathrooms. A hearty breakfast with home-made preserves
is included.

Rooms 2 rms (1 en suite) (1 pri facs) S £35-£45;
D £65-£75* **Facilities** tea/coffee Cen ht **Parking** 2
Notes LB ⊛

relax ▪ sleep ▪ explore ▪ restore

Brook Barn is a beautiful converted barn set in over an acre of gardens
which include an orchard, wildflower meadow and a beautiful chalk
stream. Brook Barn is equipped to the highest standards and is a perfect
respite for business travellers and holiday-makers alike, with the extra
luxuries you would expect to find in a chic boutique hotel. Brook Barn
offers the perfect combination of ambience and comfort typical of the
English country house with the highest standards of a top hotel.

brook barn, letcombe regis, wantage, oxfordshire, OX12 9JD
tel: 01235 766502, email: info@brookbarn.com, web: www.brookbarn.com

www.brookbarn.com

an idyllic country retreat

BURFORD — Map 5 SP21

PREMIER COLLECTION

Burford House
★★★★★ GUEST ACCOMMODATION

99 High St OX18 4QA
☎ 01993 823151 📄 01993 823240
e-mail: stay@burfordhouse.co.uk
dir: Off A40 onto A361, on right half way down hill

Under new ownership, this charming house provides superb quality with a professional and friendly welcome. Bedrooms offer very good quality, space and comfort. Wonderful lunches and afternoon teas are available daily, while dinners are available by appointment.

Rooms 8 en suite (1 fmly) (1 GF) S £110-£185; D £160-£185* Facilities STV tea/coffee Dinner available Direct Dial Cen ht Licensed Wi-fi Notes LB ⊗

The Angel at Burford
★★★★ ◉◉ RESTAURANT WITH ROOMS

14 Witney St OX18 4SN
☎ 01993 822714 📄 01993 822069
e-mail: paul@theangelatburford.co.uk
web: www.theangelatburford.co.uk
dir: Off A40 at Burford rdbt, down hill, 1st right onto Swan Ln, 1st left to Pytts Ln, left at end onto Witney St

Once a coaching inn, and built in the 16th century, this establishment is situated in the centre of Burford, the 'Gateway to The Cotswolds'. Three attractively decorated en suite bedrooms offer plentiful accessories and share a cosy residents' lounge. The award-winning restaurant is open for lunch and dinner. The peaceful courtyard and walled garden are perfect for relaxing in the summer.

The Angel at Burford

Rooms 3 en suite; D £85-£110* Facilities tea/coffee Dinner available Direct Dial Cen ht Wi-fi Notes No Children 9yrs RS Mon & Sun eve No coaches

Potters Hill Farm (SP300148)
★★★★ FARMHOUSE

Leafield OX29 9QB
☎ 01993 878018 📄 01993 878018 Mrs K Stanley
e-mail: potterabout@freenet.co.uk
dir: 4.5m NE of Burford. A361 onto B4437, 1st right, 1st left, 1.5m on left

Located on a working farm in peaceful parkland with diverse wildlife, this converted coach house stands next to the farmhouse. It has been refurbished to offer comfortable bedrooms with many original features. Breakfast served in the main farmhouse features local produce.

Rooms 3 annexe en suite (1 fmly) (2 GF) S £45-£50; D £60-£65* Facilities tea/coffee Cen ht Parking 5 Notes ⊗ 🐾 770 acres mixed/sheep

The Golden Pheasant
★★★ INN

91 High St OX18 4QA
☎ 01993 823223 📄 01993 822621
e-mail: andrew@goldenpheasant-burford.co.uk
web: www.goldenpheasant-burford.co.uk

Ideally located in the heart of this Oxfordshire town, this privately owned, 18th-century property offers comfortable accommodation for the leisure and business traveller. It is also the ideal base for exploring the surrounding Cotswold area. Meals are served in the attractive restaurant with its period fireplace.

The Golden Pheasant

Rooms 10 rms (9 en suite) (1 pri facs) S £65-£85; D £79-£110* Facilities tea/coffee Dinner available Direct Dial Cen ht Wi-fi Parking 8

CHARLBURY — Map 11 SP31

Tulip Tree House
★★★ BED AND BREAKFAST

Church St OX7 3PP
☎ 01608 810609 📄 01608 810609
dir: A44 onto B4437 into Charlbury, turn onto Church St, behind Bell Hotel

Tucked away in the market town of Charlbury, this charming property offers nicely appointed rooms, with good standards of comfort. Breakfast is served in the bright conservatory overlooking the well-tended gardens, which help to create a peaceful and charming atmosphere.

Rooms 3 rms (2 en suite) (1 pri facs) (1 fmly) Facilities TVL tea/coffee Cen ht Parking 4 Notes ⊛

CHISELHAMPTON   Map 5 SU59

Coach & Horses

★★★ 🍴 INN

Watlington Rd OX44 7UX
☎ 01865 890255   📠 01865 891995
e-mail: enquiries@coachhorsesinn.co.uk
dir: On B480

Located six miles south-east of Oxford, this 16th-century inn retains original exposed beams and open fires, while furniture styles enhance the character of the building. A wide range of imaginative food is served, and the practically equipped chalet-style bedrooms have lovely rural views.

Rooms 9 annexe en suite S £59-£68; D £68-£78*
Facilities tea/coffee Dinner available Direct Dial Cen ht
Conf Max 12 Parking 30 Notes LB

EAST HENDRED   Map 5 SU48

Mather House

★★★★ GUEST ACCOMMODATION

White Rd OX12 8JG
☎ 01235 833338   📠 01235 821632
e-mail: greensands@btconnect.com

Located within easy reach of transport networks, this newly refurbished accommodation benefits from a peaceful rural setting. Bedrooms and bathrooms are spacious and comfortably appointed whilst providing a number of thoughtful accessories. A hearty breakfast is served in the bright breakfast room. The property provides ample parking.

Rooms 4 en suite S £50-£80; D £50-£80* Facilities FTV
tea/coffee Cen ht Wi-fi Parking 10 Notes ⊗

FARINGDON   Map 5 SU29

Chowle Farmhouse Bed & Breakfast (SU272925)

★★★★ FARMHOUSE

Great Coxwell SN7 7SR
☎ 01367 241688   Mr & Mrs Muir
e-mail: info@chowlefarmhouse.co.uk
web: www.chowlefarmhouse.co.uk
dir: From Faringdon rdbt on A420, 2m W on right. From Watchfield rdbt 1.5m E on left

Chowle is a delightful modern farmhouse in a quiet setting, just off the A420. Bedrooms are very well equipped and there is a charming and airy downstairs breakfast room. Guests have use of ample parking space, and the location is ideal for visiting Oxford and Swindon. Dinner is available; pre-booking preferred.

Rooms 4 en suite (1 GF) S fr £55; D fr £75* Facilities FTV
tea/coffee Dinner available Cen ht Wi-fi ↖ ⅃ Fishing
Clay pigeon shooting, Indoor spa Parking 10 Notes LB ⊛
10 acres pedigree beef cattle

The Eagle Tavern

★★★★ INN

Little Coxwell SN7 7LW
☎ 01367 240120
e-mail: info@eagletavern.co.uk
dir: Off A420 near Faringdon signed White Horse Hill, Fernham. After 0.25m turn right to Little Coxwell

Located in the middle of the pleasant village of Little Coxwell, The Eagle Tavern offers the kind of hospitality, real pub food and ale expected of a traditional inn but with a more modern ambience. Rooms have been recently refurbished to offer good levels of quality and comfort, and include some useful extras. A range of homemade food includes a not-to-be-missed range of delicious pies served with a choice of pastry toppings and accompaniments.

Rooms 6 en suite (3 fmly) S fr £60; D fr £65*
Facilities tea/coffee Dinner available Cen ht Wi-fi Pool
Table Conf Thtr 50 Class 28 Board 20

The Trout at Tadpole Bridge

★★★★ 🍴 INN

Buckland Marsh SN7 8RF
☎ 01367 870382   📠 01367 870912
e-mail: info@troutinn.co.uk
web: www.troutinn.co.uk
dir: A420 Swindon to Oxford road, turn signed Bampton.
Inn 2m on right

The Trout is located 'where the River Thames meets the Cotswolds'. The peaceful location offers riverside walks from the door and berthing for up to six boats. Bedrooms and bathrooms are located adjacent to the inn and all rooms are very comfortable and well equipped with welcome extras. The main bar and restaurant offer an excellent selection of carefully prepared local produce at both lunch and dinner, together with cask ales and a varied choice of wines by the glass. The Trout at Tadpole Bridge is the AA Pub of the Year for England 2009-2010.

Rooms 3 en suite 3 annexe en suite (1 fmly) (4 GF)
S £75-£95; D £110-£140* Facilities FTV tea/coffee
Dinner available Cen ht Wi-fi Fishing Conf Max 20 Thtr 20
Class 20 Board 20 Parking 40 Notes LB Closed 25-26
Dec No coaches

GORING   Map 5 SU68

PREMIER COLLECTION

The Miller of Mansfield

★★★★★ 🍴 RESTAURANT WITH ROOMS

High St RG8 9AW
☎ 01491 872829   📠 01491 873100
e-mail: reservations@millerofmansfield.com
web: www.millerofmansfield.com

The frontage of this former coaching inn hides sumptuous rooms with a distinctive and individual style, an award-winning restaurant that serves appealing dishes using locally sourced ingredients and a comfortable bar, which serves real ales, fine wines, afternoon tea and a bar menu for a quick bite.

Rooms 13 en suite (2 fmly) S £100-£125;
D £125-£225* Facilities FTV tea/coffee Dinner
available Direct Dial Cen ht Wi-fi Conf Max 14 Thtr 14
Class 14 Board 14 Parking 2 Notes LB

See advert on opposite page

HAILEY   Map 5 SP31

Bird in Hand Inn

★★★★ INN

Whiteoak Green OX29 9XP
☎ 01993 868321   📠 01993 868702
e-mail: welcome@birdinhandinn.co.uk
web: www.birdinhandinn.co.uk

Situated on the edge of the Cotswolds, The Bird in Hand is ideally located to discover the natural beauty of the area plus the culture heritage of nearby Oxford. Sixteen gorgeous en suite bedrooms combine style and comfort to provide fabulous accommodation. The restaurant offers an imaginative seasonal menu using the finest, local produce and the bar serves traditional local ales.

Rooms 16 annexe en suite (2 fmly) (9 GF) S £70-£100;
D £80-£120* Facilities FTV tea/coffee Dinner available
Direct Dial Cen ht Wi-fi Conf Max 40 Thtr 40 Class 40
Board 40 Parking 100

HAMPTON POYLE   Map 11 SP51

The Bell at Hampton Poyle

Ⓤ

11 Oxford Rd OX5 2QD
☎ 01865 376242
e-mail: megan@thebellathamptonpoyle.co.uk
dir: Turn off A34 signed Kidlington, 0.25m

Currently the rating for this establishment is not confirmed. This may be due to a change of ownership or because it has only recently joined the AA rating scheme.

Rooms 9 en suite (3 GF) S £75-£95; D £85-£160 (room only)* Facilities FTV tea/coffee Dinner available Cen ht Licensed Wi-fi Conf Max 30 Parking 31 Notes LB No Children 5yrs

HENLEY-ON-THAMES
Map 5 SU78

PREMIER COLLECTION

Crowsley House
★★★★★ BED AND BREAKFAST

Crowsley Rd, Lower Shiplake RG9 3JT
☎ 0118 940 6708
e-mail: info@crowsleyhouse.co.uk
dir: A4155 onto Station Rd in Shiplake. Right onto
Crowsley Rd, 2nd house on right

Situated close to the popular village of Henley-on-
Thames and a moment's walk from Shiplake railway
station. Bedrooms are smartly appointed and very well
equipped with many thoughtful extras. A comfortable
lounge area and beautifully landscaped gardens
provide areas in which to relax. Breakfast is served
around the dining table in the well styled dual aspect
dining room. A two or three course dinner option is
available on request.

Rooms 3 rms (2 en suite) (1 pri facs) S £75-£95;
D £95-£125 **Facilities** FTV Dinner available Cen ht Wi-fi
Parking 6 **Notes** ⊗ No Children 14yrs

The Baskerville
★★★★ INN

Station Rd, Lower Shiplake RG9 3NY
☎ 0118 940 3332
e-mail: enquiries@thebaskerville.com
dir: 2m S of Henley in Lower Shiplake. Off A4155 onto
Station Rd, B&B signed

Located close to Shiplake station and just a short drive
from Henley, this smart accommodation is perfect for a
business or leisure break. It is a good base for exploring
the Oxfordshire countryside, and the enjoyable hearty
meals served in the cosy restaurant use good local
produce.

Rooms 4 en suite (1 fmly) S £75; D £85* **Facilities** tea/
coffee Dinner available Cen ht Wi-fi **Conf** Max 15 Thtr 15
Class 15 Board 15 **Parking** 15 **Notes** RS 23 Dec-2 Jan
room only No coaches

The Cherry Tree Inn
★★★★ ⊛ INN

Stoke Row RG9 5QA
☎ 01491 680430
e-mail: info@thecherrytreeinn.com
web: www.thecherrytreeinn.com
dir: W of Henley. Off B841 into Stoke Row

This stylish inn is situated in a peaceful rural setting,
just 20 minutes away from Reading and motorway
connections. Bedrooms are of a modern design, and have
spacious bathrooms with luxurious toiletries. The cosy,
contemporary dining room is the setting for imaginative
and hearty food.

Rooms 4 annexe en suite (4 GF) **Facilities** tea/coffee
Dinner available Cen ht Wi-fi **Parking** 30 **Notes** Closed
25-26 Dec No coaches

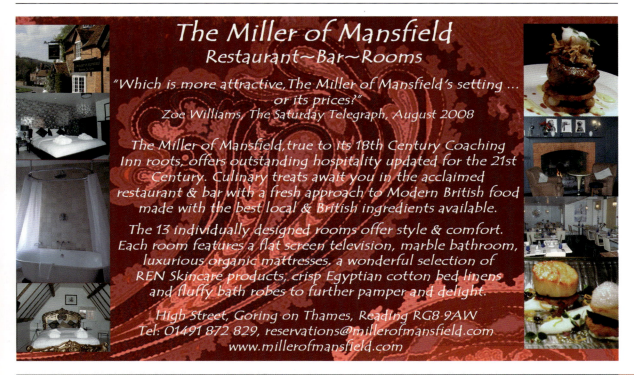

The Miller of Mansfield
Restaurant~Bar~Rooms

"Which is more attractive, The Miller of Mansfield's setting …
or its prices?"
Zoe Williams, The Saturday Telegraph, August 2008

The Miller of Mansfield, true to its 18th Century Coaching
Inn roots, offers outstanding hospitality updated for the 21st
Century. Culinary treats await you in the acclaimed
restaurant & bar with a fresh approach to Modern British food
made with the best local & British ingredients available.

The 13 individually designed rooms offer style & comfort.
Each room features a flat screen television, marble bathroom,
luxurious organic mattresses, a wonderful selection of
REN Skincare products, crisp Egyptian cotton bed linens
and fluffy bath robes to further pamper and delight.

High Street, Goring on Thames, Reading RG8 9AW
Tel: 01491 872 829, reservations@millerofmansfield.com
www.millerofmansfield.com

HENLEY-ON-THAMES *continued*

The White Hart Nettlebed

★★★★ @ GUEST ACCOMMODATION

High St, Nettlebed RG9 5DD
☎ 01491 641245 📠 01491 649018
e-mail: info@whitehartnettlebed.com
dir: On A4130, 3.5m from Henley-on-Thames towards Oxford

The combination of traditional and contemporary style at this pleasant property creates a unique and relaxing atmosphere in which to appreciate the staff's attentive service. Bedrooms are located in the main building and the courtyard, and are equipped with a host of modern comforts and thoughtful extras. A wide selection of dishes, featuring carefully sourced organic ingredients can be enjoyed in either the bar or the restaurant where the cooking could be described as delightfully straightforward.

Rooms 6 en suite 6 annexe en suite (3 fmly) (3 GF) S £125; D £125* **Facilities** tea/coffee Dinner available Cen ht Licensed Wi-fi **Conf** Max 40 Thtr 40 Class 20 Board 20 **Parking** 30 **Notes** ⊗ RS Sun eve restaurant closed

Apple Ash

★★★★ Ⓐ BED AND BREAKFAST

Woodlands Rd, Harpsden Woods RG9 4AB
☎ 01491 574198 📠 01491 578183
e-mail: appleash@fsmail.net
dir: From Henley exit A4155 towards Caversham, turn right onto Woodlands Rd, house 0.5m on right

Rooms 4 rms (3 en suite) (1 pri facs) S £50; D £70* **Facilities** tea/coffee Cen ht Wi-fi **Parking** 6 **Notes** ⊗ No Children 10yrs Closed 24-27 Dec ⊛

Slater's Farm

★★★ Ⓐ BED AND BREAKFAST

Peppard Common RG9 5JL
☎ 01491 628675
e-mail: stay@slatersfarm.co.uk
dir: 3m W of Henley. A4130 onto B481 to Rotherfield Peppard, pass The Dog pub & fork left to primary school, farm 200yds on right

Rooms 3 rms (1 pri facs) S fr £40; D fr £60* **Facilities** FTV tea/coffee Dinner available Cen ht Wi-fi 🏊 **Parking** 5 **Notes** ⊗ Closed Xmas ⊛

| HOOK NORTON | Map 11 SP33 |

The Gate Hangs High

★★★★ 🍴 INN

OX15 5DF
☎ 01608 737387 📠 01608 737870
e-mail: gatehangshigh@aol.com
dir: 0.6m N of village on x-rds

This delightful inn located between Banbury and Chipping Norton is convenient for Oxford and the Cotswolds. Stylish spacious bedrooms are situated around a courtyard in a carefully converted barn. They are comfortably furnished and extremely well-equipped. Carefully prepared food is served in the bar or the attractive restaurant.

Rooms 4 en suite (1 fmly) (4 GF) **Facilities** FTV tea/coffee Dinner available Direct Dial Cen ht Golf Riding **Parking** 40 **Notes** Closed Xmas night

---

| IDBURY | Map 10 SP21 |

Bould Farm *(SP244209)*

★★★★ FARMHOUSE

OX7 6RT
☎ 01608 658850 📠 01608 658850 Mrs L Meyrick
e-mail: meyrick@bouldfarm.co.uk
web: www.bouldfarm.co.uk
dir: Off A424 signed Idbury, through village, down hill, round two bends, on right

This delightful 17th-century farmhouse stands amid pretty gardens between Stow-on-the-Wold and Burford. The spacious bedrooms are carefully furnished and thoughtfully equipped, and some have stunning views of the surrounding countryside. Breakfast is served in the cosy dining room which features a cast-iron stove and stone-flagged floors.

Rooms 3 rms (2 en suite) (1 pri facs) (1 fmly) S £45-£50; D £65-£70* **Facilities** TVL tea/coffee Cen ht **Parking** 6 **Notes** ⊗ ⊛ 400 acres arable/sheep

---

| KINGHAM | Map 10 SP22 |

Moat End

★★★★ 🛏 BED AND BREAKFAST

The Moat OX7 6XZ
☎ 01608 658090 & 07765 278399
e-mail: info@moatend.com
web: www.moatend.co.uk
dir: Off B4450/A436 into village centre

The converted barn lies in a peaceful Cotswold village and has splendid country views. Its well-appointed bedrooms either have a Jacuzzi or large shower cubicles, one with hydro-massage jets. The attractive dining room leads to a comfortable beamed sitting room with a stone fireplace. Quality local ingredients are used in the wholesome breakfasts. The owner has won an award for

---

green tourism by reducing the impact of the business on the environment.

Rooms 3 en suite (1 fmly) S £40-£50; D £60-£70* **Facilities** TVL tea/coffee Cen ht Wi-fi **Parking** 4 **Notes** LB Closed Xmas & New Year ⊛

The Tollgate Inn & Restaurant

★★★★ 🍴 INN

Church St OX7 6YA
☎ 01608 658389
e-mail: info@thetollgate.com

Situated in the idyllic Cotswold village of Kingham, this Grade II-listed Georgian building has been lovingly restored to provide a complete home-from-home among some of the most beautiful and historic countryside in Britain. The Tollgate provides comfortable, well-equipped accommodation in pleasant surroundings. A good choice of menu for lunch and dinner is available with fine use made of fresh and local produce. You can also be sure of a hearty breakfast provided in the modern, well-equipped dining room.

Rooms 5 en suite 4 annexe en suite (1 fmly) (4 GF) **Facilities** tea/coffee Dinner available Cen ht Wi-fi **Conf** Max 15 **Parking** 12

| MILTON COMMON | Map 5 SP60 |

Byways

★★★★ 🛏 BED AND BREAKFAST

Old London Rd OX9 2JR
☎ 01844 279386 📠 01844 279386
e-mail: byways.molt@tiscali.co.uk
web: www.bywaysbedandbreakfast.co.uk
dir: Between M40 juncts 7 & 8A

A friendly welcome awaits you at Byways, situated a few minutes from the M40. Bedrooms are comfortable and tastefully decorated, and the emphasis is on a peaceful and relaxing stay away from it all. Breakfast is home produced, organic and obtained locally where possible. There is a large garden for guests to enjoy. Please note that Byways is a TV-free establishment. Sylvia Mott was a finalist for the AA Friendliest Landlady of the Year 2009-2010 Award.

Rooms 3 rms (2 en suite) (1 pri facs) (3 GF) S £35-£40; D £60-£65 **Facilities** tea/coffee Cen ht **Parking** 3 **Notes** ⊗ No Children 7yrs ⊛

PREMIER COLLECTION

Burlington House
★★★★★ ⬛ GUEST ACCOMMODATION

374 Banbury Rd, Summertown OX2 7PP
☎ 01865 513513 📄 01865 311785
e-mail: stay@burlington-house.co.uk
dir: *Opposite Oxford Conference Centre on A4165 on corner of Hernes Rd & Banbury Rd*

Guests are assured of a warm welcome and attentive service at this smart, beautifully maintained Victorian house, within walking distance of Summertown's fashionable restaurants. Elegant, contemporary bedrooms are filled with a wealth of thoughtful extras, and some open onto a pretty patio garden. Memorable breakfasts, served in the delightful dining room, include home-made preserves, fruit breads, granola and excellent coffee.

Rooms 10 en suite 2 annexe en suite (12 smoking) S £65-£74; D £85-£105* **Facilities** FTV tea/coffee Direct Dial Cen ht Wi-fi **Parking** 5 **Notes** ⊗ No Children 12yrs Closed 24 Dec-2 Jan

Gables Guest House
★★★★★ 🅰 GUEST ACCOMMODATION

6 Cumnor Hill OX2 9HA
☎ 01865 862153 📄 01865 864054
e-mail: stay@gables-oxford.co.uk
web: www.gables-guesthouse.co.uk
dir: *A34 onto A420. At rdbt take Oxford/Botley exit, right at lights, 500yds on right*

Rooms 5 en suite (1 GF) S £50-£60; D £70-£85 **Facilities** STV TVL tea/coffee Direct Dial Cen ht Wi-fi **Parking** 6 **Notes** LB ⊗ No Children 10yrs Closed 24 Dec-2 Jan

Conifers Guest House
★★★★ GUEST ACCOMMODATION

116 The Slade, Headington OX3 7DX
☎ 01865 763055 📄 01865 742232
e-mail: stay@conifersguesthouse.co.uk
web: www.conifersguesthouse.co.uk
dir: *Off ring road onto A420 towards city centre. Left onto B4495, house on left past hospital*

Located in a residential area close to the hospitals, this impressive Edwardian house has been renovated to provide attractive, pine-furnished bedrooms. Breakfast is served in a smart, front-facing dining room. Private car park.

Rooms 8 en suite (1 fmly) **Facilities** tea/coffee Cen ht **Parking** 8 **Notes** ⊗

Cotswold House
★★★★ GUEST ACCOMMODATION

363 Banbury Rd OX2 7PL
☎ 01865 310558 📄 01865 310558
e-mail: d.r.walker@talk21.com
web: www.cotswoldhouse.co.uk
dir: *A40 onto A423 into Oxford city centre, following signs to Summertown, 0.5m on right*

Situated in a leafy avenue close to the northern ring road and Summertown, this well-maintained house offers comfortable, well-equipped bedrooms and a relaxed atmosphere. Enjoy a traditional, hearty breakfast with vegetarian choice, including home-made muesli and fresh fruit, served in the bright attractive dining room.

Rooms 8 en suite (2 fmly) (2 GF) S £55-£65; D £90-£100 **Facilities** FTV tea/coffee Cen ht Wi-fi **Parking** 6 **Notes** ⊗ No Children 5yrs

Galaxie
★★★★ GUEST ACCOMMODATION

180 Banbury Rd OX2 7BT
☎ 01865 515688 📄 01865 556824
e-mail: info@galaxie.co.uk
web: www.galaxie.co.uk
dir: *1m N of Oxford centre, on right before shops in Summertown*

Situated in the popular Summertown area of the city, the Galaxie has a welcoming atmosphere and very good quality accommodation. The well-equipped bedrooms are all very comfortable and have a good range of extra

facilities. The attractive conservatory-dining room looks over the Oriental garden.

Rooms 32 rms (28 en suite) (3 fmly) **Facilities** TV31B TVL tea/coffee Direct Dial Cen ht Lift **Parking** 30 **Notes** ⊗

Marlborough House
★★★★ GUEST ACCOMMODATION

321 Woodstock Rd OX2 7NY
☎ 01865 311321 📄 01865 515329
e-mail: enquiries@marlbhouse.co.uk
web: www.marlbhouse.co.uk
dir: *1.5m N of city centre. Off junct A34 & A44 for city centre, onto A4144 (Woodstock Rd), premises on right by lights*

Marlborough House is just 1.5 miles north of Oxford's historic city centre, and is within easy reach of the M40 and the A34 ring road. Custom built in 1990 to a traditional design, the house sits comfortably alongside its Victorian neighbours in a predominantly residential area. All 17 bedrooms have en suite facilities, kitchenettes and mini-bars so guests aren't tied to any routine. Wi-fi covers the lounge and many of the rooms.

Rooms 13 en suite 4 annexe en suite (2 fmly) (4 GF) S £73-£82; D £85-£95* **Facilities** STV tea/coffee Direct Dial Cen ht Licensed Wi-fi **Parking** 6 **Notes** ⊗

OXFORD *continued*

Pickwicks

★★★★ GUEST HOUSE

15-17 London Rd, Headington OX3 7SP
☎ 01865 750487 📠 01865 742208
e-mail: pickwicks@tiscali.co.uk
web: www.pickwicksguesthouse.co.uk
dir: *Off ring road onto A420 towards city centre, Pickwicks 0.9m on right at junct with Sandfield Rd*

Just a short walk from the bustling community of Headington, this double-fronted Edwardian house has been renovated to provide good standards of overall comfort. Bedrooms offer a useful range of facilities, and an attractive breakfast room overlooks the pretty gardens.

Rooms 15 rms (13 en suite) (2 pri facs) (4 fmly) (4 GF) S £30-£55; D £70-£90* **Facilities** FTV TVL tea/coffee Direct Dial Cen ht Licensed Wi-fi **Parking** 12 **Notes** Closed 23 Dec-2 Jan

Red Mullions Guest House

★★★★ GUEST HOUSE

23 London Rd, Headington OX3 7RE
☎ 01865 742741 📠 01865 769944
e-mail: stay@redmullions.co.uk
dir: *M40 junct 8 onto A40. At Headington rdbt, 2nd exit signed Headington onto London Rd*

Red Mullions takes its name from the brick columns between the windows of the building. Modern bedrooms provide comfortable accommodation set within easy reach of motorway networks and Oxford city centre. Hearty breakfasts provide a good start to any day.

Rooms 13 rms (12 en suite) (1 pri facs) (3 fmly) (4 GF) S £65-£85; D £80-£95* **Facilities** FTV tea/coffee Cen ht Wi-fi **Parking** 9 **Notes** ⊗

Acorn Guest House

★★★ GUEST ACCOMMODATION

260-262 Iffley Rd OX4 1SE
☎ 01865 247998
e-mail: acorn@kpattullo.wanadoo.co.uk
dir: *Off ring road onto A4158 towards city centre, 1m on left after VW garage*

This double-fronted Victorian house is located between the ring road and the city centre, and offers good value accommodation. The lounge leads out to a quiet enclosed rear garden.

Rooms 15 rms (6 en suite) (1 pri facs) (1 fmly) **Facilities** tea/coffee Cen ht Lift **Parking** 6

All Seasons

★★★ GUEST ACCOMMODATION

63 Windmill Rd, Headington OX3 7BP
☎ 01865 742215 📠 01865 429667
e-mail: info@allseasonshouse.com
web: www.allseasonshouse.com
dir: *Off ring road onto A420 towards city centre. 1m left at lights onto Windmill Rd, house 300yds on left*

Within easy walking distance of the suburb of Headington, this double-fronted Victorian house provides comfortable homely bedrooms equipped with practical and thoughtful extras. The elegant dining room features an original fireplace, and secure parking is available behind the property.

Rooms 6 rms (4 en suite) S £30-£50; D £50-£80 **Facilities** FTV TVL tea/coffee Cen ht Wi-fi **Parking** 6 **Notes** ⊗ No Children 4yrs

Athena Guest House

★★★ GUEST ACCOMMODATION

255 Cowley Rd, Cowley OX4 1XQ
☎ 01865 425700 & 07748 837144 📠 01865 240566
e-mail: info@athenaguesthouse.com
web: www.athenaguesthouse.com
dir: *1.5m SE of city centre on B480*

Located close to the shops and amenities in Cowley, this Victorian brick house offers smart modern bedrooms on three floors with many useful extras. Breakfast is served in the bright and relaxing dining room, and limited parking is available.

Rooms 6 en suite (2 fmly) (2 GF) **Facilities** STV TVL tea/coffee Cen ht Wi-fi **Conf** Max 15 **Parking** 4 **Notes** ⊗

Green Gables

★★★ GUEST ACCOMMODATION

326 Abingdon Rd OX1 4TE
☎ 01865 725870 📠 01865 723115
e-mail: green.gables@virgin.net
web: www.greengables.uk.com
dir: *Off ring road onto B4144 towards city centre, Green Gables 0.5m on left*

A warm welcome is assured at this Edwardian house, located within easy walking distance of the city centre. Bedrooms are equipped with a range of practical and homely extras, and a comprehensive breakfast is served in the cosy dining room. Guests have free access to the internet in the smart conservatory-lounge and private parking is available.

Rooms 11 en suite (2 fmly) (4 GF) S £48-£52; D £68-£75* **Facilities** TVL tea/coffee Direct Dial Cen ht Wi-fi **Parking** 9 **Notes** ⊗ Closed 23-31 Dec

Heather House

★★★ GUEST ACCOMMODATION

192 Iffley Rd OX4 1SD
☎ 01865 249757 📠 01865 249757
e-mail: stay@heatherhouseoxford.com
web: www.heatherhouseoxford.com
dir: *Off A40 at Headington rdbt, S onto A4142 to Littlemore rdbt onto A4158 Iffley Rd then house 1.25m. On left after pedestrian crossing near Chester St*

A short walk from the colleges, city centre and Oxford Brookes campus, this detached Edwardian house stands in a residential area and has its own parking. The en suite bedrooms are bright and comfortable, and come complete with useful facilities including TV and CD/DVD players. There is a choice of breakfasts, Wi-fi, a computer station (with Skype) and a relaxing lounge with lots of tourist information.

Rooms 6 rms (5 en suite) (1 pri facs) (2 fmly) (1 GF) S £37-£47; D £67-£80* **Facilities** FTV TVL tea/coffee Direct Dial Cen ht Wi-fi **Parking** 4 **Notes** ⊗

Highfield

★★★ GUEST ACCOMMODATION

91 Rose Hill OX4 4HT
☎ 01865 774083
e-mail: highfield.house@tesco.net
dir: Off A4142 Eastern Bypass Rd onto A4158, continue 250yds

This attractive detached house stands in immaculate gardens close to Cowley and provides homely bedrooms equipped with quality pine furniture. The attractive front dining room is the setting for comprehensive breakfasts and there is also a spacious lounge.

Rooms 7 rms (5 en suite) (2 pri facs) (1 fmly) S £30-£48; D £60-£72* **Facilities** FTV TVL tea/coffee Cen ht Wi-fi **Parking** 6 **Notes** ⊗ Closed Xmas

Sports View Guest House

★★★ GUEST ACCOMMODATION

106-110 Abingdon Rd OX1 4PX
☎ 01865 244268 🖹 01865 249270
e-mail: stay@sportsviewguesthouse.co.uk
web: www.sportsviewguesthouse.co.uk
dir: Exit Oxford S at Kennington rdbt towards city centre, 1.25m on left

This family-run Victorian property, overlooks the Queens College sports ground. Situated south of the city it is within walking distance of the centre. Rooms are comfortable, and the property benefits from off-road parking.

Rooms 20 rms (19 en suite) (1 pri facs) (4 fmly) (5 GF) **Facilities** tea/coffee Direct Dial Cen ht Wi-fi **Parking** 10 **Notes** ⊗ No Children 3yrs

Tower House

★★★ GUEST ACCOMMODATION

15 Ship St OX1 3DA
☎ 01865 246828 🖹 01865 247508
e-mail: generalmanager.towerhousehotel@ohiml.com
dir: Follow signs to city centre, turn left onto Turl St, then right onto Ship St

A charming 17th-century house set on a quiet street in the heart of Oxford city centre. Bedrooms all individually decorated in keeping with the age of the property. A light Continental breakfast is served in the quaint breakfast room on the ground floor.

Rooms 7 rms (4 en suite) (1 fmly) **Facilities** FTV tea/coffee Cen ht Wi-fi **Notes** ⊗

Newton House

★★★ 🅰 BED AND BREAKFAST

82-84 Abingdon Rd OX1 4PL
☎ 01865 240561 🖹 01865 244647
e-mail: newton.house@btinternet.com
dir: On A4144 (Abingdon Rd)

Rooms 13 rms (2 en suite) (11 pri facs) (4 fmly) (4 GF) S £47-£78; D £56-£80 **Facilities** FTV tea/coffee Direct Dial Cen ht Wi-fi **Parking** 8 **Notes** LB ⊗

SOUTH STOKE Map 5 SU58

Perch & Pike

★★★ INN

The Street RG8 0JS
☎ 01491 872415 🖹 01491 871001
e-mail: info@perchandpike.co.uk
dir: From A4074 take B4009 S to South Stoke

Set in the quiet village of South Stoke, minutes from the River Thames, this cosy inn offers a very warm welcome. The four en suite bedrooms are comfortable and well equipped. Public areas are spacious and include a separate dining room. Enjoy local asparagus, when in season, or trout caught that day by the proprietor.

Rooms 4 en suite (1 fmly) S £90-£120; D £90-£120* **Facilities** FTV tea/coffee Dinner available Cen ht **Parking** 25 **Notes** No coaches

STADHAMPTON Map 5 SU69

PREMIER COLLECTION

The Crazy Bear

★★★★★ ⓦ ⑩⑩ GUEST ACCOMMODATION

Bear Ln OX44 7UR
☎ 01865 890714 🖹 01865 400481
e-mail: enquiries@crazybear-oxford.co.uk
web: www.crazybearhotel.co.uk
dir: M40 junct 7, A329. In 4m left after petrol station, left into Bear Lane

This popular and attractive restaurant with rooms successfully combines modern chic with old world character. Cuisine is extensive and varied, with award-winning Thai and English restaurants under the same roof (both with AA Rosettes). Those choosing to make a night of it can enjoy the concept bedrooms, all presented to a very high standard and styled with exciting themes; the 'infinity suites' have state-of-the-art facilities.

Rooms 5 en suite 12 annexe en suite (3 fmly) (4 GF) **Facilities** STV Dinner available Direct Dial Cen ht Licensed Wi-fi **Conf** Max 40 Thtr 30 Class 30 Board 30 **Parking** 100 **Notes** ⊗ Civ Wed 100

WALLINGFORD Map 5 SU68

Bed & Breakfast at Little Gables

★★★★ 🅰 BED AND BREAKFAST

166 Crowmarsh Hill OX10 8BG
☎ 01491 837834 & 07860 148882 🖹 01491 834426
e-mail: mail@littlegables.co.uk
web: www.littlegables.co.uk
dir: 1m E of Wallingford. Off A4130 at Crowmarsh Gifford rdbt onto Crowmarsh Hill & right

Rooms 3 rms (2 en suite) (1 pri facs) (3 fmly) (1 GF) S £50-£65; D £65-£75* **Facilities** FTV tea/coffee Cen ht Wi-fi **Parking** 7 **Notes** LB 🖾

WANTAGE Map 5 SU38

PREMIER COLLECTION

Brook Barn

★★★★★ ⓦ 🖭 🍴 GUEST HOUSE

Brook Barn, Letcombe Regis OX12 9JD
☎ 01235 766502 🖹 0118 329 0452
e-mail: info@brookbarn.net
web: www.brookbarn.com
dir: M4 junct 14 onto A338 to Wantage. Left onto B4507 signed Ashbury, after 1m take left signed Letcombe Regis. House 0.75m on left

A bijou country house hideaway with luxurious bedrooms. The house is set in over an acre of gardens which include an orchard, and a beautiful chalk stream so guests can enjoy the tranquillity of the Oxfordshire countryside. Brook Barn is equipped to the highest standards, and is a perfect respite for business travellers or holiday-makers alike. Mark and Sarah-Jane Ashman were runners-up for the AA Friendliest Landlady of the Year 2009-2010 Award.

Rooms 4 rms (3 en suite) (1 pri facs) (3 GF) S £65-£120; D £85-£170* **Facilities** STV FTV tea/coffee Dinner available Direct Dial Cen ht Licensed Wi-fi Outdoor hot tub **Parking** 6 **Notes** LB ⊗ No Children 16yrs

See advert on page 272

WANTAGE *continued*

Greensands Guest House

★★★ GUEST HOUSE

Reading Rd OX12 8JE
☎ 01235 833338 📄 01235 821632
e-mail: info@greensandsguesthouse.co.uk.
web: www.greensandsguesthouse.co.uk
dir: A4185 to Rowstock rdbt, take A417, 1m on right

This guest house in a peaceful rural setting has good access to local towns, attractions and transport networks. Bedrooms vary in size and are comfortably appointed. Hearty breakfasts are served overlooking the attractive gardens. Ample parking available.

Rooms 7 rms (6 en suite) (1 pri facs) (2 fmly) (3 GF)
Facilities tea/coffee Cen ht Wi-fi **Parking** 9

Down Barn Farm *(SU332852)*

★★ FARMHOUSE

Sparsholt Down OX12 9XD
☎ 01367 820272 Mrs P A Reid
e-mail: pendomeffect@aol.com
dir: 4m SW of Wantage. Off B4507 S onto Kingston Lisle-Seven Barrows road

Popular with walkers and horse riders (stabling is available), this working farm has glorious views over the Downs and is near to the famous Ridgeway. Bedrooms and public areas have a homely and comfortable aspect while home-produced veal, beef and pork can be anticipated for dinner.

Rooms 3 rms (1 en suite) (3 GF) S £30-£40; D £60-£70*
Facilities TVL Dinner available Cen ht Riding **Parking** 4
Notes LB Closed Xmas 🐾 100 acres Organic beef/pigs

WITNEY   Map 5 SP31

Corn Croft Guest House

★★★★ GUEST ACCOMMODATION

69-71 Corn St OX28 6AS
☎ 01993 773298 📄 01993 773298
e-mail: richardturner4@btconnect.com
web: www.corncroft.co.uk
dir: A40 to town centre, from Market Square onto Corn Street, 400mtrs on left

Located in the quieter end of town, yet close to the centre, Corn Croft offers comfortable well equipped accommodation in a friendly atmosphere. Substantial breakfasts featuring local produce are served in the attractive dining room.

Rooms 9 en suite (1 fmly) (2 GF) **Facilities** FTV tea/coffee Cen ht Wi-fi **Notes** Closed 24-26 Dec

The Fleece

★★★ INN

11 Church Green OX28 4AZ
☎ 01993 892270 📄 0871 8130458
e-mail: fleece@peachpubs.com
dir: A40 to Witney town centre, on Church Green

Set in the centre of Witney overlooking the church green, The Fleece offers ten well equipped en suite modern bedrooms. The popular destination pub offers food all day including breakfast, and a great selection of wines and real ales.

Rooms 7 en suite 3 annexe en suite (1 fmly) (1 GF) S fr £80; D fr £90* **Facilities** tea/coffee Dinner available Direct Dial Cen ht Wi-fi **Conf** Max 30 Thtr 25 Class 16 Board 22 **Parking** 12 **Notes** LB Closed 25 Dec

---

WOODSTOCK   Map 11 SP41

The Laurels

★★★★ 🏠 BED AND BREAKFAST

40 Hensington Rd OX20 1JL
☎ 01993 812583 📄 01993 810041
e-mail: stay@laurelsguesthouse.co.uk
dir: Off A44 onto Hensington Rd by pedestrian lights, 500yds on right opp Catholic church

Located in a peaceful area just a short walk from the historic centre, the Victorian house has been renovated to provide high standards of comfort. Bedrooms come with thoughtful extras, and the elegant period-furnished dining room is the setting for imaginative breakfasts, which feature organic produce whenever possible.

Rooms 2 en suite S £65-£70; D £75-£85 **Facilities** tea/coffee Cen ht **Notes** ⊗ No Children 10yrs Closed Dec & Jan

---

The Duke of Marlborough

A44 WOODSTOCK, OXFORD, OX20 1HT
Tel: 01993-811460

Quiet and friendly, this inn is situated on the edge of historic Woodstock, one mile from Blenheim Palace & 9 miles from Oxford.

Ample parking. All rooms are new, fitted to a high standard, en-suite & with all facilities associated with 4-stars.

e-mail: sales@dukeofmarlborough.co.uk
Website: www.dukeofmarlborough.co.uk

Duke of Marlborough Country Inn

★★★★ INN

A44, Woodleys OX20 1HT
☎ 01993 811460 📄 01993 810165
e-mail: sales@dukeofmarlborough.co.uk
dir: 1m N of Woodstock on A44 x-rds

The Duke of Marlborough is just outside the popular town of Woodstock, convenient for local attractions including Blenheim Palace. Bedrooms and bathrooms are in an adjacent lodge-style building and offer high standards of quality and comfort. Dinner includes many tempting home-cooked dishes complemented by a good selection of ales and wines.

Rooms 13 annexe en suite (2 fmly) (7 GF) **Facilities** tea/coffee Dinner available Direct Dial Cen ht Wi-fi **Conf** Max 20 Thtr 20 Class 16 Board 12 **Parking** 42 **Notes** ⊗

See advert on opposite page

Kings Head House

★★★★ GUEST ACCOMMODATION

Chapel Hill, Wootton OX20 1DX
☎ 01993 811340
e-mail: t.fay@kings-head.co.uk
web: www.kings-head.co.uk
dir: 2m N of Woodstock. Off A44 to Wootton, close to village church

Set in the pretty village of Wootton, this mellow stone house retains many original features, including exposed beams and open fireplaces. The property is currently undergoing a total refurbishment which should complete in late 2009.

Rooms 2 en suite 1 annexe en suite (1 fmly) (1 GF) S £60-£65; D £75-£85 **Facilities** tea/coffee Cen ht Wi-fi **Parking** 2 **Notes** LB ⊗ No Children 12yrs Closed Xmas

The Blenheim Guest House & Tea Rooms

★★★★ 🅐 GUEST ACCOMMODATION

17 Park St OX20 1SJ
☎ 01993 813814 📄 01993 813810
e-mail: theblenheim@aol.com
web: www.theblenheim.com
dir: Off A44 in Woodstock to County Museum, B&B after museum on left

Rooms 6 rms (5 en suite) (1 pri facs) (2 fmly) S £50; D £60-£70* **Facilities** tea/coffee Cen ht Licensed Wi-fi

Sturdys Castle

★★★ INN

Banbury Rd, Tackley OX5 3EP
☎ 01869 331328 📄 01869 331686
e-mail: enquiries@sturdyscastle.com
dir: On A4260 (Oxford to Banbury road)

Within easy reach of historic Woodstock and Blenheim Palace this well-presented inn is a good touring base. Purpose-built accommodation is located to the rear of the attractive pub where a wide range of traditional fare is on offer. Bedrooms are comfortable and well appointed.

Rooms 20 en suite (4 fmly) (10 GF) **Facilities** tea/coffee Dinner available Direct Dial Cen ht Lift **Conf** Max 50 **Parking** 40 **Notes** ⊗

WOOLSTONE — Map 5 SU28

The White Horse Inn

★★★ INN

SN7 7QL
☎ 01367 820726 📄 01367 820566
e-mail: angustucker@aol.com
web: www.whitehorsewoolstone.co.uk
dir: Just off B4507, at foot of Uffington White Horse Hill

Located in the delightful village of Woolstone, The White Horse is a traditional country inn complete with friendly staff, a resident dog in the bar and an excellent selection of real ales and carefully prepared, quality home cooking. Bedrooms are located in an annexe adjacent to the inn and are generally spacious and comfortable. In addition to the relaxing bar and dining room, guests are welcome to enjoy the outdoor seating in the warmer months.

Rooms 5 annexe en suite (5 GF) **Facilities** tea/coffee Dinner available Cen ht Wi-fi **Parking** 40

RUTLAND

CLIPSHAM — Map 11 SK91

Beech House

★★★★ ◉◉ INN

Main St LE15 7SH
☎ 01780 410355 📄 01780 410000
e-mail: rooms@theolivebranchpub.com
dir: From A1 take B668 signed Stretton & Clipsham

Beech House stands over the road from the Olive Branch restaurant. It offers very well furnished bedrooms which include DVD players. Breakfasts are served in the Olive Branch. Excellent lunches and dinners are also available.

Rooms 5 en suite 1 annexe en suite (2 fmly) (3 GF) **Facilities** tea/coffee Dinner available Direct Dial Cen ht **Parking** 10 **Notes** Closed 1 Jan No coaches

EMPINGHAM — Map 11 SK90

The White Horse Inn

★★★ INN

Main St LE15 8PS
☎ 01780 460221 📄 01780 460521
e-mail: info@whitehorserutland.co.uk
web: www.whitehorserutland.co.uk
dir: On A606 (Oakham to Stamford road)

This attractive stone-built inn, offering bright, comfortable accommodation, is conveniently located just minutes from the A1. Bedrooms in the main building are spacious and include a number of family rooms. Public areas include a well-stocked bar, a bistro and restaurant where a wide range of meals is served.

Rooms 4 en suite 9 annexe en suite (3 fmly) (5 GF) S £53-£63; D £70-£90* **Facilities** TVL tea/coffee Dinner available Direct Dial **Conf** Max 25 Thtr 25 Class 20 Board 20 **Parking** 60 **Notes** Closed 25 Dec

OAKHAM — Map 11 SK80

Kirkee House

★★★★ BED AND BREAKFAST

35 Welland Way LE15 6SL
☎ 01572 757401
e-mail: carolbeech@kirkeehouse.demon.co.uk
dir: S of town centre. Off A606 High St onto Mill St, over level crossing, 400yds on left

Located on a leafy avenue a short walk from the town centre, this immaculately maintained modern house provides comfortable bedrooms filled with homely extras. Comprehensive breakfasts, including local sausages and home-made jams, are served in the elegant conservatory-dining room, which overlooks the pretty garden.

Rooms 2 en suite; D £60-£70* **Facilities** FTV tea/coffee Cen ht **Parking** 2 **Notes** ⊗ No Children 7yrs ◉

OAKHAM *continued*

Nick's Restaurant at Lord Nelson's House

★★★★ ◉◉ 🛏 RESTAURANT WITH ROOMS

11 Market Place LE15 6HR
☎ 01572 723199
e-mail: simon@nicksrestaurant.co.uk
web: www.nicksrestaurant.co.uk
dir: *A1(M) onto A606, after 2nd rdbt, Market Place on right*

Tucked away in the corner of the market square, this restaurant with rooms offers fine dining and four individually appointed bedrooms with a range of antiques and knick-knacks. Service is attentive and helpful, and the food a delight, offering a selection of carefully crafted dishes using the best of quality seasonal produce.

Rooms 4 en suite S £55-£85; D £85-£115* Facilities tea/coffee Dinner available Direct Dial Cen ht Wi-fi Parking 3 Notes LB ⊗ No coaches

---

UPPINGHAM Map 11 SP89

The Lake Isle

★★★★ ◉◉ 🛏 RESTAURANT WITH ROOMS

16 High Street East LE15 9PZ
☎ 01572 822951 📠 01572 824400
e-mail: info@lakeisle.co.uk
web: www.lakeisle.co.uk
dir: *From A47, turn left at 2nd lights, 100yds on right*

This attractive, townhouse centres round a delightful restaurant and small elegant bar. There is also an inviting first-floor guest lounge, and the bedrooms are extremely well appointed and thoughtfully equipped; spacious split-level cottage suites situated in a quiet courtyard are also available. The imaginative cooking and an extremely impressive wine list are highlights.

Rooms 9 en suite 2 annexe rms (2 annexe pri facs) (1 fmly) Facilities FTV tea/coffee Dinner available Direct Dial Cen ht Wi-fi Conf Max 16 Parking 7 Notes No coaches

---

WING Map 11 SK80

Kings Arms Inn & Restaurant

★★★★ ◉ INN

13 Top St LE15 8SE
☎ 01572 737634 📠 01572 737255
e-mail: info@thekingsarms-wing.co.uk
web: www.thekingsarms-wing.co.uk
dir: *1.5m off A6003 in village centre*

This traditional village inn, with its open fires, flagstone floors and low beams, dates from the 17th century. The refurbished restaurant is more contemporary and offers a wide range of interesting freshly produced dishes. Service is attentive and friendly. The spacious, well-equipped

---

bedrooms are in The Old Bake House and Granny's Cottage, in the nearby courtyard.

Rooms 8 en suite (4 fmly) (4 GF) S fr £45; D fr £55 (room only)* Facilities FTV tea/coffee Dinner available Cen ht Conf Max 20 Thtr 16 Class 16 Board 16 Parking 30 Notes ⊗ RS Nov-Mar closed Mon

---

SHROPSHIRE

BISHOP'S CASTLE Map 15 SO38

The Sun at Norbury

★★★★ 🛏 🍴 INN

Norbury SY9 5DX
☎ 01588 650680
web: www.sunatnorbury.co.uk
dir: *3m NE of Bishop's Castle. Off A488/A489 into Norbury*

The delightful stone inn stands in the quiet village of Norbury. Exposed beams and log-burning stoves are enhanced by period furnishings, and the attractive, traditionally furnished bedrooms have modern facilities. Wholesome home-cooked food is available in the elegant dining room or in the popular bar.

Rooms 3 rms (2 en suite) (1 pri facs) 3 annexe en suite (1 GF); D £90-£120* Facilities tea/coffee Dinner available Cen ht Parking 20 Notes LB ⊗ No Children 14yrs No coaches

---

Shuttocks Wood

★★★★ BED AND BREAKFAST

Norbury SY9 5EA
☎ 01588 650433 📠 01588 650433
e-mail: info@shuttocks.co.uk
dir: *From A489, turn left signed Norbury 3m, on the left past Norbury school*

Peacefully located in the rural hamlet of Norbury, this modern detached house, stands on pretty mature gardens and provides good standards of comfort and facilities. Bedrooms are equipped with thoughtful extras, there is a separate self-catering annexe and breakfasts feature local fresh produce.

Rooms 3 en suite (1 fmly) (1 GF) S £30-£40; D £50-£70 Facilities tea/coffee Dinner available Cen ht Parking 10 Notes LB No Children 10yrs

---

BRIDGNORTH Map 10 SO79

PREMIER COLLECTION

The Albynes
★★★★★ BED AND BREAKFAST

Nordley WV16 4SX
☎ 01746 762261
e-mail: thealbynes@hotmail.com
dir: *In Nordley on B4373, 500yds past Nordley sign*

This imposing farmhouse features grand staircases, high ceilings and idyllic views. Melissa Woolley is a charming hostess, while husband Hayden looks after the crops and sheep. Bedrooms are comfortable, spacious and offer many thoughtful extras. Day rooms retain many original features and guests can enjoy traditional breakfasts, home-cooked on the Aga.

Rooms 3 en suite S £40-£45; D £60-£70 Facilities TVL tea/coffee Cen ht Parking 6 Notes ⊗ No Children 12yrs Closed Xmas-New Year ⊗

The Laurels

★★★★ GUEST HOUSE

Broadoak, Six Ashes WV15 6EQ
☎ 01384 221546
e-mail: george.broadoak75@btinternet.com
web: www.thelaurelsbandb.co.uk
dir: *On right 5m from Bridgnorth towards Stourbridge on A458*

Located on pretty gardens in a hamlet between Bridgnorth and Stourbridge, this immaculately maintained property provides a range of homely bedrooms, some of which are in converted stables. Breakfast is served in an attractive conservatory-dining room, and a lounge and indoor swimming pool are additional attractions.

Rooms 2 en suite 5 annexe en suite (1 fmly) (5 GF) Facilities FTV TVL tea/coffee Cen ht Wi-fi 🏊 Parking 9 Notes ⊗ Closed Xmas & New Year ⊗

Bearwood Lodge Guest House

★★★★ GUEST ACCOMMODATION

10 Kidderminster Rd WV15 6BW
☎ 01746 762159
dir: On A442, 50yds S of Bridgnorth bypass island

This friendly guest house is situated on the outskirts of Bridgnorth. It provides soundly maintained modern accommodation, including one bedroom on the ground floor. The bright and pleasant breakfast room has an adjacent conservatory, which opens onto the attractive and colourful garden. There is also a comfortable lounge.

Rooms 5 en suite (1 GF) S £45; D £60* **Facilities** TVL tea/coffee Cen ht **Parking** 8 **Notes** LB ⊛

The Swan Inn

★★★★ INN

Knowlesands WV16 5JL
☎ 01746 763424 📄 01746 764293
e-mail: info@swaninnbridgnorth.co.uk
dir: On B4555, 1m from town centre

Located on the town's outskirts, close to The River Severn and The Historic Foot Ferry, this country inn has been sympathetically renovated to provide high standards of comfort and facilities. Attractive bedrooms, furnished in minimalist style, are complimented by smart modern bathrooms and the spacious vibrant public areas are an ideal setting for accurate and imaginative cooking.

Rooms 6 en suite (1 fmly) **Facilities** tea/coffee Dinner available Cen ht Wi-fi **Conf** Max 60 Thtr 60 Class 40 Board 20 **Parking** 60 **Notes** ⊛

The Halfway House Inn

★★★ INN

Cleobury Mortimer Rd WV16 5LS
☎ 01746 762670 📄 01746 768063
e-mail: info@halfwayhouseinn.co.uk
web: www.halfwayhouseinn.co.uk
dir: 1m from town centre on A4363 to Cleobury Mortimer

Located in a rural area, this 16th-century inn has been renovated to provide good standards of comfort, while retaining original character. The bedrooms, most of which are in converted stables and cottages, are especially suitable for families and groups.

Rooms 10 en suite (10 fmly) (6 GF) S £55-£75; D £65-£95 **Facilities** FTV TVL tea/coffee Dinner available Cen ht Wi-fi Fishing Pool Table **Conf** Max 30 Thtr 30 Class 24 Board 20 **Parking** 30 **Notes** LB RS Sun eve (ex BHs)

Wyndene

★★ BED AND BREAKFAST

57 Innage Ln WV16 4HS
☎ 01746 764369 & 07977 943074
e-mail: wyndene@bridgnorth2000.freeserve.co.uk
dir: 500yds NW of town centre. Off B4373 onto Innage Ln

Situated within walking distance of the centre of Bridgnorth, this small guest house is a home from home. Bedrooms are carefully decorated and one has a four-poster bed. Home-cooked breakfasts are served in an attractive dining room and parking space is available.

Rooms 3 rms (1 en suite) S £32-£35; D £55-£60* **Facilities** TVL tea/coffee Cen ht **Parking** 3 **Notes** ⊛ ⊛

CHURCH STRETTON — Map 15 SO49

PREMIER COLLECTION

The Orchards

★★★★★ BED AND BREAKFAST

Eaton Rd, Ticklerton SY6 7DQ
☎ 01694 722268
e-mail: lnutting@btinternet.com
web: www.theorchardsticklerton.com
dir: 2m SE of Church Stretton. Off B4371 to Ticklerton

This large new house stands in the quiet hamlet of Ticklerton, two miles south-east of Church Stretton. Surrounded by four and a half acres of grounds, garden and orchard, it enjoys picturesque rural views. The comfortable accommodation is thoughtfully equipped and warm hospitality is a major strength here.

Rooms 3 rms (2 en suite) (1 pri facs) (1 fmly) **Facilities** tea/coffee Cen ht **Parking** 6 **Notes** ⊛ No Children 3yrs ⊛

PREMIER COLLECTION

Field House

★★★★★ GUEST HOUSE

Cardington Moor, Cardington SY6 7LL
☎ 01694 771485
e-mail: pjsecrett@talktalk.net
dir: A49 onto B4371 at lights in Church Stretton. After 3.5m turn left signed Cordington, after 1m turn left, 0.5m on right

This delightful old cottage is surrounded by 9 acres of grounds and gardens and is quietly located in a picturesque valley. It has been considerably renovated and extended to provide tastefully appointed, modern accommodation including a bedroom on ground-floor level. Evening meals are available and separate tables are provided in the pleasant dining room. There is also a conservatory lounge.

Rooms 3 en suite (1 GF); D £56-£70* **Facilities** tea/coffee Dinner available Direct Dial Cen ht Licensed Pool Table Table tennis **Parking** 3 **Notes** ⊛ Closed Nov-Feb ⊛

PREMIER COLLECTION

Rectory Farm (SO452985)

★★★★★ FARMHOUSE

Woolstaston SY6 6NN
☎ 01694 751306 📄 01694 751306 Mrs A Rodenhurst
e-mail: d.rodenhurst@btconnect.com
dir: 1.5m from A49 Shrewsbury to Ludlow road, turn by Copper Kettle

Located in immaculate grounds in the pretty hamlet of Woolstaston, this early 17th-century half-timbered longhouse retains many original features including a wealth of exposed beams. The spacious bedrooms feature many thoughtful extras and ground-floor areas include two sitting rooms and an elegant dining room.

Rooms 2 en suite **Facilities** TVL tea/coffee Cen ht **Parking** 6 **Notes** ⊛ No Children 12yrs ⊛ 10 acres non-working

CHURCH STRETTON *continued*

PREMIER COLLECTION

Willowfield Guest House
★★★★★ GUEST HOUSE

Lower Wood SY6 6LF
☎ **01694 751471**
e-mail: willowfieldlowerwood@tiscali.co.uk
dir: *A5 onto A49 to Leebotwood, follow sign for Lower Wood, 0.5m on left*

Set in spacious and immaculate gardens, this Edwardian house, parts of which are much older, provides high standards of comfort. The bedrooms are well equipped and have many thoughtful extras as well as stunning views, while stylish décor and period furnishings add to the charm. A comfortable lounge is available, plus two elegant dining rooms where wholesome home-cooked dinners and hearty breakfasts are served.

Rooms 6 en suite (1 GF) S £40-£45; D £60-£70*
Facilities tea/coffee Dinner available Cen ht **Parking** 6
Notes LB ⊗ ⊛

Belvedere
★★★★ GUEST HOUSE

Burway Rd SY6 6DP
☎ **01694 722232** 📠 **01694 722232**
e-mail: info@belvedereguesthouse.co.uk
dir: *Off A49 into town centre, over x-rds onto Burway Rd*

Popular with walkers and cyclists and located on the lower slopes of the Long Mynd, this impressive, well-proportioned Edwardian house has a range of homely bedrooms, equipped with practical extras and complemented by modern bathrooms. Ground-floor areas include a cottage-style dining room overlooking the pretty garden and a choice of lounges.

Rooms 7 rms (6 en suite) (2 fmly) S £32-£42;
D £54-£64* **Facilities** TVL tea/coffee Cen ht Wi-fi
Parking 9 **Notes** LB

Brereton's Farm *(S0424871)*
★★★★ FARMHOUSE

Woolston SY6 6QD
☎ **01694 781201** 📠 **01694 781201** Mrs J Brereton
e-mail: info@breretonsfarm.co.uk
web: www.breretonsfarm.co.uk
dir: *A49 N from Craven Arms, at Jewsons turn left A489. Under bridge turn right Wistonstow, top of village signed left 1.75m to Woolston. Farm on right*

Located among undulating hills in the pretty hamlet of Woolston, this impressive early-Victorian red-brick house provides thoughtfully equipped bedrooms with stunning country views. Comprehensive breakfasts are served in

an elegant dining room, and the lounge has a wood-burning fireplace.

Rooms 2 en suite S £32; D £60* **Facilities** TVL tea/coffee Dinner available Cen ht **Parking** 6 **Notes** Closed 30 Nov-Mar ⊛ 350 acres mixed

The Bucks Head
★★★★ INN

42 High St SY6 6BX
☎ **01694 722898**
e-mail: lloyd.nutting@btconnect.com
web: www.the-bucks-head.co.uk
dir: *A49 N or S, turn into Church Stretton. At top of town turn left, Bucks Head on right*

Located in the heart of this historic market town, a total renovation has transformed this period hostelry into a vibrant modern inn with high levels of comfort and facilities, whilst retaining original charm and character. Comfortable bedrooms are complimented by smart en suite bathrooms, and the attractive open-plan public areas are a perfect setting for the enjoyment of food or drinks, which is matched by warm and caring hospitality.

Rooms 4 en suite **Facilities** tea/coffee Dinner available Cen ht **Notes** ⊗ No Children 5yrs No coaches

Court Farm *(S0514951)*
★★★★ FARMHOUSE

Gretton SY6 7HU
☎ **01694 771219** 📠 **01694 771219**
dir: *Turn off B4371at Longville, left at x-rds, 1st on left*

Located in the pretty village of Gretton, this 17th-century impressive stone-built Tudor house has been sympathetically renovated to provide high standards of comfort and facilities. Bedrooms overlook the pretty gardens and are equipped with a wealth of thoughtful extras. Comprehensive breakfasts are taken in an elegant dining room and a comfortable guest lounge is also available.

Rooms 2 en suite **Facilities** TVL tea/coffee Cen ht **Parking** 4 **Notes** ⊗ No Children 12yrs ⊛ 330 acres mixed

The Mount
★★★★ BED AND BREAKFAST

Sandford Av SY6 7AA
☎ **01694 722997**
e-mail: enquiry@themount.biz

Located on a leafy residential avenue, within easy walking distance of the town centre, this elegant red brick Edwardian house has been sympathetically renovated to provide high standards of comfort and facilities. Bedrooms are equipped with lots of thoughtful extras and day rooms include an antique furnished dining

room, the setting for comprehensive breakfasts featuring quality local produce.

Rooms 3 rms (1 en suite) (2 pri facs); D £65-£70
Facilities TVL tea/coffee Cen ht Wi-fi **Parking** 6 **Notes** ⊗ RS Xmas & New Year ⊛

North Hill Farm
★★★★ BED AND BREAKFAST

Cardington SY6 7LL
☎ **01694 771532**
e-mail: cbrandon@btinternet.com
dir: *From Cardington village S onto Church Stretton road, right signed Cardington Moor, farm at top of hill on left*

This delightful house has been modernised to provide comfortable accommodation. It is located on a fairly remote 20-acre sheep-rearing holding amid the scenery of the Shropshire hills. The lounge, with exposed beams, has log fires in cold weather. Guests share one large table in the breakfast room.

Rooms 2 rms (2 pri facs) 1 annexe en suite (1 GF) S £35; D £55-£64* **Facilities** tea/coffee Cen ht **Parking** 6 **Notes** LB Closed Xmas ⊛

Malt House Farm *(S0459979)*
★★★ FARMHOUSE

Lower Wood SY6 6LF
☎ **01694 751379** 📠 **01694 751379** Mr & Mrs D Bloor
dir: *A49 N 3m, left signed Lower Wood, 0.5m to farm*

Located on an elevated position north of the town, this house was refashioned in 1772 and retains many original features. Modern bathrooms complement the homely bedrooms. Comprehensive breakfasts, which include free-range eggs, are served in the cosy dining room and a lounge is also available.

Rooms 3 en suite **Facilities** tea/coffee Dinner available Cen ht **Parking** 3 **Notes** ⊗ No Children Closed Nov-Mar ⊛ 150 acres beef/sheep

CLUN Map 9 SO38

PREMIER COLLECTION

Birches Mill
★★★★★ ● BED AND BREAKFAST

SY7 8NL
☎ 01588 640409 🖹 01588 640224
e-mail: gill@birchesmill.fsnet.co.uk
web: www.birchesmill.co.uk
dir: A488 N from Clun for Bishop's Castle, 1st left to Bicton, in Bicton 2nd left for Mainstone, pass farm & 1st right

Located in mature, pretty gardens beside a river in an Area of Outstanding Natural Beauty, this 17th-century former mill retains many original features, enhanced by the décor and furnishing schemes throughout. Bedrooms are filled with lots of thoughtful extras and a comfortable lounge is available.

Rooms 3 rms (2 en suite) (1 pri facs) Facilities TVL tea/coffee Cen ht Parking 3 Notes ⊗ No Children 12yrs Closed Nov-Mar

CRAVEN ARMS Map 9 SO48

The Firs
★★★★ BED AND BREAKFAST

Norton SY7 9LS
☎ 01588 672511 🖹 01588 672511
e-mail: thefirs@wrb.me.uk
dir: Off A49 at Craven Arms onto B4368 towards Bridgnorth. 2m right at x-rds & B&B sign to Norton. Pass farm on left to next left, house 100yds on left

Located in immaculate grounds on an elevated position in the hamlet of Norton, this impressive Victorian house retains many original features, highlighted by period furnishings and quality decor. Bedrooms are filled with thoughtful extras and have stunning views. Breakfast makes use of local produce and is served in an elegant dining room.

Rooms 3 rms (2 en suite) (1 pri facs) Facilities tea/coffee Cen ht Parking 5 Notes ⊗ ⊛

Castle View
★★★★ BED AND BREAKFAST

Stokesay SY7 9AL
☎ 01588 673712
e-mail: castleviewb_b@btinternet.com
dir: On A49 S of Craven Arms opp turning to Stokesay Castle

The Victorian cottage, extended about 20 years ago, stands in delightful gardens on the southern outskirts of Craven Arms, close to Stokesay Castle. Bedrooms are thoughtfully furnished, and breakfasts, featuring local

produce, are served in the cosy, traditionally-furnished dining room.

Rooms 3 rms (1 en suite) (2 pri facs) Facilities tea/coffee Cen ht Parking 4 Notes LB No Children 3yrs ⊛

Strefford Hall Farm (SO444856)
★★★★ FARMHOUSE

Strefford SY7 8DE
☎ 01588 672383 🖹 0870 132 3818 Mrs C Morgan
e-mail: strefford@btconnect.com
dir: A49 from Church Stretton, S for 5.5m to Strefford, 0.25m past Travellers Rest Inn signed left. Strefford Hall 0.25m on right

This well-proportioned Victorian house stands at the foot of Wenlock Edge. The spacious bedrooms, filled with homely extras, have stunning views of the surrounding countryside. Breakfast is served in the elegant dining room and a comfortable lounge is also available.

Rooms 3 en suite (1 fmly) (3 smoking) S £31-£40; D £60-£70 Facilities TVL tea/coffee Cen ht Parking 3 Notes LB ⊗ RS end Feb-end Oct ⊛ 350 acres arable/beef/sheep/pigs

DORRINGTON Map 15 SJ40

Ashton Lees
★★★★ BED AND BREAKFAST

Ashton Lees SY5 7JW
☎ 01743 718378
dir: On N edge of village on A49. From Shrewsbury, Ashton Lees on right on entering village

Located in immaculate mature gardens, this well-proportioned mid-20th-century house has been renovated to provide high standards of comfort and facilities. Bedrooms are filled with thoughtful extras, and public areas include a cosy lounge-dining room and a separate sitting room, both featuring open fires.

Rooms 3 rms (2 en suite) (1 pri facs) S £27.50-£30; D £55-£60* Facilities TVL tea/coffee Cen ht Parking 4 Notes ⊗ Closed Dec-Jan ⊛

Caro's Bed & Breakfast
★★★ BED AND BREAKFAST

1 Higher Netley SY5 7JY
☎ 01743 718790 & 07739 285263
e-mail: info@carosbandb.co.uk
dir: 1m SW of Dorrington. Off A49 in Dorrington signed Picklescott, 1m left onto driveway by stone bridge, signed Higher Netley

Self-contained guest accommodation is provided in this converted barn, south-west of Dorrington. Bedrooms, with smart modern bathrooms, are equipped with thoughtful extras and the open-plan ground-floor area contains a dining area and a comfortable lounge with a wood-burning stove.

Rooms 2 en suite Facilities tea/coffee Cen ht Wi-fi Parking 4 Notes ⊗ Closed 21-28 Dec

ELLESMERE Map 15 SJ33

Hordley Hall
★★★★ BED AND BREAKFAST

Hordley SY12 9BB
☎ 01691 622772 🖹 01691 622772
e-mail: hordleyhall@hotmail.co.uk
dir: Exit A5 at Queens Head junct signed Hordley 4m. 1st left after village sign, 1st large cream house on right

This large former farmhouse has a wealth of charm and character. Surrounded by large and attractive gardens, it is quietly located at Hordley, some three miles south-west of Ellesmere. It provides traditionally furnished, well quipped accommodation, which is equally suitable for both tourists and business visitors. Facilities include a comfortable lounge.

Rooms 4 rms (2 en suite) (2 pri facs) S £30-£35; D £60-£65* Facilities TVL tea/coffee Cen ht Conf Max 6 Parking 4 Notes LB ⊗ No Children 2yrs ⊛

HADNALL Map 15 SJ52

Hall Farm House
★★★★ BED AND BREAKFAST

Shrewsbury Rd SY4 4AG
☎ 01939 210269
e-mail: hallfarmhouse@tiscali.co.uk
web: www.hallfarmhouse.co.uk
dir: On A49 in centre of Hadnall

Parts of this elegant former farmhouse, situated in pretty, mature gardens in the village, date from the 16th century. Accommodation is offered in two thoughtfully equipped bedrooms and comprehensive breakfasts are taken in a spacious, traditionally furnished dining room.

Rooms 2 en suite S £35-£40; D £50-£60 Facilities tea/coffee Cen ht Parking 6 Notes LB ⊗ No Children 1yr ⊛

HADNALL *continued*

Saracens at Hadnall

★★★★ ⑧ RESTAURANT WITH ROOMS

Shrewsbury Rd SY4 4AG
☎ 01939 210877 ▤ 01939 210877
e-mail: reception@saracensathadnall.co.uk
web: www.saracensathadnall.co.uk
dir: *M54 onto A5, at junct of A5/A49 take A49 towards Whitchurch. Follow A49 to Hadnall, diagonally opposite church*

This Georgian Grade II listed former farmhouse and village pub has been tastefully converted into a very smart restaurant-with-rooms, without any loss of charm or character. The bedrooms are thoughtfully equipped and include a family room. Skilfully prepared meals are served in either the elegant dining room or the adjacent conservatory where there is a glass-topped well.

Rooms 5 en suite (1 fmly) S fr £45; D £60-£75*
Facilities tea/coffee Dinner available Cen ht **Parking** 20
Notes LB ⊗ RS Sun eve-Mon Closed No coaches

IRONBRIDGE Map 10 SJ60

PREMIER COLLECTION

The Library House

★★★★★ ▤ GUEST ACCOMMODATION

11 Severn Bank TF8 7AN
☎ 01952 432299
e-mail: info@libraryhouse.com
web: www.libraryhouse.com
dir: *50yds from Iron Bridge*

A warm welcome is assured at this renovated Georgian house, once the local library. Bedrooms, named after writers of note, have a wealth of thoughtful extras and the immaculate gardens and hanging baskets are stunning during spring and summer. Memorable breakfasts are served in the pine- and copper-furnished dining room and a comfortable guest lounge is also available.

Rooms 4 en suite S £65-£75; D £75-£95*
Facilities TVL tea/coffee Cen ht Licensed Wi-fi
Notes LB ⊗ No Children

Broseley House

★★★★ GUEST HOUSE

1 The Square, Broseley TF12 5EW
☎ 01952 882043 ▤ 01952 882043
e-mail: info@broseleyhouse.co.uk
web: www.broseleyhouse.co.uk
dir: *1m S of Ironbridge in Broseley town centre*

A warm welcome is assured at this impressive Georgian house in the centre of Broseley. Quality individual décor and soft furnishings highlight the many original features, and thoughtfully furnished bedrooms are equipped with a wealth of homely extras. Comprehensive breakfasts are taken in an elegant dining room and a stylish apartment is also available.

Rooms 4 en suite (1 fmly) (1 GF) **Facilities** tea/coffee Cen ht **Notes** No Children 5yrs

---

Woodlands Farm Guest House

★★★★ BED AND BREAKFAST

Beech Rd TF8 7PA
☎ 01952 432741
e-mail: woodlandsfarm@ironbridge68.fsnet.co.uk
web: www.woodlandsfarmironbridge.co.uk
dir: *Off B4373 rdbt in Ironbridge onto Church Hill & Beech Rd, house on private lane 0.5m on right*

Woodlands was originally a brick works and then a working farm before conversion to spacious comfortable en suite bedrooms. Stylish furnishing and comfortable beds feature alongside warm hospitality. Wholesome breakfast is taken overlooking the pretty garden.

Rooms 5 en suite (1 fmly) (3 GF) S £35-£70; D £50-£80
Facilities STV FTV tea/coffee Cen ht Wi-fi **Parking** 8
Notes LB No Children 5yrs Closed 24 Dec-2 Jan

KNOCKIN Map 15 SJ32

Top Farm House

★★★★ GUEST HOUSE

SY10 8HN
☎ 01691 682582 ▤ 01691 682070
e-mail: p.a.m@knockin.freeserve.co.uk
web: www.topfarmknockin.co.uk
dir: *Off B4396 in village centre*

This impressive half-timbered Tudor house, set amid pretty gardens, retains many original features including a wealth of exposed beams and open fires. Bedrooms are equipped with many thoughtful extras, and the open-plan ground-floor area includes a comfortable sitting room and elegant dining section, where imaginative comprehensive breakfasts are served.

Rooms 3 en suite (1 fmly) **Facilities** TVL tea/coffee Cen ht **Parking** 6

LLANFAIR WATERDINE Map 9 SO27

PREMIER COLLECTION

The Waterdine

★★★★★ ⑧⑧ ▤ RESTAURANT WITH ROOMS

LD7 1TU
☎ 01547 528214
e-mail: info@waterdine.com
dir: *Off B4355 into village, last property on left before church*

Standing in pretty, mature gardens in an Area of Outstanding Natural Beauty, which includes part of Offa's Dyke, this former 16th-century drovers' inn retains much of its original character. Bedrooms are filled with a wealth of thoughtful extras and have modern bathrooms. Public areas include a cosy lounge bar and an elegant restaurant, the setting for imaginative dinners that use quality, seasonal local produce.

Rooms 3 en suite; D £170* (incl.dinner) **Facilities** tea/coffee Dinner available Cen ht **Parking** 12 **Notes** LB ⊗ No Children 12yrs Closed 1wk autumn & 1wk spring RS Sun & Mon (ex BHs) Closed Sun eve & all day Mon No coaches

LUDLOW Map 10 SO57

PREMIER COLLECTION

The Clive Bar & Restaurant with Rooms
★★★★★ ◎◎ RESTAURANT WITH ROOMS

Bromfield SY8 2JR
☎ 01584 856565 & 856665 📄 01584 856661
e-mail: info@theclive.co.uk
web: www.theclive.co.uk
dir: *2m N of Ludlow on A49 in village of Bromfield*

The Clive is just two miles from the busy town of Ludlow and is a convenient base for visiting the local attractions or for business. The bedrooms are spacious and very well equipped, and some are suitable for families. Meals are available in the well-known Clive Restaurant or the Cookhouse café bar. A small meeting room is also available.

Rooms 15 annexe en suite (9 fmly) (11 GF) S £60-£85; D £85-£110* **Facilities** tea/coffee Dinner available Direct Dial Cen ht Wi-fi **Conf** Max 40 Thtr 40 Class 40 Board 24 **Parking** 100 **Notes** LB ⊗ Closed 25-26 Dec

PREMIER COLLECTION

De Greys of Ludlow
★★★★★ GUEST HOUSE

5-6 Broad St SY8 1NG
☎ 01584 872764 📄 01584 879764
e-mail: degreys@btopenworld.com
web: www.degreys.co.uk
dir: *Off A49, in town centre, 50yds beyond clock tower*

This 16th-century timber-framed property is situated in the town centre. It has recently been extensively refurbished to provide high quality accommodation with modern facilities, including two suites and one bedroom on ground floor level, all with the added confidence of an electronic security system. Careful renovation of the original beams combined with lush fabrics and beautiful wooden furniture has created a real fusion of the past and present. Breakfast is taken in the adjacent tearoom/restaurant and bakery shop.

De Greys of Ludlow

Rooms 9 en suite (1 GF) **Facilities** tea/coffee Cen ht Licensed **Notes** ⊗ Closed 26 Dec & 1 Jan

PREMIER COLLECTION

Line Farm
★★★★★ BED AND BREAKFAST

Tunnel Ln, Orleton SY8 4HY
☎ 01568 780400
dir: *Signed from A49 in Ashton. B&B signs in Tunnel Ln to Line Farm*

A warm welcome is assured at this well-maintained non-smoking farmhouse, which is set in immaculate gardens to the south of Ludlow. Bedrooms, one of which is located in a superb Scandinavian style chalet, and can also be used for self-catering, are filled with a wealth of thoughtful extras and have modern efficient bathrooms. Comprehensive breakfasts are served in an elegant dining room, and a spacious lounge is available.

Rooms 3 en suite S £50-£55; D £70-£75* **Facilities** TVL tea/coffee Direct Dial Cen ht **Parking** 6 **Notes** ⊗ No Children Closed Nov-Feb ⊗

Number Twenty Eight
★★★★ 🏠 BED AND BREAKFAST

28 Lower Broad St SY8 1PQ
☎ 01584 875466
e-mail: enquiries@no28ludlow.co.uk
web: www.no28ludlow.co.uk
dir: *In town centre. Over Ludford Bridge onto Lower Broad St, 3rd house on right*

A warm welcome is assured at this 200-year-old property just a stroll from the centre. There are two double bedrooms, each well-equipped and containing thoughtful extra welcoming touches. Day rooms include an antique furnished combined lounge/sitting room, and a small roof terrace that overlooks the pretty rear garden.

Rooms 2 en suite; D £80-£90* **Facilities** tea/coffee Cen ht **Notes** ⊗ No Children 16yrs Closed Nov-May

Angel House
★★★★ BED AND BREAKFAST

Bitterley SY8 3HT
☎ 01584 891377
e-mail: angelhousebandb@googlemail.com
dir: *On A4117, 4m E of Ludlow on Clee Hill*

Located in an elevated position five miles from Ludlow. This sympathetically renovated 17th-century former pub provides high standards of comfort and facilities. Thoughtfully furnished bedrooms have stunning rural views and comprehensive breakfasts are served in an attractive dining room. A guest lounge is also available and a warm welcome is assured.

Rooms 2 en suite (1 fmly) S £55-£65; D £65-£75* **Facilities** tea/coffee Dinner available Cen ht Wi-fi **Parking** 7 **Notes** No Children 7yrs ⊗

The Charlton Arms
★★★★ 🍽 INN

Ludford Bridge SY8 1PJ
☎ 01584 872813
dir: *From town centre onto Broad St, over Ludford Bridge, Charlton Arms on right*

This recently refurbished riverside inn is situated in the market town of Ludlow, which is home to a number of famous festivals and a wealth of historic buildings. The restaurant provides fresh, locally-sourced ingredients and as a free house also offers a fine selection of local beers. Accommodation is newly refurbished and reflects the character of this historic building whilst offering all the comforts of modern life. There is one bedroom which has a private terrace and hot tub, and there are decking areas to enjoy drinks or a meal on warmer days.

Rooms 11 en suite (2 fmly); D £80-£180* **Facilities** TV9B TVL tea/coffee Dinner available Cen ht Fishing **Conf** Max 100 Thtr 100 Class 80 Board 70 **Parking** 25

Church Inn
★★★★ INN

The Buttercross SY8 1AW
☎ 01584 872174 📄 01584 877146
web: www.thechurchinn.com
dir: *In town centre at top of Broad St*

Set right in the heart of the historic town, this Grade II listed inn has been renovated to provide quality accommodation with smart modern bathrooms, some with spa baths. Other areas include a small lounge, a well-equipped meeting room, and cosy bar areas where imaginative food and real ales are served.

Rooms 8 en suite (3 fmly) **Facilities** TVL tea/coffee Dinner available Direct Dial Cen ht **Conf** Max 38 **Notes** No coaches

LUDLOW *continued*

Moor Hall

★★★ GUEST HOUSE

Cleedownton SY8 3EG
☎ 01584 823209 🖹 08715 041324
e-mail: enquiries@moorhall.co.uk
dir: *A4117 Ludlow to Kidderminster, left to Bridgnorth. B4364, follow for 3.2m, Moor Hall on right*

This impressive Georgian house, once the home of Lord Boyne, is surrounded by extensive gardens and farmland. Bedrooms are richly decorated, well equipped, and one room has a sitting area. Public areas are spacious and comfortably furnished, and include a choice of sitting rooms and a library bar. Guests dine family-style in an elegant dining room.

Rooms 3 en suite (1 fmly) S £40-£45; D £60-£70*
Facilities tea/coffee Dinner available Cen ht Licensed Fishing **Conf** Max 14 Thtr 14 Class 14 Board 14 **Parking** 7 **Notes** LB Closed 25-26 Dec ⊛

Roebuck Inn

★★★★ ⊛⊛ INN

Brimfield SY8 4NE
☎ 01584 711230
e-mail: info@theroebuckludlow.co.uk
web: www.theroebuckinnludlow.co.uk
dir: *On A49, turn off at Brimfield*

Located in the rural village of Brimfield, this former 15th-century inn has been sympathetically renovated to provide good standards of comfort and facilities. Bedrooms offer a good range of homely extras and public areas include a lounge bar, which retains original period features and an elegant restaurant, in minimalist style, the setting for imaginative cooking.

Rooms 3 en suite **Facilities** tea/coffee Dinner available Cen ht **Conf** Max 40 **Parking** 20 **Notes** ⊗

Southcot

★★★★ GUEST HOUSE

Livesey Rd SY8 1EZ
☎ 01584 879655 & 07787 533718 🖹 01584 878372
e-mail: gillandjohn@southcotbandb.co.uk
dir: *From lights at Tesco up Station Dr, past station to next lights, left & 1st right, Southcot on left*

Southcot is located in a select residential area just five minutes walk from the historic centre. The bedrooms are comfortable, spacious and very well equipped with thoughtful extra touches and smart modern bathrooms. One ground floor room has been adapted for disabled guests. Facilities include a cosy lounge and breakfast room.

Rooms 5 en suite (1 GF) S £50-£75; D £60-£75
Facilities FTV TVL tea/coffee Cen ht **Parking** 6 **Notes** ⊗

Tean House

★★★★ BED AND BREAKFAST

8 Ledwyche Close, Middleton SY8 3EP
☎ 01584 875891
dir: *A4117 onto B4364, 0.7m on right*

Located in a small rural hamlet a few minutes drive from the town centre, this impressive modern detached house offers comfortable bedrooms equipped with a range of homely extras. Comprehensive breakfasts provide a good start to the day and a warm welcome is assured.

Rooms 3 rms (1 en suite) (1 pri facs) S £38; D £60*
Facilities TVL tea/coffee Cen ht Wi-fi **Parking** 3 **Notes** ⊗ No Children 5yrs ⊛

37 Gravel Hill

★★★★ BED AND BREAKFAST

SY8 1QR
☎ 01584 877524
dir: *Close to town centre*

This charming old house is within walking distance of the town centre. It provides good quality, thoughtfully equipped accommodation, and there is also a comfortable sitting room. Guests share one large table in the elegant breakfast room.

Rooms 2 rms (1 en suite) (1 pri facs) **Facilities** TVL tea/coffee Cen ht **Notes** ⊛

Haynall Villa (SO543674)

★★★ FARMHOUSE

Little Hereford SY8 4BG
☎ 01584 711589 🖹 01584 711589 Mrs R Edwards
e-mail: rachelmedwards@hotmail.com
web: www.haynallvilla.co.uk
dir: *A49 onto A456, at Little Hereford right signed Leysters & Middleton on the Hill. Villa 1m on right*

Located in immaculate gardens in the pretty hamlet of Little Hereford, this Victorian house retains many original features, which are enhanced by the furnishings and décor. Bedrooms are filled with lots of homely extras and the lounge has an open fire.

Rooms 3 rms (2 en suite) (1 fmly); D fr £60*
Facilities FTV TVL tea/coffee Dinner available Cen ht Fishing **Parking** 3 **Notes** No Children 6yrs Closed mid Dec-mid Jan ⊛ 72 acres arable

MARKET DRAYTON	Map 15 SJ63

PREMIER COLLECTION

Ternhill Farm House & The Cottage Restaurant

★★★★★ ⊛ 🖹 RESTAURANT WITH ROOMS

Ternhill TF9 3PX
☎ 01630 638984 🖹 01630 638752
e-mail: info@ternhillfarm.co.uk
web: www.ternhillfarm.co.uk
dir: *On junct A53 & A41, archway off A53 to back of property*

The elegant Grade II listed Georgian farmhouse stands in a large pleasant garden and has been modernised to provide quality accommodation. There is a choice of comfortable lounges, and the Cottage Restaurant features imaginative dishes using local produce. Secure parking is an additional benefit.

Rooms 5 en suite (2 fmly) S £35-£80; D £60-£80*
Facilities FTV tea/coffee Dinner available Cen ht Wi-fi **Parking** 15 **Notes** LB ⊗

The Four Alls Inn

★★★ INN

Woodseaves TF9 2AG
☎ 01630 652995 📄 01630 653930
e-mail: inn@thefouralls.com
web: www.thefouralls.com
dir: On A529 1m S of Market Drayton

This country inn provides spacious open-plan public areas and has a strong local following for its imaginative food and real ales. Bedrooms, which are in a purpose-built chalet block, offer a good balance between practicality and homeliness. Superb beer gardens adorned with attractive floral displays are a feature during the summer.

Rooms 9 annexe en suite (4 fmly) (9 GF) S fr £45; D fr £62* Facilities FTV tea/coffee Dinner available Direct Dial Cen ht Conf Max 100 Thtr 100 Class 100 Board 30 Parking 60 Notes LB ⊗ Closed 24-26 Dec

MINSTERLEY   Map 15 SJ30

Pool Cottage

★★★★ BED AND BREAKFAST

Gravels SY5 0JD
☎ 01743 891621
e-mail: reservations@poolcottage.com
dir: Off A488, signed Pool Cottage

This small, pleasant and friendly bed and breakfast is quietly located amid open countryside five miles south of Minsterley and is set well back from the A488. It provides well-maintained, modern accommodation, as well as a cosy breakfast room where guests are seated around one table.

Rooms 3 en suite (1 fmly) (1 GF) S fr £20; D fr £60* Facilities tea/coffee Cen ht Wi-fi Stabling available Parking 7 Notes ⊗ Closed Xmas ⊠

MUCH WENLOCK   Map 10 SO69

Yew Tree (SO543958)

★★★★ 🏠 FARMHOUSE

Longville In The Dale TF13 6EB
☎ 01694 771866   Mr & Mrs A Hilbery
e-mail: hilbery@tiscali.co.uk
dir: 5m SW of Much Wenlock. N off B4371 at Longville, left at pub, right at x-rds, farm 1.2m on right

Peacefully located between Much Wenlock and Church Stretton in ten acres of unspoiled countryside, where pigs, sheep and chickens are reared, and own produce is a feature on the comprehensive breakfast menu. Bedrooms are equipped with thoughtful extras and a warm welcome is assured.

Rooms 2 rms (1 en suite) (1 pri facs) S £25-£30; D £50-£60* Facilities FTV TVL tea/coffee Cen ht Parking 4 Notes LB ⊠ 10 acres small holding/sheep/pigs

Talbot Inn

★★★ 🅰 INN

High St TF13 6AA
☎ 01952 727077 📄 01952 728436
e-mail: the_talbot_inn@hotmail.com
web: www.the-talbot-inn.com
dir: In village centre on A458

Rooms 6 annexe en suite (1 GF) S £37.50-£40; D £75-£80* Facilities TVL tea/coffee Dinner available Cen ht Parking 6 Notes LB ⊗ Closed 25 Dec

MUNSLOW   Map 10 SO58

Crown Country Inn

★★★★ ◎◎ 🏠 INN

SY7 9ET
☎ 01584 841205
e-mail: info@crowncountryinn.co.uk
dir: Off B4368 into village

Located between Much Wenlock and Craven Arms, this impressive pastel-coloured and half-timbered Tudor inn is full of character and charm with stone floors, exposed beams and blazing log fires during winter. Smart pine-

---

furnished bedrooms are in a converted stable block and spacious public areas include two dining rooms.

Rooms 3 en suite (1 fmly) (1 GF) S £55-£85; D £85-£90* Facilities tea/coffee Dinner available Cen ht Wi-fi Conf Max 30 Thtr 30 Class 30 Board 20 Parking 20 Notes LB ⊗ Closed 25 Dec RS Closed Sun eve Closed Mon lunch/eve for food

NEWPORT   Map 15 SJ71

Red Gables Country B&B

★★★★ 🅰 BED AND BREAKFAST

Longford TF10 8LN
☎ 01952 811118 📄 01952 811118
e-mail: sandracorbett@red-gables.com
dir: From Newport onto Salters Ln/Longford Rd, left at T-junct, 100yds on left

Rooms 3 annexe en suite S fr £50; D £60-£70* Facilities FTV TVL tea/coffee Cen ht Wi-fi Parking 10 Notes LB ⊗ ⊠

OSWESTRY   Map 15 SJ22

PREMIER COLLECTION

Greystones

★★★★★ 🍴 BED AND BREAKFAST

Crickheath SY10 8BW
☎ 07976 740141
e-mail: enquiry@stayatgreystones.co.uk
web: www.stayatgreystones.co.uk
dir: From A483 follow B4396, turn right through village take No Through Road, Greystones on right

A warm welcome is assured at this impressive detached house, located on pretty mature gardens in the hamlet of Crickheath. Bedrooms are equipped with a wealth of thoughtful extras and smart modern bathrooms. Hearty breakfasts and imaginative dinners are available in an elegant dining room and a comfortable guest lounge is also available.

Rooms 3 en suite (2 fmly) S £65; D £90-£100* Facilities FTV TVL tea/coffee Dinner available Cen ht Licensed Wi-fi Conf Board 10 Parking 20 Notes LB ⊗ No Children 14yrs

OSWESTRY *continued*

Pear Tree Cottage

★★★★ BED AND BREAKFAST

Crickheath SY10 8BJ
☎ 01691 830766
e-mail: mike.bossen@virgin.net
web: www.stayatpeartree.co.uk
dir: *A5 onto B4396 through Knockin, left after Lloyd Animal Feed Mill onto Crickheath Ln, house on right*

This 200-year-old property, reputedly once a pub, is set in quiet gardens alongside a disused section of the Montgomery Canal, which is currently being restored. The well-maintained accommodation consists of two thoughtfully equipped bedrooms. Warm hospitality is assured and hearty breakfasts take full advantage of local produce.

Rooms 2 en suite S £40; D £60* **Facilities** TVL tea/coffee Cen ht **Parking** 3 **Notes** ⊗ No Children 12yrs ⊛

The Pentre

★★★★ 🍴 ⊕ GUEST HOUSE

Trefonen SY10 9EE
☎ 01691 653952
e-mail: helen@thepentre.com
web: www.thepentre.com
dir: *4m SW of Oswestry. Off Oswestry-Treflach road onto New Well Ln & signed The Pentre*

This 500-year-old stone farmhouse retains many original features, including a wealth of exposed beams and a superb inglenook fireplace with blazing wood burner during colder months. Bedrooms are equipped with a range of thoughtful extras, and breakfast and dinner are memorable, with quality produce cooked with flair on an Aga.

Rooms 3 en suite (1 fmly) (1 GF); D £66-£100* **Facilities** TVL tea/coffee Dinner available Cen ht **Parking** 10 **Notes** LB ⊗ ⊛

Top Farm House

★★★★ GUEST HOUSE

SY10 8HN
☎ 01691 682582 📠 01691 682070
e-mail: p.a.m@knockin.freeserve.co.uk

(For full entry see Knockin)

Ashfield Farmhouse

★★★★ GUEST ACCOMMODATION

Maesbury SY10 8JH
☎ 01691 653589 & 07989 477414
e-mail: marg@ashfieldfarmhouse.co.uk
dir: *1m off A5/A483; 1.5m S of Oswestry near Maesbury village school & tiny white church*

The farmhouse is located in the hamlet of Maesbury and dates in part from the 16th century. Original features include open fireplaces and a superb polished staircase. Bedrooms, one in a renovated coach house that can also be used for self-catering, are equipped with modern facilities and homely extras. There is a comfortable lounge, a traditionally furnished breakfast room and solar power heats the hot water supply.

Rooms 3 en suite (2 fmly) S £30-£50; D £58-£80* **Facilities** TVL tea/coffee Cen ht **Parking** 5 **Notes** LB

The Bradford Arms

★★★★ INN

Llanymynech SY22 6EJ
☎ 01691 830582 📠 01691 839009
e-mail: catelou@tesco.net
dir: *5.5m S of Oswestry on A483 in Llanymynech*

Once a coaching inn on the Earl of Bradford's estate, the Bradford Arms provides a range of carefully furnished bedrooms with a wealth of thoughtful extras. The elegant ground-floor areas include lounges, bars, and a choice of formal or conservatory restaurants, the settings for imaginative food and fine wines.

Rooms 5 en suite (2 fmly) (2 GF) S £35-£40; D £60-£80* **Facilities** FTV tea/coffee Dinner available Direct Dial Cen ht Wi-fi Golf 18 Fishing Riding Pool Table **Parking** 20

Riseholme

★★★★ BED AND BREAKFAST

4 Hampton Rd SY11 1SJ
☎ 01691 656508
e-mail: ssparnell1234@googlemail.com

Located in a residential area within easy walking distance of the town centre, via the attractive memorial gardens. Comfortable bedrooms are complemented by smart modern bathrooms at this attractive home. Comprehensive breakfasts are taken in a cosy dining room and a spacious guest lounge is also available.

Rooms 3 en suite (1 fmly) **Facilities** TVL tea/coffee Cen ht Wi-fi **Notes** No Children 12yrs ⊛

Carreg-y-big Farm

★★★ BED AND BREAKFAST

Carreg-y-big, Selattyn SY10 7HX
☎ 01691 654754
e-mail: info@carreg-y-bigfarm.co.uk
dir: *Off B4580 at Old Racecourse, signed Selattyn. 1m on right on Offa's Dyke*

Incorporated within The Oswestry Equestrian Centre on the edge of Selattyn, this former farmhouse provides a range of simply appointed bedrooms, ideal for walkers on nearby Offa's Dyke. Comprehensive breakfasts and dinners, by arrangement, are served at one pine table in an attractive beamed dining room, and a small guest lounge is also available.

Rooms 4 rms (1 pri facs) (1 GF) **Facilities** TVL Dinner available Cen ht Riding **Parking** 10 **Notes** ⊛

The Red Lion

★★★ INN

Bailey Head SY11 1PZ
☎ 01691 656077 📠 01691 655932
dir: *In town centre. Off Castle St onto Powis Place, 1st left into car park signed Red Lion Complex*

Located in the historic town square, this well-maintained inn provides spacious, well-furnished open-plan public areas, the setting for a wide range of real ales and bar meals. Bedrooms are well equipped and have modern en suite shower rooms.

Rooms 5 en suite (1 fmly) (2 smoking) S £30-£40; D £40-£50 **Facilities** tea/coffee Dinner available Cen ht Pool Table **Parking** 4 **Notes** LB ⊗

Summerfield B&B

⋃

Sarn Holdings, Sarn Ln, Rhosygadfa SY10 7AU
☎ **01691 661429**
web: www.summerfieldbandb.co.uk

Currently the rating for this establishment is not confirmed. This may be due to a change of ownership or because it has only recently joined the AA rating scheme.

Rooms 2 rms (1 en suite) (1 pri facs) S £38; D £64
Facilities FTV TVL tea/coffee Cen ht Golf 18 **Parking** 5
Notes LB Closed Xmas & New Year ⊗

RUYTON-XI-TOWNS Map 15 SJ32

Brownhill House

★★★ BED AND BREAKFAST

SY4 1LR
☎ **01939 261121** 📠 **01939 260626**
e-mail: brownhill@eleventowns.co.uk
web: www.eleventowns.co.uk
dir: A5 onto B4397, 2m to Ruyton-XI-Towns. Through village. Brownhill House on left of right-hand bend

A warm welcome is assured at this charming guest house, parts of which date from the 18th century. The large terraced garden has been painstakingly created on the side of a steep hill above the River Perry, and guests are welcome to explore. All bedrooms have modern facilities and guests share one large table in a cosy kitchen-dining room.

Rooms 3 en suite (1 GF) S £26–£28.50; D £45–£55*
Facilities TVL tea/coffee Cen ht 🐟 Fishing **Parking** 5
Notes LB ⊗ RS Xmas

SHIFNAL Map 10 SJ70

The Anvil Lodge

★★★★ GUEST ACCOMMODATION

22 Aston Rd TF11 8DU
☎ **01952 460125**
web: www.anvillodge.co.uk

A friendly welcome is assured at Anvil Lodge, just a short stroll from the market town of Shifnal. Delicious, freshly cooked breakfasts are served around the dining room table. Bedrooms are spacious, fresh in appearance and very comfortable with modern bathrooms complete with bath and separate shower. Off-road secure parking is available.

Rooms 4 annexe en suite (2 fmly) (2 GF) S fr £58*
Facilities FTV Cen ht **Parking** 8 **Notes** ⊗

SHREWSBURY Map 15 SJ41

See also Criggion (Powys), Ruyton-XI-Towns, Wem & Westbury

Fieldside

★★★★ GUEST HOUSE

38 London Rd SY2 6NX
☎ **01743 353143** 📠 **01743 354687**
e-mail: robrookes@btinternet.com
dir: A5 onto A5064, premises 1m on left

Located on manicured grounds within easy walking distance of town centre, this well maintained, early Victorian house provides a range of tastefully furnished bedrooms equipped with a wealth of thoughtful extras. Breakfast is taken in an elegant spacious dining room and a warm welcome is assured.

Rooms 8 rms (5 en suite) (3 pri facs) S £25–£45; D £50–£65* **Facilities** TV4B tea/coffee Cen ht Wi-fi
Parking 8 **Notes** No Children 10yrs ⊗

Tudor House

★★★★ 🏠 GUEST HOUSE

2 Fish St SY1 1UR
☎ **01743 351735** & **07870 653040**
e-mail: enquiry@tudorhouseshrewsbury.co.uk
web: www.tudorhouseshrewsbury.co.uk
dir: Enter town over English Bridge, ascend Wyle Cop, in 50yds take 1st right

Located in the beautiful medieval town centre, this fine 15th-century house has original beams and fireplaces, enhanced by the décor and furnishings. Bedrooms are filled with thoughtful extras and breakfast features local organic produce.

Rooms 3 rms (2 en suite) (1 pri facs) **Facilities** tea/coffee Cen ht **Notes** ⊗ No Children 11yrs ⊗

Abbey Court

★★★★ GUEST HOUSE

134 Abbey Foregate SY2 6AU
☎ **01743 364416** 📠 **01743 358559**
e-mail: info@abbeycourt.biz
web: www.abbeycourt.biz
dir: N of river off A5112

Located within easy reach of the town centre, this Grade II listed house offers a range of homely bedrooms, some of which are in an attractive extension. Comprehensive breakfasts are served in a cosy dining room and a warm welcome is assured.

Rooms 6 en suite 4 annexe en suite (1 fmly) (4 GF)
Facilities tea/coffee Direct Dial Cen ht **Parking** 10
Notes ⊗ RS 23–27 Dec room only

The Bull Inn

★★★★ INN

7 Butcher Row SY1 1UW
☎ **01743 344728**
e-mail: markglenister@btconnect.com
web: www.bull-inn.co.uk
dir: Off High St onto Butcher Row, next to Prince Rupert Hotel

Originally a slaughter house and situated in the heart of the town's pedestrianised area, this timber-framed hostelry has a wealth of charm and character. Now renovated, it provides modern equipped accommodation and spacious bar and restaurant areas, where a wide range of food is available. A pleasant beer garden is also available.

Rooms 6 rms (4 en suite) (2 pri facs) (1 fmly)
Facilities tea/coffee Dinner available Cen ht **Notes** ⊗

SHREWSBURY continued

Shenandoah Guest House

★★★ GUEST HOUSE

Sparrow Ln, Off Abbey Ln SY2 5EP
☎ 01743 363015 📠 01743 244918
web: www.shenandoah.org.uk
dir: A5 onto A5064, turn onto Abbey Foregate after 100yds right onto Sparrow Ln

Located between the Lord Hill Monument and Abbey, and within easy walking distance of the town centre, this peacefully located modern house provides a range of thoughtfully furnished bedrooms with en suite shower rooms. Hearty breakfasts are taken in an attractive dining room and a warm welcome is assured.

Rooms 4 en suite (3 fmly) S £25-£35; D £50-£65*
Facilities FTV tea/coffee Cen ht **Parking** 6 **Notes** LB

TELFORD | Map 10 SJ60

Avenue Farm

★★★★ BED AND BREAKFAST

Uppington TF6 5HW
☎ 01952 740253 & 07711 219453 📠 01952 740401
e-mail: jones@avenuefarm.fsnet.co.uk
web: www.virtual-shropshire.co.uk/avenuefarm
dir: M54 junct 7, B5061 for Atcham, 2nd left signed Uppington. Right after sawmill, farm 400yds on right

This impressive, well-proportioned period house stands in immaculate mature gardens in the hamlet of Uppington. Quality furnishings and décor highlight the many original features, and the bedrooms are equipped with thoughtful extras. Comprehensive breakfasts are taken at an antique table in the elegant dining room and a comfortable sitting room is also available.

Rooms 3 en suite (1 fmly) S £35-£40; D £55-£60*
Facilities TV2B FTV TVL tea/coffee Riding **Parking** 4
Notes Closed Xmas ⊗

Potford House

★★★ BED AND BREAKFAST

Little Bolas, Wellington TF6 6PS
☎ 01952 541362
e-mail: dsadler@potford.fsnet.co.uk
web: www.shropshirebedandbreakfast.com
dir: 7m N of Wellington on A442, turn right signed Little Bolas, 1m from pub. Potford House on left

Located in a peaceful hamlet north of Wellington, this spacious detached house provides a warm welcome and homely bedrooms with thoughtful extras. Wholesome breakfasts using local produce are served in an attractive dining room overlooking the pretty gardens.

Rooms 4 rms (1 en suite) (2 fmly) **Facilities** TV3B TVL tea/coffee Cen ht **Conf** Board 10 **Parking** 3 **Notes** ⊗ ⊗

Church Farm

Ⓤ

Wrockwardine Village, Wellington TF6 5DG
☎ 01952 251927 📠 01952 427511
e-mail: info@churchfarm-shropshire.co.uk
dir: M54 junct 7 towards Wellington, 1st left, 1st right, then right at end of road. 0.5m on left opp St Peters church

Currently the rating for this establishment is not confirmed. This may be due to a change of ownership or because it has only recently joined the AA rating scheme.

Rooms 4 rms (3 en suite) (1 pri facs) (1 fmly) S £50-£60; D £60-£70* **Facilities** FTV tea/coffee Dinner available Cen ht Wi-fi **Conf** Max 20 Thtr 20 Class 20 Board 14 **Parking** 12

WEM | Map 15 SJ52

Soulton Hall

★★★★ ⬤ GUEST ACCOMMODATION

Soulton SY4 5RS
☎ 01939 232786 📠 01939 234097
e-mail: enquiries@soultonhall.co.uk
web: www.soultonhall.co.uk
dir: A49 between Shrewsbury & Whitchurch turn onto B5065 towards Wem. Soulton Hall 2m E of Wem on B5065

Located two miles from historic Wem, this late 17th-century former manor house incorporates part of an even older building. The house stands in 560 acres and provides high levels of comfort. Bedrooms are equipped with homely extras and the ground-floor areas include a spacious hall sitting room, lounge-bar and an attractive dining room, the setting for imaginative dinners.

Rooms 4 en suite 3 annexe en suite (2 fmly) (3 GF) S £60.50-£80.50; D £90-£129* **Facilities** FTV tea/coffee Dinner available Direct Dial Cen ht Licensed Wi-fi ⬤ Fishing Birdwatching in 50 acre private woodland **Conf** Max 100 Thtr 100 Class 60 Board 50 **Parking** 52 **Notes** LB Civ Wed 100

WESTBURY | Map 15 SJ30

Barley Mow House

★★★★ BED AND BREAKFAST

Aston Rogers SY5 9HQ
☎ 01743 891234 📠 01743 891234
e-mail: colinrigby@astonrogers.fsnet.co.uk
web: www.barleymowhouse.co.uk
dir: 2m S of Westbury. Off B4386 into Aston Rogers, house 400yds opp Aston Hall

Dating in part from the 17th century and extended in the 18th century, this charming property has been restored to provide comfortable accommodation with modern facilities. The house stands in a peaceful village and is surrounded by beautifully maintained gardens.

Rooms 3 en suite (1 fmly) (1 GF) S £25-£65; D £50-£60*
Facilities FTV TVL tea/coffee Cen ht Wi-fi **Parking** 4
Notes LB ⊗

SOMERSET

BATH | Map 4 ST76

For other locations surrounding Bath see also Box (Wiltshire), Bradford on Avon (Wiltshire), Farmborough, Frome & Trowbridge (Wiltshire)

PREMIER COLLECTION

Ayrlington

★★★★★ GUEST ACCOMMODATION

24/25 Pulteney Rd BA2 4EZ
☎ 01225 425495 📠 01225 469029
e-mail: mail@ayrlington.com
web: www.ayrlington.com
dir: A4 onto A36, pass Holburne Museum, premises 200yds on right

The charm of this impressive Victorian house is evident in the attractive exterior and throughout the rooms, many of which feature Oriental artefacts and pictures. The bedrooms, some with spa baths, four-poster beds and views over Bath cricket ground, are very comfortable. Breakfast is served in the elegant dining room, which shares the enjoyable view.

Rooms 16 en suite (3 fmly) (3 GF) **Facilities** tea/coffee Cen ht Licensed Wi-fi Unlimited free golf at local golf club **Conf** Max 15 **Parking** 16 **Notes** ⊗ No Children 14yrs Closed 22 Dec-5 Jan

PREMIER COLLECTION

Bradford Old Windmill
★★★★★ ⬛ BED AND BREAKFAST

4 Masons Ln BA15 1QN
☎ 01225 866842 📄 01225 866648
e-mail: aa@bradfordoldwindmill.co.uk

(For full entry see Bradford-on-Avon)

PREMIER COLLECTION

One Three Nine
★★★★★ GUEST ACCOMMODATION

139 Wells Rd BA2 3AL
☎ 01225 314769 📄 01225 443079
e-mail: info@139bath.co.uk
dir: *M4 junct 19 onto A46. A4 towards Bath, then A367 towards Wells and Shepton Mallet. On left 500mtrs up hill*

Overlooking the historic city of Bath this quality establishment provides spacious accommodation paired with thoughtful design. Bedrooms are spacious and comfortably equipped providing a very good range of accessories to enhance guest comfort. A number of feature bathrooms add a dash of luxury. Breakfast is served in the bright and airy dining room, where an excellent choice of continental and hot items is available. Off-street parking is available for car users.

Rooms 10 en suite (2 fmly) (2 GF) D £65–£185*
Facilities FTV tea/coffee Direct Dial Cen ht Wi-fi
Parking 10 **Notes** ⊗ Closed 24-25 Dec

PREMIER COLLECTION

Apsley House
★★★★★ ⬛ BED AND BREAKFAST

Newbridge Hill BA1 3PT
☎ 01225 336966 📄 01225 425462
e-mail: info@apsley-house.co.uk
web: www.apsley-house.co.uk
dir: *1.2m W of city centre on A431*

Built in 1830 for the Duke of Wellington, Apsley House is within walking distance of the city centre. The house is extremely elegant, and the spacious bedrooms have pleasant views. There are family rooms and rooms with four-poster beds, while two rooms have direct access to the charming garden. A smart dining room and a delightful lounge are also available.

Rooms 11 en suite (2 fmly) (2 GF) S £55–£140;
D £69–£180* **Facilities** STV FTV tea/coffee Dinner available Direct Dial Cen ht Licensed Wi-fi **Parking** 12
Notes LB ⊗ Closed 3 days Xmas

PREMIER COLLECTION

Athole House
★★★★★ ⬛ GUEST ACCOMMODATION

33 Upper Oldfield Park BA2 3JX
☎ 01225 320000 📄 01225 320009
e-mail: info@atholehouse.co.uk
web: www.atholehouse.co.uk
dir: *A36 onto A367 Wells Rd, 1st right*

Appointed to offer very high standards of comfort, this detached house stands in a quiet location just a 15-minute walk from the city centre. It has modern, well-equipped bedrooms and bathrooms, and the varied breakfast menu includes fresh fruit salad and home-made bread. There is a lovely garden to enjoy in summer, and secure parking with electronic gates.

Rooms 4 en suite (1 fmly) S £58–£68; D £78–£93
Facilities STV FTV tea/coffee Direct Dial Cen ht Wi-fi
Parking 7 **Notes** LB ⊗

PREMIER COLLECTION

Cheriton House
★★★★★ GUEST ACCOMMODATION

9 Upper Oldfield Park BA2 3JX
☎ 01225 429862 📄 01225 428403
e-mail: info@cheritonhouse.co.uk
web: www.cheritonhouse.co.uk
dir: *A36 onto A367 Wells Rd, 1st right*

Expect a friendly welcome and a relaxed atmosphere at this well-presented Victorian house with panoramic views over Bath. The carefully decorated bedrooms are well equipped and include a two-bedroom suite in a converted coach house. A substantial breakfast is served in the conservatory-breakfast room overlooking the rear garden. There is also a comfortable lounge.

Rooms 11 en suite (2 fmly) (2 GF) S £60–£90;
D £85–£130 **Facilities** tea/coffee Direct Dial Cen ht
Wi-fi **Parking** 11 **Notes** LB ⊗ No Children 12yrs

See advert on page 295

PREMIER COLLECTION

Chestnuts House
★★★★★ ⬛ GUEST ACCOMMODATION

16 Henrietta Rd BA2 6LY
☎ 01225 334279 📄 01225 312236
e-mail: reservations@chestnutshouse.co.uk
web: www.chestnutshouse.co.uk

Located just a few minutes walk from the city centre and totally renovated using light shades and oak, the accommodation is fresh and airy. Bedrooms are attractively co-ordinated, well equipped and comfortable. Added enhancements, such as Wi-fi, make the rooms suitable for both business and leisure. Breakfast, which features quite an extensive buffet and daily specials, is served in the dining room that opens onto the pretty rear garden. There is a cosy lounge, and the small car park is a bonus. Antonia Pecchia was a finalist for our AA Friendliest Landlady of the Year 2009-2010 Award.

Rooms 5 en suite (1 fmly) (2 GF) **Facilities** STV FTV TVL
tea/coffee Cen ht Wi-fi Riding **Parking** 5 **Notes** ⊗

BATH *continued*

PREMIER COLLECTION

Dorian House
★★★★★ GUEST ACCOMMODATION

1 Upper Oldfield Park BA2 3JX
☎ 01225 426336 📠 01225 444699
e-mail: info@dorianhouse.co.uk
web: www.dorianhouse.co.uk
dir: *A36 onto A367 Wells Rd, right onto Upper Oldfield Park, 3rd building on left*

This elegant Victorian property has stunning views over the city. The atmosphere is welcoming and the accommodation of high quality. Several of the rooms have fine period four-poster beds and all offer a range of extra facilities. The attractive lounge has an honesty bar and views of the terraced gardens.

Rooms 11 en suite (1 fmly) (2 GF) S £55-£165; D £65-£195* **Facilities** FTV tea/coffee Direct Dial Cen ht Licensed Wi-fi **Parking** 9 **Notes** LB ⊗

PREMIER COLLECTION

Meadowland
★★★★★ GUEST ACCOMMODATION

36 Bloomfield Park BA2 2BX
☎ 01225 311079 📠 01225 580055
e-mail: stay@meadowlandbath.co.uk
dir: *A367 signed Exeter/Wells, past the Bear pub, take right fork onto Bloomfield Rd. 2nd right onto Bloomfield Park*

Peacefully located in a residential area, yet just a twenty minute stroll from Bath, Meadowland offers a relaxing retreat with plenty of quality and comfort throughout. The three bedrooms are all spacious and equipped with welcome extras. Guests are also welcome to use the very comfortable lounge. Breakfast is a highlight, with a range of carefully prepared, good quality produce.

Rooms 3 en suite S £55-£70; D £95-£120 **Facilities** tea/coffee Cen ht Wi-fi **Parking** 4 **Notes** LB ⊗ No Children 4yrs

PREMIER COLLECTION

Paradise House
★★★★★ GUEST ACCOMMODATION

Holloway BA2 4PX
☎ 01225 317723 📠 01225 482005
e-mail: info@paradise-house.co.uk
web: www.paradise-house.co.uk
dir: *A36 onto A367 Wells Rd, 3rd left, down hill onto cul-de-sac, house 200yds on left*

Set in half an acre of lovely walled gardens, this Georgian house, built of mellow Bath stone, is within walking distance of the city centre. Many bedrooms have fine views over the city, and all are decorated in opulent style. Furnishings are elegant and facilities modern. The lounge is comfortable and relaxing, and breakfast is served in the smart dining room. Hospitality and service here are friendly and professional.

Rooms 11 en suite (2 fmly) (4 GF); D £65-£180* **Facilities** FTV tea/coffee Direct Dial Cen ht Licensed Wi-fi **Parking** 11 **Notes** LB ⊗ Closed 24-25 Dec

See advert on opposite page

PREMIER COLLECTION

The Villa Magdala
★★★★★ GUEST ACCOMMODATION

Henrietta Rd BA2 6LX
☎ 01225 466329 📠 01225 483207
e-mail: office@VillaMagdala.co.uk
web: www.VillaMagdala.co.uk
dir: *A4 onto A36 Bathwick St, 2nd right*

This stylish Victorian house is just a short walk from the city's attractions and offers a haven of peace and tranquillity. There are pleasant views from the attractively furnished and spacious bedrooms, all of which are well equipped. The charming lounge and dining room overlook one of Bath's delightful parks.

Rooms 17 en suite (4 fmly) S £75-£120; D £80-£170 **Facilities** tea/coffee Direct Dial Cen ht Wi-fi **Parking** 17 **Notes** LB ⊗ No Children 5yrs

The Bailbrook Lodge
★★★★ GUEST HOUSE

35/37 London Road West BA1 7HZ
☎ 01225 859090 📠 01225 852299
e-mail: hotel@bailbrooklodge.co.uk
web: www.bailbrooklodge.co.uk
dir: *M4 junct 18, A46 S to A4 junct, left signed Batheaston. Lodge on left*

Set in extensive gardens on the east edge of the city, this imposing Georgian building provides smart accommodation. The well-equipped bedrooms include some with four-poster beds and period furniture, and service is professional and efficient. The inviting lounge has a small bar, and light snacks are available from noon until evening. Breakfast is served in the elegant dining room.

Rooms 15 rms (14 en suite) (1 pri facs) (5 fmly) (1 GF) S £60-£79; D £88-£180 **Facilities** FTV tea/coffee Cen ht Licensed Wi-fi **Conf** Max 20 Thtr 20 Class 10 Board 12 **Parking** 15 **Notes** LB ⊗

Brooks Guesthouse
★★★★ 🏠 GUEST ACCOMMODATION

1 & 1A Crescent Gardens, Upper Bristol Rd BA1 2NA
☎ 01225 425543 📠 01225 318147
e-mail: info@brooksguesthouse.com
web: www.brooksguesthouse.com
dir: *On A4, 350yds W of Queens Square, before Royal Victoria Park*

Conveniently located just a few minutes stroll from the centre of Bath, guests here will enjoy the relaxed atmosphere and welcoming hospitality. Bedrooms and bathrooms vary in size but are generally spacious and well decorated. Breakfast is served in the cosy downstairs dining room.

Rooms 21 en suite (4 fmly) (7 GF) S £65-£90; D £75-£110* **Facilities** STV FTV TVL tea/coffee Direct Dial Cen ht Licensed Wi-fi **Notes** LB ⊗ Closed 25 Dec

The Hollies
★★★★ GUEST ACCOMMODATION

Hatfield Rd BA2 2BD
☎ 01225 313366
e-mail: davcartwright@lineone.net
dir: *A36 onto A367 Wells Rd & Wellsway, 0.7m right opp Devonshire Arms*

This delightful house stands in impressive gardens overlooking a magnificent church, and is within easy reach of the city centre. Individually decorated themed bedrooms are finished to provide excellent levels of comfort and facilities. Breakfast in the elegant dining room is an enjoyable start to the day.

Rooms 3 rms (2 en suite) (1 pri facs) S £55-£65; D £65-£75* **Facilities** tea/coffee Cen ht Wi-fi **Parking** 3 **Notes** ⊗ No Children 16yrs Closed 15 Dec-Jan

Oldfields

★★★★ GUEST HOUSE

102 Wells Rd BA2 3AL
☎ 01225 317984 📠 01225 444471
e-mail: info@oldfields.co.uk
dir: 0.5m S of city centre. A36 onto A367

This accommodation has been sensitively developed both to maintain some period features and to offer guests luxurious comfort. The attractive, light and airy bedrooms, some of which have four-poster beds and Jacuzzis, are well equipped with considerate extras. The lounge has an open fire during colder days. The elegant dining room, offers a choice of dishes for breakfast.

Rooms 16 en suite (4 fmly) (2 GF) S £49-£69;
D £59-£170* **Facilities** STV tea/coffee Direct Dial Cen ht
Wi-fi **Parking** 12 **Notes** LB ⊗ Closed 24-26 Dec

The Town House

★★★★ 🏠 GUEST ACCOMMODATION

7 Bennett St BA1 2QJ
☎ 01225 422505 📠 01225 422505
e-mail: stay@thetownhousebath.co.uk
dir: 400yds N of city centre. Off A4 Roman Rd at lights onto Lansdown Hill, 2nd on left

Bath's historical attractions and shops are on the doorstep when you stay here. The Town House is located alongside the Assembly Rooms and just a stone's throw away from the Royal Crescent. This stylish Georgian accommodation offers a good level of comfort. Bedrooms are finished with many thoughtful extras and the friendly hosts are attentive. At breakfast time the atmosphere is relaxed and memorable, with a good choice of freshly prepared dishes enjoyed around a communal table.

Rooms 3 en suite S £84-£125; D £94-£125*
Facilities tea/coffee Cen ht Wi-fi **Parking** 1 **Notes** ⊗ No Children 14yrs Closed Jan

Villa Claudia

★★★★ BED AND BREAKFAST

19 Forester Rd, Bathwick BA2 6QE
☎ 01225 329670 📠 01225 329670
e-mail: claudiaamato77@aol.com
dir: From A4 onto Cleveland Place East (A36), at next rdbt take 1st exit onto Beckford Rd, then left onto Forester Rd

A beautiful Victorian property located on a quiet, tree-lined residential street within easy walking distance of the City centre's attractions and restaurants. This family-run bed and breakfast with Italian owners provides attentive and personal service. Bedrooms and bathrooms are beautifully decorated and very comfortable; a four-poster bed is available. Delicious breakfasts are served in the charming dining room at the communal table.

Rooms 3 en suite (1 fmly) S £70-£90; D £85-£95*
Facilities tea/coffee Cen ht **Parking** 4 **Notes** ⊗

Cheriton House

Charming Bed and Breakfast accommodation

9 UPPER OLDFIELD PARK, BATH BA2 3JX
Tel: (01225) 429862   Fax: (01225) 428403
e-mail: info@cheritonhouse.co.uk
Website: www.cheritonhouse.co.uk

A Victorian house in a quiet location off A367. Set in mature gardens overlooking Bath. With the benefit of a private car park we are only a short walk into the city. The attractive rooms are all individually and tastefully decorated complete with courtesy trays, telephones etc. provided for our guest's comfort. We offer an excellent breakfast choice to be enjoyed in our spacious and welcoming breakfast room where a relaxed atmosphere is guaranteed.

Paradise House

86/88 Holloway, Bath BA2 4PX
Tel: 01225 317723   Fax: 01225 482005
info@paradise-house.co.uk   www.paradise-house.co.uk

Paradise House is a listed Georgian (1735) Bath stone house perfectly situated in a quiet cul-de-sac, only ten minutes walk from the centre of Bath. The rear-facing rooms and beautiful gardens command the most magnificent views of the city and surrounding countryside. Long established and highly recommended. Parking available.
Please visit our website for full details.

BATH *continued*

Aquae Sulis

★★★★ GUEST ACCOMMODATION

174/176 Newbridge Rd BA1 3LE
☎ 01225 420061 📠 01225 446077
e-mail: enquiries@aquaesulishotel.co.uk
web: www.aquaesulishotel.co.uk
dir: On A4 1.8m W of city centre, on A4 (Upper Bristol Rd)

Located within easy reach of the city centre, this attractive Edwardian house offers a genuine welcome. Bedrooms are of a good size and well equipped with many modern facilities such as internet access. There are two inviting lounges, one with a small but well-stocked bar. Breakfast is served in the comfortable dining room.

Rooms 13 rms (11 en suite) (2 pri facs) 1 annexe en suite (5 fmly) (3 GF) S £59-£79; D £69-£120 **Facilities** STV FTV tea/coffee Direct Dial Cen ht Licensed Wi-fi **Parking** 12 **Notes** LB ⊗ Closed 24-26 Dec RS 27-30 Dec Bed only no room service

The Bath House

★★★★ GUEST ACCOMMODATION

40 Crescent Gardens BA1 2NB
☎ 0117 937 4495 📠 0117 337 6791
e-mail: info@thebathhouse.org
web: www.thebathhouse.org
dir: 100yds from Queen Sq on A441

Now refurbished to high quality specifications, this accommodation is stylish and just a few minutes level walk from the city. Bedrooms are attractive, spacious, light and airy, and equipped with modern accessories, including flat screen televisions and Wi-fi internet connection. Breakfast is room service only and a full height dining table provided in the bedroom ensures guests enjoy their meal experience. Limited parking space is available.

Rooms 5 en suite (1 GF) S £69-£99; D £79-£119*
Facilities FTV tea/coffee Cen ht Wi-fi **Parking** 4 **Notes** LB ⊗ No Children 8yrs

Bathwick Gardens

★★★★ BED AND BREAKFAST

95 Sydney Place BA2 6NE
☎ 01225 469435
e-mail: mechthild.svh@virgin.net
web: www.bathwickgardens.co.uk
dir: From A46 onto A4 for 1m. At lights turn left, pass Holburne Museum, turn left

Located close to the city centre this substantial Regency town house was used for the filming of Jane Austen's *Persuasion*. Architecturally restored with many original features, the house provides an insight into the 18th century. The en suite bedrooms are very spacious and decorated with period wallpapers. Breakfast is a choice

of traditional English or the house special, an Austrian continental breakfast. Parking is by arrangement.

Rooms 3 rms (2 en suite) S £80-£95; D fr £95
Facilities TV1B tea/coffee Cen ht Wi-fi **Parking** 2 **Notes** ⊗ 🐾

Brocks Guest House

★★★★ GUEST ACCOMMODATION

32 Brock St BA1 2LN
☎ 01225 338374 📠 01225 338425
e-mail: brocks@brocksguesthouse.co.uk
web: www.brocksguesthouse.co.uk
dir: Just off A4 between Circus & Royal Crescent

A warm welcome is extended at this delightful Georgian property, located in the heart of the city just a few hundred yards from Royal Crescent. All rooms reflect the comfortable elegance of the Georgian era. A traditional breakfast is served in the charming dining room, which also offers a lounge area with comfortable seating.

Rooms 6 en suite (2 fmly) **Facilities** FTV tea/coffee Cen ht Wi-fi **Parking** **Notes** ⊗ Closed 24 Dec-1 Jan

Cranleigh

★★★★ 🏠 BED AND BREAKFAST

159 Newbridge Hill BA1 3PX
☎ 01225 310197 📠 01225 423143
e-mail: cranleigh@btinternet.com
web: www.cranleighguesthouse.com
dir: 1.2m W of city centre on A431

This pleasant Victorian house is in a quiet location near the city centre. The well-equipped bedrooms, some on the ground floor, are decorated in the period style and two rooms have four-poster beds. Breakfast is served in the elegant dining room, and there is also an attractive garden which includes a popular hot tub.

Rooms 9 en suite (2 fmly) (2 GF) D £65-£115*
Facilities FTV tea/coffee Direct Dial Cen ht Licensed Wi-fi Garden hot tub **Parking** 5 **Notes** ⊗ No Children 5yrs Closed 25-26 Dec

Dolphin House

★★★★ BED AND BREAKFAST

8 Northend, Batheaston BA1 7EN
☎ 01225 858915
e-mail: georgeandjane@hotmail.com
dir: 2m NE of Bath. Off Batheaston High St to Northend, 100yds on right

This detached Grade II listed Georgian house is convenient for Bath and has a delightful terraced walled garden. Bedrooms, including a suite with lounge, twin bedroom and large bathroom, feature attractive period

decor. Continental breakfasts are served in the bedrooms or on the terrace.

Rooms 2 rms (1 en suite) (1 pri facs) (1 GF) S £50-£65; D ££5-£90 **Facilities** tea/coffee Cen ht Wi-fi **Parking** 2 **Notes** ⊗ No Children 12yrs Closed Xmas RS 24-27 Dec 🐾

Eagle House

★★★★ GUEST ACCOMMODATION

Church St, Bathford BA1 7RS
☎ 01225 859946 📠 01225 859430
e-mail: jonap@eagleho.demon.co.uk
web: www.eaglehouse.co.uk
dir: Off A363 onto Church St

Set in attractive gardens, this delightful Georgian house is pleasantly located on the outskirts of the city. Bedrooms are individually styled, and each has a thoughtful range of extra facilities. The impressive lounge is adorned with attractive pictures, and the dining room has views of the grounds and tennis court.

Rooms 6 en suite 2 annexe en suite (2 fmly) (2 GF) S £48-£88.50; D £62-£112 **Facilities** tea/coffee Dial Cen ht Wi-fi 🏊 ⛳ **Conf** Max 18 Thtr 18 Class 18 Board 14 **Parking** 10 **Notes** LB Closed 12 Dec-8 Jan

Grosvenor Lodge

★★★★ GUEST ACCOMMODATION

Grosvenor Place, London Rd BA1 6BA
☎ 01225 420504
e-mail: info@grosvenorlodge-bath.co.uk
dir: M4 junct 18 onto A46 then A4. Past Lambridge Rugby training ground, on left past lights

Set back from the main road leading into and out of Bath, this pleasant accommodation has undergone careful re-decoration and refurbishment by the new owners. Bedrooms offer a range of shapes and sizes and guests are also welcome to use the spacious lounge. A carefully prepared breakfast is offered in the stylish dining room.

Rooms 3 rms (1 en suite) (2 pri facs) S £50-£65; D £75-£110* **Facilities** TVL tea/coffee Cen ht Wi-fi **Parking** 3 **Notes** LB No Children 7yrs

Grove Lodge

★★★★ GUEST ACCOMMODATION

11 Lambridge BA1 6BJ
☎ 01225 310860 🖷 01225 429630
e-mail: stay@grovelodgebath.co.uk
dir: 0.6m NE of city centre. Off A4, 400yds W from junct A46

This fine Georgian house lies within easy reach of the city centre and is reached by a stone path through a neat garden surrounded by trees. The spacious bedrooms have period character and all are well equipped. There is an attractive breakfast room and parking is available in nearby side streets. Guests may venture into the city for evening meals or alternatively, a short stroll along the canalside leads to an inn, which serves food.

Rooms 5 rms (4 en suite) (1 pri facs) (1 GF) S £50–£75; D £70–£90* Facilities FTV tea/coffee Cen ht Wi-fi Notes LB ⊗ No Children 6yrs Closed Xmas & New Year

Highways House

★★★★ GUEST ACCOMMODATION

143 Wells Rd BA2 3AL
☎ 01225 421238 🖷 01225 481169
e-mail: stay@highwayshouse.co.uk
dir: A36 onto A367 Wells Rd, 300yds on left

This elegant Victorian house is just a 10-minute walk from the city centre (or alternatively, there is a frequent bus). The bedrooms are individually styled, well equipped and homely; some located on the ground floor. A spacious attractive lounge is available, and breakfast is served in the dining room at separate tables. Parking is a bonus.

Rooms 7 en suite (2 fmly) (3 GF) S £45–£60; D £72–£82* Facilities tea/coffee Cen ht Wi-fi Parking 7 Notes ⊗ No Children 8yrs

The Kennard

★★★★ 🏠 GUEST ACCOMMODATION

11 Henrietta St BA2 6LL
☎ 01225 310472 🖷 01225 460054
e-mail: reception@kennard.co.uk
web: www.kennard.co.uk
dir: A4 onto A36 Bathwick St, 2nd right onto Henrietta Rd & Henrietta St

This attractive Georgian house dates from 1794 and is situated just off famous Great Pulteney Street, making it convenient for the city centre. The house is decorated and furnished in keeping with the elegance of the architecture. Bedrooms, some located at ground floor level, vary in terms of style and space. Breakfast is served in the lower garden dining room and includes an excellent cold buffet as well as a selection of hot items.

Rooms 12 rms (10 en suite) (2 GF) Facilities STV tea/coffee Direct Dial Cen ht Licensed Wi-fi Notes ⊗ No Children 8yrs Closed 2wks Xmas

Marlborough House

★★★★ GUEST ACCOMMODATION

1 Marlborough Ln BA1 2NQ
☎ 01225 318175 🖷 01225 466127
e-mail: mars@manque.dircon.co.uk
web: www.marlborough-house.net
dir: 450yds W of city centre, at A4 junct

Marlborough House is situated opposite Royal Victoria Park and close to the Royal Crescent. Some original features remain and the rooms are decorated with period furniture and pictures. The atmosphere is relaxed, and service is attentive and friendly. The breakfast, served from an open-plan kitchen, is vegetarian and organic.

Rooms 6 en suite (2 fmly) (1 GF) S £75–£95; D £85–£135 Facilities FTV tea/coffee Direct Dial Cen ht Licensed Wi-fi Parking 3 Notes LB Closed 24-26 Dec

Number 30

★★★★ GUEST ACCOMMODATION

30 Crescent Gardens BA1 2NB
☎ 01225 337393 🖷 01225 337393
e-mail: david.greenwood12@btinternet.com
web: www.numberthirty.com
dir: 0.5m from Queens Sq towards Bristol

This cared-for accommodation is conveniently located just a stroll from the city centre. The hosts are friendly, attentive and more than happy to provide useful local information. The freshly prepared breakfast, featuring home-made preserves and some interesting specials, is served in the light, pleasant dining room which has an original fireplace. Limited parking is available.

Rooms 3 rms (2 en suite) (1 pri facs) S £70–£95; D £80–£135 Facilities tea/coffee Cen ht Wi-fi Parking 3 Notes LB ⊗ No Children 12yrs Closed 18 Dec-24 Jan

Devonshire House

★★★ GUEST ACCOMMODATION

143 Wellsway BA2 4RZ
☎ 01225 312495
e-mail: enquiries@devonshire-house.uk.com
web: www.devonshire-house.uk.com
dir: 1m S of city centre. A36 onto A367 Wells Rd & Wellsway

Located within walking distance of the city centre, this charming house maintains its Victorian style. Secure parking is available and the friendly proprietors make every effort to ensure your stay is pleasant and memorable. The attractive bedrooms, some appointed to a high quality standard, have many considerate extras. There is a small lounge area and freshly cooked breakfasts are served in the pleasant dining room.

Rooms 4 en suite (1 fmly) (1 GF) S £50–£70; D £70–£90 Facilities tea/coffee Cen ht Wi-fi Parking 6 Notes LB ⊗

Rivers Street Rooms

★★★ BED AND BREAKFAST

39 Rivers St BA1 2QA
☎ 07787 500345
e-mail: sharonabrahams3@yahoo.co.uk
dir: From Lansdown Rd, take Julian Rd & left onto Rivers St

This centrally located, five-storey, 1770s townhouse offers modern contemporary styling that blends seamlessly with the wealth of original features. There's a family suite that comprises two rooms, and a double room with king-size bed and the private use of small courtyard garden; both rooms have flat-screen Freeview TVs and refreshment trays. Breakfast is continental but very generous, offering a wide variety of delicious home-baked goodies such as mini-quiches, pastries, scones and fresh fruits.

Rooms 2 rms (1 en suite) (1 pri facs) (1 fmly); D £59–£99 Facilities FTV tea/coffee Cen ht Wi-fi Notes ⊠

BATH *continued*

The Parade Park and Lambrettas Bar

★★★ GUEST ACCOMMODATION

8, 9, 10 North Pde BA2 4AL
☎ 01225 463384 📠 01225 442322
e-mail: info@paradepark.co.uk
web: www.paradepark.co.uk
dir: *In city centre. Off A36 Pulteney Rd onto North Parade Rd & North Parade*

This attractive Georgian property was formerly the home of William Wordsworth. The restored rooms are brightly decorated, and well equipped with modern facilities. Traditional breakfasts are served in the impressive, panelled first-floor dining room. The mod, scooter-themed Lambretta bar is open to the public.

Rooms 38 rms (32 en suite) (8 fmly) (2 GF) **Facilities** tea/coffee Cen ht Licensed **Notes** ⊗ Closed Xmas

Pulteney House

★★★ GUEST ACCOMMODATION

14 Pulteney Rd BA2 4HA
☎ 01225 460991 📠 01225 460991
e-mail: pulteney@tinyworld.co.uk
web: www.pulteneyhotel.co.uk
dir: *A4 onto A36, 200yds past lights on right*

This large detached property, situated in a colourful garden is within walking distance of the city centre. Bedrooms vary in size including some annexe rooms, and are well equipped with useful facilities. Full English breakfasts are served in the dining room at individual tables. A guest lounge and car park are both welcome features.

Rooms 12 rms (11 en suite) (1 pri facs) 5 annexe en suite (6 fmly) (2 GF) S £48-£55; D £75-£130* **Facilities** TVL tea/coffee Cen ht Wi-fi **Parking** 18 **Notes** LB ⊗

Roman City Guest House

★★★ GUEST HOUSE

18 Raby Place, Bathwick Hill BA2 4EH
☎ 01225 463668
e-mail: enquire@romancityguesthouse.co.uk
dir: *A4 onto A36 Bathwick St, turn right at lights, straight on at rdbt. Turn left at St Mary's church onto Bathwick Hill*

A warm welcome is assured at this 18th-century, end of terrace house, located just a stroll from the heart of the historic city. The spacious bedrooms, some with four poster beds, are comfortable and well equipment with many extra facilities. A pleasant lounge is also available.

Rooms 4 rms (3 en suite) (1 pri facs) (2 fmly) (2 smoking) S £35-£50; D £55-£70* **Facilities** FTV tea/coffee Cen ht Wi-fi **Conf** Board 12 **Notes** LB ⊗

Waltons

★★★ GUEST HOUSE

17-19 Crescent Gardens, Upper Bristol Rd BA1 2NA
☎ 01225 426528 📠 01225 420350
e-mail: rose@waltonsguesthouse.co.uk
web: www.bathguesthouse.com
dir: *On A4 350yds W of city centre*

There is a warm welcome at Waltons, situated within strolling distance of the centre of Bath. The cosy bedrooms come with useful extra facilities, and a traditional English breakfast is served at individual tables in the dining room.

Rooms 7 en suite S £50-£85; D £69-£135 **Facilities** FTV tea/coffee Direct Dial Cen ht **Notes** ⊗ 📷

Hermitage

★★ GUEST ACCOMMODATION

Bath Rd SN13 8DT
☎ 01225 744187 📠 01225 743447
e-mail: hermitagebb@btconnect.com

(For full entry see Box (Wiltshire))

Lamp Post Villa

🅤

3 Crescent Gardens, Upper Bristol Rd BA1 2NA
☎ 01225 331221
e-mail: lamppostvilla@aol.com
dir: *350yds W of city centre on A4*

Currently the rating for this establishment is not confirmed. This may be due to a change of ownership or because it has only recently joined the AA rating scheme.

Rooms 4 en suite (1 fmly) (1 GF) **Facilities** FTV TVL tea/coffee Direct Dial Cen ht **Parking** 4 **Notes** ⊗ No Children 6yrs Closed 24-26 Dec

BECKINGTON   Map 4 ST85

Pickford House

★★★ GUEST ACCOMMODATION

23 Bath Rd BA11 6SJ
☎ 01373 830329 📠 01373 830329
e-mail: AmPritchar@aol.com
web: www.pickfordhouse.com
dir: *Off A36 (Little Chef rdbt) signed Beckington, follow for 300yds to 30mph signs by village hall, turn right then sharp left*

This peacefully located Regency-style house is set in secluded walled gardens. The proprietors are welcoming and attentive, and many guests visit this pleasant house on a regular basis. Dinner is an enjoyable experience with a 'pot luck' menu (unless you require vegetarian or special dietary dishes) and, along with the impressive wine list, provides fine dining.

Rooms 2 rms 3 annexe en suite (2 fmly) (1 GF) **Facilities** tea/coffee Dinner available Cen ht Licensed ⤨ **Parking** 15 **Notes** Closed Xmas 📷

BEERCROCOMBE   Map 4 ST32

Whittles Farm *(ST324194)*

★★★★ FARMHOUSE

TA3 6AH
☎ 01823 480301 📠 01823 480301 Mr & Mrs Mitchem
e-mail: djcm.mitchem@btinternet.com
web: www.whittlesfarm.co.uk
dir: *Off A358 through Hatch Beauchamp to Beercrocombe, keep left through village, Whittles Farm 1st lane on right, no through road*

This 16th-century farmhouse set between the Quantock and Blackdown Hills is ideal for a relaxing break. The friendly and attentive owners have been receiving guests here for over 20 years, and everyone is assured of a caring and genuine welcome. Bedrooms are spacious and comfortable with an engaging homeliness. There's a choice of lounges in which to relax and perhaps curl up beside the fire. Breakfasts are impressive and a great way to start the day.

Rooms 2 en suite S £40-£48; D £60-£68* **Facilities** FTV tea/coffee Cen ht **Parking** 4 **Notes** ⊗ No Children 12yrs Closed Dec & Jan 🐄 250 acres

BRIDGWATER   Map 4 ST23

Ash-Wembdon Farm *(ST281382)*

★★★★ FARMHOUSE

Hollow Ln, Wembdon TA5 2BD
☎ 01278 453097 📠 01278 445856 **Mr & Mrs Rowe**
e-mail: mary.rowe@btinternet.com
web: www.farmaccommodation.co.uk
dir: *M5, A38, A39 to Minehead, at rdbt 3rd exit Homeburg Way, at lights B3339, right onto Hollow Ln*

Near the Quantock Hills, this is a 17th-century farmhouse on a working beef and arable farm offering homely and comfortable accommodation. All rooms have en suite showers or private bathrooms, and English or Continental breakfasts are served in the guest dining room. Guests also have use of a lounge and landscaped garden.

Rooms 3 rms (2 en suite) (1 pri facs) S £33-£36; D £50-£60 **Facilities** tea/coffee Cen ht Wi-fi **Parking** 3 **Notes** ⊗ No Children 10yrs Closed 22 Dec-3 Jan 340 acres arable/beef

The Boat & Anchor Inn

★★★ INN

Huntworth TA7 0AQ
☎ 01278 662473 📠 01278 662542
dir: *M5 junct 24, 500yds NE to Huntworth, 0.5m N of village across canal bridge*

This popular canal-side inn offers easy access to the M5 and is a useful stopover en route for the West Country. Bedrooms vary in size and style with some offering lovely views across the canal and open fields. An impressive selection of food is offered from the blackboard menus, served either in the bar and lounge areas, or the newly added conservatory.

Rooms 11 en suite (3 fmly) **Facilities** tea/coffee Dinner available Cen ht **Conf** Thtr 80 Class 50 Board 45 **Parking** 100 **Notes** ⊗ RS Nov-Mar Mon-Thu 12-3 & 5-11 Fri-Sun all day

BROMPTON REGIS   Map 3 SS93

Holworthy Farm *(SS978308)*

★★★★ 🍽 FARMHOUSE

TA22 9NY
☎ 01398 371244 📠 01398 371244 **Mrs G Payne**
e-mail: holworthyfarm@aol.com
web: www.holworthyfarm.co.uk
dir: *2m E of Brompton Regis. Off A396 on E side of Wimbleball Lake*

Set in the south-east corner of Exmoor, this working livestock farm has spectacular views over Wimbleball Lake. Bedrooms are traditionally furnished and well equipped. The dining room overlooking the garden is the attractive setting for breakfast. Dinner is available by arrangement.

Rooms 5 rms (3 en suite) (2 pri facs) (2 fmly) (1 GF) **Facilities** TVL tea/coffee Dinner available Cen ht **Conf** Max 20 **Parking** 8 **Notes** LB ⊗ 🐄 200 acres beef/sheep

BURNHAM-ON-SEA   Map 4 ST34

Magnolia House

★★★★ GUEST HOUSE

26 Manor Rd TA8 2AS
☎ 01278 792460 📠 01278 795190
e-mail: enquiries@magnoliahouse.gb.com
web: www.magnoliahouse.gb.com
dir: *M5 junct 22, follow signs to Burnham-on-Sea, at 2nd rdbt, Magnolia House on right*

Within walking distance of the town centre and beach, this elegant Edwardian house has been totally refurbished to an impressive standard. Contemporary bedrooms offer comfort and quality with many extras such as Wi-fi and a large DVD film library. Bathrooms are also modern and stylish with invigorating showers. A family suite is offered with separate, interconnecting bedrooms. Traditional full English breakfast is served in the attractive, air-conditioned breakfast room, with vegetarian and continental options available.

Rooms 4 en suite (2 fmly) **Facilities** FTV tea/coffee Cen ht Wi-fi **Parking** 7 **Notes** LB ⊗

CASTLE CARY   Map 4 ST63

Clanville Manor *(ST618330)*

★★★★ 🏠 FARMHOUSE

BA7 7PJ
☎ 01963 350124 & 07966 512732
📠 01963 350719 **Mrs S Snook**
e-mail: info@clanvillemanor.co.uk
web: www.clanvillemanor.co.uk
dir: *A371 onto B3153, 0.75m entrance to Clanville Manor via white gate & cattle grid under bridge*

Built in 1743, Clanville Manor is situated on a beef-rearing holding, and has been owned by the Snook family since 1898. A polished oak staircase leads up to the individually decorated bedrooms, which retain a great deal of their original character. Hearty breakfasts are served in the elegant dining room, which looks out over

continued

CASTLE CARY *continued*

open meadows. There is also a spacious and comfortable sitting room.

Clanville Manor

Rooms 4 en suite S £35-£45; D £70-£90 **Facilities** FTV TVL tea/coffee Cen ht Wi-fi ✈ 🚲 **Parking** 6 **Notes** LB ⊗ No Children 12yrs Closed 21 Dec-2 Jan 165 acres beef

The Pilgrims

★★★★ 🏠 🍽 INN
- -
Lovington BA7 7PT
☎ 01963 240600
e-mail: jools@thepilgrimsatlovington.co.uk
web: www.thepilgrimsatlovington.co.uk
dir: *On B3153, 1.5m E of lights on A37 at Lydford*

This popular accommodation describes itself as "The pub that thinks it's a restaurant", which is pretty accurate. With a real emphasis on fresh, local and carefully prepared produce, both dinner and breakfast are the focus of any stay here. In addition, the resident family proprietors provide a friendly and relaxed atmosphere. Comfortable and well equipped bedrooms are available in the adjacent, converted cider barn.

Rooms 5 annexe en suite (5 GF) S £80-£95; D £80-£110* **Facilities** tea/coffee Dinner available Cen ht Wi-fi **Parking** 5 **Notes** LB No Children 14yrs RS Sun eve-Tue Restaurant & bar closed to non-residents No coaches

CATCOTT Map 4 ST33

Honeysuckle

★★★★ GUEST ACCOMMODATION
- -
King William Rd TA7 9HU
☎ 01278 722890
dir: *Off A39 to Catcott, pass King William pub, house 200yds on right*

Situated in the village centre, this delightful modern house is a good base for visiting the many attractions in the area. Bedrooms are comfortable, and there is a spacious lounge and a charming garden. Breakfast is served around a communal table in the pleasant dining room.

Rooms 3 rms (1 en suite) S £23; D £54-£63 **Facilities** tea/coffee Cen ht **Parking** 3 **Notes** ⊗ No Children 7yrs Closed 20 Dec-3 Jan 🥘

CHARD Map 4 ST30

PREMIER COLLECTION

Bellplot House
★★★★★ GUEST ACCOMMODATION

High St TA20 1QB
☎ 01460 62600 🖷 01460 62600
e-mail: info@bellplothouse.co.uk
web: www.bellplothouse.co.uk
dir: *In town centre, 500yds from Guildhall*

This grand Georgian property in the centre of town provides stylish accommodation suitable for business and leisure. There is ample parking, and the atmosphere is friendly and relaxed. Bedrooms are well equipped, and the elegant restaurant is the venue for impressive breakfasts. Wi-fi access is available.

Rooms 7 en suite (1 fmly) (2 GF) S £79.50; D £89.50 **Facilities** STV tea/coffee Direct Dial Cen ht Licensed Wi-fi Pool Table **Conf** Max 20 Thtr 20 Class 20 Board 20 **Parking** 12 **Notes** ⊗

Watermead

★★★ GUEST HOUSE
- -
83 High St TA20 1QT
☎ 01460 62834 🖷 01460 67448
e-mail: trudy@watermeadguesthouse.co.uk
dir: *On A30 in town centre*

Guests will feel at home at this family-run house, a smart establishment in a convenient location. Hearty breakfasts are served in the dining room overlooking the garden. Bedrooms are neat, and the spacious, self-contained suite is popular with families. Free Wi-fi access is available.

Rooms 9 rms (6 en suite) 1 annexe en suite (1 fmly) S £32-£45; D £60-£65* **Facilities** TVL tea/coffee Cen ht Wi-fi **Parking** 10 **Notes** LB

CHEDDAR Map 4 ST45

See also Draycott

PREMIER COLLECTION

Batts Farm *(ST462507)*
★★★★★ 🏠 FARMHOUSE

Nyland BS27 3UD
☎ 01934 741469 Mr & Mrs J Pike
e-mail: clare@batts-farm.co.uk
web: www.batts-farm.co.uk
dir: *A371 from Cheddar towards Wells, 2m right towards Nyland, Batts Farm 1m on left*

Nestled in an idyllic location at the bottom of Nyland Hill, Batts Farm is a 200-year-old property full of character. The peaceful location overlooks open farmland and the moors at the foot of the Mendips. The spacious bedrooms are all decorated and furnished to a high standard and include especially comfortable beds. Guests are welcome to use the relaxing lounge and the summerhouse in the delightful garden. Breakfast includes home-made breads and local jams.

Rooms 3 en suite 1 annexe en suite S £50-£75; D £65-£95* **Facilities** TVL tea/coffee Cen ht **Parking** 6 **Notes** LB ⊗ No Children 12yrs

Tor Farm

★★★★ GUEST ACCOMMODATION
- -
Nyland BS27 3UD
☎ 01934 743710 & 07766 026175 🖷 01934 743710
e-mail: info@torfarm.co.uk
web: www.torfarm.co.uk
dir: *A371 from Cheddar towards Wells, after 2m turn right towards Nyland. Tor Farm 1.5m on right*

Tucked away in the Somerset countryside, this attractive, comfortable accommodation has many welcome extras, including its own heated swimming pool. The smartly furnished bedrooms, including several on the ground floor, have wonderful views and some have either a private terrace or balcony. Guests can relax in the cosy lounge, or enjoy barbecues in the garden during summer months.

Rooms 8 en suite (2 fmly) (5 GF) S £70; D £70-£110* **Facilities** FTV TVL tea/coffee Cen ht Wi-fi ✈ **Conf** Class 15 **Parking** 12 **Notes** LB ⊗

CLUTTON
Map 4 ST65

The Hunters Rest
★★★★ INN

King Ln, Clutton Hill BS39 5QL
☎ 01761 452303   📠 01761 453308
e-mail: paul@huntersrest.co.uk
web: www.huntersrest.co.uk
dir: Off A37 onto A368 towards Bath, 100yds right onto lane, left at T-junct, inn 0.25m on left

This establishment was originally built around 1750 as a hunting lodge for the Earl of Warwick. Set in delightful countryside, it is ideally located for Bath, Bristol and Wells. Bedrooms and bathrooms are furnished and equipped to excellent standards, and the ground floor combines the character of a real country inn with an excellent range of home-cooked meals.

Rooms 5 en suite (1 fmly) Facilities tea/coffee Dinner available Direct Dial Cen ht Wi-fi Conf Max 40 Thtr 40 Class 25 Board 25 Parking 90

CREWKERNE
Map 4 ST40

Manor Farm
★★★ GUEST ACCOMMODATION

Wayford TA18 8QL
☎ 01460 78865 & 0776 7620031   📠 01460 78865
web: www.manorfarm.biz
dir: B3165 from Crewkerne to Lyme Regis, 3m in Clapton right onto Dunsham Ln, Manor Farm 0.5m up hill on right

Located off the beaten track, this fine Victorian country house has extensive views over Clapton towards the Axe Valley. The comfortably furnished bedrooms are well equipped, and front-facing rooms enjoy splendid views. Breakfast is served at separate tables in the dining room, and a spacious lounge is also provided.

Rooms 4 en suite 1 annexe en suite (2 fmly) S £30-£40; D £65-£70* Facilities TV4B STV FTV TVL tea/coffee Cen ht Fishing Riding Parking 14 Notes ⊗ 🖂

The George
★★★ INN

Market Square TA18 7LP
☎ 01460 73650   📠 01460 72974
e-mail: georgecrewkerne@btconnect.com
web: www.thegeorgehotelcrewkerne.co.uk
dir: In town centre on A30

Situated in the heart of town, this welcoming inn has been providing rest and sustenance for over 400 years. The atmosphere is warm and inviting, and the bar is the ideal place for a natter and a refreshing pint. Comfortable bedrooms are traditionally styled and include four-poster rooms. A choice of menus is available, served either in the bar or attractive restaurant.

Rooms 13 rms (8 en suite) (2 pri facs) (2 fmly) S £35-£100; D £55-£150* Facilities FTV TVL tea/coffee Dinner available Direct Dial Cen ht George Suite has a hydro-therapy spa bath Conf Max 100 Thtr 100 Class 100 Board 50 Notes LB

The Old Stagecoach Inn
★★★ INN

Station Rd TA18 8AL
☎ 01460 72972   📠 01460 77023
e-mail: info@stagecoach-inn.co.uk
web: www.stagecoach-inn.co.uk
dir: 1m from town centre next to station

Well located for the railway station, and just a short walk from the centre of town, this relaxing inn provides informal and welcoming accommodation. Rooms are located around a rear courtyard, motel style. The proprietors are from Belgium, and offer a fine selection of beers and cuisine from their home country.

Rooms 13 annexe en suite (3 fmly) (13 GF) (2 smoking) S £38-£48; D £58* Facilities tea/coffee Dinner available Direct Dial Cen ht Wi-fi Conf Max 25 Parking 25 Notes LB

CROSCOMBE
Map 4 ST54

Bull Terrier
★★★ INN

BA5 3QJ
☎ 01749 343658
e-mail: barry.vidler@bullterrierpub.co.uk
dir: On A371 by village cross

Located in the centre of the village, this attractive country inn has a relaxed and friendly atmosphere. The public areas are particularly enjoyable, as the character of the inn has been retained with the flagstone floors and inglenook fireplace. Bedrooms are brightly decorated and well equipped. Freshly prepared lunches and dinners are available.

Rooms 2 en suite S £30-£40; D £60-£70* Facilities tea/coffee Dinner available Cen ht Conf Max 16 Parking 3 Notes No Children 10yrs RS Oct-Mar Closed Mon

DINDER
Map 4 ST54

Crapnell Farm (ST597457)
★★★★ FARMHOUSE

BA5 3HG
☎ 01749 342683   📠 01749 342683   Mrs P J Keen
e-mail: pamkeen@yahoo.com
dir: A371 from Shepton Mallet to Wells, after Croscombe right to Dinder, sharp right before village, Crapnell Farm 1.5m

This charming farmhouse is thought to date from the 17th century. It provides attractive accommodation that includes a family bedroom. Breakfast is served in the dining room, which is equipped with period furniture, either at a communal or separate table. There is also a comfortable lounge, where log fires burn in the inglenook fireplace during cold weather. A very homely and comfortable establishment.

Rooms 3 en suite (1 fmly); D £60-£70* Facilities TVL tea/coffee Cen ht 3/4 size snooker table, Splash pool Parking 8 Notes ⊗ Closed 18 Dec-3 Jan 🖂

DRAYCOTT
Map 4 ST45

Oakland House
★★★★ 🍴 GUEST ACCOMMODATION

Wells Rd BS27 3SU
☎ 01934 744195 📠 01934 744195
e-mail: enquiries@oakland-house.co.uk
web: www.oakland-house.co.uk
dir: Off A371 at S end of village

Situated a short distance from Cheddar, this friendly home provides comfortable and spacious accommodation. There are splendid views of the Somerset moors and Glastonbury Tor from the sun lounge and the well-appointed and attractive bedrooms. Dinner features fresh fruit and vegetables from the garden.

Rooms 3 en suite (1 fmly) S £45-£65; D £70-£115*
Facilities STV TVL tea/coffee Dinner available Cen ht Pool Table **Parking** 6 **Notes** LB ⊗

DULVERTON
Map 3 SS92

See also Winsford

PREMIER COLLECTION

Tarr Farm Inn
★★★★★ 🍴 INN

Tarr Steps, Exmoor National Park TA22 9PY
☎ 01643 851507 📠 01643 851111
e-mail: enquiries@tarrfarm.co.uk
web: www.tarrfarm.co.uk
dir: 4m NW of Dulverton. Off B3223 signed Tarr Steps, signs to Tarr Farm Inn

Tarr Farm, dating from the 16th century, nestles on the lower slopes of Exmoor overlooking the famous old clapper bridge, Tarr Steps. The majority of rooms are in the bedroom block that provides very stylish and comfortable accommodation with an impressive selection of thoughtful touches. Tarr Farm Inn, with

much character and traditional charm, draws the crowds for cream teas and delicious dinners which are prepared from good local produce.

Rooms 9 en suite (4 GF) S £75-£90; D £150*
Facilities STV tea/coffee Dinner available Direct Dial Cen ht Wi-fi Fishing Riding **Conf** Max 18 **Parking** 10
Notes LB No Children 14yrs No coaches

DUNSTER
Map 3 SS94

Buttercross
★★★★ BED AND BREAKFAST

36 Saint Georges St TA24 6RS
☎ 01643 821413
e-mail: robertbuck@onetel.com
dir: Off A39 into Dunster, right after lights onto Saint Georges St, pass school & church, last white house on right

Quietly situated on the edge of an idyllic village, this welcoming family home is just a short walk from Dunster Castle and other interesting local sights. The spacious and homely accommodation is smart, well equipped and benefits from some lovely views. A hearty, cooked breakfast featuring local produce will set you up for the day.

Rooms 1 en suite (1 fmly) S £30-£35; D £55-£60*
Facilities FTV tea/coffee Cen ht **Parking** 2 **Notes** LB ⊗
No Children 5yrs Closed 21 Dec-4 Jan 🐾

FARMBOROUGH
Map 4 ST66

School Cottages Bed & Breakfast
★★★★ BED AND BREAKFAST

The Street, Near Bath BA2 0AR
☎ 01761 471167
e-mail: tim@schoolcottages.co.uk
web: www.schoolcottages.co.uk
dir: Off A39 in Farmborough onto The Street, 1st left opp village school

This lovingly restored country house is conveniently located to the south-west of Bath in the pretty Somerset village of Farmborough. Contemporary, stylish bedrooms are equipped with Wi-fi, while excellent bathrooms may include a power shower or a spa bath. Home-made jams and freshly-laid eggs add to delicious breakfasts served in a charming conservatory overlooking the garden.

Rooms 3 en suite **Facilities** tea/coffee Cen ht Wi-fi
Parking 3 **Notes** ⊗ 🐾

FROME
Map 4 ST74

PREMIER COLLECTION

Lullington House
★★★★★ BED AND BREAKFAST

Lullington BA11 2PG
☎ 01373 831406 📠 01373 831406
e-mail: info@lullingtonhouse.co.uk
web: www.lullingtonhouse.co.uk
dir: 2.5m N of Frome. Off A36 into Lullington

Built in 1866 as a rectory, this quintessentially English stone country house stands in extensive grounds and gardens which convey an air of peace, quiet and tranquillity. The luxurious large bedrooms, some with four-poster beds, are decorated to high standards using beautiful fabrics, fine antique furniture and many extras such as Wi-fi, decanters of sherry, fresh flowers and well-stocked beverage trays. Breakfast is served in the impressive dining room with an excellent selection of dishes available.

Rooms 3 en suite; D £80-£100 **Facilities** FTV tea/coffee Cen ht **Parking** 4 **Notes** ⊗ Closed Xmas & New Year 🐾

PREMIER COLLECTION

The Place To Stay
★★★★ GUEST ACCOMMODATION

Knoll Hill Farm, Trudoxhill BA11 5DP
☎ 01373 836266
web: www.theplacetostayuk.com
dir: From Frome on A361 towards Shepton Mallet. Turn left for Trudoxhill, Knoll Hill Farm on left

Set in the Somerset countryside but close to Bath, Glastonbury and Wells. These beautifully renovated farm buildings provide contemporary bedrooms and impressive bathrooms with a range of luxurious extras. A warm friendly welcome and genuine hospitality is provided from the charming owners who serve wonderful farm breakfasts in the conservatory where guests can enjoy far reaching views of the local countryside.

Rooms 5 annexe en suite (1 fmly) (5 GF) S £60-£90; D £95-£145 **Facilities** tea/coffee Cen ht Wi-fi
Parking 10 **Notes** ⊗ 🐾

The Lamb Inn

★★★★ INN

1 Christchurch St East BA11 1QA
☎ 01373 472042
e-mail: info@thelambinnfrome.co.uk
dir: On A362 in Frome

Located at the top of the hill above the pleasant town of Frome, The Lamb Inn has undergone a major refurbishment programme. A selection of seven bedrooms and bathrooms of varying shapes and sizes is available, and all have been completed to a high standard of quality and comfort. The inn is owned by the Blindmans Brewery and as might be expected, an excellent selection of real ales is served in the modern bar. A range of dishes including homemade pies is also available.

Rooms 7 en suite (3 fmly) S £50-£70; D £90-£110* **Facilities** FTV tea/coffee Dinner available Direct Dial Cen ht Wi-fi **Conf** Max 30 Class 30 Board 30 **Parking** 12 **Notes** LB ⊗ No coaches

Brookover Farm (ST775514)

★★★ FARMHOUSE

Orchardleigh BA11 2PH
☎ 01373 462806   Mr & Mrs Collingwood
e-mail: gcollingwood@btinternet.com
dir: 2m from Frome on A362, straight over x-rds and continue for 400yds, turn right, past farm buildings, 200yds on left

This farmhouse has plenty of character and a homely, friendly environment. It is ideally placed for visiting the attractions of Somerset and Wiltshire and is within easy reach of Longleat. Bedrooms vary in size and are well equipped. A traditional cooked (or continental) breakfast is served in the cosy dining room where a log fire burns during colder months. For horse lovers, there is a riding school just next door.

Rooms 3 rms (2 en suite) (1 pri facs) (2 fmly) S fr £45; D £60-£105* **Facilities** FTV tea/coffee Cen ht Golf 18 Riding **Parking** **Notes** ⊗ 38 acres arable/horses/sheep

---

GLASTONBURY   Map 4 ST53

See also Catcott & Somerton

Parsnips B&B

★★★★ BED AND BREAKFAST

99 Bere Ln BA6 8BE
☎ 01458 835599
e-mail: l.parsons@virgin.net
dir: Opposite Rural Life Museum at junct Bere Ln & Chilkwell St

Located just a short walk from the town centre and near to the Tor, this accommodation is fresh, light and airy. Bedrooms are cosy, well equipped and attractively presented. There is a comfortable lounge for guest use and the hosts extend a warm, friendly welcome. Freshly prepared breakfast is served in the conservatory dining room. There is a pleasant garden with a seating area for relaxing during those warmer months.

Rooms 3 en suite S £50-£55; D £65-£70* **Facilities** tea/coffee Cen ht Wi-fi **Parking** 3 **Notes** ⊗ ⊜

Wearyall Hill House

★★★★ BED AND BREAKFAST

78 The Roman Way BA6 8AD
☎ 01458 835510
e-mail: enquiries@wearyallhillhouse.co.uk
dir: 0.5m SW of town centre. A39 rdbt towards Street, pass B&Q on right, left onto Roman Way

Set on an elevated position on the edge of town, and close to places of interest, this delightful late Victorian residence affords sweeping views. Restored to its former glory by the present owners, the property is appropriately decorated and furnished with many extra facilities. The sumptuous breakfasts served in the attractive dining room are a highlight.

Rooms 3 en suite S fr £50; D £60* **Facilities** STV FTV TVL tea/coffee Cen ht Wi-fi **Parking** 8 **Notes** ⊗ No Children 10yrs ⊜

Belle-Vue Bed & Breakfast

★★★ GUEST ACCOMMODATION

2 Bere Ln BA6 8BA
☎ 01458 830385
e-mail: info@bellevueglastonbury.co.uk
web: www.bellevueglastonbury.co.uk
dir: M5 junct 23 onto A39, then A361 signed Glastonbury. On right, past Fisher Hill junct

This fully refurbished 1920s property close to the town centre that provides a relaxed and cosy atmosphere. All bedrooms are en suite, and some have fabulous far-reaching views; they are all decorated in a contemporary style with many extras provided. A hearty breakfast, using quality produce, is served in the charming dining room.

Rooms 6 en suite (1 fmly) (2 GF) S £30-£35; D £60-£70 **Facilities** FTV tea/coffee Cen ht Licensed Wi-fi Golf 18 Fishing Riding **Parking** 6 **Notes** LB ⊗

Cradlebridge (ST477385)

★★★ FARMHOUSE

BA16 9SD
☎ 01458 831827   Mrs J Tinney
dir: From rdbt at end of Street bypass take A39 towards Glastonbury. 1st left after garden centre signed Meare, Wedmore, farm signed 1m on left

Cradlebridge is part of a 200-acre dairy farm with pleasant views over the Somerset Levels. The relaxing farmhouse offers spacious bedrooms, which have French doors that allow greater appreciation of the tranquil surroundings. A full English breakfast is served around a communal table in the dining room.

Rooms 2 en suite (2 fmly) (2 GF) S £40; D £65* **Facilities** tea/coffee Cen ht **Parking** 6 **Notes** ⊗ No Children 5yrs ⊜ 200 acres dairy

No 1 Park Terrace

★★★ GUEST HOUSE

Street Rd BA6 9EA
☎ 01458 835845   🖶 01458 833296
e-mail: info@no1parkterrace.co.uk
dir: From High St, onto Magdalene St. At mini rdbt turn right, 100mtrs on right

A spacious and charming Victorian guest house located within walking distance of the High Street and the abbey ruins, that are close to the centre of Glastonbury. The fully licensed restaurant provides a Spanish influenced menu. The proprietors are friendly and welcoming; bedrooms are bright and airy with singles available. Limited parking is available.

Rooms 5 rms (2 en suite) (1 pri facs) S £35; D £60-£70* **Facilities** tea/coffee Dinner available Cen ht Licensed Wi-fi **Conf** Max 20 **Parking** 5 **Notes** LB ⊗

GLASTONBURY *continued*

Pilgrims B & B

Ⓤ

12/13 Norbins Rd BA6 9JE
☎ 01458 834722
e-mail: pilgrimsbb@hotmail.com
web: www.pilgrimsbb.co.uk
dir: *In town centre. From St John's Church on High St onto Archers Way, left onto St Edmunds Rd, right onto Norbins Rd*

Currently the rating for this establishment is not confirmed. This may be due to a change of ownership or because it has only recently joined the AA rating scheme. Please see the AA website for up-to-date details: the AA. com

Rooms 6 rms (3 en suite) (2 pri facs) (2 fmly) (2 GF) S £27.50-£35; D £55* **Facilities** TVL tea/coffee Cen ht Wi-fi **Notes** LB ⊗ Closed Xmas & New Year 🚭

HIGHBRIDGE   Map 4 ST34

The Greenwood

★★★★ GUEST ACCOMMODATION

76 Main Rd, West Huntspill TA9 3QU
☎ 01278 795886   📠 01278 795886
e-mail: info@the-greenwood.co.uk
web: www.the-greenwood.co.uk
dir: *On A38 in West Huntspill, between Orchard Inn & Sundowner Hotel*

Set in two acres of land, this 18th-century former farmhouse and family home offers comfortable accommodation in a friendly environment. Breakfast, featuring home-made preserves, is served in the dining room and home-cooked dinners are available by arrangement. There is a lounge for relaxation and a family dog who extends a hearty welcome.

Rooms 7 rms (6 en suite) (1 pri facs) (3 fmly) (1 GF) S £47.50; D £68* **Facilities** TVL tea/coffee Dinner available Cen ht Licensed Wi-fi Treatment room **Conf** Max 30 Thtr 30 Class 20 Board 12 **Parking** 8 **Notes** LB

HOLCOMBE   Map 4 ST64

Holcombe Inn

★★★★ 🍴 INN

Stratton Rd BA3 5EB
☎ 01761 232478   📠 01767 233737
e-mail: bookings@holcombeinn.co.uk
dir: *A367 to Stratton on The Fosse, take hidden left turn opposite Downside Abbey, signed Holcombe. Next right, 105mtrs on left*

Dating back to the 16th century this inn has views towards Downside Abbey in the distance. The attentive owners and pleasant staff create a friendly and relaxed atmosphere. Bedrooms are individually furnished and very comfortable. Real ales are served in the open-plan bar which has an attractive split-level restaurant.

Rooms 8 en suite (1 fmly) S £65; D £85* **Facilities** tea/coffee Dinner available Direct Dial Cen ht Wi-fi **Conf** Thtr 40 Class 40 **Parking** 25 **Notes** LB No coaches

ILCHESTER   Map 4 ST52

Liongate House B&B

★★★★ BED AND BREAKFAST

Liongate House, Northover BA22 8NG
☎ 01935 841741
e-mail: marlene@liongatehouse.com
dir: *0.5m from A303 junct signed to Ilchester, opposite Texaco garage*

These former stables have been developed to provide light and airy, contemporary-style accommodation. Bedrooms, one located at ground floor level, are individually designed, but each is comfortable and equipped with many considerate extras, including fresh flowers and fruit. Bathrooms are fresh and a pleasure to use. Breakfast is served in the lounge/dining room around a communal table.

Rooms 3 en suite (1 fmly) (1 GF) S £45-£60; D £60-£70 **Facilities** FTV TVL tea/coffee Cen ht Wi-fi **Parking** 3 **Notes** LB Closed 23 Dec-21 Jan

ILMINSTER   Map 4 ST31

Herne Lea Guest House

★★★★ GUEST ACCOMMODATION

15 Station Rd TA19 9BE
☎ 01460 53067
e-mail: enquiries@hernelea-ilminster.co.uk
web: www.hernelea-ilminster.co.uk
dir: *M5 junct 25 onto A358 follow signs for Ilminster, 100mtrs past Best Western hotel*

This welcoming Edwardian house has been extensively refurbished to provide impressive levels of quality and character. Bedrooms provide good levels of comfort with well appointed and stylish bathrooms. Breakfast utilises local produce and is served in the elegant dining room which opens into the conservatory lounge with lovely views towards Herne Hill.

Rooms 2 en suite (1 fmly) S £45-£50; D £60-£65 **Facilities** FTV tea/coffee Cen ht Wi-fi **Notes** LB ⊗

The New Inn

★★★★ 🍴 INN

Dowlish Wake TA19 0NZ
☎ 01460 52413
e-mail: newinn-ilminster@tiscali.co.uk
dir: *A358 or A303, follow signs for Perry's Cider, well-signed in village*

Situated in the tranquil and unspoilt village of Dowlish Wake, the New Inn is a proper local pub with a warm welcome at the convivial bar. Bedrooms are all on the ground floor, contemporary in style and located to the rear, overlooking the garden. The menu offers a range of enduring favourites and daily specials with good local produce used whenever possible. Breakfast is a substantial offering, just right for healthy appetites.

Rooms 4 annexe en suite (4 GF) **Facilities** FTV tea/coffee Dinner available Cen ht **Parking** 20

KEYNSHAM — Map 4 ST66

Grasmere Court

★★★★ GUEST HOUSE

22-24 Bath Rd BS31 1SN
☎ 0117 986 2662 ▤ 0117 986 2762
e-mail: grasmerecourt@aol.com
web: www.grasmerecourthotel.co.uk
dir: On B3116 just off A4 between Bath & Bristol

This very friendly, family-run establishment is located between Bath and Bristol. Bedrooms vary in size and one has a four-poster bed. A comfortable lounge and a well-stocked bar are available, and good-value, freshly prepared food is served in the attractive dining room.

Rooms 16 en suite (2 fmly) (4 GF) S £58-£68; D £78-£98 **Facilities** STV FTV TVL tea/coffee Dinner available Direct Dial Cen ht Licensed Wi-fi Golf 18 **Conf** Max 30 Thtr 30 Class 20 Board 20 **Parking** 11 **Notes** LB ⊗

KILVE — Map 3 ST14

Hood Arms Inn

★★★★ INN

TA5 1EA
☎ 01278 741210 ▤ 01278 741477
e-mail: info@thehoodarms.com
dir: W of Bridgwater on A39, halfway between Bridgwater & Minehead

The Hood Arms is a family-run, 17th-century coaching inn with a long history of welcoming weary travellers. This proud heritage continues with a relaxed and engaging atmosphere ensuring a rewarding stay. Bedrooms are located both in the main building and in adjacent self-contained units, all of which provide reassuring levels of comfort and quality. Three of the rooms have king-size poster beds. Local food and beers are on offer in the charming bar or smart restaurant area, while outside

there is an extensive garden with lovely views. Within the grounds there is also a separate lodge.

Hood Arms Inn

Rooms 10 en suite 2 annexe en suite (2 fmly) (2 GF) **Facilities** tea/coffee Dinner available Direct Dial Cen ht Wi-fi Boules, bar billiards **Conf** Max 20 Class 20 Board 16 **Parking** 10 **Notes** LB No coaches

LANGPORT — Map 4 ST42

The Old Pound Inn

★★★ INN

Aller TA10 0RA
☎ 01458 250469
e-mail: oldpoundinn@btconnect.com
web: www.oldpoundinn.co.uk
dir: On A372 in village centre

Situated in the heart of a charming village, just two miles from Langport, this popular inn was once a cider house, and dates back to 1571. Its long tradition of hospitality continues with a convivial and welcoming atmosphere for both locals and visitors alike. Bedrooms are soundly appointed and include a four-poster room and connecting family room. Public areas include the traditional bar, together with a 'snug' and a la carte restaurant. There is also a skittle alley for those who fancy some competition with their pint.

Rooms 8 en suite (2 fmly) S £45; D £70* **Facilities** tea/coffee Dinner available Cen ht Pool Table **Conf** Max 90 Thtr 90 Class 90 Board 90 **Parking** 15 **Notes** LB ⊗

LOWER VOBSTER — Map 4 ST74

The Vobster Inn

★★★★ ⊛ INN

BA3 5RJ
☎ 01373 812920 ▤ 01373 812920
e-mail: rdavila@btinternet.com
dir: From A361 follow signs for Whatley & Mells, then Vobster

Peacefully located in four acres of Somerset countryside, this is the ideal village inn with a real sense of personal attention and a genuine welcome from the resident proprietors. Bedrooms and bathrooms provide high levels of quality and comfort. Dinner places an emphasis on high quality, simply prepared dishes with regular seasonal changes, and includes several dishes

demonstrating the Spanish heritage of the chef proprietor.

Rooms 3 annexe en suite (2 fmly) (3 GF) S £55-£75; D £85-£95* **Facilities** FTV tea/coffee Dinner available Cen ht Wi-fi Petanque **Conf** Max 40 Thtr 25 Class 32 Board 32 **Parking** 60 **Notes** LB ⊗

LYMPSHAM — Map 4 ST35

Batch

★★★★ GUEST ACCOMMODATION

Batch Ln BS24 0EX
☎ 01934 750371 ▤ 01934 750501
web: www.batchcountryhotel.co.uk
dir: M5 junct 22, take last exit on rdbt signed A370 to Weston-Super-Mare 3.5m, left into Lympsham 1m, sign at end of road

In a rural location between Weston-Super-Mare and Burnham-on-Sea, this former farmhouse offers a relaxed, friendly and peaceful environment. The comfortable bedrooms have views to the Mendip and Quantock hills. Spacious lounges overlook the extensive, well-tended gardens and the comfortably furnished function room, together with the restaurant, make this a popular venue for wedding ceremonies.

Rooms 11 en suite (3 fmly) (1 GF) S £58-£62; D £80-£90 **Facilities** tea/coffee Direct Dial Fishing **Parking** 140 **Notes** Closed 25-26 Dec Civ Wed 260

MARTOCK — Map 4 ST41

Higher Farm

★★★★ BED AND BREAKFAST

Bladon Hill, Kingsbury Episcopi TA12 6BJ
☎ 01935 823099
e-mail: boltonali@aol.com
dir: 2m NW of Martock. Off B3165 to Kingsbury Episcopi, left at Wyndham Arms, farm on right

Located in the scenic village of Kingsbury Episcopi, Higher Farm provides comfortable accommodation with a relaxed and friendly atmosphere. Breakfast is served in the pleasant dining room which opens onto the patio and rear garden. There are two pubs serving evening meals just a 5-minute walk in opposite directions from the farm.

Rooms 2 en suite (1 fmly) S £35; D £55* **Facilities** tea/coffee Cen ht **Parking** 6 **Notes** ⊗ ⊜

MILVERTON   Map 3 ST12

The Globe

★★★ 🍽 INN

Fore St TA4 1JX

☎ 01823 400534

e-mail: adele@theglobemilverton.co.uk

web: www.theglobemilverton.co.uk

dir: M5 junct 27 follow B3277 to Milverton. In village centre

This popular village local was once a coaching inn, but has been given a contemporary styling whilst still retaining its traditional charm. The welcome is warm and genuine with a convivial atmosphere always guaranteed. Bedrooms share a similar modern style with comfy beds. The hard-working kitchen is committed to quality, with excellent locally sourced produce used in some impressive dishes. Continental breakfast is served.

Rooms 3 en suite (1 fmly) S £45-£50; D £55-£60 (room only)* **Facilities** tea/coffee Dinner available Cen ht Wi-fi **Parking** 4 **Notes** LB ⊗ Closed 20 Dec-2 Jan No coaches

MINEHEAD   Map 3 SS94

See also Dunster

Glendower House

★★★★ GUEST HOUSE

30-32 Tregonwell Rd TA24 5DU

☎ 01643 707144   📠 01643 708719

e-mail: info@glendower-house.co.uk

web: www.glendower-house.co.uk

dir: A39 into Minehead, last exit at mini rdbt, 200yds right by school onto Ponsford Rd & Tregonwell Rd

The family-run Glendower House is near the seafront, harbour and town centre. A friendly atmosphere prevails and there are comfortable bedrooms and smart bathrooms. Public areas are spacious and guests can relax in the garden in the summer. Ample parking is a bonus.

Rooms 11 en suite (2 GF) **Facilities** tea/coffee Cen ht **Parking** 14 **Notes** ⊗ Closed mid Dec-Feb

Kenella House

★★★★ GUEST ACCOMMODATION

7 Tregonwell Rd TA24 5DT

☎ 01643 703128 & 07710 889079   📠 01643 703128

e-mail: kenellahouse@fsmail.net

dir: Off A39 onto Townsend Rd & right onto Ponsford Rd & Tregonwell Rd

A warm welcome and relaxed atmosphere are found at Kenella House. Located close to the town centre, the guest house is also convenient for walkers (heated boot cupboard available) and visitors to the steam railway. The well-maintained bedrooms are very comfortable and have many extras. Home-cooked dinners, available by arrangement, and hearty breakfasts are served in the smart dining room.

Rooms 6 en suite (1 GF) D £60-£70* **Facilities** tea/coffee Dinner available Cen ht **Parking** 8 **Notes** LB ⊗ No Children 14yrs Closed 23-26 Dec 🐾

NORTH WOOTTON   Map 4 ST54

Crossways

★★★ GUEST ACCOMMODATION

Stocks Ln BA4 4EU

☎ 01749 899000   📠 01749 890476

e-mail: enquiries@thecrossways.co.uk

dir: Exit M5 junct 22 towards Shepton Mallet, 0.2m from Pilton

Family run and tucked away in a quiet lane, yet with easy access to Wells, Glastonbury and other interesting areas of Wiltshire and Somerset. The rooms are spacious and there is a large bar-restaurant and a smaller dining room where breakfast is served. The extensive menu features many home-cooked dishes.

Rooms 21 en suite (4 fmly) S £50-£60* **Facilities** tea/coffee Dinner available Cen ht Licensed Pool Table **Conf** Max 40 Thtr 40 Class 40 Board 25 **Parking** **Notes** ⊗ Closed 25 Dec RS 26 Dec-2 Jan Civ Wed 100

PORLOCK   Map 3 SS84

The Cottage

★★★★ GUEST ACCOMMODATION

High St TA24 8PU

☎ 01643 862996   📠 01643 862996

e-mail: cottageporlock@aol.com

web: www.cottageporlock.co.uk

dir: In village centre on A39

One of the oldest houses in the area, The Cottage is located right in the heart of this ancient village, and so ideally placed to enjoy village life, exploring Exmoor and walking the South West coastal path. Bedrooms are well equipped and there is a comfortable lounge solely for guest use. Breakfast is served in the pleasant dining room at the front of the house.

Rooms 4 en suite (1 fmly) S £35-£40; D £60-£80 **Facilities** tea/coffee Dinner available Cen ht **Parking** 3 **Notes** LB ⊗ Closed Jan

Glen Lodge

★★★★ 🅐 GUEST ACCOMMODATION

Hawkcombe TA24 8LN

☎ 01643 863371   📠 01643 863016

e-mail: glenlodge@gmail.com

web: www.glenlodge.net

dir: From Minehead into Porlock on A39, left at church into Parsons St. 0.5m to 'Weak Bridge' sign, left over bridge, Lodge opposite

Rooms 5 rms (1 en suite) (2 pri facs) S £55; D £80* **Facilities** TVL tea/coffee Dinner available Cen ht Wi-fi 🏊 **Parking** 6 **Notes** ⊗ Closed 24 Dec-2 Jan 🐾

RUDGE   Map 4 ST85

The Full Moon Inn

★★★ INN

BA11 2QF

☎ 01373 830936

e-mail: info@thefullmoon.co.uk

dir: From A36 S from Bath, 10m, left at Standerwick by The Bell pub. 4m from Warminster

Peacefully located in the quiet village of Rudge, this traditional inn offers a warm welcome and a proper country pub atmosphere. In the bar area, guests mix well with the locals to enjoy a selection of real ales and a log fire in the colder months. In addition to bar meals, a comfortable restaurant serving excellent home cooked dishes is also available. Bedrooms include some at the main inn and more in an adjacent annexe - all are comfortable and well equipped.

Rooms 5 en suite 12 annexe en suite (2 fmly) (3 GF) S £57.50-£62.50; D £79.50-£85* **Facilities** tea/coffee Dinner available Cen ht 🕭 **Conf** Max 65 Thtr 30 Class 12 Board 18 **Parking** 25 **Notes** LB

SHEPTON MALLET   Map 4 ST64

Cannards Grave Farmhouse

★★★★ GUEST ACCOMMODATION

Cannards Grave BA4 4LY

☎ 01749 347091   📠 01749 347091

e-mail: sue@cannardsgravefarmhouse.co.uk

web: www.cannardsgravefarmhouse.co.uk

dir: On A37 between Shepton Mallet & The Bath & West Showground, 100yds from Highwayman pub towards showground on left

Conveniently located for the Bath and West showground, Longleat, Glastonbury and Wells, this 17th-century house provides thoughtfully equipped en suite bedrooms. There is also a well-furnished lounge. The proprietors offer warm hospitality. Breakfast is served in the conservatory dining room.

Rooms 5 en suite (2 fmly) (1 GF) S £40-£60; D £60-£80* **Facilities** FTV TVL tea/coffee Cen ht Wi-fi **Parking** 6 **Notes** ⊗

Thatched Cottage

★★★★ ◉ INN

63-67 Charlton Rd BA4 5QF
☎ 01749 342058 ▯ 01749 343265
e-mail: enquiries@thatchedcottage.info
web: www.thatchedcottage.info
dir: 0.6m E of town centre on A361

This delightful Grade II listed, 17th-century hostelry has been renovated and upgraded while retaining its original character. The modern accommodation is well equipped with spacious bedrooms and the public areas are light, airy and very attractively appointed. The inn offers a good choice of carefully prepared dishes in the restaurant or lighter options in the bar.

Rooms 8 en suite S £69-£100; D £79-£140 (room only)* Facilities STV TVL tea/coffee Dinner available Direct Dial Cen ht Wi-fi Conf Max 45 Thtr 45 Class 35 Board 30 Parking 40 Notes LB

The Three Horseshoes

★★★★ ◉ INN

Batcombe BA4 6HE
☎ 01749 850359 ▯ 01749 850615
e-mail: shirley@thethreehorsesinn.co.uk
dir: 3m from Bruton signed on A359

The Three Horseshoes is a traditional freehouse that dates back to the 17th century. The long, low bar with its cream-painted beams and inglenook fireplace is a great place for a pint or a delicious meal. In the garden is an ornamental fish pond and a patio for alfresco dining. Bedrooms are very comfortable with useful facilities and charming rustic décor.

Rooms 3 rms (2 en suite) (1 pri facs) (1 fmly) S £65-£75; D £75 Facilities tea/coffee Dinner available Cen ht Parking 30 Notes RS Mon Closed No coaches

The Abbey Barn

★★★ BED AND BREAKFAST

Doulting BA4 4QD
☎ 01749 880321
e-mail: abbeybarn@btconnect.com
dir: 2m E of Shepton Mallet on A361 in Doulting centre

Situated on the edge of the Mendips in the pretty village of Doulting, this Grade II listed property is renowned for its superb friendly welcome and top quality breakfasts. A licensed cosy residents' lounge bar provides a relaxing area to enjoy a drink or two. Log fires burn in the winter, and guests can enjoy the attractive garden in the summer. Private parking is available.

Rooms 3 en suite (1 fmly) S £47-£70; D £67-£70* Facilities tea/coffee Licensed Parking 10 Notes LB ⊗ No Children

L'Abri B&B

★★★ GUEST ACCOMMODATION

Portman House, Pylle-on-the-Fosse BA4 6TA
☎ 01749 830150
e-mail: moonbase@sky.com
dir: On A37, 2m S of Shepton Mallet

Conveniently located near the Bath and West Showground, this establishment, which was formerly an inn, offers annexe bedrooms, each having their own front door leading to the back garden. Rooms are situated at ground floor level. Dinner is available by prior arrangement and features a selection of home-made dishes.

Rooms 3 en suite (3 GF) D £50* Facilities tea/coffee Dinner available Cen ht Parking 10 Notes ⊗ No Children 14yrs Closed 24-31 Dec ☺

SLOUGH GREEN Map 4 ST21

The Farmers Inn

★★★★ ⊜ INN

West Hatch TA3 5RS
☎ 01823 480480 ▯ 01823 481177
e-mail: robin@farmersinnwesthatch.co.uk
web: www.farmersinnwesthatch.co.uk
dir: M5 junct 25 onto A358, turn right at Nags Head & follow RSPCA signs for 2m

Dating back to the 16th century, this friendly and welcoming inn offers high standards of accommodation with a relaxed and engaging atmosphere. The bar is the focal point with crackling fires, cosy sofas and wooden floors adding to the charm. Bedrooms are spacious and elegantly appointed with antique furnishings and polished wooden floors, and bathrooms have deep, roll-top baths. Food is well worth sampling with a talented young kitchen team using excellent local produce to impressive effect. Pretty gardens provide a lovely place to sit, enjoy a drink and admire the wonderful Somerset countryside.

Rooms 5 en suite (5 fmly) (5 GF) D £125-£150* Facilities tea/coffee Dinner available Direct Dial Cen ht Wi-fi Parking 50 Notes LB No coaches Civ Wed 100

SOMERTON Map 4 ST42

Lower Farm (ST527309)

★★★★ FARMHOUSE

Kingweston TA11 6BA
☎ 01458 223237 ▯ 01458 223276 Mrs J Sedgman
e-mail: lowerfarm@btconnect.com
web: www.lowerfarm.net
dir: 3m NE of Somerton. On B3153 in Kingweston

Set in the heart of Somerset, this Grade II listed stone farmhouse has been home to the same family for several generations. Furnished in cottage style, the cosy bedrooms combine period charm with modern comforts and have attractive rural views. Guests are served a hearty breakfast in the Georgian dining room.

Rooms 2 en suite S £60; D £65* Facilities FTV tea/coffee Cen ht Wi-fi Conf Max 36 Thtr 36 Class 20 Board 20 Parking 8 Notes ⊗ Closed Xmas & New Year 500 acres arable

Somerton Court Country House

★★★★ GUEST ACCOMMODATION

TA11 7AH
☎ 01458 274694 ▯ 01458 274694
e-mail: enquiries@somertoncourt.com
web: www.somertoncourt.com
dir: From A303 onto A372 at Podimore rdbt. In 3m right onto B3151 to Somerton, & follow B&B signs

Dating back to the 17th century and set in extensive gardens and grounds, this house is a tranquil haven away from the pressures of modern life. The comfortable bedrooms have lovely views, and breakfast is served in a delightful dining room that overlooks the gardens.

Rooms 6 en suite (2 fmly) S £50-£65; D £80* Facilities tea/coffee Cen ht Riding Conf Max 150 Thtr 200 Class 150 Parking 30 Notes ⊗ Closed Xmas & New Year Civ Wed 150

The Devonshire Arms

★★★ ◉ INN

Long Sutton TA10 9LP
☎ 01458 241271 ▯ 01458 241037
e-mail: mail@thedevonshirearms.com
web: www.thedevonshirearms.com
dir: A303 onto A372 at Podimore rdbt. After 4m left onto B3165, signed Martock & Long Sutton

This inn has undergone a dramatic refurbishment to provide stylish public rooms and accommodation. The bedrooms have contemporary furnishings and the spacious public areas are comfortable. A choice of ales, wines and spirits, and interesting cuisine complete the picture in the bar-restaurant.

Rooms 7 rms (6 en suite) (1 pri facs) 2 annexe en suite (1 fmly) (2 GF) S £70-£120; D £80-£120* Facilities FTV tea/coffee Dinner available Cen ht Wi-fi ⟿ Parking 6 Notes LB Closed 25-26 Dec

---

SOUTH PETHERTON — Map 4 ST41

Old Harp House

★★★★ 🍴 BED AND BREAKFAST

Over Stratton TA13 5LB
☎ 01460 242301 📄 01460 242301
e-mail: anne.larpent@btinternet.com
web: www.oldharphouse.com

Peacefully located in an engaging Somerset village just a short distance from the A303, this Grade II listed farmhouse dates back to the early 17th century. Many fascinating original features have been retained, such as a Tudor hamstone fireplace and winder staircase. Bedrooms are individually styled with luxurious touches, and breakfasts (and dinners by prior arrangement) utilise local produce and are served in the elegant dining room.

Rooms 3 en suite S £60-£65; D £75-£80* Facilities FTV TVL tea/coffee Dinner available Cen ht Wi-fi Riding Parking 6 Notes ⊗ No Children 12yrs ⊜

STANTON DREW — Map 4 ST56

Greenlands (ST597636)

★★★★ FARMHOUSE

BS39 4ES
☎ 01275 333487 📄 01275 331211 Mrs J Cleverley
dir: A37 onto B3130, on right before Stanton Drew Garage

Situated near the ancient village of Stanton Drew in the heart of the Chew Valley, Greenlands is convenient for Bristol Airport and Bath, Bristol and Wells. There are comfortable, well-equipped bedrooms and a downstairs lounge, and breakfast is the highlight of any stay here.

Rooms 4 en suite Facilities STV FTV TVL tea/coffee Cen ht Parking 8 Notes No Children 12yrs ⊜ 3 acres hobby farming/poultry

---

Valley Farm

★★★★ BED AND BREAKFAST

Sandy Ln BS39 4EL
☎ 01275 332723 & 07799 768161 📄 01275 332723
e-mail: valleyfarm2000@tiscali.co.uk
dir: Off B3130 into Stanton Drew, right onto Sandy Ln

Located on a quiet country lane, Valley Farm offers relaxing and friendly accommodation. All bedrooms are comfortable and well equipped, and each has pleasant views over the countryside. Breakfast is served around a communal table in the dining room, and although dinner is not available, the village pub is just a stroll away.

Rooms 3 en suite (1 fmly) (1 GF) Facilities TVL tea/coffee Cen ht Parking 6 Notes ⊗ No Children 8yrs Closed 24-26 Dec ⊜

STAPLE FITZPAINE — Map 4 ST21

Greyhound

★★★★ 🍴 INN

TA3 5SP
☎ 01823 480227 📄 01823 481117
e-mail: thegreyhound-inn@btconnect.com
web: www.greyhoundinn.biz
dir: M5 junct 25, A358 signed Yeovil. In 3m turn right, signed Staple Fitzpaine

Set in the heart of Somerset in the Blackdown Hills, this picturesque village inn has great atmosphere and character, complete with flagstone floors and open fires. An imaginative choice of freshly-prepared seasonal dishes using locally sourced ingredients is featured on the ever-changing blackboard menu. The delightful

---

bedrooms are spacious, comfortable, and well equipped with many extra facilities.

Greyhound

Rooms 4 en suite Facilities tea/coffee Dinner available Direct Dial Cen ht Wi-fi Pool Table Conf Max 60 Thtr 60 Class 30 Board 20 Parking 40 Notes No Children 10yrs

---

STOGUMBER — Map 3 ST03

Wick House

★★★★ 🅰 GUEST HOUSE

Brook St TA4 3SZ
☎ 01984 656422
e-mail: sheila@wickhouse.co.uk
web: www.wickhouse.co.uk
dir: Off A358 into village, left at the x-rds, Wick House 3rd on left

Rooms 6 en suite (1 GF) S £40-£44; D £60-£64* Facilities TVL tea/coffee Dinner available Licensed Wi-fi Stairlift Parking 6 Notes LB ⊗

STREET — Map 4 ST43

The Birches

★★★★ BED AND BREAKFAST

13 Housman Rd BA16 0SD
☎ 01458 442902
e-mail: askins@ukonline.co.uk
dir: Off B3151 onto Portway at Cider Farm sign. 1st right onto Housman Rd

The Birches is a modern house located in a quiet residential area, just ten minutes walk from Clarks Village Outlet Centre. Bedrooms, one situated on the ground floor, are well equipped and have spacious private bathrooms. A freshly cooked breakfast, featuring home-made and garden produce is served in the pleasant dining room/lounge around a family table. A pub serving evening meals is just a stroll away.

Rooms 2 rms (2 pri facs) (1 fmly) (1 GF) S £45-£55; D fr £62* Facilities tea/coffee Cen ht Parking 2 Notes ⊗ ⊜

Kasuli

★★★ BED AND BREAKFAST

71 Somerton Rd BA16 0DN
☎ 01458 442063
dir: *B3151 from Street rdbt for Somerton, house 400yds past Street Inn on left*

This family home is located close to Clarks Village Outlet Centre and with easy access to local places of historical interest. Friendliness and a homely atmosphere are offered, and bedrooms are neatly presented. An enjoyable traditional breakfast is served in the dining room around the family dining table.

Rooms 2 rms S £24-£28; D £46-£52* **Facilities** tea/coffee Cen ht **Parking** 2 **Notes** ⊗ No Children 10yrs ⊜

TAUNTON	Map 4 ST22

See also Staple Fitzpaine

PREMIER COLLECTION

Elm Villa

★★★★★ BED AND BREAKFAST

1 Private Rd, Staplegrove Rd TA2 6AJ
☎ 01823 336165
e-mail: ferguson@elmvilla10.freeserve.co.uk
dir: *M5 junct 25, A358 (Minehead road) to Staplegrove Inn, left & left again into Private Rd*

This spacious and comfortable Victorian villa enjoys distant views of the Blackdown Hills, yet is within walking distance of the town centre, theatre, station and County Cricket Ground. All bedrooms are en suite and have plenty of facilities. Ample parking is available.

Rooms 2 en suite S £40-£45; D £56-£58 **Facilities** FTV tea/coffee Cen ht **Parking** 2 **Notes** ⊗ No Children 10yrs ⊜

Cutsey House

★★★★ GUEST ACCOMMODATION

Cutsey, Trull TA3 7NY
☎ 01823 421705 📄 01823 421294
e-mail: cutseyhouse@btconnect.com
dir: *M5 junct 26, into West Buckland, right at T-junct, 2nd left, next right*

A Victorian house set in over 20 acres of gardens and grounds with parts of the building dating back to the 15th century. The comfortable spacious bedrooms have glorious views of the countryside towards the Blackdown Hills. Dinner is available by arrangement and guests can enjoy drinks in the library.

Cutsey House

Rooms 3 en suite (1 smoking) S £35-£40; D £60-£70* **Facilities** TVL Dinner available Cen ht Snooker **Parking** 11 **Notes** ⊗ Closed Xmas-Etr ⊜

4 Elm Grove B&B

★★★★ BED AND BREAKFAST

4 Elm Grove TA1 1EG
☎ 01823 354653
e-mail: stirlings.taunton@tiscali.co.uk

Quietly located in a leafy residential area, just a short stroll from the centre of Taunton, this elegant establishment offers a warm and genuine welcome with every effort made to ensure a comfortable and relaxing stay. The tastefully appointed bedrooms offer a host of luxurious extras with modern bathrooms complete with power showers and fluffy towels. Substantial continental breakfasts are served at the dining room table.

Rooms 2 en suite S £40-£50; D £55-£65* **Facilities** TVL tea/coffee Cen ht Wi-fi **Notes** ⊗ No Children 12yrs ⊜

The Spinney

★★★★ 🍴 GUEST ACCOMMODATION

Curland TA3 5SE
☎ 01460 234362
e-mail: enquiries@spinneybedandbreakfast.co.uk
web: www.spinneybedandbreakfast.co.uk
dir: *2m W off A358 (Taunton-Ilminster road)*

A warm welcome awaits you at this delightful family home, set in well-tended gardens and having magnificent views of the Blackdown, Quantock and Mendip hills. The attractive bedrooms are equipped with modern comforts and include a ground floor room with level access. Using the best local produce, delicious dinners are available by arrangement and guests may bring their own wine.

Rooms 3 en suite (2 GF) S £50-£55; D £65-£70* **Facilities** FTV TVL tea/coffee Dinner available Cen ht Wi-fi **Parking** 6 **Notes** ⊗ No Children 10yrs Closed Xmas & New Year

Brookfield House

★★★★ GUEST HOUSE

16 Wellington Rd TA1 4EQ
☎ 01823 272786 📄 01823 272786
e-mail: info@brookfieldguesthouse.uk.com
web: www.brookfieldguesthouse.uk.com
dir: *From town centre signs to Musgrove Hospital, onto A38 Wellington Rd, on right opp turning to hospital*

This charming Grade II listed Georgian house is just a five minute, level walk from the town centre. The family take great pride in caring for guests, and the brightly decorated bedrooms are well equipped. Breakfast, featuring local ingredients, is served in the attractive dining room. The property is entirely non-smoking.

Rooms 7 en suite (1 fmly) S £50-£65; D £70-£90* **Facilities** tea/coffee Dinner available Cen ht Wi-fi **Parking** 8 **Notes** ⊗ No Children 7yrs

Creechbarn

★★★★ BED AND BREAKFAST

Vicarage Ln, Creech-St-Michael TA3 5PP
☎ 01823 443955
e-mail: mick@somersite.co.uk
dir: *M5 junct 25, A358 to Creech-St-Michael, follow canal boat signs to end Vicarage Ln. Through brick gateposts, turn right*

Located next to the canal and on a Sustrans cycle route, this traditional Somerset barn was lovingly converted by the current owners. Bedrooms are comfortable and there is a spacious sitting room with books and TV. Breakfast is carefully prepared with free-range eggs and home-made bread.

Rooms 3 rms (1 en suite) S £44-£46; D £50-£58* **Facilities** TV1B TVL tea/coffee Direct Dial Cen ht Wi-fi **Parking** 6 **Notes** LB Closed 20 Dec-6 Jan ⊜

TAUNTON *continued*

Lower Farm *(ST281241)*

★★★★ FARMHOUSE

Thornfalcon TA3 5NR
☎ 01823 443549   **Mrs D Titman**
e-mail: doreen@titman.eclipse.co.uk
web: www.somersite.co.uk
dir: *M5 junct 25, 2m SE on A358, left opp Nags Head pub, farm signed 1m on left*

This charming, thatched, 15th-century farmhouse is set in lovely gardens and is surrounded by open countryside. Hearty breakfasts, served in the farmhouse kitchen, feature home-produced eggs. Some bedrooms are located in the converted granary, some on the ground floor. There is a comfortable sitting room with a log fire.

Rooms 2 rms (1 en suite) (1 pri facs) 9 annexe rms 7 annexe en suite (2 pri facs) (2 fmly) (7 GF)
Facilities TV9B TVL tea/coffee Cen ht Wi-fi **Parking** 10
Notes ⊗ No Children 5yrs 10 acres beef/cows/poultry

Lower Marsh Farm *(ST224279)*

★★★★ FARMHOUSE

Kingston St Mary TA2 8AB
☎ 01823 451331   📠 01823 451331
Mr & Mrs J Gothard
e-mail: b&b@lowermarshfarm.co.uk
dir: *M5 junct 25. Farm between Taunton & Kingston St Mary just past King's Hall School on right*

Located at the foot of the Quantock Hills, this delightful family-run farm provides bright, comfortable bedrooms, complemented by numerous, thoughtful extra facilities. Evening meals are available by arrangement. Guests enjoy a hearty breakfast around one large table in the attractive dining room; a spacious lounge with log fire in winter is also available.

Rooms 3 en suite (1 fmly) S fr £38; D fr £70
Facilities TVL tea/coffee Dinner available Cen ht
Parking 6 **Notes** ⊗ ⊜ 300 acres arable

Meryan House

★★★★ 🍴 GUEST ACCOMMODATION

Bishop's Hull TA1 5EG
☎ 01823 337445   📠 01823 322355
e-mail: meryanhousehotel@yahoo.co.uk
web: www.meryanhouse.co.uk
dir: *1.5m W of town centre. Off A38 into Bishop's Hull*

Located in its own grounds just over a mile from the town centre, this 17th-century property has delightful individually furnished rooms. The comfortable bedrooms feature antiques along with modern facilities. Interesting dishes are available at dinner, and there is also a cosy bar and a spacious lounge.

Rooms 12 en suite (2 fmly) (2 GF) S £60-£65; D £65-£95* **Facilities** STV FTV TVL tea/coffee Dinner available Direct Dial Cen ht Licensed Wi-fi **Conf** Max 25 Thtr 25 Class 25 Board 18 **Parking** 17 **Notes** LB RS Sun No eve meal

Blorenge House

★★★ GUEST ACCOMMODATION

57 Staple Grove Rd TA1 1DG
☎ 01823 283005   📠 01823 283005
e-mail: enquiries@blorengehouse.co.uk
dir: *M5 junct 25, towards cricket ground & Morrisons on left, left at lights, right at 2nd lights, house 150yds on left*

This fine Victorian property offers spacious accommodation within walking distance of the town centre. The bedrooms (some at ground floor level and some with four-poster beds) are individually furnished and vary in size. A lounge is available, and the garden with outdoor swimming pool is open to guests during daytime hours most days of the week. There is also ample parking.

Rooms 23 rms (19 en suite) (4 pri facs) (4 fmly) (3 GF) S £65-£75; D £82-£95* **Facilities** FTV TVL tea/coffee Cen ht Wi-fi ⚡ **Conf** Max 20 **Parking** 23 **Notes** LB

The Hatch Inn

★★★ INN

Village Rd, Hatch Beauchamp TA3 6SG
☎ 01823 480245
e-mail: jamie@thehatchinn.co.uk
web: www.thehatchinn.co.uk
dir: *M5 junct 25, 3m S off A358*

With easy access to both the A303 and M5, this 18th-century, family-run coaching inn is very much the village local, complete with crackling log fires and a convivial atmosphere. Bedrooms offer good levels of comfort with well appointed bathrooms. Public areas include a choice of bars serving local ales, and the menu features honest, home-cooked cuisine with a focus upon local produce.

Rooms 5 en suite (1 fmly) **Facilities** FTV tea/coffee Dinner available Cen ht Wi-fi Pool Table skittle alley **Parking** 15 **Notes** No coaches

Higher Dipford *(ST216205)*

★★★ FARMHOUSE

Trull TA3 7NU
☎ 01823 275770 & 257916   📠 01823 275770
Mrs M Fewings
e-mail: mafewings@tesco.net
dir: *A38 S from town centre on Honiton Rd to Trull, right onto Dipford Rd, farm on left*

This Grade II listed 17th-century longhouse is part of a working farm. Steeped in character with elm beams and inglenook fireplaces, the house provides well-equipped and homely accommodation. Bedrooms are comfortable and individually decorated, and there is an honesty bar and lounge. Breakfasts and home-cooked dinners, featuring local produce, are served in the spacious dining room.

Rooms 3 en suite S £40-£50; D £65-£70* **Facilities** STV TVL tea/coffee Dinner available Cen ht Licensed **Parking** 6 **Notes** LB ⊗ ⊜ 120 acres beef

TEMPLE CLOUD   Map 4 ST65

The Old Court

★★★★ GUEST ACCOMMODATION

Main Rd BS39 5DA
☎ 01761 451101   🖨 01761 451223
e-mail: oldcourt@gifford.co.uk

This is truly a unique property was a courthouse in a previous time. Plentiful and spacious public areas include the large courtroom, now converted into a comfortable lounge with an adjoining games room. Bedrooms vary in size but all are comfortably furnished and are based in the main building. Should guests wish there is the option to stay in one of the smaller converted cells - though this may not suit everyone! Freshly prepared breakfast is a highlight, and very welcoming hospitality is assured from the resident American owner.

Rooms 5 rms (4 en suite) (1 pri facs) S £60-£125; D £70-£150* **Facilities** STV tea/coffee

TINTINHULL   Map 4 ST41

Crown & Victoria

★★★★ ⊚ INN

Farm St BA22 8PZ
☎ 01935 823341   🖨 01935 825786
e-mail: info@thecrownandvictoria.co.uk
web: www.thecrownandvictoria.co.uk
dir: Off A303, signs for Tintinhull Gardens

Appointed to a high standard, the light and airy accommodation has very well-equipped bedrooms. The staff ensure guests are cared for, and the contemporary bar and restaurant provide a good selection of carefully prepared dishes.

Rooms 5 en suite **Facilities** tea/coffee Dinner available Cen ht Wi-fi **Parking** 60 **Notes** No coaches

WATCHET   Map 3 ST04

The Georgian House

★★★★ GUEST HOUSE

28 Swain St TA23 0AD
☎ 01984 639279
e-mail: georgianhouse_watchet@virgin.net
dir: A39 over railway bridge onto Watchet main street

This elegant Georgian property is situated in the heart of this increasingly popular coastal resort and is within a short walk of the impressive new marina. Refurbished with considerable care, the comfortable bedrooms combine quality and individuality. Breakfast (and dinner by arrangement) is served in the well-appointed dining room. Additional facilities for guests include a lounge and the garden.

Rooms 3 en suite **Facilities** Dinner available Cen ht **Parking** 2 **Notes** ⊗ 🌐

The Linhay B&B

★★★★ BED AND BREAKFAST

Williton Rd TA23 0NU
☎ 01984 641252 & 07940 894009
e-mail: linhaybnb@aol.com
dir: A39 towards Minehead, 2.5m after Williton

Convenient for coastal and country attractions, Linhay offers spacious and friendly accommodation. Hospitality is a feature and guests are made to feel at home. The bedrooms are particularly well appointed and well equipped, and a hearty breakfast is served in the conservatory. There is an attractive garden with pool, a sauna and ample parking.

Rooms 3 en suite (3 GF) S £45-£55; D £60-£70* **Facilities** tea/coffee Cen ht ⤜ Sauna **Parking** 3 **Notes** LB ⊗ Closed Xmas & New Year 🌐

WATERROW   Map 3 ST02

The Rock

★★★★ ⊜ INN

TA4 2AX
☎ 01984 623293   🖨 01984 623293
e-mail: matt@rockinn.co.uk
dir: On B3227

Set in the lush greenery of the Tone Valley, this 16th-century inn, as its name suggests, is built against the rock face. There is an abundance of character and the friendly atmosphere draws both locals and visitors. A range of freshly prepared, imaginative meals is available in the bar or restaurant, including Aberdeen Angus steaks from the owner's farm. The bedrooms are comfortable, light and airy.

Rooms 8 en suite (1 fmly) S £50; D £75* **Facilities** FTV TVL tea/coffee Dinner available Direct Dial Cen ht Pool Table **Parking** 25 **Notes** LB

WELLINGTON   Map 3 ST12

Thorne Manor (ST097210)

★★★★ FARMHOUSE

Thorne St Margaret TA21 0EQ
☎ 01823 672264 Mrs P Hasell
e-mail: hasell@thornemanor.wanadoo.co.uk
web: www.thorne-manor.co.uk
dir: 3m W of Wellington. Off A38 to Thorne St Margaret

There is a tangible sense of history at this engaging
16th-century manor house which stands in a small
village near the Blackdown Hills. The centuries old front
door opens to reveal accommodation of genuine character
and good levels of comfort, with inglenook fireplaces in
the dining room and the lounge. The spacious bedroom is
well equipped and you will be well cared for by the hosts.
The well-tended garden provides space for relaxation,
and breakfast features local produce.

Rooms 1 en suite; D £64-£68* Facilities TVL tea/coffee
Wi-fi Parking 2 Notes ⊗ No Children Closed mid Dec-
mid Jan ⊛ 175 acres mixed

WELLS   Map 4 ST54

See also Croscombe

PREMIER COLLECTION

Beaconsfield Farm

★★★★★ ▤ BED AND BREAKFAST

Easton BA5 1DU
☎ 01749 870308
e-mail: carol@beaconsfieldfarm.co.uk
web: www.beaconsfieldfarm.co.uk
dir: 2.5m from Wells on A371, on right just before
Easton

Set in pleasant, well-tended gardens on the west side
of the Mendip Hills, Beaconsfield Farm is a convenient
base for visiting this attractive area. The welcoming
hosts are most friendly and attentive and many guests
return on a regular basis. Bedrooms, which are very
comfortable and equipped with many extra facilities,
are delightfully decorated with co-ordinated colours
and fabrics. A choice of well-cooked dishes featuring
fresh local produce is offered at breakfast.

Rooms 3 en suite Facilities FTV TVL tea/coffee Cen ht
Wi-fi Parking 10 Notes ⊗ No Children 8yrs Closed 22
Dec-3 Jan ⊛

Beryl

★★★★★ ⌂ BED AND BREAKFAST

Hawkers Ln BA5 3JP
☎ 01749 678738 📄 01749 670508
e-mail: stay@beryl-wells.co.uk
dir: Off B3139 Radstock Rd, signed The Horringtons, onto
Hawkers Ln to end

Rooms 9 rms (8 en suite) (1 pri facs) (2 fmly)
Facilities TVL tea/coffee Direct Dial Cen ht Lift Licensed
⛹ 🐦 childrens play area Parking 20 Notes Closed
25-26 Dec

Double-Gate Farm (ST484424)

★★★★ FARMHOUSE

Godney BA5 1RX
☎ 01458 832217 📄 01458 835612 Mrs H Millard
e-mail: doublegatefarm@aol.com
web: www.doublegatefarm.com
dir: A39 from Wells towards Glastonbury, at Polsham
right signed Godney/Polsham. 2m to x-rds, continue to
farmhouse on left after inn

Expect a warm welcome not only from the owners, but
also Jasper and Paddy, their friendly Retrievers. Set on
the banks of the River Sheppey on the Somerset Levels,
this comfortable farmhouse is well-known for its
attractive summer flower garden, as well as delicious
breakfasts. Guests have use of a games room, and free
internet access in the lounge.

Rooms 3 en suite 7 annexe en suite (5 fmly) (5 GF)
Facilities FTV TVL tea/coffee Dinner available Cen ht
Fishing Snooker Table tennis Parking 13 Notes ⊗ Closed
22 Dec-5 Jan 100 acres mixed

Riverside Grange

★★★★ BED AND BREAKFAST

Tanyard Ln, North Wootton BA4 4AE
☎ 01749 890761
e-mail: riversidegrange@hotmail.com
web: www.riversidegrange.co.uk
dir: 2.5m SE of Wells in North Wootton

A delightful restored tannery, built in 1853, the
foundations of which actually sit in the River Redlake,
which runs alongside the house. A warm welcome and
attentive service is guaranteed from the friendly
proprietor, who makes every effort to ensure guests feel
at home. The house, furnished throughout with rosewood,
is most comfortable. The bedrooms are stylishly co-
ordinated and guests may relax in the attractive garden
in summer or the cosy snug overlooking the orchard in
winter.

Rooms 2 rms (1 en suite) (1 pri facs) S £55; D £65*
Facilities tea/coffee Cen ht Wi-fi Parking 6 Notes ⊗ No
Children 10yrs Closed Xmas & New Year ⊛

The Crown at Wells

★★★★ INN

Market Place BA5 2RP
☎ 01749 673457 📄 01749 679792
e-mail: stay@crownatwells.co.uk
web: www.crownatwells.co.uk
dir: In Market Pl

Retaining its original features and period charm, this
historic inn is situated in the heart of the city, just a
short stroll from the cathedral. The building's frontage
has been used for film sets. Bedrooms, all with modern
facilities, vary in size and style. Public areas focus
around Anton's, the popular bistro, which offers a light
and airy environment and relaxed atmosphere. The Penn
Bar offers an alternative eating option and real ales.

Rooms 15 en suite (2 fmly) S £45-£90; D £90-£110*
Facilities FTV tea/coffee Dinner available Cen ht
Parking 10 Notes LB

See advert on opposite page

Glengarth House

★★★★ GUEST ACCOMMODATION

7 Glastonbury Rd BA5 1TW
☎ 01749 674792 📄 01749 674792
e-mail: glengarthhouse@tiscali.co.uk
dir: On A39 S, on left past mini-rdbt

This pleasant guest accommodation is located on the
edge of Wells, just a short walk from the central
attractions. A continental breakfast is provided in the
light and airy dining room. The comfortable bedrooms are

modern and brightly decorated, and guests will benefit from the limited off-road parking.

Rooms 5 en suite (1 fmly) S fr £35; D £60–£78*
Facilities tea/coffee Cen ht Wi-fi **Parking** 5 **Notes** LB ⊗ ♨

Highfield
★★★★ BED AND BREAKFAST

93 Portway BA5 2BR
☎ 01749 675330
dir: *Enter Wells & signs for A371 Cheddar, Highfield on Portway after last lights at top of hill*

Within walking distance of the city and cathedral, this delightful home maintains its Edwardian style and provides comfortable accommodation. A warm welcome is assured while bedrooms are well equipped. Breakfast is served at one large table in the smart dining room, which overlooks the pretty garden.

Rooms 3 en suite (1 fmly) **Facilities** tea/coffee Cen ht **Parking** 7 **Notes** ⊗ No Children 2yrs Closed 23 Dec–1 Jan ♨

Highgate Cottage
★★★★ BED AND BREAKFAST

Worth BA5 1LW
☎ 01749 674201 ▤ 01749 674201
dir: *B3139 into Worth, Pheasant pub on left, Highgate Cottage 200yds on right*

Located in the village of Worth to the west of Wells and set in two acres of land, access to this delightful stone cottage is over its own private bridge. The attractive bedrooms are comfortable and quiet. Full English breakfasts are served at individual tables in the lounge-dining room.

Rooms 2 en suite (1 fmly) **Facilities** tea/coffee Cen ht Wi-fi **Parking** 6 **Notes** Closed Dec–Jan ♨

Hollow Tree Farm
★★★★ GUEST ACCOMMODATION

Launcherley BA5 1QJ
☎ 01749 673715 & 07704 506513 ▤ 01749 673715
dir: *A39 from Wells for Glastonbury, 1st left at Brownes Garden Centre, farm 0.5m on right*

Delightfully appointed rooms with bright, cheery colour schemes and comfortable furnishings are provided at this non-working farm. Spectacular views of Wells Cathedral and Glastonbury Tor and delightful flower-filled gardens add to the charm. The friendly hosts are most welcoming and attentive, and home-baked bread, jams and marmalade are only a part of the delicious breakfast.

Rooms 2 en suite (1 fmly) (2 GF) S £30; D £50*
Facilities TVL tea/coffee Cen ht **Parking** 4 **Notes** ⊗ No Children 12yrs Closed mid Dec–mid Jan ♨

Market Place, Wells, Somerset BA5 2RP
Telephone: 01749 673457
Fax: 01749 679792
Email: stay@crownatwells.co.uk
Web: www.crownatwells.co.uk

the **Crown** *at* **Wells**
c. 1450

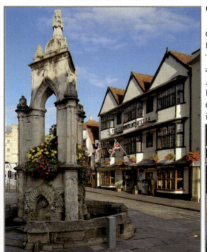

The Crown is a 15th-century coaching inn, offering affordable accommodation, in the heart of Wells, overlooking the Market Place.

Close to Wells Cathedral and the Bishop's Palace, The Crown is a great base from which to tour this fabulous part of Somerset.

There are fifteen, comfortably furnished, en-suite bedrooms, with four-poster and family rooms available.

A super variety of food and refreshments are served throughout the day in Anton's Bistrot and the Penn Bar at The Crown.

Guests are assured of good food and friendly service in a relaxed and comfortable atmosphere. Everyone is very welcome.

WELLS *continued*

Infield House

★★★★ BED AND BREAKFAST

36 Portway BA5 2BN
☎ 01749 670989   📠 01749 679093
e-mail: infield@talk21.com
web: www.infieldhouse.co.uk
dir: *500yds W of city centre on A371 Portway*

This charming Victorian house offers comfortable, spacious rooms of elegance and style. The friendly hosts are very welcoming and provide a relaxing home-from-home. Guests may bring their pets, by arrangement. Dinners, also by arrangement, are served in the pleasant dining room where good home cooking ensures an enjoyable and varied range of options.

Rooms 3 en suite; D £64-£66* **Facilities** tea/coffee Dinner available Cen ht Wi-fi **Parking** 3 **Notes** No Children 12yrs

Littlewell Farm

★★★★ GUEST ACCOMMODATION

Coxley BA5 1QP
☎ 01749 677914
e-mail: enquiries@littlewellfarm.co.uk
web: www.littlewellfarm.co.uk
dir: *A39 from Wells towards Glastonbury, farm 1m on right opp sign for Coxley*

This charming house stands in spacious gardens at Coxley, on the outskirts of Wells. It provides well-equipped accommodation and has a smart, comfortable lounge. Breakfast, featuring local produce when possible, is served in the bright, modern dining room at separate tables.

Rooms 5 rms (4 en suite) (1 pri facs) (1 GF) S £35-£40; D £60-£65* **Facilities** TVL tea/coffee Cen ht **Parking** 10 **Notes** ⊗ Closed 25 Dec 🐾

Amber House

★★★ BED AND BREAKFAST

Coxley BA5 1QZ
☎ 01749 679612
e-mail: amberhouse@wellscity27.freeserve.co.uk
dir: *On A39 in village, 0.25m S past Pound Inn on right*

Located just 1.5 miles south of the centre of Wells and ideally placed for touring the area's historic sites and countryside, this friendly family home offers a relaxed atmosphere. Bedrooms are well equipped; some look out over open countryside and farmland to the rear. A traditional English breakfast is served, at separate tables, in the cosy dining room, which guests are welcome to use at other times, if they so wish.

Rooms 2 en suite S £30; D £48-£55 **Facilities** FTV tea/coffee Cen ht **Parking** 3 **Notes** ⊗ 🐾

Birdwood House

★★★ GUEST ACCOMMODATION

Birdwood, Bath Rd BA5 3EW
☎ 01749 679250
e-mail: info@birdwood-bandb.co.uk
web: www.birdwood-bandb.co.uk
dir: *1.5m NE of city centre. On B3139 between South & West Horrington*

Set in extensive grounds and gardens just a short drive from the town centre, this imposing detached house dates from the 1850s. The bedrooms are comfortable and equipped with a number of extra facilities. Breakfast is served around a communal table in the pleasant dining room or conservatory, which is also available for guest use and enjoyment throughout the day.

Rooms 3 rms (2 en suite) (1 pri facs) (1 fmly) **Facilities** TVL tea/coffee Cen ht ♿ **Parking** 12 **Notes** LB 🐾

19 St Cuthbert Street

★★ BED AND BREAKFAST

BA5 2AW
☎ 01749 673166
dir: *At bottom of High St opp St Cuthbert's Church*

Guests are assured of a friendly welcome at this charming terrace house, which is within walking distance of the cathedral and bus station. The accommodation is fresh, light and comfortable and the atmosphere homely. Bedrooms are well appointed and there is a comfortable lounge. Breakfast, featuring home-made marmalade, is served in the dining room around a family table.

Rooms 2 rms S £30-£32.50; D fr £50* **Facilities** FTV TVL tea/coffee Cen ht **Notes** No Children 5yrs 🐾

WESTON-SUPER-MARE   Map 4 ST36

PREMIER COLLECTION

Church House

★★★★★ BED AND BREAKFAST

27 Kewstoke Rd, Kewstoke BS22 9YD
☎ 01934 633185
e-mail: churchhouse@kewstoke.net
web: www.churchhousekewstoke.co.uk
dir: *From M5 junct 21 follow signs for Kewstoke 2.5m, next to Kewstoke Church*

In a peaceful location at the foot of Monk's Hill, this delightful property enjoys wonderful views over the Bristol Channel and across to Wales on clear days. Bedrooms are stylish and spacious, with lots of thoughtful extras and well-equipped en suites. Public areas include a pleasant conservatory and an elegant dining room where impressive breakfasts are served.

Rooms 5 en suite **Facilities** tea/coffee Cen ht Wi-fi **Parking** 10 **Notes** LB

The Beaches

★★★★ GUEST ACCOMMODATION

36 Beach Rd BS23 1BG
☎ 01934 629529   📠 01934 629529
e-mail: info@beacheshotel.co.uk
dir: *M5 junct 21 onto A370, follow signs for beach*

This attractive Victorian property enjoys wonderful sea views from its front-facing bedrooms. Immaculately presented and family-run with a relaxed atmosphere, the accommodation is bright and comfortable, and parking is available at the rear.

Rooms 10 en suite (3 fmly) S £30-£35; D £55-£60* **Facilities** TVL tea/coffee Cen ht Wi-fi **Parking** 8 **Notes** LB ⊗ Closed 29 Oct-Mar

Beverley Guest House

★★★ GUEST HOUSE

11 Whitecross Rd BS23 1EP
☎ 01934 622956 📠 01934 622956
e-mail: beverley11@hushmail.com
web: www.beverleyguesthouse.co.uk
dir: Off A370 Beach Rd onto Ellenborough Park Rd South
& take 2nd right

Guests can expect to be warmly greeted at this Victorian
house which is set in a quiet residential street close to
the seafront, rail station and town centre. The
individually-styled bedrooms are thoughtfully equipped
and include a family suite. There is a small conservatory-
lounge next to the dining room, where hearty breakfasts,
using local produce, are served.

Rooms 5 en suite (3 fmly) (1 GF); D £60-£75*
Facilities tea/coffee Cen ht Wi-fi **Notes** LB ⊗ Closed
Xmas & New Year

Camellia Lodge

★★★★ BED AND BREAKFAST

76 Walliscote Rd BS23 1ED
☎ 01934 613534 📠 01934 613534
e-mail: dachefscamellia@aol.com
dir: 200yds from seafront

Guests return regularly for the warm welcome at this
immaculate Victorian family home, which is just off the
seafront and within walking distance of the town centre.
Bedrooms have a range of thoughtful touches, and
carefully prepared breakfasts are served in the relaxing
dining room. Home-cooked dinners are also available by
prior arrangement.

Rooms 5 en suite (2 fmly) S £27.50-£30; D £60-£65*
Facilities FTV tea/coffee Dinner available Cen ht Wi-fi
Notes ⊛

Jamesfield Guest House

★★★★ GUEST HOUSE

1A Ellenborough Park North BS23 1XH
☎ 01934 642898 📠 01934 624933
e-mail: jamesfield1@aol.com

A well-maintained property in an ideal location, a short
walk from the seafront and only a few minutes stroll from
town. Bedrooms are all comfortably furnished and well
decorated, and include rooms on the ground floor. Guests
are welcome to use the relaxing lounge, and the property
also benefits from its own car park.

Rooms 7 rms (6 en suite) (1 pri facs) (2 GF) S £30;
D £55* **Facilities** TVL tea/coffee Cen ht **Parking** 9
Notes ⊗

Linden Lodge Guest House

★★★★ GUEST ACCOMMODATION

27 Clevedon Rd BS23 1DA
☎ 01934 645797
e-mail: info@lindenlodge.com
dir: Follow signs to seafront. 0.5m S of grand pier turn
onto Clevedon Rd

Just a short walk from the town centre and the seafront,
Linden Lodge offers a traditional style of welcoming
hospitality and guest care. Bedrooms offer a range of
shapes and sizes and are all well decorated and
equipped. A good selection is offered at breakfast and
served in the pleasant conservatory.

Rooms 5 en suite (1 fmly) **Facilities** tea/coffee Cen ht
Parking 3 **Notes** ⊗

Oakover

★★★★ GUEST HOUSE

25 Clevedon Rd BS23 1DA
☎ 01934 620125 📠 01934 620173
e-mail: info@oakover.co.uk
web: www.oakover.co.uk
dir: Off A370 (Beach Rd) near Sea Life Aquarium onto
Clevedon Rd

Oakover is a substantial Victorian property situated a
short level walk from the town centre and seafront.
Bedrooms and bathrooms offer very good levels of quality
and comfort. A varied breakfast menu is offered in the
bright dining room. The friendly resident proprietor
maintains an easy-going and welcoming establishment.

Rooms 6 en suite (2 GF) S £42-£61.50; D £56-£82
Facilities tea/coffee Cen ht Wi-fi **Parking** 7 **Notes** ⊗ No
Children 12yrs

The Owls Crest House

★★★★ BED AND BREAKFAST

39 Kewstoke Rd, Kewstoke BS22 9YE
☎ 01934 417672
e-mail: theowlscrest1@btinternet.com
dir: M5 junct 21, A370 to Weston, 1st left towards
Kewstoke. Through 4 rdbts to T-junct in Kewstoke. Turn
left. Owls Crest House after New Inn pub

Located in the pleasant village of Kewstoke, guests will
find an especially friendly welcome from the resident Irish
hosts at this relaxed accommodation. Bedrooms and
bathrooms offer good comfort and provide plenty of useful
extras. Traditional home-cooked breakfasts are served in
the relaxing dining room. Guests are welcome to use the
comfortable lounge and a car park is also available.

Rooms 4 en suite (1 fmly) S £47-£49; D £60-£70*
Facilities TVL tea/coffee Cen ht Licensed Wi-fi **Parking** 5
Notes LB No Children 10yrs Closed 28 Dec-2 Jan &
annual holidays ⊛

Timbertop Aparthotel

Popular with business clients, golfing
parties and families. En-suite rooms, some
with micro kitchens. Also self-catering
suites for extended periods. Licensed bar
and guest lounge with wifi, access to fax
and photocopier. Speciality breakfast,
including fresh fruit (strawberries etc),
yoghurts, plus full English hot buffet. Car parking for 14 cars. Located
4½ miles J21/M5. 300 yards sea front, close to conference centre.

8 Victoria Park, Weston Super Mare, North Somerset BS23 2HZ

Contact: Rosemary Moncrieff
Tel: 01934 631178 or 424348   **Fax:** 01934 414716
Email: stay@aparthoteltimbertop.com

WESTON-SUPER-MARE *continued*

Rookery Manor

★★★★ 🍽 GUEST ACCOMMODATION

Edingworth Rd, Edingworth BS24 0JB
☎ 0845 4090909 📄 0845 4090908
e-mail: enquiries@rookery-manor.co.uk
web: www.rookery-manor.co.uk
dir: *M5 junct 22, A370 towards Weston, 2m right to Rookery Manor*

Situated in its own delightful gardens and grounds within easy reach of the M5 and all the resort attractions of Weston-Super-Mare, this 16th-century manor house is best known for its extensive wedding and conference facilities. Bedrooms, each with its own access to the garden, are modern and bright. A carte menu is offered in Truffles Restaurant.

Rooms 22 en suite (2 fmly) (10 GF) **Facilities** TVL tea/coffee Dinner available Direct Dial Cen ht Licensed 🏊 🐴 Golf 9 ⛳ Riding Snooker Pool Table **Conf** Max 800 Thtr 800 Class 120 Board 120 **Parking** 460 **Notes** LB ⊗ Civ Wed 400

Timbertop Aparthotel

★★★★ GUEST ACCOMMODATION

8 Victoria Park BS23 2HZ
☎ 01934 631178 & 424348 📄 01934 414716
e-mail: stay@aparthoteltimbertop.com
web: www.aparthoteltimbertop.com
dir: *Follow signs to pier, then 1st right after Winter Gardens, 1st left (Lower Church Rd). Left, then right to Timbertop*

Located in a quiet, mainly residential area, Timbertop offers a varied range of accommodation. All rooms are comfortably furnished and include a range of useful extras. A relaxed and friendly welcome is provided at all times by the resident proprietor. A small bar and seating area are also available.

Rooms 8 en suite 5 annexe en suite (2 fmly) **Facilities** TVL tea/coffee Cen ht Licensed Wi-fi **Parking** 15 **Notes** ⊗

See advert on page 315

Bella Vista

★★★ GUEST HOUSE

19 Upper Church Rd BS23 2DX
☎ 01934 631931 📄 01934 620126
web: www.bellavistawsm.co.uk
dir: *A370 to town and seafront, right past Grand Pier. Right after 300yds onto Upper Church Rd & right at x-rds*

Situated close to the seafront and town centre, this delightful terrace property has an attractive patio with seating at the front. The well decorated bedrooms have TVs and hospitality trays. There is a cosy dining room where full English breakfasts are served, and a large comfortable lounge is also available.

Rooms 8 en suite (3 fmly) **Facilities** TVL tea/coffee Cen ht **Notes** LB ⊗ Closed 12 Dec-2 Jan 🚭

Edelweiss Guest House

★★★ GUEST HOUSE

24 Clevedon Rd BS23 1DG
☎ 01934 624705 📄 01934 624705
e-mail: edelweissguesthouse@tiscali.co.uk
dir: *Turn onto Clevedon Rd off Beach Rd (Seafront) opposite Tropicana. Edelweiss 75yds on right*

Located in a residential area around a hundred yards from the seafront and beach, Edelweiss is a traditional and comfortable guest house run in a welcoming manner. Bedrooms vary in size but all are nicely decorated. Although dinner is not available, guests are welcome to select from a snack and beverage menu up until 10pm.

Rooms 5 rms (4 en suite) (1 pri facs) (3 fmly) (2 GF) S £25-£35; D £50-£70* **Facilities** FTV tea/coffee Cen ht **Notes** LB ⊗ Closed Xmas wk

Goodrington

★★★ GUEST HOUSE

23 Charlton Rd BS23 4HB
☎ 01934 623229
e-mail: vera.bishop@talk21.com
web: www.goodrington.info
dir: *A370 Beach Rd S onto Uphill Rd, left onto Charlton Rd*

The owners make every effort to ensure you enjoy your stay at this charming Victorian house tucked away in a quiet residential area. The bedrooms are comfortably furnished, and there is an attractive lounge. Families are especially welcome and this is a good holiday base.

Rooms 3 rms (2 en suite) (1 pri facs) (1 fmly) (1 GF) S £30-£35; D £50-£59* **Facilities** FTV TVL tea/coffee Dinner available Cen ht **Notes** LB ⊗ RS Oct-Mar 🚭

The Sunfold

★★★ GUEST ACCOMMODATION

39 Beach Rd BS23 1BG
☎ 01934 624700 📄 01934 624700
e-mail: enquiries@thesunfold.co.uk
web: www.sunfold-hotel.co.uk

Located right on the seafront opposite the Tropicana building, this family-run establishment offers a relaxed atmosphere and a friendly welcome. Traditionally-furnished bedrooms vary in size and include some with sea-facing views and a number of family rooms. Enjoyable home-cooked dinners are available in the downstairs dining room where a small bar is also open to guests.

Rooms 11 en suite (4 fmly) (2 GF) S £40-£60; D £60-£80* **Facilities** TVL tea/coffee Dinner available Cen ht Licensed **Parking** 5 **Notes** LB RS Xmas & New Year

Weston Bay Guest House

★★★ GUEST HOUSE

2-4 Clevedon Rd BS23 1DG
☎ 01934 628903 📄 01934 417661
e-mail: westonbayhotel@btinternet.com
web: www.westonbayhotel.co.uk
dir: *Opp Sea Quarium on seafront*

Located on the seafront, this family-run property has generally spacious, well-equipped bedrooms with modern en suites. The comfortable lounge and attractive breakfast room have sea views, and packed lunches are available on request. There is a small private car park.

Rooms 9 en suite (5 fmly) (1 GF) S £49-£55; D £65-£75* **Facilities** TVL tea/coffee Cen ht **Parking** 11 **Notes** LB ⊗ Closed mid Nov-mid Mar

Ynishir B&B

★★★ BED AND BREAKFAST

74 Uphill Way BS23 4TN
☎ 01934 412703 & 0771 495 0023
e-mail: simon.bilkus@homecall.co.uk
dir: *A370 follow signs to hospital (Grange Rd), right at mini-rdbt, left onto Uphill Way*

Set in pleasant countryside in the quiet village of Uphill, just a short distance from the Channel, Ynishir has one bedroom with private facilities, and would be ideal for anyone who wants to walk the Mendip Way.

Rooms 1 en suite (1 fmly) (1 GF) **Facilities** FTV TVL tea/coffee Cen ht **Parking** 1 **Notes** 🚭

Corbiere

★★ GUEST HOUSE

24 Upper Church Rd BS23 2DX
☎ 01934 629607 📄 01934 629607
e-mail: corbierehotel@aol.com
dir: *M5 junct 21 take A370 to town/seafront. Turn right for pier along Knightstone Rd, approx 300yds turn right onto Upper Church Rd & right at x-rds*

Located within walking distance of the city centre, this charming house maintains its Victorian style. Friendly proprietors make every effort to ensure a stay is pleasant and memorable, and the attractive bedrooms have many considerate extras. There is a lounge, and freshly cooked breakfasts are served in the pleasant dining room.

Rooms 10 en suite (4 fmly) (2 GF) S £20-£28; D £40-£56* **Facilities** TVL tea/coffee Dinner available Cen ht **Notes** LB ⊗ 🚭

WHEDDON CROSS
Map 3 SS93

North Wheddon Farm *(SS923385)*

★★★★ 🏠 🍴 FARMHOUSE

TA24 7EX
☎ 01643 841791   Mrs R Abraham
e-mail: rachael@go-exmoor.co.uk
web: www.go-exmoor.co.uk
dir: *500yds S of village x-rds on A396. Pass Moorland Hall on left, driveway next right*

North Wheddon Farm is a delightfully friendly and comfortable environment with great views. The tranquil grounds include a pleasant garden, and the memorable dinners and breakfasts feature local and the farm's own fresh produce. The bedrooms are thoughtfully equipped, and beds are most comfortable.

Rooms 3 rms (2 en suite) (1 pri facs) S £35-£40; D £70-£80 **Facilities** tea/coffee Dinner available Cen ht Licensed Wi-fi Riding **Parking** 5 **Notes** LB 20 acres mixed

The Rest and Be Thankful Inn

★★★★ INN

TA24 7DR
☎ 01643 841222   📠 01643 841813
e-mail: stay@restandbethankful.co.uk
dir: *M5 junct 25, A358 to Minehead, left onto B3224 at sign to Wheddon Cross*

The Rest and be Thankful stands in the highest village on Exmoor overlooking Dunkery Beacon. The comfortable bedrooms are extremely well equipped with extras such as mini-bars and trouser presses. The convivial bar, complete with crackling log fires is a popular meeting point for locals and visitors alike. A range of wholesome dishes is offered either in the bar, restaurant and outside on the patio.

Rooms 8 en suite (1 fmly) **Facilities** tea/coffee Dinner available Direct Dial Cen ht Wi-fi Pool Table Skittle alley **Conf** Max 50 Class 50 Board 50 **Parking** 10 **Notes** ⊗ Closed 25 Dec

WILLITON
Map 3 ST04

The White House

★★★★ GUEST HOUSE

11 Long St TA4 4QW
☎ 01984 632306   📠 01984 634639
e-mail: thewhitehouse@stefanroberts.orangehome.co.uk
dir: *A39 Bridgwater to Minehead, In Williton on right prior to Watchet turning*

A relaxed and easy-going atmosphere is the hallmark of this charming Georgian property. Bedrooms in the main building are more spacious than those in the courtyard, but all are well equipped with extra touches that make the White House a home-from-home.

Rooms 8 rms (7 en suite) (1 pri facs) 6 annexe en suite (2 fmly) (6 GF) S £30-£50; D £60-£80* **Facilities** FTV tea/coffee Dinner available Cen ht Licensed **Parking** 12 **Notes** LB

WINCANTON
Map 4 ST72

Brookleigh

★★★★ BED AND BREAKFAST

Holton BA9 8AE
☎ 01963 34685
e-mail: theclementss@hotmail.com
dir: *A371 from Wincanton towards Templecombe, at rdbt 1st exit onto A357, B&B signed*

Just a stone's throw from the A303, this well-kept family home is a good stopover and a useful base for touring Somerset and Wiltshire, with easy access to both Stourhead and Longleat. The clean, fresh bedrooms are attractively co-ordinated, and there is also a lounge. Breakfast, served in the conservatory dining room, features eggs laid by the neighbour's chickens.

Rooms 3 en suite S £35; D £55* **Facilities** TVL tea/coffee Cen ht **Parking** 6 **Notes** ⊗ ✉

WINSFORD
Map 3 SS93

Karslake House

★★★★ 🏆 GUEST HOUSE

Halse Ln TA24 7JE
☎ 01643 851242   📠 01643 851242
e-mail: enquiries@karslakehouse.co.uk
web: www.karslakehouse.co.uk
dir: *In village centre, past pub, up hill*

The 15th-century Karslake House stands in a peaceful Exmoor village. Its public rooms feature original beams and fireplaces, and an interesting menu of delicious dishes is available in the dining room. Bedrooms are thoughtfully furnished and have a number of extra touches.

Rooms 6 rms (5 en suite) (1 pri facs) (1 GF) **Facilities** tea/coffee Dinner available Cen ht Licensed Aromatherapist & Masseuse **Parking** 15 **Notes** No Children 12yrs Closed Feb & Mar RS Nov-Jan Limited opening by request

WITHYPOOL
Map 3 SS83

PREMIER COLLECTION

Kings Farm

★★★★★ 🖥 BED AND BREAKFAST

TA24 7RE
☎ 01643 831381   📠 01643 831381
e-mail: info@kingsfarmexmoor.co.uk
dir: *Off B3223 to Withypool, over bridge & sharp left to farm*

Over two acres of landscaped gardens beside the river form the backdrop of this delightful farmhouse, set in an idyllic valley beside the Barle. It combines all the character and charm of its 19th-century origins with every modern comfort. From the carefully planned bedrooms to the sumptuously furnished sitting room, delicious home-cooked breakfasts and the warmest of welcomes, top quality is most definitely the hallmark of Kings Farm. Stabling and fishing available.

Rooms 2 rms (1 en suite) (1 pri facs) S £58; D £85-£95* **Facilities** STV tea/coffee Cen ht Wi-fi Fishing **Parking** 3 **Notes** No Children 14yrs

WITHYPOOL *continued*

The Royal Oak Inn

★★★★ 🍴 INN

TA24 7QP
☎ 01643 831506 📄 01643 831659
e-mail: enquiries@royaloakwithypool.co.uk
dir: 7m N of Dulverton, off B3223

Set at the heart of Exmoor, this long established and popular inn continues to provide rest and sustenance for weary travellers. The atmosphere is warm and engaging with the bar always frequented by cheery locals. Bedrooms and bathrooms are stylish and very well appointed with added touches of luxury such as Egyptian cotton linen, bath robes and cosseting towels. Menus feature local produce and can be enjoyed either in the bars or in the elegant restaurant.

Rooms 8 rms (7 en suite) (1 pri facs) **Facilities** tea/coffee Dinner available Direct Dial Cen ht **Parking** 10 **Notes** LB No Children 10yrs No coaches

---

WIVELISCOMBE — Map 3 ST02

White Hart

★★★★ INN

West St TA4 2JP
☎ 01984 623344 📄 01984 624748
e-mail: reservations@whitehartwiveliscombe.co.uk
dir: M5 junct 25 then A38 to Taunton. Follow signs for A358 to Minehead then B3227 to Wiveliscombe

This establishment is the focal point of this delightful town situated near the foot of the Quantock Hills. Exmoor is on the doorstep and the coast is just a few miles drive away. Bedrooms are contemporary with a good range of facilities. Innovative dishes are offered in the restaurant and the bar has good range of locally brewed beers.

Rooms 16 en suite (2 fmly) S £55-£65; D £70-£90 **Facilities** FTV tea/coffee Dinner available Direct Dial Cen ht Wi-fi Skittle alley **Conf** Max 30 Thtr 30 Class 15 Board 15 **Parking** 12

YEOVIL — Map 4 ST51

See also Crewkerne

PREMIER COLLECTION

Little Barwick House

★★★★★ 🍴🍴🍴 RESTAURANT WITH ROOMS

Barwick Village BA22 9TD
☎ 01935 423902 📄 01935 420908
e-mail: littlebarwick@hotmail.com
dir: From Yeovil A37 towards Dorchester, left at 1st rdbt, 1st left, 0.25m on left

Situated in a quiet hamlet in three and half acres of gardens and grounds, this listed Georgian dower house is an ideal retreat for those seeking peaceful surroundings and good food. Just one of the highlights of a stay here is a meal in the restaurant, where good use is made of local ingredients. Each of the bedrooms has its own character, and a range of thoughtful extras such as fresh flowers, bottled water and magazines.

Rooms 6 en suite **Facilities** tea/coffee Dinner available Direct Dial Cen ht **Parking** 30 **Notes** LB No Children 5yrs RS Sun eve & Mon Closed No coaches

---

The Masons Arms

★★★★ 🍴🍴 INN

41 Lower Odcombe BA22 8TX
☎ 01935 862591 📄 01935 862591
e-mail: paula@masonsarmsodcombe.co.uk
web: www.masonsarmsodcombe.co.uk
dir: From A303 take A3088 to Yeovil, follow signs to Montacute after village, 3rd turning on right

Dating back to the 16th century, this charming inn claims to be the oldest building in this small country village on the outskirts of Yeovil. The spacious bedrooms are contemporary in style, with clean lines, high level of comfort and a wide range of considerate extras. The friendly hosts run their own micro-brewery, and their ales are available at the bar along with others. Public areas include the bar/restaurant, which offers a full menu of freshly prepared dishes, along with a choice of lighter snacks. There is a small caravan/touring park at the rear of the inn.

Rooms 6 en suite (1 fmly) (6 GF) S £55-£70; D £85* **Facilities** FTV tea/coffee Dinner available Direct Dial Cen ht Wi-fi **Conf** Max 15 Class 15 Board 15 **Parking** 35 **Notes** No coaches

---

The Helyar Arms

★★★★ 🍴 INN

Moor Ln, East Coker BA22 9JR
☎ 01935 862332 📄 01935 864129
e-mail: info@helyar-arms.co.uk
dir: 3m S of Yeovil. Off A30 or A37 into East Coker

A charming 15th-century inn, serving real food in the heart of a pretty Somerset village. The traditional friendly bar with hand-drawn ales retains many original features while the bedrooms offer well equipped, attractive accommodation and modern facilities.

Rooms 6 en suite (3 fmly) S £65; D £89* **Facilities** tea/coffee Dinner available Direct Dial Cen ht Wi-fi Skittle alley **Conf** Max 40 Thtr 40 Class 20 Board 30 **Parking** 40 **Notes** LB

The Halfway House Inn Country Lodge

★★★ INN

Ilchester Rd BA22 8RE
☎ 01935 840350 📄 01935 849006
e-mail: paul@halfwayhouseinn.com
web: www.halfwayhouseinn.com
dir: A303 onto A37 Yeovil road at Ilchester, inn 2m on left

This roadside inn offers comfortable accommodation, which consists of bedrooms in the main house and other contemporary style rooms, each having its own front door, in the annexe. All rooms are bright and well equipped. Meals of generous portion are available in the cosy restaurant and bar, where friendly staff ensure a warm welcome.

Rooms 11 en suite 9 annexe en suite (7 fmly) (9 GF) **Facilities** STV tea/coffee Dinner available Cen ht Wi-fi Fishing Pool Table **Conf** Max 120 Thtr 120 Class 50 Board 40 **Parking** 49 **Notes** LB

City Lodge Yeovil

★★★ GUEST ACCOMMODATION

South Western Ter BA20 1NB
☎ 01935 706655 📄 01935 424449
e-mail: yeovil@citylodge.biz
dir: In centre of Yeovil, opp Yeovale Leisure Park

A beautifully restored 18th-century building houses this modern lodge accommodation which is in walking distance of Yeovil centre. All rooms are en suite with bath and power shower along with extra modern amenities such as flat-screen TVs and free Wi-fi. Breakfast is continental and served in the privacy of your room.

Rooms 30 en suite (3 fmly) (10 GF) S £50-£54; D £54-£69 (room only) **Facilities** FTV tea/coffee Cen ht Wi-fi **Notes** ⊗

The Half Moon Inn

★★★ INN

Main St, Mudford BA21 5TF
☎ 01935 850289 📠 01935 850842
e-mail: enquiries@thehalfmooninn.co.uk
dir: A303 at Sparkford onto A359 to Yeovil, 3.5m on left

Situated north of Yeovil, this delightful village inn dates from the 17th century. It has a wealth of character, enhanced by exposed beams and flagstone floors. The inn is very popular for its extensive range of wholesome food, and there is a choice of bar and dining area. Most of the spacious, well-equipped bedrooms are on the ground floor of a separate adjacent building.

Rooms 14 en suite (4 fmly) (9 GF) S £59.95; D £64.95 (room only) Facilities STV FTV tea/coffee Dinner available Cen ht Wi-fi Parking 36 Notes ⊗ Closed 25-26 Dec

STAFFORDSHIRE

ABBOTS BROMLEY   Map 10 SK02

Marsh Farm (SK069261)

★★★★ FARMHOUSE

WS15 3EJ
☎ 01283 840323 Mrs M K Hollins
e-mail: marshfarm@meads1967.co.uk
dir: 1m N of Abbots Bromley on B5013

Guests are welcome to walk around the fields at this working farm and watch the activities. The farmhouse has been modernised and bedrooms are carefully furnished and equipped; three rooms are located in a sympathetic barn conversion. Comprehensive breakfasts are served in the spacious cottage-style dining room, which operates as a popular tea room during the summer.

Rooms 5 rms (3 en suite) (1 fmly) (1 GF) S £32-£35; D £55-£60* Facilities TVL tea/coffee Cen ht Parking 6 Notes ⊗ Closed 25-27 Dec 20 acres mixed

ALTON   Map 10 SK04

Chained Oak Farm

★★★★ GUEST ACCOMMODATION

Farley Ln ST10 4BZ
☎ 01538 702104
e-mail: cross@barn.fslife.co.uk
web: www.chainedoak.com
dir: Between Alton & Farley, opp Alton Towers

This modern detached house stands in delightful grounds including extensive woodlands and affords fine all-round views. It is very close to Alton Towers and offers spacious bedrooms, three of which are located in the renovated former stables. Families are especially welcome and warm hospitality is assured.

Rooms 1 en suite 3 annexe en suite (2 fmly) (4 GF)
Facilities TVL tea/coffee Cen ht Parking 10 Notes ⊗ ⊗

BREWOOD   Map 10 SJ80

The Old Vicarage

★★★★ BED AND BREAKFAST

Vicarage Rd ST19 9HA
☎ 01902 850210
dir: From A449 to Brewood, right onto The Pavement, then right onto Vicarage Rd, on left

Located close to the village centre, this elegant period house stands in pretty mature gardens and has been sympathetically renovated to provide modern facilities, while retaining lots of character. Bedrooms provide a wealth of thoughtful extras, and comprehensive breakfasts are taken at an antique oak table in the dining room, which overlooks the grounds.

Rooms 3 rms (2 en suite) (1 pri facs) S fr £38; D £62-£68* Facilities FTV tea/coffee Cen ht Wi-fi Parking 5 Notes ⊗ Closed Xmas & New Year ⊗

BURTON UPON TRENT   Map 10 SK22

The Delter

★★★★ GUEST ACCOMMODATION

5 Derby Rd DE14 1RU
☎ 01283 535115 📠 01283 845261
e-mail: info@delterhotel.co.uk
web: www.thedelter.co.uk
dir: A511 rdbt onto A5121 (Derby Rd), 50yds on left

This relaxing guest house is on the outskirts of Burton upon Trent, close to the famous Bass Museum. Bedrooms are thoughtfully equipped and carefully decorated, while the public areas consist of a pleasant breakfast room. Expect friendly and attentive service.

Rooms 7 en suite (2 fmly) (2 GF) Facilities FTV tea/coffee Cen ht Wi-fi Parking 8 Notes ⊗ Closed Xmas

The Edgecote

★★★★ GUEST HOUSE

179 Ashby Rd DE15 0LB
☎ 01283 568966 📠 01283 740118
e-mail: susanmccabe@hotmail.co.uk
dir: 0.5m E of town centre on A511

Located in a residential area on the outskirts of town, this impressive Edwardian house provides a range of thoughtfully-equipped bedrooms, with either en suite or with private facilities. A comprehensive breakfast is served in the oak-panelled dining room and there is a quiet lounge.

Rooms 11 rms (5 en suite) (2 pri facs) (1 fmly) S £35-£59; D £55-£69* Facilities tea/coffee Cen ht Wi-fi Parking 6 Notes ⊗

CHEDDLETON   Map 16 SJ95

PREMIER COLLECTION

Choir Cottage and Choir House

★★★★★ BED AND BREAKFAST

Ostlers Ln ST13 7HS
☎ 01538 360561 & 07719 617078
e-mail: enquiries@choircottage.co.uk
dir: Off A520 opp Red Lion onto Hollow Ln, pass church & left onto Ostlers Ln, cottage on right at top of hill

Original features complement this carefully decorated 17th-century stone cottage. The bedrooms have lots of thoughtful extras and feature four-poster beds, modern bathrooms and private entrances. Spacious lounge areas are available in an adjacent house, and the attractive dining room is the setting for breakfast.

Rooms 1 en suite 2 annexe en suite (1 fmly) (2 GF) S £50-£59; D £70-£75* Facilities tea/coffee Direct Dial Cen ht Wi-fi Parking 5 Notes LB ⊗ Closed Xmas ⊗

Prospect House

★★★★ GUEST HOUSE

334 Cheadle Rd ST13 7BW
☎ 01782 550639
e-mail: prospect@talk21.com
web: www.prospecthouseleek.co.uk
dir: 4m S of Leek on A520

Prospect House was built from local stone in 1838, and is situated between Cheddleton and Wetley Rocks. Bedrooms are in a converted coach house behind the house, and facilities include a traditionally-furnished dining room together with a cosy lounge, and a pleasant garden with a conservatory.

Rooms 4 en suite (1 GF) S £30; D £60* Facilities FTV TVL tea/coffee Dinner available Direct Dial Cen ht Wi-fi Parking 4 Notes LB ⊗

ECCLESHALL Map 15 SJ82

Slindon House Farm (SJ826324)

★★★★ FARMHOUSE

Slindon ST21 6LX
☎ 01782 791237 Mrs H Bonsall
e-mail: helenbonsall@btconnect.com
dir: 2m N of Eccleshall on A519

This large, charming, Victorian farmhouse is fronted by a lovely garden and situated on a dairy, arable and sheep farm in the village of Slindon some 2 miles from Eccleshall. It has one twin and one double-bedded room, both of which are thoughtfully equipped. Breakfast is served at individual tables in the traditionally-furnished combined breakfast room and lounge.

Rooms 2 rms (1 en suite) (1 pri facs) S £40; D £60 Facilities TVL tea/coffee Cen ht Wi-fi Parking 4 Notes ⊗ Closed 23 Dec-3 Jan ⊛ 175 acres arable/dairy/sheep/beef

EDINGALE Map 10 SK21

Oakwood Barn B&B

★★★ BED AND BREAKFAST

Oakwood Barn, Lullington Rd B79 9JA
☎ 01827 383916
e-mail: edingalequeenbee@yahoo.co.uk
dir: From Lichfield take A38, right onto A513. Left towards Croxall, then right towards Edingdale, 900mtrs on Lullington Road, B&B on right

Oakwood Barn dates back to the 16th century and is set in the wonderful Staffordshire countryside. The well equipped en suite bedrooms provide good comfort. Awake to the early morning dawn chorus of birds and enjoy a hearty breakfast with eggs supplied by the chickens in the garden.

Rooms 1 en suite 1 annexe en suite (1 GF) S £60-£65; D £70-£75* Facilities FTV tea/coffee Cen ht Wi-fi Parking 6 Notes LB ⊗ No Children Closed Xmas & New Year ⊛

FROGHALL Map 10 SK04

Hermitage Working Farm (SK037497)

★★★ FARMHOUSE

ST10 2HQ
☎ 01538 266515 📠 01538 266155 Mrs W Barlow
e-mail: wilma@hermitagefarm.co.uk
web: www.hermitagefarm.co.uk
dir: A52 onto B5053 in Froghall, farm 0.5m on left at top of hill

Parts of this charming sandstone house date from the 16th century. It is quietly located on an elevated position with panoramic views. There is traditionally-furnished accommodation in the main house as well as a converted barn that offers rooms suitable for families. Handy for visiting Alton Towers.

Rooms 3 en suite 6 annexe en suite (3 fmly) (3 GF) Facilities tea/coffee Cen ht Wi-fi Shooting Parking 13 Notes LB ⊗ 100 acres beef/sheep/poultry

KINGSLEY Map 10 SK04

The Church Farm (SK013466)

★★★★ FARMHOUSE

Holt Ln ST10 2BA
☎ 01538 754759 Mrs Jane Clowes
e-mail: thechurchfarm@yahoo.co.uk
dir: Off A52 in Kingsley onto Holt Ln, 150mtrs on right opposite school drive

A warm welcome is assured at this charming farmhouse situated in the village of Kingsley. Thoughtfully equipped bedrooms with stylish furnishing are available in the main house. A hearty breakfast is served on individual tables overlooking the cottage gardens.

Rooms 3 en suite S £28-£30; D £50-£55 Facilities TV2B FTV TVL Cen ht Parking 6 Notes ⊗ ⊛ 100 acres dairy/beef

LEEK Map 16 SJ95

Peak Weavers Rooms & Restaurant

★★★★ ⊛ GUEST ACCOMMODATION

King St ST13 5NW
☎ 01538 383729 📠 01538 387475
e-mail: info@peakweavershotel.co.uk
web: www.peakweavershotel.co.uk
dir: In town centre behind St Mary's Church, off A53

Peak Weavers, formerly a convent to the Catholic church, stands in it own grounds close to Leek town centre. Bedrooms have been modernised to provide quality accommodation. The restaurant features traditional dishes using local produce. Service is friendly and obliging.

Rooms 6 rms (5 en suite) (1 pri facs) (1 fmly) (1 GF) S £35-£60; D £80* Facilities FTV tea/coffee Dinner available Cen ht Licensed Wi-fi Conf Max 30 Thtr 30 Class 20 Board 25 Parking 15 Notes ⊗

LICHFIELD Map 10 SK10

Coppers End

★★★★ GUEST ACCOMMODATION

Walsall Rd, Muckley Corner WS14 0BG
☎ 01543 372910 📠 01543 360423
e-mail: info@coppersendguesthouse.co.uk
web: www.coppersendguesthouse.co.uk
dir: A5 onto A461 N for 100yds

Formerly the police station, this family-run guest house provides well-appointed modern accommodation. Two bedrooms are on the ground floor, and most have smart en suites. There is a comfortable lounge, and breakfast is served in a modern conservatory overlooking the pretty rear gardens.

Rooms 6 rms (4 en suite) (2 GF) S £35-£39; D £52-£58* Facilities FTV TVL tea/coffee Cen ht Wi-fi Parking 9 Notes LB ⊗ Closed Xmas & New Year

Netherstowe House

★★★★ GUEST HOUSE

Netherstowe Ln WS13 6AY
☎ 01543 254270 📠 01543 254270
e-mail: reservations@netherstowehouse.com
web: www.netherstowehouse.com
dir: A38 onto A5192, 0.3m on right, turn onto Netherstowe Ln. Take 1st left & 1st right down private drive

Located in a residential area a few minutes drive from city centre, this elegant Georgian house provides a range of bedrooms, some of which are quite spacious. Comprehensive breakfasts are taken in a cosy dining room and a comfortable guest lounge is also available.

Rooms 12 en suite 8 annexe en suite (2 fmly) (5 GF) Facilities FTV TVL tea/coffee Cen ht Wi-fi ⊛ Gymnasium Parking 35 Notes ⊗

The Hawthorns

★★★ BED AND BREAKFAST

30 Norwich Close WS13 7SJ
☎ 01543 250151
e-mail: bambrushton@hotmail.com
dir: 1m N of city centre. Off A5192 Eastern Av nr Vauxhall garage onto Norwich Clo

Located in a residential area on the outskirts of the city, this modern house provides two homely bedrooms with separate side entrance and a modern private shower room. Breakfast is taken in an attractive kitchen/dining room overlooking a pretty rear garden.

Rooms 2 en suite (2 GF) S £36; D £50 Facilities tea/coffee Cen ht Wi-fi Parking 2 Notes ⊗ No Children ⊛

The Beehive Guest House

★★★★ GUEST HOUSE

Churnet View Rd ST10 3AE
☎ **01538 702420** 📠 **01538 703735**
e-mail: thebeehiveoakamoor@btinternet.com
web: www.thebeehiveguesthouse.co.uk
dir: *Off B5417 in village N onto Eaves Ln, sharp left onto Churnet View Rd*

Standing in the centre of the village and overlooking the river, this spacious detached house offers thoughtfully equipped and comfortable bedrooms. There is also a comfortable lounge-dining room, where substantial breakfasts are served. This guest house is renowned for its hospitality.

Rooms 5 en suite (1 fmly) (1 GF) S £35-£54; D £54-£60*
Facilities TVL tea/coffee Dinner available Cen ht
Parking 6 **Notes** LB ⊗ No Children 5yrs

Crowtrees Farm (SK049459)

★★★★ FARMHOUSE

Eaves Ln ST10 3DY
☎ **01538 702260**   Mrs D Bickle
e-mail: dianne@crowtreesfarm.co.uk
web: www.crowtreesfarm.co.uk
dir: *Off B5417 in village N onto Eaves Ln, 1m on left*

This impeccably maintained 200-year-old farmhouse is convenient for the Potteries, the Peak District and Alton Towers. Bedrooms are comfortable and well equipped. It is still a working farm with splendid views, and has a variety of pets. The friendly owners create a relaxing atmosphere.

Rooms 3 en suite 5 annexe en suite (2 fmly); D £52-£55
Facilities tea/coffee Cen ht **Parking** 8 **Notes** LB ⊗
Closed 25-26 Dec 55 acres beef/sheep

The Laurels Guest House

★★★★ GUEST HOUSE

Star Bank ST10 3BN
☎ **01538 702629** 📠 **01538 702796**
e-mail: bbthelaurels@aol.com
web: www.thelaurels.co.uk
dir: *On B5147 from Cheadle, 250yds on right past Cricketers Arms public house in Oakamoor*

At the edge of Oakamoor village, offering comfortable bedrooms and a bar lounge and a spacious dining room, this friendly guest house is ideally located for families wishing to visit Alton Towers or touring rural Staffordshire and the Potteries.

Rooms 9 en suite (5 fmly) (1 GF) **Facilities** FTV TVL tea/coffee Dinner available Cen ht Licensed Pool Table **Parking** 9 **Notes** ⊗

Tenement Farm

★★★★ GUEST ACCOMMODATION

Three Lows, Ribden ST10 3BW
☎ **01538 702333** 📠 **01538 703603**
e-mail: stanleese@aol.com
web: www.tenementfarm.co.uk
dir: *2m NE of Oakamoor. Off A52 onto B5417, 1st drive on left, signed*

Families are particularly welcome at this non-smoking former farmhouse, which has been renovated to provide high standards of comfort throughout. Popular with visitors to Alton Towers, bedrooms are equipped with homely extras. Public areas include a comfortable lounge with honesty bar, an attractive dining room and a children's play room.

Rooms 8 en suite (6 fmly) (2 GF) **Facilities** TVL tea/coffee Dinner available Cen ht Licensed **Parking** 12 **Notes** ⊗ Closed Nov-Feb

Admirals House

★★★ GUEST HOUSE

Mill Rd ST10 3AG
☎ **01538 702187**
e-mail: admiralshouse@btinternet.com
dir: *A52 onto B5417. In Oakamoor opposite picnic site*

Within the heart of the village a few minutes drive from Alton Towers, this half-timbered house is a popular community meeting point for a range of tasty bar meals and real ales. Homely bedrooms are equipped with thoughtful extras and family rooms are also available.

Rooms 6 en suite (4 fmly) (1 GF) S £25-£35; D £50*
Facilities tea/coffee Dinner available Cen ht Licensed
Parking 10 **Notes** ⊗ Closed 23 Dec-3 Jan RS Nov-Mar Restaurant closed Sun & Mon eve

PREMIER COLLECTION

Colton House

★★★★★ 🏛 GUEST HOUSE

Colton WS15 3LL
☎ **01889 578580** 📠 **01889 578580**
e-mail: mail@coltonhouse.com
web: www.coltonhouse.com
dir: *1.5m N of Rugeley. Off B5013 into Colton, 0.25m on right*

Set in the pretty village of Colton, this elegant early 18th-century house has been restored to retain original character and provide high standards of comfort and facilities. Bedrooms have a wealth of thoughtful extras, there is a spacious and comfortable lounge and a 1.5 acre garden.

Rooms 6 en suite S £50-£75; D £66-£96*
Facilities FTV TVL tea/coffee Dinner available Cen ht Licensed Wi-fi **Conf** Max 15 Thtr 15 Class 15 Board 15 **Parking** 15 **Notes** ⊗ No Children 12yrs

Ye Olde Dun Cow

Ⓤ

73 High St, Colton WS15 3LG
☎ **01889 584026** 📠 **01889 570869**
e-mail: winter665@btinternet.com
dir: *M6 junct 11 towards Cannock, take A460 to Rugeley onto B5013 to Colton*

Currently the rating for this establishment is not confirmed. This may be due to a change of ownership or because it has only recently joined the AA rating scheme. For up-to-date information please see the AA website: theAA.com

Rooms 4 rms (2 en suite) (2 pri facs) S fr £45; D fr £55*
Facilities STV FTV tea/coffee Dinner available Cen ht Licensed Fishing **Parking** 32 **Notes** ⊗

STAFFORD Map 10 SJ92

Haywood Park Farm *(SJ991207)*
★★★★ FARMHOUSE

Shugborough ST17 0XA
☎ 01889 882736 ▤ 01889 882736 Mr T Nichols
e-mail: haywood.parkfarm@btopenworld.com
web: www.haywoodparkfarm.co.uk
dir: *4m SE of Stafford off A513. Brown signs to Shugborough, on right 400yds past estate exit*

Part of the Shugborough Estate, this historic house commands panoramic views over the fruit, flower and sheep farm. Delightfully furnished bedrooms have a wealth of thoughtful extras, and breakfast is served in the attractive lounge-dining room and features home grown and local produce

Rooms 2 en suite S £60-£75; D £80-£85* **Facilities** STV TVL tea/coffee Cen ht Fishing Riding **Parking** 4 **Notes** LB ⊗ No Children 14 yrs ▣ 120 acres sheep/horse livery/fruit

Leonards Croft
★★★ GUEST HOUSE

80 Lichfield Rd ST17 4LP
☎ 01785 223676 ▤ 01785 223676
e-mail: leonardscroft@hotmail.com
dir: *A34 from town centre signed Cannock, 0.5m on left*

Located south of the town centre, this well-proportioned late Victorian house has been carefully renovated to provide a range of practically furnished bedrooms, two of which are situated on the ground floor. A range of popular evening dishes is available in addition to comprehensive breakfasts, and a spacious lounge is also available. The gardens are extensive.

Rooms 9 en suite (3 fmly) (2 GF) **Facilities** TVL tea/coffee Dinner available Cen ht Licensed **Parking** 12

Old School
★★★ BED AND BREAKFAST

Newport Rd, Haughton ST18 9JH
☎ 01785 780358 ▤ 01785 780358
e-mail: info@theoldsc.co.uk
dir: *A518 W from Stafford, 3m to Haughton, Old School next to church*

Located in the heart of Haughton, this Grade II listed former Victorian school has been renovated to provide a range of modern bedrooms equipped with thoughtful extras. The three rooms include a single, a double and a twin. All three have colour TV. Breakfast is served at a family table in a cosy lounge-dining room.

Rooms 3 rms (3 GF) S £25; D £50 **Facilities** tea/coffee Cen ht **Parking** 3 **Notes** ▣

The Windsor
★★ GUEST HOUSE

69 Lichfield Rd ST17 4LW
☎ 01785 258531 ▤ 01785 246875
e-mail: info@abbeyhotelstafford.co.uk
dir: *0.6m SE of town centre on A34*

The Windsor is popular with contractors and overseas students. It has a range of practically equipped bedrooms, and a large car park. Breakfast is served in the dining room of the adjacent Abbey Hotel, which is under the same ownership.

Rooms 14 rms (3 en suite) **Facilities** FTV TVL tea/coffee Dinner available Cen ht Licensed **Parking** 16 **Notes** ⊗ Closed 21 Dec-6 Jan

STONE Map 10 SJ93

Field House
★★★ BED AND BREAKFAST

59 Stafford Rd ST15 0HE
☎ 01785 605712 ▤ 01785 605712
e-mail: fieldhouse@ntlworld.com
dir: *A34 NW into town centre, right onto Stafford Rd, opp Walton Grange*

This family home stands in secluded, pretty gardens close to the town centre. The Georgian house has traditionally furnished bedrooms, some with family

pieces. Guests breakfast together in the lounge-dining room, and hospitality is very welcoming.

Rooms 3 rms (1 en suite) (2 fmly) **Facilities** TVL tea/coffee Cen ht Art tuition on request **Parking** 4 **Notes** ⊗ ▣

TAMWORTH Map 10 SK20

PREMIER COLLECTION

Oak Tree Farm
★★★★★ GUEST ACCOMMODATION

Hints Rd, Hopwas B78 3AA
☎ 01827 56807 ▤ 01827 67271
e-mail: oaktreefarm1@aol.com
web: www.oaktreefarmhotel.co.uk
dir: *2m NW of Tamworth. Off A51 in Hopwas*

A warm welcome is assured at this sympathetically restored farmhouse, located in peaceful rural surroundings yet only a short drive from the NEC. Spacious bedrooms are filled with homely extras. The elegant dining room, adorned with Oriental artefacts, is the setting for memorable breakfasts. A small conference room is available.

Rooms 2 en suite 5 annexe en suite (2 fmly) (2 GF) S £45-£85; D £65-£105* **Facilities** TVL tea/coffee Cen ht Wi-fi ⁛ Fishing Sauna **Conf** Max 15 Thtr 15 Class 9 Board 15 **Parking** 20

Middleton House Farm
★★★★ ◮ GUEST ACCOMMODATION

Tamworth Rd, Middleton B78 2BD
☎ 01827 873474 ▤ 01827 872246
e-mail: rob.jane@tinyonline.co.uk
dir: *4m S of Tamworth on A4091*

Rooms 6 en suite **Facilities** FTV TVL tea/coffee Cen ht Wi-fi **Parking** 8 **Notes** ⊗ No Children 12yrs Closed Xmas & New Year

Globe Inn
★★★ INN

Lower Gungate B79 7AW
☎ 01827 60455 ▤ 01827 63575
e-mail: info@theglobetamworth.com

Located in the centre of Tamworth, this popular inn provides well-equipped and pleasantly decorated accommodation. The public areas include a spacious lounge bar and a relaxed dining area where a varied selection of dishes is available. There is also a function room and adjacent parking.

Rooms 18 en suite (2 fmly) (18 smoking) S fr £50; D fr £50 **Facilities** STV tea/coffee Dinner available Cen ht **Conf** Thtr 90 Class 90 Board 90 **Parking** 30 **Notes** ⊗ Closed 25 Dec

High View Cottage

★★★★ GUEST ACCOMMODATION

Toothill Rd ST14 8JU
☎ 01889 568183
e-mail: info@highviewcottage.co.uk
dir: 1m S of town centre. Off B5017 Highwood Rd onto Toothill Rd

Located on the edge of Uttoxeter and close to the racecourse, High View Cottage offers comfortable, well-equipped accommodation and a friendly atmosphere. Bedrooms are equipped with lots of thoughtful extras, and hearty breakfasts are served in the attractive Garden Room which overlooks the courtyard.

Rooms 5 en suite (2 fmly) (5 GF) S £25-£55; D £45-£60 **Facilities** FTV tea/coffee Cen ht Wi-fi Pool Table **Conf** Max 8 Board 8 **Parking** 10 **Notes** ⊗

Oldroyd Guest House & Motel

★★★ GUEST HOUSE

18-22 Bridge St ST14 8AP
☎ 01889 562763 ▤ 01889 568916
e-mail: enquiries@oldroyd-guesthouse.com
dir: On A518 near racecourse

This privately owned and personally run guest house is close to the town centre and eight miles from Alton Towers. Bedrooms have modern facilities, and some family and ground-floor rooms are available. Breakfast is served at separate tables in the bright and pleasant breakfast room.

Rooms 12 rms (10 en suite) 3 annexe en suite (7 fmly) (5 GF) **Facilities** TVL tea/coffee Cen ht **Parking** 20

Tunstall Hall Farm *(SJ771273)*

★★★★ FARMHOUSE

ST20 0NH
☎ 01785 280232 ▤ 01785 280232 **Mrs Cooke**
e-mail: isabel.cooke@btinternet.com
dir: 2m NW of Woodseaves. A41 onto A519, 1st left to Shebdon, in 3m right towards Woodseaves. Bishops Offley 1m on right

Located in a quiet hamlet, this impressive renovated farmhouse dates from the early 18th century and retains original exposed beams and open fires. The thoughtfully furnished bedrooms have smart modern shower rooms en suite, and breakfast is served in the attractive conservatory.

Rooms 2 en suite (1 fmly) S £25-£40; D £50-£60* **Facilities** TVL tea/coffee Cen ht Wi-fi **Parking** 6 **Notes** ⊗ ⊜ 280 acres mixed/dairy

The Toll House

★★★★ GUEST HOUSE

50 Victoria Rd IP15 5EJ
☎ 01728 453239 & 454474
e-mail: tollhouse@fsmail.net
web: www.tollhouse.travelbugged.com
dir: B1094 into town until rdbt, B&B on right

Expect a warm welcome at this delightful red brick property situated just a short walk from the seafront and town centre. Bedrooms are tastefully furnished, have co-ordinated fabrics and many thoughtful touches. Breakfast is served at individual tables in the smart dining room, which overlooks the garden.

Rooms 7 en suite (3 GF) **Facilities** tea/coffee Cen ht **Parking** 6 **Notes** ⊗

The Mill Inn

★★★ INN

Market Cross Place IP15 5BJ
☎ 01728 452563 ▤ 01728 452563
e-mail: peeldennisp@aol.com

A traditional seafront inn in a bustling coastal town. Public areas include a lounge bar, a restaurant and a public bar frequented by local fishermen and the lifeboat crew. Bedrooms are simply decorated and well equipped; some rooms have lovely sea views.

Rooms 4 rms **Facilities** tea/coffee Dinner available Cen ht **Notes** No Children 8yrs

Earsham Park Farm *(TM304883)*

★★★★ ▲ FARMHOUSE

Old Railway Rd, Earsham NR35 2AQ
☎ 01986 892180 ▤ 01986 894796 **Mrs B Watchorn**
e-mail: aa@earsham-parkfarm.co.uk
web: www.earsham-parkfarm.co.uk
dir: 3m SW of Bungay on A143 on N side of road

Rooms 3 en suite S £46-£65; D £72-£92* **Facilities** FTV tea/coffee Cen ht Wi-fi **Conf** Max 16 Board 16 **Parking** 11 **Notes** 589 acres arable/pigs (outdoor)

Clarice House

★★★★★ ⚛ GUEST ACCOMMODATION

Horringer Court, Horringer Rd IP29 5PH
☎ 01284 705550 ▤ 01284 716120
e-mail: bury@claricehouse.co.uk
web: www.claricehouse.co.uk
dir: 1m SW from town centre on A143 towards Horringer

A large country property set amidst pretty landscaped grounds a short drive from the historic town centre. The spacious, well-equipped bedrooms have co-ordinated fabrics and many thoughtful touches. Public rooms have a wealth of charm and include a smart lounge bar, an intimate restaurant, a further lounge and a conservatory. The property also has superb leisure facilities.

Rooms 13 en suite S £65-£105; D £100-£125 **Facilities** STV FTV tea/coffee Dinner available Direct Dial Cen ht Lift Licensed ⊛ Sauna Solarium Gymnasium Spa & Beauty facilities **Conf** Max 50 Thtr 50 Class 50 Board 50 **Parking** 85 **Notes** LB ⊗ No Children 5yrs Closed 24-26 Dec & 31 Dec-1 Jan

The Black Boy

★★★★ INN

69 Guildhall St IP33 1QD
☎ 01284 752723
dir: Off A14 to town centre

A popular inn situated in the centre of this historic town. The spacious bedrooms have co-ordinated fabrics, pine furniture and many thoughtful touches. Public areas feature a large open-plan bar with a good selection of ales and a range of bar snacks are also available.

Rooms 5 en suite **Facilities** tea/coffee Dinner available Cen ht **Parking** 6 **Notes** ⊗ No coaches

BURY ST EDMUNDS *continued*

Brambles Lodge

★★★★ BED AND BREAKFAST

Welham Ln, Risby IP28 6QS
☎ 01284 810701 📠 01284 810701
e-mail: brambleslodge.bandb@homecall.co.uk
dir: *4m W of Bury. Off A14 junct 41 into Risby. Down South St, past Crown & Castle on left into Welham Ln. 2nd drive on right*

This establishment stands amid attractive landscaped gardens in the peaceful village of Risby. Breakfast is served at a large table in the smart conservatory that overlooking the garden with its duck pond. All the bedrooms are on the ground floor level, and have tea and coffee making facilities along with colour TV.

Rooms 2 en suite 1 annexe en suite (1 fmly) (3 GF) S £40-£45; D £60-£70 **Facilities** TVL tea/coffee Cen ht **Parking** 5 **Notes** ⊗ ⊗ 🖾

The Chantry

★★★★ GUEST ACCOMMODATION

8 Sparhawk St IP33 1RY
☎ 01284 767427 📠 01284 760946
e-mail: chantryhotel1@aol.com
dir: *From cathedral S onto Crown St, turn left onto Sparhawk St*

Expect a warm welcome at this attractive Georgian property, just a short walk from the town centre. The individually decorated bedrooms are furnished with well-chosen pieces and have many thoughtful touches. Dinner and breakfast are served in the smart restaurant, and there is a cosy lounge-bar.

Rooms 12 en suite 3 annexe en suite (1 GF) S £69-£89; D £89-£99* **Facilities** FTV tea/coffee Dinner available Direct Dial Cen ht Licensed Wi-fi **Parking** 16 **Notes** LB

83 Whiting Street

★★★★ BED AND BREAKFAST

83 Whiting St IP33 1NX
☎ 01284 704153
e-mail: gordon.wagstaff@btinternet.com
dir: *In town centre*

An attractive three-storey terrace property convenient for exploring this historic town. The spacious, individually decorated bedrooms are furnished with pine and

equipped with modern facilities. Breakfast is served in the beamed dining room that features an open fireplace and a wall painting dating from 1530.

Rooms 4 en suite £45; D fr £75* **Facilities** TV3B tea/coffee Cen ht **Notes** ⊗ 🖾

The Fox & Hounds

★★★★ INN

Felsham Rd, Bradfield St George IP30 0AB
☎ 01284 386379
dir: *From A134 (Sudbury road), turn left just past Rushbrook Inn. Follow signs for Bradfield St George*

Charming inn situated in a peaceful rural location surrounded by open countryside. The well equipped bedrooms are located in a converted barn to the rear of the property; each one has lovely pine furniture and co-ordinated soft furnishings. Public rooms include a cosy bar, a smart dining room and a small conservatory.

Rooms 2 en suite 2 annexe rms (2 GF); D £65* **Facilities** FTV tea/coffee Dinner available Cen ht **Parking** 25 **Notes** No Children RS Mon closed

The Six Bells at Bardwell

★★★★ INN

The Green, Bardwell IP31 1AW
☎ 01359 250820 📠 01359 250820
e-mail: sixbellsbardwell@aol.com
web: www.sixbellsbardwell.co.uk
dir: *8m NE, off A143 on edge of viillage. Follow brown signs from A143*

This 16th-century inn lies in the peaceful village of Bardwell. The bedrooms are in a converted stable block next to the main building, and are furnished in a country style and thoughtfully equipped. Public rooms have original character and provide a choice of areas in which to relax.

Rooms 10 annexe en suite (1 fmly) (10 GF) **Facilities** FTV tea/coffee Dinner available Cen ht **Parking** 50 **Notes** Closed 25 Dec-3 Jan

The Three Kings

★★★★ INN

Hengrave Rd, Fornham All Saints IP28 6LA
☎ 01284 766979
e-mail: thethreekings@keme.co.uk
web: www.the-three-kings.com
dir: *A14 junct 42, B1106 to Fornham, left onto B1101, establishment on left*

Attractive inn situated in the pleasant village of Fornham All Saints. The bedrooms are in a building adjacent to the main property; each one is smartly furnished and thoughtfully equipped. Public rooms feature a smart lounge bar, a conservatory and a comfortable restaurant.

Rooms 9 annexe en suite (2 fmly) (6 GF) S £62; D £75-£80* **Facilities** tea/coffee Dinner available Direct Dial Cen ht Wi-fi Pool Table **Conf** Max 45 Thtr 12 Class 24 Board 24 **Parking** 28 **Notes** ⊗

Dog & Partridge, The Old Brewers House

★★★ 🍴 INN

29 Crown St IP33 1QU
☎ 01284 764792
e-mail: 1065@greeneking.co.uk
web: www.oldenglish.co.uk
dir: *In town centre. Off A134 Parkway onto Westgate St & left onto Crown St*

Charming inn situated just a short walk from the town centre. Public rooms include a smart conservatory, a lounge bar, a small dining area and a smartly decked terrace to the rear of the property for alfresco dining. Bedrooms are pleasantly decorated, have co-ordinated fabrics, natural wood furniture and many thoughtful touches.

Rooms 9 en suite (2 fmly) (3 GF) **Facilities** STV tea/coffee Dinner available Direct Dial **Parking** 11 **Notes** ⊗

Old Cannon Brewery

★★★ INN

86 Cannon St IP33 1JR
☎ 01284 768769
e-mail: stay@oldcannonbrewery.co.uk
dir: *A14 junct 43, A134 towards town centre. At rdbt after Tesco left then sharp right onto Cadney Ln, left onto Cannon St, on left*

This delightful Victorian property was originally a beer house and brewery. The current owner is continuing this tradition and the finished products can be sampled in the bar, which features a unique mirror-polished stainless-steel mash tun and boiler, which is used every Monday to produce fine ales. The smartly appointed bedrooms are in an adjacent building.

Old Cannon Brewery

Rooms 5 annexe en suite (1 GF) S £65; D £79* **Facilities** FTV tea/coffee Dinner available Cen ht Wi-fi Micro Brewery on premises, tours available **Parking** 6 **Notes** LB ⊗ No Children 14yrs RS Xmas/New Year No coaches

5/6 Orchard Street

★★★ BED AND BREAKFAST

IP33 1EH
☎ 01284 750191 & 07946 590265
e-mail: mariellascarlett@hotmail.com
dir: *In town centre near St John's Church on one-way system; Northgate St turn right onto Looms Ln, 2nd right onto Well St, straight on onto Orchard St*

Expect a warm welcome from the caring hosts at this terrace property situated just a short walk from the town centre. The pleasant bedrooms are comfortably appointed and have a good range of useful extras. Breakfast is served at a large communal table in the cosy dining room.

Rooms 3 rms S £25; D £40* **Facilities** tea/coffee Cen ht **Notes** No Children 6yrs Closed 3-27 Aug ⊜

The Abbey

★★★ GUEST ACCOMMODATION

35 Southgate St IP33 2AZ
☎ 01284 762020 ▤ 01284 724770
e-mail: 01284762020@tel-w.com
dir: *A14 junct 44, A1302 to town centre, onto Southgate St, premises 400yds*

The Abbey is well placed for visiting the historic town centre. The property is split between several historic buildings, the main core dating from the 15th century. The public rooms in the Tudor inn section feature a comfortable lounge and an informal dining area.

Bedrooms vary in size and style, but all are comfortably furnished and well equipped.

Rooms 9 en suite 3 annexe en suite (1 fmly) (2 GF) **Facilities** tea/coffee Cen ht **Parking** 12 **Notes** ⊗ No Children 3yrs

Hamilton House

★★★ BED AND BREAKFAST

4 Nelson Rd IP33 3AG
☎ 01284 703022 & 07787 146553 ▤ 01284 703022
e-mail: hamiltonhouse@hotmail.co.uk
dir: *A14 junct 43, A134, left onto Risbygate St, 1st right*

A warm welcome awaits at this relaxing Edwardian villa, which is situated in a quiet side road just a short walk from the town centre. The bedrooms are brightly decorated with co-ordinated fabrics and have a good range of facilities. Breakfast is served at a large communal table in the dining room.

Rooms 4 rms (2 en suite) (1 fmly) S £25-£35; D £50-£55* **Facilities** tea/coffee Cen ht Wi-fi **Notes** ⊗ ⊜

St Andrews Lodge

★★★ BED AND BREAKFAST

30 Saint Andrews Street North IP33 1SZ
☎ 01284 756733
e-mail: standrewslodge@hotmail.com
dir: *A14 junct 43, A134 towards town centre, left onto Saint Andrews St North, Lodge on right*

This delightful property which is ideally situated close to the A14 and town centre. The well-equipped modern bedrooms are on the ground floor of a separate purpose-built building to the rear of the house. Breakfast is served at individual tables in the smart dining room, which overlooks the neat courtyard.

Rooms 3 annexe en suite (3 GF) S £45-£47.50; D £60-£65* **Facilities** FTV tea/coffee Cen ht **Parking** 3

Dunston Guest House

★★★ Ⓐ GUEST HOUSE

8 Springfield Rd IP33 3AN
☎ 01284 767981 ▤ 01284 764574
web: www.dunstonguesthouse.co.uk
dir: *A14 from Cambridge, 1st slip road onto A1302, in 1.5m after pedestrian crossing & Falcon pub left onto Springfield Rd*

Rooms 11 rms (7 en suite) (4 pri facs) 6 annexe rms 2 annexe en suite (5 fmly) (4 GF) **Facilities** TVL tea/coffee Cen ht **Parking** 10 **Notes** ⊗ ⊜

Avery House

★★ GUEST ACCOMMODATION

2 Newmarket Rd IP33 3SN
☎ 01284 755484
dir: *1m from Bury St Edmunds West, junct off A14 towards town centre*

Large detached, purpose-built property situated on the edge of town within easy walking distance of the shops. The property is popular with contractors and offers value for money accommodation. The practically equipped bedrooms are comfortable and a full English breakfast is provided in the cafeteria style dining room.

Rooms 6 en suite (1 fmly) (3 GF) S £35-£40; D £45-£50* **Facilities** tea/coffee Cen ht **Parking** 7 **Notes** ⊗ ⊜

CLARE
Map 13 TL74

Ship Stores
★★★★ GUEST ACCOMMODATION

22 Callis St CO10 8PX
☎ 01787 277834   📠 01787 277183
e-mail: shipclare@aol.com
dir: A1092 to Clare, onto B1063, past church 100yds on right

A charming property situated in the heart of an historic market town. Bedrooms are split between the main house and a converted stable block; each room is furnished in a country style with bright, co-ordinated soft furnishings and many thoughtful touches. Public areas include a lounge with comfy sofas, and a contemporary breakfast room with a stripped pine floor.

Rooms 4 en suite 2 annexe en suite (1 fmly) (3 GF)
S £45-£60; D £59-£66* **Facilities** tea/coffee Cen ht Wi-fi
Parking 3 **Notes** LB ⊗

ELMSWELL
Map 13 TL96

Kiln Farm Guest House
★★★★ GUEST HOUSE

Kiln Ln IP30 9QR
☎ 01359 240442
e-mail: davejankilnfarm@btinternet.com
dir: Exit A14 junct 47 for A1088. Entrance to Kiln Ln off eastbound slip road

A delightful Victorian farmhouse situated in a peaceful rural location amid three acres of landscaped grounds. The bedrooms are housed in converted farm buildings; each one is smartly decorated and furnished in country style. Breakfast is served in the smart conservatory and there is also a cosy lounge and bar area.

Rooms 2 en suite 6 annexe en suite (2 fmly) (6 GF);
D £70-£90* **Facilities** TVL tea/coffee Dinner available
Cen ht Licensed Wi-fi **Parking** 20

EYE
Map 13 TM17

The White Horse Inn
★★★★ INN

Stoke Ash IP23 7ET
☎ 01379 678222   📠 01379 678800
e-mail: mail@whitehorse-suffolk.co.uk
web: www.whitehorse-suffolk.co.uk
dir: On A140 halfway between Ipswich & Norwich

A 17th-century coaching inn situated in the village of Stoke Ash. Bedrooms are located in an annexe adjacent to the main building; each one is smartly decorated in pastel shades, tastefully furnished with co-ordinated fabrics and thoughtfully equipped. An interesting choice of dishes is served in the restaurant, which features exposed beams and inglenook fireplaces.

Rooms 11 annexe en suite (1 fmly) (9 GF) (2 smoking)
S £52.50; D £55-£62.50* **Facilities** FTV tea/coffee Dinner
available Direct Dial Cen ht Wi-fi **Conf** Max 50 Thtr 50
Class 50 **Parking** 60 **Notes** LB ⊗

FRAMLINGHAM
Map 13 TM26

Woodlands Farm (TM269709)
★★★★ FARMHOUSE

Brundish IP13 8BP
☎ 01379 384444   Mrs J Graham
e-mail: jillatwoodlands@aol.com
dir: 6m N of Framlingham. Off A1120 onto B1116 N, 4th
left, 0.5m left onto no-through road

Quietly located north of the town, this charming house has a wealth of character, including original exposed beams and inglenook fireplaces in the sitting room and the elegant dining room. The pleasant bedrooms are carefully decorated and thoughtfully equipped.

Rooms 3 en suite S £30-£35; D £55-£60 **Facilities** TVL
tea/coffee Cen ht **Parking** 6 **Notes** ⊗ No Children 10yrs
Closed 24 Dec-2 Jan 🐾 4 acres smallholding

Church Farm (TM605267)
★★★ FARMHOUSE

Church Rd, Kettleburgh IP13 7LF
☎ 01728 723532   Mrs A Bater
e-mail: jbater@suffolkonline.net
dir: Off A12 to Wickham Market, signs to Easton Farm
Park & Kettleburgh 1.25m, house behind church

A charming 300-year-old farmhouse situated close to the village church amid superb grounds with a duck pond, mature shrubs and sweeping lawns. The converted property retains exposed beams and open fireplaces. Bedrooms are pleasantly decorated and equipped with useful extras, and ground-floor bedrooms are available.

Rooms 2 rms (1 en suite) (1 pri facs) 2 annexe rms 1
annexe en suite (1 pri facs) (3 GF) S £32-£35; D £64-£70
Facilities TVL tea/coffee Dinner available Cen ht Fishing
Parking 10 **Notes** 🐾 70 acres mixed

HADLEIGH
Map 13 TM04

PREMIER COLLECTION

Edge Hall
★★★★★ GUEST ACCOMMODATION

2 High St IP7 5AP
☎ 01473 822458   📠 01473 822458
e-mail: r.rolfe@edgehall.co.uk
dir: B1070 into Hadleigh. 1st property in High St on
right

This imposing 16th-century building is situated at the quiet end of High Street and has been run by the same family for over 25 years. The spacious bedrooms are individually decorated and carefully furnished in period style - one room has a superb four-poster bed. Breakfast is served in the elegant dining room and there is also a comfortable lounge.

Rooms 6 en suite 4 annexe en suite (2 fmly) (1 GF)
S £57.50-£67.50; D £85-£110 **Facilities** tea/coffee
Cen ht 🐾 **Conf** Max 12 **Parking** 20 **Notes** LB 🐾

HOLTON — Map 13 TM47

PREMIER COLLECTION

Valley Farm
★★★★★ BED AND BREAKFAST

Bungay Rd IP19 8LY
☎ 01986 874521
e-mail: mail@valleyfarmholton.co.uk
web: www.valleyfarmholton.co.uk
dir: A144 onto B1123 to Holton, left at fork in village, left at school, 500yds on left

Expect a warm welcome from the caring hosts at this charming red brick farmhouse situated in a peaceful rural location a short drive from Halesworth. The individually decorated bedrooms are tastefully appointed with co-ordinated soft furnishings and many thoughtful touches. Breakfast, which features locally sourced and home grown produce, is served at a large communal table in the smartly appointed dining room. The property has lovely landscaped grounds, a summer house, and an indoor heated swimming pool.

Rooms 2 en suite (1 fmly) S £60; D £70-£80*
Facilities FTV tea/coffee Cen ht Wi-fi ⚡ 🏊 Boule piste
Parking 15 Notes LB ⊗ 🚭

INGHAM — Map 13 TL87

The Cadogan Arms
★★★★ 🍴 INN

The Street IP31 1NG
☎ 01284 728443
e-mail: info@thecadogan.co.uk

A popular inn situated four miles from the centre of town. The smartly appointed bedrooms have been thoughtfully designed and have many useful touches such as, flat-screen TVs, Freeview and CD/radios. The open-plan public

rooms are contemporary in style; they include a range of seating areas with leather sofas and a smart restaurant.

Rooms 7 en suite S fr £65; D fr £85*

IPSWICH — Map 13 TM14

The Shipwrights Arms
★★★ INN

55-61 Wherstead Rd IP2 8JJ
☎ 01473 602261 📄 01473 604255
dir: A14 onto A137 Ipswich Centre, at West Dock, turn left at Audi garage, 50yds on right

A smartly presented inn situated just a few minutes walk from the town centre. Bedrooms are generally quite spacious; each one is smartly decorated with co-ordinated soft furnishings and has many thoughtful touches. Public rooms include a small bar area, two dining rooms and a lovely conservatory.

Rooms 9 en suite (2 fmly) (2 GF) (1 smoking) S £45-£65; D £55-£85 (room only)* Facilities TVL tea/coffee Dinner available Cen ht Wi-fi Parking 6 Notes ⊗ RS Sun Bar & rest closed No coaches

LAVENHAM — Map 13 TL94

PREMIER COLLECTION

Lavenham Great House 'Restaurant With Rooms'
★★★★★ ⚫⚫ RESTAURANT WITH ROOMS

Market Place CO10 9QZ
☎ 01787 247431 📄 01787 248007
e-mail: info@greathouse.co.uk
web: www.greathouse.co.uk
dir: Off A1141 onto Market Ln, behind cross on Market Place

The 18th-century front on Market Place conceals a 15th-century timber-framed building that houses a restaurant with rooms. The Great House remains a pocket of France offering high-quality rural cuisine served by French staff. The spacious bedrooms are individually decorated and thoughtfully equipped with many useful extras; some rooms have a separate lounge area.

Rooms 5 en suite (1 fmly) S £90-£195; D £110-£195 (room only)* Facilities FTV tea/coffee Dinner available Direct Dial Cen ht Wi-fi Free bicycle use for guests Notes LB Closed Jan RS Sun eve & Mon Restaurant closed No coaches

PREMIER COLLECTION

Lavenham Old Rectory
★★★★★ BED AND BREAKFAST

Church St CO10 9SA
☎ 01787 247572
e-mail: susie_dwright@hotmail.co.uk

After four years of restoration work, the Old Rectory has been reborn and now offers sumptuous en suite accommodation, where classic style and décor meet modern technology to suit a discerning clientele. Breakfast is served in the morning room or, weather permitting, on the terrace with breathtaking views of the rear garden.

Rooms 3 en suite S £130-£150; D £155-£190
Facilities FTV Cen ht Wi-fi Parking 10 Notes ⊗ No Children Closed 24-26 Dec

PREMIER COLLECTION

Lavenham Priory
★★★★★ BED AND BREAKFAST

Water St CO10 9RW
☎ 01787 247404 📄 01787 248472
e-mail: mail@lavenhampriory.co.uk
web: www.lavenhampriory.co.uk
dir: A1141 to Lavenham, turn by side of Swan onto Water St & right after 50yds onto private drive

This superb Grade I listed building, dating from the 15th century, once belonged to Benedictine monks and has been lovingly restored to maintain its original character. Individually decorated bedrooms are very spacious; each is beautifully furnished and thoughtfully equipped. Breakfast is served in the spectacular Merchants dining room or in the sheltered courtyard herb garden. Guests also have use of the Great Hall, with inglenook fireplace, and an adjoining lounge.

Rooms 6 en suite S £75-£85; D £100-£165*
Facilities TVL tea/coffee Cen ht Licensed Wi-fi
Parking 11 Notes No Children 10yrs Closed 21 Dec-2 Jan

LAVENHAM *continued*

Wood Hall

★★★★ BED AND BREAKFAST

Little Waldingfield CO10 0SY
☎ **01787 247362**
e-mail: susan@woodhallbnb.fsnet.co.uk
web: www.thewoodhall.com
dir: *A1141 onto B1115 into Little Waldingfield, Wood Hall 200yds on left past Swan pub*

This is a delightful 15th-century property, just a short drive from historic Lavenham. The spacious, individually decorated bedrooms are thoughtfully equipped. Breakfast is served in the elegant dining room, which features a superb inglenook fireplace with a wood-burning stove. Parking at rear.

Rooms 2 en suite S £50-£90; D £85-£90 **Facilities** tea/coffee Dinner available Cen ht Wi-fi 🏊 **Parking** 4 **Notes** ⊗ No Children 10yrs Closed 21 Dec-2 Jan

The Angel

★★★★ ⬤ RESTAURANT WITH ROOMS

Market Place CO10 9QZ
☎ **01787 247388** 📄 **01787 248344**
e-mail: angel@maypolehotels.com
web: www.maypolehotels.com
dir: *From A14 take Bury E & Sudbury turn onto A143. After 4m take A1141 to Lavenham. Off High Street*

A delightful 15th-century inn overlooking the market place in the heart of this historic medieval town. The Angel is well known for its cuisine and offers an imaginative menu based on fresh ingredients. Public rooms include a residents' lounge and open-plan bar/dining area. Bedrooms are tastefully furnished, attractively decorated and thoughtfully equipped.

Rooms 8 en suite (1 fmly) (1 GF) S fr £80; D £95-£115* **Facilities** FTV TVL tea/coffee Dinner available Direct Dial Cen ht Wi-fi **Parking** 5 **Notes** No coaches

Brett Farm

★★★★ Ⓐ BED AND BREAKFAST

The Common CO10 9PG
☎ **01787 248533**
e-mail: brettfarmbandb@aol.com
web: www.brettfarm.com
dir: *In Lavenham turn by Swan Hotel onto Water St, 4th left & 1st right over white bridge, farm on right*

Rooms 3 rms (2 en suite) (1 pri facs) (3 GF) S £40-£65; D £65-£70* **Facilities** tea/coffee Cen ht Wi-fi Carriage rides Bike hire **Parking** 6 **Notes** ⊗ ⬤

LEISTON   Map 13 TM46

Field End

★★★★ GUEST HOUSE

1 Kings Rd IP16 4DA
☎ **01728 833527** 📄 **01728 833527**
e-mail: herbert@herbertwood.wanadoo.co.uk
web: www.fieldendbedandbreakfast.co.uk
dir: *In town centre off B1122*

This Edwardian house has been appointed to a high standard and is impeccably maintained by the present owners. Bedrooms have co-ordinated soft furnishings and many thoughtful touches. Breakfast is served in an attractive dining room, which has a large sofa and a range of puzzles and games.

Rooms 5 rms (2 en suite) (1 pri facs) (1 fmly) (1 GF) S £30-£35; D fr £60* **Facilities** TVL tea/coffee Cen ht **Parking** 5 **Notes** ⊗ No Children 6mths ⬤

LOWESTOFT   Map 13 TM59

Abbe Guest House

★★★★ GUEST ACCOMMODATION

322 London Road South NR33 0BG
☎ **01502 581083**
e-mail: abbehouse@btconnect.com
web: www.abbehouse-hotel.co.uk
dir: *On A12, 1.5m from the Pakefield Water Tower rdbt, 50yds past Rectory Rd*

Expect a warm welcome from the caring hosts at this charming property situated just a short walk from the seafront and town centre. Bedrooms are pleasantly decorated, have co-ordinated soft furnishings and benefit from many thoughtful touches. Breakfast is served in the

smart dining room, and guests have the use of a cosy lounge bar.

Rooms 4 rms (3 en suite) (1 pri facs) (1 fmly) S £30-£40; D £50-£70* **Facilities** FTV TVL tea/coffee Dinner available Cen ht Licensed Wi-fi **Notes** ⊗ No Children 5yrs Closed 21 Dec-6 Jan

Katherine

★★★★ ⬤ GUEST ACCOMMODATION

49 Kirkley Cliff Rd NR33 0DF
☎ **01502 567858** 📄 **01502 581341**
e-mail: beauthaicuisine@aol.com
web: www.beauthaikatherine.co.uk
dir: *On A12 seafront road next to Kensington Garden*

This large Victorian property lies opposite the beach in the quiet part of town. The spacious public rooms include a smart lounge bar with leather sofas and an intimate restaurant serving authentic Thai cuisine. The pleasant bedrooms have co-ordinated fabrics and many thoughtful touches.

Rooms 10 en suite (5 fmly) S £35-£39; D £65-£75* **Facilities** tea/coffee Dinner available Direct Dial Cen ht Licensed **Parking** 4 **Notes** LB

Somerton House

★★★★ GUEST ACCOMMODATION

7 Kirkley Cliff NR33 0BY
☎ **01502 565665** 📄 **01502 501176**
e-mail: pippin.somerton@btinternet.com
dir: *On old A12, 100yds from Claremont Pier*

Somerton House is a Grade II Victorian terrace situated in a peaceful area of town overlooking the sea. Bedrooms are smartly furnished in a period style and have many thoughtful touches; some rooms have four poster or half-tester beds. Breakfast is served in the smart dining room and guests have the use of a cosy lounge.

Rooms 6 rms (4 en suite) (2 pri facs) (1 fmly) (1 GF) S £36-£46; D £57-£62* **Facilities** FTV TVL tea/coffee Dinner available Cen ht Licensed Wi-fi **Notes** LB Closed 25-26 Dec

Wavecrest Guest House

★★★★ GUEST HOUSE

31 Marine Pde NR33 0QN
☎ **01502 561268**
e-mail: wavecrestguesthouse@googlemail.com
dir: *On seafront just S of Lowestoft Bridge*

This Victorian terrace house is situated on the seafront, overlooking the award-winning beach and within easy walking distance of the town centre. The bedrooms are smartly decorated with co-ordinated soft furnishings and equipped with modern facilities. Public areas include an elegant dining room where breakfast is served at individual tables.

Rooms 5 rms (4 en suite) (1 pri facs) (1 fmly) S £28-£39; D £45-£60* **Facilities** tea/coffee Cen ht Wi-fi **Notes** ⊗ Closed 24-31 Dec

Fairways Bed & Breakfast

★★★★ 🅰 BED AND BREAKFAST

288 Normanston Dr, Oulton Broad NR32 2PS
☎ **01502 582756** 📄 **01502 582756**
e-mail: info@fairwaysbb.co.uk
web: www.fairwaysbb.co.uk
dir: On A1117 through Oulton Broad

Rooms 2 en suite 1 annexe en suite (1 fmly) S £45-£47.50; D £65-£70* **Facilities** FTV tea/coffee Cen ht **Parking** 5

Coventry House

★★★ GUEST HOUSE

8 Kirkley Cliff NR33 0BY
☎ **01502 573865** 📄 **01502 573865**
e-mail: gill.alden@sky.com
dir: On A12 opp Claremont Pier, 0.25m S from Harbour Bridge

An impressive Victorian terrace house, situated on the seafront opposite the pier. The pleasant bedrooms are thoughtfully equipped and many rooms have lovely sea views. Breakfast is served in the carefully appointed dining room and there is a comfortable lounge.

Rooms 7 rms (5 en suite) (2 pri facs) (3 fmly) (1 GF) **Facilities** TVL tea/coffee Cen ht **Parking** 4 **Notes** LB Closed 24-27 Dec 🐾

Edingworth

★★★ GUEST HOUSE

395 London Road South NR33 0BJ
☎ **01502 572051** 📄 **01502 572051**
e-mail: enquiries@edingworth.co.uk
web: www.edingworth.co.uk
dir: 600yds on left after start of Pakefield/Kirkley one-way system, N towards town centre

A friendly, family-run guest house situated within easy walking distance of the town centre and seafront. The spacious bedrooms are pleasantly decorated and thoughtfully equipped. Breakfast is served in the smart dining room and there is a comfortable television lounge.

Rooms 6 rms (6 pri facs) (5 fmly) (1 GF) **Facilities** STV tea/coffee Dinner available Cen ht **Parking** 3 **Notes** LB ⊗ Closed 24-26 Dec 🐾

Fairways

★★★ GUEST HOUSE

398 London Road South NR33 0BQ
☎ **01502 572659**
e-mail: amontali@netmatters.co.uk
dir: S of town centre on A12, 1m from rail & bus station

A friendly, family-run guest house located at the southern end of the town. Bedrooms come in a variety of sizes and styles; each room is pleasantly decorated and thoughtfully equipped. Breakfast is served in the smart dining room and there is also a cosy lounge.

Rooms 7 rms (4 en suite) (2 fmly) S £22-£30; D £42-£48 **Facilities** TVL tea/coffee Cen ht

Highbury House

★★★ GUEST HOUSE

397 London Road South NR33 0BJ
☎ **01502 589064** & 07760 227245
e-mail: highbury.house@hotmail.co.uk
dir: On A12 follow signs to Lowestoft then follow South Beach signs, then London Rd South. On left after St Peters Rd

A friendly, family-run guest house situated just a short walk from the town centre and seafront. Bedrooms are generally quite spacious; each one is pleasantly decorated and equipped with a good range of useful facilities. Breakfast and dinner are served at individual tables in the dining room.

Rooms 5 en suite (1 fmly) S £29-£30; D £50-£52 **Facilities** FTV tea/coffee Dinner available Cen ht **Notes** ⊗ 🐾

Kingsleigh

★★★ GUEST HOUSE

44 Marine Pde NR33 0QN
☎ **01502 572513**
e-mail: levett@kingsleigh.wanadoo.co.uk
dir: On A12 S from Lowestoft town centre, house on right, 0.25m from Harbour Bridge

A warm welcome is to be expected on arrival at this well-maintained Victorian property, situated on the south side of town just a short walk from the shops. Bedrooms are attractively decorated in pastel shades and have co-ordinated soft furnishings and many thoughtful touches. Most rooms have superb sea views.

Rooms 5 rms (3 en suite) (2 pri facs) (1 fmly) S £25-£35; D £45-£55* **Facilities** FTV tea/coffee Cen ht **Notes** 🐾

Seavilla

★★★ GUEST ACCOMMODATION

43 Kirkley Cliff Rd NR33 0DF
☎ **01502 574657** 📄 **01502 574657**
dir: A12 into town, right at South Beach, 300yds past Claremont Pier

Expect a warm welcome at the Seavilla which is situated on the southern side of town overlooking the beach. The pleasant bedrooms are thoughtfully equipped and many have superb sea views. Breakfast is served at individual tables in the attractive dining room and guests have the use of a cosy lounge.

Rooms 9 rms (5 en suite) S £25-£35; D £50-£60* **Facilities** FTV TVL tea/coffee Cen ht **Parking** 3 **Notes** LB

MENDHAM   Map 13 TM28

Weston House Farm (TM292828)

★★★★ FARMHOUSE

IP20 0PB
☎ **01986 782206** Mrs J E Holden
e-mail: holden@farmline.com
web: www.westonhousefarm.co.uk
dir: Off A143 or B1123 signed Mendham, signs from village centre

Well maintained Grade II listed, 17th-century farmhouse set in an acre of pleasant gardens in the heart of the Waveny Valley. The individually decorated bedrooms are generally quite spacious, thoughtfully furnished and well-equipped. Breakfast is served in the smart dining room which overlooks the garden.

Rooms 3 en suite (1 GF) S £34-£42; D £54-£65* **Facilities** TVL tea/coffee Cen ht **Parking** 6 **Notes** No Children 10yrs Closed Dec-Feb 🐾 600 acres mixed

NAYLAND — Map 13 TL93

Hill House

★★★★ BED AND BREAKFAST

Gravel Hill CO6 4JB
☎ 01206 262782
e-mail: heighamhillhouse@hotmail.com
dir: *In village centre. Off B1087 Birch St onto Gravel Hill. House 100yds up hill on right*

Set in secluded grounds in a peaceful village on the edge of Constable Country, this Grade II listed, 16th-century timber-framed building has a wealth of exposed beams, a flagstone hall and inglenooks. The attractive bedrooms are well equipped and overlook the pretty garden. Breakfast is served around a large communal table in the attractive, beamed dining room.

Rooms 2 en suite S £36-£40; D £65-£70 **Facilities** tea/coffee Cen ht ➥ **Parking** 4 **Notes** LB ⊗ No Children 10yrs Closed 20 Dec-1 Jan ☺

The Steam Mill House

★★★★ GUEST ACCOMMODATION

1 Fen St CO6 4HT
☎ 01206 262818 🖹 01206 262818
e-mail: brendaassing@tiscali.co.uk
web: www.thesteammillhouse.com
dir: *A134 onto B1087 into Nayland, bear right 0.5m. Fen St 1st on left*

Dating back to 1811, this house is situated in a beautiful and tranquil village in the heart of Constable Country which is an Area of Outstanding Natural Beauty. Rooms are comfortable and individually decorated. Breakfast is served in the dining room, and includes homemade jams and locally sourced produce.

Rooms 3 en suite (2 fmly) (1 GF) S £40-£45; D £60-£65* **Facilities** tea/coffee Cen ht Wi-fi **Parking** 3 **Notes** ⊗ No Children 4yrs Closed 22 Dec-3 Jan ☺

NEWMARKET — Map 12 TL66

See also Kirtling (Cambridgeshire)

The Garden Lodge

★★★★ BED AND BREAKFAST

11 Vicarage Ln, Woodditton CB8 9SG
☎ 01638 731116
e-mail: swedishgardenlodge@hotmail.com
web: www.gardenlodge.net
dir: *3m S of Newmarket in Woodditton*

A warm welcome is assured in this home-from-home, not far from the famous racecourse. The accommodation, in quality chalets, is very well equipped and features a wealth of thoughtful extras. Freshly prepared home-cooked breakfasts are served in an elegant dining room in the main house.

Rooms 3 en suite (3 GF) S £35-£40; D £60-£70* **Facilities** tea/coffee Dinner available Cen ht **Parking** 6 **Notes** ☺

ORFORD — Map 13 TM45

Jolly Sailor

★★★ INN

Quay St IP12 2NU
☎ 01394 450243
e-mail: hello@thejollysailor.net

This lovely inn dates back to the 1700s, and is ideally placed for touring the Suffolk coast. The comfortable bedrooms are smartly appointed and well equipped, some rooms have superb views of the garden and the marshes. Public areas have a wealth of character, they include a lounge bar, a dining room and open log fires.

Rooms 4 en suite S £55-£95; D £55-£105*

SAXMUNDHAM — Map 13 TM36

Sandpit Farm

★★★★ BED AND BREAKFAST

Bruisyard IP17 2EB
☎ 01728 663445
e-mail: smarshall@aldevalleybreaks.co.uk
web: www.aldevalleybreaks.co.uk
dir: *4m W of Saxmundham. A1120 onto B1120, 1st left for Bruisyard, house 1.5m on left*

Sandpit Farm is a delightful Grade II listed farmhouse set in 20 acres of grounds. Bedrooms have many thoughtful touches and lovely country views, and there are two cosy lounges to enjoy. Breakfast features quality local produce and freshly laid free-range eggs.

Rooms 2 en suite S £50-£60; D £65-£80* **Facilities** TVL tea/coffee Cen ht Wi-fi ➥ ➥ Riding **Parking** 4 **Notes** LB Closed 24-26 Dec ☺

SOUTHWOLD — Map 13 TM57

PREMIER COLLECTION

Sutherland House

★★★★★ ◉◉ RESTAURANT WITH ROOMS

56 High St IP18 6DN
☎ 01502 724544
e-mail: enquiries@sutherlandhouse.co.uk
web: www.sutherlandhouse.co.uk
dir: *A1095 into Southwold, on High St on left after Victoria St*

A delightful 16th-century house situated in the heart of the bustling town centre with a wealth of character; there are oak beams, exposed brickwork, open fireplaces and two superb ornate plasterwork ceilings. The stylish bedrooms are tastefully decorated, have co-ordinated fabrics and many thoughtful touches. Public rooms feature a large open-plan contemporary restaurant with plush furniture.

Rooms 4 en suite (1 fmly) S £120-£220; D £120-£250* **Facilities** FTV tea/coffee Dinner available Direct Dial Cen ht Wi-fi **Conf** Max 80 Thtr 80 Class 30 Board 30 **Parking** 1 **Notes** ⊗ No coaches

Home at 21 North Parade

★★★★ BED AND BREAKFAST

21 North Pde IP18 6LT
☎ 01502 722573
e-mail: pauline.archer@btconnect.com
web: www.homeat21northparade.co.uk
dir: *A12 onto B1095. At mini rdbt, left onto Pier Avenue, right onto North Parade. Premises 100yds on right*

This delightful Victorian property is situated on the promenade overlooking the sea. The stylish bedrooms have co-ordinated soft furnishings and many thoughtful touches, and some rooms have superb sea views. Breakfast, which includes fresh local produce, is served in the smart lounge/dining room at a large polished table.

Rooms 3 rms (2 en suite) (1 pri facs) S £70-£75; D £90-£100 **Facilities** FTV tea/coffee Cen ht ➥ Golf 18 **Notes** LB ⊗ No Children 10yrs Closed Xmas & New Year ☺

STOWMARKET — Map 13 TM05

PREMIER COLLECTION

Bays Farm
★★★★★ GUEST ACCOMMODATION

Forward Green IP14 5HU
☎ 01449 711286
e-mail: information@baysfarmsuffolk.co.uk
web: www.baysfarmsuffolk.co.uk
dir: A14 junct 50, onto A1120. 1m after Stowupland,
turn right at sharp left bend signed Broad Green. Bays
Farm 1st house on right

Tea and home-made cake are offered on arrival at this
delightful 17th-century former farmhouse, situated
amid four acres of mature grounds. The property has a
wealth of character. Bedrooms are carefully decorated
and have co-ordinated soft furnishings as well as
many thoughtful touches. Breakfast, which includes
locally sourced produce, is served around a large
polished table in the stylish dining room.

Rooms 3 en suite **Facilities** tea/coffee Cen ht
Parking 3 **Notes** No Children 12yrs

SUDBURY — Map 13 TL84

The Case Restaurant with Rooms
★★★★ ⒶRESTAURANT WITH ROOMS

Further St, Assington CO10 5LD
☎ 01787 210483 ▤ 01787 211725
e-mail: restaurant@thecaserestaurantwithrooms.co.uk
dir: Exit A12 at Colchester, take A134 to Sudbury. 7m
from Colchester on left

Rooms 7 en suite (2 fmly) (7 GF) **Facilities** FTV tea/coffee
Dinner available Cen ht Wi-fi **Parking** 25 **Notes** LB ⊗

WHEPSTEAD — Map 13 TL85

Folly House Bed & Breakfast
★★★★ BED AND BREAKFAST

Folly Ln IP29 4TJ
☎ 01284 735207 & 07990 943060 ▤ 01284 735207
e-mail: lowerlinda@hotmail.com
dir: Off B1066 onto Rectory Rd 1.5m, at T-junct turn
right, Folly Ln on right

This former alehouse dates back to the 1830s and is set
amid landscaped grounds in peaceful countryside. The
spacious bedroom has co-ordinated fabrics and many
thoughtful touches. Public rooms include an elegant
dining room, a conservatory-lounge and an indoor
swimming pool.

Rooms 3 rms (1 en suite) (1 fmly) S fr £35; D fr £65*
Facilities tea/coffee Dinner available Cen ht 🦮
Parking 10 **Notes** ⊗ 🐾

WINGFIELD — Map 13 TM27

Gables Farm
★★★★ BED AND BREAKFAST

Earsham St IP21 5RH
☎ 01379 586355
e-mail: enquiries@gablesfarm.co.uk
web: www.gablesfarm.co.uk
dir: B1118 left to Wingfield Green, turn right after 1m,
B&B 1.7m on right

This delightful Grade II listed farmhouse is set amid two
acres of moated gardens on the outskirts of the village.
The spacious bedrooms are carefully furnished and
thoughtfully equipped. Breakfast, which includes locally
sourced produce, is served in the smart dining room at
individual tables.

Rooms 3 en suite (1 fmly) **Facilities** TVL tea/coffee
Parking 5 **Notes** Closed 20-25 Dec ⊛

WOODBRIDGE — Map 13 TM24

Grove House
★★★ GUEST HOUSE

39 Grove Rd IP12 4LG
☎ 01394 382202
e-mail: reception@grovehousehotel.ltd.uk
dir: W of town centre on A12

A warm welcome is assured at this owner-managed
establishment on the west side of town. The bedrooms
are pleasantly decorated and thoughtfully equipped with
a good range of useful facilities. The smart public rooms
include a cosy bar, a comfortable lounge and a large
dining room with individual tables.

Rooms 10 en suite (1 fmly) (6 GF) S £55; D £65-£70*
Facilities tea/coffee Dinner available Cen ht Licensed
Wi-fi **Conf** Max 20 Thtr 20 Class 20 Board 20 **Parking** 12
Notes LB ⊗

WORLINGWORTH — Map 13 TM26

Pond Farm B&B (TM219697)
★★★ FARMHOUSE

Fingal St IP13 7PD
☎ 01728 628565 & 0798 0914768   Ms Sophie Prowse
e-mail: enquiries@featherdown.co.uk

A 16th-century, Grade II listed farmhouse set in twelve
acres of pastures and paddocks, a short drive from
Framlingham and Woodbridge. The well-equipped
bedrooms are split between the main house and new
annexe rooms adjacent to the main building. Breakfast is
served at a large communal table in the cosy dining room
and dinner is available on request.

Rooms 2 en suite (2 fmly) (2 GF) S £35-£42; D £64-£70*
Facilities STV FTV TVL tea/coffee Dinner available Direct
Dial Cen ht Fishing **Parking** 10 **Notes** LB ⊛ 100 acres
beef/pigs

YAXLEY — Map 13 TM17

PREMIER COLLECTION

The Auberge
★★★★★ ⓪⓪ RESTAURANT WITH ROOMS

Ipswich Rd IP23 8BZ
☎ 01379 783604 ▤ 01379 788486
e-mail: aubmail@the-auberge.co.uk
web: www.the-auberge.co.uk
dir: On A140 between Norwich & Ipswich at B1117
x-rds with Eye & Thornham Parva

A warm welcome awaits at this charming 15th-century
property, which has been lovingly converted by the
present owners into a smart restaurant with rooms. The
public areas have a wealth of character, such as
exposed brickwork and beams. The spacious bedrooms
are tastefully appointed and have many thoughtful
touches.

Rooms 4 en suite 7 annexe en suite (2 fmly) (6 GF)
S £65-£85; D £85-£150 **Facilities** FTV tea/coffee
Dinner available Direct Dial Cen ht Wi-fi **Conf** Max 46
Thtr 30 Class 30 Board 20 **Parking** 40 **Notes** LB ⊗ No
coaches

SURREY

BETCHWORTH — Map 6 TQ25

The Red Lion
★★★ INN

Old Rd, Buckland RH3 7DS
☎ 01737 843336 ▤ 01737 845242
e-mail: info@redlionbetchworth.co.uk
dir: Off A25 between Reigate & Dorking, turn left to
Betchworth. At rdbt turn left at T-junct, 500mtrs pub
on left

The Red Lion is conveniently located just 20 minutes from
Gatwick in the quiet village of Betchworth. The garden
and some bedrooms have views of the neighbouring
village cricket green. Bedrooms have spacious, modern
décor, all with LCD TVs and beverage-making facilities.
The pub serves lunch and dinner daily and a continental
breakfast is available.

Rooms 6 annexe en suite (3 GF) S £60-£75; D £65-£80
Facilities FTV tea/coffee Dinner available Wi-fi Cricket
pitch **Conf** Max 40 Thtr 40 Class 25 Board 25 **Parking** 40
Notes LB No coaches

CAMBERLEY | Map 6 SU86

PREMIER COLLECTION

Maywood House
★★★★★ GUEST ACCOMMODATION

Maywood Dr GU15 1LH
☎ 01276 601730 📄 0845 0540909
e-mail: reservations@maywoodhouse.com

Maywood House provides comfortable accommodation in a secluded location but convenient for the M3. Amenities include extremely well equipped bedrooms and modern bathrooms with powerful showers. Delicious breakfasts are served in the airy dining room that overlooks beautiful gardens.

Rooms 5 en suite (1 fmly) S £98.50-£127.95; D £117-£145.90* **Facilities** FTV TVL tea/coffee Dinner available Direct Dial Cen ht **Conf** Max 12 Thtr 12 Class 12 Board 12 **Parking** 10 **Notes** ⊗ Closed 22 Dec-2 Jan

Burwood House

★★★★ GUEST ACCOMMODATION

15 London Rd GU15 3UQ
☎ 01276 685686 📄 01276 62220
e-mail: enquiries@burwoodhouse.co.uk
dir: On A30 between Camberley and Bagshot

Burwood House is a very stylish establishment with individually-designed bedrooms that offer all modern conveniences including Wi-fi. Every Monday to Thursday evening the kitchen offers a varied menu full of traditional favourites, as well as seasonal house specialties. Breakfast can be taken either buffet-style or as a fresh-cooked meal prepared upon request. Public areas include a lounge, bar and garden.

Rooms 19 en suite (3 fmly) (7 GF) S £75-£95; D £95-£115* **Facilities** TVL tea/coffee Dinner available Direct Dial Cen ht Licensed Wi-fi 🎾 **Conf** Max 60 Thtr 50 Class 16 Board 20 **Parking** 22 **Notes** Closed 22 Dec-4 Jan

CHARLWOOD

For accommodation details see under Gatwick Airport (London), (Sussex, West)

CHIDDINGFOLD | Map 6 SU93

PREMIER COLLECTION

The Crown Inn
★★★★★ INN

The Green, Petworth Rd GU8 4TX
☎ 01428 682255
e-mail: enquiries@thecrownchiddingfold.com

Set in a tranquil location in a picturesque village, the inn dates back to as early as 1216. This charming property has been completely renovated and offers stylish, modern accommodation which has been tastefully renovated without losing any period features. Breakfast and dinner can be enjoyed in the oak-panelled dining room, and there is a spacious bar, outside seating and small courtyard.

Rooms 8 en suite S £100; D £125-£200* **Facilities** FTV Dinner available Direct Dial Cen ht Wi-fi **Conf** Max 40 **Notes** ⊗

The Swan Inn

Ⓤ

Petworth Rd GU8 4TY
☎ 01428 682073 📄 01428 683259
e-mail: the-swan-inn@btconnect.com
web: www.theswaninn.biz
dir: A3 onto A283 signed Milford, past village green on left

Currently the rating for this establishment is not confirmed. This may be due to a change of ownership or because it has only recently joined the AA rating scheme.

Rooms 11 en suite (1 fmly) **Facilities** tea/coffee Dinner available Direct Dial Licensed Wi-fi **Parking** 40

CHOBHAM | Map 6 SU96

Pembroke House
★★★★ GUEST ACCOMMODATION

Valley End Rd GU24 8TB
☎ 01276 857654 📄 01276 858445
e-mail: pembroke_house@btinternet.com
dir: A30 onto B383 signed Chobham, 3m right onto Valley End Rd, 1m on left

Proprietor Julia Holland takes obvious pleasure in welcoming guests to her beautifully appointed and spacious home. The elegantly proportioned public areas include an imposing entrance hall and dining room with views over the surrounding countryside. Bedrooms are restful and filled with thoughtful extras.

Rooms 4 rms (2 en suite) (2 pri facs) (1 fmly) S £40-£50; D £90-£110* **Facilities** STV tea/coffee Cen ht Wi-fi 🎾 **Parking** 10 **Notes** ⊛

CRANLEIGH | Map 6 TQ03

Brown's Bed & Breakfast

★★ BED AND BREAKFAST

Avenue Rd GU6 7LL
☎ 01483 273940
e-mail: agbrown@ukgateway.net
dir: Take Horsham Rd at east end of Cranleigh (petrol station on right), 5th road on left into Avenue Rd, B&B on left, just after Grove Rd

Brown's is a delightful establishment located a short walk from Cranleigh town centre. The two bedrooms provide good comfort levels and shared bathroom facilities are provided. An attractive TV lounge with ample local area information and reading material is available. Breakfast is served overlooking the lovely rear gardens; during summer months, breakfast is available al fresco.

Rooms 2 rms (1 pri facs) (1 fmly) S £30-£35; D £60-£65* **Facilities** TVL tea/coffee Cen ht Wi-fi **Parking** 2 **Notes** ⊗ No Ch ldren 12yrs ⊛

FARNHAM   Map 5 SU84

PREMIER COLLECTION

Bentley Mill
★★★★★ BED AND BREAKFAST

Gravel Hill Rd, Bentley GU10 5JD
☎ 01420 23301 & 07768 842729 📠 01420 22538
e-mail: ann.bentleymill@supanet.com
web: www.bentleymill.com
dir: Off A31 (Farnham-Alton road), opp Bull Inn, turn left onto Gravel Hill Rd

This delightful former corn mill, sitting beside the River Wey in beautifully tended gardens, has been expertly converted to provide two bedroom suites of the highest standard. Luxurious beds, antique furnishings and a host of thoughtful extra touches compliment the original features and maximise the immense character and charm of this Georgian property. Ann and David Hallett's hospitality knows no bounds: they do everything to ensure you enjoy their wonderful country home.

Rooms 2 annexe en suite (2 fmly) (1 GF) S £85-£100; D £105-£140* **Facilities** STV FTV tea/coffee Cen ht Wi-fi 🏊 Fishing **Parking** 6 **Notes** LB ⊗

Dares Farm House
★★★★ GUEST HOUSE

Farnham Rd, Ewshot GU10 5BB
☎ 01252 851631 📠 01252 852367
e-mail: daresfarm@tiscali.co.uk
dir: 3m NW of Farnham. M3 junct 5, A287 towards Farnham for 5m, up hill past Dares Ln, 1st left

This attractive Grade II listed, 17th-century timber-framed cottage property is within easy reach of the M3 and A31. You can expect a warm welcome and a comfortable sleep in the cosy, individually decorated bedrooms. The hearty breakfast in the farmhouse kitchen sets you up for the day.

Rooms 4 en suite S fr £40; D fr £70* **Facilities** TVL tea/coffee Cen ht **Parking** 5 **Notes** ⊗ No Children 14yrs 🍴

Sandiway
★★★ BED AND BREAKFAST

24 Shortheath Rd GU9 8SR
☎ 01252 710721
e-mail: john@shortheath.freeserve.co.uk
dir: Onto A287 Hindhead, at lights at top of hill right onto Ridgway Rd, past green on left, Sandiway 300yds on right

Guests are warmly welcomed at this delightful house, set in attractive gardens in a quiet residential area. Smart bedrooms have a thoughtful range of facilities and share a spacious, well-appointed bathroom. Guests have use of a comfortable lounge during the day and evening, which doubles as the dining room at breakfast.

Rooms 3 rms S £30-£35; D £50-£55* **Facilities** TVL tea/coffee Cen ht Wi-fi **Parking** 3 **Notes** ⊗ No Children Closed 21-31 Dec 🍴

GUILDFORD   Map 6 SU94

Asperion Hillside
★★★★ 🍴 GUEST ACCOMMODATION

Perry Hill, Worplesdon GU3 3RF
☎ 01483 232051 📠 01483 237015
e-mail: info@thehillsidehotel.com

Located just a short drive away from central Guildford this accommodation is popular with both business and leisure travellers. Bedrooms are comfortable and well equipped with good facilities. Public areas include a spacious lounge bar where dinner is served, and a bright well-styled breakfast room. Gardens are well maintained and are enhanced by a guest terrace. Intimate meetings and events can also be catered for here.

Rooms 15 en suite (6 GF) S £65; D £80-£120 **Facilities** FTV tea/coffee Dinner available Cen ht Licensed Wi-fi **Conf** Max 20 Thtr 20 Class 10 Board 12 **Parking** 15 **Notes** ⊗ Closed 21 Dec-7 Jan

Asperion
★★★★ GUEST ACCOMMODATION

73 Farnham Rd GU2 7PF
☎ 01483 579299 📠 01483 457977
e-mail: enquiries@asperion.co.uk

The stylish Asperion provides comfortable, modern, and contemporary styled bedrooms in a convenient location close to the city centre of Guildford. Car parking is available on site and meals include a healthy organic breakfast and traditional British cooking during the evening (Monday to Thursday).

Rooms 15 rms (14 en suite) (1 pri facs) (1 fmly) (9 GF) S £50-£120; D £85-£120 **Facilities** STV TVL tea/coffee Dinner available Direct Dial Cen ht Licensed **Parking** 11 **Notes** ⊗ No Children 12yrs Closed 21 Dec-5 Jan

Blanes Court Guest House
★★★ GUEST ACCOMMODATION

Albury Rd GU1 2BT
☎ 01483 573171 📠 01483 532780
e-mail: reservations@blanes.demon.co.uk
web: www.blanes.demon.co.uk
dir: 0.7m E of town centre, off A246 Epsom Rd

This large Edwardian house stands in a quiet residential area close to the town centre and has ample private parking. Public areas include a small seating area with a bar, and a conservatory overlooking the attractive rear garden. Bedrooms vary in size, but each is individually decorated and all offer a useful range of facilities.

Rooms 16 en suite (3 fmly) (6 GF) S £60-£64; D £86-£95* **Facilities** FTV tea/coffee Cen ht Licensed Wi-fi **Parking** 22 **Notes** LB ⊗ Closed 1wk Xmas

HASLEMERE   Map 6 SU93

Wheatsheaf
★★★ 🍴 INN

Grayswood Rd, Grayswood GU27 2DE
☎ 01428 644440 📠 01428 641285
e-mail: ken@thewheatsheafgrayswood.co.uk
web: www.thewheatsheafgrayswood.co.uk
dir: 1m N of Haslemere on A286 in Grayswood

Situated in a small village just outside Haslemere, this well-presented inn has a friendly atmosphere. The smart conservatory restaurant is a new addition, which complements the attractive dining area and popular bar. Bedrooms are furnished to a good standard, all but one on the ground floor.

Rooms 7 en suite (6 GF) S £55-£60; D £75-£80* **Facilities** tea/coffee Dinner available Direct Dial Cen ht Wi-fi **Parking** 21 **Notes** No coaches

HASLEMERE *continued*

Ashleigh *(SU949313)*

★★ FARMHOUSE

Fisherstreet Farm GU28 9EJ
☎ **01428 707229** 🖹 **01428 707229** **Mr & Mrs S
Thomas**
e-mail: gu284sx@yahoo.co.uk
dir: *3.5m E of Haslemere. B2131 onto A283 S*

Stephen and Madeleine Thomas make you feel like friends
at their charming farmhouse. A homely ambience is
evident throughout the spacious bedrooms, the cosy
lounge and the elegant dining room. Breakfast, served
family style, uses farm produce whenever possible.

Rooms 3 rms (1 pri facs) (1 fmly) S £27.50–£35;
D £55–£70 **Facilities** STV TVL tea/coffee Dinner available
Cen ht Wi-fi **Parking** 6 **Notes** ⊗ 🐾 450 acres beef/
arable

HORLEY

**For accommodation details see under Gatwick Airport
(London), (Sussex, West)**

RIPLEY
Map 6 TQ05

The Talbot Inn

★★★★ 🎖 🏠 INN

High St GU23 6BB
☎ **0845 4591492** 🖹 **01483 211332**
e-mail: info@thetalbotinn.com
dir: *Exit A3 signed Ripley, on left on High St*

The Talbot Inn simply oozes charm and character and has
retained many of its historical features even having
undergone a recent major transformation. Public areas
provide great comfort levels with real ales and delicious
home-cooked food on offer. Al fresco dining is available
in summer months. Traditional bedrooms are available in
the main house and more contemporary-styled rooms are
featured in the 'stable block'.

Rooms 9 en suite 30 annexe en suite (17 GF) S £79–£109;
D £89–£129* **Facilities** STV FTV tea/coffee Dinner
available Direct Dial Cen ht Wi-fi **Conf** Max 120 Thtr 120
Class 58 Board 36 **Parking** 35 **Notes** Civ Wed 120

SUSSEX, EAST

BEXHILL
Map 6 TQ70

Eves Bed and Breakfast

★★★★ 🅰 GUEST ACCOMMODATION

20 Hastings Rd TN40 2HH
☎ **01424 733268**
e-mail: evesbandb@googlemail.com
Rooms 4 en suite (2 fmly) (1 GF) S £25–£40; D £50–£65
Facilities TVL tea/coffee Dinner available Cen ht Wi-fi
Parking 4 **Notes** LB

BODIAM

Spring Farm

★★★★ BED AND BREAKFAST

Northlands TN32 5UX
☎ **01580 831222**
e-mail: springfarmbandb@tiscali.co.uk
dir: *A21, 1m S of Hurst Green, turn left, follow signs for
Bodiam Castle. After 2m continue across x-rds, 400mtrs
on left.*

Spring Farm is located just one mile from Bodiam Castle
and close to Hastings, Rye and Tenterden. Bedrooms and
bathrooms are stylishly decorated providing guests with
comfortable accommodation. Flat screen TVs and free
Wi-fi throughout. The guest lounge on the ground floor
provides additional space for guests to relax during the
day, and is where a cooked or continental breakfast is
served in the morning. There is an outdoor swimming pool
set amongst beautiful gardens.

Rooms 3 en suite S £50–£75; D £70–£85 **Facilities** tea/
coffee Cen ht Wi-fi FTV TVL 🐾 **Parking** 3 **Notes** LB ⊗ No
children 12yrs

BRIGHTON & HOVE
Map 6 TQ30

Brighton Pavilions

★★★★ GUEST ACCOMMODATION

7 Charlotte St BN2 1AG
☎ **01273 621750** 🖹 **01273 622477**
e-mail: sanchez-crespo@lineone.net
web: www.brightonpavilions.com
dir: *A23 to Brighton Pier, left onto A259 Marine Parade,
Charlotte St 15th left*

This well-run operation is in one of Brighton's Regency
streets, a short walk from the seafront and town centre.
Bedrooms have themes such as *Mikado* or *Pompeii*, and
are very smartly presented with many thoughtful extras
including room service breakfast in superior rooms and
free Wi-fi. The bright breakfast room is styled after a
Titanic garden restaurant.

Rooms 10 rms (7 en suite) (1 fmly) (1 GF) S £40–£48;
D £70–£152* **Facilities** FTV tea/coffee Direct Dial Cen ht
Wi-fi **Notes** LB

Five

★★★★ GUEST ACCOMMODATION

5 New Steine BN2 1PB
☎ **01273 686547** 🖹 **01273 625613**
e-mail: info@fivehotel.com
dir: *On A259 towards E, 8th turn on left into square*

An attractive townhouse in a traditional Georgian square
just a stone's throw from the famous Brighton beaches,
cafés and shops. Comfortable bedrooms and bathrooms
are well equipped. A copious organic breakfast is served
by cheerful hosts in the spacious, contemporary dining
room.

Rooms 10 en suite (4 fmly) S £45–£75; D £70–£140*
Facilities TVL tea/coffee Cen ht Wi-fi **Conf** Max 20 Board
20 **Notes** ⊗

Lansdowne Guest House

★★★★ 🏠 GUEST ACCOMMODATION

3 The Red House, 21 Lansdowne Rd BN3 1FE
☎ **07803 484775** 🖹 **01273 773718**
e-mail: lansdowneguesthouse@hotmail.co.uk

This modern and spacious suite is in a large 19th-century
house originally built by Lord Caernarvon and retains
much of the original charm. There are two large
bedrooms, a private sitting room, an elegant lounge and
a dining room where a substantial breakfast is served.

Rooms 2 rms (1 en suite) (1 pri facs) S £65–£75;
D £75–£85* **Facilities** FTV TVL tea/coffee Dinner available
Cen ht **Notes** LB ⊗ Closed 24-27 Dec

See advert on opposite page

New Steine

★★★★ 🏠 🍴 GUEST ACCOMMODATION

10-11 New Steine BN2 1PB
☎ **01273 695415** & **681546** 🖹 **01273 622663**
e-mail: reservation@newsteinehotel.com
dir: *A23 to Brighton Pier, left onto Marine Parade, New
Steine on left after Wentworth St*

This guest house is close to the seafront off the
Esplanade. The spacious bedrooms are well equipped and
some have sea views. There is a cosy lounge, where a
wide choice of English, vegetarian, vegan or continental

breakfasts is served. There is street parking in front of the property.

Rooms 20 rms (16 en suite) (4 fmly) (2 GF) S £39-£55; D £65-£105* **Facilities** FTV tea/coffee Dinner available Direct Dial Cen ht Licensed Wi-fi **Conf** Max 50 Thtr 50 Class 20 Board 26 **Notes** LB No Children 4yrs

The Twenty One Guest House

★★★★ GUEST ACCOMMODATION

21 Charlotte St, Marine Pde BN2 1AG
☎ 01273 686450
e-mail: enquiries@thetwentyone.co.uk
web: www.thetwentyone.co.uk
dir: *From Brighton Pier turn left onto Marine Parade, 16th turning on left*

This stylishly refurbished townhouse property is situated in Kemp Town within easy reach of clubs, bars and restaurants and just a short walk from the beach. Rooms are elegantly furnished and comfortable with an abundance of thoughtful extras provided. A smart dining room is the setting for a delicious, freshly-cooked breakfast.

Rooms 8 en suite (1 fmly) S £50-£60; D £90-£149 **Facilities** FTV tea/coffee Cen ht Wi-fi **Notes** LB ⊗

See advert on this page

The White House

★★★★ GUEST ACCOMMODATION

6 Bedford St BN2 1AN
☎ 01273 626266
e-mail: info@whitehousebrighton.com
web: www.whitehousebrighton.com
dir: *Arrive into Brighton A23 & follow signs to city centre. At rdbt opposite pier take 1st exit, continue through 2 sets of lights, turn left onto Bedford St*

The White House is a small Regency residence only 100 metres from the seafront, and a short walk from Brighton's centre. There are sea views from the south-facing rooms and a courtyard garden where guests may sit and relax. All rooms are smartly and stylishly decorated and guests can expect a relaxed atmosphere. Breakfast is served in the dining room, or al fresco. The extensive breakfast menu uses only best quality ingredients.

Rooms 10 rms (8 en suite) (2 GF) **Facilities** tea/coffee Cen ht Wi-fi **Notes** ⊗ Closed Jan

Alvia

★★★★ GUEST ACCOMMODATION

36 Upper Rock Gardens BN2 1QF
☎ 01273 682939 📄 01273 626287
e-mail: enquiries@alviahotel.co.uk
web: www.alviahotel.co.uk
dir: *A23 to Brighton Pier, left onto Marine Parade, 500yds left at lights onto Lower Rock Gdns & Upper Rock Gdns*

This fine Victorian house is just a short walk from the seafront and town centre, and offers a choice of

continued

Lansdowne Guest House, Brighton

Tel: 07803 484775   Email: lansdowneguesthouse@hotmail.co.uk

Quality, well appointed, friendly luxury accommodation. Tasteful new guest bedrooms, sound proofed, and modern. Tea, coffee-making facilities, fridge, air cooler, biscuits, fruit, television, DVD player, computer link, desk, wifi connection, toiletries, sewing & writing materials, fresh flowers and sitting area.

Sea, city centre, a wide variety of restaurants, cafes, bars, pubs nearby.

the 21 Brighton

21 Charlotte St, East Sussex, Brighton, BN2 1AG
Tel: 01273 686450
Website: www.thetwentyone.co.uk
Email: enquiries@thetwentyone.co.uk

AA

Welcome to *The Twenty One*, our refurbished Regency townhouse is located in a quiet residential side street, yet right at the heart of the lively and cosmopolitan Kemp Town area of Brighton.

We are a few steps from the seafront (our principal rooms have the benefit of oblique sea views), and within easy walking distance of all the major attractions, you will also find dozens of bars and restaurants a short walk from Charlotte Street in the St James's Street area of Kemp Town.

All rooms have flat panel TVs with freeview & DVD, hairdryer, toiletries, use of towelling bathrobes and slippers, hospitality tray, mini fridge, digital radio/alarm/iPod docks.

BRIGHTON & HOVE *continued*

comfortable and well-equipped bedrooms. Full English and vegetarian breakfasts are offered, served in the bright dining room. Some parking is available, which should be booked in advance.

Rooms 10 rms (9 en suite) (1 fmly) **Facilities** tea/coffee Cen ht Wi-fi **Parking** 4 **Notes** ⊗

Ambassador Brighton

★★★★ GUEST ACCOMMODATION

22-23 New Steine, Marine Pde BN2 1PD
☎ 01273 676869   ▤ 01273 689988
e-mail: info@ambassadorbrighton.co.uk
web: www.ambassadorbrighton.co.uk
dir: *A23 to Brighton Pier, left onto A259, 9th left, onto Garden Sq, 1st left*

At the heart of bustling Kemp Town, overlooking the attractive garden square next to the seaside, this well-established property has a friendly and relaxing atmosphere. Bedrooms are well equipped and vary in size, with the largest having the best views. A small lounge with a separate bar is available.

Rooms 24 en suite (9 fmly) (3 GF) (8 smoking)
S £36-£75; D £59-£115* **Facilities** tea/coffee Direct Dial Cen ht Licensed **Conf** Max 20 Thtr 20 Board 14 **Notes** LB

Bannings@ Number 14

★★★★ GUEST ACCOMMODATION

14 Upper Rock Gardens, Kemp Town BN2 1QE
☎ 01273 681403
e-mail: christopher.c.darnell@btinternet.com
dir: *Left onto A259 towards pier front, left at next lights, left to Tower Rock Garden, straight on to Upper Rock Gdns*

This attractive Victorian property is situated close to the seafront and just steps away from restaurants and shops. The comfortably furnished bedrooms are fresh and bright, and the cheerful dining room is the setting for a healthy breakfast. Parking tokens are available for a small charge.

Rooms 6 rms (5 en suite) (1 pri facs) (1 fmly);
D £55-£96* **Facilities** FTV tea/coffee Cen ht Wi-fi **Notes** ⊗

Brighton House

★★★★ ⬢ GUEST ACCOMMODATION

52 Regency Square BN1 2FF
☎ 01273 323282
e-mail: info@brighton-house.co.uk
web: www.brighton-house.co.uk
dir: *Opp West Pier*

Situated close to the seafront is the elegant, environmentally-friendly, Brighton House. Comfortably appointed bedrooms and bathrooms come in a variety of sizes and are located on four floors. An impressively abundant, organic continental breakfast is served in the

spacious elegant dining room. Parking is in the nearby underground car park.

Rooms 16 en suite (2 fmly) **Facilities** tea/coffee Cen ht Licensed **Notes** ⊗ No Children 12yrs

Colson House

★★★★ GUEST ACCOMMODATION

17 Upper Rock Gardens BN2 1QE
☎ 01273 694922   ▤ 01273 694922
e-mail: info@colsonhouse.co.uk
dir: *From Brighton Pier, east on A259 then left at lights*

Just a short walk from Kemp Town this listed Regency property offers a warm friendly welcome and some comfortable accommodation. Bedrooms are named after movie icons and include DVD players with films by the artiste. Breakfast is served in a light and airy dining room.

Rooms 8 en suite (1 GF); D £69-£99* **Facilities** tea/coffee Cen ht Wi-fi **Notes** ⊗ No Children 12yrs

Four Seasons Guest House

★★★★ GUEST ACCOMMODATION

3 Upper Rock Gardens BN2 1QE
☎ 01273 673574
e-mail: info@fourseasonsbrighton.com
web: www.fourseasonsbrighton.com
dir: *At rdbt take first exit proceed along Marine Parade, at lights, turn left onto Lower Rock Gdns*

Caring hosts William and Thommy provide smart accommodation with a variety of stylish contemporary bedrooms, each with ample facilities including Wi-fi and hairdryers. A healthy breakfast is served in the sunny dining room. Beaches, restaurants and shops are within close walking distance

Rooms 7 rms (6 pri facs) (1 GF) S £49-£54; D £62-£120* **Facilities** FTV tea/coffee Cen ht Wi-fi **Notes** LB ⊗ No Children 10yrs

George IV

★★★★ GUEST ACCOMMODATION

34 Regency Square BN1 2FJ
☎ 01273 321196
e-mail: info@georgeivbrighton.co.uk
web: www.georgeivbrighton.co.uk
dir: *Opp West Pier, at top of square*

Situated at the top of the prominent Regency Square overlooking the gardens and sea, this restored property provides elegantly furnished bedrooms with modern bathrooms and good facilities. There is a lift to all floors and a freshly prepared continental breakfast is served in your bedroom.

Rooms 8 en suite (1 fmly) S £45-£55; D £65-£150 (room only)* **Facilities** tea/coffee Cen ht Lift Wi-fi **Notes** ⊗ Closed Jan

Guest and the City

★★★★ GUEST ACCOMMODATION

2 Broad St BN2 1TJ
☎ 01273 698289
e-mail: info@guestandthecity.co.uk
dir: *M23 onto A23 towards pier, at rdbt left onto Manchester St then right onto Saint James St. 2nd left onto Broad St*

Guest and the City is just seconds away from the beach and famous Palace Pier and just minutes from the town centre. This refurbished boutique style townhouse offers comfortable, modern accommodation equipped with flat-screen TVs and Wi-fi. Some rooms feature custom-made stained glass windows. Breakfast is served in a contemporary dining room.

Rooms 7 rms (6 en suite) (1 pri facs) S £40-£70; D £60-£150* **Facilities** FTV TVL tea/coffee Cen ht Wi-fi **Notes** ⊗ Closed 24-26 Dec

Gullivers

★★★★ GUEST ACCOMMODATION

12a New Steine BN2 1PB
☎ 01273 681546 & 695415   ▤ 01273 622663
e-mail: reservation@gullivershotel.com
web: www.gullivershotel.com
dir: *A23 to Brighton Pier, left onto Marine Parade, premises 300yds on left*

Situated in an impressive Regency square close to the town and seafront, the New Steine has much to offer. Compact rooms use clever design and contemporary colours to ensure comfort, and some have quality shower rooms en suite. The lounge, decorated with fine art, and brasserie are super areas in which to relax and dine.

Rooms 12 rms (9 en suite) (3 pri facs) (2 GF) (4 smoking) S £29-£49; D £59-£99* **Facilities** FTV tea/coffee Dinner available Direct Dial Cen ht Licensed Wi-fi **Conf** Max 30 Thtr 30 Class 10 Board 20 **Notes** LB ⊗ No Children 4yrs

The Kelvin Guest House

★★★★ GUEST ACCOMMODATION

9 Madeira Place, Kemptown BN2 1TN
☎ 01273 603735
e-mail: enquiries@thekelvin.co.uk

The Kelvin is a Regency townhouse elegantly refurbished in a modern contemporary style with beautifully furnished bedrooms equipped with flatscreen TVs, Freeview and Wi-fi. Breakfast is served in the bright, cheery dining room, and an attractive deck patio is available for guest use. Restaurants, shops and the beach are minutes away.

Rooms 10 rms (7 en suite) (3 pri facs) (1 fmly) (1 GF)
Facilities FTV tea/coffee Cen ht Wi-fi **Notes** LB ⊗ No Children 12yrs

Marine View

★★★★ GUEST ACCOMMODATION

24 New Steine BN2 1PD
☎ 01273 603870 ▤ 01273 357257
e-mail: info@mvbrighton.co.uk
web: www.mvbrighton.co.uk
dir: From A23, left onto Marine Pde, left onto New Steine, 300mtrs

Overlooking the elegant Steine Square with the sea just a glance away, this 18th-century property offers comfortable, well designed accommodation. Plenty of accessories are provided, including free Wi-fi. A hearty breakfast is available in the bright lounge/dining room.

Rooms 11 rms (8 en suite) (1 pri facs) (2 fmly) (2 GF)
S £35-£55; D £65-£120* **Facilities** tea/coffee Cen ht Wi-fi **Notes** LB ⊗

Nineteen

★★★★ GUEST ACCOMMODATION

19 Broad St BN2 1TJ
☎ 01273 675529 ▤ 01273 675531
e-mail: info@hotelnineteen.co.uk
web: www.hotelnineteen.co.uk
dir: A23 to Brighton Pier, left onto Marine Parade, Broad St 3rd on left

This contemporary establishment lies close to the town centre, only minutes from Brighton Pier. Bedrooms are decorated with white walls, wooden floors and stylish artworks. The continental breakfast (served with champagne at the weekend) is superb, providing a fine start to the day.

Rooms 8 en suite (2 GF) **Facilities** FTV Cen ht Wi-fi Outdoor hot tub in courtyard bedroom **Conf** Max 8 Board 8 **Notes** ⊗ No Children 10yrs Closed 24-26 Dec

The Oriental

★★★★ GUEST ACCOMMODATION

9 Oriental Place BN1 2LJ
☎ 01273 205050 ▤ 01273 205050
e-mail: info@orientalbrighton.co.uk
dir: A23 right onto A259 at seafront, right into Oriental Place, on right

The Oriental is situated close to the seafront and enjoys easy access to all areas. The accommodation is comfortable and modern, and there is a licensed bar. A tasty Sussex breakfast using locally sourced produce is offered in a friendly, relaxed atmosphere.

Rooms 9 en suite (4 fmly) (1 GF) S £49-£75;
D £65-£195* **Facilities** FTV tea/coffee Cen ht Licensed Wi-fi Massage & Aromatherapy **Conf** Max 10 Thtr 10 Class 10 Board 10

Paskins Town House

★★★★ GUEST ACCOMMODATION

18/19 Charlotte St BN2 1AG
☎ 01273 601203 ▤ 01273 621973
e-mail: welcome@paskins.co.uk
web: www.paskins.co.uk
dir: A23 to pier, turn left, Charlotte St 11th left

This environmentally-friendly, family-run Victorian house is in a quiet street within walking distance of the seafront and town centre. Bedrooms are a comfortable mix of Victorian and art nouveau styles. The Art Deco breakfast room offers a variety of vegetarian and vegan dishes and traditional English breakfasts, featuring home-made vegetarian sausages and much organic produce.

Rooms 19 rms (16 en suite) (2 fmly) S £40-£60;
D £65-£140* **Facilities** FTV tea/coffee Cen ht Wi-fi **Notes** LB

Snooze

★★★★ GUEST ACCOMMODATION

25 St George Ter BN2 1JJ
☎ 01273 605797
e-mail: info@snoozebrighton.com

This splendid Victorian terraced property is close to the beach and the popular Kemp Town bars and restaurants. Bedrooms have a distinctly 'retro' feel and all are comfortably presented. A choice of hearty breakfasts is served in the spacious dining room enhanced with large bay windows. Snooze was a runner-up for the AA Funkiest B&B 2009-2010 Award.

Rooms 10 rms (9 en suite) (1 pri facs) (2 GF)
Facilities tea/coffee Cen ht Wi-fi **Notes** ⊗ No Children 12yrs

Millards

★★★ GUEST ACCOMMODATION

23 Broad St BN2 1TJ
☎ 01273 694314 ▤ 01273 676826
e-mail: info@millards-hotel-brighton.com
dir: A23 to Brighton Pier, left onto Marine Parade, left onto Manchester St, right onto St James's St & 2nd right

This attractive establishment is near to the seafront and town centre. Bedrooms are stylishly comfortable and finished with considerate extras including Freeview TV and a safe. Breakfast is served in the modern dining area next to the reception.

Rooms 8 en suite (2 GF) **Facilities** tea/coffee Direct Dial Cen ht Licensed **Notes** ⊗

Motel Schmotel

★★★ GUEST ACCOMMODATION

37 Russell Square BN1 2EF
☎ 01273 326129
e-mail: info@motelschmotel.co.uk

Charming family-run establishment situated on a quiet square just minutes away from beaches and shops. Bright en suite bedrooms include thoughtful amenities such as free Wi-fi and Freeview TV. A substantial breakfast menu uses fresh, local produce and is served in rooms.

Rooms 8 en suite (1 fmly) (2 GF) **Facilities** tea/coffee Cen ht Wi-fi **Parking** 2 **Notes** ⊗

Ainsley House

★★★ GUEST ACCOMMODATION

28 New Steine BN2 1PD
☎ 01273 605310 ▤ 01273 688604
e-mail: rooms@ainsleyhotel.com

Situated on the stylish Steine Square and with good views of the Pier, this popular property has a range of well equipped rooms; most are en suite and all are comfortably presented. Breakfast, served by the cheerful proprietor, is in the well positioned dining room with views over the square.

Rooms 12 rms (10 en suite) (3 fmly) **Facilities** TV11B TVL tea/coffee Cen ht

BRIGHTON & HOVE *continued*

Avalon

★★★ GUEST ACCOMMODATION

7 Upper Rock Gardens BN2 1QE
☎ 01273 692344 📠 01273 692344
e-mail: info@avalonbrighton.co.uk
dir: *A23 to Brighton Pier, left onto Marine Parade, 300yds at lights left onto Lower Rock Gdns, over lights Avalon on left*

A warm welcome is assured at this guest house just a short walk from the seafront and The Lanes. The en suite bedrooms vary in size and style but all are attractively presented with plenty of useful accessories including free Wi-Fi. Parking vouchers are available for purchase from the proprietor.

Rooms 7 en suite (3 fmly) (1 GF) S £49-£55; D £69-£95*
Facilities FTV tea/coffee Cen ht Wi-fi

Regency Landsdowne Guest House

★★★ GUEST ACCOMMODATION

45 Landsdowne Place BN3 1HF
☎ 01273 321830 📠 01273 777067
e-mail: regencylansdowne@aol.com
web: www.regencylansdowne.co.uk
dir: *A23 to Brighton Pier, right onto A259, 1m right onto Lansdowne Place, house on left before Western Rd*

A warm welcome is guaranteed at this Regency house, located only minutes from the seafront. Comfortable bedrooms are functionally equipped with a good range of facilities. An extensive continental breakfast is served at a communal table overlooking attractive gardens. On-road parking a short walk away.

Rooms 7 rms (5 en suite) (2 pri facs) **Facilities** FTV tea/coffee Cen ht Lift Wi-fi **Notes** ⊗

Westbourne Guest House

★★★ GUEST ACCOMMODATION

46 Upper Rock Gardens BN2 1QF
☎ 01273 686920 📠 01273 686920
e-mail: welcome@westbournehotel.net
dir: *A23 to Brighton Pier, left onto Marine Parade, 100yds left at lights, premises on right*

Just a short walk from the seafront, this Victorian house is run by friendly owners. The attractive bedrooms are bright and well furnished, and some have flat screen TVs. Spacious dining area is complimented by a large bay window.

Rooms 11 rms (7 en suite) (1 fmly) (2 GF) (2 smoking) S £25-£50; D £50-£90* **Facilities** FTV TVL tea/coffee Licensed Wi-fi **Parking** 1 **Notes** ⊗ Closed 23-30 Dec

Sandpiper Guest House

★★★ Ⓐ GUEST HOUSE

11 Russell Square BN1 2EE
☎ 01273 328202 📠 01273 329974
e-mail: sandpiper@brighton.co.uk
dir: *After conference centre on King's Rd, right onto Cannon Place. Russell Sq at end of street*

Rooms 6 rms (1 fmly) **Facilities** tea/coffee Cen ht **Notes** ⊗

The Market Inn

★★ INN

1 Market St BN1 1HH
☎ 01273 329483 📠 01273 777227
e-mail: marketinn@reallondonpubs.com
web: www.reallondonpubs.com/market.html
dir: *In city centre, on pedestrian road 50yds from junct North St & East St*

This lively period inn is within walking distance of many local attractions. Bedrooms are attractively decorated and feature a range of extra facilities. Breakfast is served in the bedrooms, and popular bar food is served at lunchtimes in the bar, which retains its original character.

Rooms 2 en suite S £40-£50; D £65-£75* **Facilities** FTV tea/coffee Dinner available Cen ht Wi-fi **Notes** LB No Children No coaches

Queensbury

★★ GUEST ACCOMMODATION

58 Regency Square BN1 2GB
☎ 01273 325558 📠 020 7373 1080
e-mail: reservations@queensburyhotel.co.uk
dir: *M23 onto A23 to seafront at Palace Pier, 3rd exit W to West Pier. Take right hand filter onto Preston St, next right onto Regency Sq*

This period accommodation is conveniently located for the promenade and town centre. Bedrooms are functional and provide basic amenities for guests, some bedrooms share bathrooms whilst others are en suite. A continental breakfast is served at individual tables in the dining room. There is a public car park in the centre of the square.

Rooms 19 rms (7 en suite) (12 pri facs) (9 fmly) (1 GF); D £39-£89 **Facilities** tea/coffee Cen ht Wi-fi **Notes** ⊗

CHIDDINGLY Map 6 TQ51

Netherwood Lodge

★★★★ BED AND BREAKFAST

Muddles Green BN8 6HS
☎ 01825 872512
e-mail: netherwoodlodge@hotmail.com
dir: *A22 at Golden Cross pub turn left. 0.5m to T-junct then sharp right at white house & round house. Down private road, Lodge 2nd on left*

Netherwood Lodge is a charming former coach house which provides a relaxing retreat for guests close to the A22, Lewes and coastal resort of Eastbourne. Well presented accommodation comprises two very well equipped bedrooms, one en suite and the other with a private bathroom. A very enjoyable, freshly cooked breakfast is served around one table in the attractive dining room which overlooks the pretty rear gardens.

Rooms 2 rms (1 en suite) (1 pri facs) (2 GF) S £50-£60; D £90* **Facilities** TVL tea/coffee Dinner available Cen ht Wi-fi **Parking** 5 **Notes** ⊗ No Children 16yrs ⊗

CROWBOROUGH Map 6 TQ53

Plough & Horses

★★★ INN

Walshes Rd TN6 3RE
☎ 01892 652614 📠 01892 652614
dir: *A26 onto B2100, under railway bridge, right onto Western Rd, over railway to Walshes Rd*

This pleasant inn has been welcoming guests for many years, and over the last two decades the present owners have made this a very attractive and popular place. The spacious bedrooms feature well-chosen pine furniture, and public rooms include a traditional bar, a restaurant, and a further lounge bar.

Rooms 15 en suite (3 fmly) **Facilities** TVL tea/coffee Dinner available Cen ht **Parking** 40 **Notes** Closed 24-25 Dec

DITCHLING
Map 6 TQ31

PREMIER COLLECTION

Tovey Lodge
★★★★★ GUEST ACCOMMODATION

Underhill Ln BN6 8XE
☎ 08456 120544
e-mail: info@sussexcountryholidays.co.uk
dir: *From Ditchling village, N on Beacon Rd. After 0.5m left onto Underhill Ln, 100yds 1st drive on left*

Set within three acres of garden and great views of the South Downs. There is an indoor swimming pool, sauna and Jacuzzi. Bedrooms and bathrooms are spacious, stylishly decorated and comfortable. Bedrooms also include Wi-fi and DVD plasma TVs. There is a guest lounge which also backs on to a patio offering additional space to relax. The lounge is spacious and features a 50" plasma TV. A cooked or continental breakfast can be enjoyed in the dining room.

Rooms 5 en suite (3 fmly) (2 GF) S £55–£80; D £80–£140* **Facilities** FTV TVL tea/coffee Dinner available Cen ht Licensed Wi-fi ⊗ Sauna **Conf** Max 12 Thtr 12 Board 12 **Parking** 28 **Notes** LB ⊜

The Bull
★★★★ ⊜ INN

2 High St BN6 8TA
☎ 01273 843147 📠 01273 843147
e-mail: info@thebullditchling.com

Dating back to 1563, the Bull is one of the oldest buildings in this famously pretty Sussex village. Owner Dominic Worrall took over in 2003, and has made this a popular venue serving home-cooked meals from a frequently-changing, modern British menu that makes the best of local produce. The huge garden commands stunning views over the South Downs. A selection of modern en suite bedrooms are stylishly decorated and comfortably furnished.

Rooms 4 en suite **Facilities** FTV Dinner available Cen ht Wi-fi **Parking** 30 **Notes** LB

EASTBOURNE
Map 6 TV69

PREMIER COLLECTION

The Manse B & B
★★★★★ BED AND BREAKFAST

7 Dittons Rd BN21 1DW
☎ 01323 737851
e-mail: anne@themansebb.com
web: www.themansebb.com
dir: *A22 to town centre railway station, onto Old Orchard Rd, right onto Arlington Rd*

This delightful home is in a quiet residential area only a five minute walk from the town centre. Built as a Presbyterian manse at the turn of the 19th century, much of the original character has been retained. The beautifully decorated bedrooms are very comfortable and have a wide range of accessories such as flat screen TV and DVD. Breakfast is served in the elegant dining room, with its stripped wooden floors and pretty courtyard view.

Rooms 3 en suite S £45–£50; D £74–£84* **Facilities** FTV tea/coffee Cen ht Wi-fi **Parking** 2

PREMIER COLLECTION

Ocklynge Manor
★★★★★ BED AND BREAKFAST

Mill Rd BN21 2PG
☎ 01323 734121 & 07979 627172
e-mail: ocklyngemanor@hotmail.com
web: www.ocklyngemanor.co.uk
dir: *From Eastbourne Hospital follow town centre/ seafront sign, 1st right onto Kings Av, Ocklynge Manor at top of road*

This charming home has seen a variety of uses through the years, including as a commanderie for the Knights of St John in the 12th century. An air of peace and relaxation is evident in the delightful public rooms, well-tended gardens and the spacious, comfortable bedrooms filled with thoughtful extras, including free Wi-fi. Hospitality is a plus and home-baked bread is just one of the delights on offer.

Rooms 3 rms (2 en suite) (1 pri facs) S £50–£80; D £80–£90* **Facilities** FTV tea/coffee Cen ht Wi-fi **Parking** 3 **Notes** ⊗ No Children 16yrs ⊜

PREMIER COLLECTION

The Berkeley
★★★★★ GUEST ACCOMMODATION

3 Lascelles Ter BN21 4BJ
☎ 01323 645055 📄 01323 400128
e-mail: info@theberkeley.net
dir: *Follow seafront from pier, take 7th turn on right*

The Berkeley's central location is convenient for seafront, theatre and the town centre. Spacious bedrooms are smartly furnished, and a stylish lounge is provided for guests to relax in. Breakfast is served in the attractive dining room.

Rooms 13 en suite (4 fmly) (1 GF) S £39–£49; D £78–£98* **Facilities** STV tea/coffee Cen ht Wi-fi

PREMIER COLLECTION

The Gables
★★★★★ BED AND BREAKFAST

21 Southfields Rd BN21 1BU
☎ 01323 644600
e-mail: info@gablesbandb.co.uk
dir: *A2270 into town centre, 2nd exit at rdbt by station, bear right into Southfields Rd*

The Gables is a splendid Edwardian property with lots of character, spacious accommodation and friendly hosts. A freshly-cooked breakfast is served in the elegant dining room. Free Wi-fi is available for guests. A short walk will take you to the station, town centre and pier. Some off-road parking is available.

Rooms 3 rms (2 en suite) (1 pri facs) **Facilities** TVL tea/coffee Cen ht Lift Wi-fi **Parking** 2 **Notes** ⊗ ⊜

EASTBOURNE continued

The Camelot Lodge

★★★★ GUEST ACCOMMODATION

35 Lewes Rd BN21 2BU
☎ 01323 725207 📄 01323 722799
e-mail: info@camelotlodgehotel.com
web: www.camelotlodgehotel.com
dir: A22 onto A2021, premises 0.5m after hospital on left

This delightful Edwardian property is within walking distance of the seafront and local amenities. The beautifully styled bedrooms feature a range of facilities including free Wi-fi access, and there is a spacious lounge-bar area. Meals are served in the conservatory dining room, and dinner is available by arrangement.

Rooms 8 en suite (3 fmly) (1 GF) S £34.95-£45; D £59.95-£80* **Facilities** FTV TVL tea/coffee Dinner available Cen ht Licensed Wi-fi **Parking** 11 **Notes** LB ⊗

Arden House

★★★★ GUEST ACCOMMODATION

17 Burlington Place BN21 4AR
☎ 01323 639639 📄 01323 417840
e-mail: info@theardenhotel.co.uk
web: www.theardenhotel.co.uk
dir: On seafront, towards W, 5th turn after pier

This attractive Regency property sits just minutes away from the seafront and town centre. Bedrooms are comfortable and bright, many with new en suite bathrooms. Guests can enjoy a hearty breakfast at the beginning of the day then relax in the cosy lounge in the evening.

Rooms 11 rms (10 en suite) (1 pri facs) (1 fmly) S £35-£39; D £58-£65 **Facilities** TVL tea/coffee Cen ht Wi-fi **Parking** 4 **Notes** LB

The Bay Lodge

★★★★ GUEST ACCOMMODATION

61-62 Royal Pde BN22 7AQ
☎ 01323 732515 📄 01323 735009
e-mail: baylodgehotel@fsmail.net
dir: From A22 follow signs to seafront. Bay Lodge on right opposite Pavilion Tea Gardens

This family-run guest house offers a warm welcome in comfortable surrounds opposite the Redoubt and Pavilion gardens. Bedrooms are bright and spacious, some with balconies. There is a sun lounge and a cosy bar overlooking the superb sea views.

Rooms 10 en suite (2 fmly) (2 GF) S £30-£39; D £56-£78* **Facilities** TVL tea/coffee Cen ht Licensed Wi-fi **Parking** 6 **Notes** LB ⊗

Bella Vista

★★★★ GUEST ACCOMMODATION

30 Redoubt Rd BN22 7DH
☎ 01323 724222
e-mail: enquiries@hotelbellavista.co.uk
dir: 500yds NE of town centre. Off A259 (Seaside Rd)

Situated on the east side of town, just off the seafront, this is an attractive flint house with the bonus of a car park. Bedrooms are generally spacious, comfortable and neatly appointed with modern facilities including free Wi-fi. There is a large lounge and dining room where dinner and breakfast is served.

Rooms 9 en suite (1 fmly) (3 GF) **Facilities** TVL tea/coffee Dinner available Cen ht Licensed **Parking** 10 **Notes** ⊗

Far End

★★★★ GUEST HOUSE

139 Royal Pde BN22 7LH
☎ 01323 725666
e-mail: ross.gowling@btconnect.com
dir: 0.5m of pier. A259 onto Channel View Rd & Royal Parade, next to Princess Park

Located north-east of the town centre, next to the popular Princess Park and the Marina, this family-run guest house offers a warm and friendly welcome. Bedrooms vary in size but are well appointed, some having sea views. Breakfast and dinner are served in the bright ground-floor dining room.

Rooms 10 rms (6 en suite) **Facilities** tea/coffee Dinner available Cen ht Licensed **Parking** 8 **Notes** No Children 6yrs

The Gladwyn

★★★★ GUEST ACCOMMODATION

16 Blackwater Rd BN21 4JD
☎ 01323 733142
e-mail: contact@thegladwyn.com
web: www.thegladwyn.com
dir: 250yds S of town centre. Off A259 South St onto Hardwick Rd & 1st right

A warm welcome is guaranteed at this delightful guest house located opposite the famous tennis courts. Art work and interesting collectables feature throughout the property, including public areas and bedrooms. Freshly prepared breakfasts are served in the cosy dining room

overlooking the attractive garden, which is available during the summer.

Rooms 10 en suite (1 fmly) (2 GF) **Facilities** TVL tea/coffee Licensed Wi-fi

Ivydene

★★★★ GUEST ACCOMMODATION

5-6 Hampden Ter, Latimer Rd BN22 7BL
☎ 01323 720547 📄 01323 411247
e-mail: ivydenehotel@hotmail.co.uk
web: www.ivydenehotel-eastbourne.co.uk
dir: From town centre/pier NE along seafront, towards Redoubt Fortress, onto St Aubyns Rd, 1st right onto Hampden Terrace

This friendly family-run property is situated a short walk from the pier and seafront. Bedrooms are bright and cheerful with comfortable, stylish furnishings. Public areas include a spacious lounge/bar, sunny conservatory and attractive dining room.

Rooms 14 en suite (2 fmly) (1 GF) S £30-£35; D £58.50-£70* **Facilities** TVL tea/coffee Dinner available Cen ht Licensed Wi-fi **Notes** LB ⊗ RS Oct-Etr No evening meal

The Mowbray

★★★★ GUEST ACCOMMODATION

2 Lascelles Ter BN21 4BJ
☎ 01323 720012 📄 01323 733579
e-mail: info@themowbray.com
dir: Opp Devonshire Park Theatre

This elegant townhouse is located opposite The Devonshire Theatre and a few minutes walk from the seafront. Bedrooms, that are accessible by a lift to all floors, vary in size, but all are attractively furnished and comfortable. There is a spacious well presented lounge, small modern bar and a stylish dining room. Breakfast is home-cooked, as are evening meals that are available by prior arrangement. Laura and Darren Weir were finalists for the AA Friendliest Landlady of the Year 2009-2010 Award.

Rooms 13 en suite (3 fmly) (1 GF) S £37-£42; D £74-£84* **Facilities** TVL tea/coffee Dinner available Cen ht Lift Licensed Wi-fi **Conf** Max 20 Thtr 20 Class 10 Board 10 **Notes** LB

The Royal

★★★★ GUEST ACCOMMODATION

8-9 Marine Pde BN21 3DX
☎ 01323 649222 ▤ 0560 1500 065
e-mail: info@royaleastbourne.org.uk
web: www.royaleastbourne.org.uk
dir: *East of pier*

This property enjoys a central seafront location close to the pier and within easy walking distance of the town centre. Spectacular uninterrupted sea views are guaranteed. Now fully renovated and eco-friendly, the comfortable bedrooms are modern with flat-screen TVs and free Wi-fi. One of the ten rooms has private facilities, while the others are fully en suite. A substantial continental breakfast is served. The Royal offers a full pet-sitting service.

Rooms 10 rms (9 en suite) (1 pri facs) (1 fmly) S £35-£47; D £70-£84* **Facilities** STV FTV tea/coffee Cen ht Wi-fi Golf Wi-fi available **Notes** LB No Children 14yrs

The Sherwood

★★★★ GUEST ACCOMMODATION

7 Lascelles Ter BN21 4BJ
☎ 01323 724002 ▤ 01323 400133
e-mail: info@thesherwood.net
dir: *Follow signs to seafront (Grand Parade). Next to Eastbourne Centre*

Attractive Victorian property just a minute's walk from the seafront, offering well-appointed bedrooms with comfortable, co-ordinated furnishings. A cosy lounge

offers a nice environment to relax in and the attractive dining room serves a robust breakfast.

Rooms 13 en suite (5 fmly) (1 GF) S £35-£41; D £70-£82* **Facilities** STV FTV TVL tea/coffee Dinner available Cen ht Licensed Wi-fi

Beach Haven

★★★ GUEST ACCOMMODATION

61 Pevensey Rd BN21 3HS
☎ 01323 726195
e-mail: enquiries@beach-haven.co.uk
web: www.beach-haven.co.uk
dir: *250yds E of town centre off A259*

The attractive terrace property is just a short walk from the seafront and attractions. Bedrooms are located on three floors, some offer en suite facilities and all have a thoughtful range of guest extras. There is also a comfortable dining room, a cosy lounge and a small private chapel.

Rooms 8 rms (3 en suite) (1 GF) S £25-£40; D £50-£80* **Facilities** tea/coffee Dinner available Cen ht **Notes** LB ⊗ No Children 1yr

Beachy Rise

★★★ GUEST HOUSE

5 Beachy Head Rd BN20 7QN
☎ 01323 639171 ▤ 01323 645006
e-mail: susanne234@hotmail.co.uk
dir: *1m SW of town centre. Off B2103 Upper Dukes Rd*

This friendly family-run guest house has a quiet residential location close to Meads Village. Bedrooms are individually styled with co-ordinated soft furnishings and feature some useful extras. Breakfast is served in the light and airy dining room overlooking the garden, which guests are welcome to use.

Rooms 4 en suite (2 fmly) S £30-£45; D £55-£70 **Facilities** tea/coffee Cen ht Wi-fi **Notes** ⊠

The Sheldon

★★★ GUEST ACCOMMODATION

9-11 Burlington Place BN21 4AS
☎ 01323 724120 ▤ 01323 430406
e-mail: sheldonhotel@tiscali.co.uk
web: www.thesheldon.co.uk
dir: *500yds SE of pier off seafront parade*

This impressive Victorian house is convenient for the town centre and only a short walk from the seafront. Bedrooms vary in size but are well equipped and cheerfully decorated. Traditional home-cooked food is served in the smart dining room.

Rooms 28 en suite (5 fmly) (2 GF) **Facilities** TVL tea/coffee Dinner available Direct Dial Cen ht Lift Licensed Wi-fi **Conf** Max 30 Board 30 **Parking** 17 **Notes** LB ⊗

HALLAND Map 6 TQ41

PREMIER COLLECTION

Tamberry Hall

★★★★★ GUEST ACCOMMODATION

Eastbourne Rd BN8 6PS
☎ 01825 880090 ▤ 01825 880090
e-mail: rosi@tamberryhall.co.uk
web: www.tamberryhall.co.uk
dir: *In Halland on A22, 200yds N of junct with B2192 at Black Lion Inn*

A warm welcome is assured at this attractive house sitting in three acres of wonderful landscaped gardens. Individually decorated bedrooms vary in size and are all equipped with a variety of thoughtful extras. An inglenook fireplace and exposed beams are a character of this establishment. Hearty breakfasts are served in a delightful dining room or on the terrace, weather permitting.

Rooms 3 en suite (1 fmly) S £65-£80; D £78-£85* **Facilities** TVL tea/coffee Cen ht **Parking** 3 **Notes** LB ⊗ RS 24-27 Dec Continental breakfast only

HALLAND *continued*

Beechwood B & B

★★★★ Ⓐ GUEST ACCOMMODATION

Eastbourne Rd BN8 6PS
☎ 01825 840936 📄 01825 840936
e-mail: chyland1956@aol.com
web: www.beechwoodbandb.co.uk
dir: *On A22*

Rooms 3 rms (1 en suite) (2 pri facs) (1 fmly)
Facilities TVL tea/coffee Cen ht Wi-fi ↘ Hot Tub
Parking 5 **Notes** LB

HASTINGS & ST LEONARDS   Map 7 TQ80

PREMIER COLLECTION

The Laindons

★★★★★ BED AND BREAKFAST

23 High St, Old Town TN34 3EY
☎ 01424 437710
e-mail: jacksonchris2007@yahoo.co.uk

The Laindons is a Georgian Townhouse, formerly a
coaching house set on this attractive high street in
Hastings. Bedrooms have been stylishly decorated
offering guests comfortable accommodation; rooms
include Freeview TV and Wi-fi. Whilst bedrooms are
spacious, there is a guest lounge providing additional
space for guests to relax. A cooked or continental
breakfast can be enjoyed in the upper floor
conservatory with views of the downs and Hastings
Church.

Rooms 3 en suite S £70-£80; D £85-£95*
Facilities STV TVL Cen ht Wi-fi **Notes** ⊗ No Children
5yrs Closed Dec-Jan

See advert on opposite page

PREMIER COLLECTION

Stream House

★★★★★ BED AND BREAKFAST

Pett Level Rd, Fairlight TN35 4ED
☎ 01424 814916 & 0794 191 1379
e-mail: info@stream-house.co.uk
web: www.stream-house.co.uk
dir: *4m NE of Hastings. Off A259 on unclassified road
between Fairlight & Cliff End*

Lovingly converted from three cottages, the house
stands in three acres of tranquil grounds, just one mile
from Winchelsea beach. The well-appointed bedrooms
are beautifully decorated. Delicious breakfasts are
served in the lounge-dining room with an original
inglenook fireplace, and during warmer months you can
enjoy the extensive garden with its rippling stream and
Koi pond.

Rooms 3 rms (2 en suite) (1 pri facs); D £70-£85
Facilities FTV TVL tea/coffee Cen ht Wi-fi Table tennis
Parking 4 **Notes** LB ⊗ No Children 10yrs Closed Dec-
Feb ♨

Parkside House

★★★★ GUEST ACCOMMODATION

59 Lower Park Rd TN34 2LD
☎ 01424 433096 📄 01424 421431
e-mail: bkentparksidehse@aol.com
dir: *A2101 to town centre, right at rdbt, 1st right*

You can expect a friendly welcome at this attractive
Victorian house overlooking Alexandra Park, just a
10-minute walk from the town centre and seafront. The
bedrooms are carefully furnished and have an abundance
of thoughtful touches including free Wi-fi and a 'tuck

shop' for midnight snackers. Breakfast is served at
individual tables in the elegant dining room.

Rooms 5 rms (4 en suite) (1 fmly) S £30-£50;
D £65-£75* **Facilities** TVL tea/coffee Cen ht Wi-fi
Notes LB ⊗

White Cottage

★★★★ GUEST ACCOMMODATION

Battery Hill, Fairlight TN35 4AP
☎ 01424 812528 📄 01424 812285
dir: *3m E off A259 (Hastings-Rye), signed Fairlight*

This modern house is set among mature gardens on the
outskirts of the peaceful village of Fairlight, between
Hastings and Rye. White Cottage offers pleasantly
decorated, thoughtfully furnished and well-equipped
bedrooms. Breakfast is served in the bright and airy
lounge-cining area which overlooks the beautiful garden.

Rooms 3 en suite (1 GF) S fr £45; D £65-£70*
Facilities tea/coffee Cen ht **Parking** 4 **Notes** LB ⊗ No
Children 12yrs Closed Dec ♨

Seaspray Bed & Breakfast

★★★★ Ⓐ GUEST HOUSE

54 Eversfield Place TN37 6DB
☎ 01424 436583
e-mail: jo@seaspraybb.co.uk
web: www.seaspraybb.co.uk
dir: *A21 to town centre & seafront, Seaspray 100yds W
of pier*

Rooms 10 rms (8 en suite) (2 pri facs) (1 fmly) (1 GF)
S £30-£50; D £65-£85 **Facilities** FTV tea/coffee Cen ht
Wi-fi **Notes** LB ⊗ Closed 10 Jan-10 Feb ♨

Foyles B&B and Tea Room

★★★ GUEST ACCOMMODATION

3 East Beach St TN34 3AR
☎ 01424 428811 & 752271
e-mail: foylesbedandbreakfast@hotmail.co.uk
dir: *A259 to Hastings old town, located on seafront*

This Grade II listed, 17th-century building is full of period
features and character, and is just opposite the beach
where the original fish market was. A delightful tea room
offers breakfast and lunch, and specialises in home-
made cream teas. The bedrooms are comfortable and
traditional, with original wooden beams. On Friday
evenings the tea room is transformed into the fully
licensed "Yoshi House", offering home-made Japanese
dishes and sushi, along with beer, sake and wine.

Rooms 4 rms (2 en suite) (2 pri facs) (1 fmly) S £35-£45;
D £55-£70* **Facilities** tea/coffee Cen ht Licensed
Notes LB ♨

HEATHFIELD
Map 6 TQ52

Holly Grove
★★★★ BED AND BREAKFAST

Little London TN21 0NU
☎ 01435 863375
e-mail: joedance@btconnect.com
dir: *A267 to Horam, turn right at Little London garage, proceed to bottom of lane*

Holly Grove is set in a quiet rural location with heated outdoor swimming pool, satellite TV, Wi-fi and parking facilities. Bedrooms are appointed to a very high standard. There is a separate lounge available for guests, and breakfast is served in the dining room or on the terrace, weather permitting.

Rooms 3 rms (2 en suite) (1 pri facs) (1 fmly) (2 GF) S £40-£70; D £60-£80* **Facilities** STV TVL tea/coffee Dinner available Cen ht Wi-fi ↘ Pool Table Table tennis, table hockey **Parking** 7 **Notes** No Children 12yrs

HERSTMONCEUX
Map 6 TQ61

PREMIER COLLECTION

Wartling Place
★★★★★ GUEST ACCOMMODATION

Wartling Place, Wartling BN27 1RY
☎ 01323 832590 📠 01323 831558
e-mail: accom@wartlingplace.prestel.co.uk
dir: *2.5m SE of Herstmonceux. Off A271 to Wartling. Wartling Place opp village church*

Located in a sleepy village, this beautiful Grade II listed country home is set in two acres of well-tended gardens. The individually decorated bedrooms, two featuring four-poster beds, are luxurious and have a host of thoughtful extras. Delicious breakfasts are served in the elegant dining room. For business travellers, there is free broadband access.

Rooms 4 en suite (1 fmly) **Facilities** tea/coffee Dinner available Cen ht **Conf** Max 12 **Parking** 10 **Notes** ⊗ 60

HOVE

See Brighton & Hove

LEWES
Map 6 TQ41

Nightingales
★★★★ GUEST ACCOMMODATION

The Avenue, Kingston BN7 3LL
☎ 01273 475673 📠 01273 475673
e-mail: jean.hudson@xln.co.uk
dir: *2m SW of Lewes. A23 onto A27 to Lewes, at Ashcombe rdbt exit for Kingston, under rail bridge, right at 30mph sign, house 2nd from end on right*

A warm welcome is assured at this delightful modern bungalow, set in beautifully kept gardens and grounds. The spacious bedrooms and bathrooms are well appointed and come with a wide range of thoughtful extras, including fresh fruit and sherry. Refreshment is

continued

THE LAINDONS
BOUTIQUE BED & BREAKFAST

23 High Street, Hastings, TN34 3EY
Tel: 01424 437710
www.thelaindons.com

The Laindons boutique bed & breakfast is located in the heart of Hastings Old Town. Originally a coaching house, this beautiful Georgian Grade II listed building has recently been refurbished, the interior is now luxurious and contemporary. The three double bedrooms have Egyptian cotton bed linen, sumptuous towels and robes and toiletries by The White Company. Multi-channel TV with DVD and WiFi access are standard.

Our guests can relax in their own private sitting room with its adjoining conservatory overlooking the Old Town and the East Hill. A perfect place to spend the night – but you'll want to stay longer!

LEWES *continued*

served on arrival in either the lounge or conservatory, both of which overlook the garden.

Rooms 2 en suite (2 GF) S £45-£65; D £65-£75*
Facilities TVL tea/coffee Cen ht **Parking** 2 **Notes** ⊗ No Children

The Blacksmiths Arms

★★★★ INN

London Rd, Offham BN7 3QD
☎ 01273 472971
e-mail: blacksmithsarms@tiscali.co.uk
web: www.theblacksmithsarms-offham.co.uk
dir: *2m N of Lewes. On A275 in Offham*

Situated just outside Lewes, this is a great location for touring the South coast, offering high quality accommodation in comfortable bedrooms. Enjoyable meals are available in the cosy bar downstairs and this is where the hearty cooked breakfast is also served.

Rooms 4 en suite **Facilities** tea/coffee Dinner available Cen ht Wi-fi **Parking** 22 **Notes** ⊗ No Children 5yrs No coaches

---

NEWHAVEN   Map 6 TQ40

The Harbourside

★★ INN

Fort Rd BN9 9EL
☎ 01273 513340   📄 01273 512372
dir: *A259 into Newhaven, signs to Fort, left onto South Rd & Fort Rd*

This Victorian inn is, as the name suggests, conveniently situated for the ferry terminals and harbour attractions. Bedrooms are spacious and a hearty meal can be enjoyed in the attractive bar and dining area. There is also a useful car park to the rear.

Rooms 10 rms (3 en suite) (5 fmly) **Facilities** tea/coffee Dinner available Cen ht Pool Table **Conf** Max 50 **Parking** 25 **Notes** ⊗

RYE   Map 7 TQ92

See also Hastings & St Leonards

PREMIER COLLECTION

Jeake's House

★★★★★ 🏠 GUEST ACCOMMODATION

Mermaid St TN31 7ET
☎ 01797 222828
e-mail: stay@jeakeshouse.com
web: www.jeakeshouse.com
dir: *Approach from High St or The Strand*

Previously a 17th-century wool store and then a 19th-century Baptist school, this delightful house stands on a cobbled street in one of the most beautiful parts of this small, bustling town. The individually decorated bedrooms combine elegance and comfort with modern facilities. Breakfast is served at separate tables in the galleried dining room, and there is an oak-beamed lounge as well as a stylish book-lined bar with old pews.

Rooms 11 rms (10 en suite) (1 pri facs) (2 fmly) S £70-£85; D £104-£128 **Facilities** FTV tea/coffee Direct Dial Cen ht Licensed Wi-fi **Parking** 20 **Notes** No Children 5yrs

---

PREMIER COLLECTION

Manor Farm Oast

★★★★★ 🛏️ 🍽️ GUEST ACCOMMODATION

Windmill Ln TN36 4WL
☎ 01424 813787   📄 01424 813787
e-mail: manor.farm.oast@lineone.net
web: www.manorfarmoast.co.uk
dir: *4m SW of Rye. A259 W past Icklesham church, left at x-rds onto Windmill Ln, after sharp left bend left into orchards*

Charming 19th-century, environmentally friendly oast house peacefully located amid orchards in open countryside. Spacious bedrooms are individually styled and include numerous thoughtful extras including free Wi-Fi. A choice of lounges is available, one heated by a roaring log fire during the winter, and locally sourced, home-produced dinners are a feature of any stay.

Rooms 3 rms (2 en suite) (1 pri facs) (1 fmly) S £56; D £99* **Facilities** tea/coffee Dinner available Cen ht Licensed Wi-fi **Conf** Max 20 Thtr 20 Board 12 **Parking** 8 **Notes** LB ⊗ No Children 11yrs Closed 23 Dec-15 Jan Civ Wed 70

PREMIER COLLECTION

Olde Moat House

★★★★★ 🛏️ GUEST ACCOMMODATION

TN29 0AZ
☎ 01797 344700   📄 01797 343919
e-mail: oldemoathouse@hotmail.com
web: www.oldemoathouse.co.uk

(For full entry see Ivychurch (Kent))

PREMIER COLLECTION

White Vine House
★★★★★ 🍴 RESTAURANT WITH ROOMS

24 High St TN31 7JF
☎ 01797 224748
e-mail: info@whitevinehouse.co.uk
dir: In centre of High Street

Situated in the heart of the ancient Cinque Port town of Rye, this property's origins go back to the 13th century. The cellar is the oldest part, but the current building dates from 1560, and boasts an impressive Georgian frontage. The original timber framework is visible in many areas, and certainly adds to the house's sense of history. The bedrooms have period furniture along with luxury bath or shower rooms; one bedroom has an antique four-poster.

Rooms 7 en suite (1 fmly) **Facilities** tea/coffee Dinner available Cen ht Wi-fi **Conf** Max 30 Thtr 30 Class 30 Board 30 **Notes** ⊗ No coaches Civ Wed 30

Oaklands
★★★★★ 🅰 GUEST ACCOMMODATION

Udimore Rd TN31 6AB
☎ 01797 229734 📠 01797 229734
e-mail: info@oaklands-rye.co.uk
web: www.oaklands-rye.co.uk
dir: Take B2089 from Rye 1.3m, Oaklands drive on right

Rooms 3 en suite; D £84-£100 **Facilities** FTV tea/coffee Cen ht ♨ **Parking** 5 **Notes** ⊗

The Rise
★★★★★ 🅰 BED AND BREAKFAST

82 Udimore Rd TN31 7DY
☎ 01797 222285
e-mail: theriserye@aol.com
dir: A21 Johns Cross take B2089 towards Rye. On right at bottom of hill

Rooms 3 en suite; D £84-£100 **Facilities** FTV tea/coffee Cen ht Wi-fi **Parking** 3 **Notes** ⊗ No Children 12yrs Closed 23 Dec-3 Jan

Strand House
★★★★ 🏠 🍴 GUEST ACCOMMODATION

Tanyards Ln, Winchelsea TN36 4JT
☎ 01797 226276 📠 01797 224806
e-mail: info@thestrandhouse.co.uk
web: www.thestrandhouse.co.uk
dir: M20 junct 10 onto A2070 to Lydd. Follow A259 through Rye to Winchelsea, 2m past Rye

This charming 15th-century house is just a few miles drive from Rye. Traditional character is maintained in comfortably appointed rooms and public areas. Local produce is a feature of the home-cooked evening meals and breakfasts.

Rooms 10 rms (9 en suite) (1 pri facs) (3 fmly) (1 GF) S £55-£75; D £65-£125* **Facilities** FTV TVL tea/coffee Dinner available Cen ht Licensed Wi-fi **Parking** 12 **Notes** LB No Children 12yrs RS wknds (high season) 2 night bookings only Civ Wed 30

Little Saltcote
★★★★ GUEST ACCOMMODATION

22 Military Rd TN31 7NY
☎ 01797 223210 📠 01797 224474
e-mail: info@littlesaltcote.co.uk
web: www.littlesaltcote.co.uk
dir: 0.5m N of town centre. Off A268 onto Military Rd signed Appledore, house 300yds on left

This delightful family-run guest house stands in quiet surroundings within walking distance of Rye town centre. The bright and airy en suite bedrooms are equipped with modern facilities including Wi-fi, and you can enjoy afternoon tea in the garden conservatory. A hearty breakfast is served at individual tables in the dining room.

Rooms 4 en suite (2 fmly) (1 GF) S £40-£75; D £65-£85 **Facilities** tea/coffee Cen ht Wi-fi **Parking** 5 **Notes** LB

The Windmill Guest House
★★★★ GUEST ACCOMMODATION

Ferry Rd TN31 7DW
☎ 01797 224027
e-mail: info@ryewindmill.co.uk
web: www.ryewindmill.co.uk

This white smock windmill has been a Rye landmark since 1820 and was more recently a bakery. Bedrooms located in the purpose-built extension have good beds and en suite facilities that are generously proportioned. Breakfast taken in the old granary is a freshly-cooked affair from well-sourced local ingredients including local butchers' sausages and some good local fruit juices.

Rooms 8 en suite (4 GF) **Facilities** FTV TVL tea/coffee Cen ht Licensed **Parking** 8 **Notes** No Children 12yrs Closed 24-26 Dec

Cliff Farm (TQ933237)
★★★ FARMHOUSE

Military Rd, Iden Lock TN31 7QE
☎ 01797 280331 📠 01797 280331 Mrs P Sullivin
e-mail: info@cliff-farm.com
dir: 2m along Military Rd to Appledore, turn left at hanging milk churn

Beautiful views and wonderful hospitality are what you'll find at this farmhouse situated in a peaceful rural location just a short drive from Rye and Hastings. Bedrooms are pleasantly decorated and comfortably furnished. Breakfast is served at individual tables in the dining room, and there is also a cosy sitting room with a wood-burning stove and TV.

Rooms 3 rms (1 fmly) S £28-£30; D £48-£50* **Facilities** TVL tea/coffee Cen ht **Parking** 6 **Notes** LB Closed Nov-Feb ⊛ 6 acres smallholding

ST LEONARDS

See Hastings & St Leonards

SEAFORD — Map 6 TV49

Ab Fab Rooms

★★★★ BED AND BREAKFAST

11 Station Rd, Bishopstone BN25 2RB
☎ 01323 895001 📄 0870 127 1624
e-mail: stay@abfabrooms.co.uk

Just a short walk from Bishopstone station and sandy beaches, this is a perfect base for visiting local sights and attractions. Contemporary-styled bedrooms offer superior comfort and amenities. Breakfast, served in the garden conservatory, includes home-made jams and local Sussex produce.

Rooms 3 en suite S £45–£50; D £65–£75* **Facilities** STV tea/coffee Cen ht Wi-fi **Parking** 2 **Notes** ⊗ 🚭

The Avondale

★★★ GUEST ACCOMMODATION

Avondale Rd BN25 1RJ
☎ 01323 890008 📄 01323 490598
e-mail: avondalehotel@btconnect.com
dir: In town centre, off A259 behind war memorial

A warm welcome is offered by the caring owners at this friendly, family-run guest accommodation which is ideally placed for the Newhaven to Dieppe ferry service. The bedrooms are pleasantly furnished and thoughtfully equipped. Breakfast is served in the attractive dining room and guests also have the use of a cosy lounge.

Rooms 14 rms (8 en suite) (4 fmly) **Facilities** TVL tea/coffee Cen ht Lift Wi-fi **Conf** Max 15 Class 15 Board 15 **Notes** ⊗

WADHURST — Map 6 TQ63

Little Tidebrook Farm (TQ621304)

★★★★ FARMHOUSE

Riseden TN5 6NY
☎ 01892 782688 **Mrs Sally Marley-Ward**
e-mail: info@littletidebrook.co.uk
web: www.littletidebrook.co.uk
dir: A267 from Tunbridge Wells to Mark Cross, left onto B2100, 2m turn right at Best Beech Inn, left after 1m, farm on left

This traditional farmhouse has cosy log fires in winter and wonderful garden dining in warm months. The imaginative décor combines with modern amenities such as Wi-fi to provide leisure and business travellers with the ideal setting. Close to Bewl Water and Royal Tunbridge Wells.

Rooms 3 rms (2 en suite) (1 pri facs) S £45–£80; D £60–£85* **Facilities** TVL tea/coffee Cen ht Wi-fi **Parking** 8 **Notes** No Children 12yrs ⊗ 40 acres horses

WILMINGTON — Map 6 TQ50

Crossways

★★★★ 🏵🏵 RESTAURANT WITH ROOMS

Lewes Rd BN26 5SG
☎ 01323 482455 📄 01323 487811
e-mail: stay@crosswayshotel.co.uk
web: www.crosswayshotel.co.uk
dir: On A27 between Lewes & Polegate, 2m E of Alfriston rdbt

Amidst stunning gardens and attractively tended grounds sits this well-established, popular restaurant. The well-presented bedrooms are tastefully decorated and provide an abundance of thoughtful amenities including free Wi-fi. Guest comfort is paramount and naturally warm hospitality ensures guests often return.

Rooms 7 en suite S £70–£79; D £120–£145 **Facilities** FTV tea/coffee Dinner available Direct Dial Cen ht Wi-fi **Parking** 30 **Notes** LB ⊗ No Children 12yrs Closed 24 Dec–23 Jan No coaches

SUSSEX, WEST

AMBERLEY — Map 6 TQ01

Stream Cottage

★★★★ BED AND BREAKFAST

The Square BN18 9SR
☎ 01798 831266 📄 01798 831266
e-mail: janet@streamcottage.co.uk
web: www.streamcottage.co.uk
dir: Off B2139 into village centre

Located on the edge of the South Downs and within easy reach of Arundel, Goodwood and Chichester, this picturesque thatched cottage has a wealth of beams and brick floors, and was reputedly built in 1587. The comfortable, well-equipped bedroom comes with a private sitting room. Breakfast is a wealth of imaginative ideas.

Rooms 1 rms (1 pri facs) (1 fmly); D £80* **Facilities** TVL tea/coffee Cen ht **Parking** 1 **Notes** LB ⊗ Closed Xmas & New Year 🚭

Woody Banks Cottage

★★★★ BED AND BREAKFAST

Crossgates BN18 9NR
☎ 01798 831295 & 07719 916703
e-mail: woodybanks@btinternet.com
web: www.woodybanks.co.uk
dir: Off B2139 into village, right at Black Horse pub, Woody Banks 0.5m on left past Sportsman pub

Located close to Arundel in an elevated position with stunning views over the Wildbrooks, this immaculately maintained house and gardens is very popular with walkers. It provides two comfortable, homely bedrooms filled with thoughtful extras. Imaginative breakfasts are served in the panoramic lounge-dining room.

Rooms 2 rms (2 pri facs) (1 fmly) S £35–£40; D £60–£65 **Facilities** TVL tea/coffee Cen ht **Parking** 3 **Notes** LB ⊗ No Children 6yrs Closed 24-27 Dec 🚭

ANGMERING — Map 6 TQ00

Angmering Manor

★★★★ 🍴 GUEST ACCOMMODATION

High St BN16 4AG
☎ 01903 859849 📄 01903 783268
e-mail: angmeringmanor@thechapmansgroup.co.uk
web: www.relaxinnz.co.uk
dir: Follow A27 towards Portsmouth, exit A280, follow signs for Angmering

This former manor house in the heart of the village has been stylishly appointed. It offers good food, a bar, an indoor pool, and good parking. Staff are friendly and helpful and rooms are very comfortable.

Rooms 17 en suite (3 fmly) **Facilities** FTV tea/coffee Dinner available Direct Dial Cen ht Licensed Wi-fi 🕸 Sauna Gymnasium Beauty salon **Conf** Max 20 Class 20 **Parking** 25 **Notes** LB ⊗ Civ Wed

ARUNDEL	Map 6 TQ00

See also Amberley

PREMIER COLLECTION

Brooklands Country Guest House
★★★★★ GUEST ACCOMMODATION

Brooklands Barn, Priory Ln BN18 0BG
☎ 01903 889515
e-mail: mail@brooklandsbarn.co.uk
dir: *A27/A284 Arundel rdbt, take Ford road, Priory Ln next right after Maxwell Rd*

Brooklands is a stunning barn conversion situated in the picturesque Arun Valley, just a short distance from the historic town of Arundel. Stylish bedrooms offer an array of extras such as Wi-fi. The dining room overlooks the fabulous gardens, and is ideal for breakfast. There is also an indoor pool.

Rooms 4 en suite (1 fmly) (2 GF) S £50-£80; D £70-£150 **Facilities** FTV tea/coffee Cen ht Wi-fi 🔄 Riding **Conf** Max 12 **Parking** 13 **Notes** LB

The Townhouse
★★★★ ⊚ RESTAURANT WITH ROOMS

65 High St BN18 9AJ
☎ 01903 883847
e-mail: enquiries@thetownhouse.co.uk
web: www.thetownhouse.co.uk
dir: *Follow A27 to Arundel, onto High Street, establishment on left at top of hill*

This an elegant, Grade II-listed Regency building overlooking Arundel Castle, just a short walk from the shops and centre of the town. Bedrooms and public areas retain the unspoilt characteristics of the building. The ceiling in the dining room is particularly spectacular and comes all the way from 16th-century Florence. The owners can be justifiably proud of the enterprise they took on just a short years ago.

Rooms 4 en suite S £70-£85; D £85-£120* **Facilities** FTV tea/coffee Dinner available Cen ht Wi-fi **Notes** ⊗ Closed 2wks Feb & 2wks Oct RS Sun-Mon Restaurant closed

Arden
★★★ GUEST ACCOMMODATION

4 Queens Ln BN18 9JN
☎ 01903 882544
e-mail: terry@ardenguesthouse.net
dir: *From station, at rdbt take turning for town centre. Take next left onto Queens Ln*

This is a comfortable guest house situated a few minutes from the town centre and station. The property has a selection of single, double and twin bedrooms, some of which are en suite. Traditional cooked breakfasts are served in the well-lit dining room. Off-street parking is available.

Rooms 8 rms (5 en suite) (2 GF) S £40-£48; D £53-£67* **Facilities** tea/coffee Cen ht **Parking** 5 **Notes** ⊗ No Children 14yrs Closed 31 Dec

BOGNOR REGIS	Map 6 SZ99

Arbor D'Oak
★★★★ BED AND BREAKFAST

221 Hawthorn Rd PO21 2UW
☎ 01243 861280
dir: *A29 to Bognor Regis, pass hospital, take last exit from rdbt Chichester Rd A259. Over lights next left onto Hawthorn Rd, past sports field*

A modern property that offers guests stylish, comfortable accommodation. Bedrooms and bathrooms are spacious with excellent quality fixtures and fittings. Useful features include hairdryers and irons in the rooms. The guest lounge on the ground floor creates additional space in which to relax. Breakfast can be enjoyed around the family-style breakfast table in the conservatory that looks out over the garden.

Rooms 2 rms (1 en suite) (1 pri facs) S fr £45; D fr £90* **Facilities** FTV TVL tea/coffee Cen ht cycle storage available **Parking** 4 **Notes** LB ⊗ No Children Closed Oct-Mar

Old Priory
★★★★ GUEST HOUSE

80 North Bersted St PO22 9AQ
☎ 01243 863580   📠 01243 826597
e-mail: old.priory@btinternet.com
web: www.old-priory.com
dir: *1.6m NW of Bognor. Off A259 (Chichester road) to North Bersted. Old Priory sign on left*

Located in the mainly residential area of North Bersted, this 400-year-old property retains many original features. Bedrooms which are all individual in style are homely and one has a four-poster waterbed and a double air bath. There is an outdoor pool and attractive grounds, perfect for the summer.

Rooms 3 rms (2 en suite) (1 pri facs) 3 annexe en suite (3 GF) S £35-£40; D £65-£100* **Facilities** STV tea/coffee Cen ht Wi-fi ⌇ Hot tub **Parking** 6 **Notes** ⊗

Trevali Guest House
★★★★ ⚫ GUEST ACCOMMODATION

Belmont St PO21 1LE
☎ 01243 862203
e-mail: info@trevaliguesthouse.co.uk
dir: *Follow signs to seafront, then Tourist Information signs*

Rooms 8 rms (5 en suite) (3 pri facs) (2 fmly) (2 GF) **Facilities** FTV tea/coffee Cen ht **Notes** ⊗

Jubilee
★★★ GUEST ACCOMMODATION

5 Gloucester Rd PO21 1NU
☎ 01243 863016   & 07702 275967   📠 01243 868017
e-mail: jubileeguesthouse@tiscali.co.uk
web: www.jubileeguesthouse.com
dir: *A259 to seafront, house opp Day Entrance to Butlins Family Entertainment Resort*

This property is close to Butlins, the seafront and the town centre. The brightly decorated and well-equipped bedrooms vary in size. A generous and freshly cooked breakfast, including provision for vegetarians, is served in the attractive dining room.

Rooms 6 rms (2 en suite) (3 fmly) S £25-£50; D £50-£100 **Facilities** tea/coffee Cen ht **Parking** 4 **Notes** LB ⊗ Closed Xmas, Jan & Feb

Sea Crest
★★★ ⚫ GUEST ACCOMMODATION

19 Nyewood Ln PO21 2QB
☎ 01243 821438
e-mail: seacrest.19@btinternet.com
Rooms 6 rms (4 en suite) (1 fmly) S fr £28; D £60-£64* **Facilities** tea/coffee Cen ht **Notes** ⊗ ⊗ 📧

BOGNOR REGIS *continued*

Regis Lodge

★★ GUEST ACCOMMODATION

3 Gloucester Rd PO21 1NU
☎ 01243 827110
e-mail: frank.regislodge@btinternet.com
web: www.regislodge.co.uk
dir: *A259 to Bognor, signs for Southcoast World, Regis Lodge opposite day visitors entrance to Southcoast World*

Located within easy walking distance of the seafront and attractions, this family-run guest house offers a high standard of hospitality. Bedrooms vary in size and are well presented and suitably equipped. The brightly decorated dining room has separate tables and a good choice is offered at breakfast.

Rooms 6 en suite (5 fmly) S £25-£35; D £50-£70
Facilities tea/coffee Cen ht **Parking** 4 **Notes** LB ⊗

BOSHAM Map 5 SU80

The Boathouse Bosham

★★★★ GUEST ACCOMMODATION

Main Rd PO18 8EH
☎ 01243 572572 📠 01243 572572
e-mail: info@bosham-boathouse.com
web: www.bosham-boathouse-bed-and-breakfast.co.uk
dir: *On A259, opp Chequers Ln*

This modern establishment, conveniently located near Bosham, Emsworth and Chichester, provides sumptuously comfortable beds and is ideal for walkers and leisure guests. A delicious home-cooked breakfast can be served outside in the attractive garden during warmer months and enjoyable evening meals are available by prior arrangement. Off-road car parking is a bonus.

Rooms 2 en suite (2 GF) S £60-£85; D £65-£99*
Facilities FTV tea/coffee Dinner available Cen ht Wi-fi
Parking 6

Charters B&B

★★★★ BED AND BREAKFAST

Bosham Ln PO18 8HG
☎ 01243 572644
e-mail: louise@chartersbandb.co.uk
dir: *A27 onto A259, 3m left at rdbt, right at T-junct, 100yds on right*

Charters B&B provides comfortable accommodation in a peaceful location close to Bosham Harbour and Goodwood race circuit. Bedrooms and bathrooms are spacious, stylish and modern with their own separate, self contained entrances. A continental breakfast is served in the comfort of guest bedrooms mid-week, and a freshly prepared hot breakfast is provided for guests on a Saturday and Sunday morning, served in the bright and airy conservatory.

Rooms 2 annexe en suite (1 GF) **Facilities** tea/coffee Cen ht **Parking** 3 **Notes** ⊗ No Children 10yrs Closed Xmas & New Year

White Barn

★★★★ BED AND BREAKFAST

Crede Ln PO18 8NX
☎ 01243 573113 📠 01243 573113
e-mail: chrissie@whitebarn.biz
web: www.whitebarn.biz
dir: *A259 Bosham rdbt, turn S signed Bosham Quay, 0.5m to T-junct, left signed White Barn, 0.25m turn left signed White Barn, 50yds turn right*

This delightful single storey property is close to Bosham Harbour, Goodwood Race Circuit, Chichester and Portsmouth, and has cosy bedrooms with colour co-ordinated soft furnishings and many thoughtful extras. The open-plan dining room overlooks an attractive garden, where breakfast is served if the weather permits.

Rooms 2 en suite 1 annexe en suite (3 GF) S £60-£65; D £75-£95* **Facilities** FTV tea/coffee Cen ht **Parking** 3 **Notes** ⊗ No Children 12yrs

---

BURGESS HILL Map 6 TQ31

Abbey House

★★★★ BED AND BREAKFAST

2 The Holt RH15 0RF
☎ 01444 233299
e-mail: info@abbey-house.biz
dir: *0.5m E of town centre. Off A2113 Folders Ln onto Kings Way, 3rd left onto The Holt*

This excellent accommodation is set in a comfortable family home, in a pleasant residential area: just a short walk from the town centre and railway station. The modern bedrooms are well equipped and include hair dryers, TVs, fridges and CD players; welcoming touches include wine and fruit. A good breakfast is served around a large communal dining table.

Rooms 4 rms (3 en suite) (1 pri facs) (1 GF) S £35-£45; D £65-£85* **Facilities** FTV tea/coffee Direct Dial Cen ht Wi-fi **Parking** 5 **Notes** ⊗ No Children 11yrs Closed 24 Dec-2 Jan

The Homestead

★★★★ 🏠 GUEST ACCOMMODATION

Homestead Ln, Valebridge Rd RH15 0RQ
☎ 01444 246899 & 0800 064 0015 📠 0870 165 6035
e-mail: homestead@burgess-hill.co.uk
web: www.burgess-hill.co.uk
dir: *0.5m N of Burgess Hill. From Wivelsfield station onto Valebridge Rd, 0.5m turn right to end of Homestead Ln*

The Homestead has a country setting surrounded by eight acres of garden and woodland just a short distance from the town centre. Bedrooms vary in size but all are well equipped and include generous extras. A great choice at breakfast includes vegetarian options. The attractive dining room overlooks the garden and there is a comfortable conservatory-lounge and good leisure facilities.

Rooms 3 en suite (2 GF) S £40; D £80 **Facilities** STV FTV tea/coffee Direct Dial Cen ht Wi-fi 🏊 Gymnasium Hot tub **Parking** 50 **Notes** ⊗ No Children 12yrs Closed 23 Dec-2 Jan

CHICHESTER   Map 5 SU80

See also Bosham, Chilgrove & West Marden

PREMIER COLLECTION

Rooks Hill
★★★★★ 🏠 GUEST HOUSE

Lavant Rd, Lavant PO18 0BQ
☎ 01243 528400
e-mail: enquiries@rookshill.co.uk

Rooks Hill occupies a convenient and picturesque location near to Goodwood and the City of Chichester. The warm and friendly proprietors create a wonderful home-from-home atmosphere for both business and leisure guests. The bedrooms are superbly finished and have powerful thermostatic showers and additional thoughtful extras. A delicious breakfast served in the stylish dining room or on the patio overlooking the pretty gardens in warmer weather provides a substantial start to the day.

Rooms 6 en suite (2 GF) S £85-£110; D £115-£165 **Facilities** FTV tea/coffee Cen ht Wi-fi **Parking** 6 **Notes** LB ⊗ No Children 12yrs

PREMIER COLLECTION

West Stoke House
★★★★★ 🍴🍴🍴 RESTAURANT WITH ROOMS

Downs Rd, West Stoke PO18 9BN
☎ 01243 575226 📠 01243 574655
e-mail: info@weststokehouse.co.uk
dir: *3m NW of Chichester. Off B286 to West Stoke, next to St Andrew's Church*

This fine country house, part Georgian and part medieval, with over five acres of lawns and gardens, lies on the edge of the South Downs. The large uncluttered bedrooms have smart modern bathrooms and great country views. The restaurant provides very good cooking in a relaxed atmosphere. Public rooms have a light-filled elegance and are adorned with an eclectic mix of period furniture and contemporary art.

Rooms 8 rms (7 en suite) (1 pri facs) (1 fmly) **Facilities** TV6B tea/coffee Dinner available Direct Dial Cen ht Wi-fi 🏊 **Conf** Max 60 Thtr 60 Class 30 Board 20 **Parking** 20 **Notes** Closed 24-28 Dec No coaches Civ Wed 60

PREMIER COLLECTION

The Royal Oak
★★★★★ ◉ INN

Pook Ln PO18 0AX
☎ 01243 527434 📠 01243 775062
e-mail: info@royaloaklavant.co.uk
dir: *2m N of Chichester. Off A286 into East Lavant centre*

Located close to the Goodwood estate and Rolls Royce HQ this delightful inn is full of character with beamed ceilings, timber floors and open fires in the public areas. Bedrooms are finished to a very high standard with comfortable beds and state of the art electronic equipment. Award winning meals are served in the popular restaurant.

Rooms 3 en suite 5 annexe en suite (1 fmly) **Facilities** STV tea/coffee Dinner available Direct Dial Cen ht Riding **Parking** 25 **Notes** No coaches

The Bull's Head
★★★★ INN

99 Fishbourne Road West PO19 3JP
☎ 01243 839895 📠 01243 774647
e-mail: julie@bullsheadfishbourne.co.uk
dir: *A27 onto A259, 0.5m on left*

The Bull's Head is a charming traditionally-styled inn which has a roaring open fire during winter months. By contrast, the accommodation is modern and contemporary and offers very good levels of comfort, spacious showers and generously sized fluffy towels. Evening meals and enjoyable breakfasts are provided daily. The establishment is perfectly located for Fishbourne Roman Palace, Goodwood, Portsmouth, Chichester Theatre and Bosham Harbour. Ideal for walkers, leisure visitors and corporate guests.

Rooms 4 en suite (1 fmly) (4 GF) S £40-£55; D £70-£95* **Facilities** FTV tea/coffee Dinner available Cen ht **Parking** 35 **Notes** LB

82 Fishbourne
★★★★ BED AND BREAKFAST

82 Fishbourne Road West PO19 3JL
☎ 07854 051013
e-mail: nik@nikwestacott.plus.com
web: www.82fishbourne.co.uk
dir: *A27 Chichester rdbt, towards Fishbourne and Bosham on A259. 0.5m on right diagonally opp Woolpack pub*

Warm and friendly hospitality abounds at 82 Fishbourne which is located only a short drive from the historic city of Chichester. Accommodation is spacious and well equipped for the business traveller or leisure guest. Breakfast provides a substantial start to the day and includes delicious fresh eggs from the free range hens which live in the back garden. Scheduled activities include 'Mushroom Hunts' and wine tastings throughout the year.

Rooms 3 en suite (1 fmly) (1 GF); D £40-£150* **Facilities** FTV tea/coffee Dinner available Cen ht Wi-fi **Parking** 3

Englewood B&B
★★★★ BED AND BREAKFAST

East Ashling PO18 9AS
☎ 01243 575407
e-mail: sjenglewood@hotmail.co.uk
dir: *Bosham rdbt A259, N exit. At T-junct turn right, next left to B2178, left again, Englewood on left*

Set well back from the main road, in an Area of Outstanding Natural Beauty (scheduled to become a National Park in 2010), Englewood has a very pretty garden, and is surrounded by pleasant lanes and footpaths. The two bedrooms have lots of thoughtful facilities and extras including bottled water, boiled sweets and fruit squash.

Rooms 2 rms (1 en suite) (1 pri facs) (2 GF) S £38-£40; D £50-£70* **Facilities** tea/coffee Cen ht **Parking** 2 **Notes** LB ⊗ No Children 🐾

Gable End
★★★★ BED AND BREAKFAST

Main Rd, Nutbourne PO18 8RT
☎ 01243 573356
e-mail: jill@po188rt.freeserve.co.uk
dir: *A259 W past Barleycorn pub on left, after 0.3m turn left & immediately right, 150yds 4th house on left, set back from road*

You are guaranteed a genuinely warm welcome at Gable End which occupies a peaceful location close to Bosham and Emsworth Marina. Enjoy a delicious home cooked breakfast in attractive surroundings with views from the rear of the property overlooking the sea and pretty garden.

Rooms 1 rms (1 pri facs); D fr £70* **Facilities** tea/coffee Dinner available Cen ht **Parking** 8 **Notes** ⊗ No Children 11yrs Closed 23 Dec-2 Jan 🐾

CHICHESTER *continued*

Horse and Groom

★★★★ INN

East Ashling PO18 9AX
☎ 01243 575339 📠 01243 575560
e-mail: info@thehorseandgroomchichester.co.uk
web: www.thehorseandgroomchichester.co.uk
dir: *3m N of Chichester, on B2178 towards Rowland's Castle*

The Horse and Groom is a unique 17th-century country pub and restaurant offering spacious and comfortable accommodation, and warm, friendly hospitality. Substantial, freshly prepared breakfasts, lunches and dinners, making good use of freshly caught fish and locally sourced ingredients, are available.

Rooms 11 en suite (11 GF) **Facilities** tea/coffee Dinner available Cen ht **Parking** 40 **Notes** RS Sun eve Bar & Restaurant close 6pm

Old Chapel Forge

★★★★ 🏠 BED AND BREAKFAST

Lower Bognor Rd, Lagness PO20 1LR
☎ 01243 264380
e-mail: info@oldchapelforge.co.uk
dir: *4m SE of Chichester. Off A27 Chichester bypass at Bognor rdbt signed Pagham/Runcton, onto B2166 Pagham Rd & Lower Bognor Rd, Old Chapel Forge on right*

Great local produce features in the hearty breakfasts at this comfortable, eco-friendly property, an idyllic 17th-century house and chapel set in mature gardens with panoramic views of the South Downs. Old Chapel Forge is a short drive from Chichester, Goodwood, Pagham Harbour Nature Reserve and the beach. Bedrooms, including suites in the chapel, are luxurious, and all have internet access.

Rooms 4 annexe en suite (2 fmly) (4 GF) S £45-£70; D £50-£110* **Facilities** FTV tea/coffee Dinner available Cen ht Wi-fi **Parking** 6 **Notes** LB

Old Orchard Guest House

★★★★ GUEST ACCOMMODATION

8 Lyndhurst Rd PO19 7PF
☎ 01243 536547
e-mail: info@oldorchardguesthouse.co.uk
dir: *In city centre, behind Old Cattle Market, follow Market Av, Stirling Rd, Caledonian Rd onto Lyndhurst Rd*

Old Orchard Guest House occupies a convenient location only a few minutes walk from the centre of the historic City of Chichester. Hospitality is genuinely warm and friendly and smart, stylish accommodation is very comfortable. A fully cooked breakfast is available served at separate tables in the bright dining room. Linda and Rupert Trotman were finalists for the AA Friendliest Landlady of the Year 2009-2010 Award.

Rooms 3 en suite S £50-£100; D £70-£100*
Facilities FTV TVL tea/coffee Cen ht **Parking** 2 **Notes** ⊗ No Children 12yrs

Trents

★★★★ GUEST ACCOMMODATION

50 South St PO19 1DS
☎ 01243 773714
e-mail: enquiries@trentchichester.co.uk
dir: *Enter Chichester from M27 Stockbridge rdbt straight ahead onto South St. Trents on right*

Trents is a friendly brasserie situated in the heart of Chichester. The sun terrace is perfect for alfresco dining, weather permitting. The contemporary bedrooms, all en suite, are very comfortable.

Rooms 5 en suite (1 fmly) S £60-£80; D £80-£109 (room only) **Facilities** tea/coffee Dinner available Direct Dial Cen ht Licensed Wi-fi **Notes** ⊗

Wilbury House

★★★★ BED AND BREAKFAST

Main Rd, Fishbourne PO18 8AT
☎ 01243 572953 📠 01243 572953
e-mail: jackiepenfold@onetel.com
dir: *Off A27 Chichester bypass onto A259 W to Fishbourne and Bosham, 1m on left from Tesco rdbt*

This modern and well-appointed house is located on the edge of the village surrounded by countryside. Personally supervised by the charming owner, the atmosphere is friendly. Bedrooms are individually decorated, nicely furnished and include two ground-floor garden rooms. A generous English breakfast is served in the kitchen, overlooking the rear garden or in the dining room.

Rooms 1 rms (1 pri facs) 2 annexe en suite (2 GF) S £45-£55; D £60-£80 **Facilities** tea/coffee Cen ht Wi-fi **Parking** 7 **Notes** ⊗ No Children 6yrs Closed mid Dec-mid Jan 🐾

The Vestry

Ⓤ

23 Southgate PO19 1ES
☎ 01243 773358 📠 01243 530633
e-mail: info@the-vestry.com

Currently the rating for this establishment is not confirmed This may be due to a change of ownership or because it has only recently joined the AA rating scheme. For up-to-date information please see the AA website: theAA.com

Rooms 11 en suite (2 fmly) S £65-£75; D £75-£95*
Facilities FTV tea/coffee Direct Dial Licensed Wi-fi
Notes Closed 24-26 Dec & 31 Dec-1 Jan

CHILGROVE   Map 5 SU81

The Fish House

[U]

PO18 9HX
☎ 01243 519444   📄 01243 519499
e-mail: info@fishhouse.co.uk
dir: *From Chichester take A286 N, turn left onto B2141 to village*

Currently the rating for this establishment is not confirmed. This may be due to a change of ownership or because it has only recently joined the AA rating scheme. For up-to-date information please see the AA website: theAA.com

Rooms 15 en suite (11 GF) S £80–£120; D £120–£150 (room only)* **Facilities** STV FTV tea/coffee Dinner available Direct Dial Cen ht Licensed Wi-fi Sauna **Conf** Max 40 Thtr 40 Class 40 Board 40 **Parking** 50 **Notes** LB Civ Wed 100

CLIMPING   Map 6 SU90

Derwent House

★★★★ BED AND BREAKFAST

Climping St BN17 5RQ
☎ 01903 726204
e-mail: jonshorrock@yahoo.co.uk
dir: *Turn S off A259 at Yapton onto Climping St*

Derwent House is situated in the Conservation Area of the Climping Gap, the last undeveloped stretch of coastline between Brighton and Bognor Regis. Guests will find a warm and friendly welcome at this attractive country house, which offers well-appointed rooms, a dining room and a cosy lounge overlooking the garden.

Rooms 2 en suite; D £70–£75 **Facilities** FTV tea/coffee Cen ht Wi-fi **Parking** 8 **Notes** LB No Children

Field Place

★★★★ 🅰 GUEST ACCOMMODATION

Church Ln BN17 5RR
☎ 01903 723200   📄 01903 724800
e-mail: info@fieldplace.org
Rooms 5 en suite S £40–£45; D £70–£90*

CRAWLEY

For accommodation details see Gatwick Airport (London)

GATWICK AIRPORT (LONDON)   Map 6 TQ24

Acorn Lodge Gatwick

★★★★ GUEST ACCOMMODATION

79 Massetts Rd RH6 7EB
☎ 01293 774550
e-mail: info@acornlodgegatwick.co.uk
web: www.acornlodgegatwick.co.uk
dir: *M23 junct 9, A23 into Horley, off A23 Brighton Rd*

This property provides a 24-hour transfer service to the airport and has on-site parking. Bedrooms are comfortably furnished, come with a practical desk area and useful touches. The breakfasts served in the comfortable dining room make a good start to the day; dinner is also available.

Rooms 15 en suite (4 fmly) (7 GF) **Facilities** FTV TVL tea/coffee Dinner available Cen ht Licensed Wi-fi **Parking** 20 **Notes** ⊗

Corner House

★★★★ GUEST ACCOMMODATION

72 Massetts Rd RH6 7ED
☎ 01293 784574   📄 01293 784620
e-mail: info@thecornerhouse.co.uk
web: www.thecornerhouse.co.uk
dir: *M23 junct 9 to Gatwick 1st rdbt, 2nd exit (straight ahead) next rdbt 4th exit signed Redhill onto A23 towards Redhill, turn off 2nd right Massetts Rd, on left*

Well located for Gatwick Airport with a 24-hour courtesy transfer service, the Corner House provides a range of thoughtfully furnished bedrooms, some in a separate house. Ground-floor areas include an attractive dining room and a comfortable lounge bar.

Rooms 19 rms (13 en suite) 12 annexe en suite (6 fmly) (9 GF) **Facilities** FTV TVL tea/coffee Dinner available Direct Dial Cen ht Licensed Golf 18 Membership to local sports centre **Conf** Max 15 Class 15 Board 15 **Parking** 12

The Lawn Guest House

★★★★ GUEST HOUSE

30 Massetts Rd RH6 7DF
☎ 01293 775751   📄 01293 821803
e-mail: info@lawnguesthouse.co.uk
web: www.lawnguesthouse.co.uk
dir: *In Massetts Rd, 200yds on left*

Once a Victorian school, this friendly guest house is well-positioned on a quiet leafy street close to Gatwick. Bedrooms are spacious with thoughtful amenities such as free Wi-fi, and fans for use in warm weather. Airport parking is available.

Rooms 12 en suite (4 fmly) S £40–£50; D £50–£60* **Facilities** STV tea/coffee Direct Dial Cen ht Wi-fi **Parking** 4

Trumbles

★★★★ GUEST ACCOMMODATION

Stan Hill RH6 0EP
☎ 01293 863418   📄 01293 862925
e-mail: stay@trumbles.co.uk
web: www.trumbles.co.uk
dir: *0.5m N of Charlwood. From village centre onto Norwoodhill Rd, 1st left onto Stan Hill*

This attractive house, within easy reach of Gatwick, enjoys a quiet and secluded setting in this charming village. Bedrooms are spacious with a good range of facilities. The conservatory offers an ideal environment for guests to relax and enjoy either continental or full English breakfast. Parking is available, along with airport transfers.

Rooms 6 en suite (2 fmly) (1 GF) S £55; D £65–£70* **Facilities** tea/coffee Cen ht Wi-fi **Parking** 20 **Notes** ⊗ Closed 24-26 Dec

Vulcan Lodge

★★★★ BED AND BREAKFAST

27 Massetts Rd RH6 7DQ
☎ 01293 771522   📄 01293 775376
e-mail: reservations@vulcan-lodge.com
dir: *M23 junct 9, A23 into Horley, off A23 Brighton Rd*

A particularly warm and friendly welcome is offered by the hosts of this charming period house, which sits back from the main road and is convenient for Gatwick Airport. Bedrooms are well equipped and feature many thoughtful extras. A choice of breakfast is offered, including vegetarian options, and is served in a delightful dining room.

Rooms 4 rms (3 en suite) (1 pri facs) (1 fmly) S £40–£45; D £60* **Facilities** FTV TVL tea/coffee Cen ht Wi-fi **Parking** 13

GATWICK AIRPORT (LONDON) *continued*

Cumberland House
★★★ GUEST HOUSE

39 Brighton Rd RH6 7HH
☎ 01293 825800
e-mail: carmel@cumberlandhs.com
web: www.cumberlandhs.com
dir: *M23 junct 9, A23 into Horley, on A23 (Brighton road) at corner of Church Rd, left & left again into car park*

This attractive and well-run guest house is convenient for Gatwick Airport. The comfortable bedrooms are carefully decorated and have a good range of facilities, and breakfast is served in the first-floor dining room. Ample off-road holiday parking.

Rooms 6 en suite (2 fmly) (1 GF) **Facilities** tea/coffee Cen ht Wi-fi Golf **Parking** 15 **Notes** ⊗

Gainsborough Lodge
★★★ GUEST HOUSE

39 Massetts Rd RH6 7DT
☎ 01293 783982 🖷 01293 785365
e-mail: enquiries@gainsborough-lodge.co.uk
dir: *2m NE of airport off A23 Brighton Rd*

Close to Gatwick, this fine Edwardian house offers a courtesy service to and from the airport. The bright bedrooms are comfortably appointed, and a varied breakfast, including a vegetarian option, is served in the cheerful conservatory-dining room. There is also an attractive lounge and bar.

Rooms 16 rms (14 en suite) 14 annexe en suite (5 fmly) (12 GF) **Facilities** TVL tea/coffee Direct Dial Cen ht Free membership of local Gym **Parking** 30 **Notes** ⊗

Gatwick White House
★★★ GUEST ACCOMMODATION

50-52 Church Rd RH6 7EX
☎ 01293 402777 & 784322 🖷 01293 424135
e-mail: hotel@gwhh.com
web: www.gwhh.com
dir: *In Horley centre off A23 (Brighton Rd)*

Convenient for the airport and major routes, this establishment offers efficient and functional accommodation. There is a bar, restaurant with good curries as well as traditional dishes, parking, and a 24-hour transfer service to Gatwick is available on request.

Rooms 27 en suite (2 fmly) (10 GF) **Facilities** TVL tea/coffee Dinner available Direct Dial Cen ht Licensed Wi-fi **Parking** 30 **Notes** ⊗

Frylands (TQ231197)
★★★★ FARMHOUSE

Wineham BN5 9BP
☎ 01403 710214   Mrs S Fowler
e-mail: b&b@frylands.co.uk
dir: *2m NE of Henfield. Off B2116 towards Wineham, 1.5m left onto Fryland Ln, Frylands 0.3m on left*

The friendly hosts offer comfortable accommodation at this delightful 16th-century timber-framed farmhouse, set in peaceful countryside. Day rooms and bedrooms are full of character and the well-appointed dining room is the setting for freshly cooked breakfasts. Ample off-road parking and free car storage for travellers using Gatwick Airport is available.

Rooms 3 rms (1 pri facs) (1 fmly) S £35-£37.50; D £57.50-£60* **Facilities** tea/coffee Cen ht Wi-fi ⌁ Fishing **Parking** 6 **Notes** Closed 20 Dec-1 Jan ⊜ 250 acres mixed

---

Denham Cottage
★★★★ BED AND BREAKFAST

1 Friday St, Warnham RH12 3QY
☎ 01403 243362
e-mail: denhamcottage@btinternet.com
dir: *From A24 into Warnham, past church on left, 2nd right, cottage 2nd on left*

Denham Cottage is situated in the picturesque village of Warnham, near Horsham on the edge of the famous deer park. Very smart and spacious accommodation with a private lounge/study adjoining and lots of useful extras, whether staying on business or for pleasure.

Rooms 1 en suite S £38; D £60* **Facilities** TVL tea/coffee Cen ht Wi-fi **Parking** 2 **Notes** ⊗ Closed Xmas ⊜

Random Hall
★★★★ GUEST ACCOMMODATION

Stane St, Slinfold RH13 0QX
☎ 01403 790558 🖷 01403 791046
e-mail: nigelrandomhall@btconnect.com
web: www.randomhall.co.uk
dir: *4m W of Horsham. On A29 W of Slinfold*

This 16th-century farmhouse combines character with good quality accommodation and service from the resident proprietors. The comfortable bedrooms are equipped with useful extras. Beams, flagstone floors and quality fabrics add style to the bar and public areas, and an enjoyable dinner is served Monday to Thursday.

Rooms 13 en suite (5 GF) S £65-£82.50; D £75-£110* **Facilities** STV tea/coffee Dinner available Direct Dial Cen ht Licensed Wi-fi Golf 18 **Conf** Max 20 Thtr 20 Class 16 Board 16 **Parking** 40 **Notes** LB ⊗

PREMIER COLLECTION

The Pilstyes
★★★★★ GUEST ACCOMMODATION

106-108 High St RH16 2HS
☎ 01444 484101 🖷 01444 484100
e-mail: carol@pontifexes.co.uk
web: www.sussex-bedandbreakfast.co.uk
dir: *On High Street (B2028), 8 houses from church*

Pilstyes is a Grade II-listed village house built around 1575. The spacious bedrooms are beautifully furnished and provide all the comforts of home. A healthy breakfast is served in the charming country kitchen or, on sunny days, in the flower-filled cottage courtyard. Carol and Roy are caring hosts providing a warm welcome and ensuring a pleasant stay.

Rooms 2 en suite S £75-£100; D £80-£105* **Facilities** FTV TVL tea/coffee Cen ht Wi-fi **Parking** 4 **Notes** ⊗ No Children 5yrs

---

Leeside
★★★★ GUEST ACCOMMODATION

Rope Walk BN17 5DE
☎ 01903 723666
e-mail: leeside1@tiscali.co.uk
dir: *Off A259. Onto Ferry Road 1m, turn right, up on right*

This bright bungalow is close to local sailing clubs, the River Arun and the beach. Visitors will enjoy a warm welcome, comfortable modern bedrooms; including free Wi-fi and flat-screen TVs, and a hearty breakfast to start the day.

Rooms 4 rms (3 en suite) (1 pri facs) (3 GF) S fr £35; D fr £60* **Facilities** FTV TVL tea/coffee Cen ht Wi-fi **Parking** 4 **Notes** ⊗ No Children 14yrs

Racing Greens

★★★★ BED AND BREAKFAST

70 South Ter BN17 5LQ
☎ 01903 732972 📠 01903 719389
e-mail: racinggreens@aol.com
web: www.littlehampton-racing-greens.co.uk
dir: *A259 onto B2187 for Littlehampton seafront, follow brown signs to seafront. B&B faces The Greens & sea, near Harbour Park Entertainment Centre*

This Victorian seafront home offers bright, spacious, comfortable accommodation. Bedroom amenities include Wi-fi and Freeview TV. Breakfast, featuring local and organic produce and a variety of breads, is served around a large table in the airy dining room overlooking the Greens.

Rooms 2 rms (1 en suite) (1 pri facs) **Facilities** FTV tea/coffee Cen ht Wi-fi **Notes** ⊗ No Children

MIDHURST   Map 6 SU82

See also Rogate

See also Rogate

PREMIER COLLECTION

Park House

★★★★★ 🏡 GUEST ACCOMMODATION

Bepton GU29 0JB
☎ 01730 819000 📠 01730 819099
e-mail: reservations@parkhousehotel.com
web: www.parkhousehotel.com
dir: *3m SW of Midhurst off A286*

This delightful, family-run guest house stands in landscaped gardens in the peaceful village of Bepton. The attractive, spacious bedrooms are thoughtfully equipped, and there is an elegant drawing room and an honesty bar. Breakfast and dinner are served in the dining room.

Rooms 21 rms (12 en suite) 3 annexe en suite (2 fmly) (1 GF) **Facilities** TV14B STV tea/coffee Dinner available Direct Dial Cen ht Licensed 🎣 ⚓ 🏌 ⚓ **Conf** Max 50 Thtr 50 Class 50 Board 25 **Parking** 30 **Notes** Civ Wed 54

PREMIER COLLECTION

Rivermead House

★★★★★ BED AND BREAKFAST

Hollist Ln GU29 9RS
☎ 01730 810907 & 07885 699479
e-mail: mail@bridgetadler.com
web: www.bridgetadler.com
dir: *1m NW of Midhurst. Off A286 towards Woolbeding*

Rivermead House is situated in a semi-rural area on the outskirts of Midhurst, in a quiet location, and offers friendly and relaxed accommodation. The spacious and comfortable guest bedroom is at the front of the house and enjoys wonderful south-facing views over the garden and farmland, with distant views of the South Downs. Breakfast is served in the farmhouse-style kitchen.

Rooms 1 en suite (1 fmly) **Facilities** tea/coffee Dinner available Cen ht Golf **Parking** 2 **Notes** ⊗ Closed 24-26 Dec 📧

Amberfold

★★★★ GUEST ACCOMMODATION

Amberfold, Heyshott GU29 0DA
☎ 01730 812385 📠 01730 813559
e-mail: erlingamberfold@aol.com
web: www.amberfold.co.uk
dir: *Off A286 signed Graffham/Heyshott, after 1.5m pass pond, Amberfold on left*

A delightful 17th-century, Grade II listed cottage, set in mature and attractive gardens in peacefully idyllic countryside. The accommodation is provided in two very different self-contained units, a cottage annexe and a modern open-plan lodge. Each bedroom is tastefully appointed with many thoughtful extras.

Rooms 5 annexe en suite (4 GF) S £60-£75; D £75-£110 **Facilities** TV2B FTV tea/coffee Cen ht **Parking** 5 **Notes** ⊗ No Children 14yrs Closed 16 Dec-8 Feb 📧

Cowdray Park Golf Club

★★★★ GUEST ACCOMMODATION

GU29 0BB
☎ 01730 813599 📠 01730 815900
e-mail: enquiries@cowdraygolf.co.uk
dir: *1m E on A272*

This renovated lodge provides contemporary bedrooms, with some rooms overlooking the internationally famous polo grounds. The immaculate golf course itself provides a challenge to members and visitors. Refreshments and meals are taken in the clubhouse which has modern facilities.

Rooms 6 en suite (1 fmly) (4 GF) S £60-£80; D £80-£120* **Facilities** FTV TVL tea/coffee Dinner available Cen ht Licensed Golf 18 🏌 Fishing **Conf** Max 60 Thtr 60 Class 60 Board 20 **Parking** 10 **Notes** LB ⊗

Holly Tree Lodge

★★★★ BED AND BREAKFAST

Easebourne St GU29 0BE
☎ 01730 813729 & 07746 523094 📠 01730 813729
e-mail: eabhamilton@yahoo.co.uk
dir: *1.5m NE of town centre. Off A272 at Easebourne church onto Easebourne St, premises on left after 600mtrs*

A warm welcome is guaranteed at this family home, set in lovely gardens, just one mile from the centre of Midhurst. One large, bright en suite bedroom can accommodate a family, and a cosy double room is also available. Breakfast is served in the sunny dining room or conservatory overlooking pretty gardens.

Rooms 2 rms (1 en suite) (2 GF); D £50-£90* **Facilities** tea/coffee Cen ht **Parking** 5 **Notes** 📧

Loves Farm *(SU912235)*

★★★★ FARMHOUSE

Easebourne St GU29 0BG
☎ 01730 813212 & 07789 228400 Mr J Renwick
e-mail: info@lovesfarm.com
dir: *2m NE of town centre. Off A272 at Easebourne church onto Easebourne St, signs for Loves Farm*

This 17th-century farmhouse is set on a 300-acre farm with wonderful views of the South Downs from the windows. The comfortable rooms have their own entrance and benefit from king size beds and en suite or private shower rooms. A great location for access to Midhurst, Cowdray Park and Goodwood.

Rooms 3 rms (2 en suite) (1 pri facs) (2 fmly) (1 GF); D £70-£80* **Facilities** tea/coffee Cen ht **Parking** 3 **Notes** ⊗ 📧 300 acres arable/sheep/horses

PETWORTH   Map 6 SU92

The Angel Inn
★★★★ 🍽 INN

Angel St GU28 0BG
☎ 01798 342153
e-mail: theangelinn@live.co.uk

Dating back to the Domesday Book, The Angel Inn offers extremely comfortable accommodation in bedrooms which are equipped with antique furniture. Some rooms feature four-poster beds and some bathrooms benefit from jacuzzi-style baths. Very good substantial meals are available in the stylish dining room and the inn provides character places to rest and relax. The Angel Inn is perfectly located for exploring Petworth House which is within walking distance.

Rooms 7 rms (7 pri facs) S £80-£150; D £80-£150
Facilities tea/coffee Dinner available

PULBOROUGH   Map 6 TQ01

Orchard Mead
★★★★ BED AND BREAKFAST

Toat Ln RH20 1BZ
☎ 01798 872640
e-mail: siggy.rutherford@ukonline.co.uk
dir: Off A29 1m N of Pulborough onto Blackgate Ln, left onto Pickhurst Ln & right onto Toat Ln, Orchard Mead at end

A long winding road leads you this delightful detached home. Set in a peaceful rural location and only a short drive from the local train station. Bedrooms are comfortably furnished with thoughtful touches. A delicious light supper or full dinner can be provided on request.

Rooms 2 en suite (2 GF) **Facilities** TVL tea/coffee Dinner available Cen ht **Parking** 2 **Notes** ⊗ No Children 12yrs Closed Xmas & Etr 🐾

Harkaway
★★★ BED AND BREAKFAST

8 Houghton Ln, Bury RH20 1PD
☎ 01798 831843
e-mail: carol@harkaway.org.uk
web: www.harkaway.org.uk
dir: 5m S of Pulborough. Off A29 into Bury, at x-rds onto Houghton Ln, on left past Coombe Crescent

Harkaway is a small family-run guest house situated at the foot of the South Downs just half a mile from the South Downs Way in the beautiful village of Bury. Guests have their own entrance. A full English, vegetarian or continental breakfast is available, and drinks-making facilities are freely available. There is a colour TV in the guests' dining room. Harkaway is a non-smoking house which is open all year round.

Rooms 3 rms (1 en suite) (1 GF) S £25-£35; D £55-£65
Facilities TVL Cen ht Wi-fi **Parking** 2 **Notes** LB ⊗ No Children 6yrs 🐾

ROGATE   Map 5 SU82

PREMIER COLLECTION

Mizzards
★★★★★ BED AND BREAKFAST

GU31 5HS
☎ 01730 821656   📠 01730 821655
e-mail: francis@mizzards.co.uk
dir: 0.6m S from Rogate x-rds, over river & signed 300yds on right

This charming 16th-century house stands near the River Rother in two acres of resplendent landscaped gardens with a lake and the proprietor's own sculptures. Relax in either the conservatory or the split-level drawing room, and the airy, well-appointed bedrooms look over the grounds. There is an entrance hall dining room, and a swimming pool is available in summer.

Rooms 3 en suite S £50-£60; D £80-£90 **Facilities** tea/coffee Cen ht 🏊 🐎 **Parking** 12 **Notes** ⊗ No Children 9yrs Closed Xmas 🐾

RUSTINGTON   Map 6 TQ00

Kenmore
★★★★ GUEST ACCOMMODATION

Claigmar Rd BN16 2NL
☎ 01903 784634   📠 01903 784634
e-mail: thekenmore@hotmail.co.uk
dir: A259 follow signs for Rustington, turn for Claigmar Rd by war memorial. Kenmore on right as Claigmar Rd bends

A warm welcome is assured at this Edwardian house, located close to the sea and convenient for touring West Sussex. Spacious bedrooms, all individually decorated, are provided with many useful extras. There is a comfortable lounge in which to relax and a bright dining room where a good choice of breakfast is served.

Rooms 7 rms (6 en suite) (2 fmly) (2 GF) **Facilities** tea/coffee Cen ht **Parking** 7

SELSEY   Map 5 SZ89

St Andrews Lodge
★★★★ GUEST ACCOMMODATION

Chichester Rd PO20 0LX
☎ 01243 606899   📠 01243 607826
e-mail: info@standrewslodge.co.uk
web: www.standrewslodge.co.uk
dir: B2145 into Selsey, on right just before church

This friendly lodge is just half a mile from the seafront. The refurbished bedrooms are bright and spacious, and have a range of useful extras. Five ground-floor rooms, one with easier access, overlook the large south-facing garden, which is perfect for a drink on a summer evening.

Rooms 5 en suite 5 annexe en suite (3 fmly) (5 GF) S £38-£55; D £68-£85 **Facilities** TVL tea/coffee Direct Dial Cen ht Licensed Wi-fi **Conf** Max 15 **Parking** 14 **Notes** LB Closed 21 Dec-11 Jan

Greenacre
★★★★ 🅰 BED AND BREAKFAST

5 Manor Farm Court PO20 0LY
☎ 01243 602912
e-mail: greenacre@zoom.co.uk
dir: B2145 to Selsey, over a small rdbt, next left (Manor Farm Court), bear left & Greenacre on left

Rooms 4 rms (3 en suite) (1 fmly) (1 GF) S £30-£50; D £65-£80* **Facilities** STV TVL tea/coffee Cen ht Wi-fi **Parking** 7

SIDLESHAM   Map 5 SZ89

PREMIER COLLECTION

The Crab & Lobster
★★★★★ ⊛ RESTAURANT WITH ROOMS

Mill Ln PO20 7NB
☎ 01243 641233
e-mail: enquiries@crab-lobster.co.uk
dir: A27 onto B2145 Selsey. Take 1st left after garage at Sidlesham onto Rookery Ln. Follow road to Crab and Lobster

Hidden away on the south coast near Pagham Harbour and only a short drive from Chichester is the stylish Crab & Lobster. Bedrooms are superbly appointed, and bathrooms are a feature with luxury toiletries and powerful 'raindrop' showers. Guests can enjoy lunch or dinner in the smart restaurant where the menu offers a range of locally caught fresh fish amongst other regionally-sourced, seasonal produce.

Rooms 4 en suite S £75-£85; D £130-£150*
Facilities FTV tea/coffee Dinner available Cen ht Wi-fi
Parking 12 **Notes** ⊗ No coaches

PREMIER COLLECTION

Landseer House
★★★★★ GUEST ACCOMMODATION

Cow Ln PO20 7LN
☎ 01243 641525   📄 01243 641525
e-mail: enq@landseerhouse.co.uk
web: www.landseerhouse.co.uk
dir: A27 Chichester bypass, take B2145 towards Selsey. After Hunston & Sidlesham, pass garage 0.5m, turn right signed Highleigh. Turn onto Keynor Ln, then 2nd left onto Cow Ln, House 0.5m last on right

Landseer House is very tranquil, and benefits from its peaceful location close to Pagham Harbour, yet only a ten minute drive from the centre of the historic Cathedral City of Chichester. The hands-on proprietors provide genuinely warm and friendly hospitality.

Bedrooms and bathrooms are furnished to an excellent standard, and breakfast is freshly cooked to order.

Landseer House

Rooms 4 rms (3 en suite) (1 pri facs) **Facilities** FTV TVL tea/coffee Cen ht Wi-fi **Parking** 14 **Notes** No Children 12yrs

The Jolly Fisherman B&B
★★★★ BED AND BREAKFAST

Selsey Rd PO20 7LS
☎ 01243 641544
e-mail: pamela.brett@btinternet.com

The Jolly Fisherman B&B benefits from its location halfway between the historic City of Chichester and Selsey. It is perfect for exploring the South coast harbours and ideal for Goodwood. Accommodation is comfortable and a traditional substantial breakfast is available in the dining room or on the rear patio overlooking fields, weather permitting.

Rooms 3 rms (1 en suite) (2 pri facs); D £65-£90*
Facilities FTV Cen ht Wi-fi Golf **Parking** 3 **Notes** ⊗ 🐾

SLINFOLD   Map 6 TQ13

The Red Lyon
★★★ 🍽 INN

The Street RH13 0RR
☎ 01403 790339   📄 01403 791863
e-mail: enquiries@theredlyon.co.uk
dir: Off A29

Located in the village centre, this delightful 18th-century inn, with parts dating from the 14th century, has a wealth of beams. Tasty meals at lunch and dinner are offered in the timber-panelled dining room. The bedrooms and bathrooms are bright, spacious and well equipped. A pleasant beer garden and ample parking are also available.

Rooms 4 en suite (1 fmly); D £50-£60 (room only)*
Facilities FTV TVL tea/coffee Dinner available Cen ht Wi-fi
Parking 30 **Notes** ⊗

SOUTH HARTING   Map 5 SU71

Torberry Cottage
★★★★ GUEST ACCOMMODATION

Hurst GU31 5RG
☎ 01730 826883   📄 01730 826883
e-mail: torberry.cottage@virgin.net
dir: 1m W of South Harting on B2146

Located in a rural setting north of the South Downs, this pleasantly furnished house offers well-equipped bedrooms and fine hospitality. Breakfasts, using fresh produce and served around a large table, are a feature. The house stands in very pleasant gardens.

Rooms 2 en suite **Facilities** tea/coffee Cen ht Wi-fi
Parking 4 **Notes** ⊗ No Children 10yrs Closed Xmas RS wknds 2 night bookings only 🐾

WEST MARDEN   Map 5 SU71

FRIENDLIEST LANDLADY OF THE YEAR 2009-2010

PREMIER COLLECTION

West Marden Farmhouse *(SU770135)*
★★★★★ FARMHOUSE

PO18 9ES
☎ 023 9263 1761   Carole M Edney
e-mail: carole.edney@btinternet.com
web: www.westmardenfarmhousebandb.co.uk

Located in the small rural village of West Marden is the delightful West Marden Farmhouse (a working arable farm) which provides extremely comfortable and stylish accommodation comprising one guest bedroom, an en suite bathroom plus shower room and a fabulous private lounge with sofas, where the log fire is lit in cooler weather. The farmhouse provides relaxation, escapism and a delicious home cooked, freshly prepared breakfast for all of its welcome visitors. Complimentary Wi-fi is available throughout. Carole Edney is the winner of the AA's Friendliest Landlady Award 2009-2010.

Rooms 1 en suite; D fr £95* **Facilities** FTV tea/coffee Cen ht Wi-fi **Parking** 5 **Notes** ⊗ Closed 23-28 Dec 🐾 1000 acres arable

WEST MARDEN *continued*

Grandwood House

★★★ GUEST ACCOMMODATION

Watergate PO18 9EG
☎ 07971 845153 & 023 9263 1436 🖷 023 9263 1436
e-mail: info@grandwoodhouse.co.uk
web: www.grandwoodhouse.co.uk

Set in the South Downs and built in 1907, Grandwood
House was originally a lodge belonging to Watergate
House, which was accidentally burnt down by troops
during WW II. Only a short walk away is the local pub in
nearby Walderton which serves lunches and evening
meals. All rooms are en suite and enjoy views of the
garden, open farmland or both. Large security gates
leading onto the driveway ensure secure parking at all
times.

Rooms 4 annexe en suite (4 GF) D £50–£85*
Facilities FTV tea/coffee Cen ht Wi-fi **Parking** 8 **Notes** LB

WORTHING   Map 6 TQ10

The Beacons

★★★★ GUEST ACCOMMODATION

18 Shelley Rd BN11 1TU
☎ 01903 230948
e-mail: thebeacons@btconnect.com
dir: *0.5m W of town centre. Off A259 Richmond Rd onto
Crescent Rd & 3rd left*

This splendid Edwardian property is ideally situated close
to the shopping centre, marine garden and pier.
Bedrooms are bright, spacious and attractively furnished
with many thoughtful amenities, including free Wi-fi.
Guests can enjoy the comfortable lounge with honesty bar
and breakfast is served in the sunny dining room.

Rooms 8 en suite (1 fmly) (3 GF) S £40–£45; D £70–£80*
Facilities tea/coffee Cen ht Licensed Wi-fi **Parking** 8

The Burlington

★★★★ GUEST ACCOMMODATION

Marine Pde BN11 3QL
☎ 01903 211222 🖷 01903 209561
e-mail: info@theburlingtonworthing.co.uk
web: www.theburlingtonworthing.co.uk
dir: *On seafront 0.5m W of Worthing Pier, Wordsworth
Rd junct*

Imposing seafront building offers a modern contemporary
look that appeals to a mainly youthful clientele. The light
spacious bar and terrace extends to a night club open at
the weekends. Bedrooms are spacious and thoughtfully
furnished with some modern touches. Friendly staff.

Rooms 26 en suite (6 fmly) **Facilities** FTV tea/coffee
Dinner available Direct Dial Cen ht Licensed Wi-fi
Conf Max 100 Thtr 50 Class 35 Board 40 **Notes** ⊗

The Conifers

★★★★ GUEST ACCOMMODATION

43 Parkfield Rd BN13 1EP
☎ 01903 265066 & 07947 321096
e-mail: conifers@hews.org.uk
dir: *A24 or A27 onto A2031 at Offington rdbt, over lights,
Parkfield Rd 5th right*

This charming home with its award-winning garden is
located in a quiet residential area within easy reach of
the town centre. Bedrooms are bright and comfortable
with plenty of thoughtful extras. A hearty English
breakfast is served by friendly host Barbara in a
traditionally furnished, oak-panelled dining room.

Rooms 2 rms (1 pri facs) (2 fmly) S £40–£50; D £80–£100
Facilities tea/coffee Cen ht **Notes** LB ⊗ No Children
12yrs Closed Xmas ⊛

John Henry's Inn

★★★★ INN

The Forge, Nepcote Ln, Findon Village BN14 0SE
☎ 01903 877277 & 07850 661230 🖷 01903 877178
e-mail: enquiries@john-henrys.com
dir: *Off A24 rdbt into Findon, over x-rds at bottom of hill,
300yds on left*

Located in a quiet village, this delightful converted
cottage provides accommodation which varies in size,
and offers comfortable beds and good facilities. A sports
room is on-site. Dinner and breakfast are served in the
bar brasserie just opposite. Parking available.

Rooms 5 en suite (3 fmly) (2 GF) **Facilities** tea/coffee
Dinner available Cen ht Pool Table **Parking** 12 **Notes** ⊗
No coaches

Moorings

★★★★ GUEST ACCOMMODATION

4 Selden Rd BN11 2LL
☎ 01903 208882
e-mail: themooringsworthing@hotmail.co.uk
dir: *0.5m E of pier off A259 towards Brighton*

This well-presented Victorian house is located in a quiet
residential street just a short walk from the seafront and
town centre. Bedrooms are attractively co-ordinated with
plenty of extras such as Wi-fi and Freeview TV. Breakfast
is served in a smart dining room and there is a small
lounge with books and games.

Rooms 6 en suite (1 fmly) S £40–£45; D £50–£60
Facilities FTV tea/coffee Direct Dial Cen ht Wi-fi **Notes** LB
⊗

Olinda Guest House

★★★★ GUEST ACCOMMODATION

199 Brighton Rd BN11 2EX
☎ 01903 206114
e-mail: info@olindaguesthouse.co.uk
web: www.olindaguesthouse.co.uk
dir: *1m E of pier on Brighton Rd along Worthing seafront*

Guests are assured a warm welcome at this
establishment which is located on the seafront just a
walk away from the town centre. The bedrooms are cosy
and comfortable, and breakfast is taken in the
attractively appointed dining room overlooking the
seafront.

Rooms 6 rms (3 en suite) **Facilities** tea/coffee Cen ht
Wi-fi **Notes** ⊗ No Children 12yrs

Tudor Guest House

★★★★ GUEST ACCOMMODATION

5 Windsor Rd BN11 2LU
☎ 01903 210265
e-mail: info@tudor-worthing.co.uk
dir: *Off A259 (seafront road)*

The Tudor Guest House is a friendly and attractive
establishment situated just off the seafront on the east
side of town. Bedrooms are generally spacious and neatly
appointed with modern facilities. Fresh organic produce
is served in the bright breakfast room.

Rooms 7 en suite (1 GF) S £35; D £70 **Facilities** tea/
coffee Cen ht **Parking** 6 **Notes** ⊗ No Children 8yrs Closed
24 Dec-3 Jan

Avalon

★★★ GUEST ACCOMMODATION

8 Windsor Rd BN11 2LX
☎ 01903 233808 🖷 01903 215201
e-mail: avalon.worthing@ntlworld.com
dir: *0.75m E from town centre off A259 (seafront road)*

This family-run guest house provides a warm welcome
and is only a stroll from the beach. Bedrooms vary in size
but all are well appointed, suiting a variety of travellers.
Hearty breakfasts are served in the bright and cheerful
ground-floor dining room.

Rooms 7 rms (2 en suite) (1 fmly) (1 GF) S £25; D £50*
Facilities tea/coffee Cen ht Wi-fi **Parking** 3 **Notes** ⊗ No
Children 5yrs

Marina Guest House

★★★ GUEST ACCOMMODATION

191 Brighton Rd BN11 2EX
☎ 01903 207844
e-mail: marinaworthing@ntlworld.com
dir: M27 onto A259 to Worthing; or M23 onto A24 to Worthing

This Victorian establishment is in a great location with uninterrupted sea views and just a short distance from the town centre. The property is well maintained with comfortable accommodation. A cooked breakfast can be enjoyed in the family-style breakfast room that looks out over the sea.

Rooms 5 rms (2 en suite) (2 fmly) S £25-£30; D £60-£65* **Facilities** tea/coffee Direct Dial Cen ht Wi-fi **Notes** ⊗

TYNE & WEAR

GATESHEAD Map 21 NZ26

PREMIER COLLECTION

The Stables Lodge

★★★★★ 🏠 GUEST HOUSE

South Farm, Lamesley NE11 0ET
☎ 0191 492 1756 📄 0191 410 6192
e-mail: janet@thestableslodge.co.uk
dir: From A1, take Team Valley/Retail World slip road and turn off towards Lamesley/Kibblesworth

The Stables Lodge is in a semi-rural setting not far from Newcastle and Gateshead, with the Metro Centre and Angel of the North only minutes away. The Stables has been thoughtfully converted with a 'Hunting Lodge' theme. Features include luxurious surroundings and excellent guest care. The Red Room has a sauna and steam room, while the Garden Room has an outside seating area. The Stables Lodge was the AA's Guest Accommodation of the Year 2008-2009.

Rooms 3 en suite (1 fmly) (1 GF) **Facilities** STV TVL tea/coffee Cen ht Sauna **Parking** 6 **Notes** ⊗

The Angel View Inn

★★★ INN

Low Eighton NE9 7UB
☎ 0191 410 3219 📄 0191 492 4350
e-mail: reception@angelviewinn.co.uk
dir: Follow brown tourist signs to Angel of the North. At rdbt, take 4th exit B1295, 1st left to Angel View Inn

The inn was originally built as a farmhouse and stables, although it has been extended and modernised to offer thoughtfully equipped accommodation, with uninterrupted views of the famous Angel of the North. Perfectly located for access to the north or south bound A1. An extensive menu is available either in the lounge bar or in the restaurant.

Rooms 19 en suite 8 annexe en suite (1 fmly) (6 GF) S £55-£65; D £70-£90 **Facilities** TVL tea/coffee Dinner available Direct Dial Cen ht Wi-fi **Conf** Max 120 Thtr 100 Class 45 Board 45 **Parking** 100 **Notes** ⊗ Closed 25 Dec

---

SOUTH SHIELDS Map 21 NZ36

Forest Guest House

★★★★ GUEST HOUSE

117 Ocean Rd NE33 2JL
☎ 0191 454 8160 📄 0191 454 8160
e-mail: enquiries@forestguesthouse.com
dir: Take A194 into South Shields to Ocean Rd

Close to parks, beaches and the town centre, this tastefully decorated house offers a variety of room sizes, all well equipped and benefiting from en suite or private bath or shower rooms. Hearty breakfasts are served in the smart open-plan kitchen/dining room. A friendly welcome is always guaranteed.

Rooms 6 rms (5 en suite) (1 pri facs) (3 fmly) S £26-£40; D £45-£55* **Facilities** STV FTV tea/coffee Cen ht Wi-fi **Notes** LB ⊗ No Children 6yrs

Ocean Breeze

★★★★ GUEST HOUSE

11 Urfa Ter NE33 2ES
☎ 0191 456 7442
e-mail: info@oceanbreezeguesthouse.co.uk
dir: A183 towards town centre, onto Lawe Rd, 3rd left

Situated just a short walk from the seafront and town centre, this smartly appointed terrace house offers modern, fully-equipped bedrooms, most with en suite shower rooms. Guests are given a genuine warm welcome and hearty breakfasts, made using fresh local ingredients are served in the pleasant dining room.

Rooms 6 rms (3 en suite) (1 fmly) **Facilities** FTV tea/coffee Cen ht Wi-fi **Notes** ⊗ No Children 5yrs Closed 16 Dec-6 Jan

---

SUNNISIDE Map 19 NZ25

PREMIER COLLECTION

Hedley Hall Country House

★★★★★ GUEST ACCOMMODATION

Hedley Ln NE16 5EH
☎ 01207 231835
e-mail: hedleyhall@aol.com
web: www.hedleyhall.com
dir: From A1 follow signs for Lanseley, at mini rdbt turn right 2m, left at Birkheads Garden/Nursery sign. Straight over x-rds, turn left to Hedley Hall Country House

Located within easy reach of Beamish, Hedley Hall Country House was once a working farm that was part of the Queen Mother's estate. A warm welcome and quality accommodation is guaranteed. The stylish modern bedrooms, one with a super-king-sized bed, are very thoughtfully equipped. Delightful day rooms include a spacious lounge with deep sofas. Breakfasts are served in the conservatory or the elegant dining room.

Rooms 3 en suite (1 fmly) **Facilities** TVL tea/coffee Dinner available Cen ht Wi-fi **Parking** 6 **Notes** LB ⊗ Closed 22 Dec-2 Jan

---

WHITLEY BAY Map 21 NZ37

Park Lodge

★★★★ GUEST HOUSE

158/160 Park Av NE26 1AU
☎ 0191 253 0288 📄 0191 252 6879
e-mail: parklodgehotel@hotmail.com
dir: From S A19 through Tyne Tunnel, right onto A1058 to seafront. Turn left, after 2m left at lights onto A191. On left

A friendly atmosphere prevails at this refurbished Victorian house, located on a leafy avenue, overlooking the park and just minutes from the town centre and coastline. Park Lodge is the ideal base for exploring the region. Bedrooms are very comfortable, stylishly furnished and feature homely extras. A hearty breakfast is served and free Wi-fi is available.

Rooms 5 en suite (1 fmly) (2 GF) S £60-£75; D £90-£95 **Facilities** FTV TVL tea/coffee Cen ht Wi-fi **Notes** ⊗ Closed 24-30 Dec

WHITLEY BAY *continued*

Lindsay Guest House

★★★★ Ⓐ GUEST HOUSE

50 Victoria Av NE26 2BA
☎ 0191 252 7341 📄 0191 252 7505
e-mail: info@lindsayguesthouse.co.uk
dir: *Off Promenade by tennis courts & bowling green*

Rooms 4 en suite (4 fmly) S £29-£35; D £55-£75
Facilities STV FTV TVL tea/coffee Cen ht **Parking** 3

Sandsides Guest House

★★★ GUEST ACCOMMODATION

122 Park Av NE26 1AY
☎ 0191 253 0399 & 07947 447695
e-mail: sandsides@btinternet.com
dir: *A19 Tyne Tunnel exit A1058. At rdbt follow A192 Whitley Bay, next rdbt turn left. Located in one-way system*

Situated opposite the park and close to the beach and town centre, Sandsides offers a variety of room sizes, two with en suite shower rooms and the others with shared facilities. Freshly cooked breakfasts are served in the dining room.

Rooms 5 rms (2 en suite) (2 fmly) S £18-£27.50; D £36-£55* **Facilities** tea/coffee Cen ht **Parking** 1 **Notes** LB ⊗ 🐾

See advert on opposite page

See advert on opposite page

WARWICKSHIRE

ATHERSTONE   Map 10 SP39

PREMIER COLLECTION

Chapel House Restaurant With Rooms

★★★★★ ⊛ RESTAURANT WITH ROOMS

Friar's Gate CV9 1EY
☎ 01827 718949 📄 01827 717702
e-mail: info@chapelhouse.eu
web: www.chapelhouse.eu
dir: *A5 to town centre, right onto Church St. Right onto Sheepy Rd & left onto Friar's Gate*

Sitting next to the church this 18th-century town house offers excellent hospitality and service while the cooking, using much local produce, is very notable. Bedrooms are well equipped and lounges are extensive; there is also a delightful walled garden for guests to use.

Rooms 12 en suite **Facilities** tea/coffee Dinner available Direct Dial Cen ht Wi-fi **Notes** LB ⊗ Closed Etr wk, Aug BH wk & Xmas wk No coaches

BAGINTON   Map 11 SP37

Old Mill

★★★★ INN

Mill Hill CV8 3AH
☎ 024 7630 2241 📄 024 7630 7070
e-mail: oldmillinn@thespiritgroup.com
dir: *In village centre (0.25m from junct A45 & A46)*

Enjoying a peaceful riverside location, yet within easy reach of the motorway networks, the Old Mill has been furnished to a high standard. Public areas include the popular Chef & Brewer bar and restaurant, with a pleasant patio for summer evenings. Spacious bedrooms are smartly appointed and well equipped.

Rooms 26 en suite (2 fmly) (10 GF); D fr £77 (room only)* **Facilities** tea/coffee Dinner available Direct Dial Cen ht Wi-fi **Conf** Max 25 Thtr 25 Class 16 Board 20 **Parking** 200 **Notes** LB ⊗

The Oak

★★★ INN

Coventry Rd CV8 3AU
☎ 024 7651 8855 📄 024 7651 8866
e-mail: thebagintonoak@aol.com
web: http://theoak.greatpubs.net

Located close to major road links and Coventry Airport, this popular inn provides a wide range of food throughout the themed, open-plan public areas. Families are especially welcome. Modern, well-equipped bedrooms are situated in a separate accommodation building.

Rooms 13 annexe en suite (1 fmly) (6 GF) S £40-£60; D £40-£60* **Facilities** FTV tea/coffee Dinner available Cen ht Wi-fi Free use of local gym **Conf** Max 40 Thtr 40 Class 40 Board 25 **Parking** 110

BARNACLE   Map 11 SP38

Park Farm House

★★★★ GUEST ACCOMMODATION

Spring Rd CV7 9LG
☎ 024 7661 2628 📄 024 7661 6010
dir: *M6 junct 2 onto B4065 to Shilton. Left at lights, left again over M69, right into Barnacle*

Excellent accommodation and hospitality in a peaceful location is provided at this delightful farmhouse which dates from 1655. The spacious bedrooms are well equipped and there is a cosy lounge. Good breakfasts are provided around a large table and dinner is available by arrangement.

Rooms 3 en suite S £48-£52; D fr £79* **Facilities** tea/coffee Dinner available Cen ht **Parking** 6 **Notes** ⊗ No Children 12yrs 🐾

COLESHILL   Map 10 SP28

Ye Olde Station

★★★ GUEST HOUSE

Church Rd, Shustoke B46 2AX
☎ 01675 481736 📄 01675 481736
e-mail: patr@freeuk.com
web: www.yeoldestationguesthouse.co.uk
dir: *2.5m NE, on B4114 300yds past Griffin pub*

This converted Victorian railway station has been modernised to provide a range of practically furnished bedrooms with efficient bathrooms. Ground-floor areas include a lounge-dining room and a games room with pool table.

Rooms 9 en suite (1 fmly) S £46; D £66* **Facilities** TVL tea/coffee Cen ht Pool Table **Parking** 16

ETTINGTON   Map 10 SP24

PREMIER COLLECTION

Fulready Manor

★★★★★ 🛏 BED AND BREAKFAST

Fulready CV37 7PE
☎ 01789 740152 📄 01789 740247
e-mail: stay@fulreadymanor.co.uk
web: www.fulreadymanor.co.uk
dir: *2.5m SE of Ettington. 0.5m S off A422 at Pillerton Priors*

Located in 120 acres of arable farmland, this impressive, new Cotswold-stone house provides very high levels of comfort. The spacious ground-floor areas are furnished with quality and flair, and feature fine furniture and art. The individually themed bedrooms have a wealth of thoughtful extras, and memorable breakfasts are served in the elegant dining room overlooking immaculate gardens.

Rooms 3 en suite; D £125-£140 **Facilities** Cen ht Wi-fi **Parking** 6 **Notes** ⊗ No Children 15yrs 🐾

GREAT WOLFORD   Map 10 SP23

PREMIER COLLECTION

The Old Coach House
★★★★★ BED AND BREAKFAST

CV36 5NQ
☎ 01608 674152
e-mail: theoldcoachhouse@thewolfords.net
web: www.theoldcoachhouseatthewolfords.co.uk
dir: Off A44/A3400 to village centre

Located in a historic Cotswold village next to a fine country inn, this former coach house has been restored to provide high levels of comfort and facilities. Bedrooms are equipped with a wealth of thoughtful extras, and quality decor and furnishings enhance the intrinsic charm of the property.

Rooms 2 en suite Facilities TVL tea/coffee Cen ht Conf Max 6 Board 6 Parking 2 Notes ⊗ No Children 10yrs

---

KENILWORTH   Map 10 SP27

Stoneleigh Park Lodge
★★★★ GUEST HOUSE

Stoneleigh Park CV8 2LZ
☎ 024 7669 0123   024 7669 0789
e-mail: info@stoneleighparklodge.com
web: www.stoneleighparklodge.com
dir: 2m E of Kenilworth in National Agricultural Centre

This house lies within the grounds of the National Agricultural Centre and provides modern, well-equipped accommodation. Meals, using local produce, are served in the Park View Restaurant overlooking the showground. Various conference and meeting facilities are available.

Rooms 58 en suite (4 fmly) (26 GF) S £70-£110; D £80-£120* Facilities FTV TVL tea/coffee Dinner available Direct Dial Cen ht Licensed Wi-fi Fishing Conf Max 10 Parking 60 Notes Closed Xmas

Victoria Lodge
★★★★ GUEST ACCOMMODATION

180 Warwick Rd CV8 1HU
☎ 01926 512020   01926 858703
e-mail: info@victorialodgehotel.co.uk
dir: 250yds SE of town centre on A452 opp St John's Church

Situated within walking distance of Kenilworth Castle and the historic town's many acclaimed restaurants, Victoria Lodge is a family-run establishment. All of the well-appointed rooms are en suite and thoughtfully furnished with homely extras. There a Victorian walled garden for guests' use, plus a car park.

Rooms 10 en suite (1 fmly) (2 GF) S £49-£62; D £72-£80* Facilities FTV tea/coffee Direct Dial Cen ht Licensed Wi-fi Parking 9 Notes ⊗ Closed 24 Dec-1 Jan

---

Avondale
★★★★ Ⓐ BED AND BREAKFAST

18 Moseley Rd CV8 2AQ
☎ 01926 859072
Rooms 3 en suite S £35-£40; D £45-£50* Facilities TVL tea/coffee Cen ht Parking 4 Notes ⊗ No Children Closed Xmas RS New Year ⊛

Hollyhurst
★★★ GUEST ACCOMMODATION

47 Priory Rd CV8 1LL
☎ 01926 853882   01926 853882
e-mail: admin@hollyhurstguesthouse.co.uk
dir: On A452 in town centre

Located on a mainly residential avenue within easy walking distance of the castle and town centre, this constantly improving establishment offers a range of bedrooms, some of which have the benefit of modern shower rooms. Ground-floor areas include a comfortable lounge in addition to an attractive dining room.

Rooms 7 rms (3 en suite) (1 pri facs) (1 fmly) S £26-£37; D £50-£57* Facilities tea/coffee Cen ht Wi-fi Parking 7 Notes ⊗ Closed Xmas & New Year ⊛

Sandsides Guest House

Whitley Bay, Tyne & Wear
Tel: 0191 253 0399
Email: sandsides@btinternet.com
Website: www.sandsides.co.uk

This family-run bed & breakfast is ideal for families and couples looking for a peaceful, relaxing place to stay whilst enjoying all that the North East of England has to offer. Whitley Bay and the surrounding area has something for everyone from award-winning beaches to attractions and shops.

• Rooms are cosy and traditionally furnished, most are ensuite.

• High standards guaranteed.

KENILWORTH *continued*

Howden House

★★★ BED AND BREAKFAST

170 Warwick Rd CV8 1HS
☎ 01926 850310
dir: *From A46 take Leamington exit onto A452, follow sign to Kenilworth*

Guests will find a warm welcome awaits them at Howden House which is situated at the end of the main street, convenient for the town centre, the National Exhibition Centre and motorway networks. The bedrooms are homely and comfortable.

Rooms 3 rms (1 en suite) (1 fmly) (1 GF) D £50-£55*
Facilities TVL tea/coffee Cen ht ⚓ Golf 36 **Parking** 1
Notes ⊗ Closed Xmas & New Year 🐾

LEAMINGTON SPA (ROYAL)　Map 10 SP36

The Adams

★★★★ GUEST ACCOMMODATION

22 Avenue Rd CV31 3PQ
☎ 01926 450742 　 📠 01926 313110
e-mail: bookings@adams-hotel.co.uk
dir: *500yds W of town centre. Off A452 (Adelaide Rd) onto Avenue Rd*

Just a short walk from the town centre, this elegant 1827 Regency house offers a relaxing setting and quality accommodation. Public areas include a lounge bar with leather armchairs, and a pretty garden. The attractive bedrooms are very well appointed, and have modem points and bathrobes.

Rooms 10 en suite (2 GF) **Facilities** tea/coffee Direct Dial Cen ht Licensed Wi-fi **Parking** 14 **Notes** ⊗ No Children 12yrs Closed 23 Dec-2 Jan

Bubbenhall House

★★★★ GUEST ACCOMMODATION

Paget's Ln CV8 3BJ
☎ 024 7630 2409 　 & 07746 282541 　 📠 024 7630 2409
e-mail: wharrison@bubbenhallhouse.freeserve.co.uk
dir: *5m NE of Leamington. Off A445 at Bubbenhall S onto Paget's Ln, 1m on single-track lane (over 4 speed humps)*

Located between Leamington Spa and Coventry in extensive mature grounds with an abundance of wildlife,

this impressive late Edwardian house was once the home of Alexander Issigonis, designer of the Mini. It contains many interesting features including a Jacobean-style staircase. Thoughtful extras are provided in the bedrooms, and public areas include an elegant dining room and choice of sumptuous lounges.

Rooms 5 en suite (1 GF) **Facilities** FTV TVL tea/coffee Cen ht Wi-fi ⚓ ⚓ **Parking** 12 **Notes** 🐾

LIGHTHORNE　Map 10 SP35

Redlands Farm

★★★★ BED AND BREAKFAST

Banbury Rd CV35 0AH
☎ 01926 651241
e-mail: redlandsfarm@btinternet.com
dir: *Off B4100, 5m S of Warwick*

Redlands Farm offers a tranquil location, conveniently located just six miles from Warwick, Leamington Spa and Stratford-upon-Avon. Bedrooms offer a comfortable stay and breakfast features fresh eggs provided by the chickens in the garden.

Rooms 3 en suite (1 fmly) S £30-£40; D £65-£70*
Facilities TVL tea/coffee Cen ht ⚓ **Parking** 7 **Notes** ⊗ No Children 7yrs Closed Xmas & New Year Civ Wed

---

LONG COMPTON　Map 10 SP23

The Red Lion

★★★★ INN

Main St CV36 5JJ
☎ 01608 684221 　 📠 01608 684968
e-mail: info@redlion-longcompton.co.uk
dir: *5m S of Shipston on Stour on A3400*

Located in the pretty rural village of Long Compton, this mid-18th-century posting house retains many original features, highlighted by rustic furniture in the public areas. A good range of ales is offered, and interesting menus make good use of quality local produce. Newly refurbished bedrooms are well appointed, and furnished with a good range of facilities.

Rooms 5 en suite (1 fmly) **Facilities** tea/coffee Dinner available Cen ht Wi-fi **Parking** 60 **Notes** No coaches

---

Tallet Barn B&B

★★★★ BED AND BREAKFAST

Yerdley Farm CV36 5LH
☎ 01603 684248 　 📠 01608 684248
e-mail: talletbarn@tiscali.co.uk
dir: *Off A3400 in village onto Vicarage Ln opp village stores, 3rd entrance on right*

This converted barn and grain store in the heart of an unspoiled Cotswold village provides comfortable bedrooms with thoughtful extras. Comprehensive breakfasts are served in the elegant beamed dining room in the main house, which also has a comfortable lounge.

Rooms 2 annexe en suite (1 fmly) (1 GF) S £40-£45; D £60-£65 **Facilities** tea/coffee Cen ht **Parking** 3 **Notes** ⊗ No Children 6yrs 🐾

NUNEATON　Map 11 SP39

Odstone Hall

★★★★★ Ⓐ GUEST ACCOMMODATION

Hall Ln, Odstone CV13 0QS
☎ 01530 260312 　 📠 01530 263936
e-mail: woodwards@odstonehall.com
web: www.odstonehall.com
dir: *M1 junct 22 onto A50 then A447, Odstone signed on right*

Rooms 5 en suite 1 annexe en suite (1 GF) S £65-£100; D £65-£100* **Facilities** FTV TVL tea/coffee Dinner available Cen ht Licensed Wi-fi ⚓ ⚓ ⚓ **Conf** Max 15 Thtr 15 Class 15 Board 14 **Parking** 15 **Notes** ⊗

SHIPSTON ON STOUR　Map 10 SP24

Holly End Bed & Breakfast

★★★★ 🏠 BED AND BREAKFAST

London Rd CV36 4EP
☎ 01608 664064
e-mail: hollyend.hunt@btinternet.com
web: www.holly-end.co.uk
dir: *0.5m S of Shipston on Stour on A3400*

Located between Oxford and Stratford-upon-Avon and a short walk from the town centre, this immaculate detached house offers bedrooms with lots of thoughtful extras. Comprehensive breakfasts use the best of local produce.

Rooms 3 rms (2 en suite) (1 pri facs) (1 fmly) S £50-£60; D £75-£90* **Facilities** FTV tea/coffee Cen ht Wi-fi **Parking** 6 **Notes** LB ⊗ No Children 9yrs 🐾

Folly Farm Cottage

★★★★ ⚴ GUEST ACCOMMODATION

Ilmington CV36 4LJ
☎ 01608 682425
e-mail: bruceandpam@follyfarm.co.uk
dir: *A3400 S of Stratford-upon-Avon, turn right signed Wimpstone/Ilmington*

Rooms 3 en suite S £55-£65; D £68-£84* **Facilities** FTV tea/coffee Dinner available Cen ht Wi-fi 🏊 **Parking** 8 **Notes** LB ⊗ No Children 18yrs

---

STRATFORD-UPON-AVON   Map 10 SP25

PREMIER COLLECTION

Cherry Trees

★★★★★ GUEST HOUSE

Swans Nest Ln CV37 7LS
☎ 01789 292989
e-mail: gotocherrytrees@aol.com
web: www.cherrytrees-stratford.co.uk
dir: *250yds SE of town centre over bridge. Off A422, next to Butterfly Farm*

Comfortably located close to the theatre and the centre of town, Cherry Trees offers spacious, luxurious, well-equipped rooms. Guests have a separate entrance and hearty breakfasts are served in the attractive upstairs dining room.

Rooms 3 en suite (3 GF) S £55-£65; D £95-£115* **Facilities** FTV tea/coffee Cen ht Wi-fi **Parking** 11 **Notes** LB ⊗ No Children 10yrs

Ambleside

★★★★ GUEST HOUSE

41 Grove Rd CV37 6PB
☎ 01789 297239 🖷 01789 295670
e-mail: ruth@amblesideguesthouse.com
dir: *On A4390 opp Firs Park*

This attractive and friendly house is situated close to the market square and town centre. The bedrooms are carefully decorated, well appointed and some have smart modern shower rooms. Breakfast is served in the light airy dining room overlooking the pretty front garden.

There is a free private car park at the rear of the house. Free Wi-fi throughout.

Ambleside

Rooms 7 rms (5 en suite) (4 fmly) (2 GF) S £28-£35; D £55-£75* **Facilities** tea/coffee Cen ht Wi-fi **Parking** 8 **Notes** ⊗ No Children 5yrs

Clopton Orchard Farm *(SP165455)*

★★★★ FARMHOUSE

Lower Clopton, Upper Quinton CV37 8LH
☎ 01386 438669 & 07765 414636
🖷 01386 438669   Mrs A Coldicott
e-mail: mail@clopton-orchard.fsnet.co.uk
dir: *6m S of Stratford on B4632. S through Lower Clopton, on right opposite farm shop*

A warm welcome is assured at this attractive modern farmhouse located between Broadway and Stratford-upon-Avon. The spacious bedrooms come with practical and thoughtful extras, and comprehensive breakfasts are served around a family table in the cosy pine-furnished first-floor dining room.

Rooms 2 en suite (1 fmly) S £45-£50; D £65-£70* **Facilities** tea/coffee Cen ht Wi-fi **Parking** 5 **Notes** LB ⊗ 300 acres arable/sheep/pigs/geese

Emsley Guest House

★★★★ GUEST ACCOMMODATION

4 Arden St CV37 6PA
☎ 01789 299557 🖷 01789 299557
e-mail: val@theemsley.co.uk
web: www.theemsley.co.uk
dir: *A46 onto A3400 into Stratford, right at lights onto A4390 Arden St*

This house is just a short walk from the town centre and railway station, and is a good base for visiting the many local attractions. Bedrooms are carefully decorated and well equipped. Substantial breakfasts, including vegetarian options, are served in the attractive dining room. There is also a comfortable lounge, and parking nearby can be arranged by the owners.

Rooms 5 en suite (3 fmly) **Facilities** TVL tea/coffee Cen ht **Parking** 20 **Notes** ⊗ Closed 24 Dec-1 Jan

Monk's Barn *(SP206516)*

★★★★ FARMHOUSE

Shipston Rd CV37 8NA
☎ 01789 293714   Mrs R M Meadows
e-mail: ritameadows@btconnect.com
dir: *2m S of Stratford on A3400, on right after bungalows on left*

With stunning views of the surrounding countryside, a warm welcome is assured at this impressive renovated house. Bedrooms, some of which are located in former outbuildings, are filled with a wealth of thoughtful extras. Memorable breakfasts are served in the spacious and cosy lounge-dining room.

Rooms 4 rms (3 en suite) (1 pri facs) 3 annexe en suite (1 fmly) (4 GF) S £27-£29.50; D £54-£59 **Facilities** TVL tea/coffee Cen ht **Parking** 7 **Notes** ⊗ Closed 25-26 Dec 75 acres mixed

Moonraker House

★★★★ GUEST ACCOMMODATION

40 Alcester Rd CV37 9DB
☎ 01789 268774 🖷 01789 268774
e-mail: info@moonrakerhouse.com
dir: *200yds from rail station on A422 (Alcester Rd)*

Just a short walk from the railway station and the central attractions, this establishment provides a range of stylish bedrooms. The sitting area during the day is the setting for the freshly cooked breakfasts. The attractive exterior is enhanced by a magnificent floral display during the warmer months.

Rooms 7 en suite (1 fmly) (2 GF) S £40-£47; D £65-£87* **Facilities** FTV tea/coffee Cen ht Wi-fi **Parking** 7 **Notes** LB ⊗ No Children 6yrs

STRATFORD-UPON-AVON *continued*

Twelfth Night

★★★★ GUEST ACCOMMODATION

13 Evesham Place CV37 6HT
☎ 01789 414595
e-mail: twelfthnight@fsmail.net
web: www.twelfthnight.co.uk
dir: *In town centre off A4390 Grove Rd*

This delightful Victorian villa is within easy walking distance of the town centre. Quality décor and furnishings enhance the charming original features, and the elegant dining room is the setting for imaginative English breakfasts.

Rooms 7 rms (6 en suite) (1 pri facs) S £40-£50; D £50-£85* **Facilities** tea/coffee Cen ht **Parking** 6 **Notes** ⊗ Closed 11-25 Feb

Victoria Spa Lodge

★★★★ GUEST HOUSE

Bishopton Ln, Bishopton CV37 9QY
☎ 01789 267985 🖷 01789 204728
e-mail: ptozer@victoriaspalodge.demon.co.uk
web: www.victoriaspa.co.uk
dir: *A3400 1.5m N to junct A46, 1st left onto Bishopton Ln, 1st house on right*

Located within immaculate mature gardens beside the canal on the outskirts of town, this impressive Victorian house retains many original features enhanced by the lovely furnishings and décor. Bedrooms are filled with thoughtful extras and the spacious dining room, furnished with quality antiques and ornaments, also contains a cosy lounge area.

Rooms 7 en suite (3 fmly) S £50-£55; D £65-£70* **Facilities** tea/coffee Cen ht Wi-fi **Parking** 12 **Notes** ⊗

Caterham House

★★★★ Ⓐ GUEST HOUSE

58-59 Rother St CV37 6LT
☎ 01789 267309
e-mail: caterhamhousehotel@btconnect.com
Rooms 10 en suite S £60-£70; D £80-£95* **Facilities** TVL tea/coffee Cen ht Licensed **Conf** Max 25 Thtr 25 Class 25 Board 25 **Parking** 10 **Notes** Closed 24-26 Dec

Heron Lodge Guest House

★★★★ Ⓐ GUEST ACCOMMODATION

260 Alcester Rd CV37 9JQ
☎ 01789 299169
e-mail: info@heronlodge.com
Rooms 5 en suite (1 fmly) S £35-£45; D £58-£68* **Facilities** FTV tea/coffee Cen ht Wi-fi **Parking** 7 **Notes** ⊗ No Children 5yrs Closed 24 Dec-1 Jan

Arden Way Guest House

★★★ GUEST HOUSE

22 Shipston Rd CV37 7LP
☎ 01789 205646 🖷 01789 205646
e-mail: info@ardenwayguesthouse.co.uk
web: www.ardenwayguesthouse.co.uk
dir: *On A3400, S of River Avon, 100mtrs on left*

A warm welcome is assured at this constantly improving no-smoking house, located within easy walking distance of the Butterfly Farm and cricket ground. The homely bedrooms are filled with lots of thoughtful extras and an attractive dining room, overlooking the pretty rear garden, is the setting for comprehensive breakfasts.

Rooms 6 rms (5 en suite) (1 pri facs) (2 fmly) (2 GF) S £28-£55; D £56-£68* **Facilities** FTV tea/coffee Cen ht Wi-fi **Parking** 6 **Notes** ⊗

Travellers Rest

★★★ GUEST ACCOMMODATION

146 Alcester Rd CV37 9DR
☎ 01789 266589
e-mail: enquiries@travellersrest.biz
web: www.travellersrest.biz
dir: *0.5m W of town centre on A422, past railway station*

Located with easy access to the town centre, this attractive semi-detached house provides cosy bedrooms, each with a modern shower room and filled with thoughtful extras. Breakfast is taken in an attractive front-facing dining room, and a warm welcome is assured.

Rooms 4 en suite (1 fmly) S £30-£50; D £55-£80* **Facilities** tea/coffee Cen ht Wi-fi **Parking** 5 **Notes** LB Closed 24-26 Dec ⊜

Cherry Blossom House

★★★ GUEST ACCOMMODATION

51 Grove Rd CV37 6PB
☎ 01789 293404
e-mail: enqs@cherryblossomhouse.com
web: www.cherryblossomhouse.com

Cherry Blossom House is situated within easy walking distance of the town centre, theatres and the many attractions of the town of Shakespeare's birth. The accommodation is comfortable with a good range of extras provided including a Wi-fi connection. There is also a ground floor bedroom. The welcoming dining room provides well spaced tables with friendly service from host Christine, who serves a hearty breakfast using fresh local ingredients. Parking is available.

Rooms 6 rms (4 en suite) (1 GF) D £50-£75 **Facilities** tea/coffee Cen ht **Parking** 4 **Notes** ⊗ No Children 12yrs

Clomendy

★★★ BED AND BREAKFAST

10 Broad Walk CV37 6HS
☎ 01789 266957
e-mail: clomendy@amserve.com
dir: *In town centre, turn left off B439 at Evesham Place*

Located on a peaceful avenue within easy walking distance of central attractions, this wonderfully maintained house offers homely, thoughtfully equipped bedrooms with modern bathrooms. Breakfast is served at a family table in the elegant dining room, which opens to the pretty rear patio garden.

Rooms 2 rms (1 en suite) (1 pri facs) S £50; D £50-£60* **Facilities** tea/coffee Cen ht **Parking** 1 **Notes** LB ⊗ No Children 5yrs ⊜

Forget-me-Not

★★★ GUEST ACCOMMODATION

18 Evesham Place CV37 6HT
☎ 01789 204907 🖷 01789 204907
e-mail: kate@forgetmenotguesthouse.co.uk
dir: *W side of town centre on A4390 ring road, near Chestnut Walk junct*

This guest house benefits from lots of care and attention applied by its enthusiastic owners. Bedrooms of varying sizes offer comfortable beds and modern shower rooms. Breakfast is offered in a pretty, bright ground-floor dining room.

Rooms 5 en suite (1 fmly) **Facilities** tea/coffee Cen ht **Parking** 2 **Notes** ⊗

The Fox & Goose Country Inn

★★★ INN

Armscote CV37 8DD
☎ 01608 682293   📠 01608 682293
e-mail: manager@foxandgoosearmscote.co.uk
web: www.foxandgoose.co.uk
dir: S of Stratford-upon-Avon. Off A3400 near church in Newbold on Stour signed Armscote 1m, bear right in village

Just a few miles from Stratford-upon-Avon in the small, quiet village of Armscote, this inn is an ideal base to explore the Heart of England. The bedrooms are well laid out and have a good range of extras. The inn provides menus that highlight good, locally sourced ingredients plus a good selection of beers from the bar. Hearty breakfasts can be enjoyed in the spacious dining area. Parking is available to the rear and there is a garden suitable for families.

Rooms 3 en suite **Facilities** tea/coffee Dinner available Cen ht **Conf** Max 20 Thtr 20 Class 20 Board 20 **Parking** 20 **Notes** ⊗ No coaches

Stretton House

★★★ GUEST ACCOMMODATION

38 Grove Rd CV37 6PB
☎ 01789 268647   📠 01789 268647
e-mail: shortpbshort@aol.com
web: www.strettonhouse.co.uk
dir: On A439 in town centre road behind police station

This attractive Edwardian terrace house is within easy walking distance of the railway station and Shakespeare's birthplace. Bedrooms are carefully decorated, well equipped, and many have modern shower rooms en suite. The pretty front garden is a very welcoming feature.

Rooms 6 rms (5 en suite) (1 pri facs) (3 fmly) (1 GF) **Facilities** tea/coffee Cen ht Wi-fi **Parking** 7

Salamander

★★★ 🅰 GUEST HOUSE

40 Grove Rd CV37 6PB
☎ 01789 205728   📠 01789 205728
e-mail: p.delin@btinternet.com
web: www.salamanderguesthouse.co.uk
dir: 250yds W of town centre on A439 ring road, opp Firs Garden

Rooms 7 rms (6 en suite) (1 pri facs) (5 fmly) (1 GF) **Facilities** tea/coffee Dinner available Cen ht Wi-fi **Parking** 12

Barbette Guest House

★★ BED AND BREAKFAST

165 Evesham Rd CV37 9BP
☎ 01789 297822
e-mail: barbette@sitgetan.demon.co.uk
dir: B439 S, 0.5m from town centre

Expect a friendly welcome at this guest house, a compact but comfortable establishment close to the main road with ample parking and a landscaped rear garden. Bedrooms are comfortable and well-equipped, and guests have use of a TV lounge.

Rooms 4 rms (1 en suite) **Facilities** FTV TVL tea/coffee Cen ht **Parking** 5 **Notes** ⊗ 🐾

WARWICK   Map 10 SP26

See also Lighthorne

Croft

★★★★ GUEST HOUSE

Haseley Knob CV35 7NL
☎ 01926 484447   📠 01926 484447
e-mail: david@croftguesthouse.co.uk
web: www.croftguesthouse.co.uk
dir: 4.5m NW of Warwick. Off A4177 into Haseley Knob, follow B&B signs

Friendly proprietors provide homely accommodation at this modern detached house, set in peaceful countryside and convenient for Warwick and the NEC, Birmingham. The conservatory dining room overlooks large well-kept gardens. Fresh eggs from home-reared chickens are used for memorable English breakfasts.

Croft

Rooms 7 rms (5 en suite) (2 pri facs) 2 annexe rms 1 annexe en suite (1 pri facs) (2 fmly) (4 GF) S £40-£45; D £60-£65* **Facilities** TVL tea/coffee Cen ht Wi-fi **Parking** 9 **Notes** Closed Xmas wk

WEST MIDLANDS
BIRMINGHAM   Map 10 SP08

PREMIER COLLECTION

Westbourne Lodge

★★★★★ GUEST ACCOMMODATION

25-31 Fountain Rd, Edgbaston B17 8NJ
☎ 0121 429 1003   📠 0121 429 7436
e-mail: info@westbournelodge.co.uk
web: www.westbournelodge.co.uk
dir: 100yds from A456

Located on a quiet residential avenue close to the Hagley Road, this well-maintained property provides a range of non-smoking, thoughtfully furnished bedrooms, some of which are on the ground floor. Breakfast, and dinner by arrangement, are served in an attractive dining room overlooking a pretty patio garden. A comfortable sitting room and lounge bar are also available.

Rooms 24 en suite (7 fmly) (3 GF) S £49.50-£59.50; D £69.50-£89.50* **Facilities** FTV TVL tea/coffee Dinner available Direct Dial Cen ht Licensed Wi-fi **Parking** 12 **Notes** Closed 24 Dec-1 Jan

Black Firs

★★★★ GUEST HOUSE

113 Coleshill Rd, Marston Green B37 7HT
☎ 0121 779 2727   📠 0121 779 2727
e-mail: julie@b-firs.co.uk
web: www.b-firs.co.uk
dir: M42 junct 6, A45 W, onto B4438, signs for Marston Green

This elegant house is set in immaculate gardens in a mainly residential area close to the NEC. Thoughtfully equipped bedrooms with Wi-fi access are complemented by smart shower rooms. Memorable breakfasts are served in an attractive dining room and a lounge is also available.

Rooms 6 en suite **Facilities** TVL tea/coffee Cen ht **Conf** Max 14 **Parking** 6 **Notes** ⊗ 🐾

BIRMINGHAM *continued*

Olton Cottage

★★★★ GUEST HOUSE

School Ln, Old Yardley Village, Yardley B33 8PD
☎ 0121 783 9249 📄 0121 789 6545
e-mail: olton.cottage@virgin.net
dir: *3.5m E of city centre. Off A45 onto A4040 to Yardley onto Stoney Ln via Yew Tree rdbt then 1m right onto Vicarage Rd, right onto Church Rd, left onto School Ln*

A warm welcome is assured at this carefully renovated Victorian house, located in a peaceful residential area close to the city centre. The cosy bedrooms contain a wealth of thoughtful extras and ground-floor areas include a cottage-style dining room and comfortable lounge overlooking the pretty enclosed garden.

Rooms 6 rms (2 en suite) (1 fmly) S fr £30; D fr £55*
Facilities TVL tea/coffee Cen ht **Parking** 2 **Notes** ⊗ 🐾

Tri-Star

★★★ GUEST ACCOMMODATION

Coventry Rd, Elmdon B26 3QR
☎ 0121 782 1010 & 782 6131 📄 0121 782 6131
dir: *On A45*

Located a short drive from the airport, the international station and the NEC, this owner-managed property provides a range of thoughtfully furnished bedrooms with modern bathrooms. The open-plan ground-floor area includes a bright, attractive dining room, a comfortable lounge bar and a separate conference room.

Rooms 15 en suite (3 fmly) (6 GF) S £42-£80;
D £52-£90* **Facilities** TVL tea/coffee Dinner available Cen ht Licensed Wi-fi Pool Table Games room **Conf** Max 20 Thtr 20 Class 10 Board 20 **Parking** 25 **Notes** ⊗

Central

★★★ GUEST HOUSE

1637 Coventry Rd, South Yardley B26 1DD
☎ 0121 706 7757 📄 0121 706 7757
e-mail: stay@centralguesthouse.com
web: www.centralguesthouse.com
dir: *3.5m SE of city centre. M42 junct 6, A45 W, past McDonalds & shops, on left*

Located between the airport and city centre, this comfortable house is made a real home-from-home by the friendly and attentive proprietors. Bedrooms are equipped with plenty of thoughtful extras. Breakfast is served in an attractive dining room and you can relax in the attractive garden.

Rooms 5 en suite (1 fmly) S £30-£35; D £45-£50*
Facilities TVL tea/coffee Cen ht **Parking** 4 **Notes** LB ⊗

Rollason Wood

★★ GUEST ACCOMMODATION

130 Wood End Rd, Erdington B24 8BJ
☎ 0121 373 1230 📄 0121 382 2578
e-mail: rollwood@globalnet.co.uk
dir: *M6 junct 6, A5127 to Erdington, right onto A4040, 0.25m on left*

Well situated for routes and the city centre, this owner-managed establishment is popular with contractors. The choice of three different bedroom styles suits most budgets, and rates include full English breakfasts. Ground-floor areas include a popular bar, cosy television lounge and a dining room.

Rooms 35 rms (11 en suite) (5 fmly) (9 smoking)
S £21.50-£39.95; D £38-£49.50 **Facilities** TVL tea/coffee Dinner available Cen ht Licensed Wi-fi Pool Table **Parking** 35

BIRMINGHAM (NATIONAL EXHIBITION CENTRE)

See Hampton-in-Arden & Solihull

COVENTRY | Map 10 SP37

Acacia Guest House

★★★★ GUEST HOUSE

11 Park Rd, Cheyles More CV1 2LE
☎ 024 7663 3622 📄 024 7663 3622
e-mail: acaciaguesthouse@hotmail.com
dir: *Off city ring road junct 6 to railway station & left*

Located within easy walking distance of the train station and city centre, the Acacia provides a range of carefully furnished bedrooms, many of which are on the ground floor. A cosy lounge bar is available.

Rooms 14 rms (13 en suite) (1 pri facs) (6 fmly) (6 GF)
Facilities TVL tea/coffee Dinner available Cen ht **Parking** 12 **Notes** ⊗ Closed Xmas 🐾

Ashdowns

★★★ 🅰 GUEST HOUSE

12 Regent St CV1 3EP
☎ 024 7622 9280
dir: *A429 to city centre, over rdbt before ring road, 1st left onto Grosvenor Rd, right onto Westminster Rd, right onto Regent St*

Rooms 8 rms (7 en suite) (3 fmly) (1 GF) S £45-£50;
D £50-£55* **Facilities** TVL tea/coffee Cen ht **Parking** 8 **Notes** LB ⊗ No Children 13yrs Closed 22 Dec-1 Jan 🐾

DORRIDGE | Map 10 SP17

The Forest

★★★★ 🎖🎖 RESTAURANT WITH ROOMS

25 Station Rd B93 8JA
☎ 01564 772120 📄 01564 732680
e-mail: info@forest-hotel.com
web: www.forest-hotel.com
dir: *In town centre near station*

The well-established and very individual establishment is well placed for routes to Birmingham, Stratford-upon-Avon and Warwick. Rooms are very well equipped with modern facilities, and imaginative food is served in the bars and intimate restaurant. A warm welcome is assured.

Rooms 12 en suite S £95-£130; D £120-£140*
Facilities FTV tea/coffee Dinner available Direct Dial Cen ht Wi-fi **Conf** Max 100 Thtr 100 Class 60 Board 40 **Parking** 50 **Notes** ⊗ RS Sun eve Restaurant closed No coaches Civ Wed 120

HAMPTON-IN-ARDEN | Map 10 SP28

The Cottage Guest House

★★★★ GUEST ACCOMMODATION

Kenilworth Rd B92 0LW
☎ 01675 442323 📄 01675 443323
e-mail: cottage.roger88@virgin.net
web: www.cottageguesthouse.net
dir: *2m SE of Hampton on A452*

A fine collection of antique memorabilia adorns the public areas of this delightful cottage, which is convenient for visiting the NEC, Birmingham, or exploring the area. Many guests return for the friendly and relaxing atmosphere and the attentive service. Freshly cooked traditional breakfasts, served in the cottage dining room, provide a good start to the day.

Rooms 9 en suite (2 GF) S £35-£45; D £55-£60* **Facilities** TVL tea/coffee Cen ht Golf 18 **Parking** 14 **Notes** Closed Xmas 🖺

SOLIHULL   Map 10 SP17

The Gate House

★★★ BED AND BREAKFAST
- -
Barston Ln, Barston B92 0JN
☎ 01675 443274
e-mail: enquiries@gatehousesolihull.co.uk
web: www.gatehousesolihull.co.uk
dir: 4m E of Solihull. Off B4101 or B4102 to Barston, on W side of village

This elegant Victorian building stands in landscaped grounds with secure parking, and is within easy driving distance of the NEC, Birmingham. The resident proprietor is most welcoming and provides spacious comfortable accommodation. Breakfast is served in an elegant dining room overlooking the pretty gardens.

Rooms 4 rms (2 en suite) S £25-£50; D £50-£80* **Facilities** tea/coffee Cen ht Wi-fi **Parking** 20 **Notes** ⊗ No Children 5yrs 🖺

SUTTON COLDFIELD   Map 10 SP19

Windrush

★★★★ 🏠 BED AND BREAKFAST
- -
337 Birmingham Rd, Wylde Green B72 1DL
☎ 0121 384 7534
e-mail: windrush59@hotmail.com
dir: M6 junct 6, on A5127 to Sutton Coldfield, pass shopping centre on left. 75yds then house just before Hawthorn's Surgery on right immediately before traffic bollards

A warm welcome is assured at this elegant Victorian house, located between the city centre and Sutton

Coldfield. Recently refurbished accommocation offers considerable luxury. Memorable breakfasts are served in an elegant dining room.

Rooms 2 rms (1 en suite) (1 pri facs) S £40-£45; D £60-£65* **Facilities** FTV tea/coffee Cen ht **Parking** 5 **Notes** ⊗ No Children 16yrs Closed 19 Dec-3 Jan 🖺

WIGHT, ISLE OF

ARRETON   Map 5 SZ58

Blandings

★★★★ BED AND BREAKFAST
- -
Horringford PO30 3AP
☎ 01983 865720 & 865331   📄 01983 862099
e-mail: robin.oulton@horringford.com
web: www.horringford.com/bedandbreakfast.htm
dir: S through Arreton (B3056), pass Stickworth Hall on right, 300yds on left farm entrance signed Horringford Gdns. U-turn to left, at end of poplar trees turn right. Blandings on left

This recently-built detached home stands in the grounds of Horringford Gardens. The bedroom has private access and has a decking area for warm summer evenings. Breakfast is a highlight with local island produce gracing the table.

Rooms 1 en suite (1 GF) **Facilities** TV1B FTV tea/coffee Cen ht **Parking** 3 **Notes** 🖺

BEMBRIDGE   Map 5 SZ68

The Crab & Lobster Inn

★★★★ INN
- -
32 Forelands Field Rd PO35 5TR
☎ 01983 872244
e-mail: crab.lobster@bluebottle.com

A traditional beamed inn enjoying a coastal location overlooking Bembridge Ledge with panoramic sea views. Bedrooms and bathrooms are traditionally fitted, comfortable and spacious, offering a good range of accessories. Locally-caught crab and lobster is the specialty during lunch and dinner at this popular dining destination.

Rooms 5 en suite (1 fmly) S £45-£70; D £75-£100* **Facilities** tea/coffee Dinner available Cen ht Wi-fi **Parking** 20 **Notes** RS 24-26 Dec No B&B available No coaches

See advert on page 367

Sheepstor Cottage

★★★★ BED AND BREAKFAST
- -
West Green, St Helens PO33 1XA
☎ 01983 873132
e-mail: sheepstor@talktalk.net
dir: A3055 onto B3330 to the Green, left onto Field Ln, 3rd house on right

A friendly welcome awaits you from the proprietor and her cats at this cosy cottage-style guest house. The attractive bedrooms are en suite, and freshly prepared breakfasts are served in the pleasant dining room, which looks over the surrounding countryside.

Rooms 2 en suite (1 fmly) S £33; D £66 **Facilities** tea/coffee Cen ht **Notes** ⊗ 🖺

The **GRANGE**
by the Sea, Isle of Wight

AA
★★★★
Guest Accommodation

'home from home'

01983 867 644
www.thegrangebythesea.com

BEMBRIDGE *continued*

The Windmill Inn

★★★★ INN

1 Steyne Rd PO35 5UH
☎ 01983 872875 📄 01983 874760
e-mail: info@windmill-inn.com
web: www.windmill-inn.com

The Windmill Inn offers a range of comfortably furnished public rooms including a smart dining area where an excellent choice of substantial food is available to suit all tastes. Al fresco dining is available during warmer months. Accommodation is well presented and equipped for both the leisure and business guest. The service is provided by helpful and friendly staff and off-road car parking is a bonus here.

Rooms 14 en suite (2 fmly) S £59-£89; D £80-£120*
Facilities TVL tea/coffee Dinner available Cen ht Wi-fi
Parking 40 **Notes** No coaches

BONCHURCH   Map 5 SZ57

PREMIER COLLECTION

Winterbourne Country House
★★★★★ GUEST HOUSE

Bonchurch Village Rd PO38 1RQ
☎ 01983 852535 📄 01983 857529
e-mail: info@winterbournehouse.co.uk
dir: *1m E of Ventnor. Off A3055 into Bonchurch village*

During his stay in 1849, Charles Dickens described Winterbourne as 'the prettiest place I ever saw in my life, at home or abroad'. Today, the comfortable bedrooms are all well equipped and differ in size, and include luxurious rooms with sea views. There are two lounges and a secluded terrace.

Rooms 7 rms (6 en suite) (1 pri facs) S £65-£150; D £110-£190* **Facilities** TVL tea/coffee Direct Dial Cen ht Licensed ⬧ **Parking** 8 **Notes** No Children 11yrs Closed Dec-Mar

BRIGHSTONE   Map 5 SZ48

Teapots
★★★ BED AND BREAKFAST

9 St Mary's Court, Main Rd PO30 4AH
☎ 01983 740998
dir: *Village centre on B3399. Entrance opposite Mace shop*

A warm welcome awaits at this modern, detached house, situated in the centre of this picturesque village. It provides thoughtfully equipped bedrooms and a pleasant breakfast room, where all share one table. There is also a very attractive garden.

Rooms 3 rms (1 pri facs) (1 fmly) S £35; D £60-£70*
Facilities TVL tea/coffee Cen ht **Parking** 2 **Notes** ⊗ Closed Xmas & New Year 🏵

CHALE   Map 5 SZ47

The Old House
★★★★ 🏠 BED AND BREAKFAST

Gotten Manor, Gotten Ln PO38 2HQ
☎ 01983 551368 & 07746 453398
e-mail: aa@gottenmanor.co.uk
web: www.gottenmanor.co.uk
dir: *1m N of Chale. Turn right off B3399 onto Gotten Ln (opp chapel), house at end*

Located in countryside close to the coast, this 17th-century house was 18th- and 19th-century additions. Restoration has created comfortable, rustic bedrooms with antique bathtubs. Comprehensive breakfasts using the finest ingredients are served in the cosy dining room, and there is a spacious lounge with an open fire.

Rooms 2 en suite S £70-£90; D £80-£100 **Facilities** STV FTV tea/coffee Cen ht Wi-fi ⬧ **Parking** 4 **Notes** LB ⊗ No Children 12yrs 🏵

COWES   Map 5 SZ49

Duke of York
★★★ INN

Mill Hill Rd PO31 7BT
☎ 01983 295171 📄 01983 295047
e-mail: dukeofyorkcowes@btconnect.com

This family-run inn is situated very close to the town centre of Cowes. Comfortable bedrooms are divided between the main building and a separate building only seconds away. Home-cooked meals, with a number of fish and seafood dishes, feature on the menu every evening and are served in the newly redecorated bar and dining area. Car parking is a bonus at this location and outdoor covered dining is also an option.

Rooms 8 en suite 5 annexe en suite (1 fmly) S £39-£70; D £59-£100* **Facilities** FTV tea/coffee Dinner available Wi-fi **Parking** 10

The Fountain Inn

Ⓤ

High St PO31 7AW
☎ 01983 292397 📄 01983 299554
e-mail: fountain.cowes@oldenglishinns.co.uk

Currently the rating for this establishment is not confirmed. This may be due to a change of ownership or because it has only recently joined the AA rating scheme.

Rooms 20 en suite **Conf** Max 30

FRESHWATER   Map 5 SZ38

Seagulls Rest
★★★★ GUEST ACCOMMODATION

Colwell Chine Rd PO40 9NP
☎ 01983 754037 & 754929
e-mail: selena.flint@btinternet.com
dir: *A3054 W from Yarmouth, 2.5m at Colwell Bay Inn right for beach, 300yds on left*

Situated just a stroll from the beach, this smart modern detached house has bright and spacious bedrooms, and there is a comfortable lounge. Breakfast and evening meals (by arrangement) are served in the cheery dining room.

Rooms 4 en suite (2 fmly) (1 GF) S £28-£40; D £56-£60*
Facilities tea/coffee Dinner available Cen ht Wi-fi
Parking 9 **Notes** LB ⊗ 🏵

Buttercup House
★★★★ GUEST ACCOMMODATION

Camp Rd PO40 9HL
☎ 01983 752772
e-mail: enquiries@buttercuphouse.co.uk

Situated on the quieter, western side of the island, this attractive stone house dates back in part to 1836. The atmosphere is relaxed and welcoming. Bedrooms are comfy and spacious and have a number of extra facilities. Breakfast is served around the dining room table, providing a tasty and satisfying start to the day, perhaps before setting off to explore on foot or bicycle.

Rooms 3 en suite (1 fmly) S £35-£45; D £50-£70*
Facilities FTV tea/coffee Cen ht **Parking** 3 **Notes** ⊗ No Children 3yrs

GODSHILL   Map 5 SZ58

PREMIER COLLECTION

Godshill Park Farm House
★★★★★ BED AND BREAKFAST

Shanklin Rd PO38 3JF
☎ 01983 840781
e-mail: info@godshillparkfarm.uk.com
web: www.godshillparkfarm.uk.com
dir: *From ferry teminal towards Newport, onto A3020 & signs to Sandown, at Blackwater Corner right to Godshill, farm on right after Griffin pub*

This delightful 200-year-old stone farmhouse is set in 270 acres of organic farmland with lakes and woodlands. Bedrooms, one with a four-poster bed and the other overlooking the millpond, are comfortably furnished with many extra facilities. Delicious full English breakfasts are served at one large table in the oak panelled Great Hall.

Rooms 2 en suite (1 fmly); D £90-£99* **Facilities** Cen ht Wi-fi Fishing **Parking** 4 **Notes** ⊗ No Children 8yrs

PREMIER COLLECTION

Koala Cottage
★★★★★ BED AND BREAKFAST

Church Hollow PO38 3DR
☎ 01983 842031
e-mail: info@koalacottage.co.uk
web: www.koalacottage.co.uk

Nestled in the quaint village of Godshill is the hidden gem which is Koala Cottage. Bedrooms and bathrooms are furnished to a luxury standard and equipped with endless thoughtful accessories. Leisure facilities include a hot tub and sauna; beauty treatments are available in the comfort of guest bedrooms by prior arrangement. Enjoy a delicious freshly cooked breakfast each morning.

Rooms 3 en suite (3 GF) **Facilities** STV FTV tea/coffee Cen ht Wi-fi Sauna Spa **Parking** 3 **Notes** LB ⊗ No Children 18yrs

'Arndale'
★★★★ BED AND BREAKFAST

High St PO38 3HH
☎ 01983 842003
e-mail: arndalebandb@aol.com
dir: On A3020 High St

Arndale is situated in the pretty village of Godshill. Expect a warm welcome from the resident dogs, Bayley and Arrow. The private lounge-dining room is where dinner is served by arrangement. Guests have access to the patio and garden.

Rooms 2 rms (2 pri facs) (2 fmly) (1 GF) S £35; D £60 **Facilities** TVL Cen ht Riding **Parking** 4 **Notes** ⊗ No Children 14yrs ⊗

NEWPORT Map 5 SZ58

Braunstone House
★★★★ GUEST ACCOMMODATION

33 Lugley St PO30 5ET
☎ 01983 822994 ⊟ 01983 526300
e-mail: lugleys@uwclub.net

Occupying a central location in Newport, this Georgian house has lots of charm. Bedrooms retain elegant proportions and ambience, and are well provided with extras. The popular brasserie restaurant has a modern aspect and well-prepared and appealing cuisine.

Rooms 5 rms (4 en suite) (1 pri facs) **Facilities** tea/coffee Dinner available Cen ht Licensed Wi-fi **Notes** LB ⊗

Castle Lodge
★★★ GUEST ACCOMMODATION

54 Castle Rd PO30 1DP
☎ 01983 527862 & 07789 228203 ⊟ 01983 559030
e-mail: castlelodge@hotmail.co.uk
web: www.castlelodgeiow.co.uk
dir: 0.5m SW of town centre. On B3323 towards Carisbrooke Castle

This well-presented establishment is located in a quiet residential area within close walking distance of the famous Carisbrooke Castle. A comfortable stay is assured with attractive and restful bedrooms together with a bright and airy dining room where a substantial breakfast can be enjoyed.

Rooms 3 rms (2 en suite) (1 pri facs) 5 annexe rms 4 annexe en suite (1 pri facs) (1 fmly) (5 GF) S £30-£35; D £60-£65* **Facilities** tea/coffee Cen ht **Parking** 8 **Notes** ⊗

NITON Map 5 SZ57

PREMIER COLLECTION

Enchanted Manor
★★★★★ GUEST ACCOMMODATION

Sandrock Rd PO38 2NG
☎ 01983 730215
e-mail: info@enchantedmanor.co.uk
web: www.enchantedmanor.co.uk

This delightful property, set in charming grounds, enjoys an enviable location within walking distance of the sea. An enchanted theme prevails throughout the beautifully appointed suites and spacious public areas that are all furnished and decorated to a very high standard. A host of extra touches are provided such as DVD players, well-stocked mini-fridges and welcome baskets. Guests are ensured of friendly, attentive personalised service and an excellent breakfast. Enchanted Manor was the AA's Funkiest B&B of the Year for 2008-2009.

Rooms 7 en suite (2 GF) **Facilities** STV FTV tea/coffee Cen ht Wi-fi ⊁ Snooker Pool Table Spa/hot tub Massage beauty treatment room **Conf** Max 30 Board 30 **Parking** 15 **Notes** LB No Children Civ Wed 50

RYDE Map 5 SZ59

1 The Lawn
★★★★ BED AND BREAKFAST

Spencer Rd PO33 2NU
☎ 01983 568742
dir: A3054, left into West St. Left at T-junct, 100yds on left up drive signed Veterinary Surgery

Attractive Victorian house in quiet area, convenient for town centre as well as hovercraft and Catamaran terminals. Off-road parking is available.

Rooms 2 rms (2 pri facs); D £60* **Facilities** TV1B tea/coffee Cen ht **Parking** 2 **Notes** ⊗ No Children 5yrs ⊗

Crab & Lobster Inn

A traditional beamed Inn enjoying a stunning coastal location overlooking Bembridge Ledge with panoramic sea views which is popular with both locals and visitors alike. There are five spacious en-suite bedrooms all recently refurbished, including a mixture of double, twin and family accommodation, which provide the location for a perfect escape. An extensive menu including lobster caught daily within sight of the pub and brought direct to the kitchen door makes this a popular dining destination. Add in a good selection of Real Ales and Wine and you have all the ingredients for a relaxed and enjoyable experience.

AA ★★★★

32 Forelands Field Rd, Bembridge PO35 5TR
Tel: 01983 872244
Website: www.crabandlobsterinn.co.uk
Email: crab.lobster@bluebottle.com

The Lawns

★★★★ GUEST ACCOMMODATION

72 Broadway PO36 9AA
☎ 01983 402549
e-mail: lawnshotel@aol.com
web: www.lawnshotelisleofwight.co.uk
dir: *On A3055 N of town centre*

The Lawns stands in grounds just a short walk from the beach, public transport and town centre. There is a comfortable lounge and bar, and evening meals (by arrangement) and breakfast are served in the bright dining room. Service is friendly and attentive, and the bedrooms are comfortably equipped.

Rooms 13 en suite (2 fmly) (2 GF) S £34-£42; D £68-£110* **Facilities** FTV TVL tea/coffee Dinner available Cen ht Licensed Wi-fi **Parking** 13 **Notes** LB ⊗ Closed Nov-Jan

Carisbrooke House

★★★★ GUEST HOUSE

11 Beachfield Rd PO36 8NA
☎ 01983 402257 📄 01983 402257
e-mail: wmch583@aol.com
dir: *Opposite Ferncliff Gardens*

Expect a friendly welcome at this family-run guest house situated opposite Ferncliff Gardens and within walking distance of the town centre and seafront. A full English breakfast is served in the dining room overlooking the sun terrace. Enjoy a drink in the bar/lounge. Dinner by arrangement.

Rooms 11 rms (9 en suite) (2 pri facs) (3 fmly) (3 GF) **Facilities** TVL tea/coffee Dinner available Cen ht Licensed Wi-fi **Parking** 3

Montague House

★★★★ GUEST HOUSE

109 Station Av PO36 8HD
☎ 01983 404295
e-mail: enquiries@montaguehousehotel.fsnet.co.uk
dir: *A3055 from Ryde to Sandown, onto Station Av, follow signs for beach*

This large, detached, late Victorian house is just a short walk from the town centre and seafront. The friendly

hosts provide good quality, well-equipped modern accommodation. Separate tables are provided in the very attractive dining room and you can relax in the pleasant conservatory.

Rooms 11 rms (9 en suite) (2 pri facs) (2 fmly) (3 GF) S £30; D £60* **Facilities** TVL tea/coffee Cen ht **Notes** LB ⊗ No Children 5yrs 🚭

Chester Lodge

★★★ GUEST HOUSE

7 Beachfield Rd PO36 8NA
☎ 01983 402773
dir: *On B3395 S from seafront/High St*

This family-run property is within walking distance of the seafront and shops. The neat bedrooms include some on the ground floor with easier access, and there is a comfortable bar and lounge. Breakfast is served in the bright dining room.

Rooms 13 en suite (3 fmly) (4 GF) **Facilities** TVL tea/coffee Dinner available Licensed **Parking** 14 **Notes** ⊗

The Sandhill

★★★ 🅰 GUEST ACCOMMODATION

6 Hill St PO36 9DB
☎ 01983 403635 📄 01983 403695
e-mail: sandhillsandown@aol.com
dir: *In Sandown proceed along main broadway, turn onto Leed St*

Rooms 16 en suite (6 fmly) (4 GF) S £25-£35; D £50-£70 **Facilities** TVL tea/coffee Dinner available Direct Dial Cen ht Licensed Wi-fi **Parking** **Notes** LB

The Avenue

★★★★ GUEST ACCOMMODATION

6 Avenue Rd PO37 7BG
☎ 01983 862746
e-mail: info@avenuehotelshanklin.co.uk
dir: *A3055 from Sandown, through Lake, right onto Avenue Rd before x-rds lights*

This friendly, family-run guest house is in a quiet location just a 5-minute walk from the town centre and beaches. The well-equipped bedrooms are generally spacious, and there is a bar-lounge, a conservatory and a comfortable breakfast room. An attractive terraced courtyard lies to the rear.

Rooms 8 en suite (2 fmly) S £31-£35; D £62-£70* **Facilities** tea/coffee Cen ht Licensed Wi-fi **Parking** 6 **Notes** LB ⊗ Closed Nov-Feb

The Bedford Lodge

★★★★ GUEST ACCOMMODATION

4 Chine Av PO37 6AA
☎ 01983 862416 📄 01983 868704
e-mail: mail@bedfordlodge.co.uk
dir: *A3055 onto Chine Av, opp Tower Cottage Gardens*

A particularly warm welcome is guaranteed here at this delightful property. The Bedford Lodge benefits from an unspoilt and quiet location with pretty gardens and is extremely close to Old Shanklin and Shanklin beach. Bedrooms are well equipped and comfortable. A delicious breakfast is served at individual dining tables in the attractive dining room; in addition a bar and lounge is available for guests' use.

Rooms 14 en suite (1 fmly) (2 GF) S £29-£45; D £52-£80* **Facilities** TVL tea/coffee Cen ht Licensed Wi-fi **Parking** 8 **Notes** LB No Children 5yrs

The Belmont

★★★★ GUEST ACCOMMODATION

8 Queens Rd PO37 6AN
☎ 01983 862864 & 867875
e-mail: enquiries@belmont-iow.co.uk
dir: *From Sandown (on A3055), half left at Fivewys lights signed Ventnor. Belmont 400mtrs on right, opp St Saviour's church*

Situated less than ten minutes walk from Shanklin beach and only five minutes from Old Shanklin Village is Belmont. This establishment offers comfortable accommodation with several rooms benefiting from stunning sea views. The Belmont is licensed and beverages and sandwiches are available during the day time and evening. Off-road car parking is provided and during summer months guests can enjoy the outdoor swimming pool.

Rooms 13 en suite (2 fmly) (2 GF) S £52-£91; D £70-£124 **Facilities** FTV tea/coffee Direct Dial Licensed Wi-fi 🐾 **Parking** 9 **Notes** LB ⊗ No Children 5yrs

Courtlands

★★★★ GUEST ACCOMMODATION

15 Paddock Rd PO37 6PA
☎ 01983 862167 🖂 01983 863308
e-mail: enquiries@courtlandshotel.co.uk
web: www.courtlandshotel.co.uk
dir: *In town centre. Off A3020 Victoria Av onto Highfield Rd, 1st left*

Located just a short walk from the High Street and the old village, this welcoming establishment offers comfortable accommodation, a spacious bar area and a lounge. Breakfast is served in the pleasant dining room.

Rooms 19 rms (18 en suite) (4 fmly) (6 GF) S £38-£42; D £76-£84 **Facilities** TVL tea/coffee Cen ht Licensed ⊀ Pool Table **Parking** 12 **Notes** LB ⊗ Closed Oct-Mar

Glendene Guest House

★★★★ GUEST HOUSE

7 Carter Av PO37 7LQ
☎ 01983 862924
e-mail: jpierceglendene@aol.com
dir: *A3020 into Shanklin, left onto St John's Rd & Brook Rd to Carter Av x-rds*

Located in the heart of Shanklin and within walking distance of the sandy beach, Glendene offers comfortable accommodation in a friendly environment. Breakfast is served in the attractive dining room and a delicious home-cooked dinner is available by arrangement.

Rooms 7 rms (4 en suite) (2 pri facs) (2 fmly) S £25-£30; D £50-£60 **Facilities** TVL tea/coffee Dinner available Wi-fi **Parking** 6 **Notes** LB ⊗

The Grange

★★★★ GUEST ACCOMMODATION

9 Eastcliff Rd PO37 6AA
☎ 01983 867644 🖂 01983 865537
e-mail: jenni@thegrangebythesea.com
web: www.thegrangebythesea.com
dir: *Off A3055, High St*

This delightful house specialises in holistic breaks and enjoys a tranquil yet convenient setting in manicured

grounds close to the seafront and village centre. Extensive refurbishment has resulted in beautifully presented bedrooms and spacious public areas. Dinner and breakfast are taken en famille (outside in fine weather).

Rooms 16 en suite (2 fmly) (6 GF) S £73-£81; D £96-£112* **Facilities** TVL tea/coffee Dinner available Cen ht Licensed Wi-fi Sauna **Parking** 8 **Notes** LB ⊗ Civ Wed 100

See advert on page 365

Hayes Barton

★★★★ ⬤ GUEST ACCOMMODATION

7 Highfield Rd PO37 6PP
☎ 01983 867747
e-mail: williams.2000@virgin.net
web: www.hayesbarton.co.uk
dir: *A3055 onto A3020 Victoria Av, 3rd left*

Hayes Barton has the relaxed atmosphere of a family home and provides well-equipped bedrooms and a range of comfortable public areas. Dinner is available from a short selection of home-cooked dishes and there is a cosy bar lounge. The old village, beach and promenade are all within walking distance.

Rooms 9 en suite (4 fmly) (2 GF) **Facilities** TVL tea/coffee Dinner available Cen ht Licensed Wi-fi **Parking** 9 **Notes** LB Closed Nov-Mar

The Richmond

★★★★ GUEST HOUSE

23 Palmerston Rd PO37 6AS
☎ 01983 862874
e-mail: info@richmondhotel-shanklin.co.uk
dir: *Off Shanklin High St at Conservative Club*

This friendly guest house is a stroll from the town centre and beach. The carefully furnished bedrooms have a good range of facilities, and the public rooms include a cosy lounge bar and an attractive dining room.

Rooms 9 en suite (3 fmly) S £28-£32; D £56-£64* **Facilities** TVL tea/coffee Dinner available Cen ht Licensed Wi-fi **Parking** 5 **Notes** LB ⊗

Rowborough

★★★★ GUEST ACCOMMODATION

32 Arthurs Hill PO37 6EX
☎ 01983 866072 & 863070 🖂 01983 867703
e-mail: susanpatricia@btconnect.com
web: www.rowboroughhotel.com
dir: *Between Sandown & Shanklin*

Located on the main road into town, this charming, family-run establishment provides comfortable bedrooms with many extra facilities. The non-smoking conservatory overlooks the garden, along with a lounge and a bar. Dinner is available by arrangement.

Rooms 9 en suite (5 fmly) (1 GF) S £32-£36; D £64-£72* **Facilities** TVL tea/coffee Dinner available Cen ht Licensed Wi-fi DVD players in all rooms **Parking** 5 **Notes** LB

St Georges House

★★★★ GUEST ACCOMMODATION

2 St Georges Rd PO37 6BA
☎ 01983 863691 🖂 01983 861597
e-mail: stgeorgesiow@isleofwight.com
web: www.stgeorgesiow.com
dir: *S from Fiveways turn 2nd right off A3055, next right*

A warm welcome is assured at this family-run property located in a quiet area between the town centre and cliff top. Bedrooms vary in size but all are comfortable and well appointed. Guests have use of the lounge and bar, and dinners are available by arrangement during the winter months.

Rooms 9 en suite (1 fmly) (1 GF) S £30-£40; D £60-£80 **Facilities** FTV TVL tea/coffee Cen ht Licensed Wi-fi **Parking** 7 **Notes** LB Closed mid Dec-mid Jan

The Braemar

★★★ GUEST HOUSE

1 Grange Rd PO37 6NN
☎ 01983 863172 🖂 01983 863172
e-mail: djsherfield@aol.com

Tucked away in Shanklins Old Village, expect a warm welcome at this family-run, licensed guest house. Bedrooms are comfortable and vary in size. Breakfast is served in the bright dining room overlooking the gardens. Home-cooked evening meals by arrangement.

Rooms 11 en suite (1 fmly) (3 GF) **Facilities** TVL tea/coffee Dinner available Cen ht Licensed Pool Table **Parking** 10

SHANKLIN *continued*

The Waterfront Inn

★★★ INN

19 Esplanade PO37 6BN
☎ 01983 863023
e-mail: norfolkhouseiow@aol.com
dir: *A3055 Sandown to Shanklin, at Arthur's Hill lights left onto Hope Rd, signed Esplanade*

Genuine hospitality is offered at this friendly, family-run establishment, located on the seafront with the beach just across the road. Bedrooms are comfortable and have many extras. There is a bar, lounge and a garden, and the proprietors here set a convivial atmosphere.

Rooms 6 en suite (1 fmly) S £25; D £80* Facilities TVL tea/coffee Dinner available Cen ht Wi-fi Notes No Children 2yrs

Perran Lodge

★★ GUEST ACCOMMODATION

2 Crescent Rd PO37 6DH
☎ 01983 862816 📠 01983 862816
e-mail: bookings@bethnabas.co.uk
dir: *Off A3055 onto Queens Rd, up hill onto Crescent Rd, Lodge on left*

Perran Lodge is a licensed establishment which occupies a convenient location only a few minutes walk from Shanklin town centre and from the beachfront. Accommodation is comfortable and adequately equipped and public areas are attractively maintained. Substantial breakfasts are prepared to order in the bright dining room.

Rooms 23 en suite (5 fmly) (5 GF) S £25-£35; D £50-£70 Facilities tea/coffee Cen ht Licensed Parking 5 Notes ⊗

TOTLAND BAY
Map 5 SZ38

The Golf House

★★★★ BED AND BREAKFAST

Alum Bay New Rd PO39 0JA
☎ 01983 753293
e-mail: sue@thegolfhouse.info
dir: *Totland B3322, at War Memorial rdbt take 2nd exit onto Church Hill 1m, entrance on right*

The Golf House is a detached house in its own grounds situated at the western tip of the Isle of Wight, with all rooms enjoying amazing views. Two bedrooms, each with televisions, comprise of a two bedroom suite with one bathroom which can accommodate up to four guests and the second bedroom has en suite facilities. Local produce is used where possible and evening snacks are available by prior arrangement. Transport to and from Yarmouth can be arranged.

Rooms 3 rms (1 en suite) (2 pri facs); D £65-£85* Facilities STV FTV TVL tea/coffee Cen ht Wi-fi Snooker Parking 3 Notes LB ⊗

The Hoo

★★★★ BED AND BREAKFAST

Colwell Rd PO39 0AB
☎ 01983 753592 📠 01983 753592
e-mail: the.hoo@btinternet.com
dir: *From Yarmouth ferry right onto A3054, 2.25m enter Colwell Common, The Hoo on corner of Colwell Rd & Warden Rd*

Located close to the port and beaches, this friendly family home provides a peaceful setting. The house has many Japanese features and guests are asked to wear slippers. The spacious bedrooms are well equipped and comfortably furnished. English breakfast is most enjoyable and is served overlooking the attractive gardens.

Rooms 3 rms (1 en suite) (2 fmly) S £25-£47; D £40-£75* Facilities FTV tea/coffee Cen ht Parking 1 Notes No Children 5yrs

The Hermitage

★★★ GUEST ACCOMMODATION

Cliff Rd PO39 0EW
☎ 01983 752518
e-mail: blake_david@btconnect.com
web: www.thehermitagebnb.co.uk
dir: *Church Hill B3322, right onto Eden Rd, left onto Cliff Rd, 0.5m on right*

The Hermitage is an extremely pet and people friendly establishment which occupies a stunning and unspoilt location near to the cliff top in Totland Bay. Extensive gardens are well maintained and off-road parking is a bonus. Accommodation is comfortable and you are assured of a genuinely warm welcome and friendly service at this traditionally styled establishment. A range of delicious items at breakfast provide a substantial start to the day.

Rooms 4 rms (3 en suite) (1 pri facs) (1 fmly) S £25-£35; D £50-£70* Facilities TVL tea/coffee Dinner available Parking 6 Notes LB

VENTNOR
Map 5 SZ57

PREMIER COLLECTION

The Hambrough

★★★★★ ◉◉◉ RESTAURANT WITH ROOMS

Hambrough Rd PO38 1SQ
☎ 01983 856333 📠 01983 857260
e-mail: info@thehambrough.com

A former Victorian villa set on the hillside above Ventnor and with memorable views out to sea, The Hambrough has a modern, stylish interior with well-equipped and comfortable bedrooms. The team's passion for food is clearly evident in the superb cuisine served in the minimalist restaurant.

Rooms 7 en suite; D £100-£200* Facilities tea/coffee Dinner available Direct Dial Cen ht Wi-fi Notes ⊗ Closed 1-13 Nov, 27 Dec-14 Jan & 19-30 Apr No coaches

PREMIER COLLECTION

The Leconfield

★★★★★ ◉ 🖃 GUEST ACCOMMODATION

85 Leeson Rd, Upper Bonchurch PO38 1PU
☎ 01983 852196 📠 01983 856525
e-mail: enquiries@leconfieldhotel.com
web: www.leconfieldhotel.com
dir: *On A3055, 3m from Old Shanklin village*

This country house is situated on an elevated position with panoramic seaviews above the historic village of Bonchurch. Luxury finished bedrooms and suites are spacious and individually styled. Public rooms include two lounges and a conservatory in addition to the Sea Scape restaurant, named after the views, where freshly prepared breakfast and imaginative dinner menus are served. Additional facilities include the outdoor pool, terrace area and ample off-road parking.

Rooms 7 en suite 5 annexe en suite (3 GF) S £48-£176; D £80-£200* Facilities tea/coffee Dinner available Cen ht Licensed Wi-fi 🕏 Parking 14 Notes LB ⊗ No Children 16yrs

Horseshoe Bay House
★★★★★ ☐ GUEST HOUSE

Shore Rd PO38 1RN
☎ 01983 856800
e-mail: howard@horseshoebayhouse.com
dir: 0.5m E of Ventnor. Off A3055 to Bonchurch, house opp pond

Set at the very edge of the beach in the pretty village of Bonchurch, this super place offers spacious accommodation in a memorable location. Hospitality is friendly and the proprietors here are attentive hosts. Bedrooms are smartly styled in tranquil colours and comfortably appointed; most rooms enjoy the spectacular views. Breakfast offers a good range of choice and provides an excellent start to the day.

Rooms 6 rms (5 en suite) (1 pri facs) (1 fmly) (1 GF)
Facilities TVL tea/coffee Cen ht Licensed Wi-fi
Parking 6 **Notes** LB ⊗ No Children 8yrs

Winterbourne Country House
★★★★★ GUEST HOUSE

Bonchurch Village Rd PO38 1RQ
☎ 01983 852535 ▤ 01983 857529
e-mail: info@winterbournehouse.co.uk

(For full entry see Bonchurch)

The Lake
★★★★ GUEST ACCOMMODATION

Shore Rd, Bonchurch PO38 1RF
☎ 01983 852613
e-mail: enquiries@lakehotel.co.uk
dir: 0.5m E of Ventnor. Off A3055 to Bonchurch, opp village pond

A warm welcome is assured at this friendly, family-run property set in two acres of well-tended gardens close to the sea. Bedrooms are equipped with modern facilities and the elegant public rooms offer a high standard of comfort. A choice of menus is offered at dinner and breakfast.

Rooms 11 en suite 9 annexe en suite (7 fmly) (4 GF)
S £36-£46; D £72-£95 **Facilities** TVL tea/coffee Dinner available Cen ht Licensed Wi-fi **Parking** 20 **Notes** LB No Children 3yrs Closed 20 Dec-2 Jan

St Augustine Villa
★★★★ GUEST ACCOMMODATION

Esplanade PO38 1TA
☎ 01983 852285 ▤ 01983 856630
e-mail: info@harbourviewhotel.co.uk
web: www.harbourviewhotel.co.uk
dir: Opp harbour

Located on an elevated position with spectacular sea views, this delightful Victorian property next to the Winter Gardens provides well-equipped and comfortable bedrooms. Public areas include a conservatory dining room, lounge, cosy bar, small garden and patio area, all with sea views.

Rooms 9 en suite S £74-£90; D £83-£99* **Facilities** STV FTV TVL tea/coffee Direct Dial Cen ht Licensed Wi-fi **Parking** 8 **Notes** ⊗ No Children 21yrs Closed 5 Jan-1 Feb

St Maur
★★★★ GUEST ACCOMMODATION

Castle Rd PO38 1LG
☎ 01983 852570 & 853645 ▤ 01983 852306
e-mail: sales@stmaur.co.uk
dir: Exit A3055 at end of Park Ave onto Castle Rd, premises 150yds on left

A warm welcome awaits guests at this Victorian villa, which is pleasantly and quietly located in an elevated position overlooking the bay. The well-equipped bedrooms are traditionally decorated while public areas include a spacious lounge and cosy residents' bar. The gardens here are a delight.

Rooms 9 en suite (2 fmly) **Facilities** STV tea/coffee Dinner available Cen ht Licensed **Parking** 9 **Notes** ⊗ No Children 5yrs Closed Dec

Gothic View B&B
★★★ ☐ ☕ BED AND BREAKFAST

Town Ln, Chale Green PO38 2JS
☎ 01983 551120
e-mail: info@gothicview.co.uk

This establishment provides comfortable accommodation in a converted gothic chapel located in the picturesque village of Chale Green. Delicious meals are prepared with guests' personal tastes fully catered for, and breakfast is also a real treat with a number of home-made, freshly created and healthy items available.

Rooms 3 rms (2 en suite) (1 pri facs) (3 GF)
Facilities tea/coffee Dinner available Cen ht **Parking** 1 **Notes** LB ⊗ ☕

Crown at Aldbourne
[U]

2 The Square SN8 2DU
☎ 01672 540214 ▤ 01672 540214
e-mail: gant12@hotmail.co.uk
web: www.crownataldbourne.co.uk
dir: M4 junct 15, N on A419, signed to Aldbourne

Currently the rating for this establishment is not confirmed. This may be due to a change of ownership or because it has only recently joined the AA rating scheme.

Rooms 4 en suite S £40-£50; D £55-£65 (room only)*
Facilities tea/coffee Dinner available Cen ht Licensed **Conf** Max 30 Thtr 20 Class 12 Board 10 **Notes** LB

Mandalay
★★★★ GUEST ACCOMMODATION

15 Stonehenge Rd SP4 7BA
☎ 01980 623733 ▤ 01980 626642
e-mail: nick.ramplin@btinternet.com
dir: 500yds W of town centre, off High St onto Church St & Stonehenge Rd

Quietly located on the edge of the town, yet within easy reach of Stonehenge and the cathedral, this delightful property provides individually decorated rooms. Freshly cooked breakfasts are served in the pleasant breakfast room, which overlooks the landscaped gardens. Please note that a 48 hour cancellation policy is in operation.

Rooms 5 en suite (2 fmly) S £45-£55; D £60-£70
Facilities TVL tea/coffee Cen ht **Parking** 5 **Notes** ⊗

AMESBURY *continued*

Park House Motel

★★★★ GUEST ACCOMMODATION

SP4 0EG
☎ 01980 629256 📠 01980 629256
e-mail: info@parkhousemotel.com
dir: *5m E of Amesbury. Junct A303 & A338*

This family-run establishment offers a warm welcome and is extremely convenient for the A303. Bedrooms are practically equipped with modern facilities and come in a variety of sizes. There is a large dining room where dinner is served during the week, and a cosy bar in which to relax.

Rooms 30 rms (27 en suite) (1 pri facs) (9 fmly) (25 GF)
Facilities STV FTV TVL tea/coffee Dinner available Cen ht Licensed Wi-fi **Parking** 40

See advert on opposite page

Catkin Lodge

★★★ BED AND BREAKFAST

93 Countess Rd SP4 7AT
☎ 01980 624810 & 622139 📠 01980 622139
e-mail: info@catkinlodge.fsnet.co.uk
web: www.catkinlodge.fsnet.co.uk
dir: *From A303 at Amesbury onto A345 (Marlborough road), 400yds on left*

Popular for business and leisure, Catkin Lodge is close to Stonehenge and offers off-road parking. The three bedrooms, including two on the ground floor, offer good levels of comfort and can accommodate children if required. The artwork of the talented proprietor is displayed around the property, adding further interest.

Rooms 3 en suite (1 fmly) (2 GF) S £35-£55; D £65-£75
Facilities FTV tea/coffee Cen ht **Parking** 7 **Notes** ⊗ No Children 7yrs 🐾

BOX Map 4 ST86

PREMIER COLLECTION

Foggam Barn Bed and Breakfast

★★★★★ BED AND BREAKFAST

Box Hill SN13 8ES
☎ 01225 744888 📠 01225 744888
e-mail: denise@foggambarn.com
web: www.foggambarn.com

Foggam Barn is a delightful, detached house with pleasant gardens and excellent views over the surrounding countryside. Chippenham and Bath are just a short drive away. The two bedrooms are very comfortably furnished and decorated, and guests are welcome to use the relaxing lounge. Breakfast, made with high quality local and home-made produce, is served in the spacious conservatory.

Rooms 2 rms (1 en suite) (1 pri facs) (4 fmly) S £70-£85; D £85-£115* **Facilities** STV TVL tea/coffee Cen ht Wi-fi **Parking** 8 **Notes** LB ⊗ No Children 14yrs

---

PREMIER COLLECTION

Spinney Cross

★★★★★ BED AND BREAKFAST

Lower Kingsdown Rd, Kingsdown SN13 8BA
☎ 01225 742019 & 461518
e-mail: dotcom@spinneycross.co.uk
dir: *Bath A4 toward Chippenham, A353 from Bathford to Bradford on Avon. Under railway bridge, left at Crown PH to Kingsdown, left at Swan PH, bear right at bottom of hill, Spinney Cross 500yds on left*

A warm welcome is assured at this delightful home located in the quiet village of Kingsdown. The views are a pleasure to behold. Bedrooms are spacious and attractively styled, and all have their own private access to the patio and garden. A varied range of tasty options is available at breakfast.

Rooms 3 rms (2 en suite) (1 fmly) (3 GF) **Facilities** tea/coffee Cen ht Wi-fi **Parking** 6 **Notes** ⊗

Lorne House

★★★★ GUEST HOUSE

London Rd SN13 8NA
☎ 01225 742597
e-mail: info@lornehousebox.co.uk
web: www.lornehousebox.co.uk
dir: *On A4 in village, E of High St next to doctors' surgery*

The bedrooms and bathrooms have now undergone a complete refurbishment with air conditioning, DVD players and luxury showers being just some of the features. At breakfast there's a good selection of carefully prepared local and home-made produce. Lorne House offers guests a high standard of quality and comfort throughout, and a genuinely warm welcome is extended by the resident proprietors. Parking is available adjacent to the house.

Rooms 5 en suite (2 fmly) (1 GF) S £50-£65; D £75-£85*
Facilities TVL tea/coffee Cen ht Licensed Wi-fi 🏊
Conf Max 12 Thtr 12 Class 12 Board 12 **Parking** 6
Notes ⊗ Closed Xmas

White Smocks

★★★★ BED AND BREAKFAST

Ashley SN13 8AJ
☎ 01225 742154 📠 01225 742212
e-mail: whitesmocksashley@hotmail.com
dir: *A4 1m W of Box turn opp The Northy, at T-junct White Smocks right of thatched cottage*

Quietly located in the pleasant village of Ashley, and just a short drive from Bath with its many attractions, White Smocks offers a relaxing escape where guests are encouraged to enjoy the pleasant garden in the summer, real fires in the winter and the Jacuzzi all year round. The two bedrooms and bathrooms are immaculately presented and comfortably furnished. Guests are also welcome to use the lounge.

Rooms 2 en suite (1 fmly) **Facilities** TVL tea/coffee Dinner available Cen ht **Parking** 3 **Notes** ⊗

Hermitage

★★ GUEST ACCOMMODATION

Bath Rd SN13 8DT
☎ 01225 744187 📄 01225 743447
e-mail: hermitagebb@btconnect.com
dir: On A4 at W end of village

This 16th-century house is located in a pleasant village five miles from Bath. The spacious bedrooms are comfortably furnished, with two rooms in a small adjacent cottage. Breakfast is served in the dining room. There is also a lounge area, and delightful gardens with a heated swimming pool.

Rooms 3 en suite 2 annexe en suite (1 fmly) (1 GF)
S £35-£45; D £55-£65* **Facilities** tea/coffee Cen ht 🐾
Parking 6 **Notes** ⊗ Closed 22 Dec-6 Jan 🍴

BRADFORD-ON-AVON   **Map 4 ST86**

PREMIER COLLECTION

Bradford Old Windmill
★★★★★ ⩳ BED AND BREAKFAST

4 Masons Ln BA15 1QN
☎ 01225 866842 📄 01225 866648
e-mail: aa@bradfordoldwindmill.co.uk
dir: N of town centre off A363. Driveway on E side of Masons Ln, no sign or number, 100mtrs before Castle public house

This unique property has been restored to retain many original features. Bedrooms are individually decorated, and include a number of interesting options such as a round room, a waterbed or a suite with minstrels' gallery. An extensive breakfast menu, featuring local and organic products whenever possible, offers a range of alternatives from devilled mushrooms or passion fruit pancakes to the more traditional choices. A comfortable lounge is also available.

Rooms 3 en suite (1 fmly) S £59-£99; D £59-£109
Facilities tea/coffee Dinner available Cen ht Wi-fi
Parking 3 **Notes** ⊗ No Children 6yrs Closed Dec-Jan RS Tue, Fri & Sun (Mar-Oct) No dinner

---

Home Farm

★★★★ BED AND BREAKFAST

Farleigh Rd, Wingfield BA14 9LG
☎ 01225 764492 📄 01225 764492
e-mail: info@homefarm-guesthouse.co.uk
dir: 2m S in Wingfield village on A366

This delightful former farmhouse offers comfortable, well-equipped accommodation. Guests are assured of a warm welcome, and are free to use the charming gardens, which have wonderful views over farmland. A full English breakfast is served at individual tables.

Rooms 3 en suite (1 fmly) (1 GF) **Facilities** tea/coffee Cen ht **Parking** 30 **Notes** ⊗

Park House Motel

Amesbury
Cholderton
SP4 0EG

Tel: 01980 629256
Email: info@parkhousemotel.com
Website: www.parkhousemotel.com

AA
★★★★
Guest Accommodation

BRADFORD-UPON-AVON *continued*

Midway Cottage

★★★★ BED AND BREAKFAST

Farleigh Wick BA15 2PU
☎ 01225 863932
e-mail: midwaycottage@btinternet.com
web: www.midwaycottage.co.uk
dir: *2m NW of Bradford on A363, next to Fox & Hounds pub*

A warm welcome is assured at this delightful Victorian cottage, located near Bradford-on-Avon and Bath. The comfortable bedrooms are equipped with a variety of thoughtful extras, and there is a pleasant garden. Breakfast is served around a communal table in the lounge-dining room.

Rooms 3 en suite (1 GF) S £50-£60; D £60-£70*
Facilities TVL tea/coffee Cen ht Wi-fi **Parking** 3 **Notes** ⊗ No Children 5yrs Closed Xmas-5 Jan

Serendipity

★★★★ BED AND BREAKFAST

19f Bradford Rd, Winsley BA15 2HW
☎ 01225 722380
e-mail: vanda.shepherd@tesco.net
dir: *A36 onto B3108, 1.5m right into Winsley, establishment on right on main road*

Set in a quiet residential area, Serendipity is convenient for visiting nearby Bath. The proprietors are friendly and welcoming, and bedrooms are brightly decorated and equipped with a range of extras. Two are on the ground floor. Guests can watch badgers and local wildlife in the gardens during the evening. Breakfast is served in the conservatory overlooking the garden.

Rooms 3 en suite (1 fmly) (2 GF) S £42-£65; D £50-£65*
Facilities FTV tea/coffee Cen ht Wi-fi 🏊 **Parking** 5 **Notes** LB ⊗ ⊕

The Tollgate Inn

★★★★ ◉◉ INN

Ham Green, Holt BA14 6PX
☎ 01225 782326   📄 01225 782805
e-mail: alison@tollgateholt.co.uk
web: www.tollgateholt.co.uk
dir: *2m E on B3107, at W end of Holt*

The Tollgate Inn combines the comforts of a traditional inn with excellent quality food served in delightful surroundings. It stands near the village green at Holt, and is only a short drive from Bath. Bedrooms, varying in size, are well decorated and thoughtfully equipped with welcome extras.

Rooms 4 en suite S £50-£80; D £80-£100* **Facilities** tea/coffee Dinner available Direct Dial Cen ht Wi-fi **Conf** Max 30 Thtr 30 Board 30 **Parking** 40 **Notes** ⊗ No Children 16yrs Closed 25-26 & 31 Dec-1 Jan No coaches

Diana Lodge Bed & Breakfast

★★★ BED AND BREAKFAST

Grathie Cottage, 72 Marshfield Rd SN15 1JR
☎ 01249 650306
dir: *500yds NW of town centre on A420, into West End Club car park*

A cheerful welcome awaits guests at this late 19th-century cottage, within walking distance of the town centre and the railway station. Comfortable bedrooms are well decorated and adjacent car parking is available.

Rooms 5 rms (3 en suite) (2 pri facs) (1 fmly) (2 GF) S £35-£45; D £50-£60* **Facilities** FTV tea/coffee Cen ht Wi-fi **Parking** 1 **Notes** ⊗

Thurlestone Lodge

★★★★ BED AND BREAKFAST

13 Prospect SN13 9AD
☎ 01249 713397   & 07815 731131
e-mail: v_ogilvie_robb@hotmail.com
web: www.thurlestone.webeden.co.uk
dir: *0.25m from Corsham Centre on B3353. 150yds on right after Great Western pub halfway between turnings to Lypiatt Rd & Dicketts Rd*

This charming Victorian house is delightfully located in the attractive town of Corsham, convenient for the countryside and attractions of the Cotswolds and Bath. Bedrooms are comfortable, spacious and well appointed. Breakfast is served in the spacious dining room and provides a hearty start to the day.

Rooms 2 en suite (1 fmly) S £48-£65; D £65-£76* **Facilities** tea/coffee Cen ht Wi-fi **Parking** 5 **Notes** ⊗ No Children 7yrs Closed Xmas & New Year RS 22 Dec-2 Jan

Pickwick Lodge Farm *(ST857708)*

★★★★ FARMHOUSE

Guyers Ln SN13 0PS
☎ 01249 712207   📄 01249 701904 Mrs G Stafford
e-mail: b&b@pickwickfarm.co.uk
web: www.pickwickfarm.co.uk
dir: *Off A4, Bath side of Corsham, onto Guyers Ln, farmhouse at end on right*

This Grade II listed, 17th-century farmhouse is peacefully located on a 300-acre beef and arable farm, within easy reach of Bath. The spacious bedrooms are well equipped with modern facilities and many thoughtful extras. A hearty breakfast using the best local produce is served at a communal table in the dining room.

Rooms 3 rms (2 en suite) (1 pri facs) S £40-£50; D £70-£75* **Facilities** FTV TVL tea/coffee Cen ht Wi-fi Fishing **Parking** 6 **Notes** LB ⊗ No Children 12yrs 300 acres arable/beef

CRICKLADE — Map 5 SU09

Upper Chelworth Farm

★★★ BED AND BREAKFAST

Upper Chelworth SN6 6HD
☎ 01793 750440
dir: 1.5m W of Cricklade. Off B4040 x-rds for Chelworth Upper Green

Close to the M4 and Swindon, Upper Chelworth Farm offers a genuinely friendly welcome in addition to comfortable bedrooms of varying sizes. There is a spacious lounge with a wood-burning stove, games room with a pool table, and a lovely garden. Breakfast is served in the dining room.

Rooms 7 rms (6 en suite) (1 fmly) S £25-£30; D £45-£50* Facilities TV6B TVL tea/coffee Cen ht Pool Table Parking 10 Notes No Children 5yrs Closed mid Dec–mid Jan ✿

DEVIZES — Map 4 SU06

PREMIER COLLECTION

Blounts Court Farm

★★★★★ BED AND BREAKFAST

Coxhill Ln, Potterne SN10 5PH
☎ 01380 727180
e-mail: carys@blountscourtfarm.co.uk
dir: A360 to Potterne, into Coxhill Ln opp George & Dragon, at fork left, follow drive to farmhouse

A warm welcome is assured at this peacefully located, delightful arable farm, overlooking the village cricket field. The character barn has been converted to provide three attractive bedrooms on the ground floor - one has a four-poster bed. The elegant décor is in keeping with the character of the house. Breakfast, which features home-made and local produce, is served in the farmhouse dining room.

Rooms 3 en suite (3 GF) S £38-£42; D £65-£72* Facilities FTV TVL tea/coffee Cen ht Wi-fi Parking 5 Notes ✿ No Children 8yrs

Summerhayes B&B

★★★★★ BED AND BREAKFAST

143 High St, Littleton Panell SN10 4EU
☎ 01380 813521
e-mail: summerhayesbandb@ukonline.co.uk
web: www.summerhayesbandb.co.uk
dir: 5m S of Devizes on A360, near x-rds with B3098

Rooms 2 rms (1 en suite) (1 pri facs) S £45-£55; D £65-£80* Facilities FTV TVL tea/coffee Cen ht Wi-fi Parking 6 Notes LB ✿ No Children 3yrs

Littleton Lodge

★★★ GUEST ACCOMMODATION

Littleton Panell (A360), West Lavington SN10 4ES
☎ 01380 813131 ▦ 01380 816969
e-mail: stay@littletonlodge.co.uk
web: www.littletonlodge.co.uk
dir: On A360 in Littleton Panell

Convenient for Stonehenge and for touring the many attractions of this pleasant area, Littleton Lodge offers spacious and comfortable accommodation and a relaxed friendly atmosphere. Breakfast is served in the stylish dining room and freshly cooked dishes provide a excellent start to the day.

Rooms 3 en suite Facilities tea/coffee Cen ht Golf Parking 4 Notes ✿

DINTON — Map 4 SU03

Marshwood Farm B&B (SU005327)

★★★★ 🅰 FARMHOUSE

SP3 5ET
☎ 01722 716334 Mrs F J Lockyer
e-mail: marshwood1@btconnect.com
dir: A30 onto B3089 into Dinton, turn right to Wylye, B&B 0.5m on left

Rooms 2 en suite (1 fmly) S £45-£60; D £60-£70 Facilities tea/coffee Cen ht ⌣ Parking 4 Notes LB ✿ 580 acres arable/sheep

FIRSDOWN — Map 5 SU23

Junipers

★★★★ BED AND BREAKFAST

3 Juniper Rd SP1 1SS
☎ 01980 862330
e-mail: junipersbedandbreakfast@btinternet.com
web: www.junipersbedandbreakfast.co.uk
dir: 5m from Salisbury on A30, A343 to London follow Junipers brown signs into Firsdown

Located in a quiet residential area, just five miles from the city, this homely accommodation is located at ground floor level. Bedrooms are well equipped with thoughtful extras. The hosts, who have craft skills, are happy to show guests their interesting items constructed in medieval style. Breakfast, featuring local produce, is served in the cosy dining room/lounge.

Rooms 3 en suite (3 GF) S £45-£50; D £65-£70 Facilities tea/coffee Cen ht Parking 6 Notes LB ✿ No Children

FONTHILL BISHOP — Map 4 ST93

The River Barn

★★★ GUEST HOUSE

SP3 5SF
☎ 01747 820232
dir: Off A303 to Tisbury/Fonthill Bishop. 1m to junct then right onto B3089, 100yds on left

Surrounded by lawns stretching down to the river, The River Barn is the central hub of the village of Fonthill Bishop. Parts of the barn are 600 years old and it has operated as a business for the last 100 years. The annexe bedrooms are spacious and well appointed. The café-bar offers sumptuous cakes and cream teas, light lunches and evening meals.

Rooms 4 annexe en suite (1 fmly) (3 GF) S £55-£75; D £75-£95* Facilities tea/coffee Dinner available Cen ht Licensed Parking 20 Notes LB

GRITTLETON — Map 4 ST88

Staddlestones

★★ BED AND BREAKFAST

SN14 6AW
☎ 01249 782458 ▦ 01249 782458
e-mail: staddlestonesbb@btinternet.com
dir: 500yds E of village x-rds

This large modern bungalow lies at the east end of the small village, and is convenient for the M4. The local pub is just a stroll away and ample parking is available.

Rooms 3 rms (3 GF) S £35-£65; D £50-£80* Facilities FTV TVL tea/coffee Cen ht Parking 5 Notes ✿

HIGHWORTH — Map 5 SU29

PREMIER COLLECTION

Jesmonds of Highworth
★★★★★ ⚙️⚙️ RESTAURANT WITH ROOMS

Jesmond House SN6 7HJ
☎ 01793 762364 🖷 01793 861201
e-mail: info@jesmondsofhighworth.com
web: www.jesmondsofhighworth.com
dir: A419 onto B4019 to Highworth, left at lights, establishment on left

Jesmonds offers high quality bedrooms and bathrooms in addition to a contemporary restaurant providing memorable cuisine. The young team of staff offer an effortless mix of professional service delivered in a relaxed and welcoming manner. In addition to a comfortable bar and separate lounge, guests are encouraged to enjoy the pleasant Zen-inspired rear garden. Head Chef William Guthrie and his team skilfully utilise high quality produce in an interesting combination of textures and flavours.

Rooms 10 en suite (2 fmly) S £100-£140; D £125-£180* **Facilities** FTV tea/coffee Dinner available Direct Dial Cen ht Wi-fi **Conf** Class 24 Board 18 **Parking** 20 **Notes** LB ⊗ No coaches

Highlands of Highworth
★★★★ GUEST HOUSE

1 Swindon Rd SN6 7DE
☎ 01793 765131
e-mail: highlandsofhighworth@yahoo.co.uk
web: www.highlandsofhighworth.co.uk
dir: A361 from Swindon, after Shell garage, last house on left before rdbt

Conveniently located on the edge of Highworth, this detached accommodation offers a range of very well decorated and equipped bedrooms including one on the ground floor. Extras such as free Wi-fi in rooms are welcome features. Ample parking is provided, and a good selection of pubs and restaurants are within easy walking distance.

Rooms 4 en suite (1 GF) S £45-£50; D £50-£60* **Facilities** FTV TVL tea/coffee Cen ht Wi-fi **Parking** 6 **Notes** LB ⊗ No Children 12yrs

HINDON — Map 4 ST93

The Lamb Inn
★★★★ ⚙️ INN

SP3 6DP
☎ 01747 820573 🖷 01747 820605
e-mail: manager@lambathindon.co.uk
dir: Off B3089 in village centre

This 17th-century coaching inn is in a pretty village within easy reach of Salisbury and Bath. It has been refurbished in an eclectic style, and some of the well-equipped bedrooms have four-poster beds. Enjoyable, freshly prepared dishes are available at lunch and dinner in the restaurant or bar, where log fires provide a welcoming atmosphere on colder days.

Rooms 14 en suite (1 fmly) (2 GF) S £50-£80; D £70-£150* **Facilities** STV tea/coffee Dinner available Direct Dial Cen ht Wi-fi Pool Table **Conf** Max 40 Thtr 40 Class 16 Board 24 **Parking** 16 **Notes** LB Civ Wed 60

LACOCK — Map 4 ST96

At the Sign of the Angel
★★★★ 🛏️ 🍽️ GUEST ACCOMMODATION

6 Church St SN15 2LB
☎ 01249 730230 🖷 01249 730527
e-mail: angel@lacock.co.uk
dir: Off A350 into Lacock, follow 'Local Traffic' sign

Visitors will be impressed by the character of this 15th-century former wool merchant's house, set in the National Trust village of Lacock. Bedrooms come in a range of sizes and styles including the atmospheric rooms in the main house and others in an adjacent new building. Excellent dinners and breakfasts are served in the beamed dining rooms, and there is also a first-floor lounge and a pleasant rear garden.

Rooms 6 en suite 4 annexe en suite (3 GF) S £82; D £120* **Facilities** FTV tea/coffee Dinner available Direct Dial Cen ht Licensed Wi-fi **Conf** Max 14 Board 14 **Parking** 6 **Notes** Closed 23-27 Dec RS Mon (ex BHs) Closed for lunch Civ Wed 24

The Old Rectory
★★★★ 🅰 GUEST ACCOMMODATION

Cantax Hill SN15 2JZ
☎ 01249 730335 🖷 01249 730166
e-mail: sexton@oldrectorylacock.co.uk
web: www.oldrectorylacock.co.uk
dir: M4 junct 17, A350 S from Chippenham, left at lights into Lacock, The Old Rectory 1st on right

Rooms 6 rms (4 en suite) (2 pri facs) (2 fmly) (1 GF) S £45-£60; D £75-£85* **Facilities** TVL tea/coffee Cen ht Wi-fi 🐦 **Conf** Max 20 Board 14 **Parking** 8 **Notes** LB No Children 10yrs Closed 24-26 Dec ⊕

LOWER CHICKSGROVE — Map 4 ST92

Compasses Inn
★★★★ ⚙️ INN

SP3 6NB
☎ 01722 714318 🖷 01722 714318
e-mail: thecompasses@aol.com
web: www.thecompassesinn.com
dir: Off A30 signed Lower Chicksgrove, 1st left onto Lagpond Ln, single-track lane to village

This charming 17th-century inn, within easy reach of Bath, Salisbury, Glastonbury and the Dorset coast, offers comfortable accommodation in a peaceful setting. Carefully prepared dinners are enjoyed in the warm atmosphere of the bar-restaurant, while breakfast is served in a separate dining room.

Rooms 5 en suite (1 fmly) S £65-£90; D £85-£90* **Facilities** FTV tea/coffee Dinner available Cen ht Wi-fi **Conf** Max 14 **Parking** 40 **Notes** LB Closed 25-26 Dec

MALMESBURY — Map 4 ST98

Lovett Farm (ST975850)
★★★★ 🅰 FARMHOUSE

Little Somerford SN15 5BP
☎ 01666 823268 & 07808 858612
🖷 01666 823268 Mrs S Barnes
e-mail: sue@lovettfarm.co.uk
web: www.lovettfarm.co.uk
dir: 3m from Malmesbury on B4042 opp 2nd turning to the Somerfords

Rooms 2 en suite S £35-£50; D £65-£80* **Facilities** FTV tea/coffee Cen ht **Parking** 4 **Notes** ⊗ No Children 12yrs 75 acres beef

The Horse & Groom Inn

[U]

The Street, Charlton SN16 9DL
☎ 01666 823904
e-mail: info@horseandgroominn.com
dir: 2m NE on B4040, through Charlton village on left

Currently the rating for this establishment is not confirmed. This may be due to a change of ownership or because it has only recently joined the AA rating scheme.

Rooms 5 en suite S £65-£99.95; D £65-£99.95*
Facilities Wi-fi

MERE Map 4 ST83

Chetcombe House

★★★★ GUEST ACCOMMODATION

Chetcombe Rd BA12 6AZ
☎ 01747 860219 📄 01747 860111
e-mail: mary.butchers@lineone.net
dir: Off A303

Chetcombe House has wonderful views across an acre of well-tended gardens towards Gillingham and the Blackmore Vale. The house, built in 1937, provides elegance and charm, and is pleasantly spacious, comfortable and fresh. The bedrooms are well equipped and are provided with many extra facilities. Breakfast is served in the attractive dining room, which overlooks the rear garden.

Rooms 5 en suite (1 fmly) S £45; D £60* **Facilities** tea/coffee Cen ht Wi-fi **Parking** 10 **Notes** ⊗ Closed Xmas & New Year ⊗

NETTLETON Map 4 ST87

Fosse Farmhouse Chambre d'Hote

★★★★ 🍽 BED AND BREAKFAST

Nettleton Shrub SN14 7NJ
☎ 01249 782286 📄 01249 783066
e-mail: caroncooper@fossefarmhouse.com
web: www.fossefarmhouse.com
dir: 1.5m N from Castle Combe on B4039, left at Gib, 1m on right

Set in quiet countryside not far from from Castle Combe, Fosse Farmhouse has well-equipped bedrooms decorated in keeping with its 18th-century origins. Excellent dinners are served in the farmhouse, and cream teas can be enjoyed in the old stables or the delightful garden.

Rooms 2 en suite (1 fmly) S £65-£75; D £90-£125*
Facilities tea/coffee Dinner available Cen ht Licensed Wi-fi Golf 18 **Conf** Max 15 Thtr 10 Class 10 Board 10 **Parking** 12 **Notes** LB

REDLYNCH Map 5 SU22

Rookseat B&B

★★★ BED AND BREAKFAST

Grove Ln SP5 2NR
☎ 01725 512522
e-mail: deanransome@btinternet.com

Expect a friendly welcome at this family-run bed and breakfast situated in the quiet New Forest village of Redlynch, perfect for visiting Salisbury and Bournemouth. Comfortable bedrooms all have en suite shower rooms. A delicious breakfast with plenty of choice is served in the dining room.

Rooms 3 en suite **Facilities** tea/coffee Cen ht **Parking** 3 **Notes** ⊗ No Children 12yrs ⊗

ROWDE Map 4 ST96

The George & Dragon

★★★★ ⊛⊛ RESTAURANT WITH ROOMS

High St SN10 2PN
☎ 01380 723053
e-mail: thegandd@tiscali.co.uk
dir: 1.5m from Devizes on A350 towards Chippenham

This is a traditional inn dating back to the 14th century when it was a meeting house. Exposed beams, wooden floors, antique rugs and open fires create a warm atmosphere in the bar and restaurant. Bedrooms and bathrooms are very well decorated and equipped with some welcome extras. Dining in the bar or restaurant should not be missed, as local produce and fresh fish deliveries from Cornwall are offered from the daily-changing blackboard menu.

Rooms 3 rms (2 en suite) (1 pri facs) (1 fmly) S £55-£85; D £65-£105* **Facilities** tea/coffee Dinner available Cen ht **Parking** 15 **Notes** ⊗ No coaches

---

SALISBURY Map 5 SU12

See also Amesbury & Stoford

St Anns House

★★★★ GUEST ACCOMMODATION

32-34 Saint Ann St SP1 2DP
☎ 01722 335657
e-mail: info@stannshouse.co.uk
web: www.stannshouse.co.uk
dir: From Brown St turn left onto St Ann St

St Ann's House is a newly refurbished former public house close to the Cathedral and city centre. Lovingly restored with many original features and modern creature comforts such as flat-screen TVs, this is a high quality operation with a friendly host.

Rooms 9 en suite (1 GF) S £55-£70; D £70-£120
Facilities FTV TVL tea/coffee Cen ht Licensed Wi-fi **Conf** Max 30 Thtr 18 Class 18 Board 18 **Notes** Closed 23 Dec-2 Jan

---

Avonlea House

★★★★ BED AND BREAKFAST

231 Castle Rd SP1 3RY
☎ 01722 338351
e-mail: guests@avonleahouse.co.uk
web: www.avonleahouse.co.uk
dir: 1.5m N of city centre. On A345 near Old Sarum

The Avonlea has very comfortable and well equipped bedrooms. Breakfast is offered with a choice of fresh local items. The property is located close to Old Sarum and within walking distance of Salisbury city centre for the Cathedral and riverside walks. There are leisure facilities close by in the shape of a swimming pool and gym, and there is easy access to Stonehenge, the New Forest and the South coast.

Rooms 3 en suite; D £55-£65* **Facilities** tea/coffee Cen ht Wi-fi **Parking** 3 **Notes** ⊗ No Children 12yrs Closed Xmas & New Year

SALISBURY *continued*

Cathedral View

★★★★ GUEST ACCOMMODATION

83 Exeter St SP1 2SE
☎ 01722 502254
e-mail: wenda.rampton@btopenworld.com
web: www.cathedral-viewbandb.co.uk
dir: *200yds E of cathedral. Off A338 ring road onto Exeter St, signs for Old George Mall*

The friendly home has views of the cathedral, which is just a two minute walk away, and provides attractive refurbished bedrooms with numerous thoughtful extras. Breakfast is a good selection served around one large table in the dining room.

Rooms 4 en suite (1 fmly); D £75-£85* **Facilities** FTV tea/coffee Cen ht Wi-fi **Notes** ⊗ No Children 10yrs 🕮

Clovelly

★★★★ GUEST HOUSE

17-19 Mill Rd SP2 7RT
☎ 01722 322055 📄 01722 327677
e-mail: info@clovellyhotel.co.uk
dir: *500yds W of market square*

The Clovelly provides quality accommodation and service within easy reach of the railway station and city centre. The proprietor is a Blue Badge Guide and offers expert advice on sightseeing. Bedrooms are neatly decorated with co-ordinated furnishings. Public areas include a delightful lounge and a light and airy breakfast room.

Rooms 14 en suite (3 fmly) **Facilities** tea/coffee Cen ht **Conf** Thtr 20 Class 20 Board 20 **Parking** 15 **Notes** ⊗ No Children

Cricket Field House

★★★★ GUEST ACCOMMODATION

Skew Bridge, Wilton Rd SP2 9NS
☎ 01722 322595 📄 01722 322595
e-mail: cricketfieldcottage@btinternet.com
web: www.cricketfieldhouse.co.uk
dir: *A36, W of Salisbury, towards Wilton & Warminster*

The 19th-century gamekeeper's cottage stands in award-winning gardens overlooking the South Wiltshire Cricket Ground. Within walking distance of the city centre and railway station, Cricket Field House provides a high level of accommodation, hospitality and customer care.

Rooms 7 en suite 10 annexe en suite (1 fmly) (10 GF) S £45-£75; D £60-£95 **Facilities** FTV tea/coffee Dinner available Cen ht Licensed Wi-fi **Conf** Thtr 20 Class 14 Board 16 **Parking** 25 **Notes** ⊗ No Children 14yrs RS 24-26 Dec room only

Newton Farmhouse *(SU230223)*

★★★★ FARMHOUSE

Southampton Rd SP5 2QL
☎ 01794 884416   Mr & Mrs Guild
e-mail: lizzie@newtonfarmhouse.com
web: www.newtonfarmhouse.com

(For full entry see Whiteparish)

The Old House

★★★★ GUEST ACCOMMODATION

161 Wilton Rd SP2 7JQ
☎ 01722 333433 📄 01722 335551
dir: *1m W of city centre on A36*

Located close to the city centre, this non-smoking property dates from the 17th century. Bedrooms have modern facilities and one room has a four-poster bed. There is a spacious lounge, cosy cellar bar, and large gardens to enjoy - weather permitting.

Rooms 7 en suite (1 fmly) S £40-£60; D £65-£70* **Facilities** TVL tea/coffee Cen ht **Parking** 10 **Notes** LB ⊗ No Children 7yrs

Salisbury Old Mill House

★★★★ BED AND BREAKFAST

Warminster Rd, South Newton SP2 0QD
☎ 01722 742458
e-mail: salisburymill@yahoo.com
dir: *4m NW of Salisbury on A36 in South Newton*

This restored watermill exudes character, and the mill machinery is still on view. Friendly and welcoming, the property offers comfortable, well-appointed bedrooms, a lounge with wood-burning stove, and a dining area where delicious dinners are available by arrangement. The garden features the original millpond.

Rooms 3 rms (2 en suite) (1 pri facs) 1 annexe en suite (1 fmly) (1 GF) S £38-£45; D £60-£85* **Facilities** tea/coffee Dinner available Cen ht Licensed Outdoor table tennis **Parking** 10 **Notes** ⊗ Closed 25 Dec & 1 Jan 🕮

2 Park Lane

★★★★ GUEST ACCOMMODATION

2 Park Ln SP1 3NP
☎ 01722 321001
web: www.2parklane.co.uk

A stylish period property that has been completely renovated, within walking distance of the city centre and its attractions. Light, airy rooms, comfortable beds and good off-road parking are available.

Rooms 6 en suite; D £65-£85* **Facilities** FTV tea/coffee Cen ht Wi-fi **Parking** 6 **Notes** ⊗ No Children 6yrs

Websters

★★★★ GUEST HOUSE

11 Hartington Rd SP2 7LG
☎ 01722 339779
e-mail: enquiries@websters-bed-breakfast.com
dir: *From city centre onto A360 Devizes Rd, 1st turning on left*

A warm welcome is assured at this delightful property, located in a quiet cul-de-sac close to the city centre. The charming, well-presented bedrooms are equipped with numerous extras including broadband. There is one ground-floor room with easier access.

Rooms 5 en suite (1 GF) S £45-£48; D £60-£65* **Facilities** TVL tea/coffee Cen ht Wi-fi **Parking** 5 **Notes** LB ⊗ No Children 12yrs Closed 31 Dec & 1 Jan RS Xmas & New Year Continental breakfast only at Xmas

Wyndham Park Lodge

★★★★ Ⓐ BED AND BREAKFAST

51 Wyndham Rd SP1 3AB
☎ 01722 416517 📠 01722 328851
e-mail: enquiries@wyndhamparklodge.co.uk
dir: Off A36 S onto Castle St towards city centre, 2nd left

Rooms 3 en suite 1 annexe en suite (1 fmly) (1 GF)
S £45-£50; D £58-£65 **Facilities** FTV tea/coffee Cen ht
Wi-fi **Parking** 3 **Notes** ⊗ Closed Xmas & New Year

City Lodge

★★★ GUEST ACCOMMODATION

33 Milford St SP1 2AP
☎ 01722 326600 📠 01722 338686
e-mail: info@citylodge.biz

City Lodge offers excellent value lodge-style
accommodation in a converted 15th-century Merchant
House in the centre of Salisbury. Newly refurbished, with
a wealth of original beams and features, the lodge also
boasts free Wi-fi, flat screen digital TVs, and en suite
bathrooms in all bedrooms. No meals are served, but
friendly helpful staff are on hand to assist with dining
recommendations.

Rooms 23 en suite (5 fmly) (5 GF) S £39-£79; D £39-£79
(room only)* **Facilities** FTV tea/coffee Cen ht Wi-fi
Notes ⊗

Byways Guest House

★★★ GUEST ACCOMMODATION

31 Fowlers Rd SP1 2QP
☎ 01722 328364 📠 01722 322146
e-mail: info@bywayshouse.co.uk
web: www.bywayshouse.co.uk
dir: 500yds E of city centre. A30 onto A36 signed
Southampton, follow Youth Hostel signs to hostel, Fowlers
Rd opp

Located in a quiet street with off-road parking, Byways is
within walking distance of the town centre. Several
bedrooms have been decorated in a Victorian style and
another two have four-poster beds. All rooms offer good
levels of comfort, with one adapted for easier access.

Rooms 23 rms (19 en suite) (6 fmly) (13 GF) S £39-£60;
D £55-£80* **Facilities** tea/coffee Cen ht Licensed Wi-fi
Conf Max 8 **Parking** 15 **Notes** Closed Xmas & New Year

Melbury House

★★★ BED AND BREAKFAST

46 Stonehenge Rd, Durrington SP4 8BP
☎ 01980 653151
e-mail: jwcw@freenet.co.uk
dir: From A303 Countess Rd rdbt, take A345. At rdbt turn
right signed Durrington 5yds, turn left onto Stonehenge
Rd

Melbury House is a traditional small bed and breakfast
with warm, friendly hosts. Rooms are fresh and
comfortable and it has a great location, handy for
Stonehenge and Salisbury. Breakfast is at a family table
and is freshly cooked to order - a good start to the day.

Rooms 2 rms (1 en suite) (1 pri facs) (2 fmly) (2 GF)
S £40; D £65-£70* **Facilities** FTV tea/coffee Cen ht
Parking 4 **Notes** ⊗ No Children 10yrs 🐾

Sarum Heights

★★★ BED AND BREAKFAST

289 Castle Rd SP1 3SB
☎ 01722 421596 & 07931 582357
e-mail: sarumheights@ntlworld.com

Sarum Heights is a large family home on the outskirts of
the city with good off-road parking. Rooms are smart,
clean and well appointed with quality beds and linen.
Freshly-cooked breakfasts are served at a family table in
the kitchen.

Rooms 3 rms (2 en suite) (1 pri facs) S £40-£44;
D £60-£66 **Facilities** tea/coffee Cen ht Wi-fi **Parking** 3
Notes LB ⊗ 🐾 🐾

Holmhurst House

★★ GUEST ACCOMMODATION

Downton Rd SP2 8AR
☎ 01722 410407 📠 01722 410407
e-mail: holmhurst@talk21.com
dir: Off ring road onto A338 S, Holmhurst on left near
Shell station

Holmhurst lies on the outskirts of the city within walking
distance of the cathedral and centre. This family-run
property provides comfortable, well-equipped bedrooms,
and a traditional breakfast is served at individual tables
in the bright dining room.

Rooms 4 rms (3 en suite) (1 pri facs) (1 fmly) S £35-£45;
D £50-£65* **Facilities** FTV tea/coffee Cen ht Wi-fi
Parking 9 **Notes** LB ⊗

Old Mill

Ⓤ

Town Path SP2 8EU
☎ 01722 327517 📠 01722 333367
e-mail: theoldmill@simonandsteve.com
web: www.simonandsteve.com
dir: Turn right from A338 onto A3094, then third turning
on right

Currently the rating for this establishment is not
confirmed. This may be due to a change of ownership or
because it has only recently joined the AA rating scheme.

Rooms 11 en suite S £55-£62.50; D £65-£110*
Facilities FTV tea/coffee Dinner available Direct Dial
Cen ht Licensed Wi-fi Fishing **Parking** 17

SHREWTON   Map 5 SU04

The Manor

★★★★ RESTAURANT WITH ROOMS

SP3 4HF
☎ 01980 620216
e-mail: info@rollestonemanor.com

This Grade II listed manor house occupies a peaceful
location close to Stonehenge and is only a 45-minute
drive from both the historic cities of Bath and Salisbury.
A range of comfortable accommodation is provided in the
original house and public areas consist of an elegant
drawing room and modern dining area. Dinner is prepared
to order every evening, and special events such as
weddings and anniversaries are regularly catered for.

Rooms 7 en suite; D £80-£130* **Facilities** tea/coffee
Dinner available Wi-fi

STAPLEFORD   Map 5 SU03

Oak Bluffs

★★★ BED AND BREAKFAST

4 Church Furlong SP3 4QE
☎ 01722 790663 & 07796 893502 📠 01722 790663
dir: In village centre off B3083

A warm and friendly welcome awaits you at this
immaculately presented bungalow situated in a delightful
village, complete with an ancient church and many
thatched properties. Well located for visiting Stonehenge,
the well appointed bedroom has its own separate
entrance, with lots of thoughtful extras provided. A couple
of pubs are within walking distance.

Rooms 1 en suite (1 GF) S £40-£45; D £55-£60*
Facilities tea/coffee Cen ht **Parking** 1 **Notes** ⊗ 🐾 🐾

STOFORD — Map 5 SU03

The Swan Inn
★★★ INN

Warminster Rd SP2 0PR
☎ 01722 790236
e-mail: info@theswanatstoford.co.uk
web: www.theswanatstoford.co.uk
dir: On A36 in village centre

This centrally located, family-run inn is ideal for touring the area. Good-sized bedrooms are available, and the newly refurbished bar and restaurant serve an excellent choice of meals with an emphasis on locally sourced produce. Other facilities include Wi-fi, private fishing on the river and a skittle alley.

Rooms 9 en suite (2 fmly) Facilities tea/coffee Dinner available Cen ht Wi-fi Fishing Pool Table Skittle alley Conf Thtr 40 Class 30 Board 20 Parking 70 Notes ⊗

STOURTON — Map 4 ST73

Spread Eagle Inn
★★★★ 🍴 INN

Church Lawn BA12 6QE
☎ 01747 840587
e-mail: enquiries@spreadeagleinn.com
web: www.spreadeagleinn.com
dir: 0.5m W off B3092 at entrance to Stourhead Gardens

Set in the beautiful grounds of Stourhead House with its Palladian temples, lakes and vistas, the Spread Eagle is an impressive red brick building with a good reputation for simple, honest, locally-sourced food. In the bedrooms, National Trust antiques sit side by side with modern comforts. The large Georgian windows, low ceilings and uneven floors give the feel of a comfortable country house.

Rooms 5 en suite S £80-£90; D £110-£125*
Facilities tea/coffee Dinner available Direct Dial Cen ht Wi-fi Conf Max 30 Thtr 30 Board 20 Notes LB ⊗

SWINDON — Map 5 SU18

Ardecca
★★★★ GUEST ACCOMMODATION

Fieldrise Farm, Kingsdown Ln, Blunsdon SN25 5DL
☎ 01793 721238 & 07791 120826
e-mail: chris-graham.ardecca@fsmail.net
web: www.ardecca-bedandbreakfast.co.uk
dir: Off A419 for Blunsdon & Swindon, onto B4019. Right at Cold Harbour pub, 1st on left

Ardecca is quietly located in sixteen acres of pastureland with easy access to Swindon and the Cotswolds. All rooms are on the ground floor and are well furnished and equipped. An especially friendly welcome is provided and freshly-cooked home-made dinners are available by arrangement. Arts and crafts workshops are available on site.

Rooms 4 rms (4 pri facs) (1 fmly) (4 GF) S £40-£45; D £60-£65* Facilities tea/coffee Dinner available Cen ht Wi-fi Art & Crafts workshops Conf Class 16 Parking 5 Notes ⊗ No Children 6yrs 🐾

The Old Post Office Guest House
★★★★ GUEST HOUSE

Thornhill Rd, South Marston SN3 4RY
☎ 01793 823114 📠 01793 823441
e-mail: theoldpostofficeguesthouse@yahoo.co.uk
web: www.theoldpostofficeguesthouse.co.uk
dir: A420 onto Thornhill Rd at Gablecross rdbt 0.75m on left before Old Vicarage Lane

Sympathetically extended, this attractive property is about two miles from Swindon. Guests are welcomed by the enthusiastic owner, a professional opera singer with a wonderful sense of humour. The comfortable bedrooms vary in size, and all are equipped with numerous facilities. An extensive choice is offered at breakfast, freshly cooked using the best of local produce.

Rooms 5 en suite (1 fmly) Facilities FTV tea/coffee Cen ht Wi-fi Parking 6 Notes ⊗

Portquin

★★★★ GUEST ACCOMMODATION

Broadbush, Broad Blunsdon SN26 7DH
☎ 01793 721261
e-mail: portquin@msn.com
dir: A419 onto B4019 at Blunsdon signed Highworth, continue 0.5m

This friendly guest house near Swindon provides a warm welcome and views of the Lambourn Downs. The rooms vary in shape and size, with six in the main house and three in an adjacent annexe. Full English breakfasts are served at two large tables in the kitchen-dining area.

Rooms 6 en suite 3 annexe en suite (2 fmly) (4 GF) S £35-£45; D £55-£70* Facilities tea/coffee Cen ht Wi-fi Conf Max 20 Thtr 20 Class 20 Board 20 Parking 12

Tawny Owl
★★★★ INN

Queen Elizabeth Dr, Taw Hill SN25 1WP
☎ 01793 706770 📠 01793 706785
e-mail: tawnyowl@arkells.com
dir: 2.5m NW of town centre, signed from A419

Expect a genuinely friendly welcome from the staff at this modern inn on the north-west outskirts of Swindon. It has comfortable, well-equipped bedrooms and bathrooms. A varied selection of enjoyable home-cooked meals is on offer at dinner, and a range of Arkells ales and wines. A private function room is available.

Rooms 5 en suite (1 fmly) Facilities TVL tea/coffee Dinner available Direct Dial Cen ht Stairlift Conf Max 55 Thtr 55 Class 55 Board 55 Parking 75 Notes ⊗ RS Xmas/New Year Civ Wed 50

Crown Inn

★★★ INN

Ermin St SN3 4NL
☎ 01793 827530 📄 01793 831683
e-mail: thecrownstratton@arkells.com
dir: A419 onto B4006 Stratton St Margaret, left onto Ermin St

This popular inn, dating back to 1868, is situated in Stratton St Margaret near to Swindon centre and the M4. Public areas are furnished in traditional style with crackling log fires that add to the character of the place. Bedrooms are located within the main building and in a newer adjacent block.

Rooms 21 en suite (7 GF) **Facilities** STV tea/coffee Dinner available Direct Dial Cen ht Wi-fi **Parking** 60 **Notes** No coaches

Fairview Guest House

★★★ GUEST HOUSE

52 Swindon Rd, Wootton Bassett SN4 8EU
☎ 01793 852283 📄 01793 848076
e-mail: fairview@woottonb.wanadoo.co.uk
web: http://fairviewguesthouse.website.orange.co.uk
dir: On A3102 to Wootton Bassett. 1.25m from M4 junct 16. 5m from Swindon centre

A welcoming, family-run property with easy access to the M4 and the town of Swindon. Bedrooms are split between the main house and the bungalow annexe, and breakfast is served in an open-plan dining/sitting room with an open fire on cooler mornings.

Rooms 8 rms (3 en suite) 4 annexe rms 3 annexe en suite (1 pri facs) (2 fmly) (4 GF) S £30-£38 **Facilities** FTV TVL tea/coffee Cen ht Wi-fi **Parking** 14 **Notes** LB ⊗

Fir Tree Lodge

★★★ GUEST ACCOMMODATION

17 Highworth Rd, Stratton St Margaret SN3 4QL
☎ 01793 822372 📄 01793 822372
e-mail: info@firtreelodge.com
dir: 1.5m NE of town centre. A419 onto B4006 signed Stratton/Town Centre, premises 200yds opp Rat Trap pub

Fir Tree Lodge is a modern building offering a range of comfortable bedrooms including rooms on the ground floor. The resident proprietors provide a relaxed and

friendly welcome. The guest house benefits from a large secure car park.

Rooms 12 en suite 2 annexe rms (2 annexe pri facs) (1 fmly) (5 GF) (2 smoking) **Facilities** FTV tea/coffee Cen ht **Parking** 13

Heart in Hand

★★★ INN

43 High St, Blunsdon SN26 7AG
☎ 01793 721314 📄 01793 727026
e-mail: leppardsteve@aol.com
dir: Off A419 at High St, 200yds on right

Located in the village centre, this family-run inn offers a relaxed and friendly welcome together with a wide selection of home-cooked food. Bedrooms are spacious, well equipped and offer a number of useful extras. A pleasant patio and rear garden with seating is also available.

Rooms 4 en suite (1 fmly) **Facilities** tea/coffee Dinner available Cen ht **Parking** 17 **Notes** ⊗

Internos B & B

★★★ BED AND BREAKFAST

3 Turnpike Rd, Blunsdon SN26 7EA
☎ 01793 721496 📄 01793 721496
web: www.internos-bedandbreakfast.co.uk
dir: 4m N of Swindon. Alongside A419 access from Cold Harbour End

Situated just off the A419 towards Cirencester, this establishment offers comfortable accommodation and a relaxed and friendly atmosphere. The gardens open onto a field, which is a haven for wildlife. Guests enjoy a freshly-cooked breakfast served in the dining room, and a cosy lounge is also available.

Rooms 3 rms (1 fmly) S £25-£27; D £42* **Facilities** FTV TVL tea/coffee Cen ht Wi-fi **Parking** 6 **Notes** ⊗ ⊜

Saracens Head

★★ INN

High St, Highworth SN6 7AG
☎ 01793 762284 📄 01793 767869
e-mail: arkells@arkells.com
dir: 5m NE of Swindon

This establishment stands on the main street of a pleasant market town, close to Swindon. It offers plenty of character, including a popular bar dating from 1828. A fine selection of real ales and home-cooked food are highlights. Bedrooms, which vary in size, are generally compact. A rear car park and a patio area are available.

Rooms 13 en suite (2 fmly) **Facilities** tea/coffee Dinner available Direct Dial Cen ht Wi-fi **Conf** Max 10 Thtr 10 Class 10 Board 10 **Parking** 30

TROWBRIDGE Map 4 ST85

Eastbrook Cottage

★★★★ BED AND BREAKFAST

Hoopers Pool, Southwick BA14 9NG
☎ 01225 764403
e-mail: enquiries@eastbrookcottage.co.uk
web: www.eastbrookcottage.co.uk
dir: 2m SW of Trowbridge. Off A361 between Rode & Southwick

This cottage, situated just off the main Frome road, offers fresh, smart accommodation. Although the bedrooms are not the most spacious, they are finished to a high level of quality and equipped with many thoughtful extras. To add to this, the host offers genuine hospitality and friendliness. Guests may not want to move from the wood-burning stove in the snug lounge. Breakfast, featuring local produce wherever possible, is enjoyed around a large oak table.

Rooms 3 rms (2 en suite) (1 pri facs) S £35-£50; D £60-£70* **Facilities** tea/coffee Cen ht Wi-fi **Parking** 5 **Notes** ⊗ No Children 10yrs ⊜

Paxcroft Cottage

★★★★ 🅰 BED AND BREAKFAST

62B Paxcroft Cottages, Devizes Rd, Hilperton BA14 6JB
☎ 01225 765838
e-mail: paxcroftcottages@hotmail.com
web: www.paxcroftcottages.pwp.blueyonder.co.uk
dir: 2m NE of Trowbridge. On A361 near Paxcroft Farm, 0.5m from Paxcroft Mead Estate

Rooms 3 en suite S £30-£40; D £50-£60* **Facilities** FTV TVL tea/coffee Cen ht **Parking** 6 **Notes** LB ⊗ ⊜

Bridge House Bed & Breakfast

★★ BED AND BREAKFAST

Canal Bridge, Semington BA14 6JT
☎ 01225 703281 & 706101 📄 01225 790888
e-mail: jeanpayneDHPS@aol.com
dir: 3m NE of Trowbridge. Off A361 into Semington, over bridge, house on right

The front garden of this charming house leads directly to the canal, which offers a wonderful opportunity for cyclists, dedicated ramblers and strollers, who may choose to travel to heritage towns such as Bradford-on-Avon. Bedrooms are pretty and well equipped. Breakfast, featuring home-made preserves, is served around a farmhouse table in the pleasant dining room, adjacent to the kitchen.

Rooms 4 rms S £27-£29; D £50-£54* **Facilities** tea/coffee Dinner available **Parking** 6 **Notes** ⊗ Closed 20 Dec-3 Jan ⊜

WARMINSTER — Map 4 ST84

Deverill End

★★★★ BED AND BREAKFAST

Sutton Veny BA12 7BY
☎ 01985 840356
e-mail: mertens.59@amserve.com
dir: *2.5m SE of Warminster. Off A36 at Heytesbury rdbt to Sutton Veny, over x-rds, 200yds on left*

This farmside B&B is located midway between Bath and Salisbury and within easy reach of Stonehenge, Longleat and Stourhead, guests are made to feel at home and invited to share the spectacular southern views and pretty garden. Bedrooms are comfortable, well equipped and all on the ground floor. Breakfast features home-grown produce (when in season) and own free range eggs.

Rooms 3 en suite (3 GF) S £55-£70; D £65-£70*
Facilities tea/coffee Cen ht **Parking** 4 **Notes** ⊗ No Children 10yrs Closed Xmas & Jan ⌨

The George Inn

★★★★ INN

Longbridge Deverill BA12 7DG
☎ 01985 840396 📠 01985 841333
web: www.thegeorgeinnlongbridgedeverill.co.uk
dir: *3m S on A350*

The George Inn combines a friendly village pub atmosphere with modern well-equipped bedrooms, one of which has a four-poster bed. In addition to the pleasant bar/restaurant, there is a cosy first floor lounge and a pleasant river garden in which to enjoy a cool summer drink. There is an extensive menu available, featuring home-cooked dishes.

Rooms 11 en suite (5 fmly) **Facilities** tea/coffee Dinner available Direct Dial Cen ht **Conf** Max 120 Thtr 50 Class 50 Board 30 **Notes** ⊗ RS Xmas Closed pm

The Granary Bed & Breakfast

★★★★ BED AND BREAKFAST

Manor Farm, Upton Scudamore BA12 0AG
☎ 01985 214835 📠 01985 214835
dir: *2m NW of Warminster. Off A350 into Upton Scudamore*

The Granary is located in the peaceful village of Upton Scudamore and has delightful country views. It offers ground-floor bedrooms, each with a private terrace, stylishly decorated with co-ordinated fabrics and comfortable furnishings. The many thoughtful extras include a fridge, and breakfast is served in your room.

Rooms 2 annexe en suite (2 GF) **Facilities** FTV tea/coffee Cen ht Wi-fi **Parking** 3 **Notes** ⊗ No Children 8yrs Closed 20 Dec-3 Jan ⌨

White Lodge

★★★★ GUEST ACCOMMODATION

22 Westbury Rd BA12 0AW
☎ 01985 212378 📠 01985 212378
e-mail: carol@lioncountry.co.uk
dir: *0.5m N of town centre. Off High St onto Portway signed Westbury, White Lodge 0.75m on left*

Situated on the outskirts of Warminster, this attractive house, with art deco features, is well placed for touring Wiltshire and Somerset. Individually styled bedrooms, which overlook well-tended grounds, are comfortable and well-appointed.

Rooms 3 rms (1 en suite) (2 pri facs) (1 fmly) S £50-£65; D £65-£68* **Facilities** tea/coffee Cen ht **Parking** 8 **Notes** ⊗ No Children 5yrs Closed Xmas RS Jan-Feb ⌨

The Dove Inn

★★★ INN

Corton BA12 0SZ
☎ 01985 850109 📠 01985 851041
e-mail: info@thedove.co.uk
dir: *5m SE of Warminster. Off A36 to Corton village*

This relaxing inn stands in the heart of a peaceful village. There are carefully furnished courtyard rooms and a conservatory, and in cooler months a roaring log fire accompanies the imaginative bar menu. Home-cooked dishes and a selection of real ales are highlights of any stay here.

Rooms 5 annexe en suite (1 fmly) (4 GF) **Facilities** tea/coffee Dinner available Cen ht **Parking** 24

WHITEPARISH — Map 5 SU22

Brayford

★★★★ BED AND BREAKFAST

Newton Ln SP5 2QQ
☎ 01794 884216
e-mail: reservations@brayford.org.uk
dir: *Off A36 at Newton x-rds onto Newton Ln towards Whiteparish, Brayford 150yds on right*

A genuine welcome awaits guests at this comfortable family home. Peacefully located with views over neighbouring farmland, the house is just a short drive off the A36. Suitable for business and leisure travellers, bedrooms are well equipped with many thoughtful extras. Guests are invited to relax in the lounge dining room, where a tasty breakfast is served.

Rooms 3 rms (2 pri facs) (1 fmly) (2 GF) S £40; D £60-£65 **Facilities** FTV TVL tea/coffee Cen ht **Parking** 2 **Notes** ⊗ Closed Xmas & New Year ⌨

Newton Farmhouse (SU230223)

★★★★ FARMHOUSE

Southampton Rd SP5 2QL
☎ 01794 884416 **Mr & Mrs Guild**
e-mail: lizzie@newtonfarmhouse.com
web: www.newtonfarmhouse.com
dir: *7m SE of Salisbury on A36, 1m S of A27 junct*

Dating back to the 16th century, this delightful farmhouse was gifted to Lord Nelson's family as part of the Trafalgar estate. The house has been thoughtfully restored and bedrooms, most with four-poster beds, have been adorned with personal touches. Delicious breakfasts are available in the relaxing conservatory. The pleasant gardens include an outdoor swimming pool.

Rooms 6 en suite 3 annexe en suite (2 fmly) (5 GF) **Facilities** FTV TVL tea/coffee Cen ht Wi-fi 🛶 🏊 **Parking** 9 **Notes** LB ⊗ 2.5 acres non-working

WHITLEY — Map 4 ST86

PREMIER COLLECTION

The Pear Tree Inn

★★★★★ ⊚⊚ RESTAURANT WITH ROOMS

Maypole Group, Top Ln SN12 8QX
☎ 01225 709131 📠 01225 702276
e-mail: peartreeinn@maypolehotels.com

This inn provides luxurious bedrooms, some in an adjoining annexe at ground floor level, and some in the main building. The restaurant draws visitors from a wide area to experience the interesting menu, the rustic atmosphere and the friendliness of the hosts.

Rooms 4 en suite 4 annexe en suite (2 fmly) (4 GF) S £95; D £125* **Facilities** FTV tea/coffee Dinner available Cen ht Wi-fi **Parking** 45

ZEALS — Map 4 ST73

Cornerways Cottage

★★★★ BED AND BREAKFAST

Longcross BA12 6LL
☎ 01747 840477
e-mail: cornerwayscottage@btinternet.com
dir: *From A303 onto B3092 signed Stourhead. At bottom of slip road, turn right under bridge & follow signs for Zeals. On left by 40mph sign*

A warm friendly welcome, comfortable rooms and hearty breakfasts await in this charming 250-year-old stone cottage. Situated right on the borders of Somerset, Dorset and Wiltshire it is ideal for visiting Longleat, Stourhead House and Gardens or for simply touring the local area. Horseriding, fishing, the Wiltshire Cycleway and plenty of great walks are all on the doorstep.

Rooms 3 rms (2 en suite) (1 pri facs) S £45-£50; D £55-£60* **Facilities** FTV TVL Cen ht **Notes** ⊗ No Children 8yrs Closed Xmas & New Year

WORCESTERSHIRE

ABBERLEY — Map 10 SO76

Orleton Court B&B

★★★★ BED AND BREAKFAST

WR6 6SU
☎ 01584 881248   📄 01584 881159
e-mail: pmspilsbury@aol.com
dir: *4m W of Abberley. A443 onto B4203 through Stanford Bridge, 1st right, 1m right into Orleton Court*

This Georgian farmhouse situated by the River Teme is part of a working hop farm. There are two comfortable en suite bedrooms. Hearty breakfasts are served in the parlour and a comfortable lounge is available. Coarse fishing, golf and shooting are available by arrangement.

Rooms 3 rms (2 en suite) (2 fmly) **Facilities** TV2B TVL tea/coffee Cen ht Fishing **Parking** 20 **Notes** ⊗ ⊜

ALVECHURCH — Map 10 SP07

Woodlands Bed and Breakfast

★★★★ BED AND BREAKFAST

Coopers Hill B48 7BX
☎ 0121 445 6774   📄 0121 505 1801
e-mail: john.impey@gmail.com
web: www.woodlands-bed-and-breakfast.com
dir: *From Red Lion, Alvechurch, enter Tanyard Ln over canal, under railway. Woodlands 2nd on left*

Woodlands is set is 18 acres of delightful countryside with extensive gardens, a heated swimming pool (in season) and croquet lawn. A warm welcome is offered by John and Amanda your hosts. Bedrooms are spacious and comfortable, and a substantial breakfast is served in the elegant dining room. Situated within 10 miles of the centre of Birmingham and a short drive from Stratford and Warwick.

Rooms 3 en suite 1 annexe en suite (2 fmly) (1 GF) S £42; D £75-£100* **Facilities** FTV tea/coffee Dinner available Cen ht Licensed Wi-fi ⛵ 🎣 Fishing Table tennis **Parking** 10 **Notes** Closed Xmas/Etr wks

Alcott Farm *(SP056739)*

★★★ 🅰 FARMHOUSE

Icknield St, Weatheroak B48 7EH
☎ 01564 824051   📄 01564 829799   Mrs J Poole
e-mail: alcottfarm@btinternet.com
web: www.alcottfarm.co.uk
dir: *2m NE of Alvechurch. M42 junct 3, A435 for Birmingham, left signed Weatheroak, left at x-rds down steep hill, left opp pub, farm 0.5m on right up long driveway*

Rooms 4 en suite (1 GF) S £40; D £60* **Facilities** TVL tea/coffee Cen ht Wi-fi Fishing **Parking** 20 **Notes** ⊗ No Children 10yrs 66 acres horses

ASTWOOD BANK — Map 10 SP06

Corner Cottage

★★★ BED AND BREAKFAST

1194 Evesham Rd B96 6AA
☎ 01527 459122
e-mail: marilyn_alan1194@hotmail.co.uk
dir: *A441 through Astwood Bank, at T-lights*

A warm welcome awaits you at Corner Cottage, a beautiful Victorian cottage set in a pristine village location within walking distance of pubs, shops and restaurants. Convenient for Statford-upon-Avon, Evesham, Warwick, Birmingham and Worcester. Marylin and Alan Harris were finalists for the AA Friendliest Landlady of the Year 2009-2010 Award.

Rooms 3 rms (2 en suite) (1 pri facs) (3 fmly) S £45; D £55* **Facilities** TVL tea/coffee Cen ht **Parking** 3 **Notes** LB ⊗ ⊜

BEWDLEY — Map 10 SO77

PREMIER COLLECTION

Number Thirty

★★★★★ 🛏 BED AND BREAKFAST

30 Gardners Meadow DY12 2DG
☎ 01299 402404   📄 01299 402404
e-mail: info@numberthirty.net
dir: *Off Load St/Bewdley bridge onto Severnside South, 2nd right*

A warm welcome is assured at this smart modern house, a short stroll from the River Severn and Georgian town centre. Bedrooms are luxuriously furnished and have lots of thoughtful extras. Comprehensive breakfasts are taken in an attractive dining room overlooking immaculate gardens and cricket ground and guests can enjoy the game from a raised sun deck. A sumptuous guest lounge is also available.

Rooms 3 en suite S fr £60; D fr £75* **Facilities** FTV TVL tea/coffee Cen ht Wi-fi **Parking** 6 **Notes** ⊗ No Children 10yrs ⊜

BEWDLEY *continued*

The Mug House Inn
★★★★ 🏵 INN

12 Severnside North DY12 2EE
☎ **01299 402543**
e-mail: drew@mughousebewdley.co.uk
web: www.mughousebewdley.co.uk
dir: *In town centre on riverfront*

Located on the opposite side of the River Severn to Bewdley Rowing Club, this 18th-century inn has been renovated to combine high standards of comfort and facilities with many original features. Bedrooms are thoughtfully furnished, there is a separate breakfast room, and imaginative dinners are served in the restaurant.

Rooms 4 en suite 3 annexe en suite (2 fmly) (1 GF) S £60-£95; D £75-£120* **Facilities** tea/coffee Dinner available Cen ht Wi-fi **Notes** ⊗ No Children 10yrs No coaches

Royal Forester Country Inn
★★★★ INN

Callow Hill DY14 9XW
☎ **01299 266286**
e-mail: contact@royalforesterinn.co.uk

Located opposite The Wyre Forest on the town's outskirts, this inn dates back to 1411 and has been sympathetically restored to provide high standards of comfort. Stylish modern bedrooms are complemented by smart bathrooms and equipped with many thoughtful extras. Décor styles throughout the public areas highlight the many retained period features and the restaurant serves imaginative food featuring locally sourced produce.

Rooms 7 en suite (2 fmly) **Facilities** STV FTV tea/coffee Dinner available Cen ht Wi-fi **Parking** 40 **Notes** No coaches

Bank House
★★★ BED AND BREAKFAST

14 Lower Park DY12 2DP
☎ **01299 402652**
e-mail: fleur.nightingale@virgin.net
web: www.bewdley-accommodation.co.uk
dir: *In town centre. From junct High St & Lax Ln, Bank House after junct on left*

Once a private bank, this Victorian house retains many original features and offers comfortable accommodation. The cosy dining room is the setting for tasty English breakfasts served at one family table. Owner Mrs Nightingale has a comprehensive knowledge of the town and its history.

Rooms 4 rms (1 fmly) S £32-£34; D £56-£58* **Facilities** tea/coffee Cen ht **Parking** 2 **Notes** ⊗ Closed 24-26 Dec 🐾

Woodcolliers Arms
★★★ INN

76 Welch Gate DY12 2AU
☎ **01299 400589** 📠 **01299 400589**
e-mail: roger@woodcolliers.co.uk
web: www.woodcolliers.co.uk
dir: *Exit A456, follow road behind church and turn left into Welch Gate (B4190)*

Dating from before 1780, the Woodcolliers is a family-run establishment located in the renowned Georgian town of Bewdley. A traditional inn offering an interesting menu with both traditional British pub food and a speciality Russian menu. Accommodation is comfortable and rooms are well equipped.

Rooms 5 rms (3 en suite) (2 pri facs) S £20-£40; D £40-£60 (room only)* **Facilities** tea/coffee Dinner available Cen ht **Parking** 2 **Notes** LB

Welchgate Guest House
Ⓤ

1 Welchgate DY12 2AT
☎ **01299 402655**
e-mail: info@welchgate-guesthouse.co.uk
web: www.welchgate-guesthouse.co.uk

Currently the rating for this establishment is not confirmed. This may be due to a change of ownership or because it has only recently joined the AA rating scheme.

Rooms 4 en suite S fr £50; D £70-£90* **Facilities** tea/coffee Cen ht Licensed Wi-fi **Parking** 4 **Notes** ⊗ No Children

---

BROADWAY Map 10 SP03

PREMIER COLLECTION

Mill Hay House
★★★★★ GUEST ACCOMMODATION

Snowshill Rd WR12 7JS
☎ **01386 852498** 📠 **01386 858038**
e-mail: millhayhouse@aol.com
web: www.millhay.co.uk
dir: *0.7m S of Broadway towards Snowshill, house on right*

Set in three acres of immaculate grounds beside a medieval watermill, this impressive early 18th-century stone house has many original features complemented by quality décor, period furniture and works of art. The spacious bedrooms are filled with thoughtful extras and one has a balcony. Imaginative breakfasts are served in the elegant dining room and there is a spacious drawing room.

Rooms 3 en suite **Facilities** FTV TVL tea/coffee Direct Dial Cen ht Wi-fi **Parking** 15 **Notes** LB ⊗ No Children 12yrs

PREMIER COLLECTION

Russell's
★★★★★ 🏵🏵 🏠 RESTAURANT WITH ROOMS

20 High St WR12 7DT
☎ **01386 853555** 📠 **01386 853555**
e-mail: info@russellsofbroadway.com
dir: *Opposite village green*

Situated in the centre of a picturesque Cotswold village this restaurant with rooms is a great base for exploring local attractions. Bedrooms, each with their own character, boast superb quality, air conditioning and a wide range of extras for guests. Cuisine is a real draw here with freshly-prepared, local produce skilfully utilised.

Rooms 4 en suite 3 annexe en suite (4 fmly) **Facilities** TV3B STV tea/coffee Dinner available Direct Dial Cen ht **Conf** Max 12 Board 12 **Parking** 16 **Notes** No coaches

Bowers Hill Farm *(SP086420)*
★★★★ FARMHOUSE

Bowers Hill, Willersey WR11 7HG
☎ **01386 334585** & **07966 171861**
📠 **01386 830234 Mr & Mrs M Bent**
e-mail: sarah@bowershillfarm.com
web: www.bowershillfarm.com
dir: *3m NW of Broadway. A44 onto B4632 to Willersey, at mini rdbt signs to Badsey/industrial estate, farm 2m on right by postbox*

An impressive Victorian house set in immaculate gardens on a diverse farm, where point-to-point horses are also bred. The house has been renovated to provide very comfortable bedrooms with modern bathrooms. Breakfast is served in the elegant dining room or the magnificent conservatory, and a lounge with an open fire is also available to guests.

Rooms 3 en suite (1 fmly) **Facilities** TVL tea/coffee Cen ht Wi-fi **Conf** Max 8 Class 8 Board 8 **Parking** 5 **Notes** LB ⊗ 40 acres horse breeding/grassland

Cowley House
★★★★ GUEST ACCOMMODATION

Church St WR12 7AE
☎ 01386 858148
e-mail: cowleyhouse.broadway@tiscali.co.uk
dir: *Follow signs for Broadway. Church St adjacent to village green, 3rd on left*

A warm welcome is assured at this 18th-century Cotswold-stone house, just a stroll from the village green. Fine period furniture enhances the interiors, and the elegant hall has a polished flagstone floor. Tastefully equipped bedrooms include thoughtful extras and smart modern shower rooms. Comprehensive breakfasts feature local produce.

Rooms 6 rms (5 en suite) (1 pri facs) (1 fmly) (2 GF) **Facilities** tea/coffee Cen ht Wi-fi **Parking** 6 **Notes** LB

Horse & Hound
★★★★ ⊜ INN

54 High St WR12 7DT
☎ 01386 852287 ▤ 01386 853784
e-mail: k2mtk@aol.com
dir: *Off A46 to Evesham*

The Horse & Hound is at the heart of this beautiful Cotswold village. A warm welcome is guaranteed whether dining in the inviting pub or staying overnight in the attractive and well-appointed bedrooms. Breakfast and dinner should not to be missed - both use carefully prepared local produce.

Rooms 5 en suite (1 fmly) **Facilities** tea/coffee Dinner available Cen ht **Parking** 15 **Notes** RS Winter Closed 3pm-6pm

Leasow House
★★★★ GUEST ACCOMMODATION

Laverton Meadows WR12 7NA
☎ 01386 584526 ▤ 01386 584596
e-mail: leasow@hotmail.com
web: www.leasow.co.uk

(For full entry see Laverton (Gloucestershire))

Mount Pleasant Farm (SP056392)
★★★★ FARMHOUSE

Childswickham WR12 7HZ
☎ 01386 853424 ▤ 01386 853424 Mrs H Perry
e-mail: helen@mountpleasantfarm.biz
dir: *Onto B4632 for Winchcombe, 50yds right to Childswickham (3m). Farm 1.5m W on left*

Located in immaculate, mature grounds in a pretty hamlet, this impressive Victorian house provides spacious, traditionally furnished bedrooms with smart modern bathrooms. Comprehensive breakfasts are served in an elegant dining room, and a comfortable lounge is available.

Rooms 3 en suite (1 fmly) S £45; D £65-£70 **Facilities** tea/coffee Cen ht Golf **Parking** 10 **Notes** ⊗ No Children 5yrs 950 acres arable

Whiteacres Guest House
★★★★ GUEST ACCOMMODATION

Station Rd WR12 7DE
☎ 01386 852320
e-mail: whiteacres@btinternet.com
web: www.broadwaybandb.com
dir: *500yds NW from E end of High St*

Located a few minutes walk from the historic village centre, this elegant Edwardian house has been lovingly renovated to provide high standards of comfort and facilities. Bedrooms are equipped with a wealth of thoughtful extras and memorable breakfasts are taken in an attractive dining room. A comfortable guest lounge is also available and a warm welcome is assured.

Rooms 5 en suite S £60-£75; D £75-£90* **Facilities** TVL tea/coffee Cen ht Wi-fi **Parking** 5 **Notes** LB No Children 5yrs

DROITWICH Map 10 SO86

The Hadley Bowling Green Inn
★★★★ ⊛⊛ INN

Hadley Heath WR9 0AR
☎ 01905 620294 ▤ 01905 620771
e-mail: info@hadleybowlinggreen.com
web: www.hadleybowlinggreen.com

Dating back to the 16th century and named after the UK's oldest bowling green, which is next door, many of the original coaching inn features have been retained. Reputedly, this was one of the meeting places for Guy

Fawkes and his fellow conspirators. The kitchen provides imaginative food from high quality local produce; service is both professional and friendly and you'll find a good selection of fine wines or real ales to complement. Bedrooms are comfortable and spacious with en suite facilities including some with feature four-poster beds.

The Hadley Bowling Green Inn

Rooms 12 en suite (4 fmly) (1 GF) S £65-£75; D £75-£85* **Facilities** FTV TVL tea/coffee Dinner available Cen ht Lift Wi-fi Crown bowling green **Conf** Max 100 Thtr 100 Class 100 Board 100 **Parking** 80 **Notes** Civ Wed 100

FLYFORD FLAVELL Map 10 SO95

The Boot Inn
★★★★ ⊜ INN

Radford Rd WR7 4BS
☎ 01386 462658 ▤ 01386 462547
e-mail: enquiries@thebootinn.com
web: www.thebootinn.com
dir: *In village centre, signed from A422*

An inn has occupied this site since the 13th century, though the Boot itself dates from the Georgian period. Modernisation has retained historic charm, while the bedrooms, furnished in antique pine, are equipped with practical extras and have modern bathrooms. A range of ales, wines and imaginative food is offered in the cosy public areas, which include an attractive conservatory and patio.

Rooms 5 annexe en suite (2 GF) S £50-£60; D £65-£90 **Facilities** tea/coffee Dinner available Cen ht Wi-fi Golf 27 Pool Table **Parking** 30 **Notes** LB

The Swan Inn

★★★★ INN

Worcester Rd WR8 0EA
☎ 01684 311870
e-mail: info@theswanhanleyswan.co.uk
web: www.theswanhanleyswan.co.uk
dir: M5 junct 7, follow signs for Three Counties Showground, 1m before

This 17th-century property, often described as a quintessential country inn, is located right on the village green, and has a warm, cosy, home-from-home atmosphere. Ideally situated at the foot of the beautiful Malvern Hills, it has easy access to local events and attractions. The five en suite bedrooms are pleasantly furnished, modern and comfortable. Dining, particularly on warmer days in the garden and the patio, is a delight. There is ample parking to the rear of the property.

Rooms 5 en suite (2 fmly) **Facilities** tea/coffee Dinner available Cen ht Wi-fi **Parking** 30

Walter de Cantelupe Inn

★★★ INN

Main Road (A38) WR5 3NA
☎ 01905 820572
e-mail: walter.depub@fsbdial.co.uk
web: www.walterdecantelupeinn.com
dir: On A38 in village centre

This inn provides cosy bedrooms with smart bathrooms, and is convenient for the M5 and Worcester. The intimate, open-plan public areas are the setting for a range of real ales, and imaginative food featuring local produce and a fine selection of British cheeses.

Rooms 3 rms (2 en suite) (1 pri facs) **Facilities** tea/coffee Dinner available Cen ht Wi-fi **Parking** 24 **Notes** No coaches

The Dell House

★★★★ BED AND BREAKFAST

Green Ln, Malvern Wells WR14 4HU
☎ 01684 564448   📄 01684 893974
e-mail: burrage@dellhouse.co.uk
web: www.dellhouse.co.uk
dir: 2m S of Great Malvern on A449. Turn left off A449 onto Green Ln. House at top of road on right, just below old church

This impressive, well-proportioned Victorian house retains many unique features, several of which were introduced by the resident scholar and vicar during the time it was a rectory. Spacious bedrooms are filled with thoughtful extras, and a comprehensive breakfast is served in an elegant dining room that has superb views over the

mature gardens to the countryside beyond. Babies under one year are catered for.

The Dell House

Rooms 3 en suite S £35-£45; D £62-£70* **Facilities** TV1B TVL tea/coffee Cen ht Wi-fi **Parking** 4 **Notes** ⊗ No Children 10yrs

Bredon House

★★★★ GUEST ACCOMMODATION

34 Worcester Rd WR14 4AA
☎ 01684 566990
e-mail: enquiries@bredonhouse.co.uk
web: www.bredonhouse.co.uk
dir: 200yds N of Great Malvern centre on A449, large fir tree in front car park

Superbly located on the east side of the Malvern Hills, with stunning views of the Vale of Evesham and the Severn valley, this elegant Regency house retains many original features. Bedrooms, some with spectacular rear views, offer both thoughtful and practical extras, and a comfortable licensed lounge is also available.

Bredon House

Rooms 10 en suite (2 fmly) (1 GF) S £50-£65; D £80-£100* **Facilities** FTV TVL tea/coffee Direct Dial Cen ht Licensed Wi-fi **Parking** 7

The Pembridge

★★★ GUEST ACCOMMODATION

114 Graham Rd WR14 2HX
☎ 01684 574813   📄 01684 566885
e-mail: info@thepembridge.co.uk
dir: A449 onto Church St, 1st left

Located on a leafy residential road close to the town centre, this large Victorian house retains many original features, including a superb staircase. Bedrooms, which include a ground-floor room, are well equipped. Other areas include a comfortable sitting room with a small bar and an elegant dining room.

Rooms 8 en suite (1 fmly) (1 GF) **Facilities** FTV TVL tea/coffee Direct Dial Cen ht Licensed **Conf** Max 8 **Parking** 10 **Notes** LB ⊗ No Children 7yrs RS 25-26 Dec No cooked English breakfast

Portocks End House

★★★ BED AND BREAKFAST

Little Clevelode WR13 6PE
☎ 01684 310276
e-mail: mpa-cameron@countryside-inter.net
dir: On B4424, 4m N of Upton-on-Severn, opposite Riverside Caravan Park

Peacefully located but convenient for Showground and major road links, this period house retains many original features, and traditional furnishing and décor styles highlight the intrinsic charm. Bedrooms are equipped with lots of thoughtful extras and breakfasts are taken in a cosy dining room, overlooking the pretty garden.

Rooms 2 rms (1 en suite) (1 pri facs) (1 fmly) S £27; D £50 **Facilities** tea/coffee **Parking** 4 **Notes** Closed Dec-Feb ⊛

Sidney House

★★★ GUEST ACCOMMODATION

40 Worcester Rd WR14 4AA
☎ 01684 574994   📄 01684 574994
e-mail: info@sidneyhouse.co.uk
web: www.sidneyhouse.co.uk
dir: On A443, 200yds N from town centre

This impressive Grade II Georgian house is close to the central attractions and has stunning views. Bedrooms are filled with thoughtful extras, and some have small shower rooms en suite. The spacious dining room overlooks the Cotswold escarpment and a comfortable lounge is also available.

Rooms 8 rms (6 en suite) (2 pri facs) (1 fmly) S £25-£55; D £59-£75* **Facilities** FTV TVL tea/coffee Cen ht Licensed Wi-fi **Parking** 9 **Notes** Closed 24 Dec-3 Jan

Wyche Inn

★★★ INN

74 Wyche Rd WR14 4EQ
☎ 01684 575396 ▤ 01684 575396
e-mail: reservations@thewycheinn.co.uk
dir: 1.5m S of Malvern. On B4218 towards Malvern & Colwall. Off A449 (Worcester to Ross/Ledbury)

Located in an elevated position on the outskirts of Malvern, with stunning countryside views, this inn is popular with both the locals and visiting walkers. Thoughtfully furnished bedrooms provide good levels of comfort and a good range of ale and food is offered; value 'specials' nights are available.

Rooms 4 en suite S fr £40; D fr £60* **Facilities** tea/coffee Dinner available Cen ht Pool Table **Parking** 4 **Notes** No coaches

Four Hedges

★★ GUEST ACCOMMODATION

The Rhydd, Hanley Castle WR8 0AD
☎ 01684 310405
e-mail: fredgies@aol.com
dir: 4m E of Malvern at junct of B4211 & B4424

Situated in a rural location, this detached house stands in mature grounds with wild birds in abundance. The bedrooms are equipped with thoughtful extras. Tasty English breakfasts, using free-range eggs, are served in a cosy dining room at a table made from a 300-year-old elm tree.

Rooms 4 rms (2 en suite) S fr £25; D fr £50 **Facilities** TVL tea/coffee Cen ht ⚓ Fishing **Parking** 5 **Notes** No Children 1yr Closed Xmas ⊗

MARTLEY — Map 10 SO76

Admiral Rodney Inn

★★★★ INN

Berrow Green WR6 6PL
☎ 01886 821375
e-mail: rodney@admiral.fslife.co.uk
dir: A44 onto B4197 at Knightwick, 2m on left

Located in the pretty village of Berrow Green, this 16th-century inn has been renovated to provide high standards of comfort and facilities. New hosts Karen and Desmond offer a warm welcome to all their customers, and provide spacious, carefully furnished bedrooms, complemented by luxurious modern bathrooms. Ground-floor areas include quality bars with log fires and a unique tiered and beamed restaurant, where imaginative dishes are served. There are also outside seating areas to front and rear, and excellent parking facilities.

Rooms 3 en suite; D £55-£65* **Facilities** tea/coffee Cen ht Wi-fi Pool Table **Parking** 40

WORCESTER — Map 10 SO85

Bants

★★★★ ⬤ INN

Worcester Rd WR7 4NN
☎ 01905 381282 ▤ 01905 381173
e-mail: info@bants.co.uk
web: www.bants.co.uk
dir: 5m E of Worcester. On A422 at Upton Snodsbury

A family-run 16th-century pub with a modern atmosphere. Bedrooms are carefully decorated and well equipped, with some rooms separate from the inn. A wide range of freshly-cooked meals is available in the free-house bar or served in the large conservatory.

Rooms 3 en suite 5 annexe en suite (3 GF); D £65-£125* **Facilities** FTV tea/coffee Dinner available Cen ht Wi-fi **Conf** Max 50 **Parking** 40 **Notes** LB ⊗ No Children 12yrs No coaches

Burgage House

★★★★ BED AND BREAKFAST

4 College Precincts WR1 2LG
☎ 01905 25396 ▤ 01905 25396
e-mail: louise.newsholme@googlemail.com
dir: M5 junct 7, A44 into city centre, after 7th set of lights left onto Edgar St, College Precincts is pedestrian only on right

Located next to the cathedral and the historic centre, this impressive Georgian house has original features, including a fine stone staircase, enhanced by the décor and furnishings. Bedrooms, including the ground-floor Cromwell Room, are spacious and homely. An elegant dining room is the setting for comprehensive English breakfasts.

Rooms 4 en suite (1 fmly) (1 GF) S £32-£36; D £60-£65* **Facilities** FTV tea/coffee Cen ht **Notes** ⊗ Closed 23-30 Dec ⊗

Oaklands B&B

★★★★ GUEST ACCOMMODATION

Claines WR3 7RS
☎ 01905 458871 ▤ 01905 759362
e-mail: barbara.gadd@zoom.co.uk
dir: M5 junct 6 onto A449. At rdbt take 1st exit signed Claines. 1st left onto School Bank. Oaklands 1st house on right

A warm welcome is guaranteed at this converted stable, which is well located in a peaceful setting just a short drive from major routes. The property stands in abundant mature gardens, and the well-appointed bedrooms are mostly spacious. There is also a snooker room and parking is available.

Rooms 4 en suite (2 fmly) S £40; D £70* **Facilities** tea/coffee Cen ht Wi-fi Snooker **Parking** 6 **Notes** LB Closed Xmas & New Year ⊗

Wyatt

★★★★ GUEST HOUSE

40 Barbourne Rd WR1 1HU
☎ 01905 26311 ▤ 01905 26311
e-mail: wyatt.guest@virgin.net
dir: On A38 0.5m N from city centre

Located within easy walking distance of shops, restaurants and central attractions, this constantly improving Victorian house provides a range of thoughtfully furnished bedrooms. Breakfast is served in an attractive dining room, a warm welcome is assured, and the attractive frontage is a regular winner in the Worcester Britain in Bloom competition.

Rooms 8 rms (7 en suite) (1 fmly) (1 GF) S £34-£40; D £52-£55* **Facilities** STV tea/coffee Cen ht Wi-fi

Croft Guest House

★★ GUEST HOUSE

Bransford WR6 5JD
☎ 01886 832227
e-mail: accom@brianporter.orangehome.co.uk
web: www.croftguesthouse.com
dir: 4m SW of Worcester. On A4103 Leigh exit at Bransford rdbt, driveway on left after 30yds

This cottage-style property, dating in parts from the 16th century, is convenient for the city centre and the Malverns. Freshly-cooked breakfasts feature homemade sausages. Bedrooms are homely and the pretty gardens have a water feature. Dogs are welcome provided they have a current vaccination certificate.

Rooms 4 rms (3 en suite) (1 fmly) S £30-£39; D £50-£64* **Facilities** TVL tea/coffee Cen ht Licensed **Parking** 5 **Notes** LB

YORKSHIRE, EAST RIDING OF

BEVERLEY
Map 17 TA03

See also Leven

PREMIER COLLECTION

Burton Mount Country House
★★★★★ GUEST ACCOMMODATION

Malton Rd, Cherry Burton HU17 7RA
☎ 01964 550541
e-mail: pg@burtonmount.co.uk
web: www.burtonmount.co.uk
dir: *3m NW of Beverley. B1248 for Malton, 2m right at x-rds, house on left*

A charming country house three miles from Beverley, set in delightful gardens and offering luxurious accommodation. Bedrooms are well equipped and have thoughtful extra touches. The spacious drawing room has a blazing fire in the cooler months, and an excellent, Aga-cooked Yorkshire breakfast is served in the morning room. Pauline Greenwood is renowned locally for her customer care, culinary skills and warm hospitality.

Rooms 3 en suite S £64; D £91* **Facilities** STV TVL tea/coffee Dinner available Cen ht Licensed Wi-fi 🐾 🎿 **Conf** Max 30 Thtr 30 Class 20 Board 20 **Parking** 20 **Notes** LB ⊗ No Children 12yrs

The Ferguson Fawsitt Arms & Country Lodge
★★★★ 🅰 INN

East End, Walkington HU17 8RX
☎ 01482 882665 📠 01482 882665
e-mail: admin@fergusonfawsitt.com
web: www.fergusonfawsitt.co.uk
dir: *M62 junct 38 onto B1230, left on A1034, right onto B1230, on left in centre of Walkington*

Rooms 10 en suite (2 fmly) (10 GF) S £60-£70; D £65-£75* **Facilities** FTV tea/coffee Dinner available Cen ht Wi-fi **Conf** Max 80 Thtr 60 Class 40 Board 20 **Parking** 120 **Notes** ⊗ RS 25-26 & 31 Dec No breakfast available

BRIDLINGTON
Map 17 TA16

PREMIER COLLECTION

Marton Grange
★★★★★ GUEST ACCOMMODATION

Flamborough Rd, Marton cum Sewerby YO15 1DU
☎ 01262 602034 📠 01262 602034
e-mail: martongrange@talk21.com
web: www.marton-grange.co.uk
dir: *2m NE of Bridlington. On B1255, 600yds W of Links golf club*

There is a welcoming atmosphere at this country guest house and the bedrooms are all of high quality, with a range of extra facilities. There are attractive lounges with views over the immaculate gardens while substantial breakfasts are served in the delightful dining room. Ground-floor rooms are available.

Rooms 11 en suite (3 GF) S £47.50-£55; D £75-£90* **Facilities** tea/coffee Cen ht Lift Licensed Wi-fi **Parking** 11 **Notes** LB No Children 12yrs Closed Dec-Feb

Burlington Quays
★★★★ GUEST ACCOMMODATION

20 Meadowfield Rd YO15 3LD
☎ 01262 676052
e-mail: burlingtonquays@axis-connect.com
dir: *A165 into Bridlington, 1st right past golf course onto Kingston Rd. Bear left to seafront, take 3rd left*

In a peaceful street close to the seafront, this spacious house features modern, well appointed bedrooms, all with en suite bath or shower rooms. Guests also have use of a comfortable lounge and a cosy, fully licensed bar. Tasty breakfasts are served in the pleasant dining room at individual tables.

Rooms 5 en suite (4 fmly) S £38-£40; D £56-£60 **Facilities** TVL tea/coffee Cen ht Licensed **Parking** 2 **Notes** LB ⊗ ⊗

Longleigh
★★★★ BED AND BREAKFAST

12 Swanland Av YO15 2HH
☎ 01262 676234 & 07980 310777
e-mail: geraldineross@hotmail.co.uk
dir: *Flamborough Rd, N past Holy Trinity Church*

In a quiet location ten minutes walk from the town centre or beach, Longleigh offers comfortable, tastefully appointed accommodation in a friendly atmosphere. Rooms are well equipped and breakfast is served in the attractive dining room.

Rooms 3 en suite S £25-£30; D £50-£56* **Facilities** TVL tea/coffee Cen ht **Notes** ⊗

The Mount
★★★★ GUEST ACCOMMODATION

2 Roundhay Rd YO15 3JY
☎ 01262 672306
e-mail: mounthotel01@btconnect.com
dir: *M62 junct 37 onto A164, pass golf course, right onto Shaftesbury Av, Roundham Rd 3rd on left, The Mount on right*

This spacious Victorian house offers friendly and attentive service. Bedrooms are attractively presented and well furnished. Home-cooked five-course meals are available with prior arrangement and are served in the bright dining room. Guests are also welcome to use the comfortable lounge that leads through to a fully licensed bar.

Rooms 8 rms (6 en suite) (2 pri facs) (2 fmly) S £27-£30; D £54-£60* **Facilities** TVL tea/coffee Dinner available Cen ht Licensed Wi-fi **Notes** LB ⊗

The Royal Bridlington
★★★★ GUEST ACCOMMODATION

1 Shaftesbury Rd YO15 3NP
☎ 01262 672433 📠 01262 672118
e-mail: info@royalhotelbrid.co.uk
dir: *A615 N to Bridlington (Kingsgate), right onto Shaftesbury Rd*

Located just off the promenade, this immaculate property has a range of thoughtfully furnished bedrooms with smart modern bathrooms. Spacious public areas include a large dining room, conservatory-sitting room, and a cosy television lounge. Freshly-cooked dinners are a feature and a warm welcome is assured.

Rooms 14 rms (13 en suite) (1 pri facs) 4 annexe en suite (7 fmly) (4 GF) S £37-£44; D £64-£78* **Facilities** FTV TVL tea/coffee Dinner available Cen ht Licensed Wi-fi **Conf** Max 85 Thtr 85 Class 20 Board 40 **Parking** 7 **Notes** LB ⊗

The Ryburn

★★★★ GUEST ACCOMMODATION

31 Flamborough Rd YO15 2JH
☎ 01262 674098 📠 01262 674098
dir: *From harbour take B1255 towards Flamborough. Ryburn 300mtrs on left after leisure centre*

This attractive Tudor-style accommodation stands in a prominent position just a short walk from the town centre. A variety of rooms are available: some suitable for families, one is on the ground floor, and one has a private balcony. Public areas include a dining room and an attractive lounge. This is a non-smoking establishment.

Rooms 7 en suite (2 fmly) (1 GF) **Facilities** TVL tea/coffee Cen ht Licensed Wi-fi **Parking** 6 **Notes** ⊗ No Children 5yrs Closed 6-27 Nov

The Tennyson

★★★ GUEST ACCOMMODATION

19 Tennyson Av YO15 2EU
☎ 01262 604382 & 07729 149729
e-mail: dianew2@live.co.uk
web: www.thetennyson-brid.co.uk
dir: *500yds NE of town centre. B1254 Promenade from town centre towards Flamborough, Tennyson Av on left*

Situated in a quiet side road close to the town centre and attractions, this friendly guest house offers attentive service, comfortable bedrooms and a cosy bar.

Rooms 8 rms (7 en suite) (1 pri facs) (2 fmly) (1 GF) S £23-£26.50; D £46-£60* **Facilities** tea/coffee Dinner available Cen ht Licensed **Notes** LB

Westward-Ho Guest House

★★★ GUEST HOUSE

8 West St YO15 3DX
☎ 01262 670110
e-mail: westward.ho@homecall.co.uk
dir: *250yds S of town centre. Off A1038 at harbour onto South Cliff Rd, right onto Windsor Crescent & West St*

Situated in a side road, close to the harbour and Spa centre, this family-owned guest house offers good hospitality. Contemporary bedrooms (including family rooms) are attractively presented and feature smart en suites or a private shower room. Hearty breakfasts are served in the open-plan guest lounge and dining room which also has a small bar.

Rooms 5 rms (4 en suite) (1 pri facs) (1 fmly) **Facilities** FTV TVL tea/coffee Cen ht Licensed **Notes** LB ⊗

Aidansdale

★★★ GUEST HOUSE

92 Trinity Rd YO15 2HF
☎ 01262 676723

This friendly family-run house is located on a street next to North Beach and is only five minutes from the town centre. The attractive bedrooms are comfortable and well equipped, with good quality en suite shower rooms. Tasty breakfasts are served in the pleasant dining room and service is very attentive.

Rooms 7 rms (6 en suite) (4 fmly) **Facilities** TVL tea/coffee Cen ht **Notes** ⊛

The Langdon

★★★ GUEST ACCOMMODATION

13-16 Pembroke Ter YO15 3BX
☎ 01262 400124 📠 01262 605377
e-mail: tcruxon@tiscali.co.uk
dir: *250yds SW of town centre. Off seafront South Marine*

Located on the seafront, the Langdon has a cosy bar and lounge where regular evening entertainment is held, and the reception rooms extend to a small garden porch. Home-cooked meals are served in the cheerful dining room or the stylish new restaurant.

Rooms 30 en suite (7 fmly) S £29.50-£34; D £69-£78* **Facilities** STV FTV TVL tea/coffee Cen ht Lift Licensed Pool Table **Conf** Max 50 Board 50 **Notes** LB ⊗ Closed Jan-Feb

Lansdowne House

★★★ GUEST ACCOMMODATION

33 Lansdowne Rd YO15 2QT
☎ 01262 604184 📠 01262 604184
e-mail: stephennunn07@aol.com
dir: *N of town centre. Off B1254 Promenade near Leisure World onto Lansdowne Rd, last house on left*

A well maintained and friendly house located close to the seafront and only a short walk from the shops and attractions. Bedrooms are comfortable and appropriately equipped. Breakfasts and evening meals (by arrangement) are served in the dining room at individual tables. There is also a licensed bar with small lounge area.

Rooms 9 rms (7 en suite) (4 fmly) S £21-£23 **Facilities** FTV TVL tea/coffee Dinner available Cen ht Licensed **Notes** LB ⊗

The Ransdale

★★★ GUEST ACCOMMODATION

30 Flamborough Rd YO15 2JQ
☎ 01262 674334
e-mail: the.ransdale@tiscali.co.uk

Close to all main attractions this establishment offers comfortable bedrooms and friendly service. Guests have use of a small, modern lounge. Evening meals and tasty breakfasts are served in the spacious dining room which also has a bar area. Limited off-street parking is also available.

Rooms 16 en suite (4 fmly) (4 GF) S £44; D £64* **Facilities** FTV TVL tea/coffee Dinner available Cen ht Licensed Wi-fi **Parking** 10 **Notes** LB ⊗

Sandra's Guest House

★★★ GUEST HOUSE

6 Summerfield Rd, South Marine Dr YO15 3LF
☎ 01262 677791
e-mail: sandra@axis-connect.com
dir: *250yds SW of town centre. Off seafront South Marine Dr*

Close to the south beach and the Spa Theatre, this friendly guest house offers very homely and comfortable accommodation with good home cooking. There is a comfortable lounge and the dining room has a bar.

Rooms 9 rms (8 en suite) (1 pri facs) (1 GF) S £25-£30; D £50-£65 **Facilities** tea/coffee Dinner available Cen ht Licensed **Notes** LB ⊗ No Children 12yrs Closed 24-27 Dec ⊛

HUGGATE Map 19 SE85

The Wolds Inn

★★★ 🍴 INN

Driffield Rd YO42 1YH
☎ 01377 288217
e-mail: huggate@woldsinn.freeserve.co.uk
dir: *Huggate signed off A166 & brown signs to Wolds Inn*

At the end of the highest village in the Yorkshire Wolds, midway between York and the coast, this ancient inn is a rural haven beside the Wolds Way walk. Substantial meals are served in the dining room and a good range of well-kept beers is available in the bar. Bedrooms, varying in size, are well equipped and comfortable.

Rooms 3 en suite S fr £40; D fr £52 (room only) **Facilities** tea/coffee Dinner available Cen ht Pool Table **Parking** 30 **Notes** ⊗

LEVEN Map 17 TA14

The New Inn

★★★ INN

44 South St HU17 5NZ
☎ 01964 542223 📄 01964 545828
dir: *Off A1035, in village centre*

This central red-brick inn was built in the early 19th century. The modern bedrooms are brightly decorated and all rooms have showers en suite. There is an attractive breakfast room and a friendly atmosphere in the bars where traditional ales are served. The property has ample parking.

Rooms 10 en suite (1 fmly) (9 smoking) S £35; D £50*
Facilities TVL tea/coffee Dinner available Cen ht Wi-fi Golf 18 Pool Table **Parking** 55

MARKET WEIGHTON Map 17 SE84

Robeanne House

★★★ GUEST ACCOMMODATION

Driffield Ln, Shiptonthorpe YO43 3PW
☎ 01430 873312 📄 01430 879142
e-mail: enquiries@robeannehouse.co.uk
web: www.robeannehouse.co.uk
dir: *1.5m NW on A614*

Set back off the A614 in a quiet location, this delightful modern family home was built as a farmhouse. York, the coast, and the Yorkshire Moors and Dales are within easy driving distance. All bedrooms have country views and include a large family room. A charming wooden chalet is available in the garden.

Rooms 2 en suite 5 annexe en suite (2 fmly) (2 GF)
S £30-£45; D £60-£65* **Facilities** TVL tea/coffee Dinner available Cen ht Wi-fi **Conf** Max 8 **Parking** 10 **Notes** LB

SOUTH CAVE Map 17 SE93

Rudstone Walk

★★★★ 🏅 🛏 GUEST ACCOMMODATION

HU15 2AH
☎ 01430 422230 📄 01430 424552
e-mail: office@rudstone-walk.co.uk
web: www.rudstone-walk.co.uk
dir: *M62 junct 38, onto B1230, over A1034, Rudstone Walk 200yds on left*

Set among 80 acres of green fields and lawns, on the edge of the Yorkshire Wolds, this converted 17th-century farm is ideal as a relaxing retreat for both tourists and conferences, and is just one mile from the M62 and a short drive from the town of Beverley. Bedrooms form a garden courtyard around the farmhouse, which is where all meals are served. Self-catering accommodation is also available.

Rooms 14 en suite (2 fmly) (10 GF) **Facilities** tea/coffee Dinner available Direct Dial Cen ht Licensed **Conf** Max 120 Thtr 50 Class 30 Board 26 **Parking** 50 **Notes** RS 24-28 Dec & 31 Dec-2 Jan Self catering only over this period Civ Wed 50

YORKSHIRE, NORTH

ALDBROUGH ST JOHN Map 19 NZ21

Lucy Cross Farm

★★★ GUEST ACCOMMODATION

DL11 7AD
☎ 01325 374319 & 07931 545985
e-mail: sally@lucycross.co.uk
web: www.lucycross.co.uk
dir: *A1 junct 56 onto B6275 at Barton, white house 3m from Barton rdbt on left towards Piercebridge*

Located close to major road links, a relaxed atmosphere and friendly welcome is assured. Traditionally furnished

bedrooms are very comfortably equipped; one is on the ground floor. A lounge is available and hearty breakfasts are served in the pleasant dining room.

Rooms 5 rms (3 en suite) (2 pri facs) (1 fmly) (1 GF)
S £35-£45; D £65-£75 **Facilities** FTV TVL tea/coffee Dinner available Cen ht Wi-fi Fishing Riding **Conf** Max 12 Board 12 **Parking** 10 **Notes** LB

AMPLEFORTH Map 19 SE57

PREMIER COLLECTION

Shallowdale House

★★★★★ 🛏 GUEST ACCOMMODATION

West End YO62 4DY
☎ 01439 788325 📄 01439 788885
e-mail: stay@shallowdalehouse.co.uk
web: www.shallowdalehouse.co.uk
dir: *Off A170 at W end of village, on turn to Hambleton*

An outstanding example of an architect-designed 1960s house, Shallowdale lies in two acres of hillside gardens. There are stunning views from every room, and the elegant public rooms include a choice of lounges. Spacious bedrooms blend traditional and 1960s style with many home comforts. Expect excellent service and genuine hospitality from Anton and Phillip. The very imaginative, freshly cooked dinners are not to be missed.

Rooms 3 rms (2 en suite) (1 pri facs) S £75-£85;
D £95-£115* **Facilities** tea/coffee Dinner available Cen ht Licensed Wi-fi **Parking** 3 **Notes** ⊗ No Children 12yrs Closed Xmas & New Year

APPLETREEWICK
Map 19 SE06

PREMIER COLLECTION

Knowles Lodge
★★★★★ BED AND BREAKFAST

BD23 6DQ
☎ 01756 720228 ▤ 01756 720381
e-mail: pam@knowleslodge.com
web: www.knowleslodge.com
dir: From Bolton Abbey B6160 3.5m, turn right after Barden Tower 1.5m, entrance on left

Located in the heart of Wharfedale and surrounded by 17 acres of meadow and woodland, this delightful Canadian-style ranch has been lovingly restored. The house is attractively furnished, with well appointed bedrooms, and whether guests are there to walk, cycle, fish, or simply relax and enjoy the scenery, they are sure to be given a warm welcome. Delicious breakfasts featuring home-made dishes are served around a large gate-leg table.

Rooms 3 en suite (1 fmly) (2 GF); D £90* Facilities TVL tea/coffee Cen ht Wi-fi ⛱ Fishing Parking 6 Notes No Children 8yrs Civ Wed 75

ASKRIGG
Map 18 SD99

Whitfield
★★★★ BED AND BREAKFAST

Helm DL8 3JF
☎ 01969 650565 ▤ 01969 650565
e-mail: bookings@askrigg-cottages.co.uk
web: www.askrigg-cottages.co.uk
dir: Off A684 at Bainbridge signed Askrigg, right at T-junct, 150yds to No Through Rd sign, left up hill 0.5m

Set high in the fells, this smart accommodation is in a carefully converted barn, built of Yorkshire limestone. Both bedrooms are homely, and have stunning views of the Wensleydale countryside. Hearty breakfasts are served around a communal table in the inviting lounge-dining room.

Rooms 2 en suite; D £54-£64* Facilities TVL tea/coffee Cen ht Parking 1 Notes LB Closed 23 Dec-2 Jan

AYSGARTH
Map 19 SE08

George & Dragon
★★★★ RESTAURANT WITH ROOMS

DL8 3AD
☎ 01969 663358 ▤ 01969 668773
e-mail: info@georgeanddragonaysgarth.co.uk
dir: A684, on main road in village

This 17th-century coaching inn offers spacious, comfortably appointed rooms. Popular with walkers, the cosy bar has a real fire and a good selection of local beers. The beamed restaurant serves hearty breakfasts

and interesting meals using fresh local produce. Service is very friendly and attentive.

Rooms 7 en suite (2 fmly) S £45-£60; D £40-£120* Facilities FTV tea/coffee Dinner available Direct Dial Cen ht Wi-fi Parking 35 Notes LB No Children

Stow House
★★★★ A GUEST ACCOMMODATION

DL8 3SR
☎ 01969 663635
e-mail: info@stowhouse.co.uk
web: www.stowhouse.co.uk
dir: 0.6m E of Aysgarth on A684

Rooms 9 en suite (1 GF) S £40-£55; D £80-£100* Facilities tea/coffee Dinner available Cen ht Licensed ⛱ Parking 10 Notes LB Closed 24-26 Dec

BEDALE
Map 19 SE28

PREMIER COLLECTION

Mill Close Farm (SE232922)
★★★★★ FARMHOUSE

Patrick Brompton DL8 1JY
☎ 01677 450257 ▤ 01748 813612 Mrs P Knox
e-mail: pat@millclose.co.uk
web: www.millclose.co.uk
dir: 3m NW of Bedale. A684 to Patrick Brompton & brown tourist signs to farm

A real home-from-home atmosphere prevails at this working farm. Bedrooms are furnished with quality and style; one has a four-poster and two have spa baths, but all rooms feature homely extras including fridges. Well-prepared breakfasts are one of the highlights of a stay and feature home-made produce cooked on the Aga of the farm kitchen.

Rooms 3 en suite S £60-£65; D £80-£90* Facilities tea/coffee Cen ht Parking 6 Notes LB ⊗ No Children 10yrs Closed Dec-Feb 240 acres mixed

Elmfield House
★★★★ GUEST HOUSE

Arrathorne DL8 1NE
☎ 01677 450558 ▤ 01677 450557
e-mail: stay@elmfieldhouse.co.uk
web: www.elmfieldhouse.co.uk
dir: 4m NW of Bedale. A684 from Bedale for Leyburn, right after Patrick Brompton towards Richmond, B&B 1.5m on right

Originally a gamekeeper's cottage, and now carefully extended, Elmfield House has uninterrupted views of the surrounding countryside. The comfortable bedrooms are generally spacious and very well equipped. The attractive public rooms are also well proportioned and offer a cosy

lounge area, as well as a conservatory-lounge and games area. Dinners are available by prior arrangement.

Rooms 7 en suite (1 fmly) (2 GF) S £60-£70; D £75-£85* Facilities FTV tea/coffee Dinner available Cen ht Licensed Wi-fi Fishing Parking 7 Notes LB ⊗

Castle Arms
★★★★ ⊟ INN

Snape DL8 2TB
☎ 01677 470270 ▤ 01677 470837
e-mail: castlearms@aol.com
dir: 2m S of Bedale. Off B6268 into Snape

Nestled in the quiet village of Snape, this former coaching inn is full of character. Bedrooms are in a converted barn, and each room is very comfortable and carefully furnished. The restaurant and public bar offer a good selection of fine ales, along with an interesting selection of freshly-prepared dishes.

Rooms 9 annexe en suite (8 GF) S £55-£65; D £65-£85* Facilities tea/coffee Dinner available Cen ht Parking 15 Notes LB No coaches

BISHOP MONKTON
Map 19 SE36

Lamb & Flag Inn
★★★★ INN

Boroughbridge Rd HG3 3QN
☎ 01765 677322
e-mail: carol@lambandflagbarn.co.uk
dir: A61 turn E onto Moor Rd crossing Knaresbrough Rd

A delightful country inn set in the countryside yet close to Harrogate, York and Leeds. The inn provides a warm welcome and freshly prepared local food. The three comfortably furnished and equipped bedrooms are a conversion from a barn and are annexed next to the pub. A continental-style breakfast is provided in your bedroom.

Rooms 3 annexe en suite (1 fmly) (3 GF) Facilities FTV tea/coffee Dinner available Cen ht Pool Table Parking 20 Notes ⊗

BOLTON ABBEY — Map 19 SE05

Howgill Lodge

★★★★ GUEST ACCOMMODATION

Barden BD23 6DJ
☎ 01756 720655
e-mail: info@howgill-lodge.co.uk
dir: B6160 from Bolton Abbey signed Burnsall, 3m right at Barden Tower signed Appletreewick, Howgill Lodge 1.25m on right at phone box

Having an idyllic position high above the valley, this converted stone granary provides a quality get-away-from-it-all experience. The uniquely styled bedrooms provide a host of thoughtful touches and are designed to feature original stonewalls, flagstone floors and timber beams. All of the rooms boast spectacular, memorable views. Breakfasts make excellent use of fresh local ingredients.

Rooms 4 en suite (1 fmly) (4 GF) S £47; D £74*
Facilities tea/coffee Cen ht **Parking** 6 **Notes** LB ⊗ Closed 24-26 Dec

BURNSALL — Map 19 SE06

Devonshire Fell

★★★★ RESTAURANT WITH ROOMS

BD23 6BT
☎ 01756 729000 📠 01756 729009
e-mail: manager@devonshirefell.co.uk
web: www.devonshirefell.co.uk
dir: On B6160, 6m from Bolton Abbey rdbt A59 junct

Located on the edge of the attractive village of Burnsall, this establishment offers comfortable, well-equipped accommodation in a relaxing atmosphere. There is an extensive menu featuring local produce, and meals can be taken either in the bar area or the more formal restaurant. A function room with views over the valley is also available.

Rooms 12 en suite (2 fmly) S £79-£108; D £142-£192* (incl.dinner) **Facilities** STV FTV tea/coffee Dinner available Direct Dial Cen ht Wi-fi Fishing **Conf** Max 50 Thtr 50 Class 30 Board 24 **Parking** 30 **Notes** LB Civ Wed 90

BYLAND ABBEY — Map 19 SE57

PREMIER COLLECTION

The Abbey Inn

★★★★★ ⚫ RESTAURANT WITH ROOMS

YO61 4BD
☎ 01347 868204 📄 01347 868678
e-mail: paul.tatham@english-heritage.org.uk
web: www.bylandabbeyinn.com

There is an abundance of history, charm and character at this romantic inn located at the foot of the Hambleton Hills and opposite the ruins of Byland Abbey. Delicious meals are prepared using high quality, local ingredients and served in the candlelit dining rooms. There are three delightfully furnished bedrooms, each with generously sized en suite bathrooms.

Rooms 3 en suite; D £95-£199* **Facilities** FTV tea/coffee Dinner available Direct Dial Cen ht **Parking** 50 **Notes** ⊗ No Children Closed 25-26 & 31 Dec RS Sun closed evening No coaches

CARPERBY — Map 19 SE08

The Wheatsheaf

★★★ Ⓐ INN

DL8 4DF
☎ 01969 663216 📠 01969 663019
e-mail: wheatsheaf@paulmit.globalnet.co.uk
dir: Off A684 signed Aysgarth Falls to village centre

Rooms 8 en suite 5 annexe en suite (1 fmly) (1 GF) **Facilities** tea/coffee Dinner available Cen ht Wi-fi Fishing **Conf** Max 20 Board 20 **Parking** 40 **Notes** RS Mon Closed for lunch

CATTERICK — Map 19 SE29

Rose Cottage

★★★ GUEST ACCOMMODATION

26 High St DL10 7LJ
☎ 01748 811164
dir: Off A1 in village centre, opp newsagents

Convenient for exploring the Dales and Moors, this well-maintained guest house lies in the middle of Catterick. Bedrooms are nicely presented and comfortable. The cosy public rooms include a cottage-style dining room adorned with Mrs Archer's paintings, and a lounge. Dinner is available by arrangement during the summer.

Rooms 4 rms (2 en suite) (1 fmly) (4 smoking) S £29-£35; D £52* **Facilities** tea/coffee Dinner available Cen ht **Parking** 4 **Notes** Closed 24-26 Dec ⊗

CLAPHAM — Map 18 SD76

Brookhouse Guest House

★★★ GUEST HOUSE

Station Rd LA2 8ER
☎ 015242 51580
e-mail: admin@brookhouseclapham.co.uk
web: www.brookhouse-clapham.co.uk
dir: Off A65 into village

Located in the pretty conservation village of Clapham beside the river, this well-maintained and friendly guest house provides thoughtfully furnished bedrooms and a popular ground-floor café, serving a selection of meals and snacks through the day.

Rooms 3 rms (2 en suite) (1 pri facs) (1 fmly) S £35-£45; D £60-£8C* **Facilities** FTV tea/coffee Dinner available Cen ht Licensed Wi-fi ⊗ Golf 18 **Notes** LB ⊗ ⊟

CLOUGHTON — Map 19 TA09

Blacksmiths Arms

★★★★ ⊜ INN

High St YO13 0AE
☎ 01723 870244
e-mail: enquiries@blacksmithsarmsinn.co.uk
dir: On A171 in village centre. 6m N of Scarborough

Located six miles north of Scarborough, this inn features smartly furnished bedrooms. Four are in converted stone buildings that have private entrances. A good range of dishes is served in the bar and dining room, which have the ambience of a country inn, including open fires and traditional furniture.

Rooms 6 en suite 4 annexe en suite (1 fmly) (4 GF) S £45-£80; D £75-£100* **Facilities** FTV tea/coffee Dinner available Cen ht Wi-fi **Parking** 35 **Notes** LB ⊗ RS 25-27 Dec No breakfast or room service No coaches

Rockhaven

★★★★ GUEST ACCOMMODATION

Newlands Rd YO13 OAR
☎ 01723 871971
e-mail: bbclevelandway@talktalk.net
dir: 6m N of Scarborough on A171. At junct of
Staintondale Rd & Hood Ln

A delightful Victorian detached house with views across
open countryside and out to sea. Superbly furnished with
comfortable beds and a spacious guest lounge,
Rockhaven offers freshly-cooked breakfasts, and is set in
ideal countryside for walking, cycling or touring.

Rooms 3 en suite (1 fmly) S £30-£35; D £60-£70*
Facilities tea/coffee Dinner available Cen ht Wi-fi
Badminton court, summer house for guests use Parking 6
Notes LB ⊗ Closed Dec-Jan RS Feb-Mar, Oct-Nov wknds
& 3 day bookings only ⊗

CRAYKE   Map 19 SE57

The Durham Ox

★★★★ 🅰 RESTAURANT WITH ROOMS

Westway YO61 4TE
☎ 01347 821506   📠 01347 823326
e-mail: enquiries@thedurhamox.com
dir: A19 to Easingwold. Through market place to Crayke,
1st left up hill

Rooms 4 annexe en suite (2 fmly) (2 GF) S £60-£100;
D £80-£140* Facilities tea/coffee Dinner available Wi-fi
Shooting, fishing, riding by arrangement Conf Max 18
Thtr 18 Board 18 Parking 35 Notes LB RS 25 Dec No food
served No coaches

FLIXTON   Map 17 TA07

Orchard Lodge

★★★★ GUEST ACCOMMODATION

North St YO11 3UA
☎ 01723 890202   📠 01723 890202
e-mail: c.pummell@btinternet.com
web: www.orchard-lodge.com
dir: Off A1039 in village centre

Located six miles south of Scarborough, just off the main
road, this establishment offers spacious and comfortable
bedrooms. It is a good base for touring the coast, the
North York Moors or the Wolds. Hearty breakfasts feature
home-made preserves.

Rooms 6 en suite S £45-£50; D £70-£80 Facilities tea/
coffee Cen ht Parking 8 Notes LB ⊗ No Children 3yrs
Closed Jan-Feb

GIGGLESWICK   Map 18 SD86

Harts Head Inn

★★★★ 🅰 INN

Belle Hill BD24 OBA
☎ 01729 822086   📠 01729 824992
e-mail: info@hartsheadinn.co.uk
web: www.hartsheadinn.co.uk
dir: On B6480, 1m from A65

Rooms 7 en suite 3 annexe en suite (1 fmly)
S £42.50-£45; D £70-£85* Facilities STV tea/coffee
Dinner available Cen ht Wi-fi Snooker Pool Table Conf Max
30 Class 30 Board 20 Parking 25 Notes LB

GOLDSBOROUGH   Map 19 SE35

PREMIER COLLECTION

Goldsborough Hall

★★★★★ GUEST ACCOMMODATION

Church St HG5 8NR
☎ 01423 867321   📠 0870 285 1327
e-mail: accommodation@goldsboroughhall.com
dir: A1(M) junct 47, take A59 to Knaresborough. Take
2nd left onto Station Rd, at T-junct left onto Church St

It's not everyday that you get the chance to stay in the
former residence of a Royal Princess, in this case HRH
Princess Mary. Hospitality at Goldsborough Hall is
second to none. Six luxury rooms have been refurbished
to the highest standards, and the bathrooms offer a
real "wow" factor. Bedrooms feature hand-made
mahogany 8ft four-poster beds, Chesterfields and 50-
inch televisions.

Rooms 6 en suite (3 fmly) S £125-£200; D £150-£700*
Facilities FTV TVL tea/coffee Dinner available Direct
Dial Cen ht Lift Licensed Wi-fi Outdoor hot tub
Conf Max 150 Thtr 150 Class 50 Board 30 Parking 50
Notes LB ⊗ Civ Wed 110

GRASSINGTON   Map 19 SE06

PREMIER COLLECTION

Ashfield House

★★★★★ 🍴 GUEST ACCOMMODATION

Summers Fold BD23 5AE
☎ 01756 752584   📠 07092 376562
e-mail: sales@ashfieldhouse.co.uk
web: www.ashfieldhouse.co.uk
dir: B6265 to village centre, main street, left onto
Summers Fold

Guests are greeted like old friends at this beautifully
maintained 17th-century house, peacefully tucked
away a few yards from the village square. The smart
lounges offer a high level of comfort and an honesty
bar. The freshly prepared three-course dinner (by
arrangement) is a highlight of any stay. The attractive
bedrooms are well furnished and thoughtfully
equipped.

Rooms 7 en suite 1 annexe en suite S £65-£89;
D £95-£106* Facilities tea/coffee Dinner available
Cen ht Licensed Wi-fi Conf Max 8 Board 8 Parking 8
Notes LB ⊗ No Children 5yrs RS Nov-Mar No Dinner on
Sun & Wed eve

GREAT AYTON   Map 19 NZ51

Royal Oak

★★★ INN

123 High St TS9 6BW
☎ 01642 722361   & 723270   📠 01642 724047
e-mail: info@royaloak-hotel.co.uk
dir: Off the A173, on High Street

This 18th-century former coaching inn is very popular
with locals and visitors to the village. Bedrooms are all
comfortably equipped. The restaurant and public bar
retain many original features and offer a good selection
of fine ales; an extensive range of food is available all
day and is served in the bar or the dining room.

Rooms 5 en suite S £35-£50; D £70* Facilities tea/coffee
Dinner available Direct Dial Cen ht Snooker Conf Max 30
Thtr 30 Class 30 Board 30

GUISBOROUGH — Map 19 NZ61

The Kings Head at Newton

★★★★ GUEST ACCOMMODATION

The Green TS9 6QR
☎ 01642 722318 📠 01642 724750
e-mail: info@kingsheadhotel.co.uk
web: www.kingsheadhotel.co.uk
dir: A171 towards Guisborough, at rdbt onto A173 to Newton under Roseberry, under Roseberry Topping landmark

Converted from a row of traditional cottages, the friendly, family-owned Kings Head offers modern accommodation with original features. The stylish modern bedrooms are thoughtfully equipped, and the adjacent restaurant offers a choice of wines, beers and a very good range of dishes.

Rooms 8 en suite (1 fmly) (2 GF) S £59.50-£85;
D £75-£110* **Facilities** FTV TVL tea/coffee Direct Dial
Cen ht Licensed Wi-fi Mountain biking **Parking** 100
Notes ⊗ Closed 25-26 Dec & 1 Jan

HACKNESS — Map 19 SE99

Troutsdale Lodge

★★★★ GUEST ACCOMMODATION

Troutsdale YO13 0BS
☎ 01723 882209
e-mail: clive@troutsdalelodge.fsnet.co.uk
web: www.troutsdalelodge.com
dir: Off A170 at Snainton signed Troutsdale

Commanding magnificent views across a peaceful valley and the forest beyond, this Edwardian house showcases many original features combined with modern art. Bedrooms offer good all-round comforts and guests receive fine hospitality from the resident owners.

Rooms 4 en suite (1 fmly) (4 GF) **Facilities** TVL tea/coffee
Dinner available Cen ht Licensed ⛳ **Parking** 8 **Notes** ✉

HARROGATE — Map 19 SE35

Cold Cotes

★★★★★ 🅰 GUEST ACCOMMODATION

Cold Cotes Rd, Felliscliffe HG3 2LW
☎ 01423 770937
e-mail: info@coldcotes.com
web: www.coldcotes.com
dir: W of Harrogate. Off A59 after Black Bull, 3rd entrance on right

Rooms 3 en suite 3 annexe en suite (2 GF);
D £78.50-£93* **Facilities** FTV tea/coffee Dinner available
Cen ht Licensed Wi-fi **Conf** Max 50 Thtr 30 Class 24 Board
14 **Parking** 20 **Notes** ⊗ No Children 12yrs

Alexa House & Stable Cottages

★★★★ GUEST HOUSE

26 Ripon Rd HG1 2JJ
☎ 01423 501988 📠 01423 504086
e-mail: enquires@alexa-house.co.uk
web: www.alexa-house.co.uk
dir: On A61, 0.25m from junct A59

This popular establishment has stylish, well-equipped bedrooms split between the main house and cottage rooms. All rooms come with homely extras. The opulent day rooms include an elegant lounge with honesty bar, and a bright dining room. The hands-on proprietors ensure high levels of customer care.

Rooms 9 en suite 4 annexe en suite (2 fmly) (4 GF)
S £55-£60; D £85-£90* **Facilities** tea/coffee Cen ht
Licensed Wi-fi **Conf** Max 10 Class 10 **Parking** 10
Notes Closed 23-26 Dec

April House

★★★★ GUEST ACCOMMODATION

3 Studley Rd HG1 5JU
☎ 01423 561879
e-mail: info@aprilhouse.com
dir: Off A59/A61 onto Kings Rd signed Harrogate
International Centre. Opposite Holiday Inn turn onto
Alexandra Rd. Establishment at top of road on right

Located in a quiet residential area just a short walk from the conference centre, this impeccable Victorian house retains many original features. The comfortable bedrooms come with an array of homely touches, and breakfast is served in an attractive dining room.

Rooms 5 rms (4 en suite) (1 pri facs) (1 fmly) S £25-£50;
D £60-£80* **Facilities** FTV tea/coffee Wi-fi **Notes** LB ⊗

Ashwood House

★★★★ GUEST ACCOMMODATION

7 Spring Grove HG1 2HS
☎ 01423 560081 📠 01423 527928
e-mail: ashwoodhouse@aol.com
web: www.ashwoodhouse.co.uk
dir: A61 Ripon Rd onto Springfield Av, 3rd left

This delightfully decorated and furnished Edwardian house is situated in a quiet area of town. The spacious bedrooms are individually styled and thoughtfully equipped, and one has a four-poster bed. There is a cosy lounge and an elegant dining room where full English breakfasts are served.

Rooms 5 en suite (1 fmly) S £35-£50; D £65-£75*
Facilities TVL tea/coffee Cen ht **Parking** 3 **Notes** LB ⊗
No Children 7yrs Closed Xmas & New Year

The Camberley

★★★★ GUEST ACCOMMODATION

52-54 Kings Rd HG1 5JR
☎ 01423 561618 📠 01423 536360
e-mail: camberleyhotelharrogate@yahoo.co.uk
dir: *Opposite Harrogate International Centre*

Located directly opposite the convention centre and with the benefit of private car parking, this constantly improving owner-managed guest house provides comfortable accommodation and a warm welcome is assured. A spacious guest lounge is available in addition to a period-themed basement dining room, the setting for comprehensive breakfasts utilising local produce.

Rooms 11 rms (9 en suite) (2 pri facs) (2 fmly) (1 GF) S £35-£45; D £65-£85 **Facilities** FTV tea/coffee Cen ht Wi-fi **Parking** 10 **Notes** LB ⊗ Closed 24-25 Dec

The Dales

★★★★ GUEST ACCOMMODATION

101 Valley Dr HG2 0JP
☎ 01423 507248
e-mail: reservations@dales-hotel.co.uk
dir: *A61 N into Harrogate, left before Bettys on Parliament St, to rdbt & 2nd exit, left onto Valley Dr*

Set in a peaceful residential area overlooking Valley Gardens, the cosy property has well-equipped bedrooms with either en suite or private facilities. Relax in the stylish lounge; an honesty bar is also available. Quality breakfasts are served in the dining room, and service is friendly and attentive.

Rooms 8 rms (6 en suite) (2 pri facs) S £40; D £70-£75 **Facilities** FTV TVL tea/coffee Cen ht Licensed Wi-fi **Notes** LB ⊗

Fountains B&B

★★★★ GUEST ACCOMMODATION

27 Kings Rd HG1 5JY
☎ 01423 530483 📠 01423 705312
e-mail: dave@fountains.fsworld.co.uk
dir: *500yds N of town centre. Off A59 Skipton Rd onto Kings Rd, 0.75m on right on corner of Coppice Dr*

This delightful guest house offers very comfortable accommodation close to the conference centre. Carefully decorated throughout, the bedrooms have co-ordinated soft fabrics, and some have period furniture. The elegant lounge is available for guests use. Substantial breakfasts are served in the breakfast room.

Rooms 10 en suite (2 GF) S £40; D £71* **Facilities** FTV tea/coffee Cen ht Wi-fi **Parking** 8 **Notes** ⊗ No Children 6yrs Closed 24 Dec-2 Jan

The Grafton

★★★★ GUEST ACCOMMODATION

1-3 Franklin Mount HG1 5EJ
☎ 01423 508491 📠 01423 523168
e-mail: enquiries@graftonhotel.co.uk
web: www.graftonhotel.co.uk
dir: *Follow signs to International Centre, onto Kings Rd with Centre on left, Franklin Mount 450yds on right*

The delightful family-run Grafton is in a quiet location just a short walk from the conference centre and town. Bedrooms are well appointed and comfortably furnished, and there are lounges with a small cosy bar. Breakfast is served in the light and spacious dining room, which overlooks the garden.

Rooms 17 en suite (3 fmly) S £40-£55; D £60-£95 **Facilities** FTV TVL tea/coffee Direct Dial Cen ht Licensed Wi-fi **Parking** 3 **Notes** LB ⊗ Closed 15-28 Dec

Harrogate Brasserie with Rooms

★★★★ GUEST ACCOMMODATION

28-30 Cheltenham Pde HG1 1DB
☎ 01423 505041 📠 01423 722300
e-mail: info@harrogatebrasserie.co.uk
web: www.harrogatebrasserie.co.uk
dir: *On A61 town centre behind theatre*

This town centre establishment is distinctly continental in style. The brasserie covers three cosy dining areas richly decorated and adorned with artefacts. Live jazz is featured on Wednesday, Friday and Sunday nights. The individual bedrooms feature period collectibles; many rooms have DVD players and all have lots to read.

Rooms 15 en suite (3 fmly) S £70* **Facilities** tea/coffee Dinner available Direct Dial Licensed **Parking** 12 **Notes** LB Closed 26 Dec-2 Jan

Shannon Court

★★★★ GUEST HOUSE

65 Dragon Av HG1 5DS
☎ 01423 509858 📠 01423 530606
e-mail: info@shannoncourtguesthouse.co.uk
web: www.shannoncourtguesthouse.co.uk
dir: *On corner of Dragon Ave & Mornington Cres, parallel to A59 (Skipton Rd)*

Situated within easy walking distance of the town centre, this friendly guest house offers individually decorated, pleasantly furnished and thoughtfully equipped bedrooms. There is a comfortable dining room where hearty breakfasts are served at individual tables and also a cosy lounge area for guests to relax in.

Rooms 8 en suite (2 fmly) S £50-£55; D £75-£80* **Facilities** tea/coffee Cen ht Wi-fi **Parking** 2 **Notes** LB ⊗ Closed 5 Dec-5 Jan

Shelbourne

★★★★ GUEST ACCOMMODATION

78 Kings Rd HG1 5JX
☎ 01423 504390 📠 01423 504390
e-mail: sue@shelbournehouse.co.uk
web: www.shelbournehouse.co.uk
dir: *Follow signs to International Centre, over lights by Moat House Hotel, premises on right*

Situated opposite the conference centre and near to the town centre, this elegant Victorian house extends a warm welcome to all guests. Bedrooms are tastefully decorated and well equipped. There is a guest's lounge and an attractive breakfast room where hearty breakfasts are served at the individual tables.

Rooms 8 en suite (2 fmly) **Facilities** TVL tea/coffee Cen ht Licensed **Conf** Board 16 **Parking** 1 **Notes** ⊗

Wynnstay House

★★★★ GUEST ACCOMMODATION

60 Franklin Rd HG1 5EE
☎ 01423 560476
e-mail: wynnstayhouse@tiscali.co.uk
web: www.wynnstayhouse.com
dir: *Off A61 in town centre onto Kings Rd, right onto Strawberry Dale, 2nd left*

Located in a residential area a short distance from the conference centre, shops and attractions, this friendly, family-run guest house is ideal for business or leisure. There is a passion for ruined castles at Wynnstay House: the attractive, well-equipped bedrooms are each named after a spectacular fortress.

Rooms 6 en suite S £47.50-£80; D £65-£85* **Facilities** FTV tea/coffee Cen ht Wi-fi **Notes** LB ⊗ No Children 14yrs

HAWES Map 18 SD88

Steppe Haugh

★★★★ GUEST ACCOMMODATION

Town Head DL8 3RH
☎ 01969 667645
e-mail: info@steppehaugh.co.uk
dir: *On A684, W side of Hawes, next to fuel station*

Over 350 years old, the stone house retains much original charm and offers a very welcoming atmosphere. The thoughtfully furnished bedrooms are cosy, and the spacious lounge has a welcoming log fire in the cooler seasons. Private parking is available.

Rooms 5 en suite S £37-£39; D £67-£70* **Facilities** TVL tea/coffee Cen ht **Parking** 5 **Notes** No Children 7yrs Closed Dec-Jan 🐾

The Inn at Hawnby
★★★★ ⬤ INN

YO62 5QS
☎ 01439 798202 📠 01439 798344
e-mail: info@innathawnby.co.uk
web: www.innathawnby.co.uk
dir: Off B1257 between Stokesley & Helmsley

A charming 19th-century inn located in a peaceful village. Service is attentive and friendly, with guests able to relax and browse menus in the cosy bar where there is a good wine list and range of ales. Delicious, home-cooked meals are served in the restaurant, overlooking the gardens and surrounding countryside. Bedrooms are well equipped with a few in the converted stables.

Rooms 6 en suite 3 annexe en suite (1 fmly) (1 GF) S £69; D £85-£89* Facilities FTV tea/coffee Dinner available Direct Dial Cen ht Fishing Riding Conf Max 9 Class 9 Parking 9 Notes LB Closed 25 Dec RS Feb & Mar No lunch service Civ Wed 30

Laskill Grange
★★★★ GUEST ACCOMMODATION

YO62 5NB
☎ 01439 798268
e-mail: laskillgrange@tiscali.co.uk
web: www.laskillgrange.co.uk
dir: From York A19 to Thirsk, A170 to Helmsley then B1257 N, after 6m sign on left to Laskill Grange

Lovers of the countryside will enjoy this charming 19th-century farmhouse. Guests can take a walk in the surrounds, fish the River Seph which runs through the grounds, or visit nearby Rievaulx Abbey. Comfortable

bedrooms are in the main house and are well furnished and supplied with many thoughtful extras.

Rooms 3 rms (2 en suite) (1 pri facs) (3 GF) S £30-£40; D £77-£80* Facilities FTV TVL tea/coffee Dinner available Cen ht Licensed Fishing Riding Outdoor activity area Conf Max 20 Parking 20 Notes LB Civ Wed 60

See also Hawnby

PREMIER COLLECTION

Shallowdale House
★★★★★ 🍴 GUEST ACCOMMODATION

West End YO62 4DY
☎ 01439 788325 📠 01439 788885
e-mail: stay@shallowdalehouse.co.uk
web: www.shallowdalehouse.co.uk

(For full entry see Ampleforth)

Plumpton Court
★★★★ GUEST ACCOMMODATION

High St, Nawton YO62 7TT
☎ 01439 771223
e-mail: mail@plumptoncourt.com
web: www.plumptoncourt.com
dir: 2.5m E of Helmsley. Off A170 in Nawton, signed

Located in the village of Nawton, in the foothills of the North Yorkshire Moors, this characteristic 17th-century, stone-built house offers a warm welcome. The cosy lounge bar has an open fire. Bedrooms are comfortable, modern and well equipped, one with a four-poster bed.

Rooms 7 en suite (1 GF) S £50; D £68-£70 Facilities FTV tea/coffee Cen ht Licensed Wi-fi Parking 8 Notes ⊗ No Children 12yrs Closed Dec-Jan

The Carlton Lodge
★★★★ 🅰 GUEST HOUSE

Bondgate YO62 5EY
☎ 01439 770557 📠 01439 772378
e-mail: enquiries@carlton-lodge.com
web: www.carlton-lodge.com
dir: 400yds E of Market Sq on A170

Rooms 8 rms (7 en suite) (1 pri facs) (1 fmly) (2 GF) S £45-£55; D £75-£95* Facilities FTV tea/coffee Dinner available Direct Dial Cen ht Licensed Wi-fi Parking 10 Notes LB

The Crown Inn
★★★★ 🅰 INN

21 Market Place YO62 5BJ
☎ 01439 770297
e-mail: info@tchh.co.uk
web: www.tchh.co.uk
dir: A19 onto A170 at the top of market square

Rooms 12 en suite 7 annexe en suite (2 fmly) (6 GF); D £70-£180* Facilities TVL tea/coffee Dinner available Cen ht Wi-fi Conf Max 30 Thtr 20 Class 30 Board 20 Parking 30 Notes LB

The New Inn Motel
★★★ GUEST ACCOMMODATION

Main St YO61 1HQ
☎ 01347 810219 📠 01347 810219
e-mail: enquiries@newinnmotel.freeserve.co.uk
web: www.newinnmotel.co.uk
dir: Off A19 E into village centre, motel on left

Located behind the New Inn, this modern motel-style accommodation has a quiet location in the village of Huby, nine miles north of York. Comfortable bedrooms are spacious and neatly furnished, and breakfast is served in the cosy dining room. The reception area hosts an array of tourist information and the resident owners provide a friendly and helpful service.

Rooms 8 en suite (3 fmly) (8 GF) S £38-£50; D £65-£75 Facilities tea/coffee Cen ht Parking 8 Notes LB Closed mid Nov-mid Dec & part Feb

The Countryman's Inn
★★★ INN

Bedale DL8 1PY
☎ 01677 450554
e-mail: tony@countrymansinn.co.uk
dir: Between Bedale & Leyburn, 2m N of A684

Set in the heart of this quiet village, the inn is popular with visitors and locals and serves good home-made food. The resident owner and staff provide warm hospitality, and the bedrooms are smartly furnished and comfortably equipped.

Rooms 3 en suite Facilities FTV TVL tea/coffee Dinner available Cen ht Wi-fi Parking 11 Notes RS Mon-Tue Restaurant closed

---

INGLETON
Map 18 SD67

Gale Green Cottage
★★★★ BED AND BREAKFAST

Westhouse LA6 3NJ
☎ 015242 41245 & 077867 82088
e-mail: jill@galegreen.com
dir: *2m NW of Ingleton. S of A65 at Masongill x-rds*

Peacefully located in a rural hamlet, this 300-year-old house has been lovingly renovated to provide modern facilities without compromising original charm and character. Thoughtfully furnished bedrooms feature smart modern en suite shower rooms and a guest lounge is also available.

Rooms 3 en suite (1 fmly) S £39; D £58* **Facilities** FTV TVL tea/coffee Cen ht **Parking** 6 **Notes** Closed Xmas & New Year ⊗

KIRKBYMOORSIDE
Map 19 SE68

Brickfields Farm *(SE704852)*
★★★★ ⒶFARMHOUSE

Kirby Mills YO62 6NS
☎ 01751 433074 Mrs J Trousdale
e-mail: janet@brickfieldsfarm.co.uk
web: www.brickfieldsfarm.co.uk
dir: *A170 E from Kirkbymoorside, 0.5m right into Kirby Mills (signed), farm 1st right*

Rooms 1 en suite 4 annexe en suite (5 GF) S £60-£82.50; D £79-£110* **Facilities** FTV tea/coffee Cen ht Wi-fi Golf 0 **Parking** 8 **Notes** LB ⊗ No Children 15 acres non-working

---

KNARESBOROUGH
Map 19 SE35

PREMIER COLLECTION

General Tarleton Inn
★★★★★ ◉◉ RESTAURANT WITH ROOMS

Boroughbridge Rd, Ferrensby HG5 0PZ
☎ 01423 340284 ▤ 01423 340288
e-mail: gfi@generaltarleton.co.uk
dir: *A1(M) junct 48 at Boroughbridge, take A6055 to Knaresborough. 4m on right*

Food is a real feature here with skilfully prepared meals served in the restaurant, traditional bar and modern conservatory. Accommodation is provided in brightly decorated and airy rooms, and the bathrooms are thoughtfully equipped. Enjoying a country location, yet close to the A1(M), the inn remains popular with both business and leisure guests.

Rooms 14 en suite (7 GF) S £75-£137; D £129-£150* **Facilities** tea/coffee Dinner available Direct Dial Cen ht Wi-fi **Conf** Max 40 Thtr 40 Class 35 Board 20 **Parking** 40 **Notes** LB ⊗ Closed 24-26 Dec, 1 Jan No coaches

---

Newton House
★★★★ 🏠 GUEST ACCOMMODATION

5-7 York Place HG5 0AD
☎ 01423 863539 ▤ 01423 869748
e-mail: newtonhouse@btinternet.com
web: www.newtonhouseyorkshire.com
dir: *On A59 in Knaresborough, 200yds from town centre*

The delightful 18th-century former coaching inn is only a short walk from the river, castle and market square. The property is entered by an archway into a courtyard. The attractive, very well-equipped bedrooms include some four-posters and also king-size doubles. There is a charming lounge, and memorable breakfasts feature local and home-made produce.

Rooms 9 rms (8 en suite) (1 pri facs) 2 annexe en suite (3 fmly) (3 GF) S £50; D £75-£100* **Facilities** FTV TVL tea/coffee Direct Dial Cen ht Licensed Wi-fi **Parking** 10 **Notes** LB Closed 1wk Xmas

---

LEEMING BAR
Map 19 SE57

Little Holtby
★★★★ Ⓐ BED AND BREAKFAST

DL7 9LH
☎ 01609 748762
e-mail: littleholtby@yahoo.co.uk
dir: *2m N of A684 (junct with A1)*

Rooms 3 en suite S £37.50-£40; D £70-£74 **Facilities** FTV TVL tea/coffee Cen ht Wi-fi **Parking** **Notes** LB ⊗ No Children 12yrs ⊗

LEYBURN
Map 19 SE19

PREMIER COLLECTION

Capple Bank Farm
★★★★★ BED AND BREAKFAST

West Witton DL8 4ND
☎ 01969 625825
e-mail: julian.smithers@btinternet.com
dir: *A1 to Bedale. Turn off onto A684 to Leyburn. Continue through Hawes & Wensley, take 1st left in West Witton. Up hill, round left bend, gates straight ahead*

Ideal for walking and touring in the Yorkshire Dales National Park, this spacious house has been recently converted and refurbished. Guests have use of a lovely lounge with a real fire lit on cooler days, and breakfast is served at a beautiful table in the open-plan kitchen and dining room.

Rooms 2 en suite S fr £45; D £65-£70* **Facilities** STV TVL tea/coffee Cen ht **Parking** 6 **Notes** ⊗ No Children 10yrs ⊗

PREMIER COLLECTION

Thorney Hall
★★★★★ BED AND BREAKFAST

Spennithorne DL8 5PW
☎ 01969 622120 & 07836 269453
e-mail: nesbit1954@btinternet.com

This beautiful, lovingly restored country house offers period features, open fireplaces and elegant furnishings. Bedrooms are well appointed and each has either a modern en suite or private bathroom. Guests receive a warm welcome and have use of an attractive lounge. Well-cooked evening meals and hearty breakfasts are served at a traditional table in the grand dining room.

Rooms 3 rms (2 en suite) (1 pri facs) (1 fmly); D £96 **Facilities** tea/coffee Dinner available Cen ht ⚘ ⚘ Golf **Parking** 10 **Notes** No Children 12yrs ⊗

The Queens Head
★★★★ 🍺 INN

Westmoor Ln, Finghill DL8 5ND
☎ 01677 450259
e-mail: enquiries@queensfinghall.co.uk
web: www.queensfinghall.co.uk
dir: *From Bedale follow A684 W towards Leyburn, just after pub & caravan park turn left signed to Finghall. Follow road, on left*

Located in the quiet village of Finghall this country inn offers a cosy pub, dating back to the 18th century, with original oak beams. A wide choice of freshly prepared meals are served in either the bar or more contemporary restaurant, which has lovely views of the surrounding countryside. Bedrooms are spacious and located in an adjacent annexe.

Rooms 3 annexe en suite (1 fmly) (3 GF) S £60-£80; D £70-£90* **Facilities** FTV TVL tea/coffee Dinner available Cen ht Pool Table **Parking** 40 **Notes** LB

LONG PRESTON
Map 18 SD85

Boars Head
★★★ INN

9 Main St BD23 4ND
☎ 01729 840217 ▤ 01729 840217
e-mail: darrenjmonks@hotmail.co.uk
web: www.hotelyorkshiredales.co.uk
dir: *On A65 between Skipton & Settle*

Located in the heart of the village the inn provides comfortable bedrooms with modern bathrooms en suite. Imaginative food and real ales are served in the spacious open-plan ground floor area and a warm welcome is assured.

Rooms 5 en suite (2 fmly) S £32-£37.50; D £50-£60* **Facilities** FTV tea/coffee Dinner available Cen ht Wi-fi Pool Table **Parking** 46 **Notes** ⊗

LOW ROW — Map 18 SD99

The Punch Bowl Inn
★★★★ INN

DL11 6PF
☎ 01748 886233 📠 01748 886945
e-mail: info@pbinn.co.uk
dir: *From Scotch Corner take A6108 to Richmond then B6270 to Low Row*

This friendly inn has recently been refurbished in a contemporary style. Real ales and freshly-cooked meals are served in either the spacious bar or dining room. The modern bedrooms are simply furnished and stylish, with well-equipped bathrooms. Guests also have use of a lounge, which like all rooms has stunning views of the Dales.

Rooms 9 en suite 2 annexe en suite (1 GF); D £85-£115*
Facilities FTV tea/coffee Dinner available Direct Dial Cen ht Wi-fi Fishing Riding **Parking** 20 **Notes** LB ⊗ Closed 25 Dec

MALHAM — Map 18 SD96

River House
★★★★ 🏠 🍴 GUEST HOUSE

BD23 4DA
☎ 01729 830315
e-mail: info@riverhousehotel.co.uk
web: www.riverhousehotel.co.uk
dir: *Off A65, N to Malham*

A warm welcome awaits you at this attractive house, which dates from 1664. The bedrooms are bright and comfortable, with one on the ground floor. Public areas include a cosy lounge and a large, well-appointed dining room. Breakfasts and evening meals really do offer excellent choice and quality.

Rooms 8 en suite (1 GF) S £45-£65; D £60-£75*
Facilities tea/coffee Dinner available Cen ht Licensed Wi-fi **Parking** 5 **Notes** LB No Children 9yrs Closed 2wks Jan

Beck Hall
★★★ GUEST HOUSE

Cove Rd BD23 4DJ
☎ 01729 830332
e-mail: alice@beckhallmalham.com
web: www.beckhallmalham.com
dir: *A65 to Gargrave, turn right to Malham. Beck Hall 100yds on right after mini rdbt*

A small stone bridge over Malham Beck leads to this delightful property. Dating from 1710, the house has true character, with bedrooms carefully furnished with four-poster beds. Delicious afternoon teas are available in the colourful garden in warmer months, while roaring log fires welcome you in the winter.

Rooms 10 rms (9 en suite) (1 pri facs) 7 annexe en suite (4 fmly) (4 GF) S £25-£60; D £48-£76 **Facilities** TV15B STV tea/coffee Dinner available Cen ht Licensed Wi-fi Fishing Riding **Conf** Max 35 Thtr 30 Class 30 Board 30 **Parking** 40 **Notes** LB

The Lister Arms
Ⓤ

BD23 4DB
☎ 01729 830330
e-mail: info@listerarms.co.uk

Currently the rating for this establishment is not confirmed. This may be due to a change of ownership or because it has only recently joined the AA rating scheme.

Rooms 9 en suite (3 fmly) **Facilities** tea/coffee Dinner available Licensed **Parking** 30 **Notes** LB

MALTON — Map 19 SE77

Green Man
★★★ INN

15 Market St YO17 7LY
☎ 01653 600370 📠 01653 696006
e-mail: greenman@englishrosehotels.co.uk
dir: *from A64 follow signs to Malton. Left into Market St, hotel on left*

This friendly inn, set in the centre of town, has an inviting reception lounge where a log fire burns in winter. There is also a cosy bar, and dining takes place in the traditional restaurant at the rear.

Rooms 24 rms (18 en suite) (4 fmly) S £36.50-£49.50; D £80-£100 **Facilities** tea/coffee Direct Dial **Parking** 40 **Notes** ⊗

MASHAM — Map 19 SE28

Bank Villa
★★★★ 🏠 🍴 GUEST HOUSE

HG4 4DB
☎ 01765 689605
e-mail: bankvilla@btopenworld.com
web: www.bankvilla.com
dir: *Enter on A6108 from Ripon, property on right*

An elegant Georgian house set in a pretty walled garden. Individually decorated bedrooms feature stripped pine, period furniture and crisp, white linen. Imaginative home-cooked meals are served in the attractive dining room. Character public rooms include a choice of lounges, or you can relax in the garden in summer.

Rooms 6 rms (4 en suite) (2 pri facs) (2 fmly)
Facilities TVL tea/coffee Dinner available Cen ht Licensed **Conf** Max 12 Thtr 12 Class 12 Board 12 **Parking** 6 **Notes** LB ⊗ No Children 5yrs

MIDDLESBROUGH — Map 19 NZ41

The Grey House
★★★★ GUEST ACCOMMODATION

79 Cambridge Rd, Linthorpe TS5 5NL
☎ 01642 817485 📠 01642 817485
e-mail: denistaylor-100@btinternet.com
web: www.greyhousehotel.co.uk
dir: *A19 N onto A1130 & A1032 Acklam Rd, right at lights*

This Edwardian mansion stands in mature gardens in a quiet residential area, and is lovingly maintained to provide a relaxing retreat. The master bedrooms are well sized, and the upper rooms, though smaller, also offer good comfort. Downstairs there is an attractive lounge and the breakfast room.

Rooms 9 en suite (1 fmly) **Facilities** FTV TVL tea/coffee Direct Dial Cen ht Wi-fi **Parking** 10

MUKER — Map 18 SD99

Oxnop Hall *(SD931973)*

★★★★ FARMHOUSE

Low Oxnop, Gunnerside DL11 6JJ
☎ 01748 886253 🖷 01748 886253 Mrs A Porter
dir: *Off B6270 between Muker & Gunnerside*

Set in beautiful Swaledale scenery, this smartly presented
17th-century farmhouse has been furnished with thought
and care. The attractive bedrooms are well equipped and
some boast original exposed beams and mullion windows.
Hearty farmhouse breakfasts are served, using local and
home-made produce where possible. A cosy lounge is also
available.

Rooms 4 en suite 1 annexe en suite (1 GF) **Facilities** FTV
tea/coffee Cen ht **Parking** 10 **Notes** ⊗ No Children 10yrs
Closed Nov-Mar ⊛ 1300 acres beef/sheep/hill farming

NORTHALLERTON — Map 19 SE39

Three Tuns

★★★★ 🍴 RESTAURANT WITH ROOMS

9 South End, Osmotherley DL6 3BN
☎ 01609 883301 🖷 01609 883988
e-mail: enquiries@threetunsrestaurant.co.uk
dir: *NE of Northallerton. Off A19 into Osmotherley*

Situated in the popular village of Osmotherley, the Three
Tuns is full of character. Bedrooms, set above the bar
and also in an adjoining building, vary in size but are
stylishly furnished in pine and equipped to meet the
needs of tourists and business travellers alike. The
restaurant offers an imaginative menu of wholesome,
modern British dishes.

Rooms 3 en suite 4 annexe en suite (1 fmly) (1 GF)
Facilities TVL tea/coffee Dinner available Direct Dial

Windsor Guest House

★★★★ GUEST HOUSE

56 South Pde DL7 8SL
☎ 01609 774100 🖷 01609 774100
e-mail: windsorguesthouse@yahoo.co.uk
dir: *On A684 at S end of High St*

This Victorian terrace house is convenient for the town
centre. The well maintained accommodation consists of
bright, cheerful, and thoughtfully equipped bedrooms
with en suite bathrooms. The attractive dining room looks
out to the back garden and is a pleasant venue for tasty
breakfasts served by the friendly proprietors.

Rooms 6 rms (5 en suite) (1 pri facs) (1 fmly) S £35-£40;
D £55-£60* **Facilities** FTV TVL tea/coffee Cen ht Wi-fi
Parking 1 **Notes** ⊗

OLDSTEAD — Map 19 SE57

The Black Swan at Oldstead

◉◉ ▣

YO61 4BL
☎ 01347 868387 & 868634
e-mail: enquiries@blackswanoldstead.co.uk
dir: *Exit A19, 3m S Thirsk for Coxwold, left in Coxwold, left
at Byland Abbey for Oldstead*

Currently the rating for this establishment is not
confirmed. This may be due to a change of ownership or
because it has only recently joined the AA rating scheme.

Rooms 4 annexe en suite (4 GF) **Facilities** FTV tea/coffee
Dinner available Cen ht Licensed Wi-fi **Parking** 4
Notes ⊗

PATELEY BRIDGE — Map 19 SE16

Roslyn House

★★★ GUEST ACCOMMODATION

9 King St HG3 5AT
☎ 01423 711374 🖷 01423 715995
e-mail: roslynhousepb@aol.com
web: www.roslynhouse.co.uk
dir: *B6165 into Pateley Bridge, end of High St turn right
at newsagents onto King Street, house 200yds on left*

You are assured of a very warm welcome at this well-
maintained guest house in the village centre. Bedrooms
are sensibly furnished and offer many homely touches. A
very comfortable lounge is available, and hearty
breakfasts set you up for the day. Roslyn House caters
well for cyclists and walkers on the famous Nidderdale
Way.

Rooms 6 en suite (6 fmly) S £45-£49; D £59-£69*
Facilities STV TVL tea/coffee Cen ht Wi-fi **Conf** Max 8
Board 8 **Parking** 4 **Notes** LB ⊗ No Children 3yrs ⊛

PICKERING — Map 19 SE78

PREMIER COLLECTION

17 Burgate

★★★★★ 🏠 GUEST ACCOMMODATION

17 Burgate YO18 7AU
☎ 01751 473463
e-mail: info@17burgate.co.uk
dir: *From A170 follow sign to Castle. 17 Burgate on
right*

An elegant market town house close to the centre and
the castle, offering comfortable individually designed
bedrooms with all modern facilities including free
broadband. Public areas include a comfortable lounge
bar, and breakfast includes a wide choice of local,
healthy foods.

Rooms 5 en suite S £70-£75; D £80-£105*
Facilities FTV tea/coffee Cen ht Licensed Wi-fi
Parking 7 **Notes** LB ⊗ No Children 10yrs

RAVENSCAR — Map 19 NZ90

Smugglers Rock Country House

★★★★ ◭ GUEST ACCOMMODATION

YO13 0ER
☎ 01723 870044
e-mail: info@smugglersrock.co.uk
dir: *0.5m S of Ravenscar. Off A171 towards Ravenscar,
opp stone windmill*

Rooms 8 en suite (3 fmly) S £37-£40; D £64-£70*
Facilities FTV TVL tea/coffee Cen ht Wi-fi **Parking** 12
Notes LB ⊗ No Children 3yrs Closed Nov-Mar RS end
Mar-early Oct

REETH — Map 19 SE09

Charles Bathurst Inn

★★★★ 🍴 INN

Arkengarthdale DL11 6EN
☎ 01748 884567 🖷 01748 884599
e-mail: info@cbinn.co.uk
dir: *B6270 to Reeth, at Buck Hotel turn N to Langthwaite,
pass church on right, inn 0.5m on right*

The CB Inn, as it is known, is surrounded by magnificent
scenery high in the Dales. Food is the focus of the pub,
where a choice of rustic eating areas makes for
atmospheric dining. The well-equipped bedrooms blend
contemporary and traditional styles and cosy lounge
areas are available. A well-equipped function suite is
also available.

Rooms 19 en suite (2 fmly) (5 GF) D £85-£122.50*
Facilities tea/coffee Dinner available Direct Dial Cen ht
Wi-fi Fishing Riding Pool Table **Conf** Max 100 Thtr 100
Class 30 Board 30 **Parking** 35 **Notes** LB ⊗ Closed 25 Dec

RICCALL — Map 16 SE63

The Park View

★★★★ GUEST ACCOMMODATION

20 Main St YO19 6PX
☎ 01757 248458 🖶 01757 249211
e-mail: mail@parkviewriccall.co.uk
web: www.parkviewriccall.co.uk
dir: A19 from Selby, left for Riccall by water tower, 100yds on right

The well-furnished and comfortable Park View stands in grounds and offers well-equipped bedrooms. There is a cosy lounge plus a small bar, while breakfasts are served in the dining room. Dinner is available midweek.

Rooms 7 en suite (1 fmly) S £49-£52; D £71-£74*
Facilities TVL tea/coffee Dinner available Cen ht Licensed Wi-fi Parking 10

Dairymans of Riccall

★★★★ A GUEST ACCOMMODATION

14 Kelfield Rd YO19 6PG
☎ 01757 248532 🖶 0871 251 3863
e-mail: bookings@dairymansriccall.co.uk
dir: Off A19 into village, off Main St onto Silver St & Kelfield Rd

Rooms 4 en suite (1 fmly) Facilities FTV TVL tea/coffee Cen ht Wi-fi Notes ⊗

White Rose Villa

★★★★ A BED AND BREAKFAST

33 York Rd YO19 6QG
☎ 01757 248115
e-mail: whiterosevilla@btinternet.com
web: www.whiterosevilla-info.com
dir: S of York, from A19, signed Riccall, 50mtrs on right

Rooms 3 en suite (2 fmly) S £30-£35; D £60-£65*
Facilities TVL tea/coffee Cen ht Wi-fi Parking 4 Notes LB ⊗ Closed 24-26 & 31Dec ⊛

RICHMOND — Map 19 NZ10

See also Reeth

Whashton Springs Farm (NZ149046)

★★★★ FARMHOUSE

DL11 7JS
☎ 01748 822884 🖶 01748 826285 Mrs J M Turnbull
e-mail: whashtonsprings@btconnect.com
dir: In Richmond N at lights towards Ravensworth, 3m down steep hill, farm at bottom on left

A friendly welcome awaits you at this farmhouse accommodation, situated in the heart of the countryside yet convenient for major routes. Bedrooms are split between the courtyard rooms and the main farmhouse. Hearty breakfasts are served in the spacious dining room overlooking the gardens. A stylish lounge is also available.

Rooms 3 en suite 5 annexe en suite (2 fmly) (5 GF) S £44-£50; D £70-£80* Facilities FTV tea/coffee Cen ht Wi-fi Conf Max 16 Board 16 Parking 10 Notes LB ⊗ No Children 3yrs Closed late Dec-Jan ⊛ 600 acres mixed/arable/beef/sheep

RIPON — Map 19 SE37

PREMIER COLLECTION

Mallard Grange (SE270704)

★★★★★ FARMHOUSE

Aldfield HG4 3BE
☎ 01765 620242 🖶 01765 620242 Mrs M Johnson
e-mail: maggie@mallardgrange.co.uk
web: www.mallardgrange.co.uk
dir: B6255 W fom Ripon, Mallard Grange 2.5m on right

Located near Fountains Abbey a genuine welcome is always guaranteed at Mallard Grange. The original features of this early 16th-century, Grade II-listed farmhouse are highlighted by quality furnishings and décor. Bedrooms, two of which are in a converted smithy, are filled with a wealth of thoughtful extras, and comprehensive breakfasts feature home-reared and local produce.

Rooms 2 en suite 2 annexe en suite (2 GF) S £60-£90; D £75-£105* Facilities tea/coffee Cen ht Wi-fi Parking 6 Notes LB ⊗ No Children 12yrs Closed Xmas & New Year 500 acres mixed/beef/sheep/arable

The Old Coach House

★★★★★ A GUEST ACCOMMODATION

2 Stable Cottages, North Stainley HG4 3HT
☎ 01765 634900 🖶 01765 635352
e-mail: enquiries@oldcoachhouse.info
web: www.oldcoachhouse.info
dir: From Ripon take A6108 to Masham. Once in North Stainley, on left opposite Staveley Arms

Rooms 8 en suite (4 GF) S £35-£45; D £69-£89*
Facilities FTV tea/coffee Direct Dial Cen ht Wi-fi Parking 8 Notes ⊗ No Children 14yrs Closed Jan

See advert on opposite page

Bay Tree Farm (SE263685)

★★★★ 🏠 FARMHOUSE

Aldfield HG4 3BE
☎ 01765 620394 📄 01765 620394 Mrs V Leeming
e-mail: val@btfarm.entadsl.com
web: www.baytreefarm.co.uk
dir: 4m W of Ripon. S off B6265 in village of Aldfield

A warm welcome awaits you at this farmhouse set in the countryside close to Fountains Abbey and Studley Park. Bedrooms are suitably equipped, there is a cosy lounge with a log-burning stove, and breakfast is traditional home-cooked fare. Dinner is available for groups of eight or more by arrangement.

Rooms 4 en suite 2 annexe en suite (1 fmly) (3 GF) S £50-£70; D £80-£95 **Facilities** tea/coffee Dinner available Cen ht **Parking** 10 **Notes** LB 400 acres beef/arable

St George's Court (SE237697)

★★★★ 🏠 FARMHOUSE

Old Home Farm, Grantley HG4 3PJ
☎ 01765 620618 Mrs Hitchen
e-mail: stgeorgescourt@bronco.co.uk
web: www.stgeorges-court.co.uk
dir: B6265 W from Ripon, up hill 1m past Risplith sign & next right, 1m on right

This renovated farmhouse is a great location to get away from it all, in the delightful countryside close to Fountains Abbey. The attractive, well-equipped, recently upgraded ground-floor bedrooms are located around a central courtyard. Imaginative breakfasts are served in the new breakfast room and a guest lounge is now available, both with views of the surrounding countryside.

Rooms 5 en suite (1 fmly) (5 GF) S £45-£55; D £70-£80* **Facilities** tea/coffee Cen ht Fishing **Conf** Max 12 **Parking** 12 **Notes** LB 20 acres beef /sheep/pigs

---

ROBIN HOOD'S BAY   **Map 19 NZ90**

The Flask Inn

★★★ INN

Fylingdales YO22 4QH
☎ 01947 880305
e-mail: admin@theflaskinn.com
dir: On A171, 7m S from Whitby

The Flask, originally a 16th-century hostel, is now a comfortable inn offering a good range of real ales and food. Thoughtfully equipped bedrooms are furnished in attractive pine and have modern shower rooms en suite. The spacious bar has a friendly atmosphere.

Rooms 6 en suite (2 fmly) S £35-£60; D £60* **Facilities** tea/coffee Dinner available Cen ht Pool Table **Conf** Max 40 **Parking** 20 **Notes** LB

Bramblewick

★★★ 🍴 RESTAURANT WITH ROOMS

2 King St YO22 4SH
☎ 01947 880960 & 880339 📄 01947 880960
e-mail: bramblewick@btinternet.com
web: www.bramblewick.org
dir: A171 onto B1447 to rdbt, straight over & down steep hill into 'Old Village', establishment at bottom on left

Only yards from the lifeboat slipway and the beach, this building dates from the 17th century. Modern en suite bedrooms have great charm with low beams, and below on the ground floor is a popular daytime café that changes in the evening to offer intimate candlelight dinners. Parking is at Bank Top, a five-minute walk from the old village; cars can stop briefly in the old village to drop off or pick up passengers.

Rooms 3 en suite S £40-£45; D £70* **Facilities** tea/coffee Dinner available Cen ht **Notes** LB ⊗ Closed 24-26 Dec No coaches

---

The Old Coach House

2 Stable Cottages, North Stainley, Ripon HG4 3HT

The Old Coach House is an accommodation jewel and one of Yorkshire's best kept secrets. The 18th century coaching house stands proud in the grounds of North Stainley Hall in the picturesque village of North Stainley, just north of Ripon.

This 5 star luxury guesthouse is nestled between The Yorkshire Dales and North Yorkshire Moors National Park and is a great location to explore these beautiful areas of outstanding natural beauty as well as The Yorkshire Wolds, Nidderdale, Harrogate and York.

The area is steeped in history with the historic city of Ripon nearby as well as countryside walks, attractions, plentiful restaurants and country pubs.

All eight rooms are en-suite and designed with modern living in mind. Each room offers a range of contemporary high quality fittings and facilities including tea/coffee, safe, telephone, hair dryer, flat screen TV, alarm clock and refrigerator.

Tel: 01765 634900 Fax: 01765 635352 Website: www.oldcoachhouse.info Email: enquiries@oldcoachhouse.info

---

ROSEDALE ABBEY   Map 19 SE79

Sevenford House

★★★★ GUEST ACCOMMODATION

YO18 8SE
☎ 01751 417283
e-mail: sevenford@aol.com
web: www.sevenford.com
dir: Off A170 at sign for Rosedale Abbey, in village turn sharp left at Coach & House Restaurant & right at White Horse

Set in the heart of the North Yorkshire National Park, this elegant Victorian house stands in a peaceful garden within walking distance of the village. The well-proportioned bedrooms are comfortable, well equipped and have stunning panoramic views. There is also an inviting lounge and a spacious breakfast room with grand piano.

Rooms 3 en suite (1 fmly) S £45; D £70* **Facilities** tea/coffee Cen ht Wi-fi **Parking** 7 **Notes** LB ⊗ ⊜

SCARBOROUGH   Map 17 TA08

PREMIER COLLECTION

Holly Croft

★★★★★ ⇔ BED AND BREAKFAST

28 Station Rd, Scalby YO13 0QA
☎ 01723 375376 & 07759 429706
e-mail: christine.goodall@tesco.net
web: www.holly-croft.co.uk
dir: A171 at Scalby x-rds, turn right at tennis courts, 500yds on right

A beautifully appointed detached Victorian house in a quiet residential area in the village of Scalby. All rooms, including the spacious bedrooms, are furnished with family antiques and thoughtful accessories are provided. Guests can relax in the lounge and there is also a billiard room and large garden.

Rooms 2 rms (1 en suite) (1 pri facs) **Facilities** TVL tea/coffee Dinner available Cen ht Wi-fi **Parking** 2 **Notes** LB ⊗ No Children 5yrs Closed Xmas & New Year ⊜

Columbus

★★★★ GUEST ACCOMMODATION

124 Columbus Ravine YO12 7QZ
☎ 01723 374634 & 07930 545964
e-mail: hotel.columbus@lineone.net
dir: On A165 towards North Bay, near Peasholm Park

Yorkshire hospitality at its best is offered here, and Bonnie Purchon is a welcoming hostess. The establishment is well located for the beach and attractions. Bedrooms are compact, well equipped and homely. A very comfortable lounge is provided. In the dining room a good breakfast is served, as are evening meals during the main season.

Rooms 10 en suite (2 fmly) S £35-£39.50; D £70-£79* **Facilities** tea/coffee Dinner available Cen ht Licensed **Parking** 8 **Notes** LB ⊗ No Children 3yrs

---

The Danielle

★★★★ GUEST ACCOMMODATION

9 Esplanade Rd, South Cliff YO11 2AS
☎ 01723 366206
e-mail: hoteldanielle@yahoo.co.uk
dir: S of town centre. Off A165 Filey Rd onto Victoria Av, left onto Esplanade, left onto Esplanade Rd

A warm welcome is assured at this elegant Victorian house situated a short walk from the Spa Cliff Lift. Bedrooms are equipped with thoughtful extras, and day rooms include an attractive dining room and a lounge.

Rooms 9 rms (7 en suite) (3 fmly) S £28-£30; D £60-£70 **Facilities** TVL tea/coffee Cen ht Licensed **Notes** LB ⊗ No Children 2yrs Closed Dec-mid Feb

---

Foulsyke Farm House B&B

★★★★ BED AND BREAKFAST

Barmoor Ln, Scalby YO13 0PG
☎ 01723 507423
e-mail: jaynepickup@btinternet.com
dir: 2.5m NW of Scarborough. Off A171 in Scalby onto Barmoor Ln & 1st right after duck pond

In the pretty village of Scalby this delightful house is situated on a farm. Recently renovated, the house offers elegantly furnished bedrooms, with thoughtful accessories and well-equipped bathrooms. A warm welcome is assured and a hearty breakfast is served in the bright, attractive dining room.

Rooms 3 rms (2 en suite) (1 pri facs) **Facilities** tea/coffee Cen ht Wi-fi Bikes for hire **Parking** 6 **Notes** ⊗ ⊜

The Hillcrest

★★★★ GUEST ACCOMMODATION

2 Peasholm Av YO12 7NE
☎ 01723 361981
e-mail: enquiries@hillcresthotel.co.uk
dir: A165 to North Bay/leisure parks, onto Peasholm Dr & Peasholm Crescent

Hillcrest s in a residential area close to Peasholm Park, within walking distance of the cricket ground and the North Bay attractions, and its individually furnished bedrooms contain many extras. There is a spacious guest lounge with video library and an attractive breakfast room.

Rooms 7 en suite (1 fmly) S £35; D £68.50 **Facilities** FTV tea/coffee Dinner available Cen ht Licensed **Parking** 2 **Notes** LB ⊗ No Children 3yrs Closed Dec-1 Feb

---

Olivers

★★★★ GUEST ACCOMMODATION

34 West St YO11 2QP
☎ 01723 368717
e-mail: info@olivershotelscarborough.co.uk
dir: Take A64 to B1427 (Margarets Rd). Right onto A165 (Filey Rd). Take 2nd left onto Granville Rd

Well-equipped, spacious bedrooms are a feature of this Victorian gentleman's residence, and one bedroom was originally the nursery. Close to the cliff lift down to the spa, beaches and gardens, and centrally located on the South Cliff.

Rooms 6 en suite (2 fmly) (1 GF) D £54-£64* **Facilities** FTV tea/coffee Dinner available Cen ht **Notes** LB ⊗ Closed 20-28 Dec

Paragon

★★★★ GUEST ACCOMMODATION

123 Queens Pde YO12 7HU
☎ 01723 372676 ▧ 01723 372676
e-mail: enquiries@paragon-hotel.fsnet.co.uk
web: www.paragonhotel.com
dir: On A64, follow signs for North Bay. Establishment on clifftop

This welcoming Victorian terrace house has been carefully renovated to provide stylish, thoughtfully equipped, non-smoking accommodation. Hearty English breakfasts are served in the attractive dining room and there is also a lounge bar with a fabulous sea view.

Rooms 14 en suite (1 fmly) S £35-£60; D £64-£70* **Facilities** tea/coffee Dinner available Direct Dial Cen ht Licensed **Parking** 6 **Notes** LB No Children 3yrs Closed 20 Nov-24 Jan

The Ramleh

★★★★ GUEST ACCOMMODATION

135 Queens Pde YO12 7HY
☎ 01723 365745
e-mail: info@theramleh.co.uk
dir: A64/A165 to North Bay & Alexandra Bowling Centre. At Bowling Centre, follow Queens Pde

Overlooking North Bay, this welcoming terrace house has a friendly atmosphere. The modern bedrooms are bright and comfortable, and tasty breakfasts are served in the spacious dining room, which also has a well-stocked bar and a stunning view.

Rooms 9 rms (8 en suite) (1 pri facs) (3 fmly) S £30-£35; D £50-£60* **Facilities** TVL tea/coffee Dinner available Cen ht Licensed **Parking** 6 **Notes** LB ⊗ Closed 20 Dec-3 Jan

The Whiteley

★★★★ GUEST ACCOMMODATION

99/101 Queens Pde YO12 7HY
☎ 01723 373514 ▧ 01723 373007
e-mail: whiteleyhotel@bigfoot.com
dir: A64/A165 to North Bay & Peasholm Park, right onto Peasholm Rd, 1st left

The Whiteley is an immaculately run, sea-facing home-from-home. Bedrooms, though compact, are carefully decorated and have many thoughtful extras. There's a small garden at the rear, a choice of lounges, and a bar. The establishment has some superb views, and the owners provide personal attention and a substantial breakfast.

Rooms 10 en suite (3 fmly) (1 GF) S £31.50-£33; D £51-£62 **Facilities** TVL tea/coffee Cen ht Licensed **Parking** 8 **Notes** LB ⊗ No Children 3yrs Closed 30 Nov-Jan

The Windmill Bed & Breakfast

★★★★ GUEST ACCOMMODATION

Mill St, Off Victoria Rd YO11 1SZ
☎ 01723 372735 ▧ 01723 377190
e-mail: info@windmill-hotel.co.uk
web: www.windmill-hotel.co.uk
dir: A64 into Scarborough, pass Sainsbury's, left onto Victoria Rd, 3rd left onto Mill St

Situated in the centre of town but having its own car park, this unique establishment has modern bedrooms situated around a courtyard next to a windmill dating from 1784. The base of the mill includes a spacious breakfast room and a toy museum which is only viewable by guests.

Rooms 11 en suite (3 fmly) (6 GF) **Facilities** tea/coffee Cen ht **Parking** 7 **Notes** ⊗

Ainsley Court Guest House

★★★★ Ⓐ GUEST HOUSE

112 North Marine Rd YO12 7JA
☎ 01723 500352
e-mail: lynn@ainsleycourt.co.uk
dir: Next to Scarborough cricket ground

Rooms 6 rms (4 en suite) (2 pri facs) (2 fmly) S £20-£26; D £35-£52* **Facilities** TVL tea/coffee Cen ht **Notes** LB ⊗

The Wharncliffe

★★★★ Ⓐ GUEST ACCOMMODATION

26 Blenheim Ter YO12 7HD
☎ 01723 374635
e-mail: info@thewharncliffescarborough.co.uk
dir: Follow signs to Castle, left onto Blenheim St, left onto Blenheim Ter

Rooms 12 en suite; D £58-£68* **Facilities** FTV TVL tea/coffee Cen ht Licensed Wi-fi **Notes** LB ⊗ No Children 18yrs

Chessington

★★★ GUEST ACCOMMODATION

The Crescent YO11 2PP
☎ 01723 365207 ▧ 01723 375206
e-mail: info@thechessington.co.uk
web: www.thechessington.co.uk
dir: A64 to town centre lights, right, left at next lights & right at next lights, Chessington on left

This Grade II listed building occupies a fine position overlooking the Crescent and is close to the town centre. The bedrooms are well equipped, and the spacious dining room is the setting for comprehensive breakfasts. A sitting room and lounge bar are available.

Rooms 10 en suite (2 fmly) S £32; D £64* **Facilities** TVL tea/coffee Cen ht Licensed **Conf** Max 10 **Notes** LB ⊗ Closed Dec & Jan

The Croft

★★★ 🏠 GUEST ACCOMMODATION

87 Queens Pde YO12 7HT
☎ 01723 373904
e-mail: information@crofthotel.co.uk
web: www.crofthotel.co.uk
dir: Follow tourist signs for North Bay seafront, along front towards castle headland, right turn up cliff, right at top, premises on left

A flexible approach to your needs is a key feature of this friendly establishment. It overlooks the bay, so you can enjoy the spectacular view from the comfortable lounge or from the patio in fine weather. Meals are served in the very pleasant well-appointed dining room.

Rooms 6 rms (5 en suite) (1 pri facs) (4 fmly) S £24-£28; D £48-£56* **Facilities** TVL tea/coffee Cen ht Licensed **Parking** 4 **Notes** LB ⊗ Closed Dec-Feb

SCARBOROUGH *continued*

Plane Tree Cottage Farm (SE999984)

★★★ FARMHOUSE

Staintondale YO13 0EY
☎ 01723 870796   Mrs M A Edmondson
dir: *A171, N from Scarborough. At Cloughton onto Staintondale road, farm 2m N of Cloughton*

The Edmondson family are welcoming hosts, and the animals on the farm include unusual breeds of sheep and hens. This is an interesting and pleasant venue, either for its tranquil, secluded setting, or as a base for walking. There is good home cooking, comfortable bedrooms, and a cosy lounge and dining room.

Rooms 3 rms (2 en suite) (1 GF); D £56* **Facilities** TVL tea/coffee Dinner available Cen ht **Parking** 3 **Notes** ⊗ No Children Closed Oct-Mar ⊛ 60 acres sheep/hens/Highland cattle

Argo

★★★ GUEST HOUSE

134 North Marine Rd YO12 7HZ
☎ 01723 375745
dir: *Close to entrance of Scarborough Cricket Ground*

This friendly house is a haven for cricket fans, with some of the comfortable bedrooms overlooking the championship ground. Day rooms include a well appointed lounge and a dining room where tasty cooked breakfasts are served at individual tables.

Rooms 8 rms (5 en suite) (2 fmly) S £17.50-£19; D £44* **Facilities** TVL tea/coffee Cen ht **Notes** ⊗ ⊛

Jalna House

★★★ GUEST ACCOMMODATION

168 North Marine Rd YO12 7HZ
☎ 01723 360668   📄 01723 360668
dir: *A165 to Peasholm Park, onto Peasholm Rd & North Marine Rd, near cricket ground*

A well-furnished guest house close to Peasholm Park and within walking distance of the North Beach attractions, cricket field and the town centre. Compact bedrooms are comfortable, there is a cosy lounge and a dining room serving tasty home-cooked meals.

Rooms 10 rms (6 en suite) (6 fmly) (2 GF) **Facilities** TVL tea/coffee Dinner available Cen ht **Notes** LB Closed 21 Dec-7 Jan ⊛

North End Farm Country Guesthouse

★★★ GUEST ACCOMMODATION

88 Main St, Seamer YO12 4RF
☎ 01723 862965
e-mail: northendfarm@tiscali.co.uk
dir: *A64 N onto B1261 through Seamer, farmhouse next to rdbt*

Located in Seamer, a village inland from Scarborough, this 18th-century farmhouse contains comfortable, well-equipped en suite bedrooms. Breakfast is served at individual tables in the smart dining room, and the cosy lounge has a large-screen TV.

Rooms 3 en suite S £30-£40; D £55-£65 **Facilities** TVL tea/coffee Cen ht **Parking** 6 **Notes** ⊛

Parmelia

★★★ GUEST ACCOMMODATION

17 West St YO11 2QN
☎ 01723 361914
e-mail: parmelia.hotel@btconnect.com
web: www.parmeliahotel.co.uk
dir: *Off A64 at The Mere onto Queen Margarets Rd, left at next T-lights (A165) onto Ramshill Rd, right for Esplanade Gdns Rd*

Only a short walk from the Esplanade on the south cliff, this large guest house provides modern co-ordinated bedrooms. Cheerful hospitality makes guests feel at home, and there is an attractive lounge for relaxation.

Rooms 15 rms (12 en suite) (1 pri facs) (4 fmly) (2 GF) S £21.50-£35; D £47-£55 **Facilities** STV FTV TVL tea/coffee Cen ht **Notes** LB No Children 4yrs Closed Dec-Feb

Peasholm Park

★★★ GUEST ACCOMMODATION

21-23 Victoria Park YO12 7TS
☎ 01723 500954
e-mail: peasholmparkhotel@btconnect.com
web: www.peasholmpark.co.uk
dir: *Opp entrance to Peasholm Park*

A warm welcome awaits you at this family-run guest house, which is within easy walking distance of the beach or the town centre. Bedrooms are comfortable, and feature homely extras. Breakfast is served at individual tables in the dining room, which looks over Peasholm Park.

Rooms 12 en suite (3 fmly) **Facilities** TVL tea/coffee Dinner available Cen ht Licensed **Parking** 2 **Notes** ⊗ No Children 4yrs RS 22 Dec-2 Jan Bed & Breakfast only

Scarborough Fayre

★★★ GUEST ACCOMMODATION

143-147 Queens Pde YO12 7HU
☎ 01723 361677
e-mail: info@scarboroughfayrehotel.com
dir: *Off N Marine Road, near cricket ground. Car park on Queens Parade*

Overlooking the North Bay, a warm welcome is assured at Scarborough Fayre, and guests have use of a comfortable lounge, fully licensed bar and spacious restaurant. Bedrooms are well equipped, most benefiting from compact en suites and some with stunning sea views.

Rooms 24 rms (23 en suite) (1 pri facs) (6 fmly) (1 GF) S £27.50-£35; D £55-£70 **Facilities** TVL tea/coffee Cen ht Licensed Wi-fi **Parking** 23 **Notes** LB ⊗

Marine View Guest House

★★★ 🅰 GUEST HOUSE

34 Blenheim Ter YO12 7HD
☎ 01723 361864
e-mail: info@marineview.co.uk
dir: *From A64 left onto B1364, turn onto Rutland Ter. After 0.1m straight onto Blenheim Ter*

Rooms 6 en suite (2 fmly) S £28-£29; D £48-£54* **Facilities** FTV TVL tea/coffee Cen ht Wi-fi **Notes** LB ⊗ No Children 3yrs

The Grosvenor

★★ GUEST ACCOMMODATION

51 Grosvenor Rd YO11 2LZ
☎ 01723 363801   📄 01723 363801
e-mail: grosvenorhotelscarborough@msn.com
web: www.grosvenor-scarborough.co.uk
dir: *Follow signs for South Bay along Valley Rd, Grosvenor Rd on right*

You can expect good hospitality from all the family at the Grosvenor, situated a short walk from the town and the seafront. Freshly cooked breakfasts are served in the lower ground floor dining room and guests also have use of a spacious lounge.

Rooms 14 en suite (3 fmly) (3 GF) S £30–£45; D £60–£80 **Facilities** FTV TVL tea/coffee Cen ht Licensed Wi-fi **Notes** LB ⊗

Warwick House

★★ GUEST ACCOMMODATION

70 Westborough YO11 1TS
☎ 01723 374343 📠 01723 374343
e-mail: warwick-house@talktalk.net
dir: On outskirts of town centre, just before railway station on left

Close to the Stephen Joseph Theatre, station and shops, this friendly guest house has some en suite bedrooms and some rooms with shared facilities. Hearty breakfasts are served in the pleasant basement dining room. Private parking is available.

Rooms 6 rms (2 en suite) (4 fmly) **Facilities** tea/coffee Cen ht Wi-fi **Parking** 5 **Notes** LB ⊚

SCOTCH CORNER Map 19 NZ20

The Vintage

★★★ 🅐 INN

DL10 6NP
☎ 01748 824424 & 822961 📠 01748 826272
e-mail: thevintagescotchcorner@btinternet.com
web: www.thevintagehotel.co.uk
dir: Leave A1 at Scotch Corner onto A66 towards Penrith, premises 200yds on left

Rooms 8 rms (5 en suite) S £23.50–£39.50; D £39.50–£49.50 (room only)* **Facilities** TVL tea/coffee Dinner available Direct Dial Cen ht **Conf** Max 48 Thtr 40 Class 24 Board 20 **Parking** 40 **Notes** LB ⊗ Closed Xmas & New Year

SETTLE Map 18 SD86

See also Clapham & Long Preston

Whitefriars Country Guesthouse

★★★★ GUEST ACCOMMODATION

Church St BD24 9JD
☎ 01729 823753
e-mail: info@whitefriars-settle.co.uk
dir: Off A65 through Settle market place, premises signed 50yds on left

This friendly, family-run house stands in peaceful gardens just a stroll from the town centre and railway station. Bedrooms, some quite spacious, are attractively furnished in a traditional style and thoughtfully equipped. A hearty breakfast is served in the traditional, beamed dining room, and a cosy lounge is available.

Rooms 10 rms (6 en suite) (1 pri facs) (1 fmly) S fr £34; D £52–£65 **Facilities** TVL tea/coffee Cen ht **Parking** 10 **Notes** ⊗ Closed 25 Dec ⊚

SKIPTON Map 18 SD95

Clay Hall

★★★★ GUEST ACCOMMODATION

Broughton Rd BD23 3AA
☎ 01756 794391
dir: On A6069, 1m from Skipton towards Broughton

A warm welcome is assured here on the outskirts of the town next to the Leeds and Liverpool canal. The house has been restored to provide carefully furnished bedrooms with smart modern shower rooms en suite, and a wealth of thoughtful extras. Comprehensive breakfasts are served in an attractive dining room.

Rooms 2 en suite S £40–£45; D £50–£55* **Facilities** tea/coffee Cen ht **Parking** 4 **Notes** ⊗ No Children 12yrs ⊚

Westfield House

★★★★ 🏠 GUEST HOUSE

50 Keighley Rd BD23 2NB
☎ 01756 790849
dir: 500yds S of town centre on A6131, S of canal bridge

Just a stroll from the town centre, this friendly, non-smoking guest house provides smart accommodation. Bedrooms are well presented and most have large beds and many accessories including bathrobes. A hearty breakfast is served in the cosy dining room, and permission to use nearby parking is a bonus. Hospitality here is warm and nothing is too much trouble for the owners.

Rooms 4 en suite; D £55–£60 **Facilities** tea/coffee Cen ht **Notes** ⊗ No Children ⊚

Rockwood House

★★★ GUEST ACCOMMODATION

14 Main St, Embsay BD23 6RE
☎ 01756 799755 & 07976 314980 📠 01756 799755
e-mail: rockwood@steadonline.co.uk
web: www.stayinyorkshire.co.uk
dir: 2m NE of Skipton. Off A59 into Embsay village centre

This Victorian terrace house has a peaceful location in the village of Embsay. Bedrooms are thoughtfully furnished, individually styled and reassuringly comfortable. The traditionally styled dining room sets the venue for hearty breakfasts. Hospitality is a feature here with a genuine and friendly welcome.

Rooms 3 en suite (1 fmly) (1 GF) S fr £35; D £60–£90* **Facilities** TVL tea/coffee Direct Dial Cen ht Wi-fi **Parking** 3 **Notes** LB ⊗

SUTTON-ON-THE-FOREST Map 19 SE56

The Blackwell Ox Inn

★★★★ ⊚ 🏠 INN

Huby Rd YO61 1DT
☎ 01347 810328 & 01904 690758 📠 01904 691529
e-mail: enquiries@blackwelloxinn.co.uk
web: www.blackwelloxinn.co.uk
dir: Off A1237, onto B1363 to Sutton-on-the-Forest. Left at T-junct, 50yds on right

Standing in the lovely village, this refurbished inn and restaurant offers very good bedrooms and pleasing public rooms. Cooking is well worth seeking out and staff are very keen and friendly.

Rooms 7 en suite S £65; D £95–£110* **Facilities** FTV TVL tea/coffee Dinner available Direct Dial Cen ht Lift **Parking** 18 **Notes** LB ⊗ No coaches

Goose Farm (SE593629)

★★★★ FARMHOUSE

Eastmoor YO61 1ET
☎ 01347 810577 📠 01347 810577 Mr G Rowson
e-mail: stay@goosefarm.fsnet.co.uk
web: www.goosefarm.co.uk
dir: York outer ring road A1237 onto B1363 N. Take 2nd right, 1st farm on left

Situated on a quiet countryside road, this 19th-century farmhouse is convenient for the many attractions of York. Guests are sure of a friendly welcome, comfortable bedrooms and hearty breakfasts.

Rooms 3 en suite S £36–£46; D £68–£80* **Facilities** tea/coffee Cen ht **Parking** 4 **Notes** ⊗ 25 acres beef

TADCASTER Map 16 SE44

The Old Presbytery Guest House

★★★ BED AND BREAKFAST

London Rd, Saxton LS24 9PU
☎ 01937 557708 & 557392 📠 01937 557392
e-mail: guest@presbytery.plus.com
web: www.presbyteryguesthouse.co.uk
dir: 4m S of Tadcaster on A162. 100yds N of Barkston Ash on E side of road

Dating from the 18th century, this former dower house has been modernised to provide comfortable accommodation with original features. The hall lounge features a wood-burning stove, and extensive breakfasts are served at an old oak dining table in a cosy breakfast room.

Rooms 4 rms (3 en suite) (1 pri facs) (1 fmly) S £40; D £76 **Facilities** TVL tea/coffee Cen ht Wi-fi Golf 18 **Conf** Max 8 Board 8 **Parking** 6 **Notes** ⊗

THIRSK — Map 19 SE48

PREMIER COLLECTION

Spital Hill
★★★★★ GUEST ACCOMMODATION

York Rd YO7 3AE
☎ 01845 522273 📄 01845 524970
e-mail: spitalhill@spitalhill.entadsl.com
web: www.spitalhill.co.uk
dir: 1.5m SE of town, set back 200yds from A19, driveway marked by 2 white posts

Set in gardens, this substantial Victorian country house is delightfully furnished. The spacious bedrooms are thoughtfully equipped with many extras, one even has a piano, but no TVs or kettles; the proprietor prefers to offer tea as a service. Delicious meals feature local and home-grown produce and are served house-party style around one table in the interesting dining room.

Rooms 3 rms (2 en suite) (1 pri facs) 2 annexe en suite (1 GF) Facilities TVL Dinner available Direct Dial Cen ht Licensed ⚓ Parking 6 Notes ⊗ No Children 12yrs

THORNTON WATLASS — Map 19 SE28

PREMIER COLLECTION

Thornton Watlass Hall
★★★★★ GUEST ACCOMMODATION

HG4 4AS
☎ 01677 422803 📄 01677 424160
e-mail: enquiries@thorntonwatlasshall.co.uk
dir: Off B6268, at N end of village

Thornton Watlass Hall dates from the 11th century and has been occupied by the same family for just under 1000 years. The Hall has featured in TV dramas over the years such as All Creatures Great and Small and it has also been the home to 'Lord Ashfordly', as Ashfordly Hall in Heartbeat. The Hall is finely furnished in period style and is unspoilt but still offers all the modern amenities. David and Liz Smith-Dodsworth offer a very friendly welcome and breakfasts are served in the grand dining room offering local produce. Relax in the palatial drawing room with its large open fireplace and honesty bar.

Rooms 6 en suite (1 fmly) S £80; D £125-£135
Facilities FTV TVL tea/coffee Direct Dial Cen ht Licensed Wi-fi ⚓ Snooker Parking 50 Notes Closed 24 Dec-1 Jan RS 2 Jan-Apr Full house parties only

Buck Inn
★★★ INN

HG4 4AH
☎ 01677 422461 📄 01677 422447
e-mail: innwatlass1@btconnect.com
web: www.thebuckinn.net
dir: From A1 at Leeming Bar take A684 towards Bedale, B6268 towards Masham 2m, turn right at x-rds to Thornton Watlass

This traditional country inn is situated on the edge of the village green overlooking the cricket pitch. Cricket prints and old photographs are found throughout and an open fire in the bar adds to the warm and intimate atmosphere. Wholesome lunches and dinners, from an extensive menu, are served in the bar or dining room. Bedrooms are brightly decorated and well equipped.

Rooms 7 rms (5 en suite) (1 fmly) (1 GF) S £65; D £80-£90* Facilities TVL tea/coffee Dinner available Cen ht Wi-fi Fishing Pool Table Quoits Conf Max 50 Thtr 50 Class 45 Board 30 Parking 10 Notes LB RS 24-25 Dec No accommodation, no food 25 Dec

WESTOW — Map 19 SE76

Woodhouse Farm (SE749637)
★★★★ FARMHOUSE

YO60 7LL
☎ 01653 618378 & 07904 293422
📄 01653 618378 Mrs S Wardle
e-mail: stay@wood-house-farm.co.uk
web: www.wood-house-farm.co.uk
dir: Off A64 to Kirkham Priory & Westow. Right at T-junct, farm drive 0.5m out of village on right

The owners of this house are a young farming family who open their home and offer caring hospitality. Home-made bread, preserves and farm produce turn breakfast into a feast, and the views from the house across open fields are splendid.

Rooms 2 en suite (1 fmly) S £40-£45; D £60-£70*
Facilities TVL tea/coffee Cen ht Wi-fi Fishing Parking 12
Notes LB ⊗ Closed Xmas, New Year & mid Mar-mid Apr
⚓ 500 acres arable/sheep

Clifton Farm (SE776463)
★★★ FARMHOUSE

YO60 7LS
☎ 01653 658557 & 07776 112530 Ms L Laughton
e-mail: lynn@cliftonfarm.co.uk
web: www.cliftonfarm.co.uk
dir: 2m SE of Westow. Off A64 signed Harton then Howsham, pass Howsham towards Leavening, over x-rds & Clifton Farm 1m on right

Situated in countryside on the edge of Leavening village, this comfortable, well-furnished farmhouse offers outstanding hospitality and service. Bedrooms are well equipped, breakfasts are hearty, and a lounge is available.

Rooms 3 rms (2 en suite) (1 pri facs) (1 fmly) S £40-£50;
D £60-£70* Facilities TVL tea/coffee Cen ht Wi-fi
Parking 6 Notes LB No Children 5yrs 120 acres mixed

WHITBY — Map 19 NZ81

See also Robin Hood's Bay

Estbek House
★★★★ ⊛⊛ RESTAURANT WITH ROOMS

East Row, Sandsend YO21 3SU
☎ 01947 893424 📄 01947 893625
e-mail: info@estbekhouse.co.uk
dir: On Cleveland Way, within Sandsend, next to East Beck

A speciality seafood restaurant on the first floor is the focus of this listed building in a small coastal village north west of Whitby. Below is a small bar and breakfast room, while up above are four individually presented bedrooms offering luxury and comfort.

Rooms 4 rms (3 en suite) (1 pri facs) Facilities tea/coffee Dinner available Cen ht Wi-fi Conf Board 20
Parking 6 Notes LB ⊗ No Children 14yrs No coaches

Netherby House

★★★★ 🏠 🍽 GUEST ACCOMMODATION

90 Coach Rd, Sleights YO22 5EQ
☎ 01947 810211 📠 01947 810211
e-mail: info@netherby-house.co.uk
web: www.netherby-house.co.uk
dir: In village of Sleights, off A169 (Whitby-Pickering road)

This fine Victorian house has been lovingly refurbished and now offers thoughtfully furnished, individually styled bedrooms together with delightful day rooms. There is a fine conservatory and the grounds are extensive, with exceptional views from the summerhouse at the bottom of the garden. Imaginative dinners feature produce from the extensive kitchen garden.

Rooms 6 en suite 5 annexe en suite (1 fmly) (5 GF) S £37-£46.50; D £74-£93* **Facilities** tea/coffee Dinner available Cen ht Licensed 🐾 **Parking** 17 **Notes** LB ⊗ No Children 2yrs Closed 25-26 Dec

Chiltern Guest House

★★★★ GUEST HOUSE

13 Normanby Ter, West Cliff YO21 3ES
☎ 01947 604981
e-mail: Jjchiltern@aol.com
dir: Whalebones next to Harbour, sea on right. Royal Hotel on left, 200yds. Royal Gardens turn left, 2nd road on left, 6th house on right

The Victorian terrace house offers a warm welcome and comfortable accommodation within walking distance of the town centre and seafront. Public areas include a smartly decorated lounge and a bright, attractive dining room. Bedrooms are thoughtfully equipped and many have modern en suites.

Rooms 9 en suite (2 fmly) S £30-£35; D £60-£70* **Facilities** TVL tea/coffee Cen ht Wi-fi Golf 18 **Notes** LB

Corra Lynn

★★★★ GUEST ACCOMMODATION

28 Crescent Av YO21 3EW
☎ 01947 602214 📠 01947 602214
dir: Corner A174 & Crescent Av

Occupying a prominent corner position, this property mixes traditional values with a trendy and artistic style. Bedrooms are thoughtfully equipped, individually furnished and have bright colour schemes, but it is the

delightful dining room with corner bar, and a wall adorned with clocks that catch the eye.

Rooms 5 en suite (1 fmly) S fr £30* **Facilities** STV tea/coffee Direct Dial Cen ht Licensed **Parking** 5 **Notes** ⊗ Closed 21 Dec-5 Jan 📶

Kimberley House

★★★★ GUEST ACCOMMODATION

7 Havelock Place YO21 3ER
☎ 01947 604125
e-mail: enquiries@kimberleyhouse.com
web: www.kimberleyhouse.com
dir: Follow signs to West Cliff, A174 onto Crescent Av, right onto Hudson St, next junct

This 19th-century house was built for a local seafaring family. It stands in a quiet residential area within walking distance of the West Cliff promenades and the historic town centre. Bedrooms are well equipped and comfortable, and a wide choice of breakfasts is available.

Rooms 8 rms (7 en suite) (1 pri facs) (1 GF) S £30; D fr £60* **Facilities** tea/coffee Cen ht **Notes** LB ⊗ No Children 12yrs 📶

Lansbury Guesthouse

★★★★ GUEST ACCOMMODATION

29 Hudson St YO21 3EP
☎ 01947 604821
e-mail: jill@lansbury44.fsnet.co.uk
dir: In town centre. Off A174 Upgang Ln onto Crescent Av, 2nd right

A short walk from the historic harbour, a warm welcome is assured at this elegant Victorian terrace house which has been renovated to provide good standards of comfort and facilities. Bedrooms are equipped with thoughtful extras, and comprehensive breakfasts using local produce are served in an attractive dining room.

Rooms 7 en suite; D £50-£65* **Facilities** FTV tea/coffee Cen ht **Parking** 3 **Notes** LB ⊗

Rosslyn Guest House

★★★★ GUEST HOUSE

11 Abbey Ter YO21 3HQ
☎ 01947 604086
e-mail: rosslynhouse@googlemail.com

Located close to the seafront this friendly house offers well furnished bedrooms, high standards of cleanliness and friendly service. A wide choice is offered for breakfast, which is served in the beautifully appointed dining room. A small kitchen area is also available for guest use.

Rooms 5 en suite (2 fmly) **Facilities** tea/coffee Cen ht Wi-fi **Parking** 3 **Notes** LB ⊗

Sandpiper Guest House

★★★★ GUEST HOUSE

4 Belle Vue Ter YO21 3EY
☎ 01947 600246
e-mail: enquiries@sandpiperhouse.wanadoo.co.uk
dir: A169, 2nd left at rdbt signed Whitby, follow signs to West Cliffe on N Prom, 4th right, take Esplanade straight onto Belle Vue Ter. B&B on left

This well presented Victorian house is just a few minutes walk from Whitby's golden sands and the quaint streets of its historic harbourside. The contemporary bedrooms vary in size with a choice of singles, twins, a four-poster room and family room available. Hearty breakfasts are served in the cheerful lower ground-floor dining room.

Rooms 7 en suite (1 fmly) (1 GF) **Facilities** tea/coffee Cen ht Wi-fi **Parking** 3 **Notes** ⊗ No Children 4yrs 📶

The Waverley

★★★★ GUEST HOUSE

17 Crescent Av YO21 3ED
☎ 01947 604389 📠 08700 063 3129
e-mail: stephen@whitbywaverley.com
dir: A174 towards Saltburn, turn right, 250mtrs on right at bend

This terraced house was originally built as a guest house in 1898 and is located on the West Cliff. Bedrooms vary in size, but all are comfortable and well equipped. Day rooms include a smartly appointed dining room and first-floor lounge. All guests are assured a warm welcome and a hearty breakfast.

Rooms 6 rms (5 en suite) (1 pri facs) (1 fmly) S £31-£34; D £62-£68* **Facilities** TVL tea/coffee Cen ht **Parking** 3 **Notes** ⊗ No Children 5yrs Closed Nov-Jan

WHITBY *continued*

Whitehaven

★★★★ GUEST ACCOMMODATION

29 Crescent Av YO21 3EW
☎ 01947 601569
e-mail: simon@whitehavenguesthouse.co.uk
web: www.whitehavenguesthouse.co.uk
dir: *Signs to West Cliff, A174 onto Crescent Av*

Occupying a corner position close to the sports complex and indoor swimming pool, this house provides colourful bedrooms in contrasting styles. All rooms have mini-fridges and most have DVD facilities. Vegetarian options are available at breakfast served in the attractive dining room.

Rooms 4 rms (3 en suite) (1 pri facs) (1 fmly);
D £65-£70* **Facilities** FTV tea/coffee Cen ht Wi-fi
Notes LB ⊗ Closed 23-26 Dec 🐾

Arundel House

★★★ GUEST ACCOMMODATION

Bagdale YO21 1QJ
☎ 01947 603645   📠 08703 121974
e-mail: arundel_house@hotmail.com
dir: *A171 town centre, onto Arundel Pl at bottom of hill*

In a prime location within walking distance of all the attractions, Arundel House's bedrooms are simply furnished and offer good value for money. Expect a helping of true Yorkshire hospitality, and look out for the unique collection of walking canes on show in the house.

Rooms 12 en suite (2 fmly) (2 GF) S £45; D £70-£90*
Facilities tea/coffee Cen ht Licensed Wi-fi **Parking** 6
Notes LB

The Sandbeck

★★★ GUEST HOUSE

1 & 2 Crescent Ter, West Cliff YO21 3EL
☎ 01947 604012   & 603349
e-mail: dysonsandbeck@tesco.net
dir: *On West Cliff opp theatre booking office*

Commanding a prominent corner position on the seafront, Sandbeck is being progressively upgraded. Bedrooms are generally well proportioned and front rooms have fine sea views. Public rooms comprise a bar, quiet lounge, and a spacious dining room offering various breakfast options.

Rooms 23 en suite (4 fmly) **Facilities** tea/coffee Cen ht
Lift Licensed **Notes** ⊗ No Children 5yrs Closed Dec

The White Horse & Griffin

★★★ ◉ RESTAURANT WITH ROOMS

Church St YO22 4BH
☎ 01947 825026   & 604857   📠 01947 604857
e-mail: info@whitehorseandgriffin.co.uk
web: www.whitehorseandgriffin.co.uk
dir: *From town centre E across Bridge St bridge, 2nd left, 50mtrs on right next to Whitby*

This historic inn, now a restaurant with rooms, is as quaint as the cobbled side street in which it lies. Cooking is good with the emphasis on fresh fish. The bedrooms, some reached by steep staircases, retain a rustic charm but are well equipped and include CD players.

Rooms 10 en suite 10 annexe rms 3 annexe en suite (7 pri facs) (1 fmly) **Facilities** TV14B tea/coffee Dinner available Cen ht Wi-fi **Conf** Max 30 Thtr 30 Class 12 Board 15 **Parking** 1 **Notes** ⊗ No coaches

---

YORK   Map 16 SE65

See also Sutton-on-the-Forest

Burswood Guest House

★★★★ 🏠 GUEST HOUSE

68 Tadcaster Rd, Dringhouses YO24 1LR
☎ 01904 702582   📠 01904 708377
e-mail: burswood.guesthouse@virgin.net
dir: *From A64 (on S side of city) take A1036 (Tadcaster Rd). House opposite racecourse stables*

Guests are sure of a warm welcome at this modern dormer bungalow. Bedrooms are richly furnished and very well equipped. Freshly cooked breakfasts are served in the conservatory/breakfast room which overlooks the well-tended garden. Good car parking is available at the front of the house and Burswood is easily accessible for the city centre and the racecourse.

Rooms 5 en suite (1 fmly) (3 GF) **Facilities** FTV tea/coffee
Cen ht **Parking** 6 **Notes** ⊗

The Hazelwood

★★★★ GUEST ACCOMMODATION

24-25 Portland St YO31 7EH
☎ 01904 626548   📠 01904 628032
e-mail: reservations@thehazelwoodyork.com
web: www.thehazelwoodyork.com
dir: *400yds N of York Minster, off inner ring road Gillygate*

A renovation of two elegant Victorian houses in a residential side street near the Minster. Bedrooms are equipped with thoughtful extras, and comprehensive breakfasts are served in an attractive dining room. There is a cosy garden-level lounge and a private car park.

Rooms 13 en suite (2 fmly) (2 GF) S £50-£105;
D £80-£125* **Facilities** tea/coffee Cen ht Licensed Wi-fi
Parking 8 **Notes** LB ⊗ No Children 8yrs

Ascot House

★★★★ GUEST ACCOMMODATION

80 East Pde YO31 7YH
☎ 01904 426826   📠 01904 431077
e-mail: admin@ascothouseyork.com
web: www.ascothouseyork.com
dir: *0.5m NE of city centre. Off A1036 Heworth Green onto Mill Ln, 2nd left*

June and Keith Wood provide friendly service at the 1869 Ascot House, a 15-minute walk from the town centre. Bedrooms are thoughtfully equipped, many with four-poster or canopy beds and other period furniture. Reception rooms include a cosy lounge that also retains its original features.

Rooms 13 rms (12 en suite) (1 pri facs) (3 fmly) (2 GF)
S £55-£70; D £70-£80 **Facilities** TVL tea/coffee Cen ht
Licensed Wi-fi Sauna **Parking** 13 **Notes** LB Closed 21-28
Dec

Ashley Guest House

★★★★ GUEST HOUSE

76 Scott St YO23 1NS
☎ 01904 647520
e-mail: taylor.philip.j@googlemail.com
dir: *Pass racecourse, turn right at 2nd lights onto Scarcroft Rd. Scott St 2nd last on right*

A Victorian end terrace that has been given a very modern treatment with stylish interiors and distinctive character. Attractively furnished bedrooms and caring hospitality are hallmarks of this well located city centre guest house.

Rooms 6 rms (5 en suite) (1 pri facs) S £35-£68; D £40-£96* **Facilities** tea/coffee Cen ht Wi-fi **Notes** ⊗ No Children 12yrs

City Guest House

★★★★ GUEST ACCOMMODATION

68 Monkgate YO31 7PF
☎ 01904 622483
e-mail: info@cityguesthouse.co.uk
dir: *NE of city centre on B1036*

Just a stroll from the historic Monk Bar, this guest house is well located for business, shopping and sightseeing. Carefully furnished bedrooms boast stylish interior design and come equipped with a host of thoughtful touches. The smart dining room is the venue for a good breakfast.

Rooms 7 en suite (1 fmly) (1 GF) S £38-£41; D £66-£72* **Facilities** tea/coffee Cen ht **Parking** 6 **Notes** ⊗ No Children 8yrs Closed Xmas & 1st 2wks Jan

The Heathers

★★★★ GUEST ACCOMMODATION

54 Shipton Rd, Clifton-Without YO30 5RQ
☎ 01904 640989 🖷 01904 640989
e-mail: aabbg@heathers-guest-house.co.uk
web: www.heathers-guest-house.co.uk
dir: *N of York on A19, halfway between A1237 ring road & York city centre*

Recent remodelling and refurbishment at this house has resulted in a most comfortable and welcoming establishment. Heather and Graham Fisher have designed each room, individually using quality fabrics and decor to provide a feeling of luxury in the bedrooms. The light and airy breakfast room looks out on to a well-tended garden area.

Rooms 6 rms (4 en suite) (2 pri facs) (2 fmly) S £52-£126; D £56-£130 **Facilities** TVL tea/coffee Cen ht Wi-fi **Parking** 9 **Notes** ⊗ No Children 10yrs Closed Xmas

Holly Lodge

★★★★ GUEST ACCOMMODATION

204-206 Fulford Rd YO10 4DD
☎ 01904 646005
e-mail: geoff@thehollylodge.co.uk
web: www.thehollylodge.co.uk
dir: *On A19 S side, 1.5m on left from A64/A19 junct, or follow A19 Selby signs from city centre to Fulford Rd*

Located just a short walk from the historic centre, this pleasant Georgian property has co-ordinated, well-equipped bedrooms. The spacious lounge houses a grand piano, and hearty breakfasts are served in the cosy dining room. You may also enjoy the delightful walled garden.

Rooms 5 en suite (1 fmly) (1 GF) S £58-£88; D £68-£98 **Facilities** tea/coffee Cen ht Wi-fi **Parking** 6 **Notes** ⊗ No Children 7yrs Closed 24-27 Dec

Midway House

★★★★ Ⓐ GUEST HOUSE

145 Fulford Rd YO10 4HG
☎ 01904 659272
e-mail: info@midwayhouseyork.co.uk
dir: *A64 to York, 3rd exit A19 to York city centre, over 2nd lights, house 50yds on right*

Rooms 12 rms (10 en suite) (3 fmly) (1 GF) S £40-£60; D £60-£80* **Facilities** TVL tea/coffee Cen ht Wi-fi **Parking** 14 **Notes** LB ⊗ No Children 6yrs Closed 23 Dec-1 Feb

Adam's House

★★★ GUEST HOUSE

5 Main St, Fulford YO10 4HJ
☎ 01904 655413 🖷 01904 643203
e-mail: adams.house2@virgin.net
dir: *A64 onto A19, 200yds on right after lights*

Adam's offers comfortable accommodation not far from York centre in the suburb of Fulford, close to the university. It has many fine period features, pleasant, well-proportioned bedrooms, and an attractive dining room. The resident owners are friendly and attentive.

Rooms 8 rms (7 en suite) (4 fmly) (2 GF) S £30-£35; D £68-£70* **Facilities** tea/coffee Cen ht **Parking** 8 **Notes** ⊗

Cumbria House

★★★ GUEST ACCOMMODATION

2 Vyner St, Haxby Rd YO31 8HS
☎ 01904 636817
e-mail: candj@cumbriahouse.freeserve.co.uk
web: www.cumbriahouse.com
dir: *A1237 onto B1363 S towards city centre, pass hospital, left at lights, 400yds on left*

Expect a warm welcome at this family-run guest house, which is ten minutes walk from the Minster. The attractive bedrooms are well furnished and equipped with many useful extras. Freshly-cooked breakfasts are served in the smart dining room at individual tables.

Rooms 6 rms (2 en suite) (2 fmly) **Facilities** tea/coffee Cen ht **Parking** 5 **Notes** LB ⊗

YORK *continued*

Dalescroft Guest House

★★★ GUEST HOUSE

10 South Lands Rd YO23 1NP
☎ 01904 626801 📠 01904 626801
e-mail: info@dalescroft-york.co.uk
web: www.dalescroft-york.co.uk
dir: *A64 until A1036 towards race course, right at Kwik-Fit onto Scarcroft Rd. Pass green on left, right onto Russell St, at top turn left onto Southlands Rd*

Originally built in 1908, this smartly appointed Victorian terrace house is located in a quiet residential area just ten minutes walk from the City of York. Bedrooms and bathrooms are comfortably furnished. Freshly cooked breakfasts are served at individual tables in the cosy dining room. Permits are available for the on-street parking.

Rooms 5 en suite (1 fmly) S £50-£55; D £60-£70 **Facilities** FTV tea/coffee Cen ht **Notes** LB No Children 12yrs

Greenside

★★★ GUEST HOUSE

124 Clifton YO30 6BQ
☎ 01904 623631 📠 01904 623631
e-mail: greenside@surfree.co.uk
web: www.greensideguesthouse.co.uk
dir: *A19 N towards city centre, over lights for Greenside, on left opp Clifton Green*

Overlooking Clifton Green, this detached house is just within walking distance of the city centre. Accommodation consists of simply furnished bedrooms and there is a cosy lounge and a dining room, where traditional breakfasts are served. It is a family home, and other families are welcome.

Rooms 6 rms (3 en suite) (2 fmly) (3 GF) S fr £30; D fr £56* **Facilities** TVL tea/coffee Cen ht Wi-fi **Parking** 6 **Notes** LB Closed Xmas & New Year 🐾

Jacobean Lodge

★★★ INN

Plainville Ln, Wigginton YO32 2RG
☎ 01904 762749
e-mail: matthewacdavison@hotmail.co.uk

This comfortable inn stands in extensive lawned gardens amid open farmland along a quiet lane and provides comfortable well-equipped bedrooms. Home-cooked meals are available in the pleasant bars or the restaurant, which are equally popular with locals and resident guests.

Rooms 8 en suite S fr £40; D fr £65* **Facilities** Dinner available **Parking**

Romley House

★★★ GUEST ACCOMMODATION

2 Mill Field Rd YO23 1NQ
☎ 01904 652822
e-mail: info@romleyhouse.co.uk

A Victorian terraced house situated on the west side of the city, within ten minutes walk of the railway station, racecourse and city centre. A wide choice of freshly cooked breakfasts are served in the dining room which also has a lounge area with satellite TV and complimentary tea and coffee.

Rooms 6 rms (2 en suite) S £32; D £54-£64* **Facilities** tea/coffee Cen ht **Notes** ⊗

St Georges

★★★ 🅰 GUEST ACCOMMODATION

6 St Georges Place, Tadcaster Rd YO24 1DR
☎ 01904 625056 📠 01904 625009
e-mail: sixstgeorg@aol.com
web: www.stgeorgesyork.com
dir: *A64 onto A1036 N to city centre, as racecourse ends, St Georges Place on left*

Rooms 10 en suite (5 fmly) (1 GF) S £35-£50; D £50-£65* **Facilities** tea/coffee Cen ht Wi-fi **Parking** 7 **Notes** LB Closed 20 Dec-2 Jan

HOOTON PAGNELL   Map 16 SE40

Rock Farm *(SE484081)*

★★★ 🏠 FARMHOUSE

DN5 7BT
☎ 01977 642200 & 07785 916 186
📠 01977 642200   Ms Harrison
e-mail: info@rockfarm.info
web: www.rockfarm.info
dir: *A1(M) junct 38, follow Wakefield signs. In 1m turn left, next left & left again. Farm 1st on right*

A few minutes from the A1, and located in the heart of this Domesday village beside "The Hostel" and the ancient butter cross, this working farmhouse offers well-equipped, spacious, beamed bedrooms and warm hospitality in a Grade II listed building with excellent fresh breakfasts.

Rooms 3 rms (1 en suite) (1 fmly) S £26-£35; D £50-£60* **Facilities** TVL tea/coffee Cen ht **Parking** 15 **Notes** ⊗ 🐾 200 acres horses/arable/beef

ROTHERHAM   Map 16 SK49

The Stonecroft

★★★★ GUEST ACCOMMODATION

138 Main St, Bramley S66 2SF
☎ 01709 540922 📠 01709 540922
e-mail: stonecrofthotel@btconnect.com
web: www.stonecrofthotel.com
dir: *3m E of Rotherham. Off A631 into Bramley village centre*

These converted stone cottages in the centre of Bramley provide a good base for visiting Rotherham or Sheffield. Some bedrooms are around a landscaped courtyard with private parking, and there is a lounge with a bar. Imaginative home-cooked meals are available.

Rooms 3 en suite 4 annexe en suite (1 fmly) (4 GF) S £50-£63; D £65-£80* **Facilities** FTV TVL tea/coffee Dinner available Cen ht Licensed Wi-fi **Parking** 7 **Notes** LB 🐾 Closed 25-26 Dec

Quarry House

★★★★ 🏠 GUEST HOUSE

Rivelin Glen Quarry, Rivelin Valley Rd S6 5SE
☎ 0114 234 0382 📠 0114 234 0382
e-mail: penelopeslack@aol.com
web: www.quarryhouse.org.uk
dir: *2.5m W of Sheffield. Off A6101 Rivelin Valley Rd at sharp bend, uphill to car park, signed*

A warm welcome is given at this delightful former quarry master's house in the picturesque Rivelin valley. Well-appointed bedrooms include many thoughtful extras. The tasty evening meals and comprehensive breakfasts have a strong organic influence, and there is a cosy lounge and a smart dining room.

Rooms 3 rms (2 en suite) (1 pri facs) (1 fmly) (1 GF)
Facilities TVL tea/coffee Dinner available Cen ht Wi-fi
Parking 8 **Notes** ⊜

Padley Farm B & B

★★★★ GUEST ACCOMMODATION

Dungworth Green S6 6HE
☎ 0114 285 1427 📠 0114 285 1427
e-mail: aandlmbestall@btinternet.com
web: www.padleyfarm.co.uk
dir: *M1 junct 33 follow ring road (A61 Barnsley), turn left onto B6077 signed Bradfield*

The barn conversion offers high quality en suite rooms with spectacular views of open countryside. An allergy free environment and warm hospitality ensure a pleasant stay.

Rooms 7 en suite (3 fmly) (2 GF) S £30-£37; D £54-£60*
Facilities FTV tea/coffee Cen ht Fishing Snooker **Conf** Max 15 Class 15 **Parking** 8 **Notes** LB ⊗

Westbourne House Guest Accommodation

★★★★ GUEST ACCOMMODATION

25 Westbourne Rd, Broomhill S10 2QQ
☎ 0114 266 0109 📠 0114 266 7778
e-mail: guests@westbournehousehotel.com
web: www.westbournehousehotel.com
dir: *A61 onto B6069 Glossop Rd, past university, after Hallamshire Hospital over lights, next left*

Westbourne House is a Victorian residence situated in beautiful gardens close to the university and hospitals. The modern bedrooms are individually furnished and decorated, and extremely well equipped. Wi-fi is available throughout the property. A comfortable lounge overlooks the terrace and garden.

Rooms 8 rms (7 en suite) (1 pri facs) (2 fmly) S £50-£75; D £79-£85* **Facilities** FTV tea/coffee Cen ht Licensed Wi-fi **Parking** 6 **Notes** ⊗ Closed Xmas

Wortley Hall

★★★ GUEST ACCOMMODATION

Worltey Village S35 7DB
☎ 0114 288 2100 📠 0114 283 0695
e-mail: info@wortleyhall.org.uk
dir: *Exit M1 junct 35a, straight over 2nd rdbt signed A616/Manchester. In 3m turn left to Wortley*

Standing in 26 acres of parkland, this listed country house has been in the custody of the Trades Union Movement for the last 50 years and displays much of their history. Bedrooms are mixed in size and quality, but all are comfortable and there are spacious day rooms reminiscent of the hall's original grandeur.

Rooms 49 en suite (7 fmly) (4 GF) **Facilities** TVL tea/coffee Dinner available Direct Dial Cen ht Lift Licensed Wi-fi **Conf** Thtr 150 Class 70 Board 30 **Parking** 60 **Notes** ⊗ Civ Wed 100

Shibden Mill

★★★★ INN

Shibden Mill Fold, Shibden HX3 7UL
☎ 01422 365840 📠 01422 362971
e-mail: enquiries@shibdenmillinn.com
web: www.shibdenmillinn.com
dir: *3m NE of Halifax off A58*

Nestling in a fold of Shibden Dale, this 17th-century inn features exposed beams and open fires. Guests can dine well in the two lounge-style bars, the restaurant, or outside in summer. The stylish bedrooms come in a variety of sizes, and all are thoughtfully equipped and have access to a free video library. Service is friendly and obliging.

Rooms 11 en suite (1 GF) **Facilities** FTV tea/coffee Dinner available Direct Dial Cen ht Wi-fi **Conf** Max 50 Thtr 50 Class 21 Board 24 **Parking** 100

Weavers Restaurant with Rooms

★★★ ⚜ RESTAURANT WITH ROOMS

13/17 West Ln BD22 8DU
☎ 01535 643822 📠 01535 644832
e-mail: weaversltd@btconnect.com
dir: *In village centre. Pass Brontë Weaving Shed on right, 100yds left to Parsonage car park*

Centrally located on the cobbled main street, this family-owned restaurant with rooms provides well-equipped, stylish and comfortable accommodation. Each of the three rooms is en suite and has many thoughtful extras. The kitchen serves both modern and traditional dishes with flair and creativity.

Rooms 3 en suite S £59.50; D £89.50-£99.50*
Facilities FTV tea/coffee Dinner available Direct Dial Cen ht Wi-fi **Notes** ⊗ Closed 24 Dec-10 Jan RS Sun & Mon No arrivals/restaurant

Holme House

★★★★★ 🅰 BED AND BREAKFAST

New Rd HX7 8AD
☎ 01422 847588 📠 01422 847354
e-mail: mail@holmehousehebdenbridge.co.uk
dir: *On A646 New Rd, in centre of Hebden Bridge, at junct with Holme St*

Rooms 3 en suite (1 fmly) (2 GF) S £55; D £70-£90*
Facilities tea/coffee Cen ht Wi-fi **Conf** Max 10 Board 10
Parking 6 **Notes** ⊗

HEBDEN BRIDGE *continued*

Moyles

★★★★ ⊕ RESTAURANT WITH ROOMS

6-10 New Rd HX7 8AD
☎ 01422 845272 🖹 01422 847663
e-mail: enquire@moyles.com
dir: *A646 to Hebden Bridge, opposite marina*

Centrally located in the charming town of Hebden Bridge, this Victorian building has been modernised to offer a high standard of contemporary accommodation. Fresh, local produce features on the imaginative menus served in the bar and in the restaurant. There's a relaxing ambience throughout.

Rooms 12 en suite (6 fmly) S £69-£119; D £79-£129*
Facilities FTV tea/coffee Dinner available Cen ht Wi-fi
Conf Max 12 Thtr 12 Class 12 Board 12 **Notes** ⊗

HOLMFIRTH   Map 16 SE10

Uppergate Farm

★★★★ 🄰 GUEST ACCOMMODATION

Hepworth HD9 1TG
☎ 01484 681369 🖹 01484 687343
e-mail: info@uppergatefarm.co.uk
dir: *0.5m off A616*

Rooms 2 en suite (1 fmly) S £50; D £75* **Facilities** TVL tea/coffee Cen ht Wi-fi 🄲 Sauna Pool Table Table tennis **Parking** 6 **Notes** LB ⊗

HUDDERSFIELD   Map 16 SE11

Weavers Shed Restaurant with Rooms

★★★★ ⊕⊕ 🛋 RESTAURANT WITH ROOMS

86-88 Knowl Rd, Golcar HD7 4AN
☎ 01484 654284 🖹 01484 650980
e-mail: info@weaversshed.co.uk
web: www.weaversshed.co.uk
dir: *3m W of Huddersfield. A62 onto B6111 to Milnsbridge & Scar Ln to Golcar, right onto Knowl Rd, signed Colne Valley Museum*

This converted house has spacious bedrooms named after local textile mills; all are extremely well equipped. An inviting bar-lounge leads into the well known restaurant where fresh produce, much from the establishment's own gardens, forms the basis of excellent meals.

Rooms 5 en suite (2 GF) S fr £80; D fr £100*
Facilities tea/coffee Dinner available Direct Dial Cen ht **Conf** Max 16 Board 16 **Parking** 20 **Notes** LB ⊗ Closed Xmas/New Year No coaches

The Huddersfield Central Lodge

★★★★ GUEST ACCOMMODATION

11/15 Beast Market HD1 1QF
☎ 01484 515551 🖹 01484 432349
e-mail: enquiries@centrallodge.com
web: www.centrallodge.com
dir: *In town centre off Lord St, signs for Beast Market from ring road*

This friendly, family-run operation offers smart spacious bedrooms with modern en suites. Some rooms are in the main building, while new rooms, many with kitchenettes, are situated across a courtyard. Public rooms include a bar and a conservatory, and there are arrangements for local restaurants to charge meals to guests' accounts. Secure complimentary parking.

Rooms 9 en suite 13 annexe en suite (2 fmly) (6 smoking) S £52-£58; D £68* **Facilities** STV TVL tea/coffee Direct Dial Cen ht Licensed Wi-fi **Parking** 50

The Woodman Inn

★★★★ INN

Thunderbridge Ln HD8 0PX
☎ 01484 605778 🖹 01484 604110
e-mail: thewoodman@connectfree.co.uk
web: www.woodman-inn.co.uk

(For full entry see Kirkburton)

Griffin Lodge Guest House

★★★ GUEST HOUSE

273 Manchester Rd HD4 5AG
☎ 01484 431042 🖹 01484 431043
e-mail: info@griffinlodge.co.uk
web: www.griffinlodge.co.uk

Located on the outskirts of Huddersfield and close to the villages of Holmfirth and Marsden, Griffin Lodge is family run and offers comfortable well appointed accommodation. Hearty breakfasts are served in the small dining room and there is secure parking to the rear.

Rooms 6 en suite (4 fmly) (6 GF) **Facilities** FTV tea/coffee Cen ht Wi-fi **Parking** 10

KIRKBURTON   Map 16 SE11

The Woodman Inn

★★★★ INN

Thunderbridge Ln HD8 0PX
☎ 01484 605778 🖹 01484 604110
e-mail: thewoodman@connectfree.co.uk
dir: *1m SW of Kirkburton. Off A629 in Thunderbridge*

The Woodman offers traditional innkeeping and is extremely popular with locals. The air-conditioned restaurant holds an extensive range of wines, while the popular bar offers a wide selection of ales and lagers. Bedrooms are comfortable and comprehensively furnished, making this an ideal base for walking, visiting the National Mining Museum, or simply escaping to the country.

Rooms 12 en suite (3 GF) **Facilities** tea/coffee Dinner available Direct Dial Cen ht Pool Table **Conf** Max 60 Thtr 50 Class 60 Board 30 **Parking** 50 **Notes** ⊗

MARSDEN   Map 16 SE01

The Olive Branch Restaurant with Rooms

★★★★ ⊕ RESTAURANT WITH ROOMS

Manchester Rd HD7 6LU
☎ 01484 844487
e-mail: mail@olivebranch.uk.com
web: www.olivebranch.uk.com
dir: *1m NE of Marsden on A62*

The Olive Branch, once a roadside inn, was developed into a popular restaurant with three comfortable bedrooms. The menu features the best of seasonal produce cooked with flair and enthusiasm. The surrounding countryside has many historic attractions and pleasant walking.

Rooms 3 en suite S £45-£55; D £70 (room only)
Facilities tea/coffee Dinner available Direct Dial Cen ht **Parking** 25 **Notes** ⊗ Closed 2-17 Jan No coaches

OSSETT
Map 16 SE22

Heath House

★★★★ GUEST ACCOMMODATION

Chancery Rd WF5 9RZ
☎ 01924 260654 📄 01924 263131
e-mail: jo.holland@amserve.net
web: www.heath-house.co.uk
dir: M1 junct 40, A638 towards Dewsbury, at end dual carriageway exit rdbt 2nd left, house 20yds on right

The spacious Victorian family home stands in four acres of tranquil gardens a short distance from the M1. It has elegant en suite bedrooms, and the courteous and friendly owners provide healthy, freshly-cooked breakfasts.

Rooms 2 en suite 2 annexe en suite (1 fmly) (2 GF)
S £25-£40; D £40-£52* Facilities tea/coffee Cen ht
Fishing small farm, sheep, hens, rabbits & ferrets
Parking 16

PONTEFRACT
Map 16 SE42

Wentvale

★★★★ GUEST ACCOMMODATION

Great North Rd, Knottingley WF11 8PF
☎ 01977 676714
e-mail: wentvale1@btconnect.com
dir: 1.5m NE of Pontefract. Off A1 S for A645, sharp right

Original features at this welcoming Victorian house include the stained-glass front door and a panelled hall. Double-glazing in the attractive, well-equipped bedrooms provides effective sound insulation. There is an elegant lounge and a charming dining room where hearty breakfasts are served.

Rooms 8 en suite 3 annexe en suite (4 GF) S £39; D £58*
Facilities TVL tea/coffee Cen ht Wi-fi Parking 15
Notes ⊗ No Children 12yrs Closed Xmas & New Year

WAKEFIELD
Map 16 SE32

Midgley Lodge Motel and Golf Course

★★★★ 🅐 GUEST ACCOMMODATION

Barr Ln, Midgley WF4 4JJ
☎ 01924 830069 📄 01924 830087
e-mail: midgleylodgemotel@tiscali.co.uk
dir: SW of Wakefield. M1 junct 38, A637 Huddersfield road to Midgley

Rooms 25 en suite (10 fmly) (13 GF) S £48; D £56 (room only)* Facilities STV TVL tea/coffee Direct Dial Cen ht Licensed Golf 9 Parking 90 Notes ⊗ Closed 25 Dec-2 Jan

Stanley View

★★★ GUEST HOUSE

226-230 Stanley Rd WF1 4AE
☎ 01924 376803 📄 01924 369123
e-mail: enquiries@stanleyviewguesthouse.co.uk
dir: M62 junct 30, follow Aberford Rd 3m. Signed on left

Part of an attractive terrace, this well established guest house is just half a mile from the city centre and has private parking at the rear. The well equipped bedrooms are brightly decorated, and there is a licensed bar and comfortable lounge. Hearty, home-cooked meals are served in the attractive dining room.

Rooms 17 rms (13 en suite) (6 fmly) (7 GF) Facilities STV TVL tea/coffee Dinner available Direct Dial Cen ht Licensed Parking 10

CHANNEL ISLANDS
JERSEY

ST AUBIN
Map 24

PREMIER COLLECTION

The Panorama
★★★★★ GUEST ACCOMMODATION

La Rue du Crocquet JE3 8BZ
☎ 01534 742429 📄 01534 745940
e-mail: info@panoramajersey.com
web: www.panoramajersey.com
dir: In village centre

Having spectacular views across St Aubin's Bay, the Panorama is a long-established favourite with visitors. The welcome is genuine and many of the well-equipped bedrooms have wonderful views; most bathrooms are newly upgraded. Public areas also look seaward and have attractive antique fireplaces. Breakfast is excellent and served in two dining areas.

Rooms 14 en suite (3 GF) S £44-£68; D £88-£135
Facilities STV tea/coffee Cen ht Wi-fi Notes ⊗ No Children 18yrs Closed mid Oct-mid Apr

Peterborough House

★★★ GUEST ACCOMMODATION

La Rue du Croquet JE3 8BZ
☎ 01534 741568 📄 01534 746787
e-mail: fernando@localdial.com
dir: A13 to St Aubin, left at La Haule Slip, 1st left. Left fork, half way down on left

Situated on the old St Aubin high street, this well-presented guest house dates back to 1690. The bedrooms are comfortably appointed and the sea-facing rooms are always in high demand. One of the two lounge areas has a bar, or guests can enjoy the view with a drink on the outdoor terrace. Breakfast has a choice of traditional and continental options.

Rooms 14 rms (12 en suite) (1 fmly) (2 GF) S £29.50-£39.70; D £49-£69.40* Facilities TVL tea/coffee Cen ht Licensed Notes LB ⊗ No Children 12yrs Closed Nov-Feb

ST HELIER — Map 24

Bay View Guest House

★★★★ GUEST ACCOMMODATION

12 Havre des Pas JE2 4UQ
☎ **01534 720950 & 07797 720100** 📄 **01532 720950**
e-mail: bayview.guesthouse@jerseymail.co.uk
dir: *Through tunnel, right at rdbt, down Green St & left, 100yds on left*

The Bay View is located across the road from the Havre des Pas Lido and beach, and just a ten minute walk from the centre of St Helier. Bedrooms are well equipped, and extra facilities include a bar and a television lounge with free Wi-fi internet access. There is a small garden terrace to the front of the establishment.

Rooms 13 rms (12 pri facs) (3 fmly) S £28-£48; D £60-£96* **Facilities** TVL tea/coffee Cen ht Licensed Wi-fi **Notes** LB ⊗

ISLE OF MAN

DOUGLAS — Map 24 SC37

Dreem Ard

★★★★ BED AND BREAKFAST

Ballanard Rd IM2 5PR
☎ **01624 621491** 📄 **01624 621491**
dir: *From St Ninian's Church along Ballanard Rd for 1m, over Johnny Watterson Ln x-rds, past farm on left, Dreem Ard on left*

Dreem Ard is a relaxing sanctuary, with superb views over the glens just to the north of Douglas. Bedrooms are spacious and well equipped, and the caring hosts are genuinely hospitable and attentive. Breakfast and dinner are served around a large table, where good food and good company go hand-in-hand.

Rooms 3 en suite (1 fmly) (2 GF) **Facilities** STV tea/coffee Dinner available Cen ht **Parking** 6 **Notes** ⊗ No Children 8yrs 🚭

All Seasons

★★★ Ⓐ GUEST HOUSE

11 Clifton Ter, Broadway IM2 3HX
☎ **0871 855 0603** 📄 **0871 855 0603**
e-mail: hansonsales@pilogene.co.uk
dir: *Off Central Promenade at Villa Marina, premises in 1st row of hotels on left*

Rooms 6 rms (4 en suite) (2 pri facs) (6 fmly) S £29.50-£55; D £54-£110* **Facilities** TVL tea/coffee Dinner available Cen ht Licensed Wi-fi 🛈 **Notes** LB ⊗ No Children 12yrs

---

PEEL — Map 24 SC28

Albany House Bed and Breakfast

★★★★ BED AND BREAKFAST

9 Albany Rd IM5 1JS
☎ **07624 483866**
e-mail: albanyhouseiom@msn.com
dir: *A1 from Douglas, on entering Peel turn right onto Albany Rd, last terraced house on right*

This charming red brick Victorian terraced house is conveniently situated overlooking the town of Peel with its maze of narrow streets. This period house has been sympathetically restored and public areas include a light-filled dining room and a stylish lounge with a real fire. The bedrooms are attractively presented and equipped with a host of thoughtful extras. Wi-fi is available. This is an ideal base from which to explore the island.

Rooms 3 en suite S £45-£65; D £60-£85 **Facilities** STV FTV TVL tea/coffee Dinner available Cen ht Wi-fi **Notes** LB ⊗

PORT ST MARY — Map 24 SC26

PREMIER COLLECTION

Aaron House

★★★★★ 🛈 GUEST HOUSE

The Promenade IM9 5DE
☎ **01624 835702** 📄 **01624 837731**
web: www.aaronhouse.co.uk
dir: *Follow signs for South & Port St Mary, left at Post Office. House in centre of Promenade*

Aaron House is truly individual. From the parlour down to the detail of the cast-iron baths, the house, overlooking the harbour, has been restored to its Victorian origins. The family work hard to offer the best quality, whether its providing luxury and comfort in the bedrooms or even to offering home-made cakes on arrival.

Rooms 4 rms (3 en suite) (1 pri facs) D £70-£118* **Facilities** TV1B TVL tea/coffee Cen ht **Notes** LB ⊗ No Children 12yrs Closed 21 Dec-3 Jan 🚭

ST JOHN'S — Map 24 SC28

Glen Helen Inn

★★★★ 🍽 INN

Glen Helen IM4 3NP
☎ **01624 801294** 📄 **01624 803294**
e-mail: info@glenheleninn.com
web: www.glenheleninn.com

This charming inn is in a glorious location in the heart of the island and close to some lovely country walks. Bedrooms are all very well planned and have a contemporary appearance. The stylish bar is ideal for pre-dinner drinks and there is also a popular restaurant which serves a wide range dishes.

Rooms 14 en suite (3 fmly) **Facilities** tea/coffee Dinner available Cen ht Wi-fi **Conf** Max 80 Thtr 80 Class 24 Board 40 **Parking** 70 **Notes** LB

Scotland

Pap of Glen Coe and Loch Leven

CITY OF ABERDEEN

ABERDEEN
Map 23 NJ90

The Jays Guest House

★★★★ GUEST HOUSE

422 King St AB24 3BR
☎ 01224 638295   📠 01224 638360
e-mail: alice@jaysguesthouse.co.uk
web: www.jaysguesthouse.co.uk
dir: *A90 from S onto Main St & Union St & A92 to King St N*

Guests are warmly welcomed to this attractive granite house on the north side of the city. Maintained in first-class order throughout, it offers attractive bedrooms, smartly furnished to appeal to business guests and tourists. Freshly prepared breakfasts are enjoyed in the carefully appointed dining room.

Rooms 10 rms (8 en suite) (2 pri facs) (1 GF) S £50-£60; D £90-£120* **Facilities** STV FTV tea/coffee Cen ht Wi-fi **Parking** 9 **Notes** ⊗ No Children 12yrs Closed mid Dec-mid Jan

Arkaig

★★★ GUEST HOUSE

43 Powis Ter AB25 3PP
☎ 01224 638872   📠 01224 622189
e-mail: info@arkaig.co.uk
dir: *On A96 at junct with Bedford Rd*

A friendly welcome and relaxed atmosphere is assured at this well-presented guest house, situated on the north side of the city close to the university and city centre. Bedrooms vary in size, are attractively decorated and are all thoughtfully equipped to appeal to business and leisure guests. There is a cosy sun lounge with magazines, and an attractive breakfast room where delicious freshly cooked breakfasts are served. Parking is also available.

Rooms 8 rms (6 en suite) (1 fmly) (5 GF) **Facilities** TVL tea/coffee Direct Dial Cen ht **Parking** 10

PETERCULTER
Map 23 NJ80

Furain

★★★ 🅰 GUEST HOUSE

92 North Deeside Rd AB14 0QN
☎ 01224 732189   📠 01224 739070
e-mail: furain@btinternet.com
dir: *7m W of city centre on A93*

Rooms 8 en suite (2 fmly) (3 GF) S £45-£50; D £56-£65* **Facilities** FTV tea/coffee Cen ht Wi-fi **Parking** 7 **Notes** Closed Xmas & New Year

ABERDEENSHIRE

BALLATER
Map 23 NO39

The Green Inn

★★★★ ⚜⚜ RESTAURANT WITH ROOMS

9 Victoria Rd AB35 5QQ
☎ 013397 55701
e-mail: info@green-inn.com
web: www.green-inn.com
dir: *In village centre*

A former temperance hotel, the Green Inn enjoys a central location in the pretty village of Ballater. Bedrooms are of a high standard and attractively presented. The restaurant has a strong reputation for its fine cuisine, which can be enjoyed in the stylish conservatory restaurant. Breakfast is equally enjoyable and not to be missed. Genuine hospitality from the enthusiastic proprietors is a real feature of any stay.

Rooms 3 en suite S £50-£60; D £70-£90 **Facilities** FTV TVL tea/coffee Dinner available Cen ht Wi-fi **Notes** Closed 1st 2wks Nov, last 2wks Jan No coaches

The Auld Kirk

★★★★ ⚜ RESTAURANT WITH ROOMS

Braemar Rd AB35 5RQ
☎ 01339 755762   & 07918 698000   📠 0700 6037 559
e-mail: info@theauldkirk.com
dir: *From A93 Braemar, on right just before town centre*

A Victorian Scottish Free Church building that is now a contemporary restaurant with rooms boasting newly refurbished and well-appointed bedrooms and bathrooms. Many original features of this kirk have been restored and incorporated in the design. The Spirit Restaurant with its high ceilings and tall windows provides a wonderful setting to enjoy the award-winning, seasonal food. There is a stylish bar with a good selection of malts and a terrace for alfresco eating when the weather permits.

Rooms 7 en suite (1 fmly) S £67.50-£85; D £100-£130* **Facilities** FTV tea/coffee Dinner available Direct Dial Cen ht Wi-fi **Conf** Max 25 Thtr 25 Class 18 Board 16 **Parking** 7 **Notes** RS Sun closed No coaches

BRAEMAR
Map 23 NO19

Callater Lodge Guest House

★★★★ GUEST HOUSE

9 Glenshee Rd AB35 5YQ
☎ 013397 41275
e-mail: info@hotel-braemar.co.uk
web: www.callaterlodge.co.uk
dir: *Next to A93, 300yds S of Braemar centre*

Located in the picturesque village of Braemar, a very well presented property under the new ownership of the Shores. Bedrooms are comfortable with many thoughtful extras provided as standard. Public areas are welcoming with a home-away-from-home feel. Breakfast is served on individual tables with local quality ingredients used. The gardens are a very pleasant feature.

Rooms 6 en suite (1 fmly) S £38-£40; D £72-£74* **Facilities** tea/coffee Cen ht Licensed **Parking** 6 **Notes** ⊗ Closed Xmas

INVERURIE
Map 23 NJ72

Kintore Arms

★★★★ INN

83 High St AB51 3QJ
☎ 01467 621367   📠 01467 625620
e-mail: manager.kintore@ohiml.com
web: www.oxfordhotelsandinns.com
dir: *From A96 at rdbt turn signed Inverurie, onto main High St, on left*

Well situated within easy walking distance from the town centre and benefiting from off-road parking, this traditional inn is currently undergoing a programme of refurbishment. The good-sized bedrooms are thoughtfully equipped for the modern traveller. Regular evening entertainment is provided.

Rooms 28 en suite (1 fmly) S £65; D £75-£85* **Facilities** FTV TVL tea/coffee Dinner available Cen ht Wi-fi **Conf** Max 150 Thtr 150 Class 75 Board 75 **Parking** 30 **Notes** C v Wed 150

OLDMELDRUM
Map 23 NJ82

Cromlet Hill

★★★★ 🅰 BED AND BREAKFAST

South Rd AB51 0AB
☎ 01651 872315   📠 01651 872164
e-mail: johnpage@cromlethill.co.uk
dir: *In town centre*

Rooms 3 en suite (1 fmly) S £36-£45; D £56-£70* **Facilities** FTV TVL tea/coffee Cen ht **Parking** 4 **Notes** ⊗ 🚲

STONEHAVEN   Map 23 NO88

Woodside Of Glasslaw

★★★★ GUEST ACCOMMODATION

AB39 3XQ
☎ 01569 763799   📄 01569 763799
e-mail: aileenpaton@hotmail.com
dir: *A90 N, 1st sign for Stonehaven, at end turn right, next left*

A warm welcome is assured at this charming guest house, which has a rural setting, yet close to major road network. The stylish bedrooms are all spacious and attractively presented. Freshly prepared breakfasts are served at individual tables and the new conservatory lounge is spacious and most comfortable. Wi-fi is available.

Rooms 6 en suite (1 fmly) (4 GF) S fr £40; D £60-£65 **Facilities** TVL tea/coffee Cen ht Wi-fi Small fitness room **Parking** 6 **Notes** Closed Xmas

ANGUS

INVERKEILOR   Map 23 NO64

Gordon's

★★★★ @@ 🍴 RESTAURANT WITH ROOMS

Main St DD11 5RN
☎ 01241 830364   📄 01241 830364
e-mail: gordonsrest@aol.com
dir: *Off A92, follow signs for Inverkeilor*

It's worth a detour off the main road to this family-run restaurant with rooms set in the centre of the village. It has earned AA Rosettes for its dinners, though the excellent breakfasts are equally memorable. A huge fire dominates the restaurant on cooler evenings and there is a small lounge with limited seating. The attractive bedrooms are tastefully decorated and thoughtfully equipped, the larger two being furnished in pine.

Rooms 4 en suite 1 annexe en suite (1 GF) S £75; D £90-£120 **Facilities** TV3B FTV Dinner available Cen ht **Parking** 6 **Notes** ⊗ No Children 12yrs Closed 2wks Jan No coaches

MONTROSE   Map 23 NO75

Oaklands

★★★ GUEST HOUSE

10 Rossie Island Rd DD10 9NN
☎ 01674 672018   📄 01674 672018
e-mail: oaklands1@btopenworld.com
dir: *On A92 at S end of town*

A genuine welcome and attentive service are assured at this smart detached house situated on the south side of the town. Bedrooms come in a variety of sizes and are neatly presented. There is a lounge on the ground floor next to the attractive dining room, where hearty breakfasts are served. Motorcycle guided tours can be

arranged with tourists travelling with their own motorbikes.

Rooms 7 en suite (1 fmly) (1 GF) S £30-£40; D £60-£75* **Facilities** FTV TVL tea/coffee Cen ht Wi-fi **Parking** 8 **Notes** ⊗

ARGYLL & BUTE

APPIN   Map 20 NM94

Pineapple House

★★★★ 🚄 GUEST HOUSE

Duror PA38 4BP
☎ 01631 740557   📄 01631 740557
e-mail: info@pineapplehouse.co.uk
web: www.pineapplehouse.co.uk
dir: *In Duror, off A828. 5m S of A82*

Ideally located just south of Glencoe and just north of Appin. This period farmhouse has been lovingly restored and is extremely well presented using a great mix of modern and traditional. Dinners are available on request and use the best local quality produce. Service is friendly and genuine making for a wonderful base to tour this area of Scotland.

Rooms 6 en suite (1 fmly) S £35-£40; D £70-£95 **Facilities** FTV tea/coffee Dinner available Cen ht Wi-fi **Parking** 10 **Notes** ⊗ No Children 7yrs

CAIRNDOW   Map 20 NN11

Cairndow Stagecoach Inn

★★★ INN

PA26 8BN
☎ 01499 600286 & 600252   📄 01499 600252
e-mail: enq@cairndowinn.com
dir: *From N, take either A82 to Tarbet, A83 to Cairndow, or A85 to Palmally, A819 to Inverary & A83 to Cairndow*

A relaxed, friendly atmosphere prevails at this 18th-century inn, overlooking the beautiful Loch Fyne. Bedrooms offer individual decor and thoughtful extras.Traditional public areas include a comfortable beamed lounge, a well-stocked bar where food is served throughout the day, and a spacious restaurant with conservatory extension. New deluxe bedrooms are currently being built to offer more space and luxury.

Rooms 13 en suite 5 annexe en suite (2 fmly) (5 GF) S £35-£85; D £65-£140* **Facilities** STV FTV tea/coffee Dinner available Direct Dial Cen ht Wi-fi Sauna Solarium **Conf** Max 30 Thtr 30 Class 30 Board 30 **Notes** LB

CARDROSS   Map 20 NS37

PREMIER COLLECTION

Kirkton House

★★★★★ GUEST ACCOMMODATION

Darleith Rd G82 5EZ
☎ 01389 841951   📄 01389 841868
e-mail: aa@kirktonhouse.co.uk
web: www.kirktonhouse.co.uk
dir: *0.5m N of village. Turn N off A814 onto Darleith Rd at W end of village. Kirkton House 0.5m on right*

Dating from the 18th century, this converted farmstead around an attractive courtyard has stunning views over the Clyde estuary from its elevated location. The individually styled bedrooms are well equipped and generally spacious, with two on the ground floor. Stone walls and large fireplaces feature in public areas, and wide choice of breakfasts using fresh produce are served in the delightful dining room.

Rooms 6 en suite (4 fmly) (2 GF) S £30-£45; D £60-£70 **Facilities** FTV TVL tea/coffee Direct Dial Cen ht Wi-fi Internet Cafe Riding **Parking** 10 **Notes** LB Closed Dec-Jan

CARRADALE   Map 20 NR83

Dunvalanree

★★★★ @ GUEST ACCOMMODATION

Port Righ Bay PA28 6SE
☎ 01583 431226
e-mail: stay@dunvalanree.com
web: www.dunvalanree.com
dir: *From centre of Carradale, turn right at x-rds, continue to end of road*

Set in stunning scenery on the Mull of Kintyre, Dunvalanree has been welcoming guests for over 70

continued

CARRADALE *continued*

years. The restaurant menu, which has earned an AA Rosette, uses local seafood and farm produce. Standing in delightful gardens on the edge of Port Righ Bay, the house enjoys splendid views over Kilbrannan Sound to the Isle of Arran.

Rooms 5 en suite (1 GF); D £142-£172* (incl.dinner) **Facilities** tea/coffee Dinner available Cen ht Licensed Wi-fi Golf 9 ⚑ Fishing **Parking** 8 Notes LB ⊗

CONNEL   Map 20 NM93

PREMIER COLLECTION

Ards House
★★★★★ 🛏 GUEST HOUSE

PA37 1PT
☎ 01631 710255 📄 01631 710857
e-mail: info@ardshouse.com
web: www.ardshouse.com
dir: On A85, 4m N of Oban

This delightful Victorian villa on the approaches to Loch Etive has stunning views over the Firth of Lorne and the Morven Hills beyond. The stylish bedrooms come with added touches such as home-made shortbread and mineral water. There is an inviting drawing room complete with piano, games and books, plus a fire on cooler evenings. The attractive dining room is the setting for delicious breakfasts.

Rooms 4 en suite **Facilities** FTV TVL tea/coffee Cen ht **Parking** 12 **Notes** LB ⊗ No Children 10yrs Closed mid Dec-mid Jan

Ronebhal Guest House
★★★★ GUEST HOUSE

PA37 1PJ
☎ 01631 710310 📄 01631 710310
e-mail: info@ronebhal.co.uk
dir: A85, W from village centre, 4th house after turn for Fort William

The Strachan family extends a friendly welcome to their lovely detached home, which has pleasant gardens and stunning views of Loch Etive. The bedrooms are well equipped and comfortably furnished in modern styles. There is a sitting room, and an attractive dining room where hearty traditional breakfasts are served at individual tables.

Rooms 5 rms (4 en suite) (1 pri facs) (1 fmly) (1 GF) S £25-£35; D £54-£90 **Facilities** FTV TVL tea/coffee Cen ht Wi-fi **Parking** 6 **Notes** LB ⊗ No Children 7yrs Closed Nov-Feb

HELENSBURGH   Map 20 NS28

See also Cardross

PREMIER COLLECTION

Lethamhill
★★★★★ GUEST ACCOMMODATION

West Dhuhill Dr G84 9AW
☎ 01436 676016 & 07974 798593
📄 01436 676016
e-mail: lethamhill@talk21.com
web: www.lethamhill.co.uk
dir: 1m N of pier/town centre. Off A818 onto West Dhuhill Dr. Cross Upper Colcough St, then 3rd entrance on right

From the red phone box in the garden to the old typewriters and slot machines inside, this fine house is an Aladdin's cave of unusual collectibles and memorabilia. The house itself offers spacious and comfortable bedrooms with superb bathrooms. The home-cooked breakfasts and delicious baking earn much praise.

Rooms 3 en suite S £65-£85; D fr £85* **Facilities** TVL tea/coffee Cen ht Wi-fi **Parking** 6 **Notes** LB ⊗

KILMARTIN   Map 20 NR89

Ford House
★★★ 🅐 GUEST ACCOMMODATION

PA31 8RH
☎ 01546 810273
e-mail: info@ford-house.com
Rooms 6 rms (5 en suite) (1 pri facs) (1 fmly) S £30-£37; D £56-£60* **Facilities** STV TVL tea/coffee Cen ht Licensed **Parking** 7 **Notes** LB ⊗ 🚫

LUSS   Map 20 NS39

The Inn at Inverbeg
★★★★ 🛏 INN

Inverbeg G83 8PD
☎ 01436 860678 📄 01436 860203
e-mail: inverbeg.reception@loch-lomond.co.uk
dir: On A82, N of Balloch

Dating back to the 18th century this inn offers very stylish, comfortable bedrooms, bathrooms and equally stylish public areas that boast open fires and cow-hide sofas. Food is as much as a feature as the property itself, serving unusual but quality dishes including deep fried Mars bars and Irn Bru sorbet. The Beach House accommodation is a real treat for that special occasion.

Rooms 12 en suite 8 annexe en suite (1 fmly) (5 GF) S £89-£149; D £99-£159* **Facilities** STV FTV TVL tea/coffee Dinner available Cen ht Wi-fi **Parking** 60 **Notes** LB ⊗ Civ Wed 60

OBAN   Map 20 NM82

PREMIER COLLECTION

Blarcreen House
★★★★★ 🛏 GUEST HOUSE

Ardchattan, Connel PA37 1RG
☎ 01631 750272
e-mail: info@blarcreenhouse.com
web: www.blarcreenhouse.com
dir: 9.5m NE of Oban. N over Connel Bridge, 1st right, 7m, pass church & Ardchattan Priory Gardens. Blarcreen House 2m

Built in 1886 this elegant Victorian farmhouse stands on the shores of Loch Etive and has lovely views of the surrounding mountains. Bedrooms are beautifully furnished and very well equipped. There is a comfortable drawing room with deep sofas, a plentiful supply of books and videos, and a log-burning fire. Delicious home-cooked fare featuring the very best of local produce is served in the dining room. Hospitality is strong and the atmosphere relaxed in this charming house.

Rooms 3 en suite S £66-£75; D £92-£110* **Facilities** STV TVL tea/coffee Dinner available Cen ht Licensed Wi-fi **Parking** 5 **Notes** LB ⊗ No Children 16yrs

Glenburnie House

★★★★ GUEST HOUSE

The Esplanade PA34 5AQ
☎ 01631 562089 📠 01631 562089
e-mail: graeme.strachan@btinternet.com
dir: On Oban seafront. Follow signs for Ganavan

This impressive seafront Victorian house has been lovingly restored to a high standard. Bedrooms (including a four-poster room and a mini-suite) are beautifully decorated and very well equipped. There is a cosy ground-floor lounge and an elegant dining room, where hearty traditional breakfasts are served at individual tables.

Rooms 12 en suite (2 GF) S £45-£50; D £80-£100*
Facilities FTV tea/coffee Cen ht Wi-fi **Parking** 12
Notes LB ⊗ No Children 12yrs Closed Nov-Mar

Alltavona House

★★★★ GUEST HOUSE

Corran Esplanade PA34 5AQ
☎ 01631 565067 & 07771 708301 📠 01631 565067
e-mail: carol@alltavona.co.uk
dir: From Oban centre along seafront past cathedral, 5th house from end of Esplanade

Alltavona is an elegant Victorian villa with a delightful location on the Corran Esplanade with stunning views over Oban Bay to the islands of Lismore and Kererra. The attractive bedrooms are individually styled and feature quality furnishings. Delicious breakfasts featuring the best of local produce are served in the charming dining room.

Rooms 6 en suite (3 fmly) **Facilities** tea/coffee Cen ht **Parking** 6 **Notes** ⊗ No Children 12yrs Closed 12-30 Dec

Braeside

★★★★ GUEST HOUSE

Kilmore PA34 4QR
☎ 01631 770243 📠 01631 770343
e-mail: braeside.guesthouse@virgin.net
web: www.braesideguesthouse.net
dir: On A816 5m from Oban

The family-run bungalow stands in gardens overlooking the spectacular Loch Feochan. Bedrooms, all en suite, are bright and airy, well equipped and have easy access. The lounge-dining room has a loch view, a bar with a range of single malts and wines, and offers a varied choice of tasty home-cooked evening meals and breakfasts.

Rooms 5 en suite (1 fmly) (5 GF) S £30-£35; D £60-£70*
Facilities tea/coffee Dinner available Cen ht Licensed Wi-fi **Parking** 6 **Notes** LB ⊗ No Children 8yrs

Corriemar House

★★★★ GUEST HOUSE

Corran Esplanade PA34 5AQ
☎ 01631 562476 📠 01631 564339
e-mail: info@corriemarhouse.co.uk
web: www.corriemarhouse.co.uk
dir: A85 to Oban. Down hill in right lane & follow sign for Gamavan at mini rdbt onto Esplanade

Billy and Sandra Russell have created a stylish haven of tranquillity at this detached Victorian house close to the town centre. Bedrooms are furnished with panache, range from massive to cosy, and even include a suite. Those to the front of the house have stunning views across Oban Bay to the Isle of Mull. Expect a substantial breakfast and friendly attentive service.

Rooms 9 en suite 4 annexe en suite (3 fmly) (1 GF)
Facilities tea/coffee Cen ht **Parking** 9 **Notes** ⊗

Greencourt

★★★★ GUEST HOUSE

Benvoullin Rd PA34 5EF
☎ 01631 563987
e-mail: relax@greencourt-oban.co.uk
dir: At Oban, left at Kings Knoll Hotel, over x-rds, follow Dalriach Rd. Pass leisure centre & bowling green on left, then left. Left again, sharp left onto lane, Greencourt 2nd house on left

This welcoming family home stands on an elevated location overlooking the bowling green and leisure centre. The delightful detached house has attractive, comfortable bedrooms of varying sizes, and all are well equipped. Freshly prepared breakfasts are served in the bright airy dining room, which has lovely views.

Rooms 6 rms (5 en suite) (1 pri facs) (6 GF) S £35-£38; D £70-£76 **Facilities** tea/coffee Cen ht Wi-fi **Parking** 6 **Notes** LB ⊗ Closed Dec-Jan

Lancaster

★★ GUEST ACCOMMODATION

Corran Esplanade PA34 5AD
☎ 01631 562587 📠 01631 562587
e-mail: lancasteroban@btconnect.com
dir: On seafront next to Columba's Cathedral

A family-run establishment on the esplanade that offers budget accommodation; many bedrooms boast lovely views out over the bay towards the Isle of Mull. Public areas include a choice of lounges and bars that also benefit from the panoramic views. A swimming pool, sauna and jacuzzi are added benefits.

Rooms 27 rms (24 en suite) (3 fmly) (27 smoking)
Facilities TVL tea/coffee Cen ht Licensed 🏊 Sauna Pool Table Jacuzzi, steam room **Conf** Max 30 Thtr 30 Class 20 Board 12 **Parking** 20 **Notes** LB

Westbourne House

★★★★ BED AND BREAKFAST

10 Dollar Rd FK13 6PA
☎ 01259 750314
e-mail: info@westbournehouse.co.uk
dir: A91 to St Andrews. Establishment on left just past mini rdbt

This former mill-owner's home, set in wooded gardens on the edge of the village, is adorned with memorabilia gathered by the owners during their travels abroad. They offer a friendly welcome and an excellent choice is offered at breakfast.

Rooms 3 rms (2 en suite) (1 pri facs) (1 fmly) (1 GF) S £35-£40; D £56-£60* **Facilities** STV TVL tea/coffee Cen ht Wi-fi 👣 **Parking** 3 **Notes** Closed Xmas-New Year

Craigadam

★★★★ 🏠 🍴 GUEST HOUSE

Craigadam DG7 3HU
☎ 01556 650233 & 650100 📠 01556 650233
e-mail: inquiry@craigadam.com
web: www.craigadam.com
dir: From Castle Douglas E on A75 to Crocketford. In Crocketford turn left on A712 for 2m. House on hill

Set on a farm, this elegant country house offers gracious living in a relaxed environment. The large bedrooms, most set around a courtyard, are strikingly individual in style. Public areas include a billiard room with comprehensive honesty bar, and the panelled dining room which features a magnificent 15-seater table, the setting for Celia Pickup's delightful meals.

Rooms 10 en suite (2 fmly) (7 GF) S £45-£80; D £90-£100* **Facilities** FTV tea/coffee Dinner available Cen ht Licensed Wi-fi 👣 Fishing Snooker Private fishing & shooting **Conf** Max 22 **Parking** 12 **Notes** LB Closed Xmas & New Year Civ Wed 150

Wallamhill House

★★★★ BED AND BREAKFAST

Kirkton DG1 1SL
☎ 01387 248249
e-mail: wallamhill@aol.com
dir: 3m N of Dumfries. Off A701 signed Kirkton, 1.5m
on right

Wallamhill House is set in well-tended gardens, in a
delightful rural area three miles from Dumfries. Bedrooms
are spacious and extremely well equipped. There is a
peaceful drawing room, and a mini health club with
sauna, steam shower and gym equipment.

Rooms 3 en suite (1 fmly) Facilities FTV TVL tea/coffee
Cen ht ⬎ Sauna Gymnasium Steam room Parking 6
Notes ⊗

Rivendell

★★★★ GUEST HOUSE

105 Edinburgh Rd DG1 1JX
☎ 01387 252251 📄 01387 263084
e-mail: info@rivendellbnb.co.uk
web: www.rivendellbnb.co.uk
dir: On A701 (Edinburgh Rd), 400yds S of A75 junct

Situated just north of the town and close to the bypass,
this lovely 1920s house, standing in extensive
landscaped gardens, has been restored to reflect the
period style of the property. Bedrooms are thoughtfully
equipped, many are spacious and all offer modern
facilities. Traditional breakfasts are served in the elegant
dining room.

Rooms 5 en suite (2 fmly) S £35-£50; D £60
Facilities FTV tea/coffee Cen ht Wi-fi Parking 12
Notes LB ⊗

Southpark House

★★★★ GUEST ACCOMMODATION

Quarry Rd, Locharbriggs DG1 1QG
☎ 01387 711188 & 0800 970 1588 📄 01387 711155
e-mail: info@southparkhouse.co.uk
web: www.southparkhouse.co.uk
dir: 3.5m NE of Dumfries. Off A701 in Locharbriggs onto
Quarry Rd, last house on left

With a peaceful location commanding stunning views,
this well-maintained property offers comfortable,
attractive and well-equipped bedrooms. The peaceful
lounge has a log fire on colder evenings, and fax and
e-mail facilities are available. Friendly proprietor Ewan
Maxwell personally oversees the hearty Scottish
breakfasts served in the conservatory breakfast room.

Rooms 4 en suite (1 fmly) S £30-£50; D £50-£70
Facilities STV FTV TVL tea/coffee Cen ht Wi-fi 2 acres of
garden Parking 13 Notes LB ⊗

Barrasgate

★★★ GUEST ACCOMMODATION

Millhill DG16 5HU
☎ 01461 337577 & 07711 661938 📄 01461 337577
e-mail: info@barrasgate.co.uk
web: www.barrasgate.co.uk
dir: From N, A74(M) junct 24, 1m E take 2nd left signed
Gretna Green, Longtown on right; From S, M6 junct 45,
A6071 towards Longtown 1m on left

This detached house lies in attractive gardens in a rural
setting near the Blacksmith Centre and motorway links.
Bedrooms are equipped with thoughtful extras and have
fine country views. Hearty breakfasts, featuring local

produce, are taken in an attractive dining room,
overlooking the gardens.

Rooms 5 en suite (2 fmly) (1 GF) S £25-£45; D £56-£65*
Facilities TV3B FTV TVL tea/coffee Cen ht Wi-fi Parking 9
Notes LB

Surrone House

★★★ GUEST ACCOMMODATION

Annan Rd DG16 5DL
☎ 01461 338341 📄 01461 338341
e-mail: enquiries@surronehouse.co.uk
web: www.surronehouse.co.uk
dir: In town centre on B721

You are assured of a warm welcome at this well-
maintained guest house set in attractive gardens well
back from the road. Bedrooms are sensibly furnished and
including a delightful honeymoon suite. Dinner, drinks
and light refreshments are available.

Rooms 7 rms (6 en suite) (1 pri facs) (3 fmly) (2 GF)
S £50; D £70* Facilities FTV TVL tea/coffee Dinner
available Cen ht Licensed Wi-fi Parking 10 Notes ⊗

Kirkcroft Guest House

★★★ 🅰 BED AND BREAKFAST

Glasgow Rd DG16 5DU
☎ 01461 337403 📄 01461 337403
e-mail: info@kirkcroft.co.uk
dir: On B7076 next to rail station, at bottom of drive to
Gretna Hall

Rooms 3 en suite S £40; D £54* Facilities FTV tea/coffee
Cen ht Parking 5 Notes LB ⊗

PREMIER COLLECTION

Well View

★★★★★ ◉◉ GUEST ACCOMMODATION

Ballplay Rd DG10 9JU
☎ 01683 220184
e-mail: johnwellview@aol.com
dir: From Moffat on A708 towards Selkirk, 0.5m left
onto Ballplay Rd. Well View 300mtrs on right

Well View is a well-established building set on an
elevated position with outstanding views. The house is
tastefully and traditionally decorated and furnished
with many personal touches. Service and attention to
detail are key features at Well View as is the fine food
that is personally cooked by the proprietors.

Rooms 3 en suite Facilities tea/coffee Dinner available
Cen ht Parking 4

Bridge House

★★★★ 🍽 GUEST HOUSE

Well Rd DG10 9JT
☎ 01683 220558 📄 01683 220558
e-mail: info@bridgehousemoffat.co.uk
dir: *Off A708 The Holm onto Burnside & Well Rd, house 0.5m on left*

A fine Victorian property, Bridge House lies in attractive gardens in a quiet residential area on the outskirts of the town. The atmosphere is very friendly and relaxed. The chef-proprietor provides interesting dinners (by arrangement) featuring local produce. The cosy guest lounge is the ideal venue for pre-dinner drinks.

Rooms 7 en suite (1 fmly) S £45-£50; D £70-£105*
Facilities FTV tea/coffee Dinner available Cen ht Licensed
Parking 7 **Notes** LB ⊗ No Children 2yrs Closed 23 Dec-13 Feb

Hartfell House & The Limetree Restaurant

★★★★ 🍴 GUEST HOUSE

Hartfell Crescent DG10 9AL
☎ 01683 220153
e-mail: enquiries@hartfellhouse.co.uk
web: www.hartfellhouse.co.uk
dir: *Off High St at war memorial onto Well St & Old Well Rd. Hartfell Crescent on right*

Built in 1850, this impressive Victorian house is in a peaceful terrace high above the town and has lovely countryside views. Beautifully maintained, the bedrooms offer high quality and comfort. The attractive dining room is transformed in the evening into the Limetree Restaurant (previously situated in the town centre) offering chef Matt Seddon's culinary delights.

Rooms 7 en suite (2 fmly) (1 GF) S £35-£40; D £60-£70*
Facilities tea/coffee Dinner available Cen ht Licensed Wi-fi **Parking** 6 **Notes** LB ⊗ Closed Xmas

Limetree House

★★★★ GUEST ACCOMMODATION

Eastgate DG10 9AE
☎ 01683 220001
e-mail: info@limetreehouse.co.uk
web: www.limetreehouse.co.uk
dir: *Off High St onto Well St, left onto Eastgate, house 100yds on left*

A warm welcome is assured at this well-maintained guest house, quietly situated behind the main high street. Recognisable by its colourful flower baskets in season, it provides an inviting lounge and bright cheerful breakfast room. Bedrooms are smartly furnished and include a large family room.

Rooms 6 en suite (1 fmly) (1 GF) S £42.50; D £65-£75*
Facilities FTV tea/coffee Cen ht Wi-fi **Parking** 3 **Notes** LB No Children 5yrs RS Xmas & New Year

The Balmoral

★★★ INN

High St DG10 9DL
☎ 01683 220288 📄 01683 220451
web: www.thebalmoralhotel-moffat.co.uk
dir: *0.5m from A/M74 junct 15, halfway up High St on right*

The Balmoral is situated in the centre of the town with free parking in the town square, a friendly welcome is guaranteed. Bar meals are available all day until 9.30pm. Bedrooms are very comfortably equipped with thoughtful extras. Moffat is aformer spa town and is within easy reach of many major tourist attractions.

Rooms 16 en suite (2 fmly) S £32.50-£45; D £53*
Facilities tea/coffee Dinner available Cen ht **Notes** ⊗

Barnhill Springs Country

★★ GUEST ACCOMMODATION

DG10 9QS
☎ 01683 220580
dir: *A74(M) junct 15, A701 towards Moffat, Barnhill Rd 50yds on right*

This former farmhouse has a quiet, rural location south of the town and within easy reach of the M74. Bedrooms are well proportioned, and have either en suite or private bathrooms. There is a comfortable lounge and separate dining room.

Rooms 5 rms (1 en suite) (2 pri facs) (1 fmly) (1 GF) S £30-£32; D £60-£64* **Facilities** TVL tea/coffee Dinner available Cen ht **Parking** 10 **Notes** ⊠

NEWTON STEWART Map 20 NX46

Galloway Arms Inn

★★★ INN

54-58 Victoria St DG8 6DB
☎ 01671 402653 📄 01671 401202
e-mail: info@gallowayarmshotel.com
dir: *In town centre, opp town clock*

Built in 1750 by an Earl of Galloway, this inn has provided accommodation for the past 250 years. Well situated on the high street and benefiting from off-road parking. Bedrooms are compact but offer good value for money. Dinner, using the finest local produce, is of a high standard, and can be eaten in several areas in the building or alfresco in the summer. Breakfast is also very enjoyable.

Rooms 17 en suite (3 GF) S £29.50-£39.50; D £70*
Facilities STV FTV TVL Dinner available Cen ht Wi-fi
Conf Max 150 Thtr 100 Class 50 Board 50 **Parking**
Notes LB

STRANRAER Map 20 NX06

Balyett Bed & Breakfast

★★★ 🅰 BED AND BREAKFAST

Cairnryan Rd DG9 8QL
☎ 01776 703395
e-mail: balyett@btconnect.com
dir: *0.5m N of Stranraer on A77 overlooking Loch Ryan*

Rooms 3 en suite S £45-£55; D £55-£75*

THORNHILL Map 21 NX89

PREMIER COLLECTION

Gillbank House

★★★★★ GUEST ACCOMMODATION

8 East Morton St DG3 5LZ
☎ 01848 330597 📄 01848 331713
e-mail: hanne@gillbank.co.uk
web: www.gillbank.co.uk
dir: *In town centre off A76*

Gillbank House was originally built for a wealthy Edinburgh merchant. Convenient for the many outdoor pursuits in this area, such as fishing and golfing, this delightful house offers comfortable and spacious bedrooms and smart shower rooms en suite. Breakfast is served at individual tables in the bright, airy dining room, which is next to the comfortable lounge.

Rooms 6 en suite (2 GF) S £45-£55; D £65-£70
Facilities tea/coffee Cen ht **Parking** 8 **Notes** ⊗ No Children 8yrs

EAST AYRSHIRE

SORN   Map 20 NS52

The Sorn Inn

★★★★ ◎◎ RESTAURANT WITH ROOMS

35 Main St KA5 6HU
☎ 01290 551305   📄 01290 553470
e-mail: craig@sorninn.com
dir: *A70 from S or A76 from N onto B743 to Sorn*

Centrally situated in this rural village, which is convenient for many of Ayrshire's attractions, this renovated inn is now a fine dining restaurant with a cosy lounge area. There is also a popular chop house with a pub-like environment. The freshly decorated bedrooms have comfortable beds and good facilities.

Rooms 4 en suite (1 fmly) S £40-£50; D £70-£95*
Facilities tea/coffee Dinner available Direct Dial Cen ht Wi-fi Fishing **Parking** 9 **Notes** Closed 2wks Jan RS Mon Closed

EAST LOTHIAN

HADDINGTON   Map 21 NT57

Eaglescairnie Mains

★★★★ 🅐 BED AND BREAKFAST

By Gifford EH41 4HN
☎ 01620 810491   📄 01620 810491
e-mail: williams.eagles@btinternet.com
dir: *3.5m S of Haddington. B6368 from Haddington signed Humbie & Bolton. Through Bolton, at top of hill fork left signed Eaglescairnie & Gifford, 0.5m on left*

Rooms 3 en suite S £40-£50; D £60-£75* **Facilities** TVL tea/coffee Cen ht Wi-fi 🏊 **Parking** 10 **Notes** Closed Xmas

CITY OF EDINBURGH

EDINBURGH   Map 21 NT27

See also East Calder (West Lothian)

PREMIER COLLECTION

Elmview

★★★★★ GUEST ACCOMMODATION

15 Glengyle Ter EH3 9LN
☎ 0131 228 1973
e-mail: nici@elmview.co.uk
web: www.elmview.co.uk
dir: *0.5m S of city centre. Off A702 Leven St onto Valleyfield St, one-way to Glengyle Terrace*

Elmview offers stylish accommodation on the lower ground level of a fine Victorian terrace house. The bedrooms and smart bathrooms are comfortable and extremely well equipped, with thoughtful extras such as safes, and fridges with fresh milk and water. Breakfasts are excellent and are served at a large, elegantly appointed table in the charming dining room.

Rooms 3 en suite (3 GF) S £60-£100; D £80-£120*
Facilities FTV tea/coffee Direct Dial Cen ht Wi-fi
Notes ⊗ No Children 15yrs Closed Dec-Feb

PREMIER COLLECTION

Kew House

★★★★★ GUEST ACCOMMODATION

1 Kew Ter, Murrayfield EH12 5JE
☎ 0131 313 0700   📄 0131 313 0747
e-mail: info@kewhouse.com
web: www.kewhouse.com
dir: *1m W of city centre A8.*

Forming part of a listed Victorian terrace, Kew House lies within walking distance of the city centre, and is convenient for Murrayfield rugby stadium and tourist attractions. Meticulously maintained throughout, it offers attractive bedrooms in a variety of sizes, all thoughtfully equipped to suit business and leisure guests. There is a comfortable lounge offering a supper and snack menu. Internet access is also available.

Rooms 6 en suite (1 fmly) (2 GF) S £75-£95; D £85-£180* **Facilities** FTV tea/coffee Direct Dial Cen ht Wi-fi **Parking** 6 **Notes** LB

PREMIER COLLECTION

The Witchery by the Castle
★★★★ @ RESTAURANT WITH ROOMS

352 Castlehill, The Royal Mile EH1 2NF
☎ 0131 225 5613 📄 0131 220 4392
e-mail: mail@thewitchery.com
web: www.thewitchery.com
dir: *Top of Royal Mile at gates of Edinburgh Castle*

Originally built in 1595, The Witchery by the Castle is situated in a historic building at the gates of Edinburgh Castle. Two of the luxurious and theatrically decorated suites are located above the restaurant and are reached via a winding stone staircase. Filled with antiques, opulently draped beds, large roll-top baths and a plethora of memorabilia, this ancient and exciting establishment is often described as one of the country's most romantic destinations.

Rooms 2 en suite 5 annexe en suite (1 GF) S £295; D £295* **Facilities** STV FTV tea/coffee Dinner available Direct Dial Cen ht **Notes** ⊗ No Children 12yrs Closed 25-26 Dec No coaches Civ Wed 60

Bonnington Guest House
★★★★ GUEST HOUSE

202 Ferry Rd EH6 4NW
☎ 0131 554 7610 📄 0131 554 7610
e-mail: booking@thebonningtonguesthouse.com
web: www.thebonningtonguesthouse.com
dir: *On A902, near corner of Ferry Rd & Newhaven Rd*

This delightful Georgian house offers individually furnished bedrooms on two floors, that retain many of their original features. Family rooms are also available. A substantial freshly prepared breakfast is served in the dining room. Off-street parking is an added bonus.

Rooms 7 rms (5 en suite) (2 pri facs) (4 fmly) (1 GF) **Facilities** FTV tea/coffee Cen ht Wi-fi **Parking** 9 **Notes** ⊗

Millers64
★★★★ BED AND BREAKFAST

64 Pilrig St EH6 5AS
☎ 0131 454 3666 📄 0131 454 3666
e-mail: millers64@hotmail.com
web: www.millers64.com
dir: *At E end of Princes St onto Leith Walk. Pilrig St, 3rd main street on left*

Situated in the heart of Edinburgh, Millers64 offers unique bed and breakfast accommodation in an extensively upgraded beautiful Victorian house. It is a small, very personal establishment, modern in style and offering a warm traditional welcome. Breakfasts are served around one table in the morning room which overlooks the garden, an interesting range of traditional Scottish and modern dishes are available.

Rooms 2 en suite (1 fmly) S £60-£100; D £80-£140* **Facilities** FTV tea/coffee Cen ht Wi-fi **Notes** ⊗ No Children 5yrs ◉

Southside
★★★★ 🏠 GUEST HOUSE

8 Newington Rd EH9 1QS
☎ 0131 668 4422 📄 0131 667 7771
e-mail: info@southsideguesthouse.co.uk
web: www.southsideguesthouse.co.uk
dir: *E end of Princes St onto North Bridge to Royal Mile, continue S, 0.5m, house on right*

Situated within easy reach of the city centre and convenient for the major attractions, Southside is an elegant sandstone house. Bedrooms are individually styled, comfortable and thoughtfully equipped. Traditional, freshly cooked Scottish breakfasts are served at individual tables in the smart ground-floor dining room.

Rooms 8 en suite (2 fmly) (1 GF) S £60-£80; D £80-£140 **Facilities** FTV tea/coffee Direct Dial Cen ht Licensed Wi-fi **Notes** LB ⊗ No Children 10yrs

**East Calder
near Edinburgh EH53 0ET**

ASHCROFT FARMHOUSE
(Derek & Elizabeth Scott)

Ashcroft Farmhouse is an award-winning golf-themed Guest House with no stairs for guests to have to carry luggage up, making it an ideal base. Derek won West Lothian Business Gardener of the Year 2008 for his beautifully landscaped garden.

All bedrooms are ensuite. Dining Room has lots of golf memorabilia including hickory golf clubs.

Breakfasts are delicious with 7 choices using local produce cooked to perfection by Elizabeth who has been providing B&B for 47 years . . . a great achievement.

Free wireless internet access

5 miles M8/M9, A720 City bypass, Airport, Free Park & Ride

No surcharge for credit cards

Tel: 01506 881810   Fax: 01506 884327
www.ashcroftfarmhouse.com
E-mail: ashcroftinfo@aol.com

AA
★★★★★

EDINBURGH *continued*

23 Mayfield

★★★★ 🏠 GUEST ACCOMMODATION

23 Mayfield Gardens EH9 2BX
☎ 0131 667 5806   📠 0131 667 6833
e-mail: info@23mayfield.co.uk
web: www.23mayfield.co.uk
dir: *A720 bypass S, follow city centre signs. Left at Craigmillar Park, 0.5m on right*

Well located on the route into Edinburgh with the added benefit of off-road parking. The spacious accommodation has retained many of the original period features. Breakfast is a real delight with the very best local produce used to give the guest a great start to their day. Many thoughtful extras are provided.

Rooms 9 en suite (2 fmly) (2 GF) S £55-£65;
D £65-£130* **Facilities** FTV tea/coffee Cen ht Wi-fi
Parking 10 **Notes** LB ⊗

Allison House

★★★★ GUEST ACCOMMODATION

17 Mayfield Gardens EH9 2AX
☎ 0131 667 8049   📠 0131 667 5001
e-mail: info@allisonhousehotel.com
web: www.allisonhousehotel.com

Part of a Victorian terrace, Allison House offers modern comforts in a splendid building. It's convenient for the city centre, theatres, tourist attractions and is on the main bus route. The attractive bedrooms are generally spacious and very well equipped. Breakfast is served at individual tables in the ground-floor dining room. Off-road parking is available.

Rooms 11 rms (10 en suite) (1 pri facs) (1 fmly) (2 GF) (2 smoking) **Facilities** tea/coffee Direct Dial Cen ht Wi-fi
Parking 6 **Notes** ⊗

Aonach Mor Guest House

★★★★ GUEST HOUSE

14 Kilmaurs Ter EH16 5DR
☎ 0131 667 8694
e-mail: info@aonachmor.com
dir: *A7 to Cameron Toll rdbt, follow city centre signs, Dalkeith Rd 5th on right*

Situated in the residential area, within easy reach of the city and major tourist attractions. Aonach Mor offers well equipped accommodation including a stylish four-poster feature bedroom which boasts its own steam room. The combined lounge dining room is available to relax in and internet access is available.

Rooms 7 rms (5 en suite) (2 fmly) **Facilities** FTV tea/coffee Cen ht Wi-fi Steam room **Notes** ⊗ No Children 3yrs

Ashlyn Guest House

★★★★ GUEST HOUSE

42 Inverleith Row EH3 5PY
☎ 0131 552 2954
e-mail: info@ashlynguesthouse.com
web: www.ashlyn-edinburgh.co.uk
dir: *Adjacent to Edinburgh Botanic Gardens, then follow signs for North Edinburgh & Botanics*

The Ashlyn Guest House is a warm and friendly Georgian home, ideally located to take advantage of Edinburgh's attractions. The city centre is within walking distance and the Royal Botanical Gardens are minutes away. Bedrooms are all individually decorated and furnished to a high standard. A generous and hearty breakfast gives a great start to the day.

Rooms 8 rms (4 en suite) (2 pri facs) (1 fmly) (1 GF) S £30-£40; D £65-£90* **Facilities** TVL tea/coffee Cen ht
Notes ⊗ No Children 7yrs Closed 23-28 Dec

The Edinburgh Lodge

★★★★ GUEST HOUSE

6 Hampton Ter, West Coates EH12 5JD
☎ 0131 337 3682   📠 0131 313 1700
e-mail: info@thelodgehotel.co.uk
dir: *On A8, 0.75m W of Princes St*

Situated at the west end of Edinburgh, benefiting from off-road parking this well presented property offers comfortable bedrooms with many thoughtful extras which are provided as standard including complimentary Wi-fi. A well-cooked breakfast is served on individual tables which overlook the well maintained gardens.

Rooms 12 en suite (2 fmly) (4 GF) S £65-£80;
D £75-£140* **Facilities** STV TVL tea/coffee Direct Dial Cen ht Licensed Wi-fi **Conf** Max 16 **Parking** 8 **Notes** ⊗

Ellesmere House

★★★★ GUEST HOUSE

11 Glengyle Ter EH3 9LN
☎ 0131 229 4823
e-mail: ruth@edinburghbandb.co.uk
web: www.edinburghbandb.co.uk
dir: *S of city centre off A702*

This delightful terrace house overlooks Bruntsfield Links and is convenient for the city centre. Benefiting from investment from the new proprietors, the attractive bedrooms vary in size and have many thoughtful touches. Breakfast, featuring the best of local produce, is enjoyed in the elegant dining room.

Rooms 4 en suite **Facilities** FTV TVL tea/coffee Cen ht Wi-fi **Notes** ⊗ ✉

Fraoch House

★★★★ GUEST ACCOMMODATION

66 Pilrig St EH6 5AS
☎ 0131 554 1353
e-mail: info@fraochhouse.com
dir: 1m from Princes St

Situated within walking distance of the city centre and convenient for many attractions, Fraoch House, which dates from the 1900s, has been appointed to offer well-equipped and thoughtfully furnished bedrooms. Delicious, freshly cooked breakfasts are served in the charming dining room on the ground floor.

Rooms 9 rms (7 en suite) (2 pri facs) (1 fmly) (1 GF)
S £30-£70; D £55-£105* **Facilities** FTV tea/coffee Cen ht Wi-fi Free use of DVDs and CDs & internet access.
Notes ⊗

Heriott Park

★★★★ GUEST HOUSE

256 Ferry Rd, Goldenacre EH5 3AN
☎ 0131 552 3456
e-mail: reservations@heriottpark.co.uk
web: www.heriottpark.co.uk
dir: 1.5m N of city centre on A902

A conversion of two adjoining properties, which retain many original features. The guest house is on the north side of the city and has lovely panoramic views of the Edinburgh skyline including the castle and Arthur's Seat. The attractive bedrooms are well equipped and have excellent en suite bathrooms.

Rooms 15 rms (14 en suite) (1 pri facs) (7 fmly) (1 GF)
S £40-£80; D £60-£110 **Facilities** FTV tea/coffee Cen ht Wi-fi **Notes** ⊗

International Guest House

★★★★ GUEST HOUSE

37 Mayfield Gardens EH9 2BX
☎ 0131 667 2511 & 0845 241 7551   📄 0131 667 1112
e-mail: intergh1@yahoo.co.uk
web: www.accommodation-edinburgh.com
dir: On A701 1.5m S of Princes St

Guests are assured of a warm and friendly welcome at this attractive Victorian terraced house situated to the south of the city centre. The smartly presented bedrooms are thoughtfully decorated, comfortably furnished and well equipped. Hearty Scottish breakfasts are served at individual tables in the traditionally styled dining room, which boasts a beautiful ornate ceiling.

Rooms 9 en suite (3 fmly) (1 GF) S £35-£75; D £65-£130
Facilities STV tea/coffee Direct Dial Cen ht Wi-fi
Parking 3 **Notes** LB ⊗

See advert on this page

Sherwood

★★★★ GUEST HOUSE

42 Minto St EH9 2BR
☎ 0131 667 1200   📄 0131 667 2344
e-mail: enquiries@sherwood-edinburgh.com
web: www.sherwood-edinburgh.com
dir: On A701, S of city centre

Lying on the south side of the city, this guest house is immaculately maintained and attractively presented throughout. Bedrooms vary in size, the smaller ones being thoughtfully appointed to make the best use of space. All include iron/board and several come with a fridge and microwave. Continental breakfast is served in the elegant dining room.

Rooms 6 rms (5 en suite) (1 pri facs) (2 fmly) (1 GF)
S £40-£65; D £55-£100* **Facilities** FTV tea/coffee Cen ht Wi-fi **Parking** 3 **Notes** LB ⊗ Closed 20-29 Dec & 5 Jan-2 Mar

The International Guesthouse

The International is an attractive stone Victorian house, situated less than a mile South of the city centre, on the main A701. Lying on a main bus route, access to all major attractions is easy. Private car park, free of charge.

The decor is outstanding, with original ornate plasterwork. The House is the ideal base for those either touring or on business. 'In Britain' magazine has rated The International as their 'find' in all Edinburgh.

The Scottish breakfasts, served on the finest bone china, are a delight. The bedrooms are beautifully furnished and in addition to full en-suite facilities, are equipped with colour TV, direct dial telephone, and tea/coffee hospitality tray. Some rooms enjoy magnificent views across to the extinct volcano of Arthur's Seat. Luxury bedroom at the Ground Floor for the limited disabled.

intergh1@yahoo.co.uk   www.accommodation-edinburgh.com

EDINBURGH *continued*

Gildun

★★★★ 🏠 GUEST HOUSE

9 Spence St EH16 5AG

☎ 0131 667 1368 📠 0131 668 4989

e-mail: gildun.edin@btinternet.com

dir: *A720 city bypass to Sheriffhall rdbt onto A7 for 4m to Cameron Toll rdbt. Under rail bridge follow A7 sign onto Dalkeith Rd. Spence St 4th left opp church*

Rooms 8 rms (6 en suite) (2 pri facs) (5 fmly) (2 GF) **Facilities** FTV tea/coffee Cen ht Wi-fi **Parking** 4 **Notes** LB

Abbotsford

★★★ GUEST HOUSE

36 Pilrig St EH6 5AL

☎ 0131 554 2706 📠 0131 555 4550

e-mail: info@abbotsfordguesthouse.co.uk

web: www.abbotsfordguesthouse.co.uk

Situated just off Leith Walk and within easy walking distance of the city centre, this charming and friendly guest house offers individually decorated, pleasantly furnished and thoughtfully equipped bedrooms. There is an elegant ground-floor dining room where hearty breakfasts are served at individual tables.

Rooms 8 rms (5 en suite) S £35-£55; D £70-£130* **Facilities** STV tea/coffee Cen ht **Notes** ⊗

Arden Guest House

★★★ GUEST HOUSE

126 Old Dalkeith Rd EH16 4SD

☎ 0131 664 3985 📠 0131 621 0866

e-mail: ardenguesthouse@btinternet.com

dir: *2m SE of city centre nr Craigmillar Castle. On A7 200yds W of hospital*

Well situated on the south south side of the city, close to the hospital. Benefiting from off-road parking and refurbishment in a number of areas. Many thoughtful extras are provided as standard including Wi-Fi. Attentive and friendly service really adds to the guest experience.

Rooms 8 en suite (2 fmly) (3 GF) S £35-£65; D £55-£99* **Facilities** STV tea/coffee Cen ht Wi-fi **Parking** 8 **Notes** Closed 22-27 Dec

Corstorphine Lodge

★★★ GUEST HOUSE

186-188 St Johns Rd, Corstorphine EH12 8SG

☎ 0131 539 4237 & 476 7116 📠 0131 539 4945

e-mail: corsthouse@aol.com

web: www.corstorphinehotels.co.uk

dir: *From M8 take city bypass N towards city centre for 1m on A8. Lodge on left before zoo*

Occupying two large detached Victorian villas, Corstorphine is convenient for the airport and the city centre. Bedrooms, which vary in size, are carefully decorated and well equipped. There is a spacious conservatory-dining room where traditional, Continental or vegetarian breakfasts can be enjoyed at individual tables. Ample off-road parking is available.

Rooms 12 en suite 5 annexe en suite (8 fmly) (5 GF) S £35-£59; D £55-£109 **Facilities** STV FTV TVL tea/coffee Cen ht Wi-fi **Parking** 14 **Notes** LB ⊗

Ecosse International

★★★ GUEST HOUSE

15 McDonald Rd EH7 4LX

☎ 0131 556 4967 📠 0131 556 7394

e-mail: erlinda@ecosseguesthouse.fsnet.co.uk

dir: *Off A900 NE of city centre*

Situated just off Leith Walk to the north, and within easy walking distance of the city centre, this well-maintained guest house offers comfortable and cheerful accommodation. The cosy lounge area and the adjacent dining room, where hearty breakfasts are served at individual tables, are situated on the lower-ground floor.

Rooms 5 en suite (3 fmly) **Facilities** TVL tea/coffee Cen ht **Notes** ⊗

Elder York Guest House

★★★ GUEST HOUSE

38 Elder St EH1 3DX

☎ 0131 556 1926 📠 0131 624 7140

e-mail: reception@elderyork.co.uk

web: www.elderyork.co.uk

dir: *Close to Princes St, next to bus station*

Centrally located just minutes from the bus station, Harvey Nichols and the St James Shopping centre. Accommodation is situated up several flights of stairs on the third and fourth floors of a Grade A listed building. Bedrooms are well appointed, with many thoughtful extras including Wi-fi. Breakfast is served on individual tables overlooking Queen Street.

Rooms 13 rms (10 en suite) (1 fmly) S £40-£70; D £80-£140* **Facilities** FTV tea/coffee Cen ht Wi-fi **Notes** ⊗

Garfield Guest House

★★★ GUEST HOUSE

264 Ferry Rd EH5 3AN

☎ 0131 552 2369

e-mail: enquiries@garfieldguesthouse.co.uk

Friendly hospitality and good value, no-frills accommodation offering modern comfortable bedrooms. Well situated within easy striking distance of the centre of Edinburgh and well serviced by a regular bus service.

Rooms 7 rms (6 en suite) (1 pri facs) (1 GF) **Facilities** tea/coffee Cen ht

The Lairg

★★★ GUEST HOUSE

11 Coates Gardens EH12 5LG

☎ 0131 337 1050 📠 0131 346 2167

e-mail: lairgmarie@aol.com

dir: *From A8 under rail bridge, stately home 150yds on left, Coates Gardens next 2nd left*

Situated in a residential area close to the Haymarket at the west end of the city, The Lairg is well located for the train station, Murrayfield, the city centre and tourist attractions. It offers attractive, generally spacious, well-equipped accommodation in a friendly relaxed environment. Breakfasts featuring the best of local produce are served at individual tables in the elegant ground-floor dining room.

Rooms 9 en suite (2 fmly) (1 GF) **Facilities** tea/coffee Direct Dial Cen ht **Notes** ⊗

Ardbrae House

★★★ 🏠 BED AND BREAKFAST

85 Drum Brae South, Corstorphine EH12 8TD

☎ 0131 467 5787

e-mail: info@ardbrae.com

dir: *From W enter Edinburgh on A8. At PC World/Drum Brae rdbt turn left, up hill, on left, adjacent to speed camera*

Rooms 3 en suite (3 GF) S £35-£55; D £50-£80* **Facilities** FTV tea/coffee Cen ht Wi-fi **Parking** 5 **Notes** LB ⊗ Closed 24-28 Dec

Charleston House

★★★ Ⓐ GUEST HOUSE

38 Minto St EH9 2BS
☎ 0131 667 6589 & 07904 022205 📠 0131 668 3800
e-mail: joan_wightman@hotmail.com
web: www.charleston-guesthouse.co.uk
dir: *1.5m SE of city centre on A701 at corner Duncan St*

Rooms 5 rms (2 en suite) (2 fmly) (1 GF) S £35-£80;
D £55-£90* **Facilities** FTV TVL tea/coffee Cen ht Wi-fi
Notes LB Closed 24-27 Dec

Classic House

★★★ Ⓐ GUEST HOUSE

50 Mayfield Rd EH9 2NH
☎ 0131 667 5847 📠 0131 662 1016
e-mail: info@classicguesthouse.co.uk
web: www.classichouse.demon.co.uk
dir: *From bypass follow signs for A701 city centre. At Liberton Brae, keep left, 0.5m on left*

Rooms 7 rms (6 en suite) (1 pri facs) (2 fmly) S £30-£50;
D £50-£90* **Facilities** TVL Cen ht **Notes** LB ⊗

Ravensdown Guest House

★★★ Ⓐ GUEST HOUSE

248 Ferry Rd EH5 3AN
☎ 0131 552 5438
e-mail: david@ravensdownhouse.com
web: www.ravensdownhouse.com
dir: *N of city centre, close to Royal Botanic Gardens*

Rooms 7 en suite (5 fmly) (1 GF) S £45-£105;
D £75-£125 **Facilities** FTV tea/coffee Cen ht Wi-fi
Parking 2 **Notes** LB ⊗

The St Valery

★★★ Ⓐ GUEST HOUSE

36 Coates Gardens, Haymarket EH12 5LE
☎ 0131 337 1893 📠 0131 346 8529
e-mail: info@stvalery.co.uk
web: www.stvalery.com
dir: *A8 towards city centre, pass Donaldson school on left, two streets before Haymarket station on left*

Rooms 11 en suite (3 fmly) (1 GF) S £28-£66;
D £50-£108* **Facilities** STV FTV TVL tea/coffee Dinner
available Direct Dial Cen ht Wi-fi **Notes** Closed 24-26 Dec

Averon City Centre Guest House

★★ GUEST HOUSE

44 Gilmore Place EH3 9NQ
☎ 0131 229 9932
e-mail: info@averon.co.uk
web: www.averon.co.uk
dir: *From W end of Princes St onto A702, right at Kings Theatre*

Situated within walking distance of the west end of the city and close to the Kings Theatre, this guest house offers comfortable, good value accommodation, with a secure car park to the rear.

Rooms 10 rms (6 en suite) (1 pri facs) (3 fmly)
Facilities tea/coffee Cen ht **Parking** 19 **Notes** ⊗

See advert on this page

The Osbourne

★★ GUEST ACCOMMODATION

51-59 York Place EH1 3JD
☎ 0131 556 5577 📠 0131 556 1012
e-mail: reservations@osbournehotel.com
web: www.osbournehotel.com

The friendly Osbourne offers budget accommodation ideally located at the east end of the city centre, close to the bus station and Harvey Nichols. The bedrooms vary in size but all offer good overall ease of use, the property also benefits from a lounge on the ground floor. Traditional breakfasts are served at individual tables in the spacious dining room.

Rooms 57 rms (54 en suite) (10 fmly) **Facilities** TVL tea/
coffee Direct Dial Cen ht Lift Wi-fi **Notes** ⊗

The Hedges

Ⓤ

19 Hillside Crescent EH7 5EB
☎ 0131 478 9555
e-mail: thehedgesguesthouse@hotmail.co.uk

Currently the rating for this establishment is not confirmed. This may be due to a change of ownership or because it has only recently joined the AA rating scheme. For up-to-date information see the AA website: the AA. com

Rooms 3 en suite (3 GF) **Facilities** tea/coffee Cen ht Wi-fi
Notes ⊗

CENTRAL EDINBURGH

AVERON GUEST HOUSE

AA
★★
Guest House

44 Gilmore Place
Central Edinburgh EH3 9NQ
PRIVATE CAR PARK
Comfortable Georgian Town House
Bed and Breakfast from £21
10 Minute Walk to Princes St. & Castle
ALL CREDIT CARDS WELCOME

0131-229-9932

e-mail: info@averon.co.uk **website:** www.averon.co.uk

FIFE

ANSTRUTHER   Map 21 NO50

The Spindrift

★★★★ 🔒 ☕ GUEST HOUSE

Pittenweem Rd KY10 3DT
☎ 01333 310573 📄 01333 310573
e-mail: info@thespindrift.co.uk
web: www.thespindrift.co.uk
dir: Enter town from W on A917, 1st building on left

This immaculate Victorian villa stands on the western edge of the village. The attractive bedrooms offer a wide range of extra touches; the Captain's Room, a replica of a wood-panelled cabin, is a particular feature. The inviting lounge has an honesty bar, while imaginative breakfasts, and enjoyable home-cooked meals by arrangement, are served in the cheerful dining room.

Rooms 8 rms (7 en suite) (1 pri facs) (2 fmly) S £45-£55; D £64-£80* **Facilities** FTV TVL tea/coffee Dinner available Direct Dial Cen ht Licensed Wi-fi **Parking** 12 **Notes** LB No Children 10yrs Closed Xmas-late Jan

The Waterfront

★★★★ 🔒 ☕ RESTAURANT WITH ROOMS

18-20 Shore St KY10 3EA
☎ 01333 312200 📄 01333 312288
e-mail: chris@anstruther-waterfront.co.uk
dir: Off A917 opposite marina

Situated overlooking the harbour, The Waterfront offers spacious, stylish, contemporary accommodation with bedrooms located in lovingly restored buildings in a courtyard behind the restaurant. There is a comfortable lounge with a smartly fitted kitchen and dining room, and laundry facilities are available in the granary. Dinner and breakfast are served in the attractive restaurant that

offers a comprehensive menu featuring the best of local produce.

Rooms 8 annexe en suite (3 fmly) (1 GF) S £20-£40; D £40-£80* **Facilities** STV TVL tea/coffee Dinner available Cen ht **Notes** LB ⊗

INVERKEITHING   Map 21 NT18

The Roods

★★★★ BED AND BREAKFAST

16 Bannerman Av KY11 1NG
☎ 01383 415049 📄 01383 415049
e-mail: isobelmarley@hotmail.com
web: www.the-roods.co.uk
dir: N of town centre off B981(Church St/Chapel Place)

This charming house stands in secluded, well-tended gardens close to the station. Bedrooms are individually styled and have state-of-the-art bathrooms. There is an inviting lounge, and breakfast is served at individual tables in an attractive conservatory.

Rooms 2 en suite (2 GF) **Facilities** TVL tea/coffee Dinner available Direct Dial Cen ht **Parking** 4 **Notes** ⊗ ⊗

LEUCHARS   Map 21 NO42

Hillpark House

★★★★ GUEST HOUSE

96 Main St KY16 0HF
☎ 01334 839280 📄 01334 839051
e-mail: enquiries@hillparkhouse.com
web: www.hillparkhouse.com
dir: Leaving Leuchars for St Michaels, house last on right

Lying peacefully on the edge of the village, Hillpark House is an impressive Edwardian home offering comfortable, well-appointed and equipped bedrooms. There is an inviting lounge, a conservatory and a peaceful dining room.

Rooms 5 rms (3 en suite) (1 pri facs) (1 fmly) S £38-£45; D £70-£110* **Facilities** TVL tea/coffee Cen ht Wi-fi Golf **Parking** 6 **Notes** ⊗

LEVEN   Map 21 NO30

Dunclutha Guest House

★★★★ GUEST HOUSE

16 Victoria Rd KY8 4EX
☎ 01333 425515 📄 01333 422311
e-mail: pam.leven@blueyonder.co.uk
web: www.dunclutha.myby.co.uk
dir: A915, B933 Glenlyon Rd into Leven, rdbt left onto Commercial Rd & Victoria Rd. Dunclutha opp church on right

Set in a quiet street close to the town centre, Dunclutha is an inviting Victorian property that was formerly the rectory for the nearby Episcopalian church. Lovingly restored and refurbished to its original splendour it offers comfortable, well-equipped accommodation. A splendid lounge adjoins the dining room where hearty breakfasts are served at individual tables.

Rooms 4 rms (3 en suite) (1 pri facs) (2 fmly) S £30-£40; D £60-£120 **Facilities** FTV TVL tea/coffee Cen ht Piano **Parking** 3 **Notes** ⊗ RS 2wks Jan annual holiday

MARKINCH   Map 21 NO20

Town House

★★★★ RESTAURANT WITH ROOMS

1 High St KY7 6DQ
☎ 01592 758459 📄 01592 755039
e-mail: townhousehotel@aol.com
web: www.townhousehotel-fife.co.uk
dir: In town centre opposite railway station

Well situated on the edge of town and close to the railway station, this friendly establishment offers well presented bedrooms with pleasant colour schemes, modern furnishings, and a good range of facilities and extras. The attractive bar-restaurant is popular with locals and serves a choice of good-value dishes.

Rooms 3 en suite (1 fmly) S £50; D £80-£90* **Facilities** FTV tea/coffee Dinner available Cen ht Wi-fi **Notes** ⊗ Closed 25-26 Dec & 1-2 Jan No coaches

NEWBURGH — Map 21 NO21

The Abbey Inn
★★★ INN

East Port KY14 6EZ
☎ 01337 840761 📠 01337 840761
e-mail: wo6whiskers04@aol.com
web: www.theabbeyinn.com
dir: On A913 High St

Located at the east end of the village, The Abbey Inn offers accommodation situated on the first floor. Bedrooms are bright and well appointed with many thoughtful extras provided as standard. There is a popular public and lounge bar where meals can be provided for residents by prior arrangement.

Rooms 3 en suite (1 fmly); D £60 Facilities FTV tea/coffee Dinner available Cen ht Pool Table Parking 1 Notes LB No coaches

PEAT INN — Map 21 NO40

PREMIER COLLECTION

The Peat Inn
★★★★★ ◉◉◉ RESTAURANT WITH ROOMS

KY15 5LH
☎ 01334 840206 📠 01334 840530
e-mail: stay@thepeatinn.co.uk
dir: At junct of B940 & B941, 5m SW of St Andrews

This 300-year-old former coaching inn enjoys a rural location yet is close to St Andrews. The spacious accommodation is very well appointed and all rooms have lounge areas. The inn is steeped in history and is a real haven for food lovers. The three dining areas create a romantic setting. Expect open fires and a relaxed ambiance.

Rooms 8 annexe en suite (2 fmly) (8 GF) Facilities FTV tea/coffee Dinner available Direct Dial Cen ht Parking 24 Notes Closed 25-26 Dec & 1-3 Jan RS Sun-Mon Closed No coaches

ST ANDREWS — Map 21 NO51

PREMIER COLLECTION

The Paddock
★★★★★ ▣ GUEST ACCOMMODATION

Sunnyside, Strathkinness KY16 9XP
☎ 01334 850888 📠 01334 850870
e-mail: thepaddock@btinternet.com
web: www.thepadd.co.uk
dir: 3m W from St Andrews off B939. The Paddock signed from village centre

Situated in a peaceful village overlooking rolling countryside, this friendly, family-run guest house offers stylish and very well-equipped bedrooms. Superb fish tanks, one freshwater, the other salt, line the entrance hall and contain beautiful and unusual fish. The lounge-dining room in the conservatory is a lovely setting for the delicious breakfasts.

Rooms 4 en suite (1 fmly) (2 GF) Facilities tea/coffee Cen ht Wi-fi Parking 8 Notes ✪ Closed 1-27 Dec

Glenderran
★★★★ GUEST HOUSE

9 Murray Park KY16 9AW
☎ 01334 477951 📠 01334 477908
e-mail: info@glenderran.com
web: www.glenderran.com
dir: In town centre. Off North St onto Murray Pl & Murray Park

This smart terrace house has a super location just minutes from the town centre, seafront, West Sands beach and the Old Course. Aviation-themed pictures and memorabilia decorate the public rooms. Well-equipped bedrooms come in a variety of sizes, and carefully prepared breakfasts are enjoyed in the ground-floor dining room.

Rooms 5 rms (4 en suite) (1 pri facs) S £35-£47; D £70-£100* Facilities FTV TVL tea/coffee Cen ht Wi-fi Notes LB ✪ No Children 12yrs Closed Jan

Nethan House
★★★★ GUEST HOUSE

17 Murray Park KY16 9AW
☎ 01334 472104 📠 01334 850870
e-mail: enquiries@nethan-standrews.com
dir: A91 towards St Andrews, over 2nd rdbt onto North St, Murray Park on left before cinema

This large Victorian terrace house is set in the heart of St Andrews; a short walk from the main tourist attractions and the famous St Andrews golf course. The bright bedrooms are stylish and well appointed. The freshly cooked breakfast is a highlight and is served in the attractive dining room.

Rooms 7 en suite (1 fmly) (1 GF) Facilities FTV TVL tea/coffee Cen ht Wi-fi Notes ✪ Closed 24-26 Dec

Craigmore
★★★★ GUEST HOUSE

3 Murray Park KY16 9AW
☎ 01334 472142 📠 01334 477963
e-mail: info@standrewscraigmore.com
web: www.standrewscraigmore.com
dir: In town centre. Off North St onto Murray Pl & Murray Park

Lying between the town centre and the seafront, this immaculately maintained guest house forms part of a Victorian row. Close to the Old Course, it is adorned with lots of amusing golfing touches. The stylish bedrooms are attractively decorated and well equipped. Breakfast is served at individual tables in the elegant lounge-dining room.

Rooms 7 en suite (4 fmly) (1 GF); D £72-£96 Facilities FTV TVL tea/coffee Cen ht Wi-fi Notes LB ✪

The Inn at Lathones
★★★★ ◉◉ INN

Largoward KY9 1JE
☎ 01334 840494 📠 01334 840694
e-mail: lathones@theinn.co.uk
web: www.theinn.co.uk
dir: 5m S of St Andrews on A915, 0.5m before village of Largoward on left just after hidden dip

This lovely country inn, parts of which are 400 years old, is full of character and individuality. The friendly staff help to create a relaxed atmosphere. Smart contemporary bedrooms are in two separate wings. The colourful, cosy restaurant is the main focus, the menu offering modern interpretations of Scottish and European dishes.

Rooms 13 annexe en suite (1 fmly) (11 GF) Facilities STV TVL tea/coffee Dinner available Direct Dial Cen ht Wi-fi Conf Max 40 Thtr 40 Class 10 Board 20 Parking 35 Notes Closed 26 Dec & 3-16 Jan RS 24 Dec Civ Wed 45

ST ANDREWS *continued*

Spinkstown Farmhouse (NO541144)

★★★★ FARMHOUSE

KY16 8PN
☎ 01334 473475 📄 01334 473475 Mrs A E Duncan
e-mail: admin@spinkstown.com
dir: *2m E on A917 to Crail, 3rd farmhouse on right*

This immaculately maintained modern farmhouse is surrounded by gently rolling countryside. Bedrooms are stylish, spacious and well-equipped. The comfortable lounge, complete with baby grand piano, overlooks the well-tended rear garden. Breakfast is served around a communal table in the dining room.

Rooms 3 en suite S £35-£40; D £62-£65* **Facilities** TVL tea/coffee Cen ht **Parking** 3 **Notes** ⊗ 250 acres arable/cattle/sheep

Lorimer House

★★★★ 🅰 GUEST HOUSE

19 Murray Park KY16 9AW
☎ 01334 476599 📄 01334 476599
e-mail: info@lorimerhouse.com
dir: *A91 to St Andrews, left onto Golf Place, right onto The Scores, right onto Murray Park*

Rooms 5 en suite (1 GF) S £40-£90; D £60-£120* **Facilities** STV FTV TVL tea/coffee Cen ht Wi-fi **Notes** ⊗ No Children 12yrs

Millhouse B&B

★★★★ 🅰 BED AND BREAKFAST

2 Cauldside Farm Steading, Strathkinness High Rd KY16 9TY
☎ 01334 850557
e-mail: stay@bandbinstandrews.co.uk
web: www.bandbinstandrews.co.uk
dir: *B939 W of St Andrews, right onto Strathkinness High Rd. After 1m, right onto farm track*

Rooms 2 en suite S £40-£50; D £60-£75* **Facilities** FTV TVL tea/coffee Cen ht Wi-fi **Parking** 3 **Notes** ⊗ No Children 12yrs

GLASGOW Map 20 NS56

The Kelvingrove

★★★★ GUEST ACCOMMODATION

944 Sauchiehall St G3 7TH
☎ 0141 339 5011 📄 0141 339 6566
e-mail: info@kelvingrovehotel.com
web: www.kelvingrove-hotel.co.uk

This friendly, well-maintained establishment is in a terrace just west of the city centre, and is easily spotted in summer with its colourful floral displays. Bedrooms, including several rooms suitable for families, are well equipped and have smart, fully tiled en suite bathrooms. There is a bright breakfast room, and the reception lounge is open 24 hours.

Rooms 22 en suite (5 fmly) (3 GF) **Facilities** tea/coffee Direct Dial Cen ht

Clifton Guest House

★★★ GUEST HOUSE

26-27 Buckingham Ter, Great Western Rd G12 8ED
☎ 0141 334 8080 📄 0141 337 3468
e-mail: kalam@cliftonhotelglasgow.co.uk
web: www.cliftonhotelglasgow.com
dir: *1.25m NW of city centre off A82 (Inverquhomery Rd)*

Located north-west of the city centre, the Clifton forms part of an elegant terrace and is ideal for business and leisure. The attractive bedrooms are spacious, and there is an elegant lounge. Hearty breakfasts are served at individual tables in the dining room.

Rooms 23 rms (17 en suite) (6 fmly) (3 GF) **Facilities** STV TVL tea/coffee Direct Dial Cen ht **Parking** 8 **Notes** ⊗

Georgian House

★★★ GUEST HOUSE

29 Buckingham Ter, Great Western Rd, Kelvinside G12 8ED
☎ 0141 339 0008 & 07973 971563
e-mail: thegeorgianhouse@yahoo.com
web: www.thegeorgianhousehotel.com
dir: *M8 junct 17 towards Dumbarton, through 4 sets of lights, right onto Queen Margaret Dr, right onto Buckingham Ter*

The friendly guest house offers good value accommodation at the west end of the city in a peaceful

tree-lined Victorian terrace near the Botanic Gardens. Bedrooms vary in size and are furnished in modern style. Continental-style breakfast is served in the first-floor lounge-dining room.

Rooms 11 rms (10 en suite) (1 pri facs) (4 fmly) (3 GF) S £30-£45; D £50-£90* **Facilities** FTV TVL tea/coffee Cen ht Wi-fi **Parking** 7 **Notes** LB

The Kelvin

★★★ GUEST HOUSE

15 Buckingham Ter, Great Western Rd, Hillhead G12 8EB
☎ 0141 339 7143 📄 0141 339 5215
e-mail: enquiries@kelvinhotel.com
web: www.kelvinhotel.com
dir: *M8 junct 17, A82 Kelvinside/Dumbarton, 1m on right before Botanic Gardens*

Two substantial Victorian terrace houses on the west side of the city have been combined to create this friendly establishment close to the Botanical Gardens. The attractive bedrooms are comfortably proportioned and well equipped. The dining room on the first floor is the setting for hearty traditional breakfasts served at individual tables.

Rooms 21 rms (9 en suite) (4 fmly) (2 GF) (14 smoking) S £30-£33; D £60-£66 **Facilities** FTV tea/coffee Cen ht Wi-fi **Parking** 5

Lomond

★★★ GUEST ACCOMMODATION

6 Buckingham Ter, Great Western Rd, Hillhead G12 8EB
☎ 0141 339 2339 📄 0141 339 0477
e-mail: info@lomondhotel.co.uk
web: www.lomondhotel.co.uk
dir: *M8 junct 17, A82 Dumbarton, 1m on right before Botanic Gardens*

Situated in the west end of the city in a tree-lined Victorian terrace, the Lomond offers well maintained, good value accommodation in a friendly environment. Bedrooms are brightly appointed and suitably equipped for leisure guests. Hearty breakfasts are served at individual tables in the bright ground-floor dining room.

Lomond

Rooms 17 rms (6 en suite) (5 fmly) (3 GF) S £20-£45; D £40-£60 **Facilities** tea/coffee Direct Dial Cen ht **Notes** LB

Craigielea House B&B

★★ 🄰 BED AND BREAKFAST

35 Westercraigs G31 2HY
☎ 0141 554 3446
e-mail: craigieleahouse@yahoo.co.uk
dir: *1m E of city centre. M8 junct 15 onto A8, left onto Duke St (pass Tennents Brewery) left into road after lights into Craigpark. 3rd left, then right into Westercraigs*

Rooms 3 rms (1 GF); D £44-£46* **Facilities** tea/coffee Cen ht Wi-fi **Parking** 3 **Notes** ⊗ No Children 3yrs ⊛

HIGHLAND

ABRIACHAN Map 23 NH53

AA GUEST ACCOMMODATION OF THE YEAR FOR SCOTLAND

PREMIER COLLECTION

Loch Ness Lodge

★★★★★ ⊛⊛ RESTAURANT WITH ROOMS

Brachla, Loch Ness-Side IV3 8LA
☎ 01456 459469 📠 01456 459439
e-mail: escape@lodgeatlochness.com
dir: *From A9 Inverness onto A82 signed Fort William, after 9m & 30mph speed sign. Lodge on right immediately after Clansman Hotel*

This purpose-built house enjoys a prominent position overlooking Loch Ness and each of the individually designed bedrooms enjoys views of the loch. The bedrooms are of the highest standard, and beautifully presented with a nice mix of traditional luxury and modern technology, including Wi-fi. There is a spa with a hot tub, sauna and a therapy room offering a variety of treatments. Evening meals are served in the award-winning restaurant, and guests have a choice of attractive lounges which feature real fires in the colder months.

Rooms 7 en suite (1 GF) S £120-£180; D £190-£280* **Facilities** Dinner available Direct Dial Cen ht Wi-fi Fishing Sauna Hot tub Therapy room **Conf** Max 14 Thtr 14 Class 10 Board 14 **Parking** 10 **Notes** LB ⊗ No Children 12yrs Closed 2-31 Jan No coaches Civ Wed 24

ARDELVE Map 22 NG82

Caberfeidh House

★★★ GUEST HOUSE

IV40 8DY
☎ 01599 555293
e-mail: info@caberfeidh.plus.com
web: www.caberfeidh.plus.com
dir: *A87 over Dornie Bridge into Ardelve, 1st left, 100yds on right*

Set in a peaceful location overlooking Lochs Alsh and Duich, Caberfeidh House offers good value, comfortable accommodation in relaxed and friendly surroundings. Bedrooms are traditionally furnished and thoughtfully equipped, and there is a cosy lounge with a wide selection of books, games and magazines. Hearty breakfasts are served at individual tables in the dining room.

Rooms 5 rms (4 en suite) (1 pri facs) (3 fmly) S £28; D £56* **Facilities** TVL tea/coffee Cen ht **Parking** 4 **Notes** ⊗ Closed 25-26 Dec

Eilean a Cheo

★★★ GUEST HOUSE

Dornie IV40 8DY
☎ 01599 555485
e-mail: stay@scothighland.com
web: www.scothighland.com
dir: *A87 N of Dornie Bridge, exit for Ardelve, 110yds on right*

Set in a quiet location overlooking Loch Duich and the famous Eilean Donan castle, this well maintained house offers well-equipped bedrooms some with lovely views. Breakfast is freshly prepared and served in the tidy breakfast room, with a real fire burning on cooler mornings.

Rooms 5 en suite (3 GF) S £36-£50; D £50-£66 **Facilities** tea/coffee Cen ht Wi-fi **Parking** 6 **Notes** ⊗

AVIEMORE Map 23 NH81

PREMIER COLLECTION

The Old Minister's House

★★★★★ GUEST HOUSE

Rothiemurchus PH22 1QH
☎ 01479 812181 📠 0871 661 9324
e-mail: kate@theoldministershouse.co.uk
web: www.theoldministershouse.co.uk
dir: *B970 from Aviemore signed Glenmore & Coylumbridge, establishment 0.75m at Inverdruie*

Built originally as a manse in 1906, The Old Minister's House stands in well-tended grounds close to Aviemore. The house is beautifully furnished and immaculately maintained. Bedrooms are spacious, attractively decorated and thoughtfully equipped. There is an inviting lounge and a dining room where hearty breakfasts are served.

Rooms 4 en suite (1 fmly) S £50-£70; D £90-£96 **Facilities** tea/coffee Cen ht Wi-fi **Parking** 4 **Notes** ⊗ No Children 10yrs

AVIEMORE *continued*

Ravenscraig

★★★★ GUEST HOUSE

Grampian Rd PH22 1RP
☎ 01479 810278 📄 01479 810210
e-mail: info@aviemoreonline.com
web: www.aviemoreonline.com
dir: *N end of main street, 250yds N of police station*

This friendly, family-run guest house is on the north side of the village, a short walk from local amenities. Bedrooms vary between the traditionally styled rooms in the main house and modern spacious rooms in a chalet-style annexe. There is a relaxing lounge and separate dining room, where freshly prepared breakfasts are served at individual tables.

Rooms 6 en suite 6 annexe en suite (6 fmly) (6 GF) S £30-£40; D £60-£80* **Facilities** TVL tea/coffee Cen ht Wi-fi **Parking** 15 **Notes** ✖

Corrour House

★★★★ 🅰 GUEST HOUSE

Inverdruie PH22 1QH
☎ 01479 810220 📄 01479 811500
e-mail: enquiries@corrourhouse.co.uk
web: www.corrourhouse.co.uk
dir: *From Aviemore take B970, signed Coylumbridge, entrance 0.5m on right*

Rooms 8 en suite (2 fmly) S £45-£55; D £80-£90*
Facilities tea/coffee Cen ht Licensed Wi-fi **Parking** 12
Notes Closed 17 Nov-29 Dec

BONAR BRIDGE   Map 23 NH69

Kyle House

★★★ GUEST ACCOMMODATION

Dornoch Rd IV24 3EB
☎ 01863 766360 📄 01863 766360
e-mail: kylehouse360@msn.com
dir: *On A949 N from village centre*

A spacious house with splendid views of the Kyle of Sutherland and the hills beyond. Bedrooms are comfortably furnished in traditional style and equipped with all the expected facilities. There is a lounge and hearty breakfasts are enjoyed in the dining room.

Rooms 5 rms (3 en suite) (2 fmly) S £30; D £60*
Facilities TVL tea/coffee Cen ht **Parking** 5 **Notes** ✖ No Children 5yrs Closed Dec-Jan RS Oct & Apr Occasional closure (phone in advance) ✉

BRORA   Map 23 NC90

PREMIER COLLECTION

Glenaveron

★★★★★ BED AND BREAKFAST

Golf Rd KW9 6QS
☎ 01408 621601
e-mail: alistair@glenaveron.co.uk
web: www.glenaveron.co.uk
dir: *A9 NE into Brora, right onto Golf Rd, 2nd house on right*

Glenaveron stands in attractive landscaped gardens a short distance from the beach and golf course. There are two lovely well proportioned bedrooms upstairs, and a ground-floor twin bedroom for easier access. The lounge is great for relaxation, and excellent breakfasts are served house-party style in the elegant dining room.

Rooms 3 en suite (1 GF) S £50-£55; D £72-£74
Facilities FTV tea/coffee Cen ht Wi-fi **Parking** 6
Notes ✖ Closed 8-23 Oct, Xmas & New Year

CARRBRIDGE   Map 23 NH92

Craigellachie Guest House

★★★★ 🅰 GUEST HOUSE

Main St PH23 3AS
☎ 01479 841641 📄 01479 841415
e-mail: info@craigellachiehouse.co.uk
web: www.craigellachiehouse.co.uk
dir: *A95 N from Aviemore, after 4m left to Carrbridge*

Rooms 6 rms (4 en suite) (2 pri facs) S £27-£28; D £54-£58 **Facilities** TVL tea/coffee Cen ht Wi-fi **Parking** 7 **Notes** LB ✖ No Children 4yrs

The Pines Country House

★★★ BED AND BREAKFAST

Duthil PH23 3ND
☎ 01479 841220 📄 01479 841220
e-mail: lynn@thepines-duthil.co.uk
dir: *2m E of Carrbridge in Duthil on A938*

A warm welcome is assured at this comfortable home in the Cairngorms National Park. The bright bedrooms are traditionally furnished and offer good amenities. Enjoyable home-cooked fare is served around a

communal table. Guests can relax in the conservatory-lounge and watch squirrels feed in the nearby wood.

Rooms 4 en suite (1 fmly) (1 GF) D £50-£55
Facilities STV tea/coffee Dinner available Cen ht Wi-fi
Parking 5 **Notes** LB

The Cairn

★★★ 🅰 INN

Main Rd PH23 3AS
☎ 01479 841212 📄 01479 841362
e-mail: info@cairnhotel.co.uk
web: www.cairnhotel.co.uk
dir: *In village centre*

Rooms 7 rms (5 en suite) (2 fmly) S £28-£56; D £56-£60
Facilities STV tea/coffee Dinner available Wi-fi Pool Table
Parking 20 **Notes** Closed 25 Dec

DORNOCH   Map 23 NH78

PREMIER COLLECTION

2 Quail Restaurant and Rooms

★★★★★ ◉◉ RESTAURANT WITH ROOMS

Castle St IV25 3SN
☎ 01862 811811
e-mail: theaa@2quail.com
dir: *On main street, 200yds from cathedral*

The saying 'small is beautiful' aptly applies to this restaurant with rooms. Set in the main street the careful renovation of its Victorian origins transports guests back in time. Cosy public rooms are ideal for conversation, but there are masses of books for those just wishing to relax. The stylish, individual bedrooms match the character of the house but are thoughtfully equipped to include DVD players. Food is the main feature however, with excellent breakfasts and set four-course dinners.

Rooms 3 en suite (1 fmly) S £60-£100; D £80-£120*
Facilities FTV tea/coffee Dinner available Direct Dial Cen ht Wi-fi Golf 18 **Notes** LB ✖ No Children 8yrs Closed Xmas & 2wks Feb/Mar RS Nov-Mar Fri-Sat only No coaches

DRUMNADROCHIT Map 23 NH53

Ferness Cottage

★★★★ BED AND BREAKFAST

Lewiston IV63 6UW
☎ 01456 450564
e-mail: info@lochnessaccommodation.co.uk
web: www.lochnessaccommodation.co.uk
dir: A82, from Inverness turn right after Esso service station; or from Fort William left before Esso service station, 100mtrs phone box on left. 100mtrs on right

This rose-covered cottage dating from the 1840s has a peaceful location and is within easy walking distance of the village centre. The two charming bedrooms are well equipped, with many thoughtful extra touches. Traditional breakfasts in the cosy lounge-dining room feature the best of local produce. Guests can use the grass area, with seating, beside the River Coiltie, where fishing is available.

Rooms 2 en suite S £40-£65; D £50-£65 Facilities tea/coffee Cen ht Wi-fi Fishing Parking 2 Notes LB ⊗ No Children 10yrs

Glen Rowan

★★★★ BED AND BREAKFAST

West Lewiston IV63 6UW
☎ 01456 450235
e-mail: info@glenrowan.co.uk
dir: From Inverness A82 to Drumnadrochit & Lewiston, right after Esso station, Glen Rowan 600yds on left

Set in a peaceful village, this friendly family home offers attractive, smartly furnished and well-equipped accommodation. Neat gardens surround the house and rooms at the rear overlook the River Coiltie. There is a choice of comfortable lounges, and a smart dining room where delicious home-cooked fare is served at individual tables. Bicycle storage and drying facilities are available.

Rooms 3 en suite (2 fmly) (3 GF) S £36-£46; D £52-£60* Facilities tea/coffee Dinner available Cen ht Wi-fi Fishing Parking 5 Notes LB ⊗

Tigh Na Bruaich

★★★★ Ⓐ BED AND BREAKFAST

Glen Urquhart IV63 6TH
☎ 01456 459341
e-mail: stay@tigh.clara.net
web: www.tigh.clara.net
dir: 3m from Drumnadrochit on A831. Left at sign, house 50yds on right

Rooms 2 rms (1 en suite) (1 pri facs) (2 GF) S £45-£60; D £55-£70* Facilities TVL tea/coffee Cen ht Wi-fi Parking 2 Notes ⊗ No Children 12yrs Closed Xmas ⊛

FORT WILLIAM Map 22 NN17

See also Spean Bridge

PREMIER COLLECTION

The Grange

★★★★★ ≋ GUEST ACCOMMODATION

Grange Rd PH33 6JF
☎ 01397 705516
e-mail: info@thegrange-scotland.co.uk
web: www.thegrange-scotland.co.uk
dir: A82 S from Fort William, 300yds from rdbt left onto Ashburn Ln, at top on left

This lovely Victorian villa stands in immaculate gardens on an elevated position with beautiful views of Loch Linnhe. Attractive decor and pretty fabrics have been used to good effect in the charming bedrooms, two of which have loch views. There is ample provision of books and fresh flowers in the carefully furnished lounge, and the elegant dining room is a lovely setting for hearty breakfasts. Joan Campbell was a Finalist for the Friendliest Landlady of the Year 2009-2010 Award.

Rooms 3 en suite; D £110-£118* Facilities tea/coffee Cen ht Wi-fi Parking 4 Notes LB ⊗ No Children 13yrs Closed Nov-Mar

Nevis Bridge, North Road, Fort William PH33 6LR

Tel: 01397 700103
Email: disthouse@aol.com
Website: stayinfortwilliam.co.uk

Distillery House

Standing at the foot of Ben Nevis on the banks of the River Nevis, just a stone's throw aay from the end of the West Highland Way, lies the Old Glenlochy Distillery, an impressive backdrop to one of the most attractive areas of Fort William in the beautiful Scottish Highlands.

Distillery House, a conversion of three former distillery workers' cottages, has operated as a four star Guest House for over ten years – you can be assured of the very best of Highland Hospitality.

Complimentary whisky and shortbread is served in the Reading Lounge, where Chesterfield sofas, freshly cut flowers and books provide a relaxing atmosphere in which to learn about local history and various whisky trails.

FORT WILLIAM *continued*

Distillery House

★★★★ GUEST HOUSE

Nevis Bridge, North Rd PH33 6LR
☎ 01397 700103
e-mail: disthouse@aol.com
dir: *A82 from Fort William towards Inverness, on left after Glen Nevis rdbt*

Situated in the grounds of the former Glenlochy Distillery, this friendly guest house was once the distillery manager's home. Bedrooms are attractively decorated, comfortably furnished and very well equipped. There is a relaxing lounge, which features a superb range of games, and a bright airy dining room where traditional Scottish breakfasts are served at individual tables.

Rooms 10 en suite (1 fmly) (1 GF) Facilities tea/coffee Cen ht Licensed Parking 21 Notes LB ⊗

See advert on page 435

Mansefield Guest House

★★★★ GUEST HOUSE

Corpach PH33 7LT
☎ 01397 772262 & 0845 6449432
e-mail: mansefield@btinternet.com
web: www.fortwilliamaccommodation.com
dir: *2m N of Fort William A82 onto A830, house 2m on A830 in Corpach*

Peacefully set in its own well-tended garden this friendly, family-run guest house provides comfortable, attractively decorated and well-equipped accommodation. There is a cosy lounge, where a roaring coal fire burns on cold evenings, and an attractive dining room where delicious, home-cooked evening meals and breakfasts are served at individual tables.

Rooms 6 en suite (1 GF) S £30-£40; D £52-£70* Facilities TVL tea/coffee Dinner available Cen ht Wi-fi Parking 7 Notes LB ⊗ No Children 12yrs

Glenlochy

★★★ GUEST ACCOMMODATION

Nevis Bridge PH33 6LP
☎ 01397 702909
e-mail: glenlochy1@aol.com
web: www.glenlochy.co.uk
dir: *A82 from Inverness, guest house on left after 2nd lights*

The well-tended garden of this friendly, family-run guest house marks the end of the famous West Highland Way. Bedrooms are pleasantly decorated and well equipped. There is a comfortable first-floor lounge and a bright, airy ground-floor dining room, where hearty breakfasts are served at individual tables.

Rooms 10 en suite 1 annexe en suite (2 fmly) (7 GF) Facilities TVL tea/coffee Cen ht Parking 13 Notes ⊗

Stobhan B&B

★★★ BED AND BREAKFAST

Fassifern Rd PH33 6BD
☎ 01397 702790 ▤ 01397 702790
e-mail: boggi@supanet.com
dir: *In town centre. A82 onto Victoria Rd beside St Mary's Church, right onto Fassifern Rd*

Stobhan B & B occupies an elevated location overlooking Loch Linnhe and offers comfortable, good-value accommodation. Bedrooms, one of which is on the ground floor, are traditionally furnished and have en suite facilities. Breakfast is served in the ground-floor dining room, which is adjacent to the lounge.

Rooms 4 en suite (1 GF) S £30-£34; D £56-£64 Facilities tea/coffee Cen ht

Lochview

★★★ Ⓐ GUEST HOUSE

Heathercroft, Argyll Rd PH33 6RE
☎ 01397 703149
e-mail: info@lochview.co.uk
dir: *Off A82 rdbt at S end of town centre onto Lundavra Rd, left onto Argyll Ter, 1st right onto Heathercroft to top*

Rooms 6 en suite S £38-£45; D £60-£70* Facilities tea/coffee Cen ht Wi-fi Parking 6 Notes ⊗ Closed Oct-Apr

Craigdarroch House

★★★★ ◉◉ RESTAURANT WITH ROOMS

IV2 6XU
☎ 01456 486400 ▤ 01456 486444
e-mail: info@hotel-loch-ness.co.uk
dir: *Take B862 from either end of loch, then B852 signed Foyers*

Craigdarroch is located in an elevated position high above Loch Ness on the south side. Bedrooms vary in style and size but all are comfortable and well equipped;

front-facing have wonderful views. Dinner should not be missed and breakfasts are also impressive.

Rooms 10 en suite Facilities FTV tea/coffee Dinner available Direct Dial Cen ht Wi-fi Parking 24 Notes No Children 12yrs No coaches Civ Wed 30

Foyers Bay Country House

★★★ GUEST HOUSE

Lochness IV2 6YB
☎ 01456 486624
e-mail: enquiries@foyersbay.co.uk
dir: *Off B852 into Lower Foyers*

Situated in sloping grounds with pines and abundant colourful rhododendrons, this delightful Victorian villa has stunning views of Loch Ness. The attractive bedrooms vary in size and are well equipped. There is a comfortable lounge next to the plant-filled conservatory-cafe, where delicious evening meals and traditional breakfasts are served.

Rooms 6 en suite (1 GF) S £45-£55; D £60-£90* Facilities FTV tea/coffee Dinner available Cen ht Licensed Wi-fi Conf Max 20 Thtr 20 Class 20 Board 20 Parking 6 Notes LB ⊗ No Children 16yrs Civ Wed 20

Lyn-Leven

★★★★ GUEST HOUSE

West Laroch PH49 4JP
☎ 01855 811392 ▤ 01855 811600
e-mail: macleodcilla@aol.com
web: www.lynleven.co.uk

(For full entry see South Ballachulish)

Scorrybreac

★★★★ GUEST ACCOMMODATION

PH49 4HT
☎ 01855 811354
e-mail: info@scorrybreac.co.uk
web: www.scorrybreac.co.uk
dir: *Off A82 just outside village, 500yds from River Coe bridge*

Having a stunning location above the village and overlooking the loch, this charming family-run guest house offers guests a warm welcome. Bedrooms are attractive, well equipped and comfortably furnished. There is a cosy lounge with plenty of books, board games and maps, and a bright airy dining room where delicious breakfasts are served at individual tables.

Rooms 6 en suite (6 GF) S £40-£46; D £50-£60* Facilities tea/coffee Cen ht Parking 8 Notes LB ⊗ Closed 25 Dec

GARVE
Map 23 NH36

Inchbae Lodge Guest House
★★ INN

Inchbae IV23 2PH
☎ 01997 455269 📄 01997 455207
e-mail: contact@inchbae.co.uk
dir: On A385, past Garve towards Ullapool

A friendly welcome is guaranteed from this family-run inn. Close to the River Blackwater and a 30-minute drive from Inverness, Inchbae Lodge is a firm favourite with fishermen and outdoor enthusiasts. The traditional style bar is full of character and has a loyal following; evening meals are served in both the bar and restaurant. Bedrooms vary is size but all are well equipped and comfortable.

Rooms 7 en suite (3 fmly) S £32-£35; D £53-£59.95 (room only)* **Facilities** STV FTV TVL tea/coffee Dinner available Direct Dial Cen ht Fishing Pool Table **Conf** Max 45 Thtr 45 Class 40 Board 40 **Parking** 14 **Notes** ⊗ Closed 25-30 Dec RS Nov-Mar

GOLSPIE
Map 23 NC80

Granite Villa Guest House
★★★★ GUEST ACCOMMODATION

Fountain Rd KW10 6TH
☎ 01408 633146
e-mail: info@granite-villa.co.uk
dir: Left from A9 (N'bound) onto Fountain Rd, immediately before pedestrian crossing lights

Originally built in 1892 for a wealthy local merchant, this traditional Victorian house has been sympathetically restored in recent years. Bedrooms are comfortable and all come with a range of thoughtful extras. Guests can relax in the large lounge, with its views over the landscaped garden where complimentary tea and coffee

is often served. A warm welcome is assured in this charming period house.

Rooms 5 en suite (1 fmly) (1 GF) (2 smoking) S £40-£60; D £60-£70* **Facilities** FTV tea/coffee Cen ht Wi-fi Golf Free access to leisure centre **Parking** 6 **Notes** ⊗

GRANTOWN-ON-SPEY
Map 23 NJ02

PREMIER COLLECTION

An Cala
★★★★★ GUEST HOUSE

Woodlands Ter PH26 3JU
☎ 01479 873293 📄 01479 873610
e-mail: ancala@globalnet.co.uk
web: www.ancala.info
dir: From Aviemore on A95 left onto B9102 at rdbt outside Grantown. After 400yds, 1st left, An Cala opposite

An Cala is an impressive Victorian house set in attractive gardens within easy walking distance of the town centre. Bedrooms are individually furnished with period pieces, attractively decorated and thoughtfully equipped. There is a comfortable lounge complete with log-burning stove and an elegant dining room where first class breakfasts (and dinners by arrangement) are served.

Rooms 4 en suite (1 fmly); D £74-£80* **Facilities** FTV TVL tea/coffee Dinner available Cen ht Wi-fi **Parking** 7 **Notes** LB ⊗ No Children 3yrs Closed Xmas RS Nov-Mar Phone/e-mail bookings only

Holmhill House
★★★★ GUEST ACCOMMODATION

Woodside Av PH26 3JR
☎ 01479 873977
e-mail: enquiries@holmhillhouse.co.uk
web: www.holmhillhouse.co.uk
dir: S of town centre off A939 Spey Av

Built in 1895, and situated in a large well-tended garden within walking distance of the town centre, Holmhill House combines Victorian character with modern comforts. The attractive bedrooms are well equipped, and are en suite. There is a games room suitable for all ages, and a ramp and lift is available for easier access plus a specially equipped bathroom. Children are also well catered for with games, toys, crayons and videos available.

Rooms 4 en suite (2 fmly); D £70-£80 **Facilities** tea/coffee Cen ht Lift Wi-fi **Parking** 9 **Notes** ⊗ Closed Nov-Mar

Dunallan House
★★★★ 🅰 GUEST HOUSE

Woodside Ave PH26 3JN
☎ 01479 872140
e-mail: enquiries@dunallan.com
dir: From Granton Square lights, opposite Co-op, follow Forest Rd, right into Woodside Ave

Rooms 7 rms (6 en suite) (1 pri facs) (1 fmly) (1 GF) S £35-£50; D £60-£80* **Facilities** TVL tea/coffee Cen ht Wi-fi **Parking** 8 **Notes** ⊗

See advert on this page

Dunallan House
Woodside Avenue, Grantown on Spey, Moray PH26 3JN

Warm hospitality, excellent service and delicious freshly cooked breakfasts await you at Dunallan, an elegant Victorian Country Villa built in the late 1800's. Lovingly restored Dunallan offers quality 4 star accommodation whilst retaining many of the Villa's original features. In addition to the use of our period sitting rooms, Dunallan offers the choice of seven beautifully appointed Guest bedrooms, six of these have superb ensuites and the seventh has its own luxury bathroom complete with Victorian 'Ball & Claw' bath and a Luxury power shower. Extensive private parking including a garage for motorbikes and cycles. We have laundry and drying facilities and there is free WiFi for all guests.

AA Associate

Tel/Fax: 01479 872140
Email: enquiries@dunallan.com
Website: www.dunallan.com

GRANTOWN-ON-SPEY *continued*

Rossmor Guest House

★★★★ Ⓐ GUEST HOUSE

Woodlands Ter PH26 3JU
☎ 01479 872201
e-mail: rossmorgrantown@yahoo.com
web: www.rossmor.co.uk
dir: *500yds SW of village centre on B9102*

Rooms 6 en suite (1 fmly); D £60-£76* **Facilities** tea/coffee Cen ht Wi-fi **Parking** 6 **Notes** ✪ No Children 6yrs

Willowbank Guest House

★★★ Ⓐ GUEST HOUSE

High St PH26 3EN
☎ 01479 872089
e-mail: info@wbgh.co.uk
dir: *200yds SW of village centre on B9102*

Rooms 9 rms (6 en suite) (1 pri facs) (2 fmly) (2 GF) S £30-£45; D £52-£59* **Facilities** tea/coffee Dinner available Cen ht Wi-fi **Parking** 8

INVERGARRY Map 22 NH30

Forest Lodge Guest House

★★★ Ⓐ GUEST HOUSE

South Laggan PH34 4EA
☎ 01809 501219 & 07790 907477
e-mail: info@flgh.co.uk
web: www.flgh.co.uk
dir: *2.5m S of Invergarry. Off A82 in South Laggan*

Rooms 8 rms (7 en suite) (1 pri facs) (3 fmly) (4 GF) S £35.50-£38.50; D £55-£58* **Facilities** TV1B TVL tea/coffee Dinner available Cen ht Wi-fi **Parking** 10 **Notes** LB Closed 20 Dec-7 Jan

INVERNESS Map 23 NH64

PREMIER COLLECTION

Daviot Lodge

★★★★★ GUEST ACCOMMODATION

Daviot Mains IV2 5ER
☎ 01463 772215 📠 01463 772099
e-mail: margaret.hutcheson@btopenworld.com
dir: *Off A9 5m S of Inverness onto B851 signed Croy. 1m on left*

Standing in 80 acres of peaceful pasture land, this impressive establishment offers attractive, well-appointed and equipped bedrooms. The master bedroom is furnished with a four-poster bed. There is a tranquil lounge with deep sofas and a real fire, and a peaceful dining room where hearty breakfasts featuring the best of local produce are served. Full disabled access for wheelchairs.

Rooms 7 en suite (1 GF) S £46-£50; D £78-£100* **Facilities** FTV TVL tea/coffee Direct Dial Cen ht Licensed Wi-fi **Parking** 10 **Notes** LB No Children 5yrs Closed 23-26 Dec

PREMIER COLLECTION

Trafford Bank

★★★★★ 🏠 GUEST HOUSE

96 Fairfield Rd IV3 5LL
☎ 01463 241414
e-mail: enquiries@invernesshotelaccommodation.co.uk
dir: *Off A82 at Kenneth St, Fairfield Rd 2nd left, 600yds on right*

This impressive Victorian house lies in a residential area close to the canal. Lorraine Freel has utilised her interior design skills to blend the best in contemporary styles with the house's period character and the results are simply stunning. Delightful public areas offer a choice of lounges, while breakfast is taken in a beautiful conservatory featuring eye-catching wrought-iron chairs. Each bedroom is unique in design and have TV/DVD/CDs, sherry, silent mini fridges and much more.

Rooms 5 en suite (2 fmly) S £60-£90; D £80-£120 **Facilities** STV FTV TVL tea/coffee Cen ht Wi-fi **Parking** 10 **Notes** LB ✪

See advert on opposite page

Avalon Guest House

★★★★ GUEST HOUSE

79 Glenurquhart Rd IV3 5PB
☎ 01463 239075 📠 01463 709827
e-mail: avalon@inverness-loch-ness.co.uk
web: www.inverness-loch-ness.co.uk
dir: *Exit A9 at Longman rdbt, 1st exit onto A82, at Telford St rdbt, 2nd exit. Right at lights onto Tomnahurich St/Glenurquhart Rd*

Avalon Guest House is just a short walk from the city centre, and five minutes drive from Loch Ness. Each bedroom has a flat-screen LCD TV with Freeview (some with DVD), Wi-fi, fluffy white towels and complimentary toiletries; bathrobes and slippers are available on request as well as various other useful items. A delicious breakfast, freshly cooked from a varied menu, is served in the dining room; most dietary requirements can be catered for. Public areas include a guest lounge; and the owners have a range of maps, guidebooks and brochures that guests can refer to.

Rooms 6 rms (5 en suite) (1 pri facs) (4 GF) S £50-£60; D £60-£85 **Facilities** FTV TVL tea/coffee Cen ht Wi-fi **Parking** 12 **Notes** LB ✪ No Children 12yrs

Ballifeary Guest House

★★★★ 🏠 GUEST HOUSE

10 Ballifeary Rd IV3 5PJ
☎ 01463 235572 📠 01463 717583
e-mail: william.gilbert@btconnect.com
web: www.ballifearyguesthouse.co.uk
dir: *Off A82, 0.5m from town centre, turn left onto Bishops Rd & sharp right onto Ballifeary Rd*

This charming detached house has a peaceful residential location within easy walking distance of the town centre and Eden Court Theatre. The attractive bedrooms are carefully appointed and well equipped. There is an elegant ground-floor drawing room and a comfortable dining room, where delicious breakfasts, featuring the best of local produce, are served at individual tables.

Rooms 6 en suite (1 GF) S £40-£65; D £60-£80 **Facilities** FTV tea/coffee Cen ht Wi-fi **Parking** 6 **Notes** LB ✪ No Children 15yrs Closed 24-28 Dec

The Ghillies Lodge

★★★★ 🏠 BED AND BREAKFAST

16 Island Bank Rd IV2 4QS
☎ 01463 232137 📠 01463 713744
e-mail: info@ghillieslodge.com
dir: *1m SW from town centre on B862, pink house facing river*

Situated on the banks of the River Ness not far from the city centre, Ghillies Lodge offers comfortable accommodation in a relaxed, peaceful environment. The attractive bedrooms, one of which is on the ground floor, are all en suite, and are individually styled and well equipped. There is a comfortable lounge-dining room, and a conservatory that overlooks the river.

Rooms 3 en suite (1 GF) **Facilities** STV TVL tea/coffee Cen ht Wi-fi **Parking** 4

Moyness House

★★★★ GUEST ACCOMMODATION

6 Bruce Gardens IV3 5EN
☎ 01463 233836 📠 01463 233836
e-mail: stay@moyness.co.uk
web: www.moyness.co.uk
dir: *Off A82 (Fort William road), almost opp Highland Regional Council headquarters*

Situated in a quiet residential area just a short distance from the city centre, this elegant Victorian villa dates from 1880 and offers beautifully decorated, comfortable bedrooms and well-appointed bathrooms. There is an attractive sitting room and an inviting dining room, where traditional Scottish breakfasts are served. Guests are welcome to use the secluded and well-maintained back garden.

Rooms 6 en suite (1 fmly) (2 GF) **Facilities** tea/coffee Cen ht Wi-fi **Parking** 10

The Alexander

★★★★ 🏠 GUEST HOUSE

16 Ness Bank IV2 4SF
☎ 01463 231151 📠 01463 232220
e-mail: info@thealexander.net
web: www.thealexander.net
dir: *On E bank of river, opposite cathedral*

Built in 1830 this impressive house has been extensively renovated by the current owners and many of the original Georgian features have been retained. Bedrooms are simply furnished and beds have luxurious mattresses dressed in fine Egyptian cotton. Public rooms include a charming lounge with views over the River Ness and the house is a short walk from the city centre.

Rooms 7 en suite 3 annexe en suite (1 GF) S £40-£55; D £70-£90* **Facilities** tea/coffee Cen ht Wi-fi **Parking** 8 **Notes** ⊗

Lyndon Guest House

★★★★ GUEST HOUSE

50 Telford St IV3 5LE
☎ 01463 232551 📠 01463 225827
e-mail: lyndonguesthouse@btopenworld.com
web: www.lyndon-guest-house.co.uk
dir: *From A9 onto A82 over Friars Bridge, right at rdbt onto Telford St. House on right*

A warm Highland welcome awaits at this family-run accommodation close to the centre of Inverness. All rooms are en suite and are equipped with plenty of useful facilities including full internet access. Gaelic Spoken.

Rooms 6 en suite (4 fmly) (2 GF) S £25-£38; D £50-£70* **Facilities** STV FTV TVL tea/coffee Cen ht Wi-fi **Parking** 6 **Notes** ⊗ Closed 20 Dec-5 Jan

Westbourne

★★★★ GUEST ACCOMMODATION

50 Huntly St IV3 5HS
☎ 01463 220700 📠 01463 220700
e-mail: richard@westbourne.org.uk
dir: *A9 onto A82 at football stadium over 3 rdbts, at 4th rdbt 1st left onto Wells St & Huntly St*

The immaculately maintained Westbourne looks across the River Ness to the city centre. This friendly, family-run house has bright modern bedrooms of varying size, all attractively furnished in pine and very well equipped. The ground-floor bedroom has been specially furnished for easier access. A relaxing lounge with internet access, books, games and puzzles is available.

Rooms 9 en suite (2 fmly) S £45-£50; D £70-£80 **Facilities** tea/coffee Cen ht Wi-fi **Parking** 6 **Notes** LB Closed Xmas & New Year

---

Trafford Bank Guest House

96 Fairfield Road, Inverness, Highland IV3 5LL   Tel: 01463 241414
E-mail: info@traffordbankhotel.co.uk   Web: www.traffordbankhotel.co.uk

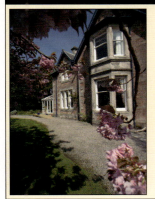

Built in 1873 Trafford Bank Guest House, this former Bishop's home, has been refurbished from top to bottom and mixes antique and contemporary furniture, some of which has been designed by Lorraine herself – an accomplished interior designer.

The home boasts a wealth of character and original features. You will be amazed by the dining room chairs, unusual lighting and original art presented throughout the house.

This guesthouse is within a few minutes walk of Inverness city centre, and the Caledonian Canal.

Luxury B&B accommodation and warm Highland hospitality go hand in hand at Trafford Bank.

The establishment is non-smoking throughout. The house is surrounded by mature gardens that the guests can enjoy and has ample parking.

Trafford Bank is ideally situated to suit both business and holiday visitors and offers guests free wireless internet connection if they have a laptop.

INVERNESS *continued*

Sunnyholm

★★★ GUEST ACCOMMODATION

12 Mayfield Rd IV2 4AE
☎ 01463 231336 📄 01463 715788
e-mail: sunnyholm@aol.com
web: www.invernessguesthouse.com
dir: *500yds SE of town centre. Off B861 Culduthel Rd onto Mayfield Rd*

Situated in a peaceful residential area within easy walking distance of the city centre, Sunnyholm offers comfortably proportioned and well-equipped bedrooms. A spacious conservatory-lounge overlooks the rear garden, and there is a another lounge next to the bright, airy dining room.

Rooms 4 en suite (4 GF) S £40-£42; D £58-£60*
Facilities tea/coffee Cen ht **Parking** 6 **Notes** ⊗ No Children 3yrs 🐾

Acorn House

★★★ GUEST HOUSE

2A Bruce Gardens IV3 5EN
☎ 01463 717021 & 240000 📄 01463 714236
e-mail: enquiries@acorn-house.freeserve.co.uk
web: www.acorn-house.freeserve.co.uk
dir: *From town centre onto A82, on W side of river, right onto Bruce Gardens*

This is an attractive detached house that is just a five-minute walk from the town centre. Bedrooms are smartly presented and well equipped. Breakfast and dinner are served at individual tables in the spacious dining room and can be followed by coffee served in the comfortable lounge.

Rooms 6 en suite (2 fmly) S £49.95; D £70-£79.90*
Facilities STV TVL tea/coffee Cen ht Wi-fi Sauna Hot tub **Parking** 7 **Notes** LB Closed 25-26 Dec

Fraser House

★★★ GUEST ACCOMMODATION

49 Huntly St IV3 5HS
☎ 01463 716488 📄 01463 716488
e-mail: fraserlea@btopenworld.com
dir: *A82 W over bridge, left onto Huntly St, house 100yds*

Situated on the west bank of the River Ness, Fraser House has a commanding position overlooking the city, and is within easy walking distance of the central amenities. Bedrooms, all en suite, vary in size and are comfortably furnished and well equipped. The ground-floor dining room is the setting for freshly cooked Scottish breakfasts.

Rooms 5 en suite (2 fmly) S £25-£35; D £50-£60*
Facilities tea/coffee Cen ht **Notes** 🐾

Royston Guest House

★★★ 🅰 GUEST HOUSE

16 Mill Burn Rd IV2 3PS
☎ 01463 231243 📄 01463 710434
e-mail: roystonguesthouse@btinternet.com
Rooms 8 en suite (2 fmly) (1 GF) S £45-£50; D £70-£80*
Facilities FTV TVL tea/coffee Cen ht Wi-fi **Parking** 16 **Notes** LB

St Ann's House

🆄

37 Harrowden Rd IV3 5QN
☎ 01463 236157 📄 01463 236157
e-mail: stannshous@aol.com
dir: *Off rdbt junct A82 & A862 on W side of bridge*

Currently the rating for this establishment is not confirmed. This may be due to a change of ownership or because it has only recently joined the AA rating scheme. For up-to-date information please see the AA website: the AA.com

Rooms 6 rms (5 en suite) (1 pri facs) (1 fmly) (1 GF)
Facilities TVL tea/coffee Cen ht Licensed **Parking** 4
Notes ⊗ 🐾

KINGUSSIE   Map 23 NH70

PREMIER COLLECTION

The Cross at Kingussie

★★★★★ 🏵🏵🏵 🍽 RESTAURANT WITH ROOMS

Tweed Mill Brae, Ardbroilach Rd PH21 1LB
☎ 01540 661166 📄 01540 661080
e-mail: relax@thecross.co.uk
dir: *From lights in Kingussie centre along Ardbroilach Rd, 300yds left onto Tweed Mill Brae*

Situated in the valley near Kingussie, this former tweed mill sits next to a river, with wild flower gardens and a sunny terrace. Hospitality and food are clearly highlights of any stay at this special restaurant with rooms. Locally sourced produce is carefully prepared with passion and skill. Bedrooms are spacious and airy, and little touches such as fluffy towels and hand-made toiletries providing extra luxury. The Cross is the AA Wine Award Winner for Wales 2009-2010.

Rooms 8 en suite (1 fmly) S £130-£195; D £180-£260* (incl.dinner) **Facilities** Dinner available Direct Dial Cen ht Wi-fi Petanque **Conf** Max 20 Thtr 20 Class 20 Board 20 **Parking** 12 **Notes** LB ⊗ No Children 8yrs Closed Xmas & Jan (ex New Year) RS Sun & Mon Accommodation/dinner not available No coaches

Allt Gynack Guest House

★★★ 🅰 GUEST HOUSE

Gynack Villa, 1 High St PH21 1HS
☎ 01540 661081
e-mail: alltgynack@tiscali.co.uk
web: www.alltgynack.com
dir: *A9 onto A86 through Newtonmore, 2m to Kingussie, on left after bridge*

Rooms 5 rms (3 en suite) (1 fmly) S £27; D £50-£54*
Facilities tea/coffee Cen ht Wi-fi Golf 18 **Parking** 5
Notes LB

LYBSTER   Map 23 ND23

Portland Arms

★★★★ 🍽 INN

Main St KW3 6BS
☎ 01593 721721 📄 01593 721722
e-mail: manager.portlandarms@ohiml.com
web: www.portlandarms.co.uk
dir: *On A99, 4m N of Thurso junct*

Originally built in the 1850 as a coaching inn, the Portland Arms has a range of stylish comfortable bedrooms with front-facing rooms having wonderful sea views. Fine dining can be enjoyed in the refurbished Library restaurant while more informal meals are served in the Farmhouse Kitchen. The residents' lounge has a range of comfortable seating and an open log fire burns brightly in the colder months.

Rooms 22 en suite (4 fmly) (4 GF) S £50-£75; D £70-£120* **Facilities** FTV tea/coffee Dinner available Direct Dial Cen ht Wi-fi **Conf** Max 150 Thtr 150 Class 150 Board 50 **Parking** 22 **Notes** LB Civ Wed 100

NAIRN	Map 23 NH85

North End

★★★★ BED AND BREAKFAST

18 Waverley Rd IV12 4RQ
☎ 01667 456338
e-mail: reservations@northendnairn.co.uk
dir: On corner of A96 (Academy St) & Waverley Rd

Built in 1895, North End is a delightful Victorian villa that has been sympathetically restored in recent years. The spacious bedrooms are comfortable and well equipped. The cosy lounge has a wood-burning stove and the original features of the house are complemented by contemporary furnishings. The house is within easy walking distance of Nairn and is a 20-minute drive from Inverness.

Rooms 3 rms (2 en suite) (1 pri facs) **Facilities** TVL tea/coffee Cen ht **Parking** 4 **Notes** ⊗ ⊗

NEWTONMORE	Map 23 NN79

PREMIER COLLECTION

Ard-Na-Coille

★★★★★ GUEST HOUSE

Kingussie Rd PH20 1AY
☎ 01540 673214 📠 01540 673214
e-mail: jacquie@ard-na-coille.co.uk
dir: Exit A9 at Newtonmore, opp Highland Folk Museum

This large period house, with landscaped grounds, is in a stunning location overlooking open fields. The spacious bedrooms are of a very high standard with a host of thoughtful extras. The public areas include a large lounge with open fires, and a light-filled dining room where delicious breakfasts are served. Jacquie Edwards was a finalist for the AA Friendliest Landlady of the Year 2009-2010 Award.

Rooms 3 en suite **Facilities** STV FTV TVL tea/coffee Direct Dial Cen ht Licensed Wi-fi Golf 18 Snooker **Parking** 10 **Notes** ⊗ No Children

Crubenbeg House

★★★★ GUEST HOUSE

Falls of Truim PH20 1BE
☎ 01540 673300
e-mail: enquiries@crubenbeghouse.com
web: www.crubenbeghouse.com
dir: 4m S of Newtonmore. Off A9 for Crubenmore, over railway bridge & right, signed

Set in peaceful rural location, Crubenbeg House has stunning country views and is well located for touring the Highlands. The attractive bedrooms are individually styled and well equipped, while the ground-floor bedroom provides easier access. Guests can enjoy a dram in front of the fire in the inviting lounge, while breakfast features the best of local produce in the adjacent dining room.

Rooms 4 rms (3 en suite) (1 pri facs) (1 GF) S £30-£36; D £50-£80 **Facilities** STV tea/coffee Dinner available Cen ht Licensed Wi-fi **Parking** 10 **Notes** LB No Children

POOLEWE	Map 22 NG88

PREMIER COLLECTION

Pool House

★★★★★ GUEST ACCOMMODATION

IV22 2LD
☎ 01445 781272 📠 01445 781403
e-mail: stay@pool-house.co.uk
dir: 6m N of Gairloch on A832 centre

Set on the shores of Loch Ewe where the river meets the bay, the understated roadside façade gives little hint of its splendid interior, nor of the views facing the bay. Memorable features are its delightful public rooms, stunningly romantic suites, each individually designed and with feature bathrooms. Pool House is run very much as a country house - the hospitality and guest care by the Harrison Family are second to none.

Rooms 5 en suite 1 annexe en suite (2 GF) S £110-£125; D £190-£220 **Facilities** tea/coffee Dinner available Direct Dial Cen ht Licensed Fishing Snooker **Parking** 12 **Notes** LB No Children 16yrs RS Mon closed

SHIEL BRIDGE	Map 22 NG91

Grants at Craigellachie

★★★★ ⑧ RESTAURANT WITH ROOMS

Craigellachie, Ratagan IV40 8HP
☎ 01599 511331
e-mail: info@housebytheloch.co.uk
dir: From A87 turn to Glenelg, 1st right to Ratagan, opp Youth Hostel sign

Sitting on the tranquil shores of Loch Duin and overlooked by the Five Sisters Mountains, Grants really does have a stunning location. The restaurant has a well deserved reputation for its fine cuisine, and the bedrooms are

stylish and have all the creature comforts. Guests are guaranteed a warm welcome at this charming house.

Rooms 2 en suite 2 annexe en suite (3 GF); D £150-£220* **Facilities** STV tea/coffee Dinner available Cen ht Wi-fi **Parking** 8 **Notes** LB No Children 12yrs Closed Dec-mid Feb RS Oct-Apr reservation only No coaches

SOUTH BALLACHULISH	Map 22 NN05

Craiglinnhe House

★★★★ GUEST HOUSE

Lettermore PH49 4JD
☎ 01855 811270
e-mail: info@craiglinnhe.co.uk
web: www.craiglinnhe.co.uk
dir: From village A82 onto A828, Craiglinnhe 1.5m on left

Built during the reign of Queen Victoria, Craiglinnhe House enjoys an elevated position with stunning views across Loch Linnhe to the village of Onich, and up to the Ballachulish Bridge and the Pap of Glencoe. The attractive bedrooms vary in size, are stylishly furnished, and are well equipped. There is a ground-floor lounge and a charming dining room where delicious breakfasts, and evening meals by arrangement, are served at individual tables.

Rooms 5 en suite S £42-£60; D £50-£80 **Facilities** tea/coffee Dinner available Cen ht Licensed Wi-fi **Parking** 5 **Notes** LB ⊗ No Children 13yrs Closed 24-26 Dec

Lyn-Leven

★★★★ GUEST HOUSE

West Laroch PH49 4JP
☎ 01855 811392 📠 01855 811600
e-mail: macleodcilla@aol.com
web: www.lynleven.co.uk
dir: Off A82 signed on left West Laroch

Genuine Highland hospitality and high standards are part of the appeal of this comfortable guest house. The attractive bedrooms vary in size, are well equipped, and offer many thoughtful extra touches. There is a spacious lounge and a smart dining room where delicious home-cooked evening meals and breakfasts are served at individual tables.

Rooms 8 en suite 4 annexe en suite (3 fmly) (12 GF) S £30-£45; D £50-£64 **Facilities** TVL tea/coffee Dinner available Cen ht Licensed **Parking** 12 **Notes** LB Closed Xmas

SPEAN BRIDGE · Map 22 NN28

Corriechoille Lodge

★★★★ 🍽 GUEST HOUSE

PH34 4EY
☎ 01397 712002
web: www.corriechoille.com
dir: Off A82 signed Corriechoille, 2.5m, left at fork
(10mph sign). At end of tarmac, turn right up hill & left

This fine country house stands above the River Spean.
There are magnificent views of the Nevis range and
surrounding mountains from the comfortable first-floor
lounge and some of the spacious, well-appointed
bedrooms. Friendly and attentive service is provided, as
are traditional breakfasts and delicious evening meals by
arrangement.

Rooms 4 en suite (2 fmly) (1 GF) S £40-£46; D £60-£72*
Facilities tea/coffee Dinner available Cen ht Licensed
Wi-fi **Parking** 7 **Notes** ⊗ No Children 7yrs Closed Nov-
Mar RS Sun-Mon closed

The Smiddy House

★★★★ 🍴🍴 🌐 RESTAURANT WITH ROOMS

Roy Bridge Rd PH34 4EU
☎ 01397 712335 📄 01397 712043
e-mail: enquiry@smiddyhouse.co.uk
web: www.smiddyhouse.co.uk
dir: In village centre, A82 onto A86

Set in the Great Glen which stretches from Fort William to
Inverness, this was once the village smithy, and is now a
friendly restaurant with rooms. The attractive bedrooms,
named after places in Scotland, are comfortably
furnished and well equipped. A relaxing garden room is
available for guest use. Delicious evening meals are
served in Russell's restaurant.

Rooms 4 en suite (1 fmly) S £60-£85; D £70-£90*
Facilities tea/coffee Dinner available Wi-fi **Parking** 15
Notes No coaches

Distant Hills Guest House

★★★★ 🅰 GUEST HOUSE

Roy Bridge Rd PH34 4EU
☎ 01397 712452
e-mail: enquiry@distanthills.com
dir: A82 onto A86 at Spean Bridge, 0.5m on right

Rooms 7 en suite (7 GF) S £46-£75; D £70-£100
Facilities TVL tea/coffee Dinner available Cen ht Wi-fi
Boules **Parking** 10 **Notes** ⊗

Achnabobane (NN195811)

★★★ FARMHOUSE

PH34 4EX
☎ 01397 712919   Mr and Mrs N Ockenden
e-mail: enquiries@achnabobane.co.uk
web: www.achnabobane.co.uk
dir: 2m S of Spean Bridge on A82

With breathtaking views of Ben Nevis, Aonach Mhor and
the Grey Corries, the farmhouse offers comfortable, good-
value accommodation in a friendly family environment.
Bedrooms are traditional in style and well equipped.
Breakfast and evening meals are served in the
conservatory-dining room. Pets are welcome.

Rooms 4 rms (1 en suite) (1 fmly) (1 GF) S fr £29; D
fr £58* **Facilities** TVL tea/coffee Dinner available Cen ht
Wi-fi **Parking** 5 **Notes** Closed Xmas

STRATHPEFFER · Map 23 NH45

Inver Lodge

★★★ GUEST HOUSE

IV14 9DL
☎ 01997 421392
e-mail: derbyshire@inverlg.fsnet.co.uk
dir: A834 through Strathpeffer centre, turn beside Spa
Pavilion signed Bowling Green, Inver Lodge on right

You are assured of a warm welcome at this Victorian
lodge, secluded in its own tree-studded gardens yet
within easy walking distance of the town centre.
Bedrooms are comfortable and well equipped, and the
cosy lounge is ideal for relaxation. Breakfasts, and
evening meals (by arrangement), are served at a
communal table.

Rooms 2 rms (1 fmly) S £30-£32.50; D £50*
Facilities tea/coffee Dinner available Cen ht **Parking** 2
Notes LB ⊗ Closed Xmas & New Year ⊛

STRATHY POINT · Map 23 NC86

Catalina

★★★★ BED AND BREAKFAST

Aultivullin KW14 7RY
☎ 01641 541395 📄 0871 900 2537
e-mail: catalina.bandb@virgin.net
dir: A836 at Strathy onto Strathy Point Rd, 1.5m then left
& 1m to end

Having a tranquil setting close to the sea, this former
croft house provides a getaway location for those seeking
relaxation. The self-contained bedroom is in a wing that
includes a dining room and a cosy lounge. Cuisine is
home-cooked and meal times are flexible.

Rooms 1 en suite (1 GF) S £37; D £56* **Facilities** STV TVL
tea/coffee Dinner available Cen ht **Parking** 2 **Notes** ⊗ No
Children ⊛

TOMATIN · Map 23 NH82

Glenan Lodge

★★★ GUEST HOUSE

IV13 7YT
☎ 01808 511217
e-mail: enquiries@glenanlodge.co.uk
web: www.glenanlodge.co.uk
dir: Off A9 to Tomatin, signed to Lodge

Peacefully located on the edge of the village, this relaxed
and homely guest house offers a warm welcome. The
comfortable bedrooms are traditionally furnished and
suitably equipped. An inviting lounge is available, and
delicious home-cooked evening meals and breakfasts are
served in the dining room. A two mile stretch of the River
Findhorn is available for fly-fishing, and golfers, walkers
and bird watchers are also well provided for locally.

Rooms 7 en suite (2 fmly) S £28-£30; D £56-£60*
Facilities TVL tea/coffee Dinner available Cen ht Licensed
Wi-fi Fishing **Parking** 7 **Notes** LB ⊗ No Children 5yrs

TORRIDON — Map 22 NG95

The Torridon Inn

★★★ 🍴 INN

IV22 2EY
☎ 01445 791242 📠 01445 712253
e-mail: inn@thetorridon.com

The Torridon Inn enjoys an idyllic location and is set in 58 acres of parkland overlooking Loch Torridon and surrounded by steep mountains on all sides. The inn is very popular with walkers, and guests can also avail themselves of the many outdoor pursuits that are provided at the Torridon Hotel. Each of the spacious bedrooms are well equipped and comfortable. Evening meals and lunches are available at the inn were over 80 whiskies, and several real ales including a local Torridon Ale are firm favourites.

Rooms 12 en suite (3 fmly) (5 GF) S £85; D £85*
Facilities STV tea/coffee Dinner available Cen ht Wi-fi 🎣 Fishing Pool Table Outdoor activities available **Conf** Max 35 Thtr 35 Board 16 **Parking** 12 **Notes** LB Closed Nov-Feb Civ Wed 40

See advert on this page

WICK — Map 23 ND35

The Clachan

★★★★ BED AND BREAKFAST

13 Randolph Place, South Rd KW1 5NJ
☎ 01955 605384
e-mail: enquiry@theclachan.co.uk
dir: Off A99 0.5m S of town centre

A warm welcome is assured at this immaculate detached home, by the main road on the south edge of the town. The bright, airy bedrooms (all on the ground floor) though compact, are attractively furnished to make good use of available space. Breakfast offers an extensive choice and is served at individual tables in the cosy dining room.

Rooms 3 en suite (3 GF) S £40-£50; D £60-£70*
Facilities FTV tea/coffee Cen ht Wi-fi **Parking** 3 **Notes** ⊗ No Children 12yrs Closed Xmas & New Year ⊗

MIDLOTHIAN

DALKEITH — Map 21 NT36

The Sun Inn

★★★★ ⊛ INN

Lothian Bridge EH22 4TR
☎ 0131 663 2456
dir: On A7 towards Galashiels, opposite Newbattle Viaduct

Dating back to 1697 and situated within easy striking distance of Edinburgh. Major refurbishment has totally transformed this property and it now has boutique-style bedrooms (one featuring a copper bath) and modern bathrooms. High quality, award-winning food is served in stylish surroundings; drinks can be enjoyed in the terraced garden area.

Rooms 5 en suite S £60-£65; D £80-£150* **Facilities** STV FTV tea/coffee Dinner available Cen ht Wi-fi Fishing **Parking** 50 **Notes** LB ⊗ RS Mon (ex BH) no food served in bar No coaches

PENICUIK — Map 21 NT25

Craigiebield House

★★★★ GUEST ACCOMMODATION

50 Bog Rd EH26 9BZ
☎ 01968 672557
e-mail: reservations.craigiebield@ohiml.com
Built in 1824 and set in its own well-tended grounds, this property offers comfortable modern accommodation with many thoughtful extras provided as standard. The bar and conservatory restaurant have enjoyed a refurbishment, and offer a relaxed and slightly more formal dining option.

Rooms 17 en suite (4 fmly) **Facilities** FTV tea/coffee Dinner available Direct Dial Cen ht Licensed Wi-fi **Conf** Max 200 Thtr 200 Class 100 Board 50 **Parking** 40 **Notes** ⊗ Civ Wed 150

ROSLIN — Map 21 NT26

The Original Roslin Inn

★★★★ INN

4 Main St EH25 9LE
☎ 0131 440 2384 📠 0131 440 2514
e-mail: enquiries@theoriginalhotel.co.uk
dir: Off city bypass at Straiton for A703 (inn near Roslin Chapel)

Whether you find yourself on the Da Vinci Code trail or in the area on business, this property a very short walk from
continued

The Torridon Inn
Stay...relax in the surroundings and rest the soul.
Restaurant...enjoy the flavours and experience the delights
Bar...Drink in the atmosphere and savour the taste
Activities...see the wilderness experience the adventures
AA Pub of the Year Scotland 2008-2009 WESTER ROSS
Tel: +44(0)1445 791242 www.thetorridon.com

ROSLIN *continued*

the famous Roslin Chapel which is well worth the visit. This delightful village inn offers well-equipped bedrooms with upgraded en suites; four of the rooms have four-poster beds. The Grail Restaurant, the lounge and conservatory offer a comprehensive selection of dining options.

Rooms 6 en suite (2 fmly) (1 smoking) S £55-£65; D £75-£85 (room only)* **Facilities** STV tea/coffee Dinner available Cen ht Wi-fi **Conf** Max 100 Thtr 100 Class 80 Board 60 **Parking** 8 **Notes** LB Civ Wed 180

NORTH AYRSHIRE

LARGS   Map 20 NS25

South Whittlieburn Farm

★★★★ 🏠 BED AND BREAKFAST

Brisbane Glen KA30 8SN
☎ 01475 675881 📠 01475 675080
e-mail: largsbandb@southwhittlieburnfarm.freeserve.co.uk
dir: *2m NE of Largs off A78 signed Brisbane Glen, after Vikingar centre*

This comfortable and welcoming farmhouse is on a working sheep farm surrounded by gently rolling countryside. The attractive bedrooms are well equipped with all having DVD and video players. There is a spacious ground-floor lounge and a bright airy dining room where delicious breakfasts are served.

Rooms 3 en suite (1 fmly) S £35-£37.50; D £59-£65* **Facilities** STV FTV TVL tea/coffee Cen ht Golf 18 **Parking** 10 **Notes** LB ⊗ RS Xmas 🐾

NORTH LANARKSHIRE

AIRDRIE   Map 21 NS76

Shawlee Cottage

★★★ GUEST HOUSE

108 Lauchope St, Chapelhall ML6 8SW
☎ 01236 753774 📠 01236 749300
e-mail: shawleecottage@blueyonder.co.uk
web: www.csaitken.fsbusiness.co.uk/index.htm
dir: *M8 junct 6, A73 to Chapelhall, left onto B799, Shawlee 600yds on right*

Shawlee Cottage is close to motorway and rail networks, and within easy reach of Edinburgh and Glasgow. This delightful cottage dates from the 19th century and has comfortable, well-equipped bedrooms with wide doors and a ramp at the entrance. Scottish breakfasts (and dinner by arrangement) are served in the attractive dining room.

Rooms 5 en suite (5 GF) S £30-£40; D £55-£65 **Facilities** tea/coffee Direct Dial Cen ht Wi-fi **Parking** 6 **Notes** ⊗

COATBRIDGE   Map 20 NS76

Auchenlea

★★★ GUEST HOUSE

153 Langmuir Rd, Bargeddie G69 7RT
☎ 0141 771 6870 & 07775 791381 📠 0141 771 6870
e-mail: helenbarr06@btinternet.com
dir: *N off A8 onto A752 for 0.4m*

Backing onto farmland, yet only a short distance from the motorway, this detached house is well placed for Glasgow and Edinburgh. Satisfying, well-cooked breakfasts are served at a communal table in the bright dining room, and there is an attractive conservatory and adjoining lounge. The bedrooms, all on the ground floor, are modern in style with one designed for easier access.

Rooms 6 en suite (1 fmly) (6 GF) S £25-£35; D £55-£60* **Facilities** FTV TVL tea/coffee Cen ht **Parking** 10 **Notes** ⊗ 🐾

PERTH & KINROSS

ALYTH   Map 23 NO24

PREMIER COLLECTION

Tigh Na Leigh Guesthouse

★★★★★ 🏠 GUEST ACCOMMODATION

22-24 Airlie St PH11 8AJ
☎ 01828 632372 📠 01828 632279
e-mail: bandcblack@yahoo.co.uk
web: www.tighnaleigh.co.uk
dir: *In town centre on B952*

Situated in the heart of this country town, Tigh Na Leigh is Gaelic for 'The House of the Doctor or Physician'. Its location and somewhat sombre façade are in stunning contrast to what lies inside. The house has been completely restored to blend its Victorian architecture with contemporary interior design. Bedrooms, including a superb suite, have state-of-the-art bathrooms. There are three entirely different lounges, while delicious meals are served in the conservatory/dining room overlooking a spectacular landscaped garden.

Rooms 5 en suite (1 GF) S £45; D £90-£115* **Facilities** FTV TVL tea/coffee Dinner available Cen ht Licensed Wi-fi **Parking** 5 **Notes** No Children 12yrs Closed Dec-Feb

BLAIRGOWRIE   Map 21 NO14

Gilmore House

★★★★ BED AND BREAKFAST

Perth Rd PH10 6EJ
☎ 01250 872791 📠 01250 872791
e-mail: jill@gilmorehouse.co.uk
dir: *On A93 S*

This Victorian villa stands in a well-tended garden on the south side of town. Sympathetically restored to enhance its period features it offers individual bedrooms tastefully furnished in antique pine, and thoughtfully equipped to include modern amenities such as Freeview TV. There are two inviting lounges, one of which has lovely views over the gardens. Hearty traditional breakfasts are served in the attractive dining room.

Rooms 3 en suite; D £56-£70 **Facilities** FTV TVL tea/coffee Cen ht Wi-fi **Parking** 3 **Notes** Closed Xmas

COUPAR ANGUS   Map 21 NO23

Enverdale House

★★★ GUEST HOUSE

6 Pleasure Rd PH13 9JB
☎ 01828 627606 📠 01828 627239

Enverdale House is located on a quiet road and is a short walk from the centre of the small market town of Coupar Angus. This family run guest house has attractively presented bedrooms, and public rooms include a large lounge bar along with spacious conference facilities. An extensive breakfast menu is provided and evening meals are served in the stylish restaurant.

Rooms 5 en suite (1 fmly) **Facilities** FTV tea/coffee Dinner available Cen ht Licensed Wi-fi **Notes** ⊗ Civ Wed 200

CRIEFF   Map 21 NN82

Merlindale

★★★★ BED AND BREAKFAST

Perth Rd PH7 3EQ
☎ 01764 655205 📠 01764 655205
e-mail: merlin.dale@virgin.net
web: www.merlindale.co.uk
dir: *On A85, 350yds from E end of High St*

Situated in a quiet residential area within walking distance of the town centre, this delightful detached house stands in well-tended grounds and offers a warm welcome. The pretty bedrooms are comfortably furnished and well equipped. There is a spacious lounge, an impressive library, and an elegant dining room where delicious evening meals and traditional breakfasts are served.

Rooms 3 en suite (1 fmly) **Facilities** STV TVL tea/coffee Dinner available Cen ht Wi-fi **Parking** 3 **Notes** ⊗ Closed 9 Dec-10 Feb 🐾

GLENDEVON　　　　　　　Map 21 NN90

An Lochan Tormaukin

★★★★ ◉ INN

FK14 7JY
☎ 01259 781252
e-mail: tormaukin@anlochan.co.uk
dir: M90 junct 6 onto A977 to Kincardine, follow signs for Stirling. Exit at Yetts of Muckart onto A823

A delightful country inn dating back to the 17th century, located in an idyllic, and secluded, setting not far from the famous Gleneagles Championship golf courses. This well-presented property is undergoing a rolling programme of refurbishment. Open log fires and bare stone walls add to the character of this property where the small team are friendly and welcoming. Food is a strong aspect here, and the kitchen makes the best use of locally sourced produce.

Rooms 13 rms (12 en suite) (4 GF) S fr £85; D fr £100*
Facilities TV12B tea/coffee Dinner available Direct Dial Cen ht Wi-fi Golf **Conf** Max 30 **Parking** 50 **Notes** LB Closed 24-25 Dec No coaches

GLENSHEE (SPITTAL OF),　　　Map 21 NO17

Dalhenzean Lodge

★★★★ BED AND BREAKFAST

PH10 7QD
☎ 01250 885217　📠 0871 733 5419
e-mail: mikepurdie@onetel.com
dir: On A93 2m S of Spittal of Glenshee

Dalhenzean Lodge was built in 1715, and is situated in the shadow of Meall Uaine, overlooking Shee Water. Some seven miles from the ski slopes at The Cairnwell, it is well located for fishing, hill walking and climbing, with the Cateran Trail nearby. Bedrooms are beautifully decorated and have many thoughtful extras. Hearty breakfasts featuring the best of local produce are served in the ground-floor dining room.

Rooms 2 rms (1 en suite) (1 pri facs); D £55-£60*
Facilities STV FTV tea/coffee Cen ht **Parking** 2 **Notes** LB ⊗

MUTHILL　　　　　　　Map 21 NN81

Barley Bree Restaurant with Rooms

★★★★ ◉ RESTAURANT WITH ROOMS

6 Willoughby St PH5 2AB
☎ 01764 681451　📠 01764 910055
e-mail: info@barleybree.com
dir: A9 onto A822 in centre of Muthill

Situated in the heart of the small village of Muthill, and is just a short drive from Crieff, genuine hospitality and quality food are obvious attractions at this charming restaurant with rooms. The property has been totally refurbished under its new owners, and the stylish

bedrooms are appointed to a very high standard. The public areas include a cosy lounge with a log burning fire.

Rooms 6 en suite (1 fmly) S £60-£65; D £85-£95*
Facilities FTV tea/coffee Dinner available Cen ht Wi-fi
Parking 10 **Notes** LB ⊗ Closed 2wks Autumn/Jan No coaches

PERTH　　　　　　　　Map 21 NO12

Cherrybank Guesthouse

★★★★ GUEST ACCOMMODATION

217-219 Glasgow Rd PH2 0NB
☎ 01738 451982　📠 01738 561336
e-mail: m.r.cherrybank@blueyonder.co.uk
dir: 1m SW of town centre on A93

Convenient for the town and major roads, Cherrybank has been extended and carefully refurbished to offer well equipped and beautifully presented bedrooms, one of which is on the ground floor. The delightful lounge is ideal for relaxation, while delicious breakfasts are served at individual tables in the bright airy dining room.

Rooms 5 rms (4 en suite) (1 pri facs) (2 fmly) (1 GF)
Facilities tea/coffee Cen ht Wi-fi **Parking** 4 **Notes** ⊗

Clunie

★★★★ GUEST HOUSE

12 Pitcullen Crescent PH2 7HT
☎ 01738 623625　📠 01738 623238
e-mail: ann@clunieguesthouse.co.uk
dir: On A94 on E side of river

Lying on the north east side of town, this family-run guest house offers a friendly welcome. The comfortable bedrooms, which vary in size, are attractively decorated and well equipped. Breakfast is served at individual tables in the elegant ground-floor dining room.

Rooms 7 en suite (1 fmly) S £30-£40; D £60-£70*
Facilities tea/coffee Cen ht Wi-fi **Parking** 8 **Notes** LB ⊗

Westview

★★★★ BED AND BREAKFAST

49 Dunkeld Rd PH1 5RP
☎ 01738 627787　📠 01738 447790
e-mail: angiewestview@aol.com
dir: On A912, 0.5m NW from town centre opp Royal Bank of Scotland

Expect a warm welcome from enthusiastic owner Angie Livingstone. She is a fan of Victoriana, and her house captures that period, one feature being the teddies on the stairs. Best use is made of available space in the bedrooms, which are full of character. Public areas include an inviting lounge and a dining room.

Rooms 5 rms (3 en suite) (1 fmly) (1 GF) **Facilities** STV TVL tea/coffee Dinner available Cen ht **Parking** 4 **Notes** ⊗

The Anglers Inn

★★★ ◉ INN

Main Rd, Guildtown PH2 6BS
☎ 01821 640329
e-mail: info@theanglersinn.co.uk
web: www.theanglersinn.co.uk
dir: 6m N of Perth on A93

This charming country inn enjoys a peaceful rural setting and yet is only a short drive from Perth city centre and is a favourite with race-goers. The inn has been totally refurbished and the accommodation comprises five tastefully styled en suite bedrooms, each equipped with flatscreen TVs and complimentary Wi-fi. The award-winning restaurant has a loyal following and the dinner menu is supplemented by nightly blackboard specials.

Rooms 5 en suite (1 fmly) S £50; D £100* **Facilities** FTV TVL tea/coffee Dinner available Cen ht Wi-fi ♨ Pool Table **Parking** 40 **Notes** LB No Children

PITLOCHRY　　　　　　Map 23 NN95

PREMIER COLLECTION

Easter Dunfallandy House

★★★★★ BED AND BREAKFAST

Logierait Rd PH16 5NA
☎ 01796 474128
e-mail: sue@dunfallandy.co.uk
web: www.dunfallandy.co.uk
dir: 1m S of Pitlochry. Off A924 Perth Rd in town onto Bridge Rd, fork left, house 1m on right

A splendid country house, Dunfallandy lies peacefully in an elevated position on the western side of the Tummel Valley. Immaculately maintained, it retains many original features including fine woodwork. The lounge is very relaxing, and the dining room, with its magnificent wood-panelled ceiling, is the setting for breakfast served to one large table. Bedrooms are well proportioned and thoughtfully equipped.

Rooms 3 en suite (1 GF) S fr £40; D fr £80
Facilities STV TVL tea/coffee Cen ht Wi-fi **Parking** 10
Notes LB Closed Xmas

PITLOCHRY *continued*

Craigroyston House

★★★★ GUEST HOUSE

2 Lower Oakfield PH16 5HQ
☎ 01796 472053 📄 01796 472053
e-mail: reservations@craigroyston.co.uk
web: www.craigroyston.co.uk
dir: *In town centre near information centre car park*

The Maxwell family delight in welcoming you to their home, an impressive detached Victorian villa set in a colourful garden. The bedrooms have pretty colour schemes and are comfortably furnished in period style. There is an inviting sitting room, complete with deep sofas for those wishing to relax and enjoy the tranquillity. Scottish breakfasts are served at individual tables in the attractive dining room.

Rooms 8 en suite (1 fmly) (1 GF); D £60-£80
Facilities tea/coffee Cen ht Wi-fi **Parking** 9 **Notes** LB ⊗
♨

Torrdarach House

★★★★ GUEST HOUSE

Golf Course Rd PH16 5AU
☎ 01796 472136 📄 01796 472136
e-mail: torrdarach@msn.com
dir: *In town centre. Off A924 Atholl Rd onto Larchwood Rd to top of hill, left, red house on right*

Torrdarach House enjoys an elevated position overlooking the Tummel Valley and the pretty town of Pitlochry. This impressive Victorian villa stands in its own secluded landscaped gardens and ample secure parking is available. The stylish bedrooms are comfortably furnished and well equipped. The lounge is spacious, very comfortable and this charming house has lots of period features.

Rooms 7 rms (6 en suite) (1 pri facs) (1 GF) S £25-£35; D £50-£70* **Facilities** TVL tea/coffee Cen ht Licensed Wi-fi **Parking** 7 **Notes** ⊗

Wellwood House

★★★★ GUEST HOUSE

13 West Moulin Rd PH16 5EA
☎ 01796 474288 📄 01796 474299
e-mail: wellwoodhouse@aol.com
web: www.wellwoodhouse.com
dir: *In town centre opp town hall*

Set in lovely grounds on an elevated position overlooking the town, Wellwood House has stunning views of the Vale of Atholl and the surrounding countryside. The comfortably proportioned bedrooms are attractively decorated and well equipped. The elegant lounge has an honesty bar and a fire on cooler evenings, and the spacious dining room is the setting for hearty breakfasts served at individual tables.

Rooms 10 rms (8 en suite) (2 pri facs) (1 fmly) (1 GF) S £40-£50; D £66-£80* **Facilities** FTV TVL tea/coffee Cen ht Licensed Wi-fi **Parking** 20 **Notes** ⊗ Closed 10 Nov-14 Feb

SCOTTISH BORDERS

BROUGHTON
Map 21 NT13

The Glenholm Centre

★★★ 🏠 GUEST ACCOMMODATION

ML12 6JF
☎ 01899 830408
e-mail: info@glenholm.co.uk
dir: *1m S of Broughton. Off A701 to Glenholm*

Surrounded by peaceful farmland, this former schoolhouse has a distinct African theme. The home-cooked meals and baking have received much praise and are served in the spacious lounge-dining room. The bright airy bedrooms are thoughtfully equipped, and the service is friendly and attentive. Computer courses are available.

Rooms 3 en suite 1 annexe en suite (1 fmly) (2 GF)
Facilities TVL tea/coffee Dinner available Cen ht Licensed Wi-fi ♨ **Conf** Max 24 Thtr 24 Class 24 Board 24
Parking 14 **Notes** Closed 20 Dec-1 Feb

CRAILING
Map 21 NT62

Crailing Old School Guest House

★★★★ 🛎 🍴 GUEST HOUSE

TD8 6TL
☎ 01835 850382
e-mail: jean.player@virgin.net
web: www.crailingoldschool.co.uk
dir: *A698 onto B6400 signed Nisbet, Crailing Old School also signed*

This delightful rural retreat, built in 1887 as the village school, has been imaginatively renovated to combine Victorian features with modern comforts. The spacious bedrooms are beautifully maintained and decorated, and filled with homely extras. The lodge annexe suite located 10 yards from the house offers easier ground-floor access. The best of local produce produces tasty breakfasts, served in the stylish lounge-dining room (evening meals by arrangement).

Rooms 3 rms (1 en suite) (1 pri facs) 1 annexe en suite (1 GF) S £38.50-£40; D £60-£80* **Facilities** FTV TVL tea/coffee Dinner available Cen ht Wi-fi **Parking** 7 **Notes** No Children 9yrs Closed 24 Dec-2 Jan, 1wk Feb & 2wks Autumn

EDDLESTON
Map 21 NT24

The Horseshoe Inn

★★★★ ⑧⑧⑧ RESTAURANT WITH ROOMS

EH45 8QP
☎ 01721 730225 📄 01721 730268
e-mail: reservations@horseshoeinn.co.uk
web: www.horseshoeinn.co.uk
dir: *A703, 5m N of Peebles*

This inn is five miles north of Peebles and only 18 miles south of Edinburgh. Originally a blacksmith's shop, it was significantly refurbished by Vivienne Steele and her partner, chef-director Patrick Bardoulet. It is now a restaurant with rooms with a very good reputation for its delightful atmosphere and its excellent classical French inspired cuisine. There are eight luxuriously appointed and individually designed bedrooms.

Rooms 8 en suite (1 fmly) (6 GF) **Facilities** tea/coffee Dinner available Direct Dial Cen ht Wi-fi **Parking** 20 **Notes** Closed 25 Dec & Mon

GALASHIELS Map 21 NT43

Over Langshaw (NT524400)

★★ FARMHOUSE

Langshaw TD1 2PE
☎ 01896 860244 📄 01896 860668 Mrs S Bergius
e-mail: overlangshaw@btconnect.com
dir: 3m N of Galashiels. A7 N from Galashiels, 1m right
signed Langshaw, right at T-junct into Langshaw, left
signed Earlston, Over Langshaw 1m, signed

There are fine panoramic views from this organic hillside
farm. It offers two comfortable and spacious bedrooms.
Hearty breakfasts are provided at individual tables in the
lounge and a friendly welcome is guaranteed.

Rooms 2 en suite (1 fmly) (1 GF) Facilities TVL tea/coffee
Cen ht Parking 4 Notes ⊗ 500 acres dairy/sheep/organic

JEDBURGH Map 21 NT62

Ferniehirst Mill Lodge

★★ GUEST HOUSE

TD8 6PQ
☎ 01835 863279
e-mail: ferniehirstmill@aol.com
web: www.ferniehirstmill.co.uk
dir: 2.5m S on A68, onto private track to end

Reached by a narrow farm track and a rustic wooden
bridge, this chalet-style house has a secluded setting by
the River Jed. Bedrooms are small and functional but
there is a comfortable lounge in which to relax. Home-
cooked dinners are available by arrangement, and hearty
breakfasts are served in the cosy dining room.

Rooms 7 en suite (1 GF) S £28; D £56* Facilities TVL tea/
coffee Dinner available Direct Dial Cen ht Fishing Riding
Parking 10

LAUDER Map 21 NT54

The Black Bull

★★★★ INN

Market Place TD2 6SR
☎ 01578 722208 📄 01578 722419
e-mail: enquiries@blackbull-lauder.com
dir: On A68 in village centre

This 18th-century coaching inn has been completely
transformed. The lovely bedrooms are furnished in period
character and thoughtfully equipped with modern
amenities. The wooden-floored, cosy bar and four dining
areas are charming, the main dining room being a former
chapel. A very good range of food makes this a popular
gastro-pub.

Rooms 8 en suite (2 fmly) S £80-£110; D £120-£150
Facilities FTV tea/coffee Dinner available Direct Dial
Cen ht Wi-fi Conf Max 40 Parking 8 Notes LB Civ Wed 40

MELROSE Map 21 NT53

PREMIER COLLECTION

Fauhope House

★★★★★ 🏠 GUEST HOUSE

Gattonside TD6 9LU
☎ 01896 823184 📄 01896 823184
e-mail: fauhope@bordernet.co.uk
dir: 0.7m N of Melrose over River Tweed. N off B6360 at
Gattonside 30mph sign (E) up long driveway

It's hard to imagine a more complete experience than a
stay at Fauhope, set high on a hillside on the north-
east edge of the village. Hospitality is first class,
breakfasts are excellent, and the delightful country
house has a splendid interior. Bedrooms are luxurious,
each individual and superbly equipped. Public areas
are elegantly decorated and furnished, and enhanced
by beautiful floral arrangements; the dining room is
particularly stunning. Fauhope House was the AA Guest
Accommodation of the Year for Scotland 2008-2009.

Rooms 3 en suite Facilities tea/coffee Dinner available
Cen ht 🛌 Riding Parking 10 Notes LB ⊗

NEWCASTLETON Map 21 NY48

Liddesdale

★★★★ INN

Douglas Sq TD9 0QD
☎ 01387 375255 📄 01387 752577
e-mail: reception@theliddesdalehotel.co.uk

Located in the peaceful 17th-century village of
Newcastleton overlooking the village square. Bedrooms
are well appointed and the public areas offer various
dining locations. The welcoming public bar is well used
by locals and residents alike. Relaxed and informal
menus use the best local produce available.

Rooms 6 en suite (2 fmly) S fr £40; D £60-£70
Facilities STV FTV TVL tea/coffee Dinner available Direct
Dial Cen ht Wi-fi 🛌 Golf 9 Fishing Pool Table Conf Max 60
Thtr 40 Class 40 Board 40 Notes LB

SWINTON Map 21 NT84

Wheatsheaf at Swinton

★★★★ 🏵🏵 RESTAURANT WITH ROOMS

TD11 3JJ
☎ 01890 860257 📄 01890 860688
e-mail: reception@wheatsheaf-swinton.co.uk
dir: In village centre on A6112

Overlooking the village green, this restaurant with rooms
has built its reputation on excellent food. Bedrooms are
stylishly furnished, all with smart en suite facilities, the
largest ones featuring a bath and separate shower
cubicle. The executive bedrooms are of a very high
standard.

Rooms 10 en suite (2 fmly) (1 GF) S £65-£95;
D £98-£148 Facilities FTV tea/coffee Dinner available
Direct Dial Cen ht Wi-fi Conf Max 18 Thtr 18 Class 18
Board 12 Parking 7 Notes LB ⊗ Closed 25-26 Dec, 31
Jan Civ Wed 50

SOUTH AYRSHIRE

AYR Map 20 NS32

See also Dunure

PREMIER COLLECTION

The Crescent

★★★★★ GUEST HOUSE

26 Bellevue Crescent KA7 2DR
☎ 01292 287329
e-mail: joyce&mike@26crescent.co.uk
web: www.26crescent.co.uk
dir: Leave A79 onto rdbt, 3rd exit onto King St. Left onto
Bellevue Crescent

Located in a quiet residential area of Ayr, close to the
seafront, town centre and race course, this guest house
offers a traditional warm welcome with well appointed
and comfortable bedrooms. Bathrooms are of a high
standard, as is the hearty breakfast served on
individual tables in the charming dining room.

Rooms 5 en suite S £50; D £70-£80* Facilities FTV
tea/coffee Cen ht Wi-fi Notes LB ⊗

AYR *continued*

Daviot House

★★★★ GUEST HOUSE

12 Queens Ter KA7 1DU
☎ 01292 269678
e-mail: daviothouse@hotmail.com
web: www.daviothouse.com
dir: *Off A719 onto Wellington Sq & Bath Place, turn right*

This well-maintained Victorian house stands in a peaceful location close to the beach and town centre. Bedrooms are modern in style and well equipped. Hearty breakfasts are served in the dining room. Daviot House is a member of Golf South Ayrshire - a golf booking service for local municipal courses, so let your hosts know if you'd like a round booked.

Rooms 5 rms (4 en suite) (1 pri facs) (1 fmly) S £35-£45; D £60-£85* **Facilities** FTV tea/coffee Cen ht Wi-fi **Notes** LB ⊗ No Children

Greenan Lodge

★★★★ BED AND BREAKFAST

39 Dunure, Doonfoot KA7 4HR
☎ 01292 443939
e-mail: helen@greenanlodge.com
dir: *2m S of town centre on A719 (coast road)*

Guests are made to feel truly welcome at this modern bungalow in a quiet residential area, convenient for the coast and attractions around Ayr. The bright, well-furnished bedrooms offer numerous extras and there is a spacious lounge. Expect a generous Scottish breakfast.

Rooms 3 en suite (3 GF) S fr £45; D fr £60* **Facilities** TVL tea/coffee Cen ht **Parking** 10 **Notes** No Children 7yrs ⊛

BALLANTRAE — Map 20 NX08

Balkissock Lodge

★★★★ 🛏️ 🍴 GUEST ACCOMMODATION

Balkissock KA26 0LP
☎ 01465 831537
e-mail: howard.balkissock@btinternet.com
dir: *S through Ballantrae (A77) over river, 1st left at campsite sign. Right at T-junct, 1.5m*

A warm and genuine welcome awaits after a scenic drive. Set in the rolling South Ayrshire countryside, surrounded by wonderful gardens, Balkissock Lodge is a perfect getaway. New owners show great hospitality and customer care in a very comfortable and well-appointed property.

Rooms 3 en suite (1 fmly) (2 GF) **Facilities** TVL tea/coffee Dinner available Cen ht **Parking** 3 **Notes** ⊗ No Children ⊛

DUNURE — Map 20 NS21

Dunduff *(NS265160)*

★★★★ FARMHOUSE

Dunure KA7 4LH
☎ 01292 500225 📠 01292 500222 Mrs A Gemmell
e-mail: gemmelldunduff@aol.com
dir: *On A719, 400yds past village school*

Parts of this working farm date from the 15th and 17th centuries. It stands on an elevated position with stunning views across the Firth of the Clyde towards Arran and the Mull of Kintyre. Bedrooms are comfortable and well-equipped, with a comfortable lounge enhancing the 'home away from home' feel. Expect genuine Scottish hospitality, and breakfast specialities including locally smoked kippers.

Rooms 3 rms (2 en suite) (1 pri facs) (2 fmly) **Facilities** TVL tea/coffee Cen ht Fishing **Parking** 10 **Notes** LB ⊗ No Children 11yrs Closed Nov-Feb 600 acres beef/sheep

---

MAYBOLE — Map 20 NS20

PREMIER COLLECTION

Ladyburn

★★★★★ 🛏️ GUEST ACCOMMODATION

KA19 7SG
☎ 01655 740585 📠 01655 740580
e-mail: jh@ladyburn.co.uk
dir: *A77 (Glasgow/Stranraer) at Maybole turn to B7023 to Crosshill and right at War Memorial. In 2m turn left for approx 1m on right*

This charming country house is the home of the Hepburn family, who take great pride in the warmth of their welcome. Sitting in open countryside with attractive gardens, it's a great place to come to relax. Classically styled bedrooms, two with four-poster beds, offer every comfort and are complemented by the library and the drawing room.

Rooms 5 en suite S £60-£70; D £110-£120 **Facilities** tea/coffee Direct Dial Cen ht Licensed Wi-fi 🍴 **Parking** 12 **Notes** ⊗ No Children 16yrs Civ Wed 60

SOUTH LANARKSHIRE

STRATHAVEN — Map 20 NS74

Rissons at Springvale

★★★ 🍴 RESTAURANT WITH ROOMS

18 Lethame Rd ML10 6AD
☎ 01357 521131 & 520234 📠 01357 521131
e-mail: rissons@msn.com
dir: *A71 into Strathaven, W of town centre off Townhead St*

Guests are assured of a warm welcome at this charming establishment close to the town centre. The bedrooms and bathrooms are stylish and well equipped. However it's the food that's the main feature, with a range of interesting, well-prepared dishes served in Rissons Restaurant.

Rooms 9 en suite (1 fmly) (1 GF) S £37.50-£42.50; D £70-£75* **Facilities** tea/coffee Dinner available Cen ht Wi-fi **Parking** 10 **Notes** ⊗ Closed 1st wk Jan No coaches

---

STIRLING

BALMAHA — Map 20 NS49

Oak Tree Inn

★★★ INN

G63 0JQ
☎ 01360 870357 📠 01360 870350
e-mail: info@oak-tree-inn.co.uk
dir: *A811 onto B837 to Balmaha*

Standing in the shade of a magnificent 500-year-old oak tree on the quiet eastern shore of Loch Lomond, this friendly family-run inn is a great base for exploring the surrounding countryside. The attractive bedrooms have been refurbished to a high standard and are individually styled and well equipped. The rustic bar is complete with beams, a roaring log fire and local memorabilia, while the dining room serves delicious home-cooked fare.

Rooms 9 en suite (1 fmly) S £75; D £75-£100*
Facilities tea/coffee Dinner available Cen ht **Parking** 6
Notes ⊗ Closed 25 Dec, 1 Jan No coaches

Annfield Guest House

★★★★ GUEST HOUSE

18 North Church St FK17 8EG
☎ 01877 330204 📄 01877 330674
e-mail: reservations@annfieldguesthouse.co.uk
dir: Off A84 Main St onto North Church St, at top on right

Situated within easy reach of the town centre, this welcoming guest house offers comfortable, good-value accommodation. The spacious bedrooms are attractively decorated and well equipped. An elegant first-floor lounge is ideal for relaxation, and hearty breakfasts are served at individual tables in the pretty dining room. Self-catering accommodation is also available.

Rooms 7 rms (4 en suite) (1 pri facs) (1 fmly) S £35-£55; D £55-£65* **Facilities** tea/coffee Cen ht Wi-fi **Parking** 7 **Notes** LB ⊗ No Children 6yrs Closed Xmas 🐾

Arden House

★★★★ 🏠 GUEST ACCOMMODATION

Bracklinn Rd FK17 8EQ
☎ 01877 330235
e-mail: ardenhouse@onetel.com
dir: Off A84 Main St onto Bracklinn Rd, house 200yds on left

This impressive Victorian villa lies in beautiful mature grounds in a peaceful area of the town. It featured in the 1960s hit TV series *Dr Finlay's Casebook* and is a friendly, welcoming house. The comfortable bedrooms are thoughtfully furnished and equipped. There is a stylish lounge in addition to the attractive breakfast room where delicious breakfasts are served at individual tables.

Rooms 6 en suite (2 GF) S £40; D £70-£80*
Facilities tea/coffee Cen ht Wi-fi ♿ **Parking** 10 **Notes** ⊗ No Children 14yrs Closed Nov-Mar

Callander Meadows

★★★★ ❀ RESTAURANT WITH ROOMS

24 Main St FK17 8BB
☎ 01877 330181
e-mail: mail@callandermeadows.co.uk
web: www.callandermeadows.co.uk
dir: M9 junct 10 onto A84 to Callander, on main street just past A81 junct

Located on the high street in Callander, this family-run business offers comfortable accommodation and a restaurant that has quickly become very popular with the locals. The bedrooms have been appointed to a high standard. Private parking is available to the rear.

Rooms 3 en suite; D £70-£80* **Facilities** tea/coffee Dinner available Cen ht Wi-fi **Parking** 4 **Notes** ⊗ RS Winter Restaurant open Thu-Sun only No coaches

Lubnaig House

★★★★ GUEST HOUSE

Leny Feus FK17 8AS
☎ 01877 330376
e-mail: info@lubnaighouse.co.uk
web: www.lubnaighouse.co.uk
dir: From town centre A84 W, right onto Leny Feus. Lubnaig House after Poppies Hotel

Lubnaig House is set in a delightful tree-lined secluded garden just a 5-minute walk from the town centre. The house, built in 1864, has been modernised to provide comfortable well-appointed bedrooms. There are two cosy lounges, and an impressive dining room where hearty traditional breakfasts are served at individual tables.

Rooms 6 en suite 2 annexe en suite S £50-£60; D £70-£84* **Facilities** tea/coffee Cen ht Wi-fi **Parking** 10 **Notes** LB ⊗ No Children 7yrs Closed Nov-Apr

Mansewood Country House

★★★★ GUEST HOUSE

FK19 8NS
☎ 01567 830213
e-mail: stay@mansewoodcountryhouse.co.uk
dir: A84 N to Lochearnhead, 1st building on left; A84 S to Lochearnhead

Mansewood Country House is a spacious former manse that dates back to the 18th century and lies in a well-tended garden to the south of the village. Bedrooms are well appointed and equipped and offer high standards of comfort. Refreshments can be enjoyed in the cosy bar or the elegant lounge, and meals prepared with flair are served in the attractive restaurant. There is also a log cabin where pets are allowed.

Rooms 6 en suite (1 GF) S £30-£45; D £54-£65
Facilities TVL tea/coffee Dinner available Cen ht Licensed Wi-fi **Parking** 6 **Notes** LB ⊗ RS Nov-Mar Phone for advance bookings

Tigh Na Crich

★★★★ BED AND BREAKFAST

FK19 8PR
☎ 01567 830235
e-mail: johntippett2@aol.com
web: www.tighnacrich.co.uk
dir: On junct of A84 & A85, next to village shop

Located in the heart of the small village of Lochearnhead and surrounded by mountains on three sides and Loch Earn on the fourth. Very well presented accommodation with many thoughtful extras provided. The generous breakfast is served in the comfortable dining room on individual tables looking out to the front of the property.

Rooms 3 en suite (1 fmly) S £38-£45; D £56-£60*
Facilities tea/coffee Cen ht **Parking** 3 **Notes** 🐾

STIRLING — Map 21 NS79

Linden Guest House

★★★★ GUEST HOUSE

22 Linden Av FK7 7PQ
☎ 01786 448850 & 07974 116573 ▤ 01786 448850
e-mail: fay@lindenguesthouse.co.uk
web: www.lindenguesthouse.co.uk
dir: 0.5m SE of city centre off A9

Situated within walking distance of the town centre, this friendly guest house offers attractive and very well-equipped bedrooms, including a large family room that sleeps five comfortably. There is a bright dining room where delicious breakfasts are served at individual tables with quality Wedgwood crockery.

Rooms 4 en suite (2 fmly) (1 GF) S £60-£70; D £70-£80* Facilities STV tea/coffee Cen ht Wi-fi Parking 2 Notes LB

STRATHYRE — Map 20 NN51

PREMIER COLLECTION

Creagan House

★★★★★ ◉◉ RESTAURANT WITH ROOMS

FK18 8ND
☎ 01877 384638 ▤ 01877 384319
e-mail: eatandstay@creaganhouse.co.uk
web: www.creaganhouse.co.uk
dir: 0.25m N of Strathyre on A84

Originally a farmhouse dating from the 17th century, Creagan House has operated as a restaurant with rooms for many years. The baronial-style dining room provides a wonderful setting for sympathetic cooking. Warm hospitality and attentive service are the highlights of any stay.

Rooms 5 en suite (1 fmly) (1 GF) S £70-£90; D £120-£140 Facilities FTV tea/coffee Dinner available Cen ht Wi-fi Conf Max 35 Thtr 35 Class 12 Board 35 Parking 26 Notes LB Closed 4-19 Nov, Xmas & 21 Jan-5 Mar RS Wed & Thu Closed

WEST DUNBARTONSHIRE

BALLOCH — Map 20 NS38

Sunnyside

★★★ BED AND BREAKFAST

35 Main St G83 9JX
☎ 01389 750282 & 07717 397548
e-mail: enquiries@sunnysidebb.co.uk
dir: From A82 take A811 then A813 for 1m, over mini-rdbt 150mtrs on left

Set in its own grounds well back from the road by Loch Lomond, Sunnyside is an attractive, traditional detached house, parts of which date back to the 1830s. Bedrooms are attractively decorated and provide comfortable modern accommodation. Free wireless internet access is also available. The dining room is located on the ground floor, and is an appropriate setting for hearty Scottish breakfasts.

Rooms 6 en suite (2 fmly) (1 GF) S £30-£45; D £46-£56* Facilities tea/coffee Dinner available Cen ht Wi-fi Parking 8

DUMBARTON

See Cardross (Argyll & Bute)

WEST LOTHIAN

BLACKBURN — Map 21 NS96

Cruachan B & B

★★★ GUEST ACCOMMODATION

78 East Main St EH47 7QS
☎ 01506 655221 ▤ 01506 652395
e-mail: enquiries@cruachan.co.uk
web: www.cruachan.co.uk
dir: On A705 in Blackburn, 1m from M8 junct 4

Ideally located for both the leisure and business traveller to central Scotland, with Edinburgh only some 30 minutes away by train and Glasgow only 35 minutes away by car. Cruachan is the comfortable, friendly home of the Harkins family. Bedrooms are bright, attractive and very well equipped. Breakfast, featuring the best of local produce is served at individual tables in the ground-floor dining room.

Rooms 4 rms (3 en suite) (1 pri facs) (1 fmly) S £35-£60; D £55-£65* Facilities FTV tea/coffee Cen ht Wi-fi Parking 5 Notes ⊗

EAST CALDER — Map 21 NT06

PREMIER COLLECTION

Ashcroft Farmhouse

★★★★★ GUEST HOUSE

EH53 0ET
☎ 01506 881810 ▤ 01506 884327
e-mail: scottashcroft7@aol.com
web: www.ashcroftfarmhouse.com
dir: On B7015, off A71, 0.5m E of East Calder, near Almondell Country Park

With over 40 years' experience in caring for guests, Derek and Elizabeth Scott ensure a stay at Ashcroft will be memorable. Their modern home sits in lovely award-winning landscaped gardens and provides attractive and well-equipped ground-floor bedrooms. The comfortable lounge includes a video and DVD library. Breakfast, featuring home-made sausages and the best of local produce, is served at individual tables in the stylish dining room. Free Wi-fi is now available, and a Park and Ride facility is nearby.

Rooms 6 en suite (2 fmly) (6 GF) S £55-£65; D £70-£80* Facilities TVL tea/coffee Cen ht Wi-fi Parking 8 Notes ⊗ No Children 12yrs

See advert on page 425

Whitecroft

★★★★ BED AND BREAKFAST

7 Raw Holdings EH53 0ET
☎ 01506 882494 ▤ 01506 882598
e-mail: lornascot@aol.com
dir: A71 onto B7015, establishment on right

A relaxed and friendly atmosphere prevails at this charming modern guest house. The bedrooms, all of which are on the ground floor, are attractively colour co-ordinated, well-equipped and contain many thoughtful extra touches. Breakfast is served at individual tables in the smart dining room.

Rooms 3 en suite (3 GF) S £40-£50; D £60-£70 **Facilities** tea/coffee Cen ht Wi-fi **Parking** 5 **Notes** ⊗ No Children 12yrs

---

FAULDHOUSE   Map 21 NS96

East Badallan Farm *(NS919598)*

★★★★ FARMHOUSE

EH47 9AG
☎ 01501 770251 **Ms Struthers**
e-mail: mary@eastbadallan.co.uk
web: www.eastbadallan.co.uk
dir: *M8 junct 3 or 4 onto B7010*

Equidistant between Edinburgh and Glasgow with great transportation links this working beef farm has been in same family since the 18th century. Well-appointed bedrooms with modern facilities provided as standard. Hospitality is a strength as is the breakfast with award winning local produce used.

Rooms 3 en suite (1 fmly) (1 GF) S £30-£40; D £60-£70* **Facilities** FTV tea/coffee Cen ht Wi-fi **Parking Notes** LB ⊗ ⊜ 127 acres beef

---

LINLITHGOW   Map 21 NS97

PREMIER COLLECTION

Arden Country House

★★★★★ GUEST ACCOMMODATION

Belsyde EH49 6QE
☎ 01506 670172   📄 01506 670172
e-mail: info@ardencountryhouse.com
dir: *1.3m SW of Linlithgow. A706 over Union Canal, entrance 200yds on left at Lodge Cottage*

Situated in the picturesque grounds of the Belsyde Country Estate and close to the Royal Burgh of Linlithgow, Arden Country House offers immaculate, stylishly furnished and spacious bedrooms. There is a cosy ground-floor lounge and a charming dining room where delicious breakfasts feature the best of local produce.

Rooms 3 en suite (1 GF) S £50-£100; D £80-£110* **Facilities** FTV tea/coffee Cen ht Wi-fi **Parking** 4 **Notes** LB ⊗ No Children 12yrs Closed 25-26 Dec

---

Belsyde House

★★★★ GUEST ACCOMMODATION

Lanark Rd EH49 6QE
☎ 01506 842098   📄 01506 842098
e-mail: hay@belsydehouse.co.uk
web: www.belsydehouse.co.uk
dir: *1.5m SW on A706, 1st left over Union Canal*

Reached by a tree-lined driveway, this welcoming farmhouse is peacefully situated in attractive grounds close to the Union Canal. There are well-proportioned double, twin and family rooms, and a cosy single. All are nicely furnished and well equipped. Breakfast, including a vegetarian menu, is served at good-sized tables in the dining room, next to the lounge.

Rooms 3 en suite (1 fmly); D £70-£90* **Facilities** TVL tea/coffee Cen ht Wi-fi **Parking** 10 **Notes** ⊗ No Children 12yrs Closed Xmas

---

Bomains Farm

★★★★ GUEST HOUSE

Bo'Ness EH49 7RQ
☎ 01506 822188 & 822861   📄 01506 824433
e-mail: bunty.kirk@onetel.net
web: www.bomains.co.uk
dir: *A706, 1.5m N towards Bo Ness, left at golf course x-rds, 1st farm on right*

From its elevated location this friendly farmhouse has stunning views of the Firth of Forth. The bedrooms which

vary in size are beautifully decorated, well equipped and enhanced by quality fabrics, with many thoughtful extra touches. Delicious home-cooked fare featuring the best of local produce is served a stylish lounge-dining room.

Rooms 5 rms (4 en suite) (1 pri facs) (1 fmly) **Facilities** STV TVL tea/coffee Cen ht Wi-fi Golf 18 Fishing **Parking** 12

Lumsdaine House

★★★★ BED AND BREAKFAST

Woodcockdale Farm, Lanark Rd EH49 6QE
☎ 01506 845001
e-mail: margaret@lumsdainehouse.co.uk
dir: *1.5m SW on A706*

Just a few minutes drive from historical town of Linlithgow this purpose built property offers modern, comfortable and spacious accommodation with some wonderful views. Hospitality is very strong and the Healthy Living Award breakfast gives the guest a great start to their day. Ample parking with large gardens.

Rooms 3 en suite S £35-£40; D £55-£60* **Facilities** TVL tea/coffee Cen ht Wi-fi **Parking** 3 **Notes** ⊗ No Children 14yrs Closed 20 Dec-1 Jan

---

LIVINGSTON   Map 21 NT06

Redcraig

★★★★ BED AND BREAKFAST

Redcraig, Midcalder EH53 0JT
☎ 01506 884249   📄 01506 884249
e-mail: jcampbelljack@aol.com
web: www.redcraigbedandbreakfast.co.uk
dir: *Off A71, turn for Morton between Lizzie Brice rdbt (Livingston) & Kirknewton traffic lights*

Enjoying a peaceful location within easy reach of central Scotland's major motorway and rail network, and situated half way between Edinburgh and Glasgow this friendly family home offers spotless, comfortable and stylish accommodation in a relaxed environment. Bedrooms are attractive and well equipped with two situated on the ground floor. Hearty breakfasts are served in the smart dining room.

Rooms 3 en suite (2 GF) S £40-£45; D £56-£65* **Facilities** tea/coffee Cen ht Wi-fi **Parking** 6 **Notes** ⊗ ⊜

Whitecroft

★★★★ BED AND BREAKFAST

7 Raw Holdings EH53 0ET
☎ 01506 882494   📄 01506 882598
e-mail: lornascot@aol.com

(For full entry see East Calder)

SCOTTISH ISLANDS
ARRAN, ISLE OF

BRODICK — Map 20 NS03

Allandale

★★★★ GUEST HOUSE

KA27 8BJ
☎ 01770 302278
e-mail: info@allandalehouse.co.uk
dir: *500yds S of Brodick Pier, off A841 towards Lamlash, up hill 2nd left at Corriegills sign*

Under enthusiastic ownership, this comfortable guest house is set in delightful gardens in beautiful countryside. Guests can relax in the lounge with its attractive garden views. Bedrooms vary in size and have pleasing colour schemes and mixed modern furnishings along with thoughtful amenities. In a peaceful location, Allandale is convenient for the CalMac ferry and Brodick centre.

Rooms 4 rms (3 en suite) (1 pri facs) 2 annexe en suite (3 fmly) (2 GF) S £46; D £74–£80 **Facilities** FTV tea/coffee Cen ht Wi-fi **Parking** 6 **Notes** LB ⊗ Closed Nov-Feb

Dunvegan House

★★★★ GUEST HOUSE

Dunvegan Shore Rd KA27 8AJ
☎ 01770 302811   📠 01770 302811
e-mail: dunveganhouse1@hotmail.com
dir: *Turn right from ferry terminal, 500yds along Shore Rd*

Dunvegan is a delightful detached home overlooking the bay towards Brodick Castle with Goat Fell beyond. The comfortable lounge and attractive dining room, as well as the pine-furnished bedrooms, enjoy the views. A daily-changing dinner menu and an interesting wine list encourage guests to dine in.

Rooms 9 en suite (1 fmly) (3 GF) S £45; D £80* **Facilities** tea/coffee Dinner available Cen ht Licensed **Parking** 10 **Notes** ⊗ Closed Xmas & New Year 🖼

HARRIS, ISLE OF

SCARISTA — Map 22 NG09

Scarista House

★★★★ ◉◉ RESTAURANT WITH ROOMS

HS3 3HX
☎ 01859 550238   📠 01859 550277
e-mail: timandpatricia@scaristahouse.com
dir: *On A859, 15m S of Tarbert*

A former manse, Scarista House is a haven for food lovers who seek to explore this magnificent island. It enjoys breathtaking views of the Atlantic and is just a short stroll from miles of golden sandy beaches. The house is run in a relaxed country-house manner by the friendly hosts. Expect wellies in the hall and masses of books and CDs in one of two lounges. Bedrooms are cosy, and delicious set dinners and memorable breakfasts are provided.

Rooms 3 en suite 2 annexe en suite (2 GF) S £125–£140; D £175–£199* **Facilities** tea/coffee Dinner available Direct Dial Cen ht **Parking** 12 **Notes** LB Closed Xmas, Jan & Feb No coaches Civ Wed 40

ISLAY, ISLE OF

BOWMORE — Map 20 NR35

PREMIER COLLECTION

The Harbour Inn and Restaurant
★★★★★ ◉ RESTAURANT WITH ROOMS

PA43 7JR
☎ 01496 810330   📠 01496 810990
e-mail: info@harbour.inn.com
dir: *Next to harbour*

No trip to Islay would be complete without experiencing a night or two at the Harbour Inn. The humble whitewashed exterior conceals the sophisticated, quality environment that draws discerning travellers from all over the world. Spacious bedrooms are appointed to a high standard and the conservatory-lounge has stunning views over Loch Indaal to the peaks of Jura. The cosy bar is popular with locals, and the smart dining room showcases some of the best seafood. Welcoming peat fires burn in cooler months.

Rooms 7 en suite (1 GF) **Facilities** tea/coffee Dinner available Direct Dial Complimentary use of local leisure centre **Notes** No Children 10yrs No coaches

ORKNEY

ST MARGARET'S HOPE — Map 24 ND49

The Creel Restaurant with Rooms

★★★★ ◉◉ RESTAURANT WITH ROOMS

Front Rd KW17 2SL
☎ 01856 831311
e-mail: alan@thecreel.freeserve.co.uk
web: www.thecreel.co.uk
dir: *Turn right from A961into village, located on seafront*

With wonderful sea views, The Creel enjoys a prominent position in the pretty fishing village of St Margaret's Hope. The award-winning restaurant has a well deserved reputation for the quality of its seafood and a window seat is a must in the charming restaurant. The stylish bedrooms have now been refurbished to a high standard and most rooms enjoy views over the bay. Breakfasts should not be missed, with local Orkney produce and freshly baked breads on the menu.

Rooms 3 en suite; D £105–£120 **Facilities** Dinner available Cen ht **Parking** 6 **Notes** ⊗ Closed mid Oct-Apr No coaches

SHETLAND

LERWICK — Map 24 HU44

Glen Orchy House

★★★★ GUEST HOUSE

20 Knab Rd ZE1 0AX
☎ 01595 692031   📠 01595 692031
e-mail: glenorchy.house@virgin.net
dir: *Next to coastguard station*

This welcoming and well-presented house lies above the town with views over the Knab, and is within easy walking distance of the town centre. Bedrooms are modern in design and there is a choice of lounges with books and board games, one with an honesty bar. Substantial breakfasts are served, and the restaurant offers a delicious Thai menu.

Rooms 24 en suite (4 fmly) (4 GF) **Facilities** STV FTV TVL tea/coffee Dinner available Cen ht Licensed Wi-fi **Parking** 10

SKYE, ISLE OF

DUNVEGAN   Map 22 NG24

Roskhill House

U

Roskhill IV55 8ZD
☎ 01470 521317
e-mail: stay@roskhillhouse.co.uk
web: www.roskhillhouse.co.uk
dir: *3m S of Dunvegan off A863 Dunvegan*

Currently the rating for this establishment is not confirmed. This may be due to a change of ownership or because it has only recently joined the AA rating scheme

Rooms 5 en suite (2 GF) S £40-£52; D £60-£78*
Facilities TVL tea/coffee Cen ht Wi-fi **Parking** 6 **Notes** No Children 9yrs Closed Nov-mid Mar

EDINBANE   Map 22 NG35

Shorefield House

★★★★ GUEST HOUSE

Edinbane IV51 9PW
☎ 01470 582444   📠 01470 582414
e-mail: stay@shorefield-house.com
dir: *12m from Portree & 8m from Dunvegan, off A850 into Edinbane, 1st on right*

Shorefield stands in the village of Edinbane and looks out to Loch Greshornish. Bedrooms range from single to family, while one ground-floor room has easier access. All rooms are thoughtfully equipped and have CD players. Breakfast is an impressive choice and there is also a child-friendly garden.

Rooms 4 en suite (1 fmly) (3 GF) D £74-£98
Facilities TVL tea/coffee Cen ht Wi-fi **Parking** 10 **Notes** LB ⊗ Closed Xmas

PORTREE   Map 22 NG44

Medina

★★★★ BED AND BREAKFAST

Coolin Hills Gardens IV51 9NB
☎ 01478 612821
e-mail: medinaskye@yahoo.co.uk
web: www.medinaskye.co.uk
dir: *From Portree centre, A855 to Staffin, at large sign for Cullin Hills Hotel turn right. Att 2nd large sign turn sharp left up hill*

A delightful bungalow quietly located in a small residential development in the former walled gardens of the Cuillin Hills Hotel. The two ground floor bedrooms are spacious, comfortable and well equipped, and guests also have the use of an elegant and comfortable lounge, where breakfast is served around a communal table.

Rooms 2 en suite (2 GF) D £68-£80* **Facilities** TVL tea/coffee Cen ht **Parking** 2 **Notes** ⊗ No Children 14yrs Closed Nov-Feb

STAFFIN   Map 22 NG46

The Glenview

★★★ ⊛ RESTAURANT WITH ROOMS

Culnacnoc IV51 9JH
☎ 01470 562248
e-mail: enquiries@glenviewskye.co.uk
web: www.glenviewskye.co.uk
dir: *12m N of Portree on A855*

The Glenview is located in one of the most beautiful parts of Skye with stunning seas views; it is close to the famous Old Man of Storr rock outcrop. The individually styled bedrooms are very comfortable and front-facing rooms enjoy the dramatic views. Evening meals should not to be missed as the restaurant has a well deserved reputation for its locally sourced produce.

Rooms 5 en suite (1 fmly) (1 GF) S £55-£65; D £80-£100* **Facilities** tea/coffee Dinner available Wi-fi

STRUAN   Map 22 NG33

PREMIER COLLECTION

Ullinish Country Lodge

★★★★★ ⊛⊛⊛ RESTAURANT WITH ROOMS

IV56 8FD
☎ 01470 572214   📠 01470 572341
e-mail: ullinish@theisleofskye.co.uk
dir: *N on A863*

Set in some of Scotland's most dramatic landscape, with views of the Black Cuillin and MacLeod's Tables, this lodge has lochs on three sides. Samuel Johnson and James Boswell stayed here in 1773 and were impressed with the hospitality even then! Hosts Brian and Pam hope to extend the same welcome to their guests today. As you would expect, all bedrooms have amazing views, and come with half-tester beds. The cuisine in the restaurant is impressive and uses the best of Skye's produce including locally sourced seafood and game.

Rooms 6 en suite S £90-£120; D £120-£160*
Facilities tea/coffee Dinner available Cen ht **Parking** 8 **Notes** LB ⊗ No Children 16yrs Closed Jan & 1wk Nov No coaches

UIG   Map 22 NG36

Woodbine House

★★★ GUEST ACCOMMODATION

IV51 9XP
☎ 01470 542243
e-mail: contact@skyeactivities.co.uk
dir: *From Portree into Uig Bay, pass Ferry Inn & right onto A855 Staffin Rd, house 300yds on right*

Built in the late 19th century, Woodbine House occupies an elevated position overlooking Uig Bay and the surrounding countryside and is well suited for walking and bird-watching enthusiasts. The ground floor dining room has lovely sea views as do the front facing bedrooms.

Rooms 4 en suite (1 fmly) S £35-£55; D £55-£59*
Facilities tea/coffee Dinner available Cen ht Wi-fi Archery, Mountain bike/sea kayak hire & boat trips **Parking** 4 **Notes** LB ⊗ ⊜

Ferry Inn

★★★ 🅰 INN

IV51 9XP
☎ 01478 611216   📠 01478 611224
e-mail: info@ferryinn.co.uk
web: www.ferryinn.co.uk
dir: *In Uig, on a loop road off A87, 1m from ferry terminal*

Rooms 6 en suite S £39-£46; D £68-£80* **Facilities** STV TVL tea/coffee Dinner available Cen ht **Parking** 10 **Notes** ⊗ No coaches

Wales

Heather on Conwy Mountains, Snowdonia National Park

ANGLESEY, ISLE OF

AMLWCH — Map 14 SH49

Lastra Farm

★★★★ GUEST ACCOMMODATION

Penrhyd LL68 9TF
☎ 01407 830906 ▤ 01407 832522
e-mail: booking@lastra-hotel.com
web: www.lastra-hotel.com
dir: *On A5025 turn left after welcome sign. Follow signs to leisure centre, Lastra Farm signed*

This 17th-century farmhouse offers pine-furnished, colourfully decorated bedrooms. There is also a comfortable lounge and a cosy bar. A wide range of good-value food is available either in the restaurant or Granary's Bistro. The establishment can cater for functions in a separate purpose-built suite and hospitality is natural and caring.

Rooms 8 en suite (1 fmly) (3 GF) Facilities FTV tea/coffee Dinner available Direct Dial Cen ht Licensed Wi-fi Conf Max 120 Thtr 120 Class 100 Board 50 Parking 50 Notes LB Civ Wed 200

BEAUMARIS — Map 14 SH67

PREMIER COLLECTION

Ye Olde Bulls Head Inn
★★★★★ ◉◉ INN

Castle St LL58 8AP
☎ 01248 810329 ▤ 01248 811294
e-mail: info@bullsheadinn.co.uk

Charles Dickens and Samuel Johnson were both regular visitors to this inn which features exposed beams and antique weaponry. Richly decorated bedrooms are well equipped and there is a spacious lounge. Meetings and small functions are catered for, and food continues to attract praise in both The Loft restaurant and the less formal brasserie.

Rooms 12 en suite 1 annexe en suite (2 GF) Facilities tea/coffee Dinner available Direct Dial Wi-fi Conf Max 16 Board 16 Parking 10 Notes ⊗

CEMAES BAY — Map 14 SH39

Hafod Country House

★★★★ BED AND BREAKFAST

LL67 0DS
☎ 01407 711645
e-mail: hbr1946@aol.com
dir: *0.5m S of Cemaes. Off A5025 Cemaes rdbt signed Llanfechell, Hafod 500yds on left*

Guests are assured of a warm welcome at this large and spacious Edwardian house, which stands in extensive gardens and is quietly located on the outskirts of the village. It provides well equipped accommodation, as well

as a comfortable lounge and an elegant dining room, the setting for comprehensive Welsh breakfasts.

Rooms 3 en suite S £40; D £60-£65* Facilities tea/coffee Cen ht Parking 3 Notes ⊗ No Children 7yrs Closed Oct-Mar

HOLYHEAD — Map 14 SH28

Wavecrest

★★ GUEST HOUSE

93 Newry St LL65 1HU
☎ 01407 763637 ▤ 01407 764862
e-mail: cwavecrest@aol.com
web: www.holyheadhotels.com
dir: *Left at end A55, 600yds turn by railings, premises 100yds up hill on right*

Well located for the Irish ferry terminals and within easy walking distance of the town centre, the Wavecrest is proving to be a popular overnight stop-off. Pretty bedrooms are equipped with satellite TV and other modern facilities. There is a comfortable lounge and evening meals may be booked in advance.

Rooms 4 rms (2 en suite) (3 fmly) S £25-£30; D £45-£60* Facilities STV TVL tea/coffee Dinner available Cen ht Wi-fi Parking 1 Notes Closed 24-31 Dec ⊗

LLANERCHYMEDD — Map 14 SH48

Tre-Wyn (SH454851)

★★★★ FARMHOUSE

Maenaddwyn LL71 8AE
☎ 01248 470875 Mrs N Bown
e-mail: nia@trewyn.fsnet.co.uk
dir: *A5025 to Benllech Bay, B5108 to Brynteg x-rds, take Llannerchymedd road 3m to Maenaddwyn. Right after 6 houses, 0.5m to farm*

An extremely friendly welcome is extended to this spacious farmhouse. Rooms are well equipped and attractively furnished. The dining room and the relaxing lounge with its log fire have wonderful views across the gardens and countryside to Bodafon Mountain.

Rooms 3 en suite (1 fmly) Facilities TVL tea/coffee Cen ht Parking 5 Notes ⊗ 240 acres arable/beef/sheep

CAERPHILLY

CAERPHILLY — Map 9 ST18

The Cottage

★★★ GUEST HOUSE

Mountain View, Pwllypant CF83 3HW
☎ 029 2086 9160 ▤ 029 2086 9160
e-mail: cottageguesthouse@tiscali.co.uk
dir: *1m N of town centre. On rdbt junct A468 & A469*

Enthusiastic proprietor Carole Beacham welcomes you to her 300-year-old home, which occupies a convenient roadside location near to the town centre. Bedrooms are thoughtfully appointed, and there is a spacious and comfortable lounge. Breakfast is served in the attractive dining room.

Rooms 7 rms (5 en suite) (1 fmly) Facilities TVL tea/coffee Cen ht Wi-fi Parking 8 Notes ⊗ ⊜

CARDIFF

CARDIFF — Map 9 ST17

Annedd Lon

★★★★ GUEST HOUSE

157 Cathedral Rd, Pontcanna CF11 9PL
☎ 029 2022 3349
web: www.anneddlon.co.uk
dir: *From Cardiff Castle, W across River Taff. 1st right into Cathedral Rd. House on left just after 4th side street*

Just a leisurely stroll from Sophia Gardens and the Millennium Stadium, this impressive Victorian house is ideally located. The house retains many original features and is attractively furnished. Elegant public areas include a comfortable lounge as well as a cosy dining room.

Rooms 6 rms (5 en suite) (2 fmly) S £40; D £55-£70* Facilities FTV tea/coffee Cen ht Wi-fi Parking 6 Notes ⊗ Closed 24-29 Dec

The Old Post Office

★★★★ ⑧ RESTAURANT WITH ROOMS

Greenwood Ln, St Fagans CF5 6EL
☎ 029 2056 5400 📠 029 2056 3400
e-mail: info@theoldpostofficerestaurant.co.uk
dir: 4m W of city centre. M4 junct 33 onto A4232, onto A48 for Cardiff & 1st left for St Fagans

Located just five miles from Cardiff in the historic village of St Fagans, this establishment offers contemporary style based on New England design. Bedrooms, like the dining room, feature striking white walls with spotlights offering a fresh, clean feel. Delicious meals include a carefully prepared selection of local produce.

Rooms 6 en suite (2 fmly) (6 GF) **Facilities** FTV tea/coffee Dinner available Cen ht Wi-fi **Parking** 20 **Notes** ⊗ Closed mid-end Jan No coaches

Tanglewood

★★★ GUEST HOUSE

4 Tygwyn Rd, Penylan CF23 5JE
☎ 029 2047 3447 & 07971 546812 📠 0870 706 1808
e-mail: reservations@tanglewoodguesthouse.com
web: www.tanglewoodguesthouse.com
dir: Towards Cardiff E & Docks. 3rd exit at rdbt. Next rdbt 1st exit. Left at lights. Right just past next lights. Establishment 120yds on right

An elegant, well-kept Edwardian house, Tanglewood is in a quiet residential district and has attractive gardens. The pleasant bedrooms are thoughtfully equipped and there is a comfortable lounge overlooking the gardens.

Rooms 4 rms (1 en suite) **Facilities** TVL tea/coffee Cen ht **Parking** 8 **Notes** ⊗ Closed 15 Dec-10 Jan ⊛

CARMARTHENSHIRE

AMMANFORD   Map 8 SN61

Bryncoch Farm

★★★ 🅰 BED AND BREAKFAST

Llandyfan SA18 2TY
☎ 01269 850480 📠 01236 850480
e-mail: robrich@bryncochfarm.co.uk
dir: M4 junct 29, A483 to Ammanford, onto A474, 0.75m left signed Trap, farm 3m

Rooms 3 en suite (1 fmly) S £25; D £45* **Facilities** FTV TVL tea/coffee Cen ht Wi-fi Fishing **Parking** 10

CARMARTHEN   Map 8 SN42

See also Cwmduad & Nantgaredig

Capel Dewi Uchaf Country House

★★★★ 🏠 BED AND BREAKFAST

Capel Dewi SA32 8AY
☎ 01267 290799 📠 01267 290003
e-mail: uchaffarm@aol.com
dir: On B4300 between Capel Dewi & junct B4310

Located in 35 acres of grounds with stunning views and private fishing in the River Towy, this Grade II listed, 16th-century house retains many magnificent features and has a wealth of character. Generous Welsh breakfasts are a feature here.

Rooms 3 en suite **Facilities** TVL tea/coffee Dinner available Cen ht Fishing Riding **Conf** Max 8 Board 8 **Parking** 10 **Notes** ⊗ Closed Xmas

Sarnau Mansion

★★★★ GUEST ACCOMMODATION

Llysonnen Rd SA33 5DZ
☎ 01267 211404 📠 01267 211404
e-mail: fernihough@so1405.force9.co.uk
web: www.sarnaumansion.co.uk
dir: 5m W of Carmarthen. Off A40 onto B4298 & Bancyfelin road, Sarnau on right

Located west of Carmarthen in 16 acres of grounds and gardens, including a tennis court, this large Grade II listed, late-Georgian house retains much original character and is stylishly decorated. There is a lounge with a log fire, an elegant dining room, and spacious bedrooms with stunning rural views.

Rooms 4 rms (3 en suite) (1 pri facs) S £45-£50; D £70-£80 **Facilities** TVL tea/coffee Dinner available Cen ht 🎱 **Parking** 10 **Notes** ⊗ No Children 5yrs

Shakeshafts

★★★★ BED AND BREAKFAST

Lower Penddaulwyn, Capel Dewi SA32 8AY
☎ 01267 290627
e-mail: elaine@shakeshafts.com
web: www.shakeshafts.com
dir: On B4300 3m E of Carmarthen

Peacefully located in the beautiful Towy Valley with three acres of grounds to the rear, Shakeshafts offers a friendly and relaxing style of accommodation. The modern bedrooms and bathrooms are newly furnished and comfortable. Guests are welcome to enjoy the surrounding gardens, or on colder days they may prefer the new conservatory.

Rooms 3 en suite (1 GF) S £30-£45; D £56-£65 **Facilities** FTV tea/coffee Cen ht 🛶 **Parking** 10 **Notes** LB ⊗ No Children 8yrs ⊛

CWMDUAD   Map 8 SN33

Neuadd-Wen

★★★ GUEST HOUSE

SA33 6XJ
☎ 01267 281438 📠 01267 281438
e-mail: goodbourn@neuaddwen.plus.com
dir: On A484, 9m N of Carmarthen, towards Cardigan

Excellent customer care is assured at this combined Post Office and guest house situated in pretty gardens in an unspoiled village. An ideal location for walkers to base themselves for exploring the surrounding areas. Bedrooms are spacious and filled with thoughtful extras. There is one area of the house which can accommodate a large family within three bedrooms and a bathroom, and ground floor bedrooms are available. There is an attractive lounge and a dining room that serves imaginative dinners using fresh local produce; hearty breakfasts are also served here to commence the day.

Rooms 9 rms (6 en suite) 1 annexe en suite (2 fmly) (2 GF) S £22-£26; D £44-£52 **Facilities** TV9B TVL tea/coffee Dinner available Direct Dial Cen ht Licensed **Parking** 12 **Notes** LB

FELINGWM UCHAF — Map 8 SN52

Allt Y Golau Farmhouse *(SN510261)*

★★★★ 🏠 FARMHOUSE

Allt Y Golau Uchaf SA32 7BB
☎ 01267 290455 📠 01267 290743 Dr C Rouse
e-mail: alltygolau@btinternet.com
web: www.alltygolau.com
dir: *A40 onto B4310, N for 2m. 1st on left after Felingwm Uchaf*

This delightful Georgian farmhouse has been furnished and decorated to a high standard by the present owners, and enjoys panoramic views over the Tywi Valley to the Black Mountains beyond. Guests are welcome to take a relaxing walk through two acres of mature garden. Many thoughtful extras are provided in the comfortable bedrooms, and there is as a separate lounge. Breakfast is provided in the cosy dining room around a communal table.

Rooms 3 rms (2 en suite) (1 pri facs) (2 GF) S £45;
D £65* **Facilities** TVL tea/coffee Cen ht **Parking** 3
Notes ⊗ Closed 20 Dec-2 Jan 🐾 2 acres small holding

LAUGHARNE — Map 8 SN31

Keepers Cottage Bed and Breakfast

★★★★ BED AND BREAKFAST

SA33 4QN
☎ 01994 427404
e-mail: info@keepers-cottage.com
web: www.keepers-cottage.com
dir: *On A4066, St Clears to Laugharne road, opp blue village sign*

Hosts Marj and Rose extend a warm welcome to this delightful cottage-style property. Bedrooms, including a ground-floor room, offer comfort with many extras. There is a lounge with stunning views which extend to The Gower Peninsular. The welcoming dining room is set with separate tables and is the venue for a hearty breakfast. The Dylan Thomas Boat House and Laugharne Castle, are both just a short walk away.

Rooms 3 en suite (1 GF) S £40-£50; D £65-£70*
Facilities FTV TVL tea/coffee Cen ht **Parking** 6 **Notes** LB
⊗ No Children 10yrs

LLANDEILO — Map 8 SN62

Blaen-Y-Garn

★★★★ 🅰 BED AND BREAKFAST

Manordeilo SA19 7BG
☎ 01550 777707
e-mail: blaenygarn@btinternet.com
dir: *On A40 between Llandeilo & Llandovery*

Rooms 2 rms (1 en suite) (1 pri facs) (1 GF) S £35;
D £55* **Facilities** FTV tea/coffee Cen ht Wi-fi **Parking** 4
Notes 🐾

LLANDOVERY — Map 9 SN73

Dan Y Parc *(SN795378)*

★★★★ 🅰 FARMHOUSE

Cynghordy SA20 0LD
☎ 01550 720401 Mrs Gillian Kilmartin
e-mail: info@danyparc.com
dir: *3m from Llandovery on A483 heading to Builth Wells*

Rooms 3 rms (2 en suite) (1 pri facs) S £28-£30;
D £56-£60* **Facilities** FTV TVL tea/coffee Dinner available
Cen ht Wi-fi **Parking** 6 **Notes** LB Closed 20-31 Dec 🐾 14
acres non-working/horses

LLANDYBIE — Map 8 SN61

Glynhir Mansion

★★★ BED AND BREAKFAST

Glynhir Rd SA18 2TD
☎ 01269 850438 📠 01269 851275
e-mail: enquiries@theglynhirestate.com
web: www.theglynhirestate.com
dir: *1m N of Ammanford on A483*

Nestling at the foot of the Black Mountains, an Area of Outstanding Beauty, Glynhir Mansion dates from the end of the 17th century. The dining room and lounge have open fires and attractive period furnishings. The 200 acres of grounds include lovely walks alongside the River Loughor, where a 30-foot waterfall is a spectacle not to be missed.

Rooms 4 en suite (1 fmly) S £50; D £80* **Facilities** TVL
Dinner available Cen ht Licensed Golf 18 Pool Table Table
tennis **Conf** Max 40 Thtr 40 Class 40 Board 30
Parking 12 **Notes** LB ⊗ Closed mid Dec-mid Jan Civ Wed
45

NANTGAREDIG — Map 8 SN42

Ty Castell - Home of the Kingfisher

★★★★ 🅰 GUEST HOUSE

Station Rd SA32 7LQ
☎ 01267 290034
e-mail: enquiries@ty-castell.co.uk
web: www.ty-castell.co.uk
dir: *M4 junct 49 onto A48, onto B4310 signed Nantgaredig. Left at junct, over bridge, 1st left, then 1st left again*

Rooms 3 en suite (1 fmly) (1 GF) S £30-£40; D £50-£60*
Facilities FTV TVL tea/coffee Dinner available Cen ht Wi-fi
Fishing **Parking** 6 **Notes** LB ⊗ No Children 10yrs

ST CLEARS — Map 8 SN21

PREMIER COLLECTION

Coedllys Country House

★★★★★ BED AND BREAKFAST

Llangynin SA33 4JY
☎ 01994 231455 📠 01994 231441
e-mail: keith@harber.fsworld.co.uk
web: www.coedllyscountryhouse.co.uk

Set in a peaceful valley with rolling countryside, Coedllys is the home of Mr and Mrs Harber, who make visitors feel like honoured guests. Bedrooms are lavishy furnished, and the thoughtful and useful extras make a stay most memorable. There is a cosy well-furnished lounge, and an extensive menu choice at breakfast is served in the pleasant dining room. For the energetic there is a fitness suite, but you can also relax in the sauna or small indoor pool which are available for guest use.

Rooms 3 en suite **Facilities** FTV tea/coffee Dinner
available Cen ht Wi-fi 🛁 Sauna Gymnasium **Parking** 6
Notes No Children 10yrs Closed Xmas

CEREDIGION

ABERAERON — Map 8 SN46

PREMIER COLLECTION

The Harbourmaster

★★★★★ ◉ 🍴 INN

Pen Cei SA46 0BA
☎ 01545 570755
e-mail: info@harbour-master.com
web: www.harbour-master.com
dir: *In town centre beside tourist office & harbour*

Located right on the harbour, this Grade II listed building was previously the harbourmaster's house. The bedrooms are delightfully furnished and have excellent showers. The proprietors and staff are very friendly and professional. Dinner and breakfast are a real treat too, a varied range of carefully prepared dishes using much local produce.

Rooms 13 rms (10 en suite) (3 pri facs) S £50-£60;
D £110-£250* **Facilities** FTV tea/coffee Dinner
available Direct Dial Cen ht Lift Wi-fi **Parking** 7
Notes LB ⊗ No Children 5yrs Closed 25 Dec No
coaches

PREMIER COLLECTION

Ty Mawr Mansion
★★★★★ ◉◉ ▤ RESTAURANT WITH ROOMS

Cilcennin SA48 8DB
☎ 01570 470033
e-mail: info@tymawrmansion.co.uk
web: www.tymawrmansion.co.uk
dir: On A482 (Lampeter to Aberaeron road), 4m from Aberaeron

Surrounded by rolling countryside in its own naturally beautiful gardens, this fine country mansion house is a haven of perfect peace and tranquillity. Careful renovation has restored it to its former glory and, combined with lush fabrics, top quality beds and sumptuous furnishings, the accommodation is spacious, superbly equipped and very comfortable. Award-winning chefs create mouth-watering dishes from local and seasonal produce. There is also a 27-seat cinema with all the authenticity of the real thing. Martin and Cath McAlpine offer the sort of welcome which makes every visit to Ty Mawr a memorable one.

Rooms 8 en suite 1 annexe en suite (1 fmly) (2 GF) S £95-£160; D £120-£280* **Facilities** FTV tea/coffee Dinner available Direct Dial Cen ht Wi-fi Fishing Outdoor hot tub, cinema **Conf** Max 25 Thtr 25 Class 25 Board 16 **Parking** 20 **Notes** LB ❸ No Children 12yrs Closed 25 Dec-8 Jan No coaches

Arosfa Harbourside Guesthouse
★★★★ ▤ GUEST HOUSE

SA46 0BU
☎ 01545 570120
e-mail: info@arosfaguesthouse.co.uk
dir: A487 in town centre onto Market St towards sea, 150yds to Arosfa. Harbourside car park

A warm welcome is assured at this renovated Georgian house, located by the historic harbour. Bedrooms are

filled with thoughtful extras and have modern bathrooms. Other areas include a cosy lounge, stairways enhanced by quality art and memorabilia, and a bright, attractive dining room is the setting for imaginative Welsh breakfasts.

Arosfa Harbourside Guesthouse

Rooms 3 en suite 1 annexe en suite (1 fmly) (1 GF) S £35-£60; D £60-£100 **Facilities** FTV tea/coffee Cen ht Wi-fi **Notes** LB ❸ ❸

ABERYSTWYTH   Map 8 SN58

PREMIER COLLECTION

Awel-Deg
★★★★★ BED AND BREAKFAST

Capel Bangor SY23 3LR
☎ 01970 880681
e-mail: awel-deg@tiscali.co.uk
web: www.awel-deg.co.uk
dir: 5m E of Aberystwyth. On A44 in Capel Bangor

Located five miles from the historic university town, this attractive bungalow, set in pretty gardens, provides high standards of hospitality, comfort and facilities. Immaculately maintained throughout, spacious bedrooms are equipped with a wealth of thoughtful extras and smart, modern en suite shower rooms. Comprehensive breakfasts are served at one table in the elegant dining room and a choice of lounges is available.

Rooms 2 en suite (2 GF) S fr £45; D £58 **Facilities** FTV TVL tea/coffee Cen ht **Parking** 8 **Notes** LB ❸ No Children 11yrs Closed 20-30 Dec ❸

Bodalwyn
★★★★ GUEST HOUSE

Queen's Av SY23 2EG
☎ 01970 612578 ▤ 01970 639261
e-mail: enquiries@bodalwyn.co.uk
web: www.bodalwyn.co.uk
dir: 500yds N of town centre. Off A487 Northgate St onto North Rd to end

Located a short walk from the promenade, this imposing Edwardian house, built for a college professor, has been totally refurbished to provide high standards of comfort and good facilities. Smart modern bathrooms complement the spacious bedrooms, which are equipped with a wealth of thoughtful extras. Family rooms are

available. Comprehensive Welsh breakfasts are served in the elegant conservatory-dining room.

Bodalwyn

Rooms 8 en suite (2 fmly) S £41-£55; D £64-£75* **Facilities** tea/coffee Cen ht Wi-fi **Notes** ❸ Closed 24 Dec-1 Jan ❸

Glyn-Garth
★★★★ GUEST HOUSE

South Rd SY23 1JS
☎ 01970 615050
e-mail: glyngarth@aol.com
web: www.glyngarth.cjb.net
dir: In town centre. Off A487 onto South Rd off South Promenade

Privately owned and personally run by the same family for over 50 years, this immaculately maintained guest house provides a range of thoughtfully furnished bedrooms with smart modern bathrooms. Breakfast is served in the attractive dining room and a lounge is also available.

Rooms 10 rms (6 en suite) (2 fmly) (1 GF) S £28-£60; D £56-£72* **Facilities** STV TVL tea/coffee Cen ht Wi-fi **Parking** 2 **Notes** ❸ Closed 2wks Xmas & New Year ❸

Llety Ceiro Country House
★★★★ GUEST HOUSE

Peggy Ln, Bow St, Llandre SY24 5AB
☎ 01970 821900 ▤ 01970 820966
e-mail: marinehotel1@btconnect.com
dir: 4m NE of Aberystwyth. Off A487 onto B4353 for 300yds

Located north of Aberystwyth, this house is well maintained throughout. Bedrooms are equipped with a range of thoughtful extras in addition to smart modern bathrooms. Morning coffees, afternoon teas and dinner are available in an attractive dining room with a conservatory extension. Bicycle hire is also available.

Rooms 11 en suite (2 fmly) (3 GF) (1 smoking) S £35-£65; D £55-£95* **Facilities** FTV TVL tea/coffee Dinner available Direct Dial Cen ht Licensed Wi-fi Free use of facilities at sister hotel **Conf** Max 60 Thtr 60 Class 40 Board 40 **Parking** 21 **Notes** LB Civ Wed 65

ABERYSTWYTH *continued*

Yr Hafod

★★★★ GUEST HOUSE

1 South Marine Ter SY23 1JX
☎ 01970 617579   📄 01970 636835
e-mail: johnyrhafod@aol.com
dir: *On south promenade between harbour & castle*

An immaculately maintained, end of terrace Victorian house in a commanding location overlooking the South Bay. The spacious bedrooms are comfortable and some have smart modern shower rooms. Breakfast is served in the attractive front-facing dining room.

Rooms 7 rms (3 en suite) S £29-£30; D £58-£80
Facilities TVL tea/coffee Cen ht Wi-fi **Parking** 1 **Notes** ⊗
Closed Xmas & New Year ⊠

Y Gelli

★★★ BED AND BREAKFAST

Dolau, Lovesgrove SY23 3HP
☎ 01970 617834
e-mail: pat.twigg@virgin.net
dir: *Off A44 2.75m E of town centre*

Located in spacious grounds on the town's outskirts, this modern detached house contains a range of practically furnished bedrooms and three further rooms are available in an adjacent Victorian property. Comprehensive breakfasts are served in the attractive dining room and a lounge is also available.

Rooms 5 rms (2 en suite) 3 annexe rms 1 annexe en suite (3 fmly) (1 GF) **Facilities** TVL tea/coffee Dinner available Cen ht Snooker Pool Table Table tennis **Conf** Thtr 30 Class 30 Board 20 **Parking** 20 **Notes** ⊗ ⊠

LAMPETER   Map 8 SN54

Haulfan

★★★★ BED AND BREAKFAST

6 Station Ter SA48 7HH
☎ 01570 422718
e-mail: haulfanguesthouse@lampeter.freeserve.co.uk
dir: *From S, A485 through town centre, right by fountain, next right*

Very popular for visitors to the nearby university, this Victorian house provides modern furnished and equipped bedrooms. There is a homely, comfortable lounge and generous breakfasts are served in the cosy dining room, where separate tables are provided. A warm welcome is assured from proprietors, who have an excellent knowledge of the area.

Rooms 3 rms (2 en suite) (1 fmly) (1 GF) S £25-£36; D £48-£55* **Facilities** TVL tea/coffee Cen ht **Parking** 1 **Notes** LB ⊗ Closed 20 Dec-mid Jan ⊠

CONWY

ABERGELE   Map 14 SH97

PREMIER COLLECTION

The Kinmel Arms

★★★★★ ◉ RESTAURANT WITH ROOMS

The Village, St George LL22 9BP
☎ 01745 832207   📄 01745 822044
e-mail: info@thekinmelarms.co.uk
dir: *From A55 junct 24a to St George. E on A55, junct 25. 1st left to Rhuddlan, then 1st right into St George. Take 2nd right*

This converted 17th-century coaching inn stands close to the church in the village of St George in the beautiful Elwy Valley. The popular restaurant specialises in produce from Wales and North West England, and the friendly and helpful staff ensures an enjoyable stay. The accommodation consists of four attractive, well-equipped suites; substantial continental breakfasts are served in the rooms.

Rooms 4 en suite (2 GF) **Facilities** STV tea/coffee Dinner available Cen ht **Parking** 8 **Notes** ⊗ No Children 16yrs Closed 25 Dec & 1 Jan RS Sun & Mon Closed Sun pm & all day Mon (ex BHs) No coaches

---

BETWS-Y-COED   Map 14 SH75

PREMIER COLLECTION

Penmachno Hall

★★★★★ ⊜ GUEST ACCOMMODATION

Penmachno LL24 0PU
☎ 01690 760410   📄 01690 760410
e-mail: stay@penmachnohall.co.uk
web: www.penmachnohall.co.uk
dir: *4m S of Betws-y-Coed. A5 onto B4406 to Penmachno, over bridge, right at Eagles pub signed Ty Mawr. 500yds at stone bridge*

Set in more than two acres of mature grounds including a mountain stream and woodland, this impressive Victorian rectory has been lovingly restored to provide high standards of comfort and facilities. Stylish décor and quality furnishings highlight the many original features throughout the ground-floor areas, and the bedrooms have a wealth of thoughtful extras. A recent addition is a superb family suite created from a sympathetic renovation of a former outhouse. Pre-booked set dinner party-style evening meals are served on Saturday night, while a buffet-style meal is served Tuesday through Friday.

Rooms 3 en suite; D £80-£95 **Facilities** tea/coffee Dinner available Cen ht Licensed Wi-fi **Parking** 5 **Notes** LB ⊗ Closed Xmas & New Year RS Sun-Mon No evening meals

PREMIER COLLECTION

Tan-y-Foel Country House
★ ★ ★ ★ ★ @@@ GUEST HOUSE

Capel Garmon LL26 0RE
☎ 01690 710507 📠 01690 710681
e-mail: enquiries@tyfhotel.co.uk
web: www.tyfhotel.co.uk
dir: *1.5m E of Betws-y-Coed. Off A5 onto A470 N, 2m right for Capel Garmon, establishment signed 1.5m on left*

Situated high above the Conwy valley and set in six acres of woodland with attractive gardens and country walks leading from the grounds, this delightful 17th-century country house has superb views in all directions. The bedrooms are individually decorated and include four-poster king, canopied and king-size beds along with modern facilities. There is a stylish sitting room and restaurant where fires burn in winter, and fresh local produce features on the small but interesting menu. Tan-y-Foel was the AA Guest Accomodation of the Year for Wales 2008-2009.

Rooms 3 en suite 2 annexe en suite (1 GF)
S £120-£160; D £150-£220 **Facilities** tea/coffee Dinner available Direct Dial Cen ht Licensed **Parking** 14
Notes LB ⊗ No Children 12yrs Closed Dec RS Jan Limited availability

Afon View Guest House
★ ★ ★ ★ GUEST HOUSE

Holyhead Rd LL24 0AN
☎ 01690 710726 📠 01690 710726
e-mail: welcome@afon-view.co.uk
web: www.afon-view.co.uk
dir: *On A5, 150yds E of HSBC bank*

A warm welcome is assured at this elegant Victorian house, located between Waterloo Bridge and village centre. Bedrooms are equipped with lots of thoughtful extras and day rooms include an attractive dining room and comfortable guest lounge. Afternoon teas are served during the summer months.

Rooms 7 en suite (1 fmly) S £40-£45; D £65-£85*
Facilities tea/coffee Cen ht Wi-fi **Parking** 7 **Notes** LB ⊗ No Children 4yrs Closed 23-26 Dec

Bryn Bella Guest House
★ ★ ★ ★ GUEST HOUSE

Lon Muriau, Llanrwst Rd LL24 0HD
☎ 01690 710627
e-mail: welcome@bryn-bella.co.uk
web: www.bryn-bella.co.uk
dir: *A5 onto A470, 0.5m right onto driveway signed Bryn Bella*

Located on an elevated position on the town's outskirts and having stunning views of the surrounding countryside, this elegant Victorian house provides a range of thoughtfully equipped bedrooms with smart modern bathrooms. A fine collection of memorabilia adorns the public areas, which include an attractive dining room and a comfortable lounge. A warm welcome is assured and guest services include a daily weather forecast.

Rooms 5 en suite (1 GF) **Facilities** FTV TVL tea/coffee Cen ht Wi-fi **Parking** 7 **Notes** LB ⊗

The Ty Gwyn Inn situated in Betws-y-Coed, at the heart of the Snowdonia National Park, is a former coaching Inn dating back to 1636. Following a recent refurbishment, all bedrooms now have en suite bathrooms two of which boast Spa Tubs in their bathrooms.

The Ty Gwyn has a very good reputation for its food, renowned locally for its international cuisine using the freshest of local produce.

The Ty Gwyn with its 3 four poster rooms and a honeymoon suite, beamed ceilings, antiques, log fires (in winter) is one of the most traditional Inns you will visit in the beautiful Snowdonia National Park.

**Ty Gwyn Inn,
Betws y Coed,
Conwy LL24 0SG**

Tel: +44 (0)1690 710383
Email: martin@tygwynhotel
Website: www.tygwynhotel.co.uk

Ty Gwyn Inn

BETWS-Y-COED *continued*

Cwmanog Isaf Farm *(SH799546)*

★★★★ FARMHOUSE

Fairy Glen LL24 0SL
☎ 01690 710225 & 07808 421634 Mrs H M Hughes
e-mail: heather.hughes3@tesco.net
dir: *1m S of Betws-y-Coed off A470 by Fairy Glen Hotel, 500yds on farm lane*

Peacefully located on 30 acres of undulating land, which also contains the renowned Fairy Glen, this 200-year-old house on a working livestock farm has been restored to provide comfortable, thoughtfully furnished bedrooms. Breakfast and dinners use home-reared or organic produce, and the raised position of the property provides stunning views of the surrounding countryside.

Rooms 3 rms (2 en suite) (1 pri facs) (1 GF) S fr £45; D £58-£66* **Facilities** STV tea/coffee Dinner available Cen ht **Parking** 4 **Notes** ⊗ No Children 15yrs Closed 15 Dec-7 Feb ⚬ 30 acres mixed

Park Hill

★★★★ GUEST HOUSE

Llanrwst Rd LL24 0HD
☎ 01690 710540 📄 01690 710540
e-mail: welcome@park-hill.co.uk
web: www.park-hill.co.uk
dir: *0.5m N of Betws-y-Coed on A470 (Llanrwst road)*

This friendly guest house benefits from a peaceful location overlooking the village. Comfortable bedrooms come in a wide range of sizes and are well equipped, one with a four-poster bed. There is a choice of lounges, a heated swimming pool, sauna and whirlpool bath for guests' use.

Rooms 9 en suite S £53-£80; D £60-£84 **Facilities** TVL tea/coffee Cen ht Licensed 🐾 Sauna **Parking** 11 **Notes** LB ⊗ No Children 8yrs

The Ferns Guest House

★★★★ 🅰 GUEST HOUSE

Holyhead Rd LL24 0AN
☎ 01690 710587
e-mail: ferns@betws-y-coed.co.uk
web: www.ferns-guesthouse.co.uk
dir: *On A5 near Waterloo Bridge*

Rooms 7 en suite (2 fmly) S £38-£45; D £60-£70* **Facilities** TVL tea/coffee Cen ht Wi-fi **Parking** 7 **Notes** ⊗ No Children 5yrs

Ty Gwyn Inn

★★★ INN

LL24 0SG
☎ 01690 710383 📄 01690 710383
e-mail: mratcl1050@aol.com
dir: *Junct of A5 & A470, by Waterloo Bridge*

Situated on the edge of the village, close to the Waterloo Bridge, this historic coaching inn retains many original features. Quality furnishing styles and memorabilia throughout enhance its intrinsic charm. Bedrooms, some of which feature antique beds, are equipped with thoughtful extras and imaginative food is provided in the cosy bars or restaurant.

Rooms 13 rms (10 en suite) (3 fmly) (1 GF) S £40-£70; D £54-£120* **Facilities** TVL tea/coffee Cen ht Wi-fi **Parking** 14 **Notes** LB Closed Mon-Wed in Jan

See advert on page 461

BYLCHAU	Map 14 SH96

PREMIER COLLECTION

Hafod Elwy Hall *(SH938562)*
★★★★★ 🍽️🍴 FARMHOUSE

LL16 5SP
☎ 01690 770345 📄 01690 770266
Mrs W Charles-Warner
e-mail: enquiries@hafodelwyhall.co.uk
web: www.hafodelwyhall.co.uk
dir: *A5 onto A543, 5.5m right onto track signed Hafod Elwy Hall*

Peacefully located with stunning views of the surrounding countryside, this 14th-century house has been sympathetically restored to provide high standards of comfort and facilities. Furnishing and décor styles include the many period features and bedrooms are equipped with many thoughtful extras. Comprehensive breakfasts include home-grown produce and a warm welcome is assured.

Rooms 3 rms (2 en suite) (1 pri facs) (1 GF) S £40-£70; D £60-£100 **Facilities** TV1B STV TVL tea/coffee Dinner available Cen ht 🐾 Fishing **Parking** 4 **Notes** LB No Children 16yrs 60 acres mixed small holding

COLWYN BAY	Map 14 SH87

Whitehall

★★★★ GUEST HOUSE

51 Cayley Promenade, Rhos-on-Sea LL28 4EP
☎ 01492 547296
e-mail: mossd.cymru@virgin.net
dir: *A55 onto B5115 (Brompton Ave), right at rdbt onto Whitehall Rd to seafront*

Overlooking Rhos-on-Sea promenade, this popular, family-run establishment is convenient for shopping and local amenities. Attractively appointed bedrooms include family rooms and a room on ground-floor level. All benefit from an excellent range of facilities such as video and CD players, as well as air-conditioning. Facilities include a bar and a foyer lounge. Home-cooked dinners are available.

Rooms 12 en suite (4 fmly) (1 GF) S £32; D £64* **Facilities** FTV TVL tea/coffee Dinner available Direct Dial Cen ht Licensed Wi-fi **Parking** 5 **Notes** LB

The Northwood

★★★ GUEST HOUSE

47 Rhos Rd, Rhos-on-Sea LL28 4RS
☎ 01492 549931
e-mail: welcome@thenorthwood.co.uk
web: www.thenorthwood.co.uk
dir: *A55 onto B5115 Brompton Av, over rdbt, 2nd right*

A short walk from the seafront and shops, The Northwood has a warm and friendly atmosphere and welcomes back many regular guests. Bedrooms are furnished in modern style and freshly prepared meals can be enjoyed in the spacious dining room/bar while light refreshments are offered in the lounge.

Rooms 11 rms (10 en suite) (1 pri facs) (3 fmly) (2 GF) **Facilities** TVL tea/coffee Dinner available Cen ht Licensed Wi-fi **Conf** Max 20 Class 20 Board 20 **Parking** 12

CONWY	Map 14 SH77

PREMIER COLLECTION

The Groes Inn
★★★★★ ◉ INN

Tyn-y-Groes LL32 8TN
☎ 01492 650545 📄 01492 650855
e-mail: enquiries@thegroes.com
web: www.groesinn.com
dir: *A55, over Old Conwy Bridge, 1st left through Castle Walls on B5106 (Trefriw Road), inn 2m on right*

Located in the picturesque Conwy Valley, this historic inn dates from 1573 and was the first licensed house in Wales. The exterior and gardens have an abundance of shrubs and seasonal flowers, and create an immediate welcome, which is matched by a friendly and professional staff. Public areas are decorated and furnished with flair to highlight the many period features, and a formal dining room is also available. Spacious bedrooms, in sympathetically renovated former outbuildings are equipped with a wealth of thoughtful extras and many have balconies overlooking the surrounding countryside.

Rooms 14 en suite (1 fmly) (6 GF) S £85-£120; D £105-£200* **Facilities** STV tea/coffee Dinner available Direct Dial Cen ht Wi-fi **Conf** Max 20 Thtr 20 Class 20 Board 20 **Parking** 100 **Notes** LB Closed Xmas

PREMIER COLLECTION

The Old Rectory Country House

★★★★★ 🏆 GUEST ACCOMMODATION

Llanrwst Rd, Llansanffraid Glan Conwy LL28 5LF
☎ 01492 580611
e-mail: info@oldrectorycountryhouse.co.uk
web: www.oldrectorycountryhouse.co.uk
dir: 0.5m S from A470/A55 junct on left, by 30mph sign

This very welcoming accommodation has fine views over the Conwy estuary and towards Snowdonia. The elegant day rooms are luxurious and afternoon tea is available in the lounge. Bedrooms share the delightful views and are thoughtfully furnished, while the genuine hospitality creates a real home from home.

Rooms 3 en suite 2 annexe en suite (1 fmly)
S £79-£119; D £99-£159 **Facilities** STV FTV tea/coffee
Direct Dial Cen ht **Parking** 10 **Notes** LB No Children
5yrs Closed 14 Dec-15 Jan

PREMIER COLLECTION

Sychnant Pass Country House

★★★★★ 🏆 GUEST ACCOMMODATION

Sychnant Pass Rd LL32 8BJ
☎ 01492 585486 📠 01492 585486
e-mail: info@sychnantpasscountryhouse.co.uk
web: www.sychnantpasscountryhouse.co.uk
dir: 1.75m W of Conwy. Off A547 Bangor Rd in town onto Mount Pleasant & Sychnant Pass Rd, 1.75m on right near top of hill

Fine views are to be had from this Edwardian house set in landscaped grounds. Bedrooms, including suites and four poster rooms, are individually furnished and equipped with a range of thoughtful extras. Lounges, warmed by open fires in the chillier months, are comfortable and inviting, and imaginative dinners and suppers are served in the attractive dining room.

Rooms 12 en suite (3 fmly) (2 GF) S £75-£160;
D £95-£180* **Facilities** tea/coffee Dinner available
Cen ht Licensed Wi-fi 🏊 Sauna Solarium Gymnasium
Parking 30 **Notes** LB Closed 24-26 Dec & Jan Civ Wed
100

Gwern Borter Country Manor

★★★★ GUEST ACCOMMODATION

Barkers Ln LL32 8YL
☎ 01492 650360 📠 01492 650360
e-mail: mail@snowdoniaholidays.co.uk
dir: From Conwy B5106 for 2.25m, right towards Rowen for 0.5m then right, left as road forks, Gwern Borter 0.5m on left

This delightful mansion has walls covered in climbing plants and is set in several acres of lawns and gardens. Children are very welcome and there is a rustic play area, games room and many farmyard pets. Bedrooms are furnished with antiques and modern facilities, and one room has an Edwardian four-poster bed. There is an elegant lounge and Victorian-style dining room, where freshly cooked breakfasts are served. Self-catering cottages are also available.

Rooms 4 rms (3 en suite) (1 pri facs) (1 fmly)
Facilities STV FTV TVL tea/coffee Cen ht Wi-fi Riding
Sauna Gymnasium Pool Table **Parking** 4 **Notes** LB ⊗ No
Children 4yrs

Glan Heulog

★★★ GUEST HOUSE

Llanrwst Rd, Woodlands LL32 8LT
☎ 01492 593845
e-mail: glanheulog@no1guesthouse.freeserve.co.uk
web: www.walesbandb.co.uk
dir: From Conwy Castle take B5106, house 0.25m on left

This late 19th-century house lies in an elevated location, with fine views over the town and castle from many rooms. Bedrooms are decorated with pretty wallpapers, are well equipped and one has a four-poster bed. A pleasant breakfast room and conservatory are provided, and hospitality from the proprietors is very friendly.

Rooms 7 rms (6 en suite) (1 pri facs) (1 fmly) S £35-£38;
D £54-£62 **Facilities** TVL tea/coffee Cen ht Wi-fi
Parking 8

Abbey Lodge

★★★★ GUEST HOUSE

14 Abbey Rd LL30 2EA
☎ 01492 878042 📠 01492 878042
e-mail: enquiries@abbeylodgeuk.com
dir: A546 to N end of town, onto Clement Av, right onto Abbey Rd

This impressive Victorian villa is on a leafy avenue within easy walking distance of the promenade. It has been lovingly restored, and stylish décor and furniture add to its charm. Bedrooms come with a wealth of thoughtful extras, and there is a choice of sumptuous lounges and an elegant dining room.

Rooms 4 en suite S £37.50; D £70-£75 **Facilities** FTV tea/
coffee Cen ht Wi-fi **Parking** 4 **Notes** ⊗ No Children 12yrs
Closed Dec-1 Mar ⊠

Brigstock House

★★★★ GUEST HOUSE

1 St David's Place LL30 2UG
☎ 01492 876416
e-mail: simon.hanson4@virgin.net
dir: A470 into Llandudno, left onto The Parade promenade, left onto Lloyd St, left onto St David's Rd & left onto St David's Place

This impressive Edwardian property is on a quiet residential cul-de-sac within easy walking distance of the seafront and central shopping area. The attractive bedrooms are well equipped, and a comfortable lounge is available. Substantial breakfasts and dinners, by arrangement, are served in the elegant dining room.

Rooms 9 rms (8 en suite) (1 pri facs) S £30-£45;
D £60-£70* **Facilities** FTV TVL tea/coffee Dinner available
Cen ht Licensed Wi-fi **Parking** 6 **Notes** LB ⊗ No Children
12yrs

LLANDUDNO *continued*

Bryn Derwen

★★★★ GUEST HOUSE

34 Abbey Rd LL30 2EE
☎ 01492 876804 ▤ 01492 876804
e-mail: brynderwen@fsmail.net
dir: *A470 into Llandudno, left at The Parade promenade to cenotaph, left, over rdbt, 4th right onto York Rd, Bryn Derwen at top*

A warm welcome is assured at this impressive Victorian house, which retains original tiled floors and some fine stained-glass windows. Quality décor and furnishings highlight the historic charm of the property, which is apparent in the sumptuous lounges and attractive dining room, the setting for imaginative breakfasts. Bedrooms are equipped with a wealth of thoughtful extras, and the establishment also has a fully-equipped beauty salon.

Rooms 9 en suite (1 fmly) S £50-£54; D £76-£96*
Facilities FTV TVL tea/coffee Cen ht Licensed Wi-fi Solarium Beauty Salon **Parking** 9 **Notes** LB ⊗ No Children 12yrs Closed Dec-Jan

Britannia Guest House

★★★★ GUEST HOUSE

Promenade, 15 Craig-y-Don Pde LL30 1BG
☎ 01492 877185
e-mail: James@jamesgraham.orangehome.co.uk
dir: *A55 onto A470 to Llandudno, at rdbt take 4th exit signed Craig-y-Don, right at promenade*

Situated at the Craig-y-Don end of Promenade, with superb sea views, this friendly owner-managed guest house provides a range of thoughtfully furnished bedrooms. Comprehensive breakfasts are taken in an attractive front-facing dining room and an attractive patio garden is a perfect setting to enjoy Llandudno Bay.

Rooms 10 rms (9 en suite) (1 pri facs) (3 fmly) (2 GF) S £40-£45; D £50-£70* **Facilities** tea/coffee Cen ht **Notes** LB ⊗ Closed 15 Dec-13 Feb

Bryn-y-Mor

★★★★ GUEST ACCOMMODATION

25 North Pde LL30 2LP
☎ 01492 876790 ▤ 01492 874990
e-mail: info@bryn-y-mor.net
web: www.bryn-y-mor.net
dir: *A55 take Llandudno junct, head for Promenade turn left, by pier on left*

Located at the foot of the Great Orme and close to the town centre and its main attractions the family-run Bryn-y-Mor offers comfortable well-equipped rooms, many with sea views. There is an attractive lounge looking over the bay to the little Orme. There is also a small bar and an outside patio which also overlooks the bay.

Rooms 12 en suite **Facilities** tea/coffee Cen ht Licensed **Notes** ⊗ No Children 16yrs Closed 15 Nov-9 Feb

Can-Y-Bae

★★★★ GUEST ACCOMMODATION

10 Mostyn Crescent, Central Promenade LL30 1AR
☎ 01492 874188 ▤ 01492 868376
e-mail: canybae@btconnect.com
web: www.can-y-baehotel.com
dir: *A55 junct 10 onto A470, signed Llandudno/Promenade. Can-Y-Bae on seafront promenade between Venue Cymru Theatre & band stand*

A warm welcome is assured at this tastefully renovated house, centrally located on the Promenade. Bedrooms are equipped with both practical and homely extras and upper floors are serviced by a modern lift. Day rooms include a panoramic lounge, cosy bar and attractive basement dining room.

Rooms 16 en suite (1 fmly) (2 GF) S £35-£45; D £80 **Facilities** tea/coffee Dinner available Direct Dial Cen ht Lift Licensed Wi-fi **Notes** LB

The Cliffbury

★★★★ GUEST HOUSE

34 St David's Rd LL30 2UH
☎ 01492 877224
e-mail: info@thecliffbury.co.uk

Located on a leafy avenue within easy walking distance of the town centre, this elegant Edwardian house has been sympathetically refurbished to provide high standards of comfort. Bedrooms, furnished in minimalist style, provide a range of practical and thoughtful extras

and smart modern bath/shower rooms are an additional benefit. Breakfast is taken in an attractive dining room and a warm welcome is assured.

Rooms 7 en suite (1 fmly) S £32.50-£35; D £60-£70* **Facilities** FTV tea/coffee Cen ht Wi-fi **Parking** 3 **Notes** LB ⊗ No Children 11yrs

Glenavon Guest House

★★★★ GUEST HOUSE

27 St Mary's Rd LL30 2UB
☎ 01492 877687 ▤ 0870 706 2247
e-mail: postmaster@glenavon.plus.com
dir: *From A470 signed Llandudno, turn left at lights onto Trinity Ave. 3rd on right into St Mary's Rd. Glenavon on right*

Supporters of Liverpool Football Club are especially welcome here and they can admire the extensive range of memorabilia throughout the comfortable day rooms. Bedrooms are equipped with thoughtful extras and Welsh breakfasts provide a good start to the day.

Rooms 7 en suite (1 fmly) S £35-£45; D £60-£75 **Facilities** FTV TVL tea/coffee Dinner available Cen ht Wi-fi **Parking** 4 **Notes** LB ⊗

St Hilary Guest House

★★★★ GUEST ACCOMMODATION

The Promenade, 16 Craig-y-Don Pde LL30 1BG
☎ 01492 875551 ▤ 01492 877538
e-mail: info@sthilaryguesthouse.co.uk
web: www.sthilaryguesthouse.co.uk
dir: *0.5m E of town centre. On B5115 seafront road near Venue Cymru Theatre*

A warm welcome is assured at this constantly improving guest house, located at the Craig-y-Don end of Promenade, and many of the thoughtfully furnished bedrooms have superb sea views. Day rooms include a spacious, attractive front-facing dining room. A cosy guest lounge is also available.

Rooms 10 rms (9 en suite) (1 pri facs) (3 fmly) (2 GF) S £38-£65; D £55-£75* **Facilities** FTV tea/coffee Cen ht Wi-fi **Notes** LB ⊗ Closed end Nov-early Feb

Ashdale Guest House

★★★★ Ⓐ GUEST HOUSE

3 St Davids Rd LL30 2UL
☎ 01492 877089 ▤ 01492 877089
e-mail: srule@btconnect.com
dir: *A470 towards town centre, continue through rdbts and keep left. After station at lights turn left, 4th right*

Rooms 8 rms (7 en suite) (1 pri facs) (1 fmly) S £26-£36; D £52-£62* **Facilities** FTV TVL tea/coffee Dinner available Cen ht **Parking** 3 **Notes** ⊗

The Kestrel

★★★ GUEST ACCOMMODATION

25 Deganwy Av LL30 2YB
☎ 01492 875108
e-mail: kestrelllandudno@msn.com
web: www.kestrelllandudno.co.uk
dir: A55 onto A546 for 4m, right onto Gloddaeth Av, Deganwy Av 4th on right

A warm welcome is assured at this Victorian terrace house close to the main shopping centre and leisure facilities. Bedrooms feature some family accommodation, and ground-floor areas include an attractive dining room with adjacent lounge bar.

Rooms 9 en suite (1 fmly) (3 smoking) S £30; D £56–£66*
Facilities FTV TVL tea/coffee Dinner available Cen ht
Licensed Parking 4 Notes LB No Children 3yrs Closed 24–28 Dec

Minion

★★★ GUEST ACCOMMODATION

21-23 Carmen Sylva Rd, Craig-y-Don LL30 1EQ
☎ 01492 877740
dir: A55 junct 19 onto A470 to Llandudno. At 4th rdbt take Craig-y-Don turn-off. 2nd right after park

Situated in a quiet residential area a few minutes walk from the eastern promenade, the Minion has been owned by the same family for over 60 years and continues to extend a warm welcome. Bedrooms are smart and comfortable, and two are on the ground floor. There is a cosy bar and a colourful garden.

Rooms 10 en suite (1 fmly) (2 GF) S £25–£29; D £50–£58* Facilities FTV TVL tea/coffee Dinner available Licensed Parking 8 Notes No Children 2yrs Closed Nov-Mar

No. 9 Guest House

★★★ GUEST HOUSE

9 Chapel St LL30 2SY
☎ 01492 877251
e-mail: no9llandudno@btinternet.com
web: www.no9llandudno.co.uk

Within easy walking distance of Promenade and town centre, this eco-friendly guest house provides a range of thoughtfully furnished bedrooms and smart modern bathrooms. Comprehensive breakfasts are taken in an attractive dining doom and a warm welcome is assured.

Rooms 6 en suite (1 fmly) S £28.50–£45; D £53–£65*
Facilities FTV TVL tea/coffee Dinner available Cen ht Wi-fi
Conf Max 14 Thtr 14 Class 14 Board 14 Notes LB

RHOS-ON-SEA Map 14 SH88

See also Colwyn Bay

PREMIER COLLECTION

Plas Rhos

★★★★★ GUEST ACCOMMODATION

Cayley Promenade LL28 4EP
☎ 01492 543698 📠 01492 540088
e-mail: info@plasrhos.co.uk
dir: A55 junct 20 onto B5115 for Rhos-on-Sea, right at rdbt onto Whitehall Rd to promenade

Stunning sea views are a feature of this renovated Victorian house, which provides high standards of comfort and hospitality. Cosy bedrooms are filled with a wealth of thoughtful extras, and public areas include a choice of sumptuous lounges featuring smart décor, quality soft furnishings and memorabilia. Breakfast is served in the attractive dining room, overlooking the pretty patio garden.

Rooms 8 en suite S £48–£65; D £70–£98*
Facilities FTV TVL tea/coffee Cen ht Licensed Wi-fi
Parking 4 Notes LB No Children 12yrs Closed 21 Dec-Jan

TREFRIW Map 14 SH76

Hafod Country House

★★★★ GUEST ACCOMMODATION

LL27 0RQ
☎ 01492 640029 📠 01492 641351
e-mail: stay@hafod-house.co.uk
dir: On B5106 entering Trefriw from S, 2nd house on right

This former farmhouse is personally run and friendly with a wealth of charm and character. The tasteful bedrooms feature period furnishings and thoughtful extras such as fresh fruit. There is a comfortable sitting room and a cosy bar. The fixed-price menu is imaginative and makes good use of fresh, local produce while the breakfast menu offers a wide choice.

Rooms 6 en suite S fr £30; D £57–£90* Facilities tea/coffee Dinner available Direct Dial Cen ht Licensed
Parking 14 Notes LB No Children 11yrs RS Jan-Mar Mon & Tue no meals for non-residents

DENBIGHSHIRE

CORWEN Map 15 SJ04

Bron-y-Graig

★★★★ GUEST HOUSE

LL21 0DR
☎ 01490 413007 📠 01490 413007
e-mail: info@north-wales-hotel.co.uk
web: www.north-wales-hotel.co.uk
dir: On A5 on E edge of Corwen

A short walk from the town centre, this impressive Victorian house retains many original features including fireplaces, stained glass and a tiled floor in the entrance hall. Bedrooms, complemented by luxurious bathrooms, are thoughtfully furnished, and two are in a renovated coach house. Ground-floor areas include a traditionally furnished dining room and a comfortable lounge. A warm welcome, attentive service and imaginative food is assured.

Rooms 8 en suite 2 annexe en suite (3 fmly) S £39–£49; D £59 Facilities STV tea/coffee Dinner available Direct Dial Cen ht Licensed Conf Max 20 Class 20 Board 15 Parking 15 Notes LB

CORWEN *continued*

Plas Derwen Country House

★★★★ GUEST ACCOMMODATION

London Rd LL21 0DR
☎ **01490 412742**
e-mail: bandb@plasderwen.supanet.com
dir: *On A5 0.5m E of Corwen*

Set in four acres of fields and mature gardens in an elevated position with superb views of the River Dee, this elegant late 18th-century house has been restored to provide high levels of comfort and facilities. Quality furnishings and décor highlight the many original features and a warm welcome is assured.

Rooms 3 rms (2 en suite) (1 pri facs) (2 fmly) S £40-£63; D £60-£66 **Facilities** FTV TVL tea/coffee Cen ht Wi-fi **Parking** 6 **Notes** ⊗ Closed Dec-Jan

| DENBIGH | Map 15 SJ06 |

See also Bylchau (Conwy)

Cayo

★★★ GUEST HOUSE

74 Vale St LL16 3BW
☎ **01745 812686**
e-mail: stay@cayo.co.uk
dir: *Off A525 into town, at lights turn up hill, supermarket on right. Guest house up hill on left*

A warm welcome is assured at this Victorian house, which is situated on the main street, just a short walk

from the town centre. Bedrooms are comfortably and thoughtfully furnished with lots of homely extras. Good home cooking is provided in a Victorian-themed dining room, and a cosy basement lounge is also available.

Rooms 4 en suite S fr £28; D fr £56 **Facilities** TVL tea/coffee Cen ht Wi-fi **Notes** Closed Xmas-New Year

| LLANDYRNOG | Map 15 SJ16 |

PREMIER COLLECTION

Pentre Mawr Country House

★★★★★ ⌂ GUEST ACCOMMODATION

LL16 4LA
☎ **01824 790732** 🖨 **01492 585486**
e-mail: info@pentremawrcountryhouse.co.uk
dir: *From Denbigh follow signs to Bodfari/Llandyrnog. Left at rdbt to Bodfari, after 50yds turn left onto country lane, follow road and Pentre Mawr on left*

Expect a warm welcome from Graham and Bre at this superb family country house set in nearly 200 acres of meadows, park and woodland. The property has been in Graham's family for over 400 years. Bedrooms are individually decorated, very spacious and each is thoughtfully equipped. Breakfast is served in either the morning room or, on warmer mornings, on the Georgian terrace. Dinner is served in the formal dining room. There is a salt water swimming pool in the walled garden. Graham and Bre were Finalists for the AA Friendliest Landlady of the Year 2009-2010 Award.

Rooms 5 en suite S £75-£130; D £95-£150* **Facilities** tea/coffee Dinner available Cen ht Licensed Wi-fi 🕯 👶 🍴 Fishing **Parking** 8 **Notes** LB No Children 13yrs Closed Nov-Feb ⊛

| LLANGOLLEN | Map 15 SJ24 |

See also Corwen

Tyn Celyn Farmhouse

★★★★ BED AND BREAKFAST

Tyndwr LL20 8AR
☎ **01978 861117** 🖨 **01978 861771**
e-mail: j.m.bather-tyncelyn@talk21.com
dir: *A5 to Llangollen, pass golf club on right, next left signed Tyndwr outdoor centre, 0.5m sharp left onto Tyndwr Rd, past outdoor centre on left. Tyn Celyn 0.5m on left*

This 300-year-old timber-framed farmhouse has stunning views over the Vale of Llangollen. Bedrooms, one of which is located on the ground floor, provide a range of thoughtful extras in addition to fine period furniture. Breakfast is served at a magnificent carved table in a spacious sitting-dining room.

Rooms 3 en suite (1 fmly) (1 GF); D £60-£64 **Facilities** TVL tea/coffee Cen ht **Parking** 5 **Notes** LB ⊗ ⊛

| RHYL | Map 14 SJ08 |

Barratt's at Ty'n Rhyl

★★★★ ⊛⊛ 🍴 RESTAURANT WITH ROOMS

Ty'n Rhyl, 167 Vale Rd LL18 2PH
☎ **01745 344138** & **0773 095 4994** 🖨 **01745 344138**
e-mail: ebarratt5@aol.com
dir: *A55 onto A525 to Rhyl, pass Sainsburys & B&Q, garden centre on left, Barratt's 400yds on right*

This delightful 16th-century house lies in a secluded location surrounded by attractive gardens. The quality of the food reflects the skill of the owner-chef. Public areas are smartly furnished and include a panelled lounge and separate bar with attractive conservatory. Bedrooms are comfortable and equipped with lots of thoughtful extras.

Rooms 3 en suite S £65; D £85* **Facilities** FTV TVL tea/coffee Dinner available Cen ht Wi-fi 🍴 **Parking** 20 **Notes** LB ⊗

| RUTHIN | Map 15 SJ15 |

PREMIER COLLECTION

Firgrove Country House B & B

★★★★★ 🍴⌂ BED AND BREAKFAST

Firgrove, Llanfwrog LL15 2LL
☎ **01824 702677** 🖨 **01824 702677**
e-mail: meadway@firgrovecountryhouse.co.uk
web: www.firgrovecountryhouse.co.uk
dir: *0.5m SW of Ruthin. A494 onto B5105, 0.25m past Llanfwrog church on right*

Standing in immaculate mature gardens in a peaceful rural location, this well-proportioned house retains many original features, highlighted by the quality décor and furnishings throughout the interior. Bedrooms, complimented by smart modern bathrooms, are equipped with a wealth of thoughtful extras and memorable breakfasts, using home-made or local produce, are served in an elegant dining room.

Imaginative dinners are also available by prior arrangement and a warm welcome is assured.

Rooms 2 en suite 1 annexe en suite (1 GF) S £45-£60; D £50-£80* **Facilities** FTV tea/coffee Dinner available Cen ht Wi-fi **Parking** 4 **Notes** ⊗ No Children Closed Nov-Feb

Eyarth Station

★★★★ GUEST ACCOMMODATION

Llanfair Dyffryn Clwyd LL15 2EE
☎ 01824 703643 📄 01824 707464
e-mail: stay@eyarthstation.com
dir: 1m S of Ruthin. Off A525 onto lane, 600yds to Eyarth Station

Until 1964 and the Beeching cuts, this was a sleepy country station. A comfortable lounge and outdoor swimming pool occupy the space once taken up by the railway and platforms. Bedrooms are carefully decorated and full of thoughtful extras. Family rooms are available, and two rooms are in the former stationmaster's house adjoining the main building.

Rooms 4 en suite 2 annexe en suite (2 fmly) (4 GF) (1 smoking) S £50; D £72-£75* **Facilities** TV1B TVL tea/coffee Dinner available Cen ht Licensed Wi-fi 🎣 **Parking** 6 **Notes** LB

Tyddyn Chambers (SJ102543)

★★★★ FARMHOUSE

Pwllglas LL15 2LS
☎ 01824 750683   Mrs E Williams
e-mail: ella.williams@btconnect.com
web: www.tyddynchambers.co.uk
dir: 3m S of Ruthin. W off A494 after Fox & Hounds pub in Pwllglas, signed

This charming little farmhouse has been extended to provide carefully appointed, modern accommodation, which includes a family room. The pleasant, traditionally furnished breakfast room has separate tables and a lounge is also available. The house stands in an elevated position with panoramic views.

Rooms 3 en suite (1 fmly) S £32-£35; D £50-£60* **Facilities** TVL tea/coffee Cen ht **Parking** 3 **Notes** LB ⊗ Closed Xmas & New Year 🐾 180 acres beef/sheep

The Wynnstay Arms

★★★★ ◉◉ RESTAURANT WITH ROOMS

Well St LL15 1AN
☎ 01824 703147 📄 01824 705428
e-mail: resevations@wynnstayarms.com
web: www.wynnstayarms.com
dir: In town centre

This former town centre period inn has been sympathetically renovated to provide good quality accommodation and a smart café-bar. Imaginative food is served in Fusions Brasserie, where the contemporary décor highlights the many retained period features.

Rooms 7 en suite (1 fmly) S £45-£60; D £65-£110* **Facilities** FTV tea/coffee Dinner available Cen ht Wi-fi **Conf** Max 30 Thtr 30 Class 20 Board 16 **Parking** 14 **Notes** LB

ST ASAPH Map 15 SJ07

AA GUEST ACCOMMODATION OF THE YEAR FOR WALES

PREMIER COLLECTION

Tan-Yr-Onnen Guest House

★★★★★ GUEST HOUSE

Waen LL17 0DU
☎ 01745 583821 📄 01745 583821
e-mail: tanyronnenvisit@aol.com
web: www.northwalesbreaks.co.uk
dir: W on A55 junct 28, turn left in 300yds

Tan-Yr-Onnen is quietly located in six acres of gardens, yet conveniently close to the A55. The very well equipped accommodation includes four ground-floor rooms with French windows opening onto the terrace with tables and chairs. Upstairs there are two luxury suites, with lounge areas. Hearty breakfasts are served in the dining room overlooking the gardens. A conservatory lounge and Wi-fi is also available.

Rooms 6 en suite (1 fmly) (4 GF) S £60-£80; D £75-£100* **Facilities** FTV tea/coffee Cen ht Licensed Wi-fi **Parking** 8

Bach-Y-Graig (SJ075713)

★★★★ FARMHOUSE

Tremeirchion LL17 0UH
☎ 01745 730627 📄 01745 730627 Mrs A Roberts
e-mail: anwen@bachygraig.co.uk
dir: 3m SE of St Asaph. Off A525 at Trefnant onto A541 to x-rds with white railings, left down hill, over bridge & then right

Dating from the 16th century, this listed building was the first brick-built house in Wales and retains many original features including a wealth of exposed beams and inglenook fireplaces. Bedrooms are furnished with fine period pieces and quality soft fabrics. Ground-floor areas include a quiet lounge and a combined sitting and dining room, featuring a superb Jacobean oak table.

Rooms 3 rms (2 en suite) (1 pri facs) (1 fmly) S £45-£50; D £70-£75* **Facilities** FTV TVL tea/coffee Cen ht Wi-fi Fishing Woodland trail **Parking** 3 **Notes** LB ⊗ Closed Xmas & New Year 200 acres dairy/mixed

---

FLINTSHIRE

NANNERCH Map 15 SJ16

The Old Mill Guest Accommodation

★★★★ GUEST ACCOMMODATION

Melin-Y-Wern, Denbigh Rd CH7 5RH
☎ 01352 741542
e-mail: mail@old-mill.co.uk
web: www.old-mill.co.uk
dir: A541, NW from Mold, 7m into Melin-Y-Wern, Old Mill on right

This converted stone stable block was once part of a Victorian watermill complex. The site also includes a restaurant and wine bar. The non-smoking guest accommodation offers modern, well-equipped bedrooms with private bathrooms, suitable for leisure and business.

Rooms 6 en suite (1 fmly) (2 GF) S £44-£60; D £56-£82* **Facilities** FTV tea/coffee Direct Dial Cen ht Wi-fi **Parking** 12 **Notes** LB ⊗ Closed 1-28 Feb

GWYNEDD

ABERDYFI   Map 14 SN69

Penmaendyfi Country House

★★★★ GUEST ACCOMMODATION

Cwrt, Pennal SY20 9LD
☎ 01654 791246
e-mail: shana@penmaendyfi.co.uk
dir: *4m W of Machynlleth on A493*

Delightfully located in sweeping grounds, Penmaendyfi offers a wealth of history in addition to stunning views over the Dyfi estuary to the mountains beyond. Bedrooms and bathrooms are particularly spacious and include one on the ground floor. Guests are welcome to use the comfortable lounge with honesty bar and the large outdoor swimming pool.

Rooms 6 en suite (2 fmly) (1 GF) S £60; D £80-£100
Facilities tea/coffee Direct Dial Cen ht ⚓ 🏊 **Parking** 10
Notes ⊗ Closed Dec-Jan

ABERSOCH   Map 14 SH32

Llysfor Guest House

★★★★ GUEST HOUSE

LL53 7AL
☎ 01758 712248 📠 01758 712248
e-mail: emma@llysforguesthouse.co.uk
web: www.llysforguesthouse.com
dir: *Take A499, at bottom of hill on right*

This large Victorian house stands opposite the harbour and is within a short walk of the beach and the town centre. It provides good quality, modern accommodation, which is complemented by a pleasant lounge and an attractive breakfast room.

Rooms 6 rms (4 en suite) (2 pri facs) S £45-£50; D £70-£80* **Facilities** tea/coffee Cen ht **Parking** 8
Notes ⊗ Closed Dec-Jan 🚭

BALA   Map 14 SH93

Erw Feurig

★★★★ GUEST HOUSE

Cefnddwysarn LL23 7LL
☎ 01678 530262 & 07786 168399 📠 01678 530262
e-mail: erwfeurig@yahoo.com
web: www.erwfeurig.com
dir: *3m NE of Bala off A494. 2nd left after x-rds at Cefnddwysarn, turn at B&B sign*

A warm welcome is assured at this delightful and peaceful farm cottage situated on a hillside with panoramic views of the Berwyn Mountains. The individually styled bedrooms have a range of additional extras, and a cosy lounge and a cheerful ground-floor breakfast room are available.

Rooms 4 rms (2 en suite) (2 pri facs) (1 GF) S £30-£40; D fr £55* **Facilities** TVL tea/coffee Cen ht Fishing **Parking** 6
Notes LB ⊗ No Children Closed Nov-Feb 🚭

Pen-Y-Bryn Farmhouse (SH967394)

★★★★ FARMHOUSE

Sarnau LL23 7LH
☎ 01678 530389   Mrs E Jones
e-mail: jonespenbryn@lineone.net
web: www.balawales.com/penbryn
dir: *3m NE of Bala off A494. Pass Cefnddwysarn, 2nd left*

A genuine welcome is assured at this stone Victorian house, located on an elevated position overlooking Sarnau and the surrounding mountains. Bedrooms are thoughtfully furnished and have modern en suite facilities. Hearty breakfasts are served in the attractive conservatory with stunning views.

Rooms 3 en suite (1 GF) S £32; D £54-£56 **Facilities** TVL tea/coffee Cen ht Bird watching, walking, cycling
Parking 8 **Notes** LB ⊗ No Children 4yrs Closed 25-26 Dec 🚭 200 acres mixed

BARMOUTH   Map 14 SH61

See also Dyffryn Ardudwy

Richmond House

★★★★ GUEST HOUSE

High St LL42 1DW
☎ 01341 281366 & 07976 833069
e-mail: info@barmouthbedandbreakfast.co.uk
web: www.barmouthbedandbreakfast.co.uk
dir: *In town centre. Car park at rear on Jubilee Rd*

A warm welcome awaits you at this lovely Victorian house, which has been modernised to provide good quality and thoughtfully equipped accommodation. Two of the bedrooms have sea views, as do the lounge and dining room, where there are separate tables. There is also a pleasant garden.

Rooms 3 en suite (1 fmly) **Facilities** tea/coffee Cen ht Wi-fi **Parking** 5 **Notes** LB ⊗

Llwyndu Farmhouse

★★★★ 🍴 GUEST ACCOMMODATION

Llanaber LL42 1RR
☎ 01341 280144
e-mail: intouch@llwyndu-farmhouse.co.uk
web: www.llwyndu-farmhouse.co.uk
dir: *A496 towards Harlech where street lights end, on outskirts of Barmouth, take next right*

This converted 16th-century farmhouse retains many original features including inglenook fireplaces, exposed beams and timbers. There is a cosy lounge and meals can be enjoyed in the licensed restaurant; two and three course dinners are offered. Bedrooms are modern and well equipped, and some have four-poster beds. Four rooms are in nearby buildings.

Rooms 3 en suite 4 annexe en suite (2 fmly); D £84-£94*
Facilities TVL tea/coffee Dinner available Cen ht Licensed
Conf Max 10 **Parking** 10 **Notes** LB Closed 25-26 Dec RS Sun No dinner

Morwendon House

★★★★ 🛏🍴 GUEST ACCOMMODATION

Llanaber LL42 1RR
☎ 01341 280566 📠 07092 197785
e-mail: info@morwendon-house.co.uk
dir: *A496 at Llanaber N of Barmouth. On Seaward side 250yds past Llanaber Church*

With its impressive position overlooking Cardigan Bay, Morwendon House is an ideal base for exploring the surrounding area and its many attractions. The bedrooms offer well-equipped accommodation, with many rooms having sea views. Dinner is available by arrangement and meals are taken in the attractive dining room overlooking the bay. There is also a comfortable lounge, again with views over the bay.

Rooms 5 en suite 1 annexe en suite (1 fmly) (1 GF) S £42-£60; D £60-£84* **Facilities** TVL tea/coffee Dinner available Cen ht Licensed **Parking** 7 **Notes** LB ⊗ No Children 5yrs

BEDDGELERT — Map 14 SH54

Tanronnen Inn

★★★★ INN

LL55 4YB

☎ 01766 890347 📠 01766 890606

This delightful inn offers comfortable, well equipped and attractively appointed accommodation, including a family room. There is also a selection of pleasant and relaxing public areas. The wide range of bar food is popular with tourists, and more formal meals are served in the restaurant.

Rooms 7 en suite (3 fmly) S £55; D £100* **Facilities** tea/coffee Dinner available Direct Dial Cen ht **Parking** 15 **Notes** LB ⊗

BETHESDA — Map 14 SH66

Snowdonia Mountain Lodge

★★ GUEST ACCOMMODATION

Nant Ffrancon LL57 3LX

☎ 01248 600500

e-mail: info@snowdoniamountainlodge.com

Located on the A5, south of Bethesda and surrounded by mountains in a stunningly beautiful area, this establishment is very popular with walkers and climbers. A World Peace Flame Monument is a feature on the attractive frontage. Bedrooms are located in chalet-style buildings and a comprehensive continental breakfast is served in an adjacent café. Specialist yoga and meditation classes are offered.

Rooms 19 en suite S £44-£49; D £59-£84* **Facilities** tea/coffee **Parking** **Notes** Closed 22nd Dec- 4th January

BETWS GARMON — Map 14 SH55

Betws Inn

★★★★ ◡ BED AND BREAKFAST

LL54 7YY

☎ 01286 650324

e-mail: stay@betws-inn.co.uk

dir: On A4085 Caernarfon to Beddgelert, opp Bryn Gloch Caravan Park

Set in the western foothills of the Snowdonia, this 17th-century former inn has been restored to create an establishment of immense charm. A warm welcome and caring service are assured. Bedrooms have a wealth of homely extras, and imaginative dinners feature local produce. Breakfast includes home-made bread and preserves.

Rooms 3 en suite S £50-£60; D £70-£80* **Facilities** TVL tea/coffee Dinner available Cen ht **Parking** 3 **Notes** ⊗

CAERNARFON — Map 14 SH46

See also Clynnog Fawr & Penygroes

Pengwern (SH459587)

★★★★ FARMHOUSE

Saron LL54 5UH

☎ 01286 831500 📠 01286 830741 Mr & Mrs G Rowlands

e-mail: janepengwern@aol.com

web: www.pengwern.net

dir: A487 S from Caernarfon, pass supermarket on right, right after bridge, 2m to Saron, over x-rds, 1st driveway on right

A beautifully maintained farmhouse surrounded by 130 acres of farmland running down to Foryd Bay, which is noted for its birdlife. Spacious bedrooms are equipped with modern, efficient bathrooms in addition to a wealth of thoughtful extras. Imaginative breakfasts are served in an elegant dining room and a lounge is also available.

Rooms 3 en suite S £55; D £60-£90 **Facilities** tea/coffee Dinner available Cen ht Licensed **Parking** 3 **Notes** LB ⊗ Closed Oct-Apr 130 acres beef/sheep

Rhiwafallen Restaurant with Rooms

★★★★ ⊛⊛ 🍴 RESTAURANT WITH ROOMS

Rhiwafallen, LLandwrog LL54 5SW

☎ 01286 830172

e-mail: ktandrobjohn@aol.com

Located south of Caernarfon on the Llyn Peninsula link, this former farmhouse has been tastefully renovated to provide high levels of comfort and facilities. Quality bedrooms are furnished in minimalist style with a wealth of thoughtful extras. The original modern art in public areas adds vibrancy to the interior. Warm hospitality and imaginative cooking ensure a memorable stay at this owner-managed establishment.

Rooms 5 en suite; D £100-£150* **Facilities** Dinner available

The Stables

★★★★ GUEST ACCOMMODATION

Llanwnda LL54 5BD

☎ 01286 830711 📠 01286 830711

dir: 3m S of Caernarfon on A499 towards Pwllheli

This privately-owned and personally-run establishment is set in 15 acres of its own land, south of Caernarfon. Very well equipped bedrooms are located within two motel-style buildings and breakfast is taken in a spacious dining room decorated with a wealth of unusual memorabilia.

Rooms 22 annexe en suite (8 fmly) (22 GF) (5 smoking); D £69* **Facilities** TVL tea/coffee Direct Dial Cen ht Licensed **Conf** Max 50 Thtr 50 Class 30 Board 30 **Parking** 40

CLYNNOG-FAWR — Map 14 SH44

Bryn Eisteddfod Country House

★★★★ GUEST HOUSE

Clynnog Fawr LL54 5DA

☎ 01286 660431

e-mail: info@bryneisteddfod.com

dir: Off A499 at village. Left turn coming off A499 slip road

This Victorian house, near the Lleyn Peninsula and Snowdonia, offers comfortable accommodation and is especially popular with golfers. The traditionally furnished bedrooms are well equipped. There is a comfortable lounge and a large attractive conservatory bar-dining room, where evening meals can be served.

Rooms 7 rms (6 en suite) (1 pri facs) (2 fmly) **Facilities** tea/coffee Dinner available Cen ht Licensed **Conf** Max 40 **Parking** 25 **Notes** ⊗

CRICCIETH — Map 14 SH43

The Abereistedd

★★★★ GUEST ACCOMMODATION

West Pde LL52 0EN
☎ 01766 522710 🖻 01766 523526
e-mail: info@abereistedd.co.uk
web: www.abereistedd.co.uk
dir: A487 through Criccieth towards Pwllheli, left 400yds after fuel station following signs for beach, on left at seafront

An extremely warm welcome is assured at this Victorian property with uninterrupted mountain and coastal views. The attractive bedrooms are very well equipped with thoughtful extras, the ground-floor lounge has a bar extension, and the bright dining room overlooks the seafront.

Rooms 12 en suite (2 fmly) S £36; D £64-£72*
Facilities tea/coffee Dinner available Direct Dial Cen ht Licensed **Parking** 9 **Notes** LB ⊗ Closed Nov-Mar

Bron Rhiw

★★★★ GUEST ACCOMMODATION

Caernarfon Rd LL52 0AP
☎ 01766 522257
e-mail: clairecriccieth@yahoo.co.uk
web: www.bronrhiwhotel.co.uk
dir: Off High St onto B4411

A warm welcome and high standards of comfort and facilities are assured at this constantly improving Victorian property, just a short walk from the seafront. Bedrooms are equipped with lots of thoughtful extras and ground-floor areas include a sumptuous lounge, a cosy bar, and an elegant dining room, the setting for imaginative breakfasts.

Rooms 9 en suite (2 fmly) S £47-£60; D £70-£74
Facilities tea/coffee Cen ht Licensed **Parking** 3 **Notes** LB ⊗ No Children 5yrs Closed Nov-Feb

Glyn-Y-Coed

★★★★ GUEST ACCOMMODATION

Porthmadog Rd LL52 0HP
☎ 01766 522870 🖻 01766 523341
e-mail: julie@glyn-y-coed.co.uk
dir: 500yds from castle on main street in village. From centre of Criccieth, walk towards Porthmadog, 1st property on left

A warm welcome is assured at this impressive refurbished Victorian house with views of Tremadog Bay and the surrounding mountains, and only a short walk from the beach. The en suite bedrooms include four-poster, king-size, family, and ground-floor options, and there is a sitting room and a south-facing patio for relaxing. Wholesome breakfasts are served in the spacious dining room, and private parking is available.

Rooms 9 en suite 1 annexe en suite (1 fmly) (1 GF) S £51-£71; D £71-£81* **Facilities** FTV tea/coffee Direct Dial Cen ht Licensed Wi-fi **Parking** 14 **Notes** LB ⊗

Cefn Uchaf Farm Guest House

★★★★ GUEST HOUSE

Garndolbenmaen LL51 9PJ
☎ 01766 530239
e-mail: enquiries@cefnuchaf.co.uk
dir: 5m N of Porthmadog. Left off A487 after Dolbenmaen. 4m N Criccieth right off B4411 Rhoslan

The large, stone-built farmhouse stands in a remote location amid stunning scenery. Some of the thoughtfully furnished modern bedrooms are ideal for families and a spacious lounge is also available. Comprehensive Welsh breakfasts are served in an attractive dining room, and a warm welcome is assured

Rooms 8 rms (7 en suite) (1 pri facs) (3 fmly) **Facilities** TVL tea/coffee Dinner available Cen ht **Parking** 12

Min y Gaer

★★★★ GUEST HOUSE

Porthmadog Rd LL52 0HP
☎ 01766 522151 🖻 01766 523540
e-mail: info@minygaer.co.uk
dir: On A497 200yds E of junct with B4411

The friendly, family-run Min y Gaer has superb views from many of the rooms. The smart, modern bedrooms are furnished in pine, and the welcoming proprietors also provide a bar and a traditionally furnished lounge.

Rooms 10 en suite (2 fmly) S £31-£32; D £62-£70*
Facilities TVL tea/coffee Cen ht Licensed Wi-fi **Parking** 12 **Notes** Closed Nov-14 Mar

DOLGELLAU — Map 14 SH71

PREMIER COLLECTION

Tyddynmawr Farmhouse (SH704159)

★★★★★ FARMHOUSE

Cader Rd, Islawrdref LL40 1TL
☎ 01341 422331 Mrs Evans
dir: From town centre left at top of square, left at garage onto Cader Rd for 3m, 1st farm on left after Gwernan Lake

A warm welcome is assured at this 18th-century farmhouse which lies at the foot of Cader Idris amidst breathtaking scenery. Bedrooms are spacious, with Welsh Oak furniture; the upper one has a balcony and the ground-floor room has a patio area. Bathrooms are large and luxurious. Superb breakfasts are a feast of home-made items; bread, preserves, muesli or smoked fish - the choice is excellent. Self-catering cottages are also available.

Rooms 3 en suite (1 GF) S fr £55; D £68-£70*
Facilities TVL tea/coffee Cen ht Fishing **Parking** 8 **Notes** ⊗ No Children Closed Jan 🐄 800 acres beef/sheep

Coed Cae

★★★★ 🍴 BED AND BREAKFAST

Taicynhaeaf LL40 2TU
☎ 01341 430628 & 07909 996983
e-mail: info@coedcae.co.uk
dir: 3m NW of Dolgellau. N off A496 opp toll bridge

A warm welcome awaits at this charming old house, which is set in its own extensive wooded grounds, overlooking spectacular views of the Mawddach Estuary. The thoughtfully equipped accommodation includes a bedroom on ground-floor level. All share one table in the spacious combined dining room and lounge, where guests can enjoy skilfully prepared, imaginative food.

Rooms 3 rms (2 en suite) (1 pri facs) (1 fmly) (1 GF) S £50-£80; D £65-£85* **Facilities** tea/coffee Dinner available Cen ht **Conf** Max 8 Board 8 **Parking** 8 **Notes** LB ⊗

Dolgun Uchaf Guesthouse

★★★ GUEST HOUSE

Dolgun Uchaf LL40 2AB
☎ 01341 422269
e-mail: dolgunuchaf@aol.com
web: www.guesthousessnowdonia.com
dir: Off A470 at Little Chef just S of Dolgellau, Dolgun Uchaf 1st property on right

Located in a peaceful area with stunning views of the surrounding countryside, this 500-year-old late medieval hall house retains many original features, including exposed beams and open fireplaces. Bedrooms are equipped with thoughtful extras and a lounge is also available.

Rooms 3 en suite 1 annexe en suite (1 GF) **Facilities** TVL tea/coffee Dinner available Cen ht Wi-fi **Parking** 6 **Notes** No Children 5yrs

Ivy House

★★★ GUEST HOUSE

Finsbury Square LL40 1RF
☎ 01341 422535 ⊟ 01341 422689
e-mail: marg.bamford@btconnect.com
dir: In town centre. Straight across top of main square, house on left after bend

Friendly hospitality is offered at this house, situated in the centre of Dolgellau at the foot of Cader Idris. Bedrooms are brightly decorated and thoughtfully equipped. Ground-floor rooms include a comfortable lounge and a spacious dining room where breakfast is served.

Rooms 6 rms (4 en suite) (1 fmly) S £42-£50; D £60-£70* **Facilities** TVL tea/coffee Cen ht Wi-fi **Notes** ⊗ Closed 24-26 Dec

---

DYFFRYN ARDUDWY Map 14 SH52

Cadwgan Inn

★★★★ INN

LL44 2HA
☎ 01341 247240
e-mail: cadwgan.hotel@virgin.net
dir: In Dyffryn Ardudwy onto Station Rd, over railway crossing

This very pleasant, privately-owned pub stands in grounds close to Dyffryn Ardudwy station, between Barmouth and Harlech. The beach is a short walk away. The good quality, well-equipped modern accommodation includes family rooms and a room with a four-poster bed. Public areas include an attractive dining room, popular bar and a beer garden.

Rooms 6 en suite (3 fmly) **Facilities** TVL tea/coffee Dinner available Cen ht Sauna Gymnasium Pool Table **Notes** ⊗ No coaches Civ Wed 60

FFESTINIOG Map 14 SH74

Ty Clwb

★★★★ BED AND BREAKFAST

The Square LL41 4LS
☎ 01766 762658 ⊟ 01766 762658
e-mail: tyclwb@talk21.com
web: www.tyclwb.co.uk
dir: On B4391 in Ffestiniog, opp church

Located opposite the historic church, this elegant house has been carefully modernised and is immaculately maintained throughout. Bedrooms are thoughtfully furnished and in addition to an attractive dining room, a spacious lounge with sun patio provides stunning views of the surrounding mountain range.

Rooms 3 en suite; D £54-£70 **Facilities** TVL tea/coffee Cen ht

Morannedd

★★★ GUEST ACCOMMODATION

Blaenau Rd LL41 4LG
☎ 01766 762734
e-mail: morannedd@talk21.com
dir: At edge of village on A470 towards Blaenau Ffestiniog

This guest house is set in the Snowdonia National Park and is well located for touring north Wales. A friendly welcome is offered and the atmosphere is relaxed and informal. Bedrooms are smart and modern and a cosy lounge is available. Hearty home cooking is a definite draw.

Rooms 4 en suite **Facilities** tea/coffee Cen ht **Notes** Closed Xmas ⊛

HARLECH Map 14 SH53

Gwrach Ynys Country

★★★★ GUEST HOUSE

Talsarnau LL47 6TS
☎ 01766 780742 ⊟ 01766 781199
e-mail: deborah@gwrachynys.co.uk
web: www.gwrachynys.co.uk
dir: 2m N of Harlech on A496

This delightful Edwardian house nestles in idyllic lawns and gardens with dramatic views of the surrounding mountains. Bedrooms are thoughtfully equipped with modern facilities. Two comfortably furnished lounges promote a home from home feel and hospitality is welcoming. Hearty meals can be enjoyed at separate tables in the dining room.

Rooms 7 rms (6 en suite) (1 pri facs) (3 fmly) **Facilities** TVL tea/coffee Cen ht **Parking** 10 **Notes** ⊗ Closed mid Nov-mid Jan ⊛

LLANBEDR Map 14 SH52

Victoria

★★★ INN

LL45 2LD
☎ 01341 241213 ⊟ 01341 241644
e-mail: junevicinn@aol.com
dir: In village centre

This former coaching inn lies beside the River Artro in a very pretty village. Many original features remain, including the Settle bar with its flagstone floor, black polished fireplace and unusual circular wooden settle. The menu is extensive and is supplemented by blackboard specials. Bedrooms are spacious and thoughtfully furnished.

Rooms 5 en suite **Facilities** tea/coffee Dinner available Cen ht **Conf** Max 30 **Parking** 75 **Notes** LB

LLANDDEINIOLEN — Map 14 SH56

Ty'n-Rhos Country House & Restaurant

★★★★★ Ⓐ GUEST ACCOMMODATION

Seion LL55 3AE
☎ 01248 670489 ▤ 01248 671772
e-mail: enquiries@tynrhos.co.uk
web: www.tynrhos.co.uk
dir: A55 junct 11 onto A5 for 50yds, right at mini-rdbt onto A4244. After 4m, take 2nd exit at rdbt, signed in 0.5m

Rooms 11 en suite 3 annexe en suite (2 fmly) (2 GF) S £65-£75; D £80-£150* Facilities FTV tea/coffee Dinner available Cen ht Licensed Wi-fi ⚓ Fishing Conf Max 60 Thtr 60 Class 40 Board 40 Parking 50 Notes Civ Wed 60

See advert on this page

PENYGROES — Map 14 SH45

Llwyndu Mawr (SH475536)

★★ FARMHOUSE

Carmel Rd LL54 6PU
☎ 01286 880419 ▤ 01286 880845 Mrs N R Williams
dir: From village onto B4418, 500yds left for Carmel, 500yds up hill after cemetery, 1st left

This hillside farmhouse dates from the 19th century and is quietly located on the outskirts of the village. Home from home hospitality is provided, with simply appointed accommodation and guests are welcome to take part in the life of this working sheep farm, where there are also boarding kennels.

Rooms 4 rms (2 en suite) (1 fmly) (1 GF) S £25-£30; D £50-£60* Facilities TVL tea/coffee Dinner available Cen ht Parking 7 Notes LB Closed 20 Dec-6 Jan ⚫ 98 acres sheep/ducks/geese/chickens

PORTHMADOG — Map 14 SH53

Tudor Lodge

★★★★ GUEST ACCOMMODATION

Tan-Yr-Onnen, Penamser Rd LL49 9NY
☎ 01766 515530
e-mail: info@tudor-lodge.co.uk
web: www.tudor-lodge.co.uk
dir: At main Porthmadog rdbt turn onto Criccieth Rd, 40mtrs on left

This large guest house is conveniently located within a short walk of the town centre. It has recently been considerably renovated to provide good quality modern accommodation, including family rooms. Separate tables are provided in the breakfast room, where a substantial self-service continental breakfast buffet is provided. There is also a pleasant garden for guests to use.

Rooms 13 en suite (3 fmly) (6 GF) S £44; D £69-£79* Facilities STV tea/coffee Cen ht Wi-fi Parking 11 Notes LB ⊗

TYWYN — Map 14 SH50

Eisteddfa (SH651055)

★★★★ FARMHOUSE

Eisteddfa, Abergynolwyn LL36 9UP
☎ 01654 782385 ▤ 01654 782385 Mrs G Pugh
e-mail: hugh.pugh01@btinternet.com
dir: 5m NE of Tywyn on B4405 nr Dolgoch Falls

Eisteddfa is a modern stone bungalow situated less than a mile from Abergynolwyn, in a spot ideal for walking or for visiting the local historic railway. Rooms are well equipped and stunning views are a feature from the attractive dining room.

Rooms 3 rms (2 en suite) (3 GF)* Facilities STV FTV TVL tea/coffee Cen ht Parking 6 Notes LB Closed Dec-Feb ⚫ 1200 acres mixed

MERTHYR TYDFIL

MERTHYR TYDFIL — Map 9 SO00

Llwyn Onn

★★★★ GUEST HOUSE

Cwmtaf CF48 2HT
☎ 01685 384384 ▤ 01685 359310
e-mail: reception@llwynonn.co.uk
dir: Off A470 2m N of Cefn Coed, overlooking Llwyn Onn Reservoir

Fronted by a large pleasant garden, this delightful house overlooks Llwyn Onn Reservoir. Newly added to this property are a further seven bedrooms which are spacious, comfortable and carefully appointed. The cosy lounge opens onto the terrace and garden, as does the bright breakfast room.

Rooms 11 en suite (3 GF) Facilities STV TVL tea/coffee Cen ht Conf Max 10 Class 10 Board 10 Parking 9 Notes ⊗ RS 2 wks Xmas

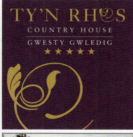

TY'N RHOS
COUNTRY HOUSE
GWESTY GWLEDIG
★★★★★

Situated in the foothills of the Snowdonia mountain range, Ty'n Rhos Country House is an ideal location for exploring the dramatic Welsh countryside. Ty'n Rhos are also winners of the coveted Visit Wales Gold Award for outstanding quality, comfort and hospitality in Wales, ensuring you a warm welcome and total luxury.

Surrounded by 50 acres of farmland, including our own lake and ample private parking, Ty'n Rhos is a 5 star establishment that offers a level of service and interior surroundings second to none. The restaurant is served by the award winning chef and proprietor, Martin James a former Dorchester chef who trained under Anton Mosimann. Martin heads a highly skilled team and serves fine dining with award winning cuisine.

Seion, Llanddeiniolen, Caernarfon LL55 3AE
Tel: 01248 670489
Email: enquiries@tynrhos.co.uk
Website: www.tynrhos.co.uk

Penrhadw Farm

★★★ GUEST HOUSE

Pontsticill CF48 2TU
☎ **01685 723481** & **722461** 📠 **01685 722461**
e-mail: treghotel@aol.com
web: www.penrhadwfarm.co.uk
dir: *5m N of Merthyr Tydfil. (Please see map on website)*

Expect a warm welcome at this former Victorian farmhouse in the glorious Brecon Beacons National Park. The house has been totally refurbished to provide quality modern accommodation. The well-equipped, spacious bedrooms include two large suites in cottages adjacent to the main building. There is also a comfortable lounge. Separate tables are provided in the cosy breakfast room.

Rooms 5 en suite 5 annexe en suite (5 fmly) (1 GF) S £45-£60; D £70-£100* **Facilities** STV FTV TVL tea/coffee Dinner available Cen ht Wi-fi **Conf** Max 10 Thtr 10 Class 10 **Parking** 22 **Notes** LB ⊗

ABERGAVENNY Map 9 SO21

Hardwick Farm *(SO306115)*

★★★★ FARMHOUSE

NP7 9BT
☎ **01873 853513** & **07773 775179**
📠 **01873 854238** **Mrs A Price**
e-mail: carol@harwickfarm.co.uk
dir: *1m from Abergavenny, off A4042, farm sign on right*

Quietly located in the Usk Valley with wonderful views, this large family-run farmhouse provides warm hospitality. The spacious bedrooms are comfortably furnished, well equipped, and include one suitable for families. Farmhouse breakfasts are served at the communal table in the traditionally furnished dining room.

Rooms 3 rms (2 en suite) (1 pri facs) (1 fmly) **Facilities** FTV tea/coffee Cen ht **Parking** 3 **Notes** LB Closed Dec-Jan 🐾 230 acres dairy/mixed

Ty-Cooke Farm *(SO310052)*

★★★★ FARMHOUSE

Mamhilad NP4 8QZ
☎ **01873 880382** 📠 **01873 880382** **Mrs M Price**
e-mail: tycookefarm@hotmail.com
dir: *Off A4042 to Mamhilad, in 2m 1st farm on left past Horseshoe Inn*

This working farm is quietly located in an attractive setting with lovely views. It is thought to date from 1700

and has a wealth of character. Breakfasts are served at one table near a magnificent ornate marble fireplace. There is also a small lounge on the ground floor of the barn accommodation which houses two upper-floor bedrooms and a ground-floor twin bedroom.

Rooms 3 en suite 3 annexe en suite (1 fmly) (1 GF) S £45-£50; D £65-£70* **Facilities** TVL tea/coffee Cen ht Wi-fi **Parking** 6 **Notes** ⊗ 135 acres beef/sheep

Black Lion Guest House

★★★★ 🅰 GUEST HOUSE

43 Hereford Rd NP7 5PY
☎ **01873 851920** 📠 **01873 857885**
e-mail: blacklionaber@aol.com
Rooms 5 rms (2 en suite) (3 pri facs) (1 fmly) S £35-£50; D £80-£90* **Facilities** STV FTV tea/coffee Dinner available Cen ht **Parking** 3 **Notes** ⊗

Pentre Court Country House

★★★ 🅰 GUEST ACCOMMODATION

Llanwenarth Citra NP7 7EW
☎ **01873 853545** 📠 **01873 851354**
e-mail: judith@pentrecourt.com
web: www.pentrecourt.com
dir: *On A40 opp Lamb and Flag Inn*

Rooms 3 en suite (1 fmly) **Facilities** TVL tea/coffee Dinner available Cen ht 🐾 🐾 **Parking** 6 **Notes** Closed 23 Dec-1 Jan 🐾

See advert on this page

Pentre Court Guest House

Pentre Court is a small Georgian country house beautifully located half a mile outside Abergavenny in South Wales. Pentre Court is surrounded by beautiful gardens and some of the most picturesque landscape to be found in the UK.

The house is beautifully set just inside the Brecon Beacons National Park in 4 acres of well-wooded gardens and paddock through which runs the stream Nantiago.

In the garden is a heated swimming pool with diving board, changing room and sun terrace.

Adjacent to the house are footpaths to the River Usk and Sugar Loaf Mountain.

Accommodation includes en-suite bedrooms, central heating, a dining room and drawing room with open fire and colour TV.

Meals include a typical British or Continental breakfast.

Evening meals can be provided by prior arrangement and packed lunches and special dietary needs can be accommodated.

Brecon Road	Tel: 01873 853545
Abergavenny	Website: www.pentrecourt.com
Monmouthshire NP7 7EW	Email: judith@pentrecourt.com

LLANDOGO Map 4 SO50

The Sloop Inn

★★★★ INN

NP25 4TW
☎ **01594 530291**
e-mail: thesloopinn@btconnect.com
dir: On A466 in village centre

This welcoming inn is centrally located close to the River Wye in an outstandingly beautiful valley. It offers a selection of traditional food, as well as friendly hospitality. The dining room has delightful views over the valley, and the spacious bedrooms and newly refurbished bathrooms are equipped for both business and leisure guests.

Rooms 4 en suite (1 fmly) S fr £35; D £60–£75*
Facilities tea/coffee Dinner available Cen ht Pool Table
Parking 50 **Notes** LB RS Mon-Fri closed between 3-6

LLANTRISANT Map 9 ST39

Greyhound Inn

★★★ [A] INN

NP15 1LE
☎ **01291 673447 & 672505** 📠 **01291 673255**
e-mail: enquiry@greyhound-inn.com
web: www.greyhound-inn.com
dir: M4 junct 24, A449, 1st exit for Usk, 2.5m from town square, follow Llantrisant signs

Rooms 10 en suite (2 fmly) (5 GF) S £56–£60; D £72–£80*
Facilities tea/coffee Direct Dial Cen ht Wi-fi **Notes** LB
Closed 25-26 Dec RS Sun eve no food No coaches

MONMOUTH Map 10 SO51

Penylan Farm

★★★★ BED AND BREAKFAST

Hendre NP25 5NL
☎ **01600 716435** 📠 **01600 719391**
e-mail: penylanfarm@gmail.com
dir: 5m NW of Monmouth. B4233 through Rockfield towards Hendre. 0.5m before Hendre turn right towards Newcastle. After 1.5m turn left, farm 0.5 m on right

This converted barn was originally part of the Hendre Estate, once owned by the Rolls family. The bedrooms are housed in a former granary, and are equipped with many thoughtful extras. There is also a self-catering accommodation which is suitable for short-term letting.

Breakfasts focus on local produce, and a lounge is available.

Penylan Farm

Rooms 5 rms (3 en suite) (1 fmly) (2 GF) **Facilities** tea/coffee Dinner available Cen ht Wi-fi 🐾 **Parking** 5
Notes LB ⊗ Closed Xmas & New Year

Church Farm

★★★ GUEST HOUSE

Mitchel Troy NP25 4HZ
☎ **01600 712176**
e-mail: info@churchfarmguesthouse.eclipse.co.uk
dir: From A40 S, left onto B4293 for Trelleck before tunnel, 150yds turn left and follow signs to Mitchel Troy. Guest House on main road, on left 200yds beyond campsite

Located in the village of Mitchel Troy, this 16th-century former farmhouse retains many original features including exposed beams and open fireplaces. There is a range of bedrooms and a spacious lounge, and breakfast is served in the traditionally furnished dining room. Dinner is available by prior arrangement.

Rooms 9 rms (7 en suite) (2 pri facs) (3 fmly) S £31–£35; D £62–£70 **Facilities** TV2B TVL tea/coffee Dinner available Cen ht **Parking** 12 **Notes** LB Closed Xmas 🐾

ROCKFIELD Map 9 SO41

The Stonemill & Steppes Farm Cottages

★★★★ ◉◉ RESTAURANT WITH ROOMS

NP25 5SW
☎ **01600 775424**
e-mail: michelle@thestonemill.co.uk
dir: A48 to Monmouth, B4233 to Rockfield. 2.6m from Monmouth town centre

Located in a small hamlet just west of Monmouth, close to the Forest of Dean and the Wye Valley, this operation

offers accommodation comprising six very well-appointed cottages. The comfortable rooms (for self-catering or on a B&B basis) are architect designed and lovingly restored with many of the original features remaining. In a separate, converted 16th-century barn is the Stonemill Restaurant with oak beams, vaulted ceilings and an old cider press. Breakfast is served in the cottages on request. This establishment's location proves handy for golfers with a choice of many courses in the area.

Rooms 6 en suite (6 fmly) (6 GF) **Facilities** TVL tea/coffee Dinner available Cen ht Free golf **Parking** 53 **Notes** LB ⊗ RS Sun eve & Mon Closed No coaches Civ Wed

SKENFRITH Map 9 SO42

PREMIER COLLECTION

The Bell at Skenfrith

★★★★★ ◉◉ RESTAURANT WITH ROOMS

NP7 8UH
☎ **01600 750235** 📠 **01600 750525**
e-mail: enquiries@skenfrith.co.uk
web: www.skenfrith.co.uk
dir: On B4521 in Skenfrith, opposite castle

The Bell is a beautifully restored, 17th-century former coaching inn which still retains much of its original charm and character. It is peacefully situated on the banks of the Monnow, a tributary of the River Wye, and is ideally placed for exploring the numerous delights of the area. Natural materials have been used to create a relaxing atmosphere, while the bedrooms, which include full suites and rooms with four-poster beds, are stylish, luxurious and equipped with DVD players. The Bell is the Winner of the AA Wine Award of the Year 2009-2010.

Rooms 11 en suite (2 fmly) S £75–£120; D £110–£220*
Facilities tea/coffee Dinner available Direct Dial Cen ht Wi-fi **Conf** Max 20 Thtr 20 Board 16 **Parking** 36
Notes No Children 8yrs Closed last wk Jan-1st wk Feb RS Nov-Mar Closed Tue No coaches

TINTERN PARVA Map 4 SO50

Parva Farmhouse Riverside Guest House

★★★★ 🍴 GUEST HOUSE

Monmouth Rd NP16 6SQ
☎ **01291 689411** 📠 **01291 689941**
e-mail: parvahoteltintern@fsmail.net
dir: On A466 at N edge of Tintern. Next to St Michael's Church on the riverside

This relaxed and friendly, family-run guest house is situated on a sweep of the River Wye with far-reaching views of the valley. Originally a farmhouse dating from the 17th century, many features have been retained, providing character and comfort in an informal atmosphere. The cosy Inglenook Restaurant is the place where quality ingredients are prepared for dinner and breakfast. The individually designed bedrooms are tastefully decorated and enjoy pleasant views; one has a four-poster.

Rooms 8 en suite (2 fmly) S £40-£65; D £60-£85*
Facilities tea/coffee Dinner available Cen ht Licensed
Parking 8 **Notes** No Children 12yrs

USK
Map 9 S030

The Newbridge

★★★★ ◉ RESTAURANT WITH ROOMS

Tredunnock NP15 1LY
☎ 01633 451000 📠 01633 451001
e-mail: newbridge@evanspubs.co.uk

This 200-year-old inn stands alongside a flowing river and provides a peaceful escape to the country. The main inn and restaurant offer tables and seating on two levels as well as some outdoor seating for warmer months. Bedrooms are located in an adjacent building and have a well furnished, contemporary style. A good selection of dishes utilising fresh local produce is served in the main restaurant at both lunch and dinner.

Rooms 6 en suite S £77; D £120* **Facilities** Dinner available Direct Dial Cen ht Wi-fi **Conf** Max 20 Thtr 20 **Parking** 50 **Notes** ⊗

WHITEBROOK
Map 4 S050

PREMIER COLLECTION

The Crown at Whitebrook
★★★★★ ◉◉ ≣ RESTAURANT WITH ROOMS

NP25 4TX
☎ 01600 860254 📠 01600 860607
e-mail: info@crownatwhitebrook.co.uk
dir: *4m from Monmouth on B4293, left at sign to Whitebrook, 2m on unmarked road, Crown on right*

In a secluded spot in the wooded valley of the River Wye, this former drover's cottage dates back to the 17th century. Refurbished, individually decorated bedrooms boast a contemporary feel with smart modern facilities. The restaurant and lounge combine many original features with a bright fresh look. Memorable cuisine features locally sourced ingredients skilfully prepared.

Rooms 8 en suite S £80-£100; D £115-£140*
Facilities FTV tea/coffee Dinner available Direct Dial Cen ht Wi-fi Fishing, Shooting **Conf** Max 12 Thtr 12 Board 12 **Parking** 20 **Notes** LB ⊗ No Children 12yrs Closed 22 Dec-4 Jan RS Sun-Tue Closed Mon & Tue No coaches

See advert on this page

NEATH PORT TALBOT

NEATH
Map 9 SS79

Cwmbach Cottages Guest House

★★★★ GUEST HOUSE

Cwmbach Rd, Cadoxton SA10 8AH
☎ 01639 639825
e-mail: l.morgan5@btinternet.com
web: www.cwmbachcottages.co.uk
dir: *1.5m NE of Neath. A465 onto A474 & A4230 towards Aberdulais, left opp Cadoxton church, guest house signed*

A terrace of former miners' cottages has been restored to provide a range of thoughtfully furnished bedrooms, with one on the ground floor for easier access. Spacious public areas include a comfortable lounge and a pleasant breakfast room with separate tables. A superb decked patio overlooks a wooded hillside rich with wildlife.

Rooms 5 en suite (1 fmly) (1 GF) S £34-£46; D £56-£66*
Facilities TVL tea/coffee Cen ht Wi-fi Golf 18 **Parking** 9
Notes LB ⊗ ➔

The Crown at Whitebrook
near Monmouthshire NP25 4TX

Tel: 01600 860254   Fax: 01600 860607
Email: info@crownatwhitebrook.co.uk
Website: www.crownatwhitebrook.co.uk

The Crown at Whitebrook is set in 3 acres of gardens surrounded by forest views in the heart of the breathtakingly beautiful Wye Valley. Eight luxurious bedrooms have been furnished to the highest standard with attention to detail throughout. Individual themes and character define each room. All boast modern en-suite bathrooms with under-floor heating, high-speed Internet access and flat screen televisions. The restaurant has a warm, relaxed ambience and a superb Modern British fine dining menu draws from the best of local ingredients.

NEWPORT

CAERLEON — Map 9 ST39

PREMIER COLLECTION

Radford House
★★★★★ BED AND BREAKFAST

Broadway NP18 1AY
☎ 01633 430101
e-mail: radfordhouse@btconnect.com
web: www.radfordhouse.co.uk
dir: In town centre opp museum & church

Located in the heart of the historic town of Caerleon, refurbished Radford House more than meets its brochure description of providing rooms of distinction for the discerning traveller. The spacious bedrooms and bathrooms have been beautifully designed and sumptuously furnished, and include fresh flowers, bottles of water, an extensive selection of teas, chocolates, fresh fruit, and flat-screen TVs. A comfortable drawing room, impressive staircase and smart breakfast room add to the air of luxury and relaxation.

Rooms 3 en suite **Facilities** FTV tea/coffee Cen ht Wi-fi **Notes** ⊗ No Children 12yrs

NEWPORT — Map 9 ST38

Labuan Guest House
★★★★ GUEST HOUSE

464 Chepstow Rd NP19 8JF
☎ 01633 664533 📠 01633 664533
e-mail: patricia.bees@ntlworld.com
dir: M4 junct 24, 1.5m on B4237

Expect a warm welcome from owners Pat and John at this delightful guest house which is set on the main road into Newport. Accommodation is comfortable and includes a ground-floor twin room. All rooms are of a good size and bathrooms feature a wide range of extras. The hearty breakfast is taken in the welcoming dining room at separate tables, where a good choice from the menu is available. Off-street parking available.

Rooms 5 rms (3 en suite) (2 pri facs) (1 GF) S £38-£45; D £68-£75* **Facilities** FTV TVL tea/coffee Dinner available Cen ht Wi-fi **Parking** 6 **Notes** LB ⊗

Kepe Lodge
★★★ GUEST HOUSE

46A Caerau Rd NP20 4HH
☎ 01633 262351 📠 01633 262351
e-mail: kepelodge@hotmail.com
dir: 500yds W of town centre. M4 junct 27, town centre signs, 2nd lights left, premises on right

This attractive guest house in a quiet residential area is set back from the road in pleasant gardens. Guests can expect attentive service and comfortable homely bedrooms. Breakfast is served at individual tables in the well-appointed dining room. A comfortable lounge is also available.

Rooms 8 rms (3 en suite) **Facilities** FTV tea/coffee Cen ht **Parking** 12 **Notes** ⊗ No Children 10yrs ⊛

The Rising Sun
★★★ INN

1 Cefn Rd, Rogerstone NP10 9AQ
☎ 01633 895126 📠 01633 891020
dir: M4 junct 27, B4591 signed Highcross, establishment 0.5m on left

Located a short drive from the M4 in the community of Rogerstone, this Edwardian inn provides high levels of comfort and facilities. Bedrooms are equipped with quality furnishings and lots of thoughtful extras. Spacious public rooms include a magnificent split-level conservatory, and the grounds feature a children's play area.

Rooms 6 rms (5 en suite) (1 pri facs) (1 fmly) (6 smoking) S £45; D £65* **Facilities** FTV tea/coffee Dinner available Cen ht Wi-fi Pool Table Childrens play area **Parking** 100 **Notes** ⊗ RS Mon-Thu 3.30-5.30pm No check in

REDWICK — Map 9 ST48

Brickhouse Country Guest House
★★★★ GUEST HOUSE

North Row NP26 3DX
☎ 01633 880230 📠 01633 882441
e-mail: brickhouse@compuserve.com
dir: M4 junct 23A, follow steelworks road for 1.5m. Left after sign for Redwick, Brickhouse 1.5m on left

This impressive country house is in a peaceful location with attractive, well-tended gardens. The friendly hosts are most attentive and provide a relaxing atmosphere. Bedrooms are spacious and traditionally furnished, while the public areas include a choice of lounges. Dinners featuring home-grown produce are sometimes available by prior arrangement. Christine Park was a Finalist for the AA Friendliest Landlady of the Year 2009-2010 Award.

Rooms 7 rms (5 en suite) (1 fmly) S £35-£45; D £60* **Facilities** TVL Dinner available Cen ht Licensed **Parking** 7 **Notes** ⊗ No Children 10yrs

PEMBROKESHIRE

FISHGUARD — Map 8 SM93

Erw-Lon (SN028325)
★★★★ 🏠 FARMHOUSE

Pontfaen SA65 9TS
☎ 01348 881297 Mrs L McAllister
e-mail: lilwenmcallister@btinternet.com
dir: 5.5m SE of Fishguard on B4313

Located in the Pembrokeshire Coast National Park, with stunning views of the Gwaun Valley, this attractive farmhouse has been converted to provide modern well-equipped bedrooms with a wealth of homely extras. The McAllisters give the warmest of welcomes, and their memorable dinners feature the finest local produce.

Rooms 3 en suite S £40; D £62-£66 **Facilities** TVL tea/coffee Dinner available Cen ht **Parking** 5 **Notes** LB ⊗ No Children 10yrs Closed Dec-Mar ⊛ 128 acres beef/sheep

HAVERFORDWEST — Map 8 SM91

See also Narberth

College Guest House

★★★★ GUEST HOUSE

93 Hill St, St Thomas Green SA61 1QL
☎ 01437 763710 📠 01437 763710
e-mail: colinlarby@aol.com
dir: *In town centre, along High St, pass church, keep in left lane. 1st exit by Stonemason Arms pub, follow signs for St Thomas Green. 300mtrs on left by No Entry sign*

Located in a mainly residential area within easy walking distance of the attractions, this impressive Georgian house has been upgraded to offer good levels of comfort and facilities. There is range of practically equipped bedrooms, along with public areas that include a spacious lounge (with internet access) and an attractive pine-furnished dining room, the setting for comprehensive breakfasts.

Rooms 8 en suite (4 fmly) S £51-£56; D £69-£76 **Facilities** FTV TVL tea/coffee Cen ht Wi-fi

Lower Haythog Farm *(SM996214)*

★★★★ FARMHOUSE

Spittal SA62 5QL
☎ 01437 731279 📠 01437 731279 Mrs N M Thomas
e-mail: nesta@lowerhaythogfarm.co.uk
web: www.lowerhaythogfarm.co.uk
dir: *5m N on B4329 to railway bridge, farmhouse entrance on right*

Located in 250 acres of unspoiled countryside, this 14th-century farmhouse with adjacent cottage provides high standards of comfort and good facilities. Bedrooms, including a two-bedroom family suite, are modern and well equipped. The elegant oak-beamed dining room is the setting for imaginative home-cooked dinners. Welcoming real fires burn during cold weather in the comfortable lounge, and a second conservatory-lounge overlooks the large, attractive garden.

Rooms 6 en suite (2 fmly) (1 GF) **Facilities** TVL tea/coffee Dinner available Cen ht Fishing **Parking** 5 **Notes** LB 😊 250 acres dairy

KILGETTY — Map 8 SN10

Manian Lodge

★★★★ GUEST HOUSE

Begelly SA68 0XE
☎ 01834 813273 📠 01834 811591
e-mail: information@manianlodge.com
dir: *A447 N onto A478, 0.5m on right in Begelly*

Manian Lodge is convenient for Tenby and the South Pembrokeshire Heritage Coast, and also the Pembroke Dock ferry terminal. The owners provide well-equipped modern bedrooms, including one on the ground floor. There is a comfortable lounge bar, a lounge, and a very attractive restaurant where a good choice of meals is offered. Self-catering accommodation is also available.

Rooms 6 en suite (1 GF) **Facilities** tea/coffee Dinner available Cen ht Licensed Wi-fi **Conf** Max 40 Thtr 40 Class 10 Board 18 **Parking** 19 **Notes** 🚫

NARBERTH — Map 8 SN11

Highland Grange Farm *(SN077154)*

★★★ FARMHOUSE

Robeston Wathen SA67 8EP
☎ 01834 860952 📠 01834 860952 Mrs N Jones
e-mail: info@highlandgrange.co.uk
web: www.highlandgrange.co.uk
dir: *2m NW of Narberth on A40 Robeston Wathen, near Bush Inn*

A warm welcome can be expected along with comfortable accommodation at this farmhouse property, where all the spacious bedrooms are on the ground floor. The property is set on the main A40 road in the small village of Robeston Wathen, between Whitland and Haverfordwest. The dining room has separate tables where a good hearty breakfast is provided. There is also a spacious and comfortable lounge where a real fire is lit in cold weather.

Rooms 3 rms (2 en suite) (1 fmly) (3 GF) **Facilities** TVL tea/coffee Dinner available Cen ht Licensed **Parking** 6 **Notes** 🚫 😊 50 acres mixed/sheep

NEVERN — Map 8 SN04

Trewern Arms

★★★★ INN

SA42 0NB
☎ 01239 820395 📠 01239 820173
e-mail: trewern.arms@virgin.net
dir: *Off A48. Midway between Cardigan & Fishguard*

Set in a peaceful and picturesque village, this charming 16th-century inn is well positioned to offer a relaxing stay. There are many original features to be seen in the two character bars and attractive restaurant, and the spacious bedrooms are appointed to a high standard and include some family rooms.

Rooms 10 en suite (4 fmly) **Facilities** TVL Cen ht Fishing Riding **Parking** 100

NEWPORT — Map 8 SN03

Llysmeddyg

★★★★ @@ RESTAURANT WITH ROOMS

East St SA42 0SY
☎ 01239 820008
e-mail: contact@llysmeddyg.com
dir: *On A487 in centre of town on Main St*

Llysmeddyg is a Georgian townhouse with a blend of old and new, elegant furnishings, deep sofas and a welcoming fire. The owners of this property have used local craftsmen to create a lovely interior that reflects an eclectic style throughout. The focus of the restaurant menu is on quality food through use of fresh seasonal ingredients sourced locally. The spacious bedrooms are comfortable and contemporary in design - the bathrooms vary in style.

Rooms 5 en suite 3 annexe en suite (3 fmly) (1 GF) S £85-£135; D £100-£150* **Facilities** tea/coffee Dinner available Cen ht Wi-fi **Conf** Max 20 Class 20 Board 20 **Parking** 8 **Notes** LB No coaches

NEWPORT *continued*

Salutation Inn

★★★ ⓐ INN

Filindre Farchog SA41 3UY
☎ 01239 820564 📄 01239 820355
e-mail: johndenley@aol.com
web: www.salutationcountryhotel.co.uk
dir: *On A487 between Cardigan & Fishguard. 3m N of Newport*

Rooms 8 en suite (2 fmly) (8 GF) S £50; D £70
Facilities tea/coffee Dinner available Direct Dial Cen ht
Wi-fi Pool Table **Conf** Max 25 Thtr 25 Class 12 Board 12
Parking 60 **Notes** LB

ST DAVID'S   Map 8 SM72

See also Solva

PREMIER COLLECTION

Ramsey House

★★★★★ ⓐ 🍽 GUEST HOUSE

Lower Moor SA62 6RP
☎ 01437 720321
e-mail: info@ramseyhouse.co.uk
web: www.ramseyhouse.co.uk
dir: *From Cross Sq in St Davids towards Porthclais, house 0.25m on left*

This pleasant guest house, under the ownership of Suzanne and Shaun Ellison offers the ideal combination of professional management and the warmth of a family-run guest house. The property is quietly located on the outskirts of St David's surrounded by unspoilt countryside. It provides modern, well-equipped bedrooms and en suite bathrooms recently refurbished to a high standard along with a good range of welcome extras. Carefully prepared dinners by award-winning chef Shaun feature quality local Welsh produce, and breakfast provides a choice of home-made items including breads and preserves.

Rooms 6 rms (5 en suite) (1 pri facs) (3 GF) S £60-£95; D £90-£95* **Facilities** FTV tea/coffee Dinner available Cen ht Licensed Wi-fi **Parking** 10 **Notes** LB ⊗

The Waterings

★★★★ BED AND BREAKFAST

Anchor Dr, High St SA62 6QH
☎ 01437 720876 📄 01437 720876
e-mail: waterings@supanet.com
web: www.waterings.co.uk
dir: *On A487 on E edge of St David's*

Situated a short walk from the centre of St David's, the Waterings offers spacious bedrooms that are accessed from a courtyard garden. Most rooms have their own separate seating area. Breakfast, from a good selection of local produce, is served in a smart dining room in the main house.

Rooms 5 annexe en suite (4 fmly) (5 GF) S £50-£80; D £75-£80* **Facilities** FTV tea/coffee Cen ht Licensed ⛵ **Conf** Max 15 Board 15 **Parking** 20 **Notes** ⊗ No Children 5yrs ♿

Y-Gorlan

★★★★ GUEST HOUSE

77 Nun St SA62 6NU
☎ 01437 720837 & 07974 108029
e-mail: mikebohlen@aol.com
dir: *In centre of St David's*

This personally-run guest house is just a stroll from the city's attractions. The well-maintained accommodation includes a family room and a room with a four-poster bed. The comfortable first-floor lounge has excellent views towards the coast across the surrounding countryside. A hearty breakfast is offered with a good choice of items available.

Rooms 5 en suite (1 fmly) S £36-£40; D £65-£75* **Facilities** STV FTV TVL tea/coffee Cen ht **Parking** 3 **Notes** ⊗ No Children 5yrs

SAUNDERSFOOT   Map 8 SN10

Vine Cottage

★★★★ GUEST HOUSE

The Ridgeway SA69 9LA
☎ 01834 814422
e-mail: enquiries@vinecottageguesthouse.co.uk
web: www.vinecottageguesthouse.co.uk
dir: *A477 S onto A478, left onto B4316, after railway bridge right signed Saundersfoot, cottage 100yds beyond 30mph sign*

A warm welcome awaits guests at this pleasant former farmhouse located on the outskirts of Saundersfoot, yet within easy walking distance of this delightful village. Set in extensive, mature gardens which include some rare and exotic plants and a summer house where guests can sit and relax on warmer evenings. Bedrooms, including a ground-floor room, are modern and well equipped, and some are suitable for families. There is a comfortable, airy lounge. Dinner, available on request, and breakfast are served in the cosy dining room.

Rooms 5 en suite (2 fmly) (1 GF) S £40-£50; D £60-£76* **Facilities** FTV tea/coffee Dinner available Cen ht **Parking** 10 **Notes** LB No Children 6yrs ♿

SOLVA   Map 8 SM82

PREMIER COLLECTION

Crug-Glas Country House

★★★★★ ⓐ 🍽 GUEST HOUSE

SA62 6XX
☎ 01348 831302
e-mail: janet@crugglas.plus.com

This house is on a mixed dairy, beef and cereal farm of approximately 600 acres, and is situated about a mile inland from the coast at the end of St David's Peninsula. This delightful property affords comfort and relaxation, along with flawless attention to detail provided by the charming host, Janet Evans. Each spacious bedroom has the hallmarks of assured design, with warm, well-chosen fabrics, grand furnishings and luxury bathrooms, each with a bath and shower. One suite on the top floor has great views. Award-winning breakfasts and dinners, using the finest local produce, are served. The sunsets in the evening are stunning.

Rooms 7 en suite (1 fmly) (2 GF) S £70; D £100-£150 **Facilities** FTV tea/coffee Dinner available Cen ht Licensed Wi-fi **Conf** Max 20 Thtr 20 Class 20 Board 20 **Parking** 10 **Notes** ⊗ No Children 12yrs Closed 24-27 Dec

PREMIER COLLECTION

Lochmeyler Farm Guest House *(SM855275)*
★★★★★ 🍴 FARMHOUSE

Llandeloy SA62 6LL
☎ 01348 837724 📠 01348 837622 Mrs M Jones
e-mail: stay@lochmeyler.co.uk
web: www.lochmeyler.co.uk
dir: *From Haverfordwest A487 (St David's road) to Pen-y-cwm, right to Llandeloy*

Located on a 220-acre dairy farm, just three miles inland from the coast, Lochmeyler provides high levels of comfort and excellent facilities. The spacious bedrooms, some in converted outbuildings, are equipped with a wealth of thoughtful extras and four have private sitting rooms. Comprehensive breakfasts are served in the dining room as well as dinner on request; a sumptuous lounge is also available.

Rooms 7 en suite 5 annexe en suite (6 GF) S £35-£50; D £70-£80* **Facilities** tea/coffee Dinner available Direct Dial Cen ht Licensed **Parking** 12 **Notes** LB No Children 10yrs 220 acres dairy

---

TENNY Map 8 SN10

Panorama
★★★★ 🛏 GUEST ACCOMMODATION

The Esplanade SA70 7DU
☎ 01834 844976 📠 01834 844976
e-mail: mail@tenby-hotel.co.uk
web: www.tenby-hotel.co.uk
dir: *A478 follow South Beach & Town Centre signs. Sharp left under railway arches, up Greenhill Rd, onto South Pde then Esplanade*

This charming property is part of a Victorian terrace, overlooking the South Beach and Caldy Island in Tenby. All the bedrooms are well equipped and comfortable. Facilities include a cosy seating area and a large elegant dining room with sea views. Breakfast offers a good selection prepared from fresh and local ingredients.

Rooms 8 en suite (1 fmly) S £45-£50; D £80-£110* **Facilities** tea/coffee Cen ht Licensed **Notes** ⊗ No Children 5yrs Closed 22-28 Dec

Rosendale Guesthouse
★★★★ GUEST HOUSE

Lydstep SA70 7SQ
☎ 01834 870040
e-mail: rosendalewales@yahoo.com
web: www.rosendalepembrokeshire.co.uk
dir: *3m SW of Tenby. A4139 W towards Pembroke. Rosendale on right after Lydstep*

A warm welcome awaits all guests at this family-run guest accommodation, ideally located on the outskirts of the pretty village of Lydstep, not far from the seaside town of Tenby. Rosendale provides modern, well-equipped bedrooms, some with coast or country views. Three rooms are on the ground floor of a separate building to the rear of the main house. The attractive dining room is the setting for breakfast, and there is also a large, comfortable lounge.

Rooms 6 en suite (3 GF) S £35-£45; D £60-£75* **Facilities** FTV tea/coffee Cen ht Wi-fi **Parking** 6 **Notes** No Children 16yrs

---

Esplanade
★★★★ GUEST ACCOMMODATION

The Esplanade SA70 7DU
☎ 01834 842760 & 843333 📠 01834 845633
e-mail: esplanadetenby@googlemail.com
web: www.esplanadetenby.co.uk
dir: *Follow signs to South Beach, premises on seafront next to town walls*

Located beside the historic town walls of Tenby and with stunning views over the sea to Caldey Island, the Esplanade provides a range of standard and luxury bedrooms, some ideal for families. Breakfast is offered in the elegant front-facing dining room, which contains a comfortable lounge-bar area.

Rooms 14 en suite (3 fmly) (1 GF) S £55-£100; D £80-£130* **Facilities** tea/coffee Direct Dial Cen ht Licensed Wi-fi **Notes** LB Closed 15-27 Dec

Giltar Grove Country House
★★★ GUEST ACCOMMODATION

Penally SA70 7RY
☎ 01834 871568
e-mail: giltarbnb@aol.com
dir: *2m SW of Tenby. Off A4139, 2nd right after railway bridge*

Just a short walk from the spectacular Pembrokeshire Coastal Path, this impressive Victorian farmhouse retains many original features. The bedrooms include rooms with four-poster beds and rooms on the ground floor. All are filled with homely extras. There is a cosy sitting room, an elegant dining room, and spacious conservatory that is used for breakfast.

Rooms 6 rms (5 en suite) (1 pri facs) (2 GF) S £25-£35; D £60-£70 **Facilities** tea/coffee Cen ht **Parking** 10 **Notes** ⊗ No Children 10yrs Closed Dec-Feb 📷

POWYS

BRECON
Map 9 SO02

See also Sennybridge

PREMIER COLLECTION

Canal Bank
★★★★★ BED AND BREAKFAST

Ty Gardd LD3 7HG
☎ 01874 623464 & 625844
e-mail: enquiries@accommodation-breconbeacons.co.uk
web: www.accommodation-breconbeacons.co.uk
dir: *B4601 signed Brecon, left over bridge before fuel station, turn right, continue to end of road*

Expect a warm welcome at this delightful property, which was developed from a row of five 18th-century cottages. It provides very high quality, comfortable and well-equipped accommodation, and stands alongside the canal in a semi-rural area on the outskirts of Brecon, yet within walking distance of the town centre. Facilities here include a comfortable lounge, a very attractive breakfast room and a lovely garden.

Rooms 3 en suite S £50-£60; D £85-£90* **Facilities** tea/coffee Cen ht Wi-fi **Parking** 5 **Notes** ⊗ No Children ⌂

PREMIER COLLECTION

The Coach House
★★★★★ GUEST ACCOMMODATION

Orchard St LD3 8AN
☎ 0844 357 1301 ▤ 01874 622454
e-mail: info@coachhousebrecon.com
dir: *From town centre W over bridge onto B4601, Coach House 200yds on right*

A warm welcome awaits you at this former coach house, now transformed into modern contemporary accommodation. The friendly and enthusiastic proprietors ensure your stay is something to remember. The bedrooms are well equipped and extremely comfortable. A selection of imaginative Welsh home-cooked breakfast items are served in the relaxing spacious dining room. The Coach House is within easy walking distance of Brecon and also benefits from a lovely garden.

Rooms 7 en suite **Facilities** STV tea/coffee Direct Dial Cen ht Licensed Wi-fi Resident holistic therapist, massage & reflexology **Conf** Max 24 Thtr 24 Board 16 **Parking** 7 **Notes** LB ⊗ No Children 16yrs

---

PREMIER COLLECTION

Peterstone Court
★★★★★ ◉◉ ▤ RESTAURANT WITH ROOMS

Llanhamlach LD3 7YB
☎ 01874 665387
e-mail: info@peterstone-court.com
dir: *3m from Brecon on A40 towards Abergavenny*

Situated on the edge of the Brecons Beacons, this establishment affords stunning views and overlooks the River Usk. The style is friendly and informal, without any unnecessary fuss. No two bedrooms are alike, but all share comparable levels of comfort, quality and elegance. Public areas reflect similar standards, eclectically styled with a blend of the contemporary and the traditional. Quality produce is cooked with care in a range of enjoyable dishes.

Rooms 8 en suite 4 annexe en suite (2 fmly) S £90-£190; D £110-£210* **Facilities** tea/coffee Dinner available Direct Dial Cen ht Wi-fi ⚼ Fishing Riding Sauna Gymnasium Pool open mid Apr-1 Oct, Spa facilities **Conf** Max 100 Thtr 100 Class 100 Board 60 **Parking** 60 **Notes** LB Civ Wed

---

The Felin Fach Griffin
★★★★ ◉◉ INN

Felin Fach LD3 0UB
☎ 01874 620111
e-mail: enquiries@eatdrinksleep.ltd.uk
dir: *4m NE of Brecon on A470*

This delightful inn stands in an extensive garden at the northern end of Felin Fach village. The public areas have a wealth of rustic charm and provide the setting for the excellent food. Service and hospitality are commendable. The bedrooms are carefully appointed and have modern equipment and facilities.

Rooms 7 en suite (1 fmly) S £65-£85; D £115-£140* **Facilities** tea/coffee Dinner available Direct Dial Cen ht ⌣ **Conf** Max 15 Board 15 **Parking** 61 **Notes** LB Closed 25-26 Dec No coaches

---

Llanddetty Hall Farm (SO124205)
★★★★ FARMHOUSE

Talybont-on-Usk LD3 7YR
☎ 01874 676415 ▤ 01874 676415 Mrs H E Atkins
dir: *SE of Brecon. Off B4558*

This impressive Grade II listed 17th-century farmhouse in the beautiful Usk valley is full of character, and the friendly proprietors ensure a comfortable stay. Bedrooms are very pleasant and feature traditional furnishings, exposed timbers and polished floorboards. Welcoming log fires are lit during cold weather in the comfortable lounge, and guests dine around one table in the dining room.

Rooms 3 rms (2 en suite) (1 pri facs) 1 annexe en suite (1 GF) S £35; D £60-£62* **Facilities** TV1B TVL tea/coffee Cen ht **Parking** 6 **Notes** ⊗ No Children 12yrs Closed 16 Dec-14 Jan RS Feb-Apr restricted service at lambing season ⌂ 48 acres sheep

---

The Usk Inn
★★★★ ◉ INN

Station Rd, Talybont-on-Usk LD3 7JE
☎ 01874 676251 ▤ 01874 676392
e-mail: stay@uskinn.co.uk
dir: *Off A40, 6m E of Brecon*

This delightful inn is personally run in a friendly manner by the new owners who have renovated the property to a high standard. The thoughtfully equipped and well-appointed bedrooms include a family room and one room with a four-poster bed. Public areas have a wealth of charm and the inn has a well-deserved reputation for its food.

Rooms 11 en suite (1 fmly) **Facilities** TVL tea/coffee Dinner available Direct Dial Cen ht **Conf** Max 60 Thtr 60 Class 40 Board 20 **Parking** 30 **Notes** LB ⊗ Closed 25-27 Dec

The Beacons Guest House

★★★ GUEST HOUSE

16 Bridge St LD3 8AH
☎ 01874 623339 📠 01874 623339
e-mail: guesthouse@thebreconbeacons.co.uk
dir: On B4601 opp Christ College.

Located west of the historic town centre over the bridge, this 17th-century former farmhouse by the river has been renovated to provide a range of homely bedrooms, some in converted barns and outbuildings. There is a guests' lounge and a cosy bar. This is a non-smoking establishment.

Rooms 11 rms (9 en suite) 3 annexe en suite (4 fmly) (3 GF) S £35-£82; D £56-£82* **Facilities** TVL tea/coffee Cen ht Licensed Wi-fi **Conf** Max 30 Thtr 30 Class 25 Board 20 **Parking** 20 **Notes** LB ⊗

Borderers

★★★ GUEST ACCOMMODATION

47 The Watton LD3 7EG
☎ 01874 623559
e-mail: info@borderers.com
web: www.borderers.com
dir: 200yds SE of town centre on B4601, opp church

This guest house was originally a 17th-century drovers' inn. The courtyard, now a car park, is surrounded by many of the bedrooms, and pretty hanging baskets are seen everywhere. The bedrooms are attractively decorated with rich floral fabrics. A room with easier access is available.

Rooms 4 rms (3 en suite) (1 pri facs) 5 annexe en suite (2 fmly) (4 GF) **Facilities** tea/coffee Cen ht Wi-fi **Parking** 6

The Lansdowne

★★★ GUEST ACCOMMODATION

The Watton LD3 7EG
☎ 01874 623321 📠 01874 610438
e-mail: reception@lansdownehotel.co.uk
dir: A40/A470 onto B4601

A privately-owned and personally-run guest house, this Georgian house is conveniently located close to the town centre. The accommodation is well equipped and includes family rooms and a bedroom on the ground floor. There is a comfortable lounge, a small bar and an attractive split-level dining room where dinner is available to residents.

Rooms 9 en suite (2 fmly) (1 GF) S £40; D £60* **Facilities** tea/coffee Dinner available Direct Dial Cen ht Licensed **Notes** LB No Children 5yrs

---

CAERSWS Map 15 SO09

PREMIER COLLECTION

The Talkhouse
★★★★★ ◉◉ RESTAURANT WITH ROOMS

Pontdolgoch SY17 5JE
☎ 01686 688919 📠 01686 689134
e-mail: info@talkhouse.co.uk
dir: 1.5m NW of Caersws on A470

A highlight of this delightful 19th-century inn is the food, home-made dishes making good use of local produce. Bedrooms offer luxury in every area and the cosy lounge, filled with sofas, is the place to while away some time with a glass of wine or a pot of tea. The bar is very welcoming with its log fire.

Rooms 3 en suite **Facilities** Dinner available Cen ht **Parking** 50 **Notes** ⊗ No Children 14yrs Closed 1st 2 wks Jan RS Sun eve & Mon open for group bookings only No coaches

---

CRICKHOWELL Map 9 SO21

PREMIER COLLECTION

Glangrwyney Court
★★★★★ BED AND BREAKFAST

NP8 1ES
☎ 01873 811288 📠 01873 810317
e-mail: info@glancourt.co.uk
web: www.glancourt.co.uk
dir: 2m SE of Crickhowell on A40 (near county boundary)

Located in extensive mature grounds, this impressive Georgian house has been renovated to provide high standards of comfort and facilities. The spacious bedrooms are equipped with a range of homely extras, and bathrooms include a jacuzzi or steam shower. The interior has been decorated with style. There are also comfortable bedrooms in an annexe with two having their own lounge and kitchen area. Comprehensive breakfasts are taken in the elegant dining room and a luxurious lounge is also provided.

Rooms 6 en suite 4 annexe en suite (1 fmly) (1 GF) S £65-£85* **Facilities** STV TVL tea/coffee Cen ht Licensed Wi-fi 🛁 Boules **Parking** 12 **Notes** LB Civ Wed 23

See advert on this page

Glangrwyney Court

Crickhowell, Powys NP8 1ES
Telephone: 01873 811288
Fax: 01873 810317

Glangrwyney Court Country House – a Georgian mansion set in four acres of established gardens and surrounded by parkland. All rooms are ensuite or have private bathrooms with fluffy towels and bathpearls. Each bedroom is individually furnished with antiques – comfortable beds and overstuffed pillows. In the winter there are log fires burning and comfortable sofas beckoning for you to relax.

CRIGGION — Map 15 SJ21

Brimford House (SJ310150)
★★★★ FARMHOUSE

SY5 9AU
☎ 01938 570235   Mrs Dawson
e-mail: info@brimford.co.uk
dir: *Off B4393 after Crew Green turn left for Criggion, Brimford 1st on left after pub*

This elegant Georgian house stands in lovely open countryside and is a good base for touring central Wales and the Marches. Bedrooms are spacious, and thoughtful extras enhance guest comfort. A cheery log fire burns in the lounge during colder weather and the hospitality is equally warm, providing a relaxing atmosphere throughout.

Rooms 3 en suite S £50-£60; D £60-£70* **Facilities** TVL tea/coffee Cen ht Fishing **Parking** 4 **Notes** LB ⊛ 250 acres arable/beef/sheep

Lane Farm (SJ305161)
★★★ ▲ FARMHOUSE

SY5 9BG
☎ 01743 884288   📄 01743 885126   Mrs L Burrowes
e-mail: lane.farm@ukgateway.net
dir: *On B4393 between Crew Green & Llandrinio*

Rooms 4 en suite (2 GF) S £30-£35; D £50-£54
Facilities tea/coffee Cen ht Fishing **Parking** 8 **Notes** LB Closed 23-27 Dec 380 acres Organic beef/sheep

See advert on opposite page

ERWOOD — Map 9 SO04

Hafod-Y-Garreg
★★★★ 🍽 BED AND BREAKFAST

LD2 3TQ
☎ 01982 560400
e-mail: john-annie@hafod-y.wanadoo.co.uk
web: www.hafodygarreg.co.uk
dir: *1m S of Erwood. Off A470 at Trericket Mill, sharp right, up track past cream farmhouse towards pine forest, through gate*

This remote Grade II listed farmhouse dates in part from 1401 and is the oldest surviving traditional house in Wales. It has tremendous character and has been furnished and decorated to befit its age, while the bedrooms have modern facilities. There is an impressive dining room and a lounge with an open fireplace. Warm hospitality from John and Annie McKay is a major strength here.

Rooms 2 en suite (1 fmly); D £65* **Facilities** STV tea/coffee Dinner available Cen ht Wi-fi **Parking** 6 **Notes** LB Closed Xmas ⊛

HAY-ON-WYE — Map 9 SO24

See also Erwood

Old Black Lion Inn
★★★★ 🍴 INN

26 Lion St HR3 5AD
☎ 01497 820841   📄 01497 822960
e-mail: info@oldblacklion.co.uk

This fine old coaching inn, with a history stretching back several centuries, has a wealth of charm and character. It was occupied by Oliver Cromwell during the siege of Hay Castle. Privately-owned and personally-run, it provides cosy and well-equipped bedrooms, some located in an adjacent building. A wide range of well-prepared food is provided, and the service is relaxed and friendly.

Rooms 6 rms (5 en suite) (1 pri facs) 4 annexe en suite (2 GF) **Facilities** STV tea/coffee Dinner available Direct Dial Cen ht **Parking** 12 **Notes** ⊛ No Children 8yrs Closed 24-26 Dec

Baskerville Arms
★★★ ▲ INN

Clyro HR3 5RZ
☎ 01497 820670   📄 0870 705 8427
e-mail: info@baskervillearms.co.uk
dir: *From Hereford follow A438 into Clyro, signed Brecon*

Rooms 13 en suite (1 fmly) S £45-£55; D £69-£85*
Facilities TVL tea/coffee Dinner available Cen ht Wi-fi
Conf Max 80 Thtr 80 Class 60 Board 40 **Parking** 12
Notes LB Civ Wed 120

LLANDRINDOD WELLS — Map 9 SO06

Guidfa House
★★★★★ 🛁 🍽 GUEST ACCOMMODATION

Crossgates LD1 6RF
☎ 01597 851241   📄 01597 851875
e-mail: guidfa@globalnet.co.uk
web: www.guidfa-house.co.uk
dir: *3m N of Llandrindod Wells, at junct of A483 & A44*

Expect a relaxed and pampered stay at this elegant Georgian house just outside the town. Comfort is the keynote here, whether in the attractive and well-equipped bedrooms or in the homely lounge, where a real fire burns in cold weather. Food is also a strength, due to the proprietor's skilful touch in the kitchen. Tony Millan was a Runner-up for the AA Friendliest Landlady of the Year 2009-2010 Award.

Rooms 5 en suite 1 annexe en suite (1 GF) S £60-£85; D £75-£100* **Facilities** FTV tea/coffee Dinner available Cen ht Licensed Wi-fi **Parking** 10 **Notes** LB ⊛ No Children 10yrs RS Sun-Tue No dinner available

Holly (SO045593)
★★★★ FARMHOUSE

Holly Farm, Howey LD1 5PP
☎ 01597 822402   📄 01597 822402   Mrs R Jones
dir: *2m S on A483 of Llandrindod Wells near Howey*

This working farm dates from Tudor times. Bedrooms are homely and full of character, and the comfortable lounge has a log fire in cooler months. Traditional home cooking using local produce can be sampled in the dining room.

Rooms 3 en suite (1 fmly) S £30-£36; D £54-£60*
Facilities TVL tea/coffee Dinner available Cen ht
Parking 4 **Notes** LB ⊛ 70 acres beef/sheep

LLANGEDWYN
Map 15 SJ12

Plas Uchaf Country Guest House
★★★★ GUEST HOUSE

SY10 9LD
☎ 01691 780588 📠 0845 280 2188
e-mail: info@plasuchaf.com
dir: *Mile End services Oswestry A483/Welshpool, 2m White Lion right, 4.5m Llangedwyn, 150yds after school on right*

Located in a superb elevated position amongst extensive mature parkland, this elegant Queen Anne house has been sympathetically renovated to provide high standards of comfort and facilities. The interior flooring is created from recycled ship timbers, which were originally part of The Armada, and furnishing styles highlight the many period features. Imaginative dinners are available and a warm welcome is assured.

Rooms 8 rms (6 en suite) (2 pri facs) 1 annexe en suite S £40-£60; D £70-£80* **Facilities** FTV tea/coffee Dinner available Cen ht Licensed Wi-fi 🦢 🦢 **Conf** Max 15 Thtr 15 Class 15 Board 15 **Parking** 30 **Notes** LB Civ Wed 50

LLANGURIG
Map 9 SN97

The Old Vicarage
★★★★ GUEST HOUSE

SY18 6RN
☎ 01686 440280 📠 01686 440280
e-mail: info@theoldvicaragellangurig.co.uk
dir: *A470 onto A44, signed*

Located on pretty mature grounds, which feature a magnificent holly tree, this elegant Victorian house provides a range of thoughtfully furnished bedrooms, some with fine period items. Breakfast is served in a spacious dining room and a comfortable guest lounge is also available. Afternoon teas are served in the garden during the warmer months.

Rooms 4 en suite (1 fmly) **Facilities** TVL tea/coffee Dinner available Cen ht Licensed Wi-fi **Parking** 6 **Notes** LB 😊

LLANIDLOES
Map 9 SN98

Mount
★★★ INN

China St SY18 6AB
☎ 01686 412247 📠 01686 412247
e-mail: mountllani@aol.com
dir: *In town centre*

This establishment is believed to occupy part of the former site of a motte and bailey castle, and started life as a coaching inn. The traditional bars are full of character, with exposed beams and timbers as well as cobbled flooring and log fires. Bedrooms, which include some in a new separate building, are carefully furnished and equipped with practical and thoughtful extras.

Rooms 3 en suite 6 annexe en suite (3 fmly) (3 GF) S £40; D £60 **Facilities** TVL tea/coffee Dinner available Cen ht Pool Table **Conf** Max 12 Board 12 **Parking** 12

Lane Farm

A warm welcome awaits on our working organic farm located between Welshpool and Shrewsbury.

Ideally situated to explore The Marches, Shropshire Hills and Mid-Wales.

Four en-suite spacious bedrooms, two on the ground floor all with central heating and TVs

Hearty farmhouse breakfasts

Criggion, Nr Shrewsbury, Powys SY5 9BG

Tel: 01743 884288 (Mrs Lesley Burrowes)

Email: lane.farm@ukgateway.net

Website: www.lanefarmbedandbreakfast.co.uk

LLANWRTYD WELLS — Map 9 SN84

Carlton Riverside

★★★★ ◉◉◉ RESTAURANT WITH ROOMS

Irfon Crescent LD5 4ST
☎ 01591 610248
e-mail: info@carltonriverside.com
dir: *In town centre beside bridge*

Guests become part of the family at this character property, set beside the river in Wales's smallest town. Carlton Riverside offers award-winning cuisine for which Mary Ann Gilchrist relies on the very best of local ingredients. The set menu is complemented by a well-chosen wine list and dinner is served in the delightfully stylish restaurant which offers a memorable blend of traditional comfort, modern design and river views. Four comfortable bedrooms have tasteful combinations of antique and contemporary furniture, along with welcome personal touches.

Rooms 4 en suite S £40–£50; D £65–£100* **Facilities** tea/coffee Dinner available Cen ht Wi-fi **Notes** LB Closed 20-30 Dec No coaches

Lasswade Country House

★★★★ ◉◉ RESTAURANT WITH ROOMS

Station Rd LD5 4RW
☎ 01591 610515   📄 01591 610611
e-mail: info@lasswadehotel.co.uk
dir: *Off A483 into Irfon Terrace, right into Station Rd, 350yds on right*

This friendly establishment on the edge of the town has impressive views over the countryside. Bedrooms are comfortably furnished and well equipped, while the public areas consist of a tastefully decorated lounge, an elegant restaurant with a bar, and an airy conservatory which looks out on to the neighbouring hills. The kitchen utilises fresh, local produce to provide an enjoyable dining experience.

Rooms 8 en suite S £55–£70; D £75–£105* **Facilities** TVL Dinner available Cen ht **Conf** Max 18 Thtr 18 Class 14 Board 14 **Parking** 6 **Notes** No coaches

LLANYMYNECH — Map 15 SJ22

The Bradford Arms

★★★★ INN

Llanymynech SY22 6EJ
☎ 01691 830582   📄 01691 839009
e-mail: catelou@tesco.net

(For full entry see Oswestry (Shropshire))

Ty-Coch Bungalow

★★★ BED AND BREAKFAST

Four Crosses SY22 6QZ
☎ 01691 830361
e-mail: bill_lee@talk21.com
dir: *1m S of Llanymynech on A483*

Built in 1984, this large bungalow provides friendly hospitality, modern accommodation and a comfortable lounge. Bedrooms provide lots of thoughtful extras and comprehensive breakfasts are taken at one table in an attractive dining room. The immaculate gardens contain a wide variety of plants, seasonal flowers and a modern gazebo.

Rooms 2 en suite (2 GF) **Facilities** TVL tea/coffee Dinner available Cen ht **Parking** 6 **Notes** LB ⊗ ⊛

MACHYNLLETH — Map 14 SH70

Yr Hen Felin (The Old Mill)

★★★★ GUEST HOUSE

Abercegir SY20 8NR
☎ 01650 511818
e-mail: yrhenfelin@tiscali.co.uk
dir: *4m E of Machynlleth. Off A489 into Abercegir, right onto unmade road after phone kiosk, over bridge.*

This converted water mill on the River Gwydol has exposed beams and superb polished timber floors. Two bedrooms overlook the river where trout and herons are often seen. There is a very comfortable lounge, and the bedrooms, in a variety of sizes, come with a wealth of thoughtful extras.

Rooms 3 en suite S £40–£43; D £60–£66* **Facilities** TVL tea/coffee Dinner available Cen ht Licensed Fishing Table tennis **Parking** 4 **Notes** LB ⊗ ⊛

Maenllwyd

★★★ GUEST HOUSE

Newtown Rd SY20 8EY
☎ 01654 702928   📄 01654 702928
e-mail: maenllwyd@btinternet.com
web: www.maenllwyd.co.uk
dir: *On A489 opp hospital*

Maenllwyd is a Victorian house set on the outskirts of this historic town, a short walk from local amenities. A warm welcome has been offered to guests here for many years and the hospitality is very enjoyable. Bedrooms are attractively decorated with modern facilities provided. There is a comfortable lounge and a separate dining room.

Rooms 8 en suite (1 fmly); D fr £65* **Facilities** TVL tea/coffee Cen ht **Parking** 11 **Notes** Closed 25-26 Dec

NEWTOWN — Map 15 SO19

The Forest Country Guest House

★★★★★ 🅰 BED AND BREAKFAST

The Forest Gilfach Ln, Kerry SY16 4DW
☎ 01686 621821
e-mail: paul@theforestkerry.co.uk
dir: *A489 from Newtown to Kerry. Turn right onto Gilfach Ln, 0.75m signed The Forest*

Rooms 5 en suite (2 fmly) S £48–£65; D £70–£90 **Facilities** STV TVL tea/coffee Cen ht Wi-fi ⌕ Riding Pool Table Table tennis, Table football **Conf** Max 10 Board 10 **Parking** 20 **Notes** LB

SENNYBRIDGE   Map 9 SN92

Maeswalter

★★★ GUEST ACCOMMODATION

Heol Senni LD3 8SU
☎ 01874 636629
e-mail: bb@maeswalter.co.uk
web: www.maeswalter.co.uk
dir: A470 onto A4215, 2.5m left for Heol Senni, 1.5m on right over cattle grid

Set in a peaceful country location with splendid views of the Senni Valley, this 17th-century farmhouse offers a friendly and relaxing place to stay. The accommodation is well maintained and includes a suite on the ground floor of an adjacent building. A lounge-dining room is provided, and freshly cooked farmhouse breakfasts are a pleasure.

Rooms 4 en suite (1 fmly) (2 GF) S £40-£45; D £60-£70 **Facilities** STV FTV TVL tea/coffee Dinner available Cen ht **Parking** 12 **Notes** LB ⊗ No Children 5yrs

WELSHPOOL   Map 15 SJ20

See also Criggion

PREMIER COLLECTION

Moors Farm B&B
★★★★★ BED AND BREAKFAST

Oswestry Rd SY21 9JR
☎ 01938 553395 & 07957 882967
e-mail: moorsfarm@tiscali.co.uk
web: www.moors-farm.com
dir: 1.5m NE of Welshpool off A483

A very warm welcome awaits you at this impressive house, parts of which date from the early 18th century. It has a wealth of character, including exposed beams and log-burning fires. Day rooms are spacious and tastefully furnished. Bedrooms feature smart modern bathrooms and are equipped with a wealth of thoughtful extras.

Rooms 5 en suite (2 fmly) **Facilities** TVL tea/coffee Cen ht **Notes** ⊗

Heath Cottage *(SJ239023)*
★★★ 🏠 FARMHOUSE

Kingswood, Forden SY21 8LX
☎ 01938 580453 📄 01938 580453 Mr & Mrs M C Payne
e-mail: heathcottagewales@tiscali.co.uk
dir: 4m S of Welshpool. Off A490 behind Forden Old Post Office, opp Parrys Garage

Furnishings and décor highlight the original features of this early 18th-century farmhouse. Bedrooms have stunning country views, and a choice of lounges, one with a log fire, is available. Memorable breakfasts feature free-range eggs and home-made preserves.

Rooms 3 en suite (1 fmly) S fr £27.50; D fr £55* **Facilities** TVL tea/coffee Cen ht **Parking** 4 **Notes** ⊗ Closed Oct-Etr 🐾 6 acres poultry/sheep

RHONDDA CYNON TAFF

PONTYPRIDD   Map 9 ST08

Tyn-Y-Wern Country House

★★★ BED AND BREAKFAST

Ynysybwl CF37 3LY
☎ 01443 790551 📄 01443 790551
e-mail: tynywern2002@yahoo.com
dir: B4273 from Pontypridd, war memorial on left. 1st right turn after row of modern terrace houses on right

This large Victorian house, once a mine manager's residence, is in a quiet location three miles from Pontypridd, and its elevated position provides good views. It has been extensively restored and provides modern yet traditionally furnished accommodation, plus an attractive dining room and a lounge. There is an extensive garden with self-catering cottages, a games room and a laundry room.

Rooms 3 rms (1 en suite) **Facilities** tea/coffee Cen ht Wi-fi Pool Table **Parking** 10 **Notes** Closed 20 Dec-6 Jan ⊛

SWANSEA

LLANGENNITH   Map 8 SS49

Kings Head

★★★★ INN

Town House SA3 1HX
☎ 01792 386212 📄 01792 386477
e-mail: info@kingsheadgower.co.uk

This establishment is made up from three 17th-century buildings set behind a splendid rough stone wall; it stands opposite the church in this coastal village. In two separate buildings the comfortable, well-equipped bedrooms, including some on the ground floor, can be found. This is an ideal base for exploring the Gower Peninsula, whether for walking, cycling or surfing. Evening meals and breakfasts can be taken in the inn.

Rooms 27 en suite (3 fmly) (14 GF) S £55-£89; D £55-£119* **Facilities** FTV tea/coffee Dinner available Direct Dial Cen ht Wi-fi Pool Table **Parking** 35 **Notes** LB

MUMBLES — Map 8 SS68

PREMIER COLLECTION

Little Langland
★★★★★ GUEST ACCOMMODATION

2 Rotherslade Rd, Langland SA3 4QN
☎ 01792 369696
e-mail: enquiries@littlelangland.co.uk
dir: Off A4067 in Mumbles onto Newton Rd, 4th left onto Langland Rd, 2nd left onto Rotherslade Rd

A total refurbishment has now been completed by proprietors, Christine and Roger Johnson. Little Langland is only five miles from Swansea's city centre and offers easy access to the stunning Gower Peninsula with its many coves and bays. The bedrooms are stylish, comfortable and include free broadband. There is a brand new café bar, ideal for a relaxing drink, and also a bar menu of freshly prepared snacks. Breakfast is served in the comfortable dining area.

Rooms 6 en suite **Facilities** FTV tea/coffee Direct Dial Cen ht Licensed **Parking** 6 **Notes** ✖ No Children 8yrs

PARKMILL (NEAR SWANSEA) — Map 8 SS58

PREMIER COLLECTION

Maes-Yr-Haf Restaurant with Rooms
★★★★★ ⑩ RESTAURANT WITH ROOMS

SA3 2EH
☎ 01792 371000 🖷 01792 234922
e-mail: enquiries@maes-yr-haf.com

This establishment offers contemporary, individually-styled bedrooms where comfort is the key along with a very good range of guest extras. Bathrooms too offer quality fixtures and fittings, and each has a bath and shower. The food is created from high quality, locally sourced ingredients; dinner is a highlight, served in the modern restaurant and breakfast provides a very good start to the day. Set in the peaceful location on The Gower in the small village of Parkmill, this property is well situated for easy access to Swansea and the coast.

Rooms 5 en suite S £65-£120; D £95-£160* **Facilities** FTV tea/coffee Dinner available Direct Dial Cen ht Wi-fi **Parking** **Notes** LB ✖ No Children 6yrs Closed 11-31 Jan

Parc-le-Breos House (SS529896)
★★★★ FARMHOUSE

SA3 2HA
☎ 01792 371636 🖷 01792 371287 Mrs O Edwards
dir: On A4118, right 300yds after Shepherds shop, next left, signed

This imposing early 19th-century house is at the end of a forest drive and set in 70 acres of delightful grounds. Many charming original features have been retained in the public rooms, which include a lounge and a games room. The bedrooms have comfortable furnishings, and many are suitable for families.

Rooms 10 en suite (7 fmly) (1 GF) **Facilities** TVL tea/coffee Dinner available Cen ht Licensed Riding Pool Table **Conf** Max 30 Thtr 30 **Parking** 12 **Notes** ✖ Closed 25-26 Dec 65 acres arable/horses/pigs/chickens

REYNOLDSTON — Map 8 SS48

PREMIER COLLECTION

Fairyhill
★★★★★ ⑩⑩ 🍴 RESTAURANT WITH ROOMS

SA3 1BS
☎ 01792 390139 🖷 01792 391358
e-mail: postbox@fairyhill.net
web: www.fairyhill.net
dir: M4 junct 47 onto A483, at next rdbt turn right onto A484. At Gowerton take B4295 10m

Peace and tranquillity are never far away at this charming Georgian mansion set in the heart of the beautiful Gower peninsula. Bedrooms are furnished with care and are filled with many thoughtful extras. There is also a range of comfortable seating areas with crackling log fires to choose from, and the smart restaurant offers menus based on local produce and complemented by an excellent wine list.

Rooms 8 en suite S £155-£255; D £175-£275 **Facilities** FTV TVL Dinner available Direct Dial Cen ht Wi-fi 🍃 Holistic treatments **Conf** Max 32 Thtr 32 Board 16 **Parking** 50 **Notes** LB No Children 8yrs Closed 26 Dec & 1-24 Jan No coaches Civ Wed 32

SWANSEA — Map 9 SS69

Hurst Dene
★★★ GUEST HOUSE

10 Sketty Rd, Uplands SA2 0LJ
☎ 01792 280920 🖷 01792 280920
e-mail: hurstdenehotel@yahoo.co.uk
dir: 1m W of city centre. A4118 through Uplands shopping area onto Sketty Rd, Hurst Dene on right

This friendly guest house has a private car park and provides soundly maintained bedrooms with modern furnishings and equipment. Facilities include an attractive breakfast room with separate tables and there is a small comfortable lounge.

Rooms 10 rms (8 en suite) (3 fmly) (1 GF) (3 smoking) S £35-£40; D £60* **Facilities** TVL tea/coffee Cen ht **Parking** 7 **Notes** ✖ Closed 22 Dec-1 Jan

See advert on opposite page

The White House
★★★ GUEST ACCOMMODATION

4 Nyanza Ter SA1 4QQ
☎ 01792 473856 🖷 01792 455300
e-mail: reception@thewhitehousehotel.co.uk
dir: On A4118, 1m W of city centre at junct with Eaton Crescent

Part of a short early Victorian terrace in fashionable Uplands, this house retains many original features. It has been restored to provide thoughtfully furnished and equipped quality accommodation. Bedrooms are filled with many extras, and the memorable Welsh breakfasts include cockles and laverbread.

Rooms 9 en suite (4 fmly) S £54-£66; D £84* **Facilities** FTV TVL tea/coffee Dinner available Direct Dial Cen ht Licensed Wi-fi **Conf** Max 16 Thtr 16 Class 16 Board 10 **Parking** 8 **Notes** LB

WREXHAM

HANMER · Map 15 SJ43

The Hanmer Arms

★★★★ INN

SY13 3DE
☎ 01948 830532 📄 01948 830740
e-mail: info@hanmerarms.co.uk
web: www.hanmerarms.co.uk
dir: On A539, just off A525 Whitchurch/Wrexham road

Located in the centre of the village and also home to the local crown green bowling club, this former farm has been sympathetically renovated to provide a good range of facilities. Well-equipped bedrooms are situated in the former stables or barns, and rustic furniture styles highlight the many period features in the public areas, which also feature an attractive first floor function room.

Rooms 12 annexe en suite (2 fmly) (8 GF) S fr £59.50; D fr £89.50* **Facilities** FTV tea/coffee Dinner available Cen ht Wi-fi **Conf** Max 140 Thtr 140 Class 100 Board 60 **Parking** 50 **Notes** LB Civ Wed 60

HORSEMAN'S GREEN · Map 15 SJ44

Murefield Bed & Breakfast

★★★★ BED AND BREAKFAST

Murefield SY13 3EA
☎ 01948 830790 📄 01948 830790
e-mail: enquiries@murefield.com
dir: Turn off A525 to Horseman's Green, in centre of village turn left for Little Arowry. 350mtrs on right

Located on immaculate gardens in a peaceful rural setting between Whitchurch and Wrexham, a modern house providing very high standards of comfort and facilities. The thoughtfully furnished bedrooms are equipped with many thoughtful extras, and feature

efficient bathrooms. Comprehensive breakfasts feature home-made produce.

Rooms 2 rms (1 en suite) (1 pri facs) (1 GF) S £37-£60; D £56-£60* **Facilities** FTV tea/coffee Cen ht Wi-fi **Parking** 2 **Notes** LB ⊗ No Children 8yrs Closed 22 Dec-3 Jan 🖃

LLANARMON DYFFRYN CEIRIOG · Map 15 SJ13

The Hand at Llanarmon

★★★★ ⊕ INN

LL20 7LD
☎ 01691 600666 📄 01691 600262
e-mail: reception@thehandhotel.co.uk
dir: Exit A5 at Chirk onto B4500 signed Ceiriog Valley, continue for 11m

Recently refurbished to a high standard, this owner managed inn provides a range of thoughtfully furnished bedrooms, with smart modern bathrooms. Public areas retain many original features including exposed beams and open fires and imaginative food utilises the finest of local produce. A warm welcome and attentive services ensure a memorable guest experience.

Rooms 13 en suite (4 GF) S £52.50-£70; D £85-£120* **Facilities** tea/coffee Dinner available Direct Dial Cen ht Wi-fi Pool Table **Conf** Max 15 Thtr 10 Class 10 Board 15 **Parking** 19 **Notes** LB RS 24-26 Dec Civ Wed 60

West Arms

★★★★ ⊕⊕ INN

LL20 7LD
☎ 01691 600665 & 600612 📄 01691 600622
e-mail: gowestarms@aol.com
dir: Off A483/A5 at Chirk, take B4500 to Ceiriog Valley. Llanamon 11m (at end of B4500)

Set in the beautiful Ceiriog Valley, this delightful 17th-century inn has a wealth of charm and character. There is a comfortable lounge, a room for private dining and two bars, as well as an elegant, award-winning restaurant offering a set-price menu of imaginative dishes, utilising quality local produce. The attractive bedrooms have a mixture of modern and period furnishings.

Rooms 15 en suite (2 fmly) (3 GF) S £53.50-£118; D £87-£225 **Facilities** tea/coffee Dinner available Direct Dial Wi-fi Fishing **Parking** 22 **Notes** Civ Wed 50

HURSTDENE GUEST HOUSE

A warm reception awaits you at this recently refurbished family run Guest House. Service is friendly, with every attention given to the comfort of our guests.

All bedrooms are tastefully appointed with most being en-suite, with colour television and welcome trays with tea- and coffee-making facilities. The Hurstdene is centrally heated. Also available are cots, highchairs, hairdryers and ironing facilities.

Also available luxury serviced SELF-CATERING APARTMENTS. Wireless Broadband.

Hurstdene emphasises quality with a warm welcome, endorsed by the Three Crowns Highly Commended Award.

10, Sketty Road, Uplands, Swansea SA2 0LJ
Tel/Fax: (01792) 280920
E-mail: hurstdenehotel@yahoo.co.uk   **Web:** www.hurstdene.co.uk

Price Guide
Single Room: Standard from £35; En Suite from £40   **Double/Twin Room:** En Suite from £60.00   **Family Room:** En suite from £75.00

Ireland

Knockmealdown Mountains, Co Tipperary

NORTHERN IRELAND
CO ANTRIM

BUSHMILLS · Map 1 C6

PREMIER COLLECTION

Whitepark House
★★★★★ GUEST ACCOMMODATION

150 Whitepark Rd, Ballintoy BT54 6NH
☎ 028 2073 1482
e-mail: bob@whiteparkhouse.com
dir: On A2 at Whitepark Bay, 6m E of Bushmills

Whitepark House nestles above a sandy beach and has super views of the ocean and Scotland's Western Isles. The house features bijouterie gathered from Far Eastern travels, while the traditional bedrooms are homely. Breakfasts are served around a central table in the open-plan hallway, and hospitality is warm and memorable.

Rooms 3 en suite S £75; D £100* **Facilities** tea/coffee Cen ht Wi-fi **Parking** 6 **Notes** ⊗ No Children 10yrs

PREMIER COLLECTION

Causeway Lodge
★★★★★ GUEST HOUSE

52 Moycraig Rd, Dunseverick BT57 8TB
☎ 028 2073 0333 ▤ 0800 7565433
e-mail: stay@causewaylodge.com

Causeway Lodge offers high quality contemporary accommodation in an idyllic peaceful setting on the North Antrim Coast. Each of the individually designed bedrooms are thoughtfully presented and the Causeway Suite is very stylish. The house is close to the Giants Causeway, Carrick-A-Rede rope bridge and the famous Bushmill's Distillery. Wi-fi is available and a warm welcome is assured from the friendly owners.

Rooms 4 rms (3 en suite) (1 pri facs); D £80-£120 **Facilities** STV FTV TVL tea/coffee Cen ht Wi-fi **Parking** 6 **Notes** ⊗

LARNE · Map 1 D5

Derrin House
★★★★ GUEST ACCOMMODATION

2 Princes Gardens BT40 1RQ
☎ 028 2827 3269 ▤ 028 2827 3269
e-mail: info@derrinhouse.co.uk
dir: Off A8 Harbour Highway onto A2 (coast route), 1st left after lights at Main St

Just a short walk from the town centre, and a short drive from the harbour, this comfortable Victorian house offers a very friendly welcome. The bedrooms are gradually being refurbished to offer smartly presented modern

facilities. Public areas are light and inviting, hearty breakfasts are offered in the stylish dining room.

Rooms 7 rms (6 en suite) (1 pri facs) (2 fmly) (2 GF) S £30-£40; D £50-£55* **Facilities** TVL tea/coffee Cen ht Wi-fi **Parking** 3 **Notes** LB

Manor
★★★★ GUEST HOUSE

23 Older Fleet Rd, Harbour Highway BT40 1AS
☎ 028 2827 3305 ▤ 028 2826 0505
e-mail: welcome@themanorguesthouse.com
dir: Near Larne ferry terminal & harbour train station

This grand Victorian house continues to prove popular with travellers thanks to its convenient location next to the ferry terminal. There is an elegant sitting room and a separate cosy breakfast room. The well-equipped bedrooms vary in size and are furnished in modern or period style. Hospitality is especially good and ensures a real home from home experience.

Rooms 8 en suite (2 fmly) **Facilities** FTV tea/coffee Cen ht Wi-fi **Parking** 6 **Notes** LB ⊗ Closed 25-26 Dec

PORTRUSH · Map 1 C6

Beulah Guest House
★★★ GUEST ACCOMMODATION

16 Causeway St BT56 8AB
☎ 028 7082 2413
e-mail: stay@beulahguesthouse.com
dir: Approach Portrush, signs for Bushmills/East Strand car park, onto Causeway St, house 300yds on left

Situated just a stroll from the East Strand and the town's attractions, this guest house offers a friendly welcome. Bright and attractive throughout, the comfortable bedrooms are well equipped. There is also a first-floor lounge and secure parking behind the house.

Rooms 9 en suite (3 fmly) S £30-£60; D £60-£80* **Facilities** TVL tea/coffee Cen ht **Parking** 10 **Notes** LB ⊗ Closed 25-26 Dec

BELFAST

BELFAST · Map 1 D5

Tara Lodge
★★★★ GUEST ACCOMMODATION

36 Cromwell Rd BT7 1JW
☎ 028 9059 0900 ▤ 028 9059 0901
e-mail: info@taralodge.com
web: www.taralodge.com
dir: M1 onto A55, left onto A1, right onto Fitzwilliam St, left onto University Rd, proceed to Botanic Ave

Friendly staff and comfortable bedrooms make this new establishment popular for tourism and business. The stylish dining room is the scene for memorable

breakfasts, while secure off-road parking is a bonus so close to the city centre.

Rooms 19 en suite 9 annexe en suite (3 GF) S £70; D £85* **Facilities** STV FTV TVL tea/coffee Direct Dial Cen ht Lift Wi-fi **Parking** 19 **Notes** LB ⊗ Closed 24-28 Dec

CO DOWN

BANGOR · Map 1 D5

PREMIER COLLECTION

Hebron House
★★★★★ BED AND BREAKFAST

68 Princetown Rd BT20 3TD
☎ 028 9146 3126 ▤ 028 9146 3126
e-mail: reception@hebron-house.com
web: www.hebron-house.com
dir: A2C onto B20 for 3m, 1st rdbt onto Princetown Rd

Hebron House stands in a peaceful elevated location within easy walking distance of the town amenities. Bedrooms are luxuriously furnished and have many thoughtful extras. The elegant lounge is richly styled and very comfortable. Breakfast offers home-made and local produce around a communal table in the smart dining room.

Rooms 3 en suite (1 GF) S £50-£80; D £75-£80* **Facilities** TVL tea/coffee Cen ht Wi-fi **Parking** 2 **Notes** ⊗ Closed 22 Dec-1 Jan

Shelleven House
★★★★ GUEST HOUSE

61 Princetown Rd BT20 3TA
☎ 028 9127 1777 ▤ 028 9127 1777
e-mail: shellevenhouse@aol.com
web: www.shellevenhouse.com
dir: A2 from Belfast, left at rail station rdbt. Onto Dufferin Av, proceed to rdbt, over to Princetown Rd

Shelleven is a large Victorian Townhouse situated in a quiet conservation area and close to the marina, the promenade and a short walk from the town centre. Bedrooms are all spacious and very comfortable, with rooms at the front of the house having wonderful sea views. There is an extensive choice available at breakfast, which is served in the elegant dining room.

Rooms 10 en suite (2 fmly) (1 GF) **Facilities** STV TVL tea/coffee Direct Dial Cen ht Licensed **Parking** 10 **Notes** ⊗

HOLYWOOD — Map 1 D5

PREMIER COLLECTION

Rayanne House
★★★★★ GUEST HOUSE

60 Desmesne Rd BT18 9EX
☎ 028 9042 5859 028 9042 5859
e-mail: rayannehouse@hotmail.com
web: www.rayannehouse.com
dir: *Exit A2 at Holywood, left onto Jacksons Rd, pass golf club, 200yds on right*

This elegant period house, set in its own grounds, is full of charm and enjoys a commanding position overlooking Belfast Lough and the Antrim Hills beyond. Bedrooms are all of a high standard and a host of thoughtful extras is provided. The house is a short drive from Belfast City centre and the City Airport. Breakfasts are not to be missed and evening meals are served in the spacious dining room.

Rooms 10 en suite (2 fmly) (1 GF) S £80-£95;
D £110-£135* **Facilities** FTV tea/coffee Dinner available Direct Dial Cen ht Licensed Wi-fi Golf 18 **Conf** Max 17 Thtr 17 Class 17 Board 17 **Parking** 15 **Notes** LB ⊗ RS 25-26 Dec no breakfast service

NEWTOWNARDS — Map 1 D5

Ballynester House
★★★★ GUEST HOUSE

1a Cardy Rd, Greyabbey BT22 2LS
☎ 028 4278 8386 028 4278 8986
e-mail: rc.davison@virgin.net
dir: *A20 S from Newtownards to Greyabbey, or A20 N from Portaferry to Greyabbey, signed at Greyabbey rdbt*

Located in the rolling hills above Strangford Lough, this stylish, modern house provides a tranquil haven and a warm welcome. Smart day rooms make the most of the super views; hearty breakfasts are served in the bright dining room. Richly furnished bedrooms include a host of thoughtful extras.

Rooms 3 en suite (1 fmly) (3 GF) S £30; D £55-£60* **Facilities** tea/coffee Cen ht Wi-fi Professional Genealogy consultation for guests **Parking** 10 **Notes** ⊗ No Children 7yrs

STRANGFORD — Map 1 D5

The Cuan Licensed Guest Inn
U

6-12 The Square BT30 7ND
☎ 028 4488 1222
e-mail: info@thecuan.com
web: www.thecuan.com
dir: *A7 to Downpatrick, follow A25 for Strangford ferry. Located in centre of village*

Currently the rating for this establishment is not confirmed. This may be due to a change of ownership or because it has only recently joined the AA rating scheme.

Rooms 9 en suite (3 fmly) S £50-£55; D £75-£85* **Facilities** FTV TVL tea/coffee Dinner available Direct Dial Licensed **Conf** Thtr 60 Class 30 Board 24 **Parking** 5 **Notes** LB ⊗

CO FERMANAGH

ENNISKILLEN — Map 1 C5

Arch House Tullyhona Farm Guest House
★★★★ GUEST HOUSE

Marble Arch Rd, Florencecourt BT92 1DE
☎ 028 6634 8452
e-mail: tullyguest60@hotmail.com
web: www.archhouse.com
dir: *A4 from Enniskillen towards Sligo, 2.5m onto A32, after 4m turn right at NT sign for Florence Court & Marble Arch Caves*

This delightful house nestles in a tranquil country setting very close to the Marble Arch Caves and Florence Court. The refurbished bedrooms are stylish, and Tullyhona's restaurant is open for all-day breakfasts, as well as a range of traditional evening meals.

Rooms 4 en suite (4 fmly) S £35-£40; D £60-£65* **Facilities** TVL Dinner available Direct Dial Cen ht Wi-fi Riding Farm tours, Trampoline, Table tennis, Badminton **Conf** Max 50 Thtr 50 Class 50 **Parking** 8 **Notes** LB

Willowbank House
★★★★ GUEST HOUSE

60 Bellvue Rd BT74 4JH
☎ 028 6632 8582 028 6632 8582
e-mail: joan@willowbankhouse.com
web: www.willowbankhouse.com
dir: *A4 from Enniskillen towards Belfast, 0.25m right after Killy Helvin Hotel signed Upper Lough Erne & Willowbank House, 2m on left*

This peacefully situated house commands an elevated position in attractive grounds just a short drive from the town. Bedrooms, all on the ground floor, vary in size and some are suitable for families. There is a comfortable lounge, and substantial breakfasts are served in the conservatory dining room, overlooking the lake.

Rooms 5 en suite (2 fmly) (5 GF) S £40-£45; D £65-£70 **Facilities** FTV TVL tea/coffee Cen ht Wi-fi **Parking** 6 **Notes** LB ⊗ Closed Xmas RS New Year

Aghnacarra Guest House
★★★ GUEST ACCOMMODATION

Carrybridge, Lisbellaw BT94 5HX
☎ 028 6638 7077
e-mail: normaensor@talk21.com
web: www.guesthouseireland.com
dir: *From Belfast A4 left to Lisbellaw-Carrybridge*

Surrounded by spacious grounds, gardens and countryside on the shores of Lough Erne, this delightful modern extended house is a haven of peace and quiet. It is understandably very popular with anglers, who may fish from the grounds. Bedrooms are well maintained, and day rooms include an elegant lounge, bright dining room and a spacious bar and games room.

Rooms 7 en suite (4 fmly) (5 GF) **Facilities** TVL tea/coffee Dinner available Cen ht Licensed Pool Table **Parking** 8 **Notes** LB ⊗

CO LONDONDERRY

COLERAINE — Map 1 C6

PREMIER COLLECTION

Greenhill House (C849210)
★★★★★ FARMHOUSE

24 Greenhill Rd, Aghadowey BT51 4EU
☎ 028 7086 8241 028 7086 8365 Mrs E Hegarty
e-mail: greenhill.house@btinternet.com
web: www.greenhill-house.co.uk
dir: *A29 from Coleraine S for 7m, left onto B66 Greenhill Rd for 300yds. House on right, AA sign at front gate*

Located in the tranquil Bann Valley, overlooking the Antrim Hills, this delightful Georgian house nestles in well-tended gardens with views to open rolling countryside. Public rooms are traditionally styled and include a comfortable lounge and an elegant dining room. The pleasant bedrooms vary in size and style and have a host of thoughtful extras.

Rooms 6 en suite (2 fmly) S fr £40; D fr £60 **Facilities** TVL tea/coffee Direct Dial Cen ht Wi-fi **Parking** 10 **Notes** ⊗ Closed Nov-Feb RS Mar-Oct 150 acres beef

COLERAINE *continued*

Bellevue Country House

★★★ GUEST HOUSE

43 Greenhill Rd, Aghadowey BT51 4EU
☎ 028 7086 8797
e-mail: info@bellevuecountryhouse.co.uk
dir: On B66 just off A29, 7m S of Coleraine

This fine country house, dating from 1840, stands in peaceful grounds. A variety of bedrooms are offered, including a family room and ground-floor accommodation, and there is also a comfortable drawing room. Generous breakfasts are freshly prepared and served around one large table.

Rooms 3 en suite (1 fmly) (1 GF) S £35; D £56–£60
Facilities TVL tea/coffee Cen ht Fishing **Parking** 9
Notes ⊗ Closed Nov-3 Mar ⊕

Heathfield *(NW012782)*

★★★★ FARMHOUSE

31 Drumcroone Rd, Killykergan BT51 4EB
☎ 028 2955 8245 📠 028 2955 8245 Ms H Torrens
e-mail: relax@heathfieldfarm.com
web: www.heathfieldfarm.com
dir: 8m S of Coleraine. On A29 nr Killykergan, 2m N of Garvagh

Heathfield is a delightful traditional farmhouse that is an integral part of a working farm. The house enjoys a rural setting and is a short drive from the towns of Garvagh and Coleraine making it an ideal base from which to explore the North Antrim Coast. Bedrooms are comfortable and all enjoy views of the surrounding countryside. Guests can enjoy a hearty breakfast in the dining room or relax in the lounge after a day's sightseeing.

Rooms 3 en suite S £40–£45; D £65* **Facilities** TVL tea/coffee Cen ht **Parking** 10 **Notes** ⊗ No Children 10yrs Closed Xmas beef/sheep

DUNGIVEN Map 1 C5

Dungiven Castle

Ⓤ

145 Main St BT47 4LE
☎ 028 7774 2428 📠 028 7774 1968
e-mail: dungivencastle@talktalkbusiness.net
web: www.dungivencastle.com

Currently the rating for this establishment is not confirmed. This may be due to a change of ownership or because it has only recently joined the AA rating scheme.

Rooms 9 en suite (1 fmly) (1 GF) S £45–£55; D £70–£100* **Facilities** FTV Dinner available Direct Dial Cen ht Licensed Wi-fi **Notes** ⊗ Civ Wed 48

LIMAVADY Map 1 C6

Ballycarton House

★★★★ GUEST HOUSE

239 Seacoast Rd BT49 0HZ
☎ 028 7775 0216 📠 028 7775 0231
e-mail: stay@ballycartonhouse.com
dir: On A2 (coast road) midway between Limavady & Castlerock

Set in the beautiful Roe Valley, Ballycarton is overlooked by Benevenagh Mountain, and is close to Magilligan Point, which has one of the longest beaches in Northern Ireland. Wi-fi is available, along with a games room, a hot tub and sauna cabin, and an honesty bar.

Rooms 5 en suite S £45; D £70* **Facilities** TVL tea/coffee Direct Dial Cen ht Wi-fi Pool Table **Parking** 8 **Notes** ⊗ No Children 5yrs Closed 25-26 Dec

LONDONDERRY Map 1 C5

Clarence House

★★★ GUEST HOUSE

15 Northland Rd BT48 7HY
☎ 028 7126 5342 & 07786 801954 📠 028 7126 5377
e-mail: clarencehouse@zoom.co.uk
web: www.guesthouseireland.biz
dir: From Belfast A6 next to University opp fire station & Radio Foyle

This long-established, family-run guest house provides charming, well-equipped bedrooms. Traditionally styled

day rooms include a spacious lounge and a smartly presented dining room where wholesome and generous meals are served.

Rooms 9 en suite (2 fmly) S £40–£45; D £75–£110*
Facilities FTV TVL tea/coffee Dinner available Direct Dial Cen ht Licensed Wi-fi

CO TYRONE

DUNGANNON Map 1 C5

PREMIER COLLECTION

Grange Lodge

★★★★★ 🏅 🍽 GUEST HOUSE

7 Grange Rd BT71 7EJ
☎ 028 8778 4212 📠 028 8778 4313
e-mail: stay@grangelodgecountryhouse.com
web: www.grangelodgecountryhouse.com
dir: M1 junct 15, A29 towards Armagh, 1m Grange Lodge signed, 1st right & 1st white-walled entrance on right

Grange Lodge dates from 1698 and nestles in 20 acres of well-tended grounds. It continues to set high standards in hospitality and food, and excellent meals are served in the bright and airy extension. Home-baked afternoon teas can be enjoyed in the sumptuous drawing room.

Rooms 5 en suite S £60–£65; D £85–£89*
Facilities STV FTV TVL tea/coffee Dinner available Direct Dial Cen ht Licensed Wi-fi 🎱 Snooker **Conf** Max 25 **Parking** 12 **Notes** ⊗ No Children 12yrs Closed 21 Dec-9 Jan

Millbrook Bed & Breakfast

★★★★ BED AND BREAKFAST

46 Moy Rd BT71 7DT
☎ 028 8772 3715
e-mail: info@millbrookonline.co.uk
dir: On A29 1m S of Dungannon, 0.25m N of M1 junct 15

This well-presented bungalow is situated just outside the town of Dungannon and close to main routes. Comfortable ground-floor bedrooms and a stylish lounge are complemented by a substantial, freshly prepared breakfast. The owners' natural hospitality is memorable.

Rooms 2 en suite (2 GF) S fr £45; D fr £65* **Facilities** TVL tea/coffee Cen ht Wi-fi **Parking** 4 **Notes** ⊗ ⊕

REPUBLIC OF IRELAND
CO CARLOW

CARLOW Map 1 C3

Barrowville Town House
★★★★ GUEST HOUSE

Kilkenny Rd
☎ **059 914 3324**
e-mail: barrowvilletownhouse@eircom.net
dir: Carlow Town, N9 Kilkenny Rd near Institute of Technology

The Smyths are the friendly owners of this carefully maintained 18th-century town house. Many of the very comfortable bedrooms are spacious, and the public rooms are elegant and relaxing. The conservatory, with its fruiting vine, is where Barrowvilles's legendary breakfasts are served, overlooking well tended gardens. Ample car parking.

Rooms 7 en suite (3 fmly) **Facilities** STV TVL tea/coffee Direct Dial Cen ht Wi-fi **Parking** 11 **Notes** ⊗ No Children 10yrs Closed 24-26 Dec

RATHVILLY Map 1 D3

Baile Ricead (S845836)
★★★★ FARMHOUSE

☎ **059 916 1120 Mrs M Corrigan**
e-mail: minacorrigan@eircom.net
dir: 5km from Rathvilly. N9 S, left at Castle Inn, left next junct, 2nd right before Graney Bridge, left after water pump, house on bend

This delightful farmhouse has comfortable bedrooms furnished to a good standard. There is a lounge, and conservatory-dining room that looks out across the delightful gardens to the Wicklow Mountains. Guests can use the barbecue in the garden.

Rooms 4 rms (2 en suite) (1 fmly) **Facilities** TVL tea/coffee Cen ht **Parking** 6 **Notes** Closed Nov-16 Mar 66 acres mixed

CO CAVAN

BALLYCONNELL Map 1 C4

Prospect Bay Lakeside Accommodation
★★★★ BED AND BREAKFAST

Brackley Lake
☎ **049 952 3930** 🖷 **049 952 3930**
e-mail: info@prospectbay.ie
dir: N87 through Ballyconnell & Bawnboy to Brackley Lake. 1st left after Lakeside car park

Prospect Bay promises you eco-friendly comfort, hospitality and home baking. The accommodation is on a 30-acre site overlooking Brackley Lake, where boats are available for fishing. Bedrooms and guest sitting/dining room are all smartly appointed and lead on to the lovely garden patio. Convenient for Slieve Russell Hotel and golf course.

Rooms 4 en suite (2 fmly) (2 GF) S €60-€70; D €70-€90* **Facilities** TVL tea/coffee Cen ht Wi-fi Fishing Clay pigeon shooting, hovercrafting, mud buggies **Parking** 5 **Notes** LB Closed 20 Dec-6 Jan

CO CLARE

BALLYVAUGHAN Map 1 B3

PREMIER COLLECTION

Rusheen Lodge
★★★★★ GUEST HOUSE

☎ **065 707 7092** 🖷 **065 707 7152**
e-mail: rusheen@iol.ie
dir: On N67, 1km from Ballyvaughan

A charming house situated on the outskirts of Ballyvaughan in the valley of The Burren, an area famous for its Arctic and Alpine plants. Karen McGann's family were founders of the famous Aillwee Cave nearby and they have a wealth of local folklore. The bedrooms are spacious and very attractively decorated, some with extra comfortable seating areas. Patio garden leads from the cosy dining room.

Rooms 9 en suite (3 fmly) (3 GF) **Facilities** STV TVL tea/coffee Direct Dial Cen ht Wi-fi **Parking** 12 **Notes** ⊗ Closed mid Nov-mid Feb

BUNRATTY Map 1 B3

Park House
★★★★ BED AND BREAKFAST

Low Rd
☎ **061 369902** 🖷 **061 369903**
e-mail: parkhouse@eircom.net
dir: From N18 take Bunratty exit, turn left at castle, pass Folk Park. Park House 4th house on left

A purpose-built guest house with spacious bedrooms within walking distance of the castle. There is a lounge and a lovely garden.

Rooms 6 en suite (3 fmly) (2 GF) **Facilities** STV tea/coffee Dinner available Cen ht Wi-fi **Parking** 6 **Notes** ⊗ Closed 25-26 Dec

CORROFIN Map 1 B3

Fergus View (R265919)
★★★ FARMHOUSE

Kilnaboy
☎ **065 6837606** 🖷 **065 6837192 Mrs M Kelleher**
e-mail: deckell@indigo.ie
dir: 3.2km N of Corofin towards Kilfenora, past ruins of Kilnaboy Church on left on R476

This fourth-generation family home is well located for touring the famous Burren area. A varied breakfast menu including home baking is on offer.

Rooms 6 rms (5 en suite) (1 fmly) S €54; D €78-€80 **Facilities** TVL Cen ht Wi-fi **Parking** 8 **Notes** ⊗ Closed 26 Oct-mid Mar 🐾 10 acres mixed

DOOLIN Map 1 B3

PREMIER COLLECTION

Ballyvara House
★★★★★ GUEST HOUSE

Ballyvara
☎ **065 7074467** 🖷 **065 7074868**
e-mail: info@ballyvarahouse.ie
dir: Left at Fitzpatrick's Bar, up hill on left

Once a 19th-century farm cottage, Ballyvara House has been transformed into a stylish guest house. Public areas and the spacious bedrooms are furnished to a high standard. Children's play area, tennis court and outdoor patio are available to guests. Set in eight hectares of unspoiled countryside close to Doolin, which is famous for traditional music, pubs and ferries to the Aran Islands.

Rooms 11 en suite (2 fmly) (5 GF) S €50-€90; D €100-€180 **Facilities** STV TVL tea/coffee Direct Dial Cen ht Licensed Wi-fi 🐾 Pool Table Childrens outdoor play area, Library **Parking** 10 **Notes** LB ⊗ Closed Oct-Apr

DOOLIN *continued*

Sea View House

★★★★ BED AND BREAKFAST

☎ 065 7074826

e-mail: darra@seaviewhouse.eu

Perched on the hillside overlooking the Atlantic and Doolin village which is renowned for traditional live music sessions and great pubs, the Hughes family home has beautifully decorated bedrooms. Guests can relax and enjoy a cup of tea on arrival in the sitting room or the deck outside while taking in the breathtaking views. Breakfast is served at one large family table and the menu includes locally smoked fish and Darra's home baking. The Cliffs of Moher and Aran Islands are close by.

Rooms 4 en suite (1 fmly) S fr €32; D fr €96* **Facilities** tea/coffee Wi-fi Riding **Parking**

Cullinan's Restaurant & Guesthouse

★★★ GUEST HOUSE

☎ 065 7074183   📄 065 7074239

e-mail: cullinans@eircom.net

dir: *In town centre at x-rds between McGanns Pub & O'Connors Pub*

This charming guest house and restaurant is situated in the village of Doolin. Bedrooms are attractively decorated and comfortable. Chef patron James features locally caught fresh fish on his dinner menu, along with steaks, lamb and vegetarian dishes and there is a popular Early Bird menu. Other facilities include a lounge, a patio, and gardens that run down to the River Aille.

Rooms 8 en suite (3 fmly) (3 GF) S €40–€80; D €70–€100 **Facilities** TV6B STV FTV TVL tea/coffee Dinner available Direct Dial Cen ht Wi-fi **Parking** 15 **Notes** ✖ Closed Jan-Feb

| KILRUSH | Map 1 B3 |

Hillcrest View

★★★★ BED AND BREAKFAST

Doonbeg Rd

☎ 065 9051986   📄 065 9051900

e-mail: ethnahynes@eircom.net

dir: *Off N67 (Kilkee road), onto Doonbeg Rd*

Within walking distance of the town centre and a short drive from the Killimer ferry, Hillcrest View has spacious and well-appointed bedrooms. There is a sitting-dining room with a breakfast conservatory, while patio seats look over the pretty garden.

Rooms 6 en suite (2 fmly) **Facilities** STV TVL tea/coffee Cen ht **Parking** 7 **Notes** ✖

Cois Na Sionna

★★★ BED AND BREAKFAST

Ferry Junction, Killimer

☎ 065 9053073   & 087 2377285   📄 065 9053073

e-mail: coisnasionna@eircom.net

dir: *On N67 at entrance to Killimer-Tarbert car ferry*

This modern house is close to the Killimer/Tarbert car ferry. Bedrooms offer good space and are bright and well appointed. There is a comfortable lounge and a traditional cooked breakfast is served in the dining room. A good base for visiting Clare and Kerry.

Rooms 4 en suite (3 fmly) **Facilities** TVL tea/coffee Cen ht **Parking** 6

| LAHINCH | Map 1 B3 |

PREMIER COLLECTION

Moy House

★★★★★ ◉ 🏠 GUEST HOUSE

☎ 065 708 2800   📄 065 708 2500

e-mail: moyhouse@eircom.net

web: www.moyhouse.com

dir: *1km from Lahinch on Miltown Malbay Rd, signed from Lahinch*

This 18th-century house overlooks Lahinch's world-famous surfing beach and championship golf links. Individually designed bedrooms are decorated with luxurious fabrics and fine antique furniture. The elegant drawing room has an open turf fire and breathtaking views. The skilful and carefully prepared dinner menu has an emphasis on local seafood and must be pre-booked. Breakfast is also a treat. This is a charming house where hospitality is memorable.

Rooms 9 en suite (2 fmly) (4 GF) S €145–€175; D €185–€360* **Facilities** STV FTV Dinner available Direct Dial Cen ht Licensed Wi-fi **Conf** Max 16 Board 16 **Parking** 30 **Notes** LB ✖ Closed Jan-13 Feb

Castleview Lodge

★★★ BED AND BREAKFAST

Ennistymon Rd

☎ 065 708 1648

e-mail: castleview_lodge@eircom.net

dir: *On N67 (Ennis-Shannon road)*

Castleview Lodge is located on the N67 within walking distance of Lahinch overlooking the golf course at the north of the town and close to the beach and Cliffs of Moher. Bedrooms are well appointed and attractively decorated. There is ample off-street car parking available.

Rooms 5 en suite **Facilities** STV FTV TVL tea/coffee Cen ht **Parking** 5 **Notes** ✖ ⬛

| NEWMARKET-ON-FERGUS | Map 1 B3 |

Carrygerry Country House

★★★ ◉ RESTAURANT WITH ROOMS

Carrygerry

☎ 061 360500   📄 061 360700

e-mail: info@carrygerryhouse.com

This charming country house was built around 1793 and has fine views over the Shannon Estuary. It has been refurbished by owners Niall and Gillian Ennis. Bedrooms in the main house feature four-poster beds and there are family rooms in the courtyard. The drawing room and cosy bar are very comfortable; the Conservatory Restaurant has the perfect ambience for a romantic dinner. Shannon Airport and Bunratty Castle are just minutes away.

Rooms 11 en suite (1 fmly) (3 GF) S €75–€95; D €115–€155* **Facilities** Dinner available Direct Dial Cen ht Wi-fi **Conf** Max 80 Thtr 60 Board 50 **Parking** 25 **Notes** LB ✖ Closed Xmas wk Civ Wed 120

| SCARRIFF | Map 1 B3 |

Clareville House

★★★★ BED AND BREAKFAST

Tuamgraney

☎ 061 922925   & 087 6867548   📄 061 922925

e-mail: clarevillehouse@ireland.com

web: www.clarevillehouse.net

dir: *On R352 in village adjacent to Scarriff*

Situated in the centre of the pretty lakeside village of Tuamgraney this purpose-built bed and breakfast is attractively decorated. The spacious bedrooms are furnished to a high standard and the cosy guest sitting room and dining room are also well furnished. Ample off-road parking is available.

Rooms 4 en suite (4 fmly) S fr €50; D fr €76* **Facilities** TVL tea/coffee Cen ht Wi-fi Golf 18 Riding **Parking** 8 **Notes** ✖ Closed 20-27 Dec

SPANISH POINT — Map 1 B3

Red Cliff Lodge

U

☎ 065 7085756 📠 065 7085775
e-mail: info@redcliff.ie
dir: R474 Ennis to Miltown Malbay, S on N67 for 1.5km

Currently the rating for this establishment is not confirmed. This may be due to a change of ownership or because it has only recently joined the AA rating scheme.

Rooms 6 annexe en suite (6 GF) **Facilities** STV TVL tea/coffee Direct Dial Cen ht Licensed **Conf** Max 12 Board 12 **Parking** 10 **Notes** ⊗ No Children Closed Dec-1 Mar

CO CORK

BANDON — Map 1 B2

Glebe Country House

★★★★ BED AND BREAKFAST

Ballinadee
☎ 021 4778294 📠 021 4778456
e-mail: glebehse@indigo.ie
dir: Off N71 at Innishannon Bridge signed Ballinadee, 8km along river bank, left after village sign

This lovely guest house stands in well-kept gardens, and is run with great attention to detail. Antique furnishings predominate throughout this comfortable house, which has a lounge and an elegant dining room. An interesting breakfast menu offers unusual options, and a country-house style dinner is available by arrangement.

Rooms 4 en suite (2 fmly) S €60-€70; D €90-€110* **Facilities** TVL tea/coffee Dinner available Direct Dial Cen ht Wi-fi **Parking** 10 **Notes** LB Closed 21 Dec-3 Jan

BLARNEY — Map 1 B2

PREMIER COLLECTION

Ashlee Lodge
★★★★★ ⇔ 🍽 GUEST HOUSE

Tower
☎ 021 4385346 📠 021 4385726
e-mail: info@ashleelodge.com
dir: 4km from Blarney on R617

Ashlee Lodge is a purpose-built guest house, situated in the village of Tower, close to Blarney and local pubs and restaurants. Bedrooms are decorated with comfort and elegance in mind, some with whirlpool baths, and one room has easier access. The extensive breakfast menu is memorable for Ann's home baking. You can unwind in the sauna or the outdoor hot tub. Transfers to the nearest airport and railway station can be arranged, and tee times can be booked at many of the nearby golf courses.

Rooms 10 en suite (2 fmly) (6 GF) **Facilities** STV FTV TVL tea/coffee Dinner available Direct Dial Cen ht Licensed Wi-fi Sauna Hot tub **Parking** 12

Killarney House

★★★★ BED AND BREAKFAST

Station Rd
☎ 021 4381841 📠 021 4381841
e-mail: info@killarneyhouseblarney.com
dir: From N20 onto R617, right after Blarney fuel station turn right, 1km on Station Rd on right

A no-smoking house with four ground-floor bedrooms in a new extension, and two on the first floor. Caroline Morgan is a charming, attentive hostess whose comfortable house is very well appointed. There is a TV lounge, drying facilities for wet gear, and off-road parking. Golf available nearby.

Rooms 6 en suite (2 fmly) (4 GF) S €40-€50; D €66-€76* **Facilities** FTV tea/coffee Cen ht Wi-fi **Parking** 8 **Notes** LB ⊗ 🐾

White House

★★★★ BED AND BREAKFAST

Shean Lower
☎ 021 4385338
e-mail: info@thewhitehouseblarney.com
web: www.thewhitehouseblarney.com
dir: On R617 (Cork-Blarney road)

Situated on an elevated position near to the town, with views of Blarney Castle, this carefully maintained bungalow is set in prize-winning gardens. Bedrooms, with modern facilities, are well appointed and have comfortable armchairs. There is a TV lounge and a breakfast room. A private car park is also available.

Rooms 6 en suite (1 fmly) (6 GF) S €50-€55; D €70-€78* **Facilities** STV tea/coffee Cen ht Wi-fi **Parking** 7 **Notes** ⊗ Closed 20 Dec-1 Jan 🐾

CLONAKILTY — Map 1 B2

PREMIER COLLECTION

An Garran Coir (W332358)
★★★★★ 🍽 FARMHOUSE

Rathbarry, Rosscarbery Coast Route
☎ 023 48236 📠 023 48236 Mr & Mrs M Calnan
e-mail: angarrancoir@eircom.net
web: www.angarrancoir.com
dir: Signed at Maxol station in Clonakilty. 6.5km W of town off N71, 1.5km on right

Situated on the coast road to Rosscarbery from Clonakilty, close to sandy beaches and the village, this comfortable farmhouse has lovely views. Bedrooms are attractively decorated to a high standard with well fitted bathrooms. Jo Calnan's cooking is a special treat, evening meals are available on request with produce from the garden and fresh eggs from the farm. A tennis court and lovely garden are available to guests.

Rooms 5 en suite (2 fmly) **Facilities** tea/coffee Dinner available Cen ht 🐾 Local leisure club available - rates negotiated **Parking** 5 **Notes** ⊗

Duvane House (W349405)

★★★★ FARMHOUSE

Ballyduvane
☎ 023 33129 Mrs N McCarthy
e-mail: duvanefarm@eircom.net
dir: 2km SW from Clonakilty on N71

This Georgian farmhouse is on the N71 Skibbereen road. Bedrooms are comfortable and include four-poster and brass beds. There is a lovely sitting room and dining room, and a wide choice is available at breakfast (dinner is available by arrangement). Local amenities include Blue Flag beaches, riding and golf.

Rooms 4 en suite (1 fmly) **Facilities** TVL tea/coffee Dinner available Cen ht 🎣 Fishing Pool Table **Parking** 20 **Notes** LB ⊗ Closed Nov-Mar 🐾 100 acres beef/dairy/mixed/sheep

Springfield House (W330342)

★★★★ FARMHOUSE

Kilkern, Rathbarry, Castlefreke
☎ 023 40622 📠 023 40622 Mr & Mrs J Callanan
e-mail: jandmcallanan@eircom.net
dir: N71 from Clonakilty for Skibbereen, 0.5km left after Pike Bar & signed for 5km

A Georgian-style farmhouse in a picturesque rural setting. Maureen and John Callanan are genuine and welcoming hosts, and their comfortable home has well-appointed bedrooms and lovely gardens. You are welcome to watch the cows being milked. Home cooking is a speciality, and dinner is available by arrangement.

Rooms 4 rms (3 en suite) (2 fmly) S €40-€55; D €70-€86 **Facilities** TV3B TVL Cen ht **Parking** 8 **Notes** LB ⊗ Closed 20-27 Dec 🐾 130 acres dairy/beef

CLONAKILTY *continued*

Desert House (W390411)

★★ FARMHOUSE

Coast Rd

☎ 023 33331 📄 023 33048 **Mrs D Jennings**

e-mail: deserthouse@eircom.net

dir: *1km E of Clonakilty. Signed on N71 at 1st rdbt, house 500mtrs on left*

This comfortable Georgian farmhouse overlooks Clonakilty Bay and is within walking distance of the town. The estuary is of great interest to bird-watching enthusiasts. It is a good base for touring west Cork and Kerry.

Rooms 5 rms (4 en suite) **Facilities** tea/coffee Cen ht **Parking** 10 **Notes** 100 acres dairy/mixed

---

CORK Map 1 B2

Crawford House

★★★★ GUEST HOUSE

Western Rd

☎ 021 4279000 📄 021 4279927

e-mail: info@crawfordguesthouse.com

dir: *0.8km from city on N22 Cork-Killarney road, opp University College*

Two adjoining Victorian houses form this friendly guest house, close to the university and city centre. Refurbished in a contemporary style, the bedrooms have refreshing natural colour schemes. The attractive dining room and conservatory overlook a colourful patio. An interesting breakfast menu is available and there is ample secure parking.

Rooms 12 en suite (2 fmly) (1 GF) S €55-€80; D €80-€100 **Facilities** STV tea/coffee Direct Dial Cen ht Wi-fi **Parking** 12 **Notes** ⊗ Closed 22 Dec-15 Jan

Garnish House

★★★★ GUEST HOUSE

1 Aldergrove, Western Rd

☎ 021 4275111 📄 021 4273872

e-mail: garnish@iol.ie

dir: *Opp Cork University College*

A stay in Garnish House is memorable for its carefully appointed rooms, with an optional jacuzzi en suite, and the extensive breakfast menu. Only five minutes walk from the city centre, and convenient for the ferry and

airport, the guest house has 24-hour reception for reservations, departures and late arrivals.

Rooms 21 en suite (4 fmly) (1 GF) (10 smoking) S €65-€99; D €79-€120* **Facilities** STV FTV TVL tea/coffee Direct Dial Cen ht **Parking** 20 **Notes** LB ⊗

Killarney

★★★★ GUEST HOUSE

Western Rd

☎ 021 4270290 📄 021 4271010

e-mail: killarneyhouse@iol.ie

dir: *On N22 Cork-Killarney opp University College*

Mrs O'Leary is the welcoming owner of this well-equipped guest house, which stands near Cork University on the N22. The bedrooms all have TVs, telephones and tea and coffee facilities. A comfortable lounge is available, and there is car parking to the rear of the house.

Rooms 19 en suite (3 fmly) **Facilities** STV TVL tea/coffee Direct Dial Cen ht Wi-fi **Parking** 15 **Notes** ⊗ Closed 24-26 Dec

---

Rose Lodge

★★★ GUEST HOUSE

Mardyke Walk, off Western Rd

☎ 021 4272958 📄 021 4274087

e-mail: info@roselodge.net

dir: *N22 from city centre, pass Jurys Hotel on left, right at University College gates, right again, Lodge on right*

This family-run guest house is close to UCC and just a 10-minute walk from the city centre. The en suite bedrooms are well appointed, and there is a comfortable sitting room and an attractive breakfast room. Limited off-road parking is available.

Rooms 16 en suite (4 fmly) **Facilities** STV TVL tea/coffee Direct Dial Cen ht **Parking** 8 **Notes** ⊗

FERMOY Map 1 B2

Abbeyville House

★★★★ BED AND BREAKFAST

Abercomby Place

☎ 025 32767 📄 025 32767

e-mail: info@abbeyvillehouse.com

dir: *N8 (Cork to Dublin road). In town centre across road from town park*

This delightful 19th-century town house is situated on the crossroads of Munster, on the Rosslare to Killarney and Cork to Dublin routes. The smart bedrooms, drawing room and dining room are furnished to a high standard. Guests have complementary use of the facilities in the Health and Fitness Club in the town park near by.

Rooms 6 en suite (2 fmly) (1 GF) **Facilities** TVL tea/coffee Cen ht Wi-fi Free use of Carrig Court Health & Fitness Club **Parking** 12 **Notes** Closed 30 Oct-1 Apr

---

GOLEEN Map 1 A1

Heron's Cove

★★★★ 🍴 BED AND BREAKFAST

The Harbour

☎ 028 35225 📄 028 35422

e-mail: suehill@eircom.net

web: www.heronscove.com

dir: *By harbour in Goleen*

There are charming views of the harbour, fast-flowing stream and inland hills from Heron's Cove, at Ireland's most south-westerly point, near Mizen Head. The restaurant and wine bar is run by chef-patron Sue Hill, where the freshest fish and local produce feature. Bedrooms are comfortable, some with balconies overlooking the harbour.

Rooms 5 en suite (2 fmly) S €50-€70; D €70-€90 **Facilities** STV tea/coffee Dinner available Direct Dial Cen ht Licensed Wi-fi **Parking** 10 **Notes** ⊗ Closed Xmas & New Year

See advert on opposite page

KINSALE Map 1 B2

PREMIER COLLECTION

Friar's Lodge

★★★★★ GUEST HOUSE

5 Friars St

☎ 086 289 5075 & 021 4777384 📄 021 4774363

e-mail: mtierney@indigo.ie

dir: *In town centre next to parish church*

This new, purpose-built property near the Friary, has been developed with every comfort in mind. Bedrooms are particularly spacious. Located on a quiet street just a short walk from the town centre, with secure parking to the rear. A very good choice is offered from the breakfast menu.

Rooms 18 en suite (2 fmly) (4 GF) (2 smoking) **Facilities** STV tea/coffee Direct Dial Cen ht Lift Wi-fi **Parking** 20 **Notes** Closed Xmas ⊗

Old Bank House
★★★★★ GUEST HOUSE

11 Pearse St
☎ 021 4774075   🖷 021 4774296
e-mail: info@oldbankhousekinsale.com
dir: On main road into Kinsale from Cork Airport (R600). House on right at start of Kinsale, next to Post Office

The Fitzgerald family has restored this delightful Georgian house to its former elegance. The en suite bedrooms, with period furniture and attractive decor, combine charm with modern comforts. Sailing, deep-sea fishing and horse riding can be arranged. Dinner is available at the sister Blue Haven Hotel.

Rooms 17 en suite (3 fmly) **Facilities** STV Direct Dial Cen ht Lift Wi-fi **Notes** ⊗ Closed 23-28 Dec

Perryville House
★★★★★ GUEST HOUSE

☎ 021 4772731   🖷 021 4772298
e-mail: sales@perryville.iol.ie

This elegant Georgian house in the centre of the town offers spacious, well-equipped accommodation. The comfortable drawing rooms are carefully decorated and the buffet breakfast is a highlight of the Perryville experience. A non-smoking property.

Rooms 26 en suite **Facilities** Direct Dial **Parking** 10 **Notes** ⊗ No Children 12yrs Closed Nov-Apr

Rivermount House
★★★★ BED AND BREAKFAST

Knocknabinny, Barrells Cross
☎ 021 4778033   🖷 021 4778225
e-mail: rivermnt@iol.ie
dir: 3km from Kinsale. R600 W towards Old Head of Kinsale, right at Barrels Cross

There are spectacular views over the Bandon River from this charming modern family home which is close to the Old Head Golf links and Kinsale. The smartly decorated bedrooms are furnished to a high standard with many thoughtful extras. Guests can relax in the contemporary conservatory lounge and sitting room where an interesting snack menu is available, Claire's breakfast and packed lunches are a speciality

Rooms 6 en suite (3 fmly) (2 GF) **Facilities** TVL tea/coffee Direct Dial Cen ht Wi-fi **Parking** 10 **Notes** ⊗ Closed Dec-Jan

Chart House Luxury Accommodation
★★★★ BED AND BREAKFAST

6 Denis Quay
☎ 021 4774568   🖷 021 4777907
e-mail: charthouse@eircom.net
dir: Off Pier Rd between Actons & Trident hotels onto Denis Quay, last house on right

This 1790 Georgian house was once a sea captain's residence. It has been lovingly restored and the comfortable bedrooms are furnished with period pieces, while two have jacuzzis. There is a cosy lobby lounge and a dining room where Mary O'Connor serves delicious breakfasts, including home-made breads. Afternoon tea and coffee are served on arrival. Being in a gourmet capital, dinner reservations can be arranged and golfing and touring trips organised.

Rooms 3 en suite S €70-€110; D €90-€150 **Facilities** STV Direct Dial Cen ht Wi-fi **Notes** ⊗ No Children 1yr Closed Xmas

Harbour Lodge
★★★★ GUEST HOUSE

Scilly
☎ 021 4772376   🖷 021 4772675
e-mail: relax@harbourlodge.com
web: www.harbourlodge.com
dir: Enter Kinsale on R600. 1st left to Scilly. At Spaniard Bar turn right, follow towards coast

This well-appointed house has superb views of Kinsale Harbour and marina. Bedrooms are smartly decorated and enhanced with quality bedding and many thoughtful extras, including some with balconies. Dinner is a particular treat, menu includes local fish, and reservations are necessary. The Tiernan family are very hospitable hosts and will help to arrange fishing trips, or golf at one of the many golf courses nearby.

Rooms 9 en suite (9 fmly) (4 GF) **Facilities** STV TVL Dinner available Direct Dial Cen ht Licensed **Conf** Max 15 Thtr 15 **Parking** 9 **Notes** ⊗ Closed 20 Dec-2 Jan

Old Presbytery
★★★★ BED AND BREAKFAST

43 Cork St
☎ 021 4772027   🖷 021 4772166
e-mail: info@oldpres.com
dir: From Cork Rd to end of Pearse St, turn left, 1st right & 1st right again, establishment on right opp parish church

This charming house, situated on a quiet street in the centre of the town, offers an elegant lounge and a delightful breakfast room. Bedrooms are traditional, with pine furnishings, brass beds and interesting memorabilia. One bedroom has external access via a staircase and is very peaceful. Sailing and sea fishing are available and there are plenty of excellent restaurants nearby. Booking is advised.

Rooms 6 en suite (1 fmly) (1 GF) **Facilities** STV FTV TVL tea/coffee Direct Dial Cen ht Wi-fi **Parking** 6 **Notes** ⊗ Closed Dec-1 Mar

The Heron's Cove™
Fresh Fish and Wine on the Harbour

Competitively priced, high-quality B&B on the Mizen Peninsula! Unique rooms, all en suite with television, direct dial telephone, tea/coffee tray and hairdryer. Enchanting views of sea harbour, fast flowing stream and inland hills. The night sky is brilliant through large all weather windows. A short stroll to Goleen village and its four pubs. A perfect home base for touring the major attractions of South west Ireland with easy access to the N71. Award winning restaurant featuring fresh fish and wine. Plan to visit The Heron's Cove – make us your destination! All credit cards welcome. Vouchers accepted.

The Harbour, Goleen, West Cork
Tel: 028-35225 Fax: 028-35422
e-mail: suehill@eircom.net
web sites: www.heronscove.com or www.heroncove.ie

AA ★★★★ Bed & Breakfast

KINSALE *continued*

Waterlands

★★★★ BED AND BREAKFAST

Cork Rd
☎ 021 477 2318 & 087 276 7917 ▤ 021 477 4873
e-mail: info@collinsbb.com
web: www.collinsbb.com
dir: *R600 to Kinsale, off at Welcome to Kinsale sign, Waterlands signed, turn right*

This house, located on an elevated position, provides luxury accommodation. A south-facing conservatory breakfast room overlooks the picturesque gardens and offers an extensive breakfast menu. The comfortable, well-decorated en suite bedrooms have electric blankets, hairdryers and clock radios.

Rooms 4 en suite (2 fmly) (4 GF) S €60; D €70-€90
Facilities TVL tea/coffee Cen ht Wi-fi **Parking** 10
Notes ⊗ Closed Dec-Feb

The White House

★★★★ ⊛ RESTAURANT WITH ROOMS

Pearse St, The Glen
☎ 021 4772125 ▤ 021 4772045
e-mail: whitehse@indigo.ie
dir: *In town centre*

Centrally located among the narrow, twisting streets of the charming town of Kinsale, this restaurant with rooms dates from 1850, and is a welcoming hostelry with modern smart, comfortable bedrooms. The bar and bistro are open for lunch and dinner, and the varied menu features local fish and beef. The courtyard makes a perfect summer setting, and there is traditional music in the bar most nights.

Rooms 10 en suite (2 fmly) S €55-€100; D €90-€200
Facilities STV tea/coffee Dinner available Direct Dial Cen ht Wi-fi **Notes** LB ⊗ Closed 24-25 Dec

Woodlands House B&B

★★★★ BED AND BREAKFAST

Cappagh
☎ 021 4772633 ▤ 021 4772649
e-mail: info@woodlandskinsale.com
dir: *R605 NW from Kinsale, pass St Multose's Church, 0.5km on left*

Situated on a height overlooking the town, about a 10-minute walk away on the Bandon road, this new house offers great comfort and the personal attention of Brian and Valerie Hosford. Rooms are individually decorated, some with views towards the harbour. Breakfast is a particular pleasure, featuring home-made breads and preserves. Free Wi-fi is also available.

Rooms 6 en suite (1 fmly) (2 GF) S €60-€80;
D €80-€100* **Facilities** TVL tea/coffee Direct Dial Cen ht Wi-fi **Parking** 8 **Notes** ⊗ Closed 16 Nov-Feb

---

Greenfield House B&B

★★★★ BED AND BREAKFAST

Navigation Rd
☎ 022 50231 & 08723 63535
e-mail: greenfieldhouse@hotmail.com
dir: *N20 at Mallow rdbt onto N72 (Killarney road), last house 300mtrs on left*

A purpose-built house, designed and furnished to the highest standards. Large, airy rooms look out over open country and all are luxuriously appointed with quality en suite facilities. Situated within walking distance of the town centre, station and Cork Racecourse. Parking facilities.

Rooms 6 en suite (3 fmly) (3 GF) **Facilities** STV TVL tea/coffee Cen ht **Parking** 10 **Notes** ⊗

PREMIER COLLECTION

Ballymaloe House

★★★★★ ⊛ GUEST HOUSE

☎ 021 4652531 ▤ 021 4652021
e-mail: res@ballymaloe.ie
dir: *From R630 at Whitegate rdbt, left onto R631, left onto Cloyne. Located on Ballycotton Rd*

This charming country house is on a 162-hectare farm, part of the Geraldine estate. Bedrooms range from one inside the old castle walls, to some in the main house and yet more in the courtyard buildings. All are well appointed to high standards. Much of the food on offer in the restaurant is produced on the farm. There is a craft shop on the estate.

Rooms 21 en suite 13 annexe rms 9 annexe en suite (4 pri facs) (2 fmly) (4 GF) **Facilities** TVL Dinner available Direct Dial Cen ht Licensed Wi-fi ᴥ ⌇ ⌇ Golf 9 ⌇ Fishing Children's sand pit/slide **Conf** Max 100 Thtr 100 Class 50 Board 50 **Parking** 30 **Notes** LB Closed 23-26 Dec Civ Wed 120

Ilenroy House

★★★ BED AND BREAKFAST

10 North St
☎ 028 22751 & 22193 ▤ 028 23228
e-mail: ilenroyhouse@oceanfree.net
dir: *90mtrs from main street on N71 (Clonakilty road)*

Conveniently situated in the centre of Skibbereen this well maintained house has comfortable bedrooms that are equipped to a high standard. This is an excellent base from which to tour South West Cork and the Islands.

Rooms 5 en suite (2 smoking) S €40-€50; D €75-€80*
Facilities STV tea/coffee Direct Dial Cen ht **Notes** ⊗

PREMIER COLLECTION

Ahernes

★★★★★ ⊛ GUEST HOUSE

163 North Main St
☎ 024 92424 ▤ 024 93633
e-mail: ahernes@eircom.net

In the same family since 1923, Ahernes offers a warm welcome, with turf fires and a traditional atmosphere. Spacious bedrooms are furnished to the highest standard and include antiques and modern facilities. There is a restaurant, well known for its daily-changing menu of the freshest seafood specialities, in addition to a cosy drawing room.

Rooms 12 en suite (2 fmly) (3 GF) **Facilities** FTV tea/coffee Dinner available Direct Dial Cen ht Licensed Wi-fi **Conf** Max 20 Thtr 20 Class 20 Board 12 **Parking** 20 **Notes** LB Closed 23-28 Dec

---

Dún Na Sí

★★★★ GUEST HOUSE

Bundoran Rd
☎ 071 985 2322
e-mail: dun-na-si@oceanfree.net
dir: *0.4km from Ballyshannon on R267*

A smart purpose-built guest house set back from the road and within walking distance of the town. The spacious bedrooms are comfortable and well equipped, and one of the two ground-floor rooms is suitable for the less mobile.

Rooms 7 en suite (2 fmly) (2 GF) **Facilities** STV tea/coffee Direct Dial Cen ht Wi-fi **Parking** 15 **Notes** ⊗

Heron's Cove

★★★★ ⊜ RESTAURANT WITH ROOMS

Creevy, Rossnowlagh Rd
☎ 071 982 2070 ▤ 071 982 2075
e-mail: info@heronscove.ie
dir: *From N side of Ballyshannon at rdbt take R231 towards Rossnowlagh 2m. Just after Creevy National School on left*

Heron's Cove is situated between Ballyshannon and Creevy Pier and is close to the sandy beach at Rossnowlagh. Bedrooms are comfortable, and there is a cosy lounge bar and charming restaurant where locally caught seafood features along with other imaginative dishes. Friendly staff and attentive service ensure a loyal local following.

Rooms 10 en suite (1 fmly) **Facilities** FTV tea/coffee Dinner available Direct Dial Cen ht **Parking** 60 **Notes** ⊗ Closed 24-28 Dec & Jan RS Oct-Mar Closed Tue-Wed

CARRIGANS   Map 1 C5

Mount Royd Country Home

★★★★ BED AND BREAKFAST

☎ 074 914 0163   🖹 074 914 0400
e-mail: jmartin@mountroyd.com
dir: *Off N13/N14 onto R236. A40 from Northern Ireland*

Set in lovely mature gardens in the pretty village and a short distance from Derry, the Mount Royd is an attractive creeper-clad house. The River Foyle runs along the back boundary. The friendly Martins have brought hospitality to new heights - nothing is too much trouble for them. Breakfast is a feast of choices. Bedrooms are very comfortable, with lots of personal touches.

Rooms 4 en suite (1 fmly) (1 GF) S €35-€40;
D €70-€80 **Facilities** TVL tea/coffee Cen ht **Parking** 7
Notes LB ⊗ No Children 12yrs Closed Jan RS Nov-Feb 🖼

DONEGAL   Map 1 B5

The Arches Country House

★★★★ BED AND BREAKFAST

Lough Eske
☎ 074 972 2029   🖹 074 972 2029
e-mail: archescountryhse@eircom.net
dir: *5km from Donegal. Signed off N15, 300mtrs from garage*

Located on an elevated site overlooking Lough Eske, this fine house is set amid beautifully manicured lawns. Each of the bedrooms shares the spectacular view, as do the breakfast room and comfortable lounge. A warm welcome is assured from the McGinty family.

Rooms 6 en suite (3 fmly) (2 GF) S €50-€55;
D €70-€80 **Facilities** STV FTV TVL tea/coffee Cen ht
Parking 10 **Notes** ⊗

Ardeevin

★★★★ BED AND BREAKFAST

Lough Eske, Barnesmore
☎ 074 972 1790   🖹 074 972 1790
e-mail: seanmcginty@eircom.net
dir: *N15 Derry road from Donegal for 5km, left at junct after garage for Ardeevin & Lough Eske & signs for Ardeevin*

Enjoying commanding views over Lough Eske, this is a very comfortable home with individually designed and decorated bedrooms with many thoughtful additional touches. The varied breakfast is tempting and features Mary McGinty's home baking.

Rooms 6 en suite (2 fmly) (2 GF) **Facilities** STV FTV TVL tea/coffee Cen ht **Parking** 10 **Notes** ⊗ No Children 9yrs Closed Dec-mid Mar 🖼

Ard Na Breatha

★★★★ GUEST HOUSE

Drumrooske Middle
☎ 074 972 2288   & 086 842 1330   🖹 074 974 0720
e-mail: info@ardnabreatha.com
web: www.ardnabreatha.com
dir: *From town centre onto Killybegs road, 2nd right, sharp right at Vivo shop*

This guest house, run by the Morrow family is just a short drive from the town centre. One of the first properties in Ireland to receive the EU Flower Award for eco-tourism, guests are assured of a warm welcome and can enjoy the peace and tranquillity of the countryside. Bedrooms are all well-appointed and very comfortable, decorated in a traditional country farmhouse style. Dinner is served in the popular split-level restaurant at weekends and during

high season. The menu makes good use of local and organic ingredients.

Rooms 6 en suite (1 fmly) (3 GF) S €50-€74;
D €80-€110 **Facilities** TVL tea/coffee Dinner available Direct Dial Cen ht Licensed **Conf** Thtr 30 Class 40 Board 20 **Parking** 16 **Notes** LB Closed Dec-Jan RS wknds Rest only open with prior reservation

DUNKINEELY   Map 1 B5

Castle Murray House and Restaurant

★★★★ ⊛ RESTAURANT WITH ROOMS

St Johns Point
☎ 074 973 7022   🖹 074 973 7330
e-mail: info@castlemurray.com
dir: *From Donegal take N56 towards Killybegs. Left to Dunkineely*

Situated on the coast road of St Johns Point, this charming family-run house and restaurant overlooks McSwynes Bay and the castle. The bedrooms are individually decorated with guest comfort very much in mind, as is the cosy bar and sun lounge. There is a strong French influence in the cooking; locally-landed fish, and prime lamb and beef are featured on the menus.

Rooms 10 en suite (2 fmly) S €70-€80; D €120-€140*
Facilities FTV tea/coffee Dinner available Direct Dial Cen ht Wi-fi **Parking** 40 **Notes** LB Closed mid Jan-mid Feb No coaches Civ Wed 30

LETTERKENNY   Map 1 C5

Ballyraine

★★★★ GUEST HOUSE

Ramelton Rd
☎ 074 912 4460   & 912 0851   🖹 074 912 0851
e-mail: ballyraineguesthouse@eircom.net
dir: *N13 onto R245*

This purpose-built guest house, five kilometres from the town centre, is well located for touring the Fanad and Inishowen Peninsula. Bedrooms are spacious and pleasantly decorated, and some are suitable for families. There is a comfortable lounge and an attractive breakfast room.

Rooms 8 en suite (1 fmly) (2 GF) **Facilities** STV TVL tea/coffee Direct Dial Cen ht **Parking** 12 **Notes** ⊗

LETTERKENNY *continued*

Larkfield B&B

★★★ BED AND BREAKFAST

Drumnahoe

☎ 074 912 1478 & 086 062 1263

e-mail: philomena21478@hotmail.com

dir: *1st left past Clanree Hotel. Signed N14 towards Letterkenny*

This house offers quiet and comfortable accommodation on the outskirts of Letterkenny. Mrs McDaid is a welcoming host and can advise on places to visit and restaurants for enjoyable evening meals. A good base for touring the Giant's Causeway and Glenveagh National Park.

Rooms 3 rms (2 en suite) (1 fmly) (3 GF) S €35–€40; D €64–€68 **Facilities** TVL tea/coffee Cen ht **Parking** 4 **Notes** LB ⊗ Closed 21 Dec–2 Jan RS 3 Jan

DUBLIN

DUBLIN	Map 1 D4

See also Howth (Co Dublin)

PREMIER COLLECTION

Aberdeen Lodge

★★★★★ GUEST HOUSE

53 Park Av, Ballsbridge

☎ 01 283 8155 ▤ 01 283 7877

e-mail: info@aberdeen-lodge.com

web: www.aberdeen-lodge.com

dir: *From city centre onto Merrion road towards Sydney Parade Dart station, 1st left onto Park Av*

This particularly fine early Edwardian house stands on one of Dublin's most prestigious roads near to the Embassy suburb and DART or bus to access the city centre. Bedrooms are very well equipped, some with four-poster beds, and there is a relaxing comfortable lounge and the breakfast room has lovely views of the colourful garden.

Rooms 16 en suite (8 fmly) **Facilities** STV tea/coffee Direct Dial Cen ht Licensed Wi-fi **Conf** Max 60 Thtr 60 Class 40 Board 40 **Parking** 16 **Notes** ⊗

PREMIER COLLECTION

Pembroke Townhouse

★★★★ GUEST HOUSE

90 Pembroke Rd, Ballsbridge

☎ 01 6600277 ▤ 01 6600291

e-mail: info@pembroketownhouse.ie

dir: *After Trinity College onto Nassan St & Northumberland Rd, onto lane to right of service station before lights, house 200mtrs on left*

Close to the city centre, three Georgian houses have been converted to make a comfortable guest house. The marble-tiled foyer, inviting lounge, and the friendly and attentive staff all combine to provide a welcoming atmosphere. The well-appointed bedrooms vary in style and some have a mezzanine sitting area. Secure parking is available behind the house.

Rooms 48 en suite (8 fmly) (10 GF) (38 smoking) S €100–€199; D €100–€310 (room only)* **Facilities** FTV TVL Direct Dial Cen ht Lift Licensed Wi-fi **Conf** Max 10 Board 10 **Parking** 20 **Notes** LB ⊗ Closed 21 Dec–5 Jan

PREMIER COLLECTION

Blakes Townhouse

★★★★★ GUEST ACCOMMODATION

50 Merrion Rd, Ballsbridge

☎ 01 6688324 ▤ 01 6684280

e-mail: info@blakestownhouse.com

dir: *Merrion Rd S to Ballsbridge, Blakes opp RDS Convention Centre*

This luxurious house has been refurbished to a very high standard. Some of the spacious, air-conditioned bedrooms have four-poster beds, others have balconies overlooking the gardens, plus all the expected facilities. Parking available.

Rooms 13 en suite (1 fmly) (2 smoking) **Facilities** STV tea/coffee Direct Dial Cen ht Licensed Wi-fi **Conf** Max 60 Thtr 60 Class 40 Board 40 **Parking** 6 **Notes** ⊗

PREMIER COLLECTION

Butlers Town House

★★★★★ GUEST ACCOMMODATION

44 Lansdowne Rd, Ballsbridge

☎ 01 6674022 ▤ 01 6673960

e-mail: reservations@butlers-hotel.com

This fine Victorian house, in the heart of Dublin's Embassy belt, has been restored and retains the charm of a gracious family home. Bedrooms are air-conditioned and individually furnished and decorated. The public areas are particularly relaxing and there is a charming and comfortable drawing room and conservatory style breakfast room. Limited off-street parking is available.

Rooms 20 en suite **Facilities** STV FTV Direct Dial Licensed Wi-fi **Parking** 14 **Notes** ⊗ Closed 22–28 Dec

PREMIER COLLECTION

Glenogra

★★★★★ GUEST HOUSE

64 Merrion Rd, Ballsbridge

☎ 01 6683661 ▤ 01 6683698

e-mail: info@glenogra.com

web: www.glenogra.com

dir: *Opp Royal Dublin Showgrounds & Four Seasons Hotel*

This fine brick house is situated in the pleasant suburb of Ballsbridge opposite the RDS and close to the city centre. Bedrooms are comfortably appointed with many thoughtful extras. There is an elegant drawing room and dining room with a rear garden where there is limited parking.

Rooms 13 en suite (1 fmly) S €70–€119; D €90–€188* **Facilities** STV TVL tea/coffee Direct Dial Cen ht Wi-fi **Parking** 10 **Notes** LB ⊗ Closed 21 Dec–5 Jan

PREMIER COLLECTION

Harrington Hall
★★★★ GUEST HOUSE

69-70 Harcourt St
☎ 01 4753497 🖷 01 4754544
e-mail: harringtonhall@eircom.net
web: www.harringtonhall.com
dir: *St Stephens Green via O'Connell St, in Earlsfort Ter pass National Concert Hall & right onto Hatch St, right onto Harcourt St*

This restored Georgian house is on a one-way street, leading to St Stephen's Green in the centre of the city. The bedrooms and bathrooms are very comfortable and include two junior suites with galleried bedroom areas, and a full suite. A lovely plasterwork ceiling adorns the relaxing drawing room. Lift, porter service and limited parking available.

Rooms 28 en suite (3 fmly) (3 GF) **Facilities** STV tea/coffee Direct Dial Cen ht Lift **Conf** Max 20 Thtr 20 Class 6 Board 12 **Parking** 8 **Notes** ⊗

PREMIER COLLECTION

Merrion Hall
★★★★★ GUEST HOUSE

54-56 Merrion Rd, Ballsbridge
☎ 01 6681426 🖷 01 6684280
e-mail: merrionhall@iol.ie
dir: *From city centre towards Dun Laoghaire Port, Ballsbridge 1.6km on main route, premises between British & US embassies*

This elegant house in Ballsbridge is convenient to the RDS and Lansdowne Road Stadium. Reception rooms are spacious, and the breakfast room overlooks the garden. The air-conditioned bedrooms are well appointed, and some rooms have balconies. Limited off-street parking is available.

Rooms 28 en suite (4 fmly) (4 GF) (2 smoking) **Facilities** STV tea/coffee Direct Dial Cen ht Lift Licensed Wi-fi **Conf** Max 60 Thtr 60 Class 40 Board 40 **Parking** 10 **Notes** ⊗

Charleville Lodge
★★★★ GUEST HOUSE

268/272 North Circular Rd, Phibsborough
☎ 01 8386633 🖷 01 8385854
e-mail: info@charlevillelodge.ie
web: www.charlevillelodge.ie
dir: *N from O'Connell St to Phibsborough, left fork at St Peter's Church, house 250mtrs on left*

Situated close to the city centre near Phoenix Park, this elegant terrace of Victorian houses has been restored to a high standard. The two interconnecting lounges are welcoming and the smart dining room offers a choice of breakfasts. Bedrooms are very comfortable with pleasant décor, and there is a secure car park.

Rooms 30 en suite (2 fmly) (4 GF) **Facilities** STV FTV TVL Direct Dial Cen ht **Conf** Max 20 Thtr 20 Class 20 Board 20 **Parking** 18 **Notes** ⊗ Closed 21-26 Dec

Eliza Lodge
★★★★ GUEST HOUSE

23/24 Wellington Quay, Temple Bar
☎ 01 6718044 🖷 01 6718362
e-mail: info@dublinlodge.com

Very smart accommodation in a completely refurbished building situated at the foot of the Millennium Bridge. Inviting, comfortable bedrooms are well equipped, and there is a lounge with a hospitality centre, and a fully licensed restaurant.

Rooms 18 en suite (2 fmly) **Facilities** STV TVL tea/coffee Direct Dial Cen ht Lift **Notes** ⊗ Closed 23 Dec-2 Jan

Glenshandan Lodge
★★★★ GUEST ACCOMMODATION

Dublin Rd, Swords
☎ 01 8408838 🖷 01 8408838
e-mail: glenshandan@eircom.net
dir: *Beside Statoil on airport side of Swords Main St*

Family and dog-friendly house with hospitable owners and good facilities including e-mail access. Bedrooms are comfortable and one room has easier access. Secure parking available. Close to pubs, restaurants, golf, airport and the Kennel Club.

Rooms 9 en suite (5 fmly) (5 GF) **Facilities** TVL tea/coffee Cen ht Wi-fi **Conf** Max 20 **Parking** 10 **Notes** Closed Xmas/New Year

Aran House
★★★ BED AND BREAKFAST

5 Home Farm Rd, Drumcondra
☎ 01 8367395
e-mail: aranhouse@eircom.net
dir: *From city centre towards airport/Drumcondra road. Past St Patrick's College and Cat & Cage pub. 1st left after Skylon Hotel*

This comfortable, red-brick terrace house is just off the main airport road close to pubs and on a bus route to the city centre. The attractive dining room is an appropriate setting for delicious breakfasts and there is a cosy guest sitting room.

Rooms 4 en suite (2 fmly) S €45-€60; D €90* **Facilities** TVL Cen ht **Notes** Closed Nov-Feb ⊛

Ardagh House
★★★ GUEST HOUSE

1 Highfield Rd, Rathgar
☎ 01 4977068 🖷 01 4973991
e-mail: enquiries@ardagh-house.ie
dir: *S of city centre through Rathmines*

Ardagh House has been refurbished and upgraded by Mary and Willie Doyle, and some of the comfortable, airy en suite rooms look over the attractive rear garden.

Rooms 19 en suite (4 fmly) (1 GF) S €65-€95; D €80-€150 **Facilities** FTV TVL tea/coffee Direct Dial Cen ht Wi-fi **Parking** 20 **Notes** ⊗ Closed 22 Dec-3 Jan

DUBLIN *continued*

Clifden

★★★ GUEST HOUSE

32 Gardiner Place
☎ 01 8746364   📠 01 8746122
e-mail: info@clifdenhouse.com
dir: *From N end of O'Connell St, around Parnell Sq & exit at church onto Gardiner Row, over lights, house 4th on right*

This city centre house is just a short walk from O'Connell Street, and close to amenities. Facilities include a comfortable sitting room, cheerfully appointed breakfast room and a car park at the rear of the house.

Rooms 15 en suite (4 fmly) (2 GF) S €25–€80; D €56–€150 **Facilities** STV TVL tea/coffee Direct Dial Cen ht **Parking** 12 **Notes** ⊗

Pairc na Bhfuiseog

★★★ BED AND BREAKFAST

55 Lorcan Crescent, Santry
☎ 01 8421318   📠 01 8421318
e-mail: rpjd@eircom.net
dir: *N1 Dublin Airport, Swords Rd to Santry, over flyover, sharp left at rdbt, to top of road. Right onto Lorcan Crescent*

An extended, modern semi-detached house, very nicely appointed throughout, with excellent en suite facilities. Convenient for Dublin Airport, ferries and city centre. The owners Ronald and Colette Downey provide a homely atmosphere and lots of local information.

Rooms 4 rms (3 en suite) (1 fmly) (1 GF) **Facilities** STV Cen ht **Parking** 4 **Notes** ⊗ No Children 18yrs Closed 21 Dec-1 Jan

St Aiden's

★★★ GUEST HOUSE

32 Brighton Rd, Rathgar
☎ 01 4902011   & 4906178   📠 01 6864946
e-mail: staidens@eircom.net
dir: *M50 junct 11, towards city centre, premises 3rd left after lights in Terenure*

A fine Victorian house situated in a residential tree-lined road just 15 minutes from the city centre. The well-proportioned reception rooms are comfortable and relaxing, and a hospitality trolley is available. Bedrooms vary from spacious family rooms to snug singles, and all have modern comforts.

Rooms 8 en suite (2 fmly) S €50–€55; D €80–€110* **Facilities** STV TVL tea/coffee Direct Dial Cen ht Wi-fi **Notes** LB ⊗

CO DUBLIN

HOWTH — Map 1 D4

Inisradharc

★★★★ BED AND BREAKFAST

Balkill Rd
☎ 01 8322306
e-mail: harbour_view@msn.com
dir: *Off R105 past Howth Yacht Club onto Abbey St, bear right of church (in middle of road), house 0.6km up hill on right*

Set in a charming fishing village of Howth with lovely views of the harbour and Dublin Bay. The breakfast room also has fine views and there is a spacious TV lounge. Well-kept gardens surround the property. Convenient for Dublin airport, ferry port and 20 minutes by DART to the city centre.

Rooms 3 en suite (1 fmly) (3 GF) **Facilities** TVL tea/coffee Cen ht **Parking** 3 **Notes** ⊗ No Children 4yrs Closed 12 Dec-8 Jan

LUSK — Map 1 D4

Brookfield Lodge

★★★ BED AND BREAKFAST

Blakescross
☎ 01 8430043
e-mail: trishb@indigo.ie
dir: *M1, R132 Donabate/Skerries for 3km, pass Esso station, at junct R132 & R129*

Set in extensive gardens, this modern bungalow offers first-class hospitality and spacious, well-appointed rooms. Breakfasts are served in a conservatory-style dining room and there is also a comfortable lounge.

Rooms 3 en suite (2 fmly) **Facilities** STV TVL tea/coffee Cen ht **Parking** 10 **Notes** ⊗ Closed 24-26 Dec

RUSH — Map 1 D4

Sandyhills Bed & Breakfast

★★★★ 🏠 BED AND BREAKFAST

Sandyhills
☎ 01 843 7148   & 086 242 3660   📠 01 843 7148
e-mail: mary@sandyhills.ie
dir: *Exit M1 onto N1, turn right to Lusk on R127. 3rd exit on rdbt in Lusk to Rush. Right towards church car park, right to Corrs Lane & then 2nd right*

Set just a stroll from the sea and the village of Rush, within easy reach of Dublin Airport, Sandyhills has spacious bedrooms, well equipped with thoughtful extra facilities. Breakfast is a special treat featuring local produce along with Mary Buckley's preserves, freshly baked cakes and breads. There is a cosy sitting room and a lovely garden with secure car parking.

Rooms 5 en suite (2 fmly) **Facilities** Direct Dial Cen ht Wi-fi **Parking** 20 **Notes** LB ⊗ No Children 12yrs

SKERRIES — Map 1 D4

Redbank House & Restaurant

★★★★ 🏵 RESTAURANT WITH ROOMS

5-7 Church St
☎ 01 849 1005   📠 01 849 1598
e-mail: sales@redbank.ie
dir: *N1 north past airport & bypass Swords. 3m N at end of dual carriageway at Esso station right towards Rush, Lusk & Skerries*

Adjacent to the well-known restaurant of the same name, this comfortable, double-fronted period town house has two reception rooms, en suite bedrooms and a secluded garden. The restaurant is the setting for quality local produce with an emphasis on fresh fish in imaginative cooking, served by friendly and attentive staff. Convenient for Dublin Airport and the ferry port.

Rooms 18 en suite (2 fmly) (7 GF) **Facilities** STV FTV TVL tea/coffee Dinner available Direct Dial Cen ht Wi-fi **Conf** Max 25 Thtr 25 Class 25 Board 25 **Notes** Closed 24-28 Dec No coaches Civ Wed 55

CO GALWAY

CLIFDEN — Map 1 A4

Buttermilk Lodge

★★★★ GUEST HOUSE

Westport Rd
☎ 095 21951   📠 095 21953
e-mail: buttermilklodge@eircom.net
web: www.buttermilklodge.com
dir: *N59 from Galway. Right at Esso station onto Westport Rd, Lodge 400mtrs from junct on left. From Westport, Lodge on right after 50km road sign*

Expect carefully decorated and appointed bedrooms, four with luxury bath en suite and the remainder with shower en suite, along with many personal touches at this large house on the edge of town. Cathriona and Patrick O'Toole are welcoming hosts who offer fresh baking, tea and coffee on arrival.

Rooms 11 en suite (2 fmly) (4 GF) **Facilities** STV FTV Direct Dial Cen ht Wi-fi **Parking** 14 **Notes** ⊗ No Children 5yrs Closed 1-27 Dec, 3 Jan-1 Mar

Ardmore House (L589523)

★★★★ FARMHOUSE

Sky Rd
☎ 095 21221 📄 095 21100 Mr & Mrs J Mullen
e-mail: info@ardmore-house.com
web: www.ardmore-house.com
dir: *5km W of Clifden. From Clifden signs for Sky Rd, pass bank onto the Abbey Glen Castle, house signed*

Ardmore is set among the wild scenery of Connemara between hills and the sea on the Sky Road. Bedrooms are attractively decorated and the house is very comfortable throughout. A pathway leads from the house to the coast. A good hearty breakfast is provided featuring Kathy's home baking.

Rooms 6 en suite (3 fmly) (6 GF); D €70-€80
Facilities STV FTV TVL tea/coffee Cen ht Wi-fi **Parking** 8
Notes LB ⊗ Closed Oct-Mar ⊜ 25 acres non-working

Faul House (L650475)

★★★★ FARMHOUSE

Ballyconneely Rd
☎ 095 21239 📄 095 21998 Mrs K Conneely
e-mail: info@ireland.com
dir: *1.5km from town right at rugby pitch signed Rockglen Hotel*

A fine modern farmhouse stands on a quiet and secluded road overlooking Clifden Bay. It is smart and comfortable with large bedrooms, all well furnished and with good views. Kathleen offers a hearty breakfast with home baking. There are Connemara ponies available for trekking.

Rooms 6 en suite (3 fmly) (3 GF) **Facilities** TVL tea/coffee Cen ht Wi-fi **Parking** 10 **Notes** ⊗ Closed Nov-26 Mar ⊜ 35 acres sheep/ponies/hens/ducks

Mallmore House

★★★★ BED AND BREAKFAST

Ballyconneely Rd
☎ 095 21460
e-mail: info@mallmore.com
dir: *1.5km from Clifden towards Ballyconneely take 1st right*

A charming Georgian-style house built in the 17th century set in fourteen hectares of woodland overlooking Clifden Bay, close to the Rock Glen Hotel. Alan and Kathy Hardman have restored the house with parquet flooring and some favourite antiques, while turf fires provide warmth and atmosphere.

Rooms 6 en suite (2 fmly) (6 GF); D €80 **Facilities** FTV tea/coffee Cen ht Wi-fi **Parking** 15 **Notes** ⊗ Closed Nov-1 Mar ⊜

Ben View House

★★★ GUEST HOUSE

Bridge St
☎ 095 21256 📄 095 21226
e-mail: benviewhouse@ireland.com
dir: *Enter town on N59, opp Esso fuel station*

This town-centre house dates from 1848 and is one of the oldest in Clifden and is a good touring base. Bedrooms offer good quality accommodation at a moderate cost.

Rooms 10 rms (9 en suite) (3 fmly) **Facilities** TV9B TVL tea/coffee Cen ht **Notes** ⊗

GALWAY   Map 1 B3

Achill Lodge

★★★★ BED AND BREAKFAST

5 Cashelmara, Upper Salthill
☎ 091 584709
e-mail: info@achill-lodge.com
web: www.achill-lodge.com
dir: *R336 from Galway City through Salthill, pass golf club*

Achill Lodge is a newly-constructed, purpose-built bed and breakfast located in the exclusive seaside resort of Salthill, just five minutes' drive from Galway. Bedrooms are carefully decorated and well equipped, with extra large en suite bathrooms. Some have lovely views over Galway Bay, as does the cosy guest sitting room and breakfast room. There is private off-road parking available.

Rooms 4 en suite (2 fmly) **Facilities** STV FTV TVL tea/coffee Cen ht Wi-fi **Parking** 8 **Notes** ⊗ Closed Nov-Feb

Almara House

★★★★ BED AND BREAKFAST

2 Merlin Gate, Merlin Park, Dublin Rd
☎ 091 755345 & 086 2451220 📄 091 771585
e-mail: info@almarahouse.com
dir: *From Martin rdbt follow signs for Merlin Park. 0.2km, Almara House on left*

Located in the eastern outskirts of Galway city, this attractive guest house offers well-appointed bedrooms with lots of thoughtful extras and Wi-fi access. Breakfast features Marie Kiernan's home baking. Almara House is well located for the Institute of Technology and off-road parking is available.

Rooms 5 en suite (2 fmly) (1 GF) **Facilities** STV FTV TVL tea/coffee Cen ht Wi-fi **Parking** 8 **Notes** ⊗ No Children 4yrs Closed 20-30 Dec

Marian Lodge

★★★★ GUEST HOUSE

Knocknacarra Rd, Salthill Upper
☎ 091 521678 📄 091 528103
e-mail: celine@iol.ie
dir: *From Galway to Salthill on R336, through Salthill, 1st right after Spinnaker Hotel onto Knocknacarra Rd*

This large modern house is only 50 metres from the seafront. The fully equipped bedrooms have orthopaedic beds and en suite facilities. There is also a lounge and separate breakfast room available.

Rooms 6 en suite (4 fmly); D €76-€120* **Facilities** STV TVL tea/coffee Direct Dial Cen ht **Parking** 10 **Notes** LB ⊗ No Children 3yrs Closed 23-28 Dec

Four Seasons

★★★ BED AND BREAKFAST

23 College Rd
☎ 091 564078 📄 091 569765
e-mail: 4season@gofree.indigo.ie
dir: *From E or S exit motorway signed Galway City East then city centre, 5th house on right after sports ground/greyhound track*

This comfortable house adjacent to the city centre is the family home of Eddie and Helen Fitzgerald who will immediately make you feel at home and help you with itineraries and sight-seeing, and will recommend restaurants for evening meals.

Rooms 5 en suite 2 annexe en suite (3 fmly) **Facilities** STV TVL tea/coffee Cen ht **Parking** 7 **Notes** ⊗

OUGHTERARD   Map 1 B4

Lakeland & Midsummer Lakehouse

★★★ BED AND BREAKFAST

Lakeland Angling Centre, Portacarron Bay
☎ 091 552121 📄 091 552146
e-mail: mayfly@eircom.net
dir: *Off N59 20 mins from Galway take 2nd right after Oughterard Golf Club sign. From Maam Cross through Oughterard, pass Gateway Hotel next left, house on lake shore*

Situated on the shores of the lough, this comfortable house offers a spacious TV lounge, and a fine dining room with views across the water. Fishing and boat trips can be arranged, and dinner is available.

Rooms 9 rms (8 en suite) (3 fmly) **Facilities** TVL tea/coffee Cen ht Fishing **Parking** 20 **Notes** ⊗ Closed 10 Dec-16 Jan

ROUNDSTONE   Map 1 A4

Ivy Rock House
★★★★ BED AND BREAKFAST

Letterdyfe
☎ 095 35872   📄 095 35959
e-mail: ivyrockhouse@eircom.net

Overlooking Bertraghboy Bay this house has been decorated to a high standard and provides comfortable accommodation. Public rooms include two adjoining reception rooms and a first-floor sitting room with spectacular views. Bedrooms are well appointed. There are good restaurants nearby.

Rooms 6 en suite (4 fmly) (3 GF) D €70* **Facilities** TV4B TVL Cen ht **Parking** 10 **Notes** LB ⊗ Closed Oct-Mar

SALTHILL   Map 1 B3

Rose Villa
★★★★ BED AND BREAKFAST

10 Cashelmara, Knocknacarra Cross
☎ 091 584200   📄 091 584200
e-mail: kevin.ohare@ireland.com
dir: 1km from Salthill Promenade in Upper Salthill on R336. On right after Golf Club before T-junct

Rose Villa enjoys lovely views over the bay especially when the sun is going down. Bedrooms are comfortable and well appointed. There is a relaxing guest lounge and Marie and Kevin O'Hara serve a good breakfast. Off-street car parking is available.

Rooms 4 en suite (3 fmly) S €50-€70; D €80-€100* **Facilities** STV FTV TVL tea/coffee Cen ht Wi-fi **Parking** 7 **Notes** ⊗ Closed 30 Nov-7 Feb

SPIDDAL (AN SPIDÉAL)   Map 1 B3

Ardmor Country House
★★★★ BED AND BREAKFAST

Greenhill
☎ 091 553145   📄 091 553596
e-mail: ardmorcountryhouse@yahoo.com
dir: On R336 (coast road) from Galway, 1km W of Spiddal

There are superb views of Galway Bay and the Aran Islands from this beautifully appointed luxury home. Bedrooms are spacious and there are relaxing lounges, a well-stocked library and delightful gardens.

Rooms 7 en suite (4 fmly) **Facilities** TVL tea/coffee Cen ht Wi-fi **Parking** 20 **Notes** ⊗ Closed Dec-Feb RS Mar-Nov ✉

Tuar Beag
★★★★ BED AND BREAKFAST

Tuar Beag
☎ 091 553422
e-mail: tuarbeagbandb@eircom.net
dir: On R336 (coast road) on W edge of Spiddal

Tuar Beag is a prominent house, much extended from the 19th-century cottage where four generations of the proprietor's family grew up. The original stone walls and fireplace have been retained and the house now offers excellent accommodation overlooking Galway Bay and the Aran Islands. Breakfast is a notable feature.

Rooms 6 en suite (6 fmly) **Facilities** TVL tea/coffee Cen ht **Parking** 20 **Notes** ⊗ No Children 2yrs Closed 16 Nov-1 Mar ✉

CO KERRY

BALLYBUNION   Map 1 A3

PREMIER COLLECTION

Cashen Course House
★★★★★ GUEST HOUSE

Golf Links Rd
☎ 068 27351   📄 068 28934
e-mail: golfstay@eircom.net
web: www.cashenguesthouse.com
dir: 200mtrs from Ballybunion Golf Club

Overlooking the Cashen links, this spacious, purpose-built house offers comfortable well-appointed bedrooms. A warm welcome is assured from the O'Brien family who are on hand to advise and assist with tee bookings. A baby grand piano is a feature of the inviting lounge. Drying facilities are available.

Rooms 9 en suite (3 fmly) (3 GF) **Facilities** STV TVL tea/coffee Direct Dial Cen ht Wi-fi Golf 18 2 golf courses opposite **Parking** 12 **Notes** ⊗ Closed Nov-Apr

CAHERDANIEL (CATHAIR DÓNALL)   Map 1 A2

Derrynane Bay House
★★★★ BED AND BREAKFAST

☎ 066 9475404 & 08723 43974   📄 066 9475436
e-mail: dbhouse@eircom.net
dir: 1km on Waterville side of Caherdaniel village on N70 overlooking Derrynane Bay

Situated on an elevated position with views over Derrynane Bay, this house is meticulously maintained. Carefully furnished throughout, there is a comfortable sitting and dining room, along with attractive bedrooms. The owner is very welcoming and offers a good breakfast menu. Walking, water sports, good beaches, fishing and golf are all nearby.

Rooms 5 rms (5 en suite) (1 pri facs) (2 fmly) (4 GF) S €50-€60; D €80* **Facilities** STV FTV TVL tea/coffee Dinner available Direct Dial Cen ht Wi-fi **Parking** 10 **Notes** ⊗ Closed Nov-Dec RS 6 Jan-20 Mar Prior bookings only

CASTLEGREGORY   Map 1 A2

PREMIER COLLECTION

Shores Country House
★★★★★ BED AND BREAKFAST

Conor Pass Rd, Cappatigue
☎ 066 713 9196 & 713 9195   📄 066 713 9196
e-mail: theshores@eircom.net
dir: N86/R560 through Stradbally, 1.6km, house on left

This charming house has panoramic views from its elevated position. Bedrooms and public rooms are all individually decorated to a very high standard. An interesting home-cooked dinner is available Monday to Friday, and features local and seasonal produce.

Rooms 6 en suite (1 fmly) (2 GF) S €45-€90; D €70-€90 **Facilities** STV TVL tea/coffee Dinner available Direct Dial Cen ht Library **Parking** 8 **Notes** LB ⊗ Closed mid Nov-mid Feb

Sea-Mount House

★★★★ BED AND BREAKFAST

Cappatigue, Conor Pass Rd
☎ 066 7139229 🖷 066 7139229
e-mail: seamount@unison.ie
web: www.seamounthouse.com
dir: *On Conor Pass road, 2.4km W of Stradbally*

Located on the Conor Pass road between Tralee and Dingle, this friendly house has great views of Brandon Bay. It is a good base for exploring the Dingle Peninsula. The cosy sitting areas and bedrooms make the most of the views, a great way to enjoy home baking and welcome tea on arrival.

Rooms 3 en suite (1 fmly) (2 GF) S €45-€55; D €70-€80* **Facilities** TVL tea/coffee Cen ht **Parking** 5 **Notes** LB ⊗ No Children 6yrs Closed Nov-Apr ⊠

Griffin's Palm Beach Country House (Q525085)

★★★ FARMHOUSE

Goulane, Conor Pass Rd
☎ 066 7139147 🖷 066 7139073 **Mrs Catherine Griffin**
e-mail: griffinspalmbeach@eircom.net
dir: *1.5km from Stradbally*

This farmhouse is a good base for exploring the Dingle Peninsula and unspoiled beaches. The comfortable bedrooms have fine views over Brandon Bay, and the delightful garden can be enjoyed from the dining room and sitting room. Mrs Griffin offers a warm welcome and her home baking is a feature on the breakfast menu.

Rooms 8 rms (6 en suite) (2 pri facs) (3 fmly) (1 GF) S €48-€50; D €80-€90* **Facilities** TVL tea/coffee Cen ht **Parking** 10 **Notes** LB Closed Nov-Feb 150 acres mixed

CASTLEMAINE Map 1 A2

Murphys Farmhouse (R801005)

★★★ FARMHOUSE

Boolteens
☎ 066 976 7337 🖷 066 976 7839 **Mrs M Murphy**
e-mail: info@murphysfarmhouse.com
dir: *From Castlemaine onto R561 (Dingle road), signed*

The elevated position of this long established house offers marvellous views of Dingle Bay. Bedrooms are very comfortable, and a choice of two lounges is available for guests. Expect a warm welcome from Mrs Mary Murphy, whose family also own a traditional pub nearby, where dinner is served.

Rooms 14 en suite (5 fmly) (6 GF) **Facilities** TVL tea/coffee Dinner available Cen ht **Parking** 16 **Notes** ⊗ Closed 23-27 Dec 30 acres dairy

CLOGHANE (AN CLOCHÁN) Map 1 A2

O'Connors Guesthouse

★★ GUEST HOUSE

☎ 066 713 8113 🖷 066 713 8270
e-mail: oconnorsguesthouse@eircom.net
dir: *In village centre*

Situated in a lovely village close to Castlegregory, this long-established, family-run house has a traditional bar and restaurant, and some of the bedrooms look over the bay and mountains.

Rooms 9 en suite (6 fmly) (2 GF) S €45-€55; D €70-€90* **Facilities** TVL tea/coffee Dinner available Direct Dial Cen ht Licensed Wi-fi **Parking** 20 **Notes** LB ⊗ Closed Nov-Feb

DINGLE (AN DAINGEAN) Map 1 A2

PREMIER COLLECTION

Emlagh House

★★★★★ GUEST ACCOMMODATION

☎ 066 9152345 🖷 066 9152369
e-mail: info@emlaghhouse.com
web: www.emlaghhouse.com
dir: *Pass fuel station at E entrance to town, turn left. House ahead*

Impressive Georgian-style house on the outskirts of Dingle, where attention to detail and luxury combine to make a stay memorable. The stylish drawing room, conservatory and dining room overlook the harbour. Bedrooms and bathrooms are individually decorated to a high standard with antique furniture, and ground floor rooms have private patios. Breakfasts make good use of fresh local produce.

Rooms 10 en suite (1 fmly) (4 GF) S €90-€120; D €160-€240 **Facilities** STV Direct Dial Cen ht Lift Licensed Wi-fi **Parking** 20 **Notes** LB ⊗ No Children 8yrs Closed 5 Nov-10 Mar

PREMIER COLLECTION

Milltown House

★★★★★ GUEST HOUSE

☎ 066 9151372 🖷 066 9151095
e-mail: info@milltownhousedingle.com
dir: *1.5km W of Dingle on Slea Head road. Cross Milltown Bridge & left*

Situated on a sea channel to the west of Dingle town, the house has been elegantly refurbished and has a warm inviting atmosphere, the Kerry family always making guests feel really welcome. Bedrooms have attractive décor and are well appointed. There is also a cosy sitting room leading to a conservatory breakfast room.

Rooms 10 en suite (1 fmly) (3 GF) **Facilities** STV tea/coffee Direct Dial Cen ht **Parking** 10 **Notes** ⊗ No Children 5yrs Closed 29 Oct-27 Apr

PREMIER COLLECTION

Castlewood House

★★★★★ GUEST HOUSE

The Wood
☎ 066 915 2788 🖷 066 915 2110
e-mail: castlewoodhouse@eircom.net
dir: *R559 from Dingle, 0.5km from Aquarium*

Located at the western edge of the town, Castlewood House has been recently built to a high specification. Each of the individually designed bedrooms is very comfortable and well equipped. There is lift access to the upper floor and a spa bath in each en suite. Both the sitting room and breakfast rooms make the most of the beautiful views.

Rooms 12 en suite (3 fmly) (4 GF) **Facilities** STV tea/coffee Direct Dial Cen ht Lift **Parking** 15 **Notes** LB ⊗ Closed 4-27 Dec, 4 Jan-4 Feb

DINGLE (AN DAINGEAN) *continued*

PREMIER COLLECTION

Gormans Clifftop House & Restaurant
★★★★★ GUEST HOUSE

Glaise Bheag, Ballydavid
☎ 066 9155162 📄 066 9155003
e-mail: info@gormans-clifftophouse.com
dir: *From Dingle harbour to rdbt W of town, over rdbt signed An Fheothanach to coast, keep left at junct*

This traditional house is in a superb location overlooking Smerwick Harbour and the vastness of the Atlantic beyond. The Gorman family offer marvellous hospitality and the food is excellent. Both the lounges and the restaurant enjoy stunning views. The comfortable bedrooms are most inviting, and one is adapted for the less mobile.

Rooms 9 en suite (2 fmly) (5 GF) **Facilities** tea/coffee Dinner available Direct Dial Cen ht Licensed Wi-fi **Parking** 15 **Notes** ⊗ Closed 24-26 Dec RS Nov-Feb reservation only

Hurleys *(Q392080)*
★★★ FARMHOUSE

An Dooneen, Kilcooley
☎ 066 9155112 Ms Mary Hurley
e-mail: andooneen@eircom.net
dir: *11km W of Dingle town on Ballydavid-Muirioch road*

Hurley's Farm is tucked away behind the church in Kilcooley, 1.5 kilometres from the beach and sheltered by Mount Brandon, a popular place for hill walkers. Accommodation includes a cosy TV room, dining room and comfortable en suite bedrooms, graced by some special pieces of high quality furniture. The whole area is rich in early historic and prehistoric relics: ogham stones, ring forts and the famous dry-stone masonry 'beehive' huts.

Rooms 4 en suite (2 GF) S €50-€60; D €80-€85* **Facilities** TVL Cen ht **Parking** 6 **Notes** LB ⊗ Closed Nov-Mar 🐾

KENMARE Map 1 B2

Annagry House
★★★★ BED AND BREAKFAST

Sneem Rd
☎ 064 6641283
e-mail: info@annagryhouse.com
dir: *500mtrs from town centre, turn left onto N70 towards Sneem on the Ring of Kerry. 400mtrs on right*

Annagry House is owned and run by the O'Sullivan family; it is situated on the Ring of Kerry road (N70) only minutes from Kenmare town. Bedrooms are spacious and comfortably furnished to accommodate families and there are two ground floor rooms. The relaxing guest sitting room has books, maps and information on the area. The extensive breakfast menu includes Fionnuala's home baking, and Danny will advise on tours and activities available

Rooms 6 en suite (3 fmly) (2 GF) **Facilities** FTV TVL tea/coffee Cen ht Wi-fi **Parking** 11 **Notes** ⊗ Closed 26 Oct-Apr 🐾

Davitts
★★★★ GUEST HOUSE

Henry St
☎ 064 6642741 📄 064 6642757
e-mail: info@davitts-kenmare.com
dir: *On N22 (Cork-Killarney rd) at Kenmare junct (R569). In town centre*

This family-run guest house is situated in the centre of the Heritage town of Kenmare. With the popular Davitts Bar Bistro at street-level serving excellent food it is the perfect ingredient for an enjoyable holiday all under one roof. The spacious, well-appointed bedrooms are decorated in a contemporary style, and there is a cosy sitting room on the first floor.

Rooms 11 en suite (1 fmly) S €45-€60; D €76-€100* **Facilities** STV TVL Dinner available Direct Dial Cen ht Licensed **Parking** 4 **Notes** ⊗ Closed 1-14 Nov & 24-26 Dec

---

Harbour View
★★★★ BED AND BREAKFAST

Castletownbere Rd, Dauros
☎ 064 6641755 📄 064 6642611
e-mail: maureenmccarthy@eircom.net
dir: *From Kenmare towards Glengarriff, onto Castletownbere Haven road (571), 1st right after bridge. Harbour View 6.5km on left on seashore*

This charming house is situated on the seashore, with lovely views of Kenmare Bay and the mountains beyond. Maureen McCarthy is a cheerful, caring hostess with infectious enthusiasm, and her attention to detail is evident throughout the comfortable bedrooms. The breakfast menu includes fresh and smoked seafood and the home baking is excellent.

Rooms 4 en suite (3 fmly) (4 GF) **Facilities** STV TVL tea/coffee Cen ht **Parking** 6 **Notes** ⊗ No Children 6yrs Closed Nov-Feb 🐾

Sea Shore Farm Guest House
★★★★ GUEST HOUSE

Tubrid
☎ 064 6641270 & 6641675 📄 064 6641270
e-mail: seashore@eircom.net
dir: *1.6km from Kenmare on N70 Ring of Kerry road. Signed at junct N70 & N71*

Overlooking Kenmare Bay on the Ring of Kerry road, this modern farm guest house is close to town and has spacious bedrooms. Ground-floor rooms open onto the patio and have easier access. Guests are welcome to enjoy the farm walks through the fields to the shore, and salmon and trout fishing on a private stretch of the Roughty River. There is a comfortable sitting room and dining room and a delightful garden.

Rooms 6 en suite (2 fmly) (2 GF) **Facilities** FTV tea/coffee Direct Dial Cen ht Wi-fi **Parking** 10 **Notes** ⊗ Closed 15 Nov-Feb

KILGARVAN · Map 1 B2

Birchwood
★★★★ BED AND BREAKFAST

Church Ground
☎ 064 6685473 📄 064 6685570
e-mail: birchwood1@eircom.net
dir: *500mtrs E of Kilgarvan on R569*

Birchwood stands in extensive gardens facing a natural forest and backed by the Mangerton Mountains, an area ideal for hill-walking and touring. The MacDonnells are caring hosts in this tranquil location, and offer comfortable and attractively decorated bedrooms. Dinner is available, and the nearby Rivers Roughty and Slaheny provide good salmon and trout fishing.

Rooms 5 en suite (3 fmly) S €40-€45; D €60*
Facilities FTV TVL tea/coffee Dinner available Cen ht Fishing **Parking** 6 **Notes** ⊗ 🚭

KILLARNEY · Map 1 B2

PREMIER COLLECTION

Fairview
★★★★★ 📄 GUEST HOUSE

College St
☎ 064 6634164 📄 064 6671777
e-mail: info@fairviewkillarney.com
dir: *In town centre off College St*

This guest house is situated in the town centre and close to the railway station. Great attention to detail has been taken in the furnishing and design to ensure guest comfort in bedrooms. There is a lift to all floors and a penthouse suite enjoys views to the mountains. Dinner is served nightly in the Fifth Season Restaurant.

Rooms 29 en suite (1 GF) (2 smoking) **Facilities** STV TVL tea/coffee Dinner available Direct Dial Cen ht Lift Licensed Wi-fi Jacuzzi suites available **Parking** 11

PREMIER COLLECTION

Foleys Town House
★★★★★ 🍴 GUEST HOUSE

22/23 High St
☎ 064 6631217 📄 064 6634683
e-mail: info@foleystownhouse.com
dir: *In town centre*

Charming, individually-designed bedrooms are a feature of this well-established house, which has good parking facilities and a comfortable lounge. Family-owned and run by Carol Hartnett who is also the chef in the adjoining restaurant that specialises in seafood.

Rooms 28 en suite S €60-€80; D €120-€150
Facilities STV TVL tea/coffee Dinner available Direct Dial Cen ht Lift Licensed Wi-fi **Parking** 60 **Notes** LB ⊗ Closed 6 Nov-16 Mar

PREMIER COLLECTION

Old Weir Lodge
★★★★★ GUEST HOUSE

Muckross Rd
☎ 064 6635593 📄 064 6635583
e-mail: oldweirlodge@eircom.net
web: www.oldweirlodge.com
dir: *On N71 (Muckross Rd), 500mtrs from Killarney*

Welcoming, purpose-built Tudor-style lodge, set in attractive gardens. Maureen loves to cook and home-baking is a feature of the breakfasts; evening meals are also available by arrangement. Dermot will help with leisure activities such as boat trips on the Killarney Lakes or golf and fishing. The comfortable bedrooms are equipped to a high standard and there is a delightful sitting room overlooking the gardens. There is also a drying room and ample off-road parking.

Rooms 30 en suite (7 fmly) (6 GF) S €70-€90; D €90-€140* **Facilities** STV TVL tea/coffee Dinner available Direct Dial Cen ht Lift Licensed **Parking** 30 **Notes** ⊗ Closed 23-26 Dec

Applecroft House
★★★★ BED AND BREAKFAST

Woodlawn Rd
☎ 064 6632782
e-mail: applecroft@eircom.net
dir: *N71 from Killarney on Muckross road for 500mtrs, left at 2nd set lights onto Woodlawn Rd for 500mtrs, sign on left*

Applecroft is a delightful home of the Brosnan family tucked away in a residential area, with beautiful landscaped gardens. Bedrooms are spacious and there is great attention to detail in the decoration. Guests can relax in the lounge or on the patio. Breakfast is served in the lovely dining room overlooking the garden.

Rooms 5 en suite (2 fmly) **Facilities** STV TVL Cen ht **Parking** 5 **Notes** ⊗ Closed Dec-Feb

KILLARNEY *continued*

Ashville

★★★★ GUEST HOUSE

Rock Rd
☎ 064 6636405 📠 064 6636778
e-mail: info@ashvillekillarney.com
dir: *In town centre. Off N end of High St onto Rock Rd*

This inviting house is just a stroll from the town centre and near the N22 Tralee road. Bedrooms are comfortably furnished and there is a relaxing sitting room and dining room. There is a private car park and tours can be arranged.

Rooms 12 en suite (4 fmly) (4 GF) **Facilities** TV10B STV FTV TVL tea/coffee Direct Dial Cen ht Wi-fi **Parking** 13 **Notes** ⊗ Closed Nov–1 Mar

Crystal Springs

★★★★ GUEST HOUSE

Ballycasheen
☎ 064 6633272 & 6635518 📠 064 6635518
e-mail: crystalsprings@eircom.net
web: www.crystalspringsbb.com
dir: *From Killarney town turn right off Cork Rd at 1st lights & Texaco. Left onto Rookery Rd, to end & Crystal Springs is across road at T-junct*

This luxurious house is on the outskirts of the town and the garden runs down to the River Flesk. It overlooks a historic mill and is close to the mountains, lakes, golf courses and Killarney National Park. Bedrooms are attractively decorated and well equipped and there is a charming lounge and dining room where delicious breakfasts are served.

Rooms 7 en suite (3 fmly) (3 GF) **Facilities** STV TVL tea/coffee Dinner available Direct Dial Cen ht Fishing **Parking** 14 **Notes** Closed 21–26 Dec

Killarney Villa Country House & Gardens

★★★★ BED AND BREAKFAST

Mallow Rd
☎ 064 6631878 📠 064 6631878
e-mail: killarneyvilla@ie-post.com
web: www.killarneyvilla.com
dir: *N22 E from Killarney, over 1st rdbt, continue after 2nd rdbt on N22 & N72 for 2km, left at rdbt, Villa 300mtrs on right*

This luxurious country home has a rooftop conservatory where complimentary beverages are available. It is situated on the outskirts of the town within easy reach of the beautiful Killarney lakes and mountains. Bedrooms are very comfortable and well equipped, and there is a lovely dining room where a variety of dishes are available at breakfast.

Rooms 6 en suite (3 fmly) S €45–€50; D €74–€84* **Facilities** STV TVL tea/coffee Cen ht **Parking** 20 **Notes** LB ⊗ No Children 6yrs Closed Nov–Etr 🍽

Kingfisher Lodge

★★★★ GUEST HOUSE

Lewis Rd
☎ 064 6637131 📠 064 6639871
e-mail: info@kingfisherlodgekillarney.com
dir: *Dublin link straight through 1st rdbt. Right at next rdbt towards town centre, Lodge on left*

This welcoming, family-run modern guest house, situated within walking distance of the town centre, has comfortable well-appointed bedrooms. A delicious breakfast is served in the attractively decorated dining room and there is also a relaxing lounge. A drying room is available for fishing and wet gear. Golf, walking and fishing trips can be arranged.

Rooms 10 en suite (1 fmly) (2 GF) S €40–€70; D €65–€110 **Facilities** FTV TVL tea/coffee Direct Dial Cen ht Wi-fi Walking, fishing, horseriding, golf can be booked **Parking** 11 **Notes** LB Closed 15 Dec–13 Feb

Redwood

★★★★ BED AND BREAKFAST

Tralee Rd
☎ 064 6634754 & 087 299 8924 📠 064 6634754
e-mail: redwd@indigo.ie
dir: *N22 N from Killarney, Redwood 3.2km from Cleeny rdbt on left*

Set in landscaped grounds 4 kilometres from the town centre, this is a very comfortable house. Bedrooms are well furnished, and the lounge and dining rooms are very spacious with picture windows framing the garden. A good choice is offered at breakfast.

Rooms 6 en suite (3 fmly) (2 GF) S €55–€70; D €72–€90 **Facilities** STV tea/coffee Cen ht Wi-fi **Parking** 6 **Notes** LB ⊗

Shraheen House

★★★★ BED AND BREAKFAST

Ballycasheen, Off Cork Rd (N22)
☎ 064 6631286
e-mail: info@shraheenhouse.com
dir: *On Ballycasheen-Woodlawn road, 1.6km off N71 at lights by Dromhall Hotel. Off N22 at Whitebridge Caravan Park Sign*

The large modern house stands in extensive grounds on a quiet road. The bedrooms are all well equipped and have attractive soft furnishings. The quiet gardens and the pleasant sun lounge are very relaxing. Within easy reach of three golf courses or local fishing.

Rooms 6 en suite (2 fmly) (3 GF) S €50–€60; D €70–€80 **Facilities** STV TVL tea/coffee Cen ht Wi-fi **Parking** 8 **Notes** ⊗ No Children 4yrs Closed Dec–Jan 🍽

PREMIER COLLECTION

Carrig House Country House & Restaurant

★★★★★ ◉ GUEST HOUSE

Caragh Lake
☎ 066 9769100 📠 066 9769166
e-mail: info@carrighouse.com

A warm and friendly atmosphere combines with a range of relaxing lounges to make a visit to Carrig House a truly memorable event. The house is in excellent condition, nestled among well-kept gardens by the shore of the lake. The spacious bedrooms are all individually decorated and many have superb views of the lake, as does the dining room, where delicious evening meals are available. The hospitality shown by hosts Mary and Frank and their team is outstanding.

Rooms 16 en suite **Facilities** TVL Dinner available Direct Dial Cen ht Licensed 🛶 Fishing **Parking** 20 **Notes** No Children 8yrs Closed Oct–Feb

Grove Lodge

★★★★ GUEST HOUSE

Killarney Rd
☎ 066 9761157 & 08720 73238 📠 066 9762330
e-mail: info@grovelodge.com
dir: *800mtrs from Killorglin Bridge on N72 (Killarney road)*

A lovely riverside house extended and developed to a high standard, with all the rooms en suite and fully equipped. Mrs Foley is an enthusiastic host who likes to please her guests and for those who just want to relax there is a patio seating area in the garden by the river.

Rooms 10 en suite (4 fmly) (4 GF) **Facilities** STV tea/coffee Direct Dial Cen ht Fishing **Parking** 15 **Notes** ⊗ Closed 22–30 Dec

Dromin Farmhouse (V806902)

★★★ FARMHOUSE

Milltown Post Office
☎ 066 9761867 Mrs M Foley
e-mail: drominfarmhouse@yahoo.com
dir: 3km from Killorglin and Milltown. Off N70 1km from Killorglin at sign after factory, continue 2km

Set on a sheep and cattle farm with fantastic mountain views, this elevated bungalow is near to local beaches, golf, fishing and horse riding. A TV lounge is available and babysitting can be arranged. The interesting High Tea menu includes local seafood. Reservations are appreciated.

Rooms 4 en suite (2 fmly) (4 GF) **Facilities** TVL tea/coffee Dinner available Cen ht **Parking** 10 **Notes** ⊗ Closed Nov-16 Mar 42 acres dairy/sheep

Hillview Farmhouse (V800908)

★★★ FARMHOUSE

☎ 066 9767117 📠 066 9767910 Ms D Stephens
e-mail: dstephens@eircom.net
dir: On N70 between Killorgin & Milltown

This working dairy and sheep farmhouse is a good base for touring Dingle and the Ring of Kerry. There are comfortable bedrooms, a cosy lounge, and a dining room where Dorothea Stephens' home baking is a speciality.

Rooms 4 en suite (3 fmly) (2 GF) S €50; D €70-€80* **Facilities** TVL Cen ht **Parking** 8 **Notes** ⊗ Closed Nov-Feb 100 acres mixed

O'Regan's Country Home & Gardens

★★★ BED AND BREAKFAST

Bansha
☎ 066 9761200 📠 066 9761200
e-mail: jeromeoregan@eircom.net
dir: 1.6km from Killorglin on N70, turn right. Beside Killorglin golf club

This dormer bungalow is set in colourful, award-winning gardens just off the N70, adjacent to Killorglin Golf Club. The bedrooms are comfortable, there is an inviting breakfast room, and the lounge overlooks the beautiful garden.

Rooms 4 en suite (1 fmly) (4 GF) S €40-€45; D €64-€68* **Facilities** TVL tea/coffee Cen ht Golf 18 **Parking** 8 **Notes** LB ⊗ Closed Nov-Feb 🐾

TRALEE Map 1 A2

Brianville

★★★★ BED AND BREAKFAST

Clogherbrien, Fenit Rd
☎ 066 7126645 📠 066 7126645
e-mail: michsmit@gofree.indigo.ie
web: www.brianville-tralee.com
dir: R558 (Tralee-Fenit road), 2km from Tralee

This welcoming large yellow bungalow, situated on the road to Fenit on the outskirts of Tralee, is within easy reach of beaches, golf and the Aqua Dome. Bedrooms vary in size and are attractively furnished with hand-crafted pine. Breakfast is served in the bright sitting/dining room overlooking the well-tended garden.

Rooms 5 en suite (1 fmly) S €40-€50; D €66-€70* **Facilities** STV TVL tea/coffee Cen ht **Parking** 10 **Notes** ⊗ 🐾

Tralee Townhouse

★★★ GUEST HOUSE

1-2 High St
☎ 066 7181111 📠 066 7181112
e-mail: traleetownhouse@eircom.net
dir: In town

Located in the town centre, close to pubs, restaurants and Splash World, this friendly guest house offers well-equipped bedrooms with a lift to all floors. Guests can relax in the comfortable lounge and Eleanor Collins serves a variety of breakfast dishes and home baked breads.

Rooms 19 en suite (2 fmly) (9 smoking) **Facilities** STV FTV TVL tea/coffee Direct Dial Cen ht Lift Wi-fi **Notes** LB ⊗ Closed 24-28 Dec

---

CO KILDARE

ATHY Map 1 C3

PREMIER COLLECTION

Coursetown Country House

★★★★★ BED AND BREAKFAST

Stradbally Rd
☎ 059 8631101 📠 059 8632740
e-mail: coursetown@hotmail.com
dir: 3km from Athy. N78 at Athy onto R428

This charming Victorian country house stands on a 100-hectare tillage farm and bird sanctuary. It has been extensively refurbished, and all bedrooms are furnished to the highest standards. Convalescent or disabled guests are especially welcome, and Iris and Jim Fox are happy to share their knowledge of the Irish countryside and its wildlife.

Rooms 5 en suite (1 GF) **Facilities** TVL tea/coffee Direct Dial Cen ht **Parking** 22 **Notes** No Children 12yrs Closed 15 Nov-15 Mar

---

CO KILKENNY

KILKENNY Map 1 C3

AA GUEST ACCOMMODATION OF THE YEAR FOR IRELAND

Rosquil House

★★★★ GUEST HOUSE

Castlecomer Rd
☎ 056 7721419 📠 056 7750398
e-mail: info@rosquilhouse.com
dir: From N77, 1km from rail & bus staions, near Newpark Hotel

Rosquil House is newly built and furnished with great attention to design and detail. Just a few minutes from the Kilkenny town centre. Bedrooms are stylishly furnished with guest comfort in mind, as are the guest sitting and breakfast rooms. There is a real treat in store at breakfast where stewed fruits and a choice of hot dishes are complimented by Rhoda Nolan's home baking. There is ample off-street parking available.

Rooms 7 en suite (1 fmly) (3 GF) **Facilities** STV tea/coffee Direct Dial Cen ht Licensed **Parking** 10 **Notes** ⊗ Closed 23-29 Dec

KILKENNY *continued*

Butler House

★★★★ GUEST HOUSE

Patrick St
☎ 056 7765707 & 7722828 ▤ 056 7765626
e-mail: res@butler.ie
web: www.butler.ie
dir: *In centre near Kilkenny Castle*

Once the dower house of Kilkenny Castle, this fine Georgian building fronts onto the main street with secluded gardens at the rear, through which you stroll to have full breakfast in Kilkenny Design Centre. A continental breakfast is served in bedrooms, which feature contemporary décor. There is a comfortable foyer lounge and conference-banqueting suites.

Rooms 13 en suite (4 fmly) S €60-€155; D €100-€225 **Facilities** STV FTV tea/coffee Direct Dial Cen ht Wi-fi **Conf** Max 120 Thtr 120 Class 40 Board 40 **Parking** 24 **Notes** LB ⊗ Closed 24-29 Dec Civ Wed 70

CO LAOIS

PORTLAOISE | Map 1 C3

O'Sullivan

★★★ BED AND BREAKFAST

8 Kelly Ville Park
☎ 0502 22774 ▤ 0502 80863
dir: *In town centre opp County Hall car park*

This family-run semi-detached house on the edge of the town offers a homely atmosphere. The en suite bedrooms are comfortable and secure parking is available.

Rooms 5 en suite (1 fmly) (2 GF) S €75; D €100* **Facilities** STV TVL Cen ht **Parking** 8 **Notes** LB ⊗ Closed 21 Dec-1 Jan ⊛

CO LIMERICK

ADARE | Map 1 B3

Berkeley Lodge

★★★★ BED AND BREAKFAST

Station Rd
☎ 061 396857 ▤ 061 396857
e-mail: berlodge@iol.ie
dir: *In village centre*

Situated just off the main street of this pretty village, Berkeley Lodge offers comfortable, well equipped and carefully decorated accommodation. The lounge leads on to an attractive conservatory-style breakfast room, which offers an extensive menu.

Rooms 6 en suite (2 fmly) (1 GF) S €60; D €80* **Facilities** TVL tea/coffee Cen ht **Parking** 6 **Notes** ⊗

Carrigane House

★★★★ BED AND BREAKFAST

Rienroe
☎ 061 396778
e-mail: carrigane.house@oceanfree.net
dir: *Off N21 rdbt 0.4km NE of Adare onto Croom road, 2nd house on right*

Guests can be assured of a warm welcome at this purpose-built house situated close to the pretty village of Adare. There is a lovely colourful garden and a relaxing lounge, while breakfast is a particular treat. Bedrooms are attractively decorated, and one is on the ground floor. Ample parking is available.

Rooms 6 en suite (3 fmly) (1 GF) S €50-€60; D €70-€78* **Facilities** TVL tea/coffee Cen ht **Parking** 10 **Notes** ⊗ Closed 15 Dec-10 Jan

Coatesland House B&B

★★★★ BED AND BREAKFAST

Tralee/Killarney Rd, Graigue
☎ 061 396372 ▤ 061 396833
e-mail: coatesfd@indigo.ie
dir: *1km from Adare on N21 Tralee Rd*

Coatesland House, situated on the main Killarney road five minutes from Adare village, is a very well appointed house featuring attractive bedrooms, all with en suite facilities. Proprietors Florence and Donal Hogan are welcoming and friendly and give superb attention to detail. Nearby activities include hunting, fishing, golf and there is also an equestrian centre.

Rooms 6 en suite **Facilities** STV FTV TVL tea/coffee Direct Dial Cen ht **Parking** 18 **Notes** Closed 8 Dec-1 Jan

BRUFF | Map 1 B3

The Old Bank Bed & Breakfast

★★★★ BED AND BREAKFAST

Main St
☎ 061 389969 ▤ 061 389969
e-mail: info@theoldbank.ie
dir: *From Limerick on R512, on right on main street*

The Old Bank is an inviting and imposing building in the town of Bruff. It has been lovingly refurbished and decorated by Miriam and Pat Sadlier-Barry. There are interconnecting family bedrooms, some with four poster beds and all are spacious and are furnished with guest comfort in mind. There is a cosy library lounge with open fire and breakfast is served where the original bank transactions took place.

Rooms 8 en suite (1 fmly) S €35-€50; D €55* **Facilities** TVL tea/coffee Cen ht Wi-fi Gymnasium **Parking** 9 **Notes** LB ⊗ Closed 24-25 Dec

KILMALLOCK | Map 1 B2

PREMIER COLLECTION

Flemingstown House (R629255)

★★★★★ FARMHOUSE

☎ 063 98093 ▤ 063 98546 Mrs I Sheedy-King
e-mail: info@flemingstown.com
dir: *On R512 Kilmallock-Fermoy route*

A lovely 18th-century farmhouse, which has been modernised to provide stylish facilities throughout. Public rooms include a comfortably furnished sitting room with antiques. At breakfast, Imelda's home baking and local produce are on offer in the delightful dining room overlooking the garden. Dinner is available by arrangement. The area is excellent for walking, horse riding, hunting, angling and golfing.

Rooms 5 en suite (2 fmly) **Facilities** tea/coffee Dinner available Cen ht Riding **Parking** 20 **Notes** No Children 8yrs Closed Nov-Feb 120 acres beef

LIMERICK | Map 1 B3

Clifton House

★★★ GUEST HOUSE

Ennis Rd
☎ 061 451166 ▤ 061 451224
e-mail: cliftonhouse@eircom.net
dir: *On N18 towards Shannon Airport, opp Woodfield House Hotel*

Providing well-equipped, attractive and very comfortable bedrooms has been the aim of the refurbishment of Michael and Mary Powell's guest house. Complimentary tea and coffee are available in the spacious, relaxing lounge.

Rooms 16 en suite **Facilities** STV TVL Direct Dial Cen ht **Parking** 22 **Notes** ⊗ Closed 21 Dec-2 Jan

CO LONGFORD

LONGFORD
Map 1 C4

Longford Country House

★★★★ BED AND BREAKFAST

Ennybegs
☎ 043 23320 🖹 043 23516
e-mail: info@longfordcountryhouse.com
web: www.longfordcountryhouse.com
dir: 3rd exit off 2nd rdbt on N4 Longford bypass, 5km, left at x-rds after Old Forge pub, 2nd house on right

A hospitable, Tudor-style house. The parlour has a wrought-iron spiral stairway to the library loft, as well as a cosy sitting room with turf fire and a dining room where dinner is served by arrangement. Other facilities include a games room and pitch and putt. Self-catering cottages are also available.

Rooms 6 rms (5 en suite) (2 fmly) **Facilities** FTV TVL tea/coffee Dinner available Cen ht Pitch & putt course Games room Aromatherapy **Parking** 20 **Notes** ⊗ RS Nov-Mar open by arrangement only

CO LOUTH

DUNDALK
Map 1 D4

Rosemount

★★★★ GUEST ACCOMMODATION

Dublin Rd
☎ 042 9335878 🖹 042 9335878
e-mail: maisieb7@eircom.net
dir: On N1 2km S of Dundalk

This handsome bungalow stands in beautiful gardens on the southern outskirts of the town close to Dundalk IT College. The nicely furnished bedrooms are attractively decorated and have many thoughtful extras. There is also a comfortable lounge and ample parking.

Rooms 6 annexe en suite (4 fmly) (6 GF) S €50; D €70* **Facilities** STV FTV TVL tea/coffee Cen ht Wi-fi **Conf** Max 20 **Parking** 8 **Notes** LB ⊗

CO MAYO

ACHILL ISLAND
Map 1 A4

Gray's

★★★★ GUEST HOUSE

Dugort
☎ 098 43244 & 43315
dir: 11km NW of Achill Sound. Off R319 to Doogort

This welcoming guest house is in Doogort, on the northern shore of Achill Island, at the foot of the Slievemore Mountains. There is a smart conservatory and various lounges, the cosy bedrooms are well appointed, and dinner is served nightly by arrangement in the cheerful

dining room. A self-contained villa, ideal for families, is also available.

Rooms 5 en suite 10 annexe en suite (4 fmly) (2 GF) **Facilities** TVL tea/coffee Dinner available Cen ht Licensed ⎚ Pool Table **Parking** 30 **Notes** Closed Oct-Feb ⊗

Lavelle's Seaside House

★★★ GUEST ACCOMMODATION

Dooega
☎ 098 45116 & 01 2828142
e-mail: info@lavellesseasidehouse.com
web: www.lavellesseasidehouse.com
dir: R319, NW from Achill Sound, Gob an Choire. Continue for 5km turn left onto L1405 Dooega/Dumma Eige junct & continue for 5km

Friendliness and good food are offered at this comfortable guest house close to the beach. Facilities include a lounge, breakfast room, and a traditional pub where seafood is available during the high season. The more-spacious bedrooms are in the new wing.

Rooms 14 en suite (5 fmly) (14 GF) S €40-€45; D €70-€80* **Facilities** TVL tea/coffee Dinner available Cen ht Licensed Pool Table **Parking** 20 **Notes** LB ⊗ Closed 2 Nov-mid Mar RS Dinner served Jul/Aug only

BALLINA
Map 1 B4

Abbey B&B

★★★ BED AND BREAKFAST

Foxford Rd
☎ 096 78499

This welcoming house is set in landscaped gardens near the train station close to the town. The first floor's individually styled bedrooms all feature comfortable beds and furniture made from reclaimed pine. The hosts are always on hand to recommend one of the many restaurants in the town.

Rooms 4 en suite S €45; D €75 **Facilities** FTV tea/coffee Cen ht **Parking** 9 **Notes** ⊗ Closed 22 Dec-1 Jan

BELMULLET
Map 1 A5

Drom Caoin Bed & Breakfast

★★★ BED AND BREAKFAST

Sraid na hEaglaise
☎ 097 81195 🖹 097 81195
e-mail: stay@dromcaoin.ie
dir: N59 to Bangor Erris, then R313 to Belmullet. 1st left off rdbt, 0.5km on left

Set in sloping gardens overlooking Blacksod Bay, Drom Caoin is the welcoming family home of Máirín and Gerry Murphy. Bedrooms are comfortable and include two spacious apartments for extended stays. The breakfast room and lounge are relaxing with good reading materials and offer good views. Drying rooms and cycle storage

facilities make this an ideal base for those who enjoy outdoor pursuits.

Rooms 5 en suite 1 annexe en suite (1 fmly) (2 GF) **Facilities** TVL tea/coffee Dinner available Cen ht Wi-fi **Parking** 7 **Notes** Closed 15 Dec-15 Jan

CASTLEBAR
Map 1 B4

Lough Lannagh Lodge

★★★ GUEST ACCOMMODATION

Old Westport Rd
☎ 094 902 7111 🖹 094 902 7295
e-mail: info@loughlannagh.ie
web: www.loughlannagh.ie
dir: N5 around Castlebar. 3rd rdbt, 2nd exit. Next left, past playground, 1st building on right

Lough Lannagh is in a delightful wooded area within walking distance of Castlebar. There is a conference centre, fitness centre, tennis, table tennis, laundry and drying facilities, a private kitchen, and many activities for children. Bedrooms are well appointed and breakfast is served in the café. Dinner is available by appointment for groups.

Rooms 24 en suite (24 fmly) (12 GF) **Facilities** FTV TVL Dinner available Direct Dial Cen ht Wi-fi ⎚ Sauna Gymnasium Steam room, table tennis, child activities Jul-Aug **Conf** Max 100 Thtr 100 Class 54 Board 34 **Parking** 24 **Notes** ⊗ Closed 10 Dec-12 Jan

WESTPORT
Map 1 B4

Carrabaun House
★★★★ BED AND BREAKFAST

Carrabaun, Leenane Rd
☎ 098 26196 📄 098 28466
e-mail: carrabaun@anu.ie
dir: On N59 S. Leave Westport town, 1.6km pass Maxol station on left, house 200mtrs

This elevated house has stunning views of Croagh Patrick and Clew Bay, situated on the outskirts of Westport town. The Gavin family are friendly hosts and serve a hearty breakfast. Bedrooms are attractively furnished and there is a comfortable guest sitting room and dining room. There is private parking, and lovely gardens surround the house.

Rooms 6 en suite (6 fmly) (1 GF) **Facilities** TVL tea/coffee Cen ht **Parking** 12 **Notes** ⊗ Closed 16-31 Dec

Bertra House (L903823)
★★★ FARMHOUSE

Thornhill, Murrisk
☎ 098 64833 📄 098 64833 Mrs M Gill
e-mail: bertrahse@eircom.net
dir: W of Westport off R335 near Croagh Patrick on L1833

This attractive bungalow overlooks the Blue Flag Bertra beach. Four bedrooms are en suite and the fifth has its own bathroom. Breakfast is generous and Mrs Gill offers tea and home-baked cakes on arrival in the cosy lounge.

Rooms 5 rms (4 en suite) (1 pri facs) (3 fmly) (5 GF) S €50-€52; D €70-€76* **Facilities** TVL tea/coffee Cen ht **Parking** 7 **Notes** LB ⊗ No Children 6yrs Closed 15 Nov-15 Mar ⊜ 40 acres beef

CO MEATH

DUNSANY
Map 1 C4

The Dunsany Lodge
★★★★ RESTAURANT WITH ROOMS

Kiltale
☎ 046 9026339 📄 046 9026342
e-mail: info@dunsanylodge.ie

Dunsany Lodge is a contemporary building located less than 30 minutes from Dublin at the gateway to the historic and picturesque Boyne Valley. The bedrooms are smart and comfortably appointed, and the Bia Restaurant offers a wide range of international dishes cooked with care; less formal fare is served in the bistro bar.

Rooms 10 en suite (10 GF) **Facilities** FTV TVL tea/coffee Dinner available Direct Dial Cen ht ♨ **Conf** Max 60 Thtr 60 Class 20 Board 20 **Parking** 70

NAVAN
Map 1 C4

Killyon
★★★★ GUEST ACCOMMODATION

Dublin Rd
☎ 046 907 1224 📄 046 907 2766
e-mail: info@killyonguesthouse.ie
dir: On N3, River Boyne side, opp Ardboyne Hotel

This luxurious house has fine views over the River Boyne from its balcony. Comfortable, well-appointed bedrooms and an inviting attractive lounge make this a popular place to stay. Owner Mrs Fogarty offers a wide range of home cooking.

Rooms 6 en suite (1 fmly) (1 GF) S €45-€50; D €70-€80* **Facilities** STV TVL Direct Dial Cen ht Wi-fi Fishing **Parking** 10 **Notes** ⊗ Closed 23-25 Dec

The Yellow House
★★★★ BED AND BREAKFAST

Springfield Glen, Dublin Rd
☎ 046 9073338
e-mail: info@theyellowhouse.ie
dir: N3 from Dublin, left at 2nd lights on approach to Navan

Located on the southern approach to the town, this friendly house is popular with return guests. It offers well-appointed rooms and a comfortable lounge reserved for residents. A number of choices are available at breakfast, and off-road parking is provided in mature gardens.

Rooms 4 rms (3 en suite) (1 pri facs) (2 fmly) **Facilities** FTV TVL tea/coffee Cen ht Wi-fi **Parking** 12 **Notes** LB ⊗

TRIM
Map 1 C4

Brogans
★★★ GUEST HOUSE

High St
☎ 046 943 1237 📄 046 943 7648
e-mail: info@brogans.ie
web: www.brogans.ie
dir: Exit M50 junct 6 at rdbt, 1st exit to Blanchardstown, N3 rdbt 2nd exit, turn 1st left, left again onto R154. Continue to High St

Situated in the designated heritage town of Trim, this guest house was built nearly two centuries ago using stone from Trim Castle. The bedrooms in the main house have been refurbished and there are new rooms in the courtyard, all are comfortable and furnished to a high standard. There is a cosy traditional bar, and dinner is available in the smart Beacon Restaurant and bar. This

guest house is convenient to New Grange, The Hill of Tara and many championship golf courses.

Rooms 18 en suite (3 fmly) (4 GF) S €55-€65; D €99-€120 **Facilities** STV TVL tea/coffee Dinner available Direct Dial Cen ht Licensed **Conf** Max 35 Thtr 35 Class 35 Board 35 **Notes** ⊗ Closed Good Fri & 25 Dec

CO SLIGO

ACLARE
Map 1 B4

Haggart Lodge
★★★ BED AND BREAKFAST

Lislea
☎ 071 9181954
e-mail: mleheny@eircom.net

Maeve Leheny welcomes guests to her comfortable home overlooking the Ox Mountains in west Sligo, near the Mayo border. Traditional country-cooked dinners are available if booked before midday, and home baking is a feature of breakfast. This is a pet friendly property, where resident dogs Tyke and Tyra will vacate their kennels if required. There are stables available nearby.

Rooms 4 rms (3 en suite) S €30-€45; D €60-€80 **Facilities** TVL Dinner available Cen ht Wi-fi **Parking** 12 **Notes** LB

BALLINTOGHER
Map 1 B5

Kingsfort Country House
★★★★ GUEST HOUSE

☎ 071 911 5111
e-mail: bernard@kingsfortcountryhouse.com
dir: From Collooney onto Ballygawley (8km), follow signs

This charming guest house is situated in the village of Ballintogher south of Sligo town. Built in 1790 as a court house, it has been magnificently restored and decorated in an understated rustic style providing all modern comforts. Two of the bedrooms are in the main house, and six, including one adapted for the less mobile, are in the courtyard building. There is a sitting room and TV lounge for guests, and dinner is available by prior arrangement.

Rooms 2 en suite 6 annexe en suite (1 fmly) (3 GF) S €70-€110; D €120-€190* **Facilities** TVL Dinner available Direct Dial Cen ht **Parking** 10 **Notes** Closed Nov-Mar

BALLYMOTE — Map 1 B4

Church View

★★★★ BED AND BREAKFAST

Main St, Gurteen
☎ 071 9182935
e-mail: info@thechurchview.com
dir: *From Ballymote at x-rds head towards Gurteen, on left beside church*

Located in the centre of Gurteen village, a half hour's drive from Knock airport, this architect designed townhouse is home to Jacci Conlon and her family. Bedrooms are spacious and individually decorated. A wide selection of breakfast options is available, served in the smart dining room.

Rooms 5 en suite (2 fmly) (1 GF) S €45-€50; D €72-€90 **Facilities** STV TVL tea/coffee Cen ht Wi-fi **Parking** 5 **Notes** ✖

BALLYSADARE — Map 1 B5

Seashore House

★★★ BED AND BREAKFAST

Lisduff
☎ 071 916 7827   🖷 071 916 7827
e-mail: seashore@oceanfree.net
dir: *N4 onto N59 W at Ballisadore, 4km Seashore signed, 0.6km right to house*

An attractive dormer bungalow in a quiet seashore location. A comfortable lounge with open turf fire and sunny conservatory dining room looking out over attractive landscaped gardens to sea and mountain scenery. Bedrooms are attractively appointed and comfortable, and there is also a tennis court and bicycle storage.

Rooms 5 rms (4 en suite) (2 fmly) (3 GF) S €50-€55; D €76-€80* **Facilities** STV TVL Cen ht 🏊 Fishing Solarium **Parking** 6 **Notes** LB ✖ No Children

BELTRA — Map 1 B5

Rafter's Woodifield Inn

★★★★ GUEST ACCOMMODATION

Larkhill
☎ 091 071916610
dir: *On N59*

This delightful property is attached to a cosy traditional pub, established in 1775, that serves bar food in the evening. Guests can relax in the conservatory lounge while enjoying the views of the Ox Mountains. Three of the bedrooms are on the ground floor and are fitted to accommodate less mobile guests; all bedrooms well furnished, individually decorated and identified by names

from the local area. Breakfast menu includes Carol's brown bread, spotted dog scones and preserves.

Rooms 5 en suite (3 fmly) (3 GF) S €45-€50; D €80 **Facilities** FTV TVL Cen ht Licensed Wi-fi **Parking** 25 **Notes** ✖ ☕

DRUMCLIFFE — Map 1 B5

Willsborough House B&B

★★★ BED AND BREAKFAST

Cullaghbeg
☎ 071 9173526
e-mail: willsboroughhouse@eircom.net
dir: *7km on N15 from Sligo, after restaurant on left, take 2nd on right*

This attractive house is tucked under Ben Bulben just off the N15 between Drumcliffe and Sligo town and within walking distance of Davis's pub and restaurant. The bedrooms are well appointed and suitable for families. Fiona and Anthony produce a fine breakfast with local produce and home baking a feature. Cycle routes, bike hire and horse riding near by.

Rooms 3 en suite (2 fmly) **Facilities** tea/coffee Cen ht Bicycle hire, Dog boarding kennels **Parking** 4 **Notes** ✖ ☕

INISHCRONE — Map 1 B5

PREMIER COLLECTION

Seasons Lodge

★★★★★ BED AND BREAKFAST

Bartragh
☎ 096 37122
e-mail: dermot@seasonslodge.ie
web: www.seasonslodge.ie
dir: *Beside Enniscrone Golf Club*

This modern guest house is next to Enniscrone Golf Course and close to the famous seaweed baths and a lovely beach. The spacious bedrooms are fitted to a high standard, are all on the ground floor and have access to the garden. There is a relaxing sitting and dining room where breakfast is served. Proprietor Dermot O'Regan is happy to arrange golf or tours.

Rooms 4 en suite (2 fmly) (4 GF) **Facilities** STV TVL Direct Dial Cen ht **Parking** 10 **Notes** ✖ No Children 8yrs Closed Dec-Jan

SLIGO — Map 1 B5

Aisling

★★★ BED AND BREAKFAST

Cairns Hill
☎ 071 916 0704   🖷 071 916 0704
e-mail: aislingsligo@eircom.net
dir: *N4 to Sligo, right at 1st lights, S from Sligo past Esso fuel station, left at lights*

This delightful home of Des and Nan Faul has a beautiful garden and is conveniently situated on the southern end of the town and close to Sligo race course. Bedrooms are comfortably furnished and there is a cosy sitting and dining room for guests to relax and enjoy mountain views.

Rooms 4 rms (3 en suite) (2 fmly) (4 GF) **Facilities** STV FTV TVL Cen ht **Parking** 6 **Notes** ✖ No Children 6yrs Closed Dec-6 Jan

TOBERCURRY — Map 1 B4

Cruckawn House

★★★ BED AND BREAKFAST

Ballymote/Boyle Rd
☎ 071 918 5188   🖷 071 918 5188
e-mail: cruckawn@esatclear.ie
dir: *300mtrs off N17 on R294, on right, overlooking golf course*

Overlooking the golf course, just a short walk from the town centre, Cruckawn House offers friendly hospitality. The dining room adjoins the comfortable sun lounge, and there is also a television lounge. Salmon and coarse fishing, horse riding and mountain climbing are all available nearby and the area is renowned for traditional Irish music.

Rooms 5 en suite (2 fmly) **Facilities** TVL Dinner available Cen ht Golf 9 ⛳ Gymnasium Pool Table Game & coarse fishing, bike hire **Parking** 8 **Notes** ✖ Closed Nov-Feb

CO TIPPERARY

CASHEL
Map 1 C3

Ard Ri House

★★★★ GUEST ACCOMMODATION

Dualla Rd
☎ 062 63143 📄 062 63037
e-mail: donalcreed@eircom.net
dir: Turn 1st right after Information Office onto R688, turn left after church onto R691, 1km on right

A warm welcome awaits you at this non-smoking house, only a short distance from the town on the Kilkenny Road. All of the bedrooms are comfortably furnished with thoughtful extras, and are on the ground floor. The breakfast served by Eileen features locally sourced ingredients from a varied menu. Facilities are available for children.

Rooms 4 en suite (1 fmly) (4 GF); D €70-€80
Facilities TVL tea/coffee Cen ht Wi-fi **Parking** 8 **Notes** ⊗ Closed Nov-Feb

Aulber House

★★★★ GUEST HOUSE

Golden Rd
☎ 062 63713 & 087 6314720 📄 062 63715
e-mail: info@aulberhouse.com
web: www.aulberhouse.com
dir: From Cashel on N74. First house on right

A newly-built guest house, set in landscaped gardens just a 5-minute walk from the Rock of Cashel and town centre. Spacious bedrooms are thoughtfully furnished and equipped, and include one fitted for the less mobile. Relax by the open fire in the sitting room, or enjoy views of the surrounding countryside and the Rock from the first-floor lounge.

Rooms 12 en suite (2 fmly) (3 GF) S €45-€80; D €80-€120* **Facilities** FTV TVL tea/coffee Direct Dial Cen ht Wi-fi **Conf** Max 40 Thtr 40 Class 30 Board 25 **Parking** 20 **Notes** ⊗ Closed 23 Dec-23 Jan

Thornbrook House

★★★★ BED AND BREAKFAST

Dualla Rd
☎ 062 62388 📄 062 61480
e-mail: thornbrookhouse@eircom.net
web: www.thornbrookhouse.com
dir: 1st right after tourist office onto Friar St, left after church onto R691, house 1km on right

Visitors to Thornbrook will relish the combined skills of the Kennedys. Mary runs this attractively appointed bungalow with great attention to detail, while the superbly landscaped gardens are the handiwork of Willie

Kennedy. Comfortable lounge and bedrooms, ample parking.

Rooms 5 rms (3 en suite) (1 fmly) (5 GF) S €50-€60; D €64-€80 **Facilities** tea/coffee Cen ht Wi-fi **Parking** 8 **Notes** ⊗ No Children 4yrs Closed Nov-Mar

Ashmore House

★★★ BED AND BREAKFAST

John St
☎ 062 61286 📄 062 62789
e-mail: info@ashmorehouse.ie
dir: Off N8 in town centre onto John St, house 100mtrs on right

Ashmore House is set in a pretty walled garden in the town centre with an enclosed car park. Guests have use of a large sitting and dining room, and bedrooms come in a variety of sizes from big family rooms to a more compact double.

Rooms 5 en suite (2 fmly) S €50-€70; D €75-€90* **Facilities** STV TVL tea/coffee Dinner available Cen ht **Parking** 10 **Notes** ⊗

NENAGH
Map 1 B3

Ashley Park House

★★★★ BED AND BREAKFAST

☎ 067 38223 & 38013 📄 067 38013
e-mail: margaret@ashleypark.com
web: www.ashleypark.com
dir: 6.5km N of Nenagh. Off N52 across lake, signed on left & left under arch

The attractive, colonial style farmhouse was built in 1770. Set in gardens that run down to Lake Ourna, it has spacious bedrooms with quality antique furnishings. Breakfast is served in the dining room overlooking the lake, and dinner is available by arrangement. There is a delightful walled garden, and a boat for the fishing on the lake is available.

Rooms 5 en suite (3 fmly) **Facilities** TVL tea/coffee Dinner available Cen ht Licensed Wi-fi Golf 18 Fishing Rowing boat on lake **Conf** Max 30 Board 30 **Parking** 30 **Notes** ⊗

THURLES
Map 1 C3

PREMIER COLLECTION

Inch House Country House & Restaurant

★★★★★ ⊕ GUEST HOUSE

☎ 0504 51348 & 51261 📄 0504 51754
e-mail: mairin@inchhouse.ie
dir: 6.5km NE of Thurles on R498

This lovely Georgian house was built in 1720 and the Egan family has restored the property. The elegant drawing room ceiling is particularly outstanding among the grand public rooms, and the spacious bedrooms are delightfully appointed. Reservations are essential in the fine restaurant, where an imaginative choice of freshly prepared dishes using local produce is on offer.

Rooms 5 en suite (1 fmly) S €70-€80; D €120-€130* **Facilities** TVL tea/coffee Dinner available Direct Dial Cen ht Licensed Wi-fi **Parking** 40 **Notes** ⊗ Closed Xmas & Etr RS Sun & Mon Restaurant closed Sun & Mon evening Civ Wed 30

PREMIER COLLECTION

The Castle

★★★★★ BED AND BREAKFAST

Twomileborris
☎ 0504 44324 📄 0504 44352
e-mail: b&b@thecastletmb.com
dir: 7km E of Thurles. On N75 200mtrs W of Twomileborris at Castle

Pierce and Joan are very welcoming hosts. Their fascinating house, sheltered by a 16th-century tower house, has been in the Duggan family for 200 years. Bedrooms are comfortable and spacious, there is a relaxing lounge, and the dining room overlooks the delightful garden. Golf, fishing, hill walking, and traditional pubs and restaurants are all nearby. Dinner is available by arrangement.

Rooms 4 en suite (3 fmly) S €50-€60; D €80-€100 **Facilities** STV FTV TVL tea/coffee Dinner available Cen ht Wi-fi 🎣 Fishing Pool Table **Conf** Max 40 Board 20 **Parking** 30 **Notes** LB ⊗

TIPPERARY   Map 1 C3

Ach-na-Sheen House
★★★ GUEST HOUSE

Clonmel Rd
☎ 062 51298   📠 062 80467
e-mail: gernoonan@eircom.net
dir: *In town centre*

This large, modern bungalow is set in a lovely garden and only five minutes walk from the main street of Tipperary town on the N24 road. Public areas include a guest sitting room and dining room and bedrooms are well appointed. There is good off-street parking.

Rooms 8 en suite (5 fmly) (6 GF) S €50-€60;
D €80-€90* **Facilities** STV tea/coffee Cen ht **Parking** 13
Notes ⊗ Closed 11 Dec-8 Jan

Aisling
★★★ BED AND BREAKFAST

Glen of Aherlow
☎ 062 33307   📠 062 82955
e-mail: ladygreg@oceanfree.net
web: www.aislingbedandbreakfast.com
dir: *In town, take R664 at T-lights at Main St*

Aisling is situated 3kms from Tipperary town on the R664 Glen of Aherlow road and close to the train station and Tipperary Golf club. Bedrooms are well furnished and attractively decorated. There is a comfortable guest sitting room and a delightful garden with patio seating. Marian and Bob will arrange day trips and have maps and good information on the locality.

Rooms 5 rms (4 en suite) (1 pri facs) (2 fmly) (5 GF) (2 smoking) S €50; D €80 **Facilities** FTV TVL tea/coffee Dinner available Cen ht Wi-fi **Parking** 4 **Notes** LB

CO WATERFORD

BALLYMACARBRY   Map 1 C2

PREMIER COLLECTION

Glasha Farmhouse (S104106)
★★★★★ 🍴 FARMHOUSE

Glasha
☎ 052 36108   📠 052 36108   Mr & Mrs P O'Gorman
e-mail: glasha@eircom.net
dir: *Signed off R671 between Clommel & Dungarvan*

Excellent accommodation and a warm welcome are assured at this comfortable country house. Two of the bedrooms are on the ground floor and all rooms are individually styled with smart furnishings and lots of personal touches. Home-cooking is a speciality and trout fishing is available on the river which runs through the grounds.

Rooms 8 en suite (5 fmly) (2 GF) **Facilities** TVL tea/coffee Dinner available Cen ht Fishing **Parking** 10
Notes ⊗ Closed 20-27 Dec 150 acres dairy

PREMIER COLLECTION

Hanoras Cottage
★★★★★ GUEST HOUSE

Nire Valley
☎ 052 6136134 & 6136442   📠 052 6136540
e-mail: hanorascottage@eircom.net
dir: *From Clonmel or Dungarvan R672 to Ballymacarbry, at Melodys Bar turn into Nire Valley, establishment by bridge beside church*

Located in the beautiful Nire Valley, Hanoras Cottage offers spacious bedrooms with Jacuzzis. Lounge areas are very comfortable and the award-winning restaurant serves fresh local produce. Mrs Wall's breakfasts are a real feast and deserve to be savoured at leisure.

Rooms 10 en suite S €95; D €150-€170*
Facilities STV FTV TVL tea/coffee Dinner available Direct Dial Cen ht Licensed **Conf** Class 40 **Parking** 15
Notes LB ⊗ No Children Closed Xmas wk RS Sun Restaurant closed Civ Wed 40

DUNGARVAN   Map 1 C2

PREMIER COLLECTION

Castle Country House (S192016)
★★★★★ FARMHOUSE

Millstreet, Cappagh
☎ 058 68049   Mrs J Nugent
e-mail: castlefm@iol.ie
dir: *15km off N25 between Dungarvan & Cappoquin. House signed on N72 & R671. From N72 take R671 for 3.5m, right at Millstreet*

This delightful house is in the west wing of a 15th-century castle. Guests are spoiled by host Joan Nugent who loves to cook and hunt out antiques for her visitors to enjoy. She is helped by her husband, Emmett, who is very proud of his high-tech dairy farm, and is a fount of local knowledge. Bedrooms are spacious and enjoy lovely views. There is a river walk and a beautiful garden to relax in.

Rooms 5 en suite (1 fmly) **Facilities** FTV tea/coffee Dinner available Cen ht Fishing Farm tour **Parking** 11
Notes Closed Dec-Feb 170 acres dairy/beef

PREMIER COLLECTION

Sliabh gCua Farmhouse (S191057)
★★★★★ 🍴 FARMHOUSE

Touraneena, Ballinamult
☎ 058 47120   Mrs B Cullinan
e-mail: breedacullinan@sliabhgcua.com
web: www.sliabhgcua.com
dir: *From Dungarvan take R672 towards Clonmel, continue for 1km to village of Touraneena*

This creeper-clad farmhouse, set in landscaped grounds, is a sign of the warm welcome offered by the Cullinan family. Rooms are comfortably appointed, each with two views of the gardens. Breakfast is a particular delight, with bread baked each morning and a great selection of fruits.

Rooms 4 en suite (1 fmly) S €50; D €90*
Facilities TVL tea/coffee Cen ht Children's playground **Parking** 6 **Notes** LB ⊗ Closed Nov-Mar 🍴 170 acres beef

DUNMORE EAST   Map 1 C2

The Beach Guest House
★★★★ GUEST HOUSE

Lower Village
☎ 051 383316   📠 051 383319
e-mail: beachouse@eircom.net
dir: *R684 from Waterford into Dunmore East, 1st left in village to sea wall, house on left*

This purpose-built guest house is family run and centrally placed facing the beach in this picturesque village. No two bedrooms are alike but all share high standards of comfort and quality with a wealth of thoughtful extras. Expect a delicious breakfast served in the conservatory-style dining room, and relax in the lounge or on the patio.

Rooms 7 en suite (1 fmly) (1 GF) **Facilities** tea/coffee Direct Dial Cen ht Wi-fi **Parking** 11 **Notes** ⊗ No Children 6yrs Closed Nov-Feb

TRAMORE   Map 1 C2

Glenorney
★★★★ BED AND BREAKFAST

Newtown
☎ 051 381056   📠 051 381103
e-mail: glenorney@iol.ie
dir: *On R675 opp Tramore Golf Club*

A beautifully spacious and luxurious home with spectacular views of Tramore Bay, located opposite a championship golf course. Great attention has been paid to detail and there is an extensive breakfast menu. Bedrooms are carefully decorated and the lounge is comfortably furnished. There is also a sun room, patio and garden.

Rooms 6 en suite (2 fmly) (3 GF) **Facilities** TVL tea/coffee Direct Dial Cen ht **Parking** 6 **Notes** ⊗ Closed Xmas

TRAMORE *continued*

Cliff House

★★★★ BED AND BREAKFAST

Cliff Rd
☎ 051 381497 & 391296 📄 051 381497
e-mail: hilary@cliffhouse.ie
dir: *Off R675, left at Ritz thatched pub*

This comfortable and spacious home of the O'Sullivan family is situated overlooking Tramore Bay and has beautiful gardens and a conservatory lounge where guests can relax while enjoying the breathtaking views. All bedrooms are decorated to a high standard, there are rooms with balconies and some rooms are suitable for families. The extensive breakfast menu offers many delicious choices.

Rooms 6 en suite (3 fmly) (3 GF) S €50-€65; D €76-€80* **Facilities** STV TVL tea/coffee Cen ht Wi-fi **Parking** 10 **Notes** LB ⊗ No Children 4yrs Closed Nov-Mar

Cloneen

★★★★ BED AND BREAKFAST

Love Ln
☎ 051 381264 📄 051 381264
e-mail: cloneen@iol.ie
dir: *N25 onto R675 to Tramore, Majestic Hotel on right, continue up hill until road bears left, take 1st left*

This pleasant family home is situated on a quiet residential area off the coast road and within walking distance of the seaside town of Tramore. Bedrooms are stylishly furnished with guest comfort in mind, some with their own patio overlooking the garden. Three rooms are on the ground floor and there are two rooms suitable for families. Guests have use of a conservatory-style sitting room and separate dining room.

Rooms 5 en suite (2 fmly) (3 GF) S €50; D €70-€80* **Facilities** STV TVL tea/coffee Cen ht Wi-fi **Parking** 8

WATERFORD   Map 1 C2

PREMIER COLLECTION

Sion Hill House & Gardens

★★★★★ GUEST ACCOMMODATION

Sion Hill, Ferrybank
☎ 051 851558 📄 051 851678
e-mail: sionhill@eircom.net
dir: *Near city centre on N25 to Rosslare*

Situated close to the city, this 18th-century residence has extensive peaceful gardens, which include a walled garden, a meadow and woodlands. Flanked by two pavilions, the house has been refurbished to provide two fine reception rooms and comfortable en suite bedrooms. The friendly owners like to mix with their guests, as the visitors' book shows.

Rooms 4 en suite (4 fmly) **Facilities** STV TVL tea/coffee Cen ht **Parking** 16 **Notes** ⊗ Closed mid Dec-early Jan

Diamond Hill Country House

★★★★ GUEST HOUSE

Diamond Hill, Slieverue
☎ 051 832855 📄 051 832254
e-mail: info@stayatdiamondhill.com
dir: *2km from Waterford off N25 to Rosslare*

Extensive refurbishment has been carried out to a very high standard at this friendly house. These include spacious new bedrooms, comfortable lounges and a private car park. Diamond Hill is a welcoming home with lovely gardens and a sun terrace.

Rooms 17 en suite (6 fmly) (9 GF) **Facilities** STV TVL tea/coffee Dinner available Direct Dial Cen ht Wi-fi **Parking** 20 **Notes** Closed 22-27 Dec

---

Belmont House

★★★ BED AND BREAKFAST

Belmont Rd, Rosslare Rd, Ferrybank
☎ 051 832174 📄 051 832174
e-mail: belmonthouse@eircom.net
dir: *2km from Waterford on N25 to Rosslare road*

The dormer bungalow is convenient for the Waterford Glass Factory, golf clubs and the city centre. There are tea and coffee facilities in the sitting room and the dining room looks out across the garden to the countryside beyond. Bedrooms are comfortably furnished.

Rooms 5 rms (4 en suite) (3 fmly) S €50-€60; D €64-€76* **Facilities** TVL Cen ht **Parking** 6 **Notes** ⊗ No Children 7yrs Closed Nov-Apr ⊛

CO WESTMEATH

ATHLONE   Map 1 C4

Wineport Lodge

★★★★ ⊛ RESTAURANT WITH ROOMS

Glasson
☎ 090 6439010
e-mail: lodge@wineport.ie
web: www.wineport.ie
dir: *From Athlone take N55 to Ballykeeran village. Fork left at Dog & Duck pub, 1m on left*

Set in a wonderful location right on the shores of the inner lakes of Lough Rea on the Shannon and three miles north of Athlone. Guests can arrive by road or water, dine on the deck or in the attractive dining room. Cuisine is modern with innovative use of the best of local produce. Most of the luxurious bedrooms and suites have balconies – the perfect setting for breakfast. There is a Canadian hot tub on the roof terrace.

Rooms 29 en suite (3 fmly) (13 GF) S €125-€195; D €150-€495* **Facilities** STV tea/coffee Dinner available Direct Dial Lift Wi-fi Fishing Spa, Hot tub **Conf** Max 60 Thtr 60 Class 60 Board 30 **Parking** 100 **Notes** LB ⊗ No coaches Civ Wed 150

HORSELEAP — Map 1 C4

Woodlands Farm House (N286426)

★★★ FARMHOUSE

Streamstown
☎ 044 9226414 Mrs M Maxwell
e-mail: maxwells.woodlandsfarm@gmail.com
dir: N6 N onto R391 at Horseleap, farm signed 4km

This very comfortable and charming farmhouse has a delightful setting on a farm. The spacious sitting and dining rooms are very relaxing, and there is a hospitality kitchen where tea and coffee are available at all times.

Rooms 5 rms (4 en suite) (1 pri facs) (2 fmly) (2 GF)
Facilities TVL Cen ht **Parking Notes** ⊗ 120 acres mixed

CO WEXFORD

BALLYHACK — Map 1 C2

Marsh Mere Lodge

★★★★ BED AND BREAKFAST

☎ 051 389186
e-mail: stay@marshmerelodge.com
dir: R733 to Ballyhack

This charming house, a short walk from the Ballyhack ferry, embodies relaxation and comfort. Each bedroom has an individual character and afternoon tea is served on the sunny veranda overlooking King's Bay and Waterford harbour.

Rooms 4 en suite (2 GF) **Facilities** TVL Cen ht **Parking** 5 **Notes** LB ⊗

CAMPILE — Map 1 C2

PREMIER COLLECTION

Kilmokea Country Manor & Gardens

★★★★★ GUEST ACCOMMODATION

Great Island
☎ 051 388109 📠 051 388776
e-mail: kilmokea@eircom.net
dir: R733 from New Ross to Campile, right before village for Great Island & Kilmokea Gardens

An 18th-century stone rectory, recently restored. Located in wooded gardens (open to the public), where peacocks wander and trout fishing is available on the lake. Comfortable bedrooms and public rooms are richly furnished, and a country-house style dinner is served nightly (booking essential). Take breakfast in the conservatory and tea overlooking the beautiful gardens.

Rooms 4 en suite 2 annexe en suite (1 fmly) (2 GF)
S €75-€180; D €180-€300 **Facilities** TV2B STV TVL tea/coffee Dinner available Direct Dial Cen ht Licensed Wi-fi 🎾 🌳 🏊 Fishing Riding Sauna Gymnasium
Conf Max 75 Thtr 40 Class 30 Board 25 **Parking** 23
Notes LB RS Nov-end Jan

ENNISCORTHY — Map 1 D3

Lemongrove House

★★★★ GUEST HOUSE

Blackstoops
☎ 05392 36115 📠 05392 36115
e-mail: lemongrovehouse@iolfree.ie
dir: 1km N of Enniscorthy at rdbt on N11

A large house set on an elevated site surrounded by gardens. Lemongrove House offers en suite bedrooms which are all individually decorated in warm, cheerful colour schemes, and there is a comfortable sitting room and breakfast room. Plenty of parking.

Rooms 9 en suite (3 fmly) (5 GF) **Facilities** STV TVL tea/coffee Direct Dial Cen ht **Parking** 12 **Notes** ⊗ Closed 20-31 Dec

GOREY — Map 1 D3

PREMIER COLLECTION

Woodlands Country House

★★★★★ BED AND BREAKFAST

Killinierin
☎ 0402 37125
e-mail: info@woodlandscountryhouse.com
dir: N11 junct 22, Arklow - Gorey bypass, sign for Gorey. Immediately after rdbt, sign for Woodlands on right opp fruit farm

The 1836 country house stands in extensive mature gardens with a courtyard of stone buildings. The O'Sullivan family offer warm hospitality and (home-made scones on arrival). Three rooms have balconies.

Rooms 6 en suite (3 fmly) **Facilities** STV FTV TVL tea/coffee Cen ht 🎱 Pool Table **Parking** 10 **Notes** LB ⊗ Closed Oct-Mar

Hillside House

★★★★ BED AND BREAKFAST

Tubberduff
☎ 053 9421726 📠 053 9422567
e-mail: hillsidehouse@eircom.net
web: www.hillsidehouse.net
dir: N11 junct 22, take Gorey/Ballymoney Rd, & follow signs for Hillside House

A pristine house with pretty garden set in a lovely rural location commanding panoramic views of mountains and the sea, only 3 kilometres from Ballymoney beach. Ann Sutherland is a good cook, providing guests with a variety of home baking. The reception rooms are spacious, bedrooms are very comfortable and attractively decorated.

Rooms 6 en suite (4 fmly) (4 GF) S €60-€70;
D €70-€90* **Facilities** STV TVL tea/coffee Cen ht Wi-fi
Parking 6 **Notes** LB ⊗ Closed 20-28 Dec

NEW ROSS — Map 1 C3

Woodlands House

★★★ BED AND BREAKFAST

Carrigbyrne
☎ 051 428287 📠 051 428287
e-mail: woodwex@eircom.net
dir: On N25 (New Ross-Wexford route), 0.4km from Cedar Lodge Hotel towards New Ross

Commanding panoramic views, this is a recently refurbished bungalow with pretty gardens. It is only a 30-minute drive to Rosslare Harbour. Snacks are available, and dinner by arrangement. Bedrooms vary in size, though all are very comfortable. There is a guest sitting room.

Rooms 4 en suite (4 GF) **Facilities** tea/coffee Dinner available Cen ht **Parking** 6 **Notes** ⊗ No Children 5yrs

ROSSLARE HARBOUR — Map 1 D2

PREMIER COLLECTION

Churchtown House

★★★★★ GUEST HOUSE

☎ 053 913 2555 📠 053 913 2577
e-mail: info@churchtownhouse.com
dir: N25 onto R736 at Tagoat, turn between Cushens pub & church, house 0.8km on left

This charming house stands in mature grounds between Rosslare Strand and the Harbour port. Individually decorated bedrooms match the comfortable and relaxing lounge areas where hosts Patricia and Austin Cody are very welcoming. Dinner is served at 8 pm by arrangement, following sherry in the lounge.

Rooms 12 en suite (1 fmly) (5 GF) S €75-€110;
D €95-€150 **Facilities** FTV TVL Dinner available Direct Dial Cen ht Licensed 🌳 **Parking** 14 **Notes** LB ⊗ Closed Nov-Feb

ROSSLARE HARBOUR *continued*

The Light House

★★★ BED AND BREAKFAST

Main Rd
☎ 053 913 3214 053 913 3214

A contemporary bungalow set in grounds, The Light House is convenient for ferry users or for the beach and golf club. There is a television lounge and breakfast room in addition to the bedrooms, all of which have excellent en suite shower rooms.

Rooms 4 en suite (4 GF) S €40* **Facilities** TVL tea/coffee Cen ht **Parking** 6 **Notes** ⊗ No Children Closed Oct-Apr

---

WEXFORD   Map 1 D3

Killiane Castle *(T058168)*

★★★★ 🏠 FARMHOUSE

Drinagh
☎ 053 915 8885 053 915 8885 Mr & Mrs J Mernagh
e-mail: killianecastle@yahoo.com
dir: *Off N25 between Wexford and Rosslare*

This 17th-century house is part of a 13th-century Norman castle where the Mernagh family run a charming house on a dairy farm close to Wexford town. The comfortable reception rooms and bedrooms are beautifully furnished. Breakfast is a real treat and includes farm produce and Kathleen's baking and preserves. There is hard tennis court, croquet lawn, a golf driving range and walks to wander through the farm. Killiane Castle was the AA Guest Accommodation of the Year for Ireland 2008-2009.

Rooms 8 en suite (2 fmly) S €70; D €100* **Facilities** TVL Cen ht Wi-fi 🐾 🐕 ⛳ Driving range **Parking** 8 **Notes** ⊗ Closed Dec-Feb 230 acres dairy

Maple Lodge

★★★★ BED AND BREAKFAST

Castlebridge
☎ 053 915 9195 053 915 9195
e-mail: sreenan@eircom.net
dir: *5km N of Wexford. On R741, N on outskirts of Castlebridge, pink house on left*

This imposing house, set in extensive mature gardens, is in a peaceful location close to Curracloe Beach. Eamonn and Margaret Sreenan offer warm hospitality in their comfortable home. There is a varied breakfast menu offered and secure parking in the grounds.

Rooms 4 en suite (2 fmly) **Facilities** STV TVL Cen ht **Parking** 5 **Notes** ⊗ No Children 10yrs Closed mid Nov-mid Mar

---

Newbay Country House & Restaurant

★★★★ ◎ RESTAURANT WITH ROOMS

Newbay, Carrick
☎ 053 42779 053 46318
e-mail: newbay@newbayhouse.com
dir: *A11 from Wexford Bridge and turn right towards N25. Turn left before Quality Hotel and next right*

Built in the 1820s, but only offering accommodation for some ten years, Newbay offers a choice of two dining areas, the casual Cellar Bistro on the lower floor, or the more formal restaurant in the original house. Unsurprisingly, seafood is a passion here. The freshest catch only has to travel a few hundred yards. The very comfortable bedrooms are situated in both the house and a wing. Some have four-posters and all have lovely views.

Rooms 11 en suite (1 fmly) (6 smoking) **Facilities** TVL tea/coffee Dinner available Cen ht Wi-fi **Notes** ⊗

Rathaspeck Manor

★★★★ BED AND BREAKFAST

Rathaspeck
☎ 053 9141672 & 086 836 5764
e-mail: mickcuddihy@eircom.net
dir: *Signed on N25, near Johnstone Castle*

Standing in grounds that feature an 18-hole par-3 golf course, this Georgian country house is 0.8 kilometres from Johnstone Castle. The comfortable, spacious bedrooms are en suite and the public rooms are appointed with period furnishings.

Rooms 4 en suite **Facilities** TVL Cen ht Wi-fi Golf 18 **Parking** 8 **Notes** ⊗ No Children 10yrs Closed 8 Nov-Jun

See advert on opposite page

Slaney Manor

★★★★ GUEST ACCOMMODATION

Ferrycarrig
☎ 053 91 20051 053 91 20510
e-mail: slaneymanor@eircom.net
dir: *On N25, 0.8km W of N11 junct*

This attractive manor house stands in 24 hectares of woodland overlooking the River Slaney. Restored by the owners, the house retains many fine features. The elegant, high-ceilinged drawing room and dining room have views of the river, and four-poster beds feature in all bedrooms. The rooms in the converted coach house can be reserved on a room only basis for those travelling on the Rosslare ferry.

Rooms 9 en suite (2 fmly) (4 GF) S €60-€105; D €90-€190* **Facilities** TVL tea/coffee Dinner available Direct Dial Cen ht Lift Licensed **Conf** Max 250 Thtr 250 Class 100 Board 100 **Parking** 30 **Notes** LB ⊗ Closed 24-26 Dec Civ Wed 200

CO WICKLOW

ARKLOW   Map 1 D3

Koliba Country Home

★★★ BED AND BREAKFAST

Beech Rd, Avoca
☎ 0402 32737 0402 32737
e-mail: koliba@eircom.net
dir: *N11 onto R772 into Arklow, right at Rover garage, house 3km on right*

Situated halfway between Avoca and Arklow, this recently renovated house has panoramic views of the Vale of Avoca. Each cosy room is individually decorated. Rose and Brendan are very hospitable hosts and ensure a warm welcome.

Rooms 4 en suite (4 fmly) (4 GF) **Facilities** TVL tea/coffee Cen ht **Parking** 8 **Notes** ⊗ Closed Nov-Mar

---

ASHFORD   Map 1 D3

Ballyknocken House & Cookery School

★★★★ 🏠🍽 GUEST HOUSE

☎ 0404 44627 0404 44696
e-mail: cfulvio@ballyknocken.com
web: www.ballyknocken.com
dir: *N11, S into Ashford, right after petrol station, house 5km on right*

This charming Victorian farmhouse stands in the foothills of the Wicklow Mountains. Catherine Fulvio is an enthusiastic hostess and reservations are necessary for dinner, which includes imaginative, freshly prepared dishes using produce from the garden and farm. The smart bedrooms are comfortable, and the farm buildings have been converted into a cookery school.

Rooms 7 en suite (1 fmly) S €69-€95; D €110-€138* **Facilities** tea/coffee Dinner available Direct Dial Cen ht Licensed 🍽 Cookery school **Conf** Max 80 Thtr 80 Class 50 Board 30 **Parking** 8 **Notes** LB ⊗ Closed 14 Dec-8 Jan

AVOCA   Map 1 D3

Cherrybrook Country Home

★★★★ BED AND BREAKFAST

☎ 0402 35179 & 08761 05027   📄 0402 35765

e-mail: cherrybandb@eircom.net

dir: *M50, N11 S to Arklow, follow signs for Vale of Avoca. From village turn right facing Fitzgeralds bar, house on right 0.5km*

Set in the village made famous by the television series *Ballykissangel*, Cherrybrook has fine gardens with a barbeque area. It is a well-presented house with a lounge and conservatory dining room. Bedrooms are attractively decorated.

Rooms 5 en suite (2 fmly) (3 GF) S €50-€60; D €70-€80 **Facilities** STV TVL tea/coffee Cen ht Wi-fi **Parking** 5 **Notes** LB ⊗ No Children 13yrs

DUNLAVIN   Map 1 C3

PREMIER COLLECTION

Rathsallagh House

★★★★★ ◎ 🏠 GUEST ACCOMMODATION

☎ 045 403112   📄 045 403343

e-mail: info@rathsallagh.com

dir: *10.5km after end of M9 left signed Dunlavin, house signed 5km*

Surrounded by its own 18-hole championship golf course this delightful house was converted from Queen Ann stables in 1798 and now has the new addition of spacious and luxurious bedrooms with conference and leisure facilities. Food is country-house cooking at its best, and there is a cosy bar and comfortable drawing room to relax in. Close to Curragh and Punchestown racecourses.

Rooms 29 en suite (11 GF) S €150-€300; D €220-€320* **Facilities** FTV TVL tea/coffee Dinner available Direct Dial Cen ht Licensed Wi-fi 🏌 🏊 Golf 18 ♣ Snooker Sauna Golf academy with driving range **Conf** Max 160 Thtr 150 Class 75 Board 40 **Parking** 150 **Notes** LB No Children 12yrs Civ Wed 100

Tynte House (N870015)

★★★★ FARMHOUSE

☎ 045 401561   📄 045 401586 Mr & Mrs J Lawler

e-mail: info@tyntehouse.com

web: www.tyntehouse.com

dir: *N81 at Hollywood Cross, right at Dunlavin, follow finger signs for Tynte House, past market house in town centre*

The 19th-century farmhouse stands in the square of this quiet country village. The friendly hosts have carried out a lot of restoration resulting in comfortable bedrooms and a relaxing guest sitting room. Breakfast is a highlight of a visit to this house, which features Caroline's home baking.

Rooms 7 en suite (2 fmly) **Facilities** TVL tea/coffee Direct Dial Cen ht Wi-fi 🏌 Golf 18 Pool Table Playground, games room **Parking** 16 **Notes** Closed 16 Dec-9 Jan 200 acres beef/tillage

WICKLOW   Map 1 D3

Kilpatrick House (T257808)

★★★★ FARMHOUSE

Redcross

☎ 0404 47137 & 087 6358325   📄 0404 47866 Mr Howard Kingston

e-mail: info@kilpatrickhouse.com

dir: *13km S, 3.2km off N11, signed from Jack Whites pub*

This elegant 18th-century Georgian residence is set on a beef and tillage farm just off the N11 north of Arklow. Bedrooms are carefully furnished and thoughtfully equipped. Dinner is available on request and the extensive breakfast menu includes Shirley's home baking and country produce. Close to Brittas Bay, there is a choice of golf courses and horse riding.

Rooms 4 rms (3 en suite) (1 pri facs) (2 fmly) S €55-€60; D €95* **Facilities** TVL tea/coffee Cen ht 🏌 Fishing **Parking** 20 **Notes** ⊗ Closed Oct-Apr 150 acres beef

---

Rathaspeck Manor

Rathaspeck, Co. Wexford, Ireland

Tel: 00353539141672
Mobile: 00353868365764
Email: reservations@rathaspeckmanor.com or golf@rathaspeckmanor.com
Website: www.rathaspeckmanor.com

A luxurious 17th-century Georgian country house and golf club

Rathaspeck Manor, with its beautiful mature grounds and spacious ensuite bedrooms provides the ideal venue for a relaxing break and the perfect base from which to explore the sunny south east. The house, surrounded by its own executive Par 3 Golf course and bursting with history, is only 5km away from Wexford Town and a number of amenities to suit all tastes.

County Maps

England

1   Bedfordshire
2   Berkshire
3   Bristol
4   Buckinghamshire
5   Cambridgeshire
6   Greater Manchester
7   Herefordshire
8   Hertfordshire
9   Leicestershire
10 Northamptonshire
11 Nottinghamshire
12 Rutland
13 Staffordshire
14 Warwickshire
15 West Midlands
16 Worcestershire

Scotland

17 City of Glasgow
18 Clackmannanshire
19 East Ayrshire
20 East Dunbartonshire
21 East Renfrewshire
22 Perth & Kinross
23 Renfrewshire
24 South Lanarkshire
25 West Dunbartonshire

Wales

26 Blaenau Gwent
27 Bridgend
28 Caerphilly
29 Denbighshire
30 Flintshire
31 Merthyr Tydfil
32 Monmouthshire
33 Neath Port Talbot
34 Newport
35 Rhondda Cynon Taff
36 Torfaen
37 Vale of Glamorgan
38 Wrexham

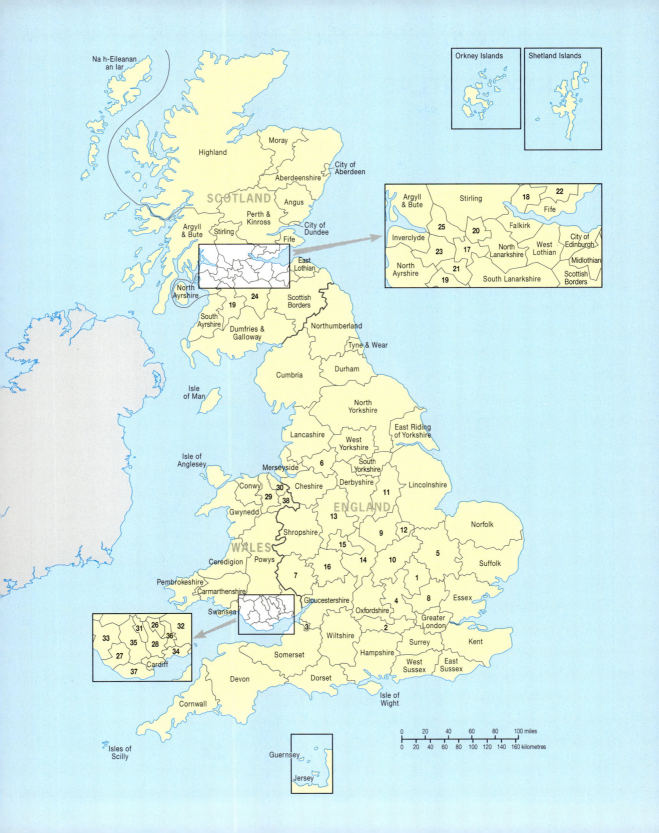

Orkney Islands

Shetland Islands

Na h-Eileanan
an Iar

Highland

Moray

City of
Aberdeen

Aberdeenshire

SCOTLAND

Angus

Perth &
Kinross

City of
Dundee

Argyll
& Bute

Stirling

Fife

Argyll
& Bute

Stirling

18

22

Fife

Inverclyde

85

20

Falkirk

City of
Edinburgh

East
Lothian

23

17

North
Lanarkshire

West
Lothian

Midlothian

North
Ayrshire

21

19

South Lanarkshire

Scottish
Borders

North
Ayrshire

19

24

Scottish
Borders

South
Ayrshire

Dumfries &
Galloway

Northumberland

Tyne & Wear

Isle
of Man

Cumbria

Durham

Isle of
Anglesey

North
Yorkshire

Lancashire

East Riding
of Yorkshire

Conwy

Merseyside

30

29

Cheshire

West
Yorkshire

6

South
Yorkshire

38

Derbyshire

Lincolnshire

Gwynedd

13

ENGLAND

11

Norfolk

Shropshire

9

12

WALES

15

Ceredigion

Powys

14

10

5

Suffolk

Pembrokeshire

7

16

1

Carmarthenshire

Gloucestershire

4

8

Essex

Swansea

3

Oxfordshire

Greater
London

31

26

32

Wiltshire

2

Surrey

Kent

33

36

Cardiff

35

28

34

Somerset

Hampshire

West
Sussex

East
Sussex

27

37

Devon

Dorset

Isle of
Wight

Cornwall

Isles of
Scilly

Guernsey

Jersey

| 0 | 20 | 40 | 60 | 80 | 100 miles |
| 0 | 20 | 40 | 60 | 80 | 100 | 120 | 140 | 160 kilometres |

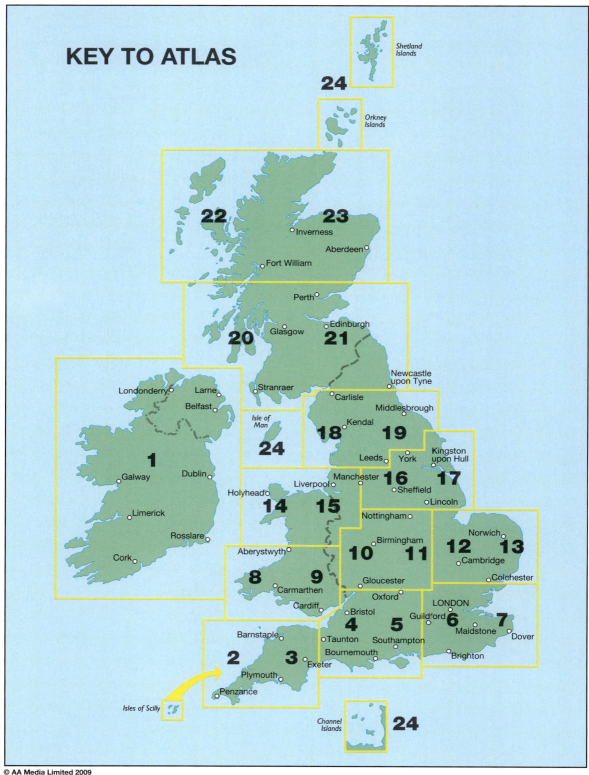

KEY TO ATLAS

Shetland Islands

24

Orkney Islands

22

23

Inverness

Aberdeen

Fort William

Perth

Glasgow

Edinburgh

20

21

Newcastle upon Tyne

Londonderry

Larne

Belfast

Stranraer

Carlisle

Middlesbrough

Isle of Man

Kendal

18

19

24

1

Leeds

York

Kingston upon Hull

Galway

Dublin

Holyhead

Liverpool

Manchester

16

17

Limerick

Sheffield

Lincoln

Rosslare

Nottingham

14

15

Cork

Birmingham

Norwich

Aberystwyth

10

11

12

13

Cambridge

8

9

Gloucester

Colchester

Carmarthen

Oxford

Cardiff

LONDON

Bristol

4

5

Guildford

6

7

Barnstaple

Taunton

Southampton

Maidstone

Dover

Bournemouth

Brighton

2

3

Exeter

Plymouth

Penzance

Isles of Scilly

Channel Islands

24

© AA Media Limited 2009

Legend

- M6 — Motorway/toll motorway
- Motorway junction full/restricted. Service area
- A33 — Primary route single/dual carriageway
- A34 — Other A road single/dual carriageway
- B2400 — B road
- Unclassified road
- V — Vehicle ferry
- C — Fast vehicle ferry or catamaran
- ● Stamford — Bed & Breakfast
- ○ King's Cliffe — Town/Village name
- National boundary
- ESSEX — English county name & boundary
- CONWY — Welsh county name & boundary
- MORAY — Scottish county name & boundary
- National Park

ISLES OF SCILLY

Bryher, New Grimsby, Tresco, St Martin's, Higher Town, PRESSO, Hugh Town, St Mary's, ISLES OF SCILLY (ST MARY'S), Middle Town, Old Town, St Agnes

SV

SW

CORNWALL

Lundy, Hartland Point, Hartland, Morwenstow, Kilkhampton, Bude, Bude Bay, Widemouth Bay, Stratton, St Gennys, Crackington Haven, Week St Mary, Boscastle, Tintagel, Delabole, Camelford, Congdon's Shop, BODMIN MOOR, Port Isaac, Pendoggett, Polzeath, Rock, St Tudy, Bolventor, Blisland, Harlyn, Padstow, Wadebridge, St Cleer, Porthcothan, Lanivet, Bodmin, Dobwalls, Mawgan Porth, St Mawgan, St Columb Major, CORNWALL, Liskeard, St Keyne, Newquay, Crantock, West Pentire, Roche, Lanlivery, Bugle, St Blazey, Lostwithiel, Par, Pelynt, Mitchell, Summercourt, St Austell, Looe, Fowey, Polruan, Polperro, Perranporth, Ladock, St Stephen, St Agnes, Marazanvose, Grampound, Pentewan, Mevagissey, Porthtowan, Portreath, St Day, Carnon Downs, Truro, Tregony, Gorran, Gorran Haven, Gwithian, St Ives Bay, Redruth, Camborne, Perranarworthal, Devoran, St Just-in-Roseland, Portloe, Veryan, St Ives, Zennor, Lelant, Hayle, Penryn, Flushing, Portscatho, St Mawes, St Hilary, Drym, Falmouth, St Just, Penzance, Marazion, Goldsithney, Helston, Constantine, Mawnan Smith, Land's End, Newlyn, Perranuthnoe, Praa Sands, Gweek, Manaccan, Sennen, St Buryan, Mousehole, Porthleven, St Keverne, Porthcurno, Treen, Mullion, Coverack, Ruan Minor, Cadgwith, Lizard, Lizard Point

For continuation pages refer to numbered arrows

For continuation pages refer to numbered arrows

For continuation pages refer to numbered arrows

For continuation pages refer to numbered arrows

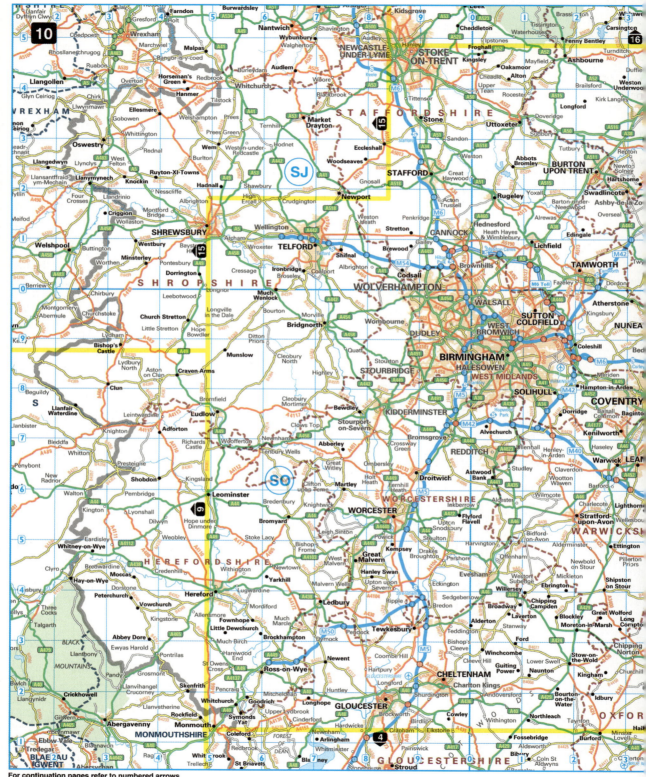

For continuation pages refer to numbered arrows

14

ISLE OF ANGLESEY

Cemaes
Amlwch
Llanerchymedd
Llanfachraeth
Holyhead
Trearddur Bay
Holy Island
Rhosneigr
Benllech
Red Wharf Bay
Llangoed
Pentraeth
Llangefni
Aberffraw
Y Felinheli
Newborough
Menai Bridge
Llanfair P.G.
Beaumaris
Bangor
Caernarfon
Llanddeiniolen
Llanrug
Llanberis
Bentnewydd
Llanwnda
Llandwrog
Betws Garmon
Penygroes
Rhyd-Ddu
Clynnog-fawr

Caernarfon Bay

Llanaelhaearn
Morfa Nefyn
Nefyn
Bodfuan
Llanystumdwy
Sarn
Pwllheli
Llanbedrog
Aberdaron
Y Rhiw
Abersoch
Bardsey Island

PENINSULA
LLEYN

Prenteg
Tremadog
Porthmadog
Criccieth
Borth-y-Gest
Harlech
Llanbedr
Dyffryn Ardudwy
Tal-y-bont
Barmouth
Fairbourne
Llwyngwril
Bryncrug
Tywyn
Pennal
Aberdyfi
Borth
Tal-y-bont
Llandre
Aberystwyth
Capel Bangor
Ponterwyd

Beddgelert
Maentwrog
Penrhyndeudraeth
Talsarnau
Trawsfynydd
Llanuwchllyn

SNOWDONIA

NATIONAL

PARK

GWYNEDD
MOUNTAINS

Ffestiniog
Blaenau Ffestiniog
Penmachno
Ganllwyd
Dinas-Mawddwy
Mallwyd
Corris
Cemmaes Road
Llanbrynmair
Machynlleth
Carno
Llanidloes

Llandudno
Deganwy
Conwy
Penmaenmawr
Llanfairfechan
Llanllechid
Bethesda
Tal-y-Bont
Capel Curig
Betws-y-Coed
Dolwyddelan
Pentrefoelas
Cerrigydrudion
Trefriw
Llanrwst
Llangernyw
Betws-yn-Rhos
Llansanffraid Glan Conwy
Rhôs-on-Sea
Colwyn Bay
Abergele
Rhyl
Llanddulas
Llansannan
Llanfair Talhaiarn
Bylchau

CONWY

Bala
Llanderfel

Cardigan Bay

Bed & Breakfast
Town/Village name

0 .... 10 miles
0 ... 10 ... 20 kilometres

SH

SN

9

For continuation pages refer to numbered arrows

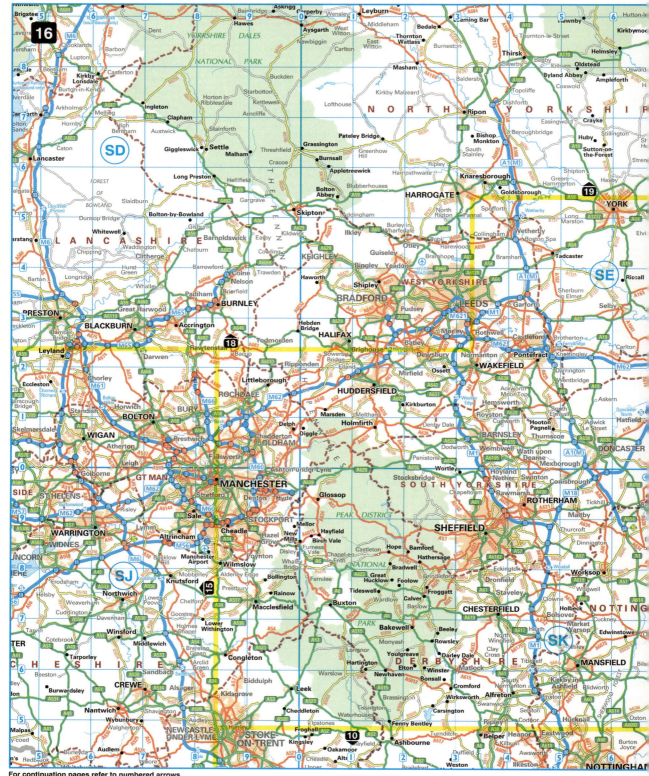

For continuation pages refer to numbered arrows

20

C EDIN	City of Edinburgh
C GLAS	City of Glasgow
CLACKS	Clackmannanshire
C DUND	City of Dundee
E DUNS	East Dunbartonshire
E RENS	East Renfrewshire
INVER	Inverclyde
MDLOTH	Midlothian
N LANS	North Lanarkshire
RENS	Renfrewshire
W DUNS	West Dunbartonshire
W LOTH	West Lothian

For continuation pages refer to numbered arrows

For continuation pages refer to numbered arrows

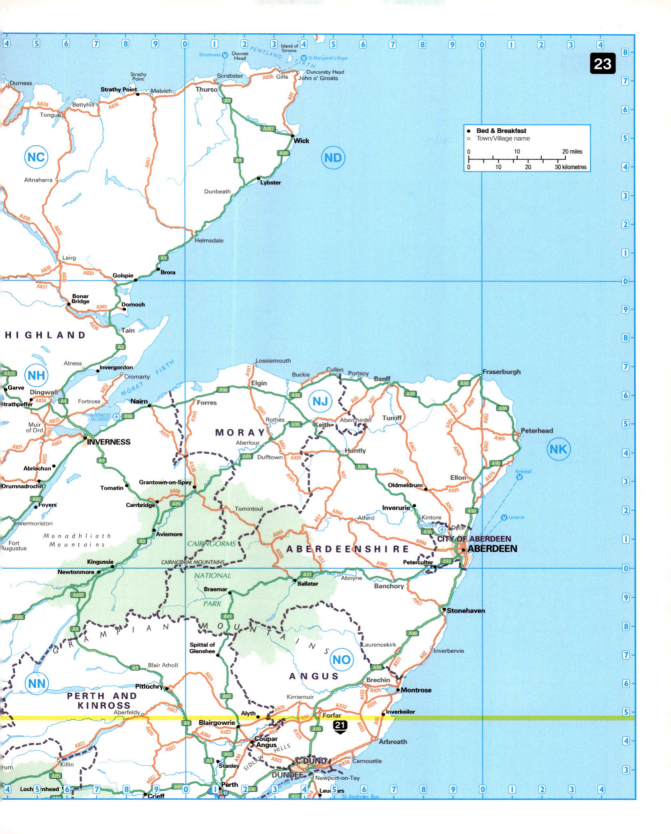

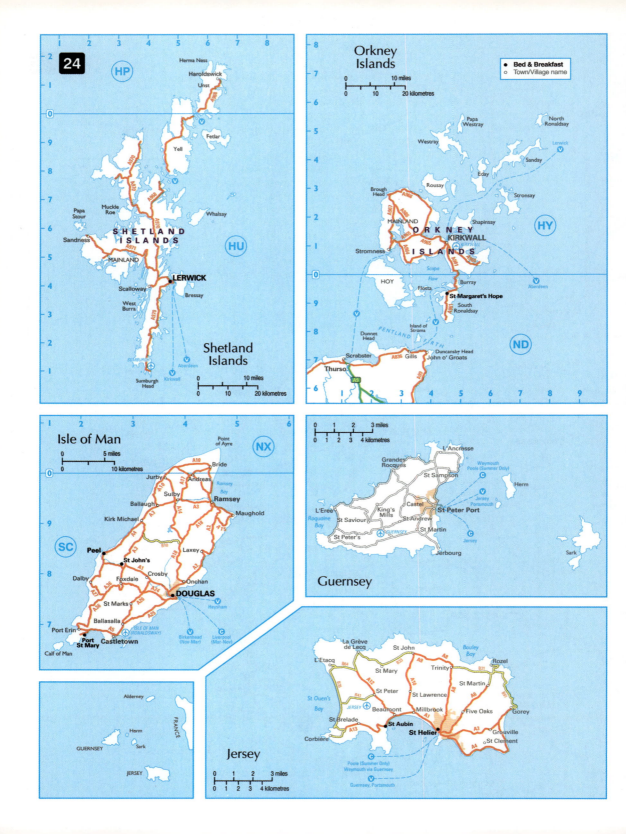

24

HP

Herma Ness
Haroldswick
Unst
A968

Fetlar

Yell
A970

HU

Muckle Roe
Papa Stour
A968
Whalsay
A971
SHETLAND ISLANDS
Sandness
MAINLAND
A971
LERWICK
Scalloway
Bressay
West Burra
A970
SUMBURGH
Sumburgh Head
Aberdeen
Kirkwall

Shetland Islands

10 miles
0   10   20 kilometres

Orkney Islands

● Bed & Breakfast
○ Town/Village name

10 miles
0   10
0   20 kilometres

Papa Westray
North Ronaldsay
Westray
Sanday
Lerwick
Rousay
Eday
Sronsay
Brough Head
A967
A966
Shapinsay
MAINLAND
ORKNEY
Stromness
A965
KIRKWALL
A961
ISLANDS
HY

Scapa Flow
HOY
Burray
Aberdeen
Flotta
St Margaret's Hope
A961
South Ronaldsay
PENTLAND FIRTH
Dunnet Head
Island of Stroma
Duncansby Head
John o' Groats
Scrabster
A836
Gills
A9
Thurso
A9
ND

Isle of Man
5 miles
0   10 kilometres

Point of Ayre
NX

A10
Bride
Jurby
A17
Andreas
A10
Sulby
Ramsey Bay
Ramsey
Ballaugh
A3
A14
Kirk Michael
A3
Maughold
A4
A18
A15
SC
A4
Laxey
Peel
B10
A2
St John's
A1
Crosby
Dalby
Foxdale
Onchan
A27
A36
A24
DOUGLAS
St Marks
A26
A25
Heysham
Ballasalla
ISLE OF MAN (RONALDSWAY)
Port Erin
A5
Birkenhead (Nov–Mar)
Liverpool (Mar–Nov)
Port St Mary
Castletown
Calf of Man

Guernsey

3 miles
0   1   2
0   1   2   3   4 kilometres

L'Ancresse
Grandes Rocques
St Sampson
Weymouth Poole (Summer Only)
Herm
L'Erée
Castel
St Peter Port
King's Mills
St Andrew
Jersey Portsmouth
Roquaine Bay
St Saviour
St Martin
GUERNSEY
St Peter's
St Peter's
Jerbourg
Jersey
Sark

Alderney
Herm
Sark
FRANCE
GUERNSEY
JERSEY

Jersey
3 miles
0   1   2
0   1   2   3   4 kilometres

La Grève de Lecq
St John
Bouley Bay
L'Etacq
B64
A8
Rozel
St Mary
A9
Trinity
B31
JERSEY
St Peter
A12
A9
St Martin
St Ouen's Bay
B41
St Lawrence
A8
A6
Beaumont
A1
Millbrook
Five Oaks
Gorey
St Brelade
A3
St Aubin
Corbière
A13
St Helier
A4
Grouville
St Clement
Poole (Summer Only)
Weymouth via Guernsey
Guernsey, Portsmouth

Central London

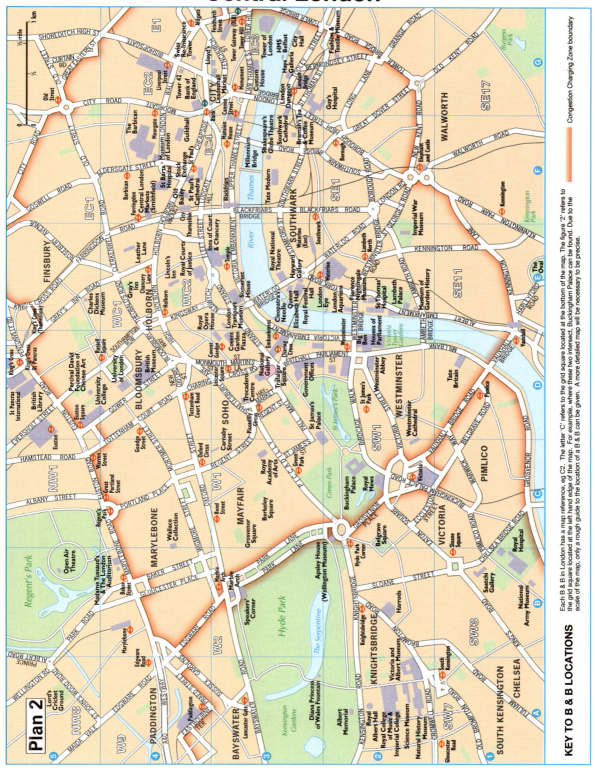

KEY TO B & B LOCATIONS

Each B & B in London has a map reference, eg C2. The letter 'C' refers to the grid square located at the bottom of the map. The figure '2' refers to the grid square located at the left hand edge of the map. For example, where these two intersect, Buckingham Palace can be found. Due to the scale of the map, only a rough guide to the location of a B & B can be given. A more detailed map will be necessary to be precise.

━━━ Congestion Charging Zone boundary

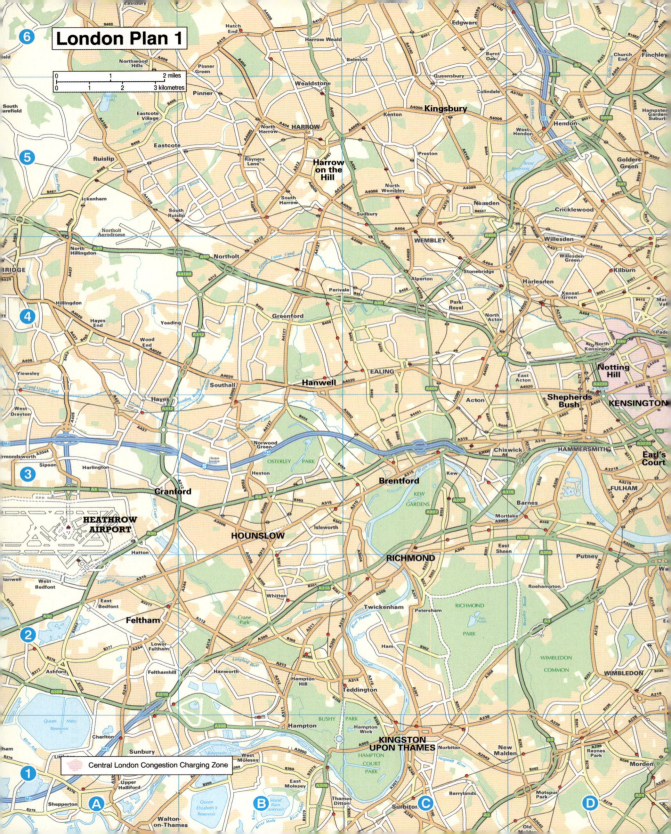

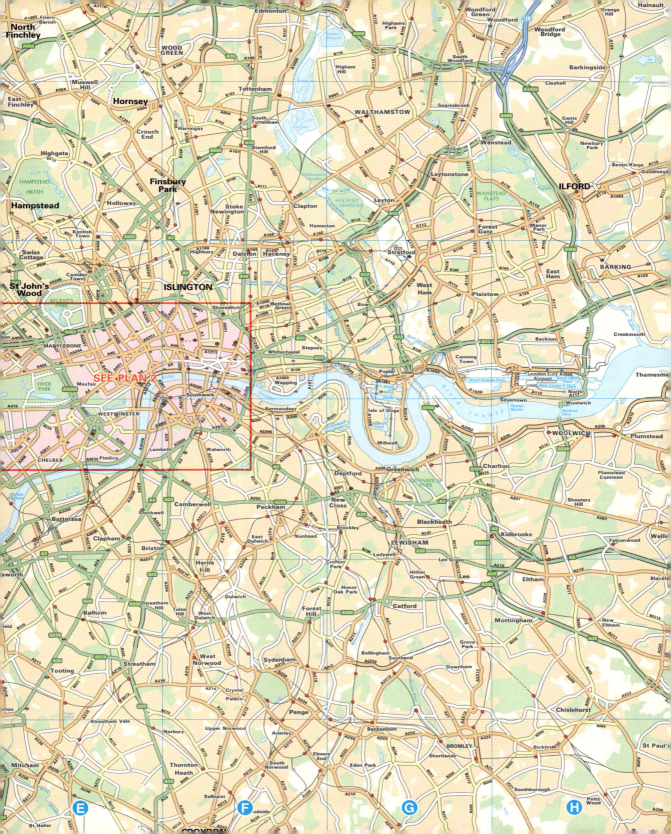

Index of Bed & Breakfasts

The Automobile Association would like to thank the following photographers and companies for their assistance in the preparation of this book.

Abbreviations for the picture credits are as follows: (t) top; (b) bottom; (l) left; (r) right; (c) centre (AA) AA World Travel Library.

1 Ees Wyke Country House; 2 Mayflower, London; 3 Foley's Town House, Killarney; 4 AA/S Montgomery; 5 The Cottage Lodge, Brockenhurst; 6 Photolibrary Group; 7 The Old Farmhouse, Sidmouth; 9 AA/M Moody; 10 Plas Rhos, Rhos-on-Sea; 11t The St Endoc Hotel Restaurant, Rock; 13t Windermere Suites; 13b The Sumner; 14l Chatton Park House; 14r Loch Ness Lodge; 15l Tan-Yr-Onnen; 15r Rosquil House; 16 Photolibrary Group; 18 Photolibrary Group; 19tl, 19r, 19c, 19b Photolibrary Group; 20 AA/K Doran; 20/1 AA/J A Tims; 22l Photolibrary Group; 22r AA/J A Tims; 23 AA/K Doran; 28/9 AA/M Kipling; 415 AA/M Kipling; 416 AA/S Anderson; 454 AA/S Lewis; 490 AA/S McBride.

Every effort has been made to trace the copyright holders, and we apologise in advance for any accidental errors. We would be happy to apply the corrections in the following edition of this publication.

Readers' Report Form

Please send this form to:–
Editor, The B&B Guide,
Lifestyle Guides,
AA Publishing,
Fanum House, FH13
Basingstoke RG21 4EA

or e-mail: lifestyleguides@theAA.com

Use this form to recommend any guest house, farmhouse or inn where you have stayed that is not already in the guide.

If you have any comments about your stay at an establishment listed in the Guide, please let us know, as feedback from readers helps to keep our Guide accurate and up to date. If you have a complaint during your stay, we recommend that you discuss the matter with the establishment.

Please note that the AA does not undertake to arbitrate between you and the establishment, to obtain compensation, or to engage in protracted correspondence.

Date

Your name (BLOCK CAPITALS)

Your address (BLOCK CAPITALS)

Post code

E-mail address

Name of hotel

Comments (Please include the name and address of the establishment)

(please attach a separate sheet if necessary)

Please tick here ☐ if you DO NOT wish to receive details of AA offers or products   PTO

Readers' Report Form *continued*

Have you bought this guide before? ☐ YES ☐ NO

What other accommodation, restaurant, pub or food guides have you bought recently?

Why did you buy this guide? (tick all that apply)
Holiday ☐   Short break ☐   Business travel ☐   Special occasion ☐   Overnight stop ☐   Conference ☐
Other (please state)

How often do you stay in B&Bs? (tick one choice)
More than once a month ☐   Once a month ☐   Once in two to three months ☐   Once in six months ☐
Once a year ☐   Less than once a year ☐

Please answer these questions to help us make improvements to the guide.
Which of these factors is most important when choosing a B&B?
Price ☐   Location ☐   Awards/ratings ☐   Service ☐   Décor/surroundings ☐
Previous experience ☐   Recommendation ☐
Other (please state)

Do you read the editorial features in the guide? ☐ YES ☐ NO

Do you use the location atlas?   ☐ YES ☐ NO

What elements of the guide do you find most useful when choosing somewhere to stay?
Description ☐   Photo ☐   Advertisement ☐   Star rating ☐

Can you suggest any improvements to the guide?

Thank you for completing and returning this form

Readers' Report Form

Please send this form to:–
Editor, The B&B Guide,
Lifestyle Guides,
AA Publishing,
Fanum House, FH13
Basingstoke RG21 4EA

or e-mail: lifestyleguides@theAA.com

Use this form to recommend any guest house, farmhouse or inn where you have stayed that is not already in the guide.

If you have any comments about your stay at an establishment listed in the Guide, please let us know, as feedback from readers helps to keep our Guide accurate and up to date. If you have a complaint during your stay, we recommend that you discuss the matter with the establishment.

Please note that the AA does not undertake to arbitrate between you and the establishment, to obtain compensation, or to engage in protracted correspondence.

Date

Your name (BLOCK CAPITALS)

Your address (BLOCK CAPITALS)

Post code

E-mail address

Name of hotel

Comments (Please include the name and address of the establishment)

(please attach a separate sheet if necessary)

Please tick here ☐ if you DO NOT wish to receive details of AA offers or products

PTO

Readers' Report Form *continued*

Have you bought this guide before? ☐ YES ☐ NO

What other accommodation, restaurant, pub or food guides have you bought recently?

....

....

....

Why did you buy this guide? (tick all that apply)
Holiday ☐   Short break ☐   Business travel ☐   Special occasion ☐   Overnight stop ☐   Conference ☐
Other (please state)

How often do you stay in B&Bs? (tick one choice)
More than once a month ☐   Once a month ☐   Once in two to three months ☐   Once in six months ☐
Once a year ☐   Less than once a year ☐

Please answer these questions to help us make improvements to the guide.
Which of these factors is most important when choosing a B&B?
Price ☐   Location ☐   Awards/ratings ☐   Service ☐   Décor/surroundings ☐
Previous experience ☐   Recommendation ☐
Other (please state)

Do you read the editorial features in the guide? ☐ YES ☐ NO

Do you use the location atlas?   ☐ YES ☐ NO

What elements of the guide do you find most useful when choosing somewhere to stay?
Description ☐   Photo ☐   Advertisement ☐   Star rating ☐

Can you suggest any improvements to the guide?

....

....

....

Thank you for completing and returning this form